Great Lives from History

The Ancient World

Prehistory - 476 C.E.

Great Lives from History

The Ancient World

Prehistory - 476 C.E.

Volume 1
Aaron-Lysippus

Editor
Christina A. Salowey
Hollins University

Editor, First Edition
Frank N. Magill

SALEM PRESS
Pasadena, California   Hackensack, New Jersey

Editor in Chief: Dawn P. Dawson
Editorial Director: Christina J. Moose
Project Editor: Rowena Wildin
Copy Editor: Leslie Ellen Jones
Copy Editor: Elizabeth Ferry Slocum
Assistant Editor: Andrea E. Miller
Editorial Assistant: Dana Garey

Photograph Editor: Philip Bader
Acquisitions Editor: Mark Rehn
Research Supervisor: Jeffry Jensen
Research Assistant: Desiree Dreeuws
Production Editor: Joyce I. Buchea
Graphics and Design: James Hutson
Layout: Eddie Murillo

Cover photos: Library of Congress

Some of the essays in this work originally appeared in the following Salem Press sets: *Dictionary of World Biography* (1998-1999, edited by Frank N. Magill) and *Great Lives from History* (1987-1995, edited by Frank N. Magill).

Library of Congress Cataloging-in-Publication Data

Great lives from history. The ancient world, prehistory-476 C.E. / editor, Christina A. Salowey, editor, Frank N. Magill.—
1st ed.
    p. cm.
Includes bibliographical references and indexes.
    ISBN 1-58765-152-1 (set : alk. paper) — ISBN 1-58765-153-X (vol. 1 : alk. paper) — ISBN 1-58765-154-8 (vol. 2 : alk. paper)
    1. Biography—To 500. 2. History, Ancient. I. Title: Ancient world, prehistory-476 C.E. II. Salowey, Christina A. III. Magill, Frank Northen 1907-1997.
CT113.G745 2004
920.03—dc22

2004000705

First Printing

CONTENTS

PUBLISHER'S NOTE

Great Lives from History: The Ancient World, Prehistory-476 C.E. is the first in a multivolume series covering the lives of important personages from the ancient world through the twenty-first century. This series is a revision of the 10-volume *Dictionary of World Biography* series (1998-1999), which was a revision and reordering of Salem Press's 30-volume *Great Lives from History* series (1987-1995). The original essays are enhanced by the addition of new entries covering a wider geographical area and including more women, updated bibliographies, succession tables, a new page design, and a section containing maps of various parts of the ancient world.

Great Lives from History: The Ancient World, Prehistory-476 C.E. gathers 260 essays from the *Dictionary of World Biography: The Ancient World* and adds 65 new biographies, creating a total of 325 essays. The date of 476 C.E., the fall of Rome, was selected by the editors as the cutoff between the ancient world and the Middle Ages. Those lives spanning this cutoff date were included if their life's work or major accomplishments fell within the period covered by this set.

The articles in this set range from 1,700 to 3,000 words in length (roughly 3 to 6 pages) and follow a standard format. Each article begins with the subject's name, as best known in the Western world, and an identifier stating the person's nationality and life role, along with reign dates if the person was a ruler. These are followed by ready-reference listings: a brief statement summarizing the person's contribution to society and later ages, his or her birth and death dates and places (including both ancient place-names and modern equivalents), other names the person might have used, and his or her areas of achievement. In some of the ready-reference material and in parenthetical material within the text, the following abbreviations have been used: "r." for "reigned," "b." for "born," "d." for "died," and "fl." for flourished.

The body of each article is divided into three parts. "Early Life," the first section, provides facts about the individual's upbringing and the environment in which he or she was reared, as well as the pronunciation of his or her name, if unusual. The heart of the article is the section entitled "Life's Work," which consists of a straightforward account of the period during which the individual's most significant achievements were made. The concluding section, "Significance," is not a recapitulation of what has been discussed but rather an overview of the individual's place in history. Each essay is supplemented by an annotated, evaluative bibliography, a starting point for further research. In addition, each essay is cross-referenced to other essays within the volume as well as to relevant essays in the companion set, *Great Events from History: The Ancient World, Prehistory-476 C.E.* (2 vols., 2004). Three essays, "Cleomenes," "Gracchi," and "Tarquins," cover 2 or 3 individuals. These essays differ slightly from those covering individuals in terms of format, but otherwise, they contain the same information, including ready-reference materials.

Accompanying the essays are about 170 illustrations (mostly line art and photographs of busts, sculptures, coins, paintings, and drawings depicting the individual) and 40 succession lists, genealogies, and other tables. Nineteen maps of portions of the ancient world appear grouped together for easy reference in the front of each volume.

The temporal and geographical scope of *Great Lives from History: The Ancient World, Prehistory-476 C.E.* is broad. Represented here are figures as ancient as the Egyptian pharaoh Zoser (c. 2700-c. 2650 B.C.E.) and as late as the Buddhist monk Bodhidharma (fifth-sixth century C.E.). Geographically, the coverage is worldwide, with individuals identified with one or more areas: 92 with Greece, 4 with Sparta, 4 with Macedonia, 66 with the Roman Empire, and 23 with the Roman Republic; 33 with Asia Minor; 7 with Mesopotamia, 7 with Persia, 21 with Israel, 6 with Assyria, and 10 with other parts of the Middle East; 22 with China, 3 with Japan, 16 with India and Sri Lanka, and 3 with Central Asia; 3 with Britain and 9 with other parts of Europe; and 26 with Egypt, 15 with Alexandria, 8 with Carthage, and 4 with other parts of Africa.

The editors have sought to provide coverage that is broad in areas of achievement as well as geography, while at the same time including the recognized shapers of history essential in any liberal arts curriculum. Major world leaders appear here—pharaohs, emperors, conquerors, kings, and khans—as well as giants of religious faith: Buddha, Moses, Zoroaster, Jesus, and the priests, monks, and saints who left their imprint on political as well as spiritual institutions. The set also includes scholars, philosophers, scientists, explorers, writers, and artists. Among these architects of today's civilization are 39 women of the ancient world—poets, scholars, leaders, and influential mothers and wives. These leaders of the world have made significant achievements in one or more fields: 131 in government and politics, 69 in war and conquest, 75 in religion, 55 in philosophy, 56 in literature, 17 in art and art patronage, 4 in music, 8 in scholarship, 15 in historiography, 7 in geography, 7 in law, 12 in architecture, 13 in science, 11 in medicine, 13 in mathematics, 9 in astronomy, and 6 in natural history.

Each set in the *Great Lives from History* series has its distinctive qualities, and several features distinguish this series as a whole from other biographical reference works. The articles combine breadth of coverage with a format that offers the user quick access to the particular information needed. For convenience of reference, this set is indexed by area of achievement, by geographical location, and by name. A chronological list of entries that places the personages of the ancient world in order of birth provides historical perspective.

The worldwide scope of *Great Lives from History* resulted in the inclusion of many names and words that must be transliterated from languages that do not use the Roman alphabet, and in some cases, there is more than one transliterated form in use. In many cases, transliterated words in this set follow the American Library Association and Library of Congress (ALA-LC) transliteration format for that language. However, if another form of a name or word was judged to be more familiar to the general audience, it is used instead. The variants for names of essay subjects are listed in ready-reference top matter and are cross-referenced in the subject and personages indexes. The Pinyin transliteration was used for Chinese topics, with Wade-Giles variants provided for major names and dynasties. In a few cases, a common name that is not Pinyin has been used (for example, "Confucius"). Sanskrit words generally follow the ALA-LC transliteration rules; although again, the more familiar form of a word is used when deemed appropriate for the general reader (for example, sutra).

Latin nomenclature uses three names: *praenomen*, *nomen* or family name, and *cognomen*. Most individuals are listed by their *nomen*, but some are listed by their common English name. For example, Marcus (*praenomen*) Tullius (*nomen*) Cicero (*cognomen*), is commonly known as Cicero. Many Roman men had at least two names, a *praenomen* and *nomen*. Roman women were given the grammatically feminine form of their father's *nomen*. For example, Cicero's daughter is Tullia. If there were two daughters, they were called Major and Minor for elder and younger. In some cases, the common English name (for example, Agrippina the Younger) has been used. In addition to the *praenomen* and *nomen*, some men had a *cognomen*. In some cases, this is the common English name of famous Romans such as Caesar, Cicero, and Scipio. A name may have more than one *cognomen*, and these are typically nicknames or titles given for military success. Notable exceptions to these basic rules are Augustus and the emperors following him. Augustus was born Gaius Octavius and by adoption became Gaius Julius Caesar Octavianus. In 27 B.C.E., he was given an honorary and quasi-religious name Augustus. All subsequent emperors took the name Caesar Augustus followed by their *praenomen*, *nomen*, and *cognomen*.

Research on the ancient world is ongoing, with contributions from historians, linguists, archaeologists, anthropologists, and other scholars supplementing and revising what is known of ancient peoples and cultures. Therefore, the dates, names, and descriptions of events in *Great Lives from History* represent a consensus of generally accepted modern scholarship.

Salem Press would like to extend its appreciation to Christina A. Salowey of Hollins University, the editor of *Great Lives from History: The Ancient World, Prehistory-476 C.E.*, and to the academicians and scholars who prepared essays for this work. Without their expert contributions, a project of this nature would not be possible. A full list of contributors and their affiliations appears in the front matter of this volume.

CONTRIBUTORS

Linda Perry Abrams
Bob Jones University

Patrick Adcock
Independent Scholar

Susan K. Allard-Nelson
Pacific Lutheran University

Amy Allison
Independent Scholar

J. Stewart Alverson
*University of Tennessee
at Chattanooga*

James A. Arieti
Hampden-Sydney College

Mike Ashley
Independent Scholar

Bryan Aubrey
Independent Scholar

Richard Badessa
University of Louisville

Silvia P. Baeza
Independent Scholar

Carl L. Bankston III
Tulane University

Iraj Bashiri
University of Minnesota

Michael E. Bauman
Hillsdale College

Tanja Bekhuis
TCB Research

Albert A. Bell, Jr.
Hope College

Richard P. Benton
Trinity College

Alan Berkowitz
Swarthmore College

Milton Berman
University of Rochester

Terry D. Bilhartz
Sam Houston State University

Cynthia A. Bily
Adrian College

Kevin Edward Birch
Salisbury University

Nicholas Birns
New School University

Edward Bleiberg
Memphis State University

Walter C. Bouzard, Jr.
Wartburg College

Gerhard Brand
*California State University,
Los Angeles*

Erica Brindley
*University of California, Santa
Barbara*

William S. Brockington, Jr.
University of South Carolina - Aiken

W. R. Brookman
North Central University

Thomas W. Buchanan
Ancilla Domini College

David D. Buck
University of Wisconsin-Milwaukee

Jeffrey L. Buller
Mary Baldwin College

Edmund M. Burke
*University of California Medical
Center*

William H. Burnside
John Brown University

Elizabeth D. Carney
Clemson University

Joan E. Carr
Washington University

Gilbert T. Cave
Lakeland Community College

James T. Chambers
Texas Christian University

Mark W. Chavalas
University of Wisconsin-La Crosse

Victor W. Chen
Chabot College

Pei-kai Cheng
Pace University

Key Ray Chong
Texas Tech University

Stefan G. Chrissanthos
University of California, Riverside

David Christiansen
Truman State University

Patricia Cook
Emory University

Owen C. Cramer
Colorado College

Frank Day
Clemson University

Kirsten Day
University of Arkansas

Nguyen Thi Dieu
Temple University

Malcolm Drew Donalson
*Alabama School of Mathematics &
Science*

Bruce L. Edwards
Independent Scholar

Michael M. Eisman
Temple University

Robert P. Ellis
Independent Scholar

Thomas L. Erskine
Salisbury University

Todd W. Ewing
William Baptist College

Randall Fegley
Pennsylvania State University

Stephen W. Felder
University of California, Irvine

Gary B. Ferngren
Oregon State University

John W. Fiero
University of Louisiana at Lafayette

Michael S. Fitzgerald
Pikeville College

Edwin D. Floyd
University of Pittsburgh

Robert J. Forman
St. John's University, New York

Douglas A. Foster
David Lipscomb College

Rita E. Freed
Memphis State University

Richard N. Frye
Harvard University

Keith Garebian
Independent Scholar

Daniel H. Garrison
Northwestern University

Elise P. Garrison
Texas A&M University

Judy E. Gaughan
Colorado State University

Donald S. Gochberg
Michigan State University

Hans Goedicke
Johns Hopkins University

Leonard J. Greenspoon
Clemson University

William S. Greenwalt
Santa Clara University

Christopher E. Guthrie
Tarleton State University

Thomas Halton
Catholic University of America

Gavin R. G. Hambly
University of Texas at Dallas

J. S. Hamilton
Old Dominion University

Wells S. Hansen
Milton Academy

Katherine Anne Harper
Loyola Marymount University

Sandra Hanby Harris
Tidewater Community College

Paul B. Harvey, Jr.
Penn State University

Peter B. Heller
Manhattan College

Diane Andrews Henningfeld
Adrian College

Michael Hernon
University of Tennessee at Martin

Charles W. Holcombe
Northeast Missouri State University

James P. Holoka
Eastern Michigan University

Tonya Huber
Wichita State University

J. Donald Hughes
University of Denver

Patrick Norman Hunt
Stanford University

Kwang-Kuo Hwang
National Taiwan University

Shakuntala Jayaswal
Independent Scholar

Amy J. Johnson
Berry College

Edward Johnson
University of New Orleans

Cynthia Lee Katona
Ohlone College

Robert B. Kebric
University of Louisville

Kenneth F. Kitchell, Jr.
Louisiana State University

Wilbur R. Knorr
Stanford University

Julian Kunnie
University of Arizona

Donald G. Kyle
University of Texas at Arlington

David H. J. Larmour
Texas Tech. University

Eugene S. Larson
Los Angeles Pierce College

John M. Lawrence
Independent Scholar

Daniel B. Levine
University of Arkansas

Leon Lewis
Appalachian State University

Thomas Tandy Lewis
College of St. Scholastica

Charles Xingzhong Li
Central Washington University

Winston W. Lo
Florida State University

Rita E. Loos
Independent Scholar

Herbert Luft
Pepperdine University

R. C. Lutz
University of the Pacific

Peter F. Macaluso
Montclair State College

CONTRIBUTORS

T. Davina McClain
Loyola University, New Orleans

Murray C. McClellan
The University Museum

C. Thomas McCullough
Centre College

Michelle C. K. McKowen
Independent Scholar

Kerrie L. MacPherson
SUNY, Buffalo

John D. Madden
University of Montana

Paul Madden
Hardin-Simmons University

Paolo Mancuso
Independent Scholar

Ralph W. Mathisen
University of South Carolina

James M. May
St. Olaf College

Lysle E. Meyer
Moorhead State University

Caitlin L. Moriarity
University of Missouri - Columbia

Ian Morris
University of Chicago

Terry R. Morris
Shorter College

B. Keith Murphy
Fort Valley State University

Terence R. Murphy
American University

Alice Myers
Simon's Rock of Bard College

Byron J. Nakamura
University of Washington

Carolyn Nelson
University of Kansas

Eric D. Nelson
Pacific Lutheran University

Frances Stickney Newman
University of Illinois

Steven M. Oberhelman
Texas A&M University

Glenn W. Olsen
University of Utah

Robert M. Otten
Marymount University

Lisa Paddock
Independent Scholar

Robert J. Paradowski
Rochester Institute of Technology

William E. Pemberton
University of Wisconsin - La Crosse

Mark Pestana
Grand Valley State University

Nis Petersen
New Jersey City University

Sara E. Phang
Independent Scholar

John R. Phillips
Purdue University Calumet

Allene Phy-Olsen
Austin Peay State University

Linda J. Piper
University of Georgia

Clifton W. Potter, Jr.
Lynchburg College

David Potter
University of Michigan

Dorothy T. Potter
Lynchburg College

David Powell
Western New Mexico University

James M. Quillin
Northwestern University

Thomas Rankin
Independent Scholar

Abe C. Ravitz
California State University, Dominguez Hills

John D. Raymer
Independent Scholar

Rosemary M. Canfield Reisman
Charleston Southern University

Clark G. Reynolds
College of Charleston

Edward A. Riedinger
Ohio State University Libraries

Francesca Rochberg-Halton
University of California, Riverside

Carl Rollyson
Baruch College, CUNY

Fiona Rose
New College

Joseph Rosenblum
University of North Carolina, Greensboro

Adriane Ruggiero
Independent Scholar

Susan Rusinko
Bloomsburg University

Thomas Ryba
Michigan State University

Stephen Satris
Clemson University

Daniel C. Scavone
University of Southern Indiana

Thomas C. Schunk
Independent Scholar

Victoria Scott
Lick Observatory

Judith Lynn Sebesta
University of South Dakota

John C. Sherwood
University of Oregon

H. J. Shey
Independent Scholar

T. A. Shippey
St. Louis University

R. Baird Shuman
*University of Illinois at Urbana-
Champaign*

Thomas J. Sienkewicz
Monmouth College

Narasingha P. Sil
Western Oregon University

Donald C. Simmons, Jr.
South Dakota Humanities Council

Donna Addkison Simmons
Independent Scholar

Sanford S. Singer
University of Dayton

Andrew C. Skinner
Brigham Young University

Ralph Smiley
Bloomsburg University

Clyde Curry Smith
University of Wisconsin

Ronald F. Smith
Independent Scholar

Larry Smolucha
Benedictine University

Norman Sobiesk
Winona State University

C. Fitzhugh Spragins
Arkansas College

Heinrich von Staden
Yale University

Kelli E. Stanley
San Francisco State University

David L. Sterling
University of Cincinnati

Leslie A. Stricker
Park University

Paul Stuewe
St. Jerome's University

Susan A. Stussy
Independent Scholar

Bruce M. Sullivan
Arizona State University

James Sullivan
California State University, Los Angeles

Roy Arthur Swanson
University of Wisconsin, Milwaukee

John E. Thorburn, Jr.
Baylor University

Jonathan L. Thorndike
Belmont University

Shelley A. Thrasher
Lamar State College - Orange

Greg Tomko-Pavia
Independent Scholar

Antonia Tripolitis
Rutgers University

Marlin Timothy Tucker
David Lipscomb College

Kriston J. Udd
Michigan Theological Seminary

Jiu-Hwa Lo Upshur
Eastern Michigan University

Larry W. Usilton
*University of North Carolina at
Wilmington*

Ruth Van der Maas
Independent Scholar

George W. Van Devender
Independent Scholar

Branko F. van Oppen de Ruiter
CUNY Graduate Center

Peter L. Viscusi
Central Missouri State University

Albert Wachtel
Pitzer College

William T. Walker
Chestnut Hill College

John Walsh
Hofstra University

Albert T. Watanabe
Louisiana State University

Thomas H. Watkins
Western Illinois University

Ronald J. Weber
University of Texas at El Paso

Winifred O. Whelan
St. Bonaventure University

Carlis C. White
Slippery Rock University

Thomas Willard
University of Arizona

Julie A. Williams
Independent Scholar

John F. Wilson
University of Hawaii - Manoa

John D. Windhausen
Saint Anselm College

Johnny Wink
Ouachita Baptist University

Michael Witkoski
University of South Carolina

Robert W. Yarbrough
Wheaton College

Clifton K. Yearley
SUNY, Buffalo

William M. Zanella
Hawaii Loa College

Janie Anne Zuber
Northwestern University

KEY TO PRONUNCIATION

Many of the names of personages covered in *Great Lives from History: The Ancient World, Prehistory-476 C.E.* may be unfamiliar to students and general readers. For these unfamiliar names, guides to pronunciation have been provided upon first mention of the names in the text. These guidelines do not purport to achieve the subtleties of the languages in question but will offer readers a rough equivalent of how English speakers may approximate the proper pronunciation.

Vowel Sounds

Symbol	Spelled (Pronounced)
a	answer (AN-suhr), laugh (laf), sample (SAM-puhl), that (that)
ah	father (FAH-thur), hospital (HAHS-pih-tuhl)
aw	awful (AW-fuhl), caught (kawt)
ay	blaze (blayz), fade (fayd), waiter (WAYT-ur), weigh (way)
eh	bed (behd), head (hehd), said (sehd)
ee	believe (bee-LEEV), cedar (SEE-dur), leader (LEED-ur), liter (LEE-tur)
ew	boot (bewt), lose (lewz)
i	buy (bi), height (hit), lie (li), surprise (sur-PRIZ)
ih	bitter (BIH-tur), pill (pihl)
o	cotton (KO-tuhn), hot (hot)
oh	below (bee-LOH), coat (koht), note (noht), wholesome (HOHL-suhm)
oo	good (good), look (look)
ow	couch (kowch), how (how)
oy	boy (boy), coin (koyn)
uh	about (uh-BOWT), butter (BUH-tuhr), enough (ee-NUHF), other (UH-thur)

Consonant Sounds

Symbol	Spelled (Pronounced)
ch	beach (beech), chimp (chihmp)
g	beg (behg), disguise (dihs-GIZ), get (geht)
j	digit (DIH-juht), edge (ehj), jet (jeht)
k	cat (kat), kitten (KIH-tuhn), hex (hehks)
s	cellar (SEHL-ur), save (sayv), scent (sehnt)
sh	champagne (sham-PAYN), issue (IH-shew), shop (shop)
ur	birth (burth), disturb (dihs-TURB), earth (urth), letter (LEH-tur)
y	useful (YEWS-fuhl), young (yuhng)
z	business (BIHZ-nehs), zest (zehst)
zh	vision (VIH-zhuhn)

COMPLETE LIST OF CONTENTS

VOLUME 1

Volume 2

LIST OF MAPS AND TABLES

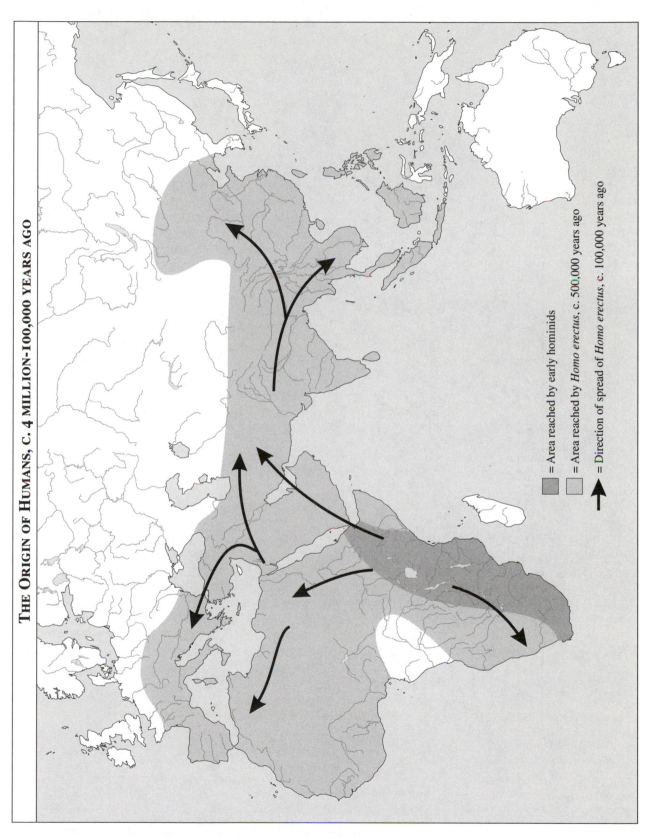

THE ORIGIN OF HUMANS, C. 4 MILLION-100,000 YEARS AGO

= Area reached by early hominids

= Area reached by *Homo erectus*, c. 500,000 years ago

= Direction of spread of *Homo erectus*, c. 100,000 years ago

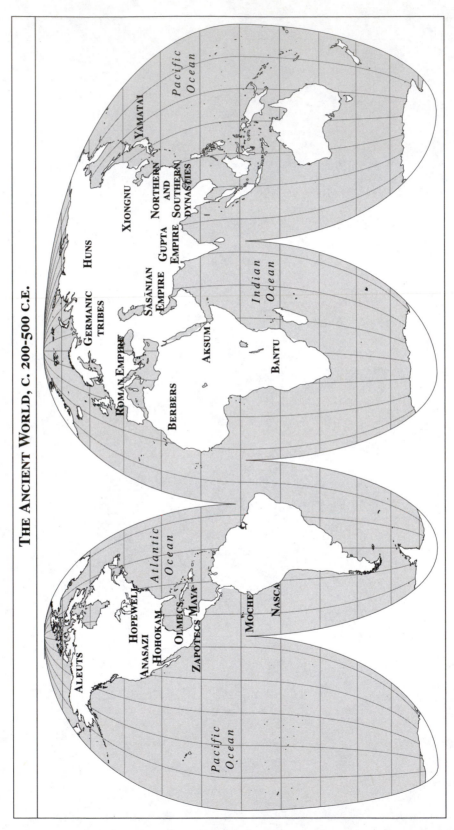

THE ANCIENT WORLD, C. 200-500 C.E.

ANCIENT NORTH AMERICA

Ipiutak

• Anangula

Norton   Onion
         Portage

ALEUTS

ARCTIC AND SUBARCTIC

PACIFIC COAST

Cape
Dorset

DORSET   Port
                              au Choix

Head-Smashed-In

Hoko River

CALIFORNIA

Casper

**GREAT
PLAINS**

Serpent   **RED
Mound   PAINT**

OLD
COPPER   • Osceola   Neville

**GREAT
BASIN**   Danger Cave   Meadowcroft

ANASAZI   • Mesa Verde   **EASTERN**   • Adena
                               HOPEWELL
               MOGOLLON
Canyon de   • Tularosa Cave   Koster   Indian Knoll
Chelly   • Bat Cave (Cochise)
HOHOKAM   Poverty Point   *WOODLAND*

*Pacific
Ocean*   *Atlantic
                                                    Ocean*

               Blackwater Draw   • Porter
               (Clovis)   Marksville

*Gulf

of

Mexico*

ZAPOTEC   **MAYA**
        OLMEC

• = Sites
Cultures indicated by **BOLD SMALL CAPS**

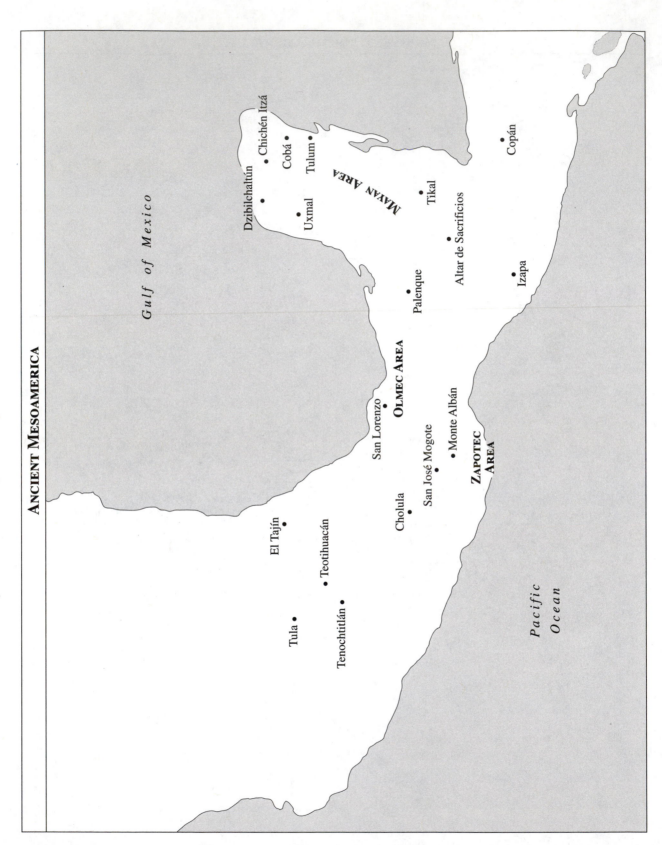

ANCIENT MESOAMERICA

Gulf of Mexico

Pacific Ocean

Tula •

Tenochtitlán •

Teotihuacán •

El Tajín •

Cholula •

San José Mogote •

San Lorenzo •

OLMEC AREA

Monte Albán •

ZAPOTEC AREA

Palenque •

MAYAN AREA

Dzibilchaltún •

Uxmal •

Cobá •

Chichén Itzá •

Tulum •

Tikal •

Altar de Sacrificios •

Izapa •

Copán •

ANCIENT SOUTH AMERICA

Valdivia

Moche

Chavín de Huántar

Recuay

Telarmachy Cave

El Paraíso
Pachacámac (Lima)

Paracas

Cahuachi (Nasca)

Lake Titicaca

Tiwanaku

Chinchorro

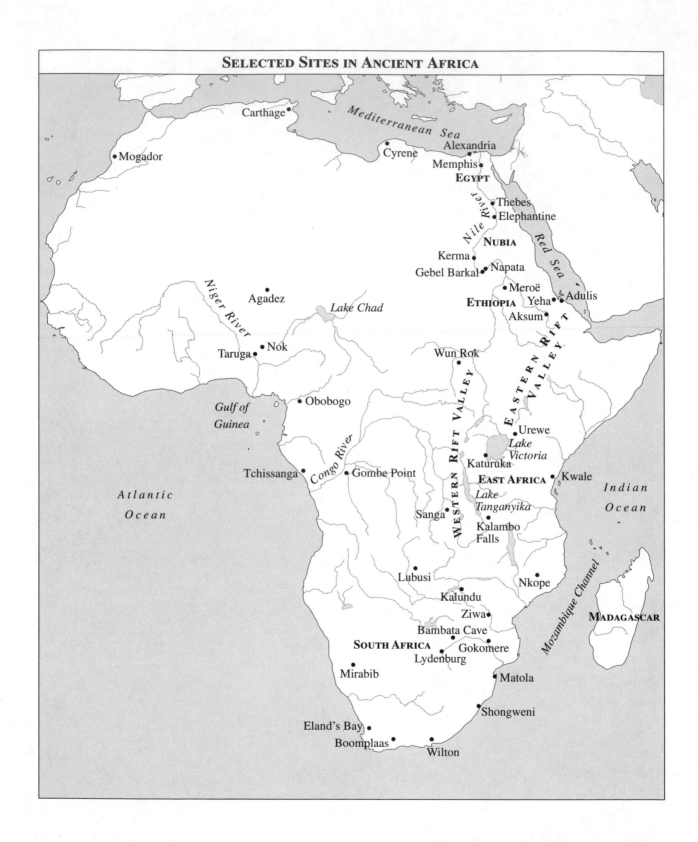

SELECTED SITES IN ANCIENT AFRICA

Mediterranean Sea

Carthage

Mogador

Cyrene

Alexandria

Memphis

EGYPT

Thebes

Elephantine

Nile River

NUBIA

Kerma

Gebel Barkal

Napata

Meroë

Red Sea

Adulis

ETHIOPIA

Yeha

Aksum

Niger River

Agadez

Lake Chad

Taruga

Nok

Wun Rok

EASTERN RIFT VALLEY

Obobogo

Gulf of Guinea

Congo River

WESTERN RIFT VALLEY

Urewe

Lake Victoria

Katuruka

EAST AFRICA

Kwale

Tchissanga

Gombe Point

Atlantic Ocean

Indian Ocean

Sanga

Lake Tanganyika

Kalambo Falls

Mozambique Channel

MADAGASCAR

Lubusi

Nkope

Kalundu

Ziwa

Bambata Cave

SOUTH AFRICA

Lydenburg

Gokomere

Mirabib

Matola

Shongweni

Eland's Bay

Boomplaas

Wilton

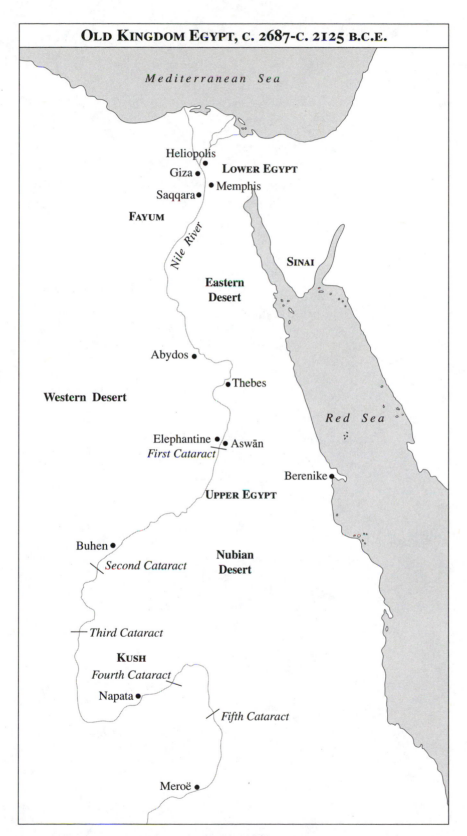

OLD KINGDOM EGYPT, C. 2687–C. 2125 B.C.E.

Mediterranean Sea

Heliopolis

Giza

LOWER EGYPT

Saqqara

Memphis

FAYUM

Nile River

SINAI

Eastern Desert

Western Desert

Abydos

Thebes

Red Sea

Elephantine

Aswān

First Cataract

UPPER EGYPT

Berenike

Buhen

Second Cataract

Nubian Desert

Third Cataract

KUSH

Fourth Cataract

Napata

Fifth Cataract

Meroë

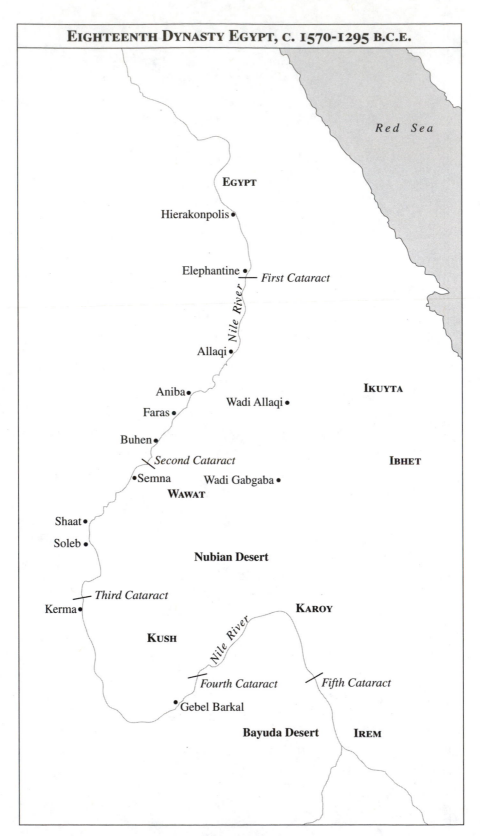

EIGHTEENTH DYNASTY EGYPT, C. 1570-1295 B.C.E.

Red Sea

EGYPT

Hierakonpolis •

Elephantine • — *First Cataract*

Nile River

Allaqi •

Aniba •   **IKUYTA**

Faras •   Wadi Allaqi •

Buhen •

     Second Cataract   **IBHET**

• Semna   Wadi Gabgaba •

WAWAT

Shaat •

Soleb •   **Nubian Desert**

— *Third Cataract*

Kerma •   **KAROY**

KUSH

Nile River

Fourth Cataract   *Fifth Cataract*

• Gebel Barkal

Bayuda Desert   **IREM**

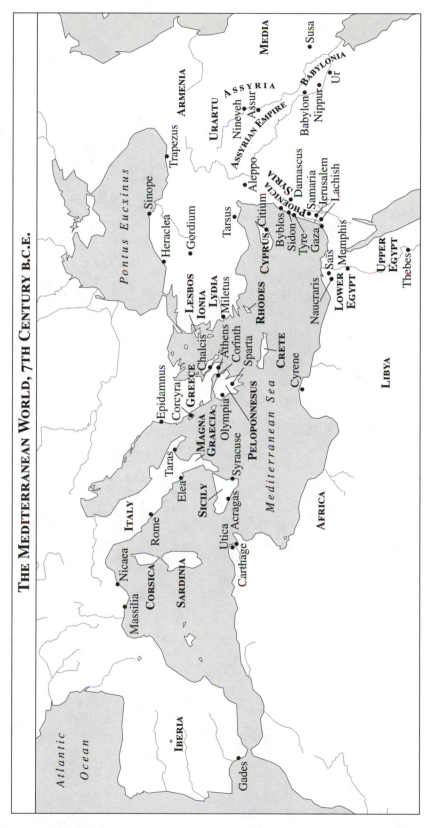

THE MEDITERRANEAN WORLD, 7TH CENTURY B.C.E.

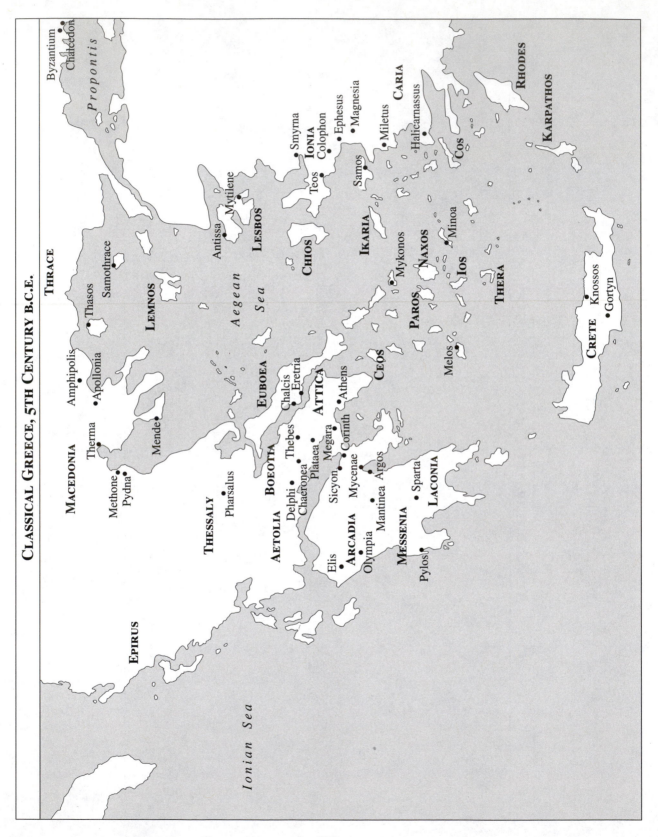

CLASSICAL GREECE, 5TH CENTURY B.C.E.

Ionian Sea

Aegean Sea

Propontis

EPIRUS

THRACE

Byzantium
Chalcedon

MACEDONIA
Amphipolis
Apollonia
Therma
Methone
Pydna
Mende

THESSALY
Pharsalus

Thasos
Samothrace

LEMNOS

Antissa
Mytilene
LESBOS

Smyrna
IONIA
Colophon
Ephesus
Magnesia
Teos

CHIOS

Miletus
CARIA
Halicarnassus

Samos
IKARIA

RHODES

KARPATHOS

Cos

Mykonos
NAXOS
Minoa
PAROS
Ios
THERA

CEOS
Melos

AETOLIA
BOEOTIA
Delphi
Thebes
Chaeronea
Chalcis
Eretria
EUBOEA
Plataea
ATTICA
Athens
Megara
Sicyon
Corinth
Mycenae
Argos
ARCADIA
Mantinea
Sparta
LACONIA
MESSENIA
Pylos
Elis
Olympia

CRETE
Knossos
Gortyn

xxx

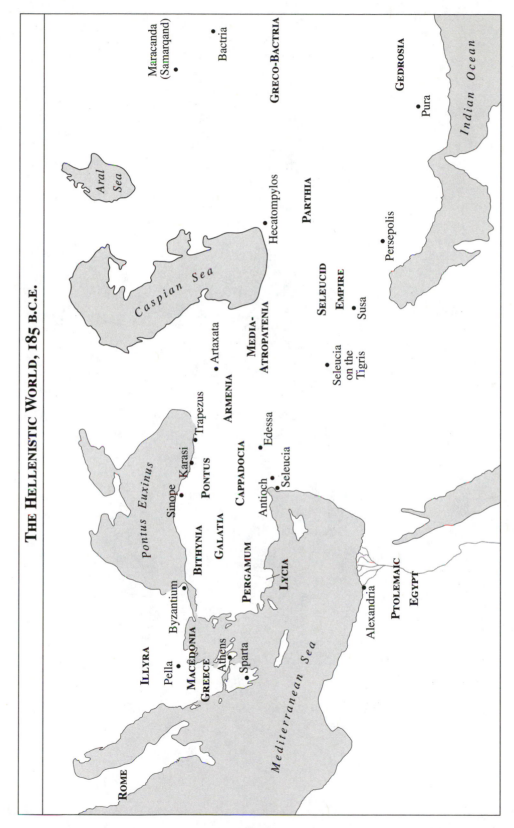

THE HELLENISTIC WORLD, 185 B.C.E.

ROME

ILLYRA

Pella

MACEDONIA

GREECE

Athens

Sparta

Byzantium

BITHYNIA

Pontus Euxinus

Sinope

Karasi

Trapezus

PONTUS

GALATIA

CAPPADOCIA

PERGAMUM

LYCIA

Antioch

Seleucia

Edessa

ARMENIA

Artaxata

MEDIA-
ATROPATENIA

Seleucia
on the
Tigris

SELEUCID
EMPIRE

Susa

PARTHIA

Hecatompylos

Persepolis

Caspian Sea

Aral
Sea

Maracanda
(Samarqand)

Bactria

GRECO-BACTRIA

GEDROSIA

Pura

Indian Ocean

Alexandria

PTOLEMAIC
EGYPT

Mediterranean Sea

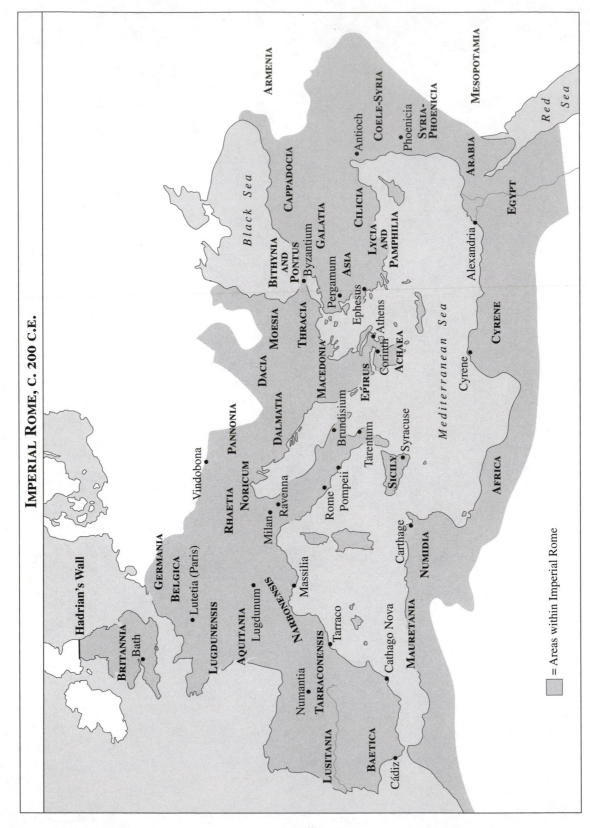

IMPERIAL ROME, C. 200 C.E.

□ = Areas within Imperial Rome

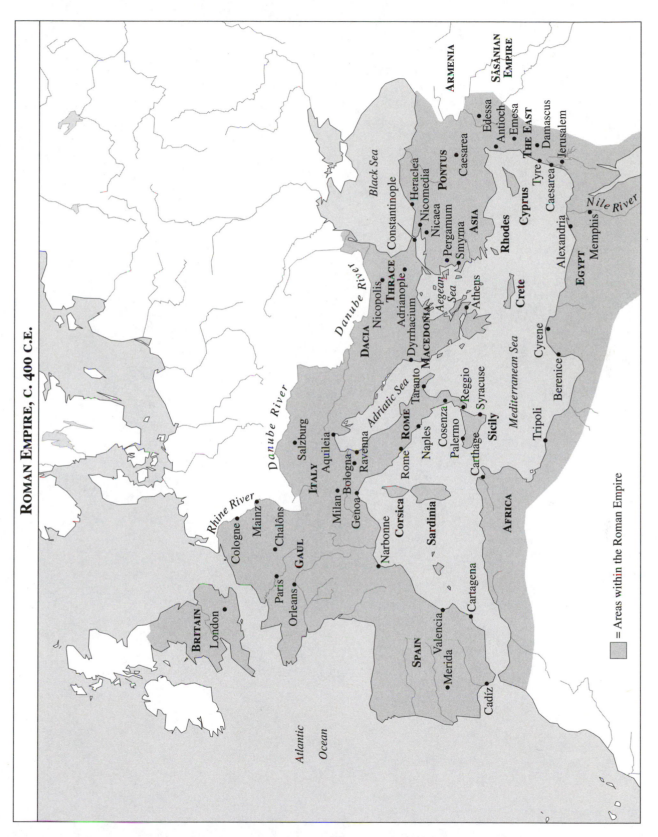

ROMAN EMPIRE, C. 400 C.E.

= Areas within the Roman Empire

Atlantic Ocean

BRITAIN
London

Rhine River

Cologne
Mainz
Chalôns
GAUL
Paris
Orleans

Narbonne
Corsica
SPAIN
Valencia
Merida
Cartagena
Cadiz
Sardinia

Salzburg
ITALY
Aquileia
Milan
Bologna
Genoa
Ravenna
ROME
Rome
Naples
Cosenza
Palermo
Sicily
Carthage
Syracuse
Reggio
Taranto
AFRICA
Tripoli

Danube River

DACIA
Nicopolis
Adrianople
THRACE
Dyrrhacium
MACEDONIA
Adriatic Sea
Athens
Aegean Sea

Black Sea

Constantinople
Heraclea
Nicomedia
Nicaea
Pergamum
Smyrna
PONTUS
Caesarea
ASIA

Mediterranean Sea

Cyrene
Berenice

Rhodes
Crete
CYPRUS
Caesarea

ARMENIA

SASANIAN EMPIRE

Edessa
Antioch
Emesa
Damascus
THE EAST
Tyre
Jerusalem

Nile River

EGYPT
Alexandria
Memphis

xxxiii

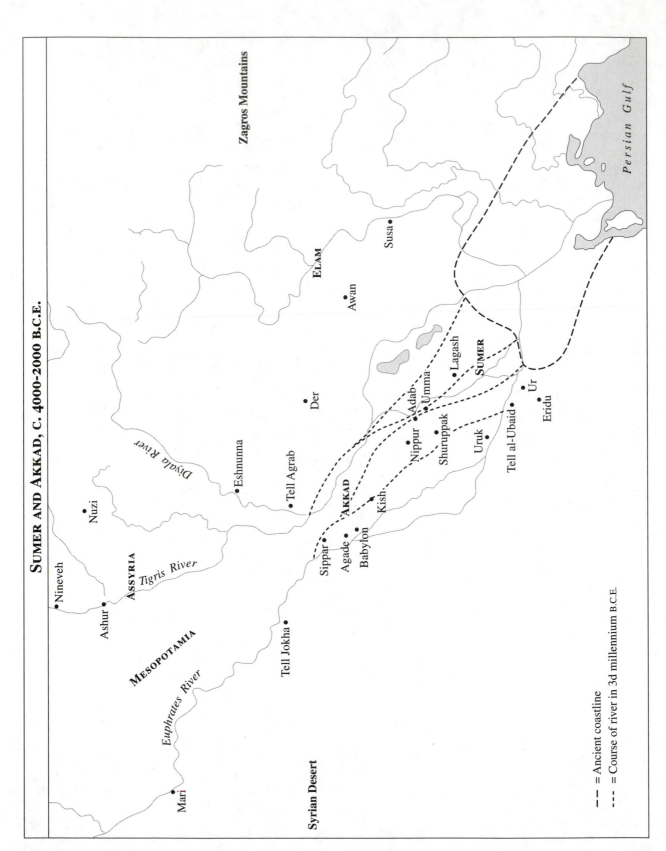

SUMER AND AKKAD, C. 4000–2000 B.C.E.

Zagros Mountains

Persian Gulf

Susa

ELAM

Awan

Der

SUMER

Lagash

Umma

Adab

Ur

Eridu

Tell al-Ubaid

Uruk

Shuruppak

Nippur

Kish

Babylon

Agade

AKKAD

Sippar

Eshnunna

Tell Agrab

Diyala River

Nuzi

ASSYRIA

Tigris River

Nineveh

Ashur

MESOPOTAMIA

Tell Jokha

Euphrates River

Syrian Desert

Mari

–– = Ancient coastline

--- = Course of river in 3d millennium B.C.E.

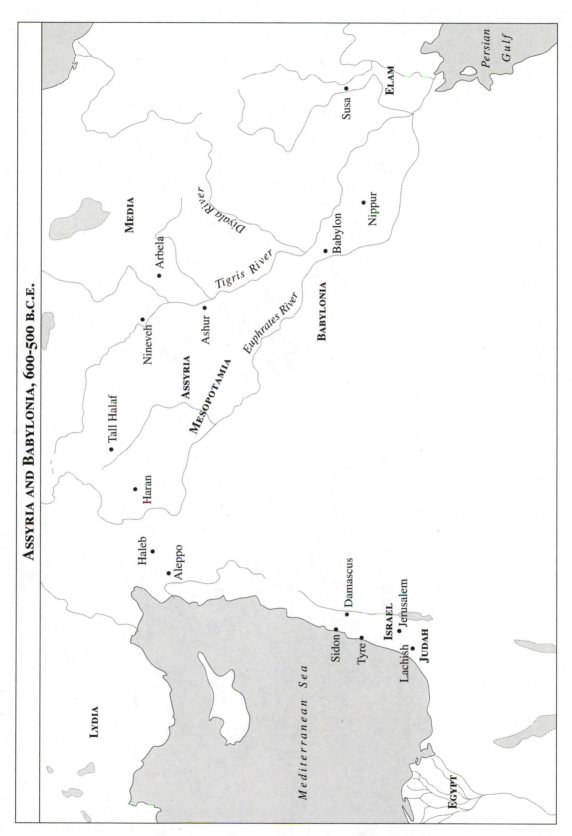

ASSYRIA AND BABYLONIA, 600–500 B.C.E.

LYDIA

Mediterranean Sea

EGYPT

Haleb
Aleppo

Damascus
Sidon
Tyre
ISRAEL
Jerusalem
Lachish
JUDAH

Haran

Tall Halaf

Nineveh
ASSYRIA
Ashur
MESOPOTAMIA
Euphrates River

Arbela
MEDIA

Tigris River

Diyala River

BABYLONIA
Babylon
Nippur

Susa
ELAM

Persian Gulf

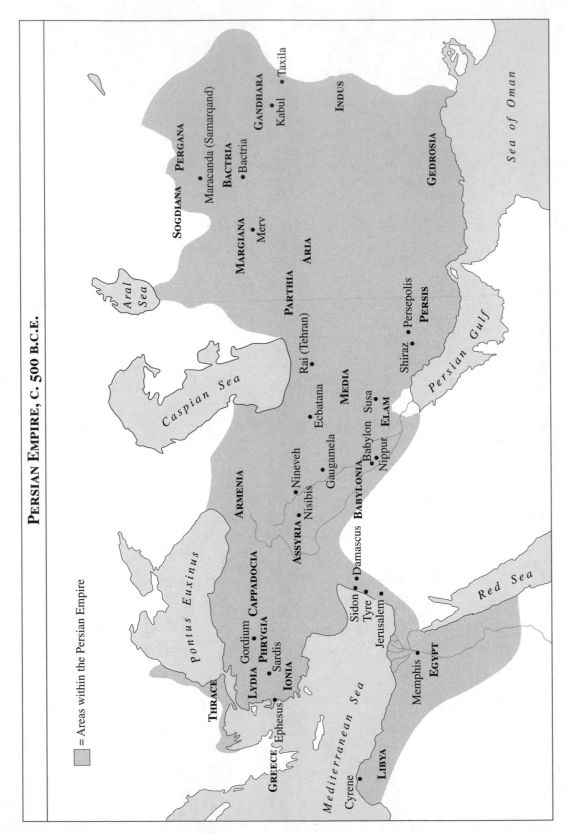

PERSIAN EMPIRE, C. 500 B.C.E.

= Areas within the Persian Empire

Aral Sea

Caspian Sea

Pontus Euxinus

Mediterranean Sea

Red Sea

Persian Gulf

Sea of Oman

SOGDIANA

PERGANA

Maracanda (Samarqand)

GANDHARA

Taxila

BACTRIA
• Bactria

Kabul

INDUS

GEDROSIA

MARGIANA
• Merv

ARIA

PARTHIA

PERSIS

Persepolis

Shiraz

Rai (Tehran)

MEDIA

Ecbatana

Susa

Babylon
Nippur

ELAM

Gaugamela

Nineveh

Nisibis

ARMENIA

ASSYRIA

CAPPADOCIA

Gordium

LYDIA
PHRYGIA

Sardis

IONIA

THRACE

Ephesus

GREECE

Damascus

Sidon
Tyre

Jerusalem

Memphis

EGYPT

LIBYA

Cyrene

BABYLONIA

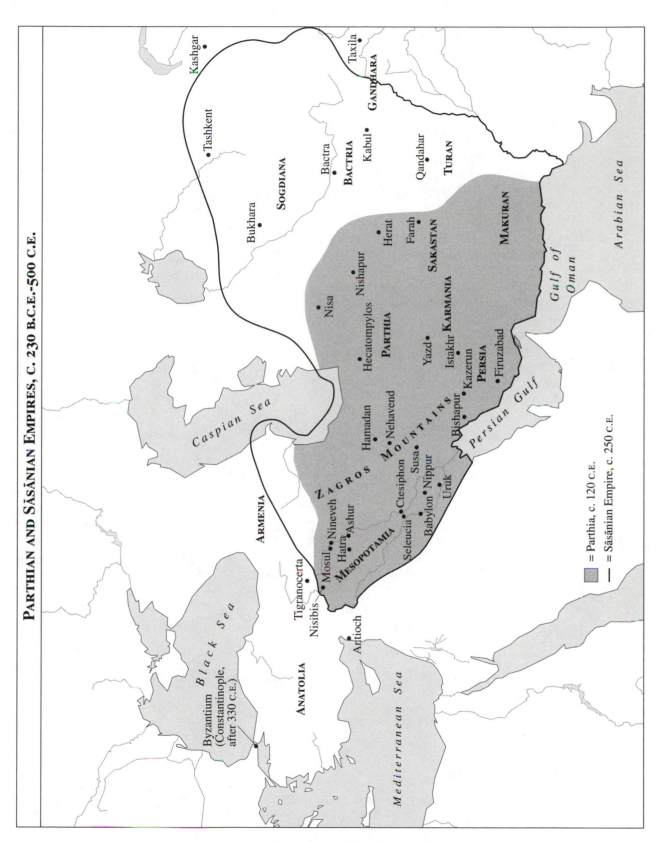

PARTHIAN AND SĀSĀNIAN EMPIRES, C. 230 B.C.E.–500 C.E.

Kashgar

Taxila

GANDHARA

Tashkent

Bactra

BACTRIA

Kabul

Qandahar

TURAN

SOGDIANA

Bukhara

MAKURAN

Herat

Farah

SAKASTAN

Nishapur

Nisa

Hecatompylos

PARTHIA

Yazd

Istakhr KARMANIA

Kazerun

PERSIA

Firuzabad

Arabian Sea

Gulf of Oman

Caspian Sea

Hamadan

Nehavend

ZAGROS MOUNTAINS

Ctesiphon

Susa

Bishapur

Persian Gulf

Seleucia

Babylon Nippur

Uruk

Mosul Nineveh

Hatra Ashur

MESOPOTAMIA

ARMENIA

Tigranocerta

Nisibis

Antioch

Black Sea

ANATOLIA

Byzantium
(Constantinople,
after 330 C.E.)

Mediterranean Sea

= Parthia, c. 120 C.E.

= Sāsānian Empire, c. 250 C.E.

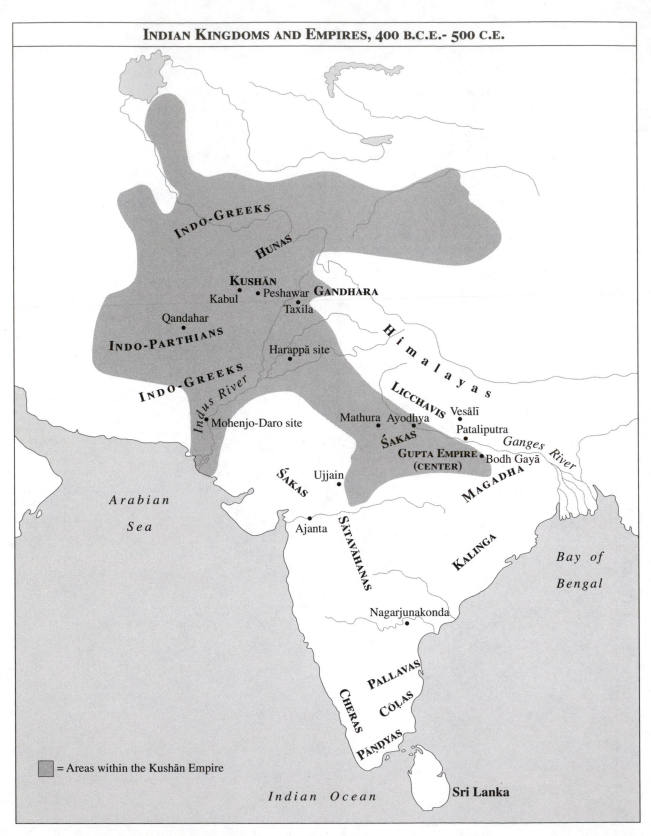

INDIAN KINGDOMS AND EMPIRES, 400 B.C.E.- 500 C.E.

INDO-GREEKS

HUNAS

KUSHĀN

Kabul • • Peshawar **GANDHARA**

Qandahar •   Taxila •

INDO-PARTHIANS

INDO-GREEKS

H i m a l a y a s

Harappā site •

Indus River

LICCHAVIS

• Vesālī

Mathura • • Ayodhya

• Mohenjo-Daro site

• Pataliputra

ŚAKAS

Ganges River

GUPTA EMPIRE
(CENTER) • Bodh Gayā

ŚAKAS
• Ujjain

MAGADHA

Arabian

Sea

Ajanta •

SĀTAVĀHANAS

KALINGA

Bay of

Bengal

Nagarjunakonda •

PALLAVAS

CHERAS **COḺAS**

PĀṆDYAS

= Areas within the Kushān Empire

Indian Ocean

Sri Lanka

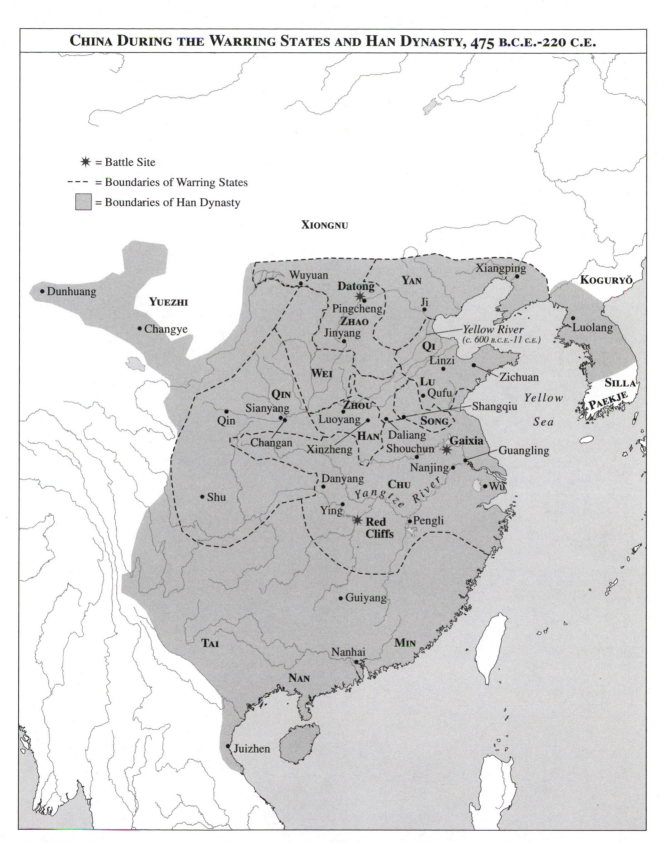

China During the Warring States and Han Dynasty, 475 B.C.E.–220 C.E.

✳ = Battle Site

- - - = Boundaries of Warring States

■ = Boundaries of Han Dynasty

XIONGNU

YUEZHI

Dunhuang

Changye

Wuyuan

Datong

Pingcheng

ZHAO

Jinyang

YAN

Ji

Xiangping

KOGURYŎ

Luolang

Yellow River
(c. 600 B.C.E.–11 C.E.)

QI

Linzi

Zichuan

SILLA

PAEKJE

WEI

QIN

Sianyang

Qin

Changan

LU

Qufu

ZHOU

Luoyang

HAN

Xinzheng

SONG

Shangqiu

Daliang

Shouchun

Gaixia

Guangling

Yellow
Sea

Shu

Danyang

Ying

Red
Cliffs

CHU

Nanjing

Wu

Pengli

Yangtze River

Guiyang

TAI

Nanhai

MIN

NAN

Juizhen

The Ancient World

Prehistory - 476 C.E.

AARON
Egypt-born Hebrew priest

According to biblical tradition, Aaron, with his brother Moses, led the Hebrews out of Egypt. During the forty years they wandered in the desert, Aaron served as high priest, teacher, and peacekeeper.

BORN: c. 1395 B.C.E.; Egypt
DIED: c. 1272 B.C.E.; Mount Hor, Edom (now in Jordan)
ALSO KNOWN AS: Aharon
AREA OF ACHIEVEMENT: Religion

EARLY LIFE

Aaron (A-ruhn) remains a figure surrounded by mystery and seeming contradiction. Even his name is questioned. Is it of Egyptian origin? Does it derive from the Hebrew word for the ark of the covenant (*arōn*) located in the Holy of Holies, that inner sanctum closed to all but the high priest? Or is it the phrase his mother, Jochebed, uttered at his birth as she lamented bearing a son: "A, harōn" (woe, alas)? (Only a few months before Aaron's birth, Pharaoh had issued his decree condemning to death all male children born to the Hebrews in Egypt.)

His parents seem to have made no effort to hide Aaron, as they would three years later with his brother, Moses, when he was born. Indeed, tradition maintains that Aaron's father, Amram, was one of Pharaoh's councillors and that the boy himself grew up in the palace before filling his father's post. Aaron was also emerging as a leader of his enslaved people, urging them to remain faithful to the God of Abraham and to hope for delivery from bondage. His marriage to Elisheba, daughter of Amminadab, allied Aaron with a distinguished family from the powerful tribe of Judah—his brother-in-law, Nahshon, was that tribe's leader—and so enhanced his already prominent position.

Consequently, when God instructed Moses to return from his self-imposed exile in Midian and lead the Jews out of Egypt, Moses urged that Aaron be assigned this task instead. Here, after all, was someone familiar with the Egyptian court and trusted by his own people, whereas Moses, having lived in another country for forty years, was a stranger. Moreover, Moses regarded his brother as the better orator. Although Moses finally accepted the primary responsibility, Aaron, too, would play a large role in the Exodus.

LIFE'S WORK

Just as God appeared to Moses and told him to return to Egypt, so he informed Aaron of his brother's imminent return and instructed him to meet Moses at the border of Midian. Together they appeared before the leaders of the Hebrews, Aaron speaking and performing signs to establish the legitimacy of their mission. Together they also appeared before Pharaoh to demand the release of the Jews. Once again, Aaron offered a sign of their divine ministry: He threw his rod onto the floor of the palace, and the stick turned into a snake. Pharaoh's magicians duplicated this feat, but Aaron bested them when his rod devoured theirs. Pharaoh remained unmoved, though, and the ten plagues began with Aaron's stretching his hand over the waters of Egypt, turning them to blood. Aaron would bring on the next two plagues—frogs and lice—as well, and with Moses he created the sixth, boils.

After the Exodus, the eighty-three-year-old Aaron seems to have become one of the triumvirate of leaders, sharing power with Moses and Hur. When the Amalekites attacked the Hebrews at Rephidim, Aaron stood on one side of Moses, with Hur on the other, to hold up Moses's hands and so ensure the victory for Joshua and his troops. When Moses ascended Mount Sinai to receive the Ten Commandments, Aaron and Hur remained behind to govern.

The strangest episode of Aaron's life occurred about this time. Moses's lengthy absence—he would be gone forty days—persuaded the Hebrews that their leader was dead, so they demanded an idol to replace him. Hur refused to comply and was killed, as were the elders opposing this wish. Alone and unsupported, Aaron instructed the people to bring him all of their gold. Was he hoping that they would be unwilling to part with their treasure? If so, he was disappointed, for they readily complied. According to the account in certain rabbinical commentaries, he cast the gold into a furnace, apparently intending only to melt it, yet a golden calf emerged, seemingly of itself. The Hebrews responded by acclaiming the calf as the god that had led them out of Egypt. Perhaps to delay any worship of this idol, Aaron declared that the next day would be a festival for the graven image; by the time Moses returned, though, the celebration had already begun.

According to some accounts, only the intervention of Moses saved Aaron's life from divine retribution. Shortly afterward, however, Aaron was designated high priest. Was he being rewarded for his efforts to delay the idolatrous worship? Might the golden calf, in fact, have represented a deity worshiped by the Hebrews in Egypt? Was Aaron's role in its creation the cause of his elevation to the priesthood? In later Jewish worship, the temple altar had two horns, and after the division of Israel into two kingdoms, Jeroboam erected golden calves at Bethel and Dan to compete with the Temple in Jerusalem. The choice of this animal suggests lingering loyalty to a bull as deity, or at least as representative of the deity.

The consecration of Aaron to the priesthood, whatever its cause, divorced religious leadership from the secular and placed priests under the power of the latter. God was to appear only to Moses in the desert, never to the high priest, and it was Moses who dictated the laws and rituals that Aaron and his sons were to follow. This subordination would become even more pronounced as political power passed from the tribe of Levi (to which both Aaron and Moses belonged) to Benjamin and then Judah after the conquest of Canaan and the establishment of the monarchy. That elevation to the post of high priest removed Aaron from political leadership did not escape his notice; with Miriam, his older sister, Aaron protested against Moses's emergence as sole leader. For her criticism, Miriam was afflicted with leprosy for seven days. Aaron escaped with a divine rebuke.

A more serious challenge came from Korah, a kinsman of Moses and Aaron. Organizing many of the tribal leaders, he attacked the brothers for assuming undue power, but this rebellion was quickly suppressed by an earthquake that destroyed the ringleaders and a plague that killed more than fourteen thousand others. The toll would have been higher had Aaron not taken his censer and arrested the plague by standing between the living and the dead.

To reinforce the message that Aaron was the divine choice for the priesthood, Moses instructed each tribal elder to bring his staff to the tabernacle (the tent of worship), and Aaron placed his own among them. The next morning they found that Aaron's staff had flowered and had produced almonds. The others removed their rods, while Aaron's remained in the tent as a warning against further rebellions.

Despite such challenges, it is clear that Aaron was popular—more popular, in fact, than the sometimes stern

Aaron. (Library of Congress)

and irascible Moses. Aaron must have been an impressive figure in the camp—his flowing white beard, his priestly garments, and the breastplate of twelve precious stones commanding reverence. He was not only respected but also loved. The famous Jewish rabbi Hillel urged his students to imitate Aaron, "loving peace and pursuing peace, loving one's fellow men and bringing them nigh to the Torah."

Freed from the role of judge and lawgiver, Aaron could devote himself to teaching and making peace. Legend says that he would go from tent to tent to instruct those unfamiliar with the law. In a similar way, when he heard that two people had quarreled, he would go to one and say, "The person you argued with deeply regrets his hasty words and actions and seeks your forgiveness." Then he would go to the other party and say the same thing, thereby effecting a reconciliation. He was famous for reuniting feuding husbands and wives, who generally named their next child for him. The eighty thousand Hebrews bearing the name of Aaron attest to his success as a marriage counselor.

Throughout the forty years that the Jews wandered in the desert, Aaron served as high priest, assisted by his two younger sons, Eleazar and Ithamar; his two older sons, Nadab and Avihu, had died when they offered "strange fire"—apparently some form of idolatry—in the sacred tent. Like his brother Moses and his sister Miriam, Aaron was not, however, destined to enter the Promised Land.

According to certain Jewish commentaries, it was, in fact, the death of Miriam at the beginning of the fortieth year of wandering that indirectly led to the punishment and death of both her brothers. Tradition holds that during Miriam's life a well had followed the Hebrews from camp to camp; as soon as she died, the well vanished. Lacking water at Meribah in the Wilderness of Zin, the Hebrews criticized Moses and Aaron for leading them into a wasteland. God commanded the two men to assemble the people and then speak to a rock, which would bring forth water. Distracted and angered by the threats and complaints of the people, Moses struck the rock instead, thus disobeying the divine order and diminishing the greatness of the miracle. For this failing, both men were condemned to die outside Canaan.

Aaron's death followed Miriam's by four months. Unwilling to reveal to his brother that God had decreed Aaron's death, Moses summoned Aaron and Eleazar to accompany him up Mount Hor. There they found a cave. Aaron removed his priestly garments and gave them to his son; the high priest then entered the cave, lay down on a couch, and died—as the story goes—by a kiss from the Shekinah, the Holy Spirit.

The people's reaction to Aaron's disappearance again reveals his popularity. When Moses and Eleazar returned, the Hebrews suspected that they had murdered Aaron out of jealousy. Tradition maintains that to save the two from being stoned, God showed Aaron lying dead in the cave, proving that he had died naturally, not violently. For thirty days all Israel mourned Aaron's passing; when Moses died eight months later the sense of loss was not so universally shared.

SIGNIFICANCE

As the first high priest and founder of the priestly caste, Aaron has served as the model of the religious leader. Christian theologians saw him as the prototype of Jesus Christ, differing only in the fact that Aaron sacrificed animals, whereas Christ offered himself to be killed. Though Aaron is less popular as an artistic subject than Moses, the French painter Jean Fouquet and the English painter John Everett Millais produced idealized portraits of him.

Nineteenth and twentieth century biblical scholars have been less kind, questioning his priestly role and, indeed, challenging his very existence. Whether he was the creation of some late biblical redactor or indeed Moses's brother, whom God chose to preside over the holy tabernacle, Aaron has assumed an important role in the Judeo-Christian tradition and has become inextricably associated with the early development of the Jewish religion.

—*Joseph Rosenblum*

FURTHER READING

Aberbach, Moses, and Leivy Smolar. "Aaron, Jeroboam, and the Golden Calves." *Journal of Biblical Literature* 86 (1967): 129-140. Points out the similarities between the biblical description of Aaron and that of Jeroboam and suggests that either the latter consciously imitated the former in the construction of the golden calves at Bethel and Dan or the story in Exodus was written by members of a non-Aaronite priesthood in Jerusalem to discredit the northern kingdom. Offers a careful examination of Aaron's role in the creation of the golden calf.

Ginzberg, Louis. *The Legends of the Jews*. 1909-1938. Reprint. Translated by Henrietta Szold. 7 vols. Baltimore: The Johns Hopkins University Press, 1998. Draws together biblical, Talmudic, and post-Talmudic sources to create a coherent narrative of Jewish history from the Creation to the time of Esther. Aaron receives extensive coverage in volumes 2 and 3, which treat life in Egypt, the Exodus, and the wanderings in the desert.

Kaufman, Yehezekel. *The Religion of Israel, from Its Beginnings to the Babylonian Exile*. Reprint. Translated by Moshe Greenberg. New York: Schocken Books, 1972. Originally published in eight volumes in Hebrew between 1937 and 1956. The English version discusses the growth of Judaism and, inter alia, examines the role that Aaron and the priesthood played in the process.

Meek, Theophile James. 1936. Reprint. *Hebrew Origins*. New York: Harper, 1960. In the fourth chapter of this work, Meek discusses the rise of the Jewish priesthood. Challenging the orthodox religious view, Meek maintains that Aaron "is clearly a supernumerary who was later introduced into the [biblical] narrative as Israelite and Judaean sagas became fused with the union of the two people."

Van Bema, David, and Emily Mitchell. "In Search of Moses." *Time* 152, no. 24 (December 14, 1998). Seeks to identify the historical Moses from an archaeological perspective; discussion includes evidence of Aaron.

SEE ALSO: Abraham; David; Moses; Solomon.
RELATED ARTICLES in *Great Events from History: The Ancient World*: c. 1280 B.C.E., Israelite Exodus from Egypt; c. 1000 B.C.E., Establishment of the United Kingdom of Israel; c. 966 B.C.E., Building of the Temple of Jerusalem; c. 950 B.C.E., Composition of the Book of Genesis; c. 922 B.C.E., Establishment of the Kingdom of Israel.

ABRAHAM
Chaldean-born settler of the land of Canaan

Abraham occupies an important place in the history of Judaism, Christianity, and Islam. According to Hebrew tradition and biblical record, he is the ancient ancestor of the people of Israel to whom God first promised territory, nationhood, and spiritual blessing. In the Qur'an, he is one of the six prophets who received God's law.

BORN: c. 2050 B.C.E.; Ur, Chaldea (now Muqaiyir, Iraq)
DIED: c. 1950 B.C.E.; Kirjath-Arba, Canaan (now Hebron, West Bank, Palestine)
ALSO KNOWN AS: Abram
AREA OF ACHIEVEMENT: Religion

EARLY LIFE
The only historical record of the life of Abraham (AY-bruh-ham) is found in the Pentateuch, the first five books of the Old Testament, one of the two divisions of the Bible whose composition is traditionally attributed to Moses. The full story of Abraham's life is contained in Genesis 11:27-25:11, although there are references to Abraham's life scattered throughout the rest of the Bible. The dating of Abraham's birth and early life is primarily informed guesswork, but archaeological consensus is that Abraham was born sometime around the twentieth century B.C.E. His father is identified as Terah in the biblical genealogy (Genesis 11:27). Evidently, Terah was a wealthy man who owned property and livestock and who worshiped the pagan gods of Chaldea. Chaldea, the ancient name for Babylonia, was a center of advanced culture and commerce in antiquity, and it is quite likely that Abraham was a highly educated, cosmopolitan citizen of this society, himself no doubt wealthy. Some archaeologists contend that it is possible that Abraham left written records of his journey to the ancient Near East that were incorporated into the Pentateuch. Most modern scholars accept the substantial historicity of these narratives.

The biblical record introduces Abraham as "Abram," which means "father" in Hebrew; later in the narrative, Abram is renamed as the better known "Abraham," which means "father of many." Abram was called by God to leave his father's house in Ur to journey to a land that God promises to him and his descendants. There is no indication in the narrative that Abram had been chosen for any particular merit or religious devotion, though later Old and New Testament writings present him as the archetypal man of faith, who serves as an example to all of the power of belief in God's sovereignty. Accompanying him on the journey were his wife, Sarah, and nephew Lot and their families.

Most startling in this sequence of events is Abraham's willingness to abandon the pagan deities of his family to embrace a seemingly new God—and thus become a declared monotheist in a decidedly polytheistic and pagan antiquity. The next episodes reported in the life of Abram trace his growing acceptance of this unique belief and center on his journey to Canaan, the land promised to him. His path takes him and his traveling companions through Egypt and the surrounding nations. In Egypt, Abram fears that his beautiful wife will be taken from him, so he claims that she is his sister and thus attempts to deceive Pharaoh and his princes. When God reveals her true identity to the Egyptian monarch, Pharaoh orders Abram and his entourage to leave. On leaving Egypt, Abram and his nephew decide to go their separate ways, Lot choosing the fertile land of Sodom and Gomorrah for settlement and Abram the northern country of Hebron. These choices become fateful in the lineage of both men.

LIFE'S WORK
The life of Abraham as it unfolds in the book of Genesis encompasses the fulfillment of the promises God had announced to him before he left Ur. Important in the light of

the birth of modern Israel is the fact that the land promised to Abraham is quite explicitly identified in the biblical record: God promises Abraham and his descendants possession of the whole land from the Euphrates River southwestward, an area, in fact, larger than the land area occupied by Israel since World War II.

The three most important episodes recounted in Genesis involve Abraham's attempt to secure an heir to receive the inheritance of God's promises, the institution of the covenant between God and Abraham sealed with the act of circumcision, and the judgment and destruction of the cities of Sodom and Gomorrah—Lot's new homeland—because of their residents' rampant rebellion and decadence. It is in these episodes that the character of Abraham as a man of faith as well as of action is established and becomes the pattern for later biblical and traditional portraits of his heroism and trust.

Soon after he and Lot part company, Abram is called on to rescue Lot; in so doing he proves himself both a good military strategist and also a devout, unselfish believer. Lot has found himself the captive of rival kings who have plundered the cities of Sodom and Gomorrah. Abram raises an army and, in saving Lot, also manages to recover all of his lost possessions and captured kinsmen. In returning from these exploits, Abram encounters the mysterious King of Salem, Melchizadek, who pronounces a blessing on Abram for his faith and his canny defeat of the treacherous armies in the land about him. Melchizadek is also a priest of "the God Most High," or "Yahweh," the same God who has called Abraham out of Ur to a special blessing. Abram pays a tithe to Melchizadek, and, when the King of Salem praises him, Abram defers the praise to God, who had blessed him with victory.

The promises to Abraham in Genesis 12 were intended to foreshadow the tapestry of events in his life, and in Genesis 15 God reiterates them as Abram continues his quest for the land. He becomes skeptical and impatient of the likelihood of their fulfillment, however, given that he is still childless because of Sarah's barrenness. Nevertheless, God renews his promise to Abram that his offspring will be as numerous as the stars in the sky and that the land and nation promised to him will indeed come to his descendants if he will only continue to trust. Thereafter, Abram is called Abraham by God, indicating the surety of His promises that he will be the father of many nations. Reluctant to wait for God's timing, Abraham proceeds to father a son by Hagar, his maidservant. This son, named Ishmael, is rejected by God; Abraham is instead exhorted to await the rightful heir with patience and confidence. In Genesis 17, the covenant between God and Abraham is proclaimed once more, and God asks Abraham and all the males of his household to be circumcised as a sign of their commitment to the covenant. The act of circumcision is ever after a peculiar sign of God's presence with the Hebrew people, not merely a hygienic practice but a religious symbol of dramatic proportion to every Hebrew family of God's blessing as well.

In the midst of Abraham's tribulations, he receives word that Lot's city Sodom will be destroyed along with Gomorrah because of its wickedness. In a famous conversation, Abraham bargains with God over the city, pleading with Him to spare the cities if He can find even ten righteous men. He cannot, and the cities are destroyed, with Lot and his family spared. On their way out of the destruc-

Abraham. (Library of Congress)

tion, however, Lot's wife—against the direct command of God—looks back at the fallen cities and is turned into a pillar of salt.

Because of their faith and righteousness, Abraham and Sarah are blessed with the birth of a son, Isaac—whose name meant "laughter," a reference to Sarah's incredulity at becoming pregnant at the age of one hundred. Some years later, Abraham faces the final test of faith in his life when God calls on him to sacrifice his son. Obedient to the end, Abraham and Isaac make the long trek to an altar far from their camp where Abraham once sacrificed animals. As he prepares to offer his son, he ties Isaac down and raises his knife, about to end the boy's life. Just before the knife is plunged into Abraham's only heir, God calls on Abraham to stop, for his faith has been shown to be full and unyielding. Because of his obedient heart, God promises him once more that he will have descendants as numerous as the grains of sand at the seashore.

Abraham eventually outlives Sarah and is blessed to see Isaac's marriage to Rebekah. Isaac and Rebekah later become the parents of Jacob and Esau, and the historical saga of Israel's development as a nation under the governance of God is initiated, a fulfillment of a divine promise to the itinerant man from Ur.

SIGNIFICANCE

Abraham occupies a unique place in the three major monotheistic traditions that have emerged as the world's dominant religions. For the Jews, it is difficult to overestimate the impact of the life of Abraham on Hebrew culture both in the ancient and medieval world and in the modern world. His acceptance of belief in one, true God, and its implications, sets him apart in the history of religions common to his time and place. It is the name of this God (Yahweh) that Moses, the champion of the Hebrews' flight from Egyptian captivity, invokes in confronting Pharaoh and in leading his people from bondage. Further, the promises made by the God of the Old Testament to Abraham have remained a part of the political and social history of the land of Israel even to this day and have played an essential part in the formation of modern Israel after World War II. To be a Jew is to trace one's ancestry back to Abraham and his sons, Isaac and Jacob. To adherents of Judaism, Abraham is the quintessential man of success, faith, and loyalty, whose stature overshadows nearly every other ancient Hebrew notable except Moses.

Abraham's character as a man of trust and perseverance has heavily influenced both Christianity and Islam to the extent that both faiths regard the biblical record of Abraham as the starting point for their own systems of doctrine. In the Qur'an, for example, Abraham (known as Ibrahim) is one of six major prophets who received the law of God, and he receives more mentions than any other prophet except Moses. Jesus Christ, according to the New Testament, claimed to be a descendant of Abraham—basing his teaching on the authority that this heritage bestowed on him—while at the same time claiming that his own life, as the eternal Son of God, is in fulfillment of God's promise to Abraham that He would bless all nations through him and his descendants. Paul, the Christian convert who wrote most of the letters of the New Testament, cites Abraham as the man who exemplifies commitment and truth for Christianity, a man who was counted "righteous" not because of his works but because of his faith. Muḥammad, the prophet of Islam, claimed Abraham as his forerunner as well, proclaiming that he and his message stood in the same historical and intellectual genealogy as that of Abraham.

The story of Abraham's willingness to sacrifice his own son in response to the call of God has long interested artists and storytellers. In the modern age, it has come to be emblematic of the piercing moment of destiny and decision making in an individual's life when he or she must make a choice that will set the pattern for the rest of his or her life. Abraham thus comes to represent to Jew and non-Jew alike the epitome of the "righteous man." His covenant with God and his faithfulness animate inhabitants of both Western and Eastern cultures in their quest for security and hope in a troubled world.

—Bruce L. Edwards

FURTHER READING

Albright, William Foxwell. *The Archaeology of Palestine.* 1932. Reprint. Gloucester, Mass.: Peter Smith, 1971. A standard work on the archaeology of the ancient world that remains a comprehensive and informed overview of the historical data gleaned from the Middle East. Provides a sense of the world from which Abraham came and the one to which he traveled.

Alexander, David, and Pat Alexander, eds. *Eerdmans' Handbook to the Bible.* Grand Rapids, Mich.: Wm. B. Eerdmans, 1987. A comprehensive handbook to biblical history and geography, with helpful charts and maps that trace Abraham's journey and illuminate the specific episodes in his life drawn from the biblical text.

Bright, John. *A History of Israel.* 4th ed. Louisville, Ky.: Westminster Press, 2000. A thorough and compelling nontheological treatment of the history of Israel in print. Includes sections on the world of the patriarchs, ancient Chaldea, Egypt, and Israel that enlighten the story of Abraham and sustain the interest of both the common reader and the scholar with helpful anecdotal commentary on life in ancient times.

Feiler, Bruce S. *Abraham: A Journey to the Heart of the Three Faiths*. New York: W. Morrow, 2002. This biography seeks to show its subject as he is portrayed in the teachings of the three great Abramaic faiths: Judaism, Christianity, and Islam. The first half of the book discusses the Qur'an and the Bible's narratives regarding Abraham, his call to monotheism, and his sons Isaac and Ishmael. The second half examines each religious tradition and how the Abraham narratives relate to contemporary religious and political conflicts.

Klinghoffer, David. *The Discovery of God: Abraham and the Birth of Monotheism*. New York: Doubleday, 2003. Biography chronicles Abraham's early years and his travels as preacher throughout the Middle East. Klinghoffer describes the many extant sites of events in the life of Abraham and depicts what they were like in ancient times; evoking details of the polytheistic culture, he shows how Abraham challenged the most fundamental beliefs of his contemporaries.

Schultz, Samuel J. *The Old Testament Speaks*. 4th ed. New York: Harper and Row, 1990. Written for the lay reader, this volume presents an objective, historical analysis of the lives of the patriarchs—including a major section on Abraham—and other characters in the evolution of ancient Israel and suggests their relevance to the study of both Christianity and Islam.

Thompson, J. A. *Handbook to Life in Bible Times*. Downers Grove, Ill.: Inter-Varsity Press, 1986. A colorful, lavishly illustrated reference tool with key sections on the domestic life, travel, family customs, and cultural preoccupations of the biblical world. This work illuminates the life and times of a person living in the twentieth century B.C.E. and thus is a helpful contextualizing volume for a study of Abraham.

SEE ALSO: Aaron; David; Jesus; Moses; Saint Paul; Solomon.

RELATED ARTICLES in *Great Events from History: The Ancient World*: c. 1280 B.C.E., Israelite Exodus from Egypt; c. 1000 B.C.E., Establishment of the United Kingdom of Israel; c. 966 B.C.E., Building of the Temple of Jerusalem; c. 950 B.C.E., Composition of the Book of Genesis; c. 922 B.C.E., Establishment of the Kingdom of Israel.

AESCHYLUS
Greek playwright

Aeschylus's dramaturgy marks a major stage in the development of Western theater, especially tragedy.

BORN: 525-524 B.C.E.; Eleusis, Greece
DIED: 456-455 B.C.E.; Gela, Sicily (now in Italy)
AREA OF ACHIEVEMENT: Literature

EARLY LIFE

Knowledge of the life of Aeschylus (EHS-kuh-luhs) is limited by minimal and unreliable sources. A Hellenistic biography surviving in the manuscript tradition of Aeschylus's plays is filled with ancient gossip, conjecture, and elaboration. The only extant portraits of the dramatist are probably not authentic.

Aeschylus was born about 525-524 B.C.E. in Eleusis, an Attic town about fourteen miles northwest of Athens. His father, Euphorion, a eupatrid, or hereditary aristocrat, had several children: at least two other sons, Cynegirus and Ameinias, and a daughter whose name is not recorded.

As the son of a eupatrid, Aeschylus belonged to one of the ancient and powerful landed families who had controlled Greece for generations but whose political power deteriorated in Aeschylus's lifetime, especially in Attica. Aeschylus's birthplace was an ancient city that had retained a sense of local pride despite its incorporation into the city-state of Athens many years before. While it is uncertain whether Aeschylus was ever initiated into the famous cult of Demeter at Eleusis, he certainly grew up within its shadow. Later in life, Aeschylus is said to have been prosecuted for revealing a mystery of Demeter in one of his plays but to have been exonerated on the grounds that he had done so unwittingly.

The young Aeschylus, benefiting from the wealth and prestige of his family, undoubtedly received a good education founded on the poetry of Homer. With such learning, Aeschylus developed a strong sense of a eupatrid's civic responsibility and authority and was exposed to the

traditional poetry, myths, and music on which his tragedies were later based.

If ancient tradition can be trusted, Aeschylus began
composing plays as a teenager. His early dramatic career
is poorly documented. Sometime between 499 and 496,
he entered the Athenian dramatic competition at the
Greater Dionysia with an unknown group of plays but did
not receive first prize. There is no record of how many
contests he entered before his first victory in 484, again
with unknown plays.

As an Athenian citizen, the young Aeschylus lived
through some of the most exciting years in that city's
history. In the tightly knit aristocratic society of late
sixth century Athens, Aeschylus would have observed at
first hand the turmoil associated with the murder of the
Athenian prince Hipparchus in 514, the expulsion of
Hipparchus's brother Hippias in 510, and the constitutional reforms of democratic Cleisthenes in 508. The
progression from tyranny to democracy in Athens inevitably meant less power for the eupatrid class. While the
political position of Aeschylus and his family in this period is uncertain, these events undoubtedly encouraged
the cautious conservatism that Aeschylus exhibited in
later years.

The young playwright was also a soldier. In the first
decade of the fifth century, the Persian Empire ruthlessly
suppressed a revolt by Ionian Greek cities along the coast
of modern Turkey and then invaded the mainland of
Greece in retaliation for support of the Ionians. In 490,
the Persian king Darius the Great was soundly defeated
by united Greek forces at the Battle of Marathon, where
Aeschylus fought and where his brother Cynegirus died.
Ten years later, during a second Persian invasion of
Greece by Darius's son, Xerxes I, Aeschylus also participated in the naval battle of Salamis, at which the Athenians defeated the Persian fleet against great odds. Accounts of Aeschylus's participation in other battles,
especially at Plataea in 479, must be dismissed as examples of biographical exaggeration. These victories permanently curtailed the threat of Persian domination of
the Greek mainland and brought about the period of
Athenian political hegemony during which Aeschylus
produced all of his extant plays.

LIFE'S WORK

While the titles of at least eighty Aeschylean plays are
known, only seven tragedies survive in the Aeschylean
corpus. As entries in the Greater Dionysia always consisted of three tragedies plus one satyr play, about three-
quarters of Aeschylus's plays were tragedies. Plots for
these plays were generally connected with the Trojan
War or with the myths of Thebes and Argos. At the height
of his dramatic career, Aeschylus, who acted in his own
plays, was extremely successful. Of the twenty-odd productions attributed to his name, he was victorious at least
thirteen times, maybe more; in addition, several of his
plays were produced after his death.

Aeschylus's earliest extant work, *Persai* (472 B.C.E.;
The Persians, 1777), was first performed in Athens in
472, together with the lost plays *Phineus* and *Glaucus
Potnieus*. This production, which won first prize, commemorated the Athenian victory at Salamis and includes
Aeschylus's own eyewitness account, placed in the
mouth of a messenger. In choosing historical rather than
mythical subject matter for this play, Aeschylus followed
a contemporary, Phrynichus, who had earlier composed
two historical dramas. Aeschylus's producer for his
plays of 472 was Pericles, but the playwright's association with this great Athenian statesman and champion of
democracy is not necessarily an indication of Aeschylus's political inclinations, for producers were assigned
by the state, not chosen by the playwright.

Shortly after 472, at the invitation of the tyrant Hiero I,
Aeschylus traveled to Syracuse in Sicily, where *The Persians* was reproduced. Hieron, a great patron of the arts,
attracted to his court not only Aeschylus but also the phi-

Aeschylus. (Library of Congress)

losopher Xenophanes and the poets Pindar, Bacchylides, and Simonides. During his stay in Sicily, which may have lasted several years, Aeschylus also produced another play, *Aetnae*, now lost. As this play celebrated Hiero's founding of the city of Aetna in 476, a visit by Aeschylus to Sicily prior to 472 was once considered to have been likely, but most scholars now believe that *Aetnae* was produced sometime shortly after 472. Aeschylus's long stay in Sicily left a permanent mark on the playwright's work, which is filled with Sicilian words and expressions.

Aeschylus was certainly back in Athens by 468, for his unknown production of that year was defeated when Sophocles won his first victory at the Greater Dionysia. In the following year, Aeschylus won the competition with a group including the lost *Laius* and *Oedipus* and the extant *Hepta epi Thēbas* (467 B.C.E.; *Seven Against Thebes*, 1777).

Sometime between 467 and 458, Aeschylus produced the so-called Danaid trilogy, composed of the extant *Hiketides* (463 B.C.E.?; *The Suppliants*, also known as *Suppliant Women*, 1777) and the lost *Egyptians* and *Danaids*. For stylistic reasons, *The Suppliants* used to be considered Aeschylus's earliest extant play, until the twentieth century publication of a papyrus fragment containing part of an ancient production notice for the play. This new evidence makes it likely that Aeschylus competed in 463 with the Danaid trilogy and was victorious over Sophocles.

In 458 Aeschylus directed his last Athenian production, which included the extant *Agamemnōn* (*Agamemnon*, 1777), *Choēphoroi* (*Libation Bearers*, 1777), and *Eumenides* (English translation, 1777) and the lost satyr play *Proteus*. Together, these three tragedies, known as the *Oresteia*, make up the only surviving connected trilogy. The *Eumenides* is filled with allusions to such events as the recent Athenian alliance with Argos and the reform of the ancient court of Areopagus by the democrat Ephialtes. This evidence has been interpreted to suggest both that Aeschylus supported and that he opposed the political agenda of Athens in the middle of the fifth century.

Shortly after this production, which won first prize, Aeschylus left Athens for Sicily, never to return. Ancients conjectured that the playwright left Athens because of political dissatisfaction or professional disappointment. None of the evidence is certain, however, and the reasons for Aeschylus's second journey to Sicily remain obscure.

Some scholars believe that the seventh play surviving in the Aeschylus corpus, *Prometheus desmōtēs* (*Prome-*

theus Bound, 1777), was composed during Aeschylus's second stay in Sicily. Others deny that the play was written by Aeschylus at all.

The playwright also wrote epigrams and elegies. Fragments of Aeschylus's elegy composed in honor of the dead at Marathon were discovered in the Athenian agora in 1933. This poem is said to have been written for a competition, at an unknown date, which Aeschylus lost to the poet Simonides.

Aeschylus died in Gela, Sicily, in 456 or 455. An ancient biography recounts the following version of Aeschylus's death: An eagle flying overhead with a tortoise in its beak mistook Aeschylus's bald head for a rock on which to shatter the shell of its prey and thus killed the poet. The Gelans erected this inscription over the poet's tomb:

This memorial hides the Athenian Aeschylus, Euphorion's son,
Who died in wheat-bearing Gela.
The sacred battlefield of Marathon may tell of his great valor.
So, too, can the long-haired Mede, who knows it well.

By tradition, Aeschylus himself is said to have requested that he be remembered only as a patriotic Athenian and not as a great playwright.

Aeschylus had at least two sons, Euphorion and Euaeon, both of whom wrote plays. In 431 Euphorion defeated both Sophocles and Euripides. A few years later, Sophocles, competing with his masterpiece, *Oidipous tyrannos* (c. 429 B.C.E.; *Oedipus Tyrannus*, 1715), was defeated by Aeschylus's nephew Philocles. After Aeschylus's death, a special decree was passed to permit revivals of his plays, which won several victories in subsequent years. In 405, the comic poet Aristophanes produced *Batrachoi* (*The Frogs*, 1780), in which the dead Aeschylus and Euripides debate the quality of each other's tragedies.

SIGNIFICANCE

Aeschylus is rightly considered the "father of Western tragedy." His works, coming at a strategic time, helped mold Greek tragedy into a great literary form. While Aristotle's statement in *De poetica* (c. 334-323 B.C.E.; *Poetics*, 1705) that Aeschylus "first introduced a second actor to tragedy and lessened the role of the chorus and made dialogue take the lead" cannot be proved, Aeschylus's extant plays do illustrate a skilled use of dialogue, which made possible the agons, or great debates between characters so important in later Greek tragedy.

Whether Aeschylus himself introduced the second actor, he almost certainly invented the connected trilogy/tetralogy. As a rule, the group of three tragedies and one satyr play that a playwright produced at the festival were not connected thematically. It was Aeschylus who first saw the brilliant potential of linking the plays together. While his first extant play, *The Persians*, was not part of a connected group, all of his other surviving plays were. No other Greek playwright was able to make use of the trilogy form as successfully as Aeschylus did.

In *The Suppliants*, Aeschylus also experimented with the use of the chorus as dramatic protagonist. Traditionally a reflective and nondramatic element in the tragedy, the chorus became in this play the central character. Similarly, in *Eumenides* the chorus played a significant role as the prosecutor of the matricidal Orestes.

Aeschylus's dramatic skills are particularly apparent in his handling of spectacular stage techniques. His plays, frequently making dramatic use of such stage trappings as altars, tombs, ghosts, and the *eccyclema*, a wheeled vehicle employed to show the interior, thus confirm Aeschylus as a master playwright who established for his successors a high standard of dramatic skill and power.

— *Thomas J. Sienkewicz*

FURTHER READING

Herington, C. J. *Aeschylus*. New Haven, Conn.: Yale University Press, 1986. An excellent introduction to Aeschylus for the general reader. One chapter is devoted to biography; includes a short annotated bibliography and a table of dates.

Lefkowitz, Mary. *The Lives of the Greek Poets*. London: Duckworth, 1981. A translation and analysis of the Hellenistic biography of Aeschylus, otherwise unavailable in English, can be found in this book, which also includes a bibliography.

Lesky, Albin. *Greek Tragedy*. Translated by H. A. Frankfort. 3d ed. New York: Barnes & Noble Books, 1979.

A scholarly introduction to Aeschylus's dramaturgy, with a brief summary of his life. A bibliography is included.

_____. *A History of Greek Literature*. Translated by James Willis and Cornelis de Heer. Indianapolis: Hackett, 1996. Aeschylus's place in the literature of ancient Greece can be traced in this standard history, which includes biographical information and a bibliography.

Podlecki, Anthony J. *The Political Background of Aeschylean Tragedy*. 2d ed. London: Bristol Classical Press, 1999. Contains an excellent life of Aeschylus in the first chapter and an interesting appendix on Aeschylus's description of the Battle of Salamis.

Rosenmeyer, Thomas G. *The Art of Aeschylus*. Berkeley: University of California Press, 1982. Primarily a literary study, this work contains a short but good appendix on the life and times of Aeschylus. There is also an excellent "comparative table of dates and events" and a select bibliography.

Smyth, Herbert Weir. Introduction to *Aeschylus: Plays and Fragments with an English Translation*. 1922-1926. Reprint. 2 vols. Cambridge, Mass.: Harvard University Press, 1963. Smyth's biography of Aeschylus, found in the introduction to volume 1, is still excellent despite being published prior to the discovery of the papyrus predating *The Suppliants*.

Spatz, Lois. *Aeschylus*. Boston: Twayne, 1982. Written for the general reader, this book includes a biography and an annotated bibliography.

SEE ALSO: Darius the Great; Homer; Phidias; Sophocles.

RELATED ARTICLES in *Great Events from History: The Ancient World*: September 17, 490 B.C.E., Battle of Marathon; 483 B.C.E., Naval Law of Themistocles Is Instituted.

AESOP
Greek sage and fabulist

Aesop invented fables for the purpose of illustrating a moral (or immoral) lesson. He probably wrote nothing himself but was rather a famous teller of tales that were later set down.

BORN: c. 620 B.C.E.; possibly Thrace, Greece
DIED: c. 560 B.C.E.; possibly Delphi, Greece
AREA OF ACHIEVEMENT: Literature

EARLY LIFE

Although some scholars claim that he is purely a legendary figure, the following assertions are most often accepted as historically true in the ancient sources pertaining to Aesop (EE-sawp): He originally came from Thrace; he was for a time a slave on the Greek island of Samos, off the coast of Asia Minor, in the service of a man named Iadmon, who later freed him; he was a contemporary of the poet Sappho in the early sixth century B.C.E.; and he was famed as a maker and teller of prose stories.

Later documents add details, of varying degrees of credibility, to Aesop's biography. For example, *The Life of Aesop*, apparently written by a Greek-speaking Egyptian in the first century C.E., states that he was very ugly, worthless as a servant, potbellied, misshapen of head, snub-nosed, swarthy, dwarfish, bandy-legged, short-armed, squint-eyed, and liver-lipped. The sources for this late biography may go back as far as the fifth century B.C.E., although that does not guarantee its authenticity. Indeed, its cumulative details relating to Aesop's life are typically as fanciful and entertaining as the fables attributed to him.

In that entertaining first century biography, Aesop was portrayed as mute until the Egyptian goddess Isis gave him speech in thanks for guiding one of her lost priestesses. Isis and the nine Muses, the patron goddesses of the arts in Greek myth, also gave him the power to conceive stories and the ability to elaborate tales in Greek that would make him famous. Aesop's sharp wit and inventive imagination contrasted greatly with his grotesque appearance and with the dullness of those about him, both his master and his fellow slaves. Rejected because of his superior intellect and unattractiveness, Aesop soon became the property of a slave dealer, who sold him promptly and cheaply to the pompous philosopher Xanthus on the island of Samos.

Aesop outwitted his master and mistress at every opportunity, usually through his verbal dexterity. There is even an episode in which Aesop had sex ten times with his master's wife, as a form of revenge. (A general mistrust of women's fidelity runs throughout the narrative.) Eventually, Xanthus was forced to grant freedom to his troublesome slave, who was the only one able to interpret an omen in which an eagle flies away with the city's official seal. Aesop interpreted the omen as an indication that powerful King Croesus of Lydia would subjugate the island. The treacherous people of Samos surrendered Aesop to Croesus, but Aesop's skillful telling of fables so pleased the king that, at Aesop's request, he did not attack Samos. Aesop then wrote down all the stories and fables that would be attached to his name and deposited them in the king's library. When he returned to the island, he was richly rewarded for having saved it from invasion. His first act in his newly exalted position on Samos was to erect a shrine to his patron goddesses—the Muses and their mother, Mnemosyne, goddess of memory—thereby insulting the Olympian god Apollo by not honoring him as leader of the Muses.

After many prosperous years in Samos, Aesop set off to see the world. Arriving in Babylon, he won the position of chamberlain to King Lycurgus of Babylon. He enabled Lycurgus to win many contests of wit with other monarchs and thereby to expand his kingdom; the most notable of these contests was with King Nectanabo of Egypt. Lycurgus was so grateful that he ordered the erection of a golden statue of Aesop and held a great celebration in honor of Aesop's wisdom.

LIFE'S WORK

Late in his life, Aesop wished to go to Delphi, the Greek city that contains the sacred oracle of Apollo. After having sworn to return to Babylon, he journeyed to other cities and gave demonstrations of his wisdom and learning. When he came to Delphi, its people enjoyed hearing him at first, but they gave him nothing. After he insulted the people of Delphi by pointing out that they were the descendants of slaves, they plotted to kill him for damaging their reputation. Their stratagem was to hide a golden cup from Apollo's temple in Aesop's baggage and then to convict him of theft from a sacred place, a capital offense. Despite Aesop's pleas of innocence and his recitation of fables indicating that the Delphians would be harmed by executing him, they stood him on the edge of the cliff at Delphi. Aesop cursed them, called on the Muses to witness that his death was unjust, and threw

Aesop. (Library of Congress)

to come forward was the grandson of Iadmon." The greatest fifth century B.C.E. comic playwright, Aristophanes, in his *Sphēkes* (422 B.C.E.; *The Wasps*, 1812), refers to the Delphians' falsely charging Aesop with theft. Perhaps the most memorably moving ancient Greek reference to Aesop occurs in the *Phaedōn* by the philosopher Plato. Aesop is describing the last day in the life of his beloved teacher Socrates in 399 B.C.E. The Athenians had sentenced Socrates to death for his critical ideas. Socrates had been spending his last hours before execution turning Aesop's fables into verse. Because no written collection of short fables would have then been available, they must have been part of the common person's memorized cultural stock. When his friends came to visit Socrates, he wondered if Aesop had ever invented a fable about the connection of pleasure and pain. The second century C.E. Greek historian Plutarch, in his series of short *Lives*, makes many references to Aesop's fables when they are relevant to the fates of his biographical subjects. Thus, whether legend or reality, the character of Aesop has been an enduring literary inspiration.

Aesopea (fourth century, B.C.E.; *Aesop's Fables*, 1484) represents the literature of the common person, in striking contrast to the aristocratic heroic mode of the dominant Homeric epics, the *Iliad* (c. 750 B.C.E.; English translation, 1611) and the *Odyssey* (c. 725 B.C.E.; English translation, 1614). The fables are part of that tradition of folk wisdom carried by the spoken word from generation to generation through such genres as parables and proverbs as well as fables. The form of the Aesopic fable is that of a brief anecdote focused on a single event, designed to teach some principle of successful living. The characters in the fables are typically animals endowed with human speech and personal qualities. Each quality fits the stereotype for that creature; for example, the fox is untrustworthy, the ass stupid, the lamb naïve and helpless, the wolf cruel, the lion noble, the ant industrious. These animals, as well as the people in the fables, become easily recognized images of human types. The concluding moral of each story, often tagged onto the text centuries later, is drawn from common human experience and, therefore, makes an easily understood lesson.

Although Aesop's language is spare and simple, the ancients did not consider the fables as intended for children. Their point of view is really adult, often satirical, and never sentimental. Aesop, for example, is reputed to have told to the Athenians the story of "The Frogs Who Asked for a King" when they expressed discontent with their ruler. The story tells of some frogs who, bothered at not having a ruler, ask Zeus to send them a king. Real-

himself over the cliff. Later, according to the first century biography, when the Delphians were afflicted with a famine, they received an oracle from Zeus, king of the gods, that they should expiate the death of Aesop. *The Life of Aesop* goes on to say that the peoples of Greece, Babylon, and Samos avenged Aesop's death, although the mode of vengeance is not specified.

There are several other ancient references to Aesop's brutal fate at Delphi. For example, the Greek "father of history," Herodotus, states that Aesop was by birth a Thracian, "the slave of Iadmon, son of Hephaestopolis of Samos. . . . When the Delphians, in obedience to the oracle's command, repeatedly advertised for someone to claim compensation for Aesop's murder, the only person

izing their stupidity, Zeus drops a log into their pool. At first, the frogs are frightened and dive to the bottom. Later, when the log floats quietly, they become contemptuous of it and climb over it. Indignant at having such an inactive ruler, the frogs bother Zeus again, asking for a change of rulers. Zeus, now angry with the frogs, this time sends a water snake who catches and eats them. "Better no rule than cruel rule," says the moral tag. The Aesopic fables are thus typical of that sort of folk literature in which people shrewdly examine their own lives, with abrasive honesty, and thus come to a better understanding of their own follies.

SIGNIFICANCE

Many phrases derived from *Aesop's Fables* are common expressions in the folk heritage of the English language: "Sour grapes," "the boy who cried 'wolf,'" "the wolf in sheep's clothing," "fishing in muddy waters," "out of the frying pan into the fire," "the dog in the manger," "the ant and the grasshopper," "the tortoise and the hare," and "the goose that laid the golden egg" are some of the better-known examples.

The Greek tradition of telling fables goes back at least as far as Hesiod's *Erga kai Emerai* (c. 700 B.C.E.; *Works and Days*, 1618). Hesiod recounts a brief episode in which a hawk carries off a whimpering nightingale in its cruel claws. The powerful hawk tells the complaining and usually proud nightingale that "I will make a meal of you if I choose, or I will let you go. Foolish is he who would match himself against those who are stronger. . . ." Hesiod's fable is told as if its content and form are already well known; there were Mesopotamian fables even older than those of the Greeks. Indeed, Aristotle, the great fourth century B.C.E. Greek philosopher, says in his *Rhetoric*, "Fables are suited to popular oratory and have this advantage that, while historical parallels are hard to find, it is comparatively easy to find fables."

The first written collection of fables in Greek attributed to Aesop is recorded as having been made by Demetrius of Phalerum in the fifth century B.C.E. Unfortunately, that collection has not survived. The oldest existing collection is a Latin version in verse done by the freedman Phaedrus in the first century C.E. The Latin verse of Phaedrus became the basis for the great seventeenth century French verse fables of Jean de La Fontaine, whose satirical verses are familiar to many generations of French schoolchildren. In the late second century C.E.,

Babrius made a version in Greek verse, thereby completing the task conceived by Socrates. Prose versions, however, have also survived the ages, dating from at least as far back as the first three centuries of the Christian era, with their roots perhaps extending to Aesop in the sixth century B.C.E. These prose fables are the primary basis of most modern English versions. The fabulist tradition remained alive in the twentieth century United States, with such fable-spinners as James Thurber and Woody Allen reinforcing the Aesopic tradition of satirical folk wisdom.

—*Donald S. Gochberg*

FURTHER READING

Aesop. *Aesop's Fables*. Translated by Laura Gibbs. New York: Oxford University Press, 2003. This compilation of six hundred fables represents all the main collections in ancient Latin and Greek. Fables are arranged according to themes and story elements.

_____. *The Fables of Aesop: Selected, Told Anew, and Their History Traced by Joseph Jacobus*. London: Macmillan, 1894. Reprint. New York: Macmillan, 1950. Skillful retellings of the fables with excellent illustrations and source notes.

Babrius. *Fabulae Aesopeae: English and Greek, Babrius and Phaedrus*. Edited and translated by Ben Edwin Perry. Cambridge, Mass.: Harvard University Press, 1990. A scholarly edition of the Greek and Latin texts, together with facing prose translations.

Daly, Lloyd W. *Aesop Without Morals: The Famous Fables, and a Life of Aesop*. New York: Thomas Yoseloff, 1961. This English translation of the *Fables* includes a translation of the first century C.E. *Life of Aesop*.

Zafiropoulos, Christos A. *Ethics in Aesop's Fables: The Augustana Collection*. Boston: Brill, 2001. Recounts the history of the fable and analyzes the theme of conflict in Aesop's fables from the perspective of ethical philosophy in ancient Greece. Argues that the fable is a form of ethical reasoning.

SEE ALSO: Quintus Ennius; Euripides; Horace; Phaedrus; Vergil.

RELATED ARTICLE in *Great Events from History: The Ancient World*: c. 736-716 B.C.E., Spartan Conquest of Messenia.

AGESILAUS II OF SPARTA
Spartan king (r. 400-360 B.C.E.)

By common consent the most powerful and illustrious Greek leader of his day, Agesilaus took Sparta to its peak of influence. Unfortunately, his policies led to a devastating defeat at Leuctra in 371 B.C.E., and at his death he left an impoverished and weakened kingdom that would never again play a dominant role in Greek affairs.

BORN: c. 444 B.C.E.; Sparta, Greece
DIED: c. 360 B.C.E.; Cyrene, Cyrenaica (now in Libya)
ALSO KNOWN AS: Agesilaos
AREAS OF ACHIEVEMENT: Government and politics, war and conquest

EARLY LIFE

When Eupolia, the young second wife of the aging Spartan king Archidamus II, gave birth to Agesilaus (uh-jehs-uh-LAY-uhs) in 444 B.C.E., her son's prospects must have seemed quite limited. Archidamus already had an heir apparent, Agis, by his first wife. Worse, Agesilaus was born lame, an egregious liability in militaristic, fitness-minded Sparta. Indeed, his very survival is remarkable, given the official inspection and possible infanticide to which the Spartan authorities subjected every infant. That he passed their scrutiny may be attributed to Sparta's growing manpower shortage, a problem that would become acute in Agesilaus's lifetime.

Because he was not considered an heir to the throne, from age seven to eighteen the boy underwent the normal Spartan training, the *agoge*. Royal heirs were normally spared this rigorous, competitive, and often violent regimen, designed to produce the bravest, most disciplined soldiers possible. Despite his lameness and small stature, Agesilaus excelled in the *agoge*. He was the first to jest at his deformity and deliberately sought out the most difficult tasks to prove that his weak leg was no real hindrance. If the young man displayed any weakness, it was excessive loyalty and favoritism to family and friends.

At some point in his youth, Agesilaus formed a relationship that would change the course of his life. It was customary that a Spartan youth cultivate a special friendship with a mature man who would guide him and advance his career. Agesilaus had the good fortune to become the special friend of Lysander, the honored and influential general who spearheaded Sparta's victory over Athens in the Peloponnesian War. Before his extreme ambition and egotism brought him discredit and demotion in 403, Lysander had initiated an aggressive style of Spartan imperialism, and he would remain a powerful advocate of Spartan expansion.

At his death in 400, after a reign of twenty-seven years, King Agis left a son and presumptive successor, Leotychides. Nevertheless, Agesilaus asserted his own claim to the throne. His participation in the *agoge* had given him a strong following among Spartan citizens. There was also some question as to the legitimacy of Leotychides, and Agesilaus made the most of it. When supporters of Leotychides recalled that an oracle had warned Spartans against the "lame kingship," Agesilaus countered that the warning was against a king of non-royal blood. Perhaps the decisive factor in this contest was the intervention of Lysander on behalf of Agesilaus. Unable to serve as king himself, Lysander championed the claim of his friend. Leotychides lost not only the kingship but also his inheritance, and Agesilaus assumed the throne in 400, when he was about forty-four years old.

Because Sparta had a curious double monarchy with two royal houses, a Spartan king had to share his royal authority with a colleague—and potential rival. During the forty-year reign of Agesilaus, exile and premature death from disease or combat brought him five comparatively short-reigned and weak colleagues in the kingship. As a result, despite some factional disputes at home, Agesilaus had an unusually free hand to lead Sparta as he saw fit.

LIFE'S WORK

Agesilaus inherited a kingdom politically and militarily supreme in Greece, but that very fact of supremacy presented potentially dangerous temptations and challenges. Specifically, Agesilaus would have to decide whether to limit Sparta's hegemony to its traditional area of dominance, southern Greece, or extend it to include central Greece or even regions beyond. He would also have to reckon with the ambitions of a former ally in central Greece, Thebes. The Thebans wanted to unify the district of Boeotia in a federal state headed by Thebes. Agesilaus could attempt to prevent this, or he could accept it and at the same time compensate by encouraging the traditional rivalry between Thebes and its neighbor Athens.

At home, Sparta had certain long-standing internal weaknesses that needed attention, most notably the decline in the number of Spartan citizens. The gradual con-

Agesilaus II of Sparta. (Library of Congress)

centration of slave-worked land in the hands of wealthy families meant that fewer Spartans could afford to pay the dues required of all citizens. Accelerated by casualties in war and natural disasters, this trend had reduced the Spartan community to no more than three thousand male citizens at the accession of Agesilaus. His performance as king must be judged by his responses to these challenges and problems.

In his first year on the throne, Agesilaus had to deal with the revolutionary conspiracy of Cinadon, a crisis that revealed the precarious position of the dwindling Spartan citizen body. Cinadon was an "inferior," one of a sizable and growing body of Spartans who had lost their citizen status because of poverty. He based his revolutionary hopes on the fact that the Spartans were dangerously outnumbered by their subjects: the free *perioikoi*, who lived in semiautonomous villages around Sparta, and the servile Helots, who lived primarily in Messenia, west of Sparta. Cinadon boasted that his supporters—Helots, freed Helots, inferiors, and *perioikoi*—hated the Spartans so much that they would be glad to eat them raw. Because of an informant who betrayed the plot in its

early stages, Agesilaus and the other Spartan authorities were able to suppress the conspiracy, but they took no steps to correct the conditions that had engendered it.

Instead, in 396, Agesilaus undertook his first military campaign to distant Asia Minor, where he challenged the power of Persia. Agesilaus may have presented this expedition as a Panhellenic crusade on behalf of the Asiatic Greeks, but others saw it as an attempt to extend Spartan hegemony. Both Athens and Thebes refused to take part, and the Thebans further offended Agesilaus by disrupting his parting sacrifices at Aulis in Boeotia. After several victories against the Persians, Agesilaus received joint command of both land and sea forces, an honor unprecedented in Spartan history. The Asian campaign won fame for Agesilaus and much treasure for Sparta, but his victories accomplished little in the military sense. Moreover, his poor choice of an incompetent brother-in-law, Peisandros, as admiral resulted in a disastrous naval defeat in 394 that seriously weakened Sparta's position overseas. How Agesilaus might have responded to this setback is uncertain, because he had already been recalled home to help Sparta face a hostile alliance of major Greek states in the so-called Corinthian War (395-386 B.C.E.).

Primarily instigated by Thebes, this war challenged Sparta's domination of central Greece and had already produced the death of the reckless Lysander and the banishment of King Pausanias, Agesilaus's first comonarch. Victory in a major battle at Coronea secured Agesilaus's safe passage through Boeotia to Sparta, but it failed to reestablish Spartan preeminence in central Greece. His vengeful frontal assault on the Theban force, moreover, needlessly risked his men and produced severe casualties, including several wounds to Agesilaus himself. In subsequent engagements, Agesilaus generally got the upper hand, although one of his companies was decimated by a tactically innovative, lightly armed force near Corinth in 390. As the war became a stalemate, Agesilaus formed an alliance with his erstwhile enemy, the Persian king. By the terms of the "King's Peace" of 386, the Asiatic Greeks were abandoned to Persian domination. In return, the Persian king promised to make war on any Greek state that violated the accord and backed Sparta as overseer and arbiter of a general peace in Greece.

By a just and conciliatory administration of the King's Peace, Agesilaus might have maintained Sparta's security and hegemony indefinitely. Instead, he intervened in the affairs of other Greek states in order to install governments friendly to Sparta. Above all, he indulged his obsessive hatred of Thebes, and he condoned—if he did not instigate—the unlawful military occupation of Thebes in 382. This act, more than any other, outraged Greek opinion and helped the Thebans to establish an alliance with their natural rivals, the Athenians. After Thebes expelled the Spartan garrison, Agesilaus twice led invasions of Boeotia in vain attempts to recapture the city. Despite serious injuries in 377 that kept him out of military action until 370, Agesilaus continued to reject the claims of Thebes to represent all of Boeotia. He presided at a peace conference in 371, and, after a bitter exchange with the Theban leader Epaminondas, he excluded Thebes from the general peace.

Then, against the advice of other Spartans, Agesilaus urged an immediate invasion of Boeotia. A momentous battle duly ensued at Leuctra, where the Spartans suffered a devastating defeat at the hands of the more tactically advanced Thebans. King Cleombrotus and four hundred of his fellow Spartans died in this conflict, the worst defeat in Spartan history.

Sparta never recovered from the setback at Leuctra. The battle itself inflicted heavy casualties on an already dangerously small Spartan citizen body and shattered the myth of Spartan invincibility. The ensuing Theban invasion of southern Greece permanently sundered Sparta's regional alliance and prompted defections among the long subordinate *perioikoi* and Helots who surrounded Sparta. In the face of the Theban advance, many Spartans panicked, while others plotted revolution. Only the energetic emergency measures of Agesilaus, who was then in his early seventies, saved the city from destruction. Worst of all in the long run, the Thebans liberated Messenia and thereby deprived Sparta of its richest agricultural district with its large number of Helot slaves.

Agesilaus refused to accept the loss of Messenia, and in the last decade of his life he pursued its recovery with a stubbornness that equaled his earlier opposition to Thebes. Unfortunately, he now ruled a weakened and impoverished Sparta with a citizen population of only one thousand. In the end, he was forced to undertake foreign mercenary service in order to finance his efforts to regain Messenia. Such was the military reputation of the aging king that rebellious Persian governors in Asia Minor and Egypt paid handsomely for his skills. In 360, after completing his final campaign in Egypt, Agesilaus set sail for home but died en route in Libya at about age eighty-four.

SIGNIFICANCE

For more than two decades, Agesilaus II was, in effect, king of Greece. Nevertheless, his reign must be seen as a failure. A general of unquestioned talent and bravery, Agesilaus shared in the Spartans' failure to keep up with the military innovations of that time. The resulting tactical backwardness of the Spartan army helps explain the defeat at Leuctra. As a statesman, Agesilaus pursued unwise policies. The attempt to extend Sparta's hegemony was unrealistic in the light of Sparta's declining manpower, while his flagrantly aggressive administration of the King's Peace needlessly alienated other Greek states and made allies for Thebes. Above all, his relentless hatred of Thebes caused a breakdown of the common peace and led directly to the disastrous confrontation at Leuctra.

Agesilaus cannot be held responsible for the structural ills of the Spartan system, but he seems to have been blind to its most glaring problem, the decline in Spartan manpower. During his reign, the number of Spartan male citizens dropped by two-thirds to a mere one thousand. He left his son a feeble kingdom that would never again play a major role in Greek affairs.

A Spartan's Spartan, a product of the *agoge*, Agesilaus sadly exemplifies Aristotle's famous critique of the Spartans: Because their whole system was directed to securing only a part of virtue, military prowess, they did well at war but failed at the higher art of peace.

—*James T. Chambers*

FURTHER READING

Cartledge, Paul. *Agesilaos and the Crisis of Sparta*. Baltimore: The Johns Hopkins University Press, 1987. This exhaustive study from a Marxist perspective places Agesilaus in the context of fourth century B.C.E. Greek history and provides an introduction to the whole political and social system of Sparta. Includes a helpful chronological table.

David, Ephraim. *Sparta Between Empire and Revolution, 404-243 B.C.: Internal Problems and Their Impact on Contemporary Greek Consciousness*. New York: Arno Press, 1981. An excellent study of the internal problems of Sparta, this book deals with the period of Agesilaus's rule in chapters 1 through 3.

Forrest, W. G. *A History of Sparta, 950-192 B.C.* 2d ed. London: Duckworth, 1980. A brief introduction to ancient Sparta. Two chapters cover the period of Agesilaus's rule.

Hamilton, Charles D. *Agesilaus and the Failure of Spartan Hegemony*. Ithaca, N.Y.: Cornell University Press, 1991. A balanced assessment that argues that Agesilaus's obsessive hatred of Thebes displaces his original genuine Panhellenic goals.

————. *Sparta's Bitter Victories: Politics and Diplomacy in the Corinthian War.* Ithaca, N.Y.: Cornell University Press, 1979. An excellent, detailed study of Greek international affairs in the period 405-386 B.C.E., this book is especially good in presenting the policies of Agesilaus and Lysander in the context of Spartan factional politics.

Plutarch. *Agesilaus and Pompey Pelopidas and Marcellus.* In *Plutarch's Lives,* translated by Beradotte Perrin. Cambridge, Mass.: Harvard University Press, 1997. This ancient source for the career of Agesilaus was written about five centuries after his death.

Xenophon. *A History of My Times (Hellenica).* Translated by George Cawkwell. New York: Penguin Books, 1979. In this work, the Athenian soldier-historian provides a contemporary narrative of the whole period of Agesilaus's rule, the only such account to survive complete. A personal friend of Agesilaus, Xenophon participated in many of the events he describes and provides revealing details. Unfortunately, he is biased in favor of Agesilaus and omits several very important events.

SEE ALSO: Alcibiades of Athens; Cimon; Cleisthenes of Athens; Draco; Epaminondas; Leonidas; Miltiades the Younger; Pausanias of Sparta; Pericles; Pisistratus; Pittacus of Mytilene; Solon; Themistocles.

RELATED ARTICLES in *Great Events from History: The Ancient World*: c. 736-716 B.C.E., Spartan Conquest of Messenia; c. 700-330 B.C.E., Phalanx Is Developed as a Military Unit; May, 431-September, 404 B.C.E., Peloponnesian War.

GNAEUS JULIUS AGRICOLA
Roman administrator and general

The governor of Britain and conqueror of Scotland was the subject of a famous biography by Roman historian Cornelius Tacitus. Agricola represented a new ideal of dutiful and modest service to Rome.

BORN: June 13, 40 C.E.; Forum Julii, Gallia Narbonensis (now Fréjus, France)
DIED: August 23, 93 C.E.; Rome (now in Italy)
AREAS OF ACHIEVEMENT: Government and politics, war and conquest

EARLY LIFE
Gnaeus Julius Agricola (uh-GRIHK-uh-luh) was the son of Lucius Julius Graecinus, a senator from Forum Julii, who was executed by Emperor Caligula (r. 37-41 C.E.). Agricola was brought up by his mother, Julia Procilla, and studied at Massilia (Marseilles). Agricola's early adulthood was marked by rapid progress through various military and administrative ranks. He was *tribunus laticlavius* in Britain around 60-61, the lowest officer rank for men of senatorial birth and a prerequisite for senate membership. Around this time Agricola married Domitia Decidiana (no relation to the emperor Domitian); of their children, only a daughter survived to marry historian Cornelius Tacitus in 77.

Agricola in 64 was quaestor (a financial official) for the governor of Asia, Salvius Titianus; next he was tribune of the plebs, a largely honorary office, and praetor (legal official) in 68. In the civil war of 69, in which his mother was killed, Agricola supported Vespasian (r. 69-79 C.E.) and recruited troops in Italy. As a reward for this support, he was appointed commander of Legio XX in Britain and successfully disciplined it.

Agricola held military commands in Britain in the early 70's under governors Vettius Bolanus and Petilius Cerialis. Tacitus in *De vita Julii Agricolae* (c. 98 C.E.; *The Life of Agricola*, 1591), the only major source on his life, claims that Bolanus was sluggish but that Cerialis assigned serious responsibilities to Agricola, who pursued them energetically. As a result, Agricola was made a patrician and governor of Aquitania in 74-77. He attained suffect consulship c. 77 at the age of about thirty-seven, some years below the official minimum age of forty-two.

LIFE'S WORK
Agricola was governor (*legatus pro praetore*) of Britain in 77 or 78 to 83 or 84, the precise dates being subject to dispute. Tacitus refers to his governorship in terms of successive summers, not absolute dates. As befits a Roman literary historian, he does not use many specific names of peoples or places, which has made the precise location of Agricola's campaigns a matter of archaeological speculation.

In his first season (77 or 78) as governor of Britain, Agricola defeated the Ordovices, a people of north Wales, almost exterminating them. He conquered the island of Mona (Anglesey). In the second season (78 or

79), Agricola consolidated the Brigantian territory in north Britain and, as governor, enforced military and administrative discipline and repressed corruption. According to Tacitus, Agricola promoted the cultural assimilation of the Britons to Roman ways. He encouraged the building of Roman-style towns and promoted Roman education for the sons of native leaders. Tacitus claims that the Britons acquired Roman dress (the toga) and Latin and even Roman vices such as baths and banquets.

In his third season (79 or 80), Agricola reached the Tay River in modern Scotland and halted to build forts. Scholars have been eager to identify all first century C.E. forts in this region as his, but this is unlikely. In his fourth season (80 or 81), Agricola reached the Forth-Clyde isthmus and consolidated the region south of it. In his fifth season (81 or 82), Agricola crossed a body of water (probably the Firth of Clyde) and conquered peoples previously unknown to the Romans, probably in southwestern Scotland. Tacitus claims that Agricola wanted to and could easily have conquered Ireland.

In his sixth season as governor (82 or 83), Agricola advanced beyond the Forth-Clyde isthmus and into the Scottish Highlands. Camps that probably were those of Agricola have been found in northeast Scotland. In the autumn of his seventh year, Agricola defeated the Scottish Britons in a pitched battle at Mons Graupius, the site of which, probably in northeast Scotland, is a matter of archaeological speculation. Details of the battle are also uncertain: Agricola fought with some twenty thousand to thirty thousand men, probably four legions and various Tungrian and Batavian auxiliaries. The Britons numbered some thirty thousand. The Romans surrounded and defeated the Britons, with some 10,000 Briton to 360 Roman losses.

Regarding Agricola's retirement and death, Tacitus is highly tendentious, representing the emperor Domitian (r. 81-96 C.E.) as a jealous tyrant and Agricola as a selfless victim. In his *Agricola*, the subject's governorship of Britain ends, and he returns to Rome. Though Agricola presents his victory in modest terms, Domitian was struck with fear and jealousy: "the qualities of a good general should be the monopoly of the emperor." The civil war of 69 had shown that great generals could make themselves emperors. Domitian appointed triumphal ornaments for Agricola, the highest military honors short of the triumph, which was reserved for the emperors. However, when Domitian offered him the governorship of Asia, which Tacitus insinuates is merely a trap set by the jealous ruler, Agricola turned it down and retired from political life.

After nine years of quiet retirement, Agricola died in 93. Tacitus reports a rumor that Agricola was poisoned by Domitian; Dio Cassius claims that he was murdered by Domitian. However, poisoning was a stock allegation in the deaths of prominent individuals when death from disease was the likely cause.

Historians have sought reasons for Agricola's retirement that do not require accepting the portrayal of Domitian as a jealous tyrant. In fact, Domitian had supported the last two or three years of Agricola's conquests. Agricola had had an unusually long tenure of office, and room had to be made for others. It is possible that Agricola's military ability was exaggerated by Tacitus; the poor fighting qualities of the Britons were remarked on even by Roman soldiers, and the wars in Dacia may have required better generals.

In general, the achievements of Agricola have been downplayed by later scholarship, which suggests that neither his military ability nor his administration was outstanding; he continued policies of Romanization that are attested to elsewhere. His conquest of Scotland was not lasting; Tacitus exaggerates when he says, *perdomita Britannia et statim omissa* ("Britain was all but conquered and immediately left aside"). Archaeology suggests that the Romans evacuated forts in northeast Scotland in 86-88 (dated by coin evidence) and retreated to the Tyne-Solway line, where Hadrian's Wall was later built. In the reign of Antoninus Pius (r. 138-161), the frontier was moved up to the Clyde-Forth line with the building of the Antonine Wall, shortly afterward abandoned.

SIGNIFICANCE

The significance of Agricola's achievements requires discussion of the nature and themes of Tacitus's *The Life of Agricola*, the famous source on his life as well as many other aspects of Roman society of the time. (A few inscriptions do survive from Roman Britain with his name and title.) *The Life of Agricola* resembles more the Greek tradition of encomiastic biography and most of all the Roman funeral *elogium* (eulogy), rather than the type of Latin biography represented by Suetonius's *De vita Caesarum* (c.120 C.E.; *History of the Twelve Caesars*, 1606). Tacitus omits the anecdotal, often scurrilous, detail of Suetonius. However, *The Life of Agricola* is too long and contains too much historical narrative for the traditional *elogium*. Agricola's personality is idealized, as Tacitus's goal was to eulogize. *The Life of Agricola* is a classic (though lacking in specific detail) depiction of the ideal Roman general and administrator. The careers of his predecessors in Britain are probably distorted to present him more favorably.

Tacitus's *The Life of Agricola* is an essay on the ideal role of the Roman administrator and general under autocracy. This political problem was also explored by Tacitus in the *Ab excessu divi Augusti* (c. 116 C.E., also known as *Annales*; *Annals*, 1598). The traditional Roman aristocrat (in the Republic, before the last century B.C.E.) was expected to win honor and *gloria* through military conquest, displaying *virtus* (courage, manliness, virtue) and earning triumphs. Winning this reputation enabled him to compete for political office. To choose not to compete, but to prefer private life (*otium*), was at best ambiguous, at worst *ignavia* (idleness, cowardice, baseness).

These formulas of conduct were redefined in the Imperial period, when one man ruled and aristocratic political competition was limited and formalized; aristocratic military glory was curtailed, triumphs reserved for the emperors; the prudent aristocrat sought a life of *otium*. However, the aristocracy revered senatorial "martyrs" who supposedly upheld ancestral *libertas* and were condemned to death by tyrannical emperors such as Tiberius, Caligula, Nero, and Domitian. In *The Life of Agricola*, Tacitus's presentation of the prudent aristocrat's inaction under autocracy is tinged with guilt and anxiety; he laments the "martyrs" and apologizes for the appearance of idleness or servility in the survivors, though he condemns those who endangered themselves by lack of prudence or modesty.

Tacitus's Agricola represents a new ideal of how to live under the autocracy. Not individual glory but dutiful service of the state is redefined as honorable. Agricola desires military glory, *militaris gloriae cupido*. However, he always shows moderation and modesty (*verecundia*) in bearing and respects his superiors. Agricola's attainment of *gloria* through conquest is limited by the alleged jealousy of Domitian, which Agricola escapes by retreating from public life (choosing *otium*), a decision that Tacitus represents as honorable. His emphasized modesty of bearing presents him almost entirely as a victim of Domitian's paranoia.

The Life of Agricola is also an important source on Roman imperialism. Besides recording conquests, it depicts the policy of "Romanization," the imposition of Roman culture on non-Roman peoples. Tacitus depicts Agricola as imposing Roman urban civilization on the Britons (temples, public squares, Roman-style houses) and promoting Roman education for sons of native leaders. Tacitus claims that Roman amenities (arcades, baths, banquets) accustomed the Britons to "servitude." This was hardly a criticism of Romanization as modern cultural imperialism; it represents the elite Roman ambivalence about luxury. Archaeological studies of Romanization suggest that acculturation also was initiated by provincials themselves (in emulation of social superiors) and that it did not usually reach the lower or rural social groups. Roman promotion of urbanization was not necessarily a mission to acculturate all provincials in the manner of the modern European civilizing mission.

The Life of Agricola, with Tacitus's *De origine et situ Germanorum* (c. 98 C.E., also known as *Germania*; *The Description of Germanie*, 1598), an ethnography of the ancient Germans, is also a key source of Roman attitudes to the "barbarian" enemy. *The Life of Agricola* contains an extended geographical and ethnographical excursus on the landscape, resources, and peoples of Britain. Tacitus depicts the Britons as "noble savages" fighting in defense of their liberty; they have not been "enervated by long peace." In a speech before Mons Graupius, Calgacus the Scottish leader rouses his men in defense of "liberty," painting a picture of Roman misrule: "they make a desert and call it peace." This speech, of course, is a rhetorical composition by Tacitus, not literal evidence. Tacitus's representations of barbarians may be veiled political statements, projecting traditional republican ideals of liberty onto the barbarians, while still depicting them as lacking self-control and moderation in "barbarian" fashion. Tacitus's representations of the Britons were not intended to be sympathetic, but to give his Roman hero an "honorable" enemy.

—*Sara E. Phang*

FURTHER READING

Braund, David. *Ruling Roman Britain: Kings, Queens, Governors, and Emperors from Julius Caesar to Agricola*. New York: Routledge, 1996. Emphasizes the cultural and literary aims of Tacitus's *The Life of Agricola*.

Hanson, W. S. *Agricola and the Conquest of the North*. New York: Barnes & Noble, 1987. Hanson takes a cautious, minimalist view of Agricola.

Jones, Brian W. *Domitian and the Senatorial Order*. Philadelphia: American Philosophical Society, 1979. This study of Domitian's relationship with the senate includes an index and a bibliography.

Mellor, Ronald. *Tacitus*. New York: Routledge, 1993. A general introduction to Tacitus's works.

Salway, Peter. *A History of Roman Britain*. New York: Oxford University Press, 1997. A more traditional view than that of Braund.

Southern, Pat. *Domitian: The Tragic Tyrant*. New York: Routledge, 1997. A traditional view of Domitian.

Tacitus. *Tacitus: "The Agricola" and "The Germania."* Edited and translated by H. Mattingly. New York: Penguin Books, 1970. Tacitus's terse, allusive Latin is expanded somewhat in translation.

SEE ALSO: Boudicca; Caligula; Nero; Tacitus; Tiberius.
RELATED ARTICLES in *Great Events from History: The Ancient World*: 43-130 C.E., Roman Conquest of Britain; c. 50 C.E., Creation of the Roman Imperial Bureaucracy; 60 C.E., Boudicca Leads Revolt Against Roman Rule; 64-67 C.E., Nero Persecutes the Christians.

MARCUS VIPSANIUS AGRIPPA
Roman administrator and engineer

Agrippa provided Emperor Augustus with the military support he needed to establish the Roman principate. Agrippa's gift for planning and building contributed to the improvement of Rome's roads, water supply, and major public buildings.

BORN: c. 63 B.C.E.; place unknown
DIED: March, 12 B.C.E.; Campania (now in Italy)
AREAS OF ACHIEVEMENT: Government and politics, war and conquest, architecture

EARLY LIFE

Marcus Vipsanius Agrippa (uh-GRIHP-uh) seems linked with Octavian (as the emperor Augustus was called before 27 B.C.E.) almost from birth. They were born into politically insignificant families in about the same year. Agrippa's equestrian (middle-class) family was obscure, and the family name, Vipsanius, was so unaristocratic that in later life he preferred not to use it at all. He and Octavian were friends from childhood and attended school together, according to the emperor's court biographer.

Nothing certain is known of Agrippa's life before 44 B.C.E. It seems safe to assume that he performed the military service that young men of his class were expected to undertake at that stage of their lives. At the time of Julius Caesar's assassination, Agrippa was with Octavian, Caesar's grandnephew, in Greece, where they had been sent to study. Agrippa seems to have been chosen by Caesar as a suitable companion for Octavian, along with Gaius Maecenas and several other solid, if unspectacular, young men. When Octavian decided to return to Rome, claim his inheritance from Caesar, and become embroiled in the political and military struggle that had been ravaging the Mediterranean world for almost a century, Agrippa accompanied him.

In spite of his youth, Agrippa helped raise an army to oppose Caesar's assassins and to give Octavian leverage against Marc Antony, who had impounded Caesar's papers and money and hoped to assume the dead dictator's place. Although Antony and Octavian reached an accord in order to pursue Caesar's assassins, relations between them soon soured. In 41, with Antony in the east, his brother Lucius revolted against Octavian's authority and in opposition to his efforts to provide land for Caesar's retiring veteran soldiers. Agrippa forced Lucius to surrender early in 40 B.C.E., the first of his many victories on Octavian's behalf.

LIFE'S WORK

Agrippa proved how indispensable he was to Octavian by filling several important offices during the following few years. As governor of Gaul, he suppressed a revolt in the strategic southern district of Aquitania. In 37 B.C.E., he was Octavian's colleague in the consulship and built up the navy to oppose Sextus, who was attacking Roman shipping from bases in Sicily in a final act of opposition to the Caesarean faction's takeover of the state. This campaign brought Agrippa's engineering abilities to the fore, as he linked Lake Avernus with the Bay of Naples to create a harbor where the new fleet could be trained. His improved grappling equipment played a significant role in Sextus's defeat.

Augustus liked to boast that he had found Rome brick and left it marble, but Agrippa's buildings were as much responsible for that accomplishment as anything the emperor did. Agrippa began making his mark by repairing and upgrading the city's aqueducts during his time as an aedile in 33 B.C.E., a responsibility that he kept in his own hands for the rest of his life. The first of his aqueducts bore the name of the Julian family, into which Octavian had been adopted by Caesar's will. Agrippa's major building contributions were the Pantheon, one of the largest domed structures erected in antiquity, and the baths that bore his name. The Pantheon, which visitors to Rome still admire, bears Agrippa's name on the frieze, but it was rebuilt by Hadrian c. 133 C.E. How much of Agrippa's original design remains is a disputed question.

Also to Agrippa's credit were a granary and a new bridge over the Tiber River. He constructed buildings and roads in the provinces as well.

If he had any political ambitions, Agrippa subordinated them to Octavian's needs. He contributed significant victories over frontier tribes in Illyria in 35 and 34 B.C.E. and should be credited with defeating Antony and Cleopatra VII at the Battle of Actium in 31 B.C.E. That victory removed Octavian's last rival and made him the undisputed ruler of Rome.

Rome had been rent by bloody civil strife since 133 B.C.E., because the Empire had outgrown the republican constitution under which it had functioned since the overthrow of the last Etruscan king in 509 B.C.E. Annually elected magistrates who shared their power and could veto one another's actions could not effectively govern an empire stretching from Spain to Syria. As Julius Caesar had found, however, the Romans would not tolerate a monarch. He had taken the illegal position of dictator for life, a stopgap measure that probably crystallized the resentment against him into a fatal conspiracy.

Octavian's problem was the same as Caesar's: to find a way for one man to govern the Roman Empire while preserving the appearance of the old Republic. Between 31 and 27 B.C.E., Octavian relied on holding the consul-

Marcus Vipsanius Agrippa. (Hulton|Archive by Getty Images)

ship, with Agrippa as his colleague in 28 and 27 B.C.E. While Octavian was away from Rome trying to stabilize affairs in the urbanized, Greek-speaking east (which resented its domination by the agricultural and Latin west), Agrippa directed governmental affairs in Italy and the west with the aid of Maecenas.

These two men seem to have been most influential in helping Octavian solve the dilemma of governing Rome. The historian Dio Cassius records a debate among the three of them, with speeches by Gaius Maecenas and Agrippa advocating, respectively, that Octavian become a constitutional monarch or restore the Republic. The speeches summarize the two philosophical points of view, but they probably have no historical validity. The settlement that Octavian worked out with the senate in 27 B.C.E. appeared on the surface to gratify the Romans' desire to see their Republic restored, but it actually granted to Octavian (by that time called Augustus) all the civilian and military powers necessary to make him an effective ruler.

This subtle monarchy, called the principate, had one flaw. Because it was not technically a legal magistracy or a hereditary monarchy, it could not be passed on to a successor designated by the princeps, the head of state. In 23 B.C.E., Augustus was taken ill and almost died. In the depths of his illness, he gave his signet ring, which served as his signature and the symbol of his power, to Agrippa, perhaps indicating his desire that his loyal friend succeed him. On his recovery, Augustus gave Agrippa proconsular power similar to his own.

In spite of his respect for Agrippa, Augustus soon realized that the aristocratic senate would never accept him as princeps because of his plebeian origins. Augustus hoped to groom some member of his own family to succeed him, but he had difficulty finding anyone suitable. He had only one child, a daughter, Julia, so he promoted the career of his nephew Marcellus by sharing the consulship with him and marrying him to Julia.

The attention showered on Marcellus provoked the first strain between Agrippa and Augustus. It was said of Agrippa that, while he did not want to be the first man in the Empire, he would be second to only one man. His departure to govern the eastern provinces, though touted as a promotion, seems to have been regarded by Agrippa as a kind of exile. He did not return to Rome until after Marcellus's untimely death in

22 B.C.E. In 20 and 19 B.C.E., Agrippa put down minor revolts in Gaul and Spain. His policy in dealing with the provinces was to defend, not expand, the borders. Soon after Agrippa's death, Augustus began listening to other advice, and Rome suffered two of its worst defeats ever in Germany.

Not all Agrippa's service to Augustus was military. In 28 B.C.E., he married Octavian's niece Marcella; in 21 B.C.E., with Augustus's approval, he divorced her to marry the widow Julia, who was then about sixteen. Augustus may have taken him as his son-in-law because Agrippa had become so powerful and so popular that he had to be taken into the Imperial family or suppressed like an enemy. With Julia, Agrippa had two daughters and three sons, two of whom Augustus adopted and promoted as possible successors.

Augustus continued to honor Agrippa and to associate him in the Imperial power. In 18 B.C.E., Agrippa was given tribunician power, one of the basic grants on which Augustus's position rested. The holder of this power could veto the actions of any other Roman magistrate. The grant was renewed in 13 B.C.E. By March of the next year, Agrippa had quieted a revolt in Pannonia (in modern Yugoslavia) and returned to Rome ill. He died by the end of the month, and his ashes were laid in the Julian family mausoleum.

SIGNIFICANCE

Marcus Vipsanius Agrippa was a remarkable man, willing to subordinate his military and engineering genius to the service of a friend who was less talented than he. Writers such as Suetonius and Cornelius Tacitus, who could find some hint of scandal to besmirch any reputation, report nothing of the kind about Agrippa. In an age when treachery and shifting alliances were common in politics, Agrippa displayed unswerving loyalty to Augustus for more than thirty years. His support enabled Augustus to defeat his rivals and assume power in the first place. His buildings and public works—many of them financed out of his personal funds—contributed to the well-being and happiness of the populace of Rome. This general good feeling was an essential element in maintaining the stability of the principate. It is extremely doubtful that Augustus could have taken power in the first place or held it for long without Agrippa's assistance.

Not only did Agrippa have a profound impact on the course of events in the first century B.C.E. and for some time after that, but he also contributed directly as the progenitor of two later emperors. His daughter Agrippina

the Elder was the mother of Caligula and the grandmother (through her daughter) of Nero. While his descendants may not have been popular leaders, Agrippa cannot be blamed for all of their flaws. Through a complex web of Imperial marriages, they also carried the genes of Augustus and Marc Antony.

Agrippa would be better known if his autobiography and his geographical commentary had survived. The latter was used to make a map, which was prominently displayed in Rome and was an important source for Strabo, Pliny the Elder, and other writers with geographic or ethnographic interests. The opinion of antiquity, that Agrippa was the noblest Roman of his day, has not been revised by later historians.

—*Albert A. Bell, Jr.*

FURTHER READING

Badian, E. "Notes on the *Laudatio* of Agrippa." *Classical Journal* 76 (1981): 97-109. This article discusses a recently discovered papyrus containing a portion of Augustus's funeral oration for Agrippa.

Buchan, J. *Augustus*. Boston: Houghton Mifflin, 1937. This slightly romantic biography of the first Roman emperor covers in detail Agrippa's contribution to his success.

Evans, H. B. "Agrippa's Water Plan." *American Journal of Archeology* 86 (1982): 401-411. A good analysis of Agrippa's contribution to Rome's system of aqueducts, which provided more water per person in Augustus's day than does the system of modern Rome.

Firth, J. B. *Augustus Caesar and the Organization of the Empire of Rome*. New York: G. P. Putnam's Sons, 1903. Helpful references to Agrippa throughout and an insightful chapter on Maecenas and Agrippa.

McKechnie, P. "Dio Cassius's Speech of Agrippa: A Realistic Alternative to Imperial Government?" *Greece and Rome* 28 (October, 1981): 150-155. Agrippa's speech is a set piece, not truly reflecting his views on democracy. In other passages, Dio describes Agrippa as an ardent supporter of monarchy.

Reinhold, M. *Marcus Agrippa*. Geneva, N.Y.: W. F. Humphrey Press, 1933. Despite some traces of hero worship, this volume is still among the most thorough studies of Agrippa available in English. It follows his career and characterizes him as a self-made man, lacking in the subtle intellect of Augustus or Maecenas but a master of practical matters of organization.

Shipley, Frederick W. *Agrippa's Building Activities in Rome*. St. Louis, Mo.: Washington University, 1933. This short book studies Agrippa's building activity by location in various districts of Rome. It also discusses the problem of determining exactly where some of the buildings were. Shipley argues that the Pantheon as Hadrian rebuilt it bears little resemblance to Agrippa's original plan.

Woodward, Christopher. *Rome: C.* New York: St. Martin's Press, 1996. Historical guide to the architecture of Rome fully describes each of two hundred buildings.

SEE ALSO: Marc Antony; Augustus; Julius Caesar; Caligula; Nero.

RELATED ARTICLES in *Great Events from History: The Ancient World*: c. 509 B.C.E., Roman Republic Replaces Monarchy; 46 B.C.E., Establishment of the Julian Calendar; 43-42 B.C.E., Second Triumvirate Enacts Proscriptions; 27-23 B.C.E., Completion of the Augustan Settlement; c. 50 C.E., Creation of the Roman Imperial Bureaucracy.

AGRIPPINA THE YOUNGER
Roman noblewoman

Julia Agrippina accumulated and exercised extensive political power during the reign of two Roman emperors in the mid-first century C.E.

BORN: November 6, c. 15 C.E.; Oppidum Ubiorum (now Cologne, Germany)

DIED: March 59 C.E.; Baiae, Campania (now near Naples, Italy)

ALSO KNOWN AS: Julia Agrippina

AREA OF ACHIEVEMENT: Government and politics

EARLY LIFE

Little is known concerning the early life of Julia Agrippina (ag-reh-PEEN-ah), or Agrippina the Younger, as she is more commonly known. The accounts of her life and deeds were recorded by ancient authors such as Cornelius Tacitus (*Ab excessu divi Augusti*, c. 116 C.E., also known as *Annales*; *Annals*, 1598), Seutonius (*De vita Caesarum*, c. 120 C.E.; *History of the Twelve Caesars*, 1606), Dio Cassius (*Romaika*, probably c. 202 C.E.; *Roman History*, 1914-1927), and Pliny the Elder (*Naturalis historia*, 77 C.E.; *Natural History*, 1938-1963). Each of these writers was highly critical of Agrippina, and the principate in general, and should be considered hostile. She was the eldest daughter of Germanicus and Agrippina the Elder. As a daughter of Germanicus, a member of the Imperial household, and possible successor to the emperor Tiberius, she would have been highly educated. Several ancient authors refer to her memoirs (now lost), attesting to her literacy and education at a time when many women were not educated beyond what was needed to manage their households.

As a child, she often accompanied her father as he traveled throughout the Empire on official duty. In fact, it was while Germanicus was serving in Germany that Agrippina was born, at the town of Oppidum Ubiorum (modern Cologne) around the year 15 C.E. She returned to Rome, along with her family, in 17 C.E. in order to celebrate her father's victories over the German tribes. Later that same year, Germanicus was sent to the East, leaving Agrippina the Younger in Rome. Germanicus died in the East in 19 C.E., having possibly been poisoned by a political rival.

After the death of her father, Agrippina the Younger lived with her mother until her marriage to Gnaeus Domitius Ahenobarbus in 28 C.E., with whom she had one son, the future emperor Nero. During the intervening years, her mother, Agrippina the Elder, worked diligently to promote the sons of Germanicus as possible candidates for the throne. In doing so, Agrippina's mother ran afoul of the sitting emperor, Tiberius. The elder Agrippina was exiled in 29 C.E., at which time Agrippina the Younger went to live with Livia, the mother of Tiberius, and wife of the late emperor Augustus. Agrippina the Elder died in exile in 33 C.E.

At the death of the emperor Tiberius in 37, Agrippina the Younger's brother Gaius Caligula became emperor. Early in Caligula's reign, Agrippina, along with her two sisters, received honors on coins, and their names were included in oaths to the welfare of the emperor. In 39 C.E., however, Agrippina was thought to have conspired against Caligula and was exiled to the island of Pontia.

Caligula was assassinated in 41 C.E. and was succeeded by Agrippina's uncle, Tiberius Claudius Caesar, commonly known as Claudius. That same year she was allowed to return to Rome. Shortly after her return, she married the wealthy Gaius Sallustus Crispus Passienus (Domitius having died the year before). The marriage was short-lived, as Passienus died sometime in the 40's. A critical event in her life occurred in 49 C.E., when she married Claudius, shortly after the execution of his third wife, Messallina. The marriage between a man and his niece was illegal according to Roman law; however, the senate quickly passed legislation allowing the emperor to marry his niece.

LIFE'S WORK

During the period of her marriage to the emperor Claudius, and thereafter, Agrippina's political skill and ambition became apparent in a variety of ways. The marriage was purely a political arrangement that helped both parties. In the years before the marriage, there were several plots against Claudius's life that created an atmosphere of political instability. Several senators were executed for treason, probably at the instigation of Claudius's third wife, Messallina. Ultimately, this political instability resulted in the execution of Messallina by Claudius be-

cause of her involvement in a conspiracy against the emperor. Claudius certainly recognized Agrippina's political skills and the stability that she would bring to his government. For Agrippina, the marriage brought her substantial political power and the chance to promote her young son, Nero, as a possible successor to the aging Claudius.

Her rising influence, and power, can best be illustrated by the many exceptional honors bestowed on her at this time. In the year 50 C.E. she received the title *Augusta*, which was the feminine form of the honorific title *Augustus* adopted by emperors. This was a signal honor in that it had never before been granted to the wife of a living emperor. Although Agrippina's image had appeared on coins during the reign of her brother, Caligula, her image was now placed, with the designation of *Augusta*, on the reverse side of coins bearing the image of Claudius. Such an honor demonstrated that she was viewed as a partner in the administration of the government. Also, her birthplace of Ubiorum Oppidum was at this time designated a Roman colony and renamed Colonia Claudia Ara Augusta Agrippinensium.

An additional honor bestowed on her was that of the *salutatio*. The *salutatio* was a daily obligation to visit, and pay respects to, important individuals in Roman society. When the important clients of the emperor came to the palace each day, they were obliged to pay their respects to Agrippina as well as Claudius.

Agrippina was able to convince Claudius to adopt her son, Nero, in 50, thus promoting Nero as a possible successor to the throne. Claudius had a son, Britannicus, by Messallina. However, Britannicus was three years younger than the thirteen-year-old Nero and therefore was not as viable a candidate for the throne. Claudius also realized that Nero, as the grandson of Germanicus, would be popular among the people of Rome. In 53 C.E., Nero's position as successor was further strengthened by his marriage to Claudius's daughter Octavia. Claudius died the following year at age sixty-four. Tacitus and Suetonius claimed that Agrippina murdered her husband by feeding him poisoned mushrooms in order to ensure that Nero would succeed before Britannicus came of age.

Agrippina the Younger. (Hulton|Archive by Getty Images)

IMPORTANT FAMILY CONNECTIONS OF AGRIPPINA THE YOUNGER

Great-granddaughter of Emperor Augustus
Granddaughter of Marcus Vipsanius Agrippa and Julia III
Daughter of Germanicus and Agrippina the Elder
Sister of Emperor Caligula
Niece and wife of Emperor Claudius I
Mother of Emperor Nero

Agrippina was a farsighted woman. She was able to exert her influence over Nero after he became emperor through his tutors, who were, at the time, among her loyal followers. She had earlier convinced Claudius to allow the exiled poet, Seneca, and the commander of the Imperial bodyguard, Burrus, to become the young boy's tutors, and they continued in this capacity after Nero became emperor. Nero purportedly allowed all of his private and public business affairs to be handled by Agrippina, while his tutors catered to his baser instincts. Even though this may be an exaggeration, it was at this time that Agrippina was at the height of her power. Women, in the highly patriarchal society of ancient Rome, were forbidden to attend senate meetings; Agrippina was said to have observed meetings of the senate from behind a curtain. In addition, she was accorded the honor of being attended by two lictors. Lictors preceded Roman magistrates on official business and carried the fasces, a symbol of authority.

Another indication of Agrippina's political power during this time is reflected in coinage. Whereas earlier her image had appeared on the reverse of the Caligula coins, now she was the first woman accorded the honor of having her image appear on the same side as that of the emperor. Her image appeared facing the image of Nero, on the coins minted in Rome. She had, in fact, appeared on coins in this manner along with her husband Claudius, but those coins were minted outside Rome.

Agrippina was certainly aware that her political power depended on her influence over her son, as well as her son remaining emperor. Several ancient authors write that Agrippina was influential in eliminating possible rivals to Nero and, therefore, rivals to her own power.

However, as the influence of Nero's tutors grew, Agrippina's influence over her son began to decrease. During the reign of Claudius, Agrippina had accompanied the emperor when he met with foreign delegations. Nero discontinued this practice and did not allow his mother this honor. Coins depicting Nero and his mother began to show Nero's head superimposed over that of Agrippina's, indicating a decline in her political power.

Some ancient writers claimed that in an attempt to regain power, Agrippina turned her attentions toward promoting Claudius's son Britannicus. Whether this is true or not, Britannicus was murdered. Some say he was poisoned at a dinner party in front of Agrippina. This violent act was purportedly carried out at the instigation of Nero to demonstrate his own power and to further indicate a decline in Agrippina's influence.

In 55 C.E. Nero had Agrippina removed from the palace, supposedly because of the number of friends and clients who visited her on a daily basis. Nero claimed that these visitations disrupted the daily routine of the palace. His motives may have been to reduce her influence within the palace. At the same time, he dismissed her Imperial guard, thus reducing her influence among the guard as well. These two actions resulted in a substantial decline in Agrippina's political power. Shortly thereafter, she was charged with treason. An investigation was held, but she was cleared of the charges. As a result of being cleared of the charges, it is believed that she may have had a brief resurgence of political power.

Unfortunately, Agrippina disappears from the historical record from 55 to 59 C.E., the year of her death. It is not known precisely why Nero decided that his mother should be murdered. What is known is that Nero's first attempts to kill Agrippina failed miserably. Nero pretended that he wanted to be reconciled with her and invited her to a festival in Baiae, near Naples. One account states that she was to stay in a bedroom that had been constructed with a collapsible ceiling. When this attempt on her life failed, Nero placed Agrippina on a boat that was designed to fall apart at sea. Agrippina, however, swam to shore. After these two failed attempts, Nero dispatched a contingent of soldiers, who executed Agrippina.

SIGNIFICANCE

Agrippina the Younger was one of a few Roman women who were able to accumulate substantial power, and have an influence on politics, in the highly patriarchal society of ancient Rome. Through her influence with two emperors, she demonstrated that some Roman women were just as intelligent and ambitious as Roman men. Although she exercised power indirectly through men, her power was publicly recognized in the Imperial coinage of the time. She served as a model for later Roman empresses, such as Pulcheria and Eudocia, who also commanded significant political power through their influence with powerful male leaders. Agrippina's exceptional abilities to form successful political alliances, and her influence on politics and governance, have earned her the right to be considered an early stateswoman.

—*Kevin Edward Birch*

FURTHER READING

Balsdon, J. P. V. D. *Roman Women: Their History and Habits*. New York: Barnes & Noble, 1962. Discusses the role of women in Roman society.

Barrett, Anthony A. *Agrippina: Sex, Power, and Politics in the Early Empire*. New Haven, Conn.: Yale University Press, 1996. An objective and comprehensive modern work concerning Agrippina the Younger. The book has helpful appendices, a bibliography, and a complete list of known citations regarding her in ancient texts.

Lefkowitz, Mary R., and Maureen B. Fant. *Women's Life in Greece and Rome*. Baltimore: The Johns Hopkins University Press, 1982. The authors provide an overview of women's role in classical society and the general attitudes toward women.

Suetonius. *The Twelve Caesars*. Translated by Robert Graves. New York: Welcome Rain, 2001. Written in the late first century or early second century C.E., Suetonius's biography of the early emperors of Rome is an important source of information about the lives of the emperors and their families. It should, however, be noted that Suetonius, like Tacitus, was biased against the Imperial families.

Tacitus. *The Annals of Imperial Rome*. Translated by Michael Grant. New York: Penguin Books, 1989. Written in the late first century or early second century C.E., Tacitus's history of the early Roman Empire is one of the few ancient accounts that survives. His bias against the Imperial family should, however, be noted.

SEE ALSO: Marcus Vipsanius Agrippa; Caligula; Claudius I; Nero; Pliny the Elder; Tacitus.

RELATED ARTICLES in *Great Events from History: The Ancient World*: c. 50 C.E., Creation of the Roman Imperial Bureaucracy; 64-67 C.E., Nero Persecutes the Christians.

AKHENATON
Egyptian king (r. 1350-c. 1334 B.C.E.)

Akhenaton is credited with the establishment of monotheism in Egypt; he built a new capital, Akhetaton, in honor of Aton, the sun god.

BORN: c. 1364 B.C.E.; Egypt
DIED: c. 1334 B.C.E.; Akhetaton (now Tell el-Amārna, Egypt)
ALSO KNOWN AS: Akhenaten; Amenhotep IV (given name); Amenophis IV; Ikhnaton
AREAS OF ACHIEVEMENT: Government and politics, religion

EARLY LIFE

Born Amenhotep IV, Akhenaton (ah-keh-NAH-tuhn) was the son and successor of Amenhotep III (also known as Amenophis III) of the Eighteenth Dynasty. Akhenaton's life and accomplishments need to be seen in the context of his family and of Egyptian history in general. Egyptian history is conventionally divided into thirty-one dynasties, which stretched from about 2925 to 332 B.C.E., and were succeeded by the Greek Ptolemies from 332 until 30 B.C.E. and the Roman emperors from 30 B.C.E. to 395 C.E. These dynasties are clumped together in groups under various designations, with the period of

Akhenaton falling into the group of dynasties known as the New Kingdom Period (c. 1570-c. 1069), approximately in the middle of ancient Egyptian history.

The New Kingdom in the fifteenth century B.C.E. covered an area almost two thousand miles from north to south, most of it centered on the Nile River. The architects of this kingdom were Thutmose I, Thutmose III, and Amenhotep II. By the time of Amenhotep II, the northern city of Memphis had been, in effect, displaced by Thebes as the center of royal power. Three hundred miles upriver from Memphis, Thebes was the home of the royal family, and the rulers of the Eighteenth Dynasty began building tombs for themselves in the desolate region west of Thebes known as the Valley of the Kings.

One consequence of Thebes's rise to power was an increase in the influence of the god Amen-Ra, whose large temple was at nearby Karnak. Amen-Ra was a powerful sun god whose name is embedded in such proper names as Tutankhamen and Amenhotep. As a result of Amen-Ra's dominance at Thebes, the city became the center of religious celebrations.

Akhenaton's father, whose reign was roughly from 1386 to 1349, controlled Egypt at the peak of its power.

He married, when quite young, a general's daughter named Tiy, but as was common, he had numerous concubines from Syria and other regions. Only the six children—two boys and four girls—of his marriage to Tiy, however, had royal significance. The second son, who became Amenhotep IV, was born around 1390.

Amenhotep III was an impressive man who achieved a reputation as a bold hunter and a gifted diplomat. He publicized his reign in a series of innovative scarab seals, each inscribed with a brief account of some historic event. Amenhotep III was also an ambitious builder; although early in his reign he continued to maintain a royal household in Memphis, he later moved to Thebes and spent the last ten years of his life directing construction projects in that city. At the same time, he had built the temple of Amen-Ra (in modern Luxor) near Karnak on the Nile River. The costs were enormous: The temple at Montu alone used 2.5 tons (2.25 metric tons) of gold and 1,250 pounds (567 kilograms) of lapis lazuli.

During these last ten years in Thebes, Amenhotep III hosted three opulent jubilees in his palace. The sybaritic life took its toll. Amenhotep III's mummy presents a fat, bald man with rotten teeth; the king died at about the age of thirty-eight and was succeeded by his second son, Amenhotep IV, or Akhenaton, as he soon came to call himself.

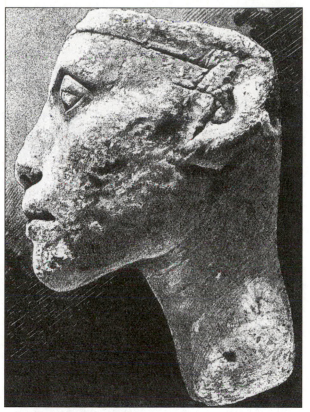

Death mask of Akhenaton. (Library of Congress)

LIFE'S WORK

His older brother apparently having died young, Amenhotep IV ascended the throne in about 1377. One peculiarity of the new king's background is his failure to appear on his father's monuments, suggesting that for some reason his existence had deliberately been downplayed. The depictions of him show a deformed body that may have been an embarrassment to his family. His sagging belly, elongated face and neck, and feminine hips all point to a pituitary condition now known as Frölich's syndrome. Although Frölich's syndrome usually results in eunuchoidism, Amenhotep IV married Nefertiti, and they had several children. Unfortunately, little is known about Nefertiti—she may have been Amenhotep's cousin—and it is not even certain that Amenhotep was the natural father of the children she bore.

For the first year of his reign, Amenhotep continued the building projects of his father. He then embarked on his own distinctive projects. He soon planned a spectacular jubilee, a surprising departure from the usual practice of hosting them only after a reign of thirty years; this jubilee was marked by the building of four large temples at nearby Karnak.

The historical record at this point is extremely sketchy for two reasons. First, when he erected his new city of Akhetaton, Amenhotep thoroughly eradicated the memorials to Amen-Ra and the other sun gods. Second, after his death, one of his successors, Horemheb, destroyed the four temples at Karnak, whose remains, in the form of blocks known as *talatat*, scholars have recently been painstakingly fitting together.

The reconstructed reliefs on these temple remains have produced several surprises for scholars. The *talatat* reveal, for example, that Amenhotep maintained a heavy military presence around himself at all times, a practice that implies insecurity. The *talatat* reliefs also celebrate Nefertiti in diverse depictions—especially surprising because Amenhotep himself appears nowhere in the decorations of his structures. No firm conclusions can be drawn, but it is impossible not to speculate on the possibility that Nefertiti played a much greater role in the royal planning than that evinced by the scanty evidence available before the *talatat* reconstructions.

After about five years at Thebes, Amenhotep suddenly abandoned that city and built a new capital farther north down the Nile River. This new capital was named Akhetaton, or "horizon of the Disk." At the same time, Amenhotep changed his name to Akhenaton (he who is useful to the Sun-disk). In keeping with his new name and devotion, Akhenaton declared Amen-Ra, the old sun god, anathema. He had Amen-Ra's name plastered over on each royal cartouche (an oblong figure enclosing a royal name or epithet), and the name of his god Aton was then inscribed on them. Throughout the kingdom, the name Amen-Ra was also at this time desecrated wherever it appeared on such objects as walls and tombs. Akhetaton was built on what is today called Tell el-Amārna, and the period of Akhetaton's dominance is designated the Amarna Age.

Akhenaton's new city was a hastily constructed affair, probably of inferior workmanship, stretching out for seven miles along the east bank of the Nile in Middle Egypt. Akhenaton's own residence was a large village at the city's north end. An unusual walled enclosure designated *Maru-aton* dominated the southern part of the city; with its pools and gardens, it was probably a site for cult observances.

Akhenaton's mother, Queen Tiy, was part of the entourage that moved to Akhetaton, and it now appears that a second wife, known as Queen Kiya, also accompanied him to the new home, although her role and status are unclear. The military guard continued as strong around Akhenaton at Akhetaton as at Thebes, but there was a complete shuffle in the important personnel at the court. The other cities, especially Thebes and Memphis, were allowed to fend for themselves; the old elite believed that they had been snubbed by the heretic king and his parvenus in the new center of the kingdom.

In about the eleventh year of Akhenaton's rule, the royal family began dying, perhaps as a result of a plague in the region. Thus by the fourteenth year, Queen Tiy, Kiya, and four of Akhenaton's six daughters were all dead. With their passing, and the king's aging, his daughter Meritaton rose in power and esteem, and by the fifteenth year, she was being depicted in statuary with her husband, Smenkhare (he whom the spirit of Ra has ennobled). The epithets devoted to Smenkhare indicate that he probably acted as the king's coregent. It is an open question whether Smenkhare ever actually ruled by himself or whether the throne went directly to Tutankhamen on Akhenaton's death around the year 1360.

What happened to Nefertiti during these last years of Akhenaton's reign is not known. The fact that she seems to have disappeared at about the same time that Smenkhare came on the scene has inspired scholarly con-

jecture that they were the same person, but the theory is burdened by too many improbabilities to be convincing. As far as is known, she survived these final years at Akhetaton but with greatly reduced royal influence.

Tutankhamen, possibly Akhenaton's son by Kiya, moved back to Thebes after three years, and the power in the kingdom was concentrated largely in the capable hands of one of Akhenaton's top officials, Ay, who himself ruled for about four years after Tutankhamen's death. Ay's successor, Horemheb, destroyed Akhenaton's temples at Karnak, and the work and innovations of the heretic king were concluded.

SIGNIFICANCE

Recent scholarship challenges the old romantic picture of a humanist Akhenaton, a pioneering champion of monotheism in whose steps Moses followed. The king was an insecure ruler, physically unattractive, thrust into a role that surrounded him with figures from his father's establishment whom he feared. His vacillation weakened Egypt's control of its northern provinces, and he left the administration of his kingdom to his military advisers. Historian Donald Redford characterizes Akhenaton as a dreamy soul devoted to cultic reforms that he did not really understand. By not replacing Amen-Ra with a significant mythology, Akhenaton was actually propagating atheism. The Sun-disk, Redford says, could never be seen as "god," and Redford spells out his conception of the real focus of Akhenaton's worship:

> What it was Akhenaton tells us plainly enough: the Disk was his father, the universal king. Significant, it seems to me, is the fact that, on the eve of Amenophis III's passing, the king who sat on Egypt's throne bore as his most popular sobriquet the title "The Dazzling Sun-disk"; on the morrow of the "revolution" the only object of veneration in the supernal realm is King Sun-disk, exalted in the heavens and ubiquitously termed by Akhenaton "my father."

Redford's contemptuous verdict on Akhenaton is that the king was an effete and slothful leader of an "aggregation of voluptuaries." Moreover, Akhenaton appears to Redford as the worst kind of totalitarian, one who demanded "universal submission" from everyone. It is a harsh verdict that Redford submits and one that more sympathetic scholars will surely challenge as they continue to study the meager evidence of the life and accomplishments of this elusive king.

—Frank Day

FURTHER READING

Aldred, Cyril. *Akhenaten and Nefertiti*. New York: Viking Press, 1973. This catalog of an exhibition at the Brooklyn Institute of Arts and Sciences, written by one of the period's most eminent scholars, is an invaluable study of the art of Akhenaton's reign. Includes illustrations, many in color, and an extensive bibliography. Fully annotated.

_____. *The Egyptians*. 3d ed. New York: Thames and Hudson, 1998. Aldred provides an excellent general history of the region, with many black-and-white and color illustrations. Includes a bibliography and indexes.

Baines, John, and Jaromir Málek. *Atlas of Ancient Egypt*. New York: Facts on File, 1984. Baines and Málek provide an especially full and detailed reference book, replete with excellent tables, summaries of the ancient hieroglyphic writing system, maps, and time lines.

Hornung, Erik. *Akhenaton and the Religion of Light*. Translated by David Lorton. Ithaca, N.Y.: Cornell University Press, 1999. This examination of Akhenaton's period extends to recent archaeological finds. Hornung emphasizes that Akhenaton's monotheism represented the earliest attempt in history to explain the entire natural and human world on the basis of a single principle, making light the "absolute reference point." Also addresses the origins of the new religion.

Redford, Donald B. *Akhenaten: The Heretic King*. Princeton, N.J.: Princeton University Press, 1984. A detailed scholarly analysis of Akhenaton and his accomplishments by the man who directed the Akhenaton Temple Project. Redford's account is one of the standard studies. Includes an index, a bibliography, and illustrations.

SEE ALSO: Amenhotep III; Nefertiti; Tiy; Tutankhamen.
RELATED ARTICLES in *Great Events from History: The Ancient World*: c. 1570 B.C.E., New Kingdom Period Begins in Egypt; c. 1450 B.C.E., International Age of Major Kingdoms Begins in the Near East; c. 1365 B.C.E., Failure of Akhenaton's Cultural Revival; 1069 B.C.E., Third Intermediate Period Begins in Egypt.

AKIBA BEN JOSEPH
Jewish sage, rabbi, and martyr

The most influential rabbi in the formation of Jewish legal tradition and Mishnah, Akiba is the one scholar most often quoted in the text. He espoused the unsuccessful cause of Bar Kokhba and died a martyr. The legends about Akiba have been almost as influential as his teachings and life.

BORN: c. 40 C.E.; probably near Lydda, Palestine (now Lod, Israel)
DIED: c. 135 C.E.; Caesarea, Palestine (now in Israel)
ALSO KNOWN AS: Aqiba ben Joseph; Akiva ben Joseph
AREA OF ACHIEVEMENT: Religion

EARLY LIFE

Akiba ben Joseph (ah-KIHV-ah behn JOH-zehf) was born to humble parents. His father's name was Joseph, but tradition has no other information about his parentage. Akiba worked as an unschooled shepherd. He was part of the lower class designated as the *am-ha-aretz* (people of the land), a term of common abuse. While working for a wealthy man of Jerusalem whose name is sometimes given as Johanan ben Joshua, Akiba fell in love with his daughter, Rachel, who returned his love.

This period of Akiba's life has been variously treated in exaggerated fashion by legendary accounts. Based on the historically most reliable traditions from the Mishnah, it appears reasonably certain that Rachel, agreeing to marry him, was disinherited by her father, and the couple lived in poor circumstances. It was only after his marriage and the birth of a son (probably at about age thirty-five) that Akiba began learning how to read. After learning the basics, Akiba (probably now age forty) left both home and occupation to attend the rabbinic academy at Yavneh, in southwestern Judaea.

In the generation after the destruction of the Temple (c. 80-100 C.E.), the rabbinic assembly at Yavneh was presided over by Rabbi Gamaliel II (an aristocrat) as *Nasi* (Ethnarch) and Rabbi Joshua ben Hananiah (a nonaristocrat) as *Ab Bet Din* (head of the rabbinic court). It was to the latter that Akiba went for instruction, but Hananiah directed him first to Rabbi Tarfon, who was in turn his teacher, friend, and then follower. Later, Akiba studied with Rabbi Nahum of Gimzo and then Hananiah himself. Thus by birth, training, and temperament, Akiba was aligned with the more liberal antiaristocratic wing of the academy, which traced its roots back to Rabbi Hillel.

Finally, Akiba studied under Rabbi Eliezer ben Hyrcanus, a leading figure of the aristocratic wing, whose tradition went back to Rabbi Shammai. Akiba's formal training came to a conclusion at Yavneh when in public debate Hananiah was defeated by Eliezer on the primacy of sacrificial duties over Sabbath rest. As the debate was being concluded, the relatively unknown Akiba entered the debate and carried the day against Eliezer. At this point, Akiba was recognized as a rabbi. He began to teach, and pupils began to seek him out.

During this thirteen-year period of study, Akiba must have spent long periods of time away from home. He was encouraged and supported by his wife. While popular legend has undoubtedly exaggerated this aspect of Akiba's life, there is an underlying truth to the material, and, more important, his love and appreciation for Rachel are reflected in his teaching.

LIFE'S WORK

In the beginning, Akiba began to teach in Yavneh and spent most of his time actively engaging in the disputes of the rabbinical assembly. These must have been vigorous, for tradition indicates that there were punishments meted out to Akiba on several occasions for his lack of respect for procedure and that at one point he left the assembly and retired to Zifron in Galilee. Akiba was later invited to return to Yavneh by Gamaliel.

Akiba was a bald, tall man, muscular from years of outdoor work. He had transformed himself into a gentle scholar who stressed the value of polite behavior and tact. This emphasis on courtesy, however, did not stop him from entering into debates and arguing passionately for his convictions. As part of his philosophy, he upheld the authority of the *Nasi*, even when he was arguing strongly against the specific ideas that the *Nasi* held.

While he was never entrusted with either of the chief offices of the assembly, he was an important member of the inner circle. When Gamaliel was removed from office because of his arrogance, it was Akiba who was chosen to inform Gamaliel. Eleazar ben Arariah was made *Nasi* in his place, but he was a figurehead, and real leadership rested with Hananiah and Akiba. Having secured dominance of the assembly, Akiba and Hananiah brought the number of the assembly members up from thirty-two to seventy-two, seating younger scholars to whom Gamaliel had refused admission because of their positions, which were similar to those of Akiba. Akiba seems also to have played an important part in the restoration of Gamaliel to the position of *Nasi*. Direction of the assembly was in the hands of Gamaliel, Eleazar, Hananiah, and Akiba. At that time, he was appointed overseer for the poor. In that capacity, he traveled widely in the area, raising funds. He traveled throughout Judaea, Cappadocia, Arabia, and Egypt.

In the fall of 95 C.E., Akiba, Gamaliel, Hananiah, and Eleazar were sent as an embassy to the Emperor Domitian to calm the Imperial displeasure over the fact that a member of the Imperial family, Flavius Clemens, had converted to Judaism. During this visit, the rabbis probably consulted the Jewish historian and Imperial freedman Flavius Josephus for advice on Imperial protocol and influence for their petition. Before this could be done, however, Domitian died, and Nerva was appointed emperor. Although there is no written record of what was done, it would have been unthinkable for the embassy not to have given the new emperor the formal greetings of the Jewish community and to have made expressions of loyalty. Nerva was seen as opening up a new era in Jewish-Roman relations.

At this point (c. 97 C.E.), Akiba was between fifty and sixty years of age. He established his own school at Bene-Berak (near modern Tel Aviv). It was during this time that Akiba's most enduring work was accomplished. In his teaching, he used a combination of demanding logic, rules of interpretation, and homely parables to put forth his ideas and ideals. He set the basic organization of what was to become the Mishnah into its six parts and developed his ideas of interpretation of the law based on the mystic significance of the text. In addition to a passion for social justice, he developed his unique positions on the role of women, marriage, and other issues. None of these positions was achieved without extensive debate and discussion in Akiba's own school and in the assembly in Yavneh. There, the new leading opponent of Akiba was Rabbi Ishmael ben Elisha. Many of the teachings of these men were later arranged into opposing debates, even when it can be shown that no such discussion took place. The two men had great respect for each other and were cordial in their relations, but they were not friends.

The first generation of Akiba's disciples—Elisha ben Abuyah, Simeon ben Azzai, and Simeon ben Zoma—did not fare well. Elisha became an apostate, Simeon ben Azzai became mad, and Simeon ben Zoma lost his life. The second generation of scholars taught by Akiba, however, provided the rabbinic leadership of the next generation. Of these, Rabbi Meir and Aquila deserve special attention. Meir, who had studied with Elisha ben Abuyah and Ishmael before coming to Akiba, was responsible for continuing the arrangement of the Mishnah following the principles of Akiba. He wrote down many of the sayings of Akiba, often giving the opposing view of Ishmael. Aquila was a Greek who converted to Judaism and studied with Akiba. With Akiba's encouragement, he made a new (or made revisions to the) Greek translation of the Hebrew scriptures. For a time, Aquila seems to have been in the confidence of both the Jews and the Roman officials.

The last phase of Akiba's life is a matter of considerable debate among scholars. Relations with Rome, never good under the best of circumstances, went through a series of radical shifts. There is no clear understanding of these years because the sources (Jewish Talmudic and Roman writers) preserve the misunderstandings of the principals. What part, if any, Akiba played in the formulation of Jewish positions is not clear until the very end of the conflict. Some indicate that he used his position as overseer of the poor to travel throughout the land and foment revolt. Others suggest that his position was essentially nonpolitical and that he did not resist until religious practices, including prayer and study, were forbidden. There is no evidence that Akiba was active in politics or any other capacity during the troubles at the end of Trajan's reign through the beginning years of Hadrian.

In about 130 C.E., to ease some of the existing tension, Hadrian sought to rebuild the Temple but insisted on placing a statue of himself in it and dedicating the temple to Jupiter Capitolinus. The implications of this position for the Jews clearly were not understood by Hadrian. There is a tradition, not in itself improbable, that the rabbis selected the now-aged Akiba to lead a delegation to Hadrian to reverse this stand. It is not known whether they reached the emperor, but their efforts, for whatever reason, were unsuccessful. Open and widespread rebellion broke out, which required five years and some of Hadrian's best military talent to quell.

Of Akiba's activities during that period, only a few events are clear. The Talmudic evidence shows that Akiba was a firm supporter of living within the restrictions of 125 C.E. that forbade circumcision and severely restricted the rights of Jewish legal courts and synagogue practices. At some point in the rebellion, Akiba joined other rabbis, including Ishmael, and gave his endorsement to Bar Kokhba. Bar Kokhba (meaning son of a star), the name taken by Simeon ben Kosiba, carried messianic implications; it was Akiba who applied the verse from Numbers 24:17, "The star rises from Jacob," to him. This stance was not without opposition. The Midrash records

that "when Rabbi Akiba beheld ben Kosiba he exclaimed, 'This is the king Messiah!' Rabbi Johanan ben Tortha retorted: 'Akiba, grass will grow in your cheeks and he will still not have come!'" (*Lamentations* 2:2). Thus, at least in the last stages, Akiba gave his support to Bar Kokhba, who claimed to be the *Nasi*, superseding the rabbinical *Nasi* at Yavneh; Akiba hailed him as Savior (Messiah).

Sometime after 130, and possibly as late as 134, Akiba was arrested and imprisoned by the consular legate, Tineius Rufus. For a while, he was allowed to have visitors and continued to teach. There is a strong element of folktale about these circumstances, and the possibility of the sources imitating the classical model of Socrates cannot be ignored. Akiba's final act of scholarship was to bring the religious calendar into order. Perhaps because these activities were too much for the Romans to allow, or because Akiba's support of Bar Kokhba made him a symbol of resistance, Rufus brought him to trial in Caesarea and ordered his execution.

SIGNIFICANCE

Akiba ben Joseph's most significant contributions were made to the organization of the Mishnah and the teachings in the Talmud. Akiba took the many rabbinic decisions and arranged them under these major headings: "zeraim" ("seeds," on agriculture), "mo'ed" ("seasons," on holidays), "nashim" ("women," on marriage and divorce), "kodashim" ("sanctities," on offerings), and "teharoth" ("purities," on defilement and purification). These headings with their tractates (subheadings) were continued by Rabbi Meir and then codified by Rabbi Judah ha-Nasi around 200. There are more than twenty-four hundred citations of Akiba in the Talmud; he is the most frequently cited authority.

Akiba championed a special method of interpretation of the text that he learned from Rabbi Nahum of Gimzo and that he retained even though the latter abandoned it. Akiba saw hidden significance in every aspect of the received text, whether it was an unusual wording, a special grammatical form, or an aberrant spelling. He was opposed on that count by Ishmael, who declared that the Torah was written in the language of men (with its possibility of error). Akiba made his points by Ishmael's method and then would extend the argument with his method. Akiba was fond of using parable to explain ethical points.

Akiba's area of special concern was marriage, where he championed attractiveness for women as a means of holding their husbands' affections and divorce for loveless matches. He opposed polygamy, which was still permitted and practiced by the aristocrats. As an extension of this stance, he fought for and gained the acceptance of the Song of Songs (*Shir ha-Shirim*) in the biblical canon, against heavy opposition.

As important as Akiba's work was, the stories about his life have exerted an equal influence on Judaism. Many of them are gross exaggerations and many are probably apocryphal, but the points that they make are consistent with the known teachings of Akiba.

—Michael M. Eisman

FURTHER READING

Aleksandrov, G. S. "The Role of Aqiba in the Bar Kochba Rebellion." In vol. 2 of *Eliezer ben Hyrcanus*, by Jacob Neusner. Leiden, Netherlands: E. J. Brill, 1973. Aleksandrov refutes the position that Akiba was active in the Bar Kokhba rebellion but admits that he could have given the rebellion moral support.

Finkelstein, Louis. *Akiba: Scholar, Saint, and Martyr.* Northvale, N.J.: Jason Aronson, 1990. Finkelstein recreates Akiba's life by taking a mildly critical look at the biographical sources and then placing the teachings of Akiba where they most easily fit into Akiba's life. Finkelstein sees Akiba representing the popular party against the aristocrats. He also sees Akiba as a pacifist to the end. Both positions are overstated and are generally not accepted by other scholars.

Goldin, Judah. "Toward a Profile of a *Tanna*, Aqiba ben Joseph." *Journal of the American Oriental Society* 96 (1976): 38-56. An important scholarly article that demonstrates that much of the biographical material about Akiba can be accepted as historical. Goldin's emphasis is on Akiba's marriage and his teachings regarding marriage, love, and divorce.

Nadich, Judah. *Rabbi Akiba and His Contemporaries.* Northvale, N.J.: Jason Aronson, 1998. Anecdotes, legends, and tales about Akiba and his friends of the second century C.E. as well as an account of the stories they themselves told.

Neusner, Jacob. *Judaism: The Evidence of the Mishnah.* 2d ed. Atlanta: Scholars Press, 1988. A distillation of Neusner's work and that of his students. He leads the critical school that rejects much of the traditional information about the rabbis' lives and questions the attribution of many teachings to specific rabbis.

Schürer, Emil. *A History of the Jewish People in the Time of Jesus Christ.* Edited and abridged by Nahum N. Glatzer. 1891. Reprint. New York: Schocken Books, 1961. While the bibliography of secondary sources is obsolete, that is the only unusable part of this excellent study. Schürer has an absolute command of the classical and talmudic sources and gives more detail about the Jewish problems of Trajan and Hadrian than one will find elsewhere.

Smallwood, E. Mary. *The Jews Under Roman Rule: From Pompey to Diocletian.* Vol. 20 in *Studies in Judaism in Late Antiquity*, edited by Jacob Neusner. Leiden, Netherlands: E. J. Brill, 1981. Solid scholarly work that should be used to update that of Schürer. Good background; understandably little on Akiba.

Strack, Hermann L. *Introduction to the Talmud and Midrash.* 1931. Reprint. Minneapolis: Fortress Press, 1996. There are many guides to the Talmud, but this is still among the best short guides.

SEE ALSO: Hadrian; Jesus; Johanen ben Zakkai; Philo of Alexandria.

RELATED ARTICLES in *Great Events from History: The Ancient World*: c. 30 C.E., Condemnation and Crucifixion of Jesus Christ; c. 30 C.E., Preaching of the Pentecostal Gospel; September 8, 70 C.E., Roman Destruction of the Temple of Jerusalem; c. 90 C.E., Synod of Jamnia; c. 110 C.E., Trajan Adopts Anti-Christian Religious Policy; 130-135 C.E., Dedication of Aelia Capitolina.

ALCIBIADES OF ATHENS
Athenian general

Although it might be argued that Alcibiades was a demagogue, a traitor, a heretic, and morally dissolute, he was a gifted politician and military leader—and certainly one of the most romantic figures of the Peloponnesian War.

BORN: c. 450 B.C.E.; Athens?, Greece
DIED: 404 B.C.E.; Phrygia, Asia Minor (now in Turkey)
ALSO KNOWN AS: Alkibiades; Son of Cleinias (Kleinias)
AREAS OF ACHIEVEMENT: Government and politics, war and conquest

EARLY LIFE

Alcibiades (al-suh-BI-uh-deez) was born around 450 B.C.E., the son of Cleinias, a wealthy aristocrat and participant in the Battle of Artemisium. His mother, Deinomache, was a member of the Alcmaeonid clan and a cousin of Pericles, in whose house the youth was raised after the death of his father in 447. Unfortunately, Alcibiades proved to be a difficult boy and failed to acquire any of his guardian's noble qualities—except, perhaps, some political ambition. Even so, according to Plutarch, Alcibiades was uniquely equipped for success. He was tall, handsome, wealthy, charming, imaginative, and one of the best orators of the day, having qualities that endeared him to the masses. At the same time, he was impious, insolent, and incurably egocentric.

Alcibiades' military training began at the outset of the Peloponnesian War. He served with distinction in battles at Potidaea (432 B.C.E.) and Delium (424 B.C.E.), and, as a result, he became quite popular in Athens and elsewhere. He acquired numerous admirers—among whom was the great philosopher Socrates, who saved the youth's life in battle and then later had the favor returned. A lasting friendship was formed, although Socrates must have found his protégé's rapacious lifestyle intolerable at times. It was during this period that Alcibiades married Hipparete of the house of Hipponius, who, after an unsuccessful attempt at divorce, closed her eyes to his infidelity and proved a dutiful wife. Together, they had a son named Axiochus, who apparently acquired some of the father's less desirable traits.

LIFE'S WORK

Alcibiades began his political career in 420 B.C.E., when he was elected one of the ten generals of the state, a position of great importance. Unlike Pericles, who had served on the same board for more than thirty years, Alcibiades was less devoted to Athens than to himself. Realizing that war with Sparta was the quickest route to fame and fortune, he cast his lot with the radicals of the state. This political decision placed him at odds with Nicias, the leader of the conservative faction, who had effected a peace treaty with the Spartans in 421. Displeased with the lull in fighting, Alcibiades formed an alliance with Argos, Elis, and Mantinea against Sparta. He was successful and was reelected in 419 to his seat on the board of generals. When the alliance with Argos eventually failed, Alcibiades' popularity suffered, and he lost his generalship. It was only through a brief political *amicitia* with his enemy Nicias that he averted ostracism.

His political demise did not last long. In 416, another opportunity presented itself when a delegation from the city of Egesta in Sicily appealed to Alcibiades and the radicals in Athens for assistance in war against the neighboring state of Selinus, which was supported by Syracuse. The promise of wealth and the possibility of a western empire struck a responsive chord in Alcibiades. Under his influence and over the strenuous objections of Nicias, Athens prepared to send a large amphibious force against Syracuse.

The expedition was doomed from the start. Alcibiades, selected as one of the leaders, was accused by his detractors of impiety; the likelihood of his acquittal, however, prompted the opposition to postpone the trial, and Alcibiades was free, for the moment, to resume his position within the triumvirate of leadership designated for the Sicilian campaign. One of those with whom he would rule was Nicias, his former political adversary. It is not surprising that their inability to agree on strategy hindered field operations. Moreover, the siege had just begun when Athens dispatched a galley to bring Alcibiades back for his trial. Although he offered no resistance, the possibility of a death sentence in Athens led Alcibiades to escape at Thurii. From Thurii he made his way to Sparta, where he would remain for two years. While there, he earned the admiration of the Spartans with abstemious behavior. He plunged into politics, urging the Spartans to assist Syracuse in its war with Athens. He also convinced the Spartans to fortify Decelea, from which they could strike into Attica.

Although Alcibiades adapted to the Spartan way and rendered valuable services, he had not abandoned all the vices of earlier years. He seduced the Spartan queen

Socrates, seated, instructs Alcibiades, standing. (F. R. Niglutsch)

while her husband, King Agis, was away at Decelea. The queen became pregnant and gave birth to a son. By the summer of 412, it was clear that Alcibiades could no longer remain in Sparta. From there, he fled to the court of the Persian satrap of Sardis, Tissaphernes, who, like others before him, was very impressed with his peripatetic guest.

Alcibiades worked hard to effect an alliance with Tissaphernes and Persia, which would prove injurious to Sparta and enable him to return to power in Athens. First the democracy must be overthrown and an oligarchy established in its place, he reasoned. In the deliberations that followed, many Athenians were receptive to the plan, and in 411 an oligarchic faction took control of the government. Unfortunately, the satrap's demands were too great, and the oligarchy quickly lost faith in Alcibiades. Even so, a number of generals remained loyal to Alcibiades, who continued to control the bulk of Athenian military forces on the island of Samos.

The threat of a Spartan invasion, however, soon threw Athens into chaos; the oligarchy was toppled, and Alci-

biades was recalled. He did not return immediately, choosing instead to remain in the eastern Aegean Sea area, where he achieved significant victories at Cynossema and Cyzicus. In the latter engagement, all Spartan ships were either destroyed or captured, and a Spartan admiral was killed. Between 410 and 408, Alcibiades enjoyed other successes—in the Bosporus Thracius, the Hellespontus, the area neighboring the Propontis Sea, and the area north of the Aegean Sea—as he struggled to keep Athenian food supplies flowing from the Black Sea area.

By the autumn of 408, Alcibiades was supreme in the Aegean area and was now ready to return triumphant to Athens. He reached the city in the following year and was given ultimate authority over Athenian military forces. It was at this time, during the peak of his power, that he probably intended to establish a tyranny. The Spartan commander Lysander, however, turned the tide of battle in the Aegean again, with a victory at Notium over one of Alcibiades' subordinates. Even though Alcibiades was not wholly responsible for the defeat, the capricious Athenians could not forgive him. Deprived of his command, Alcibiades went into exile in Thrace. Ignored by his former countrymen and hounded by his enemies, he fled to Phrygia, where, at the insistence of Lysander, he was assassinated in 404.

SIGNIFICANCE

When Pericles died in 429, a void was left in Athenian leadership. Into this void stepped Alcibiades. Endowed with the physical and intellectual requisites for greatness, he might have been the leader—indeed, the hero— for whom Athens was looking. Certainly Alcibiades was a great general whose judgment in military matters carried him from victory to victory and earned for him the admiration of Spartans, Athenians, and Persians. It might be argued that his superior generalship in the eastern Aegean prolonged the Peloponnesian War for the Athenians and, if the Athenian leadership had accepted his advice from exile in Thrace, Athens might not have lost the Battle of Aegospotami in 405 B.C.E.

However, military victories are not always sufficient to attain greatness. In the opinion of most scholars, Alcibiades, although a gifted individual, was a traitor, a heretic, and an opportunist. In all arenas, he was determined to win, regardless of the cost. In the Olympic Games of 416, he entered seven four-horse teams in the chariot race and came away with all the top prizes. He was a demagogue who tempted Athens into costly schemes—such as the Syracusan expedition of 415, which resulted in the loss of about fifty thousand men and more than two hundred triremes. He also conspired to overthrow the democracy and dreamed of the day when he might become a dictator.

—*Larry W. Usilton*

FURTHER READING

Benson, E. F. *The Life of Alcibiades*. New York: D. Appleton, 1929. The standard biography of Alcibiades, old but still very useful. Written in large part from primary materials, especially Thucydides and Plutarch. A sympathetic study that, at times, reads like a novel. Should appeal to scholars and students alike.

Bury, J. B., and Russell Meiggs. *A History of Greece to the Death of Alexander the Great*. 4th ed. New York: St. Martin's Press, 1991. An excellent one-volume survey of Greek history to the time of Alexander the Great. The main events of Alcibiades' life are treated in the chapter "The Decline and Downfall of the Athenian Empire." Includes maps, illustrations, and copious bibliographical notes.

Henderson, Bernard W. *The Great War Between Athens and Sparta: A Companion to the Military History of Thucydides*. London: Macmillan, 1927. Excellent study of the Peloponnesian War. One of the better sources for the life of Alcibiades. A sympathetic survey from boyhood to death. Written in large part from primary materials.

Meiggs, Russell. *The Athenian Empire*. New York: Oxford University Press, 1979. Excellent political and military history of the fifth century B.C.E. Athens. Treats the important events in Alcibiades' career. Includes a good bibliography.

Plutarch. *The Rise and Fall of Athens: Nine Great Lives*. Translated by I. Scott-Kilvert. Baltimore: Penguin Books, 1975. Plutarch was a first century C.E. Greek historian whose biographies of Greek and Roman heroes are an indispensable resource. This edition contains nine of those biographies, including that of Alcibiades. Especially useful for getting a sense of Alcibiades' character.

Thucydides. *The Peloponnesian War*. Translated by J. S. Rusten. New York: Cambridge University Press, 2001. Written by a famous Greek historian of the fifth century B.C.E., this book is a valuable source of information on the Peloponnesian War. Chronicles the main events of Alcibiades' life in scattered references, from his role in the alliance with Argos to the Athenian victory at Cynossema in 411. Most secondary accounts of Alcibiades begin with Thucydides and Plutarch.

SEE ALSO: Aegesilaus II of Sparta; Pericles; Socrates.

RELATED ARTICLES in *Great Events from History: The Ancient World*: c. 550 B.C.E., Construction of Trireme Changes Naval Warfare; May, 431-September, 404 B.C.E., Peloponnesian War; 399 B.C.E., Death of Socrates.

ALCMAEON
Greek philosopher and scientist

Alcmaeon was one of the earliest Greeks known to have written on medicine and the first to have practiced scientific dissection.

BORN: c. 510 B.C.E.; Croton, Magna Graecia (now in southern Italy)
DIED: c. 430 B.C.E.; place unknown
ALSO KNOWN AS: Alkmaeon
AREAS OF ACHIEVEMENT: Medicine, philosophy

EARLY LIFE

Almost nothing is known about the early life of Alcmaeon (alk-MEE-uhn) except that his father's name was Peirithous and that he was a native of Croton (Greek Crotona), a coastal town inside the "toe" of Italy. Even Alcmaeon's dates are uncertain. According to Aristotle, he lived during the old age of the philosopher Pythagoras, whose life spanned much of the sixth century B.C.E. and who died about 490 or later. It was once assumed that, as a younger contemporary of Pythagoras, Alcmaeon probably should be placed in the sixth century. It is now widely held, however, largely from the evidence of his ideas, that he probably lived in the fifth century. The evidence at the disposal of modern scholars is not sufficient to fix the date of his lifetime more precisely.

Croton was a Greek city founded by Achaeans from mainland Greece in 710 B.C.E. It had a fine harbor and enjoyed extensive commerce. As a result, it became the wealthiest and most powerful city in Magna Graecia (the Greek name for southern Italy), especially after its forces defeated and destroyed its enemy, the neighboring city of Sybaris, in 510. It boasted the most splendid temple in southern Italy, the temple of Hera Lacinia, which drew large numbers of Greeks to a great annual religious assembly. Croton was renowned for its devotion to gymnastics; one of its citizens, Milon, became the most famous athlete in Greece, having won the victory in wrestling at Olympia six times. Croton is said to have produced more Olympic victors than any other city.

Croton was also the home of a well-known school of medicine, which was perhaps the earliest in Greece and which long retained its reputation. The city enjoyed the distinction of producing the finest physicians in Greece, of whom the most prominent was Democedes, regarded as the best physician of his day (the second half of the sixth century B.C.E.). His fame carried him to Aegina, Athens, and Samos, where he was employed by the tyrant Polycrates, and to Persia (as a prisoner), where he cured both King Darius the Great and his wife, Atossa, before he escaped, returning to Croton to marry the daughter of Milon.

Croton was also known as the home of the philosopher Pythagoras and his followers. Born in Samos, Pythagoras emigrated to Croton about 530, where he formed a religious brotherhood composed of about three hundred young men. Pythagoras quickly gained influence over the political affairs of the city, but growing opposition to his order led to his retirement from Croton. In the second half of the fifth century a democratic revolution resulted in a massacre of nearly all the members of the order. Alcmaeon is said by some ancient authors to have been a disciple of Pythagoras, but it is likely that this belief was based only on inferences from the similarities of some of his doctrines to those of the Pythagoreans. Aristotle compares his theory of opposites with that of the Pythagoreans but says that Alcmaeon either borrowed this idea from them or they took it from him. There is, in fact, no definitive evidence that associates Alcmaeon with the Pythagoreans. He lived during the period in which the Pythagorean brotherhood flourished at Croton, and he probably knew of the Pythagoreans and their beliefs. His precise relationship to them, however, is not known. Diogenes Laertius reports that Alcmaeon wrote mostly on medicine, and it has been inferred from this statement that he was a physician. Given Croton's reputation as a medical center, it is not unlikely. He wrote on physics and astronomy as well, however, and in this respect he resembles the Ionian philosophers, some of whom were interested in medicine. He was certainly a natural philosopher, interested in science and medicine; he may or may not have been a physician.

LIFE'S WORK

Alcmaeon lived in the pre-Socratic period, when the study of physiology was merely a part of philosophy. Only later did Hippocrates separate medicine from philosophy. Greek medical theory, in fact, grew out of philosophical speculation rather than the practice of medicine. Alcmaeon's contributions include both cosmological conjecture and anatomical research. He was credited in antiquity with having written the first treatise on natural philosophy. The book is no longer extant, but some idea of its contents can be gleaned from portions that were summarized by later writers. In the opening sentence of the work, Alcmaeon declared that the gods alone have certain knowledge, while for humans only inference from things seen is possible. Thus, he eschewed all-encompassing, oversimplified hypotheses in favor of careful observation as the basis of understanding nature.

Nevertheless, Alcmaeon shared with the Ionian philosophers an interest in natural speculation. Thus, he posited a microcosmic-macrocosmic relationship between humans and the universe. He believed that the human soul was immortal because it was continuously in motion, like the heavenly bodies, which he thought divine and immortal because they moved continuously and eternally in circles. While the heavenly bodies are immortal, however, humans perish because "they cannot join the beginning to the end." Alcmaeon seems to mean by this that human life is not circular but linear and thus is not eternally renewed but runs down and dies when its motion ceases.

Alcmaeon developed a theory of opposites, according to which human beings have within them pairs of opposing forces, such as black and white, bitter and sweet, good and bad, large and small. He may well have been indebted to the Pythagoreans, who posited pairs of contrary qualities on mathematical lines (or they may have borrowed the notion from him). Alcmaeon, however, applied his theory particularly to health and disease. He defined health as a balance or equilibrium (*isonomia*) of op-

Alcmaeon. (Library of Congress)

posing forces in the body (for example, warm and cold, bitter and sweet, wet and dry). He explained disease as the excess or predominance (*monarchia*) of one of these qualities or pairs of opposites that upsets the balance. This predominance could be caused by an excess or deficiency of food or by such external factors as climate, locality, fatigue, or exertion. Alcmaeon probably based this theory on his observation of factional struggles in Greek city-states, and he may have been influenced by the growth of democratic political ideas. Of all Alcmaeon's theories, this concept of opposites was to be the most influential in later Greek thought. The Hippocratic treatise *Peri archaies ietrikes* (c. 430-400 B.C.E.; *On Ancient Medicine*, 1849) defends and elaborates on this explanation.

Alcmaeon's theoretical speculation was balanced by a notable empirical tendency. It is this mixture of theory and observation that gives his work a distinctive and even pioneering nature. Alcmaeon, like many pre-Socratic philosophers, was interested in physiology, but he appears to have been the first to test his theories by examination of the body. In a celebrated case, he cut out the eye of an animal (whether dead or alive is uncertain). He was apparently interested in observing the substances of which the eye was composed. Whether he dissected the eye is not known. He also discovered (or inferred the existence of) the channels that connect the eye to the brain (probably the optic nerves).

There is no evidence that Alcmaeon ever dissected human corpses, and it is unlikely that he did so. He believed that the eye contained fire (which could be seen when the eye was lit) and water (which dissection revealed to have come from the brain). He concluded that there were similar passages connecting the other sense organs to the brain, and he described the passages connecting the brain to the mouth, nose, and ears (and quite possibly was the first to discover the Eustachian tubes). He thought that these channels were hollow and carried *pneuma* (air). Alcmaeon concluded that the brain provided the sensations of sight, hearing, smell, and taste, for he noticed that when a concussion occurred, the senses were affected. Similarly, when the passages were blocked, communication between the brain and the sense organs was cut off. Plato followed Alcmaeon in holding that the brain is the central organ of thought and feeling, but Aristotle and many other philosophers continued to attribute that function to the heart. Alcmaeon also differed from most contemporary philosophers in distinguishing between sensation and thought. He observed that sensation is common to all animals, while only humans possess intelligence.

According to Alcmaeon, whether the body was awake or asleep had to do with the amount of blood in the veins. Sleep was caused by the blood retiring to the larger blood vessels, while waking was the result of the blood being rediffused throughout the body. Alcmaeon was also interested in embryology, and he opened birds' eggs and examined the development of the embryos. He believed that the head, not the heart, was the first to develop. He resorted to speculation rather than observation in holding that human semen has its origin in the brain. He explained the sterility of mules by the theory that the seed produced by the male was too fine and cold, while the womb of the female did not open, and hence conception was prevented.

SIGNIFICANCE

Alcmaeon is recognized as an important figure in the development of the biological sciences in ancient Greece. Although few details regarding either his career or his scientific methods are known, it is clear that he exercised considerable influence on subsequent Greek writers in the fields of medicine and biology. He introduced ideas that were later elaborated by Empedocles, Democritus, several Hippocratic writers, Plato, and Aristotle, among others. His idea that health is a balance of opposing forces in the body, although later modified, was accepted for many hundreds of years. Alcmaeon has often been called the father of embryology, anatomy, physiology, and experimental psychology. While such titles may be unwarranted, in each of these areas Alcmaeon did make significant contributions.

Regardless of whether Alcmaeon was a physician, he was one of the earliest Greeks to formulate medical theories. Many of his ideas were speculative and borrowed from earlier philosophers. Although influenced by the Pythagoreans, he avoided their mysticism, and he recognized the limitations of scientific inference. His medical theory did not grow out of medical practice but always retained a close affinity with philosophy; such theories tended to have little influence on the general practice of Greek medicine. Still, Alcmaeon's anatomical investigation (particularly his dissection of the eye) and his recognition that the senses are connected with the brain established him as a genuine pioneer in the development of Greek medical science.

—*Gary B. Ferngren*

FURTHER READING

Codellas, P. S. "Alcmaeon of Croton: His Life, Work, and Fragments." *Proceedings of the Royal Society of Medicine* 25 (1931/1932): 1041-1046. A brief but comprehensive discussion of Alcmaeon's life and contributions, published by the Royal Society of Medicine's Section on the History of Medicine.

Gross, Charles G. *Brain, Vision, Memory: Tales in the History of Neuroscience.* Cambridge: Massachusetts Institute of Technology Press, 1998. Alcmaeon is credited as the first neuroscientist because he correctly described the brain as the site of both cognition and sensation.

Guthrie, W. K. C. *A History of Greek Philosophy.* Vol. 1. New York: Cambridge University Press, 1978-1990. Includes a discussion of the evidence for Alcmaeon's dates and an examination of his medical, physiological, and cosmological theories (particularly his doctrine of the soul) by a leading expert on Greek philosophy.

Jones, W. H. S. *Philosophy and Medicine in Ancient Greece.* 1946. Reprint. New York: Arno Press, 1979. Provides translations of the most important sources for Alcmaeon's life and doctrines and discusses Alcmaeon's relationship to Plato and Aristotle.

Lloyd, Geoffrey. "Alcmaeon and the Early History of Dissection." *Sudhoffs Archiv* 59 (1975): 113-147. A detailed examination of the evidence for Alcmaeon's use of dissection, which Lloyd believes Alcmaeon to have practiced in a very limited manner rather than systematically. Explores as well the history of early Greek dissection after Alcmaeon.

Sigerist, Henry E., ed. *Early Greek, Hindu, and Persian Medicine.* Vol. 2 in *A History of Medicine.* New York: Oxford University Press, 1987. A general discussion of Alcmaeon and his work in the context of early Greek medicine and philosophy. Valuable for its general treatment of Greek medicine and its background.

SEE ALSO: Aretaeus of Cappadocia; Asclepiades of Bithynia; Diocles of Caristus; Pedanius Dioscorides; Erasistratus; Galen; Herophilus; Hippocrates; Pythagoras.

RELATED ARTICLES in *Great Events from History: The Ancient World*: 6th-4th century B.C.E. (traditionally, 1st millennium B.C.E.), Suśruta, Indian Physician, Writes Medical Compendium; c. 530 B.C.E., Founding of the Pythagorean Brotherhood; c. 500 B.C.E., Acupuncture Develops in China; c. 500-400 B.C.E., Greek Physicians Begin Scientific Practice of Medicine; c. 157-201 C.E., Galen Synthesizes Ancient Medical Knowledge.

ALEXANDER THE GREAT
Macedonian king, conqueror of Persia (r. 336-323 B.C.E.)

By military genius, political acumen, and cultural vision, Alexander unified and Hellenized most of the civilized ancient world and in so doing became a legendary figure in subsequent ages.

BORN: 356 B.C.E.; Pella, Macedonia (now in Greece)
DIED: June 10 or 13, 323 B.C.E.; Babylon (now in Iraq)
ALSO KNOWN AS: Alexander III of Macedonia
AREAS OF ACHIEVEMENT: Government and politics, war and conquest

EARLY LIFE

Born into royalty as the son of King Philip II of Macedonia and Olympias, daughter of King Neoptolemus of Epirus, Alexander was educated during his early teenage years by the Greek philosopher Aristotle. Although tutor and pupil later differed on political matters, such as Alexander's decision to downgrade the importance of the city-state, Aristotle performed his assigned task of preparing his young charge for undertaking campaigns against the Persian Empire as well as inculcating in him a love of learning so vital to Hellenic culture.

In 340 B.C.E., at age sixteen, Alexander's formal training ended with his appointment to administer Macedonia while Philip was absent on a campaign. Young Alexander won his first battle against a force of Thracians and in 338 distinguished himself as commander of the left wing during Philip's crushing victory over the combined Greek army at Chaeronea. A break with his father over the latter's divorce and remarriage led Alexander to flee with his mother to Epirus. Although father and son reaffirmed their ties, Alexander feared for his status as successor. Philip's assassination in 336, along with the army's support of Alexander, eliminated all doubt of his kingship, and he had the assassins and all of his apparent enemies executed.

LIFE'S WORK

At the age of twenty, Alexander proceeded to fulfill Philip's planned attack on Persia and thereby to free Greeks living under Persian rule in Asia Minor. Soon, however, he determined to place himself on the throne of Persia. Eager to represent all Greece at the head of a Pan-hellenic union, he first received the approval and military support of the Greek League at Corinth and the endorsement of the oracle at Delphi as invincible. (The Romans later called him "the Great.")

In order to consolidate his rear guard in Europe before crossing into Asia, he spent the year 335 subduing restive peoples north and west of Macedonia and crushing an Athenian-endorsed revolt of Thebes by taking and razing the city of Thebes, killing six thousand and selling the rest as slaves. His harsh policy had the desired effect of discouraging further attempts by the Greeks to undermine his authority. Alexander therefore had no need to punish Athens, center of Hellenic culture, source of the largest navy available to him, and vital to the financial administration of the territories he would conquer. Nevertheless, he remained sufficiently suspicious of the Athenians to decline employing their fleet against Persia. The only Greek city-state openly disloyal to Alexander was Sparta, but it was isolated and later brought into line by Alexander's governor of Greece.

Alexander crossed the Hellespont (Dardanelles) into Asia Minor with his army of thirty-five thousand Macedonians and Greeks in the spring of 334, intent on humbling the Persian army and gaining spoils adequate to restore the strained Macedonian treasury. Alexander's army was a superbly balanced force of all arms, based on the highly disciplined maneuvers of the Macedonian phalanx and cavalry. With its offensive wing on the right, the infantry phalanxes implemented Alexander's strategy by advancing steadily, using their longer spears and supported by light-armed archers and javelin throwers. That was in reality a holding force, however, for while it moved forward, the cavalry attacked the enemy's flank and rear. If that did not succeed, then the infantry would institute a skillful fighting withdrawal to open a gap in the enemy's line and to gain the higher ground. This difficult maneuver thus created a flank, on which Alexander's men would then rush. The key to success was timing, and Alexander's great ability was knowing where and when to strike decisively. Then he pursued the retreating enemy, who could not regroup. Alexander's tactical skills triumphed almost immediately when he met and crushed a Persian army at the river Granicus, largely as a result of his realization that victory was possible only after an interceding river was crossed.

No less a genius as a strategist, Alexander neutralized the Persian fleet by marching down the coasts of the Eastern Mediterranean, taking the enemy's seaports by land. To establish himself as a liberator, he dealt harshly only with those cities that opposed his advance, and he installed Greek-style democracies in those that yielded without a fight. Indeed, he retained local governors, customs, and taxes, insisting only on loyalty to himself instead of to King Darius III of Persia. This political policy had the additional logistical benefit of making available supplies crucial to keeping his army in the field. To provide balanced governments of occupation, however, as at Sardis, he appointed a Macedonian governor with troops, a local militia officer as fortress commander, and an Athenian overseer of monies. Also, the fact that the army was accompanied by scientists, engineers, and historians is evidence that he planned a long campaign to conquer all Persia and to gather new knowledge as inspired by Aristotle.

The conquest of Asia Minor was completed in the autumn of 333 when Alexander crushed Darius's army at Issus on the Syrian frontier, then advanced down the coast, receiving the submission of all the Phoenician cities except Tyre. Enraged by its defiance, he besieged Tyre for seven months, building a long mole (causeway) with siege towers and finally assaulting the city in July,

332. Tyre suffered the same fate as Thebes, and the rest of the coast lay open to Alexander, save for a two-month standoff at Gaza. Then Egypt welcomed him as a deliverer, whereupon he established the port city of Alexandria there. Returning to Syria, he advanced into Mesopotamia, where he routed the Grand Army of Darius at Arbela (or Gaugamela) in mid-331. One year later, Darius was killed by a rival as Alexander advanced eastward, the same year that Alexander burned down the Persian royal palace at Persepolis.

Alexander's vision of empire changed from 331 to 330 to that of a union of Macedonians and Persians under his kingship. He began to wear Persian dress, married the first of two Persian princesses after conquering the eastern provinces in 328, and later prevailed on the Macedonian troops to do the same. As his men increasingly resisted such alien practices, Alexander ordered the execution of some of the most vocal critics, notably his second in command, Parmenio, his late father's intimate counselor, who was the spokesman for the older oppo-

Alexander the Great at the Battle of Granicus. (Library of Congress)

nents of assimilation. In spite of such excesses, the army remained loyal and followed Alexander into India to his last great victory—one over local rulers at the Hydaspes River in June, 326, using native troops and methods, as well as elephants. Now his Macedonian troops, however, tired and homesick, refused to go on, and he had no choice but to end his offensive. His engineers thereupon built a fleet of more than eight hundred vessels, which ferried and accompanied the army downriver to the Indus, then to the Indian Ocean and west again to Persia. Heavy fighting, severe desert terrain, and unfavorable weather inflicted much suffering and heavy losses on his forces.

By the time he reached Susa, administrative capital of the Persian Empire, in 324, Alexander had indeed fashioned a sprawling empire. He had established numerous cities bearing his name and had infused Asia with the dynamic Hellenic culture that would influence the region for centuries to come. In addition, he now attempted greater racial intermixing, which led to another near-complete break with his fellow Macedonians. Alexander, ever more megalomaniacal, pronounced himself a god and had more of his subordinates put to death, usually during drunken sprees. These were so frequent in his last seven years that there is every reason to believe he had become a chronic alcoholic. As a result of one binge at Babylon in 323, he became ill and died ten days later; he was thirty-three years old. His empire was quickly divided among his successor generals, who eliminated his wives and two children.

SIGNIFICANCE

Inculcated by Aristotle with the superiority of high Greek culture, Alexander the Great undertook the political unification of the Greek world along Panhellenic lines, followed by its extension over the vast but internally weak Persian Empire. His tools were the superb Macedonian army inherited from his father and his own genius at command. As one success followed another, however, his horizons became broader. He identified himself with the religion and deities of each land he conquered, especially Egypt, and ultimately seems to have concluded that it was his destiny to merge most of the known world under common rule. That vision possibly included Carthage and the western Mediterranean, though death denied him further territorial acquisitions.

Alexander's shrewd administrative skills enabled him to succeed in the five major facets of statehood. In reli-

DYNASTIES THAT EMERGED FROM ALEXANDER THE GREAT'S EMPIRE		
Dynasty	*Founder*	*Reign* (B.C.E.)
Antigonid Dynasty	Antigonus I Monophthalmos	306-301
Ptolemaic Dynasty	Ptolemy Soter	305-285
Seleucid Dynasty	Seleucus I Nicator	305-281

gion, he began with the Greek pantheon but then recognized all faiths, with himself as the common godhead. Hellenic culture was also the intellectual power that drove his social ambitions and that prevailed in spite of his attempts to amalgamate it with Persian ways, leaving a predominantly Hellenistic world in his wake. In the economic sphere, he followed the Greek practices of silver-based coinage, which, with Persian gold, brought about common commercial practices and general prosperity. As one of the greatest generals in history, Alexander obtained victory with skillful tactics, flexibility, a keen sense of logistics, and superior leadership, followed by an effective system of garrisons with divided commands. His charismatic personality and vision combined all these elements into the final one—firm, dynamic, political rule. Once Alexander passed from the scene, however, the system could not be sustained. Nevertheless, his example of continental empire contributed to the eventual rise of the Roman Empire.

—*Clark G. Reynolds*

FURTHER READING

Arrianus, Flavius. *The Life of Alexander the Great*. Translated by Aubrey de Sélincourt. Baltimore: Penguin Books, 1958. An excellent, reliable study of the ancient works on Alexander, actually titled the *Anabasis*, though preoccupied with the military aspects. For the most part, it takes the form of straight narrative.

Bosworth, A. B. *Alexander and the East: The Tragedy of Triumph*. New York: Oxford University Press, 1996. Compares Alexander the Great's massacres in Central Asia and Pakistan to Spain's conquest of Mexico. Bosworth examines Alexander's concept of the universal monarch. Depictions of Alexander throughout history are surveyed. Includes maps, bibliography, and index.

Burn, A. R. *Alexander the Great and the Hellenistic Empire*. London: The English Universities Press, 1959. An almost complete rejection of Alexander as a heroic figure, denying the impact ascribed to him by most other writers.

Engels, Donald W. *Alexander the Great and the Logistics of the Macedonian Army.* Berkeley: University of California Press, 1978. A masterful use of mathematics to ascertain the four-day carrying load of Alexander's soldiers and the means by which these considerations influenced his strategy and movements.

Fox, Robin Lane. *Alexander the Great.* New York: Penguin, 1986. A direct, no-nonsense use of the sources to fashion a serious examination of Alexander, scholarly in every way except exhaustive citations and virtually ignoring Tarn's thesis, which Fox rejects.

Fuller, J. F. C. *The Generalship of Alexander the Great.* 1960. Reprint. New York: Da Capo Press, 1989. The best work on Alexander's military achievements, complete with campaign maps and battle diagrams; by a retired British general and leading military pundit of the twentieth century.

Green, Peter. *Alexander the Great.* New York: Praeger, 1970. A judicious biography, replete with illustrations of the territory that Alexander traversed, which rejects the "brotherhood of man" ascribed to Alexander's motives by others and includes many surviving legends.

Hammond, N. G. L. *Alexander the Great: King, Commander, and Statesman.* 3d ed. London: Bristol Classical Press, 1996. A good overview with an appendix on the question of Alexander's drinking and possible alcoholism.

Tarn, W. W. *Alexander the Great.* 2 vols. New York: Cambridge University Press, 1979. A complete and sympathetic biography, by a leading Hellenistic historian who views Alexander as having sought the brotherhood of man. Especially useful for its in-depth review of all the ancient authorities.

Wilcken, Ulrich. *Alexander the Great.* Translated by G. C. Richards. 1931. Reprint. New York: W. W. Norton, 1967. An excellent, balanced treatment of Alexander's life and achievements, introduced by lengthy discussions of the Greek world in the fourth century B.C.E. and of his father, Philip II.

SEE ALSO: Aristotle; Darius the Great; Olympias; Philip II of Macedonia.

RELATED ARTICLES in *Great Events from History: The Ancient World*: 8th-6th century B.C.E., Phrygian Kingdom Rises; 359-336 B.C.E., Philip II Expands and Empowers Macedonia; August 2, 338 B.C.E., Battle of Chaeronea; 336 B.C.E., Alexander the Great Begins Expansion of Macedonia; 333 B.C.E., Battle of Issus; 332 B.C.E., Founding of Alexandria; October 1, 331 B.C.E., Battle of Gaugamela; 327-325 B.C.E., Alexander the Great Invades the Indian Subcontinent; c. 323-275 B.C.E., Diadochi Divide Alexander the Great's Empire.

SAINT AMBROSE
Milanese bishop

By the practical application of Roman virtue and Christian ethics, Ambrose established the Nicene Creed as the orthodox doctrine of Christianity and asserted the spiritual authority of the church over the state.

BORN: 339 C.E.; Augusta Treverorum, Gaul (now Trier, Germany)
DIED: April 4, 397 C.E.; Milan (now in Italy)
ALSO KNOWN AS: Ambrosius (Latin name)
AREAS OF ACHIEVEMENT: Religion, government and politics

EARLY LIFE

Ambrose (AM-brohz) is a good example of why Christianity replaced traditional paganism as the official religion of the Roman Empire. The son of one of the highest civilian officials in the Roman hierarchy, he was educated in the best Roman tradition and raised in a devout Christian family. When Ambrose was born, his father, Aurelius Ambrosius, was praetorian prefect of Gaul and could offer Ambrose every advantage of Roman life. Ambrosius died when Ambrose was still an infant, and thus it was left to his mother, whose name is unknown, to raise the young Ambrose, his sister Marcellina, and his brother Satyrus. Almost immediately the family returned to Rome. Little is known about this time in Rome except that Ambrose and his brother attended the usual Roman schools, where they learned grammar and composition by reading and reciting the works of the Roman masters. Ambrose stated that he most enjoyed Cicero, Vergil, and Sallust. Later both brothers studied rhetoric and prepared for careers in the civil service.

Christianity seems to have been established within the family well before Ambrose's birth. The family boasted of a holy ancestor, a great-aunt Soteris, who had suffered martyrdom in 304 C.E. during the persecutions propagated by Diocletian. The depth of this belief first appeared on the feast of the Epiphany in 353, when Marcellina, in the presence of Pope Liberius, dedicated her virginity to God and committed herself to the practice of an ascetic life. Afterward, Marcellina continued to live in her mother's house and with her mother formed the core for one of the first groups of patrician women who renounced the world and gave themselves up to Christian study, prayer, and good works.

The effects of a Christian life were not immediately obvious in Ambrose's life. In 365, Emperor Valentinian I appointed him and Satyrus legal advocates in Sirmium at the tribunal of the praetorian prefect of Italy, Africa, and Illyria. Both men impressed successive prefects with their eloquence and intelligence and advanced quickly. As a result, in 370 both received provincial governorships. Ambrose became governor of Aemilia-Liguria in northern Italy. Because the capital of the province was at Milan, then the principal seat of the Imperial government in the West, Ambrose became known to the most important people of the time. An anecdote in the biography written after his death by his secretary Paulinus indicates how popular a governor he was. In 373, when Bishop Auxentius died, governor Ambrose, in an effort to keep the peace, addressed the bickering factions of orthodox and Arian Christians. From the crowd a child's voice was heard to call "Bishop Ambrose." It was enough to start a public outcry for his consecration as the next bishop of Milan.

LIFE'S WORK

Ambrose's whole career as bishop of Milan was directed toward defending what he called the "cause of God," which included the advocacy of an orthodox Christian doctrine, the defining of Church authority, and the disestablishment of pagan state religion. From the time of his consecration, Bishop Ambrose had made known his opposition to the Arian heresy, but he was unable to influence the Emperor Valentinian I. To maintain public order, Valentinian followed a policy of neutrality toward the different religions of the Empire, even though he himself was a Christian. Ambrose's first successes were in shaping the attitudes and programs of the Emperor Gratian. His strongly worded statement against Arianism, *De fide* (380), used extensive scriptural quotations to present the argument that orthodoxy provided a physi-

cal protection for the Empire. Ambrose pointed out that the Goths had devastated the Arian provinces of the Balkan Peninsula but that the provinces defended by the orthodox Gratian were spared. Convinced by the argument, Gratian enlisted Ambrose as an adviser and teacher. It was probably Ambrose who inspired Gratian's firm stands against heresy and his decree for the removal of the Altar of Victory from the senate house in 382. The Altar of Victory to the people of the time was a symbol of the ancient association of paganism and the Roman government.

Ambrose's relationship with Gratian proved his powers of persuasion, but it established no real authority for the Church. Since the time of Constantine the Great, emperors had freely interfered in church affairs as a legitimate function of their office. After Gratian's death in 383, Justina and her son Valentinian II represented the Imperial family in Milan. They favored Arian doctrine. At the beginning of 385 Justina ordered Ambrose to assign a church for Arian worship. Ambrose refused, saying that sacred things were not subject to the power of the emperor. He was unwilling to allow the gains made against heresy to be lost as the result of changes in the religious preference of the civil authorities. For more than a year, Ambrose resisted the queen mother's demands and the pressures of the emperor. At times he physically obstructed troops trying to occupy Christian churches. In the end he was successful for several reasons. First, Ambrose's popularity ensured broad public support for his stand. Second, while excavating for the construction of the new basilica, workmen discovered the skeletal remains of two large men. Ambrose interpreted the finds as the remains of the martyred saints Gervasius and Protasius, a sign from Heaven on the correctness of his position. The emperor found it difficult to combat a sign from God. Third, in 387 the usurper Magnus Maximus moved his armies toward Milan, and Valentinian and Justina fled. Circumstances left Ambrose in control in Milan.

The prestige that Ambrose achieved as the result of his successful resistance to Justina and Valentinian was the basis for future success in asserting church authority over the authority of the soldier emperor Theodosius the Great. In late 388, at the instigation of the local bishop, a mob looted and burned a Jewish synagogue at Callinicum in Syria. The news of the event reached Milan in a report that also told of monks destroying a chapel of a Gnostic sect. In the interest of public order, Theodosius ordered reparations. In particular he ordered the bishop to rebuild the synagogue at his own expense and to see to the restoration of the stolen articles. The offending monks were to be punished. Ambrose was appalled. In a letter written to Theodosius, he took the position that if the bishop rebuilt the place of worship for the enemies of Christ he would be guilty of apostasy. It would be better for the bishop to refuse and become a martyr for not obeying the emperor. Ambrose's position was that the maintenance of civil law is secondary to religious interests. Even Theodosius's amended order that the state rebuild the synagogue would not satisfy Ambrose. A bold sermon, delivered while Theodosius was in the congregation, demanded that there be no reparation of any kind. In the past, Ambrose stated, gross breaches of public order by pagans and Jews against Christians had gone unpunished. He had in mind the violence that had occurred during the reign of the Emperor Julian. It was perverse reasoning, but it was effective. Theodosius yielded, not because he accepted Ambrose's argument but because politically he could not afford to alienate the popular bishop. In the dispute with Justina, Ambrose had proved his ability to arouse public sentiment. Unfortunately, Ambrose's stance provided a justification for anti-Semitism throughout the Middle Ages.

This public humiliation of the emperor had a chilling effect on Ambrose's relationship with the Imperial court, and for a time Theodosius preferred the advice of others. One result was Theodosius's cruel response to a violent outburst by the citizens of the Greek city of Thessalonica. During the summer of 390, the Thessalonians became upset over the quartering of barbarian troops within the city. When Botheric, the barbarian commandant, ordered the imprisonment of a popular charioteer and refused to allow him to participate in the upcoming public games, riots erupted. An angry mob savagely attacked Botheric, killed him, and dragged his body through the streets. Theodosius was furious and yielded to counsel that he punish the city. He soon repented his anger, too late to stop a general massacre. Enticed to attend a gala exhibition in the circus, the citizens filled the arena. At a signal the gates were shut and armed soldiers rushed in, attacking and killing indiscriminately anyone they found. For three hours, no distinctions were made between citizens and visitors, guilty and not guilty, young and old. In all, at least seven thousand people died.

Ambrose's response, after a judicious delay, was to excommunicate the emperor. Tradition has it that the proclamation was made publicly and that the emperor was ordered to undergo public penance, which would have increased Theodosius's humiliation before Ambrose. The letter, however, in which Ambrose refused the Sacraments to the emperor, is a model of tact and re-

straint. Ambrose acts the part of the concerned confessor and moral guardian. His position is the sanctity of divine law over a man who has sinned grievously against God and humanity. Thus, while Theodosius again had to yield to the bishop's authority, he submitted to spiritual and not secular authority. In effect, Theodosius recognized the Church's right to preserve the fundamental principles of religion and morality over princes and people alike.

The affair actually brought Ambrose and Theodosius closer together. Thereafter, Ambrose was Theodosius's chief spiritual adviser and confidant. They were truly partners in establishing the Nicene ideals in the Western church. Together, they defined the Nicene Creed as the orthodox religion. Ambrose outlived Theodosius by only three years. He died on the Vigil of Easter.

SIGNIFICANCE

Ambrose is best known for asserting the dominance of church authority over the Emperor Theodosius. Through his example, future ministers of the Gospel confidently claimed the right to judge, condemn, punish, and pardon princes. Ambrose was not motivated by any personal desire to demonstrate priestly power over the sovereign. Even in the episode of Callinicum, which was so little to his credit, he acted according to what he saw as the interests of the Church. In his mind, church and state were dominant in two separate but mutually dependent spheres. It was the function of the church to pray for the state and to act as its spiritual leader, while the state was the secular arm of society, which facilitated the spiritual purpose of the church. His confrontations with Theodosius and other secular leaders arose from the conviction that they had crossed the line separating church and state and were interfering in spiritual affairs. These became the principles that guided both civil and papal law in the Middle Ages.

This approach was a direct result of Ambrose's Roman, Stoic upbringing. In a very practical way, he was able to use what was best of Roman values as the foundation of everyday Christian virtue. Ambrose was convinced that because of the tremendous gulf between God and humankind, the day-to-day adherence to faith was the issue of greatest importance. He was not an original thinker, preferring to use his tremendous gift for oratory as a tool for education. Concern with the details of Scripture as they applied to life situations prompted him to rely on allegory, especially in his discussions of the Old Testament. The result was a dynamic body of doctrine and a devout core of converts, the most famous of whom was Saint Augustine. Typically, as one practical way to increase the involvement of women and children in church services, Ambrose advocated a greater use of music in re-ligious services. Although not the first to use music in the liturgy, he is considered the father of liturgical music.

—*Ronald J. Weber*

FURTHER READING

Campenhausen, Hans von. *Men Who Shaped the Western Church*. Translated by Manfred Hoffman. New York: Harper and Row, 1964. A collection of short analyti-cal biographies for seven of the best-known men in Latin Christianity. The aim of this book is to depict how personality contributed to the differences be-tween the Greek and Latin churches. The biography of Ambrose highlights his contribution to the practi-cal legalism of Western Christianity.

Dudden, F. Homes. *The Life and Times of St. Ambrose*. 2 vols. Oxford, England: Clarendon Press, 1935. A thorough treatment of Ambrose's life, combining bio-graphical detail with insightful analysis and source criticism and correcting many of the mistaken ideas about Ambrose. Includes bibliography.

Gilliard, Frank D. "Senatorial Bishops in the Fourth Cen-tury." *Harvard Theological Review* 77, no. 2 (1984): 153-175. In an examination of the class origins of prominent fourth century bishops, Gilliard seeks to determine if social class aided those who attained high church office, and whether that affected the con-version of the Roman aristocracy.

McLynn, Neil B. *Ambrose of Milan: Church and Court in a Christian Capital*. Berkeley: University of Califor-nia Press, 1994. McLynn interprets the body of Am-brose's actions and writings and finds the bishop's presentation of self to be purposeful; reveals how Ambrose manipulated important events of the fourth century. Also provides insight into the complexities of the late Roman government.

Paredi, Angelo. *Saint Ambrose: His Life and Times*. Translated by Joseph Costelloe. Notre Dame, Ind.: University of Notre Dame Press, 1964. A history of the period in which Ambrose lived, not a biography. Religious in its outlook, it is more accepting of the legends and less critical of the sources than are most scholarly treatments.

Paulinus. *Life of St. Ambrose by Paulinus*. Translated by John A. Lacy. New York: Fathers of the Church, 1952. Paulinus's biography is the basic source for informa-tion about the life of Ambrose. Paulinus was enam-ored of Ambrose and considered him a saint. He re-tells fantastic events as truth.

Satterlee, Craig Alan. *Ambrose of Milan's Method of Mystagogical Preaching*. Collegevill, Minn.: Liturgi-cal Press, 2002. An account of Saint Ambrose's meth-ods in initiating new Christians.

SEE ALSO: Saint Augustine; Theodosius the Great.

RELATED ARTICLES in *Great Events from History: The Ancient World*: 313-395 C.E., Inception of Church-State Problem; 325 C.E., Adoption of the Nicene Creed; 380-392 C.E., Theodosius's Edicts Promote Christian Orthodoxy.

AMENHOTEP III
Egyptian king (r. 1386-1349 B.C.E.)

Amenhotep III oversaw a period of progress in classical Egyptian civilization. He maintained the longest reign of any ruler of this period, erected temples throughout Egypt and northern Sudan, and ushered in an era of peace and prosperity.

BORN: c. 1403 B.C.E.; Thebes, Egypt
DIED: c. 1349 B.C.E.; Thebes, Egypt
ALSO KNOWN AS: Amenophis III; Amenhotep the Magnificent; Nubmaatre
AREAS OF ACHIEVEMENT: Government and politics, architecture, religion

EARLY LIFE

Little is known about the early life of Amenhotep III (ah-mehn-HOH-tehp), who historically came to be distin-guished as Amenhotep the Magnificent. He was born at Thebes after the era of Egypt's military campaigns in west Asia under the reigns of the preceding kings Thutmose III and Amenhotep II. He was the son of Thutmose IV and Mutemwia, who was a secondary wife of Thutmose IV, not his principal queen. Thutmose IV died when the young Amenhotep III was probably six-teen years of age, which places his birth at around 1403 B.C.E.

Amenhotep III's birth was depicted as a divinely in-spired event, with the god Amen-Ra visiting Mutemwia in her palace, disguised as her husband. After Amen-Ra's real identity was disclosed, Mutemwia conceived Amen-hotep III, the heir to the throne. Amenhotep III's infancy was memorialized well, depicted in scenes on the formidable temple he constructed at Luxor, with scenes of his mother, who, as the queen-mother, was referred to as "great royal wife" according to Egyptian customs of antiquity. Mutemwia enjoyed royalty status similar to that of her son, as the status that women enjoyed was akin to that of men in ancient Egypt. Mutemwia functioned as a vice regent during the early part of Amenhotep III's reign, exerting great influence in the direction of his rule.

Early portraits of Amenhotep III's youth reflect a brilliant and handsome figure who loved hunting lions and slew 102 when he was between sixteen and twenty-six years old. A scarab described the celebration of a two-day hunt in which he felled eighty-six bulls with his own arrows.

LIFE'S WORK

In the first two years of his reign, Amenhotep III opened the Tura limestone quarry south of Cairo as well as the Deir-el-Bersha quarry, in anticipation of the sprawling building construction and expansion he intended.

In the tenth year of his reign, he married his beloved queen, Tiy, daughter of Yuya and Tuyu, two common folk, a possible arrangement by his mother, as Tiy was one of his mother's attendants. Although there is much speculation about the national and ethnic origins of Tiy, she was clearly from outside the royal circles of Amenhotep III. She was most likely from the southern region of Egypt, probably Nubia, as the Eighteenth Dynasty reflected a strong Nubian character and, in contrast to the Middle Kingdom, for example, included southerners in the administration of the province, making the lines of distinction between resident Egyptians and dominant Nubians progressively obscured. Depictions of Tiy in sphinxes and in the Sedeinga temple in Nubia point heavily in the direction of black roots. In the same year, Amenhotep III married Kirgipa, daughter of Satirna, a king of neighboring Naharin.

Amenhotep III's primary inclination in marriage was to his first wife, Tiy, and he constructed a lake in her honor and for her pleasure, the remains of which are called Birket Habu, visible south of Medinet Habu, adjacent to his palace. The lake was opened on the event of Amenhotep III's first coronation anniversary. Tiy featured centrally in the reign of Amenhotep III, being described as the king's divine and his earthly partner, in the vein of the goddess Hathor, who was mother, daughter, and wife of the god Ra. Tiy is found in most statuary depictions of Amenhotep III and stellae, seated next to him. Her name is attached to his on numerous small

objects and jewelry, and her name follows his in large scarab representations of celebratory events. Cows' horns and sun disks, associated with Hathor, were added to Tiy's headdress and to her representation as a sphinx, evincing the mutualistic ruler role that she played with her husband.

Amenhotep III built a temple in honor of Tiy at Sedeinga in Nubia, where Tiy was worshiped as a female divinity, to accompany Amenhotep III's own temple at Soleb, to the south. The dynamic role of vice regent attributed to Tiy provided the basis for the emergence of the prominent queen Nefertiti during the reign of the successor to Amenhotep III, Amenhotep IV, who subsequently changed his name to Akhenaton. Though Amenhotep III had erected other temples in Thebes, such as the temple at Mut and the temple at the northern gate of the Karnak enclosure, he paid particular attention to the temple at Soleb in Nubia, where he came to be worshiped in conjunction with worship of Amen-Ra.

Amenhotep III and Tiy had four daughters, Sitamen, Hennutaneb, Isis, and Nebetah, all of whom appear prominently in statuary formations and reliefs. In the limestone group sculpture at Medinet Habu, which stands 23 feet (7 meters) high, Amenhotep III is shown seated with Tiy and three daughters: Henuttaneb, the eldest, at the center; Nebetah on the right; and a third, whose name is indistinguishable, on the left. The elevation of the princesses was again so magnanimous that Sitamen and Isis were described as "great royal wives," most likely within the last ten years of Amenhotep III's

RULERS OF THE EIGHTEENTH DYNASTY	
Ruler	Reign (*B.C.E.*)
Ahmose I	1570-1546
Amenhotep I	1546-1524
Thutmose I	1524-1518
Thutmose II	1518-1504
Thutmose III	1504-1450
Hatshepsut	c. 1503-1482
Amenhotep II	1450-1419
Thutmose IV	1419-1386
Amenhotep III	1386-1349
Akhenaton	1350-1334
Smenkhare	1336-1334
Tutankhamen	1334-1325
Ay	1325-1321
Horemheb	1321-1295

Note: Dynastic research is ongoing; data are approximate.

rule. At the Colossi of Memnon, the mortuary site of Amenhotep III, the king is sculptured with three generations of women of royalty: Mutemwia on the left side, Tiy on the right, and an unnamed princess at the center.

It appears that Amenhotep III enjoyed three major coronation anniversary celebrations, one in the thirtieth year of his reign, the second in year thirty-four, and the third in year thirty-six. In his thirtieth year as king, the harvest was in abundance, and Amenhotep III celebrated the occasion of his coronation and the bountiful food production under his leadership, achievements that increased his popularity among the citizenry. The regional leaders of the south and the north were rewarded for this prosperous outcome, a sign of the thriving power of Egypt at that time in ancient history.

Records found in the Tomb of Kherfuf of the third jubilee of Amenhotep III's coronation indicate that he erected the column of Osiris, which is the symbol of stability. New chambers were opened in the Tura quarry in the first year of Amenhotep III's reign, which also became the place at which an incomplete statue of Amenhotep III was being sculpted by an officer of the king. Such actions all were signs of the prosperity of the time and indicative of the homage paid to Amenhotep III by his viziers and officials. Evidence from jar inscriptions found at the Malkata palace establishes that Amenhotep III celebrated his three Sed-coronation festivals at Thebes. The first Heb-Sed was celebrated in the Soleb temple of the king in Upper Nubia, at which hundreds of jars of food and drink were brought for the guests at the celebration. It appears that offerings for each successive Heb-Sed were distinct: Beer was featured for the first one, meat for the second, and wine for the third.

Amenhotep III expanded the temple complex that existed prior to his reign. At the Amen-Ra temple, he built a new entrance pylon, the Third Pylon, which incorporated the lateral axis into the Amen-Ra temple. For Opet ceremonial processions, worshipers left from behind the pylon gateway, no longer directly from in front of the entrance, where the processions honoring Hatshepsut had occurred. At the south end of the temple, he extended the lateral axis by adding another pylon, which still stands, as the base of the Tenth Pylon subsequently erected by Horemheb. He had two colossal statues of himself built outside the Third Pylon. At the north end of the Amen-Ra temple, he initiated the construction of a temple for the worship of Montu. To the south, he built a small temple adjacent to the Mut temple and even began renovating the Mut temple. This new temple was massive, with a colonnaded forecourt, most likely with a pylon gateway in front, a hypostyle hall, and a sanctuary area. Three sides of the temple were surrounded by a holy lake, called Isheru, which is there today.

It is conceivable that Amenhotep III started work on the small temple of Khonsu, at the southwestern side of the Amen-Ra temple, or could have made improvements on the existing temple. The numerous sphinxes that led from this temple toward Luxor were certainly erected by him. He pioneered the enlargement of the entire temple complex at Luxor, even while extension plans were under way on the east bank of the Nile River. Many of these works were, in all probability, in preparation for observation of the elaborate Opet festival celebrated during that time.

During Amenhotep III's reign, gold-mining operations were expanded and improved. The southern Egyptian gold mines were included under the authority of the viceroy of Kush, and evidence of Amenhotep III's viceroy, Merymose, has been found in Reddesiyeh in southern Egypt. The mine there was producing gold by the beginning of the Eighteenth Dynasty. Merymose also launched campaigns in the eastern desert area of Wawat to ensure gold production for Amenhotep's rule. Another toponym, Akuyta, emerged as a significant gold-producing location, maintained even after Amenhotep III's reign, through the successive rule of Akhenaton (Amenhotep IV), Horemheb, Ramses II, and Ramses III.

It was this economy of gold production and flourishing of international trade and commerce with neighboring powers in Babylon, Mitanni, and Asia, and even contact with Crete in the Mediterranean, that made the reign of Amenhotep III distinctively famous in that era of antiquity. There are scarabs in the Aegean with Amenhotep III's name, as well as that of Queen Tiy, suggesting that Amenhotep III was engaged in diplomatic initiatives and in developing strategic alliances to consolidate the Egyptian empire and constrain the growing Hittite threat. Amenhotep III was interested in the Aegean-Anatolia region for a portion of his reign to ensure the security of the Egyptian kingdom, and hence he built ties with the Mycenaeans. One of the ceilings of his palace at Malkata is furnished in Aegean style and reflects pottery from the final palatial period of Minoan civilization.

He administered only one major military campaign, that against rebellious groups in Kush in the fifth year of his reign, which resulted in a resounding success. He clearly loathed the pursuit of military objectives as part of his kingship. Even when the Hittites invaded Mitanni and the provinces of Egypt, shortly after the third jubilee in year thirty-six of his reign, Amenhotep III sent his troops only and did not march with his entire army, as Thutmose III would have done.

Amenhotep III's rule waned with the invading forces of the Khabiri, desert Semites, inundating neighboring Palestine and Syria. The death of the king's favorite son and his rapid aging took a devastating personal toll on him as he saw his thirty-eighth year on the throne. He was significantly weakened, and even though his brother sent him an image of the goddess Ishtar of Nineveh to expunge the evil spirits of illness, he was unable to recover. He passed away soon thereafter and was buried with his fathers in the Valley of the Kings, ending the era of Amenhotep the Magnificent. He was succeeded by Amenhotep IV, who later changed his name to Akhenaton.

SIGNIFICANCE

Amenhotep III is historic in that his reign lasted the longest of all rulers of the Eighteenth Dynasty and was distinguished by an aura of prosperity and peace, security, and well-being for the citizens of Egypt during that period, notwithstanding the traditional tribute that had to be paid to the royal state by all subjects. Amenhotep III revolutionized the Nile Valley, ushering in an era of food surpluses and economic vitality unseen before in ancient Egypt. Under his rule, there were no military penetrations into western Asia, as he industriously worked to cultivate peaceful relations among diverse international factions and powers, boosting his country's standing in global trade and commerce and elevating his status among regional leaders. He demonstrated, par excellence, that diplomacy is effective, in contrast with militarism.

As king, Amenhotep III was a pioneer architect and innovative builder. He was responsible for constructing an entire temple, the largest by any one person, in Thebes. No king of Egypt left so many monuments and temples as Amenhotep III, except for Ramses II, who took over many of the buildings constructed by Amenhotep III for himself. Amenhotep III clearly was a religious ruler, whose tribute to the gods, and to his fame, is evident in the massive stone structures that stand today, unlike those of many who preceded and succeeded him. He was the first king whose place of burial was outside the view of the Nile.

Not only was the rule of Amenhotep III characterized by a euphoric aura, in which some of the more aggressive traits of preceding and successive rulers of the Eighteenth Dynasty were absent, but he also singularly established a regime that accorded his wife coequal governing status, unprecedented in his day and unlike that of any other queen of classical Egyptian antiquity. Amenhotep III patently implemented a policy of egalitarianism for women and mutual reciprocity in relations with women, including his daughters, that served as a paradigm for future rulers and has been etched in the annals of classical history.

Finally, Amenhotep III was inclusive in his administration and heralded a new era of incorporation of multiethnic communities into a cohesive nation in Egypt, unlike preceding administrations. His embracing of the peoples of Nubia was one indication of this inclusiveness, to the point that some African-centered scholars refer to the Eighteenth Dynasty as the Black Dynasty.

—*Julian Kunnie*

FURTHER READING

Brier, Bob, and Hoyt Hobbs. *Daily Life of the Ancient Egyptians*. Westport, Conn.: Greenwood Press, 1999. This book has a listing of the kings of the New Kingdom and a section on Amenhotep III's rule.

Fletcher, Joann. *Chronicle of a Pharaoh: The Intimate Life of Amenhotep III*. New York: Oxford University Press, 2000. This attractive, richly illustrated little book relates the life of Amenhotep III, who ruled Egypt in the fourteenth century B.C.E. Covers his political skills and building of the temple of Luxor but also focuses on some of the more intimate details of Amenhotep's life.

Jenkins, Earnestine. *A Glorious Past: Ancient Egypt, Ethiopia, and Nubia*. New York: Chelsea House, 1995. Connects the histories of ancient Egypt, Ethiopia, and Nubia to African Americans and has wonderful photographs of paintings and sculptures that illustrate the foundational African character of these classic civilizations.

Manning, Stuart W. *A Test of Time: The Volcano of Thera and the Chronology and History of the Aegean and East Mediterranean in the Mid-Second Millennium B.C.* Oakville, Conn.: Oxbow Books, 1999. Illuminates the archaeological discoveries in the Aegean region from the time of Amenhotep III's rule and describes in detail the role of skilled global diplomat that Amenhotep III played.

O'Connor, David, and Eric Cline, eds. *Amenhotep III: Perspectives on His Reign*. Ann Arbor: University of Michigan Press, 1997. The authors furnish a scholastic exposition on the construction of temples and monuments under Amenhotep III's reign, funerary arts, organization of the city and the politics of government, and international relations under the ruler.

Petrie, William M. *Flinders. A History of Egypt During the XVIIth and XVIIIth Dynasties*. 4th ed. Vol. 2. Freeport, N.Y.: Books for Libraries Press, 1972. Contains an elaboration on the early life of Amenhotep III, his wife's role in ruling, his family, the monuments and temples of the king, and his officials. Provides a reliable chronology of events leading up to Amenhotep III's reign and following, accompanied by depictions of figures.

Rice, Michael. *Egypt's Making: The Origins of Ancient Egypt 5000-2000 B.C.E.* New York: Routledge, 1990. Discusses ancient Egyptian civilization and Amenhotep III's reign.

Strudwick, Nigel, and Helen Strudwick. *Thebes in Egypt: A Guide to the Tombs and Temples of Ancient Luxor*. Ithaca, N.Y.: Cornell University Press, 1999. Has instructive documentation of Amenhotep III's rule, with color photographs of temples and tombs in Luxor that illustrate the magnitude of Amenhotep III's creativity.

Trigger, B. G., B. J. Kemp, D. O'Connor, and A. B. Lloyd. *Ancient Egypt: A Social History*. New York: Cambridge University Press, 1983. Describes the intimate relationship of Egypt and Nubia, particularly during the reign of Amenhotep III, the structure of the government in the New Kingdom (1152-1069 B.C.E.), and the historic legacy that Amenhotep III left with regard to temple construction, political governance and organization, and cultic associations of kingship.

Van Sertima, Ivan, ed. *Nile Valley Civilizations; Proceedings of the Nile Valley Conference, Atlanta, September 26-30, 1985*. New Brunswick, N.J.: Journal of African Civilizations, 1985. A range of articles describing the black roots and continental African relationships of early Egyptian civilization, including sections on Nubian influences on Amenhotep III and his queen Tiy, information that is not discussed in most other books on Amenhotep III.

SEE ALSO: Akhenaton; Nefertiti; Thutmose III; Tiy.

RELATED ARTICLES in *Great Events from History: The Ancient World*: c. 1900-1527? B.C.E., Kerma Kingdom Rules Nubia; c. 1570 B.C.E., New Kingdom Period Begins in Egypt; From c. 1500 B.C.E., Dissemination of the Book of the Dead; c. 1365 B.C.E., Failure of Akhenaton's Cultural Revival.

ĀNANDA

Indian disciple and personal attendant of the Buddha

It is said that because of his prodigious memory and his having listened to all the Buddha's sermons, Ānanda was able to recite them by heart in their entirety, thus helping in their compilation at the First Buddhist Council. In addition, thanks to Ānanda's entreaties and argumentation, the Buddha consented to let women join the ranks of the Buddhist community to become nuns.

FLOURISHED: Sixth century B.C.E.; North India
ALSO KNOWN AS: Ananda
AREA OF ACHIEVEMENT: Religion

EARLY LIFE

There is very little personal information concerning the early life of Ānanda (AH-nuhn-duh). According to Buddhist tradition, since he was born on the day when Siddhārtha Gautama reached enlightenment and became the Buddha, Ānanda, which means "Rejoicing," was thus named by his elated father. Ānanda belonged to the warrior caste, within the same Śākya tribal confederation as the Buddha, of the Gautama clan in the kingdom of Kapilavastu, now in southern Nepal. He was the Buddha's first cousin, as his father, King Suklodana, was the younger brother of the Buddha's father, King Śuddhodana. It is said that Ānanda's father initially did not want him to become the Buddha's disciple, and that he thus sought to keep his son from knowing about the Buddha's presence. Eventually, on encountering the Buddha on the occasion of the Buddha's return to his father's kingdom, young Ānanda decided to follow the Buddha, thus growing up within the *Sangha* (the Buddhist community) and later becoming a *bhikkhu* (monk).

Within the multitude who joined the ranks of the order, many were Śākyan princes, and one among them was Ānanda's brother, Devadatta. Craving only power and recognition, Devadatta vied unsuccessfully for the Buddha's position as head of the congregation, and failing that, tried, again without success, to harm the Buddha during one of his journeys teaching the dharma, attended as always by Ānanda. Ānanda, on the other hand, was very much beloved by the Buddha and his followers, who were greatly impressed by his learning and mindfulness as well as his warmth, humility, and compassion. His gentle manners and handsome physique attracted female attention, causing him much difficulty throughout his life. According to one account, as he was begging for food, Ānanda, very thirsty, was met at a well by a young peasant girl, Matanga, who gave him water. Struck by the young *bhikkhu*'s good looks, Matanga followed him and would not leave him alone, tempting Ānanda greatly. It was only with the Buddha's intercession that Ānanda was prevented from breaking one of the five precepts, that of sexual misconduct.

As the Buddha aged, he needed a personal attendant who would accompany him on his trips to teach the dharma, or Buddhist law. While many disciples of the Buddha competed for this position, Ānanda remained silent but was finally selected because the Buddha had foreseen that Ānanda would later be crucial in the propagation of the dharma. Ānanda was extremely devoted to the Buddha, following him everywhere as he wandered to teach the dharma, guarding his sleep, seeing to all his needs, and acting as intermediary between the Buddha and all who wanted to consult his wisdom. Before attaining *mokśa* ("liberation without remainder") at Kuśinagara (now Kasia in Uttar Pradesh), the Buddha entrusted Ānanda with the final instructions as to the disposal of his body and the direction that the *Sangha* should take after his death. As recorded in *Mahāparinibbāna Sutta* or *The Discourse of the Great Passing Away*—part of the *Tipiṭaka* (collected c. 250 B.C.E.; English translation in *Buddhist Scriptures*, 1913)—the Buddha exclaimed:

> What, Ānanda! Does the Order expect that of me? I have taught the truth without making any distinction between exoteric and esoteric doctrines; for, with the Tathāgata there is no such thing as the closed fist of the teacher who keeps some things back. . . . So Ānanda, you must be your own lamps, be your own refuges. Take refuge in nothing outside yourselves.

Ānanda attained enlightenment only after the Buddha's passing away. It is said that Venerable Ānanda lived to be 120 years old.

LIFE'S WORK

It is impossible to speak of Ānanda without speaking of the Buddha, as Ānanda did not stand alone in Buddhist history but is inextricably linked to the life and teaching of the Buddha. As the Buddha's personal attendant, Ānanda was able to listen to every one of the Buddha's sermons and thus was the best witness of the Buddha's word. The Buddha also preached to him personally.

Ānanda was noted for his prodigious memory, a quality that made his contribution to the recording of the Buddha's teaching vital. On the Buddha's passing (reaching the final nirvana or *parinibbāna*), his disciples decided to assemble to record the sutras, as the Buddha left no writing behind. This First Council, also known as the First Communal Recitation, was really a question-and-answer exercise organized by one of the Buddha's senior disciples, Mahākassapa, held in Rajājagṛha (now Rajgir, in Bihar). It included more than four hundred arhats, monks who had attained enlightenment.

At first, Ānanda was not invited because he had not yet reached arhathood, but eventually he attained that state and was able to participate, thus bringing an invaluable contribution to the formulation of the Buddhist canon by reciting from memory the Buddha's teaching. This recitation was transcribed later to form the foundation of the *Sutta-piṭaka* or "basket of discourses (sutras)." The Buddhist canon is divided into three parts referred to as *Tipiṭaka*, the "three baskets" or "threefold collections": the *Vinaya-piṭaka* (basket of discipline), which concerns itself with the rules and procedures followed by monks and nuns; the *Sutta-piṭaka* (basket of discourses), which conveys the Buddha's teaching through sermons; and the *Abhidamma-piṭaka* (basket of commentaries), added later by the different schools of Buddhism. Ānanda's recitations, recorded primarily in the *Sutta-piṭaka*, included more than five thousand sutras that are believed to bear testimony to the Buddha's teaching over more than four decades, although this belief has been questioned by some specialists. The sutras often begin with the phrase, credited to Ānanda, "Thus have I heard. At one time. . . ."

Ānanda's other major contribution was in the domain of women's participation in the Buddhist order. At first, the Buddha did not allow women to become *bhikkhunis* (nuns) out of respect for the established socioreligious order, which considered women to be dependent on men and required them to remain within the household. He held this position despite the repeated pleadings of his aunt, Mahāpajāpatī, who had reared him following the death of his birth mother. The Buddha feared that the conflict between the dharma's discipline and the demands of attachment would upset the equilibrium of monastic life and hinder the spiritual advancement of its then-exclusively male membership. Undeterred, Mahāpajāpatī, along with five hundred women of the Śākya clan, proceeded to shave their heads and begged to be allowed to enter the order. Moved by their sufferings and impressed by their determination, Ānanda interceded with the Master by arguing that women, too, could follow the dharma and progress spiritually. Finally, the Buddha yielded, permitting women to take the robe and to join the ranks of the *Saṅgha*, on the condition that they obey a stricter code than that applied to its male members.

Later, Ānanda was responsible for organizing the order of the *bhikkhunis*. Women in many parts of the Buddhist world still can become nuns by joining their own order, separate from but theoretically under the supervision of that of the *bhikkhu*.

After the passing away of the Buddha, Ānanda succeeded Mahākassapa as the head of the *Saṅgha*. He is said to have chosen to die in the middle of the Ganges River rather than in either the kingdom of Magadha or Vesālī to prevent their contesting with each other for his remains.

SIGNIFICANCE

Within the Buddhist world, Ānanda is considered one of the ten most significant disciples of the Buddha. Just as the Buddha himself left nothing in writing, Ānanda wrote nothing. However, his name appears often in the different early Buddhist texts (in Pāli) such as the *Aṅguttara-nikāya* or *Digha-nikāya*, as the personal interlocutor of the Buddha whenever the latter expounded crucial aspects of his doctrine. It is said, for example, that *The Greater Discourse on Causes* or *Mahānidāna Sutta*, which dealt with the essential question of dependent origination, resulted from the Buddha personally preaching to Ānanda, an exchange in which Ānanda actively participated.

—*Nguyen Thi Dieu*

FURTHER READING

Bechert, Heinz, Richard Gombrich, et al. *The World of Buddhism: Buddhist Monks and Nuns in Society and Culture.* New York: Thames and Hudson, 1998. This is a compilation of articles by the foremost specialists on Buddhism from Europe and the United States on a number of aspects of Buddhist theory, evolution, and propagation. It is richly illustrated, providing the reader with colorful Buddhist iconography, religious texts, and maps. Bibliography and index.

Conze, Edward. *Buddhism: A Short History.* Oxford: Oneworld Publications, 2000. A classic of Buddhism written by one of the foremost specialists, this work provides the reader with a brief history of Buddhism covering its more than two thousand years of existence. Bibliography, glossary, and index.

Coomaraswamy, Ānanda K., and I. B. Horner. *The Living Thoughts of Gotama the Buddha.* Louisville, Ken.: Fons Vitae, 2001. This text is a specialized treatise on the Buddha's life and his viewpoints concerning diverse but complex issues such as the question of caste, illustrated by quotations from the main Buddhist texts within the Pāli school.

De Bary, William Theodore, ed. *The Buddhist Tradition in India, China, and Japan.* New York: Vintage Books, 1972. The author presents excerpts of translations of fundamental Indian, Chinese, and Japanese Buddhist texts, preceded by an introduction for each of the texts. Bibliography and index.

Harvey, Peter. *An Introduction to Buddhism: Teachings, History, and Practices.* New York: Cambridge University Press, 1990. This work, written by another great specialist, is more encompassing, as it provides the reader with a thorough and knowledgeable analysis of Buddhism, its meanings, and different practices and schools. Bibliography and index.

Skilton, Andrew. *A Concise History of Buddhism.* Birmingham, England: Windhorse Publications, 1997. Provides an in-depth, very learned study of Buddhism, its different schools, and practices in different parts of Asia. Bibliography, index, and map.

Williams, Paul, with Anthony Tribe. *Buddhist Thought: A Complete Introduction to the Indian Tradition.* New York: Routledge, 2000. Presents to the student unfamiliar with Buddhism an accessible treatment that analyzes the Indian tradition within which Buddhism developed, as well as Indian Buddhism's main tenets and schools, while using the latest interpretations. Bibliography and index.

SEE ALSO: Asanga; Aśoka; Aśvaghosa; Bodhidharma; Buddha; Chandragupta Maurya; Gośāla Maskarīputra; Kanishka; Vardhamāna; Vasubandhu; Vattagamani.

RELATED ARTICLES in *Great Events from History: The Ancient World*: 6th or 5th century B.C.E., Birth of Buddhism; c. 5th-4th centuries B.C.E., Creation of the *Jātakas*; c. 321 B.C.E., Mauryan Empire Rises in India; c. 250 B.C.E., Third Buddhist Council Convenes; c. 250 B.C.E., *Tipiṭaka* Is Compiled; 1st century B.C.E.-1st century C.E., Compilation of the *Lotus Sutra*; 1st century C.E., Fourth Buddhist Council Convenes; Late 4th-5th centuries C.E., Asanga Helps Spread Mahāyāna Buddhism; 460-477 C.E., Buddhist Temples Built at Ajanta Caves in India.

ANAXAGORAS
Greek philosopher and scientist

By devising a philosophical system to explain the origins and nature of the physical universe that overcame the paradoxes and inconsistencies of earlier systems, Anaxagoras provided an indispensable bridge between the pre-Socratic philosophers of the archaic period of Greek history and the full flowering of philosophy during the Golden Age of Greece.

BORN: c. 500 B.C.E.; Clazomenae, Anatolia (now in Turkey)

DIED: c. 428 B.C.E.; Lampsacus (now Lapseki, Turkey)

AREAS OF ACHIEVEMENT: Philosophy, natural history, science

EARLY LIFE

Virtually nothing is known of the parents of Anaxagoras (an-aks-AG-ur-uhs) or his childhood, adolescence, or education. Born into a wealthy family in an Ionian Greek city, he almost certainly was exposed to the attempts by Ionian philosophers, especially Parmenides, to explain the physical universe by postulating that everything is made from a single primordial substance. Anaxagoras apparently realized even before he was twenty years of age that such an assumption could not explain the phenomena of movement and change, and he began to devise a more satisfactory system.

He grew to adulthood during the turbulent years of the wars of the Greek city-states against the Persian Empire. His own city, Clazomenae, forced to acknowledge the suzerainty of Darius the Great in 514, joined the Athenian-aided Ionian revolt against Persia in 498. That revolt ultimately was suppressed in 493. Anaxagoras's childhood was spent during a time when the echoes of Athens's great victory over Darius at Marathon in 490 were reverberating throughout the Hellenic world.

According to tradition, Anaxagoras became a resident of Athens in 480. That a young scholar should be attracted to the intellectual and artistic center of Greek civilization is not surprising, but it is doubtful that this change of residence took place in 480. Xerxes I chose that year to attempt to realize Darius's dream of conquering the Greek polis. His plans were frustrated, and his great host scattered at the Battles of Salamis and Plataea during that same year. The next year, the Ionian cities of Asia Minor again rose in rebellion against Persia, and in 477 they joined with Athens in the Delian League. The League succeeded in expelling the Persians from the Greek states of Asia Minor. It seems more likely that the young Anaxagoras came to Athens after the alliance between the Ionian cities and the Athenians.

While in Athens, Anaxagoras became friends with the young Pericles and apparently influenced him considerably. Several classical scholars have concluded that Anaxagoras's later trial was engineered by Pericles' political rivals, in order to deprive Pericles of a trusted friend. Convicted of impiety after admitting that he thought the sun was a huge mass of "hot rock," Anaxagoras went into exile at Lampsacus, where many young Greeks came to study with him before his death, probably in 428.

LIFE'S WORK

Sometime in or shortly after 467, Anaxagoras published his only written work, apparently titled *Nature*. Of this work, only seventeen fragments totaling around twelve hundred words have survived, all recorded as quotations in the works of later generations of philosophers. That so few words could have inspired the more than fifty books and articles written about him in the twentieth century alone is ample testimony to Anaxagoras's importance in the evolution of Greek philosophy and natural science.

Anaxagoras's book was an ambitious attempt to explain the origins and nature of the universe without recourse (or so it seemed to many of his contemporaries) to any supernatural agents. Other Ionian philosophers, notably Parmenides, had preceded Anaxagoras in this endeavor, but their systems were logically unable to explain the multiplicity of "things" in the universe or to explain physical and biological change in those things because they had postulated that all things are made from the same basic "stuff." Anaxagoras overcame the logical inconsistencies of this argument by postulating an infinite variety of substances that make up the whole of the universe. Anaxagoras argued that there is something of everything in everything. By this he meant that, for example, water contains a part of every other thing in the universe, from blood to rock to air. The reason that it is perceived to be water is that most of its parts are water. A hair also contains parts of every other thing, but most of its parts are hair.

In the beginning, according to the first fragment of Anaxagoras's book, infinitely small parts of everything in equal proportions were together in a sort of primal soup. In fragment 3, he proposes a primitive version of the law of the conservation of energy, by saying that anything, no matter how small, can be divided infinitely, because it is not possible for something to become nonexistent through dividing. This idea of infinite divisibility is unique to the Anaxagorean system; no philosopher before or since has proposed it.

This universal mixture of all things acquired form and substance, according to fragment 12, through the actions of *nous*, or "mind." Mind, Anaxagoras argues, is not part of everything (though it is a part of some things), nor is a part of everything found in mind (though parts of some things are found in mind). Mind set the primal soup into rotation, and the different things began to "separate off," thus forming the universe. The rotation of the primal mixture not only separated everything according to its kind (but not perfectly, as everything still contains parts of every other thing) but also supplied heat, through friction. Among other things, friction ignited the sun and the stars. Considerable disagreement over the exact meaning Anaxagoras was trying to convey with the term "mind" has colored scholarly works on his book since Aristotle and continues to be a controversial issue.

Anaxagoras's system not only enabled him and his students to describe all existing objects, but it also permitted the explanation of physical and biological change. It was the introduction of the idea of mind and its action as a formative agent in the creation of the universe for which Anaxagoras became famous and that rejuvenated Socrates' interest and faith in philosophy.

Anaxagoras. (Hulton|Archive by Getty Images)

Sometime after 467, Anaxagoras was accused of and tried for impiety (denying the gods) and "medism" (sympathizing with the Persians). The actual date of his trial and subsequent banishment from Athens is still hotly debated among classical scholars. The traditional date accepted by most historians is 450, but this seems unlikely for several reasons. By 450, the charge of medism could hardly have been a serious one, because the Persian Wars were long since over. Also, had he been in Athens in 450, the young Socrates would almost certainly have met him personally, but Socrates' own words indicate that he knew Anaxagoras only through his book. Finally, Anaxagoras's friend Pericles would have been fully able to protect his mentor from political opponents in 450. An earlier date for his exile from Athens seems likely. Some scholars have attempted to solve this problem by postulating that Anaxagoras visited Athens one or more times after being exiled shortly after the publication of his book. This seems the most reasonable explanation to reconcile the dispute, especially because several ancient sources place him in Athens as late as 437.

One of Anaxagoras's most notable achievements during his stay in Athens was his postulation of the correct explanation for a solar eclipse. Anaxagoras was apparently the first to argue that an eclipse occurs when the moon (which he said was a large mass of cold rocks) passes between the earth and the sun (which he said was a larger mass of hot rocks). He may have reached this conclusion after the fall of a large meteorite near Aegypotomi in 467, which excited wide discussion throughout the Hellenic world.

After leaving Athens, Anaxagoras spent his remaining years as the head of a flourishing school at Lampsacus. How his philosophical system may have changed over the years between the publication of his book and the end of his life is unknown. He died at Lampsacus, probably in 428.

SIGNIFICANCE

The thesis that Anaxagoras greatly influenced Socrates and Aristotle is easily proved by their elaborate discussions of his system in their own words. Through those two most influential of all Greek thinkers, he has had a profound impact on all subsequent generations of philosophers and natural scientists in the Western world. Some of Anaxagoras's critics, both ancient and modern, accuse him of merely substituting the word "mind" for "God" or "the gods." Thus, in their estimation, his philosophy becomes merely a humanistic religion. Other critics have dismissed Anaxagoras's teachings as simplistic and unworthy of serious consideration. His supporters, from Aristotle to the present, have defended him as a pioneering thinker who provided much of the inspiration for the flowering of post-Socratic philosophy during the Golden Age of Greece and the Hellenistic world.

Early critics and supporters alike may have missed an important point in the Anaxagoras fragments. Modern scholarship on Anaxagoras points out that his concept of mind giving form to the universe is not far removed from the position of some modern physicists who argue that one's perception of the universe is determined by one's own senses, which provide an imperfect understanding at best. Anaxagoras may well have been trying to express this same concept (that without cognitive perception there is no form or substance to the universe) without possessing the technical language to do so.

—Paul Madden

FURTHER READING

Barnes, Jonathan. *The Presocratic Philosophers*. London: Routledge, 1993. Includes a chapter on Anaxagoras, reconstructing his philosophy from a careful examination of the fragments.

Davison, J. A. "Protagoras, Democritus, and Anaxagoras." *Classical Quarterly* 3 (1953): 33-45. Establishes Anaxagoras's position vis-à-vis other Greek philosophers and shows his influence on the "atomist" school that succeeded him. Also contains some information on his early life not available elsewhere in English and argues for an early date for his exile from Athens.

Gershenson, Daniel E., and Daniel A. Greenberg. *Anaxagoras and the Birth of Physics*. New York: Blaisdell, 1964. This controversial work suggests that the Anaxagoras fragments are not really the words of Anaxagoras, but rather his words as interpreted by later philosophers, notably Simplicius, who succeeded him. Contains a good, if somewhat theoretical, explanation of Anaxagoras's system.

Guthrie, W. K. C. *A History of Greek Philosophy*. Vol. 2. Cambridge, England: Cambridge University Press, 1965. Contains the most complete account available of Anaxagoras's life. Puts his life and teachings in the context of his times.

Kirk, Geoffrey S., John E. Raven, and M. Schofield. *The Presocratic Philosophers*. 2d ed. New York: Cambridge University Press, 1983. One chapter contains a scholarly account of Anaxagoras's philosophy; includes Greek text of fragments.

Mansfield, J. "The Chronology of Anaxagoras's Athenian Period and the Date of His Trial." *Mnemosyne* 33 (1980): 17-95. Offers convincing arguments concerning Anaxagoras's arrival in Athens, his trial, and his banishment. Also contains references to Anaxagoras's relationship with Pericles and the political motives behind the former's exile.

Mourelatos, Alexander P. D. *The Pre-Socratics: A Collection of Critical Essays*. Princeton, N.J.: Princeton University Press, 1993. Includes two essays by eminent scholars, Gregory Vlastos and G. B. Kerford, which attempt to reconstruct Anaxagoras's philosophy in a way that makes it logically consistent. Both focus on his materialism.

Schofield, Malcolm. *An Essay on Anaxagoras*. Cambridge, England: Cambridge University Press, 1980. A clear, witty exposition of the philosophy of Anaxagoras and his importance in the history of philosophy. Perhaps the best work on Anaxagoras's system and its meaning available in English.

SEE ALSO: Aristotle; Empedocles; Parmenides; Pericles; Socrates.

RELATED ARTICLES in *Great Events from History: The Ancient World*: September 17, 490 B.C.E., Battle of Marathon; 478-448 B.C.E., Athenian Empire Is Created; c. 450-c. 425 B.C.E., History Develops as a Scholarly Discipline; c. 440 B.C.E., Sophists Train the Greeks in Rhetoric and Politics; May, 431-September, 404 B.C.E., Peloponnesian War; September, 404-May, 403 B.C.E., Thirty Tyrants Rule Athens for Eight Months; 399 B.C.E., Death of Socrates.

ANAXIMANDER
Greek philosopher, astronomer, and cartographer

Anaximander invented the scientific use of models and maps. He also realized, contrary to the prevailing thought of his day, that the original substance of matter must be an eternal, unlimited reservoir of qualities and change.

BORN: c. 610 B.C.E.; Miletus, Greek Asia Minor (now in Turkey)
DIED: c. 547 B.C.E.; probably Miletus
AREAS OF ACHIEVEMENT: Natural history, astronomy, geography

EARLY LIFE

Anaximander (uh-nak-suh-MAN-duhr) was a fellow citizen and student of Thales, the Milesian usually credited with having inaugurated Western philosophy. Thales, some forty years older than his protégé, put none of his philosophical thought in writing and maintained no formal pedagogical associations with pupils. However, Thales' cosmological views (as reconstructed by historians) doubtless inspired Anaximander, and Anaximander finally expanded on Thales' ideas with innovative leaps in conceptual abstraction.

Anaximander was known in his day for his practical achievements and his astronomical discoveries. He is said to have been chosen by the Milesians as the leader for a new colony in Apollonia on the Black Sea. He traveled widely and was the first Greek to publish a "geographical tablet," a map of the world. The map was circular, and it was centered on the city of Delphi, because Delphi was the location of the *omphalos*, or "navel" stone, that was thought to be the center of Earth. Anaximander is also said to have designed a celestial map and to have specified the proportions of stellar orbits. In addition to the celestial map, he built a spherical model of the stars and planets, with Earth located at the center and represented as a disk or cylinder whose height was one third its diameter. The heavenly bodies were rings of hollow pipe of different sizes that were placed on circling wheels in ratios of three to six to nine, in proportion to the magnitude of Earth. This model was dynamic; the wheels could be moved at different speeds, making it possible to visualize patterns of planetary motion. Anaximander is also credited with inventing the gnomon (part of a sundial) and with having discovered the zodiac.

All these eclectic interests and discoveries illustrate, with elegance, Anaximander's particular genius, namely, his rational view of the world. This way of thinking was quite an innovation at a time when both scientific and protophilosophical thought took their content from the mythical and literary traditions, and thus were marked by vagueness and mystery. Anaximander viewed the world as steadily legible; he had the expectation of its rational intelligibility. His map of the world and his model of the heavens show his anticipation of symmetry and order. Earth, he argued, remained at rest in the center of the cosmos by reason of its equidistance at all points to the celestial circumference; it had no reason to be pulled in one direction in preference to any other. He projected the celestial orbits in perfect and pleasing proportions, and he anticipated regular motions.

Anaximander's mapping and modeling techniques themselves were products of his rationalistic thinking. Models and maps relocate some set of unified phenomena into a new level of abstraction. Implicit in map and model design is the assumption that the abstractions will preserve the intelligible relationships present in the world that they reproduce. Thus Anaximander's introduction of models and maps represents a tremendous and utterly original conceptual leap from the world "seen" to the world's operations understood and faithfully reproduced by the abstracting human mind.

LIFE'S WORK

Anaximander's rational view of the world received its fullest and most innovative expression in his philosophy of nature. Here one finds the first unified and all-encompassing picture of the world of human experience in history that is based on rational deduction and explanation of all phenomena.

In order to understand Anaximander properly, his terminology must be put into its historical context. What Anaximander (and Thales as well) understood by "nature" is not quite the same as its modern sense. In Ionian Greece, *physis* denoted the process of growth and emergence. It also denoted something's origin, or source, that from which the thing is constantly renewed. Nature, in the Ionian sense of *physis*, had nothing to do with matter; even Aristotle was mistaken in thinking that it did. In fact, no word for matter even existed in Anaximander's day. It is also important to note that Anaximander's thought is reconstructed entirely from ancient secondary sources. The one extant fragment of Anaximander's own words is the quotation of an ancient historian. Thus, any

Anaximander. (Hulton|Archive by Getty Images)

guishes the source from the world is that the source itself is "unbounded": It can have no definite shape or quality of its own but must be a reservoir from which every sort or characteristic in the world may be spawned. So Anaximander called the source of things this very name: *apeiron,* Boundlessness, or the Boundless. Anaximander designated the Boundless an *arche,* a beginning, but he did not mean a temporal beginning. The Boundless can have no beginning, nor can it pass away, for it can have no bounds, including temporal ones.

Thus the eternal source, the Boundless, functions as a storehouse of the world's qualities, such that the qualities that constitute some present state of the world have been separated out of the stock, and when their contrary qualities become manifest, they will, in turn, be reabsorbed into the reservoir. When Earth is hot, heat will come forth from the Boundless; when Earth cools, cold will come forth and heat will go back. For Anaximander, this process continued in never-ending cycles.

The cause of the alternating manifestations of contrary qualities is the subject of the single existing fragment of Anaximander's own words, the only remains of the first philosophy ever written. Out of the Boundless, Anaximander explains, the worlds arise, but

> from whatever things is the genesis of the things that are, into these they must pass away according to necessity; for they must pay the penalty and make atonement to one another for their injustice according to the ordering of Time.

History has produced no consensus of interpretation for this passage and its picturesque philosophical metaphor for the rationale of the world. Anaximander was probably thinking of a courtroom image. Each existing thing is in a state of "having-too-much," so that during the time it exists it "commits injustice" against its opposite by preventing it from existing. In retribution, the existing thing must cede its overt existence for its opposite to enjoy and pay the penalty of returning to the submerged place in the great Boundless reservoir. This cycling, he added, is how Time is ordered or measured. Time is the change, the alternating manifestation of opposites.

Here is the apotheosis of Anaximander's rational worldview. The world's workings are not simply visible and perspicuous, but neither are they whimsical and mysterious. The hidden workings of things may be revealed in the abstractions of the human mind. The world works, and is the way that it is, according to an eternal and intel-

explication of Anaximander's thought is, to some extent, conjectural and interpretive.

Anaximander's philosophy of nature arose in part as a response to Thales' ideas on nature. Thales held that water was the nature of everything. This meant, in the light of the ancient idea of *physis,* that water was the origin of everything, that everything was sustained by, and constantly renewed from, water. This notion does not have any allegorical or mythical connotations in Thales' formulation. Water is the ordinary physical stuff in the world, not some engendering god such as the Oceanus of Thales' predecessors. That is the reason Thales is the first philosopher: He had a theory about the origin of things that competed with ancient creation myths.

Anaximander agreed with Thales that the origin of the things of the world was some common stuff, but he thought that the stuff could not be some ordinary element. He rejected Thales' conception on purely logical grounds, and his reasoning was quite interesting. How could any manifestly singular stuff ever give rise to qualities that pertained to things differently constituted, such as earth and fire? What is more, if water were the source of things, would not drying destroy them? Thus, reasoned Anaximander, the thing with which the world begins cannot be identical with any of the ordinary stuff with which humans are acquainted, but it must be capable of giving rise to the wide multiplicity of things and their pairs of contrary qualities. What therefore distin-

ligible principle. What is more, this world and its workings are unified, indeed form a cosmos. The cosmos, in turn, can be understood and explained by analogy with the human world; the justice sought in the city's courts is the same justice that sustains everything that human perception finds in the universe.

SIGNIFICANCE

Classical antiquity credited Thales with having pioneered philosophy. Anaximander, with his scientific curiosity and his genius for abstract insight, poised philosophical inquiry for new vistas of exploration; his new philosophical approach inaugurated penetrating, objective analysis. His principle of the eternal Boundless as the source of the world's multifarious qualities and change forms the conceptual backdrop against which twenty-five centuries of science and natural philosophy have developed.

Two particular innovations of Anaximander have never been abandoned. First, his extension of the concept of law from human society to the physical world continues to dictate the scientific worldview. The received view in Anaximander's time—that nature was capricious and anarchic—has never again taken hold. Second, Anaximander's invention of the use of models and maps revolutionized science and navigation and continues to be indispensable, even in people's daily lives. All scientific experiments are models of a sort: They are laboratory-scale contrivances of events or circumstances in the world at large. Purely visual three-dimensional models continue to be crucial in scientific discoveries: the so-called Bohr model of the atom played a crucial role in physics; the double-helical model was important to the discovery of the structure and function of deoxyribonucleic acid (DNA). Maps are taken for granted now, but if human beings had relied on verbal descriptions of spatial localities, civilization would not have proceeded very far.

Thus, Anaximander's innovations and influence persist. Indeed, it is difficult to imagine a world without his contributions. Anaximander himself could hardly have seen all the implications of his discoveries, for even now one can only guess at the future direction of abstract thought.

—*Patricia Cook*

FURTHER READING

Brumbaugh, Robert S. *The Philosophers of Greece*. Albany: State University of New York Press, 1981. This volume contains a short, digested chapter on Anaximander's life and accomplishments. Emphasizes cartography and engineering. Includes a reproduction of the first map designed by Anaximander.

Burnet, John. *Early Greek Philosophy*. 4th ed. New York: Meridian Books/World, 1961. A detailed scholarly analysis of Anaximander's thought in the context of comparisons with, and influences on, other pre-Socratic philosophers.

Couprie, Dirk L., Robert Hahn, and Gerard Naddaf. *Anaximander in Context: New Studies in the Origins of Greek Philosophy*. Albany: State University of New York Press, 2002. Examines the social, political, cosmological, astronomical, and technological backgrounds in which Anaximander's thought developed.

Guthrie, W. K. C. *The Earlier Presocratics and the Pythagoreans*. Vol. 1 in *A History of Greek Philosophy*. New York: Cambridge University Press, 1978-1990. Contains a chapter on Anaximander's cosmology. Focuses in a very close analysis on the concepts of *apeiron* and *apeiron* as *arche*.

Hahn, Robert. *Anaximander and the Architects: The Contributions of Egyptian and Greek Architectural Technologies to the Origins of Greek Philosophy*. Albany: State University of New York Press, 2001. Posits that technologies emerging among Egyptian and Greek architects strongly impacted the development of Greek philosophy.

Kahn, Charles H. *Anaximander and the Origins of Greek Cosmology*. Indianapolis: Hackett, 1994. Surveys the documentary evidence for Anaximander's views, reconstructs a detailed cosmology from documentary texts, and devotes an entire chapter to analysis and interpretation of Anaximander's fragment.

Kirk, Geoffrey S., and John E. Raven. *The Presocratic Philosophers*. 2d ed. New York: Cambridge University Press, 1983. Contains a chapter on Anaximander and a close formal analysis of textual testimony on Anaximander's thought.

Wheelwright, Philip, ed. *The Presocratics*. New York: Odyssey Press, 1966. A primary source. Contains the Anaximander fragment in translation. Also contains testimonies from Aristotle and other Greek and Latin sources who read and commented on Anaximander's treatise.

SEE ALSO: Anaximenes of Miletus; Nabu-rimmani; Ptolemy (astronomer); Sosigenes; Thales of Miletus.

RELATED ARTICLES in *Great Events from History: The Ancient World*: c. 530 B.C.E., Founding of the Pythagorean Brotherhood; c. 500-400 B.C.E., Greek Physicians Begin Scientific Practice of Medicine; c. 320 B.C.E., Theophrastus Initiates the Study of Botany; c. 275 B.C.E., Greeks Advance Hellenistic Astronomy.

ANAXIMENES OF MILETUS
Greek philosopher

Anaximenes posited the first theory to explain a single substance capable of changing its form and the first to attribute the nature of matter entirely to physical rather than moral laws.

BORN: Early sixth century B.C.E.; probably Miletus (now in Turkey)
DIED: Second half of the sixth century B.C.E.; place unknown
AREAS OF ACHIEVEMENT: Philosophy, science

EARLY LIFE

The writings of Anaximenes (an-ak-SIHM-uh-neez) of Miletus no longer exist. Thus, knowledge of Anaximenes is based on a few statements made by Aristotle and later writers on the history of Greek philosophy, some of whom quote earlier writers whose work is now lost. A few of these earlier writers show that they had access to Anaximenes' writings, but it is difficult to determine the veracity of any of their statements. Thus, scholars have almost no reliable information about Anaximenes' life; not even his dates can be accurately ascertained, and only the most general of assumptions can be made. These biographical assumptions are usually applied to Thales and Anaximander as well as Anaximenes. These men were the most famous thinkers from Miletus, then the largest and most prosperous Greek city on the west coast of Asia Minor.

While they are known only for their philosophical work, it is believed that all three were financially secure and that philosophical thought was for them an avocation. Apparently, Anaximenes was the youngest of the three. Some sources suggest that Anaximenes was the pupil of Anaximander, while others suggest that he was a fellow student and friend. Most scholars place the work of Anaximenes after the fall of Sardis to Cyrus the Great (c. 545 B.C.E.) and before the fall of Miletus (494 B.C.E.).

LIFE'S WORK

Anaximenes' work must be viewed against the background of contemporary Miletus and the work of his predecessors. Miletus in the sixth century was a flourishing center located between the eastern kingdoms and the mainland of Greece. The city was ruled by a ruthless tyrant, Thrasybulus, whose method of control was to do away with anyone who appeared threatening.

It has been suggested that the emergence of tyranny in Miletus was the crucial factor in the emergence of phi-losophy, that the need to overthrow the existing myth-centered system of values was behind philosophical speculation. It has also been said that the emergence of philosophy coincides with the emergence of participatory forms of government, the development of written codes of law, and the expansion of the role of nonaristocrats in government through oratory, which encouraged logical argument and objective reasoning. As attractive as these theories may be, they overlook the fact that Miletus itself was under the rule of a tyrant who discouraged participatory democracy absolutely.

It seems more logical to conclude that philosophy became a means of escaping the brutality of the immediate, political world. Travel brought Milesians in contact with Egypt and Phoenicia—and eventually Mesopotamia. Milesians developed an independence of thought that led them to use their knowledge of the pragmatic world gained through observation to see the contradictions in the mythologies of different peoples and to make the leap to a nonmythological explanation of causation and the nature of matter.

The work of Anaximenes was summarized in a single book whose title is unknown. In the fourth century, Theophrastus, Aristotle's successor, is said to have noted its "simple and economical Ionic style." One supposes that this comment refers to the shift from writing in poetry to writing in prose. Clearly, Anaximenes was more concerned with content than with the conventions of poetical expression.

Anaximenes wrote that "air" was the original substance of matter. Scholars of ancient history agree, however, that the exact meaning of this statement is unclear. To take the position that all other matter was derived from air, Anaximenes must have believed that air was a changeable substance that, by rarefaction and condensation, was able to take other forms. When rarefied, it became fire; when condensed, it became wind, clouds, water, earth, and finally stones. Thus, Anaximenes had modified Thales' idea that water was the original substance and contradicted Anaximander's thesis of unchanging infinity while still staying within the Milesian monist tradition.

Having determined the nature of air and its properties, Anaximenes apparently developed other ideas by extension. Topics he addressed include the nature of hot and cold as expressions of rarefaction and condensation, the divine nature of air, the motion of air, cosmogony, and cosmological problems. Under the latter heading he seems to have commented on the nature of Earth, which he saw as flat and riding on a cushion of air, and the nature of heavenly bodies. In his consideration of meteorological phenomena, Anaximenes seems to have followed Anaximander rather closely. Anaximenes' description of air also resembles Hesiod's description of Chaos. Both Chaos and air surround Earth, persist within the developed world, and can be characterized by darkness, internal motion, divinity, immense size, and probable homogeneity.

Anaximenes, like his two predecessors, challenged the mythological world of Homer and Hesiod by introducing free and rational speculation. Anaximenes also presented a challenge by writing in prose. Prior to this, poetry had been the preferred form for serious expression—not only in literature but also in politics. By writing in prose, the early philosophers moved, in part, from the world of the aristocrat to that of the new man of Greece: the hoplite, the merchant, the small, free farmer. While this new method of thought was not accepted by the average Greek (nor even, one suspects, the average Milesian), it did gain respect and placed philosophical speculation on an elevated footing.

For Anaximenes, unlike his predecessors, however, the differences that could be observed in matter were not qualitative but quantitative. Thus it is that he was the first to suggest a consistent picture of the world as a mechanism.

SIGNIFICANCE

Any account of Anaximenes' life and ideas must by virtue of scant evidence be unsatisfactory. In spite of a lack of information about him and his ideas, his place in and contribution to intellectual development are clear. Anaximenes' methods were far more influential than his specific theories on matter. Together with Thales and Anaximander, he was the first to free speculative thought from mythology and mythological terms. The methods of these three thinkers are the foundation for all modern scientific and philosophical thought. They began with intellectual curiosity about the nature of matter and combined this curiosity with keen observation of the world around them—with little regard to prior religious explanations.

At first glance, Anaximenes' ideas about air seem regressive. When, however, the idea is seen as a more general concept—as the first theory to explain a single substance capable of changing its form—its sophistication can be appreciated. Most ancient thinkers agreed that Anaximenes provided a better explanation of natural phenomena.

It is a small step from Anaximenes' ideas of rarefaction and condensation to Empedocles' definition of matter and the atomic theories of Heraclitus of Ephesus and Democritus. Clearly, no one in the modern world would take these ideas at face value, but with a small shift in the translation of Anaximeneian terms, one approaches the modern concepts of states of matter and the relationship between energy and matter. Thus, Anaximenes is an important figure in the development of Western philosophical and scientific thought.

—Michael M. Eisman

FURTHER READING

Barnes, Jonathan. *The Presocratic Philosophers*. New York: Routledge, 1996. Contains a section on Anaximenes as well as scattered comments on his ideas. Barnes is most at home with philosophical discourse and relates ancient philosophical concepts to more modern thinkers. With bibliography and concordances of ancient sources.

Burnet, John. *Early Greek Philosophy*. 4th ed. New York: World, 1961. The major ancient texts are translated and the ideas of Anaximenes discussed in this excellent work.

Guthrie, W. K. C. *The Earlier Presocratics and the Pythagoreans*. Vol. 1 in *A History of Greek Philosophy*. New York: Cambridge University Press, 1978-1990. Contains an extended section on Anaximenes that is judicial and well balanced. Guthrie's account is used as the standard by historians. With good bibliographies and concordances of ancient sources.

Hurwit, Jeffrey M. *The Art and Culture of Early Greece, 1100-480 B.C.* Ithaca, N.Y.: Cornell University Press, 1985. An exciting analysis of Greek life that integrates studies of literature, philosophy, and art.

Kirk, G. S., and J. E. Raven. *The Presocratic Philosophers*. 2d ed. New York: Cambridge University Press, 1983. The most extensive attempt to reconstruct Anaximenes by examining all the relevant ancient references with detailed discussions of each text. The relevant Greek and Latin texts are given, with translations provided in the notes. Includes interpretation based on the texts but little or no reference to other modern scholarly ideas. Contains concordances of ancient texts.

Stokes, M. C. *The One and Many in Presocratic Philosophy*. Washington, D.C.: Center for Hellenic Studies with Harvard University Press, 1972. While this book is not about Anaximenes, he looms large in the investigation, and Stokes's ideas about him are important. Stokes investigates the relationship between Anaximander's and Anaximenes' ideas, as well as the relationship of Anaximenes to ancient Near Eastern thought and Hesiod.

Sweeney, Leo. *Infinity in the Presocratics: A Bibliographical and Philosophical Study.* The Hague, Netherlands: Martinus Nijhoff, 1972. Each of the pre-Socratics is discussed in terms of his contribution to this specific topic. Important discussions on the usability of each ancient source for Anaximenes are included.

SEE ALSO: Anaximander; Empedocles; Heraclitus of Ephesus; Thales of Miletus.

RELATED ARTICLES in *Great Events from History: The Ancient World*: c. 530 B.C.E., Founding of the Pythagorean Brotherhood; c. 500-400 B.C.E., Greek Physicians Begin Scientific Practice of Medicine; c. 320 B.C.E., Theophrastus Initiates the Study of Botany; c. 275 B.C.E., Greeks Advance Hellenistic Astronomy.

SAINT ANTHONY OF EGYPT
Egyptian hermit

A hermit renowned for his ascetic labors and Gospel teachings, Anthony became celebrated within Christendom as the founder of the eremitic movement and the father of monasticism.

BORN: c. 251 C.E.; Coma, near Memphis, Egypt (now Queman el Aroune, Egypt)

DIED: Probably January 17, 356 C.E.; Mount Kolzim, near the Red Sea, Egypt

ALSO KNOWN AS: Saint Antony of Egypt; Antonios

AREA OF ACHIEVEMENT: Religion

EARLY LIFE

Saint Anthony (AN-thuhn-ee) of Egypt was born about the year 251 in the village of Coma (the modern Queman el Aroune) in Upper Egypt. The only son of wealthy Coptic Christian parents, Anthony spent his childhood along the Nile River working on the family farm and attending the village church with his pious sister and parents. Because his father feared the worldly learning of Greek academies, Anthony never attended school and did not learn to read or write. His religious training, therefore, was limited to the instructions he received from his parents and from the local priest, who read from the Coptic Bible. While not interested in questions of theology, Anthony was deeply sensitive to spiritual matters. Even as a child, he preferred spending time alone in prayer and meditation to playing games with his friends.

At about age twenty, Anthony suffered the death of both his father and mother. Though a young man of considerable inherited wealth, Anthony became depressed and overburdened with the responsibilities of administering his 130-acre (53-hectare) estate and caring for his young sister. In church, Anthony heard the priest read the Gospel story of a rich young man who asked Jesus what he must do to attain eternal life. Jesus' reply, "If thou wilt be perfect, go, sell that thou hast and give to the poor,

and thou shalt have treasure in heaven; and come, follow me" (Matthew 19:21), haunted Anthony, for he (like the protagonist in the story) was rich, had from birth followed all the commandments of the law, and yet still lacked spiritual maturity. That day Anthony decided to respond literally to the Gospel command. He gave his personal possessions to the inhabitants of Coma, sold his estate, and gave the proceeds to the poor, reserving only a small sum for the benefit of his sister.

Soon after that event, on hearing the reading of another scriptural command, "Take therefore no thought for the morrow: for the morrow shall take thought for the things of itself" (Matthew 6:34), Anthony determined to make a complete break with his former life. Taking his sister to a convent to be educated for a religious life, he moved to a hut at the edge of the village and sought direction from a hermit on how to live a holy life. Clothed only in a camel's-hair garment, Anthony studied how to resist worldly temptations by use of prayer, fasting, mortification, and manual labor.

LIFE'S WORK

Anthony, for all of his asceticism, did not achieve sanctification without a struggle. Despite his renunciation of all earthly pleasures, memories of his former life and possessions, as well as erotic visions, disrupted his quest for spiritual fullness. According to his biographer Saint Athanasius, the devil "raised up in [Anthony's] mind a great dust-cloud of arguments, intending to make him abandon his set purpose." Anthony persevered and gradually learned to overcome the temptations of his thoughts.

After years of self-conquest on the borders of the village, Anthony was ready to attack the devil in his own territory. He left his arbor hut and moved farther into the desert, into the mortuary chamber of an Egyptian tomb. Permitting the visits of only one friend, who brought him bread and water at infrequent intervals, Anthony challenged the forces of Satan by entering the dark burial cell, which Egyptians believed was haunted by demons. In closing the door behind him, Anthony symbolically severed himself from the world of the living.

The modern mind can only interpret the accounts of Anthony's struggles with the devil in the tomb as fantasies conjured by his excessive fasting. For contemporaries of Anthony, however, his confrontation with Satan—which included battling demons disguised as bulls, serpents, scorpions, and wolves—was perceived as physical and real. When he emerged after sixteen years in the subterranean tomb, Anthony was widely renowned as a warrior of God who had fought and conquered the powers of darkness.

Anthony's thirst for solitude, which first prompted him to withdraw to the outskirts of the village and then to the burial chamber on the fringe of the desert, finally drove him into the depths of the desert. He withdrew to Mount Pispir, near the Nile. Anthony at first lived in total seclusion—praying, fasting, and weaving mats from palm leaves. Disciples brought him supplies of bread occasionally, but he fasted for days at a time. As news of Anthony's disappearance into desert isolation spread, a train of visitors followed him into the wilderness. Some went simply out of curiosity; others sought spiritual guidance. Although at first Anthony attempted to avoid the visitors, in time he acquiesced and assumed pastoral responsibilities: praying for the sick, driving out demons, offering instructions for holy living, and training seekers in the path of asceticism.

Pispir became a monastery, and in or near 313, Anthony moved still farther away, settling in a cave on Mount Kolzim, near the Red Sea. He remained in this remote setting, receiving some visitors, for the rest of his life.

Anthony's teachings generally emphasized one's interior development. Unimpressed with mere human knowledge, Anthony reminded his followers that the mind created letters, not letters the mind, and that therefore "one whose mind is sound has no need of letters." Rather than coveting worldly wisdom, Anthony urged his disciples to live every day as if it were their last, always remembering that "the whole of earth is a very little thing compared with the whole of heaven." He warned them against tak-

ing pride in their own accomplishments or in thinking that in giving up worldly pleasures they were making great sacrifices. He urged his followers constantly to inspect their spiritual progress, not worrying about things that do not last, but gathering those "that we can take with us: prudence, justice, temperance, fortitude, understanding, charity, love of the poor, faith in Christ, graciousness, hospitality." For Anthony, asceticism was not an end in itself but a necessary means to spiritual maturity.

On one occasion, probably in the year 311, Anthony visited the city of Alexandria, where he offered encouragement to Christians being persecuted under the edict of the emperor Maximinus Daia. A short time later, after Constantine emerged as head of Rome, Anthony received a letter from the newly converted Christian emperor seeking spiritual guidance. Although unable either to read the message or to pen a response, Anthony dic-

Saint Anthony of Egypt. (Library of Congress)

tated for the Roman emperor the following reply: "Practice humility and contempt of the world, and remember that on the day of judgment you will have to account for all your deeds." In 338 Anthony again left his retreat for Alexandria, allegedly to help the orthodox bishop Athanasius in his theological struggle with the Arian Christians, who denied that Christ was equal in essence with the Father. As Saint Athanasius, this church leader would write the biography of Anthony. Such contact with the outside world—with people of power—was rare. Anthony much preferred the simplicity of desert life, which did not distract him from concentrating on spiritual matters.

Saint Jerome told a story about a visit in 341 between Anthony and the 113-year-old Saint Paul of Thebes, a hermit who allegedly had not seen either man or woman for more than ninety years. While this story is no doubt apocryphal, the legend was celebrated by Christians for centuries and served as an inspiration for numerous artists, including the master of Dutch Renaissance art Lucas van Leyden.

In the year 356, Anthony—knowing that he was about to die—invited his closest followers to come to his desert hermitage in order to give them a parting farewell. To his surprise, thousands responded to the invitation. Anthony walked among this throng of pilgrims, blessed them, and asked them to persevere in their devotion to God. According to tradition, Anthony died on January 17, 356, at the age of 105.

SIGNIFICANCE

It is ironic that Saint Anthony of Egypt—an unassuming, deeply private, illiterate man, who refused to pander to crowds and who renounced the efforts of the establishment to reconcile Christianity with culture—became the celebrated founder of the eremitic movement and the father of monasticism. As a result of his ascetic example and teachings, during his lifetime and for a hundred years following his death, hermitages sprang up, and the deserts of Egypt became cluttered with cells of anchorites. Stories of his desert retreat, circulated by Saint Athanasius's biography *Vita S. Antonii* (fourth century; *The Life of Saint Anthony*, 1697), spread across the Empire to Rome, Palestine, Gaul, and Spain. Constantine and his sons wrote to him. Saint John Chrysostom in his homilies designated Anthony as the greatest man Egypt had produced since the time of the Apostles. During the third and fourth centuries, thousands of pilgrims followed Anthony's example and flocked to the desert. The exodus was so great that a traveler through Egypt and

Palestine about 394 reported that the dwellers in the desert equaled the population living in the towns.

For fifteen hundred years, the temptations of Anthony have captured the imagination of artists, who have delighted especially in picturing the more dramatic episodes of devils in hideous and alluring disguises tempting, frightening, and beating the desert saint. From Saint Athanasius to Gustave Flaubert and Anatole France, Anthony has been portrayed as the prototype of a man who suffers temptation and, through the power of renunciation, overcomes it.

In an age filled with Christological problems and theological hairsplitting, Anthony and the desert fathers proclaimed a message of righteous living and simplicity of life. His teaching—"No one of us is judged by what he does not know, and no one is called blessed because of what he has learned and knows; no, the judgment that awaits each asks this: whether he has kept the faith and faithfully observed the commandments"—offered a corrective to the tendency at the time to define Christianity in purely philosophical or religious terms. Anthony's ascetic labors and simple teachings introduced themes that would run throughout the history of the monastic movement.

—*Terry D. Bilhartz*

FURTHER READING

Athanasius, Saint. *The Life of Saint Anthony the Hermit.* Translated by Tim Vivian and Apostolos N. Athanassakis with Rowan A. Greer. Kalamazoo, Mich.: Cistercian Publications, 2003. Saint Athanasius's biography is the single most important primary source on the life of Anthony.

Chadwick, Henry. *The Early Church.* 1968. Reprint. New York: Penguin Books, 1974. The best single-volume introduction to the history of the Christian church during the first through fourth centuries.

Cowan, James. *Journey to the Inner Mountain.* London: Hodder and Stoughton, 2002. A biography of Saint Anthony of Egypt.

Nigg, Walter. *Warriors of God: The Great Religious Orders and Their Founders.* Translated and edited by Mary Ilford. New York: Alfred A. Knopf, 1959. The opening chapter provides a scholarly treatment of Anthony and his impact on the monastic movement.

Queffelec, Henri. *Saint Anthony of the Desert.* Translated by James Whitall. New York: E. P. Dutton, 1954. An entertaining biography based on Saint Athanasius's account.

Waddell, Helen. *The Desert Fathers.* New York: Henry Holt, 1936. A translation from the Latin of the writings of the desert fathers. Includes many of the sayings attributed to Anthony.

Ward, Maisie. *Saints Who Made History: The First Five Centuries.* New York: Sheed and Ward, 1959. A lively, nonscholarly account of the lives of early saints of the Church. Includes a fourteen-page treatment on Anthony.

SEE ALSO: Saint Athanasius; Saint John Chrysostom; Constantine the Great.
RELATED ARTICLES in *Great Events from History: The Ancient World*: October 28, 312 C.E., Conversion of Constantine to Christianity; 325 C.E., Adoption of the Nicene Creed; November 24, 326-May 11, 330 C.E., Constantinople Is Founded.

ANTIGONUS I MONOPHTHALMOS
Macedonian king (r. 306-301 B.C.E.)

One of Alexander the Great's successors, Antigonus failed to reunite Alexander's conquests, but he did establish an eponymous dynasty (the Antigonids), which was to rule Macedonia and exert a great influence on Greek affairs elsewhere until the Roman victory at the Battle of Pydna in 168 B.C.E.

BORN: 382 B.C.E.; probably Macedonia (now in Greece)
DIED: 301 B.C.E.; Ipsus, Phrygia, Asia Minor (now in Turkey)
ALSO KNOWN AS: Antigonus Cyclops; Antigonus Monophthalmus; Antigonus the One-Eyed
AREAS OF ACHIEVEMENT: Government and politics, war and conquest

EARLY LIFE

The father of Antigonus (an-TIHG-uh-nuhs) was an aristocrat named Philip. Beyond this fact, nothing of significance is known about Antigonus's life before his service in Alexander's army and his appointment to the governorship of Phrygia in 333 B.C.E. at the age of forty-nine.

Antigonus is known to have been a tall man; his appellation, Monophthalmos (mahn-uhf-THAL-muhs), meaning one-eyed, or Cyclops, referred to his having lost an eye. It is not known whether this blinding occurred in battle or by some other means. To conceal the handicap, Apelles, the famous artist at the Macedonian court, departed from custom and painted a portrait of Antigonus in profile.

LIFE'S WORK

Before attention is turned to the course of Antigonus's life and work, it is helpful to survey the situation immediately following the death of Alexander the Great in 323 B.C.E. Alexander left no arrangement for succession. The assembly of the Macedonian army determined that rule be given to Alexander's half brother, Philip III, and his

unborn son, Alexander IV, but the real control of Alexander's empire lay in the hands of Antipater, in Greece, and Perdiccas, in Asia. In the struggle for power that ensued (in the year 321), Antigonus sided with Antipater against Perdiccas. After Perdiccas was assassinated, Antigonus was given command of Antipater's army in Asia and continued the war against Perdiccas's brother, Alcetas, and Eumenes, satrap of Cappadocia. Antipater died in 319. Antigonus continued fighting against Eumenes until 316, when, through intrigues and deceit, he managed to have him executed. Eumenes' remains were cremated, placed in a vessel, and returned to his wife and children. Among Alexander's successors, Antigonus was now in the strongest position to reunite the lands conquered by Alexander.

Antigonus was unquestionably desirous of sole rule, and his ambition was immediately recognized by his regal adversaries, Ptolemy, Lysimachus, Cassander, and Seleucus, all of whom allied themselves against Antigonus in a war lasting from 315 to 311. The war had no clear resolution; its temporary end came after Antigonus's son, Demetrius Poliorcetes, was defeated by Seleucus and Ptolemy at the Battle of Gaza in 312. Peace was made between Antigonus and all of his adversaries ex-

MAJOR KINGS OF THE ANTIGONID DYNASTY	
Ruler	*Reign (B.C.E.)*
Antigonus I Monophthalmos	306-301
Demetrius I Poliorcetes	294-287
Antigonus II Gonatas	276-239
Demetrius II	239-229
Antigonus II Doson	229-221
Philip V	221-179
Perseus	179-168

cept Seleucus. Still, the ambitions of all involved could not be suppressed, and war broke out again one year later and lasted until Antigonus's death in 301.

In the first war, most of the fighting had taken place in Asia Minor; in the war of 310-301, the final resolution would be reached in Asia Minor at the Battle of Ipsus in Phrygia, but mainland Greece was the scene of many of the most important battles. Antigonus came to recognize, perhaps a bit too late, the importance of support from the Greek cities on the mainland. In 307, Antigonus's son, Demetrius Poliorcetes, took control of Athens from Cassander's representative, Demetrius of Phaleron, and a democratic constitution was reestablished in Athens. As an expression of gratitude, the Athenians granted divine honors to Antigonus and Demetrius. Antigonus's intervention on behalf of the Athenian democracy impressed many other Greek city-states, and by 302 most of mainland Greece had rallied in his support. Highlights of the war on mainland Greece are vividly recounted by Plutarch in his "Life of Demetrius," written in the early second century C.E. and found in Plutarch's *Bioi paralleloi* (c. 105-115; *Parallel Lives*, 1579).

In spite of some major military and naval successes in Asia Minor, the war on that front was, for Antigonus, indecisive. It was his successes against Cassander on mainland Greece, more than anything, that forced his opponents to realize that their positions would be secure only with the elderly Antigonus out of the way. Attacks on Antigonus's positions in Asia came from all sides, and the situation became so serious that he recalled Demetrius, together with his army, from mainland Greece to stand with him. The decisive battle was fought at Ipsus in 301, and Antigonus, now about eighty years of age, died in this battle. Thus, at the time of his death this great general was pursuing the same course that he had pursued throughout his life: a military resolution to a political problem.

SIGNIFICANCE

Antigonus fell between two worlds. Born and educated amid the fragmented politics of competing Greek city-states, he could have had no idea, even as a mature man, of the profound changes Alexander was to bring about. In this new world, the only exemplar of success available was Alexander's, and that was primarily military and not political. Alexander's early death prevented him from demonstrating whether his political leadership was as adept as his military leadership.

Antigonus was not alone in following Alexander's lead; all the *diadochoi* (successors to Alexander) were as quick as Antigonus to rely on the sword as the means of obtaining the power that they sought. It was Antigonus, however, who had the means to consolidate Macedonian conquests, for he was the most successful of Alexander's successors militarily. His ultimate failure to unite Alexander's conquests through force, in spite of his most advantageous situation, should have shown the futility of such an approach in the face of a coalition of equally determined, although individually less powerful, dynasts. This lesson was not learned, and the result was almost constant warfare among Hellenistic monarchs who continued to present themselves as Alexander's rightful successor until Rome's final victory in the Greek East at the Battle of Actium in 31 B.C.E. Thus, it was the ambitions and methods of Antigonus, almost as much as those of Alexander, that served for some two hundred years as an example for those who sought to control the Greek world.

—John Walsh

FURTHER READING

Austin, M. M. *The Hellenistic World from Alexander to the Roman Conquest: A Selection of Ancient Sources in Translation.* Cambridge, England: Cambridge University Press, 1981. Offers translations of and introductions to many important documentary sources, primarily epigraphical, which are not generally available. This collection of primary source material contains a number of documents that bear directly on Antigonus's attempts to unify Alexander's conquests.

Bar-Kochva, B. *The Seleucid Army.* Cambridge, England: Cambridge University Press, 1976. Describes and interprets the changes in the strategy and tactics of land warfare that led to Antigonus's military successes and the continuing domination of the Macedonians over the art of warfare until Rome's victory at Pydna in 168 B.C.E.

Billows, Richard A. *Antigonos the One-Eyed and the Creation of the Hellenistic State.* Berkeley: University of California Press, 1990. An examination of the Macedonian leader and his role in the spread of Hellenism.

De Ste. Croix, G. E. M. *The Class Struggle in the Ancient Greek World: From the Archaic Age to the Arab Conquests.* Ithaca, N.Y.: Cornell University Press, 1982. Presents a Marxist view of the decline of Greek democracies. This volume is the masterpiece of a very distinguished ancient historian; it is particularly valuable for its focus on the role of political factions in Antigonus's struggle for the support of city-states on mainland Greece and Asia.

Gardner, Jane F. *Leadership and the Cult of Personality.* London: Samuel Stevens, 1974. Emphasizes the importance of controlling armies and populations through the projection of a royal personality. It discusses both leadership theory and the concrete ways in which Alexander and those who followed him manipulated regal propaganda.

Gruen, Erich S. *The Hellenistic World and the Coming of Rome.* 2 vols. Berkeley: University of California Press, 1984. A revisionist interpretation of the course of Roman expansion in the Greek East. Gruen presents a view of Roman Imperialism that is more sympathetic to the Roman position than the position taken by most scholars. This volume contains a good review of the battle among Alexander's successors. Includes a helpful bibliography.

Simpson, R. H. "Antigonus the One-Eyed and the Greeks." *Historia* 8 (1959): 385-409. This article presents a detailed account of the relations between Antigonus and the city-states on the Greek mainland, alliances that played a decisive role in convincing Antigonus's opponents to unify against him.

Smith, R. R. R. *Hellenistic Royal Portraits.* Oxford, England: Oxford University Press, 1988. An account of the visual image of kingship that Hellenistic dynasts chose to present. This study is lavishly illustrated. Includes reproductions of portraits in varied media (including coins and marble). A valuable archaeological complement to the literary and documentary evidence.

Walbank, R. W. *The Hellenistic World.* Cambridge, Mass.: Harvard University Press, 1981. The best general account of the period, by a scholar who devoted his life to its study. It combines a narrative account of military and political events with sections on the rich and varied cultural life of the Hellenistic world.

SEE ALSO: Alexander the Great; Ptolemy Soter; Seleucus I Nicator.

RELATED ARTICLES in *Great Events from History: The Ancient World*: 323 B.C.E., Founding of the Ptolemaic Dynasty and Seleucid Kingdom; c. 323-275 B.C.E., Diadochi Divide Alexander the Great's Empire.

ANTIOCHUS THE GREAT
Seleucid king (r. 223-187 B.C.E.)

Antiochus went the furthest of any of the successors of Alexander the Great toward reuniting what had once been the vast Alexandrian Empire.

BORN: c. 242 B.C.E.; probably Antioch (now Antakya, Turkey)
DIED: 187 B.C.E.; Elymais, near Susa (now in Iran)
ALSO KNOWN AS: Antiochus III
AREA OF ACHIEVEMENT: War and conquest

EARLY LIFE

Antiochus (an-TI-uh-kuhs), who was probably born in Antioch, the capital city of the Seleucid Empire, was the younger son of Seleucus II and Laodice II. Nothing is known about his early life. When his father died in 226, his older brother, Seleucus III, fell heir to the empire and all of its problems, not the least of which was Asia Minor, formerly held by the Seleucids but now controlled by Attalus I of Pergamum. One unsuccessful attempt had already been made to regain this territory. During the second, in 223, Seleucus was assassinated by two of his own generals. Because he had no heirs, his younger brother Antiochus succeeded him.

Antiochus was eighteen years old at the time of his brother's death and living in Babylon—possibly as regent of the east, as that was the usual Seleucid practice—but many thought him too young for the throne. His cousin Achaeus, who had punished Seleucus's murderers, was popular with the army, but he remained loyal to the ruling house. Finally, Antiochus was recognized as successor under the tutelage of Seleucus's former adviser, Hermias; Achaeus was given control of military affairs in Asia Minor, and two brothers, Molon and Alexander, were sent as governors (satraps) to Media and Persia, respectively. Trouble began almost immediately: Although Achaeus remained loyal for some time and even regained much of Asia Minor from Attalus, Hermias became excessively arrogant, and in 221, the brothers in the east rebelled against Seleucid authority. These actions marked the beginning of an almost constant state of war, which would continue throughout the reign of Antiochus.

In 221, with Achaeus operating successfully in Asia Minor, the first priority for the Seleucid government was the rebellion of Molon. Hermias, who was still in control, appointed Xenon and Theodotus as commanders against Molon, while convincing the king to make war against Ptolemy IV Philopator of Egypt for possession of Coele-Syria. When Molon easily defeated his opponents and Antiochus's southern campaign proved futile, the king turned to the recovery of his eastern territories. In early spring of 220, Antiochus held a council to plan his campaign. There were two important results of this meeting: Antiochus proved himself able to choose the best strategy—the immediate crossing of the Tigris River—and in crossing the river he, for the first time, split his army in three parts, initiating what would become his standard policy for advancing his forces. The majority of Molon's army, refusing to fight a Seleucid king, surrendered to Antiochus at the first opportunity. The two rebel brothers committed suicide; Antiochus was now in full command in the east.

Three problems remained: Hermias; Achaeus, now the self-proclaimed king of Asia Minor; and the subjection of Coele-Syria. Antiochus ordered the assassination of Hermias, ignored Achaeus, whose men also refused to fight a Seleucid ruler, and marched his army south, where he was at first successful. His youthful inexperience, however, led him to delay battle against a Ptolemaic army until his opponent had the advantage, and in 217 he suffered a humiliating defeat at Raphia. Ptolemy fortunately agreed to a peace treaty, thus ending the war.

King Antiochus the Great, holding staff, meets Popillius, the Roman ambassador (right). (Hulton|Archive by Getty Images)

LIFE'S WORK

Antiochus gained the title "the Great" because, through successful military strategy and shrewd diplomacy, he managed to reunite most of the territory that had been assigned to Seleucus I after the death of Alexander the Great. His prestige had suffered a blow at Raphia, but he redeemed himself by defeating Achaeus and regaining Seleucid Asia Minor. After a long siege, the capital city of Sardis fell in 214, and the citadel was betrayed a year later. Achaeus was first mutilated and then beheaded. Some sort of understanding with Attalus of Pergamum, his other rival in Asia Minor, seems to have been reached, because by 212 Antiochus had turned his back on the west in order to attempt the restoration of his eastern dominions. The Greek historian Polybius gives a fairly comprehensive account of Antiochus's movements up to this time, although most of the war against Achaeus is

missing. Now, unfortunately, the detailed history of Antiochus ends just as he begins his eastern campaigns.

By 212, Antiochus was in Armenia, where he settled affairs by arranging the marriage of his sister Antiochis to King Xerxes I. Two years later, he had arrived at the Euphrates River and in the next year he reached the limits of the Seleucid Empire in Media. He could have stopped there, but Parthia and Bactria, once part of the empire, had seceded in 250, and his plan was to regain all the lost territories, a very expensive endeavor. It was in Ecbatana, the old summer capital of the Persian kings, that Antiochus for the first time robbed a temple treasury, an act that was to become a policy for both him and his successors.

Although the Parthians put up a stiff resistance, by 209 they had been defeated and had agreed to an alliance.

Bactria was invaded in the next year; peace came two years later with another alliance. Antiochus then continued on to India to renew Seleucid relations with the new border king, from whom he received 150 elephants. He had thought of invading Arabia, but after sailing down the Arabian coast, he abandoned the idea. He was back in Syria by 204, with a reputation second only to that of Alexander. From this time on, he would be called Antiochus the Great.

Now that the king had experience and maturity, he made his final attempt to gain Coele-Syria, this time backed by an alliance with Philip V of Macedonia. Appian (c. 160 C.E.) gives the terms of the agreement, but the sources are uniformly silent on this war, the Fifth Syrian War. Ptolemy V was still a child, but his general, Scopas, moved an army across the Sinai Peninsula. The two forces met at Panion in 200 in a battle in which Antiochus's elephants played an important role in gaining for him a decisive victory. After winning the complete submission of Palestine, including Jerusalem, Antiochus decided against an invasion of Egypt and returned to Asia Minor. Ptolemy had agreed to a treaty in which he ceded Coele-Syria to the Seleucid Empire. The war finally ended in 195, when Ptolemy promised to marry Antiochus's daughter Cleopatra (not to be confused with Cleopatra VII, who was involved with Julius Caesar and Marc Antony more than a century later).

Meanwhile, Philip V had been courting disaster in the north. Rhodes and Pergamum had allied against him and called on Rome for help. The Romans declared war on Philip in 200 but also sent an embassy to Antiochus warning him that Egypt was under Roman protection, a threat he could hardly take seriously. The embassy arrived shortly after his success at Panion. By the spring of 197, the Seleucid army was in Asia Minor, along with a navy of three hundred ships just off the southern coast. The navy was stopped for a while by a Rhodian ultimatum, but after news of Philip's defeat by the Romans in 196 arrived, the Rhodians withdrew, leaving Antiochus free to take the western coast of Asia Minor to the Troas, his original plan. The city of Lampsacus appealed to Rome, but the Seleucid army was in Thrace before the Roman ambassadors caught up with it. Antiochus's answer to Roman charges of aggression was that he did not meddle in Italian affairs and Rome had no business in Asia. Shortly after that, the king lost almost his entire fleet in a storm off the coast of Syria.

Antiochus was now at the height of his power; unfortunately, he did not know when to stop. The Aetolians, unhappy over Rome's settlement with Philip, convinced Antiochus to join an anti-Rome coalition, which never materialized. In the latter part of 192, a small Seleucid army arrived, the forerunner of a much larger contingent, at Demetrias. The Aetolians, who had promised the king their full support, were distressed by the size of his force, and both Philip and the Achaean League to the south had decided to ally with Rome. In 191 a joint Roman-Macedonian army faced the Seleucid forces at Thermopylae. Antiochus's reinforcements had not arrived, and the promised Aetolian aid proved illusory. When it became evident that he could not win, Antiochus fled, losing most of his army in what was more a skirmish than a battle.

Antiochus's loss was the result not so much of Aetolian deceit as of the failure of his officers back in Asia to send him the necessary reinforcements. Even then, as was proved by Philip's earlier losses, the clumsy phalanx was no match for the Roman legion. Antiochus discovered that for himself when the Romans invaded Asia Minor. The Roman historian Livy claims that the king, once he had escaped from Greece, believed that he had nothing more to fear from the Romans, that they would not follow him to Asia. If so, he had badly misjudged Roman determination to end the Seleucid threat forever. The Romans were also well aware that Antiochus had welcomed Hannibal, their most feared enemy, to his court. A Roman fleet first cleared the Aegean Sea of Seleucid ships, and by either late 190 or early 189 (historians do not agree on the date) Antiochus fought his last major battle in the field outside Magnesia and lost. He could do nothing more than ask for and accept whatever terms the Romans offered.

Even before Antiochus's final defeat, his eastern dominions had begun to break away. After Magnesia, the Seleucid army was no longer a threat, and the empire dissolved. As soon as the peace was signed, Antiochus appointed his son Seleucus as joint king to rule Syria, which was all the Romans had left him, while he turned again to the east. In 187, Antiochus was killed while attempting to loot a temple in the Elymaean hills. His son succeeded as Seleucus IV.

SIGNIFICANCE

With the defeat of Antiochus by the Romans, the Eastern world was lost to Western culture. The Seleucid Empire crumbled, and Rome could hold only the areas bordering the Mediterranean Sea. These were so systematically exploited by Roman policy that they almost gladly welcomed the Muslim armies of the seventh century C.E.

Antiochus was perhaps not a great king or a great general. He made the same mistake of pressing too hard with his right wing at Magnesia that he had made at Raphia, and he was very unwise in antagonizing the Romans by invading Greece. He had been raised on stories of Alexander, however, and he came closer than anyone else in his attempt to restore the empire to its original size. He could be cruel when necessary, as he was with Achaeus, but his eastern campaigns were marked by leniency and diplomacy, and he refused to hand over Hannibal when the Romans demanded it. There is no record of any domestic rebellion during his long reign. The worst charge against him is the one that led to his death. Ancient temples were also treasuries, and Antiochus was constantly in need of money. It is a sad commentary on his priorities that his last act was one of sacrilege.

—*Linda J. Piper*

FURTHER READING

Bar-Kochva, B. *The Seleucid Army: Organization and Tactics in the Great Campaigns*. New York: Cambridge University Press, 1976. This work contains several chapters giving the details from ancient sources on the major battles fought by Antiochus. Includes maps of the battlefields and interesting analyses of strategy.

Grainger, John D. *The Roman War of Antiochus the Great*. Boston: Brill, 2002. An archaeological and historical examination of the Seleucid king and his relations with Rome.

Kincaid, C. A. *Successors of Alexander*. Chicago: Argonaut, 1969. Kincaid presents brief sketches of four successors, concluding with Antiochus. A good summary of the campaigns and policies, but it excuses the weaknesses of the king.

Livy. *Rome and the Mediterranean*. Translated by H. Bettenson. Baltimore: Penguin Books, 1976. An excellent translation of the part of Livy's history concerning Rome's move toward the East. A Roman interpretation of Antiochus's actions. Includes an introduction by A. H. McDonald.

Ma, John. *Antiochus III and the Cities of Western Asia Minor*. New York: Oxford University Press, 1999. This study examines Antiochus's activities in Asia Minor. Maps and bibliography.

SEE ALSO: Alexander the Great; Hannibal.

RELATED ARTICLES in *Great Events from History: The Ancient World*: c. 245 B.C.E., Diodotus I Founds the Greco-Bactrian Kingdom; 245-140 B.C.E., Rise of Parthia; 202 B.C.E., Battle of Zama; c. 155 B.C.E., Greco-Bactrian Kingdom Reaches Zenith Under Menander.

ANTISTHENES
Greek philosopher

Founder of the philosophical school of classical Cynicism, Antisthenes regarded virtue as the sole basis of happiness and viewed self-control and rejection of materialism as the only means of achieving virtue.

BORN: c. 444 B.C.E.; Athens, Greece
DIED: c. 365 B.C.E.; Athens, Greece
AREA OF ACHIEVEMENT: Philosophy

EARLY LIFE

Antisthenes (an-TIHS-thuh-neez) was the son of an Athenian citizen, also named Antisthenes; his mother was a Thracian slave. Because both parents were not Athenian citizens, Antisthenes was not entitled to citizenship under a law passed by Pericles in 451 B.C.E., and he could not take part in Athenian politics or hold public office. He probably attended the Cynosarges gymnasium, located outside the gates of Athens and reserved for children of illegitimate unions (gymnasia were the central institutions of Greek mental as well as physical education). Antisthenes bitterly resented Athenian boasts of superiority; when Athenians asserted that they had always resided in Attica, having been born of its soil, he responded that snails and wingless locusts could make the same claim. Although not a citizen, he served in the Athenian army; Socrates congratulated him on his brave conduct at the Battle of Tanagra in 426 B.C.E. during the Peloponnesian War.

Despite any disadvantage Antisthenes experienced as a consequence of his outsider status, he remained in Athens his entire life and was a major participant in the vibrant intellectual and cultural activity of the city. When the Sophist Gorgias lectured on rhetoric and logic in Athens, the young Antisthenes attended, and he adopted the Sophist approach, writing and offering lectures on these topics himself. After Antisthenes met Socrates, however, he abandoned his own teaching to follow his new mentor, walking five miles every day from his house at the Piraeus to listen and join in the dialogues through which Socrates taught.

Although he did not live in poverty—his father had left him enough property to provide an adequate income—Antisthenes disdained luxury and prided himself on his austere lifestyle. Socrates joked that he could see Antisthenes' love of fame peeping through the holes in his cloak. Plato records that Antisthenes was one of the close friends of Socrates who attended him during his execution. After the death of Socrates in 399 B.C.E., Antisthenes returned to teaching at the Cynosarges gymnasium and developed the philosophical approach that came to be known as classical Cynicism, radicalizing and exaggerating the ideas and attitudes he had learned from Socrates.

LIFE'S WORK

Few statements can be made about Antisthenes' ideas and actions that are not contradicted by one scholar or another. During his lifetime, he reportedly produced sixty-two dialogues, orations, and essays that were collected in ten volumes; however, only brief fragments of these survive, mostly in quotations and paraphrases by later Greek and Roman authors, many of whom were critical of Antisthenes. The quotations were frequently chosen for their wit and reflect Antisthenes' liking for paradoxes that challenged accepted ideas and customs. As a result, the fragments are sufficiently ambiguous to support widely varying interpretations.

Even the origin of the name "Cynicism" is disputed. The word "cynic" derives directly from the Greek word *cunikos*, meaning "doglike." Some claim it was applied to the philosophy because of the name of the gymnasium where Antisthenes taught, interpreting the name "Cyno-sarges" as "Agile Dog" or "White Dog." Others say it came from Antisthenes' Greek nickname (which translates as "Absolute Dog"), given him derisively because of his desire to live life as a dog might, free of human restraints and conventions. This appellation was accepted by Antisthenes and his successors as an appropriate label. Another version credits the origins of the name to his follower, Diogenes of Sinope. When some men eating at a feast threw bones at him and called him a dog, Diogenes approached the men in doglike fashion and urinated on them.

From Socrates, Antisthenes had learned that virtue was the only good worth striving for and that virtue could be taught; in contrast, wealth, fame, pleasure, and power were worthless, and life should be devoted to reason, self-control, and self-sufficiency. He also learned that language should be used only to express the truth. Antisthenes proceeded to expand and exaggerate the ideas learned from Socrates and to illustrate his concepts through his manner of living. To demonstrate his self-sufficiency and contempt for materialism, he reduced his possessions to the bare minimum, walking about Athens supporting himself by a strong stick, his hair and beard uncombed, in what became the Cynic uniform: a threadbare cloak and a leather knapsack containing a few necessities.

The Cynics believed that they needed to shun what others considered desirable—possessions, wealth, honors, and position. For Antisthenes, pleasure, especially, was to be avoided; it produced the illusion of happiness, thus preventing realization of true contentment, which was obtainable only through the practice of virtue. To emphasize this point, Antisthenes expressed his view with characteristic extremism, saying he would rather be mad than feel pleasure. When he heard luxury praised, Antisthenes retorted that luxury was something to wish on the sons of one's enemy; the true Cynic should be totally self-sufficient and self-governing, owing nothing to anyone, needing nothing from anyone, and being under the control of no one.

Antisthenes constantly ridiculed and expressed his contempt for the democratic political ideas and practices of Athens. He told its citizens they might as well vote to call donkeys "horses" as to believe that they could create leaders and generals by using the ballot. A true king or leader, he said, would act well and have a bad repute—that is, he would do what was right even though it was certain to be unpopular. Like many of Socrates' followers, he admired the disciplined lifestyle of Sparta, finding it a more rational way to produce leaders and followers than democratic practices—yet even Sparta was far from perfect. The political world as a whole, with its factions, greed, cruelty, and wars, was irrational and undesirable; no country and few political practices met his standards. The wise man would be guided in his public acts not by established laws but by the laws of virtue, he said.

Nor did the speculations of the philosophers and scientists of his day please Antisthenes. He dismissed their theories as linguistic games that failed to meet the Socratic standard of absolute truthfulness. Antisthenes' focus was on practical ethics; anything beyond that he considered an illusion. He was especially scornful of the Platonic theory that ideal forms had a concrete existence outside the world of sense perception and were the unchanging reality that lay behind the world of appearances. Antisthenes is reported to have told Plato that while his horse could be seen, "equinity" (the idea of a horse) could not be seen.

Antisthenes carefully distinguished between customs created by humans and what was natural and true. Everywhere he looked, he found illusions and practices that failed to meet his test of what was natural and rational. Antisthenes liked to interpret the story of Heracles—the hero who succeeded at apparently impossible labors and whose temple abutted the Cynosarges gymnasium—allegorically, as an example of the moral virtues of hard work and perseverance. However, Antisthenes did not consider the Greek epics to be serious religious tracts. At times, he came close to espousing monotheism, arguing that "according to custom there are many gods, but in nature there is only one." He rejected the anthropomorphic approach of Greek mythology, claiming that God resembled nothing and no one. God could not be seen with the eyes and therefore could not be understood through imagery. When a priest who was celebrating the Orphic Mysteries boasted about how wonderfully he and the initiates of the Mysteries would be treated in the afterlife, Antisthenes sarcastically asked the priest why he was still alive.

Antisthenes, viewing Greek society through the eyes of an outsider, questioned and criticized many of the accepted customs and values of his day. He rejected the idea that Greeks were by nature superior to the rest of humankind. He deplored the extreme parochialism and nationalism that dominated Greek city-states and led to endless internecine warfare. He was scornful of the widely held notion that work was demeaning and that craftsmen were of lower value than intellectual workers. Instead, he viewed hard labor and perseverance as a means of achieving true virtue. Women were not necessarily inferior to men, he held; because virtue could be taught to both sexes, men and women were virtuous or vicious depending on how they had been educated. By rejecting the distinction between Greek and barbarian, Antisthenes challenged the Greek justification of slavery as a status befitting inferior human beings.

SIGNIFICANCE

Antisthenes the Cynic was far removed from today's cynic, whom the dictionary defines as a person who believes that humankind is motivated wholly by self-interest and who expects the worst from human conduct and motives. Antisthenes' philosophy stressed virtue as the true aim of all men and women. Ascetic self-control and independence of thought were the means of achieving true happiness. His ideas and practices were admired and adopted by a series of Cynics who persisted through the whole of classical antiquity.

His immediate successor, Diogenes of Sinope, became the best known of the Cynics. Although many anecdotes describe Diogenes as learning directly from Antisthenes, it is unclear whether the two actually met. In any case, Diogenes' ideas obviously derive from those of his predecessor, and his activities represent an extreme and exaggerated image of what Antisthenes had taught. Diogenes, adopting the Cynic uniform that Antisthenes had pioneered, went further; he limited his possessions to what he could carry in his leather knapsack, and he slept outdoors in a barrel to demonstrate still greater freedom from material possessions. He was even more vitriolic than Antisthenes in his condemnation of custom and society. Diogenes' successor, Crates of Thebes, continued the practice of asceticism and the public flouting of human customs of his predecessors, while avoiding the sarcastic insults that Diogenes employed.

Zeno of Citium, the founder of Stoicism, began as a Cynic follower of Crates, but by 300 B.C.E. he had begun to diverge and create his own school of philosophy. Zeno stressed the self-reliant and independent strain of Antisthenes' philosophy while eliminating the challenges to the status quo that had characterized the earlier Cynics. Of the three philosophical traditions descending from Socrates, the two deriving from Plato and Aristotle are more significant for their impact on the modern world than that pioneered by Antisthenes. In the ancient world, however, the two schools of practical morality that derive from Antisthenes, classical Cynicism and Stoicism, were of major significance in teaching people how to criticize and yet manage to live in an imperfect society.

—*Milton Berman*

FURTHER READING

Branham, R. Bracht, and Marie-Odile Goulet-Cazé, eds. *The Cynics: The Cynic Movement in Antiquity and Its Legacy.* Berkeley: University of California Press, 1996. A collection of fifteen scholarly articles on the impact of Antisthenes and his followers on Western culture from classical antiquity to the present. Includes footnotes and select annotated bibliography.

Dudley, Donald R. *A History of Cynicism: From Diogenes to the Sixth Century A.D.* 2d ed. London: Bristol Classical Press, 1998. Chapter 1, on Antisthenes, argues that he was not the founder of Cynicism, reserving that title for Diogenes of Sinope. Includes footnotes.

Guthrie, William Keith Chambers. *The Fifth-Century Enlightenment*. Vol. 3 in *A History of Greek Philosophy*. New York: Cambridge University Press, 1978-1990. The standard work on its topic discusses Antisthenes in three separate sections, describing how his ideas relate to the philosophical developments in fifth century Athens. Includes footnotes and bibliography.

Navia, Luis E. *Classical Cynicism: A Critical Study*. Westport, Conn.: Greenwood Press, 1996. Chapter 2 is an informative discussion of the life and ideas of Antisthenes. Includes footnotes and bibliography.

_____. *The Philosophy of Cynicism: An Annotated Bibliography*. Westport, Conn.: Greenwood Press, 1995. Navia provides lengthy summaries of books and articles dealing with Cynicism, including works in French, German, and Italian. The chapter on Antisthenes contains 139 items.

Rankin, H. D. *Sophists, Socratics, and Cynics*. Totowa, N.J.: Barnes & Noble, 1983. Devotes a chapter to Antisthenes, arguing that he was particularly influenced by the Sophistic movement, especially by the ideas of Gorgias. Includes brief bibliography.

SEE ALSO: Diogenes; Socrates; Zeno of Citium.

RELATED ARTICLES in *Great Events from History: The Ancient World*: 399 B.C.E., Death of Socrates; c. 380 B.C.E., Plato Develops His Theory of Ideas; c. 350 B.C.E., Diogenes Popularizes Cynicism; c. 300 B.C.E., Stoics Conceptualize Natural Law.

ANTONIA MINOR
Roman noblewoman

Through her children and her involvement in Roman Imperial politics, Antonia helped determine which of the Julio-Claudian emperors came to power.

BORN: January 31, 36 B.C.E.; place unknown
DIED: May 1, 37 C.E.; Rome (now in Italy)
ALSO KNOWN AS: Antonia the Younger
AREA OF ACHIEVEMENT: Government and politics

EARLY LIFE

Antonia (an-TOHN-ee-uh) Minor was the daughter of the triumvir Marc Antony and Octavia. Her mother was the sister of Octavian, who became the Roman emperor Augustus in 27 B.C.E. Very little can be known of Antonia's early life, and only selected incidents of her life as a whole. Her early life must have been chaotic. Her parents' marriage had been arranged to cement an alliance between Antony and Octavian/Augustus. Antony, however, preferred the Egyptian queen Cleopatra. During the first six years of Antonia's life she could have seen little of her father, who was living in Alexandria while Octavia remained in Rome. Antony committed suicide early in 30 B.C.E., after his defeat at the Battle of Actium. Although he lost the empire to Augustus, it was through Antonia that three of Antony's descendants (Caligula, Claudius, and Nero) eventually ruled Rome. In fact, the Julio-Claudian emperors might more accurately be called the Julio-Claudio-Antonians.

By Antony, Octavia had two daughters, known as Antonia Major and Minor (or Antonia the Elder and Antonia the Younger). In addition, she had a son, Marcellus, by an earlier marriage. Octavia also took into her home Antony's children by Cleopatra and a son by his first wife, Fulvia. Because it is known that women of Rome's Imperial family were well educated, it is safe to assume that Antonia received more than just basic schooling. More important, the connections established in her early years would give her a wide circle of allies and make her a significant political figure for the rest of her life. Her older sister also contributed to the dynasty-making of Augustus by providing a son who married Agrippina the Younger (the granddaughter of Antonia Minor) and became the father of the boy who became the emperor Nero.

Because he had a daughter but not a son who could succeed him, Augustus looked to his nieces, nephews, and grandchildren to find the male heir he needed. Because he was not technically the king of Rome, he had to find subtle ways of promoting members of his family to make them acceptable to the senate, the army, and the people. The succession problem remained the fundamental weakness of the Empire until its end, exacerbated by the failure of the rulers to produce male children. During the first two centuries of the Empire, only two emperors—Vespasian and Marcus Aurelius—had sons who lived to succeed them. Manipulating marriages to produce potential heirs became a full-time concern of most emperors, and women like Antonia, who were blood relatives of the emperor, came to play a major role in that process.

Augustus's only male relative, his nephew Marcellus, died in 23 B.C.E., and Augustus found it necessary to look to his female relatives to produce an heir for him. In her early teens, in one of the numerous dynastic marriages arranged by Augustus, Antonia married Nero Claudius Drusus, the stepson of Augustus. They produced several children, of whom three survived: Germanicus, Livilla, and Claudius. Germanicus became the father of the emperor Caligula, and Claudius became emperor in his own right. After Drusus died in 9 B.C.E., Antonia refused to remarry, in spite of pressure from Augustus to do so. At that point all of Augustus's grandsons had died, and his daughter was in exile. He did not want to rely on his stepson Tiberius as his successor. He disliked Tiberius and wanted a blood relative of his to rule after him. Antonia was still young enough that she could have provided the aged emperor with more potential heirs. Her refusal to remarry showed a certain courage.

LIFE'S WORK

Antonia spent her life caring for various children, in addition to her own, in the Imperial family and trying to advance the careers of her favorites. Her son Germanicus married Agrippina the Elder, granddaughter of Augustus. When Augustus finally yielded to the inevitable and regretfully adopted his stepson Tiberius and designated him as his successor, he insisted that Tiberius adopt Germanicus, to show that the line of emperors would ultimately run through Augustus's family, not Tiberius's. When Germanicus died under suspicious circumstances in 19 C.E., his wife and children—Antonia's grandchildren—became the focus of opposition to Tiberius, who was a very unpopular ruler. Eventually, Agrippina and her two older sons were put to death. The younger children, including Caligula, lived for a time with their great-grandmother, Livia, or other relatives before coming to live with Antonia.

At this time (15-20 C.E.) Antonia was also providing a home for Herod Agrippa and the children of several other eastern rulers. Antonia's movements cannot be traced with any precision, but it is known that she owned a house on the Palatine Hill in Rome and several country houses, including a villa at Bauli, on the Bay of Naples, which was excavated in the early 1900's. One ancient source notes that she had a favorite fish in her fishpond there, which she adorned with gold rings. People came from considerable distances to see this curiosity. Some of the children in her care at this time were distantly related to her through her half sister, the daughter of Cleopatra and Marc Antony. According to the biographer Sueto-

nius, it was during this period that Antonia caught Caligula in bed with one of his sisters.

To say that Antonia spent her life caring for various children is not to say that she was necessarily a loving person. Her son Claudius suffered from physical, and possibly mental, problems with which Antonia found it difficult to cope. Suetonius says she often commented that Claudius was "a monster, a man whom nature didn't finish but only began." If she wanted to say that someone was stupid, she would say he was "a bigger fool than even my son Claudius." Her interest in her family's political advancement may have made her tiresome to some of her relatives. Once he became emperor, Caligula refused to meet with her—his own grandmother—without having someone else present. Suetonius claims that Caligula's unkind treatment of Antonia prompted her to commit suicide, if the erratic young emperor did not poison her outright.

In 31 C.E. Antonia played a direct role in uncovering a conspiracy against the emperor Tiberius and saving his life. Scholars have speculated that she was more interested in preserving the throne for her own descendants than in protecting her brother-in-law. Whatever her motives, she passed along to Tiberius a warning that the praetorian prefect, Aelius Sejanus, was planning to remove Tiberius and claim power for himself. Sejanus and hundreds of his partisans were executed. One of the aftershocks of the unveiling of this plan was that Tiberius learned that Antonia's daughter Livilla had been Sejanus's mistress. The two of them were believed to have poisoned Tiberius's son Drusus. Livilla was put to death.

One of the most remarkable things about Antonia may have been the very fact that she survived as long as she did. Many women in the Roman Imperial family came to unhappy ends. Augustus's daughter Julia was banished for sexual indiscretions and starved to death. His granddaughter, also named Julia, suffered a similar fate. The elder Agrippina was banished and also died of starvation. Agrippina the Younger was murdered by her son, Nero.

Antonia, however, was given extravagant honors by both Caligula and Claudius. She was held up to the public as a paradigm of motherhood. She received the title Augusta, a college of priests was established in her honor, games were held, and her image was portrayed on coins and in statues displayed in a variety of places across the Roman Empire. In fact, more can be known today about her appearance than about the events of her life.

SIGNIFICANCE

Roman women could not hold political power directly, but they could exercise enormous influence behind the scenes. Three women—Augustus's wife Livia, Antonia, and Nero's mother, Agrippina—did as much as any emperor to direct the course of the Empire during its first seventy-five years. Livia and Agrippina often seem to have acted out of malice and ambition. Antonia, by contrast, has been called level-headed and a possessor of integrity. Perhaps with her mother as a model, she cared for a number of children in addition to her own and worked tirelessly to protect her family's interests. Without her intervention to warn the emperor Tiberius of a plot against his life, the entire course of Rome's history would have been dramatically altered.

—Albert A. Bell, Jr.

FURTHER READING

Barrett, Anthony A. *Agrippina: Sex, Power, and Politics in the Early Empire*. New Haven, Conn.: Yale University Press, 1996. Frequent references to Antonia show how her influence continued to be felt, even to her granddaughter's generation.

_____. *Caligula: The Corruption of Power*. New York: Simon and Schuster, 1989. Barrett shows Antonia's

influence on the Imperial family, leading up to Caligula's principate.

Erhart, K. P. "A Portrait of Antonia Minor in the Fogg Art Museum and Its Iconographical Tradition." *American Journal of Archaeology* 82 (1978): 193-212. The numerous images of Antonia can be divided into three large groups and their chronology established by the hairstyles portrayed.

Nichols, J. "Antonia and Sejanus." *Historia* 24 (1975): 48-58. An analysis of the sources about Antonia's role in subverting Sejanus's plot to overthrow Tiberius.

SEE ALSO: Agrippina the Younger; Marc Antony; Augustus; Caligula; Claudius I; Nero; Tiberius.

RELATED ARTICLES in *Great Events from History: The Ancient World*: 51-30 B.C.E., Cleopatra VII, Last of Ptolemies, Reigns; 43-42 B.C.E., Second Triumvirate Enacts Proscriptions; September 2, 31 B.C.E., Battle of Actium; 27-23 B.C.E., Completion of the Augustan Settlement; 9 C.E., Battle of Teutoburg Forest; 43-130 C.E., Roman Conquest of Britain; c. 50 C.E., Creation of the Roman Imperial Bureaucracy.

MARC ANTONY
Roman general

The military and political defeat of Antony by Octavian (later known as Augustus) resulted in the demise of the republican form of government in Rome and the creation of the Roman Empire, which would rule much of the known world for some five hundred years.

BORN: c. 82 B.C.E.; place unknown
DIED: 30 B.C.E.; Alexandria, Egypt
ALSO KNOWN AS: Marcus Antonius (Latin name); Mark Antony
AREAS OF ACHIEVEMENT: Government and politics, war and conquest

EARLY LIFE

Marcus Antonius, called Marc Antony (AN-tuh-nee) in English, was born into a distinguished Roman family around 82 B.C.E. His grandfather, also named Marcus Antonius, had attained the highest offices of Roman public life. Antony's father, Marcus Antonius Creticus (d. c. 72 B.C.E.), however, did not equal his father's distinction. More important for Antony's future, on his mother's side he was related to Julius Caesar. Until he was about twenty-five, Antony, not unlike many of his contemporaries, was a profligate: His moral failings and

excesses were detailed by Cicero, his enemy, in a series of attacks known as *Philippicae* (44-43 B.C.E.; *Philippics*, 1926), and his energy was no doubt wasted, as Plutarch stated, "in drinking bouts, love-affairs, and excessive spending." Antony studied rhetoric in Athens and from there turned his attention to a military career and public life. By that time, many of the characteristics (both good and bad) that constituted Antony's personality had developed: his bawdy and often self-deprecating sense of humor, his familiarity with the men under his command, his liberality, and his attraction to the Greek way of life. Antony's family claimed descent from the Greek hero Hercules, and his Roman nose and other features encouraged positive comparisons between Antony and images of Hercules. Antony also cultivated a forceful and powerful appearance in figure, dress, and demeanor at public functions.

LIFE'S WORK

Antony lost the struggle against Octavian for control of the Roman world, but this fact should not negate the accomplishments of a truly remarkable Roman who had a long and successful military and political career. Antony's failure was the result not of his character or tactics, as some of his critics believe, but of his opposition to Octavian, the most successful of all Roman politicians and one of the most astute and imposing political figures of all time. Antony's early political career was bound closely to that of Julius Caesar. In 51 B.C.E., he served as a junior officer under Caesar's command, and under Caesar's patronage he rose very quickly to a position second in importance in the Caesarean forces. After this, there is some evidence of a rift between Caesar and Antony, who seems not to have participated in Caesar's final victories over Pompey the Great. Nevertheless, Caesar and Antony were sufficiently close politically that Antony was a colleague in the consulship of 44 B.C.E., the year of Caesar's assassination.

Antony's intentions after Caesar's death are impossible to determine. His inflammatory and dramatic reading of Caesar's will may be seen as an attempt to seize control of Rome. On the other hand, such funerary demonstrations were well within the traditionally accepted bounds of political and familial behavior in the Roman Republic. Antony's attitude toward Caesar's assassins was at first ambivalent and conciliatory, but ultimately tensions between Antony and Marcus Junius Brutus, one of Caesar's assassins, led to hostilities.

At this point, Octavian, Caesar's adopted son, entered the political and military scene; he defeated Antony at Mutina in 43 B.C.E. This defeat did not destroy Antony's position—his support was too strong. The Second Triumvirate, an arrangement lasting five years, was created; the three members, Marcus Aemilius Lepidus, Antony, and Octavian, were assigned with the task of establishing the form of republican government. The Roman world was split among the triumvirs, while at Rome a reign of terror resulted, and thousands of Romans perished as the triumvirs persecuted their enemies. The most notable casualty of this reign of terror was Antony's particular adversary and critic, Cicero. Having accomplished his goals in Rome, Antony turned his attention to the East. For all of their significant differences, Antony and Octavian had a common purpose. It was to the advantage of both to move against the republican forces led by Caesar's assassins; after the victory at the Battle of Philippi (42 B.C.E.), the only opposition to the triumvirate left was Pompey the Younger, the son of Pompey the Great.

Marc Antony, top center, gives an oration over the body of Julius Caesar. (F. R. Niglutsch)

After Philippi, Antony remained in the East to restore order to the provinces. His first step was to set up Herod and his brother, Phasael, over Judaea. Antony then met with Cleopatra VII at Tarsus in 41 B.C.E. (Cleopatra's spectacular arrival in her golden barge was recorded by Plutarch and later portrayed by William Shakespeare in *Antony and Cleopatra*, c. 1606-1607.) The political significance of this meeting was underscored by the establishment of a personal relationship that would capture the imagination of subsequent generations. Antony visited Cleopatra in the winter of 41-40 B.C.E., and twins were born after his departure. The relationship continued until Antony's death, and his connection with Cleopatra was in large measure responsible for his ultimate defeat.

Antony was separated from Cleopatra from 40 to 37 B.C.E. as a result of a serious threat from old Roman enemies from the east, the Parthians. In 53 B.C.E., a Roman army under Marcus Licinius Crassus had been defeated at Carrhae, and revenge was never far from the Romans' minds. In 40 B.C.E., the Parthians moved as far west as Syria, and Antony was determined to repulse this attack. A crisis in the west intervened, and Antony was forced to return to Italy to mediate a struggle between Octavian and Antony's wife and brother. Hostilities were averted when Octavian and Antony reached an agreement at Brundisium in 40 B.C.E. In the meantime, Antony's wife, Fulvia, had died; Antony strengthened his ties to Octavian through the time-honored Roman tradition of an arranged marriage with Octavian's sister, Octavia. Antony returned to Athens with Octavia, and a daughter, Antonia, was born to them. Soon after, Antony was again forced to return to Italy, and his arrangement with Octavian was formally renewed at Brundisium for another five years. During all of this, Octavia proved a loyal and helpful wife and on occasion supported Antony against her brother.

Antony and Octavia returned to Athens, but not long after the birth of a second daughter, Octavia was sent back to Italy. Once matters at Rome were settled, Antony once again turned his attention to the campaign against the Parthians. After initial Roman victories, he decided to launch a full-scale expedition into the Parthian homeland. In preparation for this very risky enterprise, Antony sought support from the rulers of Roman client-states in the Near East. Among these rulers was Cleopatra. Their personal relationship resumed, and a son, Ptolemy Philadelphus, was born in 36 B.C.E. There was now no retreating from their personal and political alliance: Politics and love became one.

Antony's first full campaign in 36 B.C.E. against the Parthians was a disaster; it was only with great difficulty that the remaining members of the Roman force were able to escape destruction. A second campaign in 33 B.C.E. was more successful, but it fell short of complete victory. Nevertheless, Antony felt confident enough to assign dominion over much territory under Roman influence to Cleopatra and her children in a settlement known as the Alexandrian Donations. Thus, on three fronts Antony lost whatever support he may have had at Rome: military failure against the Parthians, individualistic settlement of territories under Roman influence, and rejection of Octavian's sister as his Roman wife.

Antony's independent actions in the East, together with Octavian's aggressive behavior at Rome, led to a final confrontation. Octavian sensed the weakness of Antony's position at Rome, and he made public the supposed conditions of Antony's will. Its exact text remains unknown, but the effect of its publication is certain. War followed, and Antony and Cleopatra were defeated by Octavian in a naval battle at Actium in September of 31 B.C.E. They fled to Egypt, where, about a year later, Antony, under the mistaken impression that Cleopatra had already killed herself, committed suicide and died in her arms. Some time after this, Cleopatra did the same. According to tradition, she used the poison of an asp.

SIGNIFICANCE

Literary sources present a very negative picture of Marc Antony's personality and achievements. Antony's youthful excesses made it easy for critics to claim that his failure was the result of a life devoted to pleasure and self-gratification; although there is some truth to this, it nevertheless offers a one-sided view. He was an excellent general whose soldiers responded with devotion and loyalty. His administration of the Greek East was efficient and without many of the failings of his predecessors. Antony was politically astute, but he failed to appreciate sufficiently the impact of his image at Rome as a Hellenistic potentate. His enduring relationship with Cleopatra did great harm to his standing, and some even began to believe that Antony's devotion to her led to his considering moving the seat of Imperial power from Rome to Alexandria. Octavian, a master propagandist, took advantage of this situation by contrasting his traditional Roman values with Antony's Eastern way of life.

Antony's person and career highlight the tensions present in Roman society during the last century of the Republic, between conservative Roman values and the more attractive Hellenistic way of life. As Augustus,

Octavian based his rule on a return to the old Roman values, but most of the autocrats who succeeded him followed Antony's style more closely. Indeed, the division of the Roman Empire between East and West, which Antony may have seen as inevitable, eventually became reality. The history of the Roman Empire has shown that Antony's vision and style would become the rule rather than the exception.

—John Walsh

FURTHER READING

Charlesworth, M. P., and W. W. Tarn. *Octavian, Antony, and Cleopatra*. Cambridge, England: Cambridge University Press, 1965. This is an abridged, but detailed and valuable, account of the relations among its three subjects in the years between 44 and 30 B.C.E. Originally published in volumes 9 and 10 of *The Cambridge Ancient History* (1934).

Cicero, Marcus Tullius. *Philippics*. Edited and translated by D. R. Shackleton Bailey. Chapel Hill: University of North Carolina Press, 1986. These orations, composed in 44 or 43 B.C.E., provide graphically detailed and scathingly personal attacks on Antony's character. Their tone is so hostile, however, that they cannot be taken at face value.

Huzar, Eleanor G. *Mark Antony: A Biography*. New York: Methuen, 1986. A readable account of Antony's life. Well documented, it attempts to provide a balanced view of Antony's career by separating negative propaganda from fact.

Kittredge, Mary, and Arthur M. Schlesinger. *Marc Antony*. New York: Chelsea House, 1988. A biography accessible to high school readers. Illustrations, maps, index.

Plutarch, Antonius. *Life of Antony*. Edited by C. B. R. Pelling. New York: Cambridge University Press, 1988. Written early in the second century C.E., this biography provides a complete and engaging narrative account of Antony's life. Much of it is overtly hostile to Antony, and Plutarch chose to emphasize his subject's vices.

Syme, R. *The Roman Revolution*. 1939. Reprint. New York: Oxford University Press, 2002. An eminent historian's interpretive account of the reasons for the collapse of the Republic. Syme uses prosopographical analysis to explain the ways in which relations among aristocratic Romans led to Octavian's victory.

Toynbee, Jocelyn Mary Catherine. *Roman Historical Portraits*. Ithaca, N.Y.: Cornell University Press, 1978. Effectively combines visual and literary evidence in an exploration of the historical tradition in which the portraits of Antony and Octavian must be understood.

SEE ALSO: Antonia Minor; Augustus; Marcus Junius Brutus; Cicero; Cleopatra VII; Herod the Great; Julius Caesar; Ptolemy Philadelphus.

RELATED ARTICLES in *Great Events from History: The Ancient World*: 245-140 B.C.E., Rise of Parthia; 51 B.C.E., Cicero Writes *De republica*; 51-30 B.C.E., Cleopatra VII, Last of Ptolemies, Reigns; 43-42 B.C.E., Second Triumvirate Enacts Proscriptions; September 2, 31 B.C.E., Battle of Actium.

APOLLONIUS OF PERGA
Pergan geometer

One of the ablest geometers in antiquity, Apollonius systematized the theory of conic sections. His study of circular motion established the foundation for Greek geometric astronomy.

BORN: c. 262 B.C.E.; Perga, Pamphylia, Asia Minor (now Murtana, Turkey)
DIED: c. 190 B.C.E.; Alexandria, Egypt
ALSO KNOWN AS: The Great Geometer
AREAS OF ACHIEVEMENT: Mathematics, astronomy

EARLY LIFE

Information on the life of Apollonius (ap-uh-LOH-nee-uhs) is meager. Born at Perga around the middle of the third century B.C.E., he studied mathematics with the successors of Euclid at Alexandria. His activity falls near the time of Archimedes (c. 287-212 B.C.E.), but links between their work are indirect. In his surviving work, Apollonius once mentions the Alexandria-based geometer Conon of Samos, but his principal correspondents and colleagues (Eudemus, Philonides, Dionysodorus, Attalus I) were active at Pergamum and other centers in Asia Minor. It appears that this circle benefited from the cultural ambitions of the new Attalid Dynasty during the late third and the second centuries B.C.E.

LIFE'S WORK

Apollonius's main achievement lies in his study of the conic sections. Two properties of these curves can be distinguished as basic for their conception: First, they are specified as the locus of points whose distances x, y from given lines satisfy certain second-order relations: When $x^2 = ay$ (for a constant line segment a) the curve of the locus is a parabola, when $x^2 = ay - ay^{2/b}$ the curve is an ellipse (it becomes a circle when $b = a$), and when $x^2 = ay + ay^{2/b}$ it is a hyperbola. The same curves can be produced when a plane intersects the surface of a cone: When the plane is parallel to the side of the cone, there results a parabola (a single open, or infinitely extending, curve); when the plane is not parallel to the side of the cone but cuts through only one of its two sheets, there results an ellipse (a single closed curve); and when it cuts through both sheets of the cone, there results a hyperbola (a curve consisting of two separate branches, each extending indefinitely).

Apollonius of Perga. (Library of Congress)

The curves were already known in the fourth century B.C.E., for the geometer Menaechmus introduced the locus forms of two parabolas and a hyperbola in order to solve the problem of doubling the cube. By the time of Euclid (c. 300 B.C.E.), the formation of the curves as solid sections was well understood. Euclid himself produced a major treatise on the conics, as had a geometer named Aristaeus somewhat earlier. As Archimedes often assumed theorems on conics, one supposes that his basic reference source (which he sometimes cited as the "Conic Elements") was the Euclidean or Aristaean textbook. Also in the third century, Eratosthenes of Cyrene and Conon pursued studies in the conics (these works no longer survive), as did Diocles in his writing on burning mirrors (extant in an Arabic translation).

Apollonius thus drew from more than a century of research on conics. In the eight books of his treatise, *Cōnica* (*Treatise on Conic Sections*, 1896; best known as *Conics*), he systematized the elements of this field and contributed many new findings of his own. Only the first four books survive in Greek, in the edition prepared by Eutocius of Ascalon (active at Alexandria in the early sixth century C.E.), but all of its books except for the eighth exist in an Arabic translation from the ninth century C.E.

Among the topics that Apollonius covers are these: book 1, the principal constructions and properties of the three types of conics, their tangents, conjugate diameters, and transformation of axes; book 2, properties of hyperbolas, such as their relation to their asymptotes (the straight lines they infinitely approach but never meet); book 3, properties of intersecting chords and secants drawn to conics; book 4, how conics intersect one another; book 5, on the drawing of normal lines to conics; book 6, on similar conics; book 7, properties of the conjugate diameters and principal axes of conics; book 8 (lost), problems solved via the theorems of book 7.

As Apollonius states in the prefaces to the books of his treatise, the chief application of conics is to geometric problems—that is, propositions seeking the construction of a figure satisfying specified conditions. Apollonius includes only a few examples in the *Conics*: for example, to find a cone whose section produces a conic curve of specified parameters (1: 52-56), or to draw tangents and normals to given conics (2: 49-53 and 5: 55-63). Much of the content of the *Conics*, however, deals not with problems but with theorems auxiliary to problems. This is the case with book 3, for example, which Apollonius says is especially useful for problem solving but which actually contains no problems. In his preface, he explicitly mentions the problem of the "locus relative to three (or four) lines," all cases of which, Apollonius proudly asserts, can be worked out by means of his book 3, whereas Euclid's earlier effort was incomplete.

The significance of problem solving for the Greek geometric tradition is evident in works such as Euclid's *Stoicheia* (*Elements*) and *Ta dedomena* (*Data*). In more advanced fields such as conic theory, however, the surviving evidence is only barely representative of the richness of this ancient activity. A notable exception is the *Synagōgē* (*Collection*), a massive anthology of geometry by Pappus of Alexandria (fourth century C.E.), which preserves many examples of problems. Indeed, the whole of its book 7 amounts to an extended commentary on the problem-solving tradition—what Pappus calls the "analytic corpus" (*topos analyomenos*), a group of twelve treatises by Euclid, Apollonius, and others. Of the works taken from Apollonius, two are extant—*Conics* and *Logou apotomē* (*On Cutting Off a Ratio*, 1987)—while another five are lost—*Chōriou apotomē* (cutting off an area), *Diōrismenē tomē* (determinate section), *Epaphai* (tangencies), *Neyseis* (vergings), and *Topoi epipedoi* (plane loci). Pappus's summaries and technical notes preserve the best evidence available regarding the content of these lost works. Thus it is known that in *Epaphai*, for example, Apollonius covered all possible ways of constructing a circle so as to touch any combination of three given elements (points, lines, or circles). In *Neyseis* he sought the position of a line verging toward a given point and such that a marked segment of it lies exactly between given lines or circles. In *Topoi epipedoi* circles were produced as loci satisfying stated conditions, several of these being equivalent to expressions now familiar in analytic geometry.

It is significant that these last three works were restricted to planar constructions—that is, ones requiring only circles and straight lines. Pappus classifies problems in three categories: In addition to the planar, he names the solid (solvable by conics) and the linear (solvable by special curves, such as certain curves of third order, or others, such as spirals, now termed "transcendental," composed of coordinated circular and rectilinear motions). For Pappus, this scheme is normative; a planar solution, if known, is preferable to a solid one, and, similarly, a solid solution to a linear. For example, the problems of circle quadrature, cube duplication, and angle trisection can be solved by linear curves, but the last two can also be solved by conics and so are classed as solid.

Historians often misinterpret this classification as a restriction on solutions, as if the ancients accepted only the planar constructions. To the contrary, geometers throughout antiquity so fully explored all forms of construction as to belie any such restriction. Presumably, in his three books on planar constructions, Apollonius

sought to specify as completely as possible the domain of such constructions rather than to eliminate those of the solid or linear type. In any event, from works before Apollonius there is no evidence at all of a normative conception of problem-solving methods.

There survive isolated reports of Apollonian studies bearing on the regular solids, the cylindrical spiral, irrationals, circle measurement, the arithmetic of large numbers, and other topics. For the most part, little is known of these efforts, and their significance was slight in comparison with his treatises on geometric constructions.

Ptolemy reports in *Mathēmatikē suntaxis* (c. 150 C.E.; *Almagest*) that Apollonius made a significant contribution to astronomical theory by establishing the geometric condition for a planet to appear stationary relative to the fixed stars. Since, according to Ptolemy, he proved this condition for both the epicyclic and the eccentric models of planetary motion, Apollonius seems to have had some major responsibility for the introduction of these basic models. Apollonius studied only the geometric properties of these models, however, for the project of adapting them to actual planetary data became a concern only for astronomers such as Hipparchus a few decades later in the second century B.C.E.

SIGNIFICANCE

If Apollonius of Perga did indeed institute the eccentric and epicyclic models for planetary motion, as seems likely, he merits the appellation assigned to him by historian Otto Neugebauer: "the founder of Greek mathematical astronomy." These geometric devices, when adjusted to observational data and made suitable for numerical computation, became the basis of the sophisticated Greek system of astronomy. Through its codification by Ptolemy in the *Almagest*, this system flourished among Arabic and Hindu astronomers in the Middle Ages and Latin astronomers in the West through the sixteenth century. Although Nicolaus Copernicus (1473-1543) made the significant change of replacing Ptolemy's geocentric arrangement with a heliocentric one, even he retained the basic geometric methods of the older system. Only with Johannes Kepler (1571-1630), who was first to substitute elliptical orbits for the configurations of circles in the Ptolemaic-Copernican scheme, can one speak of a clear break with the mathematical methods of ancient astronomy.

Apollonius's work in geometry fared quite differently. The fields of conics and advanced geometric constructions he so fully explored came to a virtual dead end soon after his time. The complexity of this subject, proliferating in special cases and lacking convenient notations (such as the algebraic forms, for example, of modern analytic geometry that first appeared only with François Viète, René Descartes, and Pierre de Fermat in the late sixteenth and the seventeenth centuries), must have discouraged further research among geometers in the second century B.C.E.

In later antiquity, interest in Apollonius's work revived: Pappus and Hypatia of Alexandria (fourth to early fifth century C.E.) and Eutocius (sixth century) produced commentaries on the *Conics*. Their work did not extend the field in any significant way beyond what Apollonius had done, but it proved critical for the later history of conic theory, by ensuring the survival of Apollonius's writing. When the *Conics* was translated into Arabic in the ninth century, Arabic geometers entered this field; they approached the study of Apollonius with considerable inventiveness, often devising new forms of proofs, or contributing new results where the texts at their disposal were incomplete. Alhazen (early eleventh century), for example, attempted a restoration of Apollonius's lost book 8.

In the early modern period, after the publication of the translations of Apollonius and Pappus by Federigo Commandino in 1588-1589, the study of advanced geometry received new impetus in the West. Several distinguished mathematicians in this period (François Viète, Willebrord Snel, Pierre de Fermat, Edmond Halley, and others) tried their hand at restoring lost analytic works of Apollonius. The entirely new field of projective geometry emerged from the conic researches of Gérard Desargues and Blaise Pascal in the seventeenth century. Thus, the creation of the modern field of geometry owes much to the stimulus of the *Conics* and the associated treatises of Apollonius.

—*Wilbur R. Knorr*

FURTHER READING

Apollonius. *On Cutting Off a Ratio.* Translated by Edward Macierowski. Fairfield, Conn.: Golden Hind Press, 1987. This translation is literal and provisional; a full critical edition is being prepared by Macierowski.

_____. *Treatise on Conic Sections.* Translated and edited by Thomas Little Heath. Cambridge, England: Cambridge University Press, 1896. Translation in modern notation, with extensive commentary. Heath surveys the older history of conics, including efforts by Euclid and Archimedes, and then summarizes the characteristic terminology and methods used by Apollonius. A synopsis appears in Heath's *History of Greek Mathematics* (Oxford, England: Clarendon Press, 1921), together with ample discussions of the lost Apollonian treatises described by Pappus.

Fried, Michael N. *Apollonius of Perga's "Conica": Text, Context, Subtext.* Boston: E. J. Brill, 2001. A scholarly analysis. Bibliographic references, index.

Hogemdijk, J. P. *Ibn al-Haytham's Completion of the "Conics."* New York: Springer-Verlag, 1984. This edition of the Arabic text of Alhazen's restoration of the lost book 8 of the *Conics* is accompanied by a literal English translation, a mathematical summary in modern notation, and discussions of the Greek and Arabic traditions of Apollonius's work.

Knorr, W. R. *Ancient Tradition of Geometric Problems.* Cambridge, Mass.: Birkhauser Boston, 1986. A survey of Greek geometric methods from the pre-Euclidean period to late antiquity. Chapter 7 is devoted to the work of Apollonius, including his *Conics* and lost analytic writings.

Neugebauer, Otto. *A History of Ancient Mathematical Astronomy.* New York: Springer-Verlag, 1975. The section on Apollonius in this work provides a detailed technical account of his contributions to ancient astronomy.

Pappus of Alexandria. *Book 7 of the "Collection."* Translated by A. Jones. New York: Springer-Verlag, 1986. A critical edition of Pappus's Greek text (collated with the former edition of F. Hultsch in volume 2 of *Pappi Collectionis Quae Supersunt,* 1877), with English translation and commentary. Pappus's book preserves highly valuable information on Apollonius's lost works on geometric construction. Jones surveys in detail Pappus's evidence of the lost works and modern efforts to reconstruct them.

_____, ed. *Apollonius: Conics Books V to VII: The Arabic Translation of the Lost Greek Original in the Version of the Banu Musa.* New York: Springer-Verlag, 1990. This is the first literal English translation of this work ever to be published. Based on all known manuscripts, it includes the Arabic text with a full critical apparatus, an accurate English translation, and a commentary to elucidate both mathematical and historical difficulties.

Waerden, Bartel Leendert van der. *Science Awakening.* Translated by Arnold Dresden. 4th ed. Princeton Junction, N.J.: Scholar's Bookshelf, 1988. In this highly readable survey of ancient mathematics, Waerden includes a useful synopsis of the geometric work of Apollonius.

ARCHIMEDES
Greek mathematician and engineer

The greatest mathematician of antiquity, Archimedes did his best work in geometry and also founded the disciplines of statics and hydrostatics.

BORN: c. 287 B.C.E.; Syracuse, Sicily (now in Italy)
DIED: 212 B.C.E.; Syracuse, Sicily
AREAS OF ACHIEVEMENT: Science, mathematics

EARLY LIFE

Few details are certain about the life of Archimedes (ar-kuh-MEED-eez). The birth date of 287 B.C.E. was established from a report, about fourteen hundred years after the fact, that he was seventy-five years old at his death in 212 B.C.E. Ancient writers agree in calling him a Syracusan by birth, and he himself provides the information that his father was the astronomer Phidias, the author of a treatise on the diameters of the sun and moon. His father's profession suggests an explanation for the son's early interest in astronomy and mathematics. Some scholars have characterized Archimedes as an aristocrat who actively participated in the Syracusan court and who may have been related to King Hiero II, the ruler of Syracuse. He certainly was friendly with Hiero and Hiero's son Gelon, to whom he dedicated one of his works. (Original titles of Archimedes' works are not known, but most of his books were first translated into English by Thomas L. Heath in 1897 in the volume *The Works of Archimedes*.)

Archimedes traveled to Egypt to study in Alexandria, then the center of the scientific world. Some of his teachers had, in their youth, been students of Euclid. He made two close friends in Alexandria: Conon of Samos, a gifted mathematician, and Eratosthenes of Cyrene, also a good mathematician. From the prefaces to his works, it is clear that Archimedes maintained friendly relations with several Alexandrian scholars, and he played an active role in developing the mathematical traditions of this intellectual center. It is possible that he visited Spain before returning to Syracuse, and a return trip to Egypt is also a possibility. This second visit would have been the occasion for his construction of dikes and bridges reported in some Arabian sources.

In Syracuse, Archimedes spent his time working on mathematical and mechanical problems. Although he was a remarkably ingenious inventor, his inventions were, according to Plutarch, merely diversions, the work of a geometer at play. He possessed such a lofty intellect that he considered these inventions of much less worth than his mathematical creations. Plutarch may have exaggerated Archimedes' distaste for engineering, because there is evidence that he was fascinated by mechanical problems from a practical as well as a theoretical point of view.

In the stories that multiplied about him, Archimedes became a symbol of the learned man—absentminded and unconcerned with food, clothing, and the other necessities of life. In images created long after his death, he is depicted as the quintessential sage, with a heavily bearded face, massive forehead, and contemplative mien. He had a good sense of humor. For example, he often sent his theorems to Alexandria, but to play a trick on some conceited mathematicians there, he once slipped in a few false propositions, so that these individuals, who pretended to have discovered everything by themselves, would fall into the trap of proposing theorems that were impossible.

LIFE'S WORK

The range of Archimedes' interest was wide, encompassing statics, hydrostatics, optics, astronomy, and engineering, in addition to geometry and arithmetic. It is natural that stories should tell more about his engineering inventiveness than his mathematical ability, for clever machines appealed to the average mind more than abstract mathematical theorems. Unfortunately, many of these stories are doubtful. For example, Archimedes is supposed to have invented a hollow, helical cylinder that, when rotated, could serve as a water pump, but this device, now called the Archimedean screw, antedates its supposed inventor.

In another well-known story, Archimedes boasted to King Hiero that, if he had a place on which to stand, he could move the earth. Hiero urged him to make good this boast by hauling ashore a fully loaded, three-masted merchantman of the royal fleet. Using a compound pulley, Archimedes, with modest effort, pulled the ship out of the harbor and onto the shore. The compound pulley may have been Archimedes' invention, but the story, told by Plutarch, is probably a legend.

The most famous story about Archimedes is attributed to Vitruvius, a Roman architect under Emperor Augustus. King Hieron, grateful for the success of one of his ventures, wanted to thank the gods by consecrating a golden wreath. On delivery, the wreath had the weight of the gold supplied for it, but Hiero suspected that it had been adulterated with silver. Unable to make the goldsmith confess, Hiero asked Archimedes to devise some way of testing the wreath. Because it was a consecrated object, Archimedes could not subject it to chemical analysis. He pondered the problem without success until one day, when he entered a full bath, he noticed that the deeper he descended into the tub, the more water flowed over the edge. This suggested to him that the amount of overflowed water was equal in volume to the portion of his body submerged in the bath. This observation gave him a way of solving the problem, and he was so overjoyed that he leapt out of the tub and ran home naked through the streets, shouting: "Eureka! Eureka!" Vitruvius then goes on to explain how Archimedes made use of his newly gained insight. By putting the wreath into water, he could tell by the rise in water level the volume of the wreath. He also dipped into water lumps of gold and silver, each having the same weight as the wreath. He found that the wreath caused more water to overflow than the gold and less than the silver. From this experiment, he determined the amount of silver admixed with the gold in the wreath.

As amusing and instructive as these legends are, much more reliable and interesting to modern historians of science are Archimedes' mathematical works. These treatises can be divided into three groups: studies of figures bounded by curved lines and surfaces, works on the geometrical analysis of statical and hydrostatical problems, and arithmetical works. The form in which these treatises have survived is not the form in which they left Archimedes' hand: They have all undergone transformations and emendations. Nevertheless, one still finds the spirit of Archimedes in the intricacy of the questions and the lucidity of the explanations.

In finding the areas of plane figures bounded by curved lines and the volumes of solid figures bounded by curved surfaces, Archimedes used a method originated by Eudoxus of Cnidus, unhappily called the "method of exhaustion." This indirect proof involves inscribing and circumscribing polygons to approach a length, area, or volume. The name "exhaustion" is based on the idea that, for example, a circle would finally be exhausted by inscribed polygons with a growing number of sides. In *Peri sphairas kai kylindron* (c. 240 B.C.E.; *On the Sphere and the Cylinder*, 1897), Archimedes compares perimeters of inscribed and circumscribed polygons to prove that the volume of a sphere is two-thirds the volume of its circumscribed cylinder. He also proves that the surface of any sphere is four times the area of its greatest circle.

Having successfully applied this method to the sphere and cylinder, Archimedes went on to use the technique for many other figures, including spheroids, spirals, and

Archimedes. (Library of Congress)

parabolas. *Peri konoeideon kai sphaireodeon* (c. 240 B.C.E.; *On Conoids and Spheroids*, 1897) treats the figures of revolution generated by conics. His spheroids are what are now called oblate and prolate spheroids, which are figures of revolution generated by ellipses. Archimedes' object in this work was the determination of volumes of segments cut off by planes from these conoidal and spheroidal solids. In *Peri helikon* (c. 240 B.C.E.; *On Spirals*, 1897), Archimedes studies the area enclosed between successive whorls of a spiral. He also defines a figure, now called Archimedes' spiral: If a ray from a central point rotates uniformly about this point, like the hand of a clock, and if another point moves uniformly along this line (marked by the clock hand), starting at the central point, then this linearly moving and rotating point will trace Archimedes' spiral.

Tetragonismos ten tou orthogonion konoy tomes (c. 250 B.C.E.; *On the Quadrature of the Parabola*, 1897), when translated, is not Archimedes' original title for the treatise, as "parabola" was not used in the sense of a conic section in the third century B.C.E. On the other hand, quadrature is an ancient term: It denotes the process of constructing a square equal in area to a given surface, in this case a parabolic segment. Archimedes, in this treatise, proves the theorem that the area of a parabolic segment is four-thirds the area of its greatest inscribed triangle. He was so fond of this theorem that he gave different proofs for it. One proof uses a method of exhaustion in which the parabolic segment is exhausted by a series of triangles. The other consists of establishing the quadrature of the parabola by mechanically balancing elements of the unknown area against elements of a known area. This latter method gives an insight into how Archimedes discovered theorems to be proved. His most recently discovered work, *Peri tōn mechanikon theorematon* (c. 250 B.C.E.; *On the Method of Mechanical Theorems*, 1912), provides other examples of how Archimedes mathematically balanced geometrical figures as if they were on a weighing balance. He did not consider that this mechanical method constituted a demonstration, but it allowed him to find interesting theorems, which he then proved by more rigorous geometrical methods.

Archimedes also applied geometry to statics and hydrostatics successfully. In his *Epipledon isorropion* (c. 250 B.C.E.; *On the Equilibrium of Planes*, 1897), he proves the law of the lever geometrically and then puts it to use in finding the centers of gravity of several thin sheets of different shapes. By center of gravity, Archimedes meant the point at which the object can be supported

so as to be in equilibrium under the pull of gravity. Earlier Greek mathematicians had made use of the principle of the lever in showing that a small weight at a large distance from a fulcrum would balance a large weight near the fulcrum, but Archimedes worked this principle out in mathematical detail. In his proof, the weights become geometrical magnitudes acting perpendicularly to the balance beam, which itself is conceived as a weightless geometrical line. In this way, he reduced statics to a rigorous discipline comparable to what Euclid had done for geometry.

Archimedes once more emphasizes geometrical analysis in *Peri ochoymenon* (c. 230 B.C.E.; *On Floating Bodies*, 1897). The cool logic of this treatise contrasts with his emotional discovery of the buoyancy principle. In this work, he proves that solids lighter than a fluid will, when placed in the fluid, sink to the depth where the weight of the solid will be equal to the weight of the fluid displaced. Solids heavier than the fluid will, when placed in the fluid, sink to the bottom, and they will be lighter by the weight of the displaced fluid.

Although Archimedes' investigations were primarily in geometry and mechanics, he did perform some interesting studies in numerical calculation. For example, in *Kykloy metresis* (c. 230 B.C.E.; *On the Measurement of the Circle*, 1897) he calculated, based on mathematical principles rather than direct measurement, a value for the ratio of the circumference of a circle to its diameter (this ratio was not called pi until much later). By inscribing and circumscribing regular polygons of more and more sides within and around a circle, Archimedes found that the ratio was between $223/71$ and $220/71$, the best value for π (pi) ever obtained in the classical world.

In *Psiammites* (c. 230 B.C.E.; *The Sand-Reckoner*, 1897), Archimedes devises a notation suitable for writing very large numbers. To put this new notation to a test, he sets down a number equal to the number of grains of sand it would take to fill the entire universe. Large numbers are also involved in his treatise concerned with the famous "Cattle Problem." White, black, yellow, and dappled cows and bulls are grazing on the island of Sicily. The numbers of these cows and bulls have to satisfy several conditions. The problem is to find the number of bulls and cows of each of the four colors. It is unlikely that Archimedes ever completely solved this problem in indeterminate analysis.

Toward the end of his life, Archimedes became part of a worsening political situation. His friend Hiero II had a treaty of alliance with Rome and remained faithful to it, even after the Second Punic War began. After his death, however, his grandson Hieronymus, who became king, was so impressed by Hannibal's victories in Italy that he switched sides to Carthage. Hieronymus was then assassinated, but Sicily remained allied with Carthage. Consequently, the Romans sent a fleet under the command of Marcellus to capture Syracuse. According to traditional stories, Archimedes invented devices for warding off the Roman enemy. He is supposed to have constructed large lenses to set the fleet on fire and mechanical cranes to turn ships upside down. He devised so many ingenious war machines that the Romans would flee if so much as a piece of rope appeared above a wall. These stories are grossly exaggerated, if not totally fabricated, but Archimedes may have helped in the defense of his city, and he certainly provided the Romans with a face-saving explanation for their frustratingly long siege of Syracuse.

Because of treachery by a cabal of nobles, among other things, Syracuse eventually fell. Marcellus ordered that the city be sacked, but he made it clear that his soldiers were to spare the house and person of Archimedes. Amid the confusion of the sack, however, Archimedes, while puzzling over a geometrical diagram drawn on sand in a tray, was killed by a Roman soldier. During his lifetime he had expressed the wish that on his tomb should be placed a cylinder circumscribing a sphere, together with an inscription giving the ratio between the volumes of these two bodies, a discovery of which he was especially proud. Marcellus, who was distressed by the great mathematician's death, had Archimedes' wish carried out. More than a century later, when Cicero was in Sicily, he found this tomb, overgrown with brush but with the figure of the sphere and cylinder still visible.

SIGNIFICANCE

Some scholars rank Archimedes with Sir Isaac Newton (1642-1727) and Carl Friedrich Gauss (1777-1855) as one of the three greatest mathematicians who ever lived, and historians of mathematics agree that the theorems Archimedes discovered raised Greek mathematics to a new level of understanding. He tackled very difficult and original problems and solved them through boldness and vision. His skill in using mechanical ideas in mathematics was paralleled by his ingenious use of mathematics in mechanics.

The Latin West received its knowledge of Archimedes from two sources: Byzantium and Islam. His works were translated from the Greek and Arabic into Latin in the twelfth century and played an important role in stimulating the work of medieval natural philosophers.

Knowledge of Archimedes' ideas multiplied during the Renaissance, and by the seventeenth century his insights had been almost completely absorbed into European thought and had deeply influenced the birth of modern science. For example, Galileo was inspired by Archimedes and tried to do for dynamics what Archimedes had done for statics. More than any other ancient scientist, Archimedes observed the world in a way that modern scientists from Galileo to Albert Einstein admired and sought to emulate.

—*Robert J. Paradowski*

FURTHER READING

Aaboe, Asger. *Episodes from the Early History of Mathematics*. New York: Random House, 1964. After a brief account of Archimedes' life and a survey of his works, the third chapter of this book presents three samples of Archimedean mathematics: the trisection of an angle, the construction of a regular heptagon, and the determination of a sphere's volume and surface area.

Bell, E. T. *Men of Mathematics*. New York: Simon and Schuster, 1965. A collection of biographical essays on the world's greatest mathematicians. Bell discusses Archimedes, along with Zeno of Elea and Eudoxus, in an early chapter on "Modern Minds in Ancient Bodies."

Dijksterhuis, E. J. *Archimedes*. Princeton, N.J.: Princeton University Press, 1987. This edition of the best survey in English of Archimedes' life and work also contains a valuable bibliographical essay by Wilbur R. Knorr.

Finley, Moses I. *Ancient Sicily*. Vol. 1 in *A History of Sicily*. New York: Viking Press, 1968. Finley's account of the history of Sicily from antiquity to the Arab conquest has a section explaining how the politics of the Second Punic War led to Archimedes' death.

Heath, T. L. *A History of Greek Mathematics*. 2 vols. 1921. Reprint. New York: Dover, 1981. A good general survey of ancient Greek mathematics that contains, in volume 2, a detailed account of the works of Archimedes.

Kline, Morris. *Mathematical Thought from Ancient to Modern Times*. New York: Oxford University Press, 1990. Kline's treatment of Archimedes emphasizes the themes of his work rather than the events of his life.

Stein, Sherman K. *Archimedes: What Did He Do Besides Cry Eureka?* Washington, D.C.: Mathematical Association of America, 1999. An accessible account of

Archimedes' accomplishments, as well as Archimedes' life, the 1906 discovery of his manuscript, and his methods. Includes bibliography and index.

Van der Waerden, B. L. *Science Awakening.* 4th ed. Princeton Junction, N.J.: Scholar's Bookshelf, 1988. A survey of ancient Egyptian, Babylonian, and Greek mathematics. The chapter on the Alexandrian era (330-220 B.C.E.) contains a detailed account of Archimedes' life, legends, and mathematical accomplishments.

SEE ALSO: Apollonius of Perga; Eratosthenes of Cyrene; Euclid; Eudoxus of Cnidus; Hannibal; Pappus.

RELATED ARTICLES in *Great Events from History: The Ancient World*: c. 500-400 B.C.E., Greek Physicians Begin Scientific Practice of Medicine; October 1, 331 B.C.E., Battle of Gaugamela; c. 320 B.C.E., Theophrastus Initiates the Study of Botany; c. 300 B.C.E., Euclid Compiles a Treatise on Geometry; 264-225 B.C.E., First Punic War; c. 250 B.C.E., Discoveries of Archimedes.

ARETAEUS OF CAPPADOCIA
Roman physician

Considered by many the greatest ancient physician after Hippocrates, Aretaeus wrote the best and most accurate descriptions of many diseases and made landmark studies of diabetes and neurological and mental disorders.

FLOURISHED: Probably second century C.E.; Cappadocia, Roman Empire (now in Turkey)

AREA OF ACHIEVEMENT: Medicine

EARLY LIFE

Not even the exact century of Aretaeus (ar-uh-TEE-uhs) of Cappadocia's birth is known; most scholars agree on the second century C.E., although a few offer the first or third century. Aretaeus's epithet is "Cappadocian," implying that he was born in that most eastern of Roman provinces. No other information about his life is certain. Scholars conjecture, however, that he studied in Egypt at Alexandria, founded in 331 B.C.E. as the major center for medical study, research, and teaching. Aretaeus mentions Egypt in his works and describes its geography and some diseases and therapeutics unique to that country. Some scholars believe that Aretaeus also practiced medicine in Rome; he prescribed wines known to second century Rome—namely, Falernian, Fundian, Sequine, and Surrentine.

Aretaeus was an Eclectic by practice and a Pneumatist by training. After Hippocrates in the fifth century B.C.E. there was little advance in the knowledge of disease and its treatment, although there were significant gains at Alexandria in the area of anatomy because of the dissections of human bodies. Instead, post-Hippocratic physicians tended to theorize about medicine as a philosophy and to develop various schools of medicine. Dogmatism and Empiricism were the first schools. The Dogmatists employed theoretical principles; they believed that reason and systematic studies of anatomy and physiology were necessary for the physician. The Empiricists, on the other hand, rejected theory and anatomy; they stressed experience and observation. The "tripod" of the Empiricists' knowledge was personal observation, researched historical observation, and use of analogy in analyzing unknown cases.

Two schools developed in reaction to the Dogmatists and Empiricists. Methodism, founded in the late first century B.C.E., rejected the theory of the humors so prevalent in Hippocratic medicine and advocated an atomic stance. The Methodists considered disease an interference of the normal position and motion of the atoms in the human body; treatments were prescribed to restore the proper order of the atoms—relaxants to counteract excessive tension, astringents to counteract excessive looseness.

The Pneumatic school, established around 50 C.E. by Athenaeus of Attaleia, stressed *pneuma*, meaning "vital air" or "breath." The beliefs of the Pneumatists were a combination of the Stoic philosophy, with its emphasis on primordial matter, the *pneuma*, from which all life comes, and Hippocratic pathology. Disease occurs when an imbalance of the four humors (blood, phlegm, black bile, and yellow bile) disturbs the *pneuma* in the human body.

Each of these various schools had both strengths and glaring weaknesses in its theories and practices. The knowledge of these weaknesses, coupled with Roman common sense, which rejected the Greek love of theory, led most Roman physicians, beginning with Archigenes (fl. c. 100 C.E.), to pick and choose among the various doctrines and ideas of the four schools. Such physicians

Aretaeus of Cappadocia. (Library of Congress)

were called Eclectics. That Aretaeus was an Eclectic is obvious from his work: For example, although he followed Pneumatism in its concept of the vital breath and its relation to the four humors, Aretaeus pursued anatomy and physiology avidly, as the Dogmatists did, yet he also relied heavily on observation and experience in the manner of an Empiricist. His emphasis on simple regimens and treatments recalls the Methodist school as well as Hippocrates.

LIFE'S WORK

Aretaeus refused to be dogmatic and speculative. He attempted to describe diseases in clear, scientific, and rational terms, and his writings bear the marks of careful thought and extensive clinical experience. Aretaeus wrote seven works, two of which survive: *Peri aition kai semeion oxeon kai chronion pathon* (*On the Causes and Symptoms of Acute and Chronic Diseases*, 1856) and *Oxeon kai chronion nouson therapeutikon biblion* (*Book on the Treatment of Acute and Chronic Diseases*, 1856). The lost works discussed fevers, surgery, pharmacology, gynecology, and prophylaxis. Aretaeus wrote in Ionic Greek, a dialect that had not been in use for centuries; he chose the Ionic style to imitate Hippocrates, who also wrote in that dialect.

Aretaeus followed the Methodist classification of diseases into chronic and acute; the distinction was made on the course of the disease, that is, whether the disease

lasted over a long period of time or was of a short duration and reached a "crisis" (the point in the progress of the disease when the patient recovered or died). Chronic diseases include paralysis, migraine headaches, and insanity, while examples of acute diseases are pneumonia, pleurisy, tetanus, and diphtheria. Aretaeus's descriptions of these and other diseases show him to be an accurate observer who was concerned more for the patient than for theory itself. His accounts, so important in the history of medicine, may be summarized in the following categories: anatomy and physiology, symptomatology (physical description of diseases such as diabetes, leprosy, and ulcers), neurology and psychiatry, surgery, and therapeutics.

Aretaeus devoted more attention to anatomy and physiology than most ancient physicians. As stated earlier, Aretaeus followed the Pneumatist doctrine: He believed that the body is composed of the four humors and of spirit (*pneuma*), and the proper mixture and interplay of these elements constitutes health. Blood is formed in the liver from food; phlegm is secreted by the brain into the other organs; and yellow bile comes from the liver, black bile from the spleen. The most important organ is the heart, because the heart is the site of heat and *pneuma*. The heart draws the *pneuma* from the lungs, which are stimulated by it. Respiration itself depends on the movement of the thorax and diaphragm and also on the lungs' contraction and expansion. Regarding the nervous system, nerves originate in the brain; this idea was based on the perception that the spinal cord was a prolongation of the brain. All nerves cross between their origin in the brain and their final termination in the body; Aretaeus based this belief on his startling observation that a cerebral lesion caused paralysis on the opposite side of the body.

Aretaeus knew much about circulation. The aorta, he stated, comes from the heart and is located to the left of the vena cava; the aorta carries the *pneuma* to the other organs. The veins, which originate in the liver, bring the blood to all the body. Aretaeus asserted that the content of the arteries was light-colored, that of the veins dark. The liver itself is composed mostly of blood and produces blood and bile; if it becomes inflamed, jaundice results. Aretaeus wrote remarkable accounts of the kidneys and the bile ducts. He thought of the kidneys as cavities that acted like sieves for collecting urine and were connected to the bladder by two tubes, one from each kidney. Digestion of food occurs not only in the stomach but also in the intestines. The portal vein takes the food after digestion to the liver, where it is taken out as blood by the vena cava to the heart. This scheme shows that Aretaeus was aware of nearly all circulatory processes and the direction of blood flow in the veins.

One of Aretaeus's greatest accomplishments was his practice of physical diagnosis. He used anatomical inspection, distinguishing the appearances of ulcers in the small and large bowels, for example. Also, before he discussed a disease, Aretaeus prefixed an anatomical and physiological introduction concerning the part(s) of the body afflicted by the disease (this is the method used in many modern medical textbooks). In his physical examinations, Aretaeus employed auscultation of the heart, palpitation of the body (to check for enlargement of the liver and spleen), and percussion of the abdomen. Aretaeus always noted carefully the patient's symptoms: temperature, breathing, pulse, secretions, color of skin, and condition of the pupils. In the tradition of Hippocrates, Aretaeus related diseases to foods eaten by the patient and to climate, time of year, and environment.

Aretaeus's symptomatology is considered excellent by medical historians and, in some instances, not improved on even by contemporary medicine. Especially praiseworthy are Aretaeus's accounts of hematemesis, jaundice, dropsy, tuberculosis, tetanus, epilepsy, and cardiac syncope. Aretaeus distinguished between pneumonia and pleurisy and is credited with the initial descriptions of diphtheria and asthma. He was the first European to write a symptomatic account of diabetes, and he gave the disease its name. Aretaeus correctly thought of diabetes as a progressive form of dropsy with polyuria and excessive thirst that results in emaciation of flesh. Finally, Aretaeus's accounts of leprosy are invaluable. He offered useful distinctions between the types of leprosy: elephantiasis (the tuberous form of leprosy) and the maculo-anesthetic form, which involves mutilation of the body; he also provided the first recorded instance of isolating lepers and distinguished between conveyance of disease by actual contact (contagion) and transmission of disease at a distance (infection).

Aretaeus's discussions of neurological and mental diseases are important. He divided such illnesses into acute and chronic classes. The acute diseases, as he described them, are phrenitis (a febrile delirium or, at times, meningitis), lethargy (a comatose state, or encephalitis), marasmus (atrophy), apoplexy (an acute form of paralysis), tetanus, and epileptic paroxysm. Chronic diseases include cephalaea (migraine headache), vertigo (chronic paralysis), and all forms of insanity. Especially important are Aretaeus's astute distinctions between apoplexy, paraplegia, paresis, and paralysis; the basis of division

was the extent of loss of movement and sensation. Aretaeus was the first to distinguish between spinal and cerebral paralysis: When the paralysis is spinal, it occurs on the same side as the lesion; when cerebral, the paralysis occurs on the opposite side (crossed paralysis).

Aretaeus's clear and full discussion of the different kinds of insanity has remained unsurpassed. He noted the stages by which intermittent insanity (manic depression) can become a senile melancholia that does not remit. While the former may be treated by phlebotomy, wormwood, and black hellebore (a plant that produces violent shocks to the nervous system similar to those in modern electric shock treatment), senile melancholia is incurable.

Aretaeus's book on surgery has been lost; he did, however, refer to surgery throughout his extant writings. Aretaeus recommended craniotomy (trepanning) for epilepsy and for cephalalgia and cephalaea (acute and chronic headache, respectively). He used catheters for urological diseases and mentioned surgery to remove kidney stones. It should be noted that surgery was not commonly practiced in antiquity, but when it was deemed necessary, the practicing physician usually performed it.

Aretaeus's treatments of disease are conservative. As in his discussions of the causes and forms of diseases, Aretaeus relied on experience and common sense, not abstract theory. He rejected tracheotomy and pleaded for extreme caution in the application of phlebotomy, venesection, cupping, and leeches: Aretaeus argued that only in severe cases should much blood be removed. Instead, he used purgatives, emetics, suppositories, laxatives, ointments, and poultices. Aretaeus also stressed exercise, massages, baths, temperate lifestyles, and a healthy diet including milk, fruits, vegetables, and foods without starch and fat. He also prescribed opium for people afflicted with feverish delirium.

SIGNIFICANCE

No ancient medical writer, except perhaps Hippocrates, surpassed Aretaeus of Cappadocia for vividness and clarity in the description of diseases. Aretaeus's descriptions of diabetes, tetanus, diphtheria, leprosy, asthma, and mental and neurological disorders are especially valuable and are landmarks in medical history. Aretaeus tried his best to put his symptomatology on a sound anatomical basis; for every disease, he supplied splendid accounts of anatomy. He gave therapeutics and cures for every disease, acute and chronic; his treatments are simple and rational. In his writings, Aretaeus was perhaps the most unbiased physician in antiquity, rejecting dogmatic thought, theory, and superstition. Finally, Aretaeus was unique in refusing to abandon the patient who was incurable; while even Hippocrates recommended turning away hopeless cases, Aretaeus ordered all measures to be taken, and, when those failed, he offered support and sympathy.

—*Steven M. Oberhelman*

FURTHER READING

Allbutt, Sir Thomas. *Greek Medicine in Rome*. 1921. Reprint. New York: B. Blom, 1970. Still one of the best textbooks on the medical schools and the practice of medicine in the Roman Empire. The chapter "Some Pneumatist and Eclectic Physicians" discusses Aretaeus and is superb in providing background information to the Eclectic and his writings.

Aretaeus of Cappadocia. *The Extant Works of Aretaeus the Cappadocian*. Edited and translated by Francis Adams. 1856. Reprint. Boston: Milford House, 1972. Aretaeus's work translated into English. The introduction to Aretaeus, his background, and his work is somewhat difficult for the nonspecialist, and the antiquated English of the translation is forbidding.

King, Helen. *Greek and Roman Medicine*. London: Bristol Classical Press, 2001. An overview of medicine in the Greek and Roman world.

Lloyd, Geoffrey, and Nathan Sirin. *The Way and the Word: Science and Medicine in Early China and Greece*. New Haven, Conn.: Yale University Press, 2002. A study of science and medicine in two early cultures.

SEE ALSO: Asclepiades; Galen; Hippocrates.

RELATED ARTICLE in *Great Events from History: The Ancient World*: c. 500-400 B.C.E., Greek Physicians Begin Scientific Practice of Medicine.

ARISTIPPUS
Greek philosopher

Departing from the Sophism to which he was exposed as Socrates' student, Aristippus founded the Cyrenaic school of philosophy, the hallmark of which was hedonism.

BORN: c. 435 B.C.E.; Cyrene, Cyrenaica (now in Libya)
DIED: 365 B.C.E.; Athens, Greece
AREA OF ACHIEVEMENT: Philosophy

EARLY LIFE

Because Aristippus (ar-uh-STIHP-uhs) left no writings for posterity, what is known about him is derived from secondary sources, the most notable of which is Xenophon's *Apomnēmoneumata* (c. 381-355; *Memorabilia of Socrates*, 1712). From these scant and distant sources, it appears that Aristippus was born in North Africa in the city of Cyrene, in what is currently Libya but was then Cyrenaica. His family was reputed to have had considerable influence and to have been sufficiently rich to support the young Aristippus in his travels and studies. Cyrene was at the height of its prosperity and influence during Aristippus's early life.

From all accounts, Aristippus experienced life with an ebullient enthusiasm. He was affable and had a winning personality and disposition. He was also remarkably intelligent, quick to learn, and eager to share his learning with others. He had a legendary sense of humor and was considered a bon vivant whose chief aim during his early days was to seek pleasure, broadly defined.

The existing sources agree that Aristippus went to Athens and studied under Socrates in the agora and that he also journeyed to Sicily, where he was a part of the court of Dionysius I at Syracuse. Scholars are at odds in suggesting the order in which these two occurrences took place. The *Memorabilia* suggests that Aristippus went first to Athens and then left to go to Syracuse after Socrates' death, whereas other sources suggest the opposite sequence.

It is known that Aristippus studied with Socrates, attracted to this pivotal Athenian philosopher by his obvious humanity, his fun-loving qualities, his cordiality, and, most important of all, his indisputable intellectual superiority. Aristippus spent considerable time in Athens during its golden age, its most significant period of intellectual influence.

Because Socrates died in 399 B.C.E., it is known that Aristippus probably spent part of his late twenties and early thirties in Athens. It is also known that he was in Athens in his later life, because he died there thirty-four years after Socrates' death. Aristippus also went to Syracuse, where he taught rhetoric and was associated with the court of Dionysius, an ill-tempered, often rude tyrant. Once, when Aristippus invoked Dionysius's wrath, the tyrant spat in his face. Aristippus, demonstrating his ready wit, took this indignity in stride, observing that one who is landing a big fish must expect to be splashed.

After Aristippus had taught for some time in Syracuse, he returned to his native Cyrene to begin a school of philosophy. It seems logical that the correct sequence of events is that he studied first in Athens with Socrates, that he then went to Syracuse, well equipped to teach through his studies in Athens, and that he then returned to Cyrene, where he remained for several years until his ultimate return to Athens, where he spent the remainder of his life.

LIFE'S WORK

In modern philosophical terminology, Aristippus would likely be classified as a relativist. Schooled in Sophism by Socrates, the great master of the Sophist philosophy based on dialogue and structured argument, Aristippus had been exposed continually to the prevailing Socratic theory of innate ideas—to the notion that ideal forms exist, while the objects of the "real" world are mere imitations of the ideal forms (the word "idea" is derived from a Greek word meaning "shape" or "form"). Aristippus early questioned this notion, believing rather that all individuals experience and perceive things around them in unique and individual ways. One cannot, for example, speak of a universal "red." To begin with, there are many reds; the red of human blood is not the exact red of an apple, of the sun at sunset, or of a red cabbage. Further, what is red to one person might be grey-green to someone who is color-blind but who has been conditioned to the notion that apples, human blood, and some cabbages are red.

Similarly, according to Aristippus, the nominalist concept that words such as "chair," "wheel," or "bottle" evoke a universal image is flawed, because all individuals necessarily filter their concepts of words through their own experience and consciousness, each arriving perhaps at a totally different image. In other words, for Aristippus, no physical object (table, chair), quality (blue), or concept (goodness) in the real world possesses generalized qualities detached from the specific object, quality, or concept. To him, perception, which is wholly individual and idiosyncratic, determines what any object or concept communicates to any single individual.

These notions led Aristippus to the conclusion that there exists no explicit, objective, and absolute world identically perceived by all people. He further posited that it is impossible accurately to compare the experiences of different people, because all individuals can know are their own perceptions and reactions. Aristippus further contended that, from birth, all living humans seek pleasure and avoid pain. In Aristippus's view, therefore, pleasure

and pain become polar opposites in the lives of most humans, pleasure being associated with good, pain with evil.

As Socrates' student, Aristippus surely knew that his teacher explained virtue in terms of the pleasure it brings to the virtuous, as opposed to the pain that vice brings. This was at the heart of Socrates' moral philosophy, as shown particularly in his death dialogues. Aristippus, on the other hand, contended that life must be lived in pursuit of pleasure.

His one caveat was that pleasure must be defined by all people for themselves, that there is no universal pleasure. Some people, therefore, find the greatest pleasure in leading law-abiding, virtuous lives, whereas others find it in raucous, drunken revelry. Aristippus did not make moral judgments about where individuals sought and found their pleasures.

Using the formal logic that his background in rhetoric had instilled in him, Aristippus denied that there was any universal standard of pleasurableness. Drawing on his conclusion that it is impossible to compare concepts between or among individuals, he argued that it is futile to say that some pleasures are better than others or that they possess a greater good. Aristippus also argued that the source of pleasure is always the body—which, he was quick to point out, includes the mind. For him, pleasures were most fully and satisfactorily experienced in the present. Memories of pleasures past or the contemplation of pleasures promised at some future date are weak semblances of pleasures that are immediately enjoyable.

The school of philosophy that Aristippus founded at Cyrene, based on concepts such as these, was designated the Hedonistic school, "hedonistic" being derived from the Greek word for "pleasure." Hedonism was closely akin in many ways to the Cynicism of Antisthenes, who, like Aristippus, questioned the existence of universals, claiming that the so-called universals were nothing more than names. Together, Antisthenes and Aristippus formulated the Nominalist theory of universals, which flew in the face of Socrates' and Plato's realism.

For Aristippus, the moral good dwells in the immediate, intense pleasures of the moment. These pleasures are experienced through the senses. Aristippus considered them the best and greatest pleasures, the ends toward which all moral activity is directed.

This philosophy, however, proved unworkable over time. The Cyrenaics quickly realized that considerable pain is involved in the attainment of some pleasures and that anyone who would judge the intensity and, ultimately, the moral good of that pleasure must consider as well the pain involved in achieving it.

The Cyrenaics also questioned the absoluteness with which Aristippus linked pain to evil. They came to understand that pain that in the end results in the achievement of pleasure can in itself be viewed as a good. They contended that the truly good person will do nothing evil or antisocial because of the punishments or disapproval that might accompany such actions (the avoidance of pain). Unlike Aristippus, they began to view the mental and bodily pleasures as dichotomous.

Finally, those who sought to refine Aristippus's theories arrived at the realization that the understanding of pleasure and of the pleasure/pain dichotomy required an outside, objective judge. They found such a judge in reason and wisdom, which led them to the inevitable conclusion that intelligence is a determining and indispensable component of virtue. Without this element, true happiness is impossible. Indeed, this turn in their reasoning took them back into proximity with Socrates' notions of virtue and of pleasure.

SIGNIFICANCE

Perhaps Aristippus's greatest contribution to Western thought came in his questioning of Socrates' theory of ideas. In disputing these theories, he focused on individual differences and arrived at a philosophy infinitely more relativistic than the prevailing philosophies of his day.

In a sense, Aristippus took the earliest tentative steps in a march of insurgent ideas that led inevitably to the Reformation of the sixteenth century, in which Martin Luther demanded that all people be their own priests when it came to interpreting Scripture. This movement, along with the invention of the printing press in the preceding century, much stimulated the move toward universal literacy in the Western world.

If the Cynics, under the leadership of Antisthenes, represented the school of apathy in the ancient world, the Cyrenaics, following the lead of Aristippus, represented the school of happiness. These ideas ran counter to the prevailing philosophy emerging from Athens and were considered both exotic and quixotic by the most influential thinkers of the day.

As Athens skulked into defeat and steady decline, however, many of its citizenry found Hedonism—and Epicurus's refinement of it, Epicureanism—quite to their liking. Among the Cyrenaics who introduced new concepts into Aristippus's earlier philosophy was Theodorus, who did not accept categorically that pleasure is good and pain is bad. He looked to wisdom as the true source of happiness and contentment, but not as a means of procuring pleasures.

Hegesias was essentially similar to Theodorus in his view that wisdom could not procure pleasure, but he recommended the avoidance of pain as a step toward achieving happiness. He advised people to regard dispassionately such dichotomies as wealth and poverty, slavery and freedom, life and death.

Anniceris reinstituted some of the earlier teachings of Aristippus into his version of the older Hedonist philosophy and was a closer advocate of the founder of the movement than were Theodorus and Hegesias. Ultimately, Epicurus adopted many of the ethical views of the Hedonists into Epicureanism.

—*R. Baird Shuman*

FURTHER READING

Durant, Will. *The Story of Philosophy.* New York: Simon & Schuster, 1967. In this reader-friendly history of philosophy, Durant demonstrates the relationships between Aristippus's Hedonism and that of his later followers.

Fuller, B. A. G. *A History of Ancient and Medieval Philosophy.* Revised by Sterling M. McMurrin. New York: Henry Holt, 1955. This comprehensive history of ancient and medieval philosophy offers extensive treatment of Aristippus. The presentation is clear and easily understandable to the general reader.

Hamlyn, D. W. *A History of Western Philosophy.* New York: Viking, 1987. Hamlyn deals briefly with the Cyrenaic school of philosophy and with Aristippus's founding of that school, placing it in its context within the prevalent Sophist philosophy of fifth century Athens.

Kenny, Anthony, ed. *The Oxford History of Western Philosophy.* New York: Oxford University Press, 1994. Although the presentation on Aristippus is brief, it covers the high points of his philosophy well and accurately. Places Aristippus's philosophy in sharp contrast to the philosophical outlooks that prevailed in Athens during his lifetime.

Renault, Mary. *The Last of the Wine.* New York: Random House, 1975. Renault captures better than any contemporary writer the essence of Sophism and the atmosphere of ancient Greece.

SEE ALSO: Antisthenes; Epicurus; Socrates.
RELATED ARTICLES in *Great Events from History: The Ancient World*: c. 450-c. 425 B.C.E., History Develops as a Scholarly Discipline; c. 440 B.C.E., Sophists Train the Greeks in Rhetoric and Politics; 399 B.C.E., Death of Socrates; c. 350 B.C.E., Diogenes Popularizes Cynicism.

ARISTOPHANES
Greek playwright

The highly entertaining plays of Aristophanes provide the only extant examples of Old Comedy. His writings reveal much about not only dramaturgy in late fifth century B.C.E. Athens but also the social, political, and economic conditions of the time.

BORN: c. 450 B.C.E.; Athens, Greece
DIED: c. 385 B.C.E.; Athens, Greece
AREA OF ACHIEVEMENT: Literature

EARLY LIFE

The son of Philippos, who may have been a landowner in Aegina, Greece, Aristophanes (ar-uh-STAHF-uh-neez) was born in Athens about 450 B.C.E. Though little is known about his early life, he was clearly well educated, for his plays quote or allude to many sources. These works also suggest a deep interest in public affairs, and Aristophanes was to serve as representative of his district on the Athenian Council.

His literary ability became apparent quite early: When he was between seventeen and twenty-three years old, he began participating in the annual dramatic competitions in Athens. The Lenaian Dionysia, or Lenaia, held in Gamelion (January-February), was devoted largely to comedies, whereas the Great, or City, Dionysia, established in 536 B.C.E. and celebrated in Elaphebalion (March), presented tragedies but also offered three comic plays. Both festivals were religious as well as literary, honoring Dionysus, the god of wine, who was associated with agriculture in general.

The comedies derived both their name and purpose from the ancient *komos*, or procession of rejoicing in the vital forces of nature, which supposedly drove away evil spirits and guaranteed continued fertility of the land and its inhabitants. Bawdy jokes and costumes that include large phalluses constituted part of the ritual, as did the *gamos*, or sexual union, that frequently concluded the plays. Similarly, the mockery of prominent political or cultural figures served as a liberating force that temporarily gave free rein to irrational and suppressed urges; such antics were connected with the madness of intoxication. To these satiric and sexual elements, Aristophanes added a lyricism rivaling that of any other Hellenic poet. An excellent example appears in the parabasis (choral interlude) of *Ornithes* (c. 414; *The Birds*, 1824), which begins with a summoning of the nightingale:

Musician of the Birds
Come and sing
honey-throated one!
Come, O love,
flutist of the Spring,
accompany our song.

The Chorus then presents a myth of the creation of the world through the power of Love, all told in lyrical anapests.

Only a fragment survives of Aristophanes' first play, *Daitaleis* (banqueters), which won second prize at the Lenaia of 427, yet the remains suggest that the dramatist already was treating an issue that would become important in his more mature writing. Though still a young man, he attacked Athenian youth and their new ways, especially modern modes of education. An old man sends one son to the city, while the other remains in the country. The former learns only to eat, drink, and sing bawdy songs; his body is no better trained than his mind. When he returns home, he is too weak to work and no longer cares whether he does.

Babylōnioi (Babylonians), another lost play, was produced at the Great Dionysia of 426 and won first prize. Cleon, the Athenian demagogue then in power, had undertaken a policy of mass terror to force Athens's allies to support its military efforts against Sparta in the Peloponnesian War. As a believer in peace and pan-Hellenism, Aristophanes attacked Cleon's measures. Cleon responded by taking Aristophanes to court. Despite the playwright's claim in his next comedy that during the proceedings he almost "gave up the ghost," he does not seem to have been punished severely, if at all. As is evident from his next plays, he was undeterred from speaking out against war and against Cleon.

LIFE'S WORK

Acharnēs (*The Acharnians*, 1812), which in 425 won first prize at the Lenaia, continues to attack Cleon's war policy. When the demigod Amphitheus raises the question of peace in the Athenian assembly, he is ejected. Dikaiopolis (which means "Honest Citizen" or "Just City"), a refugee farmer whose land has been ravaged by war, supports this pacific plea and sends Amphitheus to Sparta to negotiate a separate peace for himself. When the demigod returns with a thirty-year treaty, the Acharnians attack him. These old men, represented by the Chorus, have suffered in the war, but they want revenge, not peace. Dikaiopolis must defend his views while he rests his head on a chopping block, so that if he fails to persuade the Chorus that his policy is best, they can kill him at once. His speech divides the old men, who resolve to summon Lamachos, a general, to argue the matter further. The agon, or debate, ensues, allowing Aristophanes to present further arguments against the war. The Chorus finally sides with Dikaiopolis, but Lamachos leaves, vowing eternal resistance.

The farmer now sets up a market. While the play shows him prospering through peace, it also reveals the hardships of war. For example, a Megarian has become so impoverished that he is willing to sell his daughters for a pittance. The final scenes highlight the contrast between the policies of Cleon and Aristophanes: Lamachos returns from war, wounded, just as Dikaiopolis, victorious in a drinking bout, appears with two young women to celebrate wine and fertility, the gifts of Dionysus and peace.

In *Hippēs* (424; *The Knights*, 1812), which took first prize at the Lenaia, Aristophanes again attacks Cleon. A lost play, *Holkades*, presented at the next Lenaia, is still another attack on Cleon. Then, at the Great Dionysia, Aristophanes turned his attention to a different subject in *Nephelai* (423; *The Clouds*, 1708). Strepsiades (Twisterson) has fallen deeply in debt because of the extravagance of his wife and the gambling of his horse-loving son, Pheidippides. To cheat his creditors, Strepsiades resolves to send the youth to the Phrontisterion (Thinkery), the local academy run by Socrates, who can make the weaker side appear the stronger. When Pheidippides refuses to attend, his father enrolls instead. Despite his best efforts, the father cannot grasp the new learning, and at length his son agrees to enter the academy.

Now Pheidippides must choose a mentor; Dikaios Logos (Just Cause) and Adikos Logos (Unjust Cause) offer themselves, and to help Pheidippides choose they engage in a debate, or agon. Dikaios Logos speaks for the old morality and simple life, but when Adikos Logos advocates skepticism and amorality, even Dikaios Logos is converted. Pheidippides becomes certified as an adept at the new philosophy and even teaches his father enough to allow Strepsiades to outwit two of his creditors.

The old man's triumph is, however, short-lived. When Strepsiades reproves his son for singing an obscene song by Euripides, Pheidippides beats him. The father appeals to the Clouds, those symbols of obscurity and form without substance that are the deities and patrons of Socrates' school. They, however, side with the son, who has used his new skill to argue that, because Strepsiades, when he

was stronger, would beat Pheidippides, Pheidippides may now beat his father. Enraged, Strepsiades heeds the advice of Hermes and burns down the Phrontisterion.

In 399, *The Clouds* was used as evidence against Socrates, yet Aristophanes' attitude toward the philosopher may be more sympathetic than the play suggests. During its performance, Socrates is supposed to have stood up in the stadium to point out how closely the actor's mask resembled him, and Plato later included Aristophanes in the *Symposium*, where he is treated kindly. Perhaps, in fact, Socrates was among the few who actually enjoyed the piece, for it received only the third prize at the festival. Aristophanes blamed its failure on its being too intellectual for the masses.

Sphēkes (*The Wasps*, 1812), which won second prize at the Lenaia of 422, returns to political issues, as Aristophanes once more criticizes Cleon as well as the litigious nature of the Athenians. In the autumn of 422, Cleon died, and ten days after the Great Dionysia of 421 Athens concluded a peace treaty with Sparta. Aristoph-

Aristophanes. (Library of Congress)

anes' *Eirēnē* (*Peace*, 1837), which won second prize that year, celebrates the end of the fighting, as Trygaios rides to heaven on a giant dung-beetle to rescue Eirēnē from the clutches of Polemos (War). He also saves Opora (Harvest) and Theoria (Ceremony), the private and public benefits of peace. The former becomes his wife; the latter he gives to the Athenian Council. As the play ends, Trygaios regains his youth and is guaranteed perpetual fertility through his union with the goddess.

None of Aristophanes' plays from the next several years has survived, though he apparently returned to the theme of regeneration in *Geras* (c. 421) and *Amphiaraus* (c. 414). His next extant piece, *The Birds*, dates from the Great Dionysia of 414, at which it won second prize. Pisthetairos (Trusty) and Euelpides (Son of Good Hope) have tired of the corruption, fast-paced life, and litigious habits of their fellow Athenians and so resolve to find a pastoral retreat among the birds. Aristophanes demonstrates that though one can leave Athens, one cannot suppress the Athenian *polupragmosunē*, that energy, daring, curiosity, restlessness, and desire for ever-expanding empire.

Instead of basking in rural retirement, Pisthetairos and Euelpides create Nephelokokkugia (Cloudcuckooland), which chooses Athena as its patroness, builds a wall like that surrounding the Acropolis, and undertakes a blockade to keep the smoke of burnt offerings from reaching the gods. In short, these refugees from Athens create a city very much like the one they have fled, except that they are now rulers instead of subjects. Nephelokokkugia does differ from its earthly counterpart in some respects, though, for Pisthetairos expels informers, oracle-mongers, and lawyers, while he treats poets well. In other words, he eliminates those elements whom Aristophanes regarded as preying on their fellow Athenians. In the final scenes, the blockade of the gods succeeds: The Olympians surrender to the birds, Pisthetairos becomes a deity, and he marries the divine Basileia.

The success of the blockade marks another difference between Nephelokokkugia and Athens. As spectators watched *The Birds*, the Athenian fleet was sailing toward disaster in Sicily. In 413, the Peloponnesian War resumed, and, as a result, so did Aristophanes' criticism of the fighting. In the Lenaia of 411, he offered his solution to end the conflict. Women in Athens were virtually powerless, but in *Lysistratē* (English translation, 1837), they become the architects of peace by refusing to sleep with their husbands until the fighting ends. In a display of pan-Hellenism, they also recruit women from all of Greece to join the sexual embargo.

The results of this effort are soon apparent in the enlarged phalluses of the husbands. Naturally, this tumidity is comical, and the large phallus is ritualistic as well. In another sense, though, it represents all the thwarted desires of Greece: the yearning for peace, prosperity, normalcy. It also links Spartan and Athenian by showing their common humanity, a point Aristophanes emphasizes further by showing that Greeks have cooperated before and can again. The Dionysian power of sex achieves peace between the warring parties as the play ends in a reconciliatory gamos.

Thesmophoriazousai (411; *Thesmophoriazusae*, 1837) dates from about the same time as *Lysistrata* and was performed either at the Great Dionysia of 411 or during the Lenaia of the following year. The piece has little political significance; instead, it satirizes several tragedies by Euripides, who had already been a comic target of Aristophanes in several of his earlier pieces. Yet, as *The Clouds* does not imply that the dramatist disliked Socrates, so *Thesmophoriazusae* should not be read as a true condemnation of Euripides.

In fact, *Batrachoi* (405; *The Frogs*, 1780), Aristophanes' next surviving comedy and the last surviving work of Old Comedy, suggests that Aristophanes admired his fellow playwright. As the piece opens, Dionysus is preparing to go to Hades to resurrect Euripides, who had died in 406 (as had Sophocles). The god arrives just in time to judge a debate between Aeschylus and Euripides, each of whom claims to be the better writer. The succeeding agon reveals Aristophanes' keen critical sense. Euripides points out that he used common language so that the audience would understand him; Aeschylus replies that his own language is dignified and elevated to encourage spectators to aspire to lofty ideals. Euripides explains that his characters are drawn from real life; Aeschylus maintains that heroic figures are more appropriate for tragedy because ordinary people cannot serve as good examples.

Although Dionysus admires both writers, he finally decides to resurrect Aeschylus, for the older dramatist represents the values Aristophanes himself admired. Aeschylus had fought in the Battle of Marathon (490) and revered the customs and gods of Athens, whereas Euripides was modern and skeptical, embracing values Aristophanes had repeatedly attacked.

Thirteen years separate *The Frogs* and Aristophanes' next play, *Ekklesiazousai* (c. 392; *Ecclesiazusae*, 1837). As in *Lysistrata*, women here seize control of events to create a utopian society. Peace is no longer an issue, because in 404 Sparta defeated Athens and tore down the vanquished city's walls. The new philosophy is no concern, either; in 399, Socrates had been executed. Although Athens was beginning to recover from a decade of economic, political, and social turmoil—in 395, it rebuilt its walls, for example—the play reflects a new mood and new conditions. Both here and in *Ploutos* (388; *Plutus*, 1651) the role of the chorus is greatly diminished, perhaps because the city could not afford to pay for one. Gone, too, is the sharp personal satire, as is criticism of contemporary events. Instead, the plays are escapist fantasies, one promising a communistic paradise, the other a society in which all receive their just deserts.

Aristophanes died shortly after the performance of *Plutus* but left two plays that his son Araros produced. *Aiolosikōn* was presumably a parody of one of Euripides' plays that is not extant, and *Kōkalos* seems to be based on the myth of a Sicilian king, who is the hero of one of Sophocles' lost plays. *Kōkalos*, which, like *Aiolosikōn*, was produced about 385, introduces a love story involving Daedalus and one of the king's daughters, and it presents a recognition scene of some sort; both features were to become standard in New Comedy.

SIGNIFICANCE

Aristophanes, the advocate of the old order, helped to create a new kind of play. Crafty servants such as Cario in *Plutus*, lovers thwarted by their elders such as those in *Ecclesiazusae*, intrigue, disguise, and recognition scenes such as the ones believed to be in *Kōkalos* became hallmarks of New Comedy. By the first century C.E., Plutarch in his *Ethika* (after c. 100; *Moralia*, 1603) would condemn the coarseness of Old Comedy, characterizing Aristophanes' plays as resembling "a harlot who has passed her prime."

Aristophanes' plays remain historically important. Not only do they provide the only surviving record of the form and content of Old Comedy, but also they reveal much about daily life in late fifth century Athens. "Great, charming, and eloquent," Quintilian called Aristophanes' works, and the 150 extant manuscripts of *Plutus* alone attest his enduring popularity in antiquity. Modern productions, unencumbered by prudery, have demonstrated the vitality and beauty of his comedies, which, though written for a particular time and place, continue to speak to people everywhere.

—*Joseph Rosenblum*

FURTHER READING

Croiset, Maurice. *Aristophanes and the Political Parties at Athens*. Translated by James Loeb. 1909. Reprint. New York: Arno Press, 1973. Focuses on the political implications of Aristophanes' plays. He offers a good discussion of the military, political, social, and economic milieu of Aristophanes' Athens.

David, Ephraim. *Aristophanes and Athenian Society of the Early Fourth Century B.C.* Leiden, Netherlands: Brill, 1984. Seeks to fill a gap in studies of Aristophanes, which concentrate on his contributions to Old Comedy and his comments on Athens during the Peloponnesian War.

Murray, Gilbert. *Aristophanes: A Study.* Reprint. New York: Russell & Russell, 1964. Concentrates on analyzing the plays and their revelation of Aristophanes' attitudes. Also gives useful information about dramatic conventions and historical events that influenced the plays.

Reckford, Kenneth J. *Aristophanes' Old-and-New Comedy: Six Essays in Perspective.* Chapel Hill: University of North Carolina Press, 1987. Examines Aristophanes and his world from six perspectives: religious, psychological, theatrical, poetic, political, and literary-historical.

Spatz, Lois. *Aristophanes.* Boston: Twayne, 1978. After an introductory chapter on the nature of Old Comedy, Spatz presents a roughly chronological discussion of Aristophanes' contributions to this genre, focusing especially on the lesser-known works. Includes bibliography.

Strauss, Leo. *Socrates and Aristophanes.* Reprint. Chicago: University of Chicago Press, 1996. Discusses the confrontation between Socrates and Aristophanes in Aristophanes' comedies. Analyzing eleven plays, Strauss argues that this confrontation is basically one between philosophy and poetry.

Ussher, Robert Glenn. *Aristophanes.* New York: Oxford University Press, 1979. Offers an excellent brief introduction to the poet and his plays. Includes a chronology of the surviving comedies and discusses them in terms of structure, theme, character, language, staging, and performance. Includes bibliography.

SEE ALSO: Aeschylus; Euripides; Menander (dramatist); Socrates; Sophocles.

RELATED ARTICLES in *Great Events from History: The Ancient World*: 480-479 B.C.E., Persian Invasion of Greece; c. 456/455 B.C.E., Greek Tragedian Aeschylus Dies; May, 431-September, 404 B.C.E., Peloponnesian War; 406 B.C.E., Greek Dramatist Euripides Dies; 399 B.C.E., Death of Socrates; c. 385 B.C.E., Greek Playwright Aristophanes Dies.

ARISTOTLE
Greek philosopher

Building on Plato's dialogical approach, Aristotle developed what is known as the scientific method. In addition, he founded the Lyceum, which housed the first research library.

BORN: 384 B.C.E.; Stagirus, Chalcidice, Greece
DIED: 322 B.C.E.; Chalcis, Euboea, Greece
AREAS OF ACHIEVEMENT: Philosophy, natural history, science

EARLY LIFE

Aristotle (ar-uhs-TAHT-uhl) was born in the town of Stagirus, located on the northeast coast of the Chalcidice Peninsula in Greece, most likely in 384 B.C.E. His father, Nicomachus, was a physician and a member of the clan, or guild, of the Asclepiadae, as had been his ancestors. The family probably had migrated from Messenia in the eighth or seventh century B.C.E. Aristotle's mother was from Chalcis, the place where he sought refuge during the last year of his life. Both his parents died while Aristotle was very young.

Aristotle was adopted and raised by Proxenus, court physician to Amyntas II of Macedonia (an occasional source suggests that Nicomachus also held this position, but others disagree). It is likely, therefore, that young Aristotle lived part of his youth at Pella, the royal seat. He may even have learned and practiced surgery during this time.

Aristotle's early environmental influences helped determine his outlook: his detached, objective way of looking at a subject, his interest in biological science, and his universality. In his early life, Aristotle was surrounded by physicians and princes, not philosophers. When he was eighteen, he was sent to Athens for training in the best school available, Plato's Academy, where he would spend the next twenty years. Thus ended the first of the four phases of Aristotle's life.

LIFE'S WORK

Aristotle's career divides itself naturally into three periods: the twenty (some say nineteen) years at Plato's Academy, from 368 to 348; the thirteen years of travel, from 348 to 335; and the return to Athens, or the years in the Lyceum, from 335 to 323.

When young Aristotle arrived at the Academy, Plato was away on a second journey to Syracuse. When the master returned the following year, however, Aristotle became his prize student and ardent friend. Although

most of Aristotle's earlier works have been preserved only in fragments, usually in quotations within works by later scholars of the Peripatetic School, several are attributed to this period and the one that followed.

As Plato's method was dialogue, Aristotle, like other students at the Academy, began writing in dialogue. Aristotle was influenced by Plato about the time the master altered his own form, moving toward dialogues other than those with Socrates as questioner and main speaker. Aristotle, in turn, made himself the main speaker in his own dialogues.

Some scholars consider *De anima* the best of Aristotle's works from this period. Translated as *On the Soul*, this work treats the soul and immortality, and it is imitative of Plato's *Phaedōn*, which was written c. 388-366 B.C.E. (Critic Werner Jaeger believes that each of Aristotle's early dialogues was influenced by a particular Platonic dialogue, that the student was still dependent on the master as far as metaphysics was concerned but independent in the areas of methodology and logic.) Aristotle's *Protrepticus* (*Protreptics*) is named for a term designating a letter written in defense of philosophy; the method employed in this work (questions and answers by teacher and student) is from Plato, but the protreptic form is borrowed from the philosopher Isocrates, who was also at Athens during this time. In the year 348 (or 347), two events influenced Aristotle's future: the death of Plato (and possibly the choice of a new leader of the Academy), which caused Aristotle to leave Athens, and Philip II's destruction of Stagirus, which caused the philosopher to look elsewhere for a new home.

With a fellow Academic, Xenocrates, Aristotle left Athens for Mysia (modern Turkey), accepting the invitation of Hermeias, a former fellow student at the Academy who had risen from slavery to become ruler of Atarneus and Assos. Aristotle presided over his host's small Platonic circle, making of it a school modeled after the Academy. He married Pythias, niece and adopted daughter of Hermeias, after the ruler's death; they had a daughter, also named Pythias. His wife lived until late in Aristotle's so-called second Athenian period. After three years came another move, this time to Mytilene, on the nearby island of Lesbos; it is possible that Theophrastus found him a suitable place of residence there. Having begun research in marine biology at Assos, Aristotle continued this work at Mytilene. During these years, he probably wrote *De philosophia* (*On Philosophy*), *Ethica*

Eudemia (*Eudemian Ethics*), and early portions of *Physica* (*Physics*), *Metaphysica* (*Metaphysics*), and *Politica* (*Politics*).

In 343, Aristotle accepted Philip's invitation to move to Pella and become tutor to his thirteen-year-old, Alexander (the Great). The tutoring lasted until Alexander became regent in 340. It is uncertain whether Aristotle remained in Pella or moved to Stagirus, which had been rebuilt by Philip in honor of Aristotle. With the assassination of Philip in 335 and the resultant accession of Alexander, Aristotle returned to Athens.

This time Aristotle's purpose was not to attend the Academy but to found its greatest competitor. The Lyceum was situated on rented property just outside the city, as an outsider could not own Athenian land. In addition to the marine specimens Aristotle had collected, the school housed many more. It is said that Alexander became his old teacher's benefactor, donating eight hun-

dred talents and instructing all under his command throughout the world to preserve for Aristotle any unusual biological specimens. The site was probably to the northeast of the city, where lay a grave sacred to Apollo Lyceius and the Muses, a place where Socrates had enjoyed walking.

In addition to specimens, the Lyceum housed hundreds of manuscripts and numerous maps. The objects in the museum were used to illustrate Aristotle's lectures and discussions. In the mornings, he utilized the peripatetic (walking) method by strolling through the trees, discussing with more advanced students difficult (esoteric) subjects; in the evenings, he would lecture to larger groups on popular (exoteric) subjects. Logic, physics, and metaphysics were discussed; lectures included rhetoric, Sophism, and politics. In turn, Aristotle seems to have prepared and made available two types of notes: preliminary ones, from which he lectured, and more polished treatises, based on the discussions. Many of these have survived as his later, published works. They are in the form of treatises rather than dialogues.

In his later years at Athens, Aristotle is described as well-dressed, enjoying the easy life of self-indulgence; he was bald and thin-legged, with small eyes; he spoke with a lisp and had a mocking disposition and a ready wit. After the death of his wife, he lived with a mistress, Herpyllis, in a permanent but nonlegal relationship. Together, they had a son, whom Aristotle named Nicomachus, after his father. With the death of Alexander and the rise of feelings in Athens against Macedonians, especially those who had been close to Alexander, Aristotle left Athens for his mother's birthplace of Chalcis, where he died a year later of a disease that had afflicted him for some time.

SIGNIFICANCE

Aristotle developed through the earliest stage for about seventeen or eighteen years, moving in circles with doctors and princes. He then spent the next twenty years at the Academy with Plato, both imitating and growing away from his great master. Aristotle learned the method of dialogue while he moved toward his own method; he respected and loved Plato but questioned some Platonic thought, such as the theory of forms (dualistic being).

Aristotle. (Library of Congress)

During the next thirteen or fourteen years in Asia Minor, he established a smaller academy and did biological research, continuing the writing of dialogues as he had done at Athens but developing his own method of writing treatises. For three years he was tutor to Alexander, becoming lifelong friends with the future conqueror and ruler of the Mediterranean world but failing to impart his own political views to his student.

When Aristotle returned to Athens to found and preside over the Lyceum, he perfected his scientific method of examining specimens and establishing logical systems of substantiation before arriving at tentative conclusions, a method that has continued to modern times. Through his teaching, he influenced a few advanced students and the large public groups who heard his lectures. Through the Peripatetic school, his work continued for centuries, and many of his writings were preserved to influence even later centuries. He learned from and used the thought of Greek philosophers from Thales to Plato, extending their ideas and synthesizing them. He perfected the method of Socrates (who had intended such an extension himself) by reaching conclusions rather than probing endlessly. Plato and Aristotle have been more influential than all other Western philosophers, advancing Greek philosophy to its greatest height.

—*George W. Van Devender*

FURTHER READING

Ackrill, J. L. *Essays on Plato and Aristotle.* New York: Oxford University Press, 1997. This work contains important and insightful reflections on two of the most influential thinkers in Western philosophy.

Adler, Mortimer J. *Aristotle for Everybody: Difficult Thought Made Easy.* New York: Scribner's, 1997. A reliable interpreter provides an account that introduces Aristotle's thought in accessible fashion.

Bar On, Bat-Ami, ed. *Engendering Origins: Critical Feminist Readings in Plato and Aristotle.* Albany: State University of New York Press, 1994. Feminist perspectives are brought to bear on Aristotle's philosophy in significant ways.

Barnes, Jonathan. *Aristotle.* New York: Oxford University Press, 1982. A reliable study designed for readers who want an introduction to Aristotle's thought.

_____, ed. *The Cambridge Companion to Aristotle.* New York: Cambridge University Press, 1995. An excellent guide to Aristotle's thought, which features significant essays on major aspects of his work.

Edel, Abraham. *Aristotle and His Philosophy.* New Brunswick, N.J.: Transaction Books, 1996. A careful and helpful study by a veteran interpreter of Western thought.

Ferguson, John. *Aristotle.* Boston: Twayne, 1972. Assisting the general reader in the study of Aristotle's works, this book discusses Aristotle's life and his views about nature and psychology and also offers perspectives on Aristotle's lasting influence.

Lear, Jonathan. *Aristotle and Logical Theory.* New York: Cambridge University Press, 1980. A detailed study of Aristotle's views on logic and their continuing significance for understanding human reasoning.

McLeisch, Kenneth. *Aristotle.* New York: Routledge, 1999. An excellent biographical introduction to the thoughts of the philosopher, clearly presented and requiring no special background. Includes bibliography.

Robinson, Timothy A. *Aristotle in Outline.* Indianapolis, Ind.: Hackett, 1995. Accessible to beginning students, this clearly written survey covers Aristotle's full range of thought.

Rorty, Amélie Oksenberg, ed. *Essays on Aristotle's "Ethics."* Berkeley: University of California Press, 1981. An important collection of essays that concentrates on various facets of Aristotle's influential moral philosophy.

Strathern, Paul. *Aristotle in Ninety Minutes.* Chicago: Ivan Dee, 1996. A brief, easily accessible, introductory overview of Aristotle's philosophy.

SEE ALSO: Alexander the Great; Plato; Socrates; Thales of Miletus.

RELATED ARTICLES in *Great Events from History: The Ancient World*: c. 500-400 B.C.E., Greek Physicians Begin Scientific Practice of Medicine; 399 B.C.E., Death of Socrates; c. 380 B.C.E., Plato Develops His Theory of Ideas; 336 B.C.E., Alexander the Great Begins Expansion of Macedonia; c. 335-323 B.C.E., Aristotle Writes the *Politics*.

ARISTOXENUS
Greek philosopher and music theorist

The theoretical writings on music by Aristoxenus established a foundation on which modern music theory is based.

BORN: 375-360 B.C.E.; Tarentum (now Taranto, Italy)
DIED: Date unknown; probably Athens, Greece
AREAS OF ACHIEVEMENT: Music, philosophy

EARLY LIFE

Aristoxenus (ar-ihs-TAWK-see-nuhs), born in Tarentum, was a Greek philosopher and music theorist who flourished during the fourth century B.C.E. He received his earliest musical training at the hands of his father, Spintharus, who enjoyed some reputation as a musician. He later studied with Lamprus of Erythrae, of whom little is known. In time Aristoxenus moved to Athens, where he studied with the Pythagorean Xenophilus—important in view of the position he was to take in his theoretical treatises. He also studied at the Lyceum with Aristotle. Because Aristoxenus later competed, although unsuccessfully, with Theophrastus, a colleague, for headship of the Lyceum around 322, it may be assumed that Aristoxenus was a superior student and respected in scholarly circles.

LIFE'S WORK

Aristoxenus was apparently a prolific writer, with one source attributing more than 450 works to him, although only a few Aristoxenus fragments have survived. The writings, which cover a variety of topics, including works on music, biography, history, and philosophy, reflect the diversity of his studies. All the fragments are of interest, but the most important of the extant fragments pertain to music: Aristoxenus made his truly original contribution as he challenged the way that theorists, past and contemporary with him, had studied and written about music. So great was his influence that theorists and philosophers on music who followed him were compelled to address his arguments.

Numbering among the music fragments that survive are parts of three books titled *Harmonika stoicheia* (*The Harmonics*, 1902), the contents of which are believed to have been derived from Aristoxenus's earlier writings on the subject. Much of what is known about ancient Greek theory comes from his writings and those of later writers, such as Plutarch, Cleonides, and Aristides, who expounded on Aristoxenus's principles.

In addition to *The Harmonics*, there is a fragment on rhythm, consisting of approximately 250 lines, which was treated by Aristides several centuries later. While Aristoxenus's work reveals a man who could be rather pompous and contentious, his writings are clearly the product of a first-rate mind.

Aristoxenian theory was about melody and articulated a system that addressed the issues of pitch, intervals, genera, systems, modes, and modulation as they applied to melody. The smallest consonant interval recognized in his system was a perfect fourth, which also formed the fixed outer boundary of a four-note unit called a tetrachord. The tetrachord was a kind of building block, which, in combination with other tetrachords, formed larger structures. The tetrachord could belong to one of three types, or genera: diatonic, enharmonic, or chromatic. This system was determined according to the placement of the two inner notes that fell within the boundary of the fixed interval of the fourth, which was formed by the two outer notes of the tetrachord. The varied placements of the two inner notes of the tetrachord were known as shadings, or colors. Aristoxenus recognized two alternative positions of the inner notes in the diatonic genus and three in the chromatic, although he accepted that the variety of shadings was theoretically infinite.

The tetrachords could be combined, either sharing a common note and called conjunct, or, if a whole step separated the two tetrachords, called disjunct. The combining of the tetrachords produced three important larger theoretical structures known as the Greater Perfect System, the Lesser Perfect System, and the Immutable System.

The Greater Perfect System consisted of two pairs of conjunct tetrachords with an added note, or, in modern terminology, it can be seen in its diatonic form as a two-octave scale ranging from A to a′, as seen on the piano keyboard. The range most used for the writing of Greek melodies, however, appears to have been the octave e′ to e, and the Greater Perfect System was probably regarded as a central octave from e′ to e lying within the A to a′ range previously noted and with a conjunct tetrachord on each end and an added note on the bottom. The Greater Perfect System produced seven different species of the octave, because a different intervallic sequence would occur for the octave scale built on each of the seven different pitches represented in the system as it is brought within the central octave of e′ to e.

The Lesser Perfect System consisted of three conjunct tetrachords with an added note that, using the piano keyboard for purposes of illustration, had the range of A to d′. The Lesser Perfect System is believed to have assisted in the function of change, or modulation, from one species to another.

The Immutable System was a combination of the Lesser Perfect and Greater Perfect systems and could be performed at various pitch levels. Such a structure was called a *tonos*. Aristoxenus identified thirteen different *tonoi*. The term is not without ambiguity, and scholars are not exactly sure what the term meant to Aristoxenus. It is, however, generally believed that the octave species and the *tonos* were one and the same during the time of Aristoxenus.

Aristoxenus's approach to the theory of music, conceived around 320 B.C.E., was unique for his time. A superior student of Aristotelian logic who was familiar with the "new math," geometry, Aristoxenus turned both logic and geometry to his advantage as he defined the way subsequent theorists were to look at the discipline of music. His treatise was not simply an exercise in abstract logic. He elevated the musician's "ear" to a level equal with the intellect. By doing so, he recognized the value and importance of the commonsense judgment of the practicing musician.

Aristoxenus's writings clearly challenged both the teachings of Pythagoras, who flourished around 530 B.C.E. and whose reputation and writings were legendary by the time of Aristoxenus, and those of a group known as the Harmonists. The supporters of Pythagoras's theories about music were scientists and mathematicians who were not interested in explanations or observations about the interplay of musical elements or about the science of music itself. They believed that understanding numbers was central to understanding the universe, and, therefore, it was quite logical to express musical intervals, of key importance to the Pythagoreans, in terms of mathematical ratios.

The Harmonists, criticized by Aristoxenus for failing to establish a rigorous system, were interested in the practical and empirical aspects of music theory but fell short of articulating an acceptable system. They were preoccupied with the identification and measurement of microintervals, which emphasized the study of certain scales to the exclusion of others.

A key factor in Aristoxenus's approach was his description of sound as a continuum, or line, along which the pitch could come to rest at any point, permitting him the freedom to create intervals of varying sizes without regard to whether the interval could be expressed using rational numbers. While abstract mathematical expression of a musical interval had become most important to the Pythagoreans and the Harmonists, Aristoxenus focused instead on the development of a system that would afford him the freedom and flexibility to identify subtleties of scalar structure. He based his system on judgments made by the ear and then represented it through geometric application.

SIGNIFICANCE

Aristoxenus was the earliest writer on music theory known to address practical musical concerns. When he took the unique position that the ear, along with the intellect, should be used in the study of music, he established a precedent that ultimately altered the course of music theory. In effect, he redefined what music theory was, taking it out of the hands of the scientists and mathematicians and creating a new discipline that focused only on the interrelationship of musical elements. His arguments, which owed much to Aristotelian influence and methodology, enabled him to produce a clearly defined and organized system of music theory.

—*Michael Hernon*

FURTHER READING

Aristoxenus. *Aristoxenou harmonika stoicheia = The Harmonics of Aristoxenus*, edited by Henry Stewart Macran. New York: Olms, 1990. An English translation of Aristoxenus's main work; also contains some commentary and some biographical material.

Barker, Andrew. "Music and Perception: A Study in Aristoxenus." *Journal of Hellenic Studies* 98 (1978): 9-16. Examines Aristoxenus's approach to music theory through an attempt to clarify the exact role the ear plays in relation to the intellect and also with respect to mathematics.

Crocker, Richard. "Aristoxenus and Greek Mathematics." In *Aspects of Medieval and Renaissance Music*, edited by Jan LaRue. New York: Pendragon Press, 1978. An excellent article that discusses the key aspects of Aristoxenus's theories on music. Compares and explains Pythagorean arithmetic with Aristoxenus's use of geometric principles to illustrate and explain his new theories on music.

Henderson, Isobel. "Ancient Greek Music." In *Ancient and Oriental Music*, edited by Egon Wellesz. Vol. 1 in *The New Oxford History of Music*. 2d ed. New York: Oxford University Press, 1990. An excellent study of ancient Greek music, with considerable treatment of Aristoxenus. There is a brief discussion of the Harmonists and the Pythagoreans. The history, issues, and elements of Greek music are all discussed.

Lippman, Edward. *Musical Thought in Ancient Greece.* New York: Da Capo Press, 1975. It is not necessary to be a practicing musician or theorist to appreciate or understand this book. There is an excellent treatment of Greek ethics, philosophy, and aesthetics of music.

Rowell, Lewis. "Aristoxenus on Rhythm." *Journal of Music Theory* 23 (Spring, 1979): 63-79. Provides a translation of Aristoxenus's fragment on rhythm. Rowell identifies the fragment as being in an Aristotelian format and discusses Aristoxenus's concept of rhythm.

Winnington-Ingram, R. P. "Aristoxenus." In *New Grove Dictionary of Music and Musicians*, edited by Stanley Sadie. 2d ed. New York: Grove's Dictionaries, 2001. The article contains important biographical material. The author discusses the philosophical differences between Aristoxenus and the Pythagoreans. He also provides a summary of Aristoxenus's contribution to theory. Includes bibliography.

SEE ALSO: Aristotle; Pythagoras; Theophrastus.
RELATED ARTICLE in *Great Events from History: The Ancient World*: c. 500-400 B.C.E., Greek Physicians Begin Scientific Practice of Medicine.

ARMINIUS
Germanic military leader

Arminius's unification of various Germanic tribes prevented the Roman conquest and colonization of Germany.

BORN: c. 17 B.C.E.; place unknown
DIED: 19 C.E.; place unknown
ALSO KNOWN AS: Armin; Hermann the Cheruscan
AREA OF ACHIEVEMENT: War and conquest

EARLY LIFE

Not much is known about the early life of Arminius (ahr-MIHN-ee-uhs), including his precise year of birth, which was around 17 B.C.E. He was the son of the Germanic tribal chieftain Segimer, one of those Germanic leaders who favored cooperation with the Romans.

Arminius, or Hermann the Cheruscan, as the Germans refer to him, grew up in a time when the Roman Empire controlled much of the known world. The borders of the Empire stretched from Mesopotamia to Northern Africa, embracing the Balkans as well as present-day Spain, France, and England. Julius Caesar had just extended Roman control over Gaul (France) and England, both areas inhabited by Celtic people. The one major area in northern Europe that resisted Roman colonization was the land east of the Rhine and north of the Danube Rivers. It was inhabited by various tribes of a non-Celtic ethnic group the Romans called the Germans. These Germanic tribes had migrated from Scandinavia to central Europe. Information on these early Germanic peoples is scant. One of the few contemporary sources on the early Germans is a short pamphlet titled *De origine et situ Germanorum* (c. 98 C.E., also known as *Germania*; *The*

Description of Germanie, 1598) by Rome's leading historian, Cornelius Tacitus. *Germania* is the length of a present-day newspaper article. In it, Tacitus describes the Germans as a hardy warrior people. In cultural development they were at a stage between the nomadic and sedentary lifestyles and organized by tribes. They had no written language and worshiped the forces of nature.

The Roman Empire was unable to extend its control over the jungle-like territory of Germany with its fierce inhabitants. While the Rhine and Danube Rivers were natural frontiers between civilization and barbarism, Germanic tribes often raided Roman colonized territory, such as Gaul. In the hope of controlling these restless people on its frontier, Rome made an effort to train and romanize the sons of Germanic tribal chieftains. Thus, they invited several to come to Rome to receive military training. Arminius and his brother Flavus (their Roman names), sons of the Cherusci chieftain Segimer, were two of those chosen to go to Rome. Following military training, both brothers received Roman citizenship, were elevated to Roman nobility, and were given officers' commissions in the Roman army. It was the hope of Rome that these younger Germanic leaders could convince their countrymen of the superiority of Roman civilization and lifestyle over their own primitive ways. Eventually, it was hoped, the Germanic lands would become a Roman province.

LIFE'S WORK

It is in the foregoing historical context that Arminius's major contribution occurred. In 7 C.E. Arminius returned to Germany and was assigned to command Germanic mercenary troops attached to a Roman occupational army that started to extend control over Germanic peoples in the regions bordering the Roman Empire. General Publius Quinctilius Varus was leading these troops. The majority of the Germanic tribes, however, did not wish to come under Roman domination, yet they were too disunited to offer effective resistance to Roman encroachment. Arminius stopped this infighting, united the tribes, and planned an attack on the Roman troops under General Varus.

In the fall of 9 C.E., General Varus and his three Roman legions, after a campaign against Germanic tribes on the Weser River, returned to their winter quarters at Fort Aliso on the Lippe River. Arminius, whom Varus trusted, offered Germanic scouts to guide the Roman legions back to their fort. Arminius's familiarity with Roman military tactics enabled him to plan an ambush designed to annihilate these troops. His scouts led the Roman army through the Teutoburg Forest, a swampy and densely wooded region in an area now called Westphalia. In the terrain the legions had to break formation, their heavy baggage and cavalry were stuck in the swamps, and trees

further hampered maneuverability. It was there that Arminius and his Germanic warriors, using guerrilla tactics of fighting, killed about twenty thousand Romans in a bloody, three-day battle. On realizing his utter defeat, General Varus and many of his officers committed suicide on the battlefield by throwing themselves onto their swords. Caesar Augustus never reconstituted the three defeated elite legions XVII, XVIII, and XIX.

The Battle of Teutoburg Forest halted, for the time being, Roman efforts to conquer the Germanic tribes. Emperor Augustus's successor was Emperor Tiberius. He commissioned his nephew Gaius Julius Caesar Germanicus—so named because he fought the Germans—to undo the shame of the defeat of the Battle of Teutoburg Forest and to make a renewed attempt to conquer the Germanic tribes. Arminius again led the resistance. Germanicus's three successive campaigns in the years 14, 15, and 16 C.E., despite a few victorious battles, did not lead to Roman mastery over the Germanic peoples and their lands. Thereupon the Romans decided to give up the pursuit of colonizing Germany. Instead, the Romans built a fortified wall, called the Limes, to keep the Germanic tribes from raiding Roman territory.

Arminius consults the prophetess. (F. R. Niglutsch)

Arminius was unable to use his status as hero to unify the German tribes beyond military resistance against the Romans. Strife among the tribes was renewed, in the course of which Hermann was murdered by a relative.

SIGNIFICANCE

Without Arminius's leadership of the Germanic resistance, Germany probably would have been colonized, much like Gaul. Only from around 900 C.E. onward did a German nation and a German state emerge. Arminius became its first national hero. The memory of his defeat of the Roman military machine with barbarian warriors is used throughout German history to rouse its people to war against any encroacher on the nation.

Especially in the early 1800's, during the Napoleonic occupation of Germany, Arminius's battle of 9 C.E. is cited as the historic precedent in overthrowing foreign domination. The argument used by German nationalists was: "Since Roman times, Germans never were slaves of another." It was the ideological preparation for the disunited three hundred German autonomous states—some of midget size—to cooperate in the War of Liberation (1813). It ended French domination over the Germanies and ushered in Napoleon's downfall.

Nationalism in the nineteenth century burned especially fiercely among intellectuals in the German states and, unlike the patriotism of other peoples, had racial overtones. It culminated in the unification of Germany under the Prussian chancellor Otto von Bismarck in 1871. Arminius played a prominent role in the rise of German nationalism as many legends were woven into his biography to make him larger than life. As such, he was used and misused by all extreme German nationalists and racists, including the Nazis.

—*Herbert Luft*

FURTHER READING

Detwiler, Donald S. *Germany: A Short History*. 3d ed. Carbondale: Southern Illinois University Press, 1999. Provides the reader with context in German history.

Herwig, Holger H. *Hammer or Anvil?* Lexington, Mass.: D. C. Heath, 1994. Another work providing a helpful background in German history.

Kuehnemund, Richard. *Arminius: Or, The Rise of a National Symbol in Literature (from Hutten to Grabbe)*. New York: AMS Press, 1966. From the University of North Carolina studies in the Germanic languages and literature series. Includes bibliographical references.

Tacitus, Cornelius. *The Annals of Imperial Rome*. Translated with an introduction by Michael Grant. Rev. ed. New York: Penguin Books, 1996. Includes the fullest description available of Arminius's exploits. This translation includes maps, genealogy tables, bibliography, and index.

_____. *Germania*. Translated, with introduction and commentary, by J. B. Rives. New York: Oxford University Press, 1999. Tacitus's tract is helpful in describing Germanic tribal life in the first century C.E.

SEE ALSO: Augustus; Boudicca; Tacitus; Tiberius; Vercingetorix.

RELATED ARTICLES in *Great Events from History: The Ancient World*: 58-51 B.C.E., Caesar Conquers Gaul; 15 B.C.E.-15 C.E., Rhine-Danube Frontier Is Established; 1st-5th centuries C.E., Alani Gain Power; 9 C.E., Battle of Teutoburg Forest; 43-130 C.E., Roman Conquest of Britain; c. 50 C.E., Creation of the Roman Imperial Bureaucracy; 60 C.E., Boudicca Leads Revolt Against Roman Rule; c. 3d-4th century C.E., Huns Begin Migration West from Central Asia; 449 C.E., Saxon Settlement of Britain Begins.

ARRIA THE ELDER
Roman noblewoman

Arria the Elder exemplified wifely devotion in her support of her husband, who was executed for his participation in a plot to overthrow Emperor Claudius.

BORN: c. 1 C.E.; place unknown
DIED: 42 C.E.; place unknown
ALSO KNOWN AS: Arria Major
AREA OF ACHIEVEMENT: Government and politics

EARLY LIFE

Nothing is known about Arria (AHR-ree-uh) the Elder's parents or childhood. At some point, either because of the way she was raised or because of her marriage to Aulus Caecina Paetus, she adopted a way of life consistent with Stoic philosophy, a life of restraint and respect for the political institutions of Rome, especially the senate. What is known of her comes from the writings of the statesman Gaius Plinius Caecilius Secundus (better known as Pliny the Younger), the historian Cornelius Tacitus, and the most famous piece, an epigram by the poet Marcus Valerius Martialis (better known as Martial). Pliny the Younger states that the information he has about Arria the Elder came from her granddaughter Fannia, who presumably learned it from Arria the Younger, her mother and the daughter of Arria the Elder.

LIFE'S WORK

Arria the Elder's husband was a man who held office and achieved consular rank. Although little is known about his political career, more is known about Arria's personal devotion to her husband and her children. Pliny the Younger recounts a story that reveals her ability to maintain control in Stoic fashion and her determination to look to the best interests of others: When her husband and son fell ill, she nursed them both. When her son died, she concealed his death from her ill husband, afraid that grief would carry him away as well. To Paetus's questions about his son's health, she offered responses that left him comforted and then left his presence to express her pain and give voice to her own grief. She managed to arrange and conduct her son's funeral without arousing her husband's suspicion. By keeping her son's death a secret, she made sure her husband would recover. Pliny the Younger praises these actions: "Without the expectation of future recognition, without expectation of fame, what a greater act it was to hide her tears, to cover her grief and to act like a mother after her son had died." Pliny's com-

ments reveal a clear admiration for the self-control and the selfless devotion displayed by Arria.

More famous were her actions as a participant in an attempted military uprising against the new Emperor Claudius (r. 41-54 C.E.). Because the Roman senate appeared to have less and less authority, a number of men began to conspire to overthrow the emperor. Arria and her husband, therefore, traveled to Illyria (modern Albania) to support a revolt led by Lucius Arruntius Camillus Scribonianus. The two legions in Illyria under Scribonianus's command refused to march on Rome, however, and turned on the leaders of the conspiracy, killing Scribonianus and capturing Paetus. When the soldiers loaded the prisoners on a ship to take them to Rome for trial, Arria begged to be allowed to go, if only as a slave, to take care of her husband. The soldiers refused, so Arria followed the ship in a small boat that she hired to carry her to Rome. Once there, she went to the Imperial palace to be with her husband. In the palace, she met Vibia, the wife of Scribonianus, who had just offered testimony against the conspirators. When Vibia tried to approach her, Arria turned her back, declaring, "Shall I listen to you who are still alive after Scribonianus died in your embrace?" Although Arria was also reputed to be a friend of Valeria Messallina, the wife of the Emperor Claudius, there is no hint that she sought Messallina's help in her husband's defense or that this friendship interfered in her determination to support her husband in his fight against the emperor.

When it became clear that Paetus would be convicted and executed, Arria let it be known to her family that she would die with her husband. Her daughter's husband, Publius Clodius Thrasea Paetus, urged her to change her mind, asking if she would want her daughter to kill herself if he should likewise be convicted of a crime. Arria responded, "If she will have lived as long and as happily with you as I have with Paetus, I do wish it." In response, her family began watching her, hoping to prevent her from doing herself harm. Once she realized what they were doing, she declared that there was no way they could stop her; they could only make things worse. To prove her point, she began beating her head against the wall until she knocked herself unconscious. When she awoke, she told her family, "I had told you that I would find some harsh path to death if you would deny me the easy way." Soon afterward, Arria stood by her husband's side when the time came for them to die. When he seemed to hesitate, Arria seized the sword, plunged it into her own breast, drew the blade out and handed it to her husband. The poet Martial records the scene: "When chaste Arria handed to Paetus the sword she had drawn from her own breast, she said, 'If you believe me, the wound I made does not hurt, but the one you are going to make, that one, Paetus, hurts me.'"

SIGNIFICANCE

In the time of the Roman Empire, many men and women were condemned for real or imagined plots against the emperors. Among these, the stories of Arria the Elder and her daughter, Arria the Younger, gained the attention of historians, politicians, and poets for their devotion to their husbands and to the principles of Stoicism that shaped their political beliefs and actions. The stories of this mother and daughter demonstrate the roles that women played in establishing political and philosophical networks among aristocratic families during the early Roman Empire.

—*T. Davina McClain*

FURTHER READING

Lefkowitz, Mary R., and Maureen B. Fant. *Women's Life in Greece and Rome: A Source Book in Translation*. 2d ed. Baltimore: The Johns Hopkins University Press, 1992. This work offers some of the documentary evidence, namely the letters of Pliny the Younger. Includes bibliography and index.

Lightman, Marjorie, and Benjamin Lightman. *Biographical Dictionary of Ancient Greek and Roman Women*. New York: Checkmark Books, 2000. This work gives details on the lives of a vast number of Greek and Roman women, including Arria the Elder, Arria the Younger, and Fannia. Includes bibliography and index.

Suetonius. *The Lives of the Twelve Caesars*. Translated by Robert Graves. New York: Welcome Rain, 2001. Suetonius's accounts of the lives of Vespasian and Domitian include information about the times in which Arria the Elder and Arria the Younger lived.

Tacitus, Cornelius. *Complete Works of Tacitus*. Edited by Moses Hadas and translated by Alfred John Church and William Jackson Brodribb. New York: Random House, 1942. Tacitus's historical works cover the periods during which Arria the Elder and Arria the Younger lived.

Treggiari, Susan. *Roman Marriage: Iusti Coniuges from the Time of Cicero to the Time of Ulpian*. New York: Oxford University Press, 1991. Treggiari explores the nature of marriage and the partnership between men and women like Arria the Elder and Thrasea. Includes bibliography and index.

SEE ALSO: Antonia Minor; Arria the Younger; Boudicca; Claudius I; Cleopatra VII; Hatshepsut; Valeria Messallina; Nefertari; Nefertiti; Tiy.

RELATED ARTICLES in *Great Events from History: The Ancient World*: 509 B.C.E., Rape of Lucretia; c. 509 B.C.E., Roman Republic Replaces Monarchy; c. 300 B.C.E., Stoics Conceptualize Natural Law; 51-30 B.C.E., Cleopatra VII, Last of Ptolemies, Reigns; 27-23 B.C.E., Completion of the Augustan Settlement; c. 50 C.E., Creation of the Roman Imperial Bureaucracy.

ARRIA THE YOUNGER
Roman noblewoman

Arria the Younger's support of her husband, Thrasea, and her son-in-law, Helvidius, both of whom were condemned by Rome, was noted by Pliny the Younger as well as other historians, politicians, and poets.

BORN: c. 21-28 C.E.; Rome (now in Italy)
DIED: c. 97-106 C.E.; Rome
ALSO KNOWN AS: Arria Minor
AREA OF ACHIEVEMENT: Government and politics

EARLY LIFE

As the daughter of Arria the Elder and Aulus Caecina Paetus, Arria (AHR-ree-uh) the Younger was raised in a household that practiced Stoicism, a philosophy that in its ethical aspect argued that the most important thing was to strive for excellence (*virtus* in Latin) and in its personal application argued that rationalism should rule over emotionalism. No details are known of Arria the Younger's early life other than that she had a brother who died young and that sometime before 42 C.E., she married Publius Clodius Thrasea Paetus, a young man who shared the same devotion to Stoicism. What is known of her comes from the writings of the statesman Gaius Plinius Caecilius Secundus (better known as Pliny the Younger) and the historian Cornelius Tacitus. Pliny the Younger expresses his devotion to Fannia, Arria the Younger's daughter, as well as his admiration for Arria the Younger and Arria the Elder.

LIFE'S WORK

Arria the Younger saw her parents play out their Stoic beliefs in their fierce defense of what they believed was best for the Roman state (through the attempted coup of Emperor Claudius) and in her mother's determination that an honorable suicide was preferable to a dishonorable and destitute widowhood. Thrasea, Arria the Younger's husband, came to earn the disapproval of the Emperor Nero Claudius Caesar, better known as Nero (r. 54-68 C.E.). Thrasea had begun his career by working with the then-new emperor, even serving in 56 C.E. as a consul suffectus (an honorary office given to two men toward the end of a year, in contrast to the consul ordinarius, two of whom were appointed at the beginning of the year and therefore, in the Roman system, gave their names to the year).

When Nero began to force the senate into accepting his crimes, Thrasea held true to his beliefs. The historian Cornelius Tacitus states in *Ab excessu divi Augusti* (c. 116 C.E., also known as *Annales*; *Annals*, 1598) that in 59 C.E. Thrasea walked out of the senate rather than listen to a letter sent by Nero detailing why he had executed his mother, Agrippina the Younger. When Nero gave games, the Iuvenalia, to commemorate his first beard, Thrasea did not participate, even though Nero encouraged members of the upper class to perform. Thrasea did, however, sing in games at Patavium, his birthplace, thereby proving that his objection was not to performing but to honoring Nero. Because Thrasea had also alienated a certain Capito Cossutianus, Capito started proceedings against Thrasea for treason against the emperor. He was joined by Marcellus Epirus, who instigated the prosecution of others, including that of Helvidius Priscus, the son-in-law of Arria and Thrasea.

Although Thrasea refused to admit any guilt and sent a letter to Nero asking for the opportunity to defend himself, he was sentenced to death, and Helvidius was sentenced to exile as Thrasea's supporter. When Arria the Younger learned that her husband was to die, she resolved to follow the example of her mother and die with him, but Thrasea succeeded in persuading her to remain alive to provide support and comfort for their daughter Fannia. Thrasea then retired to a room with Helvidius and the philosopher Demetrius, where Thrasea opened his veins and died.

Arria then accompanied Fannia and Helvidius into exile, where they remained until the death of Nero in 68. They returned to Rome during the reign of the new emperor Galba (r. 68 C.E.), and Helvidius began proceedings against Marcellus Epirus for his false accusations but withdrew his case when it seemed he could not win in the

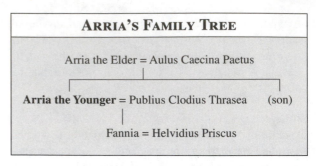

```
              ARRIA'S FAMILY TREE

        Arria the Elder = Aulus Caecina Paetus
                          |
   ┌──────────────────────┴──────────────────────┐
   Arria the Younger = Publius Clodius Thrasea      (son)
                          |
          Fannia = Helvidius Priscus
```

senate. He did, however, continue attempting to prosecute Epirus in other venues, until the new emperor Titus Flavius Vespasianus (r. 69-79 C.E.), better known as Vespasian, exiled him in 75. He was accompanied by Arria and Fannia. Helvidius was executed in exile sometime before 79.

After Vespasian's death in 79, Arria and Fannia again returned to Rome. While in the city, they again became involved in the political wrangling that had cost Arria her husband. In 93 the new emperor Titus Flavius Domitianus (Domitian, r. 81-96 C.E.) exiled all philosophers and those who sympathized with them. The strength of Arria's devotion to Stoicism and the continued admiration expressed for her husband, Thrasea, and her son-in-law Helvidius brought Arria and Fannia into the emperor's displeasure. Further, without Arria's knowledge, Fannia had provided materials to the writer Herennius Senecio to create a biography of Helvidius Priscus. Arria and Fannia again went into exile but only until Domitian's death in 96, when they returned to Rome for the last time.

Sometime before 93, Arria and Fannia developed a strong friendship with Pliny the Younger, who appears to have offered them his financial, legal, and emotional support both during their exile and after their final return to Rome. Pliny's praise for the two women conveys an admiration for their strength and a genuine affection for them. When Fannia became ill in 107, Pliny declared,

> That she is ill so pains and tortures me because I seem again to be losing her mother [Arria the Younger], that mother—I can say nothing more praiseworthy—of this so great a woman, a mother whom even as this woman gives and brings her back to us, so she will also take her away with her own death, something that will afflict me equally with a new and a reopened wound.

SIGNIFICANCE

Like that of her mother, Arria the Elder, the story of Arria the Younger captured the imagination of historians, politicians, and poets as well as of Pliny the Younger. Arria's support of her husband was matched by her devotion to her daughter's family. Arria's devotion to Stoicism remained strong even at a time when Emperor Domitian forced all philosophers and those who sympathized with them into exile. Her example illuminates the role that some women played in establishing political and philosophical networks among aristocratic families during the early Roman Empire.

—*T. Davina McClain*

FURTHER READING

Lefkowitz, Mary R., and Maureen B. Fant. *Women's Life in Greece and Rome: A Source Book in Translation.* 2d ed. Baltimore: The Johns Hopkins University Press, 1992. This work offers some of the documentary evidence of Arria the Younger's life, namely the letters of Pliny the Younger. Includes bibliography and index.

Lightman, Marjorie, and Benjamin Lightman. *Biographical Dictionary of Ancient Greek and Roman Women.* New York: Checkmark Books, 2000. This work gives details on the lives of a vast number of Greek and Roman women, including Arria the Elder, Arria the Younger, and Fannia. Includes bibliography and index.

Suetonius. *The Lives of the Twelve Caesars.* Translated by Robert Graves. New York: Welcome Rain, 2001.

Suetonius's accounts of the lives of Vespasian and Domitian include information about the times in which Arria the Elder and Arria the Younger lived.

Tacitus, Cornelius. *Complete Works of Tacitus.* Edited by Moses Hadas and translated by Alfred John Church and William Jackson Brodribb. New York: Random House, 1942. Tacitus's historical works cover the periods during which Arria the Elder and Arria the Younger lived.

Treggiari, Susan. *Roman Marriage: Iusti Coniuges from the Time of Cicero to the Time of Ulpian.* New York: Oxford University Press, 1991. Treggiari explores the nature of marriage and the partnership between men and women like Arria the Younger and Helvidius. Includes bibliography and index.

SEE ALSO: Agrippina the Younger; Antonia Minor; Arria the Elder; Claudius I; Cleopatra VII; Hatshepsut; Valeria Messallina; Nefertari; Nefertiti; Tiy.

RELATED ARTICLES in *Great Events from History: The Ancient World*: 509 B.C.E., Rape of Lucretia; c. 509 B.C.E., Roman Republic Replaces Monarchy; c. 300 B.C.E., Stoics Conceptualize Natural Law; 51-30 B.C.E., Cleopatra VII, Last of Ptolemies, Reigns; 27-23 B.C.E., Completion of the Augustan Settlement; c. 50 C.E., Creation of the Roman Imperial Bureaucracy.

ARSINOE II PHILADELPHUS
Hellenistic queen

A thrice-married queen, respectively of Thrace, Macedonia, and Egypt, Arsinoe was one of the first women in the ancient Mediterranean region to be deified within her lifetime.

BORN: c. 316 B.C.E.; Alexandria, Egypt
DIED: July, 270 B.C.E.; Alexandria, Egypt
ALSO KNOWN AS: Arsinoë II Philadelphus
AREA OF ACHIEVEMENT: Government and politics

EARLY LIFE

Arsinoe II Philadelphus (ar-SIH-no-ay fil-uh-DEHL-fuhs), the daughter of Ptolemy Soter and Berenice, was married about 300-299 B.C.E. by her father to one of Alexander the Great's generals, Lysimachus, who had become king of Thrace (r. 323-281), northern Asia Minor (r. 301-281), and Macedonia (r. 285-281). Because she cannot have been much younger than fifteen at the time of her first marriage, her birth may be dated around 316-

315. Nothing is known of her childhood before her wedding. It would seem a mistake to believe the ancient reports that the old king married Arsinoe out of love or that he separated from his Persian wife Amastris in order to marry Arsinoe. Lysimachus is not known to have married additional women in the remaining two decades of his life. With Arsinoe, the king had three sons born in a span of about five years: Ptolemy, Lysimachus, and Philip. He reportedly had more than ten children with other women.

LIFE'S WORK

When the Persian princess Amastris was murdered by her own sons (293-289? B.C.E.), Arsinoe was able to gain territory from Lysimachus in Pontus (later Anatolia) that had belonged to the princess, such as the cities Heraclea, Tius, and Amastris. It is said that in Heraclea, Arsinoe had one Heraclides of Cyme govern with a strong hand. Lysimachus later granted her other cities and founded or renamed cities in her honor. Ephesus was renamed Arsinoea after Lysimachus recaptured the city from Demetrius Poliorcetes in 289-288. In fact, coins from this period until the mid-third century B.C.E. seem to represent Arsinoe as the city goddess. If so, they represent some of the earliest coinage to depict a deified woman in the ancient world. Another city, Aetolian Conopa, was renamed in Arsinoe's honor. Although the Greek historian Strabo, writing more than two centuries later, appears to date the occasion to the time when Arsinoe was married to her brother Ptolemy II (as his second wife after his marriage with Arsinoe I), the city's proximity to Lysimachea has led some scholars to believe that the refoundation occurred during Lysimachus's lifetime, about 285-284. Inscriptions from Delos not only demonstrate political ties between Thrace and the island but also reveal the assimilation of Arsinoe with Agathe Tyche (the goddess of good fortune). Such public display of honor for a royal wife was exceptional for the times and gives clear indication of Arsinoe's position among the wives at the Thracian court.

As the latest of Lysimachus's wives, Arsinoe was understandably afraid that her children would be passed over in favor of Agathocles, who seemed to have been his father's preferred heir. Possibly her jealousy was fueled even more when her older half sister, Lysandra, was married to Agathocles in 294. Arsinoe's position was complicated further still around 285-284, when her husband Lysimachus and her father, Ptolemy I, wished to renew their ties and Lysimachus's daughter, also called Arsinoe (and known as Arinsoe I), was married to Ptolemy's son Ptolemy II Philadelphus (Arsinoe's full brother), the newly appointed Lagid heir.

Pausanias offers the rather dramatic detail that Arsinoe now contrived to seduce Agathocles in an effort to secure the positions of her own children. Pausanias maintains that Arsinoe's advances were unrequited. When she eventually conspired against Agathocles, her motive may simply have been to remove the threat to her own ambition. Proclaiming, one assumes, that he had tried to seduce her, she convinced Lysimachus to have Agathocles killed. Arsinoe II's eldest son, Ptolemy, who had most to gain from the death of his elder half brother, may very well have executed the murder. It is of interest that about the same time he erected a statue of his mother in the Greek city of Thebes, on behalf of his father. After the assassination of her husband, Lysandra immediately fled with her children and her full brothers Ptolemy and Meleager to the court of King Seleucus I Nicator in Syrian Antioch.

The Syrian king subsequently used Lysimachus's nefarious crime to further his own case against the Thracian king, whose territory in Asia Minor encroached on Seleucus's holdings. Lysimachus's allies abandoned him, subject cities might even have been revolting against him, and now Seleucus declared war on him. When their armies met at Corupedium in Lydia, the old general Lysimachus, seventy or eighty years of age, died in battle (281). Arsinoe had stayed behind in the city named after her, Arsinoea-Ephesus. When Lysimachus's troops defected and more cities came over to Seleucus, Arsinoe was no longer safe. The Greek scholar Polyaenus (second century C.E.) narrates the stratagem by which she managed to escape the Seleucid forces: She slipped out of the city to the shore dressed in rags, with her face besmeared, and while she sailed off to Macedonia, a maid dressed in royal robes was mistaken for Arsinoe and slain. Arsinoe secured herself in Cassandrea, where she gathered a mercenary army with her immense wealth.

In the meantime (late summer, 281), Arsinoe's half brother Ptolemy (not to be confused with her full brother or her eldest son)—who would receive the surname Ceraunus ("Thunderbolt") for his violent character—had stabbed Seleucus to death, allegedly to avenge the death of Lysimachus. He then appeared before the army and proclaimed himself king of Macedonia and Thrace. Soon he advanced to Cassandrea and, it is said, feigning to act out of love, Ptolemy Ceraunus offered to marry his half sister Arsinoe, to declare her queen of Macedonia and Thrace, and to adopt her children. The Roman historian Justin (third century C.E.) provides an epitome of Pompeius Trogus that gives a substantial, though dramatized, description of the ceremony in the presence of the assembled army. Arsinoe was proclaimed queen, and she invited Ptolemy Ceraunus into Cassandrea, where the celebration was continued with a banquet for the entire population.

The marriage with Lysimachus's widow could have provided Ceraunus the leverage to legitimize his claim to the Thracian throne. Nevertheless, his immediate concern was to deprive Arsinoe's children of their claim to the same throne. He ordered his troops to seize the city's citadel and to kill her sons, who fled to their mother. Arsinoe's eldest son, Ptolemy, mistrusting Ceraunus, had already fled to the Illyrian king, Monunius. According to Justin's sensationalist account, Arsinoe's younger sons, Lysimachus and Philip, were slaughtered on her lap.

Ceraunus was soon deprived of his kingdom when a Celtic army attacked Macedonia. He engaged the Celts in battle, but when the elephant on which he rode was

Arsinoe II Philadelphus (left). (F. R. Niglutsch)

wounded, he was captured and killed in early 279 B.C.E. The Celts carried his head affixed on a spear as they pillaged Macedonia—"as he had deserved," Justin added. Arsinoe's eldest son, Ptolemy, tried in vain to gain power during the period of anarchy in Macedonia. The kingdom would ultimately fall to the Antigonids in 277-276. Eventually, Ptolemy and his descendants would govern the Ptolemaic domain in Lycian Telmessus until 190 B.C.E.

Arsinoe had to flee in exile once more and found refuge on the island of Samothrace. In her honor a rotunda was built, the largest circular building of its time, known as the Arsinoeum. Here, "Queen Arsinoe, daughter of King Ptolemy, wife of King Lysimachus," set up an inscription, "as a vow to the Great Gods" of Samothrace. She left the island, in all likelihood still in 279, for her brother's palace at Alexandria. If her life at the Thracian court reads like a tragedy—seducing her stepson like Phaedra, witnessing the murder of her children like Clytemnestra—in Egypt her life would take on mythic proportions—marrying her brother like Hera, being worshiped as Aphrodite. At the royal court in Alexandria, Arsinoe's full brother Ptolemy II had been living with his wife, Arsinoe I, the daughter of Lysimachus, since their marriage in 285 or 283. This Arsinoe had borne the king three children, Ptolemy (who would eventually succeed his father), Lysimachus, and Berenice. Little else is known about Arsinoe I but that she was supposedly discovered in conspiracy and afterward banished to Koptos (now Qeft) in Upper Egypt. She evidently continued to live there in comfort and liberty, for a court official com-

memorated her with an honorary inscription. Perhaps Ptolemy II's first wife fell victim to his sister's ambition, but her exile did not involve a formal repudiation.

Soon Ptolemy and his full sister Arsinoe II married and celebrated their wedding with public pomp (commemorated by the poet Callimachus). One can only speculate who instigated this unprecedented violation of ancient customs. The date of the wedding is not known either but seems to have taken place before 274-273, when the Pithom stele refers to Arsinoe as queen, wife, and sister of Ptolemy II. Whether in mock or as flattery, their sibling marriage occasioned comparison to Zeus's union with his sister and spouse, Hera. Ancient authors believed Ptolemy and Arsinoe followed Egyptian traditions, but little evidence is found for full sibling marriage in Pharaonic times. As such close endogamy certainly breached Greco-Macedonian mores, it is all the more remarkable that Arsinoe received the cultic epitheton *Philadelphus* ("Who Loves Her Brother"), which also assimilated her with the Egyptian goddess Isis, sister and spouse of Osiris. Together, Arsinoe and Ptolemy were worshiped as the *Theoi Adelphoi* ("Sibling Gods") after 272-271. At Alexandria their cult was incorporated into that of the deified Alexander the Great. The office of the cult's eponymous priesthood (used in dating formulae), the highest of the country, was held by prominent individuals, such as army officers, court advisers, and members of the royal family.

Because of the unfortunate scarcity of sources for the last decade of her life, Arsinoe's political influence at the Ptolemaic court is difficult to assess—even if one may assume it, based on her character. According to the Pithom stele, Arsinoe accompanied the king during his campaign in 274-273 to defend the border of the Ptolemaic Empire against the Seleucid Antiochus I. As a poem by Theocritus reveals, she evidently promoted the cult of the fertility god Adonis with public festivals at the royal palace and elsewhere. In classical Athens this festival had been exclusively for women and had been derided by men, but Arsinoe raised its prestige with her patronage. The queen's care for Adonis also allowed for comparison with Aphrodite, Adonis's lover. Perhaps while he held office as priest of the Sibling Gods, admiral Callicrates established the cult of Arsinoe-Aphrodite Zephyritis-Cypris on Cape Zephyreum, east of Alexandria (commemorated in Hellenistic poetry). Additional evidence for her influence may be gleaned from an Attic decree that states that she supported preparations for the Chremonidean War (266-261). Probably for this reason, the Athenians erected statues of Arsinoe and Ptolemy in front of the Odeum.

After her death in July of 270, Arsinoe's popularity continued in many forms of posthumous veneration. Callimachus composed a poem on the apotheosis of Arsinoe. An individual eponymous priesthood, the *canephorus* ("basket-carrier") of Arsinoe Philadelphus, was added to the cult of Alexander the Great and the Sibling Gods by at least 268. Heavy silver and gold coins were issued for about 150 years, featuring her deified portrait on the obverse and a double horn of plenty on the reverse, with the legend "Of Arsinoe Philadelphus." As *synnaos theos* ("temple-sharing deity") she was the first of the Lagid Dynasty to be incorporated into the local worship of Greek and Egyptian deities throughout the country down to Nubia. A temple (Arsinoeum) and an annual religious festival (Arsinoea) were established in her honor at Alexandria. Shrines were erected for her throughout the country. In fact, she is the only queen for whom individual Egyptian priesthoods are recorded. A tax on vines and fruits (*apomoira*) was diverted to her cult in order to pay for its expenses. Districts, cities, city quarters, and streets were named after her, often denoting her divinity (in assimilation with goddesses such as Aphrodite, Demeter, and Isis). While the cults of most Ptolemaic kings and queens declined from the late second century B.C.E., worship of the deified Arsinoe survived even after the Roman conquest and into the common era.

SIGNIFICANCE

Like Olympias before and Cleopatra VII after her, Arsinoe Philadelphus was an ambitious queen, who gathered her own army and whose political influence strengthened the monarchies with which she was associated. She patronized art and public religion. Her full-sibling marriage set the precedent for many subsequent close-kin marriages among the Ptolemies. Her importance and popularity are reflected in the widespread public and private veneration she received during her lifetime and long after.

—*Branko F. van Oppen de Ruiter*

FURTHER READING

Burstein, Stanley M. "Arsinoe II Philadelphus: A Revisionist View." In *Philip II, Alexander the Great, and the Macedonian Heritage*, edited by W. L. Adams and E. N. Borza. Washington: University Press of America, 1982. Questions the influence of Arsinoe at the Ptolemaic court in the light of silence in reliable ancient historiography.

Longega, Gabriella. *Arsinoë II*. Rome: Bretschneider, 1968. Analyzes literary sources relevant for Arsinoe's life and influence. Includes index.

Macurdy, Grace H. *Hellenistic Queens: A Study of Woman-Power in Macedonia, Seleucid Syria, and Ptolemaic Egypt*. Baltimore: The Johns Hopkins University Press, 1932. Reprint. New York: AMS Press, 1977. First monograph devoted to the political significance of Macedonian queens and their successors. Includes bibliography and index.

Pomeroy, Sarah B. *Women in Hellenistic Egypt*. New York: Schocken Books, 1984. First study of social history of women in Hellenistic Egypt, with a chapter on the Ptolemaic queens—incidentally rebutting Burstein's revisionism by pointing out Egyptian sources that reveal Arsinoe's influence and popularity. Includes bibliography and index.

ARTEMISIA I
Ionian Greek queen (r. c. 480 B.C.E.)

Artemisia I was a brilliant military strategist and commander who advised Xerxes I during his campaigns in the Persian Wars.

BORN: Late sixth century B.C.E.; probably Halicarnassus, Caria, Asia Minor (now Bodrum, Turkey)
DIED: Probably mid-fifth century B.C.E.; place unknown
ALSO KNOWN AS: Artemisia of Halicarnassus
AREAS OF ACHIEVEMENT: War and conquest, government and politics

EARLY LIFE

Nearly all the information on Artemisia I of Halicarnassus (AR-teh-MEE-see-ah) comes from Herodotus, also of Halicarnassus, the historian who wrote about the Persian Wars in *Historiai Herodotou* (c. 424 B.C.E.; *The History*, 1709). Halicarnassus was one of the city-states under the Persian Empire that was culturally Greek. (In the eighth century B.C.E., many of the Greek city-states had sent out colonies to Asia Minor. Eventually the majority of those colonies were conquered and incorporated into the Persian Empire.) Artemisia was the daughter of Lygdamis, ruler of Halicarnassus. She also reportedly had a brother, Pigres. Herodotus also says that Artemisia's mother was Cretan. Artemisia assumed the throne of Halicarnassus on the death of her husband, whose name is unknown.

Herodotus does not supply her date of birth but does report that Artemisia had a grown son at the time of the Battle of Salamis (480 B.C.E.). Therefore, she was probably in her mid-thirties during the Persian Wars; thus Darius the Great would have come to power in Persia during Artemisia's youth. In 521 B.C.E. Darius seized the Persian throne and ruled until 486. Darius's reign was characterized by many changes meant to strengthen the Persian Empire. He centralized the government and moved the capital to Persepolis as well as creating an administrative and financial infrastructure stable enough to last for two centuries. He built a canal that linked the Nile River and the Red Sea, thus improving trade and commerce. He was the first Persian king to mint his own coins. Darius expanded his borders to the Indus River and Gandhara in the west and conquered Thrace.

LIFE'S WORK

Artemisia is best known for her role in the Persian Wars, most notably the naval Battle of Salamis. In 499 several city-states on the Greek mainland, most notably Athens, supported a revolt of the Ionian Greek city-states against their overlord Darius. After quelling the rebellion, Darius invaded mainland Greece in 490 in retaliation. He was utterly defeated at the Battle of Marathon by a coalition of Greek city-states. Ten years later, in 480, the new king, Darius's son Xerxes I, invaded Greece again. Artemisia, as queen of Halicarnassus, personally led a fleet of five ships in Xerxes' navy.

Before the battle, Xerxes asked all of his chief admirals their opinion on whether he should attack Salamis. All of them urged him to attack, except for Artemisia. After reminding her audience that she had fought bravely at Euboea, Artemisia, as recorded by Herodotus, advised Xerxes not to attack the Greeks by sea:

> Master, my past services give me the right to advise you now upon the course which I believe to be most to your advantage. It is this: spare your ships and do not fight at sea, for the Greeks are infinitely superior to us in naval matters—the difference between men and women is hardly greater. In any case, what pressing need have you to risk further actions at sea? Have you not taken Athens, the main objective of the war? Is not the rest of Greece in your power? There is no one now to resist you—those who did resist have fared as they deserved. Let me tell you how I think things will now go with the enemy; if only you are not in too great a hurry to fight at sea—if you keep the fleet on the coast where it now is—then, whether you stay here or advance into the Peloponnese, you will easily accomplish your purpose. . . . I hear they have no supplies in the island where they now are; and the Peloponnesian contingents, at least, are not likely to be very easy in their minds if you march with the army towards their country—they will hardly like the idea of fighting in defence of Athens. If on the other hand, you rush into a naval action, my fear is that the defeat of your fleet may involve the army, too.

Thus, Artemisia gave not only her recommended course of action but also the reasoning behind it. After she gave Xerxes this advice, Artemisia's allies feared that Xerxes would be angry with her, but instead her counsel pleased him. However, he chose to listen to the majority of his advisers and attack Salamis.

During the Battle of Salamis, Artemisia distinguished herself by sinking what Xerxes believed to be an enemy vessel. In actuality, Artemisia, finding herself surrounded by Athenian ships, used a clever and ruthless trick to ensure the survival of her crew. She deliberately rammed the ship of Damasithymus, king of the Calyndians, another ally of Persia. The Calyndian ship was lost with all hands. This convinced the Athenians on the ship pursuing her that she was actually an Athenian ally. Xerxes, seeing only that Artemisia had sunk a ship while surrounded by Athenians, believed her to have destroyed an enemy ship and praised her for her bravery.

Apparently Aminias of Pallene, the general who pursued Artemisia's ship, would not have stopped his pursuit had he known that Artemisia herself was on that ship. The Athenians, offended and outraged that a woman would go to war against them, offered a reward of ten thousand drachmas for her capture. Also, according to Plutarch in his biography of Themistocles, when Ariamenes, Xerxes' brother and one of his admirals, was killed at the Battle of Salamis, it was Artemisia who recognized the body and brought it back to Xerxes.

After the Persians' disastrous defeat at Salamis, Xerxes again called on his commanders to advise him. This time he singled out Artemisia for consultation because she alone had given him wise advice the previous time. Xerxes presented Artemisia with two possible courses of action and asked her which she recommended: Either Xerxes would lead troops to the Peloponnese himself, or he would withdraw from Greece and leave his general Mardonius in charge. According to Herodotus, Artemisia responded as follows:

> I think that you yourself should quit this country and leave Mardonius behind with the force he asks for, if that is what he really wants, and if he has really undertaken to do as he has said. If his design prospers and success attends his arms, it will be your work, master—for your slaves performed it. And even if things go wrong with him, it will be no great matter, so long as you yourself are safe and no danger threatens anything that concerns your house. While you and yours survive, the Greeks will have to run many a painful race for their lives and land; but who cares if Mardonius come to grief? He is only your slave, and the Greeks will have but a poor triumph if they kill him. As for yourself, you will be going home with the object for you campaign accomplished—for you have burnt Athens.

Once again, Artemisia had given the reasoning behind her advice, which appeared to be sound. After Xerxes decided to take her advice, he asked her to accompany his illegitimate children to Ephesus. This is the end of Herodotus's account of Artemisia, but she also appears in other ancient sources.

Thessalus, a son of Hippocrates, described her in a speech as a cowardly pirate. In his speech, he relates that Artemisia led a fleet of ships to the Isle of Cos to hunt down and slaughter the Coans, but the gods intervened. After Artemisia's ships were destroyed by lightning and she hallucinated visions of great heroes, she fled Cos with her purpose unfulfilled. According to Polyaenus, Artemisia carried two different standards on her vessels and would fly the Persian standard while chasing Greeks but would fly a Greek standard when she was being chased.

The only account of Artemisia's death is a rather dubious one. Apparently, she fell in love with a younger man and threw herself off a cliff after he broke her heart. It is improbable that a woman strong enough to rule in her own right and lead soldiers in battle would do such a thing. Because ancient literature is full of myths of women who commit suicide because of unrequited love, it seems more likely that the author adapted Artemisia's story to fit the literary traditions of the time. It is known that her grandson, named Lygdamis after her father, ruled Halicarnassus in time and was the reason Herodotus had to flee the city.

SIGNIFICANCE

In an era in which the dominant culture limited the roles of women to those of wife and mother, Artemisia successfully assumed the throne of Halicarnassus after the death of her husband, ruled the kingdom, and led troops in battle. She was highly intelligent, as evidenced by her tactics in the Battle of Salamis and her advice to Xerxes. Xerxes recognized her intelligence and rewarded it. She was not afraid of giving tactically sound advice, even at the risk of angering her overlord or sounding cowardly. The fact that her grandson later ruled Halicarnassus suggests that her rule was stable and, if not well liked, at least tolerated. Too often historians are apt to generalize about the roles of women in the ancient world. The accounts of Artemisia and others like her show that exceptional women could attain and hold power.

—*Caitlin L. Moriarity*

FURTHER READING

Cook, J. M. *The Persian Empire*. New York: Schocken Books, 1983. This history provides a thorough background on the Persian Empire of the fifth century and the Achaemenid Dynasty.

Dewald, C. "Women and Culture in Herodotus's Histories." In *Reflections of Women in Antiquity*, edited by Helene P. Foley. New York: Gordon and Breach

Science, 1981. Discusses Herodotus's attitudes toward women as evidenced by his descriptions of them, with a special emphasis on Artemisia.

Gera, Deborah. *Warrior Women: The Anonymous Tractatus de Mulieribus*. New York: E. J. Brill, 1997. Examines fourteen remarkable women of the ancient world, focusing primarily on ruling queens. The author uses the majority of the available ancient sources to draw a fairly complete picture of Artemisia and the other women.

Green, Peter. *Xerxes at Salamis*. New York: Praeger, 1970. Also published under the title *The Year of Salamis*, this exhaustive but entertaining account of Xerxes' invasion of mainland Greece gives all the details that make a story interesting, including Artemisia's role in the proceedings.

Herodotus. *The History of Herodotus*. Translated by Robin Wakefield. New York: Oxford University Press, 1998. The primary source on Artemisia I. Includes maps, bibliography, and index.

Munson, Rosaria Vignolo. "Artemisia in Herodotus." *Classical Antiquity* 7 (1988): 91-106. Discusses every appearance of Artemisia in Herodotus's *The History* in depth.

SEE ALSO: Arsinoe II Philadelphus; Boudicca; Cleopatra VII; Darius the Great; Dido; Valeria Messallina; Xerxes I; Zenobia.

RELATED ARTICLES in *Great Events from History: The Ancient World*: c. 550 B.C.E., Construction of Trireme Changes Naval Warfare; 520-518 B.C.E., Scylax of Caryanda Voyages the Indian Ocean; 499-494 B.C.E., Ionian Revolt; September 17, 490 B.C.E., Battle of Marathon; 483 B.C.E., Naval Law of Themistocles Is Instituted; 480-479 B.C.E., Persian Invasion of Greece.

ASANGA
Indian philosopher and Buddhist monk

Asanga is revered by Buddhists as the enlightened sage who revived Māhayāna Buddhism. He was a founder of the Yogācāra School.

BORN: c. 365 C.E.; Purusapura, Gandhara, India (now Peshawar, Pakistan)

DIED: c. 440 C.E.; Rajagriha, Magadha (now Rajgir, Bihar, India)

ALSO KNOWN AS: Arya Asanga or "The Noble Asanga"; Aryasanga

AREAS OF ACHIEVEMENT: Philosophy, religion

EARLY LIFE

Arya Asanga (AHR-yuh uh-SUHNG-guh) was an Indian Buddhist monk and philosopher who lived during the fourth and fifth centuries C.E. *Arya* means "Noble One" and is a title of respect; *Asanga* means "untouched" or "unfettered." He is sometimes referred to as one of the doctors of early Buddhism because of his profound erudition. He was a founder of the Yogācāra School of Buddhism, along with his guru, Maitreyanātha, and his half brother Vasubandhu. Yogācāra is a form of Mahāyāna Buddhism.

Most of what is known about Asanga's life rests on legendary accounts—primarily Bu-ston's *Chos-byung* (*History of Buddhism by Buston*, 1931) and Tāranātha's *Rgya gar chos 'byun* (1608; *History of Buddhism in India*, 1970). Some information comes from the Indian sage Paramārtha, who wrote during the sixth century an authoritative historical account of Vasubandhu's life. He also translated important Yogācāra works into Chinese.

According to legend, Asanga's mother was a Brahman of the Kausika clan. In an earlier life, she had been a monk who verbally wounded another during debate. For this unkindness, the monk was punished by many incarnations as a woman. During the time of incarnation as Asanga's mother, many people had turned from the dharma, or teaching of Buddha. She offered help in her prayers to Lord Avalokita, a bodhisattva, or one who seeks enlightenment and is the embodiment of compassion. Subsequently, she had three sons: Asanga, Vasubandhu, and Virincivatsa, all of whom joined the Hīnayāna or "Lesser Vehicle" School of Buddhism. They lived in Purusapura, Gandhara, India (now Peshawar, Pakistan).

Traditional accounts relate that Asanga was a precocious child who became a monk at an early age. He belonged to the Mahīshāsakas, a sect that valued meditation and believed that only the present has reality. He studied with Pindola, an arhat, or worthy one, who had conquered hatred, desire, and delusion, the three unwholesome roots of future suffering. An arhat embodies the sought-after ideal in the Hīnayāna, the most ancient school of Buddhism, of one who has attained the highest level of enlightenment before nirvana, or escape from the cycle of rebirth. The ideal for Mahāyāna Buddhism, a school that developed after the Hīnayāna, is the bodhisattva. For the Hīnayānist, the focus of spiritual development is on liberation of the individual from suffering, whereas for the Mahāyānist, the focus is on liberation of all beings. This is accomplished by repeatedly forgoing nirvana for oneself; the bodhisattva tends, with selfless compassion over many lifetimes, to others. Compassion for suffering beings became a theme in Asanga's eventual philosophy.

Under Pindola's guidance, Asanga learned all the sutras of the Buddha's discourse, reading the scriptures of Hīnayāna as well as some of Mahāyāna, or "Greater Vehicle" Buddhism. (The term "Hīnayāna" was originally a derogatory term used by Mahāyānists; the term "Theravāda," or "Doctrine of the Elders," is preferred today for the sole surviving Hīnayāna School.) While Pindola was Asanga's teacher on earth, his "tutelary deity" was Lord Maitreya Buddha. Maitreya is the aspect of Buddha that is love.

Eventually, Asanga left Pindola to meditate in a mountain cave for twelve years to propitiate Maitreya. He emerged at three-year intervals, totally disheartened. When he observed stones slowly worn down by birds' wings or by single drops of water, or iron needles made by a patient old man, he was encouraged to try again. At the end of twelve years he emerged from his cave, still unenlightened and brokenhearted. When he came on a dog whose hindquarters were infested with worms, he was filled with compassion. Rather than kill the worms, however, he intended to lure them to a piece of flesh sliced from his thigh. Just then, the Lord Maitreya appeared in place of the dog. Asanga cried out in wonder: Why did Maitreya appear now and not before? Maitreya answered that he always had been with him, but Asanga could see him only when his fervor was balanced with compassion.

At Maitreya's behest, Asanga asked to help educate the people about Mahāyāna doctrine. In response, he was transported to Tuśita heaven, where all the bodhisattvas reside until their final incarnations as buddhas. Asanga studied all of Mahāyāna scripture with Lord Maitreya in Tuśita heaven—some legends say for six months, others for fifty-three years. Asanga had attained the third stage of a bodhisattva—there are ten stages according to the Mahāyāna—therefore, he was called *Prabhākarī*, or "Light-giving."

LIFE'S WORK

According to legend, after Asanga returned to earth, he devoted himself to all living beings with complete compassion. He opened shelters for monks to stay in during the rainy season and wrote down what he had learned from Maitreya in the "Five Books." After this, he wrote his own texts and then converted his half brother, Vasubandhu, from Hīnayāna to Mahāyāna Buddhism. He also taught Hīnayāna monks about Mahāyāna doctrine. When his fame for profound erudition spread, King Gambhīrapaksa helped Asanga establish monasteries, which revived Mahāyāna Buddhism.

Early Mahāyāna Buddhism (c. 100 B.C.E.-100 C.E.) broadened the number of avenues to enlightenment, offering escape from samsāra (eternal wandering) and the cycle of rebirth. Its doctrine blended ideas about devotion, contemplation, and compassion. For example, one who desires to be a bodhisattva must first worship the various forms of the Buddha. Moreover, he or she must live a contemplative life by practicing the pāramitās, or the six perfections: generosity, morality, patience, courage, meditation, and wisdom. This path, unlike that of the Hīnayāna or Theravāda, is open to everyone, not just the *saṅgha* (order of monks and nuns). The coupling of self-discipline with compassion for others derives from a core ethical concern in Mahāyāna philosophy.

An early sage of the Mahāyāna was Nāgārjuna (c. second or third century C.E.). Nāgārjuna and Āryadeva founded the Mādhyamaka, or "Middle School," based on the Doctrine of Emptiness, a principal tenet that all phenomena are empty of being. If so, the only logical difference between nirvana and samsāra is one's perception of the two states. Hence, nirvana is here and now. Spiritual development depends on seeing the emptiness in all things, thereby eliminating the craving or desire that is the source of suffering. Asanga modified Nāgārjuna's views in favor of a philosophy of idealism that informs the Yogācāra School. Asanga's central tenet is that consciousness is real, but material objects have no existence beyond the conscious realm.

In the *Mahāyānasaṁgraha* (fourth century C.E.; *The Summary of the Great Vehicle*, 1992), Asanga explicated basic concepts of Yogācāra, such as the storehouse consciousness, essence of existence, and reality as pure ideation; mind-only doctrine; pāramitās; bhūmis; ethical guidelines, or shīla; meditation; wisdom; and the three Buddha bodies, or trikāya. Cittamātra (mind-only) is fundamental to Yogācāra philosophy. *Citta* means "storehouse consciousness" or "pure thought" and is the origin of all thought and sensation. The concept of the storehouse consciousness is a key to understanding karma, the universal law of cause and effect; it is where all impressions have been stored and where the seeds of moral or immoral deeds ripen and reach fruition, usually beyond one's lifetime. Hence, a cycle of rebirth occurs.

The Yogācāra, or "Application of Yoga," School is also called the Vijñānavāda, or "School That Teaches Knowing." Followers practice yoga as meditation in an effort to improve themselves on the path to Buddhahood, or perfect enlightenment. Early opponents of Yogācāra were from the Mādhyamaka School, although both are variants of Mahāyāna Buddhism.

Works attributed to Asanga and Maitreya or to Maitreyanātha include the *Abhidharmasamuccaya*, or "Collection of the Abhidharma" (*Abhidharma Samuccaya of Asanga*, 1950); the *Mahāyānasūtralankāra*, or "Ornament of the Sutras of the Mahāyāna" (fourth century C.E.; *Mahayanasutralankara of Asanga*, 1989); the *Madhyāntavibhāga*, or "Differentiation of the Middle and the Extremes" (*Discourse on Discrimination Between Middle and Extremes*, 1936); the *Yogācāra-bhūmi-shāstra*, or "Treatise on the Stages of the Yogācāra" (fourth century C.E.); and the *Mahāyānasaṃgraha*.

According to legendary accounts, the Lord Maitreya inspired Asanga to write many key texts in the Yogācāra canon. However, scholars debate whether Maitreya was a mythical or historical figure. If mythical, Maitreya is the "Future Buddha" in Buddhist cosmology, and if historic, he is the author or coauthor of important texts, such as the "Five Books." The historic person is called Maitreyanātha (c. fourth and fifth centuries C.E.) and is believed to have been Asanga's master.

Traditionally, the encyclopedic *Yogācāra-bhūmi-shāstra*, a fundamental work of the Yogācāra School of Buddhism, is believed to have been revealed by Maitreya to Asanga. It is a multivolume work divided into five parts and written in prose with some short verses; it presents all of Yogācāra doctrine. The main part describes the bhūmis, or stages of spiritual development. The second part interprets the stages. The third is about the sutras that are the basis for Yogācāra doctrine. The fourth is about the classes within the sutras. The fifth includes topics from the canon. Asanga also wrote a shorter version titled *Aryashāsana-prakarana*, or "Proof of the Sacred Doctrine." Although the original Sanskrit text of the *Yogācārabhūmi* survives as a fragment, complete translations exist in Chinese and Tibetan.

The *Bodhisattvabhūmi*, or "Stages of the Bodhisattva" is the fifteenth volume of the first part of the *Yogācāra-bhūmi-shāstra* and is particularly revered. The

text was immediately successful. Tibetan and Chinese editions were produced in the early fifth century C.E., whereas other volumes of the *Yogācāra-bhūmi-shāstra* were translated more than one hundred years later. The *Bodhisattvabhūmi* is a standard text in Mahāyāna monasteries. It instructs bodhisattvas how to interpret and move through the stages of spiritual development and includes information on proper behavior, meditation, and the teachings of the Buddha.

Arya Asanga died in Rajagriha, India (near modern-day Patna on the Ganges River). Rajagriha was the capital of Magadha, an ancient kingdom in India (now in the modern state Bihar, India).

SIGNIFICANCE

To understand the philosophical roots and the religious practices of the Mahāyānists, it is necessary to study the Yogācāra School of Maitreyanātha, Asanga, and Vasubandhu. This was an important branch of Buddhism that reached its zenith during the sixth century C.E. During that period, Nālāndā, the monastic university in northern India near modern-day Patna, was the center of Yogācāra Buddhism. Later Yogācārins attempted to reconcile the idealism of Asanga, the supposed nihilism of Nāgārjuna, and the relative realism of the Hīnayānists.

After the thirteenth century C.E., Buddhism in India nearly died out. However, it is still one of the world's great religions. Beginning in the third century, Buddhism spread to other countries. The Hīnayāna form spread from southern India to Ceylon (now Sri Lanka), Siam (now Thailand), Burma (now Myanmar), Laos, and Cambodia; the Mahāyāna form spread from northern India to China, Japan, Korea, and Vietnam. Today there are thousands of practicing Mahāyānists whose beliefs rest, in part, on the philosophy and call to compassion of Asanga.

—*Tanja Bekhuis*

FURTHER READING

Griffiths, Paul J., Noriaki Hakamaya, John P. Keenan, and Paul L. Swanson. *The Realm of Awakening: A Translation and Study of the Tenth Chapter of Asanga's "Mahāyānasaṃgraha."* New York: Oxford University Press, 1989. Introduction describes Yogācāra philosophy of consciousness in the context of religious experience. Includes English translation and discussion of Asanga's chapter on wisdom as well as romanized versions of Sanskrit and Tibetan texts. Bibliography and index.

Harvey, Peter. *An Introduction to Buddhism: Teachings, History, and Practices.* New York: Cambridge University Press, 1990. Good historical review; chapters

on early schools of Buddhism, including the Mahāyāna and Yogācāra. Includes photos and appendix
listing Pāli, Chinese, and Tibetan scriptural texts.
Contains bibliography for various subjects, including
Yogācāra, concept and name indexes.

Keown, Damien. *Buddhism: A Very Short Introduction.*
New York: Oxford University Press, 1996. Accessible review of Buddhist ideas and history. Includes
chapter on the Mahāyāna School, with mention of
Yogācāra. Maps, illustrations, time line, index, and
good list of resources for further study.

Smart, Ninian. *The Religious Experience.* 5th ed. Upper
Saddle River, N.J.: Prentice Hall, 1996. Chapter titled
"The Early Indian Experience" includes a nontechnical comparison of Hīnayāna and Mahāyāna (including Yogācāra) Schools of Buddhism in terms of six-
dimensional model of religion. Includes photos,
maps, and index.

Willis, Janice Dean. *On Knowing Reality: The Tattvārtha
Chapter of Asanga's Bodhisattvabhūmi.* New York:
Columbia University Press, 1979. Introduction relates legendary and historical accounts of Asanga's
life and work. *Tattvārtha* chapter discussed as a key to
understanding Asanga's view of the nature of reality.
Includes glossary and bibliography.

SEE ALSO: Bodhidharma; Buddha; Vardhamāna; Vasubandhu.

RELATED ARTICLES in *Great Events from History: The
Ancient World*: 6th or 5th century B.C.E., Birth of Bud-
dhism; c. 250 B.C.E., Third Buddhist Council Con-
venes; c. 250 B.C.E., *Tipiṭaka* Is Compiled; c. 247-207
B.C.E., Buddhism Established in Sri Lanka; c. 1st
century B.C.E., Indian Buddhist Nuns Compile the
Therigatha; 1st century B.C.E.-1st century C.E., Com-
pilation of the *Lotus Sutra*; 1st century C.E., Fourth
Buddhist Council Convenes; Late 4th-5th centuries
C.E., Asanga Helps Spread Mahāyāna Buddhism;
c. 380-c. 415 C.E., Gupta Dynasty Reaches Its Peak
Under Chandragupta II.

ASCLEPIADES OF BITHYNIA
Roman physician

*Asclepiades was the first physician to establish Greek
medicine in Rome.*

BORN: 124 B.C.E.; Prusa (Cios), Bithynia (now Bursa,
Turkey)
DIED: c. 44 B.C.E.; Rome (now in Italy)
ALSO KNOWN AS: Asklepiades
AREA OF ACHIEVEMENT: Medicine

EARLY LIFE

Asclepiades (as-klee-PI-uh-deez), whose father was probably Andreas, a noted physiologist of the time, was born
in Prusa, also called Cios, in Bithynia, Asia Minor. A
widely read man, he seems to have had a liberal education in his youth. Apparently, there was enough money
for him to be able to travel and study.

After studying rhetoric and medicine in Athens and
Alexandria, he practiced medicine, first in Parion, a
town on the Hellespont (Dardanelles), and later in Athens. After extensive traveling, in the year 91 B.C.E. he
settled in Rome, where he may have become a Roman citizen. A man of amiable manners, good fortune,
and worldly prosperity, Asclepiades formed friendships
with such prominent individuals as Cicero and Marc
Antony.

Preferring the freedom of a solitary life in a suburban
villa, Asclepiades refused the invitation of King Mithra-
dates of Pontus to join his court. Though he did not participate in public debates, he was not afraid to disagree
with others. He condemned all those who thought that
anatomy and physiology were the foundation of medicine. He was responsible for introducing Democritus's
atomistic philosophy to Rome.

His daily routine included three basic activities: visiting and treating the sick throughout the city, giving written advice, and writing books. Although he was a prodigious author, little remains of the twenty or more treatises
he prepared. Specific dates of his works are not known;
the fragments that remain have been assigned English titles according to their subject matter. He wrote one book
of definitions, one commentary on some of the short and
obscure works of Hippocrates, one treatise on fevers, and
three on febrile, inflammatory, and acute diseases. He
also wrote *Common Aids*, a precursor of modern guides
to healthy living; *On Enemas*, which was frequently
quoted by Aulus Cornelius Celsus in *De medicina* (c. 30
C.E.; English translation, 1830); and *On the Use of Wine*.

Asclepiades also offered public lectures on medicine
and had a large number of students. Applying many of

his principles, these students, led by Themison of Laodicea, later founded the Methodist school, which emphasized diet and exercise in the treatment of illness.

By the age of thirty, Asclepiades was already famous. Some of that fame had grown from a story about him that circulated in Rome. According to this story, one day Asclepiades encountered a funeral procession. Just as the corpse was placed on the pyre and the fire was about to be lit, he ordered the ceremony stopped, had the body taken down and delivered to his home, administered restoratives, and soon revived the man.

A statue excavated in Rome in 1700 was assumed to be a correct likeness of Asclepiades. From this, it would appear that he was a man of slender stature who possessed a rather tranquil countenance.

LIFE'S WORK

Asclepiades was one of the foremost physicians of his century, exhibiting rich practical and philosophical attainments, versatility of mind, and an ability to make rapid diagnoses. Opposing the Hippocratic idea that morbid conditions resulted from a disturbance of the humors of the body, he held that nothing happened without a cause and that the causes of events were always mechanical—that is, dependent on matter and motion.

The medical practice that Asclepiades founded was based on a modification of the atomic, or corpuscular, theory of Democritus, the Greek philosopher, according to which disease resulted from an irregular or inharmonious motion of the corpuscles of the body. Asclepiades believed that these masses were in continual motion, splitting into fragments of different shapes and sizes that then re-formed to create perceptible bodies. These particles were separated by invisible gaps, or pores. Friction between the particles created normal body heat; jamming the pores, or obstruction, was the cause of fever and inflammatory disorders. Fainting, lethargy, weakness, and similar complaints were attributed to an abnormal relaxation of the pores. Because disease was attributed to either constricted or relaxed conditions of the body's solid particles, Asclepiades founded his therapy on the efficacy of systematic interference, as opposed to the healing power of nature. The regimens that he prescribed incorporated such therapies as fresh air, light, appropriate diet, hydrotherapy, massage, clysters or enemas, local applications, and, occasionally, very small amounts of medication.

For those complaints that he believed to be caused by obstruction, he proposed various kinds of exercise to relax the pores; in this way, the free transmission of the in-

Asclepiades of Bithynia. (Library of Congress)

terrupted atoms or molecules would be facilitated. For pain, localized venesection might be cautiously practiced but only for instant relief, because bleeding tended to draw off the finer, more vital atoms first and leave the coarser atoms behind. Rigor, or rigidity of the body, might result.

He believed that dropsy, an excessive accumulation of fluid in the tissues, resulted from an infinite number of small holes in the flesh that converted all the food received into water. How such a conversion might occur, however, he did not explain. To illustrate that the brain was the seat of the finest atoms, he performed decapitation experiments on animals such as eels, tortoises, and goats.

Asclepiades condemned purgatives, emetics, and drugs. Instead, he relied greatly on changes in diet, accompanied by friction, bathing, and exercise. He paid special attention to the patient's pulse. His remedies were directed to the restoration of harmony, based on the fundamental principle that treatments should be given promptly, safely, and pleasantly. For relaxants, he used wine and massage; to stimulate patients, he used wine, cold water, vinegar, and narcotics. He taught that patients tolerated diseases differently. Exercise, in his view, was unnecessary for healthy people. In cases of dropsy, he recommended making small cuts near the ankles to release the fluid. He advised that, when tapping was done to remove fluid, the opening be made as small as possible.

Asclepiades was particularly interested in psychiatric cases. He placed these patients in brightly lit, well-ventilated rooms, used occupational therapy, prescribed exercises for improving the memory and increasing attention, soothed them with music, and used wine to induce sleep.

According to Pliny the Elder, the Roman naturalist and writer, Asclepiades had three principal modes of cure. The early stages of illness often called for "gestation," which consisted of being transported in some way, such as a boat or litter, to exhaust the patient's strength and cause fever. Asclepiades also used suspended beds that could be rocked, as well as hanging baths and other forms of hydrotherapy. He firmly believed and taught that one fever was to be cured by another. The second mode was friction, or massage. The third mode was wine, which he gave to febrile patients and used as a stimulant in cases of lethargy. He believed that it was necessary to force a patient to endure thirst. All patients were required to fast during the first three days of illness. In later stages, wine and moderate amounts of food were allowed.

Asclepiades showed great accuracy in distinguishing among various diseases, describing and dividing them into acute and chronic classes. For example, he gave a correct description of malaria; he also observed the psychic complications that occurred in cases of pneumonia and pleurisy. His special attention was devoted to chronic diseases, conditions that had been somewhat neglected by Hippocrates.

Asclepiades wagered that he would never die of disease; indeed, he is not known ever to have fallen ill. His death, at an advanced age, was the result of an accidental fall down a flight of stairs.

SIGNIFICANCE

Asclepiades of Bithynia may be ranked as the first physician to introduce Greek medicine to Rome. A full assessment of his merits cannot be made because most of his writings have been lost. The fragments of them that have surfaced in later literature deal with subjects such as the pulse, respiration, heart disease, ulcers, climate, drugs, and the preparation of remedies.

By the fourth century, Asclepiades was almost forgotten. His critics had characterized him as a man of natural talents acquainted with human nature and possessed of considerable shrewdness but little scientific or professional skill. Galen strongly opposed him because Asclepiades had been the first to attack and repudiate the humoral teachings of Hippocrates. Pliny also disliked him and regarded him as a charlatan.

On the other hand, Celsus, the first compiler of medical history and procedures, admitted that he learned much from Asclepiades. Galen grudgingly credited Asclepiades as having pioneered two surgical procedures, laryngectomy and tracheotomy. As has been noted, his ideas were influential in the development of the Methodist school, with its emphasis on diet and exercise. Furthermore, Asclepiades was a pioneer in the humane treatment of mental patients.

—*Rita E. Loos*

FURTHER READING

Allbutt, Sir Thomas C. *Greek Medicine in Rome: The Fitzpatrick Lectures on the History of Medicine Delivered at the Royal College of Physicians of London in 1909-10.* Reprint. New York: B. Blom, 1970. This series of lectures presents a complete medical history of the period, with extensive commentary on all major figures but only one brief chapter on Asclepiades. Includes excellent illustrations, bibliography, and chronology.

Cumston, Charles Greene. *An Introduction to the History of Medicine: From the Time of the Pharaohs to the End of the Nineteenth Century.* 1926. Reprint. London: Dawsons, 1968. This volume, which contains only one brief chapter on Asclepiades, is a compilation of numerous essential contributions to the general subject of a history of medicine. Written for the general reader.

Gordon, Benjamin Lee. *Medicine Throughout Antiquity.* Philadelphia: F. A. Davis, 1949. Gordon's book contains only a very brief section on Asclepiades, along with scattered page references. Includes brief reference notes and a few illustrations but no chronology or bibliography.

Green, Robert M., ed. and trans. *Asclepiades, His Life and Writings: A Translation of Cocchi's "Life of Asclepiades" and Gumpert's "Fragments of Asclepiades."* New Haven, Conn.: Elizabeth Licht, 1955. Green has prepared a complete translation of *Discorso primo di Antonio Cocchi sopra Asclepiade* (c. 1740) and of selections from Christian Gumpert's *Fragmenta* (1794), a compilation of extant writings of Asclepiades. This volume contains detailed information available in English for the general reader, although it lacks reference notes and a bibliography.

Major, Ralph. "Medicine in the Roman Empire." In *A History of Medicine*. Springfield, Ill.: Charles C Thomas, 1954. This chapter includes a brief section on Asclepiades. There is no presumption of background knowledge about medical history.

Rawson, Elizabeth. "The Life and Death of Asclepiades of Bithynia." *Classical Quarterly* 32, no. 2 (1982): 358-370. Rawson presents a critical analysis of the information known about Asclepiades. It presumes extensive background knowledge concerning Asclepiades as well as the period in which he lived.

Vallance, J. T. *The Lost Theory of Asclepiades of Bithynia*. New York: Oxford University Press, 1990. Examines how Asclepiades of Bithynia reformed traditional Hippocratic practice with his own physical theory.

SEE ALSO: Marc Antony; Aulus Cornelius Celsus; Cicero; Democritus; Galen; Hippocrates; Pliny the Elder.

RELATED ARTICLES in *Great Events from History: The Ancient World*: 6th-4th century B.C.E. (traditionally, 1st millennium B.C.E.), Suśruta, Indian Physician, Writes Medical Compendium; c. 500-400 B.C.E., Greek Physicians Begin Scientific Practice of Medicine; c. 250 B.C.E., Discoveries of Archimedes; c. 157-201 C.E., Galen Synthesizes Ancient Medical Knowledge.

ASHURBANIPAL
Assyrian king (r. 669-627 B.C.E.)

The last great king of ancient Assyria, Ashurbanipal lived within a generation of its annihilation. Inside his exquisitely decorated palace, he brought together a magnificent library of cuneiform writing on clay tablets, which included materials from twenty-five hundred years of achievement by Sumerians, Akkadians, Babylonians, and Assyrians.

BORN: c. 685 B.C.E.; Nineveh, Assyria (now in Iraq)
DIED: 627 B.C.E.; Nineveh, Assyria
ALSO KNOWN AS: Ashur-bani-apli; Assurbanipal; Asurbanipal
AREAS OF ACHIEVEMENT: Government and politics, architecture, art and art patronage, literature

EARLY LIFE

Ashurbanipal (ah-shur-BA-neh-pal) was born toward the end of a fifteen-hundred-year period of Assyrian ascendancy. His name in Assyrian is Ashur-bani-apli (the god Ashur has made a[nother] son), affirming that he was not intended to stand in the line of royal accession.

His father, Esarhaddon, youngest son of Sennacherib, had become heir when the crown prince, Ashur-nadin-shumi, was deposed by rebels from his position as vassal for Babylon. Esarhaddon was not the son of Sennacherib's queen, Tashmetum-sharrat, but of the West Semitic "palace woman" Zakutu, known by her native name, Naqi'a. The only queen known for Esarhaddon was Ashur-hamat, who died in 672 B.C.E.

Ashurbanipal grew up in the small palace called *bit reduti* (house of succession), built by Sennacherib when he was crown prince in the northern quadrant of Nineveh. In 694, Sennacherib had completed the "Palace Without Rival" at the southwest corner of the acropolis, obliterating most of the older structures. The "House of Succession" had become the palace of Esarhaddon, the crown prince. In this house, Ashurbanipal's grandfather was assassinated by uncles identified only from the biblical account as Adrammelek and Sharezer. From this conspiracy, Esarhaddon emerged as king in 681. He proceeded to rebuild as his residence the *bit masharti* (weapons house, or arsenal). The "House of Succession" was left to his mother and the younger children, including Ashurbanipal.

The names of five brothers and one sister are known. Sin-iddin-apli, the intended crown prince, died prior to 672. Not having been expected to become heir to the throne, Ashurbanipal was trained in scholarly pursuits as well as the usual horsemanship, hunting, chariotry, soldierliness, craftsmanship, and royal decorum. In a unique autobiographical statement, Ashurbanipal specified his youthful scholarly pursuits as having included oil divination, mathematics, and reading and writing. Ashurbanipal was the only Assyrian king who learned how to read and write.

In 672, on the death of his queen, Esarhaddon reorganized the line of succession at the instigation of his mother. He used the submission of Median chieftains to draft a treaty. The chieftains swore that if Esarhaddon died while his sons were still minors, they and their descendants would guarantee the succession of Ashurbanipal as king of Assyria and Shamash-shum-ukin as king of Babylon. A monumental stela set up two years later in a northwestern province portrays Esarhaddon in high relief on its face and each of the sons on a side. These portraits, the earliest dated for Ashurbanipal and his brother, show both with the full beard of maturity.

The princes pursued diverse educations thereafter. Extant letters from Shamash-shum-ukin offer his father reports of the situation in Babylon; Ashurbanipal at home received letters as crown prince. The situation came to an immediate crisis in 669, when Esarhaddon, on campaign to Egypt, died suddenly. Ashurbanipal did not accede to the kingship of Assyria until late in the year. His grandmother required all to support his sole claim to the throne. The official ceremonies of coronation came in the second month of the new year, and within the same year (668), Ashurbanipal installed his brother as king of Babylon. The transition took place smoothly, and the dual monarchy of the youthful brothers began. Texts describe their relationship as if they were twins. It was clear, however, that Ashurbanipal, as king of Assyria, like his fathers before him, was also "king of the universe."

LIFE'S WORK

One of the first challenges that Ashurbanipal had to face was a rebellion in a region of Egypt over which Esarhaddon had established Assyrian sovereignty. In 667, the ousted king Taharqa came as far north as Memphis, which he recaptured. The Assyrian army rushed south to defeat him, but he again fled. Ashurbanipal enlisted new troops from Syria and followed, capturing Thebes. Three vassals were found guilty of plotting against Assyria, and they were sent to Nineveh. One of them, Necho, convinced Ashurbanipal of his personal loyalty and was returned to his position in Sais in the Nile River Delta.

After Taharqa's death, Tanutamon tried to drive out the Assyrians. He captured Memphis and drove the Assyrian vassals into the Delta. With the return of Ashurbanipal and the Assyrian army, Tanutamon fled back to Thebes, which again fell to the Assyrians. In the course of this war, Necho had fallen, and his son Psamtik I was installed as vassal at Sais; he became king of all Egypt on the death of Tanutamon.

These events in Egypt, and Ashurbanipal's success in maintaining his position, made a considerable impression on the contemporary world. The Phoenician states, such as Sidon, quieted down. In Anatolia, Gyges, king of Lydia, sought Ashurbanipal's help against the Cimmerians, offering to acknowledge Assyrian suzerainty. There

Ashurbanipal. (Library of Congress)

was a similar gesture from the Urartian king. Ashurbanipal did not, however, succumb to the temptation to get entangled in an impossible war with the Cimmerians.

Rather, he turned against the Elamites. In the campaign against their capital at Susa, the Elamite army was routed, and their king, Tept-Humban (Teumman), was killed. This event was portrayed afterward in a chamber of Sennacherib's "Palace Without Rival," which had become Ashurbanipal's residence on accession. In Teumman's place, a prince, Ummannish, who had earlier fled to the Assyrian court, became king.

The Assyrian Empire stretched from Egypt to Urartu, from Lydia to Susa, along the full extent of both the Tigris and the Euphrates Rivers. Shamash-shum-ukin could not help feeling overshadowed by his brother, who, though technically his equal, treated him as another vassal. Messengers went out secretly from Babylon to other discontented states; in 651, Shamash-shum-ukin initiated a full revolt, together with Gyges of Lydia, Ummanigash of Elam, Arabians, and others. Ashurbanipal implored the gods to save him. The chronicle of his inscriptions reflects the new situation created by the revolt; the one who had been called his "full brother" became the "faithless, hostile brother."

The army from Arabia was delayed, so that Shamash-shum-ukin had to face the entire Assyrian army alone. He withdrew into the fortified cities in Babylonia. The Assyrians proceeded to lay siege to one after another. In 648, realizing that all was lost, Shamash-shum-ukin threw himself into the fire that consumed his palace at Babylon. For the remainder of Ashurbanipal's reign, Babylon was held directly by Assyria. The official in charge, according to all subsequent Babylonian sources, was named Kandalanu; he is impossible to identify further, unless the name is a Babylonian throne name for Ashurbanipal. Kandalanu disappeared in the same year in which Ashurbanipal died.

Ashurbanipal undertook several more campaigns between 648 and 642, including at least two against Elam. He penetrated to Susa and sacked it thoroughly. There was one final campaign against the Arabs, fought as a running battle between his cavalry and the Arabs' mounted camel corps. Ashurbanipal returned from these forays with ample spoils to finance the construction of his grand new palace on the site of the old "House of Succession."

In decorating the walls of this palace, Ashurbanipal repeated the artistic narration of the earlier defeat of Teumman, giving thereby a second version to that in Sennacherib's palace. The most intriguing detail is the final celebration of the victory, in which Ashurbanipal, with his queen, are served a repast outdoors under some grapevines, within which hangs the severed head of the disobedient vassal. Fully illustrated are the victories over Shamash-shum-ukin in 648, the Elamites in 642, and the Arabians. More noteworthy are the extensive scenes of a rather boyish Ashurbanipal hunting—none more exquisitely rendered than the one in which he single-handedly slaughters a pride of lions. Visitors to his palace got a clear impression that this king of Assyria was not merely a great king but indeed "king of the universe."

From any later perspective, the destructive events of the 640's may be judged as contributory to the final end of Assyria. However, the last fifteen years of reign appear so quiescent that Ashurbanipal went to his grave assured of the permanence of the land of Ashur that had been his inheritance.

SIGNIFICANCE

Ashurbanipal left behind an impressive legacy in architecture, in artistic decoration, and in the collection of the literary treasures of the past, which he greatly enjoyed personally. This is borne out not merely by inscriptional claim but also by lengthy colophons that he personally added to a wide variety of texts, gathered for the library at Nineveh from all parts of Mesopotamia and from all periods of time, going beyond the Babylonia of Hammurabi to what Ashurbanipal called the "obscure Akkadian and even more difficult Sumerian" on tablets he thought to have come "from before the Flood."

The letters he wrote to request manuscripts indicate that he knew where older collections existed and what they contained: the scholarly apparatus for reading and writing the cuneiform script, including multilingual dictionaries; collections of omens, essential for prognostication of every element of the royal life; and cycles of conjurations, incantations, and prayers, often with interlinear translation of the original Sumerian. To these essentials were added epics of gods or heroes, including previous kings; collections of fables, proverbial wisdom, and unusual tales, some humorous; and a miscellany reflecting the operations of the scribal school and its scholarship, especially in law.

Ashur-etil-ilani and Sin-shar-ishkun, two of his sons, succeeded him but immediately faced increasing pressure from many opponents. The last Assyrian ruler was an army general, Ashur-uballit II, who held off as long as he could the final destruction of the Assyrian state by retreating to Harran, after the capitals fell to the combined strength of the Medes and Babylonians.

The biblical tradition recalled Ashurbanipal as "the great and noble Asnappar" who had "deported and settled, in the cities of Samaria and in the rest of the province called 'Beyond-the-River,'" various conquered peoples from Babylonia and Elam. The Greek tradition conflated Ashurbanipal with his brother Shamash-shum-ukin into a cowardly, effeminate "Sardanapalus" who presided over Assyria's destruction and committed suicide. Sardanapalus became well known through George Gordon, Lord Byron's verse drama *Sardanapalus* (1821) and Eugène Delacroix's 1827 painting *Death of Sardanapalus*. Neither of these is characterized by historical veracity, as they were both products of the Romantic era, which immediately preceded the archaeological rediscovery of the real Ashurbanipal.

—*Clyde Curry Smith*

FURTHER READING

Attila, Raija. *Legal Transactions of the Royal Court of Nineveh: Assurbanipal Through Sin-Sarru-Iskun.* Helsinki: Helsinki University Press, 2002. Part of the series of critical text editions of the state archives of the Assyrian Empire, primarily from Nineveh, edited by the Neo-Assyrian Text Corpus Project in Helsinki.

Barnett, R. D. *Sculptures from the North Palace of Ashurbanipal at Nineveh (668-627)*. London: British Museum, 1976. The history of the excavations and of the reconstruction of the plans of the palace is covered, with an explanation of the location within the chambers of all known sculpted slabs. Photographs and drawings are laid out to illustrate the slabs in their discovered configuration in this massive folio.

Cole, Steven W., and Peter Machinist, eds. *Letters from Priests to the Kings Esarhaddon and Assurbanipal*. Helsinki: Helsinki University Press, 1999. From the State Archives of Assyria Series of the Neo-Assyrian Text Corpus Project in Helsinki.

Grayson, A. K. "The Chronology of the Reign of Ashurbanipal." *Zeitschrift für Assyriologie* 70 (1980): 227-245. This study serves as a guide to the texts, historiographically evaluated, and to the correlation of detail within the various text editions to the actual events and their dates. It does not address the problems of the conclusion of the reign.

Luckenbill, Daniel David, trans. *From Sargon to the End*. Vol. 2 of *Ancient Records of Assyria and Babylonia*. Chicago: University of Chicago Press, 1927. An English translation of the inscriptions of the kings of Assyria, this volume covers Ashurbanipal and his three predecessors, Sargon II, Sennacherib, and Esarhaddon.

Oates, J. "Assyrian Chronology, 631-612 B.C." *Iraq* 27 (1965): 135-159. This effort to identify the sources and define the issues related to the conclusion of Ashurbanipal's reign judiciously sifts the conflict of opinion that has dominated Assyriology. Extensive bibliographical notes and internal catalogs of data guide the reader.

Olmstead, A. T. *History of Assyria*. 1923. Reprint. New York: Charles Scribner's Sons, 1960. Written in the immediate wake of World War I, this comprehensive history was selected for reprinting for its mastery of Assyrian materials and their critical evaluation. Ashurbanipal and his capital receive extensive treatment in chapters 30-34.

SEE ALSO: Ashurnasirpal II; Hammurabi; Sennacherib.

RELATED ARTICLES in *Great Events from History: The Ancient World*: c. 3000-c. 500 B.C.E., Elamite Empire Rises in Near East; c. 1770 B.C.E., Promulgation of Hammurabi's Code; c. 1450 B.C.E., International Age of Major Kingdoms Begins in the Near East; c. 883-c. 824 B.C.E., Second Assyrian Empire Displays Military Prowess; 745 B.C.E., Tiglath-pileser III Rules Assyria.

ASHURNASIRPAL II
Assyrian king (r. c. 883-859 B.C.E.)

Ashurnasirpal II created the Neo-Assyrian Empire, expanding its boundaries to the Mediterranean coast and into the mountainous regions north and west of the Tigris homeland. At Kalhu, he built an enormous fortress capped by his magnificent palace, which featured the first extensive use of decorated bas-relief.

BORN: c. 915 B.C.E.; Ashur, Assyria (now Ash Sharqāṭ, Iraq)

DIED: 859 B.C.E.; Kalhu, Assyria (now Nimrud, Iraq)

ALSO KNOWN AS: Ashur-nasir-apli

AREAS OF ACHIEVEMENT: War and conquest, government and politics, architecture, art and art patronage

EARLY LIFE

The royal name Ashur-nasir-apli means "the god Ashur protects the son (as heir)." On each decorative slab in his palace, Ashurnasirpal (ah-shewr-NAH-zihr-pahl) II noted the names of his father, Tukulti-Ninurta II, and his grandfather, Adad-nirâri II, along with a summary of his military and architectural achievements. He knew that his great-grandfather Ashur-dan II had "freed cities and founded temples," setting in motion the process of reorganizing and expanding the Assyrian Empire, which had been reduced to the capital area.

Adad-nirâri II had made the first Assyrian attack to the east, into the Tigris River's tributary basin. South of the Diyala River, he had defeated the Babylonian king, precipitating a revolution in Babylon and ensuring the perpetuation of the peace treaty by intermarriage. By treaty renewal during a period of eighty years, from the reign of Tukulti-Ninurta II through that of Ashurnasirpal's grandson, Shamshi-Adad V, parity was maintained by Assyria and Babylonia, which secured Assyria's southern front.

Adad-nirâri II told of making new plows throughout

Ashur-land, heaping up grain, and increasing the breed and quantity of horses. Tukulti-Ninurta II had continued this economic development, which served as a base for serious expansion.

The Nairi states to the north were fragmented remains of the Hurrian kingdom, which had been demolished by royal Assyrian predecessors five centuries earlier. These states were related to the territory known as Hanigalbat and to the important Urartian mountain kingdom around Lake Van. To the northwest were Aramaean tribal states, related to peoples beyond the Euphrates River. It was against these states that Tukulti-Ninurta had begun campaigning when his reign prematurely ended.

LIFE'S WORK

Ashurnasirpal II came relatively young to the throne, but he continued the expansion begun by his grandfather and father with unparalleled energy. The army was reorganized, with cavalry units introduced for the first time to supplement infantry, which were accompanied by chariotry. The latter afforded mobility during long treks. The bas-relief art of Ashurnasirpal portrays improved vehicles of six-spoked wheels pulled by four horses, with three men standing on the armored platform. Ashurnasirpal fired bow and arrow from such a chariot, and the increased firepower was a significant development for his military strategy and tactics. The army was furnished with battering rams and other siege machines. The former appear as a kind of pointed-nosed tank with four wheels, propelled against city gates by the strength of the many men who could be sheltered under its armored top and sides. It was during Ashurnasirpal's reign that elephants were first employed by a king on campaign.

With Ashurnasirpal came an advanced art of beleaguering cities, and few were prepared to withstand his attack. Sculptures show these sieges, the prodigious amounts of tribute garnered, and a propagandistic expression of the requisite levels of brutality. In his inscriptions, Ashurnasirpal claimed to have employed this brutality so that conquered domains would not again rebel by withholding tribute. Minor princes saw the better part of valor in paying the requisite tribute before the siege and annually thereafter.

Ashurnasirpal's army employed its innovative tactics in continuous campaigns throughout his reign, although specific details are fully documented only for his initial years, from 883 to 878 B.C.E. Some scattered, undated events of the following decade and a half can be identified, but during this later period, the main energy of the king was given over to architectural construction

RULERS OF THE ASSYRIAN EMPIRE	
Ruler	*Reign (B.C.E.)*
Shamshi-Adad I	c. 1814-1782
Ishme-Dagan I	1782-1741
Ashur-uballit I	c. 1363-1330
Ashur-dan II	934-912
Adad-nirâri II	c. 911-891
Tukulti-Ninurta II	c. 890-884
Ashurnasirpal II	c. 883-859
Shalmaneser III	c. 858-824
Shamshi-Adad V	823-811
Adad-nirâri III	810-783

and artistic enterprises recording the events of the first years.

Of the surrounding lands, only Babylonia in the south was not invaded during Ashurnasirpal's reign. The most significant results of Ashurnasirpal's campaigns were in the north and northwest. The land of Nairi (later Armenia) and the Habur region were secured. He forced the ruler of Bit-Adini on the Euphrates to pay tribute and thus secured a bridgehead across that river, allowing not merely his army but also his merchant envoys to pass without duty. Later campaigns took him as far as the Mediterranean, where in a traditional gesture he dipped his weapon into the sea to symbolize its incorporation within his empire.

The methods of drawing conquered peoples into the Assyrian Empire were redefined. Adopting the words of an ancient predecessor Tukulti-apal-Esharra I (also called Tiglath-pileser), Ashurnasirpal affirmed, "To Ashur's land I added land, to Ashur's people I added people." His annexation proceeded in three ways. First, peripheral states were assumed to owe lavish tribute, which was collected whenever the Assyrian army was at their borders. Second, interim states submitting directly to Assyria paid yearly, nonruinous tribute and retained native rulers and almost complete self-government. The Assyrian official who remained to see that tribute was sent regularly to the capital could call on the army to enforce compliance. Third, conquered neighboring states became direct provinces, receiving an appointed governor supported by a military garrison. These states were under the same administrative system as Assyria itself and were required to pay the same taxes in goods or in conscripted labor and military service.

To control an empire conceived in these new ways with enlarged levels of displayed military power required not only a new capital city but also a revised conception of its fortresslike structure. The new capital at Kalhu was laid out by Ashurnasirpal on the east bank of the Tigris, nineteen miles north of its junction with the Greater Zab; its walls enclosed an irregular rectangle some 7,000 feet east to west by 5,500 feet north to south, an area of 884 acres (358 hectares).

Two citadels formed the southeast and southwest corners within the walls that Ashurnasirpal completed. The *ekal masharti*, or arsenal, occupied the somewhat lower southeast citadel, but it was not fully completed until the days of his son Shalmaneser III (named for Shalmaneser I, whom Ashurnasirpal knew to have begun the original fortifications on the site of Kalhu).

On a height some 65 feet (20 meters) above the plain, the original acropolis of the southwest citadel formed an irregular rectangle because of the abutment of its western edge along the original bed of the Tigris. In the northwest corner, the remains of the ziggurat rose to a conical peak 100 feet (30 meters) high; at its base Ashurnasirpal built the temple for the war god Ninurta.

To the south of the ziggurat and accompanying temple, a huge palace complex occupied 6.5 acres (2.6 hectares); on its rediscovery in the mid-nineteenth century it was dubbed the Northwest Palace of Ashurnasirpal II. At its northern end was the administrative wing, with a variety of bureaucratic chambers, including a records repository, surrounding a great open court area used for ceremonial and reception functions. At the southern end were the domestic suites, including harem quarters. In neither of these wings were the walls decorated with bas-relief slabs.

Beginning from the south side of the great open court of the northern administrative wing, stretching southward to the southern domestic wing, was a central ceremonial block, which opened impressively off the southern side of the great courtyard through two massive, magnificently decorated gateways leading to the largest room of the palace, the throne room. With the exception of one built by Sennacherib at Ninua (Nineveh), the room is the largest within any Assyrian palace, measuring 154 feet by 33 feet (47 meters by 10 meters). Tribute bearers from all parts of the empire were led into this room, as the bas-relief slabs of the entrance document, with details such as the type of tribute borne and the garments worn by the divergent ethnic representatives.

On the south side of the throne room lay an inner courtyard. Beyond, through a series of gateways, was a maze of chambers, many of them decorated, like the throne room, with huge bas-relief slabs standing at least

7 feet (2 meters) high from floor level. Only the throne room walls portray the fury of the king as hunter of lions and destroyer of cities. Another nine rooms have slabs with a single large relief, cut across the middle by a band of inscription right over the figures. Each room shows minor variations in lines of text or exact detail of royal campaigns during the first six years, reflecting the sequence in the construction process. In one corridor leading to the throne room, an inscribed stela of 864 B.C.E., with a relief portraying the king, records a celebration of the completion of the great palace and an exotic arboretum—a banquet at which 69,574 people from the extent of the empire, including the 16,000 inhabitants of Kalhu and 1,500 palace officials, were in attendance. The menu was varied and prodigious, and the feast lasted ten days.

Ashurnasirpal II. (Library of Congress)

When Ashurnasirpal died in 859 B.C.E., his body was laid to rest in a gigantic sarcophagus made from a single block of diorite weighing 18 tons, at the old capital of Ashur, the source of the Assyrian royal tradition. His inscribed memorial stela was placed in the row with those of his predecessors.

SIGNIFICANCE

Numerous portraits of the king came from the sculptured rooms. Sections of this bas-relief have been excavated and sent to many parts of the world, making Ashurnasirpal's face the best known of all Assyrian kings'. A variety of quasihuman, quasidivine creatures are shown accompanying the king in the performance of ritual duties. The inner core of the ceremonial midsection of the palace was the setting for a peculiar mix of propagandistically displayed belligerence, formally arranged processionals, and mysterious rites of purification. The effect was that the farther the king and his advisers penetrated into the inner chambers, the more they perceived the need for exorcism. Fearful things of humans and gods surrounded Ashurnasirpal II. Empire was an awesome matter, even for its creator.

He was succeeded by his son Shalmaneser III, grandson Shamshi-Adad V, and great-grandson Adad-nirâri III, who attempted to match the achievements of their distinguished predecessor. At a later date, Sargon II remodeled a section of the great palace for his own use, leaving inscriptional tribute to his ancestor. Esarhaddon rebuilt the *ekal masharti* and the canal that provided water from the Zab, but was, at his death, in the process of dismantling the Northwest Palace so that he might use the reverse of its wall slabs in the decoration of a palace that he had only begun to construct. Ashurbanipal reconstructed the Ehulhul Temple at Harran, which Ashurnasirpal II had founded, and honored the earlier king's work. Then began that silence from which his memory was not disinterred until A. H. Layard began excavations at Kalhu on November 9, 1845, and brought to light the remarkable bas-reliefs, the inscriptions, and the monumental buildings of Ashurnasirpal II.

—*Clyde Curry Smith*

FURTHER READING

Brinkman, J. A. *A Political History of Post-Kassite Babylonia, 1158-722 B.C.* Rome: Pontificium Institutum Biblicum, 1968. This standard of historiographic excellence mines all material pertinent to the period, with enormous bibliographic detail in its extensive notes.

Grayson, A. K. *From Tiglath-pileser I to Ashur-nasir-apli II.* Vol. 2 in *Assyrian Royal Inscriptions.* Wiesbaden, Germany: Otto Harrassowitz, 1976. A complete reediting in English translation of all source materials is the intention of this series. A consideration of Ashurnasirpal II occupies about half of this volume.

Mallowan, M. E. L. *Nimrud and Its Remains.* 3 vols. New York: Dodd, Mead, 1966. Sir Max Mallowan reexcavated the principal features of Kalhu between 1949 and 1962. These volumes, the third of which contains maps and plans, detail the history of the site, the previous excavations, and the materials found in the remains of Ashurnasirpal's Northwest Palace.

Oates, Joan, and David Oates. *Nimrud: An Assyrian Imperial City Revealed.* London: British School of Archaeology in Iraq, 2001. Written by two of the excavators from the Kalhu site, this volume is copiously illustrated and summarizes the history of Nimrud as revealed by excavations from the 1800's to the early twenty-first century.

Paley, S. M. *King of the World: Ashur-nasir-pal II of Assyria 883-859 B.C.* Brooklyn, N.Y.: Brooklyn Museum, 1976. Many museums around the world received examples of the bas-relief slabs from the Northwest Palace. The Brooklyn Museum used the occasion of publishing its own holdings to reconstruct the plan of the palace and identify the original location of all known examples.

Stearns, J. B. *Reliefs from the Palace of Ashurnasirpal II.* Osnabrück, Germany: Biblio, 1984. Stearns began the effort to identify all surviving examples of Ashurnasirpal palace relief slabs held in museum collections around the world and to classify their types and functions.

SEE ALSO: Ashurbanipal; Tiglath-pileser III.

RELATED ARTICLES in *Great Events from History: The Ancient World*: c. 883-c. 824 B.C.E., Second Assyrian Empire Displays Military Prowess; 745 B.C.E., Tiglath-pileser III Rules Assyria; 701 B.C.E., Sennacherib Invades Syro-Palestine.

AŚOKA
Indian king (r. c. 273/265-c. 238 B.C.E.)

Through energetic and enlightened administration of his kingdom, Aśoka spread the Buddhist faith in all directions and, by means of his Rock, Pillar, and Cave edicts, provided India, the districts surrounding India, and, ultimately, the entire world with an example of regal compassion that is as admirable as it is rare.

BORN: c. 302 B.C.E.; probably near Pataliputra, Magadha, India
DIED: c. 238 B.C.E.; place unknown
ALSO KNOWN AS: Aśoka the Great; Ashoka
AREAS OF ACHIEVEMENT: Government and politics, religion

EARLY LIFE

What can be known of the life of Aśoka (ah-SOH-kah) derives from two primary sources: first, the legends that sprang up during and after his death (and which are often suspected of helping to grind certain zealous religious axes); second, Aśoka's own "sermons in stone," the thirty-five edicts that he began issuing in 260 B.C.E. and that were inscribed on rocks, pillars hewn from sandstone, and the walls of caves in the Barabar Hills of ancient Magadha. Therefore, only a very fragmentary early life can be pieced together. There is much to be left to conjecture and little to be known with certainty.

Aśoka was the son of Bindusara and the grandson of Chandragupta Maurya, the founder of the Mauryan Dynasty and consolidator of a great empire that included all northern India as far west as the Hindu Kush. A charming legend is told of the naming of Aśoka. His mother, who may have been named Subhadrangi, was supposedly kept away from the king's bed by party politics. After finally having gained access to the bed, she bore the king a son and said thereafter, "I am without sorrow," which is to say, in Sanskrit, "Aśoka."

Aśoka is reputed to have been ungainly in appearance and, perhaps, to have been disliked by his father. In his early manhood, however, he was called on by Bindusara to put down a revolt in Taxila and from there to proceed to Ujjain to act as a viceroy.

Aśoka appears to have had numerous brothers and sisters, and, if certain Ceylonese legends are accepted, he was most cruel to his brothers in the process of jockeying for the succession to the throne, murdering ninety-nine of them before becoming king. Such an account, however, may well be part of the tradition of Chand Aśoka (Black Aśoka), the epithet intended to indicate that, be-

fore his conversion to Buddhism, he was a man whose ruthlessness and cruelty knew no bounds. That there was a struggle for the throne is supported by the fact that Aśoka's accession to it (c. 273) occurred four years before his coronation. That blood might have been shed in the process of Aśoka's becoming king seems not unlikely.

Xuanzang (Hsüan Tsang), a Chinese Buddhist pilgrim who traveled in India in the seventh century C.E., reports having seen a high pillar that commemorated the site of what had been called "Aśoka's Hell," a prison that housed a series of elaborate torture chambers. According to one of the legends, Aśoka's enlightenment came about when he beheld a Buddhist holy man whose imperviousness to torture moved him to become aware in a painful way of his cruelty, to destroy the prison, and to relax the laws against criminals. Solider evidence, however, indicates that Aśoka's conversion may rather have been the consequence of his beholding the extreme destructibility of the Kalinga people in southeastern India.

In 262, Aśoka fought and won a war against the Kalingas; in Rock Edict 13, referring to himself as "Priyadarsi, Beloved of the Gods," he chronicled his conversion, noting that 150,000 persons were captured, 100,000 were slain, and many times that number had died from the general effects of the war. The havoc that the war had wreaked had caused Aśoka to become intensely devoted to the study, love, and inculcation of dharma. This intense devotion, coupled with his sorrow and regret, had led him to desire "security, self-control, impartiality, and cheerfulness for all living creatures." He went on in the edict to announce a radical new program for his empire: He would abandon military conquest and would try to effect moral conquest in and among people.

LIFE'S WORK

In 260, Aśoka issued the first of the Rock Edicts and made his first "pious tour." Both edict and tour were part of his plan to endow his people with dharma. The concept of dharma is a complex one generally, and it becomes no simpler in Aśoka's use of it. For him, it had to do both with his Buddhist underpinnings and with morality and righteousness in general. Dharma was something he did out of Buddhist piety; it was also a complex of responses to life available to non-Buddhists. It was a kind of ecosystem, a recognition that one's well-being was closely and eternally connected with the well-being of everyone else. Aśoka's attempt to promulgate this understanding represents a tremendous evolution in the moral development of humankind.

Aśoka had the edict written in the languages of the districts where they were to be placed. Monumental Prakrit, a kind of *lingua franca* for India at the time, was the primary language of the edicts, but on the western frontier of the kingdom, edicts written in Greek and Aramaic have been found. Noting that in past times rulers had made great pleasure trips through the land, Aśoka determined to embark on another series of tours, during which he would talk to people about dharma, visit the aged, and give gifts and money to those in need.

In 257, Aśoka appointed the first *dharma-mahamatras*, the officers of an institution charged with traveling about the kingdom and helping to spread the concept of dharma.

Aśoka. (Hulton|Archive by Getty Images)

Interestingly, these men were responsible for spreading the Aśokan notion of dharma through all sects; they were not supposed to attempt sectarian conversions but were rather to supervise the distribution of various gifts and to help promote conformity to the ideals of compassion, liberality, truthfulness, purity, gentleness, and goodness.

Aśoka worried about the almost reflexive tendency of people dedicated to a particular religion to quarrel over dogma, and some of his sternest statements in the edicts address this problem. In one inscription, he baldly proclaims that dissident nuns and monks must be expelled from their order. Aśoka recognized two ways in which people could advance in dharma: moral prescription and meditation. The teachers of any religion, be it Buddhism, Christianity, Islam, or any other, are always ready to provide moral prescription. So, in fact, was Aśoka, and he did so in the edicts. In Pillar Edict 7, however, he acknowledged that people make greater progress in dharma through practicing meditation than through heeding moral prescription.

There has been considerable argument concerning the precise nature of Aśoka's religion. The edicts have little to say of doctrinaire Buddhism. Aśoka's tolerance of other religions is declared clearly and eloquently in the inscriptions. He often spoke of *svarga* (Heaven) and the possibility of obtaining it through dharma. He had nothing to say on stone or pillar of nirvana, a veritable plank in the Buddhist platform. Some scholars have been led by these facts to suggest that Aśoka was—as Akbar was to be almost two thousand years later—a practitioner of some sort of universal religion. In many other ways, however, Aśoka strongly supported and promoted dharma as revealed in and through Buddhism, and his religion's spread through western Asia during his reign was certainly in part a result of those tremendous administrative energies that helped further his humanitarian purposes.

Throughout the 250's, Aśoka made moral tours, erected Buddhist shrines, and commissioned edicts. In 258-257, he issued in one body the fourteen Major Rock Edicts and granted cave dwellings to the Ajivikas, an order of Buddhist monks. In 250, he made a pilgrimage to Lumbinī Garden, the birthplace of the Buddha, and erected there a commemorative pillar. In 243-242, he issued the Pillar Edicts.

According to one account of Aśoka's last days, by 238 he had lost his power to the high officials of the court. In his old age, Aśoka supposedly nominated as his successor Samprati, one of his grandsons. Under the influence of the usurping officers, Samprati proceeded to abuse his grandfather, reducing Aśoka's allowances so drastically that, finally, for dinner the aging king would be sent only half an amalaka fruit on an earthen plate. How or where Aśoka died remains a matter of conjecture but that he died in straitened circumstances seems likely.

SIGNIFICANCE

That might makes right is an idea that has been taken for granted by such historical leaders as Alexander the Great, Julius Caesar, and Genghis Khan. What made Aśoka great was his grasping another truth and giving it life in third century India. In Rock Edict 13, he asserted that "the chiefest conquest is the conquest of Right and not of Might," and he went on to make his deeds commensurate with his rock-inscribed words. He abolished war within his empire immediately after he had subdued the Kalingas. He never fought another one.

That he desired to civilize both his people and neighboring peoples is made clear by the testimony of the edicts; the usual formula, however, the one that equates civilization of a people with subjugation, did not apply. Aśoka did not give up entirely the idea that chastisement may on occasion be necessary, though, for he reminded the forest people who had come under his sway that they must grow in dharma, and he reserved the right to exercise punishment, despite having repented of his violent ways, in order to make them cease their criminal behavior. The edicts of Aśoka reveal a fascinating blend of the practical and the ideal, the proud and the humble; they record the workings of a complex mind.

Writing of Aśoka in *The Outline of History* (1921), H. G. Wells judged:

Amidst the tens of thousands of names of monarchs that crowd the columns of history, their majesties and graciousnesses and serenities and royal highnesses and the like, the name of Aśoka shines, and shines almost alone, a star. From the Volga to Japan his name is still honoured. China, Tibet, and even India, though it has left his doctrine, preserve the tradition of his greatness. More living men cherish his memory to-day than have ever heard the names of Constantine or Charlemagne.

The high-flown rhetoric of this passage ought not to bias one against the beauty of its vision. If most people do not today cherish the memory of Aśoka above the memories of Constantine the Great and Charlemagne, that fact is perhaps a measure of the modern world's bad taste in heroes.

—Johnny Wink

FURTHER READING

Bhandarkar, D. R. *Aśoka*. Ottawa: Laurier Books, 2001. A spirited and, at times, combative rehearsal of Aśoka's life and works, dealing especially well with the Aśokan concept of dharma and according Aśoka a high place in history. Contains translations of the Rock and Pillar Edicts accompanied by detailed notes.

Campbell, Joseph. *The Masks of God: Oriental Mythology*. New York: Penguin, 1976. This volume contains a brief but luminous discussion of Aśoka, comparing the destiny of Buddhism under Aśoka to that of Christianity under Constantine the Great and noting the absence from the Rock Edicts of certain fundamental Buddhist doctrines.

Durant, Will. *Our Oriental Heritage*. New York: MJF, 1992. Durant presents a respectful but slightly skeptical account of the life of Aśoka, seeing the seeds of the downfall of the Mauryas in the very piety of Aśoka that is so admired. Provides an especially vivid description, by way of Xuanzang, of "Aśoka's Hell."

Mookerji, Radhakumud. *Aśoka*. 3d ed. Delhi: Motilal Banarsidass, 1962. A scholarly biography that, like Bhandarkar's book, accords Aśoka a high place in the moral annals of humankind. It contains copiously annotated translations of the Rock and Pillar Edicts and three cave inscriptions as well as appendices concerning the chronology of the edicts and the scripts, dialects, and grammar of the texts.

Nikam, N. A., and Richard McKeon. *The Edicts of Aśoka*. Chicago: University of Chicago Press, 1978. This handy translation of all the edicts, except for the Queen's Edict and some variants of the minor edicts, also features a brief introduction that makes interesting comparisons between Aśoka and other great world figures such as Hammurabi, Charlemagne, Akbar, and Marcus Aurelius.

Thapar, Romila. *Aśoka and the Decline of the Mauryas*. Rev. ed. New York: Oxford University Press, 1997. A thorough study of the life and times of Aśoka, featuring an account of the disrepair into which his empire fell after his death. Includes numerous valuable appendices concerning the historical record of Aśoka's period based on pottery and coins, the geographical locations of the edicts, and the titles of Aśoka. Includes a translation of the edicts.

Wells, H. G. *The Outline of History*. Rev. ed. Garden City, N.Y.: Doubleday, 1971. A vivid and highly laudatory account of Aśoka, allotting him a more significant place in history than that of Alexander the Great

and arguing that the epithet "great" is more properly applied to Aśoka.

SEE ALSO: Buddha; Chandragupta Maurya.

RELATED ARTICLES in *Great Events from History: The Ancient World*: c. 273/265-c. 238 B.C.E., Aśoka Reigns over India; c. 250 B.C.E., Third Buddhist Council Convenes.

ASPASIA OF MILETUS

Greek *hetaera*

Aspasia's role as companion to the Athenian statesman Pericles made her the target of contemporary abuse and criticism. Her reputation for skill in rhetoric made her a philosophic and historical ideal of the independent, educated, influential woman.

BORN: c. 475 B.C.E.; Miletus, Asia Minor (now in Turkey)

DIED: After 428 B.C.E.; probably Athens, Greece

AREAS OF ACHIEVEMENT: Government and politics, philosophy

EARLY LIFE

Aspasia (as-PAY-shih-uh) was born in the ancient Greek city of Miletus. Her father was named Axiochus; her mother's name is unknown. Located on the southwest coast of Asia Minor (modern Turkey), Miletus enjoyed a reputation for wealth based on extensive seaborne trade and for philosophic inquiry into the nature of the universe.

The city suffered severely in a Persian attack of 494 B.C.E. It is therefore not surprising that Miletus in 479 joined the Athenian-led league against Persia. The political and military relationship of Miletus with Athens was, however, problematic. For some years after 450, an Athenian garrison occupied the city, and toward the end (after 411) of the long-term war of Athens with Sparta, Miletus was suspected of collusion with Athens's enemies. Nevertheless, during this same period, several Milesians left their home city to achieve prominence in Athens. Those emigrants included the city planner Hippodamus, the poet and musician Timotheus, and the most famous woman of fifth century Athens, Aspasia.

LIFE'S WORK

The surviving ancient sources for fifth century Athenian history do not permit a connected biography of Aspasia.

The most reliable sources are a few notices in contemporary Athenian comic literature and several references to Aspasia by Socrates' pupils (including Plato). Many details are offered by the Greek biographer Plutarch in his life of Pericles in *Bioi paralleloi* (c. 105-115 C.E.; *Parallel Lives*, 1579), but that brief account was written more than five hundred years after Aspasia's lifetime.

Aspasia must have come from Miletus to Athens before c. 450 B.C.E. She first appears in the historical record about 445, when the prominent Athenian politician and military leader Pericles divorced—under, it was asserted, amicable circumstances—the mother of his two sons. Soon thereafter, Pericles began living and appearing in public with Aspasia. Ancient sources consistently identify her as a *hetaera*, a Greek term literally meaning "female companion" and used of women (often of slave or freedwoman status and usually of foreign origin) who were sexual, social, and occasionally intellectual nonmarital companions of prominent Athenian men.

Because of her status as a foreign-born, intelligent, articulate companion of Pericles, Aspasia was, throughout Pericles' later political career, consistently attacked as a malign influence on his public policies and his political and military leadership. She was, for example, viewed by Pericles' enemies as responsible for his leadership in a war Athens fought with the island of Samos, a traditional rival of Miletus. The Athenian comic poet Aristophanes, in his play *Acharnēs* (425 B.C.E.; *The Acharnians*, 1812), which amusingly, but quite seriously, expressed the Athenian longing for a peaceful resolution to military conflicts, represented Aspasia as partially responsible for provoking the Peloponnesian War between Athens and Sparta. Another Athenian comic poet, Aristophanes' peer Cratinus, referred to Aspasia on the stage as nothing but a shameless prostitute who influ-

Aspasia of Miletus. (Library of Congress)

reported to have had a similar woman companion.

More significant than the political abuse she attracted as Pericles' partner is the strong tradition that Aspasia was skilled at oratorical composition, instruction, and philosophic conversation. Pericles is recorded as praising her wisdom and sense of politics. Thus, several ancient authorities imply or allege that Aspasia advised Pericles on his acclaimed public speeches (including the famous funeral oration of 430, reported in the works of Thucydides), and several sources state that she participated in philosophic argument with Socrates.

Aspasia had a son by Pericles. The son's irregular status had been defined by Pericles' own law denying Athenian citizenship to anyone who did not have two Athenian citizens as parents. Xanthippus, Pericles' eldest son, with whom he was said to have had a tense relationship, died in the great plague that struck Athens in 429. Before Pericles' death later that year, therefore, the Athenian democracy bestowed a special exemption so that his son born of Aspasia could become an Athenian citizen. Pericles the Younger, as he was called, grew to maturity and served the Athenian democracy as a general at the naval victory of Arginusae in 406 B.C.E. Soon thereafter, however, he was among the generals executed by the Athenians for having failed to rescue naval crews after the battle.

After Pericles' death, Aspasia virtually disappears from the historical record. A single reference mentions that she became the companion of another rising politician, a man named Lysicles, who died in 428 B.C.E.

enced Pericles with her sex. A third Athenian comedian, Hermippus, also abused Aspasia publicly and was said to have prosecuted her for impiety in an Athenian court; Pericles, in turn, reportedly offered in court an emotional, tearful defense of his mistress. These legal episodes, however, are almost certainly apocryphal, prompted by later generations' overly literal readings of Hermippus's comedies.

All these accusations simply reflect the perceived influence of a woman of independent judgment, education, intelligence, and resourcefulness. She may well have been, as were other *hetaerae*, the owner and operator of a brothel. She was certainly Pericles' mistress, but other prominent Athenian men of the time also enjoyed relationships with similar "companions." For example, Pericles' political opponent, the great Cimon—whose own sister, Elpinice, had once been the object of Pericles' attention—reportedly had liaisons with two *hetaerae*. In a later generation, the Athenian rhetorician Isocrates was

SIGNIFICANCE

In his philosophic dialogue *Menexenos* (*Menexenus*, 1804), written 388-368 B.C.E. and therefore after the life and prominence of its characters, Plato portrayed Socrates as praising Aspasia's literary and oratorical skills. Indeed, Plato presented Socrates as reciting a brief funeral oration claimed as Aspasia's composition. Plato's depiction of Aspasia in this dialogue is sarcastic—Aspasia is said to have composed speeches well, for a woman—and typical. Plato manifestly enjoyed pretending that some aspects of his master Socrates' knowledge were derived from sources other Athenians would have thought unlikely. Thus, in his dialogue *Symposion* (388-368 B.C.E.; *Symposium*, 1701), Plato asserted that Socrates learned the philosophic basis for and logical consequences of love from Diotima, a probably fictitious woman identified as coming from a rural Greek setting. Plato's mention of Aspasia, and the rhetorical exercise he attributed to her—along with the tradition about Aspasia maintained by other contemporaries in the circle of Socrates—turned her memory into a rhetorical commonplace: She became the ideal philosophic woman, one who could influence statesmen and converse on equal terms with philosophers.

This process of idealization began with Socrates' students Antisthenes and Aeschines, both of whom wrote philosophic dialogues titled "Aspasia." The process continued in Greek philosophical and rhetorical schools down through the fourth century. Aspasia's likeness adorned Roman gardens; much later, in the nineteenth century, she became the idealized figure of an educated ancient Greek woman and was represented in numerous academic paintings and historical novels. More recently, she became a symbol of independence for the North American feminist movement; for example, Aspasia is prominently depicted in artist Judy Chicago's multimedia work *The Dinner Party* (1979).

—*Paul B. Harvey, Jr.*

FURTHER READING

De Ste. Croix, G. E. M. *The Origins of the Peloponnesian War*. Ithaca, N.Y.: Cornell University Press, 1972. A scholarly, detailed, and convincing discussion of the issues that led to the Peloponnesian War. The policies and personality of Pericles are treated prominently throughout. The accusations made against Aspasia regarding her influence on Pericles are discussed in pages 235-243.

Dover, K. J. "The Freedom of the Intellectual in Greek Society." In *Greeks and Their Legacy*. Oxford, England: Blackwell, 1988. A critical examination of the tradition of Aspasia's trial for impiety. Pays full attention to social context and to the ancient evidence.

Ehrenberg, Victor. *The People of Aristophanes*. New York: Barnes & Noble, 1974. A classic introduction to Athenian society and social history in the age of Aspasia and Pericles. Ehrenberg provides (especially in pages 177-181) a reliable, lively treatment of what is known of the *hetaera* in Athenian society, and he discusses throughout what the Greek comic dramatists of fifth century Athens can—and cannot—tell modern readers about the realities of Greek life.

Henry, Madeleine M. *Prisoner of History: Aspasia of Miletus and Her Biographical Tradition*. New York: Oxford University Press, 1997. The first several chapters provide a scholarly account of Aspasia, with a critical review of the evidence for reconstructing her biography. The remainder of the book is an entertaining introduction to how Aspasia has been represented by primarily male interpreters in the literary, philosophic, and pictorial traditions of Western European society.

Kebric, Robert B. *Greek People*. Mountain View, Calif.: Mayfield, 1989. A reliable account of classical Greek history presented in terms of biographical portraits. Chapter 6 offers a highly readable but very traditional perception of Aspasia as a participant in fifth century aristocratic Athenian society.

Richter, G. M. A. *The Portraits of the Greeks*. Revised by R. R. R. Smith. Ithaca, N.Y.: Cornell University Press, 1984. Pages 99-100 show a Roman portrait of Aspasia. The accompanying discussion is an important supplement to Henry's work.

Stadter, Philip A. *Commentary on Plutarch's Pericles*. Chapel Hill: University of North Carolina Press, 1989. Stadter's commentary is a good introduction to the historical and historiographic issues surrounding Plutarch's presentation of Pericles and Aspasia.

SEE ALSO: Aristophanes; Cimon; Hypatia; Pericles; Socrates.

RELATED ARTICLES in *Great Events from History: The Ancient World*: 480-479 B.C.E., Persian Invasion of Greece; May, 431-September, 404 B.C.E., Peloponnesian War.

AŚVAGHOSA
Indian poet and religious historian

Aśvaghosa wrote the first comprehensive account of Buddha's life and two related Buddhist works, depicting the foundations of Buddhism and how the religion was perceived by contemporary Indians.

BORN: c. 80 C.E.; Ajodhya, India
DIED: c. 150 C.E.; Peshawar (now in Pakistan)
ALSO KNOWN AS: Asvagosa; Ashvagosa; Ashvaghosha; Aśvaghoṣa
AREAS OF ACHIEVEMENT: Historiography, literature, religion

EARLY LIFE

Aśvaghosa (AHSH-vuhg-oh-suh) is considered to be a great Buddhist scholar, the father of Sanskrit drama, and one of the best of all known Indian poets. He did not write about himself, and he had no biographers. As a result, very little is known about the details of Aśvaghosa's life. However, Aśvaghosa's reported life span—some seventy years—is based on several clear lines of written evidence. Among the most compelling is that his works were edited by a Central Asian writer whose writing style, which overlays the original Sanskrit text, fits within this time frame.

Aśvaghosa was most likely born in Ajodhya into a family of the Brahman caste. Therefore, Aśvaghosa's education is believed to have been that of a Brahman scholar, trained in religion and in all of the contemporary arts and sciences. According to most sources, Aśvaghosa became one of the most distinguished of Buddhist scholars during the reign of the Kushān king, Kanishka (d. c. 152 C.E.). Kanishka was the Indo-Scythian conqueror of North India whose reign began c. 127 C.E. At that time Aśvaghosa would have been in his late twenties. Kanishka, a very devout Buddhist, valued him highly and subsequently Aśvaghosa became both the king's trusted counselor and the twelfth Buddhist patriarch.

Aśvaghosa was originally a militant Brahman and was converted to Buddhism after losing a debate on the relative merits of Buddhism and Vedantic religion with Kanishka's religious adviser Parsva. After this conversion, Aśvaghosa reportedly did his best to overthrow Brahmanism.

LIFE'S WORK

Aśvaghosa is credited with writing two important Buddhist works: the *Buddhacarita* (first or second century C.E.; *Buddhacharitam*, 1911), a life of Buddha, and the *Saundarānanda* (first or second century C.E.; *Saundarananda of Asvaghosa*, 1928), which relates the conversion to Buddhism of Buddha's half brother Nanda. The colophons of these works state that Aśvaghosa is their author, and the works are stylistically interconnected in ways that prove their authorship by one individual. References to and citations of Aśvaghosa's works by other writers who lived during Kanishka's reign are testimony to their great importance.

Aśvaghosa is said to have entered Kanishka's service after the king conquered the city of Benāres, where Aśvaghosa lived at that time. Kanishka is supposed to have shown the great worth of Aśvaghosa's ideas by starving several horses for a week, then taking them to hear Aśvaghosa preach and giving them food. The horses supposedly shed tears on hearing Aśvaghosa preach and refused to eat. Aśvaghosa's name, which means "voice of the horse," is said to have come from this incident.

Aśvaghosa's writings and sermons contain allusions to ideas that some deem to derive from the early Christianity of his time. Two of these are the idea of universal salvation, and of the power of *bodhi* ("awakening" or "enlightenment"), which led to the development of Mahāyāna Buddhism in the first century C.E. Mahāyāna Buddhism (which includes, among others, modern Zen Buddhism) teaches that many paths can lead to nirvana and that all human beings have the Buddha nature (enlightenment potential). Some special people, known as bodhisattvas, attain nirvana and help others to do so. More traditional schools such as Theravāda and Hīnayāna Buddhism embrace Buddha's original monkish lifestyle of meditation and hold that humans are reborn over and over, collecting karma and reaching nirvana only by following Buddhist teaching.

Aśvaghosa is believed to have traveled very widely throughout India to collect stories about the life of Buddha and the other important founders of Buddhism, as well as in his capacity as the twelfth Buddhist patriarch. He gained a reputation as a preacher-musician and was said to have taken a troupe of skilled musicians with him on his travels. He is supposed to have converted a great many people to Buddhism through the combined persuasiveness of his poetry, preaching, and pleasant musical efforts. He also used his great writing skill to weave the stories into the *Buddhacarita*, using the vehicle of Sanskrit poetry and popularizing the poetic style known as *kavya*. Aśvaghosa's works were so important to Buddhists that the *Buddhacarita* eventually was translated into Chinese, Tibetan, Japanese, and English.

The *Buddhacarita* depicts the life of Buddha in twenty-eight cantos. Twenty-five percent of canto 1, all of cantos 2 to 13, and the first quarter of canto 14 are extant in the original Sanskrit form. The rest are found in complete Chinese and Tibetan translations. The *Buddhacarita* begins with Buddha's conception, describes his life, and closes with an account of the war over his relics, the first Buddhist council, and the reign of Aśoka (c. 302–c. 238 B.C.E.), who was a great supporter of Buddhism. The *Saundarānanda*, with eighteen extant cantos, deals with conversion of Buddha's half brother Nanda and sets out at length Aśvaghosa's view of the path to enlightenment attributed to Buddha. Aśvaghosa's reputation was so great that many later, less significant writers attempted to capture some of his glory for their works by using his name as a pen name. As a result, several other works that were once attributed to Aśvaghosa have been determined to be forgeries on modern analysis.

SIGNIFICANCE

Buddhism, founded in the sixth century B.C.E. by the Indian prince Siddhārtha Gautama, uses his life and teaching (dharma) to model religious life. Before Aśvaghosa wrote the *Buddhacarita*, no comprehensive account of Buddha's life existed. According to history, and Aśvaghosa, Siddhārtha realized that pleasure only temporarily masks suffering. He left his family to fast and meditate under a bodhi tree, attained nirvana (enlightenment), and became able to explain the causes of suffering and the way to find release from it. As Buddha, Siddhārtha taught the intertwined Four Noble Truths, the Eightfold Path, and the Middle Way. The truths are: Life is suffering; suffering is due to desire; desire can be ended; and the way to do so is by following the Eightfold Path and Middle Way. Nirvana is achieved by following tenets that include right views, intentions, speech, actions, livelihood, endeavor, mindfulness, and meditation. Buddha advocated celibacy, moderate living, and equanimity based on meditation and morality.

Aśvaghosa's works were most significant because they explained Buddhism to average readers. Some of Aśvaghosa's statements about Buddha's life and teaching appear in the commentary of his contemporaries, while others, not extant elsewhere, provide additions to understanding the history of Indian thought. Furthermore, Aśvaghosa's artistic, historical, religious, and scientific references, the result of his extensive Brahman education, provide insights into contemporary science, theater, and art unavailable from other sources. Aśvaghosa's work also incorporated some aspects of Christian belief into Buddhism, further distinguishing it from Brahmanism.

While Aśvaghosa was revered as a superb writer, he was not an original teacher or philosopher. At the end of the *Buddhacarita*, he stated that he wrote it not as a learned work, but for the happiness of the world. In this light, many authorities see it as a manual that described the viewpoint of pious, first century C.E. Indian Buddhists who respected Buddhist scripture and were devoted to Buddha.

—*Sanford S. Singer*

FURTHER READING

Aśvaghosa. *The "Buddhacarita" or Acts of the Buddha: Complete Sanskrit Text with English Translation.* Translated by E. H. Johnston. Delhi, India: Motilal Banarsidass, 1998. This detailed current work provides a great deal of information on Aśvaghosa. It includes description and analysis of the great Sanskrit poet's history and works, the extant Sanskrit cantos, and translation based on the earlier Chinese and Tibetan versions of the work.

Law, Bimala Churin. *Asvaghosa.* Calcutta, India: Royal Asiatic Society of Bengal, 1945. This very interesting monograph gives a good deal of information on Aśvaghosa as a writer, as a man, as a poet, and as a teacher. References throughout the book explain and help to clarify misconceptions on the great Buddhist.

Rosenfeld, John M. *The Dynastic Arts of the Kushans.* 1967. Reprint. Columbia, Mo.: South Asia Books, 1993. Chapter 2 in particular covers Aśvaghosa's association with Kanishka.

Thomas, Edward J. *The Life of Buddha: As Legend and History.* New York: Dover, 2000. Summarizes the state of knowledge about Buddha's life and assesses the sources for his biography. Helps to contextualize Aśvaghosa's work and compares it with the works of others.

Wilson, Epiphanius. *Sacred Books of the East.* New York: Wiley, 1945. This book includes the late nineteenth century English translation of Aśvaghosa's "Life of Buddha" (by Samuel Beal) from the Chinese version by Dharmaraksha (420 C.E.).

SEE ALSO: Ānanda; Asanga; Aśoka; Bodhidharma; Buddha; Chandragupta Maurya; Gośāla Maskarīputra; Kanishka; Vardhamāna; Vasubandhu; Vattagamani.

SAINT ATHANASIUS OF ALEXANDRIA
Alexandrian bishop and writer

For half a century, Athanasius helped to maintain Christian orthodoxy in the Eastern church from his position as bishop of Alexandria. His defense of the doctrine of the Trinity was influential in the formulation of the Nicene Creed.

BORN: c. 293 C.E.; Alexandria, Egypt
DIED: May 2, 373 C.E.; Alexandria, Egypt
AREAS OF ACHIEVEMENT: Religion, historiography

EARLY LIFE

Athanasius (ath-uh-NAY-zhee-uhs) was born about 293 C.E. in Alexandria, one of the leading cities of Egypt. Since its founding in 332 B.C.E. by Alexander the Great, Alexandria had been a focal point of the Greco-Roman world. Its beautiful harbor served as a center for extensive trade with all parts of the Mediterranean region. The native flax of Egypt was woven into linen, which was shipped as far away as Britain, and Alexandria enjoyed a world monopoly on the papyrus plant and its products—not only writing materials but also sails, mats, and sandals.

With a population of a million or more in Athanasius's time, Alexandria was not only a commercial and administrative center but also one of the greatest centers of learning in the ancient world. The Alexandrian library preserved documents from all parts of the ancient Near East and accommodated scholars from the entire Mediterranean area. It was there that the Greek Old Testament, the Septuagint, had been translated from the original Hebrew by Jewish scholars. Alexandria was a cosmopolitan city with large populations of Egyptians, Jews, Greeks, and Romans. Its array of palaces and public buildings, gardens and groves, pagan temples and Christian churches, made Alexandria one of the wonders of the Roman Empire.

Athanasius's parents, who were moderately wealthy, provided him with a liberal education, typical of the Greek culture in which he lived. He learned Greek, Latin, Egyptian antiquities, philosophy, and religion, but it was the Holy Scriptures that impressed him most. Alexandria was a focal point of intense persecution of Christians during the reign of Diocletian and Galerius, and several of Athanasius's teachers, along with many church leaders, suffered martyrdom. Athanasius well understood the seriousness of converting to the Christian faith.

Athanasius was an earnest and diligent young man who early came to the attention of Alexander, the bishop of Alexandria from 312 to 328. The bishop helped in the boy's education, and eventually Athanasius became his secretary and a presbyter under his supervision.

Athanasius was very small of stature, rather stooped, and somewhat emaciated in appearance. He had a forceful personality and sharpness of intellect. Though he was gentle and meek of spirit, he was driven by a determination to keep the orthodox Christian faith no matter what the cost, no matter how many opposed him. His inner intensity made him quick of movement and constantly active. He was known for his deep faith in God, and he manifested an ability to inspire steadfast loyalty in the congregations he served, despite persecution, exile, and denunciations.

LIFE'S WORK

The fierce persecution of the Church abruptly changed when Constantine became emperor and began to favor Christianity throughout the Empire. Such a sudden change must have been difficult for Athanasius and his fellow Christians to comprehend. The amazement and incredulity that they experienced is reflected in Eusebius of Caesarea's description of a church council:

> No bishop was absent from the table of the emperor. Bodyguards and soldiers stood guard, with sharp swords drawn, around the outer court of the palace, but among them the men of God could walk fearlessly and enter the deepest parts of the palace. At dinner [they ate with the emperor.] Easily one could imagine this to be the kingdom of Christ or regard it as a dream rather than reality.

Some of those who enjoyed Constantine's favor bore scars from the Diocletian era, such as Bishop Paphnutius from Egypt, who had lost an eye in that persecution, and Paul of Caesarea, who had been tortured with a red-hot iron under Licinius and was crippled in both hands. A disadvantage of Constantine's patronage of the Church, however, was that the power of the state would be used to enforce church discipline, as Athanasius learned later when he was exiled by Constantine to the Rhineland region of Germany.

The Roman emperor called the first ecumenical council of the Church, which met at Nicaea, in Asia Minor, in 325. ("Ecumenical" literally means "of the empire.") Constantine himself presided over the beginning sessions of this great assembly of the leadership of the Church and, in so doing, set an important precedent of involvement between church and state that lasted throughout the European Middle Ages and into modern times: Decisions of church councils were to be enforced by political authorities. For many years there had been local and regional synods or councils, but the idea of bringing together the entire Church, East and West, was new.

The Nicene Council met only twenty miles from the Imperial palace of Nicomedia, easily accessible by sea and land from all parts of the Roman Empire. Some three hundred bishops and more than one thousand presbyters and laymen assembled in an effort to bring unity to the Church. Most of these people were from the Eastern church; only seven came from Europe. At least one, a Persian bishop, was from outside the Roman Empire. The council met from mid-June to the end of July, discussing theology and matters ecclesiastical in Latin and translating speeches into Greek.

Athanasius, a young archdeacon at the time, accompanied his bishop, Alexander, and spoke often at the council, demonstrating a brilliant intellect and impressive eloquence. Though only twenty-seven at the time, Athanasius set forth an influential defense of the orthodox position that Christ was God from all eternity, uncreated and equal to God the Father. The result was the Nicene Creed, recited today by millions of Christians worldwide in their liturgy:

We believe in One God, the Father Almighty,
Maker of all things visible and invisible,
and in one Lord Jesus Christ, the Son of God, . . .
begotten not made, One in essence with the Father,
by Whom all things were made, both things in Heaven
and things in Earth. . . .

The Nicene Creed is acknowledged by Eastern Orthodox, Roman Catholic, and Protestant churches alike. The Greek Orthodox Church annually observes (on the Sunday before Pentecost) a special feast in memory of the Council of Nicaea.

In 328, Athanasius succeeded Alexander as bishop of Alexandria and remained in that position, except for five exiles, for forty-six years. As a defender of the orthodox

Saint Athanasius of Alexandria. (Library of Congress)

faith, he was popular in the Alexandrian church where he ministered. He was, however, opposed by the Arians, those who thought of Christ as a great teacher but less than God himself. Emperor Constantine, more interested in unity than in truth, thought the matter merely one of theological semantics. Hoping to have more uniformity and less discord in the Church, he removed Athanasius from his office and banished him from Alexandria.

When Constantine died in 337, Athanasius returned, but soon he was exiled a second time for seven years, which he spent in Rome, where the orthodox position was strongly affirmed. The sons of Constantine, acting on the suggestion of Julius, bishop of Rome, convened another church council at Sardica in 343. There Athanasius was reinstated as bishop.

Before long it became apparent that the differences between the Arian bishops and the orthodox leaders were more than doctrinal. The Arians gained support from the Roman Emperor Constantius because of their belief that the Church should submit to the emperor in doctrinal as well as administrative matters. Arguing from Scripture, Athanasius insisted on the independence of the Church in doctrine. As a result, Athanasius in 356 was again sent into exile, this time for six years in the Egyptian desert, where he became a close acquaintance of the famed Anthony, who helped begin the Western system of monasteries.

In 361, the pagan Emperor Julian recalled banished bishops on both sides of the controversy. By diligent and wise administration, Athanasius restored harmony to his diocese, but Julian exiled him for a fourth time and sent two hired assassins to kill him on board an Imperial ship. Athanasius, however, managed to escape from the ship while it was sailing up the Nile River.

Athanasius returned to Alexandria after Julian's death but endured yet a fifth and final brief exile under the Emperor Valens. He spent the last seven years of his life mostly undisturbed in his diocese. He continued writing, content to see the vindication of the orthodox position in the Church. He died in 373; his epitaph, *Athanasius contra mundum* (Athanasius against the world), reflected the steadfastness with which he had stood his ground against all opposition.

Throughout his tumultuous life, Athanasius was a prolific writer. He was noted for his theological depth, intellectual precision, and clarity of style; he wrote to make his meaning plain, not to embellish or entertain. He incisively demolished his opponents' arguments and methodically built a logical structure for his own position. Most of his works were written in response to some pressing matter or in defense of an action or position. Though he wrote in Greek, his works are now known solely by their Latin titles.

Athanasius's writings fall into several categories. For example, he produced apologetical works in defense of Christianity, such as *De incarnatione Verbi Dei* (before 325; *On the Incarnation of the Word of God*, 1880). Many of his theological works were written to defend the orthodox Nicene faith. For example, he wrote a letter in this regard to the bishops of Egypt and Libya (356) and a commentary on the decrees of the Council of Nicaea (352), *Contra Arianos* (350; *An Apology Against the Arians*, 1873) and *Apologia ad Constantinum* (356; *An Apology to Constantius*, 1892). Athanasius also wrote exegetical works interpreting Scripture; in his commentary on the Psalms, he followed the allegorizing style of the Alexandrian school in identifying in these Hebrew worship songs many types of Christ and the Church. Also in this category is his synopsis of the Bible. Of his devotional works, his *Epistolae festales* (329-373; *The Festal Epistles*, 1854) are most interesting. During the Easter season, these letters were read in the churches to edify and exhort the congregations.

SIGNIFICANCE

Athanasius was not a historian, but many of his writings provide important primary source materials for historians. His *Historia Arianorum* (358; *History of the Arians*, 1892) is a good example, as is *An Apology Against the Arians*. Athanasius is noted for his great accuracy and his practice of documenting his assertions. Thus, later generations were indebted to him not only for his histories but also for the compilation of many documents of the fourth century.

Athanasius's biography *Vita S. Antonii* (fourth century; *The Life of Anthony*, 1697) helped to extend the monastic system into Europe. Anthony, a native of Upper Egypt, lived a completely solitary life for a time in the Egyptian desert. Others who followed his example became known as monks, from the Greek word *monachoi* (people who live alone). Athanasius was impressed by Anthony's deep spirituality, and it was through Athanasius that Anthony began to realize that he needed to take more interest in the welfare of the Church. When Athanasius visited Rome in 340, during his second exile, he explained to the Roman Christians the lifestyle of the Egyptian monks and thus introduced monasticism into the Western church.

Because of the early period in which he lived, Athanasius's listing of the canon of Scripture has been of.

great interest to later theologians. His thirty-ninth Festal Epistle of Easter, 367, made mention of all the books now included in the New Testament but in the older order of the Gospels, Acts, the General Epistles, Paul's Epistles (including Hebrews), and the Apocalypse. His Old Testament canon comprised twenty-two books, as in the Alexandrian Jewish system, not the older Talmudic listing of twenty-four. The Apocrypha, accepted by the later Roman Catholic Church, was not included in Athanasius's list.

Throughout his long life, Athanasius demonstrated a remarkable lack of self-interest and ambition. Though he held one of the great bishoprics of the Eastern church, he never compromised what he was convinced to be the truth. His manner was humble and conciliatory, but for him, truth was not subject to political compromise. His contemporaries were strengthened by his stability, consistency, and courage in the midst of tribulation, and the later Church is indebted to him for the clarity of his theology.

—William H. Burnside

FURTHER READING

Athanasius: Select Works and Letters. Vol. 4 in *A Select Library of Nicene and Post-Nicene Fathers of the Christian Church*. 1891. Reprint. Grand Rapids, Mich.: Wm. B. Eerdmans, 1978. This six-hundred-page book is indispensable for understanding Athanasius. It contains a detailed account of his extant writings, with helpful editorial notes. Contains index, tables, and appendix.

Athanasius, Saint. *The Coptic Life of Anthony*. Translated by Tim Vivian. San Francisco: International Scholars, 1995. This brief volume brings insight into the thinking of a man who had a great influence on Athanasius—the Egyptian hermit Saint Anthony.

Bruce, F. F. *The Spreading Flame: The Rise and Progress of Christianity from Its First Beginnings to the Conversion of the English*. Grand Rapids, Mich.: Wm. B. Eerdmans, 1982. An excellent, detailed history of the early Church. There are many references to Athanasius, but the principal value of this book is in providing the historical context in which Athanasius lived.

Frend, W. H. C. *The Rise of Christianity*. Philadelphia: Fortress Press, 1984. A useful introduction to Church history. Includes a seventy-five-page chart that gives a synopsis of events in three categories from 63 B.C.E. to 615 C.E. Also includes five unusual maps that shed light on the text. Frend makes many references to Athanasius.

Latourette, Kenneth Scott. *A History of Christianity*. Rev. ed. New York: Harper and Row, 1975. The first three hundred pages of this classic fifteen-hundred-page history of Christianity are useful in interpreting Athanasius's role in the early Church and later Roman Empire.

Schaff, Philip. *Nicene and Post-Nicene Christianity, A.D. 311-600*. Vol. 3 in *History of the Christian Church*. 3d ed. Peabody, Mass.: Hendrickson, 1996. An exhaustive church history. The section on Athanasius, Constantine, and the Nicene Council are absolutely indispensable for an understanding of the life and influence of Athanasius. Schaff is noted for the thoroughness of his history and the detailed precision of his narrative.

Shelley, Bruce. *Church History in Plain Language*. Waco, Tex.: Word Books, 1995. Though this volume is rather sparse on Athanasius, it is valuable for its accessibility. Recommended for those with little background in church history. Makes clear what the conversion of Constantine meant to the Church.

SEE ALSO: Saint Anthony of Egypt; Constantine the Great; Eusebius of Caesarea.

RELATED ARTICLES in *Great Events from History: The Ancient World*: 313-395 C.E., Inception of Church-State Problem; 325 C.E., Adoption of the Nicene Creed; 361-363 C.E., Failure of Julian's Pagan Revival.

ATOSSA
Persian queen

As the daughter, the wife, and the mother of Persian kings, Atossa had great influence in the rule of ancient Persia.

BORN: c. 545 B.C.E.; Persia (now in Iran)
DIED: Possibly c. 479 B.C.E.; Persia
ALSO KNOWN AS: Hutaosâ (Old Persian)
AREA OF ACHIEVEMENT: Government and politics

EARLY LIFE

The writings of the Greek historian Herodotus are the main source of biographical information on Atossa (ah-TOH-sah). Persian sources are rare, and those that have survived do not include Atossa. For instance, the royal inscriptions do not mention Atossa or any mortal women, and women are excluded from the palace reliefs of Persepolis. There is agreement, however, that Herodotus's *Historiai Herodotou* (c. 424 B.C.E.; *The History*, 1709) provides an accurate picture of the essential facts of Atossa's life.

Atossa was the daughter of Cyrus the Great, who founded the first Persian Empire, the Achaemenid Dynasty (sixth to fourth century B.C.E.). Cyrus ruled from 559 B.C.E. until his death c. 530 while fighting in the region of the Oxus and Jaxartes Rivers on the eastern frontier. During his reign, Cyrus greatly expanded Persia by conquering Lydia, which controlled the Greek city-states along the western coast of Asia Minor, and finally Babylon.

After Cyrus's death, his son Cambyses II (r. 529-522) ascended the throne. Cambyses II wanted to marry his sister Atossa, according to ancient Egyptian custom, but marriage to siblings was not a Persian practice. Cambyses gathered all the Persian royal judges and asked them if there were a law that permitted a man to wed his sister. The judges could not find such a law, but they knew of the law that said that the king of Persia could do whatever he wanted. Thus, the judges gave Cambyses a legitimate basis for marrying Atossa.

In 525 B.C.E., Cambyses conducted a war against Egypt and was victorious. However, his investment of troops and material in the Egyptian campaign led him to worry about maintaining power at home and the potential rivalry of his and Atossa's brother Bardiya (Smerdis). Following the paranoid logic of absolute monarchy, Cambyses had their brother killed and tried to keep the murder secret. However, this led to another kind of vulnerability for Atossa's brother and husband. Because

Bardiya's death was kept secret, the general public did not question his "reappearance" in the form of an impostor, Smerdis the Magian, who actually resembled Bardiya, or Smerdis, the son of Cyrus. This impostor, the false Smerdis, led a rebellion in Persia in 522 and usurped the throne. To make matters worse, the impostor offered his supporters three years of tax relief, which increased his popularity to the point that he was able to seize control of several provinces. In the ensuing crisis, Cambyses, who was rushing back to reassert his authority, lost his life, probably from an infection after an accidental cut from his own sword or, possibly, suicide. One of the late Cambyses' most important generals was Darius (son of Hystaspes and a prince from another branch of the royal Achaemenids), who immediately took over leadership of the Persian army and continued its homeward march.

However, another complication had arisen for Atossa. When the impostor, pretending to be her murdered brother Smerdis, seized the throne, he took Atossa as his wife, as well as Cambyses' other wives. After he returned with his army, Prince Darius and six other leading Achaemenid nobles overthrew the impostor, and they declared that Darius was the rightful heir to the throne.

Along with the political authority and wealth, Darius also acquired the harem of the previous rulers and so became Atossa's third husband. Darius also married Atossa's sister Artystone and Atossa's niece Parmys, the daughter of the murdered Smerdis, son of Cyrus. After a year of bitter fighting (522-521), Darius was able to subdue the groups who had supported the pretender and bring peace back to the empire. He then began to establish a stable and organized government, including regular taxation. According to his royal inscriptions, he wished to be remembered as a lawgiver and organizer.

Although Atossa had no official role in the governance of Darius's kingdom, she had great influence and power stemming from her closeness to the king, her royal lineage, and her firsthand knowledge of the actions of the two previous rulers.

LIFE'S WORK

Herodotus also provides an interesting story showing Atossa's influence on Darius. Democedes, the Greek physician from Croton, was taken to Persia during the Achaemenians' war in Asia Minor. He became a court physician after successfully treating Darius. When he helped heal a growth on Atossa's body, she promised him any honorable favor he wished. Democedes requested that she convince Darius to consider war with Greece and send Democedes with an exploratory group to Greece, so that he could return home. His plan was to escape during this trip. The following is what Herodotus records Atossa as having said to persuade Darius to invade Greece:

> My lord, you have very great power and yet you sit idle. You have not added any nation or power to the empire of Persia. It is but right for a man who is young and is master of great wealth to achieve something for all to see, that the Persians may know that he who rules them is truly a man. Indeed there is a double benefit in such a course; the Persians will know that their leader is a man, and also they themselves will be worn down by the war and will not plot against you—as they might, were they at leisure. And it is now you should do this, while you are young. For as the body grows, so the mind grows with it; and as the body grows old, so does the wit grow old and is blunted toward all matters alike.

Darius listened to her advice and proceeded to send a reconnaissance group, including Democedes, to Greece c. 519 B.C.E.

According to Herodotus, as Darius prepared for an expedition and war against both Egypt and Athens, Persian law required him to name an heir to the throne. Darius's two oldest sons (by different mothers) fought over the throne. Darius had fathered three sons with his former wife, the daughter of Gobryas, before he became king. Their oldest son was named Artobazanes, who argued that according to custom, the first-born son should succeed the king. After Darius became king, he had four sons by Atossa, the eldest being Xerxes, born in 519. At this time, Demaratus, a former Spartan king, advised Xerxes that he should be the next king because in Sparta, the son born after the father attained the throne would be the successor. Herodotus reports that Darius accepted Xerxes' plea, and Xerxes was designated the official heir.

Herdotus comments, "But I myself believe that, even without the advice, Xerxes would have become King. For Atossa had all the power." This power would indicate that Atossa had some influence and authority in the royal court. As the daughter of Cyrus the Great and wife of three kings, she had experience and expertise in government or state affairs. When Xerxes ascended the throne, she very likely had influence as the queen mother. As crown prince, Xerxes ruled as the king's governor in Babylon and reigned as king from 486 until 465, when

harem intrigues led to his assassination. Atossa's other sons by Darius held important military and administrative positions.

Another Greek source is Aeschylus's famous tragedy *Persai* (472 B.C.E.; *The Persians*, 1777), performed in Athens eight years after the Greek victory against Xerxes at Salamis. In 481, Xerxes had begun land and sea invasions of Greece but ultimately was not successful. The Battle of Salamis in 480 was a major defeat for the Persian fleet and the turning point in the Persian Wars, after which Xerxes returned home, leaving another in charge of operations.

Although never referred to by name, Atossa is a leading character in this play. She is the "Queen of Persia, wife of Darius, mother of Xerxes." The setting is a scene with the palace of Xerxes in the background and the tomb of Darius in the center foreground. The play begins with a chorus of Persian elders and the queen awaiting news about the battle. After the news of the Persian defeat, the queen invokes the ghost of Darius. Finally Xerxes returns, and the play ends with a lament.

Although it is a historical play based on a contemporary event, and written by someone who had fought in the Battle of Salamis, *The Persians* is obviously fictional in many ways and cannot be assumed to be a factual or realistic portrayal of Atossa. In the play, she is inquisitive and asks the royal councillor questions about the power structure of Athens and the Greek armies and about what wealth or treasures the Athenians possessed. Her character is that of the emotional, caring queen mother. Although it is not known how much knowledge the Greeks actually had of Persian royalty, Atossa was a known personality, significant enough to be a main character in Aeschylus's famous play. It has been noted that the play is unique in its unexpected, sympathetic portrayal of the defeated enemy as noble. The play does support that Atossa was alive at the time of Xerxes' return to Persia c. 479, so she probably lived into her seventies. There is no record of when or how she died.

SIGNIFICANCE

Atossa played a prominent role during the Achaemenid period in ancient Persia. She was the daughter of Cyrus II, who founded the first Persian Empire. Later she was the wife of two kings, Cambyses and Darius, as well as of an impostor king, and finally the mother of King Xerxes. With her royal lineage and relationship to kings, she was an integral part of the rise and the beginning of the collapse of the Persian Empire. Although the Persian sources are scarce, Greek historiography has provided enough of a portrait to make Atossa the most renowned woman from ancient Persia.

According to Herodotus, she had power that guaranteed her son Xerxes' ascension to the throne on Darius's death, and she was able to persuade Darius to consider war with Greece. Although clearly fictional drama based on a true historical event, Aeschylus's *The Persians* confirms the existence of a memorable and interesting queen.

—*Alice Myers*

FURTHER READING

Aeschylus. *The Complete Greek Tragedies*. Edited by David Grene and Richmond Lattimore. Chicago: University of Chicago Press, 1991. This collection includes S. G. Bernardete's translation of *The Persians*, in which Atossa is a main character. The introduction provides useful background information and critical commentary on the play.

Green, Peter. *Xerxes at Salamis*. New York: Praeger, 1970. A scholarly work on the significant victory by the Greek states against the powerful Persian Empire. Includes illustrations, maps, photographs, notes, bibliography, and an index.

Herodotus. *The History*. Translated by David Grene. Chicago: University of Chicago Press, 1987. This is an English translation by one of the best-known translators of the Greek classics. Herodotus's work is the main source of information on Atossa.

_____. *The Persian Wars*. Translated by George Rawlinson. New York: The Modern Library, 1947. These selections from Herodotus's *The History* give detailed historical information on the Persians and the Achaemenid kings, and there are references to Atossa.

Sancisi-Weerdenburg, Heleen. "Exit Atossa: Images of Women in Greek Historiography on Persia." In *Images of Women in Antiquity*, edited by Averil Cameron and Amelie Kuhrt. Detroit: Wayne State University Press, 1983. This chapter is informative, because mentions of mortal women are nonexistent among the Persian sources.

SEE ALSO: Aeschylus; Agrippina the Younger; Antonia Minor; Arria the Elder; Arria the Younger; Arsinoe II Philadelphus; Bathsheba; Berenice II; Boudicca; Cleopatra VII; Cyrus the Great; Darius the Great; Hatshepsut; Julia Domna; Julia Mamaea; Julia Soaemias; Julia III; Lucretia; Valeria Messallina; Nefertari; Nefertiti; Poppaea Sabina; Tiy; Xerxes I; Zenobia.

RELATED ARTICLES in *Great Events from History: The Ancient World*: 547 B.C.E., Cyrus the Great Founds the Persian Empire; 520-518 B.C.E., Darius the Great Conquers the Indus Valley; 520-518 B.C.E., Scylax of Caryanda Voyages the Indian Ocean; September 17, 490 B.C.E., Battle of Marathon; 480-479 B.C.E., Persian Invasion of Greece; c. 456/455 B.C.E., Greek Tragedian Aeschylus Dies.

ATTILA
Hunnish khan (r. 435-453 C.E.)

By uniting all the Hunnish tribes from the northern Caucasus to the upper Danube River, rendering the Romans a tributary state, Attila fashioned the most powerful empire of the West in the fifth century.

BORN: c. 406 C.E.; Pannonia? (now primarily in Hungary)
DIED: 453 C.E.; probably Jazberin (now in Hungary)
ALSO KNOWN AS: Attila the Hun; Flagellum Dei (Latin for "Scourge of God")
AREAS OF ACHIEVEMENT: Government and politics, war and conquest

EARLY LIFE

The movement of the Huns from Asia westward through the steppes in the fourth century caused the Great Migration of Germans and Alans into Europe. By 420, the Huns had found a home in Pannonia, the seat of the main body of the nation, which was divided into three ulus, each ruled by a khan. Here was a strategic base for later operations in Italy and the Balkans. The Huns' superior cavalry tactics were well publicized, and the Romans of the East and West soon realized the need to appease them.

When Khan Roila died in 435 C.E., two of his nephews, Attila (AT-tih-lah) and his brother Bleda, were elected as joint rulers. Nothing is known of the early life of Attila or of his grandparents and mother. He was the son of Mundjuk, brother of Roila and Oktar. Mundjuk may have been a co-khan with Roila, but the evidence is unclear. What is certain is that Mundjuk and Oktar died before Roila did and that Attila became the chief khan, subordinating his older brother from the start.

The Roman statesman and writer Cassiodorus described Attila as Asian in appearance, beardless, flat-nosed, and swarthy. His body was short and square, with broad shoulders. He was adept at terrorizing enemies with the use of his deep-set eyes. Edward Gibbon, in *History of the Decline and Fall of the Roman Empire* (1776-1788), says that he was feared as much for his magic as for his militarism.

LIFE'S WORK

The death of Roila brought relief to Constantinople, because the king of the Huns had been planning an invasion of Eastern Rome. Bishops attributed his death to the intervention of God. Attila quickly exhibited a genius for leadership and statesmanship. His first task was to settle the disputes with the Romans at Constantinople, demanding an end to the use of Huns in their service. Attila and Bleda met Roman envoys from both empires at the River Morava to sign a treaty in 434. Negotiating from horseback, as was the Hunnic custom, they secured from Emperor Theodosius II the promise to end the use of Hunnish warriors, the return of those in his service, free access to border towns for Hunnish merchants, and the doubling of the annual tribute of gold from 350 to 700 pounds. Two of the fugitives handed back to the Huns were young boys, Mama and Atakam, relatives of the khans, who summarily were crucified. The Roman Flavius Aetius continued to use Huns and Alans against Germans in the West.

After this treaty of Margus with Theodosius, Attila and Bleda devoted their efforts to consolidating the eastern possessions. Striving to unite all the ulus under their rule, the khans forged an empire from the northern Caucasus to central Europe. Within five years this objective was reached, and the brothers divided their administration into two sections.

Meanwhile Persians attacked Roman Armenia in 438 in a war that lasted fifteen years, and the Romans were hoping to recover Carthage in North Africa from the Vandals, who posed a danger to Roman shipping. Partly because of other problems, the Roman emperor neglected payments to the Hun and was preparing new operations against the Vandal Gaiseric, or Genseric and the Sāsān-ian shah in Persia, allies of Attila. With the opportunity at hand, Attila launched an invasion of the Eastern Roman Empire in 441. Gibbon says that this move was prompted by Genseric. In any case, Attila's forces moved rapidly across the Morava, seizing Margus, Constantia, Singidunum (Belgrade), and Sirmium, the key to the defense of the Danube. A puzzling one-year truce fol-

Attila, shown on white horse. (Library of Congress)

lowed, enabling the Romans to prepare for defense. An angry Attila launched a new offensive in 443, destroying Ratiaria and Naissus, birthplace of Constantine, and Sardica (Sophia), thus opening the highway to the capital. Roman armies led by Aspar, an Alan, contested the Huns but were no match for the swiftly moving forces of Attila. Although Constantinople was well defended by troops and terrain, Theodosius decided to sue for peace and so paid six thousand pounds of gold to Attila to make up for his arrears of tribute. The treaty of Anatolius was signed on August 27, 443.

Within two years, Bleda was officially removed from power and soon after was killed by Attila himself. No details exist about the power struggle between the brothers. Attila was master of the entire Hunnish world empire and would have no more rivals.

The location of Attila's court is only educated conjecture. Hungarians argue that it was located about thirty-six miles west of Buda, at Jazberin. Others suggest that the location was at Tokay or Agria, all in the plains of upper Hungary. This court included a wooden palace on a hill as well as another for his chief wife, Queen Cerca, houses for his adjutants, storehouses, service buildings, and even a stone bathhouse. All were enclosed by a wooden wall. At table, Attila ate only meat, used wooden utensils, and never tasted bread. Inside the spacious palace were servants of many nationalities: Alans, Greeks, Germans, Romans, and Slavs.

The same international character prevailed within the Hunnish borders, as Attila's policy of no taxation attracted many settlers. Taxation was unnecessary, owing to the large tribute from Constantinople and annual collections of booty from warfare. Even the army comprised other nationalities. Persian engineers from the shah and deserters from the Romans helped Attila's forces prepare for siege warfare against stone walls. Slavs, taught the methods of warfare by the Huns, formed special detachments in the khan's armies, evidenced by references to the troops drinking kvass.

The Huns invaded Rome again in 447, but there are no sources indicating the motive—perhaps Attila needed more plunder. The Eastern Romans were besieged by famine and plagues and were not disposed to provoke the Huns. Nevertheless, Attila invaded with armies of subject peoples augmenting his Huns. In the midst of the campaign, a fierce earthquake struck the Eastern Roman world, destroying sections of the walls around Constantinople. The people summoned the determination to rebuild the fortifications hastily and even constructed another, outer wall to ward off the Huns. West of the capital a pitched battle took place at Utus. Although the Huns won the battle, it was fought so energetically by the Romans that the Huns suffered serious losses. Choosing to bypass the capital, Attila contented himself with enormous plunder in the Balkans. This would be his last victory over Roman forces.

That same year, the khan received news of a renegade Hunnish nation in Scythia. The Acatziri were corresponding with the emperor at Constantinople, posing a danger to Attila's rearguard position. Consequently, Attila's forces crushed the rebels, and Ellac, Attila's son, was sent to rule over them. There followed the second peace of Anatolius, in 448.

Attila found it necessary to construct an intelligence network to combat Roman espionage. At one point his German agent, Edecon, was drawn into a scheme to assassinate Attila in 448. Sent to Constantinople on business, he was "bribed" by a Roman official of the emperor, the eunuch Chrysaphius, to join the plot. Loyal to Attila,

Edecon feigned acceptance and exposed the affair to the khan, who then exploited the matter to obtain more tribute from Constantinople.

Attila next considered a plan to marry Honoria, the sister of Emperor Valentinian III. The Roman princess herself initiated the idea, perhaps in bitterness after having been placed in confinement by her mother for many years following a teenage pregnancy, or to avoid marrying an old Roman courtier and friend of her brother. The khan saw an opportunity to demand one-half of the Imperial lands as dowry for the marriage. When the emperor's expected refusal arrived, Attila prepared for war. Honoria was sent to Ravenna, Italy, by Valentinian, who called on Aetius to defend the Imperial borders. Both sides sought allies as Aetius gained the support of Visigoths, Burgundians, and most of the Franks. Attila won the support of the younger of the two Frankish brother-rulers, as well as the Ostrogoths, Vandals, and Alans.

The Alans of Gaul were compelled to accede to Aetius, and the great battle of the nations (also known as the Battle of the Catalaunian Plains) occurred at Châlons in July, 451. The Huns were disheartened for failure to capture the city of Orléans and then weakened by guerrilla tactics as they made their way to plains more suited to their cavalry. Attila delivered an inspiring address to his soldiers on the eve of battle, but the opposing armies were strong. The coalitions fought a bloody encounter but the result was indecisive. Attila led his forces back to the Danube, and the Visigoths retreated to Toulouse. His plan to take the Western Empire failed, so Attila prepared to invade Italy. Aetius found it more difficult to defend this region because he feared the consequences of bringing Visigoths to Italy. In 452, Attila invaded across the Alps, coming to Milan, where he met Pope Leo (the Great) and two Roman senators, who convinced him to turn back. It was unlikely that idealism was the issue; rather, the epidemic of dysentery among his troops and the imminent arrival of Aetius's forces via Ravenna more likely encouraged the retreat. It is also probable that Leo gave ransom for the release of prominent prisoners. Nevertheless, the Huns devastated the plains of Lombardy, forcing many to flee to the lagoons of the Adriatic Sea, where the Venetian republic arose. Returning home, Attila wished instead to strike at Byzantium.

Once back in the Danubian country, however, the khan, who had numerous wives, married again, this time to a German named Ildico. After the usual wedding party, Attila lay down to rest and was later found dead in his bed

(453). Despite rumors that he was stabbed or poisoned by Ildico (who was found at his bedside), it is more likely that he simply choked to death on vomit or blood from a hemorrhage. Hunnish warriors immediately cut off part of their own hair and disfigured their own faces with deep wounds, as was their mourning custom.

The khanate was divided among Attila's three sons: Dengizik, Ernack, and Ellac. The latter was killed the next year, when a rebellion occurred; the other two brothers took their ulus to Dacia and Bessarabia for a time. Other bands of Huns penetrated the right bank of the Danube, settling in the Roman world as allies. Most of the Alans supported the Byzantines when the forces of Dengizik were crushed in a war of 468-469. The Great Bulgarian nation of the Huns disintegrated in the East as well, as some joined Slavs to find their way to the southern Balkans to a land that bears their Hunnish name. Other Bulgar descendants of the Huns settled for a while on the upper Volga River until they were absorbed into the nomad empire of the Khazars.

SIGNIFICANCE

Attila was never a divine-right monarch in the sense of a Persian shah or even the Macedonian Alexander the Great. He never posed as a god before his people but, rather, wore simple clothing without jewelry, mixing with his people—often without bodyguards. Attila did not create a permanent administrative structure for the Hunnish nation; his influence, while truly awesome, was temporary for the Huns. He seemed to profit little from cultural contacts with the Romans of the East or West; most artistic objects traced to Hunnish origins have been discovered in the Ukraine or Volga River regions, not from the Danubian plains. Nor did Attila's Huns adopt the Roman proclivity for the plow, as some eastern Huns did.

Attila's empire helped to hasten the fall of the Roman Empire in the West. Although his forces did not destroy the Roman Imperial structure, they weakened the mystique of Rome by their continuous exactions of tribute. In the steppelands of the East, they destroyed the German and Iranian control of the Russian world, preparing the way for the next nomad empire, that of the Khazars, and even teaching the hitherto peaceful Slavs how to defend themselves from future invaders.

Ironically, by 451 the Roman tribute had ceased, and the aura of Attila's invincibility had vanished. His armies had failed at Châlons, he could no longer intimidate subject nations, and his resources were quickly disappearing. Then, when the Italian campaign was cut short, his allies grew restive without the gold and booty of former days. Perhaps his timely death preserved his historical reputation.

—*John D. Windhausen*

FURTHER READING

Gibbon, Edward. *History of the Decline and Fall of the Roman Empire*. 1776-1788. Reprint. Edited by David Womersley. New York: Penguin, 1994. A vivid picture of Attila's personality and his court is presented by this master eighteenth century historian, who culled a wealth of detail from limited sources.

Gordon, G. D. *The Age of Attila: Fifth Century Byzantium and the Barbarians*. Ann Arbor: University of Michigan Press, 1966. This work cleverly arranges selections of primary sources to relate the history of Attila's age.

Howarth, Patrick. *Attila, King of the Huns: The Man and the Myth*. New York: Barnes & Noble, 1995. Life of Attila details his eighteen-year rule, his accomplishments, and his character.

Ingram, Scott. *Attila the Hun*. Detroit: Blackbirch, 2002. Examines the collapse of the Roman Empire at the hands of the barbarian hordes led by Attila as well as Attila's legacy. Aimed at young readers.

Jones, A. H. M. *The Decline of the Ancient World*. New York: Holt, Rinehart and Winston, 1966. Jones's work includes a short but useful presentation of the relationships among Attila, Aetius, and Theodosius.

Mänchen-Helfen, Otto J. *The World of the Huns: Studies in Their History and Culture*. Edited by Max Knight. Berkeley: University of California Press, 1973. A scholarly treatment of the subject by a recognized authority who died before completing the manuscript. It is replete with excellent linguistic analysis of the sources.

Nicolle, David. *Attila and the Nomad Hordes*. Illustrated by Angus McBride. London: Osprey, 1990. A concise (64-page) overview of Attila's short-lived empire and its aftermath. Chronology, illustrations.

Thompson, E. A. *A History of Attila and the Huns*. 1948. Reprint. Westport, Conn.: Greenwood Press, 1975. A readable and clear presentation of the life of Attila. Its scholarly treatment holds up well under later academic scrutiny.

Vernadsky, George. *Ancient Russia*. 5 vols. New Haven, Conn.: Yale University Press, 1943-1969. The chapter on the Huns is a short but remarkably complete story that is not limited to the settlements in Southern Russia.

SAINT AUGUSTINE
Numidian bishop

Renowned for his original interpretations of Scripture and extensive writings, Augustine was the greatest Christian theologian of the ancient world.

BORN: November 13, 354; Tagaste, Numidia (now Souk-Ahras, Algeria)

DIED: August 28, 430; Hippo Regius, Numidia (now Annaba, Algeria)

ALSO KNOWN AS: Aurelius Augustinus (given name)

AREAS OF ACHIEVEMENT: Religion, philosophy

EARLY LIFE

Augustine (AW-guh-steen) was born Aurelius Augustinus to middle-class parents, Patricius and Monica, in the Roman province of Numidia (now Algeria). His pious mother imbued him with a reverence for Christ, but as he excelled in school he found the Church's teachings and practices unsatisfactory. As he studied at nearby Madauros and then Carthage, he was swayed by various philosophies. From 370 to 383, with the exception of one year spent in Tagaste, he taught rhetoric in Carthage. Part of these early years were wasted (he later regretted) on womanizing, but this experience created in him a lifelong sensitivity to overcoming the desires of the flesh.

On the birth of an illegitimate son, Adeodatus, in 373, Augustine identified himself with the prophet Mani, who had preached a belief in the spiritual forces of light and darkness, which also included Christ as the Redeemer. Hoping to explore the tension in this dualism, Augustine was disappointed by the shallow intellect of the Manichaean bishop Faustus and became disillusioned with that faith.

Desirous of a fresh outlook and a better teaching position, Augustine sailed to Rome in 383 and the next year began teaching rhetoric in Milan. There he was awakened to the potential of Christian theology by the sermons of Saint Ambrose and, in particular, the Neoplatonism of Plotinus. In this philosophy—the beliefs of Plato adapted to Christianity by Plotinus—the individual can only know true existence and the one God by searching within, to attain unity with God's love. Only spiritual faith, and not reason or physical appearances, could provide the ultimate answers. At first a skeptic, Augustine began his inner search and in 386 had a mystical experience in which he believed he had discovered God. Resigning his teaching position, Augustine converted completely to Christianity and was baptized by Ambrose at Milan in the spring of 387.

LIFE'S WORK

Augustine plunged into the cause of discovering and articulating God's will as a Christian philosopher. He did so with such zeal that a steady stream of treatises flowed from his pen. He returned to Numidia in 389 and established a monastery at Hippo, intending to live there quietly and write. He was ordained as a priest in 391, and he became bishop of Hippo in 396. Thus, instead of developing his theological ideas systematically, Augustine revealed them in sermons, letters in reply to queries for guidance, tracts against separatists, and books. In addition, he wrote a lengthy autobiography of his early life, *Confessiones* (397-400; *Confessions*, 1620).

God, in Augustine's view, is at the center of all events and explanations. Such a theocentric philosophy depends on Holy Scripture; for Augustine, the Psalms, Genesis, and the First Letter of John were especially important. His commentaries on the first two sources are famous treatises, along with *De Trinitate* (c. 419; *On the Trinity*, 1875) and *De civitate Dei* (412-427; *The City of God*, 1610).

God, as "the author of all existences" and "the illuminator of all truth," is Wisdom itself and therefore the highest level of reality. The second level is the human soul, which includes memory, understanding, and will. By looking to God, the individual discovers the true knowledge that God has already bestowed on him or her. All things emanate from that ultimate authority; through faith, one gains truth, the use of reason being only secondary. The third and lowest level of reality is the human body, whose greatest ethical happiness can only be realized by aspiring to God's love. Human beings are endowed with the free choice to do good or evil, but God, by divine grace, may bestow the greater freedom of enabling a person to escape an attraction to evil. Similarly, revelation frees the mind from skepticism. By grappling with the elusive problem of evil, Augustine managed to bring better focus to an issue of universal concern to all religions.

Saint Augustine. (Library of Congress)

Also a practical thinker, Augustine was an acute observer of the natural universe. By focusing on God in nature, however, and believing that true knowledge came only through spiritual introspection, he came to regard physical things as least important and science as having little utility, concluding that faith rather than reason provides the ultimate truth. By the same token, Augustine viewed history optimistically; humankind was saved by Christ's sacrifice on the cross, the premier event of the past.

The collapse of Roman hegemony to barbarian invasions, even as Augustine preached his sermons on faith, caused many doubters to blame Christianity for Rome's decline. Augustine refuted this accusation in *The City of God*. He envisioned two cities, the heavenly City of God and the other one an earthly entity, patterned respectively after the biblical examples of Jerusalem—which means "Vision of Peace"—and Babylon, permeated with evil. Whereas perfection is the hallmark of the City of God, Augustine offered important guidelines for the conduct of human cities. Earthly "peace" he defined as harmonious order, a condition whereby a person, a community, or a state operates by the ideals of felicity (good intentions) and virtue (good acts) without suffering under or imposing dominion.

No pacifist, Augustine believed that a nation might go to war—but only on the authority of God and then to achieve a "peace of the just." "Good men undertake wars," he wrote to Faustus the Manichaean in 398, to oppose evil enemies: "The real evils in war are love of violence, revengeful cruelty, fierce and implacable enmity, wild resistance, and the lust of power."

The greatest challenge to Augustine's teachings centered on the issue of how the individual might escape the evils of the flesh—whether by one's own choice or by the initiative of God through divine grace. Augustine insisted on the latter and regarded the Pelagians as heretics for arguing the former view. As Saint Paul taught, each person is guilty of Original Sin, must admit it, and can only accept salvation from God's grace through the Holy Spirit. Indeed, Augustine concluded early in his episcopate that God decides which elected souls will receive divine grace—a clear belief in the predestination of each individual. The barbarian army of the Vandals was at the gates of Hippo when Augustine died.

SIGNIFICANCE

Saint Augustine was, by any measure, a genius of Christian philosophy and has been so venerated since his death. That all subsequent Christian thinkers owe him an immense debt is evident from the continuous outpouring of reprints of his vast works and discussions concerning his ideas. He brought focus to the major issues that continue to challenge the Church to the present day, and he motivated key figures to adopt aspects of his thinking outright. In the early Middle Ages, Charlemagne founded the Holy Roman Empire in the mistaken belief that Augustine's *The City of God* had been written as a blueprint for a divine kingdom on earth. Saint Thomas Aquinas accepted Augustine's notions of predestination for the later Middle Ages, as did John Calvin during the Protestant Reformation. The power of Augustine's theology has remained undiminished through the ages.

—*Clark G. Reynolds*

FURTHER READING

Bourke, Vernon J. *The Essential Augustine*. Indianapolis, Ind.: Hackett, 1974. An excellent collection of excerpts from Augustine's principal writings, introduced topically by this Thomist writer. Includes a bibliography.

Brown, Peter. *Augustine of Hippo*. Berkeley: University of California Press, 2000. One of the best biographical accounts of Augustine, which uses the chronological approach to show Augustine's writings as they evolved during his lifetime. Heavily annotated.

Chadwick, Henry. *Augustine*. New York: Oxford University Press, 2001. This volume in the Past Masters series provides a concise introduction to Augustine's thought.

Deane, Herbert A. *The Political and Social Ideas of St. Augustine*. New York: Columbia University Press, 1966. A treatment of the theology and psychology behind Augustine's notion of "Fallen Man." Focuses on morality and justice, the state and order, war and relations among states, the church, state, heresy, and Augustine's view of history.

Gilson, Étienne. *The Christian Philosophy of Saint Augustine*. Translated by L. E. M. Lynch. Rev. ed. New York: Vintage Books, 1967. Among the best and most scholarly works on Augustine's philosophy. A translation of the 1943 version in French, more than half of which is annotations. Gilson regards Augustinianism as the discovery of humility, built on charity.

Lawless, George P. *Augustine of Hippo and His Monastic Rule*. New York: Oxford University Press, 1987. An excellent summary of the lifetime work of the late Luc Verbraken, tracing the monastic orientation of Augustine's life and showing how his love of friends in a community setting established the monastic tradition in the Christian West.

Markus, R. A., ed. *Augustine: A Collection of Critical Essays*. Garden City, N.Y.: Anchor, 1972. An anthology of in-depth essays by prominent interpreters of Augustine, extensive in its coverage of his various interests.

Meer, F. G. L. van der. *Augustine the Bishop*. New York: Harper & Row, 1965. Reviews Augustine's adult life after he became bishop of Hippo. Augmented by archaeological information from North African digs.

O'Daly, Gerard. *Augustine's Philosophy of the Mind*. Berkeley: University of California Press, 1987. The first monograph in more than a century to analyze Augustine's arguments about the mind.

Wills, Garry. *Saint Augustine: A Penguin Life*. New York: Viking Penguin, 1999. Examines Saint Augustine's early days, his writings on the human condition, and age in which he lived.

SEE ALSO: Saint Ambrose; Saint Jerome; Jesus; Saint Paul; Plotinus.

RELATED ARTICLES in *Great Events from History: The Ancient World*: c. 6 B.C.E., Birth of Jesus Christ; c. 30 C.E., Condemnation and Crucifixion of Jesus Christ; 200 C.E., Christian Apologists Develop Concept of Theology; 313-395 C.E., Inception of Church-State Problem; 325 C.E., Adoption of the Nicene Creed; 380-392 C.E., Theodosius's Edicts Promote Christian Orthodoxy; c. 382-c. 405 C.E., Saint Jerome Creates the Vulgate; 413-427 C.E., Saint Augustine Writes *The City of God*; 428-431 C.E., Nestorian Controversy; October 8-25, 451 C.E., Council of Chalcedon.

AUGUSTUS

Roman emperor (r. 27 B.C.E.-14 C.E.)

Through his political skill and intelligence, Augustus transformed the chaos that followed the assassination of Julius Caesar into the long-lasting Roman Empire.

BORN: September 23, 63 B.C.E.; Rome (now in Italy)
DIED: August 19, 14 C.E.; Nola (now in Italy)
ALSO KNOWN AS: Gaius Octavius (given name); Augustus Caesar; Caesar Augustus; Gaius Julius Caesar; Gaius Julius Caesar Octavianus; Gaius Octavian; Octavian
AREA OF ACHIEVEMENT: Government and politics

EARLY LIFE

Augustus (uh-GUHS-tuhs), the first emperor of Rome, was born Gaius Octavius, and during his youth he was known to history as Octavian. His family was an old and wealthy one from the small town of Velitrae (Velletri), about twenty miles southeast of Rome. The Octavii were not, however, a noble family; they were of the equestrian order, which meant that they did not sit in the Roman senate and thus could not hold the higher offices of the state. Octavian's father, a supporter of Julius Caesar, was the first of the family to achieve those distinctions; he died when Octavian was four.

Octavian's great-uncle was that same Julius Caesar whom he so admired, and Caesar discerned in the young man possibilities of future greatness. At sixteen, Octavian planned to accompany Caesar to Spain in his campaign against the forces of Pompey the Great, Caesar's enemy in the civil wars. Delayed by illness, Octavian followed Caesar, risking considerable hardship along the way, including a shipwreck from which he narrowly escaped. Although he arrived after the hostilities had ended, his daring and initiative greatly impressed Caesar.

In 44 B.C.E., while Caesar was preparing his campaign against the Parthian Empire in the east, Octavian went on ahead, intending to join the army en route. He was in Apollonia, on the Adriatic coast, when he learned that Caesar had been assassinated in Rome on the ides of March (March 15). Along with this shocking news, he soon learned that in his will Caesar had named him heir to the bulk of the dictator's vast estate and, much more significantly, had adopted him. Although it was impossible to transmit political office or power through inheritance, Caesar had clearly signaled his choice of successor. Octavian, in turn, indicated his determination to claim his rights by an immediate return to Italy and by taking the name Gaius Julius Caesar. At eighteen he was prepared to contest control of the Roman world.

Portrait busts, statues, and the writings of historians have left a clear picture of the first emperor. He was of average height and wore lifts in his sandals to appear taller. His hair was blondish, and his teeth were small and widely spaced. The ancient historian Suetonius describes Octavian as handsome, and other writers have remarked on his calm, quiet expression. He had clear, bright eyes and liked to believe that a certain divine radiance could be seen in them. Throughout his life he was bothered by a number of illnesses, some of them quite serious. Perhaps because of his poor health he was temperate in his habits, drinking little and eating lightly. Although a conscientious administrator, he hated to rise early, and his chief pastime was gambling with his friends. More than anything else, his actions and achievements clearly indicate that he was a man of great ambition and clear intelligence, with a profound perception of the qualities of others.

LIFE'S WORK

When Octavian returned to Italy, he had two immediate goals: to claim his inheritance from Caesar and to avenge his adoptive father's death. He first tried to establish an alliance with Marc Antony, a close associate and colleague of Caesar, but Antony took a harsh attitude toward the much younger man and even blocked the implementation of Caesar's will. As a result, Octavian went over to the side of the senate, which was attempting to regain control of the state. With the help of Octavian and an army raised largely from Caesar's veterans, the senatorial forces defeated Antony at Mutina (Modena, northern Italy) in 43 B.C.E. Octavian quickly realized, however, that the senate planned to use him to remove Antony as a threat and then discard him. The orator Cicero summed up their plan for Octavian: "The young man is to be praised, honored, and exalted." In Latin the last word can be understood as a pun for "removed."

Sensing this design, Octavian arranged a meeting with Antony and Marcus Aemilius Lepidus, another associate of Caesar. The three formed the Second Triumvirate, patterned on the earlier alliance of Caesar, Marcus Licinius Crassus, and Pompey. Both triumvirates became the effective power of the Roman world, largely because of their command of military forces. The Second Triumvirate was sealed by marriage: Octavian wed the daughter of Antony's wife; later, Antony would marry Octavian's sister.

The triumvirs quickly had themselves voted unlimited powers and began to eradicate their opposition, especially those associated with the murder of Caesar. A proscription was proclaimed, and hundreds of Romans, including Cicero, were put to death. Octavian and Antony then confronted the army of Marcus Junius Brutus and Cassius, the leaders of the conspiracy against Caesar. In the Battle of Philippi in Greece (October 23 and November 14, 42 B.C.E.), the last forces capable of restoring the Republic were smashed.

Octavian and Antony divided the Roman world between them, Octavian taking the west, Antony the east. Lepidus was shunted aside and sank into obscurity, eventually ending his life under house arrest. Relations between the two major partners steadily deteriorated. The alliance was patched up by marriage, and in 36 the two cooperated in the defeat of Sextus Pompeius (son of Pompey the Great) in Sicily. Developments after that, however, led to inevitable conflict.

Augustus. (Hulton|Archive by Getty Images)

While in the east, Antony formed a close liaison with Cleopatra, queen of Egypt and former lover of Caesar. Antony granted her territories once held by Egypt but now subject to Rome, and he displayed signs of establishing an independent monarchy in Asia. Octavian skillfully exploited the antiforeign sentiments that these actions aroused, and in 32 B.C.E. Rome declared war on Antony and Cleopatra.

Octavian gathered a fleet and an army and moved east. Under his friend Marcus Vipsanius Agrippa, the Roman forces defeated those of Antony and Cleopatra at the naval battle of Actium, off the Greek coast, on September 2, 31. The two lovers escaped to Egypt, but when surrounded by Octavian's forces, they committed suicide. Octavian annexed Egypt as a Roman province; he was now sole ruler of the Roman state.

His position was still precarious, however, and for the rest of his life he had to balance the reality of his power carefully with the appearance of a restored Republic. Although briefly considering a true return to the Republic, Octavian realized that it was impossible and would lead to bloody civil war. Instead of claiming or accepting offices of overt power—such as the dictatorship—which had brought about the death of Caesar, Octavian was content to serve in more traditional ways, such as consul (thirteen times in all) or tribune. His most frequently used title was an innovation: *princeps* (short for *princeps civitatis*, "first citizen"); this appellation was vague enough not to offend, yet sufficient to preserve his authority.

In 27 B.C.E. Octavian was granted the title Augustus by the senate, indicating the religious aspect of his position. Throughout his reign, Augustus artfully underscored the moral need for a strong ruler to end centuries of internecine bloodshed. It is as Augustus that he is best known to history.

As ruler, Augustus's major concerns were internal reform and external defense. In Rome, he revised the senate roll, striking off many who were unfit to serve. He vigorously enforced laws against immorality, even sending his own daughter into exile for her numerous and blatant adulteries. His life was less circumscribed. He stole his wife, Livia, from her first husband and was married to her while she was pregnant; he was known later for his many affairs, showing a particular preference for young virgins.

Nevertheless, he was careful in his observance of ancient Roman religious rituals and in 12 C.E. was elected *pontifex maximus*, or head priest. Whenever possible, he revived old customs and mores, attempting to strengthen

FIRST TEN EMPERORS OF IMPERIAL ROME

Ruler	Reign
Augustus	27 B.C.E.-14 C.E.
Tiberius	14-37
Caligula	37-41
Claudius	41-54
Nero	54-68
Galba	68-69
Otho	69
Vitellius	69
Vespasian	69-79
Titus	79-81

patriotism and social order. His many building projects, especially in Rome, repaired years of neglect and greatly improved life in the city.

Along the borders, Augustus was content to maintain existing boundaries for most of the Empire. In Germany, he made an effort to extend the limits of Roman rule to the Elbe River. These attempts were abruptly ended in 6 B.C.E., when German tribes ambushed and massacred three legions under the command of Publius Quinctilius Varus. The disaster caused Augustus to fix the boundaries at the Rhine River; for a long time afterward he could be heard crying out in his palace, "Varus, give me back my legions!"

As he grew older, Augustus attempted to fix the succession of power, realizing that he must provide for an orderly transition lest his accomplishments be destroyed in another round of civil war. When his three grandsons either died or proved unfit, he was forced to turn to Tiberius, Livia's son by her first husband. Tiberius had long served Augustus in civil and military posts and had been advanced as heir on several occasions, only to be set aside for a candidate more suitable to Augustus's needs. At last, however, he was adopted by Augustus and served as his colleague and virtual coemperor until Augustus's death.

Augustus died in 14, and the fact that Tiberius succeeded him without a renewal of internal strife and disastrous civil war is perhaps the best indication of Augustus's success in creating a new and lasting political order—the Roman Empire.

SIGNIFICANCE

One of the sayings attributed to Augustus is that he found Rome a city of brick and left it one of marble. This is literally true: His extensive renovation and construction transformed Rome from top to bottom—from its temples to its sewer system. A similar transformation was wrought by Augustus in the whole of the Roman world.

He found a state that was wracked by internal unrest, one that was seemingly incapable of ruling itself without resorting to self-destructive civil war. Through patience, tact, and, when necessary, force, he translated the ruins of the Republic into the edifice of the Empire. So difficult a task, to refound the Roman state, was made all the harder by the need to disguise its true nature. Throughout his reign, Augustus carefully retained the forms and procedures of a republic, deferring to the senate, refusing extravagant titles, and being careful to allow others a measure of honor and prestige—although never enough to threaten his preeminent position.

Augustus's major accomplishments were to establish the Roman Empire and to become its first emperor, almost without public notice. While all knew that power had shifted into the hands of one man, the shift had been accomplished in such a gradual, subtle fashion, and with such positive results, that few openly complained. Most Romans probably approved of the changes made by Augustus. There was security, increasing prosperity, and, above all, peace. The arts flourished, and the golden age of Roman literature under Augustus produced such lasting writers as Horace, Ovid, Livy, and Vergil.

Augustus restored peace to a society that badly needed it. Conflicts continued on the borders, but internal warfare came to an end. In one of his most significant acts, Augustus closed the gates to the temple of Janus, an act done only when Rome was formally at peace. Before his time, the gates had been shut only twice in Rome's long history. More than anything else it was this peace, this Pax Romana and the blessings it brought, that caused a grateful senate to accord Augustus the title *pater patriae*—father of his country.

—*Michael Witkoski*

FURTHER READING

Grant, Michael. *The Roman Emperors: A Biographical Guide to the Rulers of Rome, 31 B.C.-A.D. 476.* New York: Charles Scribner's Sons, 1985. A lucid, compressed review of the life and times of Augustus, placing him within the context of his society.

_____. *The Twelve Caesars.* New York: Charles Scribner's Sons, 1983. This volume takes the ancient biographer Suetonius as its starting point but goes far beyond him in its exploration and explanation of the difficulties and accomplishments of Augustus. Especially good in delineating the agonizingly careful line Augustus had to trace in establishing an empire on the ruins of a fallen, but still potent, republic.

Jones, A. H. *Augustus*. Edited by M. I. Finley. New York: W. W. Norton, 1971. A well-researched and well-presented overview of Augustus's life and career, giving equal attention to both.

Massie, Allan. *The Caesars*. New York: Franklin Watts, 1984. A popular biography of Rome's Imperial rulers. The section on the first emperor is well done and provides several interesting views of his task in setting up the Imperial system.

Southern, Pat. *Augustus*. New York: Routledge, 2001. Biography focuses on Augustus the man. Covers the life of the emperor in chronological order.

Suetonius, Gaius Tranquillus. *Lives of the Twelve Caesars*. Translated by Robert Graves. Rev. ed. New York: Welcome Rain, 2001. Suetonius is long on incident and short on evaluation, but his lively portrait of Augustus has never been surpassed. While other, later authors have given more facts about the founder of the Roman Empire, Suetonius presents him as a human being. This work certainly deserves its reputation as a classic.

SEE ALSO: Marcus Vipsanius Agrippa; Marc Antony; Marcus Junius Brutus; Julius Caesar; Cassius; Hadrian; Julia III; Livia Drusilla; Tiberius.

RELATED ARTICLES in *Great Events from History: The Ancient World*: 43-42 B.C.E., Second Triumvirate Enacts Proscriptions; 27-23 B.C.E., Completion of the Augustan Settlement; November 27, 8 B.C.E., Roman Lyric Poet Horace Dies; 9 C.E., Battle of Teutoburg Forest; c. 50 C.E., Creation of the Roman Imperial Bureaucracy.

BAN GU
Chinese historian

Through his compilation of a history of the Han Dynasty, Ban Gu created a full, well-documented record for this vital period of Chinese history and set the standard for all subsequent dynastic histories of China.

BORN: 32 C.E.; Shanxi, China
DIED: 92 C.E.; Shanxi, China
ALSO KNOWN AS: Pan Ku (Wade-Giles); Ban Mengjian (Pinyin), Pan Meng-chien (Wade-Giles)
AREA OF ACHIEVEMENT: Historiography

EARLY LIFE

Ban Gu (bahn gew) was a member of the illustrious Ban family of Han China (206 B.C.E. to 220 C.E.). Since the generation of his great-great-grandfather, the Bans had distinguished themselves in scholarship, serving the Han imperial government in both court and provincial posts. His grand-aunt had been a favorite concubine of Emperor Cheng (Ch'eng; r. 32-7 B.C.E.). Gu's twin brother, Chao (Ch'ao), assigned the title of Marquess for Establishing the Remote Regions, won for himself immortal fame by reestablishing Chinese hegemony in Central Asia. His younger sister, Zhao (Chao), much respected in court circles as the tutor of imperial princesses, was one of China's foremost women scholars; she wrote the *Nu jie* (c. 99-105 C.E.; *The Chinese Book of Etiquette and Conduct for Women and Girls*, 1900; also known as *Lessons for Women*), the first textbook ever written for teaching Chinese women.

LIFE'S WORK

Despite having such illustrious forebears and siblings, the young Ban Gu had a hard time finding his niche in the world. The Ban family had no automatic right to high office. Gu's father, Biao (Pan Piao), though fairly successful in his official career, died when his sons were still relatively young and unestablished. He did, however, bequeath to Gu a project that was to secure for the Ban family a hallowed place in China's literary tradition: the writing of a complete history of the Former Han Dynasty, the *Han Shu* (also known as *Qian Han Shu*, completed first century C.E.; *The History of the Former Han Dynasty*, 1938-1955). Gu's efforts in writing the history were brought to the attention of Emperor Ming (r. 58-75), who appreciated his merits and made him a gentleman-in-waiting (*lang*). In this capacity, Gu had access to government archives that facilitated his writing efforts.

Besides writing *The History of the Former Han Dynasty*, Gu was given other writing assignments such as to report on the proceedings at the Bohu (Po-hu) Pavilion, in which an enclave of Confucian erudites gathered to deliberate on the correct interpretations of Confucian classics bearing on the ritual aspects of the Chinese monarchy. In addition, he found time to indulge his poetic propensities. His two *fu* (rhymed prose essays or rhapsodies) on the two capitals of the Han Dynasty established him as the foremost poet of his time.

Although other people had a hand in the compilation of *The History of the Former Han Dynasty*, notably his father Biao, his younger sister Zhao, and the scholar Ma Zu (Ma Hsü), there is no question that the main credit has to go to Gu. He gave the book its definitive form and was personally responsible for writing most of the text. Thus, it is appropriate to credit Ban Gu as the author of *The History of the Former Han Dynasty*.

Traditionally, Ban Gu's name came to be linked to that of Sima Qian (Ssu-ma Ch'ien)—often the two were referred to by the dual name Ma-Ban—to suggest the highest standard in historiographical writing. There is no denying Gu's indebtedness to Sima Qian. In fact, *The History of the Former Han Dynasty* cannot be meaningfully discussed apart from the historiographical context that Sima Qian and his masterpiece, *Shiji* (first century B.C.E.; *Records of the Grand Historian of China*, 1960, rev. ed. 1993), provided.

Before Sima Qian's time (c. 145-c. 86 B.C.E.), historical works had not been formally or conceptually differentiated from other forms of serious literature, which all purported to be authentic words and deeds of the ancients. To the extent that conscious attempts to write history were made, the only available framework into which records of the past could be fitted was the *biannian* (annals), as exemplified by the *Chunqiu* (fifth century B.C.E.; *The Ch'un Ts'ew with the Tso Chuen*, 1872; commonly known as *Spring and Summer Annals*) edited by Confucius. This was a strictly chronological listing of events as they transpired, recorded from the point of view of some court historian. The disadvantages of this format are obvious. In treatments of events that had to be recorded close to the time they occurred, they often appear to be abstracted from their context, unless substantial digression and background materials were incorporated. To catch the attention of the recorder, events had to be of a spectacular nature—battles, diplomatic alliances, and the accession or death of rulers. Long-term changes such as population growth or technological development occurred too slowly to be noticed. Moreover, the format could not accommodate matters such as social or cultural history that had no immediate bearing on the government.

Sima Qian lived at a time when vast changes had overtaken China. The decentralized feudal China of the time of Confucius had given way to the centralized bureaucratic empire under the Qin (Ch'in; 221-206 B.C.E.). The Qin Dynasty, ruling over a unified China for the first time in history, was undone by excessive tyranny and was overthrown by a universal revolt. The ensuing struggle to succeed to the throne of China ended with the triumph of the House of Han, which was to rule for more than four hundred years. Meanwhile, the quest for empire was taking the Chinese into Mongolia and Central Asia. The economy was expanding, and enormous fortunes were made. Myriad individuals had played important roles in the unfolding drama. The times called for a new historiography that would be capable of portraying these vast changes and doing justice to these individuals and their contributions.

In writing the *Records of the Grand Historian of China*, Sima Qian overcame the limitations of the old historiography by developing a composite format. The seventy chapters of the *Records of the Grand Historian of China* are divided into five sections, each representing a distinct style of historical writing. The first section, known as "Basic Annals" (*benji*), essentially follows the *biannian* style of the old historiography, being a chronicle of events recorded from the viewpoint of the paramount ruler of China. The longest section is the "Biographies" (*liezhuan*). Here, attention is given to individuals, ranging from successful generals and ministers to unconventional characters such as the would-be assassin Qingke (Ch'ing K'o), as well as physicians, diviners, entertainers, and entrepreneurs. Sima Qian chose people who exemplified in their words or deeds patterns of human endeavor that were to be commended. The biographical section also gave the historian the flexibility to reconcile the two moral imperatives of his profession: objectivity in reporting, and praising the worthy and castigating evildoers. Since the annals and the biographies sections together constitute the bulk of the *Records of the Grand Historian of China*, the *shiji* format of historiography is often known as the *jizhuan* style.

The section of hereditary houses (*shijia*) deals with the history of the *de facto* sovereign states during the period preceding the Qin unification. The section on chronological tables (*biao*) traces the genealogy of the prominent families and furnishes a convenient scheme for correlating the chronologies of the various feudal states. The most distinctive section of the *Records of the Grand Historian of China* is the one titled "Monographs" (*shu*), which comprises eight chapters dealing with such wide-ranging matters as rites, music, pitched pipes, the calendar, astronomy, state sacrifices, rivers and canals, and the economy.

Sima Qian lived during the reign of Wudi (Wu-ti; 140-87 B.C.E.), during the heyday of the Former Han Dynasty. By 9 C.E., however, Wudi's descendants had been edged out of the succession by the usurper Wang Mang, who founded the Xin Dynasty (Hsin; 9-23 C.E.). Wang Mang, however, was unable to consolidate his regime, and his dynasty fell amid a revolt by starving peasants and disgruntled landlords, precipitating another scramble for the throne of China. The man who emerged triumphant in this contest, Liu Xiu (Liu Hsiu; posthumous title Guang Wudi, r. 25-57 C.E.), who was descended from the founder of the Western Han Dynasty, claimed that his dynasty was a continuation or restoration of the Great Han. As his capital was located at Luoyang (Lo-yang), to the east of the Western Han capital, Chang'an (now Xi'an), historians refer to the restored dynasty as the Eastern, or Later, Han.

To scholars living at the court of the Eastern Han, the period from the founding of the first Han Dynasty to the final overthrow of the usurper Wang Mang constituted a natural unit of history. Emulating the success of Sima Qian, several of them (among them Ban Biao, Gu's father) had tried to write its history. Apart from determining the overall design and collecting source materials for the project, however, Biao apparently had done little actual writing. Though Gu received the idea of writing *The History of the Former Han Dynasty* from his father, and though he was apparently deeply moved by the Confucian value of filial piety, he saw no need to be bound by his father's design. Whereas his father had had no use for the majority of Sima Qian's innovations, Gu retained almost all the sections of the *Records of the Grand Historian of China*, with the exception of "Hereditary Houses" (for the obvious reason that in the centralized bureaucratic polity of Han China there were no authentic hereditary houses apart from that of the imperial family).

Records of the Grand Historian of China not only was the model for Ban Gu's *The History of the Former Han Dynasty* but also constituted his single most important source. Materials from the *Records of the Grand Historian of China* pertaining to the first hundred years of the

Former Han Dynasty, in which the coverage of the two works overlaps, were copied almost verbatim into *The History of the Former Han Dynasty*. Nevertheless, Gu was no mere imitator; wherever possible, he sought to develop the potentialities of the model he had inherited. Sima Qian, for example, had invented the category of monographs to expand the scope of historiography to encompass ritual, social, and economic as well as political history. Ban Gu went one step further. In the section on monographs (which he renamed *zhi* instead of *shu*), he retained all the *Records of the Grand Historian of China* chapters on ritual matters but vastly expanded the scope of administrative history, adding new chapters on penal law and geography. The monograph on geography gives detailed population figures for the administrative subdivisions of the empire, thus yielding the first complete census of China, for the year 2 C.E. In addition, he ventured into the domain of intellectual history. The monograph on literature (*yiwenzhi*) was more than a systematic account of Chinese intellectual history; it also contained the first complete catalog of all Chinese books extant at that time.

Although Gu's character was amiable and accommodating, he had the misfortune late in life to be caught up in the factional strife of the Han court. He joined the staff of General Dou Xian (Tou Hsien) as his confidential secretary on the eve of the latter's punitive expedition against the Xiongnu (Hsiung-nu). On his return, the general was impeached for treason, and members of his retinue were also implicated. Gu was cast into prison, where he died before his friends could rescue him.

SIGNIFICANCE

Through *The History of the Former Han Dynasty*, Ban Gu had a great impact on Chinese historiography and on Chinese political consciousness. He developed the possibilities of the *jizhuan* format, bringing it into the mainstream of Chinese official historiography. His contribution in this regard is twofold. First, he produced a monumental work, in one hundred chapters, in the style of Sima Qian's new historiography, thus helping to popularize the form. Indeed, it is doubtful whether Sima Qian's legacy could have survived if Ban Gu had not written *The History of the Former Han Dynasty* in support of it. There is evidence that until the Tang Dynasty (T'ang; 618-907 C.E.), the *Records of the Grand Historian of China* was an extremely rare book and that it was primarily thanks to Ban Gu's *The History of the Former Han Dynasty* that scholars became acquainted with the *jizhuan* style of historiography. Second, Ban Gu was the one who arranged for the new historiography to be wedded to the salient feature of Chinese history, the dynastic cycle. Although dynasties varied in length and in the circumstances of their rise and fall, generally speaking, each dynasty marked a distinct period, an era with its own characteristics. After the time of Ban Gu, as soon as a new dynasty had consolidated its power, one of the first things its scholars did was compile an official history of the dynasty that had preceded it, signifying in this way that that dynasty was indeed defunct. The precedent for this practice was established by Ban Gu, who also set the tone for the writing of these official dynastic histories: impersonal, objective, and dignified.

—*Winston W. Lo*

FURTHER READING

Hughes, E. R. *Two Chinese Poets: Vignettes of Han Life and Thought*. 1960. Reprint. Westport, Conn.: Greenwood Press, 1977. The author examines two sets of rhapsodies on the two Han capitals, by Ban Gu and Zhang Heng (Chang Heng), respectively. While the book is informative with regard to the nature of Han rhapsodies and the descriptions of the two capitals, the main purpose of the author is to highlight, through exploring the minds of the two poets, the contrasting style and ethos of the two Han dynasties. Indispensable for understanding Ban Gu's ideology and worldview.

Hulsewé, A. F. P. *China in Central Asia: An Annotated Translation of Chapters Sixty-one and Ninety-six of "The History of the Former Han Dynasty."* New York: E. J. Brill, 1979. Particularly useful is the seventy-page introductory chapter by M. A. N. Loewe. Loewe comments on the materials on which the original copy of *The History of the Former Han Dynasty* was written (wood or bamboo slips) and discusses the relationship between the *Records of the Grand Historian of China* and *The History of the Former Han Dynasty*. He argues, contrary to previous assumptions, that at least in one case the *Records of the Grand Historian of China* text is not the source for *The History of the Former Han Dynasty* but indeed derivative from it.

_____. "Notes on the Historiography of the Han Period." In *Historians of China and Japan*, edited by W. G. Beasley and E. G. Pulleyblank. New York: Oxford University Press, 1961. A general but authoritative survey on the authors of the *Records of the Grand Historian of China* and *The History of the Former Han Dynasty* and other works of historiography of the Han period.

Ssu-ma Ch'ien. *The Grand Scribe's Records*. Translated by Weiguo Cao, Scott W. Galer, and David W. Pankenier, edited by William H. Neinhauser, Jr. Vols. 1, 2, and 7. Bloomington: Indiana University Press, 1994-2002. A modern translation of Sima Qian's history, with copious notes and commentary. These three volumes are the sections published to date; eventually the entire work will be available in nine volumes.

Swann, Nancy Lee. *Pan Chao, Foremost Woman Scholar of China*. 1932. Reprint. Ann Arbor, Mich.: Center for Chinese Studies, 2001. Still the most important source on Ban Gu's life. The author traces the genealogy of the Ban family, discusses the career of some of Gu's forebears, and assesses the contributions that Gu's father and younger sister and others made toward the completion of *The History of the Former Han Dynasty*. A meticulous scholar, Swann utilizes all available primary and secondary sources in arriving at her conclusions.

Twitchett, Denis, and Michael Loewe, eds. *The Ch'in and Han Empires: 221 B.C. to A.D. 220*. Vol. 1 in *The Cambridge History of China*. New York: Cambridge University Press, 1986. Among the most comprehensive and authoritative histories of the Han period. Includes essays on sociocultural as well as historical events.

Watson, Burton. *Ssu-ma Ch'ien, Grand Historian of China*. New York: Columbia University Press, 1958. Not only the most authoritative study on the *Records of the Grand Historian of China* but also indispensable for any serious work on *The History of the Former Han Dynasty*; the author often makes insightful comments on the relative merits of the *Records of the Grand Historian of China* and *The History of the Former Han Dynasty* and their respective authors.

SEE ALSO: Ban Zhao; Sima Qian; Wudi.

RELATED ARTICLES in *Great Events from History: The Ancient World*: 5th century B.C.E., Composition of the *Spring and Autumn Annals*; c. 450-c. 425 B.C.E., History Develops as a Scholarly Discipline; 206 B.C.E., Liu Bang Captures Qin Capital, Founds Han Dynasty; 140-87 B.C.E., Wudi Rules Han Dynasty China; 1st century B.C.E., Sima Qian Writes Chinese History; c. 99-105 C.E., Ban Zhao Writes Behavior Guide for Young Women.

BAN ZHAO
Chinese historian, poet, and scholar

Imperial China's greatest woman scholar, Ban Zhao wrote a guide that formulated ideal precepts for the conduct of women.

BORN: c. 45 C.E.; Anling, Fufeng County (now near Xianyang, Shaanxi Province), China

DIED: c. 120 C.E.; China

ALSO KNOWN AS: Pan Chao (Wade-Giles); Cao Dagu (Pinyin), Ts'ao Ta-ku (Wade-Giles); Cao Shishu qi (Pinyin), Ts'ao Shih-shu ch'i (Wade-Giles); Cao Shou qi (Pinying), Ts'ao Shou ch'i (Wade-Giles)

AREAS OF ACHIEVEMENT: Literature, scholarship, philosophy

EARLY LIFE

Ban Zhao (bahn jaw) was one of the most erudite and the most eminent persons of her time, a renowned scholar and poet who was one of traditional China's most illustrious women. She came from a family of distinguished literati. Her grand-aunt, known as Ban Jieyu (Pan Chiehyü; c. 48-c. 6 B.C.E.), the "Favored Beauty Ban" on account of her rank as the most distinguished concubine of

Emperor Cheng (Ch'eng; r. 32-7 B.C.E.), was a woman of great literary abilities and strong moral character. Her father Ban Biao (Pan Piao; 3-54 C.E.) was an accomplished scholar-official and historian. One of her twin older brothers, Ban Chao (Pan Ch'ao; 32-101 C.E.), was a famous explorer and campaigner in the border regions of far western China. Her other elder brother, Ban Gu (Pan Ku; 32-92 C.E.), was a great literary talent, best known for his lengthy and intricate rhapsodies (*fu*) and, especially, for his lifelong project on the history of the Former Han Dynasty, the *Han Shu* (also known as *Qian Han Shu*, completed first century C.E.; *The History of the Former Han Dynasty*, 1938-1955), a project that had been begun by his father. Ban Gu had not yet completed his great history when was dismissed from office and imprisoned, accused of being a supporter of a dishonored general; he died in prison and the project was finished by his learned sister Ban Zhao, in accordance with the emperor's personal directive. Ban Zhao's official biography is in the section of the *Hou Han ji* (fourth century C.E.; "record of the Later Han") devoted to "Illustrious Women," where she is referred to as "the wife of Cao Shishu" (Ts'ao Shih-shu, an otherwise undistinguished lesser official). Ban Zhao often is referred to in this manner, that is, by her social position. Ban Zhao was married at age fourteen; after her husband died young, she never remarried. As tutor to the empress and the palace ladies, Ban Zhao came to be known as Cao Dagu, or "Respected Elder Aunt Cao," the name by which she equally is known in Chinese sources.

LIFE'S WORK

When Ban Zhao's brother Gu died, Emperor He (Ho-ti; r. 88-105 C.E.) commanded her to work in the imperial library to complete her brother's great historical project. Although there is disagreement on how much she actually completed herself, she usually is credited with having composed at least the eight tables and the "Treatise on the Heavens." When Ban Zhao completed the work, many were unable to completely absorb it; Ma Rong (Ma Jung; 79-166 C.E.), who would come to be known as one of the literary luminaries of his age, was appointed to study the work with her in the library as her apprentice. Emperor He invited Ban Zhao to provide personal instruction to his wife, Empress Deng, and her entourage, and to compose descriptive poetic eulogies about the various treasures and curiosities that came as tribute to the court. Ban Zhao was a learned scholar, practiced in literary and historical composition, but she apparently also was a savvy player in government affairs. After the emperor passed away in 105, young Empress Deng held sway over the court until her death in 121, and it is said that Ban Zhao was her confidante, with whom she would confer on matters of politics and administration. The empress so favored Ban Zhao that she granted Zhao's son Cao Cheng (Ts'ao Ch'eng) with a title of enfeoffment and a high court appointment.

Ban Zhao may best be known for a treatise she wrote concerning the proper conduct of women, especially in their position as wives and members of the husband's family. Her *Nu jie* (c. 99-105 C.E.; *The Chinese Book of Etiquette and Conduct for Women and Girls*, 1900; also known as *Lessons for Women*) is included in her biography, written ostensibly for the edification of her own daughters; she tells in her exceedingly humble introduction that they should each write out a copy and strive to put into practice the principles discussed in the essay. *Lessons for Women* addressed personal cultivation and appropriate conduct with respect to relations within the husband's family, expounding on correct feminine attitudes and comportment within a largely Confucian value

system. Her text finds many corroborations in the Confucian classics for canonical authority; nevertheless, one modern scholar has suggested that much also is owed to Daoist texts and texts on military strategy. Perhaps the most consequential precept in the treatise is uncompromised fidelity to the husband, including an injunction not to remarry; throughout all subsequent dynasties, "chaste widows" were held up as paragons of virtuous conduct. The *Lessons for Women* comprises seven sections plus an introduction. The sections are "Humility and Compliance," "Husband and Wife," "Respect and Judiciousness," "Womanly Conduct," "Single-minded Devotion," "Yielding and Following," and "According with Younger In-laws."

Ban Zhao's *Lessons for Women* had a certain influence in its day and had immense influence over the centuries of Imperial China, continuing even into the present, but it also has had its critics. In many ways Ban Zhao's text came to be seen as the authority on proper conduct for women. Ban Zhao's student Ma Rong had his wife and daughters study it, and women over the next two millennia were praised for emulating the ideal feminine values and conduct described in Zhao's short treatise. Still, the younger sister of Ban Zhao's daughter-in-law apparently took her to task and wrote her own countertreatise.

Some modern critics have argued that the *Lessons for Women* has had a profoundly negative influence on women through the centuries by promoting what they see as subservience, obedience, humility, devotion, self-abnegation, and other aspects that they relate to negative expectations for a woman's conduct. Others, including the majority in imperial times, have praised it for promoting the education of women; for marking a path for upright conduct in the largely oppressive and sometimes treacherous realities of concubines and wives of the scholar-official class; and for providing a framework for the type of genteel femininity that has been praised and emulated in the characterization of women in traditional Chinese culture.

Ban Zhao's *Lessons for Women* spurred numerous derivative compositions and books on female propriety over the centuries, and Ban Zhao herself sometimes is portrayed within the conceit of a dialogue, where she serves as arbiter and provides instruction to an individual or group in a question/response format. An example is the *Nü xiao jing* (*Classic of Filial Piety for Women*, 1932) of the Tang Dynasty (618-907 C.E.).

Ban Zhao's copious and wide-ranging writings were collected by her daughter-in-law, surnamed Ding, who also composed a now-lost eulogy for her. The collection of Ban Zhao's writings was in sixteen sections, and included rhapsodies, eulogies, threnodies, memorial inscriptions, poems, propositions, commentaries, laments, letters, treatises, memorials, and bequeathals. Ban Zhao's collected writings remained intact for several centuries, but now only a few of her works remain. After the *Lessons for Women*, Ban Zhao's most important extant writing is her "Traveling Eastward," an elegant poetic account of her trip when she accompanied her son to his first posting in 95 C.E. (the year of the journey has been emended from 113 C.E., on the basis of contextual historical evidence), which includes her reflections on the moral associations of the places passed in her travel. In addition to these famous writings, Ban Zhao's extant works include two carefully wrought and persuasive memorials to the throne and rhapsodies on the sewing needle and thread, on the cicada, and on an ostrich sent back by her brother from Central Asia. Ban Zhao also usually is credited with having annotated or otherwise edited *Lienü zhuan* (late first century B.C.E.-early second century C.E.; *Biographies of Illustrious Women*, 1945).

SIGNIFICANCE

Ban Zhao often is called China's foremost woman scholar, a rare example of a woman known to her contemporaries and to posterity for her erudition. Her *Lessons for Women* set the model for the ideal comportment of women in traditional Chinese culture. In this treatise, Ban Zhao advocated education for women, outlined her views of a woman's proper conduct to her husband and in-laws, and established that a woman should not remarry. *Lessons for Women* is the first integral writing on the ethics of womanhood, a treatise pairing philosophical principles with practical applications. This text became an essential and indispensable part of the education for women in traditional China.

—*Alan Berkowitz*

FURTHER READING

Chen, Yu-shih. "The Historical Template of Pan Chao's *Nü chieh.*" *T'oung Pao* 82 (1996): 229-257. A recontextualization of Ban Zhao's *Lessons for Women*.

Cutter, Robert Joe, and William Gordon Crowell. *Empresses and Consorts*. Honolulu: University of Hawaii Press, 1999. Best scholarship on diverse aspects of women in early and early medieval China.

Dull, Jack L. "Marriage and Divorce in Han China: A Glimpse at 'Pre-Confucian' Society." In *Chinese Family Law and Social Change in Historical and Comparative Perspective*, edited by David C. Buxbaum. Seattle: University of Washington Press, 1978. Still the best exposition of these practices, with all data and examples coming directly from primary sources.

Hinsch, Bret. *Women in Early Imperial China*. Lanham, Md.: Rowman and Littlefield, 2002. A topical presentation of female experience, illustrating Ban Zhao's lasting influence.

Knapp, Bettina L. "Pan Chao: Poet, Historian, and Moralist." In *Images of Chinese Women: A Westerner's View*. Troy, N.Y.: Whitston, 1992. Fair treatment of Ban Zhao, including translations of Ban Zhao's works done by Nancy Swann.

Lee, Lily Xiao Hong. "Ban Zhao (48-c. 120): Her Role in the Formulation of Controls Imposed Upon Women in Traditional China." In *The Virtue of Yin: Studies on Chinese Women*. Broadway, NSW, Australia: Wild Peony, 1994. Concise, contextual, and analytic treatment.

Martin-Liao, Tienchi. "Traditional Handbooks of Women's Education." In *Woman and Literature in China*, edited by Anna Gerstlacher et al. Bochum: Brockmeyer, 1985. Good introduction to and summary of the topic.

Raphaels, Lisa. *Sharing the Light: Representations of Women and Virtue in Early China*. Albany: State University of New York Press, 1998. Excellent treatment of many diverse facets of philosophical and cultural discussions concerning womanhood in early China, especially concerning the role of virtue as expressed in the literature about exemplary women.

Swann, Nancy Lee. *Pan Chao: Foremost Woman Scholar of China*. 1932. Reprint. Ann Arbor: University of Michigan Press, 2001. See this book first; by far the best and most thorough account of Ban Zhao and her work.

SEE ALSO: Ban Gu; Hypatia.

RELATED ARTICLES in *Great Events from History: The Ancient World*: c. 2300 B.C.E., Enheduanna Becomes First Named Author; c. 580 B.C.E., Greek Poet Sappho Dies; c. 99-105 C.E., Ban Zhao Writes Behavior Guide for Young Women; c. 220 C.E., Cai Yan Composes Poetry About Her Capture by Nomads.

BATHSHEBA

Israeli noblewoman

Bathsheba wielded occasional power behind the thrones of Israel's second and third monarchs. According to the New Testament, she was an ancestor of Jesus Christ.

FLOURISHED: Tenth century B.C.E.; Israel
ALSO KNOWN AS: Bathshua; Bethsabee
AREA OF ACHIEVEMENT: Religion

EARLY LIFE

Few details are known of the life of Bathsheba (bath-SHEE-bah), yet her story, as narrated in passages from First Kings, Second Samuel, and First Chronicles of the Hebrew Bible, is dramatically tantalizing. Though rabbinical sages and church fathers make reference to her from time to time, only the salient facts of her career are known. According to their usual practice, biblical writers make no attempt to enter her mind or explore her emotions the way a modern biographer or novelist would. Her motivations may be discerned solely from her actions, and they lend themselves to different interpretations.

Bathsheba was the daughter of Eliam, a figure otherwise unidentified in the biblical record. Ancient Hebrew names generally had either literal or metaphoric descriptive significance. Hers probably meant "daughter of Sheba" or "daughter of abundance." Ironically, her name has always reminded English speakers of the action for which she is best remembered; for the artists who would later paint her, she would be "the woman who bathes."

LIFE'S WORK

Bathsheba is first introduced in the Bible as the wife of Uriah the Hittite. Her husband, a man of foreign lineage, is a consistently noble warrior, unwaveringly loyal to David, king of Israel. Though it is the time of year when kings are expected to set forth in battle, King David is found shirking his duty on the fateful day he first glimpses Bathsheba. Lounging on the rooftop of his palace in Jerusalem, the king spies Uriah's wife bathing on her own roof, evidently performing her mikveh, the ritual purification. Smitten by her beauty, David orders that she be brought to his palace. Her own wishes are never clear. Possibly she is an innocent prize claimed by a tyrant, while her husband is serving him. However, the suspicion lingers that she may have schemed all along to catch the lustful eye of the king. Without a hint of coercion, she quickly becomes David's partner in adultery. Whatever his intentions may originally have been, David's life becomes complicated when she sends him a message a short time later that she is with child. Though he will later come to cherish the ill-begotten son, his first impulse is to pass it off as the offspring of her lawful husband. Uriah is recalled from the battlefield and told to return to the comforts of his home. Uriah, however, upholds the soldier's code; while his fellows endure the dangers of battle he will neither feast nor lie with his wife. David's next plan succeeds; he arranges for Uriah to be isolated and slain in battle.

Again, Bathsheba's possible complicity in these calculations remains obscure. She performs the proper mourning rites for her husband, probably for the duration of a week. Then David makes haste to take her as one of his wives, an especially privileged member of his harem. Their son is duly born but does not flourish. David is depicted as an agonized father, fasting and praying that his child may live. When the infant perishes, the king accepts God's punishment for his crimes, remarking that while his son will never return to him, he too is mortal and will someday join the child in death.

Bathsheba's maternal grief is never detailed. The Bible states simply that David consoled her and with her begat another child, Solomon. The narrator or narrators of their story do not place blame on Bathsheba; they make it clear that this is the king's saga. David is fiercely reprimanded by the enraged prophet Nathan. He learns that his acts of adultery and murder have so angered God, who chose him for the throne, that the rest of his reign will be troubled: The sword will never depart from David's house, and his children by other wives will betray him and scheme against one another. Nevertheless, out of his initially sinful relationship, God will bring forth good. Solomon will preside over Israel's golden age.

For a number of years, Bathsheba largely vanishes from the history of King David's reign. When she reappears, the king is old, and she is now a venerable lady of the royal harem. Her character and personality appear to have changed. Perhaps the years in a royal court have made her shrewd and bold, or perhaps her true nature is revealed when the artifices of youth are stripped away. No longer a passive object of the king's pleasure, she emerges as a forceful participant in events, intent on gaining every advantage for her son. Furthermore, Nathan the prophet, who had earlier found David's adultery with her so repellant, is now her confederate. She will secure the throne for Solomon, although he is neither the elder nor the most popular of David's sons. According to ancient custom, the king is free to choose his successor among his family members. Along with Nathan and other partisans of Solomon, Bathsheba reminds the aging king of an earlier promise to bestow the throne on her son. Whether or not an earlier promise had indeed been made is never clear, but Bathsheba convincingly approaches the now exhausted old man as he lies shivering in bed beside Abishag, a virgin concubine who has been brought into the royal chamber merely to provide youthful warmth to the dying monarch. David, who can still be moved by Bathsheba, readily grants her request. Nathan, too, is satisfied because he sees God's providence at work in these events. Later rabbinical and ecclesiastical teachers will concur, designating Bathsheba a repentant adulteress transformed into God's instrument.

There is a single remaining event in Bathsheba's story that is recorded, her motivations as ambiguous as ever. Recognizing her as a power behind the throne of the new king, Adonijah, an older son of David, approaches her with a request. Though he has been passed over for kingship, Adonijah feels entitled to some consolation. He asks the queen mother to relay to Solomon his desire that Abishag, the last concubine of David, be given to him as a wife. Bathsheba easily approaches her son with the request of his half brother. Rightly or wrongly, Solomon interprets the message as a challenge to his throne and orders the execution of Adonijah. While a modern reader is likely to view the unfortunate Adonijah as a lovelorn young man with a possibly incestuous desire for a woman who had belonged to his late father, an ancient Israelite would probably have understood the request as did Solomon, who saw in it an attempt to claim the prerogatives of kingship.

Scholars question what her request reveals of Bathsheba herself. Was she simply a charitable petitioner on behalf of a family member, or did she also see Adonijah, who still had a strong following at court, as a threat to Solomon's power? Did she thus knowingly set in motion Adonijah's death sentence? It is even possible that her feelings were more complicated still, that even in these mature years she experienced pangs of jealousy. In her last recorded audience with David, she saw him lying beside Abishag, though he was exhausted beyond lust. Perhaps this scene painfully reminded her of the time she was so ardently coveted by the king.

SIGNIFICANCE

Bathsheba provides a dominant note of pathos in the great epic of David, shepherd king and psalmist of Israel.

On earlier occasions David had demonstrated his ability to rise above the violence that characterized his age in acts of courage, charity, and justice. Although his obsession with Bathsheba led him to defy the decrees of God, Bathsheba is remembered as no mere fallen woman but as the mother of Solomon. She is revered as a matriarch of Israel. The early Christian theologians sometimes marveled that with such soiled flesh as this the lineage of the promised messiah could be established. Curiously, and perhaps appropriately, even in the New Testament genealogy of Jesus, Bathsheba remains "the wife of Uriah the Hittite," the one unlawfully seized.

Despite, and possibly because of, his very human failings, David remains the most beloved of Hebrew kings. There is a single instance in the Bible where a woman is said to be in love with a man. This woman is the princess Michal, an earlier wife given David by his predecessor, King Saul, in exchange for the curious bride price of the foreskins of one hundred Philistines. David is also called "a man after God's own heart." While both a king's daughter and God Almighty openly proclaim their love for David, the nature and degree of Bathsheba's feelings for him are never revealed.

Biblical narrators refrained from physical descriptions of people. The imaginations of later writers and artists have shown no such restraint. When later Europeans invented courtly love in fourteenth century Provence, the figures of David and Bathsheba intrigued them as they reinterpreted events from an ancient, alien milieu in the light of their own glorification of forbidden love. Still, Bathsheba played a relatively insignificant part in European literature, less evident than other biblical women such as Rachel, Ruth, or even Delilah. Her story continues to interest writers, though no universally acclaimed imaginative portrait, certainly none on the order of John Milton's Delilah, has been called forth.

—*Allene Phy-Olsen*

FURTHER READING

Alter, Robert. *The David Story: A Translation with Commentary of 1 and 2 Samuel.* New York: W. W. Norton, 1999. A literary scholar thoroughly versed in Hebrew elucidates the conventions of biblical narrative, providing both historical and rabbinical frameworks for understanding the story.

Meyers, Carol, ed. *Women in Scripture.* Grand Rapids, Mich.: Wm. B. Eerdmans, 2000. A comprehensive examination of the roles of all the women, both named and unnamed, in both the Jewish and Christian Bibles. Lively, informative reading.

Rogerson, John. *Chronicle of the Old Testament Kings: The Reign-by-Reign Record of the Rulers of Ancient Israel*. London: Thames and Hudson, 1999. An enjoyable, lavishly illustrated examination of all the kings of Israel and Judah, putting into historical perspective the reigns of David and Solomon.

Sternberg, Meir. *The Poetics of Biblical Narrative*. Bloomington: Indiana University Press, 1985. A fine introduction to the literary features of biblical narrative.

SEE ALSO: Arsinoe II Philadelphus; Artemesia I; Atossa; Cleopatra VII; David; Deborah; Dido; Jesus; Mary; Moses; Solomon.

RELATED ARTICLES in *Great Events from History: The Ancient World*: c. 1000 B.C.E., Establishment of the United Kingdom of Israel; c. 966 B.C.E., Building of the Temple of Jerusalem; c. 922 B.C.E., Establishment of the Kingdom of Israel; c. 6 B.C.E., Birth of Jesus Christ.

BERENICE II
Ptolemaic (Macedonian) queen of Egypt

Berenice staged a palace coup in her native Cyrene that allowed for her marriage to Ptolemy III Euergetes, thus bringing Cyrene under Ptolemaic control.

BORN: c. 273 B.C.E.; Cyrene, Cyrenaica (now in Libya)
DIED: 221 B.C.E.; Egypt
ALSO KNOWN AS: Berenice II Euergetes; Berenike
AREA OF ACHIEVEMENT: Government and politics

EARLY LIFE

Information concerning the early life of Berenice's (beh-ruh-NI-see) is sketchy and somewhat contradictory. Aside from some fragments of a poem by Callimachus, a native of Cyrene who served in Alexandria as a kind of court poet for Ptolemy II Philadelphus and Ptolemy III Euergetes, all of the literary evidence for her comes from the Roman period. Still, it can be established that she was the female heir to the throne of Cyrene at a time when the Seleucid and Ptolemaic Empires were competing for control of the Middle East. This made her choice of husbands a highly political issue.

Cyrene was a Greek colony on the southern shores of the Mediterranean that was founded as early as 630 B.C.E. Though the Greek colonists did, at times, marry Libyan natives and though they were influenced by the culture of North Africa and Egypt, their civilization was essentially Hellenic. Cyrene and the surrounding region, sometimes known as Cyrenaica, supported Alexander the Great, but soon after his death (323 B.C.E.) and following a small revolt, the region became a dependency of the Ptolemaic kingdom of Egypt.

Berenice's father was Magas, the ruler of Cyrene, who owed his position, at least in part, to a pact with Ptolemy II Philadelphus. Though he died while Berenice was still a teenager, Magas apparently had betrothed her to Ptolemy III Euergetes. He probably intended to solidify

the relationship between Cyrene and Egypt by marrying the Cyrenean heiress to the Egyptian heir. It may also have been customary for Hellenistic kings to marry the heiress to her closest male relative not her brother, which in this case may have been Ptolemy III. In any case, the proposed union would have had important political consequences, bringing Cyrene under more direct Ptolemaic control. It would have been important for Ptolemaic Egypt in that it secured the western flank of the empire and prevented the Seleucids from gaining a foothold on the southern shore of the Mediterranean Sea. It may have had advantages for Cyrene as well, in maintaining important economic and military ties with Ptolemaic Egypt, which provided funding for numerous public projects throughout Cyrenaica.

Although Berenice was betrothed to Ptolemy III, on her father's death her mother, Apama, made different plans. The sources are unclear on the details of the marital relationships of the Cyrenean queens, but it seems that Apama betrothed Berenice to Demetrius "the Fair" (so called because of his good looks). Demetrius was the son of Demetrius Poliorcetes and the half brother of Antigonus Gonatas, who had formed an alliance with the Seleucid Empire, the Ptolemies' chief rivals. It is probably not coincidental that Apama supported an alliance with the Seleucids over the Ptolemies; she was the daughter of Antiochus I, who ruled the Seleucid Empire in Asia Minor, and Stratonice, who, before marrying Antiochus, was the (much younger) wife of Seleucus I, the founder of the Seleucid Empire in the era immediately following the death of Alexander the Great. Apama's plan was probably also supported by the more independent-minded citizens of Cyrene, who did not want to become vassals of Ptolemaic Egypt. It seems that an independent federation of cities, probably headed by Cyrene,

157

had been established by Demophanes and Ecdelus following the death of Magas.

Whether Demetrius the Fair actually married Berenice or was merely betrothed to her, he soon became Apama's lover. According to one ancient source, Berenice had her soldiers storm her mother's bedroom, where they found Demetrius with Apama in a compromising situation. Though Apama tried to protect Demetrius by wrapping her body around his, the soldiers killed him. However,

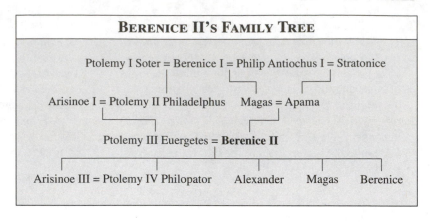

BERENICE II'S FAMILY TREE

Ptolemy I Soter = Berenice I = Philip Antiochus I = Stratonice

Arisinoe I = Ptolemy II Philadelphus   Magas = Apama

Ptolemy III Euergetes = **Berenice II**

Arisinoe III = Ptolemy IV Philopator   Alexander   Magas   Berenice

Berenice spared her mother's life, giving the soldiers directions not to harm her. Once Demetrius was eliminated, Berenice continued with her father's original plan and married Ptolemy III.

Graphic and passionate as this tale is, politics may have had as much, or more, to do with Berenice's assassination of Demetrius as jealousy or moral repugnance. By marrying Ptolemy III she was able to bring Cyrene under Ptolemaic control without risking war. She also was able to provide herself, as the queen of Egypt, with a position of much greater influence and power than she would have enjoyed as the queen of Cyrene. Seen in this light, her assassination of Demetrius may have been more of a revolt, or palace coup, than simply the actions of a jealous fiancé. This view is supported by the description of Callimachus, preserved in a Latin version of his poem by Catullus, who characterizes her as "bold" and "brave" for the manner in which she gained a "royal consort."

LIFE'S WORK

In spite of the political nature of her marriage, Berenice is known as an especially devoted wife. Early in their marriage Ptolemy III was called to battle in Syria to rescue and then avenge his sister, also called Berenice, who was murdered as the result of political intrigue in the Seleucid kingdom. (This precipitated a much larger conflict known to historians as the Third Syrian War.) Concerned for his safety, Berenice went to the temple of Arsinoe Aphrodite and pledged a lock of her hair to the goddess in exchange for the safe return of her husband. Her pledge was seen by her contemporaries as an unmistakable sign of her genuine affection for Ptolemy. He did return safely, and so Berenice devoted a lock of her hair to the goddess.

The story does not end there. According to Callimachus (as preserved in Catullus's Latin version), the lock

of hair disappeared from the temple, and the court astronomer, Conon, "discovered" it as a new constellation, henceforth known to astronomers as Coma Berenices (which means "hair of Berenice"). Today this constellation is well known as containing one of the densest clusters of galaxies in the local universe.

Berenice is also known for her compassion and influence over Ptolemy. In one story, Ptolemy was playing dice as a court official read to him a list of condemned prisoners to see if the king would approve their execution. Observing this, Berenice intervened, arguing that on matters as important as life and death the king should not be distracted by games but should devote his entire mental faculties to such decisions. Ptolemy was pleased with her response and made it his practice to give such matters his full attention.

The Cyrenean elites were known as experts in breeding and training horses for the chariot races, and Berenice was no exception. She was known as a horsewoman who sponsored several winning chariot teams. She also is remembered as patron of the Alexandrian perfume industry, which flourished during her reign.

Along with her husband, she was deified in the dynastic cult as a "benefactor" (Euergetes) god, and, according to the *Canopus Decree*, her daughter, also called Berenice, who died in childhood, was deified according to traditional Egyptian practice and belief. Similarly, Ptolemy and Berenice are portrayed in traditional Egyptian costumes and poses in engravings and reliefs found in numerous Egyptian temples. This probably reflects the renewed support of the Ptolemaic Dynasty by native Egyptians. Ptolemy's father, Ptolemy II Philadelphus, had been known, especially toward the end of his reign, as a profligate and exploitive ruler. Scholars have suggested that his extravagant displays had begun to impoverish local Egyptian institutions. This trend was reversed by the patronage of Ptolemy III Euergetes and Berenice, who built and restored several temples and supported public projects.

It was probably these displays of generosity and support, along with her reputation as a devoted wife and queen, that explain why in some Demotic (native Egyptian) inscriptions Berenice was known as "the female Pharaoh." Evidence from Egyptian coins suggests that she was widely admired and accepted by virtually all levels of Egyptian society—a significant achievement that made her a model of queenship for her successors and probably helped legitimate the role of the Ptolemaic queens in Egyptian society.

Following the death of Ptolemy III, Berenice's surviving children (at least those about whom we know anything) became involved in a struggle for power that would eventually lead to Berenice's death. It was thought that Berenice favored her son Magas as the heir to the Ptolemaic throne, but her other son, Ptolemy IV (Philopator), wanted that position for himself. He married his sister, Berenice's surviving daughter Arsinoe III, and seems to have ordered his brother's murder; Magas was scalded to death in his bath. Subsequently Berenice, who, though a woman, may have been considered a rival to her son, Ptolemy, was reportedly poisoned to death, at the behest of either Ptolemy himself or his adviser Sosibius. Perhaps as evidence of her continued popularity, about a decade after her death Ptolemy IV established an eponymous priesthood in her honor.

SIGNIFICANCE

Berenice II was one of the most celebrated queens of the Hellenistic era. She is depicted on vase-paintings, on coins, and in political inscriptions as an important, beloved, and devoted queen in an age when many of her predecessors and successors were criticized for their excesses and treacheries.

Berenice's assassination of Demetrius the Fair, which allowed her to marry Ptolemy III Euergetes, had the effect of returning Cyrene to Ptolemaic control. The dedication of her hair to the goddess Arsinoe Aphrodite led to her immortalization in the stars, lending her name to the constellation Coma Berenices.

—Stephen W. Felder

FURTHER READING

Macurdy, Grace Harriett. *Hellenistic Queens: A Study of Woman-Power in Macedonia, Seleucid Syria, and Ptolemaic Egypt*. 1932. Reprint. New York: Ares, 1985. Focuses on the ways Macedonian queens established and exercised power. This remains an excellent source for a narrative account of Berenice's life. It is especially useful because of the way Macurdy situates Berenice within the tradition of Macedonian queenship in Egypt and the Middle East.

Pomeroy, Sarah B. *Women in Hellenistic Egypt: From Alexander to Cleopatra*. New York: Schocken Books, 1985. Reprint. Detroit: Wayne State University Press, 1990. Attempts to provide an overall history of women and their lives in Hellenistic Egypt. Using inscriptions, images, and papyri, Pomeroy brings women of all social classes "to life." Includes a short discussion of Berenice and the other important Ptolemaic queens. Though her treatment of Berenice is shorter than that of Macurdy, Pomeroy's analysis is more in tune with more recent feminist approaches to the study of women in antiquity.

SEE ALSO: Arsinoe II Philadelphus; Callimachus; Ptolemy II Philadelphus; Sophonisba of Numidia.

RELATED ARTICLES in *Great Events from History: The Ancient World*: 323 B.C.E., Founding of the Ptolemaic Dynasty and Seleucid Kingdom; c. 323-275 B.C.E., Diadochi Divide Alexander the Great's Empire; c. 275 B.C.E., Greeks Advance Hellenistic Astronomy.

BODHIDHARMA
Buddhist monk

Bodhidharma is credited with originating Chan (Zen) Buddhism in China.

BORN: fifth century C.E.; India
DIED: sixth century C.E.; China
ALSO KNOWN AS: Putidamo (Pinyin); P'u-t'i-ta-mo (Wade-Giles); Damo (Pinyin); Ta-mo (Wade-Giles); Bodaidaruma (Japanese); Daruma (Japanese)
AREA OF ACHIEVEMENT: Religion

EARLY LIFE

From the standpoint of modern history of religion, nothing definite can be said about the early life of Bodhidharma (boh-dee-DAR-mah). Stories about his life have long played a central role in the practice of the Chan Buddhism he is traditionally credited with having brought to China. For that contribution, he is called First Patriarch of Zen, as well as (by most counts) Twenty-eighth Patriarch of Buddhism generally. As anthologists Nelson Foster and Jack Shoemaker remark: "That Bodhidharma . . . lived seems reasonably certain, but if scholarly standards of evidence are maintained, everything else about him is subject to question, including his role, if any, in the establishment of Ch'an."

According to the earliest biography by Tanlin (T'anlin), written in the early sixth century C.E., Bodhidharma was the third son of an Indian king. Attracted to Buddhism, he became a monk and after some years went to China as a missionary. "Why did Bodhidharma come from the West?" became a standard Zen meditation puzzle, or koan. The answer, to some extent, defines one's understanding of the nature of Zen. D. T. Suzuki, for example, proposes that Bodhidharma's coming

> was simply to introduce this satori [enlightenment] element into the body of Buddhism, whose advocates were then so engrossed in subtleties of philosophical discussion or in the mere literary observance of rituals and disciplinary rules.

The traditional account has Bodhidharma coming to South China (modern Canton) around 520 C.E., where he is said to have had an interview with Emperor Wudi (Wuti; r. 502-557 C.E.), which may have been the single most dramatic encounter in the history of Zen Buddhism. Accounts of the interview vary, but it seems to have consisted essentially of three brief questions and three cryptic answers.

As his first question, the emperor, who had devoted much money, time, and effort to supporting Buddhist enterprises, asked Bodhidharma what religious merit he (Wu) had earned through this zealous support. "No merit," replied Bodhidharma. To understand Bodhidharma's response, it is important to keep in mind that, as Buddhism developed, the tendency to divinize the Buddha grew, generating an elaborate mythology.

As historian Xingu Liu notes:

> All the new deities were willing to share with their worshipers the merit they accumulated. Consequently, Buddhist literature increasingly stressed worship and donation, which ultimately became the major route to enlightenment. . . . That the Bodhisattva could save other people through the merit he accumulated implied that merit, like goods, could be transferred and exchanged. Merit was no longer restricted to what an individual could achieve through his own efforts.

The emperor probably would have agreed with the doctrine that "A king who builds a palace of precious materials for a Buddha has the full right to claim Buddhahood by virtue of this act of merit." A different conception of spiritual merit is found in Bodhidharma texts, as translated by Red Pine: "If you don't see your nature, invoking buddhas, reciting sutras, making offerings, and keeping precepts are all useless."

Puzzled by Bodhidharma's response, the emperor inquired about the meaning of holy doctrine. "Emptiness," Bodhidharma replied, "no holiness." In interpreting the central idea of emptiness, Buddhist philosophers have always had to struggle against turning processes—including those constitutive of the self—into things (reification). Another Bodhidharma text advises: "Our mortal nature is our buddha-nature. Beyond this nature there's no buddha. . . . Don't think about buddhas. . . . At every moment, where language can't go, that's your mind."

Finally, the emperor asked the identity of this perplexing person before him. Bodhidharma's reply: "Don't know." In a more talkative mood, he might have added, as another Bodhidharma text puts it:

> You ask. That's your mind. I answer. That's my mind. . . . To search for enlightenment or nirvana beyond this mind is impossible. . . . The truth is, there's nothing to find. But to reach such an understanding you need a teacher and you need to struggle to make yourself understand.

LIFE'S WORK

Bodhidharma, evidently not the right teacher for Emperor Wu, left and, according to the traditional story, traveled to North China, crossing the Yangtze River on a reed (raft, presumably). He settled at the Shaolin monastery near Loyang (famous in American popular culture because of its associations with the 1970's television show *Kung Fu*), where he is said to have taught the *Lankāvatāra Sūtra* and practiced "wall gaze" (*pi kuan*) for nine years. What this was, or even how "wall" is to be understood (whether the wall of a chamber, wall of the mind, or wall of mountains), remains uncertain.

The work most often attributed to Bodhidharma, and possibly the only text that can attributed to him, is a short treatise, *Er jing ru* (c. 6th c. C.E.; *The Two Ways of Entrance*, 1986). According to this text, the two ways are entrance by principle or reason (*li ru*) and entrance by practice (*xing ru*).

Entrance by principle or reason involves a condition of cognitive indifferentiation, in which the unity of things outweighs their differences—a kind of mystical state growing out of Bodhidharma's practice of meditation, or "wall gaze":

> When one . . . abides in *Pi-kuan*, one finds that there is neither selfhood nor otherness, that the masses and the worthies are of one essence. . . . He will not then be guided by any literary instructions, for he is . . . free from conceptual discrimination, for he is serene and non-acting. This is called "Entrance by Reason."

A famous koan describes the disciple Huike (Hui-k'o) asking Bodhidharma to calm his mind. Bodhidharma tells him: "Go get your mind and bring it here, and I will calm it." After a while, Huike has to admit that he cannot locate his mind. "I have calmed your mind," says Bodhidharma. Huike is thereupon enlightened.

Practice, the second entrance described in the Bodhidharma treatise, involves four key ideas: karma—accepting that suffering is rooted in one's past; impermanence—accepting that all things, including life's satisfactions, depend on changing conditions; acquiescence—quelling the desire that things be otherwise than they are; and, finally, dharma—being virtuous, in particular treating others generously.

How are the concepts of principle and reason connected to these four elements of practice, which compose the basic ethos of Buddhism? The first entrance (*li ru*) involves recognizing in contemplation the emptiness of conventional conceptual categories. The second entrance (*xing ru*) involves recognizing in practice the emptiness of conventional motivations. Accepting responsibility for difficulties encountered, declining credit for (and so accepting gratefully) life's gratifications, ceasing to try to change the nature of things, and contenting oneself with simple service to others—these allow one to live harmoniously in the light of what principle or reason reveals.

In addition to his role as First Patriarch of Zen, Bodhidharma often has been claimed as founder of various martial arts traditions, usually based on nothing more substantive than "what my instructor told me." Oral tradition has value, but only high scholarly standards can guard against misinterpretation, exaggeration, self-deception, and fabrication. The idea that Bodhidharma was an innovator in the martial arts exerts a perennial fascination, and the claim continues to be made. It probably cannot be shown to be impossible, but because there is prestige (and therefore profit) in such associations, skepticism is in order.

In fact, a skeptical view seems appropriate in several aspects of the colorful mythology surrounding Bodhidharma's name. He is said, for example, to have cut off his eyelids to stay awake while meditating (his eyelids turned to tea leaves as they fluttered down to the ground, establishing the use of tea as an aid to concentration during meditation), and his legs are said to have withered away during his protracted sitting meditation. The former is unlikely, and the latter is quite fantastic, as well as inconsistent with other parts of his legend (such as that he was encountered, albeit posthumously, walking back to India with one shoe). The Bodhidharma lore is various, and has him ending his sojourn to China by being poisoned, or returning to the West, or going on to Japan.

SIGNIFICANCE

Within Zen, Bodhidharma is revered as the conveyor of a spiritual line that began with the Buddha's wordless transmission to Mahakashyapa, who smiled when Śākyamuni silently presented a flower in place of a sermon. This event is celebrated in four lines traditionally attributed to Bodhidharma (but now usually thought to date from several centuries later):

> A special transmission outside the scriptures,
> Not founded upon words and letters;
> By pointing directly to mind
> It lets one see into nature and attain Buddhahood.

These lines, which, as Heinrich Dumoulin says, have represented for later generations "the quintessence of Zen as embodied in the figure of Bodhidharma," indicate, like a finger pointing at the moon, Zen's transmission beyond, even if through, words of a realization that the differences the conceptual mind draws between things are ultimately empty, or superficial: never more than useful, often less.

Although little is known about Bodhidharma, and certainly much less than has often been claimed, he is still an intriguing figure, floating among the koans with blue eyes and red beard. Despite all historical disputes, the story of Bodhidharma remains, as Dumoulin concedes, "a legend without which it would be altogether impossible to understand the history of Zen."

—Edward Johnson

FURTHER READING

Bodhidharma. *The Zen Teachings of Bodhidharma.* Translated by Red Pine. San Francisco: North Point Press, 1989. Translation of four sermons traditionally ascribed to Bodhidharma. Includes Chinese text, brief introduction, and notes.

Broughton, Jeffrey L. *The Bodhidharma Anthology: The Earliest Records of Zen.* Berkeley: University of California Press, 1999. Translation of and commentary on essential Chan texts from the cache found in Dunhuang (Tun-huang) early in the twentieth century. The author's revisionist account emphasizes the importance of a previously unknown Master Yuan mentioned in these manuscripts. Includes glossary, bibliography, and index.

Dumoulin, Heinrich. *India and China.* Vol. 1 in *Zen Buddhism: A History.* Translated from German by James W. Heisig and Paul Knitter. Englewood Cliffs, N.J.: Prentice Hall, 1994. This revised edition of a standard history of Zen Buddhism includes a substantial supplement on the Northern School of Chinese Zen. Chapter 6 provides a cautious discussion of what (little) can be said to be known about Bodhidharma. Includes glossary, chronological and genealogical tables, and index.

Foster, Nelson, and Jack Shoemaker, eds. *The Roaring Stream: A New Zen Reader.* New York: HarperCollins, 1996. This outstanding anthology of Zen material devotes its first chapter to Bodhidharma. Includes bibliography.

Kalupahana, David J. *A History of Buddhist Philosophy: Continuities and Discontinuities.* Honolulu: University of Hawaii Press, 1992. Chapter 23 situates Bodhidharma in the context of earlier and later disagreements within Buddhist philosophy. Includes bibliography and index.

Liu, Xingu. *Ancient India and Ancient China: Trade and Religious Exchanges, A.D. 1-600.* New York: Oxford University Press, 1988. Provides insight into the mutual influence of religious practice and economic trade between India and China during the period in which Bodhidharma is supposed to have undertaken his mission. Includes bibliography, index, and appendices.

McRae, John R. *The Northern School and the Formation of Early Ch'an Buddhism.* Honolulu: University of Hawaii Press, 1986. This influential study of the early (northern) Chan school, obscured by the southern school of Huineng and Shenhui, revised understanding of the context of the gradual-versus-sudden enlightenment debate in Chinese Buddhism. Includes translations of important texts, bibliography, and index.

Suzuki, D. T. *Essays in Zen Buddhism.* First Series. 1927. Reprint. London: Rider, 1949. This classic, along with many other books by Suzuki, played a major role in popularizing Zen in the West during the twentieth century and exerted some influence on the East as well. Suzuki's traditional, ahistorical account has been much criticized in recent decades. Includes index and illustrations.

Wong, Kiew Kit. *The Complete Book of Zen.* Boston: Tuttle, 2002. A recent popular account of Zen, and of Bodhidharma, representing the perspective of a contemporary martial arts practitioner.

BOUDICCA
British queen and military leader

Having endured flogging and the violation of her daughters, Boudicca led a rebellion of the Britons against the Roman invaders. The Romans were caught by surprise and lost three cities burned by the rebels before the uprising was quelled.

BORN: First century C.E.; Britain
DIED: 60 C.E.; central Britain
ALSO KNOWN AS: Boadicca; Boadicea; Boudica
AREA OF ACHIEVEMENT: War and conquest

EARLY LIFE

Boudicca (boo-DIHK-uh) was born and grew up in Iron Age Britain, which was in the process of subjugation and colonization by Imperial Rome. Her place and date of birth and her parentage are not known; nor, in fact, are any details of her early life except that she married Prasutagus, who was allowed by the Romans to rule his tribe, the Iceni, as a client king. With him, she had two daughters who were probably teenagers by 60 C.E. It seems likely that Boudicca was born between 20 and 30.

Two classical works provide the known extended written accounts of Boudicca: *De vita Julii Agricolae* (c. 98; *The Life of Agricola*, 1591) and *Ab excessu divi Augusti* (c. 116, also known as *Annales*; *Annals*, 1598) by Cornelius Tacitus and *Romaika* (probably c. 202 C.E.; *Roman History*, 1914-1927) by Dio Cassius. Many archaeological finds—coins, pottery, and ruins of forts and other buildings—have tended to confirm the written accounts. Tacitus is generally accepted as the more reliable historian, because he wrote only forty years after the events and because his father-in-law, Julius Agricola, was a high official in the colonial administration at the time of Boudicca's revolt. Also, the work of Dio Cassius has survived only in the form of a summary, or "epitome," made by the monk Xiphilinus of Trapezus in the eleventh century.

The first Roman military adventure in Britain was that of Julius Caesar in 55 B.C.E. After several skirmishes with the Britons in which the Romans were largely victorious, Caesar withdrew, only to return again the next year with additional troops and cavalry. Some Britons, fearing destruction, made peace and agreed to pay tribute to Rome. Others in more remote regions held out fiercely. Distracted by signs of trouble in Gaul, Caesar withdrew again, leaving further conquests to others in the reign of the emperor Claudius, more than a hundred years later.

In 43 C.E., Roman legions led by Aulus Plautius landed in Britain and campaigned against the many tribes of the island in order to bring them under Roman rule. In awe of Roman might, and seeking advantage over other tribes, some leaders made deals with Rome and were allowed to rule as client kings. Others withdrew to the west, into Wales, to wage guerrilla warfare.

The most effective leader of resistance against the Romans was Caratacus, who continued to rally support for his cause even after a decisive Roman victory near the river Medway. These events occurred during the girlhood and young womanhood of Boudicca. Her husband, Prasutagus, was allowed to rule his tribe, the Iceni, as a client king, a sort of intermediary between the Romans, who were the real rulers, and the people.

When Aulus Plautius retired, he was replaced by the experienced and stern general Publius Ostorius Scapula, who arrived in Britain just in time to confront serious uprisings in the West, led by Caratacus. In order to prevent an attack from behind while chasing Caratacus, Scapula ordered all the British tribes to be disarmed, and he established a colony of retired military men at Camulodunum (modern Colchester) that he hoped would be a stabilizing influence. These measures were resented by the Britons, more so because the Romans of the colony lorded it over them, taking their property and treating them as slaves. Eventually, Caratacus fled to the north and was betrayed to the Romans by Queen Cartimandua, who needed to curry Roman favor in return for protection against other tribes. In 51 C.E., Caratacus was taken to Rome in chains. About this time, Scapula died and was succeeded by Didius Gallus, who remained as governor until 58 C.E.

Gallus had to deal with uprisings in the north and with continual trouble with the Silures, a tribe in Wales. On the death of Emperor Claudius, Gallus retired in favor of Veranius, who died within a year but not before waging a vigorous campaign against the Silures. His efforts were continued and expanded by the next governor, Suetonius Paulinus, who had served with distinction in North Africa and who was a specialist in mountain warfare. The death of Prasutagus in 59 C.E. brought on the events for which his widow, Boudicca, has become famous.

LIFE'S WORK

Prasutagus had become wealthy and knew of the Romans' greed and contempt for the rights of the Britons. He made a will leaving half of his estate to the Emperor Nero, thinking thus to protect the enforcement of the will and to preserve some of the estate for his wife and his daughters. Nevertheless, the local Roman officials, under command of the procurator Catus Decianus, sought to plunder the estate for their own benefit. Boudicca's objections were met with brutality; she was scourged, and her daughters were raped.

Far from the quietus they had sought, the Romans soon found they had stirred a hornet's nest. The Iceni and their allies gathered in a horde that may have numbered in the tens of thousands. They descended on the hated encampment of Camulodunum, where a huge temple to the recently deified Claudius was under construction, built with British taxes and British slave labor. In spite of the arrival of two hundred Roman troops, the defenders of Camulodunum were driven into the temple of Claudius and annihilated, their whole town burned and looted. A legion commanded by Petillius Cerealis marched to the relief of Camulodunum but was ambushed and suffered severe losses, Cerealis barely escaping with his life.

The Britons, excited by victory and looting, approached London, which was little more than a village with few defenses. Meanwhile, Suetonius Paulinus had been in the far west on the island of Mona (Anglesey), where his forces had destroyed a druid stronghold and cut down the sacred groves of the cult. He sped to London to see what could be done, but he decided that the city had to be abandoned to the rebels. Catus Decianus fled to Gaul to save himself from the common fate.

Boudicca and her forces burned London to the ground and slew everyone they found there, including Britons they regarded as turncoats. Even today, there is a layer of ashes about seventeen feet beneath the surface in London testifying to the holocaust. The rebels then turned to Verulamium (St. Albans) and sacked it, massacring the occupants, mostly Britons who had befriended the Romans.

Meanwhile, Suetonius Paulinus withdrew to the west and north of London because he needed time to gather provisions. He also sought reinforcements from the legion commanded by Poenius Posthumus stationed near Exeter. Preparing for the approach of the Britons, Paulinus moved his forces to a carefully chosen battlefield in a canyon with a forest behind it. The exact location is unknown, but it may have been near Mancetter, where the horde of Britons confronted the ordered ranks of the Romans. So confident were the Britons that all their families were drawn up behind them in wagons to watch the battle. Boudicca rode on a chariot with her daughters and exhorted the men and women of her army, reciting her grievances against the Romans and urging the Britons to fight for freedom.

Tall and serious in mien, Boudicca was an impressive figure, with fair, waist-long hair, dressed in a multicolored tunic and long cloak. Suetonius Paulinus told his men to ignore the cries of the attacking savages and to press on with their spears and swords, forgetting thoughts of plunder but intent on victory and the glory it would bring.

The Britons attacked with wild, warlike shouting and trumpet blasts, brandishing their yard-long swords, some of them naked

Boudicca, shown in helmet. (Hulton|Archive by Getty Images)

with their skins painted with intricate designs in blue. The Romans waited in orderly ranks, wearing armor of steel and leather strips and equipped with shields, spears, and short, thick swords.

The Romans carried the day by superior discipline and benefit of the terrain. After showering the rebels with spears, the Roman phalanx drove ahead, forcing the Britons back into their wagons. In the rout that followed, the Romans put to death anyone they could catch, including the pack animals. Boudicca took poison and died rather than accept capture and humiliation. The Roman reinforcements from Exeter failed to arrive in time for the battle, depriving them and their commander, Poenius Posthumus, from a share in the glory of victory. It is not known whether Posthumus delayed because he feared being ambushed on the way or because he was involved in other military actions. In any event, he felt sufficient shame that he killed himself by falling on his sword. It is asserted that eighty thousand people died in the battle.

In revenge for the uprising, Paulinus and his army swept through the lands of the Iceni, burning crops, looting, and killing anyone they suspected of aiding the rebels. Boudicca was reportedly buried in a magnificent tomb, which has never been found.

SIGNIFICANCE

Boudicca's rebellion and its aftermath were probably the bloodiest events ever to occur on British soil. The Romans were forced to the realization that their terror tactics had led to unacceptable losses and that a more diplomatic policy was needed. Many more years were required for the pacification of Britain, and the Caledonians in the north were never completely subdued. Increased trade and the wealth it brought to cooperative Britons was a major factor in pacification.

The memory of Boudicca turned to the stuff of legend, and she became the symbol of freedom and independence for the British. Her story was retold many times in literature by such authors as Ben Jonson, William Cowper, Alfred, Lord Tennyson, and others.

Queen Elizabeth I and Queen Victoria were both compared with Boudicca, and it is thought that the name *Boudicca* (also spelled Boadicca, Boadicea, and Boudica) probably means "victory" in the Celtic language. In London, a statue of Boudicca by Thomas Thornycroft was placed near the Houses of Parliament in 1902. It depicts the heroine and her daughters on a huge chariot, quite unlike the small Celtic war chariots described by Julius Caesar.

—John R. Phillips

FURTHER READING

Dio Cassius. *Dio's Roman History*. Translated by E. Cary. Cambridge, Mass.: Harvard University Press, 1961. Boudicca's revolt is discussed in volume 8.

Dudley, D. R., and G. Webster. *The Rebellion of Boudicca*. New York: Barnes & Noble, 1962. This and Webster's book (cited below) are major works devoted solely to Boudicca. Legends and traditions are covered as well as history. Portions of Tacitus's *Annals* and *Agricola* describing the rebellion are quoted at length in an appendix, both in the original Latin and in translation.

Fraser, Antonia. *The Warrior Queens*. New York: Alfred A. Knopf, 1989. Interesting account of women who assumed roles of power usually reserved for men. Boudicca is considered the archetypal "warrior queen" and is discussed alongside Cleopatra, Golda Meir, Margaret Thatcher, and others.

Harrison, Arjae. *Boudicca*. New York: iUniverse, 2000. Biography uses known historical facts as well as the beliefs, customs, and mores of the Celts.

Ireland, S. *Roman Britain: A Sourcebook*. London: Routledge, 1996. Translations are provided for selections from Tacitus and Dio Cassius.

Salway, Peter. *Roman Britain*. New York: Oxford University Press, 2000. Scholarly account of history (55 B.C.E. to 449 C.E.), culture, economy, and religion. Includes extensive bibliography and maps.

Tacitus, Cornelius. *Tacitus on Britain and Germany*. Translated by H. Mattingly. Baltimore: Penguin, 1965. Pages 64-67 treat the revolt of Boudicca.

_____. *Tacitus on Imperial Rome*. Translated by M. Grant. Baltimore: Penguin, 1956. Pages 317-321 provide the most reliable classical source for Boudicca's revolt.

Webster, Graham. *Boudica: The British Revolt Against Rome, A.D. 60*. London: Routledge, 1999. The 1962 book by Dudley and Webster cited above, updated to incorporate extensive new archaeological findings from excavations at London, Verulamium, and Colchester. Includes photographs of coins, inscriptions, and other artifacts and views of sites observed from aircraft.

SEE ALSO: Gnaeus Julius Agricola; Julius Caesar; Tacitus.

MARCUS JUNIUS BRUTUS
Roman official

As leader and conscience of the conspiracy that assassinated the dictator Julius Caesar, Brutus attempted to restore the Roman Republic but instead ushered in the Roman Empire.

BORN: 85 B.C.E.; probably Rome (now in Italy)
DIED: October 23, 42 B.C.E.; Philippi, Macedonia (now in Greece)
ALSO KNOWN AS: Quintus Caepia Brutus
AREAS OF ACHIEVEMENT: Government and politics, war and conquest

EARLY LIFE

According to his family's traditions, Marcus Junius Brutus (BROO-tuhs) was a descendant of the legendary Lucius Junius Brutus, who had founded the Roman Republic. According to these accounts, in 509 B.C.E. Lucius Brutus expelled the last of the early Roman kings, Tarquinius Superbus (Tarquin the Proud), and established the Republic, serving as its first consul. So devoted to liberty and the new Republic was Junius Brutus, according to Plutarch and other biographers, that he condemned to death his own sons when they plotted to restore Tarquinius and the monarchy. The family line continued, Plutarch explained, because only the two older sons were condemned; an innocent younger brother survived to be the ancestor of Marcus Brutus.

The Junius family continued its active role in Roman life. Marcus Junius's father, of the same name, was an adherent of Gaius Marius during the civil wars with Cornelius Sulla. In 77 B.C.E. the elder Brutus surrendered to the Sullustian general Gaius Pompeius (better known as Pompey Magnus, or Pompey the Great) and was put to death. Despite this, in later years Brutus's son would be allied with Pompey against Julius Caesar, believing Pompey to be a champion of the Republic.

Marcus Brutus was connected with other famous republican figures of Roman history. Through the family of his mother, Servilia, he was related to Servilius Ahala, who had killed a potential tyrant in fifth century Rome. His uncle on his mother's side was the famous Cato Uticensis (Cato of Utica), who was one of the most notable of the opponents of Julius Caesar and who committed suicide amid the ruins of Utica following the collapse of the Republic. Following the death of her first husband, Servilia married D. Junius Silanus and had three daughters. The eldest of them, Junia, married M. Aemilius Lepidus, who became a member of the Second Triumvirate with Gaius Octavian (later the emperor Augustus) and Marc Antony. A second daughter, Junia Tertia, married Cassius, along with Brutus a key conspirator in the plot against Julius Caesar; thus, Brutus and Cassius were brothers-in-law.

Marcus Brutus followed the traditional course of studies for an aristocratic Roman. He was well educated in Greek literature and philosophy and in Latin rhetoric. He continued his schooling in Athens, where his teacher, Pammenes, was described by the famous orator Marcus Tullius Cicero as the most eloquent man in Greece. While in Athens, Brutus was exposed to the philosophical schools of the Stoics and the Platonists; the latter had an especially profound influence on him.

LIFE'S WORK

His education complete, Brutus returned to Rome to pursue the *cursus honorum* (literally, the "course of honor"), which took members of the patrician class, such as Brutus, through a series of public offices and duties to the highest rank of all, the consulship. Among his earlier offices, Brutus was in charge of the mint—where, significantly, he issued coins with the head of Liberty on one side and a portrait of his ancestor Lucius Brutus on the other. He was a quaestor for the province of Cilicia in Asia Minor, and he became increasingly known as a successful advocate in the Roman law courts. In 54 B.C.E., he married Claudia, daughter of Appius Claudius; he divorced her in 45 and married his cousin Porcia, daughter of Cato.

In this marriage and in his public life, Brutus had positioned himself with the opponents of Julius Caesar. When the antagonism between Caesar and Pompey erupted into outright civil war, Brutus sided with Pompey as being the defender, such as he was, of the traditional Republic. He fought in Pompey's army at the decisive Battle of Pharsalus in 48 B.C.E., but after that defeat he quickly settled with Caesar and received a pardon.

Despite his Pompeian associations and his family's traditional hostility, Brutus was highly regarded by Caesar, who arranged for his continued advance, including service in 46 B.C.E. as proconsul of Cisalpine Gaul, one of Rome's most important strategic provinces. In 44 B.C.E. Caesar appointed Brutus *praetor urbanus*, the highest official in Rome itself.

It was during this period that the conspiracy against Caesar was taking shape. Following the defeat and death of Pompey and the destruction of his remaining forces,

Julius Caesar had become preeminent in the Roman world. In February of 44 B.C.E., he was appointed dictator for life, an unprecedented step. Along with this came outward marks of almost monarchical dignity, including a statue among the Roman kings, a special seat at the theater, a raised throne in the senate house, religious rites associated with him, and the naming of a month, July, in his honor. All these struck at the traditional liberties of Rome; perhaps worse for men such as Brutus and Cassius, they destroyed their prospects for advancing on the *cursus honorum.*

According to the historians Plutarch and Appian, Cassius was the leader of the conspiracy against Caesar and pressured Brutus into joining, knowing that to Brutus, his reputation for honesty and virtue was essential. The writer Dio Cassius, on the other hand, says that Brutus himself took the lead from the beginning, inspired largely by the memory of his family's active opposition to tyranny.

Eventually there were some sixty conspirators involved; their motives were mixed and their goals uncertain. Brutus and Cassius seem to have thought that once Caesar was dead, the traditional Republic would naturally return. In this, they ignored more than half a century

Marcus Junius Brutus. (Library of Congress)

of vicious civil war, first between Marius and Sulla and then between Caesar and Pompey. When the conspirators struck on the ides of March in 44 B.C.E., they succeeded in killing Julius Caesar, but they signally failed to kill caesarism.

For several months following the assassination, Brutus remained on his estates outside Rome. During this time, Marc Antony and Gaius Octavian, Caesar's grandnephew, who had been adopted in the dictator's will and who therefore styled himself as Gaius Caesar, began to forge an alliance against the conspirators. In 43 B.C.E. Brutus and Cassius left Italy for the eastern provinces, Brutus going to Athens and Cassius to Syria. Moving with considerable speed, Brutus raised an army and took effective control of the provinces of Greece, Illyria, and Macedonia. He was soon joined by Cassius with additional troops from Asia Minor.

In Italy, Antony, after an initial defeat, had linked with Octavian, and the two had consolidated their hold over Rome. Joining with Lepidus, Brutus's brother-in-law and Caesar's former master of the horse (second in command), they formed the Second Triumvirate. It was about this time, according to Plutarch and other writers, that Brutus's wife Porcia committed suicide, either by swallowing live coals or from breathing charcoal fumes until she was overcome. Her suicide, and Brutus's calm acceptance of it, became famous examples of traditional Roman Stoicism in the face of great personal adversity.

In the spring of 42 B.C.E., both the republicans under Brutus and Cassius and the triumvirs Antony and Octavian had moved armies into Macedonia. In October, after months of maneuvering, the opposing forces met near the town of Philippi. According to his biographers, on the march there Brutus had been awakened in his tent by an apparition. Some claimed it was the ghost of Caesar; others, Brutus's evil genius. All agreed the specter warned Brutus, "I will see you again at Philippi."

There were two battles at Philippi, both marked by confusion. In the first battle, Brutus's forces defeated the troops under the command of Octavian and captured his camp, although Octavian escaped. At the same time, however, Antony's troops had overwhelmed those of Cassius, who, unaware of Brutus's victory, retreated into the hills and killed himself rather than be captured. As the fighting died away, Brutus collected the republican forces and held his position.

The second and decisive battle of Philippi came relatively shortly thereafter. The joint army of Antony and Octavian appeared to be in a bad situation, short of supplies and suffering from the inclement weather. After three weeks, Brutus, urged on by his lieutenants and the ardor of his troops, launched an attack that was initially successful but that could not be sustained. By the end of the day, the forces of Antony and Octavian had completely routed the republicans. Fleeing from the battlefield, Brutus escaped the vengeance of the triumvirs by committing suicide by falling on his sword.

In a scene made famous by William Shakespeare's play *Julius Caesar* (c. 1599-1600), Antony and Octavian praised Brutus as "the noblest Roman of them all" and promised an honorable funeral. According to Plutarch, this is indeed what happened, and the assassin's ashes were carried back to his mother, Servilia. The historian Suetonius, however, asserts that Octavian had Brutus's head sent back to Rome to be thrown at the feet of a statue of Julius Caesar. Dio Cassius further embroiders this tale by adding that the head never reached Rome: During a storm, the superstitious sailors in the vessel carrying the head cast it overboard, fearing it was bringing them bad luck. Whatever the ultimate fate of Brutus's body, with his death came the effective end of the Roman Republic.

SIGNIFICANCE

Marcus Junius Brutus is one of the most ambiguous figures of classical antiquity. During his lifetime, he was acclaimed by many, Cicero among them, as one of the noblest figures of the dying Republic, and he was seen as representing one of its last, best hopes for revival. Yet he was unable to transform his commitment to those historic principles into effective action. His role in the assassination of Caesar could be seen either as a selfless action to restore the old and proper order or as the result of a self-centered and selfish vision of a member of the patrician order intent only on personal and family honor. In later years, Brutus would be honored by the French Revolution (1789) as the first of the champions of humankind. Centuries earlier, Dante Alighieri in *La divina commedia* (c. 1320; *The Divine Comedy*, 1802) had placed Brutus and Cassius, along with Judas Iscariot, in the mouth of Satan as among the foremost sinners and ingrates of all creation for the murder of Julius Caesar, the divinely ordained founder of the Roman Empire.

Whatever Brutus's reputation, the immediate and enduring impact of his deed was undeniable: The assassination of Julius Caesar ended the danger a single individual posed to the Republic, but it also revealed how corrupt and weakened the Republic had become and made its fall inevitable. Where Caesar had openly asserted his desire for power and prominence, his nephew and successor Octavian, later the first emperor, Caesar Augustus, was more circumspect and more successful. Where Caesar had flirted with the hated title of king, Augustus was content with the more modest "princeps," or first among equals. This pretense of republican forms masking the reality of Imperial rule was the most lasting and certainly the most unintended legacy of Marcus Junius Brutus.

—*Michael Witkoski*

FURTHER READING

Clarke, M. L. *The Noblest Roman*. Ithaca, N.Y.: Cornell University Press, 1981. Provides an outstanding brief biography of Brutus the man and a survey of his reputation over the centuries.

Grant, Michael. *Caesar*. Chicago: Follett, 1975. An excellent introduction both to the lives of Caesar, Brutus, and other major figures and to the milieu of the late Republic. Copiously and carefully illustrated.

Heitland, William E. *The Roman Republic*. 1909. Reprint. Holmes Beach, Fla.: Gaunt, 1998. The chapters on the efforts of Brutus, Cassius, and others to restore the Roman Republic after the assassination of Caesar are of considerable help in understanding the fundamental changes that swept the Roman world and led, eventually, from Republic to Empire.

Plutarch. *Lives*. New York: E. P. Dutton, 1962. The classic account of the life, deeds, and death of Brutus. This brief biography gives the modern reader a sense of what Brutus's contemporaries thought of him and how they viewed their world.

Syme, Ronald. *The Roman Revolution*. 1939. Reprint. New York: Oxford University Press, 2002. The fundamental modern study of the transformation of the state and society of Rome between 60 B.C.E. and 14 C.E. Does an excellent job of placing Brutus within the context of his time.

Wistrand, Erik. *The Policy of Brutus the Tyrannicide*. Goteborg, Sweden: Kungl, 1981. An in-depth examination of Brutus's motives and expectations in the assassination of Julius Caesar; especially good in its study of the relationship between Brutus and Cicero.

SEE ALSO: Marc Antony; Augustus; Julius Caesar; Cassius; Cato the Younger; Cicero; Dio Cassius; Pompey the Great; Tarquins.

RELATED ARTICLES in *Great Events from History: The Ancient World*: 51 B.C.E., Cicero Writes *De republica*; 51-30 B.C.E., Cleopatra VII, Last of Ptolemies, Reigns; 46 B.C.E., Establishment of the Julian Calendar; 43-42 B.C.E., Second Triumvirate Enacts Proscriptions; September 2, 31 B.C.E., Battle of Actium; 27-23 B.C.E., Completion of the Augustan Settlement.

BUDDHA
Indian religious leader and philosopher

By his own example and teaching, Buddha showed that all people can attain an enlightened state of mind by cultivating a combination of compassion (loving-kindness toward all beings without exception) and wisdom (seeing things as they really are).

BORN: c. 566 B.C.E.; Lumbinī, near Kapilavastu (now Rummindei, Nepal)
DIED: c. 486 B.C.E.; Kuśinagara (now in India)
ALSO KNOWN AS: Siddhārtha Gautama (given name); Gautama; Siddhārtha; Śākyamuni; Siddhattha Gotama; the Enlightened One; Tathāgata; Bhagwān
AREAS OF ACHIEVEMENT: Religion, philosophy

EARLY LIFE

The historical Buddha (BEW-duh)—known variously as Gautama, Siddhārtha, and Śākyamuni—was born in Lumbinī, in the Himālayan foothills of what is now Nepal. His father, Śuddhodana, was king of nearby Kapilavastu, a town whose archaeological remains have yet to be found. His mother, Māyā, died seven days after giving birth to the young prince; Śuddhodana then married her sister, who brought up the boy.

According to legend, the infant's conception and birth were accompanied by unusual signs, and he walked and talked at birth. Legend also has it that an ancient sage prophesied that the young prince would become either a Buddha (an enlightened one) or a universal monarch. Śuddhodana, determined on the latter career, kept his son confined within the palace walls to prevent him from seeing unpleasant sights that might cause him to renounce the world and take up the religious life of a wandering mendicant.

The Buddha's given name was Siddhārtha (he who has achieved his goal). Later, he was called Śākyamuni (Sage of the Śākyas), because his family was part of the warrior (*kṣatriya*) Śākya clan, which also used the Brahman clan name Gautama (descendant of the sage Gotama). He is described as a handsome, black-haired boy.

The oldest Buddhist canon is in the Pāli language and was transmitted orally for several hundred years after the Buddha's death; it was written down on palm leaves on the orders of the Sri Lankan king Vattagamani (d. c. 77 B.C.E.). The Pāli Canon records few details about Siddhārtha's early years, but it does mention that he spontaneously entered a state of meditation while sitting under a tree watching his father plowing. It also recounts his becoming aware of the inevitability of old age, illness, and

death, supposedly by seeing his first old man, ill man, and corpse on clandestine trips outside the palace gates.

When he came of age, Siddhārtha was married to Yaśodharā. They had a son who was named Rāhula ("fetter"), perhaps because Siddhārtha was already turning away from householder life. Indeed, at the age of twenty-nine, he left home forever to seek enlightenment, initially by studying with two teachers, then through extended fasting and other austerities, in which he was joined by five other ascetics. At the age of thirty-five, having failed to attain his goal, he ate enough to regain strength and sat under a tree (later known as the Bodhi Tree) at Uruvelā, near Benares (modern-day Varanasi), vowing to stay there until he reached enlightenment.

The Pāli Canon includes several different descriptions of the enlightenment that followed, "as though one were to describe a tree from above, from below and from various sides, or a journey by land, by water and by air" (Ñāṇamoli, *Life of the Buddha According to the Pali Canon*, 1972). What these accounts have in common is Śākyamuni's claim of having attained direct knowledge of the final nature of mind itself.

Examining the mind via meditation, Śākyamuni found it empty of independent existence. In combination with compassion (an altruistic attitude toward everyone, especially one's "enemies"), this knowledge led to Buddhahood. It was this discovery that Gautama Buddha would spend the rest of his life setting forth to those who came to listen to him teach.

LIFE'S WORK

The newly enlightened Buddha's first impulse was not to disseminate the truth that he had worked so diligently to uncover. He realized that every human being had the potential to attain enlightenment, just as he himself had done, but he also knew that enlightenment could not be bestowed by anyone else; each person had to reach it himself. Thus the Buddha is said to have hesitated to propagate his dharma ("truth" or "law"), thinking that it would be too difficult for beings still deluded by craving to understand. Only his compassion for the suffering of all beings eventually convinced him to do so.

Accordingly, the Buddha set out to find the five ascetics with whom he had practiced austerities. They were not immediately convinced of his enlightenment, so he elucidated the Middle Way of avoiding both sensual and ascetic extremes. At this point the Buddha is said to have

Buddha. (Library of Congress)

ultimately, manifestations of Buddha nature or enlightened mind. Thus Buddhists take refuge in what is called the Three Jewels or Triple Gem: the Buddha as a representation of enlightenment; the dharma, or teaching of how to attain enlightenment; and the *sangha*, the community of fellow aspirants on the path.

The Buddha continued to teach for the next forty-five years, which he spent journeying around the central Gangetic plain, giving discourses (*sutras*), establishing monastic guidelines (*vinaya*) as the need arose for them, and answering any questions put to him.

Śākyamuni was not concerned with metaphysical questions about the origins of the world, explaining that a man with an arrow in his chest is more sensible to address himself to removing it than to ask how it got there. The Buddha had found a way to end mental and physical suffering, by developing inner clarity and peace; to him, questions of how and why were not useful in progressing toward that goal.

According to the law of karma (the law of cause and effect), to which the Buddha subscribed, wholesome actions eventually lead to good results, while unwholesome or harmful deeds result in suffering, in this or a future life. By cultivating wholesome actions of body, speech, and mind, the Buddha maintained that anyone can experience enlightenment. To do this, the Buddha advocated dissolving the obstacles of craving, anger, and ignorance by cultivating ethical conduct, moral discipline, and wisdom.

The Buddha was not immune to death, but he remained fearless and lucid when the time came. Having become ill in his eightieth year, he told one of his foremost disciples, his cousin Ānanda, that he would soon die. He then asked the assembled monks three times whether they had any doubts or questions, but they remained silent. The Buddha's last words summarized his teaching: "Conditioned things are perishable by nature. Diligently seek realization." He died in meditation.

SIGNIFICANCE

Śākyamuni elucidated seminal ideas and methods whose effect can only be compared to the teachings of Moses, Jesus, and Muhammad. He rejected some key elements

first taught the Four Noble Truths—namely, that life inevitably involves suffering or woefulness (*dukkha*), that the cause of suffering is craving or grasping, that there is a way for craving to cease, and that the way consists of the Eightfold Path of right view, right intention, right speech, right action, right livelihood, right effort, right mindfulness, and right concentration.

During this talk, which took place 4 miles (6.5 kilometers) north of Benares, in the Deer Park at Isipatana, one of the five ascetics realized that all conditioned (interdependent) things are impermanent, and he became enlightened. The remaining four soon followed suit; other wanderers and householders from all walks of life, including Rāhula and Śākyamuni's stepmother/aunt, did the same.

The formula that distinguishes a Buddhist from a non-Buddhist evolved during this time. The Buddha taught that "oneself is one's own refuge" and that all beings are,

of the Hindu worldview of his era—notably the caste system, the idea of a permanent self (*ātman*), and the practice of austerities—but retained the notions of karma and rebirth. To these he added his unique insight into what is worthwhile: an altruistic aspiration to enlightenment for the sake of all beings.

Although Buddhism declined and eventually disappeared in India (where it is experiencing a revival today), it spread to Southeast and Central Asia, China, Korea, and Japan. Today there are many different schools of Buddhism, whose styles range from the baroque iconography of Tibetan tantrism to the stark simplicity of Zen. All recognize subsequent adepts on the Buddhist path and reflect the different cultures in which they have developed. All Buddhist traditions, however, trace their lineage and the common essence of their teaching to Śākyamuni, the man who, in recorded history, first became an enlightened one, a Buddha.

—Victoria Scott

FURTHER READING

Davidson, Ronald M. *Indian Esoteric Buddhism*. New York: Columbia University Press, 2003. Discusses the evolution of Buddhism in medieval India.

Gowans, Christopher. *Philosophy of the Buddha: An Introduction*. New York: Routledge, 2003. A clear introduction to Buddhist thought. Covers basic concepts, history, theological concerns, comparisons with other religions, and practical aspects of practice. Includes a list of Internet resources and a glossary of Pāli terms.

Heine, Steven, Charles S. Prebish, and David J. Walbert, eds. *Buddhism in the Modern World: Adaptations of an Ancient Tradition*. New York: Oxford University Press, 2003. A collection of nine essays that discuss the ways in which Buddhism has maintained its doctrinal purity yet managed to adapt throughout Asia in the face of modern science, philosophy, and lifestyle.

Robinson, Richard H., and Willard L. Johnson. *The Buddhist Religion: A Historical Introduction*. 5th ed. Belmont, Calif.: Wadsworth Publishing, 2004. An overview that traces the antecedents of Buddhism, describes the Buddha's life, and explains the development of Buddhism both in India and in Southeast Asia, Tibet, East Asia, and the West. Includes a glossary of key Sanskrit terms, an essay on meditation, and a list of selected readings.

Smith, Huston, and Philip Novak. *Buddhism: A Concise Introduction*. San Francisco: HarperSanFrancisco, 2003. An overview coauthored by a major religious historian. Covers both the historical development of Buddhism and the evolution of its various forms, and the status and practice of Buddhism in the modern world. A useful chart illuminates the differences between the major schools. Includes an annotated bibliography and index.

Williams, Paul, and Anthony Tribe. *Buddhist Thought: A Complete Introduction to the Indian Tradition*. New York: Routledge, 2000. Begins by contextualizing Buddha's life within Brahmanic tradition, and then traces the development of Mahāyāna Buddhism in India. Includes bibliography and index.

SEE ALSO: Ānanda; Asanga; Aśoka; Aśvaghosa; Bodhidharma; Chandragupta Maurya; Gośāla Maskarīputra; Kaniṣka; Vardhamāna; Vasubandhu; Vattagamani.

RELATED ARTICLES in *Great Events from History: The Ancient World*: 6th or 5th century B.C.E., Birth of Buddhism; c. 5th-4th centuries B.C.E., Creation of the *Jātakas*; c. 321 B.C.E., Mauryan Empire Rises in India; 300 B.C.E.-600 C.E., Construction of the Māhabodhi Temple; c. 250 B.C.E., Third Buddhist Council Convenes; c. 250 B.C.E., *Tipiṭaka* Is Compiled; c. 247-207 B.C.E., Buddhism Established in Sri Lanka; c. 1st century B.C.E., Indian Buddhist Nuns Compile the *Therigatha*; 1st century B.C.E.-1st century C.E., Compilation of the *Lotus Sutra*; 1st century C.E., Fourth Buddhist Council Convenes; Late 4th-5th centuries C.E., Asanga Helps Spread Mahāyāna Buddhism; 460-477 C.E., Buddhist Temples Built at Ajanta Caves in India.

JULIUS CAESAR
Roman emperor (r. 49-44 B.C.E.)

With his conquest of Gaul, Caesar expanded Roman rule into northern Europe. He then won a desperate civil war to establish himself as sole ruler of the Roman world, ending the Republic and preparing the stage for the Empire.

BORN: July 12/13, 100 B.C.E.; Rome (now in Italy)
DIED: March 15, 44 B.C.E.; Rome
ALSO KNOWN AS: Gaius Julius Caesar (full name)
AREAS OF ACHIEVEMENT: Government and politics, war and conquest, literature

EARLY LIFE

The family of Gaius Julius, later known as Julius Caesar (JEWL-yuhs SEE-zur), was of great antiquity and nobility in Roman history; Caesar claimed descent not only from the ancient kings of the city but also from Aeneas, its legendary founder, and his mother, the goddess Venus. In actual life, however, the Julian clan had more history than money and tended to favor the cause of the common people rather than the aristocrats. The twin pressures of finance and popular politics were the dominant forces that shaped the life and career of Julius Caesar.

During the first century B.C.E., the city-state of Rome had become the dominant power in the Mediterranean world, and with this expansion had come enormous wealth, immense military strength, and a gradual but unmistakable decline in the old Republic. By the time of Caesar's birth, the political factions in Rome had coalesced into two major camps. The *populares* were led by Gaius Marius, who was married to Caesar's aunt Julia; this group championed the cause of the middle and lower classes. Their opponents, the *optimates*, favored the upper classes and the traditional rule of the senate; they found their leader in Lucius Cornelius Sulla. The bloody civil war between the two sides ended with Sulla's victory and assumption of the dictatorship.

In 84 B.C.E. Caesar married Cornelia, the daughter of a leading follower of Marius. This action so angered Sulla that Caesar found it prudent to secure a diplomatic post at the court of Nicomedes, the king of Bithynia in northeastern Asia Minor. Caesar did not return to Rome until after Sulla's death.

Once back, he embarked on a daring and ambitious course of bringing charges against the leading members of the *optimates*, in the hope of winning renown and establishing his support among the followers of Marius. Unsuccessful in these attempts, Caesar journeyed to Rhodes to study oratory—an art essential to any successful Roman politician. On the voyage, Caesar was captured by pirates and held for ransom. Insulted by the small amount they demanded, Caesar had them increase it and promised that when he was freed he would return to crucify them. He was good to his word, but according to his biographer Suetonius, Caesar mercifully cut the throats of the pirates before crucifixion.

In 70 B.C.E. Caesar fully entered public life with his funeral oration for his aunt Julia. It was in this speech that he traced his family ancestry to the goddess Venus; more important, he launched a searing attack on the conservative party in Rome, announcing his intent to challenge their rule. The rest of his life would be spent in making good that challenge.

According to ancient writers, Caesar was tall and fair-complexioned, with a full face and keen black eyes. He enjoyed excellent health until the last years of his life, when he was subject to fainting fits that may have been epileptic. He was bald early and quite vain about it; Suetonius says that of all the honors granted him, the one Caesar used most was the privilege of wearing a laurel wreath at all times.

In his private life, Caesar was noted for his incessant womanizing; even amid the somewhat lax morality of the late Republic, his escapades were cause for widespread comment. He was also exceedingly avaricious, but this may have been less a character flaw than a political necessity.

Caesar's main characteristic was his amazing energy, both physical and mental. He endured the dangers and fatigues of military campaigns without complaint or distress, and he composed his lucid, fast-moving *Comentarii de bello Gallico* (45 B.C.E.; *The Gallic Wars*) and *Comentarii de bello civili* (52-51 B.C.E.; *The Civil Wars*; the two are translated together as *Commentaries*, 1609) almost before his battles were ended. He was so brilliant, in so many areas, that his contemporaries were dazzled, and historians continue to be fascinated by him.

LIFE'S WORK

It is impossible to tell if Caesar wished to destroy the last remnants of the old Republic and replace it with a formal autocracy or whether he merely intended to become the leading citizen—although one without rivals—in the Roman world. In the end, the result was the same, for Caesar for a brief time did become supreme ruler, and the Republic was destroyed. Although it was Caesar's nephew and heir Octavian (later known as Augustus) who became the first Roman emperor, it was Caesar who made the Empire possible.

Following a term as quaestor (a junior military officer) in Spain in 69 B.C.E., Caesar returned to Rome and allied himself with Marcus Licinius Crassus and Pompey the Great; the first was the richest man in Rome, the second its leading general. Together, these three formed the First Triumvirate, which was to become the real power in the Roman world.

In 61 B.C.E., Caesar was appointed governor of Farther Spain and honored with a triumph for his military campaigns there. The next year, he was elected as one of the two consuls who headed the Roman government; his term of office began in 59 B.C.E. The rest of Caesar's career stems, directly or indirectly, from this consulship.

As one of two consuls, Caesar had to deal with his colleague, a conservative opponent. Impatient with this and other obstructions, Caesar initiated numerous highly irregular, sometimes illegal, actions. These were designed to benefit Pompey's discharged veterans, increase the wealth of Crassus, and advance the general aims of the Triumvirate. So blatant, however, were the offenses—including violence against officials whose positions made them virtually sacred—that Caesar knew that his enemies would not rest until he had been prosecuted, convicted, and condemned.

His only recourse was to remain in office, because then he would be immune from trial. He secured the provinces of Cisalpine Gaul (now northern Italy) and Illyricum (the coast of modern Yugoslavia) and soon added Transalpine Gaul (southern France), which bordered on lands unconquered by Rome.

Caesar wasted no time in finding an excuse to wage war against the Gauls, and for the next eight years he was embroiled in the Gallic Wars, which are vividly recounted in his commentaries. During his campaigns, he crossed the Rhine River to drive back the German tribes and twice launched an invasion of Britain. Al-

though his attempts on the island were unsuccessful, his second fleet numbered eight hundred ships—the largest channel invasion armada until the Allied Normandy invasion in World War II.

In 52 B.C.E., the recently subdued Gauls revolted against the Romans and, led by Vercingetorix, came close to undoing Caesar's great conquests. By brilliant generalship and extraordinary efforts, Caesar pinned the Gauls in their fortress town of Alesia (Aliese-Sainte-Reine) and destroyed their army, finally ending the Gallic Wars. According to Caesar, he had fought thirty battles, captured eight hundred towns, and defeated three million enemies, of whom almost a million had been slain, another million captured. Although these figures

Julius Caesar. (Library of Congress)

are surely exaggerated, they do illustrate the extent of Caesar's victory. Its long-lasting effect was the opening of northern Europe to the influence of Greek and Roman culture and the rich heritage of the Mediterranean civilization.

Caesar's Gallic victories, however, had not secured his position in Rome. The Triumvirate had drifted apart, and Pompey was now allied with the senate and the conservatives. They demanded that Caesar give up his governorship and return to Rome. Knowing that such a move would be fatal, Caesar instead attacked his opponents. In January, 49 B.C.E., he led his troops across the Rubicon, the narrow stream that marked the border of his province. He took this irrevocable step with a gambler's daring, remarking, "Jacta alea est" (the die is cast).

Pompey and the senatorial forces were caught by surprise, and within three months they had been driven from Italy to Greece. Caesar turned west and seized Sicily to secure Rome's grain supply, then attacked Pompey's supporters in Spain. He trapped their army near the Ebro River at Ilerda (now Lerida), and when they surrendered, he showed considerable clemency in pardoning them, in marked contrast to his earlier harsh treatment of the Gauls.

Returning to Rome, Caesar became dictator for the first time and proceeded to tackle numerous social problems, especially that of widespread debt, caused by the breakdown of the Republic. In 48 B.C.E., he daringly crossed the Adriatic Sea in winter and besieged Pompey's larger forces at their base of Dyrrachium (Durazzo). Forced to retire into Thessaly, Caesar turned and defeated Pompey at the Battle of Pharsalus, destroying his army. Pompey fled to Egypt, hoping to rally support, but instead was murdered; the whole Roman world was in Caesar's grasp.

Following Pompey to Egypt, Caesar intervened in a power struggle between Cleopatra VII and her younger brother. In this, the Alexandrian War, Caesar narrowly escaped death on several occasions but was successful in placing Cleopatra on the throne. There followed an intense affair between the young queen and Caesar, and the son born in September, 48 B.C.E., was named Caesarion.

After more campaigns against foreign states in the east and the remnants of Pompey's supporters, Caesar returned to Rome in 46 B.C.E. to celebrate four triumphs: over Gaul, Egypt, Pontus, and Africa. Cleopatra arrived soon after to take up residence in the city; perhaps along with her came the eminent Egyptian astronomer Sosigenes of Alexandria, who aided Caesar in his reform of the calendar. This Julian calendar is the basis of the modern system.

Caesar was active in other areas. He settled many of his veterans in colonies throughout the Empire, and with them many of the poor and unemployed of Rome, thus reducing the strain on the public economy. Numerous other civic reforms were instituted, many of them laudable, but most of them giving increased power to Caesar alone. Although he publicly rejected the offer of kingship, he did accept the dictatorship for life in February, 44 B.C.E.

This action brought together a group of about sixty conspirators, led by Cassius and Marcus Junius Brutus. Brutus may have been Caesar's son; certainly he was an avowed, almost fanatic devotee of the Republic who thought it his duty to kill Caesar.

Realizing that Caesar planned to depart on March 18 for a lengthy campaign against the Parthian Empire in the east, the conspirators decided to strike. On March 15, the ides of March, they attacked Caesar as he entered the Theater of Pompey for a meeting of the senate. As he fell, mortally wounded, his last words are reported to have been either "Et tu, Brute?" (and you too, Brutus?) or, in Greek, "And you too, my child?"

SIGNIFICANCE

"Veni, vidi, vinci"—"I came, I saw, I conquered"—is one of the most famous military dispatches of all time, and totally characteristic of Julius Caesar. He sent it to Rome after his defeat of King Pharnaces of Pontus in 47 B.C.E., a campaign that added greatly to Rome's eastern power but which represented almost an interlude between Caesar's victories in Egypt and his final triumph in the civil war. The message captures the essence of Caesar, that almost superhuman mix of energy, ability, and ambition.

This mixture fascinated his contemporaries and has enthralled the world ever since. Caesar was ambitious, but so were others, Pompey among them. He was bold, but many other bold Romans had their schemes come to nothing. He was certainly able, but the Roman world was full of men of ability.

It was Caesar, however, who united all these qualities and had them in so much fuller measure than his contemporaries that he was unique. As a writer or speaker, he could easily hold his own against acknowledged masters such as Cicero; in statesmanship and politics, he was unsurpassed; in military skill, he had no peer. When all of these qualities were brought together, they amounted to an almost transcendent genius that seemed to give

Julius Caesar powers and abilities far beyond those of mortal men.

The central question, in 44 B.C.E. and today, is to what use—good or bad—did Caesar put those qualities and abilities? Clearly, Brutus, Cassius, and the other conspirators believed that he had perverted his qualities and subverted the state and thus must be destroyed. In later years, the term "Caesarism" has been applied to those who wished to gain supreme power for themselves, disregarding the laws and careless of the rights of others. Viewed from this perspective, Caesar destroyed the last remnants of the Roman Republic and thus stamped out what liberty and freedom remained.

From another view, he was the creator, or at least the forerunner, of a new and better system, the Empire, which brought order from chaos, peace from endless civil war. The ancient Republic had already disappeared in all but name, had become empty form without real substance, and it was for the general good that it finally disappeared. This is the view of Caesar as archetypal ruler and dispenser of order, the view that made his very name a title of monarchs—the Caesars of Rome, the kaisers of Germany, the czars of Russia.

In the end, a sensible view of Caesar must combine a mixture of these two perspectives, seeing both his faults and virtues. He accomplished much during his lifetime, and his achievements have endured for millennia after his assassination. Even in death, Caesar is best described in the words of Shakespeare: "He doth bestride this narrow world like a colossus."

—*Michael Witkoski*

FURTHER READING

Caesar, Gaius Julius. *Seven Commentaries on the Gallic War.* Translated by Carolyn Hammond. New York: Oxford University Press, 1998. Caesar's own version of his conquest of Gaul and struggle in the civil war against Pompey. One of the masterpieces of classical literature, this work gives a vivid and exciting view of truly world-changing events by the major actor of his time. Indispensable for a full understanding of the period.

Fuller, J. F. C. *Julius Caesar: Man, Soldier, and Tyrant.* New Brunswick, N.J.: Rutgers University Press, 1965.

Written by a distinguished soldier and military theorist, this work concentrates on Caesar's achievements on the battlefield, and why he was such an outstanding and innovative commander. The study, which is generally free of technical obscurities and military jargon, helps the reader understand the difficulties of Caesar's triumphs.

Grant, Michael. *Caesar.* Chicago: Follett, 1975. Grant is one of the outstanding modern historians of ancient Rome. A well-written, well-researched biography of Caesar and his time, careful to place Caesar within the context of the fall of the Roman Republic. Caesar's accomplishments become even more impressive when viewed as part of a larger whole, and this Grant does extremely well. The volume is well illustrated.

_____. *The Roman Emperors: A Biographical Guide to the Rulers of Imperial Rome.* London: Weidenfeld & Nicholson, 1996. A brief introductory sketch of Caesar can be found in this volume. Although relatively short, it provides all the necessary information to begin an investigation of the man's life and accomplishments.

_____. *The Twelve Caesars.* New York: Penguin, 1989. Both a continuation of Suetonius's classical biography and a commentary on it. Gives the reader a thorough understanding of what Caesar accomplished and an insight into why and how those accomplishments occurred.

Suetonius. *Lives of the Twelve Caesars.* Translated by Robert Graves. New York: Welcome Rain, 2001. Suetonius's work is the essential starting point for any study of the early Roman emperors. His biography of Caesar may lack historical rigor and objectivity, but it is a fascinating source of anecdotes and character traits.

SEE ALSO: Marc Antony; Augustus; Marcus Junius Brutus; Cassius; Cleopatra VII; Gaius Marius; Pompey the Great; Lucius Cornelius Sulla; Vercingetorix.

RELATED ARTICLES in *Great Events from History: The Ancient World*: 58-51 B.C.E., Caesar Conquers Gaul; 51-30 B.C.E., Cleopatra VII, Last of Ptolemies, Reigns; 46 B.C.E., Establishment of the Julian Calendar; 43-130 C.E., Roman Conquest of Britain.

CALIGULA
Roman emperor (r. 37-41 C.E.)

The third ruler of the Julio-Claudian Dynasty, Caligula did much during his short reign to transform the position of Roman emperor into an institution of absolute monarchy.

BORN: August 31, 12 C.E.; probably Antium, Latium (now Anzio, Italy)
DIED: January 24, 41 C.E.; Rome (now in Italy)
ALSO KNOWN AS: Gaius Caesar (given name); Gaius Caesar Germanicus
AREA OF ACHIEVEMENT: Government and politics

EARLY LIFE

Gaius Caesar was born in the resort town of Antium (modern Anzio) on August 31, 12 C.E., the third son of Germanicus Caesar, nephew of the future emperor Tiberius, and his wife Agrippina the Elder, granddaughter of the contemporary emperor Augustus. As a toddler, Gaius spent time in northern Europe and Syria, accompanying his father during his various military and diplomatic assignments. In fact, it was during a stay at a military installation near the Rhine River that Gaius received the nickname Caligula from his father's soldiers. Agrippina often dressed up her young son as a legionnaire, and the nickname came from the small version of soldiers' hob-nailed boots (*caliga*) that he wore. "Caligula" means "little boots."

Imperial politics at this time were unsettled and volatile. Augustus, after his victory at the Battle of Actium in 31 B.C.E., had emerged as the undisputed master of Rome, but he accepted only the title of *princeps* (which implied that he was the first official among equals) and preferred to exercise power in an indirect fashion by exploiting existing republican offices and institutions. He employed this cautious method of governing because he feared that too blatant a disregard for Roman republican traditions might offend the sensibilities of his subjects and thereby jeopardize the stability of the Empire.

In keeping with this fiction, Augustus hesitated to set up a clear-cut succession system that would pass on power in a hereditary fashion. Therefore, when Augustus died in 14 C.E., his designated successor, his stepson Tiberius, had to accept the position from the senate and secure the support of the army and Praetorian Guard (the ruler's personal bodyguard) before he could assume power. For a long time, Tiberius hesitated to designate his choice as successor. Caligula's father, Germanicus, was the most likely candidate because of his general pop-

ularity and the fact that he was the grandson of Augustus. Tiberius, however, appears to have been jealous of his nephew's fame and kept him out of Rome on various military and diplomatic missions. It was on one such mission to the Middle East that Germanicus died in 19 C.E., under suspicious circumstances. His widow, Agrippina, was convinced that her husband had been poisoned by the governor of Syria on the orders of Tiberius. While no hard evidence has ever appeared to link Tiberius with the death of Germanicus, from that point forward Agrippina became the emperor's bitter enemy.

With the death of Germanicus, Tiberius began to groom the latter's two eldest sons, Nero and Drusus, for power. However, both young men, as well as their mother, fell victim to the plots of Lucius Aelius Sejanus, Tiberius's evil prefect of the Praetorian Guard, who wanted to eliminate the family of Germanicus in order to strengthen his power over the emperor. He fabricated evidence that charged both Nero and Agrippina with involvement in plots against the emperor's life, and both were banished to remote islands where they subsequently died. Sejanus then accused Drusus of various sexual crimes and, as a result, Drusus was imprisoned in a cell below the palace (where he also would die in 33 C.E.).

After the banishment of his mother in 27 C.E., Caligula lived first with Livia Drusilla, his great-grandmother and the widow of Augustus; after her death in 29 C.E., he lived with Antonia, the sister of Augustus, Caligula's paternal grandmother. Although he had originally been too young to warrant the attention of Sejanus, the elimination of his two older brothers made Caligula the next target for the prefect's machinations. Fortunately for the young man, Sejanus fell from power and was executed in 31 C.E. Tiberius then took Caligula into his household (the emperor now lived on the island of Capri) and began to groom him as his successor.

LIFE'S WORK

The Roman historian Suetonius argues that Tiberius took Caligula under his wing because the boy's interests, which were already depraved, coincided with his own. Other historians, however, have offered less sensationalistic explanations for the decision. Tiberius had promised Augustus to promote the interests of the children of Germanicus and, if possible, to name one as his successor, and Tiberius, despite his other possible faults, was a man who kept his word. In addition, the new prefect of the Praetorian Guard, Naevius Cordus Sutorius Macro, saw a brilliant future for himself with the ascension of Caligula and actively campaigned for his official designation as heir. As the engineer of the fall of Sejanus, Macro already had the emperor's ear. He strengthened his relationship with Caligula by flattering the young man and even encouraging him to have an affair with his wife.

Tiberius was also intelligent enough to recognize Caligula's weaknesses. This was the most likely reason for his final decision regarding the succession. He named Caligula as co-heir along with his young grandson, Tiberius Gemellus. Thus when the old emperor finally died in 37 C.E. (Suetonius recorded that Macro and Caligula smothered him with a pillow on his sickbed), the twenty-six-year-old Caligula and his ten-year-old cousin assumed power in Rome.

Caligula never had any intention of sharing power with Gemellus. With the skillful aid of Macro, he moved rapidly to consolidate his position at his cousin's ex-

pense. Two days after the death of Tiberius, the senate hailed Caligula as "Imperator" and granted him, in one block, all the powers that both Augustus and Tiberius had only gradually assumed. Gemellus was left isolated and powerless.

At the time that he assumed power, Caligula was, by most accounts, an unattractive man. He was very tall, with thin legs and a pasty complexion. He had small, deep-set eyes and a broad forehead. His hair was thin, and he already had a large bald spot at the back of his head. Suetonius reports that he was so self-conscious of his baldness that he made it a crime punishable by death to look at him from above. He had married Junia Claudilla in 33 C.E., but he engaged in numerous affairs with other women and with men. It was rumored that he routinely committed incest with his sister Drusilla, and he may have also done so with his other two sisters. An inveterate gambler on chariot races, Caligula developed such a fondness for his favorite horse, Incitatus, that he had the animal attend senate meetings and even wanted to make him a consul.

Caligula, shown seated. (Library of Congress)

At the beginning of his reign, however, Caligula made an effort to be a popular ruler. He treated the senate with respect, put on lavish entertainments for the Roman populace, abolished the crime of *maiestas*, or speaking or acting against the *princeps*, which Tiberius had used to punish personal enemies, and destroyed incriminating records that Tiberius had kept on many notable Romans. In late September, 37 C.E., however, Caligula fell ill, and when he recovered in late October, his reign took a dramatic turn for the worse.

Caligula emerged from his illness convinced that there was a conspiracy against him. Determined to eliminate it, he ordered the deaths of Gemellus and his father-in-law, Junius Silanus. He then divorced his wife and married Livia Orestilla. This marriage also ended in divorce within a year, whereupon he married Lollia Paulina. His third marriage lasted less than a year. On his divorce from Lollia in 39 C.E., Caligula married Caesonia, who was already pregnant by him. She gave birth to a daughter, Drusilla, a month after the wedding.

Meanwhile, Caligula continued to go after his real and imagined enemies. The emperor forced the devious Macro and his wife to commit suicide in early 38 C.E. He accused his former best friend and lover, Marcus Lepidus, of conspiring against him with the military commander Gaetulicus and had them both executed in 39 C.E. He reintroduced the crime of *maiestas* that same year, thereby opening the door to many more executions of prominent Romans. He even went as far as to accuse his two surviving sisters, Agrippina and Livilla (Drusilla had died in 38 C.E.), of trying to overthrow him and had them both banished from Rome.

During this same period, Caligula also began to claim that he was a god. He ordered statues erected to him throughout the Empire and even demanded that one be placed in the main Jewish synagogue in Jerusalem (this order does not seem to have been carried out). Once, on a military expedition in northern Europe, Caligula claimed to have been offended by the god Neptune and declared war on him. He reportedly ordered his troops to march into the English Channel and flay the water with their swords. He then declared victory and had his men collect seashells along the shore as tribute from the defeated god.

Caligula was also extravagant in his spending. Even though he inherited a budget surplus from Tiberius of approximately 2,500 million *sesterces*, he managed to spend it all in less than a year. To gain additional revenue, he forced all rich Romans to name him as their heir and then often found reasons to have them executed. He imposed a number of new direct taxes and, according to several sources, even opened a brothel in his palace staffed by the daughters and wives of noble Romans.

Caligula's increasingly erratic and bizarre behavior finally did give rise to the conspiracy he so feared. Organized by several prominent senators and an officer in the Praetorian Guard, Cassius Chaerea, the assassins separated Caligula from his German bodyguards as he left the games celebrating the holiday of Ludi Palatini in 41 C.E. Caligula was stabbed at least thirty times, and the assassins killed his wife and daughter shortly thereafter. After a brief period of confusion, the Praetorian Guard named Caligula's uncle Claudius the new emperor, and the senate ratified the selection the next day.

SIGNIFICANCE

Augustus, the first *princeps*, pretended not to be a monarch, even though he was one in reality. Tiberius had more or less continued this tradition. During his short reign, Caligula, through his blatantly excessive and autocratic behavior, destroyed the last remnants of the fiction surrounding the position. Although he was not a good ruler in many important respects, Caligula nevertheless clearly demonstrated to the Roman people that the Republic was over and that a new era of Imperial monarchy had begun.

—Christopher E. Guthrie

FURTHER READING

Balsdon, V. D. *The Emperor Gaius.* Oxford, England: Oxford University Press, 1934. Until the 1990 publication of the Anthony Barret book discussed below, this work was the standard treatment in English on Caligula. Although the author uncritically repeats many negative stories from Suetonius and others, he also argues that the Roman senate was as guilty as the emperor himself for many of the abuses committed during Caligula's reign.

Barrett, Anthony. *Agrippina: Sex, Power, and Politics in the Early Empire.* New Haven, Conn.: Yale University Press, 1996. Although its subject is Caligula's sister, Agrippina the Younger, this volume provides an excellent examination of Caligula's reign, his relationship with his family, and the question of whether or not he committed incest with his sisters.

_____. *Caligula: The Corruption of Power.* New Haven, Conn.: Yale University Press, 1998. A biography of Caligula that argues that although the emperor was morally irresponsible, insufferably arrogant, and emotionally unequipped to rule, he was not the psychotic maniac of popular imagination.

Sandison, A. T. "The Madness of the Emperor Caligula." *Medical History* 2 (1958): 202-209. Discusses the various possible causes for Caligula's illness in 37 C.E. and examines whether the experience caused his mind to snap.

Suetonius. *Lives of the Twelve Caesars*. Translated by Robert Graves. New York: Welcome Rain, 2001. Chapter 5 deals with the life of Caligula and is the source of many of the most bizarre stories about the emperor. Given the biases of the author, however, many of these stories should not be taken at face value.

Wells, Colin. *The Roman Empire*. Stanford, Calif.: Stanford University Press, 1984. An excellent examination of the institution of Roman emperor as it evolved from Augustus to Diocletian. The author's treatment of Caligula is balanced and perceptive.

SEE ALSO: Agrippina the Younger; Augustus; Claudius I; Livia Drusilla; Tiberius.

RELATED ARTICLES in *Great Events from History: The Ancient World*: September 2, 31 B.C.E., Battle of Actium; 27-23 B.C.E., Completion of the Augustan Settlement; c. 50 C.E., Creation of the Roman Imperial Bureaucracy.

CALLIMACHUS
Greek poet

Although most of Callimachus's work has been lost, his hymns and epigrams—incorporating drama, sophistication, and a sense of history—survive as masterpieces of their kind. He set an ideal of tone and content that has influenced poets for centuries.

BORN: c. 305 B.C.E.; Cyrene, Cyrenaica (now in Libya)
DIED: c. 240 B.C.E.; Alexandria, Egypt
AREA OF ACHIEVEMENT: Literature

EARLY LIFE
The world into which Callimachus (kuh-LIHM-uh-kuhs) was born was a very different one from the world of the great poets and prose writers of fifth century B.C.E. Greece. Alexander the Great's empire had eclipsed and absorbed the old city-states and in turn had been divided into smaller warring empires after his death. Egypt had become the center of a new Greek state ruled by the Greek Ptolemies, and Alexandria had become not only a major political and commercial center and royal capital but also the center of a new and flourishing Greek culture, as rich as the old but somewhat diffident about its ability to live up to the glories of the past. Callimachus himself came from the Greek colony of Cyrene in Libya, a somewhat uneasy vassal of the Ptolemies. Although he was of a distinguished family that claimed Cyrene's founder Battus as an ancestor, it was natural for Callimachus to be drawn to Alexandria, with its promise of literary friends and royal patronage.

Callimachus began as a teacher of grammar in the suburb of Eleusis, but at length he attracted royal notice and received an appointment in the great library, which with the museum, a sort of "university complex" with lecture halls and roofed walks, was the center for the literary and scientific life of the city. Euclid and Archimedes flourished there. Not much is known of Callimachus's duties—only that he never became chief librarian and that he regarded a big book as a big evil—but the list of his lost prose works ("Catalog of Writers Eminent in All Fields of Literature," "Local Names of Months," "Rivers of the World," and so on) suggests an industrious cataloger. Compliments scattered through his work indicate royal patronage throughout his life.

LIFE'S WORK
The scanty evidence in his poems suggests that, once secure of royal patronage, Callimachus led a long, agreeable, and productive life in Alexandria. Symposia must have been frequent, although Callimachus prided himself on being a moderate drinker. Only one of his erotic poems was written to a woman, and he was almost certainly a bachelor. He valued the didactic poet Aratus for sharing his preference for brevity and craftsmanship. He may have been ambivalent toward Apollonius of Rhodes, a former pupil, for attempting a full-scale epic on the Argonauts. He wrote a romantic poem to one Theocritus, who is believed to be the inventor of pastoral poetry.

It is said that Callimachus wrote poems in every meter and that his books amounted to eight hundred (although this sum probably means counting parts of books as individual works). Callimachus sometimes brought together his shorter works under a loose framework—hence his most notable work, the *Aitiōn* (*Aetia*, 1958), in which a whole series of local rituals are described and explained, somewhat in the manner of Ovid's *Metamorphoses* (c. 8 C.E.; English translation, 1567), which indeed it influenced.

The *Aetia* shows Callimachus's cataloging zeal as well as his interest in religious matters and in local affairs. The revised version begins with an apology in the manner of Alexander Pope in which Callimachus satirizes the works of his Rhodian critics, including Apollonius, who bray like donkeys while his own muse chirps like the cicada. The *Aetia*, which must have been a lengthy collection, included stories of the Graces, Hercules, the Argonauts, Ariadne, and much else. Only two episodes survive in substantial form: the charming love story of Acontius and Cydippe and a court poem, *Lock of Berenice* (1755), which is the remote inspiration of Alexander Pope's *The Rape of the Lock* (1712, 1714). Berenice II was a real queen and a native of Cyrene.

Callimachus wrote a transitional poem to lead from the *Aetia* into his other great collection, the *Iamboi* (*Iambi*, 1958), of which only tantalizing fragments exist. Written in Greek iambic—a conversational meter used not only for drama but also for fables and lampoons— Callimachus's *Iambi* sounds as much like Pope's *The Dunciad* (1728-1743) as anything else. It included an Aesopian fable about the origin of language, a quarrel between the Laurel and the Olive, a satire on a pederastic schoolmaster, a poem in honor of a victor in the jar race, a serious poem honoring a friend's daughter, and finally an answer to those who criticized Callimachus for failing to specialize. There was another invective poem, the "Ibis," possibly directed at Apollonius, but of this little remains.

The *Aetia* and the *Iambi* were Callimachus's longest poems. He was also a practitioner of the *epyllion*, or little epic, which differed from the full-scale epic not only in length but also in subject matter: The central episode might indeed be heroic, but the emphasis might be on some unheroic character. Thus, in *Ekalē* (*Hecale*, 1958) the ostensible subject is Theseus's taming the bull of Marathon, but most of the poem told how Theseus sheltered in the hut of an old peasant woman, Hecale.

Of all Callimachus's works, the least frustrating are the hymns—to Zeus, Apollo, Artemis, Delos, the Bath of Pallas, and Demeter—which are nearly intact. There seems no reason to doubt that these were designed to be performed as part of religious ceremonies and that they embody genuine religious feeling as well as a feeling for nature and Callimachus's usual curiosity about local customs and traditions. The hymns *Eis Loutra tēs Pallados*

(*The Bath of Pallas*, 1755) and *In Delum* (*To Delos*, 1755) are particularly striking.

Callimachus's epigrams, of which a fair number have survived in *Epigrammata* (*Epigrams*, 1793) and other sources, including a Roman wall, contain epitaphs, votive dedications, love lyrics, and other miscellaneous short poems. Many seem to be occasional poems written as a favor to friends or patrons and have the limited appeal of occasional poetry, such as the following lament for the poet Heraclitus:

> They told me, Heraclitus, they told me you were dead;
> They brought me bitter news to hear and bitter tears to shed.
> I wept, as I remember'd how often you and I
> Had tired the sun with talking and sent him down the sky.
> And now that thou art lying, my dear old Carian guest,
> A handful of grey ashes, long, long ago at rest,
> Still are thy pleasant voices, thy nightingales, awake,
> For Death, he taketh all away, but them he cannot take.

William Cory's translation, "Heraclitus," published in 1858, lacks the conciseness that was Callimachus's ideal but is otherwise worthy of the original. Some of the epitaphs have grace and dignity that rise above the immediate occasion:

> Shipwrecked stranger, Leóntikhos found your
> Anonymous corpse and gave you burial
> On the seabeach here. His tears, though, were for
> His own mortality. Restless sailor,
> He beats over the sea like a flashing gull.

Because most of Callimachus's work is lost, his epigrams are prized. With any other poet, these occasional poems would be treated as an appendix rather than a central portion of the lifework. Scholarly editions of Callimachus, however, include dozens of isolated quotations, often mere phrases quoted in a dictionary, for the sake of preserving a rare word from this master.

SIGNIFICANCE

Callimachus was a far greater poet than the surviving fragments would indicate; in the Greek and Roman world, which knew his work in its entirety, his prestige was enormous. When modern scholars piece together what is left of Callimachus's work, they can conjure up the ghosts of the *Hecale*, the *Aetia*, and the *Iambi*. They can prove how great these poems were and even give something of their flavor, but in the end they can only point to how much of Callimachus's distinguished poetry is lost. (On the other hand, if the prose works had survived, perhaps they would have only a historical interest.)

The hymns are impressive even in translation and would have been even more impressive in their liturgical setting. The epigrams, however, seldom translate well and too often depend on some figure or allusion that must be elaborately footnoted. A reader who knows Greek literature thoroughly and who can work with the available parallel editions (original Greek and English translation on facing pages) has a better chance of enjoying Callimachus; for others, there is still hope. Every so often papyruses containing fragments of Callimachus's work are found in Egypt, and perhaps a less fragmentary manuscript of the *Hecale* or the *Aetia* will surface. If that happens, Callimachus will be read as much as his rival Apollonius.

—John C. Sherwood

FURTHER READING

Blum, Rudolph. *Kallimachos: The Alexandrian Library and the Origins of Bibliography*. Translated by Hans H. Wellisch. Madison: University of Wisconsin Press, 1991. In his study of the Alexandrian Library, Blum argues that Callimachus, the second director of the library, was the inventor of two essential scholarly tools: the library catalog and the biobibliographical reference work.

Callimachus. *Aetia, Iambi, Lyric Poems, Hecale, Minor Epic and Elegiac Poems, and Other Fragments*. Translated by C. A. Trypanis. Cambridge, Mass.: Harvard University Press, 1978. Provides a Greek text, a serviceable prose translation, and excellent notes.

_____. *The Poems of Callimachus*. Translated by Frank Nisetich. New York: Oxford University Press, 2001. This translation of Callimachus's extant works and major fragments includes an introduction that discusses the poet's life, his achievements, and the difficulties in the way of modern appreciation. Presents fragments as integral parts of the poetry books in which they originally were contained.

De Romilly, Jaqueline. *A Short History of Greek Literature*. Translated by Lillian Doherty. Chicago: University of Chicago Press, 1985. Includes excellent impressionistic accounts of Callimachus and Apollonius. De Romilly doubts that Callimachus shared the "simple faith" of the Homeric hymns.

Ferguson, John. *Callimachus*. Boston: Twayne, 1980. A general survey of Callimachus, this work is interesting and thorough. Ferguson pieces together fragments of gossip to make a coherent life of Callimachus, and he includes the fragments of the poems. Callimachus's social and cultural background is treated. Contains an excellent bibliography.

Kerkhecker, Arnd. *Callimachus' Book of Iambi*. New York: Oxford University Press, 1999. An extended discussion of Callimachus's collected Iambi, arguably one of the earliest surviving Greek "books of poetry."

SEE ALSO: Berenice II; Heraclitus of Ephesus.

RELATED ARTICLES in *Great Events from History: The Ancient World*: c. 750 B.C.E., Homer Composes the *Iliad*; c. 700 B.C.E., Hesiod Composes *Theogony* and *Works and Days*; c. 580 B.C.E., Greek Poet Sappho Dies; c. 438 B.C.E., Greek Lyric Poet Pindar Dies; 336 B.C.E., Alexander the Great Begins Expansion of Macedonia; 332 B.C.E., Founding of Alexandria; 54 B.C.E., Roman Poet Catullus Dies; 19 B.C.E., Roman Poet Vergil Dies; November 27, 8 B.C.E., Roman Lyric Poet Horace Dies.

CAO CAO

Chinese politician, military strategist, and soldier-poet

Cao Cao unified North China at the close of the Later Han Dynasty, popularized agricultural colonies, and wrote poems that intiated the Jian An literary period.

BORN: 155 C.E.; Qiao County (now Hao County, Anhui Province), China

DIED: 220 C.E.; Luoyang, China

ALSO KNOWN AS: Ts'ao Ts'ao (Wade-Giles); Mengde (Pinyin, literary name), Meng-te (Wade-Giles, literary name); Aman (infant name)

AREAS OF ACHIEVEMENT: Government and politics, war and conquest, literature

EARLY LIFE

Cao Cao (tsow tsow) was born in the last days of the tottering Eastern, or Later, Han Dynasty (25-220 C.E.). China was on the verge of its second disintegration after a more than four-hundred-year unification of the Qin and Han Dynasties since the period of the Warring States (475-221 B.C.E.). This period witnessed merciless power struggles between court eunuchs and external relatives of the consort families, rampant political corruption, strategic obfuscation in dealing with territorial insurrections and autonomies, successive dynastic usurpations, continuous barbarian invasions, widespread famine and pestilence, and destructive civil wars.

In this political chaos, Cao Cao's father Cao Song (Ts'ao Sung)—a son of a Xiahou (Hsiahou) family and an adopted son of Cao Teng (Ts'ao T'eng), an influential eunuch during the reign of Emperor Shun (r. 126-144 C.E.)—held the position of minister of finance and, through influence and bribery, the position of commander in chief during the reign of Emperor Ling (156-189 C.E.). Cao Cao himself held several middle-range positions in the reign of Emperor Xian (Hsien; 181-234 C.E.). Despite their ranks, Cao Cao belonged to neither the literati nor the consort families of the Han house, so when the Yellow Turbans Uprising broke out in 184 C.E., he sought to strengthen his position at the expense of the insurgents and then of the military generals who cracked down on the peasant insurrections. Several officials and landlords also sought to expand their own forces in the insurrection-suppressing turmoil and developed into new territorial sovereigns, notably Liu Bei (Liu Pei; 161-223 C.E.) and Sun Quan (Sun Ch'üan; 182-252 C.E.), both of whom were to become Cao Cao's major rivals.

The year 192 saw Cao Cao's small army take the prefecture of Yan in the west of today's Shandong Province. In the prefecture of Qing, the east of Shandong, he was able to lure 300,000 Yellow Turbans into surrender and restructure them into his Qing Prefecture Army. With this military success, Emperor Xian appointed him East-Guarding General. Thereafter Cao Cao was able to take an independent position in the face of the ongoing political turmoil.

LIFE'S WORK

Political disorder evolved to its peak in Cao Cao's age. Its roots could be traced back to 107 C.E., when Emperor An was enthroned at the age of thirteen as Empress Deng's puppet and was worsened all the way through the reigns of successive emperors Shao, Shun, Chong, Zi, Huan, and Ling, some being mere infant-emperors whose power lasted no more than a year. In 189 C.E., General He Jin (Ho Chin) was murdered by eunuchs, and General Yuan Shao (Yüan Shao) avenged him by assassinating more than two thousand eunuchs overnight. This was immediately followed by a military *coup d'état*. Dong Zhuo (Tung Cho), a frontier general, led troops into the capital Luoyang (Lo-yang) and dethroned Emperor Shao, whom He Jin had newly put on the throne. He then enthroned a puppet emperor, a boy of eight known as Emperor Xian (Hsien; 181-234 C.E.), and proclaimed himself regent, leaving the legitimate Later Han Dynasty to continue in name only until its final ruin.

Later, Dong Zhuo burned the capital and relocated the court to Changan (now Xi'an), a move that met nationwide resistance. Cao Cao, allied with Yuan Shao, the most powerful general at the time, launched a punitive expedition again the usurper. Dong Zhuo did not hold his power long and was assassinated by his own adopted son, General Lü Bu (Lü Pu), a victim of personal father-son discord sowed by Prime Minister Wang Yun (Wang Yün). A scramble to control the emperor ensued, and fighting among the old and new warlords resumed.

The year 196 C.E. witnessed a critical turning point in Cao Cao's political career. That year, Emperor Xian was obliged to leave Changan and take refuge in Luoyang. Cao Cao was able to win the emperor's confidence and invited him to Cao Cao's territory Douxu (now Xuchang, Henan Province), thus gaining the advantage of managing the court in the emperor's name. Cao Cao reduced penalties and taxation and popularized large-scale agricultural colonies known as *tuntian* to support his growing army and keep the state under his control. His administration provided soldiers and peasant refugees with cattle and seeds for them to cultivate war-ravaged land and build irrigation projects; in return, they received about half of the harvest. Meanwhile, Cao Cao launched a series of campaigns to eliminate rival powers. He first defeated Lü Bu's separatist army and several weak rival powers and then was challenged by the powerful general Yuan Shao, who had a jurisdiction of four prefectures—Ji (Chi), Qing (Ch'ing), Yu (You), and Bing (Ping)—covering virtually the whole north of China. Capitalizing on his strong military force, Yuan Shao led his army of more than 100,000 soldiers southward in 199 C.E. and made war with Cao Cao. Cao Cao's army, one fifth the size of Yuan Shao's, resisted the enemy at Guandu (Kuantu, now the northwest of Zhongmu County, Henan Province). Cao Cao took advantage of Yuan Shao's arrogance, twice mounting sneak attacks on the enemy's logistics services and burning their grain supply centers, which greatly shook the enemy's morale. Cao Cao's army then advanced on the crest of the victories, put the enemy to rout all along the line, and wiped out Yuan Shao's crack troops. The Battle of Guandu set up a brilliant example of pitting the few against the many. In the following years, Cao Cao swept out the remaining powers of Generals Yuan Shu and Yuan Tan, defeated the barbarian invasions at the northern and western frontiers, and eventually unified northern China.

Meanwhile, Liu Bei (Liu Pei), a collateral branch of the Han house, had refused to submit to Cao Cao and had built up a regime known as the Shu in the Prefecture of Yi (I, now Sichuan and the south of Shaanxi and Gansu provinces) and most of Hunan and Hubei Provinces. To the southeast of the Yangtse River, Sun Quan had set up a third regime, known as the Wu. This triangular political situation prompted numerous seesaw battles. In 208 C.E., Cao Cao's supporters proclaimed him prime minister of the Later Han, and together they made war with the Wu, who then allied with the Shu at the Red Cliff by the Yangtse River (now the Red Rocky Mountain to the west of Wuchang County, Hubei Province). Cao's soldiers and generals, however, were not good at naval battles, so they chained all their warships together for short-term military training. This turned out to be a fatal decision. The allied forces lost no time, launched a fire attack, burned Cao Cao's warships, and defeated his troops. In the ensuing years, Cao Cao never ceased his goal of unifying the Later Han and launched several wars with Liu Bei and Sun Quan, but none succeeded due to the natural barrier of the Yangtse River and the long distance from the Yi Prefecture.

Cao Cao died in 220 C.E. at the age of sixty-six. In the same year, Cao Cao's son Cao Pei (Ts'ao P'ei) deposed Emperor Xian. He named Cao Cao's territory the Kingdom of Wei, conferred on his father the posthumous title of Emperor Weiwu, and proclaimed himself Emperor Weiwen, establishing his capital in Luoyang, thus formerly ending the Later Han. In 221 C.E., Liu Bei proclaimed himself emperor, naming his kingdom Han or Shu-Han—Sichuan was also styled Shu. In 229 C.E., Sun Quan also proclaimed himself emperor, naming his kingdom Wu, with its capital in Jianye (Chienyeh, now Nanjing). Thus China was split into three spheres of political influence, called the Three Kingdoms, which would only be reunified under the Jin Dynasty about forty years later.

Cao Cao showed versatile talents. As a brilliant administrator, he selected his associates by ability but not birth, thus recruiting an increasing number of virtuous advisers and brave soldiers under his banner. As a military strategist, he wrote *Sunzi Luejie* (late second-early third century C.E.; an annotation of the art of war by Sun Zi) and *Bingshu Jieyao* (late second-early third century C.E.; essentials of the art of war). As a soldier-poet, he managed to compose many memorable poems and essays. For example, his "Xie Lu Xing" (dew on the shallots) depicts the ruin of the Han and condemns those responsible. His "Duan Ge Xing" (a short song) reveals his innermost feelings about the transience of human life, like the morning dew, with a sense of creeping pessimism, which only drinking and singing can dispel. In "Gui Sui Shou" (though the tortoise lives long) he compares himself to a horse in stall, which, though now aging, still dreams of galloping mile after mile for glory and for the unification of China.

SIGNIFICANCE

For nearly two thousand years, Cao Cao has remained a household word in China, and he is an important figure in the novel *San guo zhi* (third century; *San Kuo: Or, Romance of the Three Kingdoms*, 1925) and the many plays based on it, portrayed as one of the most dynamic personalities in Chinese history. He was the first to have annotated *Sunzi Bingfa* (probably 475-221 B.C.E.; *Sun Tzu: On the Art of War*, 1910), which was his constant companion. As an extremely successful soldier and commander, he never hesitated to kill but always avoided massacres. His flexible strategies and tactics have long given rise to the saying, "Talk of Cao Cao, and he is here," the Chinese equivalent of "Speak of the devil." His agricultural colonies helped restore production after the destruction of war and promoted the economic development of North China.

As a soldier, politician, and poet, his poems played a pioneering role in initiating a new literary period called Jian An, after the reign-period name of Emperor Xian. This literary school represented a serious philosophical departure from the declining Han Confucianism at that time, especially from the two Confucian ideals of *xiao* (filiality) and *lian* (incorruptibility). The departure found expression not only in Cao Cao's casting off of the old hereditary system and advocating a merit-based promotion policy but also in his poetry of self-awareness, capturing what a poet saw, did, and aspired to accomplish as well as the consciousness of the misery of the people in ceaseless warfare. Cao Cao, along with his sons Cao Pei and Cao Zhi (Ts'ao Chih), was recognized as "Three Caos," playing a groundbreaking role in Jian An literature. For the first time, Chinese literature began to reveal the writer's own voice, expressed at his discretion, without external direction.

—Charles Xingzhong Li

FURTHER READING

Ch'en, Shou-yi. *Chinese Literature: A Historical Introduction*. New York: Ronald Press, 1961. An account of Chinese literature from a Chinese point of view, beginning with its earliest records and ending in the mid-twentieth century, with brief explanations of philosophical backgrounds in Chinese literary periods.

De Crespigny, Rafe. *Man from the Margin: Cao Cao and the Three Kingdoms*. Fifty-first George Ernest Morrison Lecture in Ethnology. Canberra: Australian National University, 1990. Poses and answers, from the perspective of a serious historian, the question of what it is that has made Cao Cao, his associates, his rival heroes, and the entire history of the Three Kingdoms so special.

Hall, Eleanor J. *Ancient Chinese Dynasties*. San Diego, Calif.: Lucent Books, 2000. Focuses on early Chinese civilization up to the fall of the Eastern Han Dynasty and provides a helpful time line of early Chinese dynasties and a short but useful glossary.

Mair, Victor H., ed. *The Columbia History of Chinese Literature*. New York: Columbia University Press, 2001. Contains two chapters that discuss the Jian An literary period and the novel *Romance of the Three Kingdoms:* Chapter 13, "Poetry from 200 B.C.E. to 600 C.E.," and Chapter 35, "Full-length Vernacular Fiction."

Yap, Yong, and Arthur Cotterell. *The Early Civilization of China*. New York: G. P. Putnam's Sons, 1975. An abridged account of Chinese history from earliest times (500,000 B.C.E.) up to the Yuan Dynasty (1279-1368 C.E.), illustrated by a wide range of photographs, maps, and drawings.

SEE ALSO: Ashurnasirpal II; Constantine the Great; Cyrus the Great; Piye; Sargon II.

RELATED ARTICLES in *Great Events from History: The Ancient World*: c. 5th-3d century B.C.E., Composition of *The Art of War*; 184-204 C.E., Yellow Turbans Rebellion; 220 C.E., Three Kingdoms Period Begins in China.

CASSIUS
Roman military leader

As a diehard republican, Cassius distrusted Julius Caesar's ambition to control the Roman government. With his brother-in-law Marcus Brutus and others, Cassius organized Caesar's assassination on the ides of March in 44 B.C.E.

BORN: Date unknown; probably Rome (now in Italy)
DIED: 42 B.C.E.; Philippi, Macedonia (now in Greece)
ALSO KNOWN AS: Gaius Cassius Longinus (given name)
AREAS OF ACHIEVEMENT: Government and politics, war and conquest

EARLY LIFE

Little is known about the early life of Cassius (KA-see-uhs). Because he was born into a family long prominent in Roman history, Cassius almost certainly received the traditional education of a late Roman republican aristocrat and slave owner. Plutarch credited Cassius with a fluent command of the Greek language, which was employed by most Roman aristocrats during the Hellenistic Age for all important cultural and scholarly activities. Cassius would later correspond with the gifted lawyer and rhetorician Marcus Tullius Cicero, as both men wished to preserve the republican form of government in Rome and prevent the concentration of power in the hands of a dictator or oligarchical group.

Before he became an assassin, Cassius held several important positions in the Roman government and significant military commands fighting against the Parthians. In 49 B.C.E., Cassius was tribune when civil war broke out between Julius Caesar and Pompey, and he supported Pompey. Cassius surrendered to Caesar after Pompey lost the Battle of Pharsalus in 48 B.C.E. Given Caesar's strong position, his pardon of Cassius was generous. Cassius, however, still harbored a smoldering resentment against Caesar as a would-be king of Rome.

LIFE'S WORK

Cassius was a respected military leader. He first achieved public recognition in 53 B.C.E. while serving under Marcus Crassus in his campaign against the Parthians. After surviving the Roman defeat at Carrhae, he was able to secure Syria against the Parthians by 51 B.C.E. After receiving the pardon from Caesar, Cassius enjoyed a respected public position despite the fact that Caesar and others continued to question his motives.

Despite the generosity of Caesar, Cassius became alarmed as Caesar acquired more and more governmental power. In addition, Caesar appropriated some lions that Cassius had donated to the city of Megara, and Cassius may have held a long-term grudge over this issue. For whatever reasons, Cassius organized the assassination of Caesar on March 15, 44, and he recruited Marcus Junius Brutus in order to give moral credibility to the plot. Although Cassius may have resented the fact that Caesar had given an important praetorship to Brutus instead of to him (and even Caesar had said that Cassius had been the better-qualified candidate), Cassius subordinated his own personal concerns to the political end he wished to achieve. Members of the conspiracy included Casca, one of two contemporaries named Cinna, Decimus Brutus, and Tullius Cimber. Some sources say that as many as sixty individuals were involved in the assassination plot.

Plutarch indicates that the Cnidian teacher Artemidorus may have unsuccessfully tried to warn Caesar on the day of Caesar's death, and Caesar may have held an unread written warning in his hands as he died. Initially after the murder, the conspirators had reason to believe that they had been successful in the goals they had set in the assassination of Caesar. After Caesar died, Brutus gave a successful speech explaining the reasons behind the assassination. At first, it appeared as though the conspiracy would have the political impact Cassius and his allies had desired. Although the senate promptly recognized Caesar as a god, to help appease the military veterans of his campaigns a general amnesty was declared, and Brutus and Cassius both initially received honors and politically and militarily significant posts.

While Cassius needed to have Brutus involved in the assassination plot in order to give it credibility, Brutus lacked Cassius's ability to plan ahead for Roman government after the death of Caesar. Brutus foolishly insisted that the conspirators spare Marc Antony, whose funeral oration for Caesar turned the bulk of public opinion against the conspirators, particularly when the crowds learned that Caesar's will had left a bequest to every Roman citizen. Popular anger led to the murder of the Cinna who had not been involved in the conspiracy.

The conspirators thus found themselves increasingly isolated in Italy. As a result, Brutus departed for Macedonia and Cassius for Syria, where he had earlier successful experience as a Roman general and hoped to rally support. Cassius put his military prowess to efficient use, and in 43 B.C.E. he defeated an army led by Dolabella, whom Marc Antony had sent east to oppose him.

Despite his military successes and the addition to his army of troops brought by Brutus, who joined him, Cassius found himself in a difficult situation in 42 B.C.E., when Marc Antony and Caesar's great-nephew Octavian marched east to oppose Brutus and Cassius. Cassius attempted to confront the military test he faced at the Battle of Philippi with courage. As a convinced Epicurean, Cassius apparently distrusted the influence of the senses, especially when individuals were under stress. According to Plutarch's account, the more rational Cassius reassured Brutus when Brutus claimed to have seen an evil spirit that threatened to meet him at Philippi. Unlike Brutus, Cassius did not believe in spirits; at least, he doubted their power to affect the living and take on a human appearance.

At Philippi, Antony and Octavian had twenty-eight legions to oppose nineteen legions under the command of the co-conspirators. Brutus and Cassius faced a difficult military situation, and Cassius wished to postpone battle in order to take advantage of his troops' superior supplies. Brutus and Cassius did not consider their situation hopeless when they parted to assume their respective battle commands, although they decided that they would kill themselves if they were defeated. Miscalculation played a large role in the fact that Cassius lay dead at the end of the battle, having committed suicide by running on the sword he had used to kill Caesar. For many years, Cassius's Parthian freedman Pindarus had been pledged to assist in Cassius's suicide if requested, and Cassius decided to die when he thought, erroneously, that the initial battle had gone as badly for Brutus as it had for him.

Because he survived Cassius, Brutus performed the last rites for his co-conspirator, having his body wrapped and sent to Thaos for burial. A somber Brutus mourned Cassius as a man whose like would not be seen again, and Cassius's death probably marked a dramatic turning point in Roman history. The republican form of government, which had followed the overthrow of the early monarchy by a purported ancestor of Brutus, gave way to a more efficient Imperial form of government.

While no verifiable statement survives of the political ideals that brought Cassius to Philippi, a speech attrib-

The assassination of Julius Caesar. (F. R. Niglutsch)

uted by Appian to Cassius does. In the speech, Cassius reviewed the events of the preceding three years and honored the bond between soldiers and their leaders. Cassius claimed that the tyrannicides held no personal enmity for Caesar but possessed a justified concern for the preservation of Roman republican institutions.

SIGNIFICANCE

In modern terms, Cassius might be compared to senators who aspire to the presidency and never quite achieve their goal. He sincerely believed in the traditional republican ideals that had governed the Roman Republic for centuries, despite the fact that the acquisition of an empire logically necessitated changes in Rome's governmental structure to govern unruly subject peoples. With Cassius's suicide, the old Roman Republic was doomed. His ally Brutus died three weeks later, as Brutus followed Cassius's example in taking his own life. Despite the fact that Octavian, later Augustus, represented the future of Rome, Cassius was not forgotten. Among the ancient historians, however, only Appian showed respect for him as a political as well as a military leader.

Cassius's namesake descendant in the following century, who became a noted legal scholar, was exiled from Rome by Nero for his devotion to outmoded republican ideals, although he managed to die peacefully in Rome under the more moderate Vespasian. In later centuries, those seeking to justify assassination often turned to the example of Brutus and Cassius, although Cassius never obtained the respect widely granted Brutus. William Shakespeare's fictional description of Cassius as a "lean and hungry" man has remained the characteristic view of Cassius held by later generations.

—*Susan A. Stussy*

FURTHER READING

Cicero, Marcus Tullius. *Selected Letters*. Translated, with an introduction, by D. R. H. Shackleton Bailey. New York: Penguin Books, 1986. Cassius and his co-conspirator Marcus Brutus corresponded with Cicero. They shared a similar devotion to traditional Roman republican ideals and an aversion to Julius Caesar. Cicero approved of the assassination of Caesar; he did, however, regret that Caesar's assassins had left the apparatus necessary to create a monarchy intact. A January 45 B.C.E. letter from Cassius to Cicero reveals the former's basic philosophical convictions. In a cogent expression of Epicurean philosophy, Cassius holds that one cannot attain pleasure without living rightly and justly.

Dio Cassius. *The Roman History: The Reign of Augustus*. Translated by Ian Scott-Kilvert. New York: Penguin Books, 1987. In this history, Dio Cassius covers the period immediately after the deaths of Brutus and Cassius. He claims that Agrippa threatened Octavian (Augustus) with the fate of Julius Caesar unless he proceeded toward monarchy. Agrippa warned Octavian that he would find his own Brutus and Cassius unless he moved resolutely to consolidate power.

Plutarch. *Fall of the Roman Republic: Six Lives*. Translated by Rex Warner. New York: Penguin Books, 1981. Plutarch discusses Cassius in his life of Julius Caesar. In this selection, Plutarch has Caesar describe both Brutus and Cassius as "pale and thin." In his sketch of Caesar, Plutarch refers his readers to his "Life of Brutus." He also stresses that Cassius employed the dagger he had used against Caesar to kill himself and discusses the many supernatural signs that purportedly surrounded the death of Caesar.

_____. *Makers of Rome: Nine Lives*. Translated, with an introduction, by Ian Scott-Kilvert. New York: Dorset Press, 1985. This selection includes the life of Brutus, the respected co-conspirator Cassius recruited to assassinate Caesar. According to Plutarch's account, Brutus hated the concentration of power in Caesar's hands, and Cassius hated Caesar. Plutarch also describes Cassius's suicide at Philippi and how it may have been prompted by poor eyesight and error.

Shakespeare, William. *The Tragedy of Julius Caesar, with Related Readings*. Edited by Dom Saliani, Chris Ferguson, and Tim Scott. Mason, Ohio: South-Western College, 1997. A dramatic portrayal of Caesar's assassination. Shakespeare's account was based on Plutarch and perhaps on Appian. In addition, Shakespeare may have consulted portrayals of the same events by other Elizabethan dramatists. Shakespeare presents Brutus as noble in his motivations for tyrannicide but implies that Cassius was correctly described by Caesar as "lean and hungry" and motivated by ambition.

SEE ALSO: Marc Antony; Augustus; Marcus Junius Brutus; Julius Caesar; Cicero; Epicurus.

RELATED ARTICLES in *Great Events from History: The Ancient World*: 51 B.C.E., Cicero Writes *De republica*; 51-30 B.C.E., Cleopatra VII, Last of Ptolemies, Reigns; 46 B.C.E., Establishment of the Julian Calendar; 43-42 B.C.E., Second Triumvirate Enacts Proscriptions; September 2, 31 B.C.E., Battle of Actium; 27-23 B.C.E., Completion of the Augustan Settlement.

CATILINE
Roman statesman

In an attempt to overthrow the Roman government in 63 B.C.E., Catiline led an unsuccessful conspiracy.

BORN: c. 108 B.C.E.; place unknown
DIED: Early January, 62 B.C.E.; near Pistoria, Etruria (now Pistoia, Italy)
ALSO KNOWN AS: Lucius Sergius Catilina (full name)
AREA OF ACHIEVEMENT: Government and politics

EARLY LIFE
Modern understanding of the life and career of Lucius Sergius Catilina, or Catiline (CA-tuh-lin), is hampered by a lack of reliable historical sources. Two prominent Roman authors recount many details of his life, yet the integrity of their comments is suspect. The Roman politician Cicero wrote of Catiline in several speeches, vilifying his political rival. The historian Sallust provides important information about Catiline, but his account is hostile. For Sallust, Catiline was the embodiment of Rome's moral decay. Despite these problems, however, modern scholarship has pieced together the main details of Catiline's career.

Catiline was born to an aristocratic family in approximately the year 108 B.C.E. Although his ancestors included prominent politicians and distinguished military leaders, in recent years his family had fallen into obscurity. Little is know of his parents or his childhood, other than a suggestion that his father had to face financial difficulties.

The first public mention of Catiline occurs in 89 B.C.E. when he served in the army of Gnaeus Pompeius Strabo. Like many other young Roman aristocrats, Catiline served as a junior officer in order to receive military experience, normally a prerequisite for a successful political career. Among his fellow officers were Strabo's son, Pompey, who would go on to become one of the preeminent generals in Roman history, and Cicero, who would later contend with Catiline for political office. As one of the two Roman consuls for the year 89 B.C.E., Strabo led a successful campaign on Italian cities rebelling against the domination of Rome.

Catiline's activities for the next several years are uncertain, but he reappears in 83 B.C.E., when he supported Sulla in his confrontation with the senate. As a lieutenant in Sulla's army, Catiline apparently shared the general's propensity toward violence, participating in the systematic assassinations of Sulla's opponents. Various authors provide details about Catiline's activities, but their com-

ments cannot always be accepted as credible. One commonly accepted story indicates that he murdered several individuals, most notably Marcus Marius Gratidianus, a relative of Cicero and perhaps his own brother-in-law. Catiline is also said to have decapitated Gratidianus and carried his head throughout the city before delivering it to Sulla at the temple of Apollo. Other authors claimed that Catiline murdered his own brother.

In addition to persistent tales of the youthful Catiline's eagerness for violence, sources provide several stories about his sexual indiscretions. He was accused of violating the chastity of the Vestal Virgin Fabia, the half sister of Cicero's wife (Fabia was brought to trial in 73 B.C.E. and acquitted of the charge; it is unknown whether Catiline was also brought to trial). Catiline was also accused of marrying his own daughter, the product of an adulterous affair. This young woman was probably Aurelia Orestilla, around whom a second story was told. Orestilla refused to marry Catiline because she did not want to live with a grownup stepson (the product of Catiline's previous marriage). Consequently, Catiline is said to have murdered his son to win her hand.

LIFE'S WORK
Despite the scandalous stories that surrounded him, Catiline pursued an active political career in his adulthood. Along with other ambitious Roman senators, he aspired to a series of political offices that would culminate in his being chosen as one of the year's two consuls. This goal became a directing force in his life. After serving abroad in the early 70's, in 69 B.C.E. he was elected praetor, one of the eight officials who oversaw the law courts in Rome. After he completed his one-year term, he followed tradition by leaving the city to rule as governor in one of the provinces conquered by Rome. For the following two years he remained in northern Africa, ensuring Roman interests in the region and preparing to stand for the consulship in 66 B.C.E.

Even while he was serving as governor in Africa, delegates from his province traveled to Rome and accused Catiline of extortion. When he returned to declare his candidacy, charges were brought against him for his behavior, and election officials barred him from standing as consul. He stood trial and was eventually acquitted, having received the support of several eminent politicians who spoke on his behalf. However, his acquittal came too late for him to stand as consul in the following year, so he set his sights on the election in 64 B.C.E. Some ancient sources suggest that Catiline was a member of a conspiracy in 66 and 65 B.C.E. that planned to murder the consuls, but this charge is uncertain and probably the result of his rivals spreading stories about his behavior.

As Catiline planned his campaign for the consulship, he surrounded himself with a retinue of supporters and bodyguards. According to Sallust and Cicero, many of these were young men easily seduced by the attention and gifts that Catiline showered on them. It is also likely at this time that Catiline received the covert support of two influential politicians. Marcus Crassus, a former consul, used his exceptional wealth to fund Catiline's campaign; Julius Caesar used his growing reputation among the senators and the people to support his candidacy. The two men undoubtedly expected that Catiline, if he were elected consul, would support legislation benefiting their interests. The election proved to be extremely close, with Cicero being elected the senior consul and an aristocrat named Gaius Antonius narrowly defeating Catiline for the second position.

As Catiline prepared to campaign for the consulship in the following year, he was charged with murder stemming from his actions while supporting Sulla twenty years earlier. He was acquitted in time to stand for the consulship in 63 B.C.E., but by then he had lost the patronage of Crassus and Caesar. Nevertheless, he was confident of his chances. He spent lavishly on bribes and anticipated support among the lower classes because of his calls for agrarian reform and debt relief. However, his arrogant behavior alienated the senate and greatly frightened the consul Cicero. After Cicero spoke out against him, the senate postponed the normal July elections until August or September in order to take additional precautions against any actions that Catiline might take. Once the election day arrived, Catiline was convincingly defeated. Now believing that he had failed in his last opportunity to achieve the consulship, and suffering from a great amount of debt, Catiline resolved to overthrow the government through violent measures.

He courted the support of dissatisfied fellow senators and wealthy businessmen who were eager for political change. He proposed to instigate a widespread insurrection in Rome and Italy by taking advantage of dissatisfaction among the masses, many of whom were overwhelmed by debt and demanded relief. Catiline planned to raise an army among the impoverished veterans of Sulla in the countryside and to march on Rome as conspirators in the city revolted. Few details are known of what he intended to accomplish after he came to power,

other than his intention to cancel debts, proscribe his enemies, and seize their property. Unfortunately, even the ultimate political objectives of Catiline are uncertain: Many modern scholars feel that he merely wanted to seize power for himself, while others claim that he was a true populist bent on providing relief for citizens overwhelmed by debt.

Through September and October the conspiracy proceeded as Catiline dispatched men into surrounding villages in order to recruit an army; he and others focused on gaining support in Rome itself. Rumors about the conspiracy soon began to circulate throughout the city and by the middle of October news reached Rome that an army was being raised in the region of Etruria. On October 21 the senate, fearing Cicero's dire predictions about Catiline's intentions, passed emergency measures that granted the consul special powers to protect the state. Catiline was formally charged under a law dealing with violence, but no solid evidence could be brought forth, and so he was able to continue his preparations. Cicero, however, remained vigilant and tried to gather more information on the conspiracy.

Early in the morning of November 7, a pair of conspirators unsuccessfully attempted to assassinate Cicero at his home. The next day the consul delivered a dramatic speech in the senate, publicly accusing Catiline of treason. That evening Catiline fled Rome, joining the rebel army that had been raised in Etruria, and began making his final preparations for an open rebellion. However, events began overtaking his plan, and the conspiracy quickly unraveled. In the middle of November he was declared a public enemy, and Cicero prepared defenses throughout Rome. On December 3 the consul arrested several conspirators who confessed and provided evidence about Catline's activities; documents seized on the arrested men confirmed their story. After a short debate over punishment, the conspirators were executed on December 5.

Throughout December Catiline prepared his forces outside Rome. When news reached him that the conspiracy had been unmasked and that Cicero had firm control of Rome, he decided to withdraw his army to Gaul (modern-day France). However, loyal forces soon boxed him in at the foot of the Apennines, and, though greatly outnumbered, he was forced into battle. In early January, near the city of Pistoria (modern Pistoia, Italy), his army was defeated, and he was killed. According to the historian Sallust, at the end of the battle the dying Catiline was discovered far in advance of his own troops, surrounded by the bodies of those he had slain, defiant to his last breath.

SIGNIFICANCE

Although Catiline's quest to become consul failed, his career and bold attempt to overthrow the government have remained matters of great interest among historians and classicists. According to Cicero and Sallust, Catiline was a paradox. Both men acknowledged that he possessed remarkable talents, yet his actions were often monstrous. For Sallust, Catiline's career could be explained by the collapse of traditional moral standards that had begun in the previous century once Rome had vanquished its Carthaginian rivals. According to Sallust, Catiline represented a breed of man corrupted by the prosperity engendered by security and wealth. Among modern scholars, he is closely identified with the political competition and violence that ultimately undermined Rome's republican government.

—*David Christiansen*

FURTHER READING

Everitt, Anthony. *Cicero: The Life and Times of Rome's Greatest Politician*. New York: Random House, 2001. Everitt recounts Catiline's life primarily as it pertained to the consulship of Cicero and the conspiracy.

Gruen, Erich. *The Last Generation of the Roman Republic*. Berkeley: University of California Press, 1995. Gruen's account of the last years of the Roman Republic provides a context for understanding the career and motivations of Catiline. Although Catiline is often not the exclusive focus of Gruen's comments, this book successfully presents the turbulent political world in which Catiline was active.

Hutchinson, Lester. *The Conspiracy of Catiline*. New York: Barnes and Noble, 1967. Hutchinson develops a picture of Catiline's activities, starting with his relationship with Sulla. Unlike most modern scholars, he accepts Sallust's claim that Catiline began planning his conspiracy in 64 B.C.E.

Marshal, B. A. *A Historical Commentary on Asconius*. Columbia: University of Missouri Press, 1985. Marshall provides many details of Catiline's career. Extensive references are given to all the ancient authors who mentioned Catiline.

Syme, Ronald. *Sallust*. Reprint. Berkeley: University of California Press, 2002. This book offers one of the best summaries of Catiline's entire career, including his poorly documented early life. Syme excels in distinguishing between rumor and actual events.

SEE ALSO: Julius Caesar; Cicero; Pompey the Great; Sallust; Strabo; Lucius Cornelius Sulla.

RELATED ARTICLES in *Great Events from History: The Ancient World*: 264-225 B.C.E., First Punic War; 218-201 B.C.E., Second Punic War; 180 B.C.E., Establishment of the *Cursus honorum*; 149-146 B.C.E., Third Punic War; 73-71 B.C.E., Spartacus Leads Slave Revolt; Late 63-January 62 B.C.E., Catiline Conspiracy; 51 B.C.E., Cicero Writes *De republica*; 27-23 B.C.E., Completion of the Augustan Settlement.

CATO THE CENSOR
Roman administrator and orator

Through his public example, the offices he served, and his writings, Cato advocated an ideal of a powerful, prosperous state populated with self-reliant, active citizens.

BORN: 234 B.C.E.; Tusculum, Latium (now in Italy)
DIED: 149 B.C.E.; Rome (now in Italy)
ALSO KNOWN AS: Marcus Porcius Cato (given name); Cato the Elder
AREA OF ACHIEVEMENT: Government and politics

EARLY LIFE

Marcus Porcius Cato (KAY-toh) was born in Tusculum, about fifteen miles outside Rome. Little is known about his family except that his father, Marcus, and great-grandfather Cato were well-respected soldiers. The name Cato, meaning "accomplished," was given to a *novus homo* (new man) who came to public attention by his own achievements rather than by connection to a distinguished family. Young Cato spent his youth on an estate in the Sabine territory, where he learned farming, viticulture, and other agricultural skills.

When Cato was seventeen, the Carthaginian general Hannibal invaded Italy and defeated several Roman armies, inflicting huge losses. More than fifty thousand Romans died at the Battle of Cannae in 216 B.C.E. Cato enlisted soon after Cannae and served with distinction for more than a decade. He fought in major battles in Sicily and Italy, including the siege of Syracuse and the defeat of Hasdrubal (Hannibal's brother) at Metaurus in 207. By the time Hannibal fled Italy and Carthage surrendered, around 201, Cato's personality and career had been shaped. He had proved heroic and fearless in combat. He carried an implacable hatred for Carthage. He displayed leadership, being elected a military tribune responsible for the soldiers' welfare in and out of battle.

Cato now entered public life and held a series of elective offices. In 204 he became quaestor, the official charged with watching over public expenditures. In this capacity he accompanied the army of Scipio Africanus in its attack on Carthaginian soil. In 199 Cato became a plebeian aedile, one who administered public buildings, streets, temples, and the marketplace. A year later, Cato was one of four praetors chosen; praetor was a more significant post that included the power to dispense justice and to command an army. Cato spent his praetorship as governor of Sardinia, where he gained a reputation for honest and frugal administration.

Important patrons as well as ordinary voters were attracted to Cato and readily supported his advancing career. The Greek historian Plutarch described Cato at this time as a man with a ruddy complexion, gray eyes, and unusual public speaking skills. Cato's quick mind—his knack for striking analogies and turns of phrase—and fearless attitude made him a successful orator, valued as an ally and feared as an opponent.

LIFE'S WORK

Cato's election as consul in 195 began a period of forty-six years during which he exerted significant influence in both domestic politics and foreign affairs. Cato's leadership coincided with a period of profound change in Roman manners at home and in Roman policies toward other world powers. By the time of Cato's death, Rome had defeated its Imperial rivals, conquering Greece and Macedonia and destroying Carthage, burning the city to the ground. Military and political supremacy brought Rome economic supremacy, and great wealth poured into a country where simplicity and austerity were traditional. Wealth became the basis of a leisured culture that looked to Greece for social values—a culture more intellectual, aesthetic, and self-indulgent than traditional Rome. None of these changes occurred quickly or without dispute. Cato participated in the major controversies of the era, speculating on whether Rome could dominate other nations without exploiting them, whether Romans could maintain a work ethic amid unprecedented luxury, and whether Greek attitudes would supplant Roman ones.

Cato served as one of the two consuls appointed annually. Consuls were the senior Roman magistrates who ex-

Cato the Censor. (Library of Congress)

ecuted the senate's will in political and military affairs. Soon after he took office, Cato went to Spain to lead the effort to subdue several tribes in rebellion since 197. Drilling inexperienced troops rigorously, Cato prepared them so effectively that they routed a veteran Spanish force at Emporiae. Cato showed mercy to the survivors and successfully induced other rebel groups and cities to surrender. On his return to a triumph in Rome, Cato boasted that he had captured more towns than he had spent days in Spain. Soon afterward he married a senator's daughter, a sign that a *novus homo* was now acceptable to the aristocracy.

Four years later, Cato went to Greece as military tribune with the army advancing against Antiochus, Rome's chief threat in Greece and Hannibal's protector. The army's march was blocked at the pass of Thermopylae (where three centuries before, Spartan troops had held off invading Persians) until Cato led a cohort over rocks and crags to take the enemy rearguard by surprise. Cato claimed as much credit as Glabrio, the Roman commander, for the successful campaign. For years afterward, the two were political rivals.

In 189, Cato ran for the office of censor but was defeated. A censor ranked just below consul: He oversaw public morals, carried out the census, selected new members for the senate, expelled unfit senators, and conducted religious services. Previously, Cato had involved himself in important public debates about morality and ethics, such as the controversies surrounding the Oppian law and the Junian law. In the first, Cato argued for continuing a ban on ostentatious displays of wealth; in the second, he opposed repealing interest-rate limits. Already he was known as a champion of austerity and self-discipline in financial matters, both for the individual and for the state.

At the next election for censor in 184, Cato triumphed. Immediately he implemented the stern, rigorous platform on which he had campaigned. Though his program involved him in lawsuits for years to come, his supporters regarded his censorship as a landmark effort to reverse a perceived laxness in public standards. Cato and his cocensor expelled seven senators for unfitness, imposed a heavy tax on luxury goods, demolished private buildings encroaching on government property, fined those who neglected farms or vineyards, and renegotiated state contracts with private suppliers to reach better deals. Though contemporaries stressed the stringency of his actions, it is important to note that he executed his duties meticulously. He was careful to respect the letter as well as the spirit of the laws. For Cato, the primary goal was to see Rome thrive and prosper. Unlike many aristocratic Romans, Cato believed that public prosperity did not result from exploiting individuals—and he also believed that individuals ought not to thrive at public expense.

Certain individuals resented Cato's stern censorship and became enemies. Before his death he fought at least forty-four indictments and suits filed against him; none is recorded as successful. Each accusation became an occasion for Cato to display his well-honed oratorical skills, thereby leaving a rich rhetorical legacy for later generations. Cato took the unusual and self-confident step of publishing his speeches.

Though never elected censor again, Cato used his position in the senate to defend high standards and accountability for public officials. He prosecuted a provincial governor in 171 for manipulating corn prices; twenty years later, while in his eighties, Cato spoke against a special envoy and another governor who used their posts for profit. In 169, Cato led the supporters of the Voconian law to keep inheritances concentrated rather than wastefully fragmented. In the same year, he argued against a triumph for a general whose troops complained of cruel treatment. In 153, Cato supported a proposal to prevent a consul from serving a second term, lest a man find public office too profitable to do without.

Cato exercised leadership in the senate through his oratory and among the educated class through his writings. Some scholars call Cato the father of Latin prose literature because of the volume and influence of his writing. The major works, which exist only in fragments (except for the treatise on agriculture), are *Ad filium*, a compendium of precepts on practical issues written for his son; *De re militari*, a manual of military training; *De agricultura* (c. 160 B.C.E.; *On Agriculture*, 1913), a how-to guide for managing a prosperous farm; and *Origines* (168-149 B.C.E.), a seven-book history of Rome. They are didactic works, displaying common sense rather than imagination. They suggest, however, that Cato possessed a reflective side to complement his pragmatic side: He addressed what to do and why it was worth doing. His literary works embody the moral vision of his censorship and his oratory: Knowledgeable, self-reliant individuals best lead the austere, just state.

In foreign policy, Cato seems to have advocated the restrained display of Rome's unchallenged military power. After victory in the Third Macedonian War (172-167), Cato sided with those eager to see Macedonia a free ally rather than a subjugated client state. He consistently argued that smaller competitor nations and reluctant allies be treated leniently.

The one exception to Cato's usual moderation made him legendary. All of his life, Cato feared the resurgence of Carthage. Leading a senatorial delegation to Africa in 152, he saw signs there of economic and military recovery. Henceforward, Cato argued that Rome must destroy the ancient rival before it grew powerful. *Carthago delenda est* ("Carthage must be destroyed") became the injunction repeatedly brought to the senate. War broke out in 149; Carthage was razed in 146. Cato died soon after the declaration of war, relieved that, this time, war's devastation would occur on enemy soil.

SIGNIFICANCE

Because Cato the Censor's insistence that Carthage be destroyed dominated his last years, it has often been seen as the climactic event of his career. Without a doubt Cato was influential in securing war, and without a doubt that war changed the course of Roman history by extending Rome's dominion into northern Africa. Remembering Cato as a spokesman of steely, merciless national self-interest was easy for subsequent generations. It was—and is—too narrow an estimate of the man.

Cato's memorable reign as censor was also easy to recall, so easy that it gave the name by which history calls him. Rome reigned supreme for nearly six hundred years after Cato's death. Its life span as a great state encompassed extensive conquest, civil war, the transition from Republic to Empire, the acquisition of incalculable wealth, and profound social change. In times of crisis, many citizens remembered Cato. He was an emblem of personal self-control and public austerity. He knew the difference between public good and private welfare, between national prosperity and enervating materialism, between commonsensical good and rationalized failings. In subsequent neoclassical periods—Italy in the sixteenth century, England in the late seventeenth century, France and the United States in the late eighteenth century—Cato the Censor was a model of political leadership. He represented the highest civic virtue, the leader who rallied citizens by example and by eloquence to identify the public good with wise, orderly, and restrained government.

As dramatic as Cato's censorship was in combating obvious abuses, his time in office was one brief episode in a career. One must remember his lifetime of service to a civic ideal. He was not like the Old Testament prophets, men who lived obscurely until some crisis called them from obscurity to lead their people from darkness into light. His was not a lonely voice crying in the wilderness. He provided constant leadership in articulating a vision of the good state that, for the span of his life, most Romans held in common.

—Robert M. Otten

FURTHER READING

Astin, Alan E. *Cato the Censor*. New York: Oxford University Press, 1978. This study analyzes Cato as soldier, politician, orator, and writer. Astin admires his subject's rugged individualism and active public service. Astin disputes the image of Cato as a puritanical traditionalist and asserts that he is important for much more than his final act of destroying Carthage.

Livy, Titus. *The History of Rome from Its Foundations*. Translated by Audrey de Sélincourt. New York: Penguin Books, 2002. The section of Livy's landmark history called "Rome and the Mediterranean" describes Rome's competition with Macedonia after the Second Punic War with Carthage. It covers the period from 210 to 167, during which Cato was consul, censor, and senator. Working from Cato's own writings, now lost, Livy presents vivid accounts of Cato's campaign in Spain, his support for the Oppian law, and his term as censor.

Plutarch. *The Lives of the Noble Grecians and Romans*. Translated by John Dryden. New York: Modern Library, 1992. Writing as a moralist, rather than a biographer, Plutarch analyzes the strengths and weaknesses of Cato's character. The moralist praises Cato for old-fashioned virtues of temperance, public service, and frank speaking but faults him for avariciousness. By selling aging slaves and urging others to farm for profit, Plutarch charges, Cato dehumanized the social fabric he tried to save.

Scullard, H. H. *Roman Politics, 220-150 B.C.* 1951. Reprint. Westport, Conn.: Greenwood Press, 1982. This scholarly study documents the competition for political power between the son of an aristocratic family, such as Scipio Africanus, and the *novus homo*, such as Cato. Scullard provides detailed information about Cato's duties as censor, consul, and senator. He makes clear who supported Cato's policies, who opposed them, and why contemporaries took one side or the other.

SEE ALSO: Antiochus the Great; Cato the Younger; Hannibal.

CATO THE YOUNGER
Roman philosopher

Cato the Younger was a Stoic philosopher who represented the conservative Senatorial Party in Roman politics. He sought to preserve the dying Roman Republic at a time of rising military dictatorships.

BORN: 95 B.C.E.; Rome (now in Italy)
DIED: 46 B.C.E.; Utica, Africa (now in Tunisia)
ALSO KNOWN AS: Cato Uticensis
AREAS OF ACHIEVEMENT: Government and politics, philosophy

EARLY LIFE

Cato (KAY-toh) the Younger, also known as Cato Uticensis from the place of his death, was born in Rome in 95 B.C.E. He was the great-grandson of Cato the Censor, who remained an inspiration for the younger Cato throughout his life. Cato the Younger was orphaned at an early age and grew up in the household of his maternal uncle Marcus Livius Drusus. Cato idealized the early Republic. He cultivated the old Roman virtues of simplicity and frugality, in contrast to the materialism of his own day. He studied the philosophy of Stoicism, from which he came to believe that true freedom comes from within. According to the Stoics, the human body was merely a shell, and whatever happened to it was without consequence in the great world order.

Cato was known for the austerity of his life. He accustomed his body to labor and hard exercise. He traveled on foot everywhere. In taking journeys with friends who rode on horseback, he would remain on foot, conversing with one, then another, along the way. He bore illnesses with patience. He seldom laughed. He learned the art of oratory and spoke in a deep, full voice without refinements.

Cato first saw military service in 72 B.C.E., serving in the ranks against the slave revolt led by Spartacus. He distinguished himself to the extent that his commander wished to bestow a prize on him, but Cato refused, saying that he did no more than others. In 67-66 B.C.E. he served as a military tribune in Macedonia. As commander of a legion, he shared the hardships with his troops. He ate the same food, wore the same clothing, and marched on foot with the soldiers in the ranks, even when his staff rode on horseback. After completing his term of military service, Cato traveled through the cities of Asia and brought back the Stoic philosopher Athenodorus with him when he returned to Rome.

LIFE'S WORK

At the outset of his political career, Cato was elected to the office of *quaestor,* or finance minister, in 64 B.C.E. During his year in office, he kept exact records of accounts, collected old debts, and dismissed and prosecuted clerks in the treasury who for years had been stealing from the public funds. The following year, Cato won the election for tribune. As tribune-elect, he made a powerful speech in the senate denouncing the Catilinarian conspirators, whose plot to overthrow the government had been uncovered by the consul Cicero. Cato's speech, which called for the death penalty for the conspirators, carried the day despite a plea by Julius Caesar for a lesser punishment. In the same year, Cato prosecuted the consul-elect Lucinius Murena for bribery in winning the election to the consulship for 62 B.C.E., but Murena was acquitted.

In subsequent years, Cato became the leader of the conservative senatorial faction that opposed any threat to the established order. When Pompey the Great returned from the East at the end of 62 B.C.E. seeking ratification for his treaties and land for his veterans, Cato rigidly opposed Pompey's requests. Cato also prevented the passage of a bill that would have revised the tax codes for Asia. In opposing this measure, Cato antagonized both the equestrian class that stood to profit by the new tax revisions as well as Marcus Licinius Crassus, who had invested heavily in the publican tax companies. The equestrians withdrew their support from the Senatorial Party, and Cicero's hope that the equestrian class would act in harmony with the Senatorial Party was destroyed.

When Caesar returned from Spain in 60 B.C.E. seeking a triumph, he asked permission to run for the consulship in absentia while he remained with the army outside the city. The senate refused, with Cato speaking all day to prevent approval. Caesar gave up his triumph and entered the city as an ordinary citizen to stand for the consulship. Pompey, Caesar, and Crassus now joined forces, and the First Triumvirate was born. The three men agreed to work together toward their common goals.

With the support of Pompey and Crassus, Caesar won the consulship for the year 59 B.C.E. Caesar soon paid off his political debts with proposals for the ratification of Pompey's treaties in the east, a land-distribution bill for Pompey's veterans and some of the poor in Rome, and a revision of the tax codes for Asia. Cato vigorously opposed all these measures but was unable to block their passage in the Assembly. When the Assembly passed a bill giving Caesar the military command of Cisalpine Gaul and Illyricum for five years, Cato protested so strongly that Caesar had him arrested for a brief time.

In 58 B.C.E., the Triumvirate decided to rid themselves of Cato by securing his appointment as commissioner to oversee the annexation of Cyprus and to reconcile two opposing factions in Byzantium. At the time, Cyprus was ruled as a client state of Rome by King Ptolemy, the brother of Ptolemy XII, pharaoh of Egypt. Cato realized that he was being relegated to the backwaters of Roman politics but accepted the assignment out of a sense of duty. He was given only two secretaries and neither a ship nor money for the undertaking. Cato first traveled to Byzantium, where he brought about a peaceful settlement between conflicting parties. At Cyprus, the problem was resolved when King Ptolemy committed suicide. Cato supervised the inventory of the royal treasures and sent a precious cargo worth seven thousand talents of silver back to Rome.

Cato returned to Rome in 56 B.C.E. In the years that followed, he continued to oppose the political ambitions of the Triumvirate but with little success. In 54 B.C.E., Cato was elected to the office of praetor, or judge. During his one-year term, he rendered his decisions from the praetor's bench with fairness and integrity. In 51 B.C.E., he stood for the consulship but was unsuccessful; he refused to resort to bribery or other corrupt practices that had become part of Roman politics.

When the civil war between Pompey and Caesar began in 49 B.C.E., Cato sided with Pompey as the best hope for saving the Republic. Pompey had been moving closer to the senate since the death of Crassus during an unsuccessful invasion of Parthia in 53 B.C.E. Cato now viewed Pompey as a counterforce to the growing power of Caesar in Gaul. As Caesar swept down the Italian peninsula, Pompey and the senatorial forces retreated to Greece. Cato was entrusted with the defense of Sicily but was forced to withdraw from the island after the arrival of Caesarean forces. Cato joined Pompey in Greece and was with him at the Battle of Dyrrhachium in western Greece, where Caesar's forces were repulsed.

Pompey followed Caesar into the interior of Greece but was defeated at the Battle of Pharsalus in 48 B.C.E. Cato was not present at Pharsalus. He was given command of fifteen cohorts and garrisoned Dyrrhachium, which held Pompey's weapons and stores as well as the civilians in Pompey's camp.

When news of Pompey's defeat reached Cato, he brought his forces to the island of Corcyra (modern-day Corfu), where he joined Pompey's fleet. Correctly surmising that Pompey had fled to North Africa, Cato sailed with ten thousand troops and landed at Cyrene, only to learn of Pompey's death in Egypt. Cato now marched his troops westward through the Libyan deserts and eventually reached Utica, where he joined forces with other remnants of Pompey's army under Metellus Scipio, Titus Labienus, and King Juba of Numidia. As proconsul, Metellus Scipio was given command of the Pompeian forces. While Cato commanded the camp at Utica, Scipio met Caesar at the Battle of Thapsus in 46 B.C.E. and suffered a severe defeat.

Cato remained unperturbed when the news of Scipio's defeat reached Utica. He readied ships in the harbor and made certain that those who might wish to flee would be able to do so. With Caesar and his army only a day's march away, Cato spent the evening at dinner engaging in philosophic discussions with his friends. After dinner, he retired to his room and read Plato's *Phaedōn*, on the immortality of the soul. When he saw that his sword had been removed from its usual place near his bed, he called his servants and ordered that it be returned. Cato then slept for a few hours. In the early hours, before dawn he rose and suddenly stabbed himself with his sword in the abdomen. His servants heard him fall; entering the room, they found him still alive, lying in blood with his intestines protruding from his stomach. A physician pushed back the intestines, which were not pierced, and bandaged the wound. When left alone again, Cato removed the bandages, pulled open his wound, and died soon afterward; he was forty-eight years old. When Caesar arrived the next day, he grieved that Cato had deprived him of the glory of granting a pardon to his defeated adversary.

SIGNIFICANCE

Cato is remembered as a man of principle whose honesty and integrity were unquestioned in an age conspicuous for its political corruption and opportunism. He idealized the virtues of the early Republic and dedicated his life to preserving those traditions and values on which the Republic was founded. Like the ancient fathers of the early Republic, he found monarchy to be an abomination. Ironically, Cato's uncompromising opposition to the early demands of Pompey, Crassus, and Caesar had the effect of driving the three of them together to form the First Triumvirate. In the years that followed, Cato remained an obstructionist but could no longer control the sequence of events. When Cato died at Utica, the Republic died with him. Julius Caesar emerged as the sole power of the Roman world, but Cato's life and the manner of his death became an inspiration for later generations of republicans.

—*Norman Sobiesk*

FURTHER READING

Gruen, Erich S. *The Last Generation of the Roman Republic.* Berkeley: University of California Press, 1995. A highly interpretive study that seeks to show the continuity of Roman political institutions into the age of Cicero. Valuable insights on the life of Cato the Younger in the context of the historical background. Useful notes and bibliography.

Plutarch. *Lives of the Noble Greeks and Romans.* Translated by John Dryden. New York: The Modern Library, 1992. The indispensable primary source for the study of Cato the Younger. Plutarch's life of Cato provides a detailed narrative on Cato's life. Plutarch includes numerous anecdotes that serve to highlight Cato's character.

Scullard, H. H. *From the Gracchi to Nero.* New York: Routledge, 1988. Useful for the background of the last century of the Roman Republic. Highly readable and assembled with sound scholarly judgment. Numerous references to Cato the Younger and his role in Roman politics. Extensive notes, with references for additional study.

Syme, Ronald. *The Roman Revolution.* 1939. Reprint. New York: Oxford University Press, 2002. The classic study of the transformation of Roman government from an oligarchy to one-man rule. Covers the years from 60 B.C.E. to 14 C.E. Contains details of Cato's political career as the leader of the Senatorial Party.

SEE ALSO: Marcus Junius Brutus; Julius Caesar; Cato the Censor; Cicero; Pompey the Great; Spartacus.

RELATED ARTICLES in *Great Events from History: The Ancient World*: 73-71 B.C.E., Spartacus Leads Slave Revolt; Late 63-January 62 B.C.E., Catiline Conspiracy; 58-51 B.C.E., Caesar Conquers Gaul; 51 B.C.E., Cicero Writes *De republica*; 43-42 B.C.E., Second Triumvirate Enacts Proscriptions.

CATULLUS
Roman poet

Catullus was the leader of a group of poets who created a native idiom for Roman poetry. Intensely personal, epigrammatic, and more colloquial than epic or dramatic, this style of poetry set the standards for the literary achievements of the Augustan Age.

BORN: c. 85 B.C.E.; Verona, Cisalpine Gaul (now in Italy)
DIED: c. 54 B.C.E.; probably Rome (now in Italy)
ALSO KNOWN AS: Gaius Valerius Catullus (full name)
AREA OF ACHIEVEMENT: Literature

EARLY LIFE

Like most figures of Greek and Roman antiquity, Catullus (ka-TUH-luhs) provides little information about his early life, and the ancient sources add few facts. His family was prominent in Verona, which was then a part of the province of Cisalpine Gaul. They also owned a villa on the peninsula of Sirmio (modern Sermione) in the Lago di Garda, about twenty miles east of Verona. Catullus's later references to this country home reveal his deep attachment to the family seat. Suetonius's biography of Julius Caesar records that Catullus's father was prominent enough to entertain Caesar during the latter's governorship of that province in the early 50's B.C.E.

Although his views about family ties were firmly traditional, Catullus makes no reference to either of his parents. An emotional tribute to his brother, who died near Troy, is the only mention of a relative, but it strengthens the inference that Catullus's family was closely knit.

The usual education of a wealthy and talented provincial is likely to have included study in Athens, and although there is no record of an educational sojourn in Greece, Catullus's poetry is that of a young man thoroughly imbued with Greek poetry from Homer to Callimachus. His many attachments to friends from northern Italy, however, including several of the *novi poetae*, suggest that unlike the Augustans Vergil and Horace, Catullus did not completely detach himself from his provincial origins to become a Hellenized Roman. The demotic, vernacular coloring of his poetry is symptomatic of a mind that resisted imitation of the accepted Greco-Roman literary canons.

LIFE'S WORK

Catullus's reputation as one of the greatest poets of all Roman literature is even more remarkable because it is based on a collection of poems smaller than a fourth of Vergil's *Aeneid* (c. 29-19 B.C.E.; English translation, 1553) and because this collection survived antiquity in only a single copy. The 113 poems range in length from epigrams of two lines to a miniature epic of 408 lines. The near extinction of this great poet is attributable to the audacious and racy subject matter of some of his poems, which made them unsuitable for use in the schools.

It is impossible to reconstruct a dependable chronology of Catullus's poetic career on the basis of the poems themselves, and, as previously noted, the ancient sources provide little additional information. Clearly, the shortness of his life means that his oeuvre represents the work of a young poet, but nothing in it could be described as juvenilia. The poems appear to have been selected by him for publication. Poem 1 of the collection now extant refers to a "slim volume" (*libellus*) which he is dedicating to his friend the historian Cornelius Nepos, but there is no evidence that this slim volume is the same as the extant collection. There exists a scrap of another dedication also, apparently part of another collection.

The existing collection is divided into three parts on purely formal grounds. The first group, poems 1 through 60, are in a variety of meters; hence, they are called the polymetric poems. The favorite meter of this group is the hendecasyllabic, or Phalaecian, an eleven-syllable line of Greek origin that lends itself well to the colloquial tone of his work. The second group consists of eight long poems in various meters, two of them the dactylic hexameter familiar to epic poetry. The third group is written in elegiac couplets, a meter that had become popular in Hellenistic epigrams but was on its way to becoming the medium of the Latin love elegy. Yet not all Catullus's elegiac poems are on love. He wrote a poem to his dead brother as well as a number of purely satirical pieces.

Judging from what has survived, scholars agree that the elegiac couplet was Catullus's favorite medium. Within the three sections of the now-canonical collection, there is evidence of design in the ordering of the poems. The collection is not organized chronologically or by subject matter, but it betrays a subtly designed miscellany of moods and subjects, each poem contrasting with or corresponding to its neighbors in ways that sustain the reader's interest.

Because there is no known chronology, one good way to perceive the work of Catullus is through the people about whom and to whom he wrote his poems. The social character of his poetry, much of which is addressed to

Catullus. (Library of Congress)

somebody specific, is also well served by this approach. The most visible and intense of the poet's personal relationships is with a woman he calls Lesbia, mentioned in some twenty-five of Catullus's love poems. Lucius Apuleius wrote that her real name was Clodia, and it is generally believed that she was a married woman ten years older than the poet. If Apuleius's testimony is correct, Clodia was the sister of Cicero's enemy P. Clodius Pulcher and wife (later the widow) of Q. Metellus Celer, who governed Cisalpine Gaul between 64 and 62 B.C.E. For her, the affair she had with Catullus was casual, one of many. For Catullus, it was the cause of both euphoria and anguish, with little middle ground. This stormy relationship lasted about six years, from perhaps 58 or 59 to 55 or 54 B.C.E. The Lesbia poems are the best known of Catullus's work.

A second episode in Catullus's life, one whose dates are known more definitely, was his year of public service on the staff of C. Memmius, the Roman governor of Bithynia. Such tours of duty were a normal part of the life of young Romans of rank, and although Catullus complains loudly in his poems about Memmius's tight-fisted policies and writes eloquently of the pleasure of returning home, this year of furlough from the stresses of his affair with Lesbia/Clodia and the high life of Rome (from 57 to 56 B.C.E.) may have contributed much to Catullus's achievement as a poet. It is a reasonable inference that the job itself was not demanding and that in his enforced isolation on the southern shore of the Black Sea Catullus had ample opportunity to study, write, and revise.

A significant part of Catullus's poetry may be described as occasional verse, that which commemorates an event of no great objective importance in such a way as to bring out its humor, irony, or emotional significance. The Greek tradition in which he chose to write was satirical, and a large number of the poems of the collection expand on the foibles of people whom the poet wished to embarrass. Some of these were amatory rivals, some were social climbers or nuisances (such as Asinius Marrucinus, the napkin thief of poem 12). Others, including the orator Cicero, the politician Julius Caesar, and Caesar's protégé Mamurra, were public figures. In spite of attacks of varying intensity (in poems 29, 57, and 93), Caesar remained an admirer of Catullus; according to Suetonius, Catullus eventually apologized for his attacks (in one of which he accuses Caesar of sexually molesting little girls) and was invited to dine with Caesar the same day.

Traditional serious poetry also exerted its attraction for Catullus. In the course of what might be viewed as a licentious life of pleasure and scandal, Catullus composed three long wedding hymns (poems 61, 62, and 63) that show every sign of a deep belief in the institution of marriage. In addition, there is an impressive long poem about the religious frenzy of a legendary young Greek named Attis, who emasculates himself in order to serve the Asiatic goddess Cybele. Notwithstanding the emphasis of the Neoterics on short poetry in a native poetic idiom, epic remained the medium of choice for the highest achievement. Catullus's effort in this genre, the miniature epic or epyllion on the wedding of Peleus and Thetis, with its digression on Theseus's abandonment of Ariadne (poem 64), ranks with his best work. Parts of it, such as Ariadne's lament, are unsurpassed in Latin literature.

SIGNIFICANCE

Although it remains the slimmest volume on a bookshelf of classical works, the poetry of Catullus is a unique testament to the power of a young poet working in a still-raw language. As Cicero, writing a decade later, found Latin a poor vehicle for philosophy, poets of Catullus's generation had none of the vocabulary and native traditions that Greek had developed over the course of seven centuries. Instead of borrowing Greek vocabulary, themes, and genres wholesale to produce feeble imitations, Catullus set out to create a genuinely Latin poetry. The only Roman model of significant use to him was the comedian Plautus, the Umbrian stagehand-turned-playwright who transformed Greek comedies into lively shows for untutored audiences. Though inevitably indebted to Greek inspiration for most of what he wrote, Catullus put Latin poetry on a more independent course and set the agenda for Augustan poetry: to write what Horace was to call a *Latinum carmen*, or Latin song.

Specifically, this agenda meant adapting Greek poetic rhetoric to the more subjective taste of a Roman audience, reducing the dependence on words borrowed from the Greek, modifying the rigid syntactic structure of formal Latin to gain the flexibility that Greek had long enjoyed, and broadening the range of subjects that were acceptable for poets to essay. By succeeding as conspicuously as he did in these tasks, Catullus opened the way for Latin poetry to become a worthy successor to Greek rather than a mere imitator.

Ultimately more interesting to the average reader than his place in the history of Roman poetry is the vibrant and colorful picture Catullus gives of private life in the Rome of Cicero and Caesar. As it happens, Catullus wrote for all time, but his poetry is an intimate portrait of life in his own time, written with an art that few successors dared imitate.

—Daniel H. Garrison

FURTHER READING

Fordyce, C. J. *Catullus: A Commentary.* Oxford, England: Clarendon Press, 1965. An extensive and illuminating commentary in English on the Latin text, flawed by the author's refusal to print or discuss some thirty-two poems "which do not lend themselves to comment in English."

Garrison, Daniel H. *Student's Catullus.* New York: Routledge, 1996. Provides notes on vocabulary, grammar, and mythology along with translations of the poems.

Quinn, Kenneth, ed. *Catullus: The Poems.* 2d ed. New York: St. Martin's Press, 1977. This scholarly commentary is somewhat idiosyncratic but suitable for college-level readers. The Latin text of all poems is presented with introduction and commentary in English. A short bibliographical guide for further study of each of the poems is included.

Small, Stuart G. P. *Catullus: A Reader's Guide to the Poems*. Lanham, Md.: University Press of America, 1983. A running narrative, not of the poet's life but of his poetic achievement. Divided by topic, with sane judgments on matters of literary and scholarly controversy. Small supplements a reading of the poems by giving topical overviews. Includes bibliography.

Wilder, Thornton. *The Ides of March*. New York: S. French, 1971. The classic historical novel on the Rome of Cicero, Catullus, Clodius, and his sister—and Julius Caesar, the emperor whose life ended on the title day in 44 B.C.E.

Wiseman, Timothy Peter. *Catullus and His World: A Reappraisal*. New York: Cambridge University Press, 1987. A highly readable reconstruction of the social and political context, informative not only about Catullus but also about late republican Rome and its personalities. Richly documented, with eight pages of bibliography.

SEE ALSO: Julius Caesar; Cicero; Clodia; Horace; Plautus; Vergil.

RELATED ARTICLES in *Great Events from History: The Ancient World*: 54 B.C.E., Roman Poet Catullus Dies; 51 B.C.E., Cicero Writes *De republica*; 19 B.C.E., Roman Poet Vergil Dies; November 27, 8 B.C.E., Roman Lyric Poet Horace Dies; 8 C.E., Ovid's *Metamorphoses* Is Published; 100-127 C.E., Roman Juvenal Composes *Satires*.

AULUS CORNELIUS CELSUS
Roman medical writer

Celsus wrote the first complete history of medicine and the first comprehensive account of medical and surgical procedures.

BORN: c. 25 B.C.E.; possibly near Narbo Martius, Gaul (now Narbonne, France)
DIED: c. 50 C.E.; probably Rome (now in Italy)
AREAS OF ACHIEVEMENT: Historiography, medicine

EARLY LIFE

Aulus Cornelius Celsus (SEHL-suhs) probably lived during the Augustan Age and the reign of Tiberius. He is thought to have been a member of the patrician family of Cornelius. Patricians were the ruling class of Rome, nobles of wealth and influence, and they considered the practice of medicine beneath their dignity. Consequently, it is highly unlikely that Celsus was a practicing physician. Still, some knowledge of medicine was customary among the educated men of Rome. The head of the household usually practiced domestic medicine on the family, slaves, and livestock. Celsus may have followed this custom.

He was an avid reader and certainly knew both Greek and Latin. Records for the years 25 and 26 C.E. clearly indicate that he lived in Rome. Quintilian, the Roman rhetorician and critic, and Gaius Pliny, or Pliny the Elder, the Roman naturalist and writer, mention Celsus with considerable praise. Celsus was never referred to as a physi-

cian, only as an author or compiler. His literary interests were apparently comprehensive in scope and resulted in an encyclopedia called *De artibus* (25-35 C.E.). There is no clear idea of the contents and arrangement of *De artibus*. It is certain, however, that there were five books on agriculture and also sections of unknown length on military science, rhetoric, history, philosophy, government, and law.

The only portion of this encyclopedia to survive is *De medicina* (c. 30 C.E.; *The Eight Books of Medicine*, 1830; better known as *De medicina*, 1935-1938). It was a compilation from various sources such as Hippocrates' *Corpus Hippocraticum* (written during the fifth century B.C.E.) and from the lost works of Asclepiades of Bithynia, Heracleides Ponticus, Erasistratus, and others.

LIFE'S WORK

De medicina was intended primarily for practitioners. Celsus set down a guiding principle for physicians in any age: that an accurate diagnosis must precede treatment. Celsus noted the errors of both Empiricists and Methodists. He rejected the inflexible doctrines of the Empiricists, who advocated the use of drugs, and the Methodists, who stressed diet and exercise. He was influenced by Asclepiades, who established Greek medicine in Rome, and adopted many of the physiological concepts of the Alexandrian school.

The introduction to *De medicina* constitutes a first attempt at a history of medicine and includes references to eighty medical authors, some of whom are known only through this book. Celsus gave an account of the Alexandrian school, the part played by Hippocrates, and the contributions of Asclepiades.

The book, actually eight books in one, is divided into three parts. Section 1 contains a general introduction on the efficacy of diet and hygiene. Two main chapters consider the subject of general and local diseases governed by diet. Section 2 considers diseases treated with drugs. Discussed at length are different remedies, divided into various groups according to their effects: purgatives, diaphoretics, diuretics, emetics, and narcotics. There is also an examination of those diseases that require immediate treatment, diseases presenting acute or chronic manifestations, accidental or traumatic manifestations, and diseases with external symptoms. Section 3 is devoted to surgical diseases. One division concentrates on the organs, the other on orthopedics, or bones.

Celsus held strictly to the teachings of Hippocrates concerning pathological concepts and etiology, or the study of the causes of disease. He took into consideration the influence of the seasons, the weather, the patient's age and constitution, and any sudden weight changes, increases and decreases.

Diseases of the stomach are considered at length. Treatment generally consisted of diet, massage, and baths. Celsus believed that it was better to keep the bowels open by diet rather than by purgatives. Where diarrhea and fever existed, fast was the prescription. Celsus believed in the doctrine of critical days for diseases, that is, the disease's peak within a certain number of days, after which the patient would begin to recover.

In *De medicina*, Celsus addressed pneumonia, arthritis, dysentery, tonsilitis, cancer, kidney and liver diseases, tuberculosis, hemorrhoids, and diabetes. Symptoms were accurately reported for a number of diseases, such as epilepsy, and mental illnesses, such as paranoia, a form of mental illness characterized by delusions. He clearly depicted the way in which malaria attacks occurred, giving a very detailed and highly accurate account of malarial fever. According to Celsus, the fever was an effort to eliminate morbid material from the body. He was the first to name the four cardinal signs of inflammation: heat, pain, swelling, and redness.

The arguments of Celsus against taking the pulse of the patient as a criterion in the identification of disease are interesting. He regarded the pulse as an uncertain in-

Aulus Cornelius Celsus. (Library of Congress)

dication of the health of a person, because its frequency varied considerably with the sex, age, and constitution of the patient. The pulse also varied because of the patient's nervousness when in the presence of the doctor. For these reasons, the pulse was not to be examined on the doctor's first visit.

In Celsus's time, surgery was performed on all parts of the body: goiters, fistulas, tonsils, and gallstones. Cancerous growths on lips and breasts were removed. He described ulcers, tumors, amputation, and trepanation, or the removal of part of the skull, which he regarded as a treatment of last resort.

Celsus carefully reported on plastic surgery for the repair of the nose, lips, and ears and described some dental surgery, including the wiring of teeth. He also suggested lithotomy, an operation for crushing stones in the bladder; discussed ligature, or how to tie off an artery; and presented methods for stopping hemorrhages. He was very much aware of the dangers of gangrene.

Celsus was concerned with the treatment of wounds, necrosis (decaying tissues), fractures, and dislocations. His book contains an excellent account of the treatment of various fractures and dislocations. For fractures, he recommended wooden splints held in place by wax and advocated exercise after the fracture healed. Thus, he was a forerunner to modern rehabilitative therapy. In addition, Celsus described the widely used painkillers, such as opium, and anesthetics, such as the root of the mandragora plant. The root of the plant, which contained narcotics such as scopolamine, was soaked in wine, and the wine was given to the patient to induce a deep sleep.

Celsus paid particular attention to headaches, which he regarded as coming from various sources, and approved the treatment of insomnia by oil massage, which he credited directly to Asclepiades. Celsus recommended removing snake poison from a wound by sucking and correctly claimed that the venom was lethal only when absorbed into the wound, not when swallowed (although, clearly, modern physicians would regard such behavior as extremely dangerous).

Celsus clearly recognized the importance of anatomy in medicine. He attended autopsies, and his anatomical descriptions are brief but clear, including information that shows that he knew about sutures of the cranium. He distinguished between veins and arteries and favored dissection as a means to discovering more about internal organs.

In short, Celsus taught that diagnosis and prognosis must precede treatment. In so doing, he confirmed the sound doctrine of the Hippocratic school. Celsus also advocated different types of baths, massage, hygiene, and dietary rules. He relied somewhat on drugs for treatment but emphasized the benefits of sports, such as hunting, fishing, and sailing.

SIGNIFICANCE

Galen, a Greek philosopher and writer, prepared a medical encyclopedia that remained the standard authority until the sixteenth century. When Pope Nicholas V discovered Aulus Cornelius Celsus's work in the Vatican Library, he arranged to have it published in 1478. Thus, *De medicina* was the first classical book on medicine to be printed. It was also the first translation of Greek medical terms into Latin. The Latin nomenclature used in the book has dominated Western medicine for two thousand years.

The book is of interest for two reasons: its literary skill and the techniques presented. From a literary point of view, his work is outstanding. Celsus ranks as Rome's most important master of the encyclopedic literary form. As the first comprehensive account of surgical procedures by a Roman writer, *De medicina* provides much useful information on medicine of the Hellenistic period and on Alexandrian surgery. It includes a careful description of more than one hundred different types of surgical instruments.

Celsus's ideas on malaria, the treatment of fractures, and plastic surgery were ahead of his time. He was a dis-

ciple of Asclepiades, but unlike Asclepiades, Celsus was a great admirer of Hippocrates and was among the first to introduce Hippocrates' teaching to the Romans. During the first century, it was typical for medicine and other sciences to draw on many sources. Celsus followed this custom and can thus be regarded as a true eclectic.

—*Rita E. Loos*

FURTHER READING

Allbutt, Sir Thomas C. *Greek Medicine in Rome: The Fitzpatrick Lectures on the History of Medicine Delivered at the Royal College of Physicians of London in 1909-1910*. Reprint. New York: B. Blom, 1970. This series of lectures may be too abstract for the general reader. It is a complete medical history of the period, with extensive commentary on all major figures. Includes excellent illustrations, bibliography, and chronology.

Castiglioni, Arturo. *A History of Medicine*. Translated by E. B. Krumbhaar. 2d ed. New York: Alfred A. Knopf, 1947. Considered a classic reference for the period, this volume contains a full translation of Castiglioni's work. Included are numerous illustrations, chronology, and bibliography for each chapter. Designed for the general reader, it contains information relating to the content of *De medicina*.

Celsus, Aulus Cornelius. *De medicina*. Translated by W. G. Spencer. 3 vols. Cambridge, Mass.: Harvard University Press, 1960-1961. This work includes both the original Latin text and a full translation of Celsus's work. It is a major source of information about the history of medicine, as well as medical and surgical procedures for the Hellenistic period.

Cumston, Charles Greene. *An Introduction to the History of Medicine: From the Time of the Pharaohs to the End of the Nineteenth Century*. 1926. Reprint. London: Dawsons, 1968. A compilation of numerous essential contributions to the general subject of a history of medicine. Written for the general reader.

Gordon, Benjamin Lee. *Medicine Throughout Antiquity*. Philadelphia: F. A. Davis, 1949. Gordon's book contains only a very brief section on Celsus, along with scattered page references. Includes brief reference notes and a few illustrations but no chronology or bibliography.

Langslow, D. R. *Medical Latin in the Roman Empire*. New York: Oxford University Press, 2000. Systematic account of the language of Latin medical texts that includes a detailed linguistic profile of the medical terminology of Celsus and Scribonius Largus (first century C.E.) and Theodorus Priscianus and Cassius Felix (fifth century C.E.).

Lipsett, W. G. "Celsus, First Medical Historian." *Science Digest* 48 (October, 1960): 83-87. Gives very complete information about the various divisions of *De medicina* but concentrates on the surgical chapters. A very brief article that is perhaps too simplistic in language and approach, it does have appeal to the general reader.

Major, Ralph. "Medicine in the Roman Empire." In *A History of Medicine.* Springfield, Ill.: Charles C Thomas, 1954. This book requires no background

knowledge about medical history. Very limited information is presented, and few illustrations are given.

SEE ALSO: Asclepiades of Bithynia; Erasistratus; Galen; Hippocrates.

RELATED ARTICLES in *Great Events from History: The Ancient World*: 6th-4th century B.C.E. (traditionally, 1st millennium B.C.E.), Suśruta, Indian Physician, Writes Medical Compendium; c. 500-400 B.C.E., Greek Physicians Begin Scientific Practice of Medicine; 332 B.C.E., Founding of Alexandria; c. 157-201 C.E., Galen Synthesizes Ancient Medical Knowledge.

CHANDRAGUPTA MAURYA
Indian emperor (r. c. 321-301 B.C.E.)

Chandragupta Maurya established the Mauryan Dynasty and empire in India. He and his successors were the first to establish near unity in the subcontinent.

BORN: c. 346 B.C.E.; Magadha (now in India)
DIED: 298 B.C.E.; Mysore (now Karnataka, India)
ALSO KNOWN AS: Candra Gupta; Maurya; Sandrocottus
AREAS OF ACHIEVEMENT: Government and politics, war and conquest

EARLY LIFE

In the fourth century B.C.E., the Indian subcontinent was divided into more than a dozen kingdoms stretching east to west, from the Ganges to the Indus. The most powerful of these kingdoms was Magadha, based on its capital Pataliputra (the modern Patna) on the Ganges River. Chandragupta Maurya (CHUHN-druh-GEWP-tuh MAW-oor-yuh) was born here around 346 B.C.E. Despite his importance, very little information has survived concerning the early life of Chandragupta. His social status is often disputed, but it is possible he was related to the ruling Nanda Dynasty (c. 420-321 B.C.E.).

LIFE'S WORK

Around 327 B.C.E., Chandragupta apparently rose up in rebellion against the Magadha *raja* (king) Dhanananda (also known as Chandramas Nanda, and Agrammes or Xandramas to the Greeks; d. c. 321 B.C.E.). The rebellion failed and Chandragupta fled west. He found refuge with the *raja* Porus (d. c. 318 B.C.E.). Further information comes not from Indian but from Greek sources. During this same period, great events had been happening in the west, beyond the Hindu Kush Mountains. For more than

two centuries, the greatest empire on earth had been that of Persia, stretching all the way from Egypt and the borders of Greece in the west, into India itself. At this time, reports arrived in India bringing the news that a great king from Yavanna (Greece) had conquered the Persians. This king was the Macedonian Alexander the Great (r. 336-323 B.C.E.). However, Alexander was not content with the conquest of Persia, but in fact intended to conquer the entire world. (The Greeks' geographical knowledge was faulty; they believed the world ended somewhere in India.)

In 330 B.C.E., Alexander set out for the east. After difficult fighting, he entered India in 327. Porus was the first Indian *raja* to challenge Alexander, and a great battle was fought at the Hydaspes River in 326. After a difficult struggle, Alexander was victorious. However, following the battle his men refused to go any farther. They had marched for eight years and an estimated 17,000 miles (27,000 kilometers). Now they wanted to return home to enjoy their newfound wealth. They had also heard rumors that India was far larger than previously believed.

They were told that there were hundreds of thousands of infantrymen, thousands of cavalrymen, and worst of all, thousands of war elephants waiting for them farther down the road. These numbers were actually fairly accurate for the unified India that would arise a short time later during Chandragupta's rule. Despite their victory at the Hydaspes, the Macedonian soldiers did not want to face elephants in battle again. They forced Alexander to turn back. This did not mean Alexander intended to give up the territories he conquered in India. Before leaving, Alexander made arrangements for Macedonian rule in the subcontinent. Porus was allowed to keep his kingdom, though he would now be subordinate to Alexander. The other regions Alexander had conquered would be run by Macedonian governors, backed by Macedonian garrisons. Alexander left India never to return. By 323 he was dead. Immediately, there was a struggle for power among Alexander's generals. His governors in India returned to the west to participate in a struggle that would drag on for decades.

It was in this unsettled situation that Chandragupta, whom the Greeks called Sandrocottus, began his spectacular rise to power. Apparently, he was with Porus during the struggle with Alexander. Legends even suggest that Alexander and Chandragupta met at this time. Supposedly, Alexander was dismissive of the youth. Nevertheless, Chandragupta may have been inspired by Alexander's successes and his attempt to unify the world. At the very least, he took advantage of the unsettled conditions created by Alexander's campaigns in western India. Though the exact circumstances are unknown, Chandragupta raised an army, possibly with the help of Porus. The army consisted of infantry soldiers, war elephants, and archers with 5-foot (1.5-meter) bows and 9-foot (2.7-meter) arrows. Beginning in 324 B.C.E., Chandragupta conquered substantial territory in western India, driving out the remaining Macedonians in the process. By 321, he felt strong enough to attack his homeland of Magadha. He captured the capital of Pataliputra and Dhanananda was killed, bringing the Nanda Dynasty to an end. Chandragupta established the Mauryan Dynasty and empire, which stretched in a crescent along India's two great rivers, the Ganges and the Indus, from the Bay of Bengal to the Arabian Sea. This was the first time in history such a large part of the subcontinent and such a large percentage of its people had been under one government.

Unfortunately, Indian sources again fail; there is no information concerning Chandragupta's activities during the next sixteen years. It is presumed that he spent this time wisely consolidating his power. Chandragupta again appears in 305 B.C.E., and once again the information derives from Greek sources. In the west, after almost twenty years of fighting, a number of Alexander's generals had established themselves in positions of power throughout Alexander's old empire. The most powerful of Alexander's *epigoni* ("successors" in Greek) was Seleucus I Nicator (c. 358/354-281 B.C.E.). His kingdom stretched across the Middle East to the Hindu Kush Mountains. Since he had inherited Alexander's power in these regions, he also claimed hegemony over Alexander's provinces in India, which had since been lost. In

305, Seleucus felt secure enough in the west to attempt to regain the lost territories in India. Seleucus then moved into the Punjab with an army. However, unlike Alexander, Seleucus did not find a divided subcontinent. Instead, much of India was now unified under Mauryan rule. Seleucus found himself confronted by an Indian army, which included 500,000 infantry, 50,000 cavalry, and 9,000 war elephants. Unfortunately, even the Greek sources are sketchy. It is unclear whether a battle was actually fought; all that is known is that a peace treaty was signed that was highly favorable to Chandragupta. Seleucus renounced all claims to Alexander's Indian provinces (in fact, the Greeks would never return to India). Seleucus gave up all the passes through the Hindu Kush as well as the satrapies (provinces) Gedrosia and Arachosia (now in southern Afghanistan and Pakistan) on the western side of the mountains that had long been part of the old Persian Empire. Mauryan power now stretched beyond the subcontinent. Last but not least, Seleucus gave his daughter in marriage to Chandragupta.

Seleucus did, however, receive two important things in return. First, there was lasting peace between the Seleucid and Mauryan Empires. This allowed Seleucus to concentrate on what were, for him, more important matters in the west. Second, Chandragupta gave Seleucus five hundred war elephants. A short time later, Seleucus fought one of the major battles of his career, the Battle of Ipsus in 301 B.C.E. At this battle, Chandragupta's elephants proved decisive. The victory doubled the size of Seleucus's empire and led to the death of Antigonus I Monophthalmos (382-301 B.C.E.), the last man actively attempting to reunify all of Alexander's former empire. Though Seleucus was now the most powerful ruler in the western world, it is important to remember he had been humbled by the might of Chandragupta.

THE KINGS OF THE MAURYAN DYNASTY

Ruler	Reign (B.C.E.)
Chandragupta Maurya	c. 321-301
Bindusāra	298-273
Aśoka	273/265-238
Kunala	232-225
Daśaratha	232-225
Samprati	225-215
Salisuka	215-202
Devavarman	202-195
Satadhanvan	195-187
Bṛhadratha	187-185

Seleucus's relations with Chandragupta provide another valuable glimpse into the India of the time. Sometime around 300 B.C.E., Seleucus sent an ambassador named Megasthenes (c. 350-c. 290 B.C.E.) to the court of Chandragupta at Pataliputra. Megasthenes composed a number of reports on India. Unfortunately the originals have been lost, but some information survived in later authors. Megasthenes provided details about the capital. He reported that, among other interesting facts, the city walls of Pataliputra were about 21 miles (34 kilometers) in length. Megasthenes also described in detail Indian society, noting, among other things, the seven ranks into which that society was divided.

Another, possibly contemporary native source also provides information on Chandragupta's India. The *Arthaśāstra* (c. fourth century B.C.E.-c. third century C.E.; *Treatise on the Good*, 1961) was supposedly, at least in part, written by Chandragupta's chief adviser Kauṭilya. This work is a manual designed to teach rulers how to increase their own power at the expense of their enemies. It also describes in some detail the political, military, and economic situation in India. Unfortunately, much of it may have been composed after Chandragupta's reign and therefore does not shed much light on Chandragupta himself or on his specific contribution to Indian politics.

The lack of information that has plagued the study of Chandragupta follows him into old age. One tradition states that Chandragupta was a Jain. This Indian religion taught, among other things, that self-torture and starvation were the best ways to attain peace in the afterlife, a peace similar to nirvana. According to this legend, Chandragupta voluntarily abdicated the throne in 301, allowing his son Bindusāra (r. c. 298-273 B.C.E.) to become the next emperor. Chandragupta then retired to a Jain monastery in Karnataka in southern India. There, in 298 B.C.E., he starved himself to death in accordance with Jain tradition.

SIGNIFICANCE

Chandragupta Maurya established the first great Indian state. Though little information has survived, his son Bindusāra continued the expansion of the empire, apparently conquering the Deccan Plateau. The zenith of the empire was reached during the reign of Chandragupta's grandson Aśoka (c. 302-c. 238 B.C.E.; r. c. 273/265-238 B.C.E.). He gained the throne only after winning a civil war and eliminating his numerous brothers. In 261, he completed the expansion of the empire by adding Kalinga along India's eastern coast. This resulted in 100,000 deaths and 150,000 refugees. He was so horrified by his own acts that he converted to Buddhism. He spent the rest of his reign attempting to live up to the Buddha's teachings.

After Aśoka's reign, the empire began to falter. Indian sources do not even agree on the identities of later Mauryan emperors. The Mauryan Dynasty came to an end in 184 B.C.E. The last emperor, Bṛhadratha, was assassinated by one of his own generals. Altogether, the Mauryan Dynasty lasted almost 140 years and provided India with unity and peace for the first time. The Mauryan Dynasty would be a model and inspiration for all the dynasties that followed, from the Guptas to the Mughals and beyond. This was the achievement of Chandragupta.

—*Stefan G. Chrissanthos*

FURTHER READING

Bongard-Levin, G. *Mauryan India*. New Delhi: Stosius, 1985. Provides a comprehensive look at the entire Mauryan Dynasty, from its rise under Chandragupta to its zenith under Aśoka to its eventual demise.

Kulke, Hermann, and Dietmar Rothermund. *History of India*. New York: Routledge, 1998. Provides an overview of Indian history, allowing the reader a look at the centuries preceding Chandragupta's rise to power and the development of India socially, religiously, and economically.

Mookerji, R. K. *Chandragupta Maurya and His Times*. Delhi: Motilal Banarsidass, 1960. The best and most detailed biography of Chandragupta in English.

Sastri, K. A. *The Age of the Nandas and Mauryas*. Benares: Motilal Banarsidass, 1952. This book not only focuses on the Mauryans but also provides one of the few detailed looks at the Nanda Dynasty, which created a powerful state along the Ganges in eastern India and to some extent helped set the stage for Chandragupta's unification.

Thapar, R. *The Mauryas Revisited*. Calcutta: K. P. Bagchi, 1987. Provides a detailed survey of the Mauryans.

Wolpert, Stanley. *A New History of India*. 6th ed. New York: Oxford University Press, 1999. Another fine introduction to Indian history with an eye to the later impact of the country's first imperial ruler.

SEE ALSO: Alexander the Great; Aśoka; Kanishka; Menander (Greco-Bactrian king); Seleucus I Nicator; Vardhamāna.

RELATED ARTICLES in *Great Events from History: The Ancient World*: 527 B.C.E., Death of Vardhamāna, Founder of Jainism; 327-325 B.C.E., Alexander the Great Invades the Indian Subcontinent; c. 4th century B.C.E.-3d century C.E., Kauṭilya Compiles a Treatise on Practical Statecraft; c. 273/265-c. 238 B.C.E., Aśoka Reigns over India.

SAINT CHRISTOPHER
Christian martyr

Although a legendary figure, Saint Christopher has long been a popular Christian saint, known as the patron of travelers and ferrymen.

BORN: Possibly third century; Asia Minor (now in Turkey)
DIED: c. 250 C.E.; possibly Lycia, Asia Minor (now in Turkey)
AREA OF ACHIEVEMENT: Religion

EARLY LIFE

Virtually nothing is known about the early life of Saint Christopher (KRIHS-toh-fuhr). Indeed, the historical documentation for his life is so scant that some scholars question whether he actually even lived. The stories of Saint Christopher's life belong to a genre known as vitae, or saints' lives. The purpose of a vita is to present the life of a saint in such a way that it will inspire believers and persuade nonbelievers.

Saint Christopher belongs to a group of very early saints known as martyrs. Martyrs, including those early Christians who were persecuted in Rome, gave their lives for their faith. The early Christian church kept records of those who died as a result of the persecution. There is evidence to suggest that as early as the second century, the church commemorated and venerated martyrs by memorializing the dates of their deaths. Saint Christopher's name appears on early lists of martyrs known as martyrologies. As early as 452 C.E., a church in Bithynia was dedicated to him. Saint Christopher's cult is ancient in both the West and the East.

The stories of Saint Christopher's life are internally inconsistent and offer no insight as to his birth or his childhood. In an early Greek vita, Saint Christopher was described as a monster with a dog's head who ate people. His name before his baptism was listed as Reprobus in some sources and Offeros in others. By all accounts, Saint Christopher was a very large man, or even a giant, with a fearsome face. In addition, most sources suggest that he was descended from the Canaanites.

LIFE'S WORK

Most accounts of Saint Christopher available in English are retellings of Jacobus de Voragine's *Legenda aurea* (*The Golden Legend*, 1483). William Caxton, the first printer in England, translated this one of the most popular of all medieval books. This life of Saint Christopher follows a predictable pattern. First, there is a description of Saint Christopher's early pagan life, followed by the details of his conversion. Next, the writer describes with great flourish the miracles of the saint and his ability to convert others. Finally, the story of the persecution and martyrdom of the saint at the hands of a temporal king and by a description of posthumous miracles closes the account.

According to *The Golden Legend*, Saint Christopher was in the service of a great Christian king. It was Christopher's desire to serve the most powerful of all kings. When the name of the devil was spoken, however, the king crossed himself. Christopher, discovering that there was someone whom the powerful king feared, went in search of the devil.

When Christopher found the devil, he pledged himself to his service. However, one day the devil demonstrated his fear of a cross by the side of the road. Christopher demanded to know why the devil was afraid, and the devil admitted, "There was a man called Christ which was hanged on the cross, and when I see His sign I am sore afraid and flee from it wheresoever I see it." When Christopher heard this, he vowed to find Christ and serve him, because any man who gave the devil fear must be stronger than the devil himself.

In his search for Jesus Christ, according to *The Golden Legend*, Christopher met a hermit. The hermit preached to Christopher about Christ, telling him that he should fast and pray on awakening. Christopher replied that he could not fast, because it would cause him to lose his great strength. In addition, Christopher said he did not know how to pray. Therefore, the hermit told Christopher to go to a dangerous river and there carry people across the river as his service to Christ.

Certainly the most famous of all stories about Saint Christopher is connected to his service as a ferryman. *The Golden Legend* recounts that one night while Christopher slept, he heard a voice that awoke him, asking him for passage across the river. When he went outside, he found no one. This happened a second and a third time. On the third entreaty, Christopher once again went outside, where he found a child who wanted to be carried across the river. He put the child on his shoulders and started across the river. It was a difficult passage that grew more dangerous with each step. As he walked, the river swelled. The child grew heavier and heavier, and Christopher feared for his life. When he reached the other side, he told the child that he was the greatest bur-

Saint Christopher. (Library of Congress)

Christopher was reputed to have converted more than eight thousand people. In addition, saints' lives usually include a description of some sort of contest between the saint and a temporal, or earthly, king. In this case, Saint Christopher was arrested by a king called Dagnus and subjected to many temptations and persecutions. One temptation included two women, Nicaea and Aquilina, who were sent by the king to seduce Saint Christopher. Christopher did not waver in his faith, however. He converted both of the women, who were subsequently tortured and killed.

The king then began his torture of Saint Christopher, but to no avail; Saint Christopher could not be injured, even by arrows aimed at him by soldiers. One of the arrows turned back on the king and blinded him. Christopher said to the king, "Tyrant, I shall die tomorrow. Make a little clay, mixed with my blood, and anoint therewith thine eye, and thou shalt receive health." On the next day, the king had Saint Christopher beheaded. As Saint Christopher had predicted before his death, his own blood mixed with mud healed the king's eyes. Because of this miracle, the king converted to Christianity.

Although *The Golden Legend* calls the king who persecuted Saint Christopher "Dagnus," the Roman martyrologies report that Saint Christopher suffered at the hands of Decius. The Roman emperor Decius did, in fact, start a wave of persecution in 250, the traditional year of Saint Christopher's death. Other scholars attribute Saint Christopher's martyrdom to the emperor Diocletian.

SIGNIFICANCE

The stories of Saint Christopher were well known throughout the Christian West and East. Out of these stories grew the belief that Saint Christopher was the patron saint of travelers and ferrymen. His name was invoked as protection against water hazards, storms, and plagues. There was also the belief that anyone who looked at an image of the saint would not be injured or hurt on that day. Many churches erected large statues or frescoes of Saint Christopher so that their parishioners would be pro-

den that he had ever carried. The child responded that he was the Christ child and that he was so heavy because he carried the weight of the whole world on his shoulders.

As a result of this legend, medieval and Renaissance artists painted Saint Christopher with a staff in one hand and a child on his shoulders. The image of Saint Christopher and the child has been a popular one since the Middle Ages, and many paintings and artworks survive, including a famous woodcut of this event by artist Albrecht Dürer. The name "Christopher" means "Christ-bearer," and thus it is thought that this incident gave rise to his name. However, it is equally possible that the saint's name gave rise to the legend.

Saints' lives also usually include stories of the saint's ability to convert people to the Christian faith. Saint

tected. This belief, and the general popularity of Saint Christopher's cult, resulted in the many paintings and drawings of the saint made throughout the Middle Ages and Renaissance.

Further, as travel became easier through the years, Saint Christopher's popularity grew. Many Catholics wore Saint Christopher medals and placed statues of Saint Christopher on the dashboards of their cars. The Catholic Church, however, in an effort to honor only those saints for whom they could establish a historical basis for sainthood, removed Saint Christopher's feast day (July 25) from the liturgical calendar in 1969. The removal caused an uproar among Catholics, and many continued to honor the saint by wearing medallions and maintaining statues in their vehicles. The significance of this veneration is striking and demonstrates an important point about popular sainthood. Regardless of official church rulings, and regardless of historical documentation, believers continue to believe and pray for intercession in times of need. The importance of Saint Christopher is not in whatever life he may or may not have led in the distant past but rather in what Christians have chosen to believe about him through the centuries.

—*Diane Andrews Henningfeld*

FURTHER READING

Butler, Alban. *Butler's Lives of the Saints*. Revised by Peter Doyle. Tunbridge Wells, Kent, England: Burns & Oates/Search Press, 1999. Updated version of Butler's eighteenth century work. Contains index, bibliography, and liturgical calendar. A standard source for lives of the saints.

Cunningham, Lawrence. *The Meaning of Saints*. San Francisco: Harper & Row, 1980. An excellent general introduction to the idea of sainthood, demonstrating the way historical reality can be transformed into popular belief. Includes some interesting summary statements on Saint Christopher and a bibliography.

De Voragine, Jacobus. *The Golden Legend: Readings on the Saints*, edited by William Ryan Granger. 2 vols. Princeton, N.J.: Princeton University Press, 1993. This edition of the English version of *The Golden Legend* includes index and bibliography.

"The Heavenly Jobless." *Time*, June 20, 1969, 70-71. A contemporary account of the furor that arose over the demotion of a number of popular saints, including Saint Christopher.

Hodges, Margaret. *Saint Christopher*. Grand Rapids, Mich.: W. B. Erdmans, 1997. An illustrated adaptation of Caxton's version of the life of Saint Christopher found in *The Golden Legend*. Although a juvenile work, a good starting place for the student looking for the basics of the Saint Christopher legend.

New Catholic Encyclopedia. 15 vols. 2d ed. Detroit: Thomson/Gale, 2003. This reference work provides a complete and accessible source for any student beginning a study of saints' lives. Included are a number of iconographic images of Saint Christopher.

Weinstein, Donald, and Rudolph M. Bell. *Saints and Society: The Two Worlds of Western Christendom*. Chicago: University of Chicago Press, 1982. A classic scholarly discussion of the role of sainthood in medieval society. Includes both statistical detail and thorough analysis useful for providing a cultural context for the idea of sainthood.

White, Helen. *Tudor Books of Saints and Martyrs*. Madison: University of Wisconsin Press, 1963. Includes a comprehensive, chapter-length discussion of the history and impact of Caxton's *The Golden Legend* and a long bibliography of both primary and secondary sources.

Wilson, Stephen, ed. *Saints and Their Cults: Studies in Religious Sociology, Folklore, and History*. New York: Cambridge University Press, 1983. A collection of essays written by major scholars on sainthood. Most useful is a chapter by Evelyne Patlagean, "Ancient Byzantine Hagiography and Social History," in which she analyzes the genre of the saint's life in the Eastern tradition. Includes bibliography.

SEE ALSO: Saint Ambrose; Saint Anthony of Egypt; Saint Athanasius of Alexandria; Saint Augustine; Saint John Chrysostom; Saint Denis; Diocletian; Saint Helena; Saint Irenaeus; Saint Jerome; Jesus; John the Apostle; Saint Paul; Saint Peter; Saint Simeon Stylites; Saint Siricius; Saint Stephen; Saint Thomas; Saint Vincent of Lérins.

RELATED ARTICLES in *Great Events from History: The Ancient World*: c. 6 B.C.E., Birth of Jesus Christ; c. 30 C.E., Condemnation and Crucifixion of Jesus Christ; c. 30 C.E., Preaching of the Pentecostal Gospel; January-March, 55 or 56 C.E., Paul Writes His Letter to the Romans; 250 C.E., Outbreak of the Decian Persecution; c. 250 C.E., Saint Denis Converts Paris to Christianity; c. 286 C.E., Saint Anthony of Egypt Begins Ascetic Life; October 28, 312 C.E., Conversion of Constantine to Christianity; c. 382-c. 405 C.E., Saint Jerome Creates the Vulgate.

SAINT JOHN CHRYSOSTOM
Archbishop of Constantinople

John Chrysostom, the greatest homiletic preacher of the Greek church, became the patron saint of preachers.

BORN: c. 354 C.E.; Antioch, Syria (now Antakya, Turkey)

DIED: September 14, 407 C.E.; Comana, Pontus (now in Turkey)

AREAS OF ACHIEVEMENT: Literature, religion

EARLY LIFE

John Chrysostom (KRIHS-uhs-tuhm), which means "golden mouth," was raised by a devout mother, Anthousa, who had been widowed at the age of twenty. He received a first-rate education, especially in rhetoric, and his teachers are supposed to have included the renowned orator Libanius and the philosopher Andragathius. Libanius, when asked on his deathbed who should succeed him as head of his school of rhetoric, is said to have replied: "John, if the Christians had not stolen him from us." John's theological studies were undertaken at the renowned exegetical school of Antioch under one of the most illustrious scholars of the period, Diodore of Tarsus. The school favored literal rather than allegorical interpretation of the Bible.

LIFE'S WORK

According to Palladius's *Dialogus de vita S. Joannis Chrysostomi* (c. 408; *Dialogue on the Life of St. John Chrysostom*, 1921), "when [John] was eighteen, a mere boy in years, he revolted against the sophists of word-mongering, for he had arrived at man's estate and thirsted for living knowledge." Like many early Christians, Chrysostom did not receive baptism until he was about twenty years old. He became a deacon in 381 under Bishop Meletius, a native of Armenia, whose protégé Chrysostom quickly became. To this period of deaconship (381-386) probably belongs his six-book *De sacerdotio* (*On the Priesthood*, 1728), a classic on the subject and one of the jewels of patristic literature. Book 5 is of particular interest because, like book 4 of Saint Augustine's *De doctrina Christiana* (426; *On Christian Doctrine*, 1875), it constitutes a veritable monograph on the art and science of preaching. Book 6 is also of interest in that it contrasts the active with the contemplative life. Chrysostom had already been attracted to the rigors of the latter; he had spent four years in the mountains sharing ascetic life with an old hermit. This ascetic interlude is reflected

in several treatises he wrote on monastic life, including two exhortations to his friend Theodore, later bishop of Mopsuestia, who was growing tired of the monastic way of life, and the three-book *Adversus subintroductas*, which defended monasticism. In the sixth book of *On the Priesthood*, however, Chrysostom spoke out in favor of the active life, arguing that saving the souls of others demands more effort and generosity than merely saving one's own. He was ordained to the priesthood in 386 and remained in Antioch until 398; most of his great homilies belong to this period. They include more than seventy homilies on Genesis, six on Isaiah, and a particularly fine commentary on fifty-eight selected psalms. Also surviving are ninety homilies on the Gospel of Matthew, eighty-eight on the Gospel of John, fifty-five on the Acts of the Apostles, and thirty-two on Romans, this latter the finest of all his works. Almost half his surviving homilies are expositions of the Epistles of Saint Paul, his lifelong model. A series of seven homilies in praise of Paul survive among his many panegyrics on the saints of the Old and New Testaments.

Chrysostom's reputation as a pulpit orator became so widespread during his Antioch years that he was chosen to succeed Nectarius, archbishop of Constantinople, on the latter's death; he was consecrated on February 26, 398, by Theophilus, bishop of Alexandria. According to Palladius, Theophilus disliked John, "for his custom all along was not to ordain good and shrewd men lest he make a mistake. He wished to have them all weak-willed men whom he could influence."

Despite this ominous installation, Chrysostom entered on a comprehensive program of reform of church officials and church revenues; he even criticized abuses in the Imperial court. He used church revenues to set up hospitals and to aid the poor, leading a life of great simplicity himself. He was particularly critical of the luxury and wealth of the upper classes. His outspokenness soon incurred the wrath of the Empress Eudoxia, to whom Chrysostom's enemies suggested that she was the real target of his strictures.

After a synod in Ephesus in 401, when Chrysostom had six simoniac bishops deposed, some neighboring bishops made an alliance with Theophilus in a bid to unseat the archbishop. At the Oak Synod in 403, attended by thirty-six bishops, Chrysostom was deposed and sentenced to exile by order of the emperor. He was recalled the following day because of riots in his support in Constantinople, but after an uneasy peace of a few months, the emperor banished him to Cucusus in Lesser Armenia. To his three-year period there belong more than two hundred extant letters, which testify to his continuing pastoral zeal and interest in reform. This continued "meddling" proved unacceptable to his enemies, who had him transferred to the more distant Pityus, a city on the eastern shore of the Black Sea. Worn out, John Chrysostom died on his way there, at Comana in Pontus, on September 14, 407.

SIGNIFICANCE

John Chrysostom is considered one of the four great fathers of the Eastern church and one of the three ecumenical doctors of the church. He has always been regarded as the most outstanding preacher of the Greek church and one of its greatest exegetes; his eloquence had already earned for him the title "Golden Mouth" in the sixth century. He shares with Origen the reputation of being the most prolific writer of the East. His surviving works extend through eighteen volumes of J.-P. Migne's great *Patrologia Graeca* (1857-1866), and there are still others, notably *De inani gloria et de educandis liberis* (*On Vainglory and the Right Way for Parents to Bring Up Children*, 1951). Chrysostom's recently discovered baptismal homilies add to church historians' knowledge of practices surrounding Christian rites of initiation at the end of the fourth century. His homilies are interesting more for their rhetorical brilliance than for any philosophical or theological profundity; they reflect the simple faith of his audience more than the contemporary struggles with Arianism and Apollinarianism. *On the Priesthood* is deservedly a classic, setting forth the most exacting standards for the clerical life. John Chrysostom's life is eloquent proof that he practiced what he preached.

—*Thomas Halton*

FURTHER READING

Chrysostom, John. *Apologist*. Translated by Margaret A. Schatkin and Paul W. Harkins. Washington, D.C.: Catholic University of America Press, 1983. Contains first translations of two works, one extolling the martyred Babylas and one upholding the divinity of Christ. These renderings by two seasoned Chrysostom scholars are generally reliable. Includes succinct notes and helpful bibliographies.

_____. *On Marriage and Family Life*. Translated by Catharine P. Roth and David Anderson. Crestwood, N.Y.: St. Vladimir's Seminary Press, 1986. Includes two hitherto untranslated homilies, with a good intro-

duction showing that Chrysostom, who has often been accused of misogyny, had a better theology of marriage than commonly has been thought.

Kelly, J. N. D. *Golden Mouth: The Story of John Chrysostoma: Ascetic, Preacher, Bishop*. Ithaca, N.Y.: Cornell University Press, 1995. Recounts the entire story of Chrysostom's life.

Mayer, Wendy, and Pauline Allen. *John Chrysostom*. New York: Routledge, 2000. Evaluates the subject's role as a preacher and his pastoral activities. A valuable introduction to the processes of early Christianization.

Palladius. *Dialogue on the Life of St. John Chrysostom*. Translated and edited by Robert T. Meyer. New York: Paulist Press, 1985. Though clearly partial to Chrysostom, this work has value for having been written by a contemporary who was actually present at the Synod of the Oak. Vivid descriptions of the intrigues and violence of Constantinople that led to Chrysostom's downfall and exile.

Wilken, Robert. *John Chrysostom and the Jews: Rhetoric and Reality in the Late Fourth Century*. Berkeley: University of California Press, 1983. Particularly useful in its attempt to separate rhetoric from reality in Chrysostom's *Adversus Iudaeos* (c. 386; *Homilies Against the Jews*, 1889). These were aimed at Judaizing Christians in his congregation who were still attracted to meetings in the synagogue. Chrysostom is seen as a master of invective, and Judaism emerges as a continuing social and religious force in Antioch.

SEE ALSO: Saint Ambrose; Saint Anthony of Egypt; Saint Athanasius of Alexandria; Saint Augustine; Saint Denis; Saint Helena; Saint Irenaeus; Saint Jerome; Jesus; John the Apostle; Saint Paul; Saint Peter; Saint Simeon Stylites; Saint Siricius; Saint Stephen; Theodore of Mopsuestia; Saint Thomas; Saint Vincent of Lérins.

RELATED ARTICLES in *Great Events from History: The Ancient World*: c. 6 B.C.E., Birth of Jesus Christ; c. 30 C.E., Condemnation and Crucifixion of Jesus Christ; c. 30 C.E., Preaching of the Pentecostal Gospel; January-March, 55 or 56 C.E., Paul Writes His Letter to the Romans; 250 C.E., Outbreak of the Decian Persecution; c. 250 C.E., Saint Denis Converts Paris to Christianity; c. 286 C.E., Saint Anthony of Egypt Begins Ascetic Life; October 28, 312 C.E., Conversion of Constantine to Christianity; c. 382-c. 405 C.E., Saint Jerome Creates the Vulgate.

CICERO
Roman orator and rhetorician

With courageous and principled statesmanship, Cicero guided Rome through a series of severe crises. While he was not able to save the Republic, he transmitted its political and cultural values in speeches and treatises that became models of style for posterity.

BORN: January 3, 106 B.C.E.; Arpinum, Latium (now Arpino, Italy)
DIED: December 7, 43 B.C.E.; Formiae, Latium (now Formia, Italy)
ALSO KNOWN AS: Marcus Tullius Cicero (full name)
AREAS OF ACHIEVEMENT: Government and politics, law, literature, philosophy

EARLY LIFE

Marcus Tullius Cicero (SIHS-ur-oh), the elder son of Marcus Tullius Cicero and Helvia, was born a few miles from Arpinum, a small town in Latium, southeast of Rome. Long established in the district, his family had, like many other Roman families, a rather undignified source for its name: *Cicer* is Latin for chickpea, or garbanzo. According to one story, "Cicero" originated as the nickname of a wart-nosed ancestor. The Tullius clan was of equestrian, or knightly, rank—that is, they were well-to-do but their members had never served in the senate. Cicero was to be the first in the family to attain nobility as a magistrate.

Centuries earlier, Arpinum had been a stronghold of the Volscians in their unsuccessful struggle to avoid subjugation by Rome. For nearly one hundred years before Cicero's birth, however, the people of Arpinum had enjoyed full Roman citizenship. Cicero took pride in his local origins as well as in his Roman citizenship, and he sometimes referred to his "two fatherlands." His description in *Cato maior de senectute* (44 B.C.E.; *On Old Age*, 1481) of the slow, well-regulated growth of Arpinum's figs and grapes suggests the influence of his birthplace on his politics at Rome: He was a lifelong defender of order and gradual change, an enemy of both mob violence and aristocratic privilege.

Cicero's first exposure to learning came through the papyrus scrolls in his father's library at Arpinum. While still very young, both Cicero and his brother, Quintus, showed such zeal to study philosophy and oratory that their father took them to Rome to seek the best instruction available. This move to Carinae Street in the capital, coinciding with his father's retirement from active life, presented young Cicero with an opportunity to excel academically and advance socially.

Latin literature had yet to come into its own. Early Roman poets such as Livius Andrònicus and Quintus Ennius simply did not compare well with Homer, and the educators of the day made heavy use of Greek poetic works to teach elocution and rhetoric. One of Cicero's teachers was the Greek poet Aulus Licinius Archias, who had gone to Rome in 102 B.C.E. and whom Cicero afterward credited with having sparked his interest in literature. Cicero adapted the cadences of Greek and Latin poetry to his original orations, developing a complex but supple rhetorical and literary style that became a standard for his own time and for the Renaissance, fifteen hundred years later. In retrospect, however, Cicero faulted the education of his youth for not teaching how to obtain practical results through rhetoric—a problem he set himself to solve through legal studies.

In 89 B.C.E., at age seventeen, he interrupted these studies to serve on Rome's side in the Social War, a rebellion by Rome's Italian allies. His brief role in this disastrous ten-year conflict aroused in him a lifelong hatred of military service. He became more convinced than ever that his success would lie in progressing through the prescribed sequence of public offices, as it had for his models at the time, the orators Lucius Licinius Crassus and Marcus Antonius Creticus (grandfather of Marc Antony). He continued to study rhetoric and also resumed his legal studies under Quintus Mucius Scaevola, the augur (priest of the state religion), who had been consul some twenty-eight years previously.

LIFE'S WORK

Among Cicero's important achievements was a series of celebrated orations in connection with legal cases. His oratorical skills aided him in the pursuit of public office and helped secure his place in history as the savior of Rome.

Cicero launched his career as an orator and advocate in 81 B.C.E., during the dictatorship of Lucius Cornelius Sulla. Under that regime no one's life was safe; to become conspicuous through forensics was especially dangerous. Not only did Cicero confront this risk, but from his earliest cases onward he also often bravely opposed the established leaders. *Pro Quinctio* (81 B.C.E.; *For Publius Quintius*, 1741), his first speech in a court of law, had little importance in itself; in taking on this case, however, Cicero pitted himself against the leading advocate of the day, Quintus Hortensius Hortalus.

The following year, in *Pro Roscio Amerino* (80 B.C.E.; *For Sertus Roscius of America*, 1741), Cicero defended a young man accused of parricide by Chrysogonus, a favorite of Sulla. After the father of Roscius was murdered, Chrysogonus had fabricated a charge to get the dead man's name on Sulla's list of proscribed citizens—those banished from Rome for certain offenses. By law the property of a proscribed person, dead or alive, was put up at auction; Chrysogonus wanted to buy the dead father's property cheaply. He later conspired to make Roscius appear responsible for the murder. It was a bold and dangerous step to reveal in a public speech this evil scheme of Sulla's favorite. However, Cicero resolutely undertook the defense of Roscius and carried it off so effectively that his reputation was immediately established. Suddenly his services as advocate were in great demand, and Cicero sought to capitalize on this trend by publishing some of his forensic speeches.

Cicero. (Library of Congress)

Apparently Sulla bore Cicero no ill will; in any case, the dictator abdicated in 79. The next two years, however, Cicero spent away from Rome, studying philosophy and oratory in Greece and Rhodes under Molo, who had also taught Julius Caesar. During this period, Cicero regained his health; it was also during this time that he formed the great friendship of his life, with Titus Pomponius Atticus, to whom he would address some of his best-known letters.

In 77, Cicero returned to Rome and married Terentia, the daughter of a well-to-do and socially prominent family. He was old enough to campaign for quaestor, or financial officer, the first rung of the public-office ladder. Elected at the minimum age of thirty in 76, Cicero served in Sicily and distinguished himself in office by sending large supplies of grain to the capital in a time of near famine. In gratitude, the senate admitted him to membership.

Meanwhile, Cicero continued to offer his services as orator and advocate, as Roman law prescribed an interim between terms of service as a magistrate. In 70 came another noteworthy event in his career: his impeachment of Gaius Verres, governor of Sicily from 73 to 71. Most provincial governors pursued a policy of extortion to enrich themselves, but Verres had been uncommonly greedy and cruel. Having spent two months preparing a painstakingly well-documented case, Cicero prosecuted Verres so vigorously that the defendant's legal adviser—the same Hortensius whose primacy Cicero had challenged ten years earlier—gave up the defense, and Verres went into voluntary exile.

Cicero's skill as a speaker in public trials was an important factor in his election to public office, especially because he was not from one of Rome's leading aristocratic families. He won by a landslide the office of aedile (roughly, superintendent of public works) in 69. Two years later, he was chosen praetor, or judicial officer, and in 63 came the supreme honor: election as consul, Rome's chief executive. Two consuls were elected each year, and Cicero's colleague in office, Gaius Antonius Hybrida, was politically insignificant. Essentially, he allowed Cicero complete control during what became a year of crisis.

First, Cicero felt compelled to oppose a bill that ordered the distribution of state-owned land to the poor. The real significance of this particular bill lay in the powers it accorded to a commission that would be appointed to implement it. Sponsoring the bill were two wealthy aristocrats, Crassus and Julius Caesar. Cicero, a professed "man of the people," soundly defeated the measure but at the cost of appearing to be an ally of the moneyed, landowning classes, while Caesar seemed a champion of the masses.

An aristocrat was similarly responsible for the next crisis, the Catilinarian conspiracy. After losing several bids for high office, Catiline, in desperation, began plotting a coup. He recruited popular support by promising to cancel all debts and proscribe the wealthy if he came to power. When Catiline tried to enlist a group of tribal delegates from Roman Gaul, however, they informed Cicero, who arranged that they should be arrested while carrying incriminating letters from the plotters. The evidence was incontrovertible, and Cicero called for summary execution.

This bold move proved a serious mistake that almost destroyed Cicero's political career. Roman law provided that no citizen should be put to death without the privilege of final appeal to the people. Cicero, in his fourth Catilinarian oration, held that those who had plotted against their country were no longer citizens and thus had lost the right of final appeal. Despite the danger to the Republic—Catiline's supporters outside Rome were virtually in a state of rebellion—Cicero pressed for an arbitrary interpretation of the law. He had the power to do so, for in October, because of the crisis, the senate had practically given him dictatorial power. Catiline escaped but was soon killed in the battle that finally ended the conspiracy. Cicero prevailed on the senate to pass the death sentence on the other ringleaders. Thereafter, he was hailed as a savior and "father of the fatherland." Nevertheless, there were to be reprisals.

Publius Clodius Pulcher, a favorite of Caesar and a private enemy of Cicero, introduced a bill to exile anyone who had put Roman citizens to death without the right of public appeal. Cicero was not named, but the measure was clearly aimed at him. His attempts to block it failed, and in 58, stricken with grief, he was forced to leave Rome. Clodius and his followers tore down Cicero's house in Rome and persecuted Terentia.

Cicero was recalled to the capital, however, after eighteen months. Perhaps as a reaction to Clodius's excesses, the people gave Cicero a hero's welcome. His house and wealth were restored, and Caesar courted him as a potential ally. Cicero's dream at this time, however, was to save the Republic by detaching Pompey the Great from the First Triumvirate. Caesar and Pompey did indeed fall out, but the breakup of the triumvirate did not save the Republic. During the years between 57 and 51, Cicero lived in retirement and concentrated on philosophical

and rhetorical studies and the writing of treatises in these fields, works in which he articulated the political and moral philosophy he had tried to exemplify in his life. In 51, sick of living in ignominious luxury, he leaped at the opportunity to govern the province of Cilicia as proconsul. Unlike most provincial governors, he was a just, sympathetic administrator, sincerely desirous of improving the lot of the Cilicians, who had been severely exploited by his predecessors.

Cicero never forgave Caesar for putting an end to the Republic, though he took no part in Caesar's assassination in 44. Afterward, he expected to see the Republic restored, but he soon came to fear Antony as a second Caesar. When the Second Triumvirate was formed by Antony, Octavian (later Augustus), and Marcus Aemilius Lepidus, Cicero and other defenders of the old Republic were proscribed. Antony's supporters hunted down Cicero and killed him in Formiae, Latium, on December 7, 43. To disgrace him, Antony had his head and hands mounted on the Rostra at Rome.

SIGNIFICANCE

It was for his political acts that Cicero most wanted to be remembered, and, having acted courageously and decisively at certain critical moments—notably during the Catilinarian conspiracy—he was viewed in his own time as the savior of Rome. Nevertheless, Rome as Cicero knew it—the Republic—could not be saved. Though Cicero did often set an example of personal courage for his contemporaries, his more lasting value is in having articulated the political and moral ideals of the Roman Republic at the very moment when their realization was no longer possible. Through his writings, Cicero also helped to shape the form and style of a literature that was just coming into its own. In his orations and philosophical essays, he showed that the Latin language could be employed with the same grace and elegance as Greek. Though his philosophical reasoning was seldom profound, it adequately served his avowed practical purpose—in literature as in life—of helping humanity find a way of life and a consistent purpose. By recording the ideals of republican Rome, Cicero may have ensured their availability in other times when their realization would be more feasible.

—*Thomas Rankin*

FURTHER READING

Bailey, D. R. Shackleton. *Cicero*. New York: Charles Scribner's Sons, 1972. Provides a detailed biography of Cicero and discusses his writings in the context of his life. Part of the Classical Life and Letters series.

Cicero. *Letters of Cicero: A Selection in Translation.* Compiled and translated by L. P. Wilkinson. New York: W. W. Norton, 1968. Provides translations of Cicero's important letters from the year after his consulship to the end of his life, with an informative introduction.

Everitt, Anthony. *Cicero: The Life and Times of Rome's Greatest Politician.* New York: Random House, 2002. Places Cicero's life and career amid the context of the political intrigue and civil unrest of the Roman Republic.

Mackail, J. W. *Latin Literature.* Edited with an introduction by Harry C. Schnur. New York: Collier Books, 1962. Contains a chapter with literary evaluations of Cicero's forensic oratory, political philosophy, philosophy, and epistolary prose. Includes a bibliography.

May, James M. *Brill's Companion to Cicero: Oratory and Rhetoric.* Boston: Brill Academic, 2002. This volume of history and criticism includes bibliography and index.

Sihler, Ernest G. *Cicero of Arpinum: A Political and Literary Biography.* 1914. Reprint. New York: Cooper Square, 1969. A classicist's approach to the study of Cicero's life and character. Special emphasis is placed on Cicero's writings.

SEE ALSO: Marc Antony; Julius Caesar; Cato the Censor; Cato the Younger; Pompey the Great; Lucius Cornelius Sulla.

RELATED ARTICLES in *Great Events from History: The Ancient World*: c. 300 B.C.E., Stoics Conceptualize Natural Law; Late 63-January 62 B.C.E., Catiline Conspiracy; 51 B.C.E., Cicero Writes *De republica*.

CIMON
Athenian general and statesman

Through skillful military leadership and diplomacy, Cimon became an important force behind the establishment of the Delian League—a Greek alliance against the Persians—and its later transformation into the Athenian Empire. Domestically, he struggled unsuccessfully against the extension of democracy in ancient Athens.

BORN: c. 510 B.C.E.; place unknown
DIED: c. 451 B.C.E.; near Citium (now Larnaca), Cyprus
AREAS OF ACHIEVEMENT: Government and politics, war and conquest

EARLY LIFE

As the oldest child of Miltiades the Younger, the victor of the Battle of Marathon, and Hegesipyle, the daughter of King Olorus of Thrace, Cimon (SI-muhn) inherited the political leadership and influence of one of the most ancient and respected aristocratic families in Athens, the Philaidae clan. He received a traditional Athenian education, emphasizing simple literacy skills and athletic prowess, as opposed to the stress on rhetoric and speculative philosophy that would prevail in later generations. As a youth, however, Cimon disappointed his fellow clan members and other Philaidae supporters by his dissolute behavior. His riotous living and heavy drinking recalled to Athenian minds the infamous conduct of his grandfather and namesake, Cimon, nicknamed *koalemos* (the "nincompoop"). The younger Cimon's irresponsible attitudes threatened to cast the Philaidae clan into obscurity in an Athenian political arena in which familial relationships and alliances counted for much in the competition for power.

Although Cimon possessed the personal assets essential to successful political leadership—high intelligence and an impressive physical appearance—he also entered manhood in the 480's with crippling liabilities. His father's conviction in 489 for "deceiving the people" had cast disrepute on the Philaidae, while responsibility for the enormous fine imposed at the trial impoverished Cimon for several years after Miltiades' death. Inability to provide a dowry for his beautiful sister, Elpinice, forced him to support her in his own household under circumstances that incited rumors of incestuous relations. (Ancient and modern historians have debated the nature of Cimon's relationship with Elpinice. Many believe that she was his half sister, and thereby, appropriately married to Cimon under Athenian law and custom, which allowed such unions.) Cimon's hopes for a successful political career appeared dim.

Persia's invasion of Greece in 480 thrust Cimon into the limelight and decidedly reversed his political fortunes. When the Persian king Xerxes I invaded Attica and threatened Athens, the city's leaders had difficulty persuading the populace to adhere to the previously agreed-on strategy: evacuation of noncombatants and concentration of military resources and personnel with the fleet in the Bay of Salamis. Cimon resolved to set an example for the young aristocrats who traditionally formed the small, Athenian cavalry contingent. He led his comrades up to the Acropolis, where he was the first to dedicate his horse's bridle on the altar of Athena. Seizing a shield from the wall of the sanctuary, he then joined the fleet at Salamis as a simple hoplite. His actions inspired his fellow Athenians. After fighting courageously at the subsequent Battle of Salamis, Cimon emerged a hero from the Great Persian War. He was not slow to utilize his refurbished reputation.

LIFE'S WORK

About 480, Cimon was married to Isodice, an Athenian woman from the Alcmaeonidae clan. Together, they had at least three sons: twins, Lakedaimonios and Oulios, and Thettalos. According to some ancient sources, Cimon also had three other sons—Cimon, Miltiades, and Peisianax—although most modern historians are skeptical of the existence of these children. Marriage to Isodice promised important political advantages, yet Cimon also loved her passionately, and the depth of his devotion to her was unusual enough to induce comment from contemporary observers and ancient historians.

Shortly after his own marriage, Cimon was able to find a husband for Elpinice. She was betrothed to Callias of Alopeke, a member of the Hipponikos clan and the richest man in Athens. This new brother-in-law assisted Cimon in paying his father's fine and recouping the Philaidae clan's finances. More important, the marriages of Cimon and Elpinice forged an alliance among three of the most politically important clan-factions in Athens: the Philaidae, Alcmaeonidae, and Hipponikos. This coalition may have been directed against Themistocles, who had emerged from the Great Persian War as the leading Athenian politician; his skilled courting of the populace engendered defensive reactions from fellow aristocrats.

Although Cleisthenes of Athens had instituted democratic reforms to the Athenian constitution, aristocratic clan-factions, especially those based in Athens itself, still exerted considerable influence over the city's political life. Because payment for public officials was as yet unknown in Athens, only men of independent financial means could spare the time and energy necessary to state service. Ordinary Athenian voters tended to coalesce around aristocratic leaders, who could assist them with financial and judicial problems. In the 470's and 460's, Cimon was especially renowned for his skillful use of this "politics of largesse," that is, the disbursement of monetary and commodity gratuities in the hope of securing votes.

Changes in Athenian constitutional practices during the 480's strengthened aristocratic influences on government. The prestige of the Areopagus—a judicial-administrative body composed of former archons drawn from the upper classes—increased during the Persian War because of its skilled handling of the crisis. Moreover, the decision in 488/487 to select archons by lot actually enhanced the ability of the aristocracy to direct Athenian politics, because consequently the *strategoi* (board of generals) increasingly assumed leadership of the Assembly and the Council of Five Hundred. Unlike the archons, the *strategoi* could be elected to office consecutively and as many times as possible. During the 470's and 460's, aristocratic defenders of the status quo, such as Cimon and Aristides, served as *strategoi* for years, dominating Athenian foreign policy and influencing domestic developments.

These years also witnessed the establishment of the Delian League, an alliance between Athens and numerous Ionian and Aegean city-states, by which continuous war was vigorously pursued against the Persian Empire. In the 470's, Cimon's fair treatment of Athens's allies in the league spread his fame over the Greek world and ensured for him perennial command of major military expeditions. Between 476 and 469, he expelled from Byzantium the renegade Spartan commander Pausanias, seized Eion on the Strymon River from the Persians, and conquered Scyros from Dolopian pirates and colonized it with Athenians. During the latter expedition, Cimon discovered and transported to Athens the supposed bones of Theseus, the mythical founder of the Athenian state, an act that fulfilled an ancient oracle and won for him great applause.

Cimon's finest military achievement, however, took place at the mouth of the Eurymedon River in 466. There, utilizing a self-designed trireme that accommodated a greater number of hoplites, Cimon destroyed a large Persian fleet and defeated an accompanying army on land. A Phoenician fleet sailing to reinforce the Persians was similarly devastated by the new triremes. Cimon had brought Athens and the league to the pinnacle of success. Persian presence in the Aegean, in Ionia, and on the shores of southern Asia Minor had been obliterated. Cimon's foreign policy—peace with Sparta and other Greeks and concentration on the traditional Persian enemy—had proved its value.

Cimon. (Library of Congress)

The leader of the Philaidae, nevertheless, teetered dangerously on the brink of political disaster, as his tremendous success had aroused the jealousies of aristocratic rivals. Following Cimon's successful siege of Thasos—a city-state that had attempted to secede from the Delian League—and his conquest of the Persian-occupied Chersonese, he was brought to trial for allegedly accepting a bribe from Alexander I of Macedon not to attack his territory. Although Cimon was acquitted, the charge was an ominous portent of difficulties to come: The accusation had been brought by a young Pericles and other aristocrats intent on further democratizing the Athenian state to their own political advantage.

During the trial, Cimon had convincingly pleaded his incorruptibility by citing his long tenure as *proxenos* (a Greek who officially represented the interests of another city-state to his fellow citizens) for Sparta, whose citizens were known for their self-imposed poverty and inability to provide large monetary rewards for services rendered. Cimon's admiration for Spartan culture and military institutions was well known to his fellow Athenians, but previously his loyalty to his own city-state had gone unquestioned. Worsening relations between Athens and Sparta would soon cast suspicion on Cimon and his

pro-Spartan foreign policy and thereby wreck his political career.

By the late 460's, an earlier spirit of cooperation and friendship between Athens and Sparta, proceeding from the Persian War, had been replaced by fear and hostility. The tremendous growth of Athens's power—realized through the gradual conversion of the Delian League into an Athenian Empire—was largely responsible for this change. The Spartans so greatly resented Athenian usurpation of their traditional leadership role in Greece that they promised Thasos an invasion of Attica to support the Thasian secession attempt. Before the Spartans were able to execute their plan, however, Laconia was struck by a severe earthquake and a widespread helot (serf) rebellion. Sparta was forced to call on other Greek cities, including Athens, for aid.

Among the Athenians, the debate over aid to Sparta grew acrimonious. The so-called democratic party, led by Ephialtes, strongly opposed assisting the Spartans, regarding them as dangerous rivals. Cimon, on the other hand, argued that abandoning the Spartans would weaken all Greece, while he referred to Sparta as Athens's "yokefellow." In the end, his position prevailed, because the Athenians had not yet learned of Spartan complicity in the Thasian revolt. In 462, Cimon led a large Athenian army into Laconia to assist in the suppression of the helots.

With Cimon away on this expedition, Ephialtes and Pericles moved to weaken the foundations of conservative rule in Athens. They began by bringing forth accusations of malfeasance against prominent members of the Areopagus. Meanwhile, in Laconia, Cimon and his army suffered the ignominy of a curt dismissal by the Spartans, who probably feared that progressive Athenian political ideas would exacerbate Sparta's current problems with subject peoples. When Cimon returned to Athens, he faced the wrath of prideful Athenians, distrustful of Sparta and humiliated by the recent events in Laconia. With emotions running high against the Spartans, Cimon's admiration for them appeared treasonous to many Athenians. In 461, he was ostracized, a formal, political procedure by which leaders considered dangerous to Athens were exiled for ten years. In Cimon's absence, Ephialtes and Pericles stripped the Areopagus of nearly all of its judicial and administrative powers and strengthened those of the Assembly, the Council of Five Hundred, and the law courts. Athens had entered the final, radical phase of democratization.

With Cimon in exile and his pro-Spartan policies thoroughly discredited, relations between Athens and Sparta deteriorated. In 459, war broke out between the two cities and their allies. This conflict, known as the Great Peloponnesian War, lasted until 445. Initially, the Athenians enjoyed success, despite the fact that the war with Persia continued in Cyprus and Egypt, and necessitated the dispersal of Athens's resources over several theaters of action. In 457, however, the Spartans and their allies counterattacked by invading central Greece and directly threatening to invade Attica.

The Athenians, Spartans, and their respective allies met at Tanagra, a small city in southern Boeotia. Athenian morale was low because of pervasive rumors of a pro-Spartan conspiracy by Cimon's supporters and other clan-factions against the new democratic state. Nevertheless, before the battle began, Cimon appeared fully armed and offered his services to the Athenian generals. Although suspicion of Cimon's motives caused his offer to be spurned, the leader of the Philaidae exhorted his friends and relatives along the Athenian battle line to give their greatest efforts to demonstrate their loyalty to Athens. In the subsequent battle, the Philaidae faction fought courageously, making up a disproportionate number of the Athenian dead. Sympathy for Cimon revived in Athens.

While Cimon's gift for political theatrics rejuvenated his public image, events elsewhere set the stage for his return to Athens. In 454, the large Athenian expeditionary force in Egypt was annihilated by the Persians. This reversal of fortunes incited several revolts against Athenian rule in Ionia and the Aegean region. Cimon was recalled from exile as the statesman who could best attenuate Athens's overextended military commitments by making peace with Sparta. In 451, he returned to Athens and negotiated a five-year truce with the Spartans. In the next year, serving again as *strategos*, Cimon led an expedition to Cyprus, where he died while besieging Citium, fighting once again the Persians.

SIGNIFICANCE

Although as fiercely competitive as any Greek aristocrat, Cimon was extraordinary in his dedication to principle and loyalty to his city-state. By adhering to three policies—aristocratic predominance in Athenian democracy, peace and fair-dealing with fellow Greeks, and war against the Persians—he remained unusually consistent over a long career. His political style transcended the personal and clan rivalries that had structured Athenian politics for centuries and presaged a reshaping of political competition along ideological lines in the latter fifth and fourth centuries.

—*Michael S. Fitzgerald*

216

FURTHER READING

Burn, A. R. *Pericles and Athens*. London: English Universities Press, 1948. Contains useful material on the relationship between Cimon and Pericles. Burn's depiction of Cimon as a myopic, obtuse conservative is overdrawn. It was Cimon, after all, not Pericles, who stressed Greek unity against the Persians, in anticipation of similar fourth century visions.

Kagan, Donald. *The Outbreak of the Peloponnesian War*. Ithaca, N.Y.: Cornell University Press, 1969. Serves well as an introduction to interstate relations in the Aegean and eastern Mediterranean worlds during the period of Cimon's career. Important chapters on Spartan and Athenian internal politics show the relationships between domestic developments in these city-states and the growth of hostility between them. May also be used as a guide to the ancient sources on Cimon and his times.

Laistner, M. L. W. *A History of the Greek World from 479 to 323 B.C.* London: Methuen, 1962. This introductory book should be consulted first by those unfamiliar with Cimon's era. It is also useful as a broad outline of ideological interpretations of Athenian politics after the Great Persian War.

McGregor, Malcolm F. *The Athenians and Their Empire*. Vancouver: University of British Columbia Press, 1987. Written especially for students and nonprofessional historians, this is a very useful introduction to its subject. Although lacking footnotes, the information is highly reliable. Numerous maps, appendices, charts, and a glossary of Greek political terminology make this volume required reading for beginners.

Meiggs, Russell. *The Athenian Empire*. Oxford, England: Clarendon Press, 1972. This is the standard, scholarly work on its subject, replete with footnotes that can be used to guide the reader to ancient sources. Also contains detailed discussions of the controversial issues surrounding the Athenian Empire.

Plutarch. *The Rise and Fall of Athens: Nine Greek Lives*. Translated by Ian Scott-Kilvert. Harmondsworth, England: Penguin Books, 1960. An adaptation of Plutarch's famous *Bioi parallēloi* (c. 105-115 C.E.; *Parallel Lives*), this volume contains the biographies of nine important Athenians. Plutarch's "Life of Cimon," contained herein, is the most significant source of information on him and the place to start serious research. Use Plutarch only in conjunction with modern histories, however, because his love of a good story often led him to errors, which later historians have corrected.

Schreiner, Johan Henrik. *Hellanikos, Thukydides and the Era of Kimon.* Oakville, Conn.: Aarhus University Press, 1997. History includes bibliography and index.

Sealey, Raphael. *A History of the Greek City-States, c. 700-338 B.C.* Berkeley: University of California Press, 1976. Written by a prominent proponent of the prosopographical approach to Greek politics, that is, the concept that personal and familial relations overrode ideological issues in shaping events. Includes discussion of major aspects of Cimon's life and times, with ancient sources referenced. Most historians have not found Sealey's interpretation of Athenian politics in the era 480 to 450 to be persuasive, because ideology does seem to have structured political behavior much more clearly after the Great Persian War than before.

Thucydides. *The Landmark Thucydides: A Comprehensive Guide to the Peloponnesian War.* Edited by Robert B. Strassler. New York: Simon & Schuster, 1998. Contains Thucydides' famous account of the period between the Great Persian War and the outbreak of the Peloponnesian War. While recounting the development of hostility between Athens and Sparta, Thucydides reveals much about the Athenian Empire and Cimon's role in its establishment and expansion.

SEE ALSO: Aegesilaus II of Sparta; Cleisthenes of Athens; Militiades the Younger; Pericles; Themistocles; Xerxes I.

RELATED ARTICLES in *Great Events from History: The Ancient World*: c. 550 B.C.E., Construction of Trireme Changes Naval Warfare; 508-507 B.C.E., Reforms of Cleisthenes; September 17, 490 B.C.E., Battle of Marathon; 483 B.C.E., Naval Law of Themistocles Is Instituted; 480-479 B.C.E., Persian Invasion of Greece; 478-448 B.C.E., Athenian Empire Is Created; May, 431-September, 404 B.C.E., Peloponnesian War.

CLAUDIUS I
Roman emperor (r. 41-54 C.E.)

Coming to power after the politically and financially devastating reign of Caligula, Claudius I completed the centralizing tendencies of Roman Imperial government by creating a bureaucracy that was totally professional in training and totally loyal in its devotion to the Imperial concept of government.

BORN: August 1, 10 B.C.E.; Lugdunum, Gaul (now Lyon, France)

DIED: October 13, 54 C.E.; Rome (now in Italy)

ALSO KNOWN AS: Tiberius Claudius Drusus Nero Germanicus (full name)

AREAS OF ACHIEVEMENT: Government and politics, literature, war and conquest

EARLY LIFE

Tiberius Claudius (KLAW-dee-uhs) Drusus Nero Germanicus was born in Lugdunum, Gaul (modern Lyon, France), the youngest son of the elder Drusus and Antonia Minor. The father of Claudius was the stepson of the emperor Augustus, and his mother was Augustus's niece. Despite such illustrious parentage, Claudius was never expected to hold any important government office or military post. Although his elder brother Germanicus was adopted into the Imperial family by his uncle, the future emperor Tiberius, Claudius was not considered to be in line for the throne because he was physically handicapped. In an age when physical beauty and perfection were admired, he was an embarrassment to the Imperial family.

Claudius's multiple handicaps and infirmities were readily apparent. He had weak knees, trembling hands, and a wobbly head; he dragged his right foot, walked with a limp, stuttered when he spoke, and drooled uncontrollably. Desiring to preserve an image of power and authority in the eyes of the Roman people, the Imperial family kept Claudius's public appearances to a minimum. Although not permitted a career in government service, Claudius received an excellent education. As he grew older, he became more and more interested in historical studies and wrote numerous scholarly works on Roman, Etruscan, and Carthaginian history. In addition, he wrote an apology for Cicero and composed an autobiography. Not content to limit himself to historical work, Claudius studied philological problems of Latin and introduced three new letters into the Latin alphabet.

During the reigns of Augustus and Tiberius, Claudius continued to have little part in affairs of state. When his nephew Caligula ascended the throne, however, Claudius's life changed dramatically. In July, 37 C.E., Claudius became consul along with Caligula. Although consuls lacked any real power, they enjoyed considerable prestige. Still, such public recognition only made life more difficult for Claudius. Even though he was related to the reigning emperor, Claudius was the frequent butt of cruel jokes and insults, the ever-present, easy target for court jesters and practical jokers. Indeed, this was probably the most difficult and dangerous time of his life. To protect himself from the murderous whims of his mad nephew, Claudius endured the insults and played the fool. People were all too ready to believe him mentally as well as physically handicapped. The role of the simpleton was a convenient ruse that saved Claudius's life on more than one occasion.

LIFE'S WORK

When Caligula became so autocratic as to attempt the establishment of a Hellenistic-style monarchy, assassins killed him along with his wife and daughter. While searching the Imperial palace, a soldier of the Praetorian Guard discovered Claudius hiding behind a curtain. After dragging Claudius to the Praetorian camp, the soldiers quickly realized the advantage to them of perpetuating the Imperial system. Thus, the Praetorian Guard hailed Claudius emperor on January 25, 41 C.E., while the senate was still trying to decide what to do.

Despite the unusual circumstances of his coming to the throne, Claudius was not a revolutionary. He wasted no time in capturing and punishing the assassins of Caligula while simultaneously distancing himself from his predecessor's policies. As emperor, Claudius looked on Augustus as his role model, following his lead in attempting to revive the traditional religious practices and political institutions of the Roman Republic. Despite his amicable overtures toward the senate, Claudius learned what Augustus had learned: The senate, never having renounced its claim to state leadership, was resentful of being dominated by an emperor. Claudius tried to show respect for the senate by giving back provinces that Tiberius had made Imperial (Achaea and Macedonia), appointing Imperial legates of senatorial rank, allowing the senate to issue copper coinage in the provinces, and enforcing senatorial resolutions. Despite all of his efforts at coopera-

tion, the senate was not very receptive. Eventually, this lack of response led Claudius to work against the senate and to concentrate all the power of the government in his own hands.

After a lapse of sixty-eight years during which the office of censor had gone unoccupied, Claudius temporarily restored and held it for eighteen months in 47-48 C.E. As a result of his censorship, numerous old senatorial families were discredited and expelled from the senate, while many new provincial families were admitted. Imperial oversight of the senate also extended to those aspects of government that had been traditionally controlled by the senate. The *aerarium Saturni* and the *fiscus*

Idealized depiction of Claudius I. (Library of Congress)

were both brought under close Imperial supervision through the Imperial appointment or nomination of the officials who ran these treasuries.

Not able to rely on the old senatorial aristocracy for administrative support, Claudius set himself the task of creating an executive staff manned by freedmen who were to be obedient only to the emperor. While freedmen had been used in government since the reign of Augustus, Claudius made more extensive use of them by placing them in charge of government departments and entrusting them with confidential tasks. This practice guaranteed the emperor's independence from the senate and antagonized the aristocratic elite of Rome. The freedmen Narcissus and Pallas became rich and powerful as Claudius's closest and most trusted advisers. With the establishment of a centralized administration directly under the emperor's control, Claudius was able to extend his jurisdiction into senatorial provinces.

At the same time, Claudius sought uniformity of administration and equal status for the provinces. Historically, Rome and Italy had enjoyed privileged positions within the Empire, while the provinces' status had been inferior. Claudius tried to eliminate this inequality by extending citizenship rights to various provincial communities and by establishing Roman colonies, particularly in the newer Imperial provinces such as Britain and Mauretania. This policy, while politically and militarily motivated, had the effect of quickening the pace of provincial Romanization.

Claudius was as aware as Augustus had been that the army was the real power base of the Roman government. Although he lacked military experience, Claudius needed to assume the image of a military leader and so was hailed *imperator* twenty-seven times. While not known in history for his military exploits, Claudius did expand the Empire. Under Claudius, Rome conquered Mauretania in 41 C.E., Britain in 43, and Thrace in 46. In addition, Claudius established the province of Lycia in 43 and the province of Judaea in 44.

In an effort to improve communications and the movement of troops, Claudius instituted a great road-building program. Not only did these roads tie the provinces closer to Rome, but they also stimulated trade between and among the provinces. Whenever Claudius saw an opportunity to expand trade and commerce, he immediately improved area roads and port facilities and built warehouses. The level of trade within the Empire and with foreign lands increased dramatically under Claudius.

Despite his emphasis on improving the economic condition of the provinces, Claudius did not neglect It-

aly, in general, or Rome, in particular. In central Italy, Claudius employed thirty thousand men for eleven years to drain the Fucine Marsh and reclaim much-needed arable land. What Julius Caesar and Augustus had only planned, Claudius accomplished. To increase the water supply of the capital, Claudius completed an aqueduct, begun by Caligula, which brought water to Rome from a distance of 62 miles (100 kilometers). He also built the Aqua Claudia, which brought water from 45 miles (73 kilometers) away. To guarantee Rome a secure supply of grain all year round, Claudius insured grain shippers against any loss so that they would continue to sail in the winter months. If a ship owner put his ships in the service of the grain trade for six years, he was granted full Roman citizenship. In order to handle the increased volume of trade, Claudius rebuilt the port of Ostia and built the new port of Portus, outfitting both ports with appropriate warehouses.

Keeping true to his Augustan ideals, Claudius tried to rekindle the old republican virtues through a religious restoration. By reviving ancient religious rites and linking them to Rome's glorious past, he tried to instill in the Romans of the Empire both the patriotism and the religious belief of an earlier generation. Claudius founded a College of Haruspices and held the Secular Games for Rome's eight hundredth birthday. To keep the religion of Rome focused on the traditional gods, Claudius extended the *pomerium* (religious boundary) and expelled Jews from the city. Religion as practiced outside Rome, however, was a different matter. With the exception of Druidism (because of its practice of human sacrifice), religious practices indigenous to the provinces were allowed to flourish.

If Claudius had a failing, it was in his relationships with his wives. Despite marrying four times, Claudius was unable to achieve marital happiness. His first two marriages, to Plautia Urgulanilla and Aelia Paetina, ended in divorce. His marriage to Valeria Messallina produced two children, Octavia (who later married Nero) and Britannicus. Messallina was executed in 48 C.E. as a result of the intrigues of Narcissus. Claudius's fourth marriage was to his niece Agrippina the Younger, whose cause was championed by Pallas. Agrippina succeeded, in 50 C.E., in getting Claudius to adopt her son Nero (from an earlier marriage) as his heir and the guardian of his own son, Britannicus.

Having lived his early life as a scholarly historian, Claudius ended his days as a very involved ruler of one of the greatest empires in history. A dish of poisoned mushrooms offered to him by Agrippina was the cause of his death. Although Claudius had pulled Rome from the brink of chaos after the disastrous reign of Caligula, he did not show the same acumen in leaving Rome in the hands of Nero. While Nero was not as outrageous as Caligula, he proved to be such a major disappointment to the Romans that he was the last of the Julio-Claudians to rule.

SIGNIFICANCE

Claudius, a man never intended to assume control of Rome, a man having symptoms of what may have been cerebral palsy, a man more comfortable in a scholar's library than in an emperor's palace, ruled and profoundly changed the Roman Empire. While trying to maintain an Empire-wide approach to the administration of the Empire, Claudius was, nevertheless, a major contributor to the evolution of a highly centralized and autocratic governmental administration.

Claudius's reforming tendencies and his emphasis on equality and justice show a basic contradiction in thinking. In trying to bring about equality by admitting provincials to the senate, Claudius was perpetuating the inequality of the old republican class structure. While honoring the senate in various ways, he actively worked to undermine it by creating an executive staff that guaranteed that all would be under the emperor's control. Thus, even though Claudius was attempting new approaches to old problems, he was bound too closely to Augustan tradition to be a strong champion of the new ideals of his age.

—Peter L. Viscusi

FURTHER READING

Graves, Robert. *I, Claudius: From the Autobiography of Tiberius Claudius, Born 10 B.C., Murdered and Deified A.D. 54.* Vancouver, Wash.: Vintage Books, 1989. Although this acclaimed work is a historical novel, it captures the essence of a famous period in history.

Levick, B. M. "Antiquarian or Revolutionary? Claudius Caesar's Conception of his Principate." *American Journal of Philology* 99 (1978): 79-105. The author maintains that Claudius was not a disinterested observer of contemporary events before his accession to the throne. As a historian, Claudius developed his own ideas on how the Imperial government should be organized. Levick believes that Claudius used Julius Caesar as his role model rather than Augustus.

Momigliano, Arnaldo D. *Claudius: The Emperor and His Achievement.* Reprint. Westport, Conn.: Greenwood Press, 1981. Momigliano believes that Claudius modeled himself on Augustus and tried to find some common ground with the senate. The centralization of the Imperial administration was the direct result of the senate's rejection of Claudius's offer of cooperation. Despite its brevity, this book is one of the seminal works on Claudius.

Scramuzza, Vincent M. *The Emperor Claudius.* Cambridge, Mass.: Harvard University Press, 1940. The first full-scale biography of Claudius to appear in English. The author has gathered and analyzed all the available archaeological, epigraphic, and literary evidence on the life of Claudius and has presented it in a most readable form. The coverage is comprehensive, thorough, and sound.

Scullard, H. H. *From the Gracchi to Nero: A History of Rome from 133 B.C. to A.D. 68.* New York: Routledge, 1988. Gives a straightforward account of Roman history during the last century of the Roman Republic and the first century of the Roman Empire. Scullard shows the financial and administrative problems caused by Gaius (Caligula) and the important changes that occurred under Claudius.

Suetonius. *Lives of the Twelve Caesars.* Revised and translated by Robert Graves. New York: Welcome Rain, 2001. Contains a chapter on Claudius, together with other chapters on his predecessors and successors. While Suetonius is one of the most important sources of information on Claudius, he is not always reliable. Still, he is useful because he preserves much contemporary detail that otherwise would be lost.

SEE ALSO: Agrippina the Younger; Antonia Minor; Augustus; Boudicca; Caligula; Valeria Messallina; Nero; Tiberius.

RELATED ARTICLES in *Great Events from History: The Ancient World*: 58-51 B.C.E., Caesar Conquers Gaul; 15 B.C.E.-15 C.E., Rhine-Danube Frontier Is Established; 43-130 C.E., Roman Conquest of Britain; c. 50 C.E., Creation of the Roman Imperial Bureaucracy; 60 C.E., Boudicca Leads Revolt Against Roman Rule.

CLEISTHENES OF ATHENS
Athenian statesman

The famous lawgiver and reformer Cleisthenes was the real architect of Athenian democracy. His statesmanship created radical innovations in the constitution: the representative principle and the idea of political equality.

BORN: c. 570 B.C.E.; place unknown
DIED: After 507 B.C.E.; place unknown
AREAS OF ACHIEVEMENT: Government and politics, law

EARLY LIFE

Cleisthenes (KLIZ-thah-neez) was a son of the Athenian Megacles, a member of the illustrious Alcmaeonid family, and a non-Athenian, Agariste, daughter of Cleisthenes of Sicyon. Little is known of his personal life. The Alcmaeonidae had been in exile during the tyranny of Pisistratus but regained favor by their generosity in the rebuilding of the temples, and the oracle of Delphi pressed on the Spartan king, Cleomenes I, for their reinstatement. Hippias, the tyrant leader of Athens, was overthrown by the Spartans in 510 B.C.E., leaving Athens at the mercy of the powerful families.

Cleisthenes returned to Athens and realized that he would not be accepted as a leader of another oligarchy, nor would the people tolerate another tyranny. Cleisthenes did not covet personal power but wanted to benefit the city. Although the way seemed open for Athenian self-government, the problem of competing families or clans would have to be overcome. His initial attempt at reform met with aristocratic resistance. Cleisthenes had to retreat but returned after the opposing Cleomenes and Isagoras were forced out by the *demos*, that is, the people.

LIFE'S WORK

Unlike Solon and Pisistratus, Cleisthenes did not work within the existing system but introduced a completely new scheme that he thought out in detail. He did not abolish or destroy existing institutions; instead, he insisted that the government function within the new plan. He systematically introduced into the constitution a well-coordinated and harmonic operation of government founded on political equality of all the citizens and the representation and participation of all.

The age-old division of Attica into four tribes, each with three brotherhoods and ninety clans, based on blood, led to many conflicts of loyalties. Cleisthenes' objective was to direct Athenian loyalty to the community.

A long period of time would seem necessary for this transfer of loyalty, but Cleisthenes brought the transfer very quickly. He developed an artificial plan for public loyalty.

Cleisthenes' basic plan abolished the four ancient tribes and created ten new ones in their place. He also persuaded the god Apollo to tell him after what legendary heroes he was to name them. The new tribes represented national, not local, interests and unity. The marketplace of Athens had a statue of each tribal hero. Each tribe also had its own shrine and its own hero cult but was not controlled by a particular family or local group.

Cleisthenes was able to destroy the old territorial loyalties of the Coast, the Plain, and the Hill. Before Cleisthenes' reform, the adult citizen population was 10,800. After the changes introduced by Cleisthenes, fifth century Athens numbered between 20,000 and 30,000 citizens.

To take the place of the old ship districts, Cleisthenes created a new unit of local government called the *deme*, or village. More than one hundred such villages were established, divided into ten groups to correspond with the ten tribes. Membership in the *deme* was made hereditary, and a family maintained its name wherever it moved. Blood ties were weakened, because one was now recognized as "Cleisthenes of Athens," for example, rather than as "son of Megacles." This artificial arrangement separated and weakened the authority of strong families and encouraged the enrollment of new citizens. The old, established aristocracy, with its agricultural concerns, would gradually have to share its influence with the seafaring commercial population of the coast.

Each of the ten tribes was made up of three *trittyes* (thirds), and the *trittyes* of *demes*. The *deme* corresponded geographically to a district of the city and was the local administrative unit. Membership in the *deme* guaranteed citizenship. The *trittyes* were divided into three geographical groups—coastal, inland, and city—and each tribe contained one from each group. The city itself had six *demes* in five different tribes, and the other five tribes were in the suburbs and the coast.

The Athenians were mistrustful of entrenched representatives or experts; they preferred that the government be run by intelligent amateurs. According to Athenians, the person of ordinary intelligence was capable of political responsibility. Thus, the people were the supreme authority and gave in the assembly their vote to all acts. All business was discussed prior to the assembly in the Boule, or council, and passed on to the assembly for ratification. The council was composed of five hundred members elected annually, fifty from each tribe. Each *deme*, according to the number of citizens on its rolls, elected candidates for the council, and from these candidates, council members were elected by lot, fifty being selected from each tribe. The council was divided into ten committees, one of which was on duty for the tenth part of each year. This committee of fifty members, called a *prytany*, held office for a tenth of the year under a chairman who sat for one day and was chosen by lot. He was acting head of the government and had the keys to the Acropolis, the state seal, and the archives. He could not be reelected. Part of the *prytany* remained on duty day and night, eating and sleeping in the Tholos, a round building provided for this purpose. The council prepared matters for the assembly and was also responsible for fiscal policy, receiving an account from all civil officials leaving office.

Cleisthenes established ostracism in a systematic manner as a safeguard against conflict. The assembly voted once a year whether to have an ostracism. An affirmative vote meant that each member would write on a piece of pottery, *ostrakon*, the member he would like to see exiled. The person who received the most votes, six thousand or more, went into honorable exile for a period of ten years without loss of property. This measure may well have been a deterrent in neutralizing opposition; there is no record of its being used until 487 B.C.E., after Cleisthenes' time.

Legislative powers were in the *ecclesia*, or assembly that discussed and passed laws. Judicial authority was with the *heliaea*, the court of popular representatives, elected by the tribes in the same manner as the council. Judicial functions were controlled by people's juries, selected from an annual panel of six thousand citizens chosen by lot from the same units.

The magistrates, the nine archons, and the *colacietae* and *strategoi* were elected from among the wealthier citizens. The former were concerned with finance; the latter commanded ten companies of militia. This organization may have been reasonable, as the state did not pay citizens in discharging their public duties.

Each tribe supported a regiment of infantry and a squadron of cavalry who were commanded by elective officers, called *taxiarchi* and *hipparchi*. Each of the ten *strategoi* commanded the army in turn. The army was similar to a national militia. Cleisthenes, however, did not reform the navy.

SIGNIFICANCE

The constitution of Cleisthenes of Athens was put into effect in 502 B.C.E. While it did not end the conflict between parties or the unequal distribution of wealth, it did mitigate many of the problems. The government was no longer something external or alien but identified with the life and goals of each citizen. At the time of Cleisthenes' death, the *demes* were the real rulers of Athens, although they were led by the aristocracy. Cleisthenes created a strong and well-organized state and constitution. At the end of the Peloponnesian War there was a brief oligarchic reaction, but Cleisthenes' reforms were restored in 403.

Cleisthenes is credited with the complete breakdown of the patriarchal idea of the state as a corporation. It was never restored in Athens. He established new tribes, enrolled aliens as new citizens, and contributed to the idea of free communication and interchange between different peoples. This idea, together with the principles of representation and of political equality, strengthened democracy.

—*Peter F. Macaluso*

FURTHER READING

Aristotle. *The Athenian Constitution*. Translated by P. J. Rhodes. New York: Penguin, 1984. Contains the great philosopher's brief history and description of the Athenian state with a helpful commentary. This 208-page work is an essential source for the workings of Cleisthenes' constitution. Aristotle provides a good introduction to study of Cleisthenes.

Davies, John Kenyon. *Democracy and Classical Greece*. 2d ed. Stanford, Calif.: Stanford University Press, 1993. This study was the clearest reexamination of the present state of knowledge about democratic ideas in Athens. It emphasizes archaeological evidence in social and political history.

Ehrenberg, Victor. *From Solon to Socrates: Greek History and Civilization During the Sixth and Fifth Centuries B.C.* New York: Methuen, 1973. An excellent illustrated political textbook on the central period of Greek history during the sixth and fifth centuries B.C.E. Contains good references to primary and secondary sources.

Forrest, William G. *The Emergence of Greek Democracy, 800-400 B.C.* New York: McGraw-Hill, 1966. This work is a clear, lively interpretation of the reforms of Cleisthenes and provides a general account of his time. It is written in an interesting style and describes the social and political developments and the transition from aristocracy to democracy in Athens. The notes are especially good.

Highnett, Charles. *A History of the Athenian Constitution to the End of the Fifth Century B.C.* Oxford, England: Clarendon Press, 1975. Scholarly treatment of the development of the Athenian constitution, discussing its successive phases of growth from the early monarchy and aristocracy to the decline of the Athenian Empire. An important and thought-provoking analysis of the beginnings of Athenian democracy.

Staveley, E. S. *Greek and Roman Voting and Elections.* Ithaca, N.Y.: Cornell University Press, 1972. This study illuminates many practices in the Athenian government and the spirit of public service over several centuries.

Zimmern, Alfred. *The Greek Commonwealth: Politics and Economics in Fifth Century Athens.* 5th ed. New York: Oxford University Press, 1961. This classic work presents an interesting analysis of fifth century Athens but lacks an adequate bibliography. Important aspects of Cleisthenes' career and the cultural background of this period are discussed.

SEE ALSO: Cimon; Plato; Solon.

RELATED ARTICLES in *Great Events from History: The Ancient World*: 600-500 B.C.E., Greek Philosophers Formulate Theories of the Cosmos; c. 594-580 B.C.E., Legislation of Solon; c. 550 B.C.E., Construction of Trireme Changes Naval Warfare; c. 530 B.C.E., Founding of the Pythagorean Brotherhood; 508-507 B.C.E., Reforms of Cleisthenes; 483 B.C.E., Naval Law of Themistocles Is Instituted; 478-448 B.C.E., Athenian Empire Is Created; May, 431-September, 404 B.C.E., Peloponnesian War; September, 404-May, 403 B.C.E., Thirty Tyrants Rule Athens for Eight Months.

CLEMENT I
Roman bishop

Clement was the first of the Apostolic Fathers about whom anything is known and, according to tradition, was the third successor to Peter as bishop of Rome. Clement was also the author of the earliest and most valuable surviving example of Christian literature not included in the New Testament.

BORN: Date unknown; perhaps Rome (now in Italy)
DIED: c. 99 C.E.; perhaps in the Crimea (now in Ukraine)
ALSO KNOWN AS: Clemens Romanus (Latin); Clement of Rome; Saint Clement
AREA OF ACHIEVEMENT: Religion

EARLY LIFE
Of the life of Clement (CLEH-mehnt) very little is known with absolute certainty. He is called Clement of Rome (Clemens Romanus) to distinguish him from the later Clement of Alexandria (Clemens Alexandrinus). No reliable source gives even the approximate date or place of his birth. An early Christian work attributed to him titled *Recognitions* (third century C.E.) states that he was born in the city of Rome and that he was from his early youth given to meditating and sober reflection on such serious subjects as the nature of life, whether there was a preexistence, and the possibility of immortality. According to that work, he was converted to Christianity by the disciple Barnabas, who came to Rome to preach and thereafter introduced him to Peter, who received him with great joy.

Such a story is not inconsistent with other information now known about Clement. Nevertheless, true authorship of *Recognitions* cannot be ascribed to Clement himself because most scholars believe that it was penned more than a century after his time. Despite this doubt, however, the work is not completely without value; indeed, it seems to preserve traditions that contain some kernels of truth.

Undoubtedly, Clement was a younger contemporary of Peter and Paul. The early church scholars and theologians Origen (c. 185-254), Eusebius of Caesarea (c. 260-339), Epiphanius (c. 315-403), and Saint Jerome (c. 331/347-420) all identify Clement of Rome as the Clement spoken of in Philippians 4:3. This Scripture calls him Paul's fellow laborer. Similarly, Saint Irenaeus (c. 120/140-202) states that Clement saw the Apostles and talked with them, that their preaching was so fresh in his mind at the time he rose to prominence that it still rang in his ears, and that many of Clement's generation had been taught personally by the Apostles. Clement himself intimates that he was closely associated with Peter and Paul.

Clement was probably of Jewish descent. His close association with the Apostles, who were all Jewish, and his wide use of and familiarity with the Old Testament, as demonstrated in the one surviving authentic Clementine work, lend support to this inference. Clement's style of writing is colored with Hebraisms, but he probably possessed no real understanding of Hebrew, knowing only the Septuagint (Greek) translation of the Old Testament, as many Jews of the day did.

An ancient tradition identifies Clement with a certain Flavius Clemens, a distinguished Roman nobleman who held the office of consul in 95 C.E. and was the nephew of the emperor Vespasian. It is difficult to believe that the same man held both the consulship and the bishopric, as these times were difficult ones for the Church because of Roman antagonism.

It is also unlikely that the Hellenistic Jewish style of Clement's epistle would be as prominent if Clement came from the Roman classical culture of a court circle. It is more likely, then, that the future church leader was a freedman or former slave belonging to the house of Clemens and that, in accordance with custom, he assumed the name of his patron when fully liberated.

LIFE'S WORK

At some point in his life, Clement became a leader in the Roman church and was ultimately ordained bishop of that Christian community about the year 90 C.E. While Tertullian, writing about 199 C.E., says that Clement was ordained by Peter before the Apostle's death (c. 64 C.E.), other ancient, reliable authorities state that Clement was preceded by two other successors to Peter (Linus and Anacletus) and thus was the fourth bishop of Rome. Clement's fame rests on both his designation as the first known Apostolic Father and his authorship of the epistle to the Corinthian church.

The expression "Apostolic Fathers" seems to have been used first by Severus of Antioch, patriarch of Alexandria in the sixth century and scholar of early Christian literature. The phrase referred to those who were not Apostles but disciples of the Apostles and who authored writings contemporaneous with or prior to those of Irenaeus in the second century. The Apostolic Fathers, then, were the earliest orthodox writers outside the New Testament. Clement was the first, chronologically, of this group, which includes Ignatius of Antioch, Polycarp, Barnabas, and Hermas. *Klementos pros Korinthious epistola prōtē* (first century C.E.; *The First Epistle of Clement to the Corinthians*, also known as *First Clement*, 1647) is the earliest extant Christian document outside the New Testament.

The epistle to the Corinthians was Clement's most important achievement. Although Clement's name is not

Clement I. (Library of Congress)

mentioned in the letter, he seems to have been from the first recognized as its author. About 170 C.E., Dionysius, bishop of Corinth, while acknowledging another letter written from the church of Rome to the church of Corinth, mentions that the letter written by Clement was still read from time to time in their Sunday assemblies. Eusebius also speaks of the epistle to the Corinthians as being Clement's, as do Irenaeus, Origen, and Clement of Alexandria.

Clement wrote his epistle sometime after he became bishop of Rome, though the exact date of its composition is not known. The second century Christian historian Hegesippus, who visited the Corinthian church on a trip to Rome, learned that the letter was written during the reign of Domitian (81-96 C.E.). If one considers an allusion Clement makes in the epistle to the persecutions of Christians that took place at Rome under Domitian in 93 C.E., the date of the epistle can be placed between the years 93 and 96 C.E.

Clement's main objective in writing *The First Epistle of Clement to the Corinthians* was to restore peace and unity to that Greek branch of the Church. The Corinthians had been led by some young, rebellious individuals to rise up against their lawfully appointed presbyters. The significance of Clement's epistle is twofold. First, it outlines the organization, or structure, of the apostolic church. Second, it seems to have helped lay the foundation for the birth of the Roman Catholic papacy and papal theory.

Clement states that the action taken by the seditious persons at Corinth was inexcusable. He declares that Christ was sent forth by God, the Apostles were sent by Christ, and the Apostles, preaching throughout the known world, appointed the first fruits of their proselytizing activity to be bishops after having proved them by the Spirit. Clement also says that the Apostles gave instructions that when these bishops appointed by them should die, other approved men should succeed them in their ministry by appointment from the Apostles or other eminent men, with the consent of the whole church. He urges the schismatics at Corinth to return to the true order of the church, to put away strife, disorder, jealousy, and pride.

While no claim is made by the Roman church leader to interfere with another on any grounds of superior rank, the unmistakably authoritative tone of the letter gives its author more than merely a peacemaker's role. Using Clement's epistle as a precedent, Roman bishops of the second century began to assume preeminent authority to resolve general Christian disputes. By the mid-third century, the practice had arisen of reckoning Peter not only as chief Apostle but also as first bishop of Rome. Gradually, the term "pope" or "father" (Latin *papa*), which had been used for any bishop in Western Europe, began to be directed toward the bishop of Rome exclusively.

Clement served as bishop of Rome about nine years. During his time as head of one of Christianity's most important communities, Clement wrote his epistle and was occupied with duties centering on proselytism, exhortation, keeping the Church unified, and helping it to survive attacks and persecutions such as the one promoted by Domitian.

There are conflicting tales concerning the death of Clement. According to Eusebius and Jerome, he died a natural death in the third year of the reign of the emperor Trajan. Other traditions, however, reckon him among the martyrs. The apocryphal *Acts of the Martyrs* relates how, toward the end of his life and tenure of office, Clement converted more than four hundred Romans of rank; as a result, Trajan banished the bishop to the Chersonese Peninsula in the Black Sea area. There Clement set to work

converting the people of the country (two thousand in number), who built seventy-five churches. Trajan then had Clement thrown into the sea with an iron anchor around his neck. This story circulated for many years until around 868, when Saint Cyril, Apostle to the Slavs, dug up some bones and an anchor in the Crimea. Hailed as the relics of Clement, these remains were carried back to Rome and deposited by Pope Adrian II with the relics of Ignatius of Antioch in the Basilica of Saint Clement in Rome.

SIGNIFICANCE

Next to the Apostles themselves, Clement was for many generations the most esteemed figure in the Church. Clement of Alexandria called him an Apostle. Jerome referred to him as an apostolic man, and Rufinus said that he was almost an Apostle.

Clement's letter to the church at Corinth was for centuries considered canonical by many and on a par with the epistles of Paul. Eusebius speaks of the public reading of Clement's letter as the ancient custom of many churches down to his own time. The list of ancient Christian authorities and leaders who quoted *The First Epistle of Clement to the Corinthians* includes Polycarp and Ignatius, themselves Apostolic Fathers.

Numerous spurious writings have been attributed to Clement. The most celebrated among these was probably the second century *The Second Epistle of Clement to the Corinthians* (translated 1693), purporting to supplement the first. This second letter was also held in great respect by early Christians. It is interesting to note that the two epistles disappeared from the Western Church in the sixth century. They were rediscovered in the year 1628, when an ancient manuscript of the Greek Bible was presented to King Charles I of England by the patriarch Cyril Lukaris.

—Andrew C. Skinner

FURTHER READING

Apostolic Fathers. *The Apostolic Fathers: Greek Texts and English Translations of Their Writings.* Translated and edited by J. B. Lightfoot and J. R. Harmer. 2d ed. Revised by Michael W. Holmes. Grand Rapids, Mich.: Baker Book House, 1999. An extensive and authoritative work that covers Clement and his writing. It presents a facsimile of the actual Greek texts of the two epistles along with translations, notes, and commentaries on the texts. Lightfoot synthesizes and distills all the references to Clement in ancient literature and history to attempt to fill in the gaps concerning his life.

Clemens Romanus. *The First Epistle of Clement to the Corinthians*. Edited by W. K. Lowther Clarke. London: Society for the Promotion of Christian Knowledge, 1963. Contains introductory notes and a translation of Clement's authentic epistle. The explanations of the text illuminate Clement's life and the historical context of the letter.

Grant, Robert M. *The Apostolic Fathers*. 6 vols. New York: Thomas Nelson and Sons, 1964-1968. Vol. 1 is among the most accessible works on the Apostolic Fathers and their world. It discusses who the Apostolic Fathers were and their historical circumstances, theological outlook, and writings. The relationship between Clement and the other Apostolic Fathers is also discussed. Vol. 2, *First and Second Clement*, includes a translation (in idiomatic English) of, and commentary on, the two epistles ascribed to Clement. Includes detailed annotations and cross-references for virtually every verse of the two epistles.

Richardson, Cyril C., ed. *Early Christian Fathers*. Vol. 1 in *The Library of Christian Classics*. Philadelphia: Westminster Press, 1953. This first volume in a series on the classic documents of Christianity contains a fine translation of both epistles as well as a brief but thorough introduction to Clement and his writing. Its greatest value is the extensive bibliography on Clement and his work.

Staniforth, Maxwell. *Early Christian Writings*. New York: Dorset Press, 1986. A readable introduction to the Apostolic Fathers and their writings. The section on Clement contains an introduction to the man and his work and a translation of the two epistles. The introduction discusses the significance of Clement's bishopric for the Church. Includes helpful footnotes.

SEE ALSO: Eusebius of Caesarea; Saint Jerome; Origen; Saint Paul; Saint Peter; Trajan.

RELATED ARTICLES in *Great Events from History: The Ancient World*: 64-67 C.E., Nero Persecutes the Christians; c. 110 C.E., Trajan Adopts Anti-Christian Religious Policy; 200 C.E., Christian Apologists Develop Concept of Theology.

CLEOMENES
Spartan kings

Through a number of military victories and even in defeat, Cleomenes I strengthened Sparta as no ruler had before him. Cleomenes II ruled Sparta during a difficult and trying time. He managed to hold a beaten city-state together and ally it with neighboring powers. Cleomenes III instituted social reforms in Sparta that canceled debt, registered hundreds of new citizens, and redistributed lands.

CLEOMENES I (r. c. 519-c. 490 B.C.E.)

BORN: Date unknown; Sparta, Greece
DIED: c. 490 B.C.E.; Sparta, Greece
AREAS OF ACHIEVEMENT: Government and politics, war and conquest

EARLY LIFE

Cleomenes I (klee-AHM-uh-neez) succeeded his father, King Anaxandrides, to the throne around 519 B.C.E. Initially, his half brother Dorieus challenged his ascendancy, but Cleomenes was planted firmly in power when Dorieus left Sparta to establish a colony elsewhere.

LIFE'S WORK

Cleomenes I wanted to fight against Athens's tyranny and to expand Sparta's boundaries and influence outward, even into Greece. After a naval failure, he led a land expedition against Athens that succeeded in trapping the Athenian dictator, Hippias, and members of his government on the Acropolis. Spartans captured Hippias's children as they were being smuggled out of Athens and ransomed them to force Hippias to accede to the Spartans' demands and leave the city.

Overseen by Cleomenes I, Cleisthenes and Isagoras ruled Athens. Years later, when a struggle between them threatened civil war, Cleomenes ordered Cleisthenes out of Athens. He exiled seven hundred supporting Athenian families and threatened to replace Cleisthenes' council of five hundred with a three-hundred-member council supportive of Isagoras. Isagoras was Cleomenes' protégé, and Athenians did not appreciate his efforts to install him on their throne. Struggles continued until Isagoras's entire party was executed. Isagoras was able to escape.

Cleisthenes and his seven hundred supporting families returned to Athens and began negotiations with Darius of Persia for a possible alliance. On hearing of Athens's deceit, Cleomenes gathered an army to attack the city. Cleomenes' co-monarch, Demaratus, joined the military forces to demonstrate unanimous Spartan support for the campaign. Cleomenes' main goal for the attack on Athens was to return Isagoras to the throne, not to punish it for its recent negotiations with Persia, as many thought. When Demaratus discovered the true nature of the campaign, the two monarchs argued. Corinthian forces who had joined the Spartans refused to participate and went home. The campaign failed.

Early in the fifth century, Sparta's ancient enemy, Argos, refused to pay tribute. Cleomenes led his armies northward to Argosian territory to re-establish Sparta's authority. Before crossing the Erasinos River, Spartans offered sacrifices to the gods for support. Believing the sacrifices did not satisfy the gods, Cleomenes boarded his men on ships and instead attacked the Argosians at Sepeia. His victory was complete by about 494, but, in a controversial move, Cleomenes pursued a number of Argosians to a grove where they had taken refuge. Calling them out under the pretense of arranging for their ransom, Cleomenes executed fifty of Argos's leading citizens. Again citing religious reasons, he decided not to attack Argos and went home.

Three years later, a Persian invasion of Athens appeared imminent. Cleomenes received word that a number of local islands were paying homage to King Darius the Great of Persia, in particular the strategically located Aegina. Athens appealed to Cleomenes for support. Cleomenes led military forces to Aegina in 491 B.C.E. to arrest leading members of the offending parties. He was met by Krio, known as "the Ram." Krio refused to acknowledge Cleomenes' power to arrest, stating that he did not have Spartan governmental support for his campaign. If Sparta supported his cause, Krio asserted, both Spartan kings would have come to Aegina. Because of arguments between the monarchs in the struggle against Athens, Spartan law forbade any two rulers from participating together in the same campaign.

Cleomenes believed his co-king, Demaratus, was behind Krio's words and decided to try to remove him from office. He revived old rumors that Demaratus was illegitimate and therefore had no claim to the Spartan throne. When the oracle at Delphi was consulted as to his paternity, she affirmed his illegitimate status, and Spartans replaced Demaratus with his enemy Leotychides. Rumors began that Cleomenes had bribed the prophetess.

For a few months, Cleomenes and Leotychides worked well together. They further strengthened the Peloponnese against the Persian threat and managed to arrest Aeginetan leaders who opposed them. However, reports of Cleomenes' bribery of the Delphic oracle grew. Cleomenes became so unpopular that he was forced to flee to Thessaly and later Arcadia. While in Arcadia, Cleomenes put together a military force to retake his own city. He was recalled to Sparta where, on his return, his family had him arrested. Cleomenes reportedly stabbed himself to death; however, it is also possible that his Ephorian enemies killed him.

SIGNIFICANCE

Though some historians claim that Cleomenes I suffered from intermittent mental illness, his actions in office and on the military front show him to have been a capable strategist. Rumors of madness may have been spread by his enemies to justify forcing him out of Sparta. Though he may not have spread Spartan rule as far as he desired, Cleomenes increased Sparta's power more than any ruler before him.

CLEOMENES II (r. 370-c. 309 B.C.E.)

BORN: Date unknown; Sparta, Greece
DIED: c. 309 B.C.E.; Sparta, Greece
AREAS OF ACHIEVEMENT: Government and politics, war and conquest

EARLY LIFE

A year before Cleomenes II ascended the throne in 370, the great city-state of Sparta was brutally defeated at the Battle of Leuctra in Boeotia. What was once the most feared of cities had been reduced to a seemingly benign town. Under Cleomenes II, Sparta did not try to expand so much as to defend the territory it still had.

LIFE'S WORK

In 362, Thebes threatened the peninsula. After some initial successes in relieving Sparta of some of her possessions, the Theban threat encouraged Spartans to form a new coalition with their neighbors to fight their common enemy. Sparta was defeated during the ensuing battle, but Theban armies lost their leader and, with him, the will to continue.

SIGNIFICANCE

Afterward, negotiations over the reunification of the peninsula continued. After years of arguing and contending for power, Sparta rejoined the Achaean League in 332. Cleomenes II reigned during a time of great trouble, and perhaps his greatest accomplishment was to have held the defeated city together and thus prepare it for a resurgence of power.

CLEOMENES III (r. 235-219 B.C.E.)

BORN: Date unknown; Sparta, Greece
DIED: 219 B.C.E.; Alexandria, Egypt
AREAS OF ACHIEVEMENT: Government and politics, war and conquest

EARLY LIFE

Cleomenes III was the son of Leonidas II, who ruled Sparta from 254 to 235. Leonidas and his co-monarch, Agis IV, had ascended the Spartan throne during a time of financial crisis. Agis IV attempted to institute a program of social reform in Sparta. He believed that returning to a Lycurgan form of government would help Sparta regain its former glory. He proposed land redistribution so that every freeman would share equally in the city. To reform the financial situation, Agis called for the cancellation of all debts, a measure supported by many Spartans who owed creditors and by landowners who had mortgaged their properties.

While Agis was away at war, his support diminished in Sparta. Leonidas believed part of Agis's reform strategy included removing him from office. With Leonidas's consent, Agis was tried and executed. Though Leonidas

was banished and forced into exile, he later returned and regained the throne. In an effort to bring unity to the city, Leonidas induced Agis's widow, Agiatis, to marry his son, Cleomenes III. Though the marriage was arranged, Cleomenes III fell in love with his wife and was swayed by her former husband's political ideas.

LIFE'S WORK

When Cleomenes III ascended the throne in 235, he rededicated himself to instituting Agis IV's social reforms and restoring a Lycurgan constitution. The people of Sparta were calling for change. Most of Sparta's land was held by only one hundred families. Fewer and fewer people in the city, only about seven hundred men, could declare themselves full citizens. As years passed, increasing numbers of poor called for more equitable land distributions and cancellation of debts.

By conducting a few successful military skirmishes, Cleomenes III strengthened Sparta's position in the Achaean League and earned support from the military. His reform ideas and relatively austere lifestyle gained him support from the people; however, his reforms were strongly opposed by rich landowners. The Gerousia, the governing body of Sparta, refused to pass his measures. In 237, Cleomenes III staged a governmental coup and rearranged Sparta's government. He abolished the Gerousia on the grounds that Lycurgus never sanctioned its creation. In addition, Cleomenes killed or exiled many of those who opposed him. He liberated thousands of serfs by allowing them to purchase their freedom for a fee, thus increasing the treasury as well. He succeeded in canceling debts and redistributing four thousand lots of land. At the same time, Cleomenes attracted and registered thousands of new citizens.

After the liberation of the serfs, three thousand men joined Cleomenes' phalanx of soldiers. He reintroduced traditional discipline into the military, preparing them to extend Sparta's influence throughout the Peloponnese. Agis IV had strengthened Sparta's position in the Achaean League by joining Aratus of Sicyon in a joint Peloponnesian defense against the Aetolians. However, when Cleomenes III wanted to be named commander in chief of the Achaean forces, Aratus refused to acquiesce to his demands. Cleomenes quarreled with the Achaean League and then set out to break it up. The same Aratus who had assisted Agis IV against the Aetolians called on Antigonus Doson of Macedon to help the league in the impending attack from Sparta.

In the meantime, Cleomenes gained support for his cause from various Peloponnesian cities. He succeeded

Cleomenes III. (Library of Congress)

in taking Corinth, Hermione, Troezen, Pellene, Argos, Epidaurus, Philius, and Aratus. Commoners in these cities hoped that Cleomenes III would bring his social reforms with him and redistribute land as he had in Sparta; they surrendered without a fight.

In 222, Cleomenes met Doson at Sellasia in the hills of north Sparta. Doson defeated the Spartan forces and forced Cleomenes to flee to Alexandria, where he hoped to find refuge with Egyptian ruler Ptolemy III. Cleomenes, however, failed to win support among the Egyptian people. He was reportedly killed in 219 during the palace purges that surrounded the accession of Ptolemy IV.

SIGNIFICANCE

Many commoners saw Cleomenes III as liberating them from their oppressive rulers. After the death of Cleomenes, the oligarchic regime was reinstated in Sparta. Doson and his armies later occupied Sparta and revoked Cleomenes' social reform projects.

—*Leslie A. Stricker*

FURTHER READING

Boardman, John, Jasper Griffin, and Oswyn Murray, eds. *The Oxford History of Greece and the Hellenistic World.* New York: Oxford University Press, 2001. Discusses the Persian Wars and the involvement of Cleomenes I, as well as art, life, religion, and politics in the Hellenistic Age.

Forrest, W. G. *A History of Sparta 950-192 B.C.* 2d ed. London: Duckworth, 1980. Chapter 8 discusses the life and times of Cleomenes I and Cleomenes III (referred to as "Kleomenes I" and "Kleomenes III").

Grimal, Pierre. *Hellenism and the Rise of Rome.* New York: Delacorte Press, 1968. Chapter 3 describes some of the social reforms instituted by Cleomenes III and discusses his motivations.

Huxley, G. L. *Early Sparta.* New York: Barnes & Noble, 1970. Chapters 6 and 7 describe the military campaigns, career, and ultimate fall from power of Cleomenes I and the history of Sparta to 490 B.C.E.

Walbank, F. W. *The Hellenistic World.* Rev. ed. Cambridge, Mass.: Harvard University Press, 1993. Discusses how Cleomenes III came to power and the influences of his wife, the former wife of Agis IV, on his political views.

SEE ALSO: Agesilaus II of Sparta; Cleisthenes of Athens; Darius the Great; Leonidas.

RELATED ARTICLES in *Great Events from History: The Ancient World*: 499-494 B.C.E., Ionian Revolt; 480-479 B.C.E., Persian Invasion of Greece.

CLEOPATRA VII
Egyptian queen (r. 51-30 B.C.E.)

Cleopatra VII, as the last of the Ptolemaic Greek rulers of an independent Egypt, tried to come to terms with the ceaseless expansion of the Roman Empire throughout the Mediterranean region and at her death left behind a rich Imperial province that continued to flourish as a center of commerce, science, and learning under Roman rule.

BORN: 69 B.C.E.; Alexandria, Egypt
DIED: August 3, 30 B.C.E.; Alexandria, Egypt
ALSO KNOWN AS: Cleopatra Philopater
AREA OF ACHIEVEMENT: Government and politics

EARLY LIFE

Cleopatra (klee-oh-PAT-truh) VII was the daughter of Ptolemy XII Auletes and (possibly) of his sister and wife, Cleopatra Tryphaena. Such brother-sister marriages were common among the members of the Egyptian ruling house. It is believed that Cleopatra had three sisters, two older and one younger, and two younger brothers. Her representation with Nubian features by Michelangelo and her depiction as an Egyptian in cult paintings conceal her Macedonian ancestry; her family traced its lineage back to the Macedonian house of the Lagid Ptolemies, which had succeeded to the Egyptian throne after the untimely death of Alexander the Great in the early fourth century B.C.E. The Ptolemaic rule of Egypt was centered in Alexandria, the beautiful and populous city Alexander had founded to the west of the delta of the Nile River when he invaded Egypt in 332 B.C.E.

Cleopatra was raised in a court beset by violence, murder, and corruption and dominated by the reality of Roman military might—all of which had played an important role in her father's accession to the throne. In 80 B.C.E., on the death of Ptolemy IX Soter II, the only legitimate male Ptolemaic heir came to the throne as Ptolemy XI Alexander II. He was confirmed in power by the Romans but after murdering his wife, Berenice III, was himself murdered. Two illegitimate sons of Ptolemy IX Soter II were then claimants to the kingship.

The Romans put one brother in control of Cyprus. The other, Cleopatra's father, Ptolemy XII Neus Dionysos or, as he was known to the Alexandrians, Ptolemy XII Auletes (the Flute Player), succeeded to the throne of Egypt. His relations with his subjects were difficult, in part because he recognized, unlike them, the growing power of Rome throughout the Mediterranean area and realized that the only way to secure his position was to maintain close contact with the rulers of the world. During a visit to Rome, when he was hoping by means of massive bribes to secure the aid of the Roman army, his daughter, Berenice, in alliance with Archilaus, son of Mithridates, seized the throne, only to be put to death by her father on his return.

When Ptolemy XII Auletes died in 51 B.C.E., after nearly thirty stormy years in office, he willed the kingdom of Egypt to his seventeen-year-old daughter and his ten-year-old son, who ruled jointly as Cleopatra VII and Ptolemy XIII. The young Ptolemy, however, soon fell under the influence of his advisers—Pothinus, a eunuch; Theodotus, a rhetorician; and Achillas the army commander—who must have found the boy king far more manipulable than his older sister, the intelligent, headstrong, energetic Cleopatra. As a result, Cleopatra was driven from Alexandria. When Julius Caesar arrived in Egypt, in pursuit of Pompey after the Battle of Pharsalus in 48 B.C.E., Cleopatra was in Pelusium, on the eastern frontier of Egypt, with her newly acquired army preparing to attack her brother and his associates.

Caesar, as Rome's official representative, was in a position to arbitrate between the siblings, and his plan to reconcile Cleopatra and Ptolemy might have worked had not Ptolemy's advisers decided that power should remain in their own grasp. In the resulting showdown, known as the Alexandrian War, Caesar was victorious—but not without a struggle. Pothinus, Achillas, and Ptolemy were all killed, and Cleopatra was restored by Caesar to the throne, this time with Ptolemy XIV, her younger brother, as consort. By late 48 B.C.E., Cleopatra was in control of Egypt.

LIFE'S WORK

From this point onward, Cleopatra's future is inexorably intertwined with that of Rome and its leaders. In their

Cleopatra VII is unrolled from a carpet in front of Julius Caesar. (F. R. Niglutsch)

writings, Plutarch and Suetonius dwell on the love affair that developed between Julius Caesar, then in his fifties, and the twenty-one-year-old Cleopatra. In spite of the arguments to the contrary, the child born to Cleopatra shortly after Caesar left Egypt on his eastern campaign was probably Caesar's son. At any rate, Cleopatra, by naming the child Caesarion, was claiming that her son was indeed the son of the Roman conqueror. Moreover, young Octavian (later called Augustus), Caesar's heir, who had most to fear if Julius Caesar had a genuine son, had Caesarion put to death in 30 B.C.E., immediately after the death of Cleopatra.

Little is known about Cleopatra's rule of Egypt, although there is evidence that she tried to win the favor of the farmers by reducing their taxes. From 46 B.C.E., she was living in Rome with Caesarion and Ptolemy XIV. The reason stated for her visit was that she had come to ask the senate for confirmation of her father's treaty of friendship; yet she was lodged by Caesar, along with Caesarion and Ptolemy XIV, in his villa in Trastevere, where she attempted to cultivate good relations with as many influential Romans as possible. Caesar also put a golden statue of Cleopatra in the temple of Venus Genetrix at Rome, thus associating her with the goddess who was in legend the mother of Aeneas and thus of the Julian line. He may have planned to gain special permission from the Roman people to contract a legal marriage with her, as his Roman wife was childless. The plans were frustrated by Caesar's assassination in 44 B.C.E., and Cleopatra probably left Rome shortly afterward.

Egypt's wealth did not pass unnoticed by the Romans, so it is not surprising that during Marc Antony's eastern campaign after the Battle of Philippi in 42 B.C.E. he saw the chance of subsidizing his wars by taxing Cleopatra's subjects. Cleopatra was shrewd enough to realize that her personal charms would be far more effective in preserving her kingdom than would open confrontation. Plutarch's account of the meeting between Antony and Cleopatra brilliantly describes both the fabulous wealth of the monarch and her grace. Just as Cleopatra had captivated Julius Caesar in earlier days, when she "was green in judgment," she now in her maturity set out to win the heart of Antony.

After the formation of the so-called Second Triumvirate among Antony, Octavian, and Lepidus, which was sealed by Antony's marriage to Octavian's half sister Octavia, Cleopatra was left to rule Egypt. In 37 B.C.E., however, Antony's march eastward led to renewed friendship and an understanding between the two, which made available to Antony the resources of Egypt. From this time onward, Cleopatra's influence over Antony grew. She also assumed Egyptian dress that represented the goddess Isis and is reported to have adopted the following oath: "As surely as I shall one day dispense judgment in the Roman Capitol." When Antony arranged for Caesarion and his own three children with Cleopatra to share in ruling both Egypt and Roman provinces in Asia Minor and formally divorced Octavia, Octavian declared war not only against his fellow Roman Antony but also against Cleopatra. He must have realized that Antony could not help but join Cleopatra.

At the Battle of Actium in 31 B.C.E., Cleopatra's Egyptian forces, together with Antony's Roman forces, faced Octavian's fleet, commanded by Marcus Vipsanius Agrippa. When Cleopatra retreated, she was quickly followed by Antony. Cleopatra's suicide in 30 B.C.E. marked the end of Ptolemaic rule and the beginning of direct Roman rule in what was now an Imperial province.

SIGNIFICANCE

The historical picture of Cleopatra VII is one-sided. Very little is known of her apart from her association with the two Roman generals, Julius Caesar and Marc Antony. As one might expect, the Roman writers do little to enhance her reputation. In the work of Augustan poets, she is never mentioned by name but merely as "the queen," "the woman," or "that one." She is chiefly seen as a crazy drunkard, surrounded by wrinkled eunuchs. Horace also pays tribute to her courage, but he, Vergil, and Sextus Propertius, whose livelihood depended on Octavian's bounty, quite clearly toe the party line in suggesting that she received no more than she deserved.

William Shakespeare's depiction of her in *Antony and Cleopatra* (pr., pb. 1617) as high-spirited, shrewd, sensuous, and fickle is based on that found in Plutarch, a Greek biographer, who mentions her only in association with his two heroes, Caesar and Antony. Plutarch also depicts her as a highly intelligent woman who, unlike her Ptolemaic predecessors, actually went to the trouble of learning the language of her subjects. He reports, moreover, that she could converse easily with "Ethiopians, Troglodytes, Hebrews, Arabians, Syrians, Medes, or Parthians" in their own languages.

Although Cleopatra is often imagined as a ravishing beauty because of the ease with which she seduced experienced and mature soldiers such as Caesar and Antony, a few coins survive depicting her as large-nosed, sharp-chinned, and determined. She was also ruthless. After the Alexandrian War, Caesar thought it sufficient to expel Cleopatra's sister, Arsinoe, for her part in the uprising; Cleopatra later had her put to death.

Plutarch in fact describes not so much Cleopatra's beauty as her charm, humor, and ability to amuse and delight her company. She probably made a powerful impression on the Romans with her intelligence and political ambition. The Roman political system was in a period of transition. Republican government had proved inadequate. Egypt in Cleopatra's time and afterward was essential as a source of wheat for the Roman populace, and its master, if properly armed, could dictate his or her terms to Italy and the Roman senate.

As the creation of Alexander the Great and the place where he was buried, Alexandria provided an obvious starting point for the revival of his empire and its extension even as far as India. The capital of the Roman Empire would eventually be shifted to the east anyway, by Diocletian and Constantine the Great. Legend related that the Romans' ancestor Aeneas originated from Troy in Asia Minor. There may well be some truth in the stories that Caesar intended, if he had lived, to remove the capital to the old site of Troy, and Antony may have been captivated by his dead commander's vision. Cleopatra gambled that, with the aid of such Roman generals, she could make her dynasty a partner in a new eastern empire that would reduce Rome to second place. Like Caesar and Antony, she failed because she was ahead of her time. Her failure has fascinated many throughout the centuries—including Shakespeare and George Bernard Shaw—who have felt the romance and energy of her ambitions.

—Frances Stickney Newman

FURTHER READING

Bevan, Edwyn. *The House of Ptolemy: A History of Egypt Under the Ptolemaic Dynasty.* 1927. Rev. ed. Chicago: Argonaut, 1968. In chapter 13, Bevan offers a brief account of the final days of Ptolemaic rule. Includes illustrations of coins depicting Cleopatra.

Essex, Karen. *Kleopatra.* 2 vols. New York: Warner Books, 2001-2002. This biography examines Cleopatra's political ambition and her connection to Greek culture. Provides good background of the ancient world's culture and political machinations.

Fraser, P. M. *Ptolemaic Alexandria.* 3 vols. Oxford, England: Clarendon Press, 1972. The most comprehensive and scholarly treatment of the entire period of Ptolemaic rule. Especially valuable for the massively detailed citation of primary sources.

Marlowe, John. *The Golden Age of Alexandria.* London: Victor Gollancz, 1971. A popular treatment of one of the most famous cities, from antiquity to its capture in the sixth century C.E. Includes a discussion of Cleopatra.

Plutarch. "Caesar." In *Fall of the Roman Republic, Six Lives: Marius, Sulla, Crassus, Pompey, Caesar, Cicero,* translated by Rex Warner. Rev. ed. Harmondsworth, England: Penguin Books, 1981. The meeting of Caesar and Cleopatra is recounted in chapters 48 and 49. Plutarch accepts Caesar's paternity of Caesarion.

_____. "Mark Antony." In *Makers of Rome, Nine Lives: Coriolanus, Fabius Maximus, Marcellus, Cato the Elder, Tiberius Gracchus, Gaius Gracchus, Sertorius, Brutus, Mark Antony,* translated by Ian Scott-Kilvert. New York: Dorset Press, 1985. Offers a good depiction of the intelligence, vivaciousness, shrewdness, cunning, and ruthlessness of Cleopatra. This life of Antony was used to great effect by William Shakespeare in his famous play.

Pomeroy, Sarah B. *Women in Hellenistic Egypt: From Alexander to Cleopatra.* New York: Schocken Books, 1984. Chapter 1, which discusses the queens of Ptolemaic Egypt, places Cleopatra in a historical context. Pomeroy's discussion of married women, slaves, and women of the capital city of Alexandria—and the overall role of women in the economy in Cleopatra's time—brilliantly depicts the women subjects of this great queen.

Weigall, Arthur. *The Life and Times of Cleopatra, Queen of Egypt.* 1914. Reprint. New York: Greenwood Press, 1968. Although dated, this book gives a shrewd assessment of Cleopatra's relationship with Julius Caesar and Marc Antony. Weigall argues that Caesar was quite clearly intending to move the center of Roman power to the east and that in Cleopatra he had found an ally uniquely qualified to help him realize his plans.

SEE ALSO: Marcus Vipsanius Agrippa; Alexander the Great; Marc Antony; Augustus; Julius Caesar; Hatshepsut; Nefertari; Nefertiti; Tiy.

RELATED ARTICLES in *Great Events from History: The Ancient World*: 332 B.C.E., Founding of Alexandria; 323 B.C.E., Founding of the Ptolemaic Dynasty and Seleucid Kingdom; 58-51 B.C.E., Caesar Conquers Gaul; 51-30 B.C.E., Cleopatra VII, Last of Ptolemies, Reigns; September 2, 31 B.C.E., Battle of Actium.

CLODIA
Roman political figure

Clodia was an important political helper to her brother, Publius Clodius Pulcher, as well as the inspiration for much of Catullus's lyric poetry.

BORN: c. 95 B.C.E.; Rome (now in Italy)
DIED: after 45 B.C.E.; Rome
ALSO KNOWN AS: Lesbia
AREA OF ACHIEVEMENT: Government and politics

EARLY LIFE

As is the case with many figures of the ancient world, especially women, very little is definitively known about Clodia (KLOH-dee-ah), the second of three daughters of Appius Claudius Pulcher. Much of what is known about her is based on hearsay, gossip, and the testimony of hostile sources.

The Claudian family was one of the oldest and most respected patrician clans in Rome: Clodia's father, uncle, grandfather, great-grandfather, great-great-grandfather, and great-great-great-grandfather were all consuls and therefore high office holders in republican Rome. One of her ancestors, Appius Claudius Caecus ("The Blind"), had built the first Roman aqueduct and began the first portion of the Via Appia, named in his honor.

After her younger brother, Publius Clodius Pulcher, transferred himself out of the patrician class and began to spell his name in the plebeian or common fashion, Clodia imitated him as a gesture of political support. She undoubtedly received a strong education, grounded in Greek and Latin literature and philosophy. Like other aristocratic and cultivated women of the time, she probably played a lyre, danced, and delighted in droll sayings and witticisms. Cicero, the great Roman statesman and orator, calls her a poetess in his speech *Pro Caelio* (56 B.C.E.; English translation in *The Orations*, 1741-1743), a defense speech that he transforms into a vituperative attack on what he calls Clodia's loose morals and promiscuous sexuality. Though her brothers enjoyed the tutoring of Ateius Praetextatus, a famous Latin grammarian and teacher of rhetoric, Clodia, as a woman, would not have been schooled in public speaking or oratory.

Her particular branch of the Claudian family was renowned for its beauty—hence, the surname Pulcher—and Clodia was, from all accounts, an attractive woman. Though probably married at a much younger age some years before, Clodia had wed her first cousin, Quintus Caecilius Metellus, by 62 B.C.E., according to Cicero, who frequently mentions her in his letters. Though her politically ambitious husband served as consul in 60, Clodia's support was centered mostly on her brother.

Clodius had come to prominence in 65, after an embezzlement prosecution of Catiline, the future "revolutionary." In 61, however, Clodius faced potentially lethal political fallout when he tried to infiltrate an all-women religious festival, that of the *Bona Dea*, or Good Goddess. Clodius had sneaked into the ritual disguised as a woman and was subsequently charged with sacrilege. Narrowly acquitted by a (probably bribed) jury, he forever afterward loathed Cicero, whom he had asked to provide an alibi and who had refused. Their subsequent mutual antipathy contributed much to Cicero's unflattering and vindictive portrait of Clodia in the *Pro Caelio*.

During this period, sometime before 59, another man entered Clodia's life. The poet Gaius Valerius Catullus revolutionized Latin poetry with his passionate lyric and personal style. Most authorities agree that the mistress of whom he writes in both tender and terrible fashion—his "Lesbia"—was none other than Clodia. Although the facts behind their affair are obscured by the question of how much of Catullus's poetic persona was autobiographical, his verse describes a tumultuous relationship that ends bitterly, prompting him to write scathing invective in place of tributes to beauty and charm.

In 59, Clodia's husband Caecilius died suddenly, and three years later, in the *Pro Caelio*, Cicero suggested that Clodia had poisoned him. This, like much of Cicero's portrait in this speech, is character assassination and must be approached very critically. The following year brought Clodia and her brother into even more prominence, when Clodius was elected tribune of the Plebs. This position, eminently suitable for a rabble-rousing demagogue like Clodius, enabled him finally to enact revenge on Cicero. He secured the passage of a law that sent into exile anyone guilty of condemning a Roman citizen to death without trial. Cicero had, during his consulship of 63, ordered conspirators in the so-called Catiline Conspiracy to be killed without a hearing. The orator was forced into exile, while Clodius and his henchmen burned down his house.

During his enemy's absence, Clodius's power grew. He enlisted mobs of troublemakers to disrupt governmental proceedings, while growing ever more popular with the common people. Clodia's personal influence must have increased as well; by now she had replaced Catullus with another lover, the politico Marcus Caelius Rufus, and was famous for her luxurious parties, glittering salons, and indolent pleasure-seeking.

LIFE'S WORK

When Cicero returned from exile in 57, he soon found an opportunity for avenging himself on Clodius. Marcus Caelius Rufus, an up-and-coming political force, young blade, and protégé of Cicero, was brought up on charges of immorality, theft, and attempted murder by none other than his former lover Clodia. Cicero, rather than attacking the merits of the case, deflected attention from his client's notorious reputation by attacking, with unsurpassed rhetoric, pungent wit, and biting sarcasm, Clodia herself.

The very fact that Cicero chose to attack Clodia reveals the undoubted power and unprecedented influence she wielded politically as well as her vulnerability to such public visibility. As a woman, she could not defend herself, and Cicero, not wishing to play the bully, cleverly employed humor and ridicule to humiliate her, rather than attack her directly. Clodius was beyond his reach, but Clodia was within his sights.

Cicero constantly refers to her as the organizer and source of the prosecution scheme and even attributes the acquittal of Sextus Cloelius, one of Publius's goons and the arsonist of Cicero's own house, to Clodia's feminine influence. Certainly, it may be inferred, Clodia was at the height of her political power, and Cicero was keen to destroy her.

A masterpiece of biting invective, the *Pro Caelio* depicts Clodia as a thoroughly depraved woman, a monster driven by sexual appetites and even the incestuous lover of her younger brother. Cicero calls her a whore, a "Medusa of the Palatine" (the fashionable district where she lived) who attracted the naturally rambunctious Marcus Caelius with her profligate ways and sexual allure. Cicero claims that Clodia threw indecent parties and that she reveled in a garden she created along the banks of the river Tiber, where she watched the young men bathe nude and chose lovers whenever she wanted. In short, he castigates her sexual freedom, power, and assertiveness and mocks her wealthy, independent, pleasure-loving lifestyle.

Although most early historians were eager to accept his attacks at face value, Cicero's real message is more important metaphorically than literally: Women were not supposed to interfere in politics, and neither were they to initiate sexual encounters. Both activities were reserved for men. Because Clodia's political power resided in her influence, reputation, and social standing, Cicero could not attack her politically, as he could her brother. Instead, he exploited the metaphor of her aggressive sexuality to substitute for her true crime: political involvement.

Whether or not Clodia was as sexually adventurous as Cicero suggests is a matter of speculation. However, the orator's criticisms were amplified by those of Catullus, who, after the termination of his affair with Clodia (apparently broken off by her), viciously attacked his former lover. In several poems, he complains of her infidelity; in others, he abuses her with violent and obscene verse.

Again, the portrait that emerges must be attributed to not only a jilted and jealous lover but also a carefully crafted poetic persona. The true details will never be known, as Clodia—like virtually every woman in the ancient world—does not speak in her own voice. However, Catullus's poetry was certainly published and circulated in her time, and the hostile combination of orator and poet effectively eliminated Clodia's political career. She nearly disappears from even Cicero's correspondence after the debacle of the *Pro Caelio*.

Catullus died only a few years later, probably about 54 B.C.E. Clodius continued his street-fighting, gangland style politics; he vacillated in support between Caesar and Pompey and truly stood for no one but himself. His increasingly violent tactics may have been due, in part, to the loss of social influence he suffered at the hands of Cicero, after which Clodia could no longer be such a visible partner in his schemes. On January 18, 53, Clodius was murdered on the Appian Way by the gang of a rival demagogue, Titus Annius Milo. The plebeians rioted in the Forum and burned the Senate House as his funeral pyre.

Clodia reappears in the historical record toward the end of Cicero's life (he died in 43). In a letter to his friend Atticus, he remarks that Clodia owned some property he would like to buy and comments that she does not need the money. Ironically, he and Clodia had been on friendly terms prior to the *Pro Caelio*; Plutarch claims she wanted Cicero to marry her and that his wife, Terentia, was jealous of the beautiful society woman.

Clodia's biography reveals more of male attitudes toward assertiveness in women than it does of her own motivations and activities. As a Roman woman, she bequeathed no record to posterity, no poems or speeches in rebuttal or confession. Her importance stands in relief against the background of hostility with which she is described.

SIGNIFICANCE

Clodia's significance is that of her characterization. Catullus's poetry is timeless; lyrical and tawdry, emotional and contemplative, his "Lesbia" motif served as a model for other, later poets, most notably Sextus Propertius, who wished to find their own mistress-muse to immortalize. Most scholars accept Apuleius's attribution of Lesbia as Clodia, and she was very likely identified with the poems up through his era (c. 125-170 C.E.). The poetry served to emblemize Clodia/Lesbia as the prototypical "bad" woman, the sexual adventurer who ruined young men. This misogynistic view permeated later love poetry and writing about women—the sixth of Juvenal's *Saturae* (100-127 C.E.; *Satires*, 1693), for example—through the modern era. Scholarship has often accepted Catullus's construction of Clodia/Lesbia at face value, thus minimizing the poet's own inventiveness and unfairly condemning Clodia.

The influence of Cicero on later historians guaranteed that his metaphor—sexual license substituting for political boundary-crossing—would live on. His depiction of Clodia can be glimpsed in works of the later historians Tacitus and Suetonius, most notably in portraits of Imperial women like Valeria Messallina, Agrippina the Younger, and Poppaea Sabina. By the time of Tacitus (c. 56-120 C.E.), the specter of sexually voracious women wreaking havoc, uncontrolled and uncontrollable, was a standard of historiography. Weak or unsuccessful rulers were inevitably dominated by lusty female viragos. Cicero's implication about Clodia—that she did not shrink from murder—becomes standard fare with the later ladies.

Perhaps the most pernicious significance of the Clodia portrait has been in the realm of classical scholarship. For far too long, scholars blindly and unquestioningly accepted the testimony of her hostile male biographers. Clodia's own voice will never be recovered, but the shrill shouts of ancient critics should not be amplified by the acquiescent drones of their contemporaries. This characterization of Clodia has held sway for too long; it is up to current and future scholars to ensure than Clodia herself attains the significance her alter ego has long enjoyed. Fortunately, with the advent of feminist theory, academics have begun to search for a more balanced view.

Indeed, for many feminists, Clodia the woman—she who wielded power and defied public convention, on whatever level—is inspirational, reminding one to analyze, investigate, and continually question one's sources, contemporary and ancient. After more than two thousand years, Clodia may yet find a seat at the table.

—*Kelli E. Stanley*

FURTHER READING

Dixon, Suzanne. *Reading Roman Women: Sources, Genres, and Real Life*. London: Duckworth, 2001. Chapter 9 is devoted to Clodia, an excellent source that discusses the difficulty in reconstructing accurate biographies of ancient women. Includes index, map, and bibliography.

Gruen, Erich S. *The Last Generation of the Roman Republic*. Berkeley: University of California Press, 1974. The foremost history of this turbulent era by an eminent historian. Gruen reveals the political machinations of Cicero, Clodius, and Clodia. Includes index and bibliography.

Lefkowitz, Mary R., and Maureen B. Fant. *Women's Life in Ancient Greece and Rome: A Source Book in Translation*. Baltimore: The Johns Hopkins University Press, 1992. An invaluable compendium of primary sources in translation, with background information and analysis. Contains selections from Cicero's *Pro Caelio*. Includes index and bibliography.

Skinner, Marilyn B. "Clodia Metelli." *Transactions of the American Philological Association* 113 (1983): 273-287. A seminal feminist analysis and reconstruction of Clodia that discusses Cicero's motives and Catullus's anger.

Wiseman, T. P. *Catullus and His World: A Reappraisal*. New York: Cambridge University Press, 1985. Discusses the poet's affair with Clodia in chapter 2. Includes index and bibliography.

SEE ALSO: Agrippina the Younger; Boudicca; Catullus; Cicero; Cleopatra VII; Hatshepsut; Juvenal; Valeria Messallina; Nefertari; Nefertiti; Poppaea Sabina; Sextus Propertius; Tiy.

RELATED ARTICLES in *Great Events from History: The Ancient World*: Late 63-January 62 B.C.E., Catiline Conspiracy; 54 B.C.E., Roman Poet Catullus Dies; 51 B.C.E., Cicero Writes *De republica*; 100-127 C.E., Roman Juvenal Composes *Satires*.

CONFUCIUS
Chinese philosopher, ethicist, and teacher

Confucius's teachings had little impact on his own times, but through his disciples and followers, Confucianism became China's official state philosophy in the second century B.C.E., and its texts became the basis of formal education. Confucianism remained the dominant philosophy of China until the early twentieth century and still has a major influence on people throughout East Asia.

BORN: 551 B.C.E.; state of Lu (now in Shandong Province), China
DIED: 479 B.C.E.; Qufu, state of Lu (now in Shandong Province), China
ALSO KNOWN AS: Kong Qiu (Pinyin), K'ung Ch'iu (Wade-Giles); Kongfuzi (Pinyin, formal name), K'ung-Fu-Tzu (Wade-Giles, formal name); Kongzi (Pinyin), K'ung-Tzu (Wade-Giles)
AREA OF ACHIEVEMENT: Philosophy

EARLY LIFE

The name Confucius (kuhn-FYEW-shuhs) is the latinized version of a formal title, Kongfuzi, meaning "The Master Kong." He was born as Kong Qiu somewhere in the state of Lu (in the present-day province of Shandong), into a family that was part of the official class but had fallen on hard times. It is said that his great-grandparents had emigrated from the neighboring state of Song. Confucius is believed to have lost his father when still a small child and to have been raised in poverty by his mother.

Nevertheless, Confucius learned the arts of a courtier, including archery and charioteering; at age fifteen, he began to study ancient texts. In his mid-twenties, Confucius held minor posts in Lu, first as a bookkeeper and later as a supervisor of royal herds. His approach to the problems of statecraft may have begun in his thirties, but he is best known for the period after the age of fifty when he was an established teacher or philosopher-master to young men. The actual teachings that have been handed down are contained in epigraphic and somewhat disjointed form in the *Lunyu* (late sixth or early fifth century B.C.E.; *The Analects*, 1861). The book is a compilation of moral teachings, usually in the form of brief dialogues between Confucius and a questioner, who might be either a high feudal lord or one of Confucius's own disciples. Tradition holds that Confucius had an ungainly personal appearance, but nothing is actually known about his looks. He was married and had a son.

During Confucius's lifetime, China was divided into contending states under the nominal rule of the Zhou (Chou) Dynasty. By the eighth century B.C.E., the Zhou rulers had lost all effective control over their subordinate lords, who became independent rulers. By Confucius's day, these rulers often were themselves figureheads, controlled by powerful individuals or families close to the throne. Murder, intrigue, and double-dealing had become the common coin of political exchange. Moreover, established authority and traditional social distinctions were violated in daily life. In this atmosphere of treachery and uncertainty, Confucius emerged as a teacher who valued constancy, trustworthiness, and the reestablishment of the rational feudal order contained in the codes of the Zhou Dynasty.

LIFE'S WORK

Confucius was already known as a teacher, but he desired to become an adviser or government minister when, sometime before his fiftieth year, he went to live in the powerful neighboring state of Qi. The duke of Qi honored Confucius as a moral teacher but did not give him an important position in the government; eventually, Confucius returned to Lu.

When the ruler of Qi asked Confucius the best way to govern, he replied, "Let the ruler be a ruler, the subject a subject, the father a father, and the son a son." The ideas contained in this moral maxim are central to Confucius's teaching. He taught that social order and stability could be achieved at societal and personal levels if individuals studied and followed the proper standards of behavior. Confucius taught that if one acted properly in terms of one's own social role, others would be influenced positively by the good example. That worked for a ruler in state and for an individual in his or her daily life. Thus, Confucianism, from its earliest teachings, contained an approach useful for both practical living and governing.

Virtue (*de*) displayed by living properly brought one into harmony with the correct human order, called "the Way" (*dao*). Confucius acknowledged the existence of an overarching force in life called Heaven (*tian*) but did not accept any concept of a God or gods. He specifically opposed the belief in spirits and was not interested in the immortality of the soul. For Confucius, the human order and human character are fundamentally good, but there is a tendency to slip away from proper behavior through laxity and lack of understanding. A primary responsibility of leaders and elders is to uphold the social ideals through positive demonstration in their own lives. In Confucianism, the most complete statement of this approach is called the doctrine of the Rectification of Names (*zhengming*). One begins with study to establish the original meaning of the Zhou feudal order. Once that understanding is gained, individuals should alter their behavior in order to fulfill completely and sincerely the social roles they are assigned, such as those of minister, father, or brother. This entire process constitutes the Rectification of Names, which Confucius believed would restore the ideal social order.

On his return to Lu around the year 500, Confucius took up an official position under the sponsorship of Ji Huanzi, the head of the Ji clan, who were the real power holders. His post was not an important one, and Confucius resigned shortly over a question of improper conduct of ritual sacrifices. Ritual (*li*) plays a central role in Confucius's teachings. He downplayed the supernatural or religious aspects of ritual but taught that meticulous and sincere observance of rituals imparted moral improvement.

The state of Lu, where Confucius lived, derived from a collateral line of the Zhou Dynasty and was known for careful preservation of Zhou ritual practices. Confucius used this tradition as a proof of the importance of rituals. In addition to the moral training acquired by the mastery of ritual, Confucius taught ritual as a means to acquire the practical skills needed to carry out the functions of high office.

In 497, after his resignation over the ritual issue, Confucius set out, with a few disciples, as a wandering philosopher-teacher, looking for a ruler who would try his methods of governing. This long trek, which lasted from 497 to 484, led to his enhanced reputation for uprightness and wisdom, but he never obtained a significant office. In his mid-sixties, he was called back to Lu, possibly through the influence of his disciple Ran Qiu, who had become the chief steward of the Ji family. On his return, however, Confucius denounced Ran Qiu's tax policies as exploitative of the common people.

Confucius's approach to government stressed that the ruler should be benevolent and sincerely concerned about the well-being of his subjects. In Confucius's hierarchical concep-

tion of the social order, the ruler's concern for his subjects would be repaid by obedience and support. Confucius believed that the same hierarchical yet reciprocal principles applied to all social relationships.

Although later Confucius came to be deified as a sage of infinite powers, in *The Analects* he appears as a dignified, austere, but gentle man who suffered ordinary human disappointments. Significantly, his ideas are colored by a strong humanism. His teachings as recorded in *The Analects* emphasize benevolence (*ren*), meaning a love of humankind, as the key virtue of the ideal man, whom he referred to as a "gentleman" (*zhunzi*). Benevolence begins with straightforwardness (*zhi*) of character and then is trained or modified through practice of the rituals. Ritual and music impart the inner character needed by a gentleman. Confucius taught that a gentleman would

Confucius plays a lute in this twelfth century drawing. (Library of Congress)

have other virtues as well, such as loyalty (*zhong*), righteousness (*yi*), altruism (*shu*), and filial piety (*xiao*). This last virtue—the love and concern of a child for his parents, which expresses itself in dutiful and sincere concern for their well-being—became particularly important in Chinese and East Asian civilizations. All Confucius's teachings about social relationships demand the subordination of the individual; thus, Confucius was neither an egalitarian nor a libertarian.

During his last years, Confucius lived in Lu and was often consulted by the titular ruler, Duke Ai, and the new head of the dominant Ji clan, Ji Kangzi, but still never was an important minister. Many of his statements from this period are preserved in summary form and enhance the elliptical tone of *The Analects*.

Confucius, before his death at the age of seventy-two, completed the editing of several ancient texts. Both tradition and modern scholarship connect him with three classical texts. These are the *Shujing* (compiled after first century B.C.E.; English translation in *The Chinese Classics*, vol. 5, parts 1 and 2, 1872; commonly known as *Classic of History*), which contains pronouncements by the founders of the Zhou Dynasty, the *Shijing* (compiled fifth century B.C.E.; *The Book of Songs*, 1937), which preserves 305 songs from the time before 600 B.C.E., and the *Chunqiu* (fifth century B.C.E.; *The Ch'un Ts'ew with the Tso Chuen*, 1872; commonly known as *Spring and Autumn Annals*). The last is a terse chronicle of events in the state of Lu from 722 to 481 B.C.E. and has been closely studied through the centuries, for it was believed that Confucius edited it with the intent of transmitting moral messages about good government. Confucius also studied the *Yijing* (eighth to third century B.C.E.; English translation, 1876; also known as *Book of Changes*, 1986), but the tradition that he edited that cryptic ancient book of divination is not widely accepted today.

Confucius's concern to compile correct versions of ancient texts fits the image of him that survives in *The Analects*. There Confucius stressed his own role as simply a transmitter of the knowledge and ways from the past. Confucius's model from history was the duke of Zhou, who acted as regent for the infant King Cheng, "The Completed King," who reigned from 1104 to 1067. Confucius taught that the duke of Zhou was the perfect minister who served his ruler and carried out his duties in complete accord with the feudal codes of the Zhou. The story of the duke of Zhou, as a good regent and loyal minister, emphasizes the exercise of power in accord with the established social codes. Much of the appeal of Confu-

cianism to later dynasties can be found in Confucius's emphasis on loyalty to proper authority.

At the same time, Confucius's teachings have been seen as democratic, in that what he valued in others was their good character, benevolence, humanity, and learning rather than their social position, cunning, or strength of will. His teaching that anyone may become a gentleman, or good person, with proper training and devotion established the important Chinese social ideal of personal cultivation through study.

SIGNIFICANCE

Confucius died in 479, disappointed in his own career, upset at some disciples for their inability to follow his high standards of conduct, and saddened by the deaths of both his son and his favorite disciple, Yan Hui. Like Socrates, Confucius became known primarily as a teacher through the preservation of his teachings by his disciples. Some of those disciples went on to government service and others took up their master's calling as teachers.

By the second century B.C.E., the study of Confucian texts had become the norm for those aspiring to official posts. Young men were trained to memorize a set group of Confucian texts. That educational regime remained the heart of learning in China until the early twentieth century. The flourishing of his pedagogical approach is eloquent testimony to Confucius's genius. His concepts of the goodness of humankind and the importance of benevolence and humanity in political and personal affairs were developed by Mencius and given a more practical and realistic interpretation by the philosopher Xunzi. By the second century B.C.E., students of Confucian teachings were highly valued for their skills in ritual, knowledge of ancient texts, and mastery of other learning that rulers needed to regulate their courts and administer their states. During the Western Han Dynasty (206 B.C.E.-8 C.E.), Confucianism became the official court philosophy and then was elevated to a state cult. Confucianism continues to be a powerful philosophy in China, Japan, and other states of East Asia.

—*David D. Buck*

FURTHER READING

Confucius. *The Analects (Lun-yü)*. Translated by D. C. Lau. 2d ed. Hong Kong: Chinese University Press, 1992. An excellent translation of the *Lunyu*, with a good introduction to Confucius's ideas and his life.

Creel, H. G. *Chinese Thought from Confucius to Mao Tse-tung*. Chicago: University of Chicago Press, 1962. A readable, nontechnical summary that puts Confucius in the overall context of Chinese philosophy.

Dawson, Raymond. *Confucius*. New York: Hill and Wang, 1982. A short, general introduction and biography of Confucius written for a series on great individuals. Stresses Confucius's ethical and moral influence.

Fingarette, Herbert. *Confucius: The Secular as Sacred*. Prospect Heights, Ill.: Waveland Press, 1998. An interpretive essay that attempts to explain Confucius's attention to ritual (*li*) and to show how this can be reconciled with his humanism.

Schwartz, Benjamin I. *The World of Thought in Ancient China*. Cambridge, Mass.: Belknap Press of Harvard University Press, 1985. Contains a long chapter on Confucius that includes extensive comparisons with ancient Western philosophers. Schwartz emphasizes Confucius's role as a teacher who was both a perpetuator of tradition and an innovator.

Ssu-ma Ch'ien. *Records of the Historian*. Translated by Tang Nguok Kiong. Singapore: Asiapac, 1990. Contains a translation of the biography of Confucius written c. 90 B.C.E.

SEE ALSO: Mencius; Xunxi.

RELATED ARTICLES in *Great Events from History: The Ancient World*: 5th century B.C.E., Composition of the *Spring and Autumn Annals*; 479 B.C.E., Confucius's Death Leads to the Creation of *The Analects*; 475-221 B.C.E., China Enters Chaotic Warring States Period; c. 285-c. 255 B.C.E., Xunzi Develops Teachings That Lead to Legalism.

CONSTANTINE THE GREAT
Roman emperor (r. 324-337 C.E.)

As the first Christian emperor of Rome, Constantine was primarily responsible for initiating the great changes that in a few decades turned the pagan empire into a Christian one. Constantine refounded the old Greek city of Byzantium as the New Rome, which, as Constantinople, became Europe's greatest city during the following millennium.

BORN: February 17 or 27, c. 272-285 C.E.; Naissus, Moesia (now Niš, Serbia)

DIED: May 22, 337 C.E.; Nicomedia, Bithynia (now İzmit, Turkey)

ALSO KNOWN AS: Flavius Valerius Constantinus (full name)

AREAS OF ACHIEVEMENT: Government and politics, war and conquest, religion

EARLY LIFE

Flavius Valerius Constantinus, or Constantine (KAHN-stuhn-teen), was born at a crucial time in the long history of Rome. According to the eighteenth century English historian Edward Gibbon, the second century C.E. had been a golden age, but the third century saw economic decline, barbarian invasions, and political instability, the last often brought about by the ambitions of Rome's many generals. Constantine's father, Constantius Chlorus, born in the militarily crucial Danubian provinces, was a successful general who rose to high political position. Constantine's mother, Helena, came from a lower-class background and was probably not married to Constantius, who himself later married a daughter of Marcus Aurelius Valerius Maximianus (Maximian), with whom he had several additional children. Little is known of Constantine's early life; even the year of his birth is unknown, but it was probably between 272 and 285 C.E.

In 293, the emperor Gaius Aurelius Valerius Diocletianus (Diocletian), in a continuing attempt to stem the long Imperial decline, created a tetrarchy for administrative and defensive reasons. He retained the position of augustus in the east and appointed Maximian as augustus in the west. Constantius became Maximian's caesar, or assistant, and Gaius Galerius Valerius Maximianus (Galerius) was caesar to Diocletian. During the years that followed, young Constantine remained in the east at Diocletian's Imperial court, possibly as a guarantee of good behavior by Constantius. What type of formal education Constantine received is unknown, and historians have long argued over his intellectual abilities. There is, however, no question that he successfully learned the military arts.

Diocletian abdicated his throne in 305, forcing Maximian to do the same. Galerius became augustus in the east, as did Constantius in the west. When the latter requested that Constantine be allowed to join him, Galerius was reluctant, but in 306 Constantine was reunited with Constantius in Britain. When Constantius died later that year in York, Constantine was acclaimed the new western augustus by his army. Galerius, however, only re-

ROMAN EMPERORS	
CONSTANTINE THE GREAT TO THEODOSIUS THE GREAT	
Ruler	*Reign (C.E.)*
Constantine the Great (East)	306-337
Licinius (East)	308-324
Constantine the Great (all)	324-337
Constantine II (West)	337-340
Constans I (West)	337-350
Constantius II (East)	337-361
Magnentius (West, usurper)	350-353
Julian (all)	361-363
Jovian (all)	363-364
Valentinian I (West)	364-375
Valens (East)	364-378
Procopius (East)	365-366
Gratian (West)	375-383
Valentinian II (West)	375-392
Theodosius I (all)	379-395

luctantly granted Constantine the lesser rank of caesar, the position of the western augustus going to one of Galerius's favorites.

Conflict dominated the next several years, as a result of the ambitions of the Empire's many leaders. Maximian's son, Marcus Aurelius Valerius Maxentius, seized power in Rome with the help of his father. They joined forces with Constantine and resisted attempts at deposition by Galerius. Maximian, who had earlier given his daughter, Fausta, in marriage to Constantine, then attempted to seize power himself, first from his son and then from his son-in-law, Constantine, but the latter forced him to commit suicide. In the east, Galerius still ruled, joined by Valerius Licinianus Licinius, who had also become an augustus. In the west, Maxentius and Constantine survived as rivals, each claiming the rank of augustus. Diocletian's tetrarchy no longer had subordinate caesars, only ambitious and warring augusti.

LIFE'S WORK

Despite his important role in furthering Christianity, Constantine's religious beliefs remain uncertain. During the previous century the worship of the sun, Sol Invictus, had spread throughout the Empire, and that religion seemed more important to Constantius and Constantine than the traditional pantheon of Roman gods. Christianity had also taken root in parts of the Empire, although it was still a movement that lacked general acceptability.

After several decades of toleration, Diocletian instituted a period of Christian persecution, but in the west, Constantius apparently refused to pursue that policy. The connection, or the confusion, between the Christian God and Sol Invictus is still unclear as regards Constantine's beliefs.

Whatever his religious convictions were, they soon became inextricably tied to his political ambitions. After Galerius died in 311, Constantine invaded Italy in early 312, hoping to unite the Empire under his rule. Constantine and Licinius became allies through Licinius's marriage to Constantine's sister, and Maxentius seemed reluctant to face Constantine on the battlefield. Favorable omens from the gods eventually encouraged Maxentius, and on October 28, 312, he led his army out of the city gates of Rome and across the Tiber River on the Milvian Bridge. Constantine's army fought with the sign of the Christian cross on their shields and banners, and at battle's end, Maxentius lay drowned in the Tiber, leaving Constantine sole ruler in the west.

When Constantine and Licinius met at Milan in 313, just prior to Licinius's struggle against the other eastern augustus, Galerius, they granted religious toleration to all sects. This edict especially benefited the Christian minority, the primary victims of persecution during the past decade. In his subsequent victory against Galerius, Licinius upheld the cause of monotheism against the traditional Roman gods. It had become impossible to divide politics and war from religion.

There is considerable difficulty when it comes to determining Constantine's religious beliefs at the Battle of the Milvian Bridge. In the first biography of Constantine, the *Vita Constantini* (339; *Life of Constantine*, 1845) by Bishop Eusebius of Caesarea, written after the emperor's death, Eusebius recalls that Constantine told him of a vision he had on his journey from Gaul to Italy in 312. He saw a cross in the sky, an apparition visible to his entire army. Later he said that he had a dream in which Christ appeared with the cross. Another version, by Lactantius, writing only a few years after 312, tells that Constantine, on the very eve of the battle at Milvian Bridge, had a dream in which he was told to put the sign of the cross on the shields of his soldiers. Some later historians have accepted those stories as sufficient evidence of Constantine's Christian commitment before his conquest of Rome, and they have argued that he was a sincere believer. Others have expressed doubts, contending instead that he was always primarily a hypocritical opportunist. Also, the depth of Constantine's perception of the Christian beliefs is still in question. Did he have a fundamental knowledge of the doctrines of Christianity in 312, or were his actions merely a superstitious adoption of a new god of battle against other, older gods?

What is not in question is that in the years that followed, Constantine favored more and more the Christian religion and its adherents. Property seized during the persecutions was returned, Christian bishops were freed from taxes and certain public obligations in order to pursue their religious calling, and Christian advisers at court became commonplace. Other religions and their followers were not immediately discriminated against or proscribed. In Rome, in particular, where the old religion was so much a part of the political and social fabric of the city, the upper classes remained generally in favor of the traditional gods. Many of the soldiers in Constantine's armies probably remained pagan, and he never dispensed entirely, even among his close advisers, with some who opposed, peacefully, the new religion.

Two continuing disputes between Christian factions, the Donatist and the Arian heresies, posed the greatest problems to Constantine in the years that followed his victory. In North Africa, the Donatists, who believed that the efficacy of Christianity depended on the sanctity of the priest or bishop, argued that those Christian clerics who had surrendered holy writings during the period of persecution were unfit either to consecrate other clergy or to distribute the sacraments to believers. The opposition claimed that the institution of the church itself was sufficient, not the personal holiness of the individual cleric. Constantine sided against the Donatists, for he believed that the church should be inclusive, or catholic, an attitude largely based on his belief that both his well-being and that of the Empire depended on a unified church. The issue remained unresolved.

Meanwhile, in the east, in a dispute over the relationship between Christ and God, the Arians argued that the Son was subordinate to the Father. Constantine partici-

The conversion of Constantine the Great. (Library of Congress)

pated at the first general church council in Nicaea in 325, which issued the Nicene Creed and condemned the Arian position as a heresy. Until the end of his reign, however, Constantine was to waver between the two positions, often influenced by whichever advocate had last caught his ear. Constantine was the first Christian emperor of Rome, but it was often easier to win victories on the battlefield than over one's fellow believers.

Licinius, who still ruled the eastern part of the Empire, acknowledged Constantine's position as senior augustus, but Constantine refused to accept permanently such a division, even with his brother-in-law. The friction continued for many years, sometimes resulting in war, usually at Constantine's instigation. When Licinius began to persecute Christians, possibly in reaction to Constantine's active support of Christianity, Constantine found justification for a final confrontation, from which he emerged victorious. In 324, Licinius was allowed to abdicate, but within a short time he was executed. Constantine stood alone as ruler of the Empire.

Following Licinius's defeat, Constantine, as befitting a great conqueror, founded a New Rome in the east. For more than a century, Rome had not been the effective capital of the Empire; a government positioned closer to the Rhine and Danube Rivers was better able to defend against the ever-threatening barbarian tribes. In addition, Rome had proved to be less tractable to Constantine's rule and religion. The site picked for the New Rome was the old Greek city of Byzantium, a natural crossroads between Europe and Asia Minor and between the Mediterranean Sea and the Black Sea, rededicated as Constantinople in 330. Unlike Rome, Constantinople was a Christian city, and the emperor spent lavishly on his new creation, as he had in constructing churches throughout the Empire, particularly in Jerusalem, where basilicas were erected to commemorate Christian holy places. Constantine's New Rome became in time the greatest city in Europe.

Initially, Constantine intended to be buried in Rome, but after the founding of Constantinople he made the decision to be buried there, and he directed the building of his own tomb in the Church of the Holy Apostles in Constantinople. As was usual in his era, he was only baptized a Christian on the eve of his death. He had hoped to have that ceremony performed in the Jordan River, but in the spring of 337, his health began to fail. He left Constantinople in order to seek a cure at the springs of Helenopolis, named after his mother, who on a pilgrimage to the Holy Land had purportedly discovered the cross on which Christ had been crucified. On his return to Con-

stantinople, Constantine worsened in Nicomedia, was baptized there, and died on May 22.

SIGNIFICANCE

The Empire under Constantine's rule was prosperous and secure, at least in comparison to the previous century, if not to Gibbon's golden age of the second century C.E. By the time he died, Constantine had eliminated his rivals, so that there were only members of his family, sons and nephews, to inherit the Empire; heredity was to determine once again the ruler, or rulers, of Rome. In 326 he had ordered the execution of his eldest son, Crispus, and then his own wife, Fausta, in reaction to an unknown scandal. After Constantine's death, his nephews were summarily executed, leaving the Empire divided among his three surviving sons. Constantine II was killed by his brother, Constans, in 340, who in turn was killed in 350. The last brother, Constantius II, died while suppressing a rebellion by Julian, the son of one of Constantine's half brothers.

At the time of his death, the force of Constantine's influence was yet to be realized. Militarily, he had created a reserve force, mobile and supposedly better able to respond to the barbarian threat than the less mobile legions. Perhaps more ominously, increasing numbers of German barbarians were enlisted in the Empire's armies. This was not new, but it was a portent for the future. Constantinople was still a secondary city, whose ultimate importance would arrive only after the sack of Rome in 410, the fall of the Western Roman Empire in 476, and the consolidation of the Eastern Roman Empire under Justinian in the sixth century. Julian, who succeeded Constantius II, followed the old gods of Rome, and the various heretical movements within the Church continued long after 337. Julian, however, was the last of the pagan emperors, and the Empire, governed from Constantine's New Rome, survived to protect the west and to preserve the ancient heritage for the next thousand years before falling to Islam in 1453. As the first Christian emperor of the Roman Empire, Constantine became, for better or worse, one of the founders of the medieval world.

—Eugene S. Larson

FURTHER READING

Baker, G. P. *Constantine the Great: And the Christian Revolution*. New York: Cooper Square Press, 2001. Examines the dynamics of the Roman world and the rise of Christianity and its significance for the governing of the Empire.

Barnes, Timothy D. *Constantine and Eusebius*. Cambridge, Mass.: Harvard University Press, 1981. The author accepts the reality and the sincerity of Constantine's religious commitments and his desire to create a Christian empire. Concentrates particularly on religious issues, using as a focus Constantine's contemporary biographer, Eusebius of Caesarea, and the various issues, doctrinal and otherwise, which affected the Church and Empire, especially in the east.

Baynes, Norman H. *Constantine the Great and the Christian Church*. Reprint. New York: Haskell House, 1975. The author argues that Constantine was a sincere Christian who believed that he had a mission to maintain unity in the Church and convert the nonbelievers to his new faith, in part because of his belief that his future and that of Rome depended on the Christian God.

Burckhardt, Jacob. *The Age of Constantine the Great*. 1852. Reprint. Berkeley: University of California Press, 1983. Burckhardt portrays Constantine not as a sincere Christian but rather as a worldly and accomplished politician who aimed only at success and whose religious beliefs were a combination of superstition and opportunism.

Eadie, John W., ed. *The Conversion of Constantine*. Huntington, N.Y.: R. E. Krieger, 1977. The author has collected and edited a number of historical works, from the fourth century onward, which discuss the question of the meaning and importance of Constantine's religious beliefs. An excellent summary of different viewpoints on one of the central issues of his reign.

Gibbon, Edward. *History of the Decline and Fall of the Roman Empire*. 1828. Reprint. New York: Penguin, 1994. This elegantly written work by the eighteenth century historian is one of the literary classics of Western civilization. Gibbon's writings have posed questions about the fall of empires that historians have been pursuing ever since. Reflecting the Enlightenment era, Gibbon has little empathy with any religious movement, thus Constantine is pictured finally in negative terms.

Jones, A. H. M. *Constantine and the Conversion of Europe*. New York: Collier Books, 1967. This work, by an eminent scholar, was written for the general reader. Jones argues that Constantine was not a great ruler, that his major abilities were military, but his impact on religion and politics was profound because of his control over both church and state as the first Christian emperor.

MacMullen, Ramsay. *Constantine*. New York: Croom Helm, 1987. This well-written biography of Constantine by a serious scholar is written for the general reader. An excellent summary of the various aspects of the life of the emperor, including war, politics, and religion. The author sees Constantine in many ways as a traditional Roman emperor, but of great significance because he was the first Christian emperor.

Pelikan, Jaroslav. *The Excellent Empire: The Fall of Rome and the Triumph of the Church*. San Francisco: Harper and Row, 1987. In this provocative series of lectures, Constantine's establishment of Christianity is perceived as the key to both fall and triumph. The author particularly focuses on the ideas and writings of Saint Augustine of Hippo and Edward Gibbon.

SEE ALSO: Saint Anthony of Egypt; Diocletian; Eusebius of Caesarea; Saint Helena.

RELATED ARTICLES in *Great Events from History: The Ancient World*: 309-379 C.E., Shāpūr II Reigns over Sāsānian Empire; October 28, 312 C.E., Conversion of Constantine to Christianity; 313-395 C.E., Inception of Church-State Problem; 325 C.E., Adoption of the Nicene Creed; November 24, 326-May 11, 330 C.E., Constantinople Is Founded.

CROESUS
Lydian king (r. c. 560-546 B.C.E.)

The last king of Lydia, defeated by Cyrus the Great of Persia, Croesus became a legendary figure to serve as an example to the Greeks of the fate of the proud.

BORN: c. 595 B.C.E.; Lydia, Asia Minor (now in Turkey)
DIED: 546 B.C.E.; Sardis, Asia Minor (now in Turkey)
ALSO KNOWN AS: Kroisos; Croisos
AREA OF ACHIEVEMENT: War and conquest

EARLY LIFE

Croesus (KREE-suhs), the last king of the Mermnad Dynasty, is famous more as a legendary image than a historical figure. The primary source for his life and the period is the Greek historian Herodotus, who traces a convoluted account of the Lydian kingdom as background material for the Greco-Persian Wars. In the process, he mixes together various traditions and legends to create his history. Despite the legendary additions, the basic outline of Lydian history can probably be trusted. No specific details, however, are given about Croesus's early life, other than a mention that his mother was a Carian. The traditional date given for his assumption of the throne is 560 B.C.E.

LIFE'S WORK

The kingdom of Lydia in Asia Minor had emerged in the power vacuum created by the collapse of the kingdom of Phrygia when barbarians from Thrace known as the Cimmerians swept into northern Turkey. With its capital at Sardis, Lydia dominated the trade along the Hermus and Cayster Rivers, acting as an important conduit for the exchange of Anatolian and Greek goods. The wealth of the region was such that even its first king, Gyges, gained a legendary status of wealth in an early poem fragment of disdain by the Greek poet Archilochus.

Croesus continued the expansionist policies of his ancestors, especially those of his father, Alyattes, toward the coast. An ongoing war with Miletus had come to an end, according to the Herodotus legend, when a temple to Athena caught fire during the siege. Alyattes became ill and, after inquiring of the oracle at Delphi, received instructions to rebuild the structure. The truce that followed eventually turned into a peace treaty, which continued under Croesus's reign. Alyattes had also established his eastern boundary along the Halys River after a border skirmish with Cyaxerxes of the Medes ended during an eclipse. The eclipse of 585 B.C.E., purportedly predicted by Thales of Miletus, unnerved the armies and

ended the fighting. Eventually, a Lydian-Median alliance formed, sealed by a marriage arrangement of the young Croesus with a Median daughter. Alyattes left Croesus an economically thriving empire. Indeed, the first appearance of coinage seems to have been prompted by Alyattes as a means of facilitating trade between the Lydians and the Ionians.

Alyattes' death initiated a brief power struggle between Croesus and Pantaleon, his half brother born to a Greek woman. Although the legal heir, Croesus supposedly removed any possible resistance by capturing Pantaleon and torturing him to death by dragging him over a carding comb, a board with points to comb cotton fibers before spinning. After coming to the throne, Croesus initiated the final stage of Lydian expansion by conquering Ephesus and then expanding north until all of the Ionian and Aeolian Greek cities fell under his control. He apparently initiated a large shipbuilding program in order to establish his dominion over Asia Minor's coastal islands. According to Greek tradition, one of his subjects advised him of the danger of his army, dependent on its great cavalry arm, of being caught at sea in the face of those whose strength rested in their maritime prowess. Croesus discontinued the program and actually seems to have established a pact of friendship instead.

If the traditions given by Herodotus have validity, Croesus's life was marred by tragedy. One of his sons was apparently deaf and mute. The other son, Atys, lost his life in a hunting accident. When Cyrus the Great conquered Astyges of Media in 549, Croesus appealed to the oracle at Delphi and, after receiving a favorable response, invaded Cappadocia in 547. He did so on the pretext of avenging his brother-in-law.

Tradition indicates that Thales engineered the crossing of the Halys River by diverting its bed around the army, but even Herodotus doubts the veracity of the story. After an initial campaign in the region of Pteria ended in stalemate, Croesus withdrew to Sardis with the intention of gathering reinforcements from his allies, Amasis of Egypt, Nabonidus of Babylon, and possibly the Spartans from Greece. Cyrus mounted a surprise assault on the city and conquered it and, according to the Nabonidus Chronicle from Babylon, killed Croesus.

SIGNIFICANCE

In the Greek world, Croesus became the subject of various object lessons. The first, in connection with the death of his son, emphasized that one cannot escape a divinely decreed fate. In a dream, Croesus learned that his son Atys faced death by means of an iron spearhead. On awakening, he ordered the removal of all spears and weapons from the men's quarters to prevent an accident. Then he removed Atys from commanding troops on the field. After some time, a group of Mysians appeared and requested help from Atys in dispatching a giant boar that terrorized the people and damaged crops. Croesus, who had just arranged a marriage for his son, excused him from going on the grounds that he was a newlywed. The ambassadors departed with other troops, but Atys complained to his father and, as no military operations would endanger him, Croesus allowed him to join the hunting expedition. A young man, Adrastus, who was a refugee from Phrygia, having murdered his brother, had found asylum in Lydia and had befriended Atys. Adrastus accompanied the hunting party. Unbeknownst to all, he carried an iron-tipped spear. In the confusion of trying to kill the boar, Adrastus missed and accidentally struck Atys, who succumbed to the wound.

The second object lesson deals with the issue of hubris, the sin of pride. According to the tradition, Solon the Idealist, of Athens, visited Sardis and stayed as a guest in the palace. In the course of the visit, he received a grand tour of the royal complex and its treasury. When asked by Croesus if he had ever met a happier man, Solon responded that he indeed had. He referred to one, Tellus of Athens, who had great wealth, fine sons, and after being killed in battle, received honors from the city. When asked about the second happiest, Solon told the tale of two athletes from Argos who, after performing amazing feats of strength, were honored by the city, and their mother requested from the goddess Hera the best thing a human could have; they died in their sleep.

In the angry dispute that followed, Solon emphasized that one should not tempt the gods with pride in wealth. Wealthy people, he said, can be struck with misfortune and loss; thus, it is better to live day by day and die well with what wealth one has intact, as opposed to seeing a day when one loses everything. Solon's words of wisdom were lost on Croesus until the day of his own defeat. After Cyrus the Great conquered the city, he supposedly desired to sacrifice Croesus on a pyre to thank the gods for the victory. Croesus, in the midst of the flames, uttered Solon's name three times and acknowledged the wisdom of his words. Cyrus, hearing the utterances, asked an interpreter to have Croesus explain himself. After hearing the story, and struck by a realization of his own mortality, Cyrus ordered the flames to be extinguished. When Croesus saw his would-be rescuers' intent, as well as their inability to arrest the flames, he called on Apollo to remember the many valuable gifts that had been given to Delphi. The god then sent a storm that doused the fire. Seeing the divine favor given to honor Croesus's humility, Cyrus appointed him as an adviser.

This story, with its obviously legendary tone, belies any historicity, first, because of

Croesus, standing, faces Cyrus the Great. (Hulton|Archive by Getty Images)

chronological difficulties. Solon the Idealist was prominent in Athens as a political reformer and poet between 600 and 590, slightly earlier than Croesus. Second, the Persians did not practice any religious rites that would require the burning of a human sacrifice. The third object lesson that Croesus provides is a proof of the power of the Delphic oracle. When Cyrus the Great had first conquered the Median Empire, Croesus contemplated war, but he desired divine affirmation. As a test, he devised a plan to dispatch messengers to all of the known oracles. He told them to mark the one hundredth day after their departure from Sardis and then inquire of the oracles what Croesus was doing on that particular day. The answers were to be written down and returned to the king. On the one hundredth day, he prepared a stew of tortoise and lamb meat in a bronze pot. The only oracles that responded with the correct answer were at Delphi and Amphiaraus.

With confirmation of the fame of Delphi, he lavished expensive gifts and wealth on its temple and then made two other requests. He asked for advice about attacking Cyrus, and the oracle responded that if he did so, he would destroy a great empire. His second question was about the length of his reign. To that, the oracle responded by saying that Croesus would rule until a mule sat on the throne of Persia. Full of confidence, Croesus instigated his war with the Persians. Despite his defeat, the oracle claimed that it had given the correct answers; Croesus had merely misinterpreted them. Indeed, a great empire was destroyed (his own), and a mule (Cyrus was half Persian and half Median) did sit on the throne.

An unrelated oracle from Delphi was also said to have provided the truth. When Croesus asked about his mute son, he was told that the day he heard his son's voice would be the day of his misfortune. According to the legend, during the sack of Sardis, Cyrus had issued orders that Croesus be taken alive. A soldier, however, did not recognize the king and prepared to kill him, but the mute boy suddenly cried out Croesus's identity and saved his life.

Two other legends emerged about his connection to Delphi and Apollo. Another version of Croesus's fate related that he built a funeral pyre himself and threw himself and his family into it to escape death by Cyrus's hand. However, Zeus sent a storm, doused the flames, and had Apollo carry them off to the land of the Hyperboreans, a sort of paradise for his worshipers. The tradition of Croesus being saved by Cyrus ends with his gift of his chains to the oracle and the question as to why the gods had rewarded his many gifts in such a manner. The response, tying back to a supposed prophecy that Gyges would be punished for his crimes in the fourth generation, was used to prove the power of the oracle of Delphi. Thus, Croesus became an appropriate closing chapter to the story of the Lydian kingdom.

—*Todd W. Ewing*

FURTHER READING

Dunstan, William. *Ancient Greece*. New York: Harcourt, 2000. This college-level text gives brief references to Lydia, dealing with its contacts with Greek history.

Fine, John. *The Ancient Greeks: A Critical History*. Cambridge, Mass.: Harvard University Press, 1983. An excellent overview of the Lydian Dynasty, with critical commentary on the historicity of the traditions and myths.

Herodotus. *The Histories*. Translated by Robin Waterfield. New York: Oxford University Press, 1998. The relevant sections of the history of the Lydian Empire are found in book 1, sections 6-94.

Olmstead, A. T. *History of the Persian Empire*. Chicago: University of Chicago Press, 1959. In this overview of the Median and Persian Empires, the foregoing events are discussed from the perspective of Cyrus the Great.

SEE ALSO: Cyrus the Great.

RELATED ARTICLES in *Great Events from History: The Ancient World*: c. 645-546 B.C.E., Lydia Rises to Power Under the Mermnad Family; 547 B.C.E., Cyrus the Great Founds the Persian Empire.

CTESIBIUS OF ALEXANDRIA
Alexandrian inventor

One of the great mechanical geniuses and inventors of antiquity, Ctesibius was the father of pneumatics, the first to employ compressed air to run his devices. He is credited with a number of inventions, including a water pump, a water organ, a precise water clock, and bronze spring and pneumatic catapults.

BORN: c. 290 B.C.E.; Alexandria, Egypt
DIED: Probably after 250 B.C.E.; Alexandria, Egypt
ALSO KNOWN AS: Ktesibios
AREA OF ACHIEVEMENT: Science

EARLY LIFE

Biographical details about Ctesibius (tee-SIHB-ee-uhs) are scarce. He was from Alexandria in Egypt and would have grown up during the reign of Ptolemy Soter, who, following the death of Alexander the Great, founded the Ptolemaic Dynasty in Egypt in 322. Ctesibius's father was a barber, a trade he apparently taught his son. Ctesibius is said to have married a woman named Thais.

Vitruvius, the first century B.C.E. architect and military engineer who utilized Ctesibius's lost treatise on pneumatics, describes him as an industrious youth, endowed with great natural ability, who occupied much of his time amusing himself with the ingenious devices he routinely fashioned. The most famous anecdote about Ctesibius has him devising a counterweight system to raise and lower a mirror in his father's barbershop. As the counterweight moved rapidly through a narrow channel, it compressed trapped air, which escaped with a loud noise. The sounds and tones created supposedly gave Ctesibius the idea for his water organ, for which he used pipes of different lengths to vary pitch and water to pressurize the air.

The same barbershop experiment apparently also inspired Ctesibius's water pump, which consisted of two vertical cylinders, each with a plunger worked reciprocally by a rocker arm. Water was drawn into a cylinder chamber through a valve connected to a water source when its plunger was raised and then was forced out in the direction desired through another valve when its plunger was lowered. Continuous pumping on the rocker arm handle guaranteed a steady flow of water.

LIFE'S WORK

Much of Ctesibius's adult life was spent during the reign of Ptolemy Philadelphus, for whom he fashioned a singing cornucopia for a statue of Arsinoe, the king's deified

wife, about 270. Because of his mechanical skills, it can be safely assumed that he was often employed by Ptolemy to produce other machines, both serious and amusing (for example, singing birds to grace water clocks and call out the hour).

Alexandria at that time had become the cultural center of the Hellenistic world. The Ptolemaic court was never more brilliant than under Ptolemy Philadelphus, who, while expanding Egyptian power overseas, was responsible for the Great Library and Museum and one of the Seven Wonders of the Ancient World, the lighthouse on the island of Pharos at the entrance to Alexandria's harbor. This was almost certainly the period of Ctesibius's greatest achievements, which, because his own work is lost, are known primarily through three later technical writers—Vitruvius (*De architectura*, after 27 B.C.E.; *On Architecture*, 1914), Philon of Byzantium (*Mechanikē syntaxis*, third century B.C.E.), and Hero of Alexandria (*Pneumatica*, c. 62 C.E.; *The Pneumatics of Hero of Alexandria*, 1851).

In addition to inventing the water organ and pump, Ctesibius perfected the first accurate water clock. Previous water clocks did not keep precise time because the flow of water to the clock could not be correctly regulated. Ctesibius first fashioned orifices of gold or other substances that would not be worn by the action of water and did not collect dirt. Having guaranteed an uninterrupted water flow into the first chamber of the clock, Ctesibius then devised a way to keep the water level in that chamber constant. An automatic valve, worked by a float, shut off the supply when the water in the chamber rose too high and opened it again as soon as enough water had drained into the clock's second chamber. The flow of water from the first chamber to the second, consequently, was always the same, and the passage of a certain amount of water represented the passage of so much time. On the simplest of water clocks, elapsed time could be determined by noting the markings on the side of the second chamber. More elaborate water clocks had complex and imaginative ways of denoting the time.

SIGNIFICANCE

While perhaps not as familiar today as some of his famous scientific and technological contemporaries, Ctesibius of Alexandria was one of the greatest Hellenistic inventors and the founder of pneumatics. Primarily a craftsman, Ctesibius had little interest in theoretical issues, but he was a mechanical genius of the first rank. He was influenced by and contributed to the cultural and intellectual atmosphere characterizing the reigns of Ptolemy Soter and especially Ptolemy Philadelphus, by whom he was employed. Over his lifetime, he produced several important devices that would have lasting value, among them a water pump, a water organ, the first accurate water clocks, and improvements to artillery.

—*Robert B. Kebric*

FURTHER READING

Cohen, M. R., and I. E. Drabkin. *A Source Book in Greek Science.* Cambridge, Mass.: Harvard University Press, 1966. A compilation of passages from ancient writers about science and technology. Includes references to Ctesibius.

Drachmann, A. G. *The Mechanical Technology of Greek and Roman Antiquity.* Madison: University of Wisconsin Press, 1963. The standard study of the literary sources for Greek and Roman technology, particularly Hero of Alexandria's *Mechanica* (c. 62 C.E.).

Landels, J. G. *Engineering in the Ancient World.* Rev. ed. Berkeley: University of California Press, 2000. An excellent survey of ancient engineering. Includes discussion of Ctesibius's contributions, some illustrated.

Lloyd, G. E. R. *Greek Science After Aristotle.* New York: W. W. Norton, 1973. A good brief survey of ancient science, beginning with the Hellenistic period. Discusses Ctesibius's work, with some illustrations.

Sarton, George. *A History of Science.* 2 vols. New York: W. W. Norton, 1970. A standard survey of the history of Hellenistic science and culture. Ctesibius's achievements are considered.

Vitruvius Pollio. *Vitruvius: Ten Books on Architecture.* Translated by Ingrid D. Rowland. New York: Cambridge University Press, 1999. In books 9 and 10, Vitruvius provides more details about Ctesibius and his work than any other ancient writer.

SEE ALSO: Arsinoe II Philadelphus; Hero of Alexandria; Ptolemy Philadelphus; Ptolemy Soter.

RELATED ARTICLE in *Great Events from History: The Ancient World*: c. 275 B.C.E., Greeks Advance Hellenistic Astronomy.

CYRUS THE GREAT
Persian king (r. c. 559-c. 530 B.C.E.)

Cyrus conquered Media and brought Persia into the arena of world leadership by defeating the Neo-Babylonians (Chaldeans) in Babylon (c. 539 B.C.E.). He created a Persian Empire—the Achaemenian dynastic empire—stretching from Turkey to India. His unusually beneficent treatment of conquered peoples was widely praised throughout the ancient Near East as well as the later Greco-Roman world.

BORN: c. 601-590 B.C.E.; Media (now in Iran)
DIED: c. 530 B.C.E.; Scythia (now in Russia)
ALSO KNOWN AS: Cyrus II
AREAS OF ACHIEVEMENT: Government and politics, war and conquest

EARLY LIFE

The lengthiest accounts of the early life of Cyrus (SI-ruhs) are found in the works of Greek historians Xenophon and Herodotus. Xenophon's *Kyrou paideia* (fifth century B.C.E.; *The Cyropaedia: Or, Education of Cyrus,* 1560-1567), however, is not so much a biography of Cyrus as a "historical romance," that is, largely fiction, with only a few bits of factual information. Most of the valuable information in Xenophon is that concerning Cyrus's conquest of Babylon; the information covering Cyrus's early life is of little value or interest.

In like manner, the information in Herodotus's *Historiai Herodotou* (c. 425 B.C.E.; *The History,* 1709) contains speculative legends about the birth and youth of Cyrus that were most likely borrowed from earlier legends, such as those surrounding the birth of Sargon of Akkad from the twenty-fourth century B.C.E. There is even some similarity to the legends about Romulus, the founder of Rome in the eighth century B.C.E. Therefore, little confidence can be placed in Herodotus's account of Cyrus's early life. That Cyrus was half Median and half Persian, however, seems to be quite likely, and he probably spent part of his youth in Media with his grandfather, Astyages. Cyrus's father was a Persian named Cambyses, and his mother, Mandane, was a Median.

LIFE'S WORK

Most of Herodotus's and Xenophon's accounts of Cyrus deal with his military campaigns, which were widespread throughout Media, Lydia (western Turkey), former provinces of the Neo-Assyrian and Neo-Babylonian Empires, including Babylon itself, and later the unsuccessful campaign against the Massagetae, a nomadic tribe in Scythia.

Cyrus began his military rule over the Persians about 559 B.C.E., and by 550 he had taken over neighboring Media and added it to his kingdom. The decisive battle over the Medes was probably at Pasargadae, the city that was to become Cyrus's capital. He also conquered the capital city of Media, Ecbatana.

Of considerable interest to Herodotus was Cyrus's first contact with the Greek world when he defeated Croesus, king of Sardis, in Lydia in 546. Shortly afterward the Greeks of the regions of Aeolia and Ionia (also in western Turkey) submitted to the rule of Cyrus. A revolt in the city of Miletus in 499 was to bring on the famous conflict between the Greeks of the mainland and the Persian Empire.

Between 546 and 540, Cyrus campaigned primarily in the Near East. The famous Behistun Inscription of the Persian Darius the Great mentions that by 520 several areas were already under Persian rule, many of which were probably added while Cyrus was still alive, including Parthia, Bactria, and Sogdiana.

The most famous conquest by Cyrus was that of Babylon in 539. Considerable information dealing with this battle is known from the Bible, Babylonian cuneiform, and the writings of Xenophon and Herodotus. Isaiah 45:13 records the prediction that Cyrus would set the Jews free from their slavery in Babylon. The same theme of Jewish return was mentioned by other biblical prophets, including Jeremiah (16:14-15; 23:7-8; 25:12-14; 50:8-10), Ezekiel (11:14-21; 28:24-26; 34:11-16; 37:1-39:29), Daniel (6:28; 10:1), and the work *Bel and the Dragon* of the Apocrypha.

The Judeo-Roman historian Flavius Josephus (c. 37-c. 100 C.E.) said that Cyrus was so impressed with these predictions that he decided to free the Jews on the basis of them (*Antiquitates Judaicae*, 93 C.E.; *The Antiquities of the Jews*, 1773). For whatever reason Cyrus made his decision, one should not assume that his treatment of the Jews was unique. One of the most notable features of Cyrus's reign was his benevolent treatment of former captive peoples who had served as provincial servants of the Neo-Assyrians and later of the Neo-Babylonians. Their former plight was in marked contrast to conditions under Cyrus's rule. Little wonder, then, that Cyrus was admired by many of his new subjects as being a benevolent ruler.

The benevolent rule of Cyrus in the biblical texts is correlated in the ancient cuneiform sources called the "Nabonidus Chronicle," the "Cyrus Cylinder," and the poem "Persian Verse Account." These sources mention

Cyrus the Great. (Hulton|Archive by Getty Images)

that Nabonidus, the last of the Neo-Babylonian rulers, was so preoccupied with the worship of the moon god Sin that he neglected the worship and state-cult of Marduk. This infuriated the priests of Marduk and much of the population of Babylon. Therefore, when Cyrus and his generals attacked that great city, they probably had assistance from defectors of Babylon. In fact, the "Cyrus Cylinder" mentions that Marduk specifically chose Cyrus as a champion of the rights of the Babylonian people.

In the classical Greek sources Herodotus and Xenophon, Cyrus was described as an ideal general, politician, and diplomat. In later times, Cicero and Scipio Africanus expressed admiration for the military exploits of Cyrus. In spite of all the great military victories of Cyrus, his death was at the hands of a nomadic tribe, the Massagetae of Scythia. To make matters more embarrassing for the great king of Persia, the Massagetae were led in battle by a woman, Queen Tomyris. According to Herodotus, Tomyris decapitated Cyrus, dipped his head in a skin full of human blood and gore, and said that Cyrus could now have his fill of blood.

SIGNIFICANCE

The remarkable interest in the life and influence of Cyrus the Great exhibited by the Hebrews, Babylonians, and, later, the Greek historians can be explained most easily

KINGS OF THE ACHAEMENIAN DYNASTY	
Ruler	Reign (B.C.E.)
Cyrus the Great	c. 559-c. 530
Cambyses II	529-522
Smerdis the Magian*	522
Darius the Great	522-486
Xerxes I	486-465
Artaxerxes I	465-423
Darius II	424-405

*Impostor pretending to be Smerdis, son of Cyrus and deceased brother of Cambyses II

by first describing the harshness of earlier rule by the Assyrians and Babylonians. Both the Assyrians and the Babylonians were oppressive in their collection of tribute, taxes, and gifts in honor of state events. On occasion, quotas of military men were required of conquered provinces. In addition to these humiliations, the rulers sometimes destroyed temples and shrines of the subjected provinces and forced the people to make an oath of allegiance, under "divine" penalty if the oath was broken.

Therefore, Cyrus's popularity arose from his restoration of native religious observances; his tolerance of their cults was a welcome relief from earlier oppression. The famous biblical example of such tolerance found in the "Cyrus Decree" in Ezra 1:1-4, which mentions that the Jews (former captives of the Babylonians) could return home to Jerusalem in Judah and rebuild their temple, is typical of Cyrus's policies. Cyrus's burial monument in Pasargadae was humble by ancient standards. It was inscribed with words to the effect that he wanted to be remembered as founder of the Persian Empire and master of Asia.

—*John M. Lawrence*

FURTHER READING

Abbott, Jacob. *Cyrus the Great*. 1880. Reprint. New York: Simon, 2001. Biography includes illustrations and maps.

Dougherty, Raymond Philip. *Nabonidus and Belshazzar: A Study of the Closing Events of the Neo-Babylonian Empire*. 1929. Reprint. New York: AMS Press, 1980. Dougherty arranges the cuneiform evidence in probable chronological order, showing the sequence of events leading to Cyrus's capture of Babylon.

Drews, Robert. "Sargon, Cyrus, and Mesopotamian Folk History." *Journal of Near Eastern Studies* 33 (October, 1974): 387-393. Compares the legendary birth accounts of Sargon and Cyrus and concludes that the Greek historians borrowed oral legends about Cyrus's birth and early life.

Gordon, Cyrus H., and Gary A. Rendsburg. *The Bible and the Ancient Near East*. New York: W. W. Norton, 1998. An account of the historical context for the Hebrew Bible explores the origins of stories, such as the liberation of the Jews, in the cultures of the ancient Near East. Parallels in the foundational stories told in the Egyptian, Persian, Greek, and Hebrew cultures of the time are examined.

Lawrence, John M. "Cyrus: Messiah, Politician, and General." *Near East Archaeological Society Bulletin*, n.s. 25 (1985): 5-28. An attempted comparison and harmonization of the accounts of Cyrus from the biblical, cuneiform, and classical sources.

_____. "Neo-Assyrian and Neo-Babylonian Attitudes Towards Foreigners and Their Religion." *Near East Archaeological Society Bulletin*, n.s. 19 (1982): 27-40. Describes the cruelty and oppression of the Assyrians and Babylonians prior to Cyrus's freeing of countless provinces of their former captives and the stark contrast of Cyrus's benevolent rule.

Mallowan, Max. "Cyrus the Great (558-529 B.C.)." *Iran* 10 (1972): 1-17. Provides a chronology of the conquests by Cyrus and a linguistic-historical analysis of some of the cuneiform inscriptions that mention him.

Vogelsang, W. J. *Rise and Organisation of the Achaemenid Empire: The Eastern Iranian Evidence*. New York: Brill, 1992. Examines the eastern part of the Persian Achaemenid Empire, which was founded in the sixth century B.C.E. by Cyrus the Great.

Wiseman, Donald J. *The Chronicles of the Chaldaean Kings (626-556 B.C.) in the British Museum*. London: Trustees of the British Museum, 1961. Includes historical background for the struggle between the Assyrian and Babylonian Empires shortly before Cyrus conquered Babylon.

SEE ALSO: Atossa; Croesus; Darius the Great; Flavius Josephus; Xerxes I.

RELATED ARTICLES in *Great Events from History: The Ancient World*: 547 B.C.E., Cyrus the Great Founds the Persian Empire; October, 539 B.C.E., Fall of Babylon.

DARIUS THE GREAT
Persian king (r. 522-486 B.C.E.)

Darius consolidated and expanded the Persian Empire through humane, wise, and judicious administration. He respected the languages, religions, and cultures of his subject nations, and in return they fought his battles, built lavish palaces for him, and brought him precious gifts.

BORN: 550 B.C.E.; place unknown
DIED: 486 B.C.E.; Persepolis, Persia (now in Iran)
ALSO KNOWN AS: Darius I
AREAS OF ACHIEVEMENT: Government and politics, war and conquest

EARLY LIFE

According to his own account in the Behistun friezes, somewhat different from that of Herodotus in *Historiai Herodotou* (c. 424 B.C.E.; *The History*, 1709), Darius (da-REE-uhs) was the son of Hystaspes, grandson of Arsames, and great-grandson of Ariaramnes. This genealogy is important: Ariaramnes and Cyrus I were grandsons of Achaemenes, the eponymous ancestor of the Achaemenian Dynasty.

On the death of their father, Teispes, Cyrus I became the ruler of Anshan; Ariaramnes inherited the principality of Parsua. By the time of Cyrus the Great, Ariaramnes' son, Arsames, ruled Parsua. Cyrus the Great deposed Arsames and annexed Parsua to his own share of the inheritance, calling himself the king of Anshan and Parsua. A charismatic leader, Cyrus expanded his small kingdom to imperial heights within a short time by defeating Media (which included Assyria) and capturing Sardis in Asia Minor. Babylonia, his neighbor and ally, capitulated to his rule soon afterward. Cyrus's star rose in power and prestige, while that of Ariaramnes fell.

Before his death, Cyrus made plans to capture Egypt and Ethiopia. Grain from Egypt and ivory from Ethiopia were necessary commodities for the upkeep of the empire that Cyrus envisaged. After Cyrus's death, Cambyses II continued his father's plans for expansion. He captured Egypt and remained there in the hope of adding Ethiopia, the oasis of Ammon, and Carthage to the empire. He succeeded, however, only in subjugating the Greeks of Libya.

The king's long absence prompted a severe sociopolitical upheaval in Persia and Media. A usurper—either the king's brother Smerdis (also called Bardiya) or a pretender—assumed rulership and gained public sanction. When Cambyses, returning hastily to Persia, died in Syria from a self-inflicted wound, Darius appeared in Media to claim his Achaemenian divine right. With the help of six Persian noblemen, his father-in-law Gobryas among them, he invaded the palace of the pretender and ended his rule after seven months. It is not clear who the pretender was; according to Darius, he was Gaumata, a Magian. Smerdis, Darius explained, had already been slain by Cambyses in secret.

Thus, ten years after the death of Cyrus, the twenty-eight-year-old son of Hystaspes returned the Achaemenian throne to the house of Ariaramnes. There is no information on Darius's childhood and early youth. It is assumed that, as the son of a satrap, he was educated in the basic disciplines and in the martial arts. As a youth, he was ambitious; Cyrus suspected him of treason. After Cyrus's death, Darius commanded the prestigious ten thousand Immortals and served as the new king's spear bearer and bodyguard in Egypt. Tall, with long, curly hair and a long beard, he cut an impressive figure.

Darius's claim to legitimacy was slender. As descendants of Achaemenes, his immediate ancestors had lost the *farr* (divine sanction), and both Arsames and Hystaspes were still living. During the reign of Cambyses II, Darius's father, Hystaspes, had been the satrap of Parthia and Hyrcania. Darius had to create legitimacy; he had to provide visible proof that the god Ahura Mazda favored him and his family. During the first year of his rule, he married Atossa, the daughter of Cyrus the Great, and he fought nineteen battles and captured nine rebel leaders.

A gigantic bas-relief commemorating the end of his ordeal depicts the nine rulers standing crestfallen before the king. The king has his foot on the slain Gaumata. Ahura Mazda, the king's helper and embodiment of legitimacy, hovers above the assembly. Columns of cuneiform writing inform the spectator that the rebellious provinces included Persia, Elam, Media, Assyria, Egypt, Parthia, Margiana, and Scythia, and that the strategically important provinces were brought within the fold quickly, while the subjugation of Scythia and Egypt took a while longer. Some provinces did not give up after the first defeat. Susa, for example, rose up three times before it was completely crushed. When the resistance finally ran its course and tranquillity returned to the land, Darius became convinced that his rulership was undisputed and set his sights on expansion of his empire.

LIFE'S WORK

Subjugation of the unruly elements in the empire had taken about three years. After tranquillity had returned, the only threat Darius could envision was an external threat: an invasion of the northern provinces of the empire by the Scythian tribes who had fought and killed Cyrus the Great. To prevent this, Darius attacked the Scythians to the east of the Caspian Sea and pushed them far back into Sogdia. He also captured the fertile Indus Valley, adding this region to the empire for the first time.

By 518, the empire was tranquil enough for Darius to visit Egypt as king. The visit to this ancient and important land fulfilled two objectives: adding to the king's prestige at home and consolidating Persian rule in Egypt, the empire's southwestern flank, which had been neglected since the death of Cambyses.

Darius lived at a time when it was thought possible to unify the world and to rule it with justice. Darius, duty-bound to expand Zoroastrianism, also considered himself obliged to subjugate the Greeks and to put an end to their intrigue in lands under Persian domination in Asia Minor. In 513, therefore, he crossed the Bosporus and the Danube River and pushed the Scythians so far into Europe that he eventually had to abandon the campaign for lack of provisions. Thrace and Macedonia were subjugated by Persian satraps.

With the lifeline of the Greek islands in his hands, Darius decided to postpone any further campaigns in Europe and return to Persia. His return, however, did not preclude a systematic invasion of Attica at a later date. While he knew that he had shown enough might to intimidate Greece for the present, he also knew that the Greeks would continue to incite riots in Persia's Greek settlements in Asia Minor and force him to return to the battlefield.

Darius's decision to return to Persia, rather than engage his troops in a new European theater, was wise. He lacked sufficient information to formulate a coherent strategy. Intelligence on the naval capability of Greece was especially crucial, because without it, Darius could not address the question of logistics or establish a stable supply line between his land army and his navy. Furthermore, to take on Greece and her neighbors, he needed a better equipped and stronger military and naval force than Persia could afford at the time. Additionally, he was not sure that his subjects would be able to withstand the trauma of a prolonged war. After all, the young empire comprised diverse religious and cultural entities, some of which, such as Egypt and Babylonia, had enjoyed a glorious past.

Darius the Great. (Library of Congress)

Darius's forte was administration. He now brought this strength to bear on the problem of bringing Europe under Persian rule. Following Cyrus's lead, he had allowed his subjects to retain their languages, religions, and cultures. He instituted the rule of justice under the divine right of kings throughout the empire. This rule of justice would require numerous changes in the makeup of the empire. These changes were implemented with a reform of the tax system—the amount of tax was measured by ability and by the yield of the land—and the introduction of a monetary system based on the darik to replace payment in kind.

The introduction of currency led not only to further use of the mineral wealth of Persia but also to the institution of a simple system of banking. The guardianship of wealth, hitherto the sole privilege of the royal court and of the priests, was gradually turned over to the people. More money in the hands of the populace meant better *qanats* (subterranean water conduits) and canals for agriculture, better roads for trade, and overall a more unified kingdom. To free the weak from the bondage of the strong further, Darius instituted a fixed system of wages. Tablets discovered at Persepolis indicate the rates at which men, women, and children were paid for their labor.

The vast empire of Darius stretched from Macedonia and Egypt to the Jaxartes River and the Indus Valley. It could not be managed by one person. His three long years of struggle to establish his credibility had proved to Darius that he needed trustworthy men to help him rule. Toward this end, he revamped the satrap system introduced by Cyrus, increasing the number of satraps to twenty. The satraps were chosen from among the Persians of royal blood and appointed to the provinces. Each satrapy had a governor (the satrap) and a secretary to organize the affairs of the state. The secretary had a small army attached to his office. When necessary, the secretary could mobilize this army to unseat an ambitious satrap. The satrapy was also assigned a tax collector and a military general, both of whom reported to the king.

In order to safeguard his position further, Darius appointed a fifth person, an individual referred to as the "eyes and ears" of the king, to each satrapy. This officer kept the king abreast of events in his part of the empire and reported on abuses of power and activities that bordered on treason. An inspector would arrive unannounced to examine the satrapy's books and file a report at court.

Such an elaborate administrative machine could not function without a similarly elaborate communications system. Darius therefore built a royal road, 1,677 miles (2,705 kilometers) in length, to connect Sardis to Susa. A similar road connected Babylon to the Indus Valley. Royal *chapars* (messengers) carried the king's messages on fresh horses provided at 111 stations. In addition, Darius completed the construction of the 125-mile (202-kilometer) canal in the Nile Delta, a project that had been abandoned by the pharaoh Necos.

In 499, incited by Greece and Eretria, the Ionians of Asia Minor revolted against Darius and set the city of Sardis on fire. The insurrection was quickly suppressed. Seven years later, Darius's son-in-law Mardonius was sent on an expedition to subjugate Eretria and Athens. When Mardonius's fleet was destroyed in a storm near Mount Athos, Darius sent another expedition under Datis, a Mede. Datis conquered Eretria but failed to impress its population. His maltreatment of the Eretrians convinced the Greeks that they should prevent any further Persian advance in Europe. Datis's actions thus roused the Greek states to join forces and defeat the Persians.

After a defeat at Marathon, Darius could no longer focus his efforts on a final assault on Europe. Internal problems plagued the empire. Chief among them were two: the question of succession and a revolt in Egypt. The competition regarding succession had pitted Xerxes, Darius's son by Atossa, against Artabazanes, his eldest son by the daughter of Gobryas. Darius chose Xerxes to succeed him. The more pressing problem of Greek infiltration in the uppermost stratum of Persian administration, infiltration that had resulted in revolt in Egypt, remained unresolved. Darius died, after thirty-six years as the king of kings of Persia, in 486.

Darius had worn the Achaemenian crown and the royal robes very well. As a king, he was wise, determined, and a good judge of human character. More than anything, he was a builder in both the physical and the abstract senses of the word. The foundation of his empire survived not only Alexander's invasion but also the Arab invasion of Iran.

SIGNIFICANCE

Because of the dubious validity of his claim to the throne, Darius had to impose his rule by force. Once his credibility was established and order was restored, he launched a series of reforms that improved agriculture and trade. These reforms provided a solid foundation for notable military triumphs and expansion of the Persian Empire.

Darius had a deep concern for the welfare of the individual. He studied the most reliable literature available at his time, the civil law code of Hammurabi, and devised his own set of rules for the Persian Empire. In the satrapies, such as Egypt, he provided guidance for the priests, who wrote the local codes.

Though according to some sources Darius was the ruler who imposed the Zoroastrian religion on the Persians, he did not force his subject nations to follow the dictates of Ahura Mazda. On the contrary, in Egypt he built a temple to Amen and endowed another. In 519, following Cyrus's long-neglected decree, he ordered that work be resumed on rebuilding the temple at Jerusalem.

Darius was fond of massive building projects. Indeed, he used these projects as a means to unify the country. For example, in building Persepolis, the palace wherein he received foreign dignitaries on the occasion of the Now Ruz (Persian new year), he employed the full spectrum of human and mineral resources of the empire so that everyone could have a share in the product. Babylonian bricklayers, Median and Egyptian goldsmiths and designers, Ionian and Carian carpenters, and others cooperated. They gathered a wealth of material—ivory from Ethiopia, cedar from Lebanon, turquoise from Khorazmia, and gold from Lydia—and constructed Persepolis as a genuinely cosmopolitan landmark.

Darius, however, failed to do for his nation-states what he did for his individual subjects. He did not allow subject nations such as Egypt and Babylonia to participate in the administration of the empire. In time, this policy drove the frustrated elites of those societies to conspiracy and revolt. Furthermore, Darius underestimated Greece, which, making capital use of the king's vulnerability, had sown discord in Asia Minor and Egypt before the burning of Sardis, which incited Darius to march on its territories. Greek policy, therefore, should be credited for both the defeat of Darius's military might at Marathon and the establishment of Western superiority over the empire of the East.

—*Iraj Bashiri*

FURTHER READING

Burn, A. R. *Persia and the Greeks: The Defense of the West c. 546-478 B.C.* London: Arnold, 1962. Contains detailed discussion of the campaigns of Darius in Europe. The book includes maps, charts illustrating battle formations, and genealogies for the major figures.

Cook, J. M. "The Rise of the Achaemenids and Establishment of Their Empire." In *The Cambridge History of Iran*, vol. 2, edited by Ilya Gershevitch. Cambridge, England: Cambridge University Press, 1985. This article examines the principal sources on ancient Iran and the extent and composition of the empire. Toward the end, an assessment is made of the leadership that raised Persia to the head of the world's first empire.

Frye, Richard N. *The Heritage of Persia*. New York: New American Library, 1966. Frye's account of ancient Iran is unique. It focuses on the eastern provinces of the ancient kingdom but, unlike other accounts, it draws on cultural, religious, and literary sources. The book is illustrated; it includes an index, maps, genealogies, and an informative bibliography.

Ghirshman, Roman. *Iran from the Earliest Times to the Islamic Conquest*. New York: Penguin Books, 1954. In this account of prehistory to Islamic times in Iran, Ghirshman juxtaposes textual information and archaeological data to place ancient Iran in proper perspective. The book is illustrated with text figures as well as with plates. It includes an index and a selected bibliography.

Herodotus. *The Histories*. Translated by Robin Wakefield. New York: Oxford University Press, 1998. This, the most comprehensive classical account of the rise of Darius to kingship, also includes information on his administrative reforms, campaigns in Europe, and defeat at Marathon. This book should be read alongside other authoritative sources. The Penguin edition features poor maps but a good index.

Kent, Roland G. *Old Persian: Grammar, Texts, Lexicon*. New Haven, Conn.: American Oriental Society, 1950. Although set forth as a textbook, this volume provides an English translation of the most important Old Persian texts left for posterity by the Achaemenian kings, especially by King Darius.

Olmstead, Albert T. *History of the Persian Empire, Achaemenid Period*. 3d ed. Chicago: University of Chicago Press, 1966. This detailed history of the Achaemenid period remains the chief secondary source for the study of ancient Iran. The book includes a topographical index, maps, and many carefully selected illustrations.

Robinson, B. W. *The Persian Book of Kings: An Epitome of the Shahnama of Firdausi*. London: Routledge-Curzon, 2002. This adaptation of Iran's major epic provides a wealth of information on ancient Iranian religion, social hierarchy, and military organization. It especially underscores the role of the king—an absolute ruler carrying out a divine decree.

Wilber, Donald N. *Persepolis: The Archaeology of Parsa, Seat of the Persian Kings*. Princeton, N.J.: Darwin Press, 1989. Wilber provides an account of Achaemenian history and of the monuments at Persepolis built by Darius and his successors. He discusses the layout of the palaces and their division into the *apadana*, harem, and throne hall.

SEE ALSO: Alexander the Great; Atossa; Cyrus the Great; Xerxes I.

RELATED ARTICLES in *Great Events from History: The Ancient World*: 1069 B.C.E., Third Intermediate Period Begins in Egypt; c. 733 B.C.E., Founding of Syracuse; 520-518 B.C.E., Darius the Great Conquers the Indus Valley; 520-518 B.C.E., Scylax of Caryanda Voyages the Indian Ocean; 499-494 B.C.E., Ionian Revolt; September 17, 490 B.C.E., Battle of Marathon; 480-479 B.C.E., Persian Invasion of Greece.

DAVID

Hebrew king (r. c. 1000-c. 962 B.C.E.)

According to Hebrew tradition and the biblical record, David was the greatest king of Israel. It was prophesied of him that through his lineage the promise of a latter-day Messiah and other spiritual blessings would be fulfilled, making him a key monarch in the history of Israel and of importance to the development of both Christianity and Judaism.

BORN: c. 1030 B.C.E.; Bethlehem, Judah (now in Palestine)

DIED: c. 962 B.C.E.; Jerusalem, Israel

AREAS OF ACHIEVEMENT: Religion, literature

EARLY LIFE

The record of the life of David (DAY-vihd) is found in the Bible in the historical writings of 1 Samuel 16 through 1 Kings 2, with some material repeated in 1 Chronicles 2-29 and in selected psalms attributed to him in the Old Testament. The early story of David's life is contained in 1 Samuel 18-19, though there are references to his life scattered throughout the rest of the Old Testament and in the New Testament. In the latter book, the birth of Jesus of Nazareth is specifically linked with the line of David and serves as one of the criteria Jesus and his later followers used to proclaim him the Messiah and King of the Jews. Most modern scholars accept the substantial historicity of these narratives.

The dating of David's birth and early life is primarily informed guesswork, but archaeological consensus is that David was born sometime around the second half of the eleventh century B.C.E. The great-grandson of Ruth and Boaz, David was the youngest of eight sons of Jesse, evidently a wealthy man who owned property and livestock and faithfully worshiped Yahweh, the god of Abraham, Isaac, and Jacob. As part of the lineage of Judah, David was qualified by Jewish tribal tradition for rulership in Israel. In the Bible, he alone is named David, symbolic of his prominence and importance in sacred history to both Jews and Christians.

David's early fame and preparation for kingship arose from his humble shepherding and his affinity for music; he was said to be a boy who could tame both beasts and the belligerent with his sweet tones. When Saul, the king of Israel, was to be deposed as a result of his lack of obedience to God, the prophet Samuel was commissioned by God to anoint the young David, much to the jealous chagrin of his elder brothers. There ensued from this set of events much intrigue between David and Saul, as the rejected king's fall from the throne was accompanied by an apparent madness or manic-depressive state that affected his ability to govern even himself, a malady that the young shepherd-musician was called on to soothe with his music.

After David was put to the test in his legendary confrontation with the giant Philistine, Goliath, his stature as a leader began to overshadow that of Saul. In this familiar tale, David kills the taunting adversary with his slingshot and then beheads him, giving the glory of the victory to God.

As the reputation of David spread from this heroic exploit, Saul became less enamored of the young shepherd boy who had befriended his son Jonathan, and he began to see David as a bitter rival, ignorant of the fact that God had already chosen David to be his successor. Soon David was under siege, as attempts were made on his life. He was saved from one plot against him by the ingenuity of his wife Michal, one of Saul's daughters. (An irony of these court intrigues was the support David received from Saul's household through Jonathan and Michal.) The next stages in the life of David were marked by finding refuge from Saul, while awaiting the former king's demise and his own coronation as king. During this time, David wrote many of the psalms attributed to him in the Book of Psalms, autobiographical poems and songs that reveal the inner conflict he experienced while trying to evade the plots on his life that were initiated by Saul and his followers.

LIFE'S WORK

As the reign of Saul came to an end, David had two opportunities to assassinate Saul and assume the throne immediately, but he chose to spare the king's life. In battle against the Philistines, Jonathan as well as Saul's other two sons were killed. Himself mortally wounded, Saul committed suicide rather than fall into the hands of the enemy. When David learned of their deaths, he tore his clothes and wept. David was eventually anointed by his own tribesmen and established his reign in Hebron at the age of thirty. He remained in Hebron for seven and a half years.

Eventually, after a fierce but brief civil war between supporters of David and the remaining followers of Saul, he moved the capital to Jerusalem. David's reign in Jerusalem lasted more than thirty-three years, and the early decades of it were quite successful and were seen as blessed by God. With David's skillful military leadership, Israel conquered many of its enemies, including the ever-threatening Philistines and neighboring rivals Moab, Ammon, and Edom. During David's reign, Israel's dominance grew from the Egyptian boundaries to the upper Euphrates River. Major roads were built for travel and trade, and the kingdom prospered mightily. David was motivated, however, by more than a desire for military conquest and social prosperity for his people. At the center of his commitment was a religious devotion to God, who he believed had brought him to power.

In response to his devotional impulses, David won back from the Philistines the Ark of the Covenant, a sacred vessel that housed the tablets on which the Ten Commandments had been written and other sacred relics of Israel's history. It was then returned to a special tabernacle prepared for it in Jerusalem. This acquisition gave Jerusalem even more prominence in a time when Israel was just coming to maturity as a nation-state and looking for a center of influence. The irony of David's laudable motivations to restore these important religious artifacts to Israel, and thus to inspire Israel to greater faith and devotion, is that his adultery with Bathsheba and the arranged murder of her husband occurred in this time period.

The biblical record suggests that while gazing from his palace, David saw below the figure of Bathsheba, who bathed seductively in open view. Acting on his lust, David committed adultery, and a child was conceived.

David, at left. (Library of Congress)

David then ordered her soldier-husband, Uriah, to the front lines, where he was killed. The prophet Nathan, commissioned by God to confront David with his sins, told the king a parable of a rich man who stole a lamb from a poor man. David was crushed by the weight of his sin and the subsequent death of the child born to Bathsheba. Bathsheba gave birth to another child of David, Solomon, who later succeeded his father on the throne. David's reign, however, never quite recovered from this act, and it symbolized the turning point in his kingship. Absalom, David's son by his wife Maacah, began to plot against his father to take over the throne but was defeated by David's loyal commander, Joab. David's last days as king were marred by the internecine warfare between Adonijah and Solomon for his throne.

The one triumph of his career that would have meant most to David was the construction of a temple of worship to Yahweh in Jerusalem. This privilege, however, was ironically denied to David, the master of ode, music, and song, "the sweet psalmist of Israel" (2 Sam. 23:1), and left for his son Solomon. David was denied this honor because he had been a man of war. David died, however, with the reassuring words of the prophet Nathan on his heart:

> When your days are fulfilled and you lie down with your fathers, I will raise up your offspring after you, who shall come forth from your body, and I will establish his kingdom. He shall build a house for my name, and I will establish the throne of his kingdom for ever. (2 Sam. 7:12-13)

Many later Christian writers interpret this prophecy as messianic, as pointing to the coming of Jesus. In the Book of Acts, the Apostle Peter, in his first message after the ascension of Christ, refers to many of David's deeds and words as being fulfilled in the life of Jesus.

SIGNIFICANCE

David is clearly a pivotal figure in the history of ancient Israel and in the development of Christianity. In regard to the latter, he is repeatedly mentioned as an ancestor, forerunner, and foreshadower of Jesus Christ. David's impact and influence can be directly related to his personality, at once winsome and capable. His understanding of military strategy and administrative decision-making allowed him to achieve innumerable successes. He also clearly had a flawed character, however, one given to momentary flights of wild misjudgment, including lust, which magnified the instability of his family life. In a time of polygamy, David fared no better than most men in maintaining multiple households, often engendering much strife among his sets of children, and in his notorious relationship with Bathsheba.

Nevertheless, it was David and the city he built, Jerusalem, to which Israel's people repeatedly turned for inspiration. When later generations sought relief from foreign domination or unwise kings, they longed for a king like David and looked forward to a time when the Messiah, promised to David himself, would sit on his throne and reign over Israel.

No summary of David's life would be complete without a discussion of the many psalms that are attributed to him in the Old Testament's Book of Psalms. While it is difficult to determine how many of the psalms were actually composed by him, a number of them can be seen as true reflections of a man of many triumphs and sorrows. Perhaps the two most famous psalms attributed to David are Psalm 23 and Psalm 51. The former is the famous "shepherd psalm," in which David compares his relationship to God with that of a sheep to a shepherd. Psalm 51 is an intensely autobiographical poem that details David's adultery with Bathsheba and his confession of that sin. In this most personal, psychologically complex psalm, the writer calls out desperately for mercy, recognizing that what is needed is not another animal sacrifice but a "broken spirit."

Many generations of Jewish and Christian believers have been enriched by the psalmic literature attributed to David. The psalms have formed the basis for many Christian hymns and prayer books since their compilation in the late centuries B.C.E. The confessional nature of many of these psalms also has inspired religious writers from Saint Augustine to Anne Bradstreet to John Bunyan to create autobiographical narratives detailing their estrangement from and reconciliation with God.

—*Bruce L. Edwards*

FURTHER READING

Albright, William Foxwell. *The Archaeology of Palestine*. Cambridge, Mass.: American Schools of Oriental Research, 1974. This standard work on the archaeology of the ancient world remains a comprehensive and informed overview of the historical data gleaned from that time. Overall, it provides the reader with an authentic sense of the civilization from which David originated and the one in which he became a prominent ruler.

Alexander, David, and Pat Alexander, eds. *Eerdmans' Handbook to the Bible*. Rev. ed. Grand Rapids, Mich.: Wm. B. Eerdmans, 1987. A comprehensive handbook to biblical history and geography with historical interpretations that trace David's rise to power in the kingdom of Israel and illuminate for the lay reader the specific episodes in his life drawn from the biblical text.

Alter, Robert. *The David Story: A Translation with Commentary of 1 and 2 Samuel*. New York: W. W. Norton, 1999. This biography of David contains extensive footnotes covering all aspects of life in David's times.

Bright, John. *A History of Israel*. 4th ed. Louisville, Ky.: Westminster J. Knox Press, 2000. A thorough and compelling, nontheological treatment of the history of Israel. Sections on the world of the kingdoms and civilizations contemporary with the rule of David shed light on the story of his life and sustain the interest of both the common reader and the scholar. Includes helpful anecdotal commentary on life in ancient times.

Bruce, F. F. *Israel and the Nations: The History of Israel from the Exodus to the Fall of the Second Temple*. Carlisle, Cumbria, England: Paternoster Press, 1997. A comprehensive historical analysis of the kings of Israel beginning with Saul and David and continuing through the Davidic line. Provides a clear and succinct overview of the reign of David and the impact of David's rule throughout Israeli history.

Halpern, Baruch. *David's Secret Demons: Messiah, Murderer, Traitor, King*. Grand Rapids, Mich.: Wm. B. Eerdmans, 2001. Halpern analyzes the story of David from textual, historical, and archaeological perspectives. He methodically destroys the positive image of David, calling him a killer, thug, mercenary, adulterer, assassin, bandit, brigand, and predator.

Harrison, R. K. *An Introduction to the Old Testament*. Grand Rapids, Mich.: Wm. B. Eerdmans, 1972. A complete overview of the origin, message, and impact of each book of the Old Testament, speaking directly to the issues of the chronology and authenticity of the biblical narrative of David's life and discussing his influence both in ancient Israel and in the present. A massive, comprehensive scholarly work with extensive documentation.

Kidner, Derek. *The Psalms*. 2 vols. Downers Grove, Ill.: Inter-Varsity Press, 1976. Comprehensive overview and interpretation of the psalms written by David.

Kitchen, K. A. *The Bible in Its World*. Downers Grove, Ill.: Inter-Varsity Press, 1977. An insider's look at the world of archaeology and how it functions in validating ancient records and narratives. It is particularly helpful in its extensive examination of antiquity's cultural artifacts and social conditions against the backdrop of the age of Saul, David, and Solomon, and the remainder of David's lineage.

Schultz, Samuel J. *The Old Testament Speaks*. 5th ed. San Francisco: HarperSanFrancisco, 2000. Written for the lay reader, this cogent and lucidly written volume presents an objective, historical analysis of the lives of the patriarchs, including a major section on David and the kings of Israel and their role in the evolution of ancient Israel.

Thompson, J. A. *Handbook to Life in Bible Times*. Downers Grove, Ill.: Inter-Varsity Press, 1986. A colorful, lavishly illustrated reference tool with key sections on the domestic life, travel, family customs, and cultural preoccupations of the biblical world. Illuminates the life and times of Israel and its kings in the period between 1400 and 1000 B.C.E., and thus is a helpful contextualizing volume for a study of David.

SEE ALSO: Bathsheba; Jesus; Solomon.

RELATED ARTICLES in *Great Events from History: The Ancient World*: c. 1000 B.C.E., Establishment of the United Kingdom of Israel; c. 966 B.C.E., Building of the Temple of Jerusalem; c. 922 B.C.E., Establishment of the Kingdom of Israel; c. 6 B.C.E., Birth of Jesus Christ.

DEBORAH
Israeli prophet and military leader

Deborah rallied Israelite tribes to defeat oppressors as she had prophesied; her victory poem is considered one of the Bible's most ancient texts.

FLOURISHED: c. 1200 B.C.E.-1125 B.C.E.; central Israel
AREAS OF ACHIEVEMENT: Religion, war and conquest

EARLY LIFE
The biblical figure named Deborah (DEHB-oh-rah) is believed to have lived between 1200 B.C.E. and 1125 B.C.E. These years, falling between the death of Joshua and the institution of the monarchy in ancient Israel, are recounted in the biblical book of Judges. Tradition assigns Joshua as Moses's successor, charged with leading the loose federation of Hebrew tribes that were resettling ancestral lands in the area then known as Canaan. Whether or not the initial stage of resettlement proceeded as a unified military effort under Joshua, instability marked the years chronicled in Judges. Archaeological evidence supports a scenario of periods of war and crisis alternating with peaceful intervals during the twelfth and eleventh centuries B.C.E. Most towns in the region apparently suffered destruction, indicating a time of turmoil and uncertainty.

ently suffered destruction, indicating a time of turmoil and uncertainty.

The Bible views the era as a cycle of lapses into idolatry, punished by Yahweh (the god of Abraham) through the agency of outside aggressors, followed by repentance and subsequent deliverance by divinely appointed leaders, or "judges." In Deborah's lifetime, the Israelites had become enslaved to Jabin, the king of Canaan. Scripture states that following the death of the judge Ehud, the people had fallen under the sway of gods other than Yahweh, who, in turn, had given them up to their Canaanite oppressors.

The vulnerability of the Israelite population during Deborah's formative years would have highlighted her role as childbearer, particularly in a patriarchal society in which a man could sell his daughter as payment for debts. The primacy of survival, however, also required that women labor alongside men for the good of the community. Deborah's development may have been affected by her tribal affiliation. Residing in the hill country in what is now central Israel, she was most likely a member of the tribe of Ephraim. The central position of that tribe's area of settlement, along with the fact that the religious center of Shiloh was located in the territory, engendered in the Ephraimites a proud and even militant spirit.

LIFE'S WORK

The fourth chapter of the biblical book of Judges introduces Deborah as a prophet to whom people came to settle controversies. She is described as bestowing her counsel under a palm tree, apparently a sacred site popularly associated with the burial place of Deborah, the nurse of the matriarch Rebecca.

Some see in this image the *kahin* (or *kahina*), known from nomadic Arabic tribes as a kind of magician or fortune-teller holding court and dispensing judgments in a sanctified place. A common phenomenon in antiquity, prophecy was essentially oracular; that is, it involved communication of the divine will regarding a specific matter. The prophet thus played a prominent role in the political life of a community by delivering messages in the name of a god. Nothing in the biblical account indicates that Deborah as a woman functioned in the role of prophet any differently than would a man. Nevertheless, it has been suggested that, as a woman whose priority was childrearing, her calling was, at best, part-time during her childbearing years and may not even have begun until later in life.

As one to whom they came with their troubles and concerns, Deborah was no doubt keenly aware of her people's suffering under Jabin. Headed by Jabin's field commander, Sisera, the Canaanite army was equipped with iron chariots, giving them considerable military superiority over the Israelites, who were still technologically in the Bronze Age. This advantage enabled the Canaanites to control the passage through the valleys that separated the mountain tribes in the center of the land—including Ephraim, where Deborah resided—and those in the north, in Galilee, thus ensuring their subjugation of the Israelites.

Despite this obstacle, after twenty years of domination, Deborah initiated a war of liberation by summoning a military commander, a man named Barak, out of Kedesh-Naphtali in the northern reaches of the territory. Because of the similarity of meaning between the name Barak ("lightning") and that of Deborah's apparent husband, Lapidoth ("torches"), some medieval commentators identify Barak as her spouse. Most commentators, however, fail to find this identification borne out by the context. Based on the ambiguity stemming from the Hebrew word *esheth*, signifying either "woman" or "wife,"

and the question of whether or not *Lapidoth* is a proper noun, at least one commentator, Pseudo-Philo, in *Liber antiquitatum biblicarum* (first century C.E.; *Biblical Antiquities*, 1917) interprets *esheth lapidoth* to mean "fiery woman," or "enlightener." The phrase therefore refers to Deborah herself and not her marital status (though given the social conventions of the time, it is doubtful that Deborah was unmarried, whether or not her husband is named in the biblical account).

In any event, in her role as prophet and now as judge, Deborah relayed Yahweh's command that Barak gather a force of ten thousand volunteers to Mount Tabor, at the boundary of the territories of the northern tribes of Zebulun, Naphtali, and Issachar. Barak, convinced of Deborah's power and influence, refused to act unless she accompanied him. She agreed, declaring that Sisera would suffer defeat at the hand of a woman.

True to Deborah's reckoning, Sisera and his army approached Mount Tabor from the south, along the valley of the river Kishon. The strategy of the poorly armed Israelite tribes was to exploit the flooding of the riverbed and lure Sisera and his nine hundred iron chariots into the muddy river valley. The Israelites descended the mountain and engaged the enemy in Taanach, by the waters of Megiddo, a Canaanite town located near a tributary of the Kishon. As the Israelites had planned, the Canaanites' chariots sank deep in the mire, leaving their troops to be routed by the Israelites. Not one of Sisera's camp escaped, though Sisera himself fled by foot to the tent of Jael, wife of Heber, a Kenite with whom Jabin was apparently at peace. Offering Sisera hospitality, Jael then proceeded to drive a nail into his head as he slept. There Barak tracked Sisera down, defeated, as Deborah had said, by a woman—by herself as well as Jael, many would argue. The victory over Sisera that Deborah had inspired ushered in a forty-year span of prosperity for Israel, twice the years of their oppression.

The narrative in Judges 4 names only the tribes of Naphtali and Zebulun as fighting in the battle against Sisera. The account of the victory in poetic form that follows in chapter 5, however, cites numerous tribes, either extolling their participation (Ephraim, Benjamin, and Issachar as well as Naphtali and Zebulun) or condemning their absence (Reuben, Dan, and Asher). This hymn of triumph is said to be sung by Deborah and Barak, though the Hebrew verb is in the feminine form. Also in support of the claim that what has become known as the "Song of Deborah" was indeed authored by a woman, commentators note the presence of many feminine images. Chief among them is Deborah as "a mother in Israel." Her bold actions are understood to be that of a mother fiercely protective of her family—metaphorically, the family of her people. Female authorship is supported as well by the fact that more of the text is devoted to the actions of Jael and Sisera's mother—imagined as anxiously awaiting her son's return—than to a recapitulation of the battle.

SIGNIFICANCE

The defeat of Sisera, instigated by Deborah, proved decisive in the decline of the Canaanite kingdom, thus easing the resettlement of the area by the Israelites. This proved significant in the history of religion, as both Judaism and Christianity developed from the nation that formed from Israelite expansion into the territory. Deborah's poetic reconstruction of the defeat has also made a mark in literary history. The Song of Deborah is intensively studied as one of the most ancient texts in Scripture, and it also forms part of the Jewish liturgy.

Commentators have noted how unremarkable Deborah's judgeship appears in the biblical text. While the Scripture portrays Deborah as a woman of power and influence, interpreters of the biblical tradition have often blunted her impact. Flavius Josephus, in his first century account of Jewish history (*Antiquitates Judaicae*, 93 C.E.; *The Antiquities of the Jews*, 1773), omits any mention of Deborah's role as military strategist or judge, displaying a discomfort with a woman exercising authority over men that appears in rabbinical commentaries as well. The rabbis actually chastise Deborah for sending for Barak rather than going to him.

"We never hear sermons pointing women to the heroic virtues of Deborah as worthy of their imitation," bemoaned nineteenth century American suffragist Elizabeth Cady Stanton. Instead, she noted, "the lessons doled out to women" exhorted "meekness and self-abnegation." Today, the precedent set by Deborah has taken on new significance—in large part as a result of the rise of the women's movement and the rebirth of the state of Israel, whose fourth prime minister was a woman and whose women have, from the nation's beginning, served in its military.

—*Amy Allison*

FURTHER READING

Bird, Phyllis. "Images of Women in the Old Testament." In *Religion and Sexism: Images of Woman in the Jewish and Christian Traditions*, edited by Rosemary Radford Ruether. New York: Simon and Schuster, 1974. Writing from a feminist perspective, Bird views Deborah as an exceptional woman whose story is recounted in a book that portrays a man's world, that is, a world dominated by war and issues of power and control.

Brown, Cheryl Anne. *No Longer Be Silent: First Century Portraits of Biblical Women*. Gender and the Biblical Tradition Series. Louisville, Ky.: Westminster/John Knox Press, 1992. Examines references to Deborah in Pseudo-Philo's *Biblical Antiquities* and Flavius Josephus's *Jewish Antiquities*, retellings of the biblical narrative composed during Judaism's and Christianity's formative years. Brown's discussion demonstrates the variability of Deborah's image in Western religious tradition. Includes bibliography, index, and endnotes.

Klein, Lillian R. *From Deborah to Esther: Sexual Politics in the Hebrew Bible*. Minneapolis, Minn.: Fortress Press, 2003. Examines biblical portraits of women, including Deborah, and the dynamics of gender, honor, and power therein.

Lacks, Roslyn. *Women and Judaism: Myth, History, and Struggle*. New York: Doubleday, 1980. Concludes that Deborah's story counteracts conventional assumptions about women derived from elsewhere in the Bible as well as from rabbinic literature. Includes bibliography, index, and endnotes.

Phipps, William E. *Assertive Biblical Women*. Westport, Conn.: Greenwood Press, 1992. Briefly examines Deborah in her various leadership roles. Contends that ancient societies practiced gender egalitarianism to a greater degree than did later generations. Offers endnotes as well as an index and select bibliography.

Williams, James G. *Women Recounted: Narrative Thinking and the God of Israel*. Sheffield, England: Almond Press, 1982. Views the biblical texts from a literary perspective, so that the figure of Deborah owes less to historical accuracy than to ancient literary conventions. Contains a bibliography, endnotes, and an index of biblical passages.

SEE ALSO: Flavius Josephus.

RELATED ARTICLES in *Great Events from History: The Ancient World*: c. 1280 B.C.E., Israelite Exodus from Egypt; c. 1000 B.C.E., Establishment of the United Kingdom of Israel; c. 922 B.C.E., Establishment of the Kingdom of Israel.

DEMOCRITUS
Greek philosopher

Democritus worked out a far-reaching atomism, which he applied to science, metaphysics, and ethics. His view that the world is made up of changing combinations of unchanging atoms was addressed to one of the central questions of his age, how change was possible, and provided a model of reasoning that was mechanistic, materialist, and nonsupernatural.

BORN: c. 460 B.C.E.; Abdera, Thrace (now Avdira, Greece)
DIED: c. 370 B.C.E.; Abdera, Thrace
AREAS OF ACHIEVEMENT: Philosophy, science

EARLY LIFE

Democritus (dih-MAHK-ruht-uhs) was born, probably to wealthy parents, in the city of Abdera, Thrace. Although Leucippus, the philosopher who became his teacher, can properly be regarded as the founder of Greek atomism, Leucippus himself wrote very little, and very little is known about him. Democritus, however, was a prolific writer who developed a well-reasoned atomistic view and applied it to a wide variety of fields, including science, metaphysics, and ethics.

As a young man, Democritus traveled to Egypt, Persia, and Babylonia. Some ancient sources hold that he went as far south as Ethiopia and as far east as India, but modern scholars consider this doubtful. It is reported that Democritus boasted that he had visited more foreign lands and carried out more extensive inquiries and investigations than anyone else of his time. He traveled both for the "broadening" experience that falls to any inquisitive traveler and in order to receive instruction from those who were considered wise in many lands. When he returned to Greek soil, he himself earned a reputation for wisdom. He carried with him an aura of the exotic, having delved into cultures that the Greeks thought of as exotic and foreign: the cultures of Egypt, Persia, and Babylonia.

In character, Democritus is reported to have been a man of serenity, strength, and cheerfulness. The ancient Romans referred to him as "the laughing philosopher," alluding, perhaps, to his attitude toward the typically human fault of taking oneself too seriously. As a thinker and writer, he addressed the most pressing philosophical and intellectual issues of the age in his works, which numbered at least fifty. Unfortunately, his texts have survived only in fragmentary form.

LIFE'S WORK

During the years following his travels, when Democritus began to develop his philosophical system, the Greek intellectual world was occupied with grave difficulties arising from the philosophy of Parmenides of Elea and his followers, the Eleatics. Parmenides was a practitioner of strict deductive logic. Taking premises that he thought would be generally acceptable, he argued logically to necessary conclusions. Many people admired his strong reliance on reason and thought; nevertheless, Parmenides arrived at conclusions that were deeply problematic. He concluded that there is no such thing as change and that no more than one thing exists. This clearly conflicts with common experience, which seems to show constant change and plurality. Still, Parmenides held fast to logic and reasoning as sources of knowledge that are more reliable than sense experience. If reason rules out change and plurality, he thought, then change and plurality do not exist.

The basis of his argument—an argument with which Democritus and Leucippus had no choice but to grapple—is the idea that reason either apprehends something or it apprehends nothing. If it apprehends nothing, then it is not reason (that is, not an apprehending) after all. Thus, reason apprehends what exists, not nothing. Now if things came into existence or passed out of existence, or if things changed their qualities over time, then reason would have to think of the things or qualities as not existing at some time (that is, before coming into existence or after passing out of existence). Reason would then, however, be apprehending nothing—and this, it was said, cannot occur. Similarly, if more than one thing existed, and there was empty space between the things, reason would again have to apprehend nothing. The conclusion is that only one thing exists, and this one thing is eternal, never coming into existence, never passing out of existence, and never changing. This one thing Parmenides called "the One."

One of the great achievements of Democritus and the atomists lies in overcoming this argument—an argument that probably seemed much more convincing to the ancient Greeks than to modern thinkers—while retaining some of its logical points and, at the same time, acknowledging the reality of change, plurality, and other commonsense ideas that Parmenides apparently denied.

It is a fundamental principle of Democritean atomism that "nothing exists but the atoms and the void." The atoms (literally, in Greek, "the indivisibles" or "the

Democritus. (Library of Congress)

countless worlds, many of which must also contain stars, planets, and living things.

The atomism of Democritus was a reaffirmation of the reality of change as experienced in everyday life, yet it agreed with Parmenides' concept of the unchanging reality that lies behind observed phenomena. The theory attempted to do justice to both experience and reason, change and permanence. Democritus envisioned a world in which combinations and configurations of atoms change within the void, but the atoms themselves never undergo internal change. Thus, it is the void that makes change possible. Ironically, it could be said that in the theory of Greek atomism, it is really the void (and not the atoms) that is innovative and enables the theory to escape from the unpalatable conclusions of Parmenides and the Eleatics.

Democritus also addressed questions raised by an entirely new movement in Greek thought. Before the time of Democritus, Greek philosophers had been almost exclusively concerned with physical and metaphysical questions—for example, questions about being and change. Around the time of Democritus, however, a revolution in philosophy was brought about by the Sophists and Socrates, who raised questions about human nature, society, and morality, rather than questions that focused on the physical world.

Democritus approached all these questions through his atomism. The soul, he surmised, is made up of highly mobile spherical atoms, which disperse at death. He hypothesized that people who seem to die but who "come back to life" have actually retained their atomic integrity all the while; they did not really die and come back to life. Eventually, in a real death, the atoms in the body begin to lose their connections with one another. This process is gradual, however, so that hair and fingernails might grow for a while even after the life-breath (and the necessary spherical atoms) was gone. Then, as the atoms lose their connections, the entire body decays.

Democritus taught that people should have no fear or apprehension concerning supernatural matters or an afterlife. Because the totality of reality consists of the atoms and the void, when the atoms of a person disperse and the person dies, the person no longer exists. Therefore, according to Democritus, there is nothing to fear in death. The corollary conclusion is that people should not delay pleasures in anticipation of an afterlife; it is in this life—this arrangement of atoms—that human beings can find their only fulfillment and happiness.

The best life is one that is characterized by contentedness and cheerfulness, said Democritus. He believed that

uncuttables") are the smallest units of matter, the smallest pieces of being, which cannot be further divided. The void, considered nonbeing, is thought to be just as real as the atoms. It was very important for Democritus that both exist: being and nonbeing, the atoms and the void. In a sense, the atoms are individually much like the One of Parmenides. They do not come into existence or pass out of existence, and they do not change (internally). Nevertheless, the void—a necessary feature of atomism—makes it possible for the atoms to combine and separate and recombine in changing arrangements.

As Democritus envisioned them, atoms differ from one another only in shape, size, and position. Qualities such as color and flavor were said to arise from the particular arrangements of (inherently colorless and flavorless) atoms and their interaction with the senses of the observer.

Atoms are constantly in motion, according to Democritus's theory, and they do not require any force or intelligence to put them into motion. Surrounded by the void, they are not held in any one position but move quite freely. Atoms crash into one another, become entangled with one another, and sometimes establish regular motions or streams of motion. There is no limit to the void or to the number of atoms, and Democritus thought that the universe visible to human beings was only one among

passions are powerful, disturbing factors that tend to upset the natural harmony and balance in the arrangement of atoms in human beings. Democritus used his atomism to support traditional Greek views that strong passions can cause much trouble and that moderation is best. The key to moderation and to the achievement of happiness in life is knowledge. Knowledge determines one's proper goals and activities, while passion is a threat.

It is important, however, to distinguish Democritus's knowledge-passion polarity from that of many later Platonic thinkers. Platonic thinkers (and some Christian Neoplatonists) are dualists. They distinguish between one's spiritual or intellectual part—the seat of reason, which is divine and immortal—and one's physical or irrational part—the seat of passion, which is animal and mortal. The first is the spiritual soul and lives forever; the second is the body, which suffers death and decay. In contrast, Democritus was a thoroughgoing naturalist and materialist; he believed that all the atoms disperse at death and nothing survives. Knowledge was seen as important, and passion was seen as a threat, not for religious or supernatural reasons but because of their import for human contentedness and cheerfulness.

Ancient sources agree that Democritus lived to a remarkably advanced age. Few details of his later life, however, are known. The legend that he blinded himself (in order to root out lustful desires, according to Tertullian) is denied by Plutarch. Democritus is thought to have died in Thrace around the year 370 B.C.E.

SIGNIFICANCE

The theory of atomism was not favored by Plato (c. 427-347 B.C.E.) and Aristotle (384-322 B.C.E.), the two major Greek philosophers who followed Democritus, but it was adopted by the Greek Epicurus (341-270 B.C.E.) and the Roman Lucretius (c. 98-55 B.C.E.). Epicurus was attracted to the moral teaching of Democritus and held that human well-being is best achieved by eliminating pain and the painful desire for things that people cannot (or cannot easily) obtain. Consequently, he aimed to live a life of utmost simplicity. Both Epicurus and Lucretius followed Democritus in denying supernatural influences on human life and rejecting the idea of an afterlife. Moreover, all these thinkers believed that their position on these points was not only true but also useful in freeing people from superstitions that lead to pain and suffering.

Atomism, as an essentially physical and mechanical account of the world that leaves no place for "higher purposes" or "meanings," was particularly unacceptable to religious and theological writers of the Christian tradition, which dominated Western philosophy from about the fourth to the fourteenth century. In the wake of the Renaissance and the scientific revolution (that is, since about the fifteenth and sixteenth centuries), however, the influence of Democritus again became apparent in philosophy and science. Modern science, like ancient Democritean atomism, tends to conceive of the world purely in terms of physical objects operating according to natural laws; the question of higher purposes or meanings is considered to lie beyond the scope of science. In some points of detail, there is significant agreement between ancient atomism and the modern scientific view. On both accounts, for example, qualities such as the color of a book or the taste of a cup of coffee are thought to be attached not to individual atoms—there are no red atoms or coffee-flavored atoms—but to combinations of atoms in interaction with a perceiver. One obvious difference between the two forms of atomism, however, is that in the Democritean view atoms cannot be split, while the modern scientific view upholds the existence of many kinds of subatomic particles and has even led to the development of atom-splitting technology that can unleash great power.

However, the atomism of Democritus is not a scientific theory and does not pretend to be based on experiment, experience, and observation. It is basically a philosophical theory, based on argument, which was designed to refute the theory and the arguments of Parmenides and the Eleatics. Thus, interesting as it is to compare ancient and modern atomism, it is not really appropriate to think of the two views as competing in the same arena. Democritus and the Greek atomists succeeded in developing an attitude toward the world that enabled them to look on it as thoroughly physical and mechanical, and it is this attitude, or significant aspects of it, that many modern scientists have shared. According to this view, observable phenomena are explainable in terms of unseen movements that occur according to natural (not supernatural) law.

—*Stephen Satris*

FURTHER READING

Bailey, Cyril. *The Greek Atomists and Epicurus*. 1928. Reprint. New York: Russell & Russell, 1964. Contains a thorough historical account of the origins of Greek atomism, the contributions and elaborations that derive specifically from Democritus, and the further adaptation of the view at the hands of Epicurus.

Brumbaugh, Robert S. *The Philosophers of Greece*. Albany: State University of New York Press, 1981. Chapter 11 covers Democritus, atomism, and the development of materialism. Brumbaugh compares Greek, Roman, and modern atomisms. The chapter is brief, but Brumbaugh shows the place of Democritus and the atomists within Greek philosophical history.

Burnet, John. *Greek Philosophy: Thales to Plato*. 1914. Reprint. New York: St. Martin's Press, 1964. A classic work that has been reprinted many times. Scholarly, with indexes of both English and Greek terms.

Cartledge, Paul. *Democritus*. New York: Routledge, 1999. In this 64-page introduction to Democritus, Cartledge places the philosopher and his ideas in historical perspective.

Guthrie, W. K. C. *A History of Greek Philosophy*. 6 vols. New York: Cambridge University Press, 1978-1990. Contains more than one hundred pages on Democritus, an appendix on atomism, a bibliography, and three indexes. Democritus has been called an encyclopedic thinker, and Guthrie shows the truth of this remark by exploring a great number of areas with which Democritus was concerned.

Kirk, G. S., and J. E. Raven. *The Presocratic Philosophers*. 2d ed. New York: Cambridge University Press, 1983. Covers Leucippus, Democritus, and the theory of atomism. This book contains the actual Greek texts of the philosophers, accompanied by English translations and explanations. Kirk and Raven concentrate on the physics of atomism; the ethics of atomism is treated very briefly.

Pyle, Andrew. *Atomism and Its Critics: From Democritus to Newton*. South Bend, Ind.: St. Augustine's Press, 1995. Details the history of the study of matter and voids, from a philosophical as well as a scientific perspective, in contexts ranging from that of the ancient world to that of the age of Isaac Newton.

SEE ALSO: Aristotle; Epicurus; Lucretius; Parmenides; Plato; Socrates.

RELATED ARTICLES in *Great Events from History: The Ancient World*: 600-500 B.C.E., Greek Philosophers Formulate Theories of the Cosmos; c. 500-400 B.C.E., Greek Physicians Begin Scientific Practice of Medicine; c. 440 B.C.E., Sophists Train the Greeks in Rhetoric and Politics; 399 B.C.E., Death of Socrates; c. 380 B.C.E., Plato Develops His Theory of Ideas; c. 350 B.C.E., Diogenes Popularizes Cynicism; c. 300 B.C.E., Stoics Conceptualize Natural Law.

DEMOSTHENES
Greek orator

The life of Demosthenes and his career as an orator were consumed by his titanic struggle with Philip II of Macedonia and by his efforts to recall Athenian spirit and vigor to its former greatness. The single-mindedness, sincerity, and intense patriotism of Demosthenes—combined with his consummate genius and mastery of oratorical technique—make him one of the most notable personalities of antiquity.

BORN: 384 B.C.E.; Athens, Greece
DIED: 322 B.C.E.; Calauria, Greece
AREAS OF ACHIEVEMENT: Law, government and politics

EARLY LIFE

Demosthenes (dih-MAHS-thuh-neez) was born in Athens in 384 B.C.E., the son of Demosthenes, an Athenian citizen of the deme of Paeania, and Cleobule, the daughter of Gylon. The elder Demosthenes, the owner of a lucrative weapons workshop, died when his son was only seven, bequeathing him a substantial fortune. Most of this patrimony, however, was embezzled by the child's three guardians, Aphobus, Demophon, and Theryppides, who handed over to the young Demosthenes, when he came of age, only a fraction of his inheritance. As a boy, Demosthenes had witnessed the orator Callistratus win a stunning victory in the courtroom and had thereupon vowed to become an orator himself. He had turned his attention to the art of oratory and studied with Isaeus, an orator known for his acumen in cases involving questions of inheritance. This early training was now to bear fruit: Demosthenes, at only eighteen years of age, brought a series of actions against his guardians and secured a decisive victory. It is unlikely, however, that he recovered more than a little of what was owed him.

Employing his knowledge of the law and oratory, Demosthenes turned to professional speech writing (logography) and enjoyed success as a composer of orations for others. His own speaking debut before the Assembly, however, met with little approval from the people, for he was short of breath, weak in voice, and hampered by some sort of speech impediment. Chagrined, Demosthenes then began the legendary regimen of oratorical training that has become for subsequent generations a paradigm of the efficacy of hard work and perseverance in overcoming the defects or shortcomings of nature. He pronounced periods with pebbles in his mouth, declaimed to the waves over the roar of the sea, spoke while running up hill, and shaved one side of his head so that his humiliating appearance would confine him to his underground practice studio for several months at a time.

By the age of thirty, with physical impediments overcome and oratorical skills honed nearly to perfection, Demosthenes found himself increasingly involved in legal cases whose character was essentially political in nature. In 354 he delivered his first major speech before the Assembly, wherein he countered the rumored threat of war against Athens by the king of Persia, cautioned against rash action, and proposed an elaborate revision of the method for outfitting the navy. In this speech, as well as others written and delivered during this period, Demosthenes tended to support the conservative program of Eubulus, leader of the dominant party in Athens at the time, who advocated peace abroad and financial security at home. The impact of these orations thrust Demosthenes dramatically into the arena of politics and statesmanship, from which he retired only at his death.

LIFE'S WORK

It was to the north that Demosthenes directed his attention, troubled, like many of the Greeks, by the startling and unexpected ascendancy of Philip II of Macedonia in Thrace and Thessaly. Henceforth the story of Demosthenes' life was to be the drama of his all-consuming struggle to persuade the Athenians and the rest of the Greeks to oppose the Macedonian threat to their freedom. Encroaching southward, Philip had run roughshod over Athenian interests and sources of supply in Amphipolis and the Thermaicus Sinus.

Alarmed by these acts of aggression, in 351 Demosthenes delivered the impassioned *Kata Philippou A* (*First Philippic*, 1570), rousing his fellow citizens to take notice of the threat posed by Philip and calling them to military preparedness. This speech, injected with a newfound vigor and intensity, made clear his rejection of the policy of Eubulus and established the orator as leader of the opposition to Macedonia's infringement on Athenian and Greek liberty.

Philip's subsequent advance on Olynthus spurred the orator to respond with three stirring speeches, known as the *Olunthiakos* (*Olynthiacs*) in 349 and 348, aimed at securing aid for Olynthus. Demosthenes urged the Athe-

nians to resist the onslaught of Philip with all of their physical and financial resources, going so far as to propose that the Theoric Fund (the public dole that paid for the poor's admission to the theater) be made available for the necessities of war. The Athenians did respond—but too late and with too little assistance. Olynthus and several of the confederate towns were razed by Philip in 348.

Seeing that Athens was weak, vulnerable, and in need of time to collect its resources and strength, Demosthenes acceded to peace talks with Philip. In February of 346, he, along with several other ambassadors, including Aeschines and Philocrates, was sent to negotiate a treaty. Demosthenes' rhetorical collapse before Philip proved to be one of the most embarrassing ordeals in the orator's life and marked the beginning of enmity between him and Aeschines, to whom Philip apparently directed his reply. Nevertheless, it was Demosthenes who had been able to detect Philip's real intentions; thus, he condemned the terms of the treaty to his fellow citizens. Aeschines, on the other hand, rashly assured the Athenians of Philip's goodwill. Demosthenes' worst fears were realized when Philip, dallying before taking the final oath of ratification, secured more territory, crushed Phocis, assumed a place on the Amphictionic Council, and took from Athens the right of precedence in consulting the oracle at Delphi.

In response to the growing bitterness of the Athenians over Philip's continued successes, and perhaps to deflect criticism aimed at his conduct during the peace negotiations, Demosthenes impeached his rival Aeschines in 343. Charged with having caused grave injury to Athens by delaying the embassy, rendering false reports, giving bad advice, disobeying orders, and opening himself to bribery, Aeschines counterattacked with a speech and, with the support of Eubulus and other pro-Macedonians in Athens, was narrowly acquitted. It was clear, however, that the pro-Macedonian party had lost ground and that Demosthenes' hard-line anti-Macedonian stance was finally beginning to win support among the Athenians.

By 342 Philip had firmly incorporated Thrace in his kingdom and was now turning his eye toward the Chersonese, an area vital to Athens because of its geographically strategic location on the supply route from the Black Sea. In his speech "Peri tōn en Cherronesoi" (341; "On the Chersonese," 1757), Demosthenes countered Philip's complaints about Athenian-supported activity in this area. Shortly thereafter, he reiterated his plea for support of the Chersonese; in the *Kata Philippou G* (*Third Philippic*, 1570) Demosthenes was at his oratorical best, arguing that Philip's actions had already amounted to a violation of the peace and a declaration of war and passionately insisting on a union of all Greeks under the leadership of Athens.

The years immediately following represent the high point in Demosthenes' career. The naval reforms that he had earlier proposed were effected, and his eloquence and indefatigable energy finally prevailed to secure an alliance of almost all Greek states with Athens at its head. After Philip's declaration of war in 340, Demosthenes moved to suspend the allocation of surplus funds to the Theoric Fund and managed at length to secure an alliance between Athens and her traditional enemy, Thebes. For his actions during this time, the Athenians honored him, now their recognized leader, with two golden crowns, one in 340 and another in 339.

Demosthenes' dream of a unified Greek front, temporarily realized, was short-lived. In 338, Philip crushed the Greek allied forces on the battlefield of Chaeronea. Demosthenes, who took part in the battle, was said by his enemies to have fled disgracefully, but back in Athens it was Demosthenes who organized the city's defenses and

who, in fact, was called on by the citizens to deliver the funeral oration over those who had fallen in the fray.

To the surprise of some, Philip treated his enemies graciously in victory and refrained from occupying Athens. Nevertheless, such clemency failed to secure the goodwill or cooperation of Demosthenes. On the contrary, after Philip's assassination in 336, Demosthenes once again urged his countrymen to rally their support against Macedonia, reassured by rumors about the demise of Alexander (known later as Alexander the Great), Philip's son and successor. When Alexander's quick and decisive action against a rebellious Thebes (335) proved him to be as formidable a foe as his father, it was only through the agency of a special embassy that Demosthenes and other anti-Macedonian statesmen were spared.

In 336 a man named Ctesiphon proposed that Demosthenes should be awarded a crown at the festival of the Greater Dionysia because, in service to the state, "he continually speaks and does what is best for the people." Aeschines, bent on prolonging his feud with the orator, immediately charged Ctesiphon with an illegal action,

Demosthenes, at left. (F. R. Niglutsch)

thereby preventing the award of the crown. After several delays the case finally came to trial in 330 in what was, perhaps, the most celebrated oratorical contest of all time. Demosthenes' defense of Ctesiphon, "Peri tou Stephanou" ("On the Crown," 1732), in reality an apologia for himself and his entire political career, is not only the orator's masterpiece but also, in the judgment of many scholars throughout the centuries, the most sublime oratorical work of antiquity. To Demosthenes' repeated question, "What else could I have done?" the Athenian jury answered resoundingly with an overwhelming verdict in his favor. Aeschines, who received less than one-fifth of the votes, was forced into exile.

Some six years later, in 324, Demosthenes' shining victory was tarnished by charges of having accepted a bribe from Alexander's fugitive treasurer, Harpalus. Although the precise details of the case are obscure, Demosthenes was convicted of the charge and fined fifty talents. Unable to pay, he escaped from prison and fled into exile. In the following year, however, Alexander's death occasioned a dramatic reversal for the orator: He was recalled to Athens in triumph, and his fine was paid by the citizens who offered him fifty talents for preparing and adorning the altar for the sacrifice to Zeus the Savior. Macedonian power seemed broken, but once again Demosthenes and the Athenians were deluded: Antipater, Alexander's successor, defeated the Greeks in the Lamian War and demanded that Demosthenes be handed over to him. The orator fled to the island of Calauria, off the coast of Argolis, and there, on the approach of Antipater's minions in 322, committed suicide by drinking poison concealed in his stylus.

SIGNIFICANCE

To the ancients, Demosthenes was simply "the orator," in much the same way Homer had always been "the poet." His singleness of purpose, the compelling vehemence and force of his argumentation, his sincerity and intensity, and the lucidity, rapidity, flexibility, and variety of his style established him as the model for subsequent speakers, including the great Roman orator Cicero. For many he has symbolized the patriot par excellence, the champion of a lost cause, fighting to preserve the Athenian democracy in its death throes, a tragic hero and an eloquent spokesman battling for political freedom against the tyrannical threats and designs of the Macedonian aggressor. Others have had little sympathy for his policies, sharing Aeschines' view of him as a humorless "water-bibber" among wine drinkers, a stiff-necked politician whose stubbornness in the face of a new order and

a powerful, inevitable force brought destruction on himself and his homeland.

In the final analysis, no matter what judgment is rendered regarding his policies as a statesman, Demosthenes' ability to persuade is unquestionable. In his life and career he accomplished what few orators have ever been able to approach. Although a consummate master of every rule and artifice of rhetoric, Demosthenes rejected their use as ends in themselves in a mere show of rhetorical relativism. Rather, the entire force of his oratorical talent was directed as a means to greater ends, namely the recovery of the public spirit, the restoration of public vigor, the preservation of the Athenian democracy and its institutions, and the reestablishment of Athens's preeminent influence and reputation among the Greek cities. In pursuit of that goal, Demosthenes lived, spoke, and died.

—James M. May

FURTHER READING

Adams, Charles Darwin. *Demosthenes and His Influence.* New York: Cooper Square, 1963. In addition to chapters on the life and oratory of Demosthenes, Adams includes important chapters on the influence of Demosthenes in antiquity, modern Europe, and on English and American oratory.

Hansen, Mogen Herman. *The Athenian Democracy in the Age of Demosthenes: Structure, Principles, and Ideology.* Norman: University of Oklahoma Press, 1999. Examining the years 403-322 B.C.E., which coincide with the political career of Demosthenes, Hansen focuses on a crucial period of Athenian democracy. He discusses how, for Athenians, liberty was both the ability to participate in the decision-making process and the right to live without oppression from the state or from other citizens.

Jaeger, Werner W. *Demosthenes: The Origin and Growth of His Policy.* New York: Octagon Books, 1977. Systematic attempt to reconstruct the origin and growth of Demosthenes' policy, considering his youth, education, early career, turn to politics, and the development of his political thought.

Kennedy, George A. *Art of Persuasion in Greece.* Princeton, N.J.: Princeton University Press, 1994. Standard handbook on Greek rhetorical theory and practice that offers perceptive analyses of Demosthenes' major orations and places them in their proper historical and rhetorical contexts.

Murphy, James J., ed. *Demosthenes' "On the Crown": A Critical Case Study of a Masterpiece of Ancient Ora-*

tory. Davis, Calif.: Hermagoras Press, 1983. Includes Plutarch's biography of Demosthenes, an analysis of Demosthenes' oratorical career by George Kennedy, John J. Keaney's excellent translation of "On the Crown," and an examination of the background, style, and argument of the speech.

Pearson, Lionel. *The Art of Demosthenes*. Chico, Calif.: Scholars Press, 1981. Concerned with Demosthenes the orator, Pearson attempts to provide analysis and exposition of the speaker's technique, including his command of argumentation and his skill in narrative. Both forensic and deliberative speeches are examined.

Pickard-Cambridge, A. W. *Demosthenes and the Last Days of Greek Freedom*. 1914. Reprint. New York: Arno Press, 1979. A sympathetic but balanced and reliable view of Demosthenes' life and career set in its historical and political context. Contains a chronological table (404-322 B.C.E.), illustrations, maps, and diagrams of battles.

SEE ALSO: Alexander the Great; Cicero; Philip II of Macedonia.

RELATED ARTICLES in *Great Events from History: The Ancient World*: May, 431-September, 404 B.C.E., Peloponnesian War; June, 415-September, 413 B.C.E., Athenian Invasion of Sicily; 359-336 B.C.E., Philip II Expands and Empowers Macedonia; August 2, 338 B.C.E., Battle of Chaeronea; 336 B.C.E., Alexander the Great Begins Expansion of Macedonia.

SAINT DENIS
Roman bishop

Saint Denis converted the Gauls to Christianity around the area of Paris, thereby establishing the foundation of what would later become one of the leading centers of the Christian faith in Europe.

BORN: Date unknown; possibly Rome (now in Italy)
DIED: c. 250 C.E.; near Lutetia, Gaul (now Paris, France)
ALSO KNOWN AS: Dionysius (given name); Dionysius of Paris; Denys; Dennis; Dionis
AREA OF ACHIEVEMENT: Religion

EARLY LIFE

Saint Denis (deh-nee) was originally named Dionysius. He was a Christian bishop in Italy and a citizen of the Roman Empire. The name "Dionysius" is related to the Greek god Dionysus, known as Bacchus in Roman mythology. The use of such a name among early Christians is an example of how some pagan nomenclature continued in Christian culture and would be passed on in variant forms in many European languages.

Saint Denis lived during the first half of the third century. This period was dominated by increasing instability in the government of the Roman Empire. Emperors of the time had very short reigns. More and more frequently, their reigns ended with their assassinations by military guards who precariously succeeded them. After two centuries of growth, Christianity was an increasingly strong, even aggressive, element within the Empire. Christianity existed throughout the eastern Mediterranean region and in northern Africa, had advanced in Italy, and was entering into the farthest European reaches of the realm.

To the Imperial government, this growth and spread were very dangerous. Christians would not worship the emperor as a god. They were, therefore, contributing to the decline of Roman society and government, which was already enfeebled and threatened. During the third century, in unstable fits and starts, Roman officials became more desperate to stamp out Christianity. Bishops, the leaders of Christian communities, were especially the targets of government persecution.

Such persecution, however, was strengthening Christianity, creating a powerful corps of heroic Christian martyrs and saints. Many popes, who were the bishops of Rome, were martyred. In this atmosphere, Saint Denis and several other bishops set out in the middle of the third century on an evangelizing mission to the Gauls along the northwestern edge of the Empire.

LIFE'S WORK

In Gaul, the name "Dionysius" was transformed into "Denis." (The name was also rendered as "Denys," "Dennis," and "Dionis.") In addition, Saint Denis was later sometimes referred to as "Dionysius of Paris." Along with several colleagues, he evangelized in and around the Roman outpost of Lutetia, which later became Paris. The city was then a village on an island (today the Île de la Cité, the center of Paris) in the Seine River. The area was inhabited by members of the Parisii tribe. With its bridges connecting to the mainland, Lutetia was convenient as a location from which Roman troops and traders could move on their way up and down Gaul, and it could be defended from barbarian invaders. To Christians, it was a strategic frontier point.

Lutetia was located in Middle Gaul, one of the three provinces of Gaul that Julius Caesar conquered and described. The outpost was administered from the Roman capital of the province, the city of Lugdunum (later Lyons). The first Christians are thought to have appeared in the province in the latter half of the second century.

When Saint Denis and his colleagues arrived in Lutetia, they were under direct Roman scrutiny. They engaged in missionary activities, attempting to increase the Christian population. Saint Denis was a successful preacher and leader of the Christian community, and he engaged in extensive pastoral activities. He was the first bishop of Paris, and he came to be considered the founder of Christianity in France. He not only enlarged the community of lay Christians but also ordained new members of the clergy.

His success attracted Roman retaliation. During the reigns of the emperors Decius (249-251) and Valerian (253-260), renewed and brutal attempts were made to eliminate Christianity throughout the Empire. It was at some time during these reigns that Saint Denis and two of his assistants, the priest Rusticus and the deacon Eleutherius, were imprisoned. According to legend, they refused, in spite of torture, to deny their Christianity and were beheaded on October 9 at Martyrs' Hill, which is today the Montmartre district of Paris. In the third century, Montmartre was a separate district just north of Lutetia.

The bodies of the three martyrs were retrieved by the faithful and buried in a chapel, which became the site of the Benedictine Abbey of Saint Denis in Montmartre. The abbey church later became the burial site of the kings of France. As was customary at the time, Christians immediately venerated martyrs as saints. In later history, the Church would initiate a formal bureaucratic process for the canonization of saints. The burial site of Saint Denis became a place of worship and intercession and over the centuries became the center of a powerful cult. The date of the deaths of Saint Denis, Saint Rusticus, and Saint Eleutherius became a feast day of the Church.

While there is no reliable visual evidence of what Saint Denis looked like, he is usually depicted as a

Saint Denis. (Hulton|Archive by Getty Images)

bearded man in the vestments of a Catholic bishop. These clothes are sometimes etched with the fleur-de-lis, the stylized lily or iris that is a symbol of France and French royalty. As a beheaded martyr, he is often depicted holding his head, still wearing a mitre, the peaked ritual headpiece of a bishop. He is portrayed in this manner in paintings and stained-glass windows in many French and English churches, including Canterbury Cathedral.

Christian legends sometimes related that beheaded martyrs walked to their grave sites bearing their heads. Imagined scenes of Saint Denis's martyrdom were portrayed in murals at the English Benedictine Abbey of Wilton. Considerable veneration of Saint Denis occurred in England in the Benedictine monasteries founded there after the French Norman Conquest in the eleventh century. The English name Dennis and its feminine variant, Denise, also became popular.

As French history developed and Paris became the residence of the king and the political and religious center of the country, Saint Denis came to be considered the patron saint of France. He shares this honor with, among others, Saint Joan of Arc and Saint Martin of Tours. Medieval French armies appealed to Saint Denis for support in battle, much as the English did to Saint George. Saint Denis came also to be considered protector of the French crown.

There is sparse factual data about Saint Denis. The most reliable source comes from the sixth century French historian Saint Gregory, who was bishop of Tours, France. Much other inaccurate information about Saint Denis has resulted from the confusion of him with religious figures of other periods having the same name. For example, several centuries after he died, Saint Denis began to be confused with Saint Dionysius the Areopagite, a disciple of Saint Paul in the mid-first century who is mentioned in the Acts of the Apostles ("Areopagite" refers to a small hill near the Acropolis in Athens, Greece, where Saint Paul preached).

Thus confused with Dionysius the Areopagite, Saint Denis was sometimes thought to have been sent to Gaul by Pope Clement I at the end of the first century C.E., near the end of apostolic times. Because Dionysius the Areopagite was considered the first Christian bishop of Athens, Saint Denis is sometimes portrayed, even in France, in the vestments of an Orthodox bishop.

Further confusion about the life of Saint Denis ensued after he was identified as the author of certain writings of Dionysius the Areopagite that appeared in the fifth century. These writings were treatises and letters dealing with mysticism and religion that became widely popular in the medieval period. Long after their appearance, it was proved that they were not actually written by Dionysius the Areopagite. However, their early attribution to Saint Denis greatly contributed to his fame and further enhanced the reputation of the abbey named after him. The actual author came to be identified as "Pseudo-Dionysius."

In the high Middle Ages, Saint Denis was the subject of several religious plays. In these works, he was always viewed as the combined character of Dionysius the Areopagite and the historical Saint Denis. A striking feature of the plays was the extent to which they focused on the sequence of tortures he endured before his martyrdom. In these plays, he and his companions valiantly resist torment, affirming the strength of their faith. Such a sequence was the standard script for recounting the life and death of martyrs.

SIGNIFICANCE

The life of Saint Denis provides a telling example of the difficulties inherent in attempting to understand the lives of even the most significant figures of ancient times. His case illustrates a common problem that complicates efforts to study and write about such individuals: Names often have several variations, and one or more of these can be easily mistaken with those of another person or other persons. Furthermore, certain mistakes sometimes become entrenched because they are advantageous for later individuals and institutions associated with a historical figure. In the case of Saint Denis, his followers benefited from the belief that he was an associate of the Apostles and that he was the author of widely influential religious writings. French kings, especially, benefited from these distinctions of their patron, and they thereby encouraged belief in them. The problem of understanding the life of Saint Denis—and those of so many other saints and heroic figures—is complicated by the need to separate layers of legend or myth from kernels of fact.

Despite the limited facts available about him, and despite the confusion and ambiguity that surround his memory, several things are quite apparent about Saint Denis. He confronted difficult, unknown, and dangerous circumstances, and he was resolute and effective in following his beliefs. Moreover, his life and work had great significance in the advance of Christianity and in the historical development of France and of Europe as a whole.

—*Edward A. Riedinger*

FURTHER READING

Brogan, Olden. *Roman Gaul.* Cambridge, Mass.: Harvard University Press, 1953. This description of Gaul as a part of the Roman Empire sheds light on the world in which Saint Denis lived and worked. Includes illustrations.

Drinkwater, J. F. *The Gallic Empire: Separatism and Continuity in the Northwestern Provinces of the Roman Empire, A.D. 260-274.* Stuttgart, Germany: Franz Steiner Verlag, 1987. This work focuses on the immediate social, political, and military conditions in which Saint Denis lived. Includes maps. This author has also written *Roman Gaul: The Three Provinces, 58 B.C.-A.D. 260.* (Ithaca, N.Y.: Cornell University Press, 1983).

Gregory of Tours, Saint. *Glory of the Martyrs.* Liverpool, England: Liverpool University Press, 1988. Relates stories of saintly miracles in the early Church, especially in France, some of which were associated with Saint Denis.

King, Anthony. *Roman Gaul and Germany.* Berkeley: University of California Press, 1990. An examination of the Roman provincial, colonial environment before and after the time of Saint Denis, based on archaeological excavations.

Lacaze, Charlotte. *The "Vie de Saint Denis" Manuscript.* New York: Garland, 1979. An annotated translation of a manuscript in the French National Library that makes up the most extensive narrative on, and pictorial representation of, Saint Denis and his era. Numerous illustrations.

Van Dam, Raymond. *Leadership and Community in Late Antique Gaul.* Berkeley: University of California Press, 1992. Outlines the social and political environment in which Saint Denis operated and functioned. Includes maps and a bibliography.

SEE ALSO: Saint Ambrose; Saint Anthony of Egypt; Saint Athanasius of Alexandria; Saint Augustine; Saint John Chrysostom; Saint Helena; Saint Irenaeus; Saint Jerome; Jesus; John the Apostle; Saint Paul; Saint Pe-

ter; Saint Simeon Stylites; Saint Siricius; Saint Stephen; Theodore of Mopsuestia; Saint Thomas; Saint Vincent of Lérins.

RELATED ARTICLES in *Great Events from History: The Ancient World*: 64-67 C.E., Nero Persecutes the Christians; 68-69 C.E., Year of the Four Emperors; 200 C.E., Christian Apologists Develop Concept of Theology; 250 C.E., Outbreak of the Decian Persecution; c. 250 C.E., Saint Denis Converts Paris to Christianity; October 28, 312 C.E., Conversion of Constantine to Christianity; 325 C.E., Adoption of the Nicene Creed; August 9, 378 C.E., Battle of Adrianople; c. 450 C.E., Conversion of Ireland to Christianity.

DIDO
Carthaginian queen

Dido founded the city of Carthage in northern Africa, a city that was to play a crucial role in the expansion of Phoenician power throughout the Mediterranean region.

BORN: Mid-ninth century B.C.E.; Tyre, Phoenicia (now Tyre, Lebanon)
DIED: Late eighth or early ninth century B.C.E.; Carthage (now Tunisia)
ALSO KNOWN AS: Elisha; Aliyisha
AREA OF ACHIEVEMENT: Government and politics

EARLY LIFE
Information concerning the life of Dido (DI-doh) comes from a variety of sources, including Greek and Roman histories, ancient poetry, and the royal chronicles of Dido's home city, Tyre. The Tyrian royal chronicles, translated into Greek in the Hellenistic period, record that in 820 B.C.E. King Matton was succeeded by his son, Pumayatton, who was then eleven years old. The same chronicles record that King Pumayatton ("Pygmalion" in Greek) had a sister called Elisha or Aliyisha. The Greeks and Romans called Elisha "Dido," and it is by that name that she is best known today.

Tyre was the bustling metropolis of the Phoenician kingdom, which occupied the lands of modern Lebanon, Syria, and Jordan. The Phoenicians were renowned (and sometimes reviled) throughout the Mediterranean world as intrepid seafarers, skilled engineers, clever merchants, talented artisans, and learned scribes—who passed on their alphabet to ancient neighbors and, eventually, to

modern Western civilization. Phoenician society in the ninth century B.C.E. was rich and prosperous. Although a king presided, evidence suggests that a council of elders, and later a senate, allowed adult male citizens to participate in governing Tyre. The rest of the population consisted of free men and women and slaves.

As a princess in the royal court of Phoenicia, Dido would have enjoyed a privileged upbringing. She was born into a wealthy family whose rulers had built many magnificent buildings, including temples and palaces. The royal palace at Tyre was a prominent landmark with its kingly residence, archives, and treasuries. If Dido was formally educated, it is likely that she was schooled privately. Some women of Phoenicia's aristocracy were trained in the official duties of the priesthood of Astarte, goddess of fertility and fecundity. Traditionally, the priestess of the cult of Astarte was drawn from the royal family—often, like Dido, a female descendant of the queen or queen mother.

At some point after the death of King Matton, the Roman writer Justin reports, Dido was married to her mother's brother, Zakar-baal (Sychaeus in some versions). Dido would have been young, by modern standards, at the time of her marriage, and it is likely that her mother or brother arranged the match for her. Zakar-baal was the chief priest of Melqart (a god similar in character and properties to the Greek Herakles), and therefore he was second in line to the throne. Justin writes that King Pygmalion became very greedy and sought to seize the wealth and possessions of Zakar-baal, who was murdered at the order of the king. The death of her husband prompted Dido to flee Tyre, whence she began the Mediterranean voyage that led to the foundation of a new city and made her famous in the ancient world not as Elisha but as Dido, a name that has not been satisfactorily explained by modern scholars but which may have roots in a Greek word for "wanderer" or a Latin word for "virile woman."

LIFE'S WORK

Much of what happened after Dido fled Tyre is shrouded in myth. Greek and Latin authors are generally unanimous in reporting that Dido left Tyre accompanied by members of the city's aristocracy, who had joined with Dido in their opposition to Pygmalion. Their first stop was Cyprus, where they sought help from the local priest of Juno. In exchange for hospitality and provisions, Dido promised to continue the cult of Juno in her new town. At Cyprus the Tyrian refugees took on eighty virgins who were destined for sacred prostitution in the local temple to Venus. The young women were to serve the practical purpose of peopling the new settlement and were of symbolic significance because their rescue from sacred prostitution signaled Dido's piety (or cunning, to those later critics who read malfeasance in her expansionist endeavor).

Sailing from Cyprus, Dido and her retinue crossed the Mediterranean Sea and, after wandering for some time, landed in northern Africa, on a peninsula within the Gulf of Tunis that is today part of Tunisia. The mythical tradition has it that Dido bought land from the local people to give her colonists a place to live. The agreement was that she would pay the price of a plot of land large enough to be covered by an ox hide. The enterprising queen cut the hide into very thin strips and encircled the entire base of the hill on which her people had settled. Seeing that they had been outsmarted, the natives allowed Dido more land for her city. Dido called her new town Qart Hadasht, a name that comes from two Phoenician words: *qart* (city) and *hadasht* (new). The name was rendered into Latin as *Karthago*, from which came "Carthage." The hill that Dido bought with the ox hide lay at the center of the city and was called Byrsa—from the Greek word for "ox skin." The year of the city's founding is traditionally given as 814 B.C.E. At its peak, Dido's city covered about seven square miles; the walls of Carthage,

the Roman writer Livy reports, were greater than twenty miles in circumference.

Carthage grew into an important and influential city. Religious and artistic practices from Carthage's mother city, Tyre, continued. From Carthage, Phoenician culture spread to neighboring ethnic groups in northern Africa. Over time, however, Carthage developed its own cultural identity, which is recognized today as "Punic" (from the Latin name for the Carthaginians, Poeni—related to "Phoenician"). Carthage rapidly became the leading Phoenician colony in the central Mediterranean region, so strong that it was able to impose its authority on the other Phoenician colonies of northern Africa.

The success of Carthage earned Dido respect as well as resentment. According to two ancient writers, Justin and Timaeus of Taormina, the king of the Libyans—a man called Iarbas—wished to unite his kingdom with Dido's new city and so sought her hand in marriage. Loyal to the memory of her husband, and reluctant to allow Carthage to be ruled by Iarbas, Dido escaped the king's entreaties by sacrificing herself on a large funerary pyre, which she had ordered to be built under pretense of fulfilling a vow.

Dido. (Hulton|Archive by Getty Images)

Out of reverence for Dido's sacrifice, and believing that the queen's act pleased the gods and led to great prosperity for Carthage, Carthaginians continued the practice of human sacrifice well into the second century B.C.E., sometimes demanding that citizens offer their own children as sacrificial victims. The legend of Dido's death gained popularity when the Latin poet Vergil, writing c. 29-19 B.C.E., used her story in his epic the *Aeneid* (English translation, 1553). In this poem, a survivor of the Trojan War called Aeneas lands at Carthage with his companions and receives a warm welcome from Dido and her people. The queen falls in love with Aeneas and reneges on her vow of chastity to her late husband by taking Aeneas as her lover. Compelled by destiny, Aeneas announces that he must leave Carthage and go to Italy to found the city of Rome. Despondent, Dido builds and lights a huge funeral pyre, large enough for Aeneas to see from his departing ship, and sacrifices herself on top of it.

Vergil purposely adjusted chronology to bring together Dido and Aeneas in his epic: The Greek historical tradition had clearly established that Dido lived several decades before Aeneas fled Troy, and Vergil was aware of this. In joining the figures in a love story, he created a poetic reason for the animosity between Carthage and Rome that was, by his day, long-standing. Carthage and Rome fought for control of the Mediterranean region, and tensions came to a head with the First (264-241 B.C.E.) and Second (218-202 B.C.E.) Punic Wars. Although these wars took place long after her death, the image of Dido was still so potent some seven centuries later that Roman politicians demonized her, portraying the queen as the source of all "Punic barbarism." In 146 B.C.E. Roman soldiers razed Carthage.

Dido has inspired writers, artists, and performers for generations, and besides the *Aeneid*, her story lives on in two classics: the play *Dido, Queen of Carthage*, by Christopher Marlowe and Thomas Nashe (c. 1586-1587) and the opera *Dido and Aeneas* by Henry Purcell (before December, 1689). Both works were written at a time when it was popular to make flattering comparisons between Queen Elizabeth I of England and Queen Dido of Carthage—two women celebrated for establishing overseas colonies. Despite, or perhaps because of, the promotion of the mythical version of Dido's story, archaeologists and historians stress alternative explanations for what she did, why she left Tyre, and who she was. One explanation for why she left Tyre, an alternative to the story of internecine conflict, is that Dido and her companions were escaping harsh tributes imposed on the Phoenicians by Assyrian invaders. Similarly, alternative dates have been offered for the founding of the city: Because archaeologists have found no evidence for Phoenician settlement from 814 B.C.E., they propose that the city was actually founded in the mid-eighth century B.C.E.

SIGNIFICANCE

Dido is important for what she represents as well as what she did. The city that she founded left a considerable mark on the cultural and economic development of the ancient Mediterranean region. Carthage's expansion into Spain, western Africa, and Sicily brought Punic culture, the Phoenician alphabet, and new socioeconomic practices to these areas. The decision to leave Tyre spurred Phoenician interest in colonization, and waves of merchants and immigrants left in her wake. Dido's descendants, Hasdrubal and Hannibal, led Carthage in wars against Rome—wars that allowed victorious Rome to begin the territorial expansion that culminated with the Roman Empire. Dido and Carthage provided the discursive enemy that Rome needed to justify its takeover of Sicily, Spain, and northern Africa. As a woman founder of a city, Dido represents the independence, pride, and sagacity that the Greeks and Romans feared in women and offers a rare example of an ancient woman establishing a superpower. In legend and art, Dido represents a tragic figure who, despite her success as queen of Carthage, was felled by her pride and heartsickness.

—Fiona Rose

FURTHER READING

Burden, Michael, ed. *A Woman Scorn'd: Responses to the Dido Myth*. London: Faber and Faber, 1998. This is a collection of essays written by scholars of history, literature, and music, who focus on the figure of Dido as she is presented in a variety of genres. The essays on the historicity of the Dido myth are particularly useful for sifting through facts and legends and arriving at a more accurate picture of Dido's life.

Desmond, Marilynn. *Reading Dido: Gender, Textuality and the Medieval Aeneid*. Minneapolis: University of Minnesota Press, 1994. An excellent resource for those interested in how the legendary character of Dido has been received and reinterpreted in English and French literature.

Lancel, Serge. *Carthage: A History*. Cambridge, Mass.: Blackwell, 1995. Lancel provides a thorough history of the city of Carthage, beginning with its foundation as a Phoenician colony and ending with its destruction by the Romans. Religion, politics, and trade relations of Carthage are discussed, and there are good sections on Dido.

Markoe, Glenn. *Phoenicians*. London: British Museum Press, 2000. Markoe examines the history, economy, religion, and material culture of the Phoenicians. He provides useful information on Dido's cultural background and clarifies the historical and political significance of Phoenician overseas expansion. The maps at the beginning of the book illustrate the spread of Phoenicians and Carthaginians from the Near East to Spain.

SEE ALSO: Arsinoe II Philadelphus; Artemesia I; Berenice II; Boudicca; Cleopatra VII; Clodia; Enheduanna; Hannibal; Hatshepsut; Lucretia; Nefertari; Nefertiti; Olympias; Sophonisba of Numidia; Zenobia.

RELATED ARTICLES in *Great Events from History: The Ancient World*: c. 2300 B.C.E., Enheduanna Becomes First Named Author; c. 1450 B.C.E., International Age of Major Kingdoms Begins in the Near East; c. 1250 B.C.E., Fall of Troy Marks End of Trojan War; c. 1200-c. 1050 B.C.E., Sea Peoples Contribute to Mediterranean Upheaval; c. 800 B.C.E., Phoenicians from Tyre Found Carthage; c. 750 B.C.E., Homer Composes the *Iliad*; 264-225 B.C.E., First Punic War; 218-201 B.C.E., Second Punic War; 149-146 B.C.E., Third Punic War; 51-30 B.C.E., Cleopatra VII, Last of Ptolemies, Reigns; 19 B.C.E., Roman Poet Vergil Dies; 439 C.E., Vandals Seize Carthage.

DIO CASSIUS
Greek-Roman historian, senator, and administrator

Dio Cassius wrote an important history of Rome and its empire, with eighty volumes about Roman politics and major events from the mythical beginning of the city until 229 C.E.

BORN: c. 150 C.E.; Nicaea, Bithynia (now İznik, Turkey)
DIED: c. 235 C.E.; probably Nicaea, Bithynia
ALSO KNOWN AS: Dio Cassius Cocceianus (full name); Dion Cassius
AREA OF ACHIEVEMENT: Historiography

EARLY LIFE
Most of the details known about the life of Dio Cassius (DI-oh KASH-ee-uhs) come from his historical writings, which include numerous statements about his experiences in Rome and his various political offices. Although these writings provide only sketchy information about his early life, they indicate that he was raised in a wealthy and politically powerful family in Nicaea. His father, Cassius Apronianus, was a senator who served for several years as governor of Cilicia and Dalmatia. Probably Dio was a near relative of the famous orator and teacher of rhetoric Dio Chrysostom.

Dio Cassius apparently lived most of his formative years in his native city of Nicaea, a prosperous commercial center and a vital crossroads for the military forces of the Empire. His writings suggest that he sometimes stayed with his father in other provinces when his father was serving as governor. Dio's native language was Greek, which would remain the language of his writings, although his position also required a fluent command of Latin. He was educated primarily by sophists, a term that then referred generally to persons with special training and skills in the art of rhetoric. Such an educational emphasis was common among the Greek-Roman governing elite, who would expect to use rhetorical arts in their later careers. Dio frequently expressed a bias against speculative philosophy, which was probably not a significant part of his education.

There is indirect evidence that Dio had a wife and children, although the details are uncertain. Because his works contain several references to the delights of marriage, it is considered likely that he had a happy family life. While identifying primarily with Greek cultural life, Dio expressed a strong sense of loyalty toward the Roman Empire and took pride in its power and achievements. Apparently this pro-Roman point of view was more common among the Greek-speaking elite than among the masses of Greek speakers in the rural areas. Dio's interests would always center in the eastern portions of the Empire. While participating in the governing of the Empire, his roots would remain in his native region. There is no evidence that he ever ventured west of Rome.

LIFE'S WORK
Following his father's death (c. 180), Dio Cassius moved to Rome. At that time or shortly thereafter, he became a member of the senate. Thus, his entrance into politics occurred at approximately the same time that Marcus Aurelius (the last of the "five good emperors") died and

was succeeded by the unstable and dictatorial Commodus, whose reign was characterized by dangerous intrigue and civil conflict. Even after Commodus was strangled in 192, Dio continued to live under unstable governments during most of his political career, experiencing a succession of short-term emperors. His career had its lows and highs depending on which emperor was in power. Living during a period when life was very precarious for members of the senate, he managed to avoid intrigues and was never disgraced or involved in any major controversy.

Shortly after Pertinax became emperor in 193, Dio was appointed to serve as praetor (or military magistrate). Although Pertinax's reign lasted less than a year, Dio continued as praetor for the next decade. He enthusiastically supported the ascension of Lucius Septimius Severus, and he was rewarded with the title of consul in 204. Within two years, however, he retired temporarily from public life, probably because he disagreed with Severus's polices. While in temporary retirement, Dio spent most of his time doing research and writing his history. He returned to political life after Caracalla became emperor, and in 216, he served as a member of Caracalla's staff during a major campaign in the eastern provinces.

In 217, Emperor Macrinus appointed Dio curator (or supervisor) of cities in Pergamum and Smyrna, a position he held for more than six years. Severus Alexander, whose reign lasted from 222 to 235, appointed Dio to even more important positions, first as proconsul of Africa and then as governor of Dalmatia and Upper Pannonia, which were both military provinces. Dio was one of the few Greeks to have governed military provinces in central Europe. The province of Upper Pannonia was especially known for its fierce and disorderly population, requiring Dio, contrary to his mild temperament, to employ strict discipline and military coercion.

In addition to personal competence, Dio's rise to prominence was a result of the resurgence of the senate's power and prestige. In 229, he became consul for the second time, an honor achieved by very few Greeks. Later that same year, due to failing health, he wrote that he was retiring from politics in order to spend the rest of his life in Bithynia, which he called his native land. The cessation of his writing suggests that he probably did not live much longer after this date.

Dio is remembered much more for his historical work than for his political career. He apparently began to write history in the year 193, with the publication of a short booklet that contained the story of dreams and omens

foretelling the future greatness of Emperor Septimius Severus. Most likely Dio obtained this information directly from the emperor himself. Both the emperor and the public favorably received the book, and soon thereafter Dio resolved to write a full history of Rome and its empire. At this time, most literate persons believed that the field of history dealt chiefly with political and military affairs. Another common assumption was that a participant in public affairs, a man like Dio, was especially qualified to write about such matters.

Dio's most significant work was his voluminous *Romaika* (probably c. 202 C.E.; *Roman History*, 1914-1927), which originally encompassed the thousand years from Rome's legendary founding until Dio's final retirement. For models, he tried to combine the works of Thucydides, the historian, and Demosthenes, the orator. In preparation for writing his history, Dio claimed to have spent ten years gathering information and reading the available sources, which included Livy, Tacitus, Seneca, Suetonius, Julius Caesar, Plutarch, and Aulus Cremutius Cordus. After his research, Dio then spent twelve years in the writing of his history. It is possible that portions of the *Roman History* were first written as separate accounts of particular reigns. Less than half of Dio's historical work has been preserved, but it should be noted that in the ancient world a large percentage of such works disappeared altogether.

The *Roman History* was divided into three main periods of time. The first was the era of the Republic, when power resided primarily in the senate and with the citizens. The second era extended from the establishment of the monarchy under Caesar Augustus until the death of

ROMAN EMPERORS DURING DIO CASSIUS'S CAREER

Emperor	Reign (C.E.)
Marcus Aurelius	161-180
Lucius Verus	161-169
Commodus	180-192
Pertinax	193
Didius Julianus	193
Septimius Severus	193-211
Pescennius Niger	193-194
Caracalla	211-217
Geta	211-212
Macrinus	217-218
Elagabalus	218-222
Severus Alexander	222-235

Marcus Aurelius. The third period was that of Dio's own age, about which he had firsthand knowledge. Like many Roman historians, Dio often used the traditional organization of the annalists, in which all the events of a given year, regardless of where they occurred, were grouped together. He was not consistent, however, in following the annalist organization, and he abandoned it almost completely when writing about his own era.

From the modern perspective of objective historiography, the value of Dio's history is diminished by two of his theoretical perspectives. First, Dio, like many others at that time, was committed to being a rhetorician as well as a historian. Thus, if the bare facts did not appear to be sufficiently dramatic, he did not hesitate to adorn or modify them to make them more memorable. It should not be surprising, therefore, that many of the speeches quoted or summarized in his works are not considered authentic. For instance, one of his chapters included an alleged speech of Maecenas to Augustus that was really a political pamphlet defending Dio's theory of government. Second, Dio was interested primarily in the larger significance of historical events, not in details and personal anecdotes. For this reason, his discussions of events sometimes omitted any reference to particular names, accurate dates, exact numbers, and geographical descriptions. When desiring to make a political or ethical point, moreover, he would project the Imperial situation of his own day on the earlier periods of time, which tended to produce distortions about what had actually happened in the past.

Dio wrote history from the point of view of the Greco-Roman aristocracy. While consistently defending the prerogatives of the senate, he was also a strong believer in the monarchy, and he was critical of people such as Cicero who opposed monarchical institutions. Like most of his fellow aristocrats, moreover, Dio distrusted the common people and the idea of democracy.

While emphasizing politics, Dio took a great deal of interest in the religions of the Empire. When discussing Pompey's capture of Jerusalem in 63 B.C.E., for example, he included a rather long digression about the Jewish religion. Dio's writings never mentioned Christianity, even though it was growing and attracting considerable attention during his lifetime. In discussing the burning of Rome in 64 C.E., he simply assumed that Nero was responsible, without any references to the possible guilt of the Christians. When recounting the "miracle of the rainstorm" that presumably saved a Roman army under Marcus Aurelius, Dio repeated the official version, which attributed the miracle to an Egyptian magus, Arnuphis.

Although a skeptic when examining historical sources, Dio appeared to adhere fervently to the major pagan beliefs and practices of the Empire. He accepted the notion that portents (such as dreams and omens) were valid predictors of the future, and he frequently referred to his personal dreams in which divine forces or deities accurately predicted future events. He often visited pagan temples, and he actively participated in their religious rituals. At the temple of Mallos, for instance, he said a prayer while throwing frankincense in the river Aoos, and he explained that one's prayers would be granted if the river accepted the frankincense.

SIGNIFICANCE

Because of limitations in accuracy and analysis, Dio Cassius is usually classified as one of the second-class historians of the ancient world. His historical work, nevertheless, is valuable for its corroboration of other ancient works and for the additional details it provides. His treatment of the Empire is considered more dependable than what he wrote about the earlier Republic. Some modern historians believe that his account of Caesar Augustus's regime is the best extant discussion of that era. Dio's personal observations about Roman personalities, politics, and daily life during his own period are considered to be especially valuable. Following his death, his work had little influence on his immediate successors, but it later became a standard source under the Byzantine Empire, which is the reason so much of it was preserved.

—*Thomas Tandy Lewis*

FURTHER READING

Barnes, Timothy. "The Composition of Dio Cassius's *Roman History*." *Phoenix* 38 (1984): 240-255. An excellent introduction to Dio's historical theories and methods.

Cary, Earnest. Introduction to vol. 1 of *Dio's Roman History*, by Dio Cassius. Translated by Earnest Cary. Cambridge, Mass.: Harvard University Press, 1961. Cary's introduction provides a relatively short, readable, and dependable introduction to Dio's career and historical writings.

Gowing, Alain. *The Triumviral Narratives of Appian and Dio Cassius*. Ann Arbor: University of Michigan Press, 1992. A scholarly comparison of the historical work of two contemporary Greek historians, with a more favorable judgment toward Appian's work.

Grant, Michael. *Greek and Roman Historians: Information and Misinformation*. New York: Routledge, 1995. By concentrating on the nature of historiography during Dio's period, Grant's book helps place his work in its historical context so that modern readers can appreciate its strengths and weaknesses.

Millar, Fergus. *A Study of Dio Cassius*. Oxford, England: Clarendon Press, 1964. A pioneering study of Dio's ideas, methods, and historical writings. While much of the book is for scholars, the first chapter provides a readable and interesting biography.

Murison, Charles. *Rebellion and Reconstruction: Galba to Domitian*. Atlanta: Scholars Press, 1999. One of a series of eleven proposed volumes designed to make it easier for readers to appreciate and understand Dio's history. Murison's introduction is especially good.

SEE ALSO: Augustus; Julius Caesar; Cicero; Demosthenes; Livy; Nero; Plutarch; Pompey the Great; Tacitus; Thucydides.

RELATED ARTICLES in *Great Events from History: The Ancient World*: 64-67 C.E., Nero Persecutes the Christians; September 8, 70 C.E., Roman Destruction of the Temple of Jerusalem.

DIOCLES OF CARYSTUS
Greek physician

Diocles was a Greek physician who was regarded in antiquity as second only to Hippocrates. He wrote several medical works, including the first separate treatise on anatomy and the first herbal. His best-known contributions to medicine are in the area of hygiene.

BORN: c. 375 B.C.E.; Carystus, Greece
DIED: c. 295 B.C.E.; Athens?, Greece
AREA OF ACHIEVEMENT: Medicine

EARLY LIFE

Not much is known of the early life of Diocles of Carystus (DI-uh-kleez of kuh-RIHS-tuhs). His father's name was Archidamos, and Diocles was a native of Carystus, a small town on the southern tip of the island of Euboea, off the eastern coast of mainland Greece. According to the Roman writer Pliny, Diocles was second in age and fame to the famous physician Hippocrates (c. 460-370 B.C.E.). He has traditionally been placed in the first half of the fourth century B.C.E. It has been observed, however, that the language of his extant writings points to the later rather than to the earlier half of the fourth century B.C.E. It is likely that he was a younger contemporary of Aristotle (384-322 B.C.E.) and thus was active until 300 or perhaps later. Diocles is the only physician between Hippocrates' time and the Hellenistic period about whom very much is known.

Diocles probably learned his trade from his father, who was a physician, for medicine in the ancient world was a craft that was often passed from father to son. The ordinary physician acquired his skill and knowledge through an apprenticeship in which he learned the elements of traditional practice. Diocles wrote a work titled *Arkhidamos* (date unknown), dedicated to his father's memory, in which he argued against his father's condemnation of the practice of rubbing the body down with oil because he believed that it overheated the body. Diocles suggested instead that in the summer a mixture of oil and water be employed, while in the winter only oil be used.

There is good evidence, on the basis of Diocles' language and thought, that he was a pupil of the philosopher Aristotle, who founded his philosophical school, the Lyceum, in Athens in 334. Whether Diocles came to Athens specifically to study at the Lyceum or had earlier established residence there is not known. He was the first Greek to write medical treatises in Attic Greek rather than in Ionic, which was the dialect normally employed by medical writers. He seems to have belonged to the same generation of Aristotle's pupils as Theophrastus and Strato, who provide the earliest evidence for Diocles' work.

Diocles employs Aristotelian terminology and shows the influence of Aristotle's ethics, for example, in his use of the ideas of proportion and suitability in his theory of diet. On the other hand, it is quite possible that Diocles in turn influenced his master, perhaps as a source for Aristotle's zoological works. Although Diocles was apparently closely associated with the Peripatetic school, which was the chief center of scientific research in the Greek world until the founding of the Museum at Alexandria, Aristotle was not the only source of his ideas. He apparently had access to a collection of Hippocratic treatises and may, in fact, have been the first medical writer to assemble such a collection. His indebtedness to Hippocratic medicine is indicated by his treatises, some of which resemble Hippocratic works in title and subject matter. Diocles' thought also shows a debt to the Sicilian school of medicine, which was dominated by the philosopher and physician Empedocles (c. 490-430 B.C.E.).

A later member of the school, Philistion of Locri (427-347 B.C.E.), who was a contemporary of Plato, also influenced him. Nevertheless, Diocles was no slavish follower of Aristotle or of any medical or philosophical system. He borrowed elements from Hippocratic medicine, from the Sicilian school, and from Aristotle, all the while maintaining his own independence and making original contributions.

LIFE'S WORK

Diocles was a prolific writer. The titles of seventeen of his medical treatises are known, including *Peri puros kai aeros* (*On Fire and Air*), *Anatomē* (*Anatomy*), *Hugieina pros Pleistarkhon* (*Directions on Health for Plistarchus*), *Peri pepeseōs* (*On Digestion*), *Peri puretōn* (*On Fevers*), *Peri gunaikeiōn* (*On Women's Diseases*), *Peri epideomōn* (*On Bandages*), *Peri tōn kat iētreion* (*On the Equipment of a Surgery*), *Prognōstikon* (*Prognostic*), *Peri therapeiōn* (*On Treatment*), *Pathos aitia therapeia* (*Sickness, Causes, and Treatment*), *Rhizotomika, Peri lakhanōn* (*On Vegetables*), *Peri thanasimōn pharmakōn* (*On Lethal Drugs*; this and all preceding titles translated in 2000), *Arkhidamos*, and *Dioklēs epistolē prophulaktikē* (*Epistle of Diocles unto King Antigonus*, c. 1550). Of these works, more than 190 fragments have been preserved by later medical writers. Diocles' style is polished, with some literary pretensions, and shows the influence of rhetorical devices (for example, the avoidance of hiatus), while maintaining a deliberately simple style that reflects the influence of Aristotle.

According to the physician Galen (129-c. 199 C.E.), Diocles' *Anatomy* was the first book written on that subject. In it, he described the heart, lungs, gall bladder, ureters, ovaries, Fallopian tubes, and ileocecal valve. Diocles' *Anatomy* was based on the observation of animals and not human beings (he is said to have dissected animals). Nevertheless, his work marked a significant turning point in the study of human anatomy, and other writers after him began to produce treatises on the subject. Diocles was indebted to Empedocles for his views on embryology. He believed that both the male and the female contributed seed, which originated in the brain and spinal marrow, to the embryo. The embryo, he believed, required forty days to develop fully; boys, who he said developed on the warmer, right side of the uterus, grew more quickly than girls. Diocles was interested in the problem of sterility and dissected mules to determine the causes of infertility. He also wrote on gynecology. From Empedocles he adopted the view that menstruation began at fourteen and lasted until sixty in all women. He

also described signs of expected miscarriage and suggested causes of difficult birth.

In physiology, Diocles was also indebted to Empedocles, perhaps by way of Philistion. Like Empedocles, he believed that there were four elements (fire, air, water, and earth), which he equated with the four qualities (heat, cold, moisture, and dryness) that were responsible for the processes of the body. The body, possessing an innate heat, altered food that was consumed, producing the four humors (blood, phlegm, yellow bile, and black bile). Health was the result of an equilibrium of the four qualities, while disease was the result of an excess or deficiency of one of them.

Diocles wrote that health and disease also depended on external factors (for example, wounds, nourishment, or sores) and on pneuma (air), inhaled or absorbed into the body through the pores in the skin. Pneuma then went to the heart, the central organ, from which it was distributed throughout the body by means of veins. Pneuma was essential to life, and if its passage was blocked, a humor disease or death would result. The heart was believed to be the chief organ of sensation and thought and the source of blood in the body. Diocles' theory of pneuma was also taken over from Empedocles and came to exercise much influence in Greek medical thought. Diocles recognized that fever was not itself a disease but rather the symptom of a disease. He also distinguished between pneumonia, which is a disease of the lungs, and pleurisy, which is an inflammation of the pleura (the lining over the lung).

Diocles wrote as well on botany and pharmacology. He compiled the first Greek herbal, *Rhizotomika*, which described the nutritional and medical value of plants. This treatise was widely used by later writers on the subject until replaced in the first century C.E. by the definitive work of Pedanius Dioscorides. While herbal drugs had been mentioned in the Hippocratic treatises, before Diocles no descriptions had been given of the plants themselves. Diocles' work on botany was no doubt influenced by his teacher's interest in the subject, and his work was apparently known to Theophrastus, a fellow student at the Lyceum and Aristotle's successor, who founded scientific botany.

It was in dietetics and hygiene that Diocles made his greatest contribution to Greek medicine. In the late fifth century, dietetic medicine had become a means of maintaining health rather than (as it had been earlier) a method of treating disease by restoring the proper balance to the body. Treatises appeared on hygiene containing detailed instructions for a daily regimen that regulated food and drink, rest and sleep, swimming, massage, gymnastic exercise, physical cleanliness, and sexual activity. Diocles treated the subject of hygiene in several partially extant works. In *Directions on Health for Plistarchus* (written after 300), addressed to a Macedonian prince who was the son of Antipater, a general of Alexander the Great, Diocles reproduced (with some variations) the recommendations of earlier Hippocratic works on the subject of regimen. In an earlier work, *Dioklēs epistolē prophulaktikē* (c. 305-301), addressed to King Antigonus, another of Alexander's generals (which is quoted by the Byzantine writer Paul of Aegina), Diocles discussed, among other subjects, the matter of diet, advising that food and drink be adjusted to the seasons in order to counteract the effects of seasonal variation.

Diocles also wrote a treatise on diet that is preserved in fragments quoted by Oribasius, who was the physician to the Roman emperor Julian from 361 to 363 C.E. The treatise describes a complete routine, from rising to bedtime, for one typical day of each of the four seasons of the year. Gymnastic exercise in both morning and evening plays an important part in Diocles' regimen. This work reveals the influence of Aristotle's concepts of the mean and suitability to the individual and his circumstances. Although Diocles prescribes an ideal regimen, chiefly intended for a man of means and leisure, it is one that can be adapted to the needs of those who have less time as well as to those of different ages.

SIGNIFICANCE

Diocles was an important medical figure in his own day, as his reputation as a "second Hippocrates" indicates, and he forms a significant link between Hippocratic and Hellenistic medicine. He was indebted to the Sicilian school, particularly in his pneumatic pathology, but his work also shows the influence of Hippocratic medicine in hygiene and therapeutics. No mere compiler, he synthesized and improved on the work of his predecessors. Like the Hippocratics, he realized the importance of prognosis. Some later writers considered Diocles to have been a leading member of the Dogmatic sect, which sought "hidden causes" in medicine and supplemented experience with reason and speculation. He lived too early to be labeled a Dogmatic, however, and his independent and synthetic approach to medicine would in any event seem to rule out this possibility.

Diocles wrote on a number of medical subjects: dietetics, embryology, anatomy, botany, pharmacology, and gynecology. He also invented a device, called the "spoon of Diocles," for extracting barbed arrows. He influenced subsequent medical writers, beginning with his own pupil, Praxagoras of Cos, who became head of the Hippocratic school, and he is quoted by Galen, Oribasius, Caelius Aurelianus, and Paul of Aegina. Galen praises him as a "physician and rhetorician" and credits him with having arranged Hippocratic medicine in a more logical form. Diocles appears as well to have been, like many of the early Peripatetics, something of a Renaissance man, whose interests extended beyond medicine to botany, meteorology, zoology, and even mineralogy.

—*Gary B. Ferngren*

FURTHER READING

Edelstein, Ludwig. *Ancient Medicine: Selected Papers of Ludwig Edelstein*. Edited by Owsei Temkin and C. Lilian Temkin. Translated by C. Lilian Temkin. Baltimore: The Johns Hopkins University Press, 1994. This work includes discussions of the dates of Diocles and the importance of dietetics to Greek ideas of health and medicine.

Jaeger, Werner. *Aristotle: Fundamentals of the History of His Development*. 2d ed. Oxford, England: Oxford University Press, 1962. A detailed argument for dating Diocles in the late fourth and early third centuries and a discussion of Aristotle's influence on Diocles.

_____. *The Conflict of Cultural Ideals in the Age of Plato*. Vol. 3 in *Paideia: The Ideals of Greek Culture*. 3 vols. Translated by Gilbert Highet. New York: Oxford University Press, 1969. A fine discussion of the Greek ideal of health and the place of Diocles and his views on dietetic medicine in the context of the Greek emphasis on health.

Phillips, E. D. *Aspects of Greek Medicine*. Philadelphia: Charles Press, 1987. A summary of Diocles' medical doctrines. Includes a list of the titles of his known works.

Sigerist, Henry. *Early Greek, Hindu, and Persian Medicine*. Vol. 2 in *A History of Medicine*. New York: Oxford University Press, 1967. A summary of Diocles' views on diet and hygiene, set against the background of Greek views of hygiene.

Van der Eijk, Philip J., ed. *Diocles of Carystus*. 2 vols. New York: Brill, 2000. The collected fragments of Diocles, translated. Includes commentary.

SEE ALSO: Aristotle; Pedanius Dioscorides; Empedocles; Galen; Hippocrates; Theophrastus.

RELATED ARTICLES in *Great Events from History: The Ancient World*: c. 500-400 B.C.E., Greek Physicians Begin Scientific Practice of Medicine; c. 320 B.C.E., Theophrastus Initiates the Study of Botany.

DIOCLETIAN
Roman emperor (r. 284/285-305 C.E.)

Diocletian put an end to the disastrous phase of Roman history known as the Military Anarchy or the Imperial Crisis and laid the foundation for the later Eastern Roman Empire, known as the Byzantine Empire. His reforms ensured the continuity of the Empire in the East for more than a thousand years to follow.

BORN: c. 245 C.E.; possibly Salonae, Dalmatia (now Solin, Croatia)

DIED: December 3, 316 C.E.; Salonae, Dalmatia

ALSO KNOWN AS: Diocles (given name); Gaius Aurelius Valerius Diocletianus (Latin full name)

AREA OF ACHIEVEMENT: Government and politics

EARLY LIFE

Little is known for certain about the early life of Diocletian (di-uh-KLEE-shuhn). He was a native of the Dalmatian coast, was of very humble birth, and was originally named Diocles. He was either the son of a freedman or a slave by birth who was later set free. His father may have been a scribe. He grew up in the household of the senator Anullinus, and it is unlikely that he received much education beyond the elementary literacy he may have learned from his father. The scanty evidence suggests that he was deeply imbued with religious piety. Later coin portraits give an impression of his appearance: They show a close-cropped beard in the contemporary Illyrian style, a wide forehead, and eyes spaced far apart. He had a wife, Prisca, and a daughter, Valeria, both of whom reputedly were Christians.

During Diocletian's early life, the Roman Empire was in the midst of turmoil. In the early years of the third century, emperors who were increasingly insecure on their thrones had granted inflationary pay raises to the soldiers. The additional costs could be met only by debasing the silver coinage, which soon became worthless, causing the ruin of the Roman economy. The only meaningful income the soldiers then received was in the form of gold donatives granted by other leaders. This practice served to encourage emperor-making. Beginning in 235, armies throughout the Empire began to set up their generals as rival emperors.

The resultant civil wars opened up the Empire to invasion in both the north, by the Franks, Alemanni, and Goths, and the east, by the Sāsānian Persians. Another reason for the unrest in the army was the great gap between the social backgrounds of the common soldiers, who were recruited from the more backward provinces of the Empire, such as Illyria, and the officer corps, made up largely of cultured senators. As of the 250's, however, this situation began to change. Many legionnaires made their way to high rank. Beginning in 268, some even were acclaimed emperors themselves. These individuals, the so-called Illyrian or soldier emperors, gradually were able to bring the army back under control, even though their newfound status aroused enmity against them from the senators.

Like many of his countrymen, Diocletian sought his fortune in the army. He showed himself to be a shrewd, able, and ambitious individual. He soon rose to high rank. He is first attested as duke of Moesia (an area on the banks of the lower Danube River), with responsibility for border defense. He was a prudent and methodical officer, a seeker of victory rather than glory. In 282, the legions of the upper Danube proclaimed the praetorian prefect Carus emperor. Diocletian found favor under the new emperor and was promoted to count of the domestics, the commander of the cavalry arm of the Imperial bodyguard. In 283 he was granted the honor of a consulate.

In 283, in the midst of a campaign against the Persians, Carus was killed, struck by a bolt of lightning that one writer noted might have been forged in a legionary armory. That left the Empire in the hands of his two young sons, Numerian in the east and Carinus in the west. Soon thereafter, Numerian died under mysterious circumstances near Nicomedia, and Diocletian—who had by this time changed his name from Diocles to Diocletian—was acclaimed emperor in his place. In 285, Carinus was killed in a battle near Belgrade, and Diocletian gained control of the entire empire.

LIFE'S WORK

As emperor, Diocletian was faced with many problems. His most immediate concerns were to bring the mutinous and increasingly barbarized Roman armies back under control and to make the frontiers once again secure from invasion. His long-term goals were to restore effective government and economic prosperity to the Empire. Diocletian concluded that stern measures were necessary if these objectives were to be met. More than earlier emperors, he believed that it was the responsibility of the Imperial government to take whatever steps were necessary, no matter how harsh or unorthodox, to bring the Empire back under control. Earlier emperors, with typical Roman conservatism, had attempted to apply the methods instituted by Emperor Augustus (r. 27 B.C.E.-14 C.E.), even those no longer appropriate for the times. Diocletian believed that contemporary needs required him to abandon the Augustan "Principate" and to strike out on his own.

Diocletian was able to bring the army back under control by making several changes. He subdivided the roughly fifty existing provinces into approximately one hundred, thereby putting less authority into the hands of each governor. The provinces also were apportioned among twelve dioceses, each under a vicar, and later also among four prefectures, each under a praetorian prefect. As a result, the Imperial bureaucracy became increasingly bloated. He institutionalized the policy of separating civil and military careers, so that provincial governors would not also be the commanders of armies. He divided the army itself into so-called border troops, actually an ineffective citizen militia, and palace troops, the real field army, which often were led by the emperor in person.

Following the precedent of Emperor Aurelian (r. 270-275), Diocletian transformed the emperorship into an out-and-out oriental monarchy. The emperor now became a truly august, godlike figure, removed from the rest of society. He wore gold and purple robes and a pearl diadem. Access to him became restricted; he now was addressed not as "princeps" (first citizen) or the soldierly "imperator" (general), but as "dominus noster" (lord and master). Those in audience were required to prostrate themselves on the ground before him.

Diocletian also concluded that the Empire was too large and complex to be ruled by only a single emperor. Therefore, in order to provide an Imperial presence throughout the Empire, he introduced the Tetrarchy, or Rule by Four. In 285, he named his lieutenant Maximian

"caesar," or "junior emperor," and assigned him the western half of the Empire. This practice began the process that would culminate with the de facto split of the Empire in 395. Both Diocletian and Maximian adopted divine attributes. Diocletian was identified with Jupiter and Maximian with Hercules. In 286, Diocletian promoted Maximian to the rank of augustus, "senior emperor," and in 293 he appointed two new caesars, Constantius (the father of Constantine I, the Great), who was given Gaul and Britain in the west, and Galerius, who was assigned the Balkans in the east.

By instituting his Tetrarchy, Diocletian also hoped to solve another problem. In the Augustan Principate, there had been no constitutional method for choosing new emperors. The result of this, especially in the third century, had been civil wars when different armies named their own generals as the next emperor. According to Diocletian's plan, the successor of each augustus would be the respective caesar, who then would name a new caesar. Initially, the Tetrarchy operated smoothly and effectively. Even though Diocletian and Maximian technically were of equal rank, it always was clear that Diocletian really was in charge.

Once the army was under control, Diocletian turned his attention to other problems. The borders were restored and strengthened. In the early years of his reign, Diocletian and his subordinates were able to defeat foreign enemies such as Alemanni, Sarmatians, Saracens, Franks, and Persians, and to put down rebellions in Britain and Egypt. The eastern frontier was actually expanded.

The economy remained in a sorry state. The coinage had become so debased as to be virtually worthless. Diocletian's attempt to reissue good gold and silver coins failed because there simply was not enough gold and silver available to restore confidence in the currency. A Maximum Price Edict issued in 301, intended to curb inflation, served only to drive goods onto the black market. Diocletian finally accepted the ruin of the money economy and revised the tax system so that it was based on payments in kind (the annona) rather than in the now-worthless money. The annona came to be recalculated in periodic reassessments (indications) every fifteen years. The soldiers, too, came to be paid in kind. Their only salary of value eventually became donatives issued at five-year intervals in gold and silver.

In order to assure the long-term survival of the Empire, Diocletian identified certain occupations that he believed would have to be performed. These were known as the compulsory services. They included such occupations as soldiers, bakers, members of town councils (the

ROMAN EMPERORS FROM CARUS TO CONSTANTINE THE GREAT	
Ruler	*Reign (C.E.)*
Carus	282-283
Numerian (East)	283-284
Carinus (West)	283-285
Diocletian (East)	284-305
Maximian (West)	293-305
Constantius (West)	305-306
Galerius (East)	305-315
Severus (West)	306-307
Maxentius (West)	306-312
Constantine the Great (East)	306-337
Licinius (East)	308-324
Constantine the Great (all)	324-337

decurions), and tenant farmers (the coloni, who evolved into the serfs of the Middle Ages). These functions became hereditary, and those engaging in them were inhibited from changing their careers. The repetitious nature of these laws, however, suggests that they were not widely obeyed. Diocletian also expanded the policy of third century emperors of restricting the entry of senators into high-ranking governmental posts, especially military ones.

Like Augustus and Decius (249-251), Diocletian attempted to use the state religion as a unifying element. Encouraged by the caesar Galerius, Diocletian in 303 issued a series of four increasingly harsh decrees designed to compel the Christians to take part in the Imperial cult, the traditional means by which allegiance was pledged to the Empire. This began the so-called Great Persecution.

On May 1, 305, wearied by his twenty years in office and determined to implement his method for the Imperial succession, Diocletian abdicated. He compelled his co-regent, Maximian, to do the same. Constantius and Galerius then became the new augusti, and two new caesars were selected, Maxentius in the east and Severus in the west. Diocletian then retired to his palace at Split on the Yugoslavian coast. In 308 he declined an offer to resume the purple, and the aged former emperor died in 316 C.E.

SIGNIFICANCE

Diocletian recognized that the Empire as it had been established by Augustus simply did not meet the needs of his own time. He therefore instituted many administrative reforms. Not all of them, however, were completely successful. His Tetrarchy, for example, in the choice of new emperors, bypassed obvious dynastic choices. As a result, another round of civil wars swept the Empire. Constantine, the son of Constantius, emerged as the victor. Diocletian's retention of the ineffective border troops created a great drain on the treasury, and his abandonment of the money economy meant the ruin of much of the private business in the Empire. The Great Persecution ended in failure in 311, and soon afterward Constantine the Great identified Christianity itself as a more viable unifying factor.

Diocletian's successes, however, greatly outweighed his failures. He was much more skilled as an administrator than as a general, but an administrator was just what the Empire needed at that time. The pattern he established was maintained, and expanded, after his death. Emperors continued to claim absolute authority in all matters and to try to solve problems by legislative decree. Diocletian's reforms brought the Empire back from the brink of extinction and laid the foundation for the Byzantine Empire.

—*Ralph W. Mathisen*

FURTHER READING

Arnheim, M. T. W. *The Senatorial Aristocracy in the Later Roman Empire*. Oxford, England: Clarendon Press, 1972. A detailed discussion of the evolution of the ruling class of the Empire under Diocletian and his successors. Uses the methodology known as "prosopography," or "collective biography."

Barnes, Timothy D. *The New Empire of Diocletian and Constantine*. Cambridge, Mass.: Harvard University Press, 1982. An investigation of the administrative restructuring of the Empire that occurred under Diocletian.

Brauer, George C. *The Age of the Soldier Emperors: Imperial Rome, A.D. 244-284*. Park Ridge, N.J.: Noyes Press, 1975. A clear discussion of the Illyrian emperors of the third century, culminating in the reign of Diocletian. Particular use is made of the numismatic evidence.

Brown, Peter. *The World of Late Antiquity: From Marcus Aurelius to Mohammed*. New York: Norton, 1989. A very broad and well-illustrated discussion of the social and cultural background of the new age that began in the later part of the third century.

Jones, Arnold H. M. *The Later Roman Empire, 284-602: A Social, Economic, and Administrative Survey*. Baltimore: The Johns Hopkins University Press, 1986. The standard scholarly discussion of the Roman world beginning with the restructuring that occurred during the time of Diocletian. Places Diocletian's reforms in their broader context. Fully annotated.

Williams, Stephen. *Diocletian and the Roman Recovery*. New York: Routledge, 1997. A detailed, chronological biography of Diocletian. Includes an extensive bibliography of other scholarship on Diocletian as well as some illustrations.

SEE ALSO: Augustus; Clement I; Constantine the Great.
RELATED ARTICLES in *Great Events from History: The Ancient World*: 27-23 B.C.E., Completion of the Augustan Settlement; c. 50 C.E., Creation of the Roman Imperial Bureaucracy; 64-67 C.E., Nero Persecutes the Christians; 68-69 C.E., Year of the Four Emperors; c. 250 C.E., Saint Denis Converts Paris to Christianity; 284 C.E., Inauguration of the Dominate in Rome; October 28, 312 C.E., Conversion of Constantine to Christianity; 313-395 C.E., Inception of Church-State Problem; November 24, 326-May 11, 330 C.E., Constantinople Is Founded.

DIOGENES
Greek philosopher

The most famous and colorful of the Cynic philosophers, Diogenes lived in extreme poverty and shunned all comforts in his quest for a virtuous life.

BORN: c. 412-403 B.C.E.; Sinope, Paphlygonia (now in Turkey)
DIED: c. 324-321 B.C.E.; probably Corinth, Greece
AREA OF ACHIEVEMENT: Philosophy

EARLY LIFE

Diogenes (di-AWJ-uh-neez) was born in Sinope, an ancient Milesian community on the southern coast of the Black Sea. The colony of Miletus was ruled by Persian kings from 495 B.C.E. until Alexander the Great's conquest in 331 B.C.E. Diogenes himself was probably Greek, of Milesian roots. Little is known about his early life, although it is probable that he came from an educated and well-to-do family. His father, Hicesias, was a banker in charge of issuing the city's currency; coins minted between 360 and 320 B.C.E. and bearing what is presumed to be Hicesias's name have been found in Sinopean archaeological digs.

The first known accounts of Diogenes all relate to his exile from Sinope, an event that was somehow related to an episode of tampering with the Sinopean currency. Several versions of the story exist, variously incriminating Diogenes, his father, or both. How they were involved and what exactly they did—whether defacing coins, counterfeiting currency, or altering the stamping process of coins—is not certain; in any case, it was an illegal activity resulting in exile.

This event is linked to another important story in Diogenes' life that is much less probable but is recounted in various sources. To consult an oracle, supposedly Diogenes traveled to Delphi or Delos, places where those in search of guidance or answers to difficult questions came to receive answers or prophecies from people considered to be divinely inspired. The reply to Diogenes' query was "falsify the currency." (The word for "falsify" can also be translated as "counterfeit," "deface," or "alter.") One suggestion is that when Diogenes heard this, he went back to Sinope and literally did what he was told. Another idea is that this event occurred after his exile and that Diogenes took the command allegorically. In any event, Diogenes' exile was a key event in his becoming a philosopher and adopting a life of asceticism. It seems that by the time he appeared in Athens, he was already leading an ascetic life.

LIFE'S WORK

Diogenes' main goal was to "deface the currency" or to "put false currency out of circulation." The Greek word for "currency" can also be translated to mean "social rules of conduct." In "defacing the currency," then, Diogenes sought to rebel against conventional norms that he felt to be false and contrived and to encourage people to live a life adhering to the rules of nature. Unlike other philosophers, he did not teach a group of students (although he did have students at various times) or engage in intellectual study; rather, he taught by the example of his lifestyle. He believed that virtue produced happiness. Self-sufficiency was the key to virtue, and self-sufficiency was attained by ridding oneself of money, possessions, physical comforts, traditional values, associations, and internal emotions and desires. These were all unnecessary creations of humanity that kept people from being self-sufficient and, therefore, happy; only by breaking these bonds could one return to a natural life. Diogenes thus lived a bare-minimum, instinctive existence, focusing on complete mastery of his only possession, his soul.

Diogenes looked to animals and their ways of life for inspiration; one story, for example, says that Diogenes was converted after watching a mouse darting about, not having any sure place to sleep or any guaranteed source of food or warmth. Diogenes earned the nickname "the Dog" soon after his arrival in Athens, and much of his behavior was doglike in its disregard for social norms. He practiced indifference to criticism and therefore felt free to say or do as he pleased. He slept in an earthenware barrel, had a ragged appearance, and acquired food wherever he could. He relieved himself wherever he felt the need and was known to eat raw meat. He was biting in his criticism and actions toward most other people, finding them loathsome. He also belittled other philosophers, finding fault with them all. He continually sought to change people's values by criticizing them and shouting at them.

Diogenes also carried a great disdain for the state and civic responsibility. Many stories depict him suffering through self-inflicted physical hardships such as rolling in hot sand, walking on snow, or embracing a bronze statue in the cold of winter. These acts were designed to test the mind and body and achieve mastery over them, for through this training, he believed, virtue could be achieved.

On first glance, it appears that Diogenes had an intense hatred for people; however, he supposedly claimed that it was because of his love of his fellow humans that he sought to change their ways to something he felt was far superior. His standards for a "good man" were extremely high, and probably few could ever hope to meet them.

Though Cynicism is most commonly associated with Diogenes, he was preceded by an earlier Cynic, Antisthenes (c. 444 B.C.E.-c. 365 B.C.E.). Antisthenes, who was influenced by Socrates, is considered the founder of Cynicism, while Diogenes brought the essence of classical Cynicism to fruition. Antisthenes taught that traditional intellectual training and discourse did not necessarily produce enlightenment. For enlightenment to occur, he said, one needed to live a virtuous life, and by self-sufficiency of mind, one could become wise. This idea of virtue is central to Cynicism, and the lifestyle traits associated with it all center on the quest for virtue. Antisthenes showed indifference to material possessions, had no particular ties to society, and criticized many of the standards of his day.

Some sources claim that Diogenes was a pupil of Antisthenes, though others argue that this is a chronological impossibility. It is more likely that Diogenes read or heard about Antisthenes' ideas. Diogenes' lifestyle and actions were those of Antisthenes, carried to extremes. Indeed, Diogenes was critical of his predecessor, whose writings drew on various philosophical and metaphysical ideas, who lived a life of simplicity but not abject poverty, and who derived his living from teaching. Diogenes advocated complete asceticism and uncompromising contempt for intellectualism. It is possible that Cynicism derives its name from Diogenes' nickname, "the Dog." *Cynos* is the Greek word for "dog," and the Cynics were in many respects doglike in their lifestyles and attitudes.

Understanding Diogenes' life is difficult for several reasons. First, none of his writings still exist, only quotes and paraphrases by other writers and philosophers. Whether these writings were actually written by him is another question; opinion varies. Moreover, the legend that grew around the man after his death has probably obscured accurate factual data about him. Diogenes is referenced and described by a plethora of authors, but the information often conflicts. Many of the accounts attribute wise sayings and amazing anecdotes to him, and his eccentric nature perhaps encouraged some authors to exaggerate. It is therefore difficult to separate fact from fiction, but one can assume that the accounts point to the general essence of who Diogenes truly was.

Diogenes.   (Hulton|Archive by Getty Images)

One well-known story involves his walking around in daylight with a lantern looking for true human being— or, as has been added in modern times, "an honest man." In another story, Alexander the Great encounters Diogenes and offers him anything he desires; Diogenes asks Alexander to step aside, as he is blocking the sunshine. Another account claims that Diogenes was captured by pirates and sold as a slave to a Corinthian named Xeniades. Diogenes asked the slave auctioneer to announce his skill as "governing men." When Xeniades bought him, Diogenes told his new master that he would have to obey Diogenes. Diogenes lived in Xeniades' house for several years and taught his sons his ideas. All these stories, regardless of whether they are entirely truthful in their accounts, portray Diogenes as self-sufficient, a slave to no person or land, and an overseer of others.

Despite his ascetic life, Diogenes is portrayed in a small minority of writings as more of a hedonist than an ascetic. This view points to Diogenes living as a professional beggar, denouncing wealth but accepting comforts so long as they were given to him and he was not forced to work for them. It is also clear that some people thought him to be psychopathic. His assuredness that he was always right and everyone else wrong, his extreme indifference to others' opinions, and his disregard for social norms such as work and dress proved him crazy to some, including the philosopher Plato.

Diogenes is believed to have traveled extensively, but Athens and Corinth were his two main residences. He lived to a relatively old age and most likely died in Corinth, where he was living in a gymnasium called the *Craneum*. The cause of death has been variously reported as natural death, suicide by holding his breath, illness brought on by eating raw octopus, fever, and dog bite. Most reports state that the citizens of Corinth buried Diogenes in a tomb marked with an inscription and a marble effigy of a dog.

SIGNIFICANCE

Marking a departure from the philosophical and moral standards of the time, Diogenes sought to promote a radical and rebellious return to a "natural" world by the example of his own lifestyle. By clinging to what he felt was virtuous (though it involved hardship and suffering) and condemning what he felt to be pretentious and worthless, he showed his commitment to honesty amid an often-hostile environment. Diogenes became a legend as much after his death as in his own time, and he set the stage for many important Cynics who succeeded him, such as his disciple Crates.

—*Michelle C. K. McKowen*

FURTHER READING

Brehier, Emile. *The History of Philosophy*. 7 vols. Chicago: University of Chicago Press, 1963-1969. Contains a short yet clear and revealing portrait of Diogenes and Cynicism. Includes many quotations from primary sources.

Dudley, D. R. *A History of Cynicism from Diogenes to the Sixth Century A.D.* 2d ed. London: Bristol Classical Press, 1998. A detailed history of Cynicism. The chapter on Diogenes cites primary source accounts of his life. Diogenes' disciples are also described.

Gomperz, Theodor. *Greek Thinkers: A History of Ancient Philosophy*. 4 vols. 1901-1912. Reprint. Bristol, England: Thoemmes Press, 1996. Contains a concise account of Diogenes' life in the perspective of other concurrent events.

Navia, Luis E. *Classical Cynicism: A Critical Study*. Westport, Conn.: Greenwood Press, 1996. A comprehensive study of Cynicism that features a long and exhaustive study of Diogenes. Other chapters compare and contrast Diogenes with predecessors and successors, placing him in a historical and philosophical framework. His life is explored in detail, and every attempt is made to distinguish between fact and supposition.

Sayre, Farrand. *Diogenes of Sinope: A Study of Greek Cynicism*. Baltimore: J. H. Furst, 1938. Contains extensive writing on Diogenes' life and spends one chapter exploring the legends and myths surrounding him.

SEE ALSO: Alexander the Great; Antisthenes; Plato; Socrates.

RELATED ARTICLES in *Great Events from History: The Ancient World*: 600-500 B.C.E., Greek Philosophers Formulate Theories of the Cosmos; c. 500-400 B.C.E., Greek Physicians Begin Scientific Practice of Medicine; c. 440 B.C.E., Sophists Train the Greeks in Rhetoric and Politics; c. 380 B.C.E., Plato Develops His Theory of Ideas; c. 350 B.C.E., Diogenes Popularizes Cynicism; c. 335-323 B.C.E., Aristotle Writes the *Politics*; c. 300 B.C.E., Stoics Conceptualize Natural Law.

DIOPHANTUS
Greek mathematician

Diophantus wrote a treatise on arithmetic that represents the most complete collection of problems dating from Greek times involving solutions of determinate and indeterminate equations. This work was the basis of much medieval Arabic and European Renaissance algebra.

FLOURISHED: c. 250 C.E.; place unknown
AREA OF ACHIEVEMENT: Mathematics

EARLY LIFE

Almost nothing is known about the life of Diophantus (di-oh-FAHN-tuhs), and there is no mention of him by any of his contemporaries. A reference to the mathematician by Hypsicles (active around 170 B.C.E.) in his tract on polygonal numbers and a mention of him by Theon of Alexandria (fl. 365-390 C.E.) give respectively a lower and an upper bound for the period in which Diophantus lived. There is also evidence that points to the middle of the third century C.E. as the flourishing period of Diophantus. Indeed, the Byzantine Michael Psellus (latter part of the eleventh century) asserts in a letter that Anatolius, bishop of Laodicea around 280 C.E., wrote a brief work on the Diophantine art of reckoning. Psellus's remark seems to fit well with the dedication of Diophantus's masterpiece *Arithmētika* (*Arithmetica*, 1885) to a certain Dionysius, who might possibly be identified with Saint Dionysius, bishop of Alexandria after 247. The only dates known about Diophantus's life are obtained as a solution to an arithmetical riddle contained in the *Greek Anthology*, which gives thirty-three for his wedding age, thirty-eight for when he became a father, and eighty-four for the age of his death. The trustworthiness of the riddle is hard to determine. During his life, Diophantus wrote the *Arithmetica*, the *Porismata*, the *Moriastica*, and the tract on polygonal numbers.

LIFE'S WORK

Diophantus's main achievement was the *Arithmetica*, a collection of arithmetical problems involving the solution of determinate and indeterminate equations. A determinate equation is an equation with a fixed number of solutions, such as the equation $x^2 - 2x + 1 = 0$, which admits only 1 as a solution. An indeterminate equation usually contains more than one variable, as for example the equation $x + 2y = 8$. The name indeterminate is motivated by the fact that such equations often admit an infinite number of solutions. The degree of an equation is the

degree of its highest degree term; a term in several variables has degree equal to the sum of the exponents of its variables. For example, $x^2 + x = 0$ is of degree two, and $x^3 + x^2y^4 + 3 = 0$ is of degree six but of degree three in x and degree four in y.

Although Diophantus presents solutions to arithmetic problems employing methods of varying degrees of generality, his work cannot be fairly described as a systematic exposition of the theory of solution of determinate and indeterminate equations. The *Arithmetica* is in fact merely a collection of problems and lacks any deductive structure whatsoever. Moreover, it is extremely hard to pinpoint exactly which general methods may constitute a key for reading the *Arithmetica*. This observation, however, by no means diminishes Diophantus's achievements. The *Arithmetica* represents the first systematic collection of such problems in Greek mathematics and thus by itself must be considered a major step toward recognizing the unity of the field of mathematics dealing with determinate and indeterminate equations and their solutions, in short, the field of Diophantine problems.

The *Arithmetica* was originally divided into thirteen books. Only six of them were known until 1971, when the discovery of four lost books in Arabic translation greatly increased knowledge of the work. The six books that were known before that discovery were transmitted to the West through Greek manuscripts dating from the thirteenth century (these will be referred to as books IG-VIG). The four books in Arabic translation (henceforth IVA-VIIA) represent a translation from the Greek attributed to Qustā ibn Lūqā al-Baʾlabakkī (fl. mid-ninth century). The Arabic books present themselves as books 4 through 7 of the *Arithmetica*. Because none of the Greek books overlaps with the Arabic books, a reorganization of the Diophantine corpus is necessary.

Scholars agree that the four Arabic books should probably be spliced between IIIG and IVG on grounds of internal coherence: The techniques used to solve the problems in IVA-VIIA presuppose only the knowledge of IG-IIIG, whereas the techniques used in IVG through VIG are radically different and more complicated than those found in IVA-VIIA. There is also compelling external evidence that this is the right order. The organization of problems in al-Karaji's *al-Fakhri* (c. 1010), an Islamic textbook of algebra heavily dependent on Diophantus, shows that the problems taken from IG-IIIG are immediately followed by problems found in IVA. The most interesting difference between IG-VIG and IVA-VIIA consists in the fact that in the Greek books, after having found the sought solutions (analysis), Diophantus never checks the correctness of the results obtained; in the Arabic books, the analysis is always followed by a computation establishing the correctness of the solution obtained (synthesis).

Before delving into some of the contents of the *Arithmetica*, the reader must remember that in Diophantus's work the term "arithmetic" takes a whole new meaning. The Greek tradition sharply distinguished between arithmetic and logistics. Arithmetic dealt with abstract properties of numbers, whereas logistics meant the computational techniques of reckoning. Diophantus dropped this distinction because he realized that although he was working with numerical examples, the techniques he used were quite general. Diophantus has often been called "the father of algebra," but this is inaccurate: Diophantus merely uses definitional abbreviations and not a system of notation that is completely symbolic. At the outset of the *Arithmetica*, Diophantus gives his notation for powers of the unknown x, called *arithmoi* (and indicated by the symbol σ), and for their reciprocals. (For example, x^2 is denoted by Δ^v and x^3 by K^v.) Diophantus has no signs for addition and multiplication, although he has a special sign for minus and a special word for "divided by."

It is impossible to summarize the rich content of the 290 problems of the *Arithmetica* (189 in the Greek and 101 in the Arabic books), but from the technical point of view a very rough description of the books can be given as follows: IG deals mainly with determinate equations of the first and second degree; IIG and IIIG address many problems that involve determinate and indeterminate equations of degree no higher than two; IVA to VIIA are mainly devoted to consolidating the knowledge acquired in IG-IIIG; and IVG to VIG address problems involving the use of indeterminate equations of degree higher than two.

Throughout the *Arithmetica*, Diophantus admits only positive rational solutions (that is, solutions of the form p/q where p and q are natural numbers). Although negative numbers are used in his work, he seems to make sense of them only with respect to some positive quantity and not as having a meaning on their own. For example, in VG.2 (where 2 refers to problem 2 of VG), the equation $4 = 4x + 20$ is considered absurd because the only solution is -4.

In IG are found many problems involving pure determinate equations, such as equations in which the unknown is present only in one power. The solution to IG.30, for example, requires solution of the equation

$100 - x^2 = 96$, which gives $x = 2$. Note that Diophantus is not interested in the solution $x = -2$. Diophantus gives a general rule for solving pure equations:

> Next, if there results from a problem an equation in which certain terms are equal to terms of the same species, but with different coefficients, it will be necessary to subtract like from like on both sides until one term is found equal to one term. If perchance there be on either side or on both sides any negative terms, it will be necessary to add the negative terms on both sides, until the terms on both sides become positive, and again to subtract like from like until on each side only one term is left.

In other words, Diophantus reduces the equation to the normal form $ax^m = c$. If the result were a mixed quadratic,

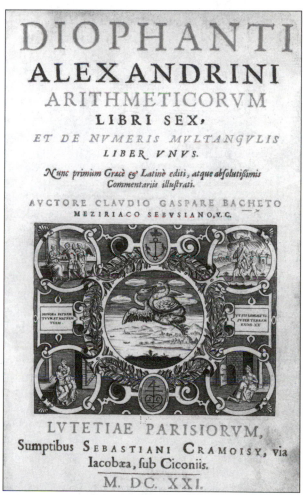

Title page from an edition of Diophantus's Arithmetica. *(Library of Congress)*

however, such as $ax^2 + bx + c = 0$, Diophantus might have solved it by using a general method of solution similar to the one commonly learned in high school. As an example, problem VIG.9 can be reduced to finding the solution of $630x^2 - 73x = 6$, for which Diophantus merely states the solution to be $x = 6/35$. Although the possibility that Diophantus might have solved these problems by trial and error is open, internal evidence strongly suggests that he knew more than is relayed in the *Arithmetica*. In fact, the passage immediately following the above quote reads, "we will show you afterwards how, in the case also when two terms are left equal to a single term, such an equation can be solved." The promised solution may be in the lost three books.

Diophantus also solves problems involving equations (or systems of equations) of the form

(a) $a_nx^n + a_{n-1}x^{n-1} + \ldots + a_1x - a_0 = y^2$
(where n is at most 6)
(b) $a_nx^n + a_{n-1}x^{n-1} + \ldots + a_1x - a_0 = y^2$
(where n is at most 3)

The methods are seldom general, however, and rely on special cases of the above equations as found in VIG.19, where one finds the system given by the two equations $4x + 2 = y^3$ and $2x + 1 = z^2$. (The reader is reminded that Diophantus always works with numerical cases and so equations in abstract form are not to be found in his work.)

In many problems, Diophantus needs to find solutions that are subject to certain limits imposed by a condition of the problem at hand. He often uses some very interesting techniques to deal with such situations (so-called methods of limits and approximation to limits).

The tract on polygonal numbers has been transmitted in incomplete form. Whereas the *Arithmetica* used methods that could be called algebraic, the treatise on polygonal numbers follows the geometrical method, in which numbers are represented by geometrical objects.

Of the other two works, *Porismata* and *Moriastica*, virtually nothing is known. The *Moriastica* was mentioned by Iamblichus (fourth century C.E.) and seems to have been merely a compendium of rules for computing with fractions similar (or identical) to the one found in IG. The *Porismata* is referred to often by Diophantus himself. In the *Arithmetica*, he often appeals to some results of number theoretic nature and refers to the *Porismata* for their proofs. It is unclear, as in the case of the *Moriastica*, whether the *Porismata* was part of the *Arithmetica* or a different work. There are other number theoretic statements that are used by Diophantus in the *Arithmetica* and that might have been part of the *Porismata*. They concern the expressibility of numbers as sums of two, three, or four squares. For example, Diophantus certainly knew that numbers of the form $4n + 3$ cannot be odd and that numbers of the form $8n + 7$ cannot be written as sums of three squares. It was in commenting on these insights of Diophantus that the distinguished mathematician Pierre de Fermat (1601-1665) gave some of his most famous number theoretic statements.

SIGNIFICANCE

Diophantus's *Arithmetica* represents the most extensive treatment of arithmetic problems involving determinate and indeterminate equations from Greek times. It is clear from the sources that Diophantus did not create the field anew but was heavily dependent on the older Greek tradition. Although it is difficult to assess how much he improved on his predecessors' results, his creativeness in solving so many problems by exploiting new stratagems to supplement the few general techniques at his disposal was impressive.

The *Arithmetica* was instrumental in the development of algebra in the medieval Islamic world and Renaissance Europe. The Arabic writers al-Khazin (fl. c. 940), Abul Wefa (940-998), and al-Karaji (fl. c. 1010), among others, were deeply influenced by Diophantus's work and incorporated many of his problems in their algebra textbooks. The Greek books have come to the West through Byzantium. The Byzantine monk Maximus Planudes (c. 1260-c. 1310) wrote a commentary on the first two Greek books and collected several extant manuscripts of Diophantus that were brought to Italy by Cardinal Bessarion. Apart from a few sporadic quotations, there was no extensive work on the *Arithmetica* until the Italian algebraist Rafael Bombelli ventured into a translation (with Antonio Maria Pazzi), which was never published, and used most of the problems found in IG-VIG in his *Algebra*, published in 1572. François Viète, the famous French algebraist, also made use of several problems from Diophantus in his *Zetetica* (1593). In 1575, the first Latin translation, by Wilhelm Holtzmann (who grecized his name as Xylander), appeared with a commentary. In 1621, the Greek text was published with a Latin translation by Claude-Gaspar Bachet. This volume became the standard edition until the end of the nineteenth century, when Paul Tannery's edition became available. A new French-Greek edition of the Greek books is planned since the Tannery edition is long outdated.

—Wilbur R. Knorr and Paolo Mancuso

FURTHER READING

Bashmakova, Isabella G. *Diophantus and Diophantine Equations*. Translated by Abe Shenitzer. Washington, D.C.: Mathematical Association of America, 1997. A discussion of the methods of Diophantus, accessible to readers who have taken some university mathematics. It includes the elementary facts of algebraic geometry indispensable for its understanding. Examines the development of Diophantine methods during the Renaissance and in the work of Pierre de Fermat.

Heath, Thomas L. *Diophantos of Alexandria: A Study in the History of Greek Algebra*. Cambridge, England: Cambridge University Press, 1885. This volume is still the major reference work on Diophantus in English. It gives an extensive treatment of the sources, the works, and the influence of Diophantus. The appendix contains translations and a good sample of problems from IG-VIG of the *Arithmetica* and translations from the tract on polygonal numbers.

_____. *A History of Greek Mathematics*. 2 vols. 1921. Reprint. New York: Dover Press, 1981. The second volume of this classic study contains a thorough exposition of Diophantus's work with a rich analysis of types of problems from the *Arithmetica*.

Sesiano, Jacques. *Books IV to VII of Diophantus's Arithmetica: In the Arabic Translation Attributed to Qusta Ibn Luqa*. New York: Springer-Verlag, 1982. A detailed analysis of the Arabic books with a translation and a commentary on the text. The introduction presents a summary of the textual history of arithmetic theory in Greek and Arabic. The English translation and the commentary are followed by an edition of the Arabic text. Other features include an Arabic index, an appendix that gives a conspectus of the problems in the *Arithmetica*, and an extensive bibliography.

Thomas, Ivor, ed. *Greek Mathematical Works*. 2 vols. Cambridge, Mass.: Harvard University Press, 1980. Volume 2 of this work contains selections from the *Arithmetica* and the quotations from the *Greek Anthology*, Psellus, and Theon of Alexandria that are relevant for Diophantus's dates. Greek texts with English translation.

Vogel, Kurt. "Diophantus of Alexandria." In *Concise Dictionary of Scientific Biography*, vol. 4. New York: Scribner's, 2000. A survey of Diophantus's life and works, with an extensive selection of types of problems and solutions found in the *Arithmetica*.

SEE ALSO: Apollonius of Perga; Euclid; Eudoxus of Cyrene; Hero of Alexandria; Hypatia; Pappus.

RELATED ARTICLES in *Great Events from History: The Ancient World*: c. 300 B.C.E., Euclid Compiles a Treatise on Geometry; 415 C.E., Mathematician and Philosopher Hypatia Is Killed in Alexandria.

PEDANIUS DIOSCORIDES
Roman physician and author

Through wide travel and much observation, Dioscorides compiled, organized, and published the most comprehensive pharmacological text produced in the ancient world. The work remained a standard reference work for herbalists and physicians for some sixteen hundred years.

BORN: c. 40 C.E.; Anazarbus, Roman Cilicia (now in Turkey)
DIED: c. 90 C.E.; place unknown
AREA OF ACHIEVEMENT: Medicine

EARLY LIFE

Pedanius Dioscorides (di-uhs-KOHR-uh-deez) came from the city of Anazarbus, located along the banks of the Pyramus River in Roman Cilicia, in the far southeastern corner of Asia Minor. In his day, Anazarbus considered itself a worthy rival to its more famous neighbor Tarsus for preeminence in this province. Other than for Dioscorides, Anazarbus is most famous for its red stone buildings and for having produced the poet Oppian in the second century C.E.

Dioscorides probably received his early education and medical training in Tarsus, a city famous for its pharmacologists (experts in the preparation, administration, and effects of drugs). Scholars have inferred that Dioscorides was schooled in Tarsus, not only because of Tarsus's reputation but also because Dioscorides dedicated his *De materia medica* (c. 78 C.E.; *The Greek Herbal of Dioscorides*, 1934, best known as *De materia medica*) to the physician Arius of Tarsus, from whom he seems to have received his medical training. It is also worth noting that Galen, the most famous of all Greek medical writers, referred to Dioscorides as Dioscorides of Tarsus, rather than of Anazarbus, indicating that Dioscorides was closely associated with the medical traditions of Tarsus in the minds of later scholars.

It may also have been in Tarsus that Dioscorides acquired his Roman name, or nomen, Pedanius. Even after the Romans had made the entire Mediterranean area part of their vast empire, it remained common for Greeks to have only one name. However, it was also common for provincials who were granted Roman citizenship to recognize their Roman patrons by adopting their names. Most likely, Dioscorides took his name from a connection with a member of the gens, or family, of the Pedanii (one of whom, Pedanius Secundus, had served as governor in the neighboring Roman province of Asia in the 50's).

There is some debate over whether—and in what capacity and for what duration—Dioscorides served in the Roman military. It is quite possible that Dioscorides did serve in the military; if he did, it would account for some of his wide travels and would probably have brought him into contact with people from distant parts of the Roman world. His military experience would not account for his genius, however, and his later work does not greatly reflect the most pressing concerns of a field surgeon: treating wounds. It will suffice to say that his military experience was not an obstacle to his later career.

LIFE'S WORK

Virtually all that is known about Dioscorides comes from the single source of his lasting fame, his great book on the medical properties of plants and other natural agents, *De materia medica*, which he wrote in Greek. In this book, a pharmacological text that describes hundreds of plants—as well as animals and minerals—and their properties when employed as drugs, Dioscorides reveals himself to be high-minded and genuinely concerned with the physician's essential task of healing. Although Dioscorides may have been associated with the empirical school of medicine, his writing shows no trace of the contentious spirit or rancor so prevalent elsewhere in the ancient medical corpus. He was, almost without question, a physician himself rather than, as has sometimes been suggested, a traveling drug dealer. Selling drugs was a highly lucrative profession during Dioscorides' time, and quackery was a serious problem, as pharmacists and so-called root-cutters competed for business with physicians. There were no licensing boards to protect patients from malpractice or fraud in the ancient world, and the motto of the day was *caveat emptor*, "let the buyer beware." Dioscorides, by producing his encyclopedic reference book on pharmacy, did much to alleviate this problem.

Dioscorides' system of classifying plants based on their pharmaceutical properties is an original one. He divided his study into five books, each concerned with a different broad group of medicinal agents. Within these books, he then discussed each plant, animal, or mineral in its own chapter. He methodically lists the plant's name (including common variants or synonyms), presents a drawing of it, gives its habitat and a botanical descrip-

Pendanius Dioscorides. (Library of Congress)

tion, and then discusses its properties as a drug. He not only discusses positive qualities of these drugs but also warns of dangerous side effects. He instructs his readers on how and when to harvest, prepare, and store each plant or compound. He hastens to add in most cases that he has traveled extensively through the eastern Mediterranean and as far afield as India, Arabia, North Africa, Spain, and Gaul to examine these plants personally.

Book 1 of *De materia medica* deals with aromatics, oils, salves, trees, and shrubs. Book 2 covers animals, their parts and products, cereals, pot herbs, and sharp herbs. Book 3 is devoted to roots, juices, herbs, and seeds, while book 4 continues with more roots and herbs. Finally, in book 5, Dioscorides deals with wines and minerals. Throughout his work, Dioscorides stresses the importance of observation. Plants are living organisms, and they have different properties in youth and decay, when flowering and in seed, and they are affected by both the changing weather of the seasons and the local environment. A physician cannot expect plants gathered at different stages of growth and in different seasons to have the same effect on patients. Naturally, he also stresses the importance of observing the action of these medicaments on each and every patient. The body of medical knowledge must constantly be updated.

Dioscorides is notable for two characteristics. One is simply his excellence. Because he was a gifted empirical observer, his work was particularly valuable. Beyond that, he was moving toward a systematic classification of drugs based on their actions. If Dioscorides is compared, for example, to his near contemporary Scribonius Largus, the difference in outlook is immediately evident. Scribonius organized his book of drugs, called the *Compositiones* (c. 43-50 C.E.), based on ailments. He begins with compounds useful for headaches and proceeds downward to the patient's feet. Dioscorides, on the other hand, is concerned with what effect a particular drug has. Much as a modern physician's reference book classifies drugs into categories such as analgesics, anesthetics, antibiotics, decongestants, and so on, Dioscorides was concerned with whether a particular drug had a warming effect, was an astringent, was a laxative, and so on. Once its properties were established, its medical applications could be discussed. Thus, plants are organized not so much by botanical similarity—as many later writers supposed—as by similar pharmacological properties.

Unfortunately, although the usefulness of Dioscorides' *De materia medica* was recognized at once, the potential medical and scientific implications of his attempt at classification were not. By the end of the Roman Empire, his work had been reissued in new editions in which the plants had been arranged alphabetically, undermining the basic principles that Dioscorides had laid out. Thus, while his work continued to receive study, it came to be seen as the culmination of a process rather than the beginning that its author intended. Had this not been the case, the progress of medical science in the next thousand years might well have been drastically different.

SIGNIFICANCE

The medical arts in the ancient world had progressed fitfully at best. Despite the genius of individual physicians such as Hippocrates and Galen, the medical profession was often disrupted by internal disputes between rival schools. Pedanius Dioscorides is one of the few writers of his day to rise above such personal concerns and produce a reference work of use to members of all medical schools. His great herbal was a landmark achievement and an instant success.

In terms of his influence, Dioscorides can rightly be placed amid the greatest of ancient medical writers. If he is not to be classed with Hippocrates and Galen, he certainly belongs in the distinguished company of such authorities as Aulus Cornelius Celsus and Pliny the Elder. Until his classification was supplanted by that of Carolus Linnaeus in the eighteenth century, he stood as the foremost authority on pharmacy for more than sixteen hundred years. He was recognized not only by later Roman and Byzantine writers but also by Islamic scholars. Throughout the Middle Ages, his writings were a veritable gold mine of information for herbalists, who often copied his work—in true medieval fashion—without citing their debt to him. Nevertheless, *De materia medica* was first published as a printed book in 1478, barely twenty years after Johann Gutenberg perfected the use of movable type, and by the sixteenth century, Dioscorides' writings had found a central position in the curriculum of virtually every university in Europe.

If Dioscorides' reputation was tarnished by Linnaeus and subsequent followers of "scientific medicine," it was at least in part because they did not genuinely understand his system. Moreover, it is likely that in years to come Dioscorides will once again be studied and his fame will once again be widespread. In the modern age, many doctors and scientists have become increasingly aware that traditional remedies do, in fact, possess medicinal properties. The plant kingdom, as Dioscorides well knew in the first century, is a giant pharmacopoeia, waiting to be used for the benefit of humankind.

—*J. S. Hamilton*

FURTHER READING

Allbutt, T. Clifford. *Greek Medicine in Rome*. Reprint. New York: Benjamin Blom, 1970. A very readable, standard survey of Roman medicine by a pioneer in the field. Particularly valuable for an appreciation of Dioscorides is chapter 17, "Pharmacy and Toxicology."

Collins, Minta. *Medieval Herbals: The Illustrative Traditions*. Buffalo, N.Y.: University of Toronto Press, 2000. Shows that treatises on the medical uses of plants date back to the work of Dioscorides, whose teachings formed the basis of Western herbal writings for a millennium and a half.

Gunther, Robert T., ed. *The Greek Herbal of Dioscorides*. Oxford, England: Oxford University Press, 1934. Based on the translation made by John Goodyer in 1655, this work is the only complete translation of Dioscorides' *De materia medica*. Includes some 396 illustrations taken from a sixth century C.E. Byzantine manuscript.

Hamilton, J. S. "Scribonius Largus on the Medical Profession." *Bulletin of the History of Medicine* 60 (1986): 209-216. A translation of and commentary on the preface to the *Compositiones* of Scribonius Largus, a contemporary of Dioscorides, who addressed many of the same concerns as Dioscorides. He was particularly concerned with the ethical and practical issues relating to the administration of drugs by physicians and with the many internal divisions by which the medical profession of his day was riven.

Riddle, John M. "Dioscorides." In *Catalogus Translationum et Commentariorum: Medieval and Renaissance Latin Translations and Commentaries, Annotated Lists, and Guides*, edited by F. Edward Cranz and Paul Oskar Kristeller. Washington, D.C.: Catholic University Press, 1980. The first dozen pages of this article provide a clear and concise synopsis of Dioscorides' life, career, and influence. The following 130 pages trace his great work, *De materia medica*, through its tortuous history of subsequent editions and commentaries. This is meant for specialist scholars but will provide students of all levels with insight into the remarkable—and tenuous—process by which knowledge of the ancient world has been preserved.

_____. *Dioscorides on Pharmacy and Medicine*. Austin: University of Texas Press, 1985. This book not only contains an excellent analysis of the work of Dioscorides but also evaluates the sources of information available for the life of the distinguished pharmacologist. The book is made even more valuable by its extensive bibliography. Contains a number of instructive diagrams and illustrations.

Sadek, M. M. *The Arabic "Materia medica" of Dioscorides*. Quebec: Éditions du Sphinx, 1983. Provides a brief illustration of the extent to which Dioscorides' writings had an impact on Arab medicine in the Middle Ages, a period in which Arab physicians equaled or excelled their Western counterparts.

Scarborough, John. *Roman Medicine*. Ithaca, N.Y.: Cornell University Press, 1969. An excellent brief overview of the development and status of the medical profession in the Roman world. The book is extensively illustrated and contains a useful appendix of very brief biographical sketches of Greek and Roman medical writers and practitioners.

Scarborough, John, and Vivian Nutton. "The Preface of Dioscorides' *De materia medica*: Introduction, Translation, Commentary." *Transactions and Studies of the College of Physicians of Philadelphia* 4 (September, 1982): 187-227. This article provides an accurate English translation of Dioscorides' own preface to *De materia medica*, along with an extensive commentary. The preface is particularly important because, in it, Dioscorides explains his system of classifying plants and drugs and also reveals virtually all that is known of his own life and medical education.

SEE ALSO: Alcmaeon; Aretaeus of Cappadocia; Asclepiades of Bithynia; Aulus Cornelius Celsus; Erasistratus; Galen; Herophilus; Hippocrates; Pliny the Elder.

RELATED ARTICLES in *Great Events from History: The Ancient World*: 6th-4th century B.C.E. (traditionally, 1st millennium B.C.E.), Suśruta, Indian Physician, Writes Medical Compendium; c. 500 B.C.E., Acupuncture Develops in China; c. 500-400 B.C.E., Greek Physicians Begin Scientific Practice of Medicine; c. 320 B.C.E., Theophrastus Initiates the Study of Botany; c. 157-201 C.E., Galen Synthesizes Ancient Medical Knowledge.

DRACO

Athenian statesman and lawgiver

Draco produced the first written codification of law for the ancient city-state of Athens. His effort is remembered primarily for the harshness of its penalties and for its differentiation among various homicidal acts. Draco was the first to assert that the state should be responsible for the punishment of homicide.

FLOURISHED: Perhaps seventh century B.C.E.; perhaps Athens, Greece
ALSO KNOWN AS: Dracon
AREAS OF ACHIEVEMENT: Government and politics, law

EARLY LIFE

Little is known about Draco (DRAY-koh) the individual. He is clearly an example of a man who was made a leader by the context of the historical moment in which he found himself. It is important to understand, therefore, what was happening in ancient Greece just prior to Draco's arrival on the historical scene.

Justice has not always been dispensed by judges operating under a written or common law equally applicable to all. In early Athens, justice was not a matter of applying a written standard to any situation or dispute. There were no explicitly written sentencing guides or judicial precedents on which to call. Rather, the victims themselves were responsible for exacting retribution or compensation for any crime. If the victim was dead, the family was left to take revenge or seek compensation. These blood feuds could last for generations as families sought to avenge a loss, rarely admitting fault and always seeking absolution.

As time wore on, groups of citizens came together to consider en masse how to prevent transgressions or punish criminals from other areas and thus avoid protracted wars based on blood feuds. Popular assemblies were called for this purpose in instances where the action affected the community as a whole. Over the years, leaders within the aristocracy of Athens began issuing the rulings. This system was not without its problems, as these "chiefs" were often the recipients of bribes.

Ten years before Draco would be called on to serve his fellow Athenians, Cylon, a member of a noble Athenian family, married the daughter of Theagenes. Theagenes was the tyrant of Megara, and his power soon infected his son-in-law. With his help, Cylon attempted to make himself the ruler of Athens. He plotted to seize the Acropolis on the greatest festival day of Zeus, as he had been in-structed by the oracle at Delphi. His first effort failed. A second attempt, aided by select young nobles and members of the Megarian military, was successful. However, Cylon quickly lost any sympathy he might have mustered when the Athenian people witnessed the taking of the Acropolis by these foreigners.

After being blockaded in the citadel, Cylon escaped with his brother, and the remaining conspirators were forced to seek shelter in the temple of Athena Polias. In exchange for their surrender, these conspirators were promised that their lives would be spared. For whatever reason, Megacles, who was in charge at the time, betrayed the promises and ordered the conspirators killed. In line with beliefs surrounding the act of murder and in the tradition of blood feuds, Athenians deemed this act a great pollution to their city. Those who killed the surrendering conspirators were ordered into exile, and their property was confiscated.

As a result of these actions and the ensuing war with Megara, conditions for the lower economic classes deteriorated over the next ten years. In the context of an increasingly complex society, the people began to call for written laws so that they might be protected from the corruption seeping into the courts. In 621 B.C.E., Draco (also known historically as Dracon) was charged with the unenviable task of sorting through traditions and "laws" to produce a written code of law.

LIFE'S WORK

Draco, as a citizen and lawyer of the city-state of Athens, was thus selected to draft a comprehensive written code of law for the people of Athens. While his work did not change the Greek constitution, this extraordinary legislator did bring some semblance of organization to the laws and prescribe punishments for their violation. His written code was built on the premise that the state should be the primary entity responsible for the prosecution and punishment of crimes.

Draco's code mixed religious, civil, and moral ordinances. His code made no attempt to separate religion from law or morality from law. In fact, Draco emphasized in certain cases the link between human action and the glorification of the Greek deities. Particularly in the area of homicide, Draco pointed to the defiling nature of murder to the gods and to the Athenian community. Murder was a crime not only against the victim but also against all things of religious significance to the early

Greeks. Draco thus introduced the Ephetae, a council of fifty-one judges that was convened to hear cases of bloodshed. Depending on the charge in question, the court was held in one of three places: Delphinian Apollo, Palladion of Phaleron, and Phreatto, which was reserved for the consideration of manslaughter cases originating outside Athens.

Draco also gave considerable attention to the relationship between the debtor and the creditor. Again, his sentences against debtors in default were severe. A creditor could go so far as to lay claim to the person of an insolvent debtor. Nevertheless, establishing the expectations of this relationship was of tremendous benefit to the Athenian poor.

A conviction for many of the crimes enumerated in Draco's written code meant death for the accused. It was said by Athenians at the time that Draco's laws were so harsh that they were written not in ink but in blood. So severe were the penalties for crimes ranging from murder to the theft of vegetables that a word based on Draco's name, "draconian," is still used to denote unreasonably harsh laws or regimes.

Despite the harshness of his code, Draco was apparently admired by his fellow Athenians. In fact, he may have been "loved to death." According to one account, a reception was held to honor Draco; as he entered the facility, the shower of hats and cloaks thrown in appreciation of his work buried him. Draco smothered before he could be rescued from the pile of clothes.

Much of Draco's work was undone by Solon, who succeeded him. Solon did, however, incorporate Draco's laws regarding homicide or murder into his own decisions. In an effort to prevent a return to the blood feuds of the previous decades, Solon left the responsibility for punishing murderers in the hands of the state.

SIGNIFICANCE

Although only a few portions of Draco's code are extant, it is recognized for being progressive in one important aspect. Draco, for the first time, defined homicide and introduced definitions of various shades of this crime, ranging from murder with intent to accidental and justifiable homicide.

Many Western concepts of law and order originated with the efforts of Draco and his contemporaries. By establishing regular processes of law and government, the ancient Athenians contributed to the creation of a tradition to which modern governments still look for guidance in the equitable distribution of justice before the law. With the writing of this first comprehensive code of law, civilization took another step forward. Moving away from the arbitrary dispersal of justice, Athens set the stage for the creation of an independent judiciary and a state responsible for the safety and well-being of its citizens.

—*Donna Addkison Simmons*

FURTHER READING

Bury, J. B. *A History of Greece to the Death of Alexander the Great*. 4th ed. New York: St. Martin's Press, 1991. Useful for understanding the historical context into which Draco's code was introduced.

Carawan, Edwin. *Rhetoric and the Law of Draco*. New York: Oxford University Press, 1998. A scholarly examination of the treatment of homicide in Greek legal tradition, with particular reference to Draco's code. Includes bibliography and index.

Gagarin, Michael. *Drakon and Early Athenian Homicide Law*. New Haven, Conn.: Yale University Press, 1981. Provides a thorough discussion of Draco and his role in the evolution of homicide laws in early Greece. Includes bibliography and index.

Maine, Sir Henry Sumner. *Ancient Law*. Reprint. New Brunswick, N.J.: Transaction, 2002. Examines the legal traditions of the ancient world, including those of Athens and Draco.

Stroud, Ronald S. *Drakon's Law on Homicide*. Berkeley: University of California Press, 1968. A transcription, with English translation and commentary, of a fifth century B.C.E. version of Draconian precepts. Taken from the inscription found on a marble stele now in the collection of the Epigraphical Musuem in Athens. Includes bibliography.

SEE ALSO: Cicero; Cleisthenes of Athens; Darius the Great; Hammurabi; Solon.

RELATED ARTICLES in *Great Events from History: The Ancient World*: c. 2340 B.C.E., Sumerian Uruk-Agina Makes Social and Political Reforms; c. 2112 B.C.E., Ur-Nammu Establishes a Code of Law; c. 1770 B.C.E., Promulgation of Hammurabi's Code; 621 or 620 B.C.E., Draco's Code Is Instituted; c. 594-580 B.C.E., Legislation of Solon; 508-507 B.C.E., Reforms of Cleisthenes; 494/493 B.C.E., Institution of the Plebeian Tribunate; 451-449 B.C.E., Twelve Tables of Roman Law Are Formulated; 445 B.C.E., Establishment of the Canuleian Law; 287 B.C.E., *Lex Hortensia* Reforms the Roman Constitution; 90 B.C.E., Julian Law Expands Roman Citizenship; c. 165 C.E., Gaius Creates Edition of the *Institutes* of Roman Law.

EMPEDOCLES
Greek philosopher

Empedocles was one of the earliest of the Greek philosophers to provide a unified theory of the nature of the world and the cosmos.

BORN: c. 490 B.C.E.; Acragas, Sicily (now in Italy)
DIED: c. 430 B.C.E.; in the Peloponnese, Greece
AREAS OF ACHIEVEMENT: Philosophy, science, natural history

EARLY LIFE

Born c. 490 in Acragas, Empedocles (ehm-PEHD-uh-kleez) was a member of the aristocracy. Much of his life has become shrouded in legend; fact is more difficult to discover. It is known that he spent some time with Zeno and Parmenides in the city of Elea; some time after that, he studied with the school of Pythagoras. Later, he left the Pythagoreans for reasons that are not completely clear and returned to Acragas.

In Acragas, he became a political figure, eventually participating in a movement to depose a tyrant, despite his aristocratic background. He made enemies, however, and they used their influence, while he was absent from Acragas, to banish him from his home. He would spend much of his life in exile.

LIFE'S WORK

Empedocles' two main works, *Peri physeōs* (fifth century B.C.E.; *On Nature*, 1908) and *Katharmoi* (fifth century B.C.E.; *Purifications*, 1908), exist only in fragments. *On Nature* is an expression of Empedocles as a cosmic philosopher and as one of the earliest natural scientists. *On Nature*, an essay on the ability of humans to experience the world, in general describes Empedocles' theory of the cosmology of the world. Parmenides believed that the world can be apprehended through the use of reason; Empedocles, however, believed that neither reason nor the senses can provide a clear picture of reality: Reason is a better instrument for dealing with abstraction, and the physical senses are best suited for the phenomenological world.

Unlike Parmenides, Empedocles assumed that the universe is in motion and that it is composed of a multitude of separate parts but that their nature is such that the senses can perceive neither the motion nor the great plurality of living and spiritual forms that inhabit the natural world. In his conception, the basic building blocks of true reality lie in the four archaic "roots": earth, air, fire, and water. In the abstract, these four elements are also repre-sented by spiritual beings: Aidoneus is associated with earth, Hera with air, Zeus with fire, and Nestis with water. The elements can neither be added to the natural world nor deleted from it: The universe is a closed system. The elements can be mixed with one another, however, and the mixture of these elements in various proportions constitutes the stuff of the perceived world.

Every physical entity is a composite of the four elements, in varying forms and degrees of mixture. Empedocles' own analogy was that the blending of the elements could be likened to the creation of a painting: A few basic colors on the palette could be blended in such a manner that all the colors of the rainbow could be achieved.

He saw living things as only a matter of appearance: While they live, they have control over their corporeal forms and assume that the forms of life are as they perceive them. At the time of their death, when the bonds that hold together the elements of which they are composed are loosened, they die.

Empedocles believed that two opposing principles, Love and Strife (also variously called Love and Hate, Harmony and Disharmony, and Attraction and Repulsion), are engaged in a constant struggle in the universe, a process that gives rise to a continual mixing and shifting of the basic particles of earth, air, fire, and water. The two powers alternate in their dominance in a great cosmic cycle that involves the whole universe. When Love dominates, the particles of matter are brought into a homogeneous mass. When Strife is in the ascendant, the effect is to separate the mixed elements into four separate and discrete masses. These alternating states form the poles of existence; the periods when neither dominated were times of flux during which the power of one gradually increased as the power of the other waned. The human world is one where Strife is in the process of slowly overcoming Love: a place of relative disintegration.

In the beginning of the cycle, the elements are separated, under the control of Strife. As the powers of Love manifest themselves, the integrative process creates from the earth random or unattached portions of animals. These combine in various haphazard ways, creating monsters. A similar integrative process creates unattached human parts: disembodied heads, shoulderless arms, unattached eyes. Through chance wanderings, the parts begin to join, creating human monsters, such as many-handed creatures with double faces, cattle with human faces, and people with the faces of oxen.

Nevertheless, some join in a manner that allows them to survive. As time and chance do their work, more and more improvements allow certain forms to prosper; eventually, human form, because of its relatively high survival value, becomes established and flourishes. The same process brings about the various orders of beasts.

After a relatively short period, the flux begins again. Strife becomes gradually more powerful, and the cycle eventually is completed. Empedocles may have meant his theory of Love and Strife to apply to human experience as well: These two forces, acting in the world of humans, are the causes of the harmony of friendship and the disharmony of hatred.

Empedocles thought that every entity in the universe was endowed with particular consciousness. In addition to being conscious of each other, Love and Strife are aware of their effect on the elements. The elements in turn are conscious of the workings of Love and Strife. Finally, the four elements—fire, air, earth, and water—are aware of one another, both pure and in their various mixtures, and thus humans have consciousness, if only on a lower level, as well. Everything in the world constantly gives off emanations into the atmosphere, consisting of the particles of which they are made. As these particles pass through the air, humans absorb them (through their pores), transmitting them through the body by the blood.

In addition, the four elements and their combinations are aware of themselves; for example, the water in the air is conscious of the water in a human body. A particle that enters the human body is eventually transported to the heart, which is a particularly sensitive organ: It is closely associated with the creation and perception of human thought. The blood is the prime medium for this transfer, because it contains equal proportions of the four elements. The operation of the senses also is based on the awareness of the elements: The particles in the air are perceived differently by the particles in the sense organs.

After Empedocles had completed *On Nature*, he apparently changed many of his beliefs—probably after he had studied among the Pythagoreans. Especially attractive was the Pythagorean doctrine concerning the transmigration of the soul. Earlier, Empedocles seems to have thought that the human, having been formed from the four elements, died, both body and soul. In *Purifications*, however, Empedocles seems to have adopted the Pythagorean idea that an individual's soul survives physically, going through a series of incarnations. Each soul has to pass through a cycle somewhat like the cosmic cycle of Love and Strife.

Sinfulness, as conceived in Christian thought, was not a factor in the Greek world. Nevertheless, *Purifications* reflects a concept of sin and atonement. The most likely source for such an abstraction would be the Buddhist Middle East, and Empedocles was probably aware of certain Buddhist doctrines.

Empedocles linked his cycle of incarnations with the concept of sin. The soul is initially in a state of sinlessness when it enters the world. In this stage, it is pure mind—a beatific state. As it resides in the world, the soul becomes tainted, especially by the sin of shedding the blood of humans or animals. The sinful soul is condemned to undergo a series of physical incarnations for thirty thousand years (an indeterminate period of time; Empedocles never defined the length of a season). The soul is incarnated in bodily forms that are in turn derived from air (such as a cloud), water, earth, and fire. Empedocles recounted some of his own incarnations: He was a boy; in another life he was a girl; he was also a bird, a bush, and a fish at various times. Each successive incarnation allows the sincere soul an opportunity to better itself. Declaring that he had progressed to the company of

Empedocles. (Library of Congress)

such people as doctors, prophets, and princes, Empedocles hoped to be reborn among the gods.

One interesting facet of Empedocles' greatness is his pioneering work in the field of biology. Implicit in his observations on anatomy is the assumption that he conducted experiments on the bodies of animals and humans. He conjectured that blood circulates throughout the body in a system powered by the heart, that respiration occurs through the pores of the skin, and that some of the organs of the human body are similar in function to the organs of animals. He also observed that the embryo is clearly human in form in the seventh week of pregnancy.

Most interesting of Empedocles' theories is his concept of evolution. In *On Nature*, he assumed that the first creatures were monstrosities, crudely formed; some of these were, by chance, better adapted to survive than others. As the millennia passed, certain mutations (Empedocles did not use the word) made some forms more efficient in basic matters, such as eating and digesting and adapting their anatomy to catch and kill prey. In the passage of time, the successful body forms became nearly perfectly adapted to living in a particular environment.

Despite the great differences in the forms of various animals, Empedocles still saw unity in the whole of life. All organisms adapted safeguards against predation; all reproduced and took in sustenance; and all had a particular consciousness—they rejoiced in the act of living and grieved at physical death.

Empedocles seems to have been many-faceted. According to contemporary accounts, his wardrobe was idiosyncratic, and some of his actions were bizarre. In his own works, and according to other testimony, he claimed to be a god. This claim seems to have gained credence: He boasted that crowds of people followed him, entreating him to use his magical healing powers. He claimed to be able to resurrect the dead as well as to have some control over the weather.

Several versions of Empedocles' death have survived: He hanged himself; he fell and broke his thigh; he fell from a ship and was drowned. From the second century B.C.E., one version superseded all others: He disappeared in a brilliant light when a voice called his name. The best-known version, however, is that made famous by Matthew Arnold in his poem *Empedocles on Etna* (1852), in which Empedocles jumped into the crater of the volcano, apparently to prove that he was immortal.

SIGNIFICANCE

In many ways, Empedocles influenced medieval and Renaissance conceptions of science and anticipated modern theories. For example, despite some criticism, Plato and Aristotle adopted his biological theories; his conception of the four elements, probably derived from the work of Hippocrates, thus had influence until the scientific revolution in the seventeenth century. Finally, his ideas on human and animal evolution foreshadow modern theories, and his conception of a universe in which elements maintained a constant though ever-changing presence presages the law of the conservation of energy.

His accomplishments were honored by his contemporaries, and his memory was revered. Aristotle called him the father of rhetoric, and Galen considered him the founder of the medical arts. According to Lucretius, Empedocles was a master poet, and the extant fragments of his works support this claim. His main contribution was philosophical, however, and his two works were an important influence on early Greek philosophy.

—*Richard Badessa*

FURTHER READING

Empedocles. *Empedocles: The Extant Fragments*. Edited by M. R. Wright. Indianapolis, Ind.: Hackett, 1995. This modern critical work includes the Greek text of Empedocles' works, a translation, an introduction, a concordance, a bibliography, and a closely written and copious set of notes.

Kirk, Geoffrey S., and John E. Raven. *The Presocratic Philosophers*. 2d ed. New York: Cambridge University Press, 1983. Much of the material on pre-Socratic philosophers is subject to interpretation; this book presents both sides of dozens of equivocal topics. It has a useful chapter on Empedocles.

Lambridis, Helle. *Empedocles: A Philosophical Investigation*. University: University of Alabama Press, 1976. This book begins with a preface by Marshall McLuhan, titled "Empedocles and T. S. Eliot." The book itself serves two useful purposes: It is a good and comprehensive survey, and it is the best analysis of the poetry of Empedocles. Both modern and ancient Greek criteria are brought to bear on the poetry.

Millerd, Clara E. *On the Interpretation of Empedocles*. Chicago: University of Chicago Press, 1908. Reprint. New York: Garland, 1980. This important study discusses a number of topics concerning the intellectual background and development of Empedocles' ideas. The discussions are well written and knowledgeable. Though by no means obsolete, the book is somewhat dated.

O'Brien, D. *Empedocles' Cosmic Cycle*. London: Cambridge University Press, 1969. The most comprehensive and scholarly discussion of Empedocles' *On Nature*. Contains a useful section of notes, following the text, in which relatively minor but interesting topics are discussed. Its exhaustive annotated bibliography is as valuable in itself as is the text.

SEE ALSO: Parmenides; Pythagoras.

RELATED ARTICLES in *Great Events from History: The Ancient World*: 600-500 B.C.E., Greek Philosophers Formulate Theories of the Cosmos; c. 530 B.C.E., Founding of the Pythagorean Brotherhood; c. 500-400 B.C.E., Greek Physicians Begin Scientific Practice of Medicine.

ENHEDUANNA
Akkadian poet

Poetry by Enheduanna to the moon god, Nanna, and the goddess Inanna is among the earliest poetry in existence and is the earliest body of poetry composed by a woman.

BORN: c. 2320 B.C.E.; Akkad, Mesopotamia (now in Iraq)

DIED: c. 2250 B.C.E.; Akkad?, Mesopotamia

ALSO KNOWN AS: Enkheduanna; Heduanna

AREAS OF ACHIEVEMENT: Literature, religion

EARLY LIFE

Aside from what sparse biographical information is gleaned from her 153-line hymn to Nanna and a few other resources, little detailed information exists about the life of Enheduanna (ehn-hee-dew-AHN-ah). It has been verified that she was the daughter of Sargon, founder of the Akkad Dynasty that flourished under his leadership from 2334 B.C.E. to 2279 B.C.E. Sargon, also known as Sharrukin, a longtime king of Akkad in Mesopotamia, lived to a considerable age. Toward the end of his reign, the jurisdictions under his rule revolted against him and besieged him in Akkad. Sargon, however, despite his years, withstood the siege and defeated the rebels. His victory was attributed to the mystical intervention of Nanna and Inanna.

It became customary in Mesopotamia around this time for affluent families to send one daughter into a cloister as a high priestess (*entum*) to pray for her family's welfare. These young women were awarded generous dowries that might include livestock, a house, land, household slaves, and other valuables. Enheduanna, the first such *entum*-priestess, was appointed to her post by her father, the king, to add legitimacy to his rule by demonstrating his family's submission to and reverence for the gods.

King Sargon was the first monarch to appoint a daughter to serve as high priestess to the moon god, Nanna. Following this appointment, a succession of royal princesses served as priestesses to Nanna over the next one thousand years, a custom that did not end until the reign of Nabonidus, the last king of Babylonia. Enheduanna was relatively young when she became a priestess. Her early years were presumably cloistered, as were her later ones, and were filled with prayer and with producing an impressive body of poetry and an extensive number of hymns.

Two seals uncovered by archaeologists mention her name. These seals are designed in a typical classical Akkadian style and bear marked similarities to seals that have been attributed to the early Akkadian period, close to the beginning of Sargon's reign. Archaeologist Rainer Michael Boehmer, however, on inspecting these seals, considered it impossible to place them chronologically as early as the other seals dating to Sargon's early kingship. He finds it more likely that Enheduanna's seals are products of a later period within her father's reign.

One long poem by Enheduanna to Inanna, preserved in cuneiform on clay tablets, has been translated and is among the oldest pieces of literature in existence anywhere in the world. Although the dates of Enheduanna's birth and death can only be conjectured, she is thought to have been born in Akkad some fifty miles north of Baghdad in what is today Iraq. None of the sources currently available to scholars provides any information about her mother or her siblings. It is thought that she was high priestess for at least twenty-five years during her father's reign. She outlived her father and continued as high priestess for many years after he died in 2279 B.C.E.

LIFE'S WORK

The position as high priestess was a choice one, as was the position of scribe, to which Enheduanna's father also appointed his daughter. Scribes, who were usually men, were among the best-remunerated people in the kingdom. Because of the complexity of making cuneiform impressions on clay tablets, their work was highly specialized. Women who served as high priestesses sometimes were married but more frequently, like Enheduanna, were unmarried and celibate. Like Enheduanna, most of them were cloistered.

Generally, ancient cuneiform literature has been viewed as anonymous, but such was not the case with Sumerian and Akkadian cuneiform works, which have colophons much like the title pages of modern books. Although these colophons do not contain authors' names, separate lists of such names exist, connecting these names either with those of the kings they served, which helps to date their work, or with works generally attributed to them, although these attributions are frequently undependable. Some cuneiform works divulge the names of their authors within their texts, as is the case in Enheduanna's hymn to Inanna.

Fortunately, three kinds of sources—archaeological, historical, and literary—serve to document Enheduanna's remarkable career. The aforementioned seals are among the archaeological sources that have been carefully examined. A realistic depiction of Enheduanna was found on a limestone disc from Ur. Inscriptions from Ur reviewed by two eminent archaeological scholars, Ignace J. Gelb and H. Hirsch, confirm that Enheduanna was the daughter of Sargon, the king, and served as the high priestess of Nanna of Ur, the moon god.

Actually, Enheduanna's original name was Heduanna. The *en-* that precedes this name is an honorific term of reverence and indicates her position as high priestess. All the extant writing attributed to her was produced under her later name, indicating that she began her writing career after she was appointed high priestess.

Enheduanna is the first among a long procession of royalty who held the office of high priestess in Akkad and other Near East venues throughout the next millennium. It is known that Enheduanna continued to function in her position after her father died but that toward the end of his reign, when revolts against him shook his kingdom, she was forced out of office for a time. She resumed her services as high priestess during the reign of her nephew, Naram-Sin. Typically, high priestesses served for considerable lengths of time, their tenures generally assumed to be for life. Presumably Enheduanna occupied her position throughout most of her lifetime up until her death, save for the period when she was forced out of office.

A record of her difficulties when her father's subjects attempted to overturn his rule is found in her hymn "The Indictment of Nanna," in which she relates in some detail how she was forced from her position toward the end of her father's reign. She escaped to Ur but seemingly returned to her cloister and to her writing shortly after Sargon died in 2279 B.C.E.

Everything would point to her ending her days there, although no existing account assigns a definite date of death to her or recounts the final days of her life. It is altogether possible that she lived to be nearly seventy, perhaps even older.

Enheduanna's writing style was sufficiently distinctive that an existing cycle of hymns to the temples of Sumer and Akkad seem clearly to be from her hand. The colophon of this significant theological piece from Mesopotamia suggests that she was its author. A poem titled "In-min-me-hus-a" ("The Myth of Inanna and Ebih"), while not specifically identified as having been written by Enheduanna, is in her style and was likely written by her.

This poem deals with the revolt of Jebel Hamrin against Enheduanna's nephew, Naram-Sin, under whose reign Enheduanna was restored to her post as high priestess. In this poem, in which Enheduanna slips into the first person singular at one point, the writer points to Inanna's omnipotence and unyielding control over all aspects of human existence.

The 153-line hymn to Inanna is probably the product of Enheduanna's more mature years, possibly of her old age. Much of what is revealed in it shows an acquaintance with the revolts of the people against Sargon and later against Naram-Sin as recorded in hymns whose authorship has not conclusively been identified, but whose style, subject matter, and subtlety of expression resemble writing known to be by Enheduanna.

If the early hymns were, as seems likely, composed by Enheduanna, they reveal an author steeped in the traditional theological thinking of the times. As her writing continued, however, Enheduanna changed her views of the traditional theological tenets of her era in subtle ways. In the hymns to Inanna, the author's voice is impassioned, losing some of the detached objectivity found in the earlier works. She presents the goddess in ways that allow audiences of common people to relate to her, thereby humanizing considerably the thrust of her writing and of her theological position. One might conclude from reading the hymns to Inanna that Enheduanna had mellowed in her later years. She appeared surely to be moving away from a lockstep theology to one that could bend to accommodate the common people of Sumer and Akkad.

SIGNIFICANCE

Among the significant aspects of Enheduanna's life is that she, with the help of her father, established the convention of having influential families consign one daughter to be a high priestess and to pray for the family's welfare. This practice continued in parts of the Near East for the next thousand years. It later served as a model for cloistered Christian nuns. The *Ancrene Wisse* (early thirteenth century), an important medieval document composed in Britain that currently exists in nine manuscripts written variously in English, Latin, and French, outlines what the life of an anchoress should be, and many of its mandates are remarkably similar to the Sumerian and Akkadian conceptions of how a high priestess would conduct her life.

Also of great significance is the poetic writing of Enheduanna, which for centuries provided models for aspiring writers. Throughout the millennium following her life, Enheduanna's writing was copied by those in training to be scribes. That Enheduanna served as a scribe is worth noting because she was among the first women throughout history to break into a profession that traditionally had been an all-male stronghold.

Enheduanna was a bright, powerful woman blessed with a remarkable gift for writing. Years after her death she was still venerated, almost deified, in writings that omit the *en-* honorific from her name. Spending most of her life cloistered allowed her time to think deeply and to write. She stands today among the earliest of feminists, demonstrating her feminist activism in her poem "The Indictment of Nanna."

—*R. Baird Shuman*

FURTHER READING

Hallo, William W., and J. J. A. Van Dijk. *The Exaltation of Inanna*. New Haven, Conn.: Yale University Press, 1968. This translation and scholarly consideration of Enheduanna's hymn to Inanna is thorough and helpful, although not for the beginner. Its biographical presentation of Enheduanna is the most extensive in print, although it is sparse. The literary analyses of Enheduanna's writing offer keen insights.

Postgate, J. N. *Early Mesopotamia: Society and Economy at the Dawn of History*. New York: Routledge, 1992. Provides a socioeconomic backdrop that helps readers understand the society of Enheduanna and her father, King Sargon. Part 3, "The Written Record," and Part 14, "Religion and Politics," are especially relevant for students of Enheduanna's work.

Toorn, Karel van der. *From Her Cradle to Her Grave: The Role of Religion in the Life of the Israelite and the Babylonian Woman*. Sheffield, England: JSOT Press, 1994. Toorn provides a context for understanding the religious context of Enheduanna's era. The comparisons between Israelite and Babylonian women present sharp contrasts between the groups.

Vivante, Bella, ed. *Women's Roles in Ancient Civilizations: A Reference Guide*. Westport, Conn.: Greenwood Press, 1999. The relevant chapters in this collection are those by Karen Rhea Nemet-Nejat, "Women in Ancient Mesopotamia," and Mayer I. Gruber, "Women in the Ancient Levant," both of which provide more biographical information about Enheduanna than most available sources. One might question some of the dates ascribed to Enheduanna and her work, but overall the assessments are clear and useful. A sensible starting point for nonexperts.

Wolkstein, Diane, and Samuel Noah Kramer. *Inanna: Queen of Heaven and Earth*. New York: Harper and Row, 1983. This volume includes a selective compilation of Sumerian poetry written about Inanna, including some by Enheduanna. A helpful background resource for increasing one's understanding of the role that Inanna played in Sumerian/Akkadian literature and religion.

QUINTUS ENNIUS
Roman poet

Known as the father of Latin poetry, Ennius extended the Latin language into areas previously reserved for Greek, offering explanations for Roman origins. He thus paved the way for the Golden Age of Latin poetry and influenced poets ranging from Lucretius to Vergil.

BORN: 239 B.C.E.; Rudiae, Calabria (now in Italy)
DIED: 169 B.C.E.?; Rome (now in Italy)
AREA OF ACHIEVEMENT: Literature

EARLY LIFE

Not much is known concerning the early life of Quintus Ennius (EHN-ih-uhs) aside from the material he included in his own works. Because of the popularity of his writings, it is likely that this information is accurate: His contemporaries could easily have contradicted him. It is clear that Ennius was born in Calabria and that his circumstances were humble. His origins were a point of personal pride that he would conscientiously maintain throughout his life. Even when established at Rome as a teacher and recognized poet, Ennius lived with somewhat awkward simplicity in the wealthy surroundings of the Aventine and employed but a single servant.

Ennius began his career as a soldier rather than as a poet and served with distinction during the Second Punic War. It was, paradoxically, his military talent rather than his skill in writing verse that first brought him to the attention of Cato the Censor, whose surname and hatred for Carthage made him a symbol of stern discipline and morality, even in his own time. It was during these years, while stationed in Sardinia, that Cato, then serving as military quaestor (a post with many of the same duties as quartermaster), tutored Ennius, his centurion, in Greek. Cato introduced Ennius to Scipio Africanus and Fulvius Nobilior; these men would further Ennius's interests after he went to Rome. Ennius subsequently served on Fulvius's staff during the Anatolian campaign, and in 184 B.C.E. Fulvius's son, with the approval of the Roman people, awarded Ennius a lot among the *triumviri coloniae deducendae*. This award constituted a grant of citizenship, though it brought him no personal wealth. Scipio, too, remained friends with his junior officer, and (at least according to tradition) asked that a bust of Ennius be placed next to his tomb.

Copies of this bust from the tomb of the Scipios may surprise the person who imagines Ennius as an old Roman ascetic. If this bust is, indeed, of Ennius (and some would disagree), he was full-faced, with an aquiline nose, thick lips, and generally provincial features. His hair is close-cropped in the republican mode but with straight locks rather than the "crab-claw," curled ones found in Imperial sculpture. He wears the expected laurel wreath, but, again unlike Imperial sculpture, the artist has made no attempt to idealize his subject. One should contrast this frank rendering of Ennius with the sensitive, idealized (also suspect) sculptures of his successor Vergil. These are products of Augustan Rome and present Vergil as an idealized poet of an idealized city.

LIFE'S WORK

At first, Ennius supported himself in Rome after his military service by teaching, armed with impressive recommendations from Cato, Scipio, and Fulvius; these were essential to attract good students, and Ennius, no doubt, attracted the best. Even so, Ennius must always have had intentions of making his mark in literature, and he wrote from his first arrival in the city.

Circumstances favored his efforts. The dramatist Livius Andronicus died in 204, and his colleague Gnaeus Naevius retired soon after, thus leaving a place to be filled. Ennius began writing dramas, all penned c. 204-169 B.C.E., primarily on mythic themes related to the Trojan War: *Achilles, Aiax* (*Ajax*, 1935), *Andromacha* (*Andromache*, 1935), *Hectoris lytra* (*The Ransom of Hector*, 1935), and *Hecuba*. He seems also to have chosen mythic subjects that would allow one to draw moral lessons on the folly of excess and pride: *Alexander, Andromeda, Athamas, Erechtheus, Eumenides, Iphigenia, Medea*, and *Thyestes*. Clearly, the Trojan War plays would have been very popular among republican audiences. Rome wistfully traced its uncertain origins to an amalgam of Trojan, Latin, and native Italic stock and consequently saw its history in its myth. Similarly, moralizing was popular in republican Rome; at least, high moral standards were officially privileged. The second group of subjects provided fertile ground for this. Unfortunately, these works (indeed, all of Ennius's writings) survive only as fragments quoted by subsequent authors. Even order of composition and dates of first performances are uncertain.

What is clear is that Ennius became popular quickly after 204 and that he was versatile. Though he continued to write drama throughout his life, he is best known as an analyst historian, that is, one who chronicled Roman history by using the *Annales Maximi*, official lists of significant events recorded year by year from the traditional date of Rome's founding, 753. His own now-fragmentary *Annales* (204-169 B.C.E.; *Annals*, 1935) was originally written in eighteen books of verse and spanned Roman history from the legendary period of Aeneas's arrival in Italy to Ennius's own day. This work was begun sometime after his success as a playwright and occupied him throughout his middle years until his death.

Its eighteen books were originally circulated in groups of three and almost immediately became a part of the school curriculum. In part, they satisfied a need for material on Rome's past. They also were elegantly written style models and were patriotic in tone. If the content of the lost sections can be judged from extant passages such as the "Dream of Ilia" (the daughter of Aeneas) and the "Auspices of Romulus and Remus," each about ten lines, the *Annals* must have struck a responsive note in the hearts of patriotic Romans. In fact, Ennius's patriotic themes, combined with his sophisticated use of the Latin language, not only made his works subject matter studied by Roman youth but also won for him the title "father of Latin poetry." His simple manner of living, even amid the luxury of the Aventine, served to support the popularly held notion of his personal ethos and integrity.

Widespread early acceptance of his works likely encouraged Ennius to write at least one *praetexta* (a historical drama played in Roman dress), known as *Sabinae*, on the rape of the Sabine women, and perhaps another, the *Ambracia*, in praise of Fulvius, though the authorship of these works is open to question. If Ennius did indeed write *praetextae*, he would then have been trying his hand at a form to that time associated with Andronicus and Naevius. Only a few lines of these *praetextae* remain, not enough to establish his certain authorship.

Ennius's prolific writing, accomplished in his comfortable but simple quarters in Rome, kept him for the most part out of the public arena even as it made him a popular literary figure. He never possessed great wealth, though his old Roman simplicity did not prevent his living well. Personal references in his works note his longtime suffering with gout. Unfortunately for those interested in his private life during these middle years, such mundane asides in his works are rare. It is clear, however, that he was struggling at this time, with varying degrees of success, to fashion Latin epic and dramatic meters that could worthily mirror their Greek antecedents. This struggle to make the Latin tongue literary sums up the contradictory impulses of Ennius himself: distrustful of Greeks and all non-Romans, yet an admirer of Greek literature and art, in this sense a grecophile; an innovator in his use of the Latin language, yet one who consistently portrayed himself as an upholder of Roman tradition.

Despite his incontestable patriotism, Ennius was fond of saying that he "possessed three hearts" (that he could speak three languages—Greek, Latin, and Oscan—and was at home in each culture). He saw no particular difficulty in maintaining both his cosmopolitanism and his staunch Roman loyalties. Indeed, Roman audiences took pleasure in his Latin adaptations of the Greek dramatists, and his *Annals* made him the "Roman Homer."

Recognition and success in drama and historical epic allowed Ennius to devote considerable energy in the last third of his life to his *Saturae* (204-169 B.C.E.; *Miscellanies*, 1935). This work is a collection of miscellaneous poems in various meters on everything from Pythagorean philosophy (specifically that of Epicharmus) and the Pythagorean mythology of Euhemerus to gastronomy and assorted personal reflections. It is in this work and in Ennius's epigrams that personal content is greatest, though both *Miscellanies* and the epigrams are fragmentary. What personal information survives concerns Ennius's early life.

SIGNIFICANCE

One of the best known of Quintus Ennius's epigrams is a panegyric to the Roman military hero Scipio Africanus. Scipio is precisely the kind of personality Ennius would favor, and in a sense he sums up Ennius's ideas of well-lived Roman life. Ennius, too, made his mark in military affairs, but he made an easy transition to the literary world and used his considerable skills to write sophisticated Latin verse. Though he used Greek models, particularly for his plays, and prided himself on his sophistication, he nevertheless fashioned poetry appropriate to the high morality and ethical standards of the Roman Republic.

Ennius is most associated with Roman history, though *Annals* is actually a historical epic that inspired subsequent Roman poets as diverse as Lucretius (author of the philosophical epic *De rerum natura*, c. 60 B.C.E., *On the Nature of Things*, 1682) and Vergil, whose *Aeneid* (c. 29-19 B.C.E.; English translation, 1553) often quotes, modifies, and improves on Ennian verse.

In the second century B.C.E., the critic Volcacius Sedigitus drew up a list of the ten best poets up to that time. He included Ennius and supposedly did so only because of his antiquity. This action indicates that Ennius was not considered the equal of his fellows in drama. His greatest contribution to Latin literature, recognized in his own times as well, is his historicizing of Roman myth in the *Annals*. The Roman historian Suetonius called

Ennius "semi-Graecus," because origins and long residence in southern Italy had made Ennius culturally a Hellenized Roman. In spirit, however, as well as in his verse, Ennius could not have been more Roman, even if he had been born within the walls of the city.

—*Robert J. Forman*

FURTHER READING

Beare, W. *The Roman Stage: A Short History of Latin Drama in the Time of the Republic*. 3d ed. London: Methuen, 1965. This is a scholarly history of the development of Roman drama with chapters on playwrights and the various genres of dramatic poetry. It discusses Ennius as successor of Livius Andronicus and Naevius and considers the mechanics of drama production as well.

Duff, J. Wight, and A. M. Duff. *A Literary History of Rome in the Silver Age: From Tiberius to Hadrian*. 3d ed. Westport, Conn.: Greenwood Press, 1979. Chapter 3 discusses at some length Livius Andronicus, Naevius, and Ennius, and chapter 5 considers Roman tragedy after Ennius, with emphasis on Pacuvius, Accius, and the *praetextae*. Analysis of the fragments appears as well as what is known about the lives of the playwrights.

Hose, Martin. "Post-colonial Theory and Greek Literature in Rome." *Greek, Roman and Byzantine Studies* 40, no. 4 (Winter, 1999): 303-326. Hose addresses the consequences of a defeat of the Romans over Alexander for the history of literature; he discusses the *Annals*, Ennius, and Ennius's presentation of Roman history.

Skutsch, Otto. *Studia Enniana*. London: Athlone Press, 1968. This is a collection, in quite readable English, of previously published articles on all areas of Ennian studies. All were written by Skutsch, and those on the *Annals* are excellent.

Warmington, E. H., trans. *Remains of Old Latin*. Vol. 1. Cambridge, Mass.: Harvard University Press, 1979. This volume, one of four in this set on the earliest Latin writers, contains all the extant Ennian fragments in its first half with English and Latin texts on facing pages.

SEE ALSO: Cato the Censor; Catullus; Cicero; Dio Cassius; Homer; Horace; Livy; Lucretius; Martial; Ovid; Plautus; Scipio Africanus; Sulpicia; Vergil.

RELATED ARTICLES in *Great Events from History: The Ancient World*: 218-201 B.C.E., Second Punic War; 54 B.C.E., Roman Poet Catullus Dies; 19 B.C.E., Roman Poet Vergil Dies; November 27, 8 B.C.E., Roman Lyric Poet Horace Dies; 8 C.E., Ovid's *Metamorphoses* Is Published; 100-127 C.E., Roman Juvenal Composes *Satires*; 159 B.C.E., Roman Playwright Terence Dies.

EPAMINONDAS
Theban general

The greatest military tactician of the classical Greek period, Epaminondas broke the hegemony of Sparta and made Thebes the most powerful state in Greece.

BORN: c. 410 B.C.E.; Thebes, Greece
DIED: 362 B.C.E.; Mantinea, Greece
AREAS OF ACHIEVEMENT: Government and politics, war and conquest

EARLY LIFE

Little is known of the early life of Epaminondas (ee-PAM-ih-nahn-dahs). His father, Polymnis, was from a distinguished yet impoverished Theban family, and the relative poverty of his youth may explain the simple lifestyle for which Epaminondas was later famous. The young man displayed an intellectual bent and formed a close attachment to the Pythagorean philosopher Lysis of Tarentum, who served as his primary tutor. Another close friend was Pelopidas, with whom he would eventually share the leadership of Thebes. While the ancient writers' contrast between the rich, athletic, daring family man—Pelopidas—and the reflective, frugal bachelor—Epaminondas—is no doubt overdrawn, it may reflect something of their characters and relationship. If the story is true that the young Epaminondas saved the life of his wounded friend during battle in 385, then he was probably born about 410.

Epaminondas's city-state, the home of the legendary Cadmus and Oedipus, was the largest of the dozen or so towns in Boeotia, a district in central Greece whose inhabitants shared a distinct dialect and ethnic identity. Because its central location so often made Boeotia the arena for battles between the major Greek city-states, Epaminondas referred to his land as "the dancing floor of Ares." Although in the fifth century Thebes rose to considerable influence as head of a federation of Boeotian towns, the city remained a secondary power behind Athens and Sparta.

The Thebans sided with Sparta in the Peloponnesian War (431-404 B.C.E.), which destroyed the Athenian Empire and made Sparta supreme in Greece, but they were quickly disillusioned by Sparta's selfish settlement of the war. As Sparta aggressively exercised its hegemony and extended its area of control, Thebes led Athens and other resentful city-states against Sparta in the Corinthian War (395-386 B.C.E.). Sparta's superior military capabilities gave it the upper hand in the war, however, and an accommodation with Artaxerxes II of Persia allowed Sparta to force its opponents to accept the "King's Peace" on terms favorable to Sparta.

Thebes was the biggest victim of this settlement, which did not recognize the Boeotian confederacy. Thebans, among them the maturing Epaminondas, then had to watch as Sparta dismembered the federation and installed pro-Spartan oligarchies in the newly autonomous towns of Boeotia. The nadir of Theban fortunes came in 382, when a faction headed by Leontiades betrayed the city to a Spartan force. Backed by a Spartan garrison, Leontiades' pro-Spartan oligarchy ruled the city for three years, and many anti-Spartan Thebans, including Pelopidas, went into exile. Perhaps because he was not yet politically active, Epaminondas remained in Thebes without suffering harm.

LIFE'S WORK

When Pelopidas returned with other exiles in 379 to liberate the city, Epaminondas made his political debut in a decisive fashion. As the exiles entered the city at night to begin their revolt, Epaminondas came to their aid with a group of armed men whom he had recruited. The next day, he presented the exiles to the Theban assembly and rallied citizens to support the revolution. Following the liberation, the Thebans formed an alliance with Athens and, despite repeated Spartan invasions of Boeotia, gradually reconstituted the Boeotian federation on a democratic basis. By 373, citizens from practically all the Boeotian towns voted at Thebes in a common assembly and annually elected seven Boeotarchs who had wide powers as the primary administrative, diplomatic, and military officials of the confederacy. Epaminondas's role in these developments is not clear, but it is likely that he honed his military skills in various operations with the federal army. By 371, his reputation was such that he was elected Boeotarch, a position he subsequently would hold almost every year.

As a member of the Boeotian delegation to the peace conference at Sparta in 371, Epaminondas faced a dilemma. If he acquiesced in the Spartan refusal to recognize the Boeotian League and signed the treaty for Thebes alone, the newly reconstructed federation would crumble, and Sparta would again be able to dominate the individual towns of Boeotia. If, on the other hand, he refused to sign except as representing all Boeotia, he would place Thebes in a precarious position: A Spartan army was already poised on the frontier of Boeotia, and Athens had deserted Thebes in favor of reconciliation with Sparta. Apparently Epaminondas wavered and at first signed the peace treaty for Thebes alone. Before the conference ended, however, he spoke out strongly against Spartan arrogance and infuriated King Agesilaus II of Sparta by asserting that Thebes would dissolve its confederacy when Agesilaus made independent the many Laconian towns dominated by Sparta. Agesilaus immediately excluded Thebes from the peace agreement, and Epaminondas hastened home to prepare for the impending Spartan attack.

At Leuctra in July, 371, Epaminondas stunned the Greek world when he led a smaller Boeotian force to victory over the heretofore invincible Spartan army. By his innovative use of an unequally weighted battle line in an oblique attack, Epaminondas overwhelmed the strongest part of the enemy formation, and his troops killed four hundred Spartans, among them the junior king Cleombrotus. This victory made Epaminondas famous throughout Greece and encouraged a number of Sparta's southern allies to defect.

While some Boeotians were now content to consolidate the confederacy's position in central Greece, others, including Epaminondas, successfully argued for a more aggressive policy toward Sparta. Consequently, Boeotia joined in alliance with those southern city-states that had defected from the Spartan alliance after Leuctra, and in the winter of 370 Epaminondas took the federal army south to aid these states against Spartan retaliation. This campaign was to be a short one in defense of allies, but, on discovering the extent of Sparta's weakness, Epaminondas seized the opportunity to strike at Sparta itself.

When his fellow Boeotarchs objected that extending the campaign would be illegal, Epaminondas promised to take full responsibility and led the army in a daring invasion of Sparta's home district of Laconia. Although he did not dare assault the city itself, he secured the defection of many Laconian towns around Sparta and ravaged a rich land that had not seen an invader in centuries.

Epaminondas, standing, center. (F. R. Niglutsch)

Worst of all for the future of Sparta, Epaminondas liberated Messenia, the rich agricultural district west of Sparta, where the bulk of Sparta's huge slave population resided. He then organized the freed Messenians into an autonomous city-state and oversaw the construction of a marvelously fortified capital city. The freeing of Messenia impoverished Sparta and presented it with a hostile new neighbor.

By his victory at Leuctra and the invasion of Laconia, Epaminondas had broken Sparta's hold over Greece. He then undertook to establish the hegemony of Thebes in its place. Some Thebans opposed this effort, but his enormous prestige usually allowed Epaminondas to pursue his goals as he saw fit. When a political rival brought him to trial for his illegal extension of the campaign against Sparta, Epaminondas made no defense and agreed to accept the death penalty—provided his tombstone bear a list of his accomplishments, which he proudly enumerated. On hearing this, the judges laughed the case out of court, and Pelopidas soon obtained the banishment of Epaminondas's accuser.

The two friends shared the conduct of Boeotian foreign policy. While Pelopidas secured the northern frontier with his operations in Thessaly, Epaminondas devoted his attentions to the southern alliance. Twice he led invasions designed to force further defections from the Spartan league and strengthen the band of allies that hemmed in Sparta. One notable success of the second invasion was the founding of Megalópolis, a great fortified city in Arcadia that permanently blocked Spartan access to Messenia.

Epaminondas's efforts reached their peak of success in 365, when Sparta's most powerful traditional ally, Corinth, along with several of its neighbors, made peace with Thebes on terms that recognized the autonomy of Messenia. Athens and Sparta refused to accept Theban ascendancy, but the Persian king looked on Thebes as the preeminent state of Greece and subsidized the construction of a Boeotian fleet with which Epaminondas hoped to disrupt Athens's revived naval league.

Within a year, however, the Theban position began to deteriorate. To be sure, Epaminondas was given warm receptions by three of Athens's most important naval allies when he sailed with the new Boeotian fleet in 364. His expedition failed to defeat the Athenian naval league, however, and the Persians suspended their subsidy of the Boeotian fleet, which never sailed again. On returning home, Epaminondas learned that Pelopidas had met his death in battle in Thessaly. He also discovered that in his absence the Thebans had destroyed the Boeotian town of Orchomenus. Provoked by an oligarchic conspiracy and fed by an ancient rivalry, this act of vengeance engendered suspicion and criticism from abroad. Worst of all, Epaminondas had to reckon with serious dissension among his southern allies. Resentful of Theban preeminence, the Arcadians had formed an alliance with Athens and now waged a territorial war that led Elis, the westernmost member of the anti-Spartan alliance, to renew its tie with Sparta. Complicating matters further, Arcadian democrats struggled against the resurgent Arcadian oligarchs of Mantinea, who also reestablished links with Sparta.

To prevent the complete collapse of his anti-Spartan coalition, in June of 362 Epaminondas undertook his fourth invasion of southern Greece. Aware that the combined might of his opponents would be formidable, he sought to confront and destroy them one by one, before they could unite. Unfortunately, misinformation led him to abandon the ambush he had set for the Athenians near Corinth, and the treachery of a deserter prevented him from taking Sparta unguarded. Consequently, near Mantinea Epaminondas drew up his force for a conflict that would involve contingents from every major Greek city-state. Against the combined forces of Sparta, Athens, Mantinea, and their allies, he employed the same tactics that had brought him victory at Leuctra but on a far grander scale in this battle, which involved nearly fifty thousand men. Catching his enemy off guard, Epaminondas opened the battle with an effective attack of his excellent cavalry and then crushed the Spartan formation with an oblique strike by his massively overbalanced left wing.

Tragically, as his troops stood poised to pursue the broken enemy and complete a brilliant victory, Epaminondas himself fell, mortally wounded. At the news of their leader's fall, the stunned Boeotians immediately abandoned the fight and allowed the beaten enemy to escape. When he was informed of the seriousness of his wound, Epaminondas reportedly advised the Thebans to make a speedy peace. The loss of Epaminondas completely nullified any gains that this well-fought battle brought and marked the end of the Theban ascendancy.

SIGNIFICANCE

A brave and resourceful general, Epaminondas was without question the outstanding tactician of the Greek classical period. His masterful use of cavalry and his oblique, unbalanced battle formation won for him two great victories and transformed the Greek art of war. He successfully employed his military skills to break the oppressive hegemony of Sparta and to make Thebes the most powerful state in Greece. The victory at Leuctra, the liberation of Messenia, and the foundation of Megalópolis ensured that Sparta would never again dominate Greece.

To his credit, Epaminondas did not imitate the earlier imperial practices of Athens and Sparta: He respected the autonomy of his allies and refused to impose garrisons or levy tribute. Unfortunately, his attempt to rule Greece could not succeed without some institutional means of expressing consensus and resolving disputes among the many autonomous Greek city-states. A formal league headed by Thebes could have been a viable vehicle, but Epaminondas's simple anti-Spartan alliance inevitably required repeated armed interventions of the kind that led to the conflict at Mantinea. If he failed to envision a new political order for Greece, his achievements were nevertheless substantial. They are well expressed in the funeral verses that the Thebans inscribed on his statue:

> This came from my counsel:
> Sparta has cut the hair of her glory:
> Messene takes her children in:
> a wreath of the spears of Thebes
> has crowned Megalopolis:
> Greece is free.

—James T. Chambers

FURTHER READING

Adcock, Frank E. *The Greek and Macedonian Art of War.* Berkeley: University of California Press, 1962. This short volume provides an excellent brief introduction to Greek warfare, with appropriate references to Epaminondas.

Anderson, John K. *Military Theory and Practice in the Age of Xenophon.* Berkeley: University of California Press, 1970. This work provides a thorough analysis of military developments during Epaminondas's time. It includes plates and battle diagrams. See especially chapter 10 on the Battle of Leuctra, with a diagram and discussion of the sources.

Boardman, John, et al., eds. *The Cambridge Ancient History.* New York: Cambridge University Press, 2000.

Chapters 2 through 4 of volume 6 provide a detailed treatment of Spartan, Athenian, and Theban developments during Epaminondas's time.

Buckler, John. *The Theban Hegemony, 371-362 B.C.* Cambridge, Mass.: Harvard University Press, 1980. This thorough work is the starting point for serious study of Epaminondas's career. It provides excellent analysis of the political and constitutional questions and full treatment of the diplomatic and military developments. Includes an evaluation of the sources for Boeotian history in this period and a full bibliography of modern works.

Pausanias. *Guide to Greece.* Translated by Peter Levi. 2 vols. New York: Penguin, 1979. In book 9 this first century traveler preserves valuable details of Epaminondas's life, probably largely derived from Plutarch's lost biography.

Plutarch. "Pelopidas." In *Plutarch's Lives,* translated by Bernadotte Perrin. Cambridge, Mass.: Harvard University Press, 1982-1990. This brief (fifty-page) biography describes the friendship of Pelopidas and Epaminondas and provides important details of Epaminondas's early life and his role in the liberation of Thebes, as well as a description of the Battle of Leuctra.

Xenophon. *A History of My Times.* Translated by Rex Warner. New York: Penguin Books, 1978. In this work, the Athenian soldier-historian provides a contemporary narrative of Epaminondas's life, the only such account to survive complete. Xenophon participated in many of the events he describes and provides many revealing details. Unfortunately, he is biased in favor of Sparta and suppresses many of Epaminondas's accomplishments. Note especially the descriptions of the Battles of Leuctra and Mantinea.

SEE ALSO: Agesilaus II of Sparta; Pausanias the Traveler.

RELATED ARTICLES in *Great Events from History: The Ancient World*: c. 700-330 B.C.E., Phalanx Is Developed as a Military Unit; c. 550 B.C.E., Construction of Trireme Changes Naval Warfare; 480-479 B.C.E., Persian Invasion of Greece; 478-448 B.C.E., Athenian Empire Is Created; May, 431-September, 404 B.C.E., Peloponnesian War; 386 B.C.E., King's Peace Ends Corinthian War.

EPICURUS
Greek philosopher

Epicurus founded The Garden, a school of Greek philosophy, which has had a significant influence on Western philosophers, statesmen, and literary figures.

BORN: 341 B.C.E.; Island of Samos, Greece
DIED: 270 B.C.E.; Athens, Greece
AREA OF ACHIEVEMENT: Philosophy

EARLY LIFE
Epicurus (ehp-ih-KYUR-uhs) was born on the Greek island of Samos, about two miles off the coast of Turkey. His father, Neocles, was an immigrant from an old Athenian family who had moved to the distant island for economic reasons and who made his living as an elementary school teacher. Epicurus was forever disadvantaged in the eyes of the men of Athens because of his rustic birth and the low social status of his father's occupation. To make matters worse, his mother was reputedly a fortune-teller. His experiences as her apprentice might well account for Epicurus's later criticism of all kinds of superstitions and even for his controversial renunciation of the ancient Greek myths and stories.

Epicurus shared a happy family life with his parents and three brothers, Neocles, Chaeredemus, and Aristobulus, who would eventually become his disciples. It is recorded by Diogenes Laertius that he began to study philosophy at the age of fourteen, because he was unsatisfied with his schoolmasters' explanations of the meaning of "chaos" in Hesiod. Others contend that he was drawn to philosophy by the works of Democritus, echoes of which can be seen in Epicurus's later writings.

At eighteen, Epicurus served his two years of compulsory military duty in Athens, at an exciting time when both Xenocrates and Aristotle were lecturing. He clearly familiarized himself with the works of Aristippus, Socrates, and Pyrrhon of Elis. He served in the garrison with the future playwright Menander, with whom he established a close friendship. Many critics believe that they see the impress of Epicurus's ideas on Menander's later plays.

After his military service, Epicurus rejoined his family, who, with other Athenian colonists, had been expelled from Samos by a dictator and had subsequently moved to Colophon. Not much is known of the ten years that Epicurus spent at Colophon, but it might be surmised that he spent much of his time in study and contemplation, perhaps even visiting the intellectual center of Rhodes. At around the age of thirty he moved to Mytilene, on the island of Lesbos, to become a teacher. As he developed his own philosophy, he came into conflict with the numerous followers of Plato and Aristotle on that island, and after only a short stay, he left. He took with him, however, Hermarchus, a man who would become a lifetime friend and, perhaps more important, after Epicurus's death, the head of his Athenian school.

Hermarchus and Epicurus moved to Lampsacus on the Hellespont for the fertile years between 310 and 306 B.C.E. At Lampsacus, Epicurus gathered around him the devoted disciples and the influential patrons who would make it possible for him, at the age of thirty-five, to move to Athens and begin the major stage of his career. They presented to him the house and the garden in the outskirts of Athens that would be both his school and his home for the rest of his life.

LIFE'S WORK

Once established in Athens, Epicurus founded his school, called The Garden, after the practice of the resident members, who, in almost monastic fashion, provided for their own food by gardening. The many statues, statuettes, and engraved gems that bear the image of Epicurus's long, narrow, intelligent face, with its furrowed brows and full beard, attest the devotion of his followers and the unusually enduring influence of his ideas.

Epicurus organized his Garden school in a strict hierarchical system, at the apex of which stood only himself: The Master. One of the common slogans of the school was "Do all things as if Epicurus were looking at you." While this motto may sound dictatorial, it represented a benevolent tyranny to which all the disciples and students of Epicurus happily adhered, and it no doubt accounts for the consistently accurate promotion of his philosophical ideas, even after his death.

Three men—Metrodorus, Hermarchus, and Plyaenus—reached the rank of associate leaders in The Garden and were understood to follow in their master's footsteps so closely that they might teach the Epicurean doctrine in its purest form. Beneath them were the many assistant leaders, unknown to modern scholars by name, and the numerous students. Among Epicurus's students were women (for example, the distinguished Leontion) and slaves (Epicurus's own slave Mys was one of his favorite students). The accessibility of the Epicurean phi-

losophy, which eschewed most classical learning, ensured a remarkably heterogeneous following.

Despite many later slanders against him, by writers who misconstrued his emphasis on pleasure as a license for sensory excess, the overwhelming evidence supports the idea that Epicurus lived in his Garden school simply and privately, following his own dictate to "live unobtrusively." His health, which was delicate and complicated by a bladder or kidney stone, would certainly not have survived the riotous living ascribed to him by his detractors.

Fortunately, both Epicurus and his closest disciples were prolific writers, and in some ways the home of Epicurus was a kind of publishing house for their works. Still, only a small portion of that original writing is extant, and an even smaller part is translated into English. Of Epicurus's three hundred or more books (it is best to think of them as scrolls), all that remains are some fragments of his central work *De natura* (c. 296 B.C.E.; *On Nature*, in *Epicurus: The Extant Remains*, 1926), three important letters recorded by Diogenes Laertius in the early third century B.C.E., and some miscellaneous correspondence, which shows Epicurus's affectionate relationship with his friends. As Plato had his Socrates, Epicurus had the Roman poet Lucretius, from whose

Epicurus. (Library of Congress)

book *De rerum natura* (c. 60 B.C.E.; *On the Nature of Things*, 1682) most modern understanding of Epicurus's ideas comes.

Through Lucretius's works one is introduced to Epicurus's theories on matter and space, the movements and the shapes of atoms, life and the mind, sensation and sex, cosmology and sociology, and meteorology and geology. In addition to Epicurus's atomic theory, which in some interesting respects presages modern physics, the parts of Epicurus's philosophy that still have the power to move people are the simple axioms of behavior around which he organized life at The Garden.

Rejecting much of traditional education because it did not foster happiness through tranquillity (which was the ultimate goal of life), Epicurus had a more profound respect for common sense than for classical learning. Prudence was an important virtue, and the senses were the ultimate sources of all knowledge. The highest good in life was attaining a secure and lasting pleasure. To Epicurus, pleasure was not unbridled sensuality but freedom from pain and peace of mind. These two goods could easily be obtained by simple living, curbing one's unnecessary desires, and avoiding the stresses and compromises of a public life. It might even be profitable to avoid love, marriage, and parenting, he said, because they usually bring more pain than pleasure. Friendship, on the other hand, was regarded as one of the highest and most secure forms of pleasure.

Epicurus thought that the great aim of philosophy was to free people of their fears. He was not an atheist, but he considered the gods to be very remote—living in Epicurean serenity—and not likely to be tampering viciously with the lives of mortals. For Epicureans, the soul dies with the body and, therefore, not even death was to be feared.

Perhaps the most salient criticisms of Epicurus's ethics of self-reliance and free will are that they are very negative (viewing wisdom as an escape from an active, hazardous, but possibly full life) and very selfish (placing the good of the individual above the needs of society or the state). While these criticisms may be valid, the life of Epicurus showed that there was much everyday merit in his philosophy. He was blessed with many lifelong friendships, and his enthusiastic followers kept his ideas alive long into the fourth century. Even on his deathbed, he exhibited that almost Eastern detachment and calm that was the major goal of his philosophy. In a letter that he wrote to friends at his last hour, he commented that the extreme pain of his abdomen was considerably relieved by the happy thoughts he had of his talks with them.

Significance

Epicurus's thought outlived most other important Greek philosophical systems, but it too was finally overwhelmed in the fourth century by Christianity, which considered it just another pagan creed. Some critics believe, however, that the writer of Ecclesiastes in the Old Testament was likely a member of the school and that the Epistles of Saint Paul in the New Testament were strongly influenced by Epicurean thought.

Ironically, it was a French priest, Pierre Gassendi, who revived interest in Epicurus in the seventeenth century with his short treatise *De vita et moribus Epicuri libri octo* (1647; eight books on the life and manners of Epicurus). This interest was manifested in English by Walter Charleton and further fueled by Sir William Temple, a renowned seventeenth century English essayist. In the early nineteenth century, the United States had an avowed Epicurean as its president: Thomas Jefferson.

Discoveries of inscriptions and manuscripts in Asia Minor and Herculaneum have kept scholars debating the issues raised in the works of Epicurus up to the present day. Richard W. Hibler, for example, has studied Epicurus, focusing on what he has to teach about pedagogy. There is no question that as long as humans worry about ethics, strive after the good life, or try to make sense of the universe, the voice of Epicurus will continue to be heard.

—Cynthia Lee Katona

Further Reading

Diogenes Laertius. *Lives of Eminent Philosophers*. Cambridge, Mass.: Harvard University Press, 1972. The most valuable parts of this early third century work are the many quoted extracts directly from the writings of Epicurus. Diogenes' unusual focus on the ancient philosophers as living men gives an interesting view of Epicurus, who is, surprisingly, treated more extensively in this work than is Socrates.

Durant, Will. *The Life of Greece*. 1939. Reprint. New York: MJF Books, 1992. Contains an excellent chapter, "The Epicurean Escape," that places Epicurus in the context of his times and also evaluates the tenets of his philosophy.

Edwards, Paul, ed. *The Encyclopedia of Philosophy*. 4 vols. New York: Macmillan, 1972. Contains a lucid short explanation of Epicurus's complex theory and a definitive scholarly bibliography.

Epicurus. *The Essential Epicurus: Letters, Principal Doctrines, Vatican Sayings, and Fragments*. Translated by Eugene Michael O'Connor. Buffalo, N.Y.:

Prometheus Books, 1993. Translation of works; includes bibliography.

Hibler, Richard W. *Happiness Through Tranquillity: The School of Epicurus*. Lanham, Md.: University Press of America, 1984. Hibler's interest in Epicurus is primarily as a great teacher; consequently, he follows his discussion of the philosopher's life and works with a summary of twenty points that are especially relevant to readers who wish to know more about Epicurus's educational methodology.

Hicks, R. D. *Stoic and Epicurean*. 1910. Reprint. New York: Russell and Russell, 1961. Hicks compares the Stoics with the Epicureans. He gives an excellent, extended account of Epicurus's theory. Includes useful chronological table and index.

Lucretius. *On the Nature of the Universe*. Translated by Ronald Latham. Baltimore: Penguin Books, 1964. This philosophical poem forms the basis of the modern reading of Epicurus. Lucretius, in true Epicurean fashion, avoided the usual occupations of his times—war and politics—to devote himself to an extensive exposition of Epicurus's teachings.

Rist, J. M. *Epicurus: An Introduction*. New York: Cambridge University Press, 1972. Rist describes his book as an unambitious and elementary account of the philosophy of Epicurus. It is, in fact, a fine introduction to the thought of Epicurus and takes full advantage of the most important developments in Epicurean scholarship.

SEE ALSO: Aristippus; Lucretius; Menander (dramatist); Saint Paul.

RELATED ARTICLES in *Great Events from History: The Ancient World*: 447-438 B.C.E., Building of the Parthenon; 399 B.C.E., Death of Socrates; c. 380 B.C.E., Plato Develops His Theory of Ideas; c. 350 B.C.E., Diogenes Popularizes Cynicism; c. 335-323 B.C.E., Aristotle Writes the *Politics*; c. 300 B.C.E., Stoics Conceptualize Natural Law; January-March, 55 or 56 C.E., Paul Writes His Letter to the Romans.

ERASISTRATUS
Greek physician

Erasistratus made numerous physiological and anatomical discoveries, perhaps using an exceptional combination of human and animal dissection (and possibly vivisection) to explore the structure and workings of the human body.

BORN: c. 325 B.C.E.; Iulis, Island of Ceos (now Keos), Greece
DIED: c. 250 B.C.E.; place unknown
AREA OF ACHIEVEMENT: Medicine

EARLY LIFE

Already during his childhood on the rocky, forested Aegean island Ceos (now Keos), Erasistratus (er-ah-SIHS-trah-tuhs) was no stranger to medicine. His father, Cleombrotus, was a physician, as was his mother's brother Medius (or Medias). His brother, Cleophantus, joined this family tradition as well. Erasistratus apparently left Iulis for apprenticeships, perhaps with the doctor Metrodorus (whom one ancient source identifies as the third husband of Aristotle's daughter Pythias) and Metrodorus's teacher Chrysippus of Cnidus, whom Erasistratus regarded as his main mentor. He may also have attended lectures by Theophrastus, Aristotle's successor as leader of the Peripatetic school of philosophy in Athens, and come under the philosophical influence of Theophrastus's successor, Strato of Lampsacus, but this remains a matter of dispute.

Where Erasistratus subsequently practiced and conducted his research has become a controversial issue, but the ancient evidence suggests that he was at the court of the Seleucid rulers in Syrian Antioch (founded on the Orontes River in 300 B.C.E.) for at least some time in the late 290's. Several ancient sources report that Erasistratus cured a mysteriously ill, suicidal Antiochus (the future King Antiochus I Soter) in Antioch. Through imaginative observation of the patient's face, demeanor, heart, and pulse, it is said, the physician correctly diagnosed that young Antiochus was in love with his stepmother Stratonice. Erasistratus subtly persuaded Antiochus's father, King Seleucus I Nicator, to give up Stratonice in order to save his son; the king promptly arranged the marriage of his wife and son.

Whether Erasistratus also practiced in Alexandria, as many modern historians have assumed, is less certain. No ancient evidence explicitly confirms his presence in Alexandria, but there is suggestive indirect evidence that he may have worked in Alexandria for at least some time during the lifetime of Herophilus.

LIFE'S WORK

Erasistratus's ingenuity as a physiologist overshadows his anatomical discoveries, but the two are closely linked. By dissecting animals—and possibly, like his brilliant contemporary Herophilus, by dissecting and vivisecting humans, as one ancient source claims—Erasistratus made major anatomical and physiological discoveries. Among his achievements, two, in particular, won high praise from later authors. First, he described the heart valves (more accurately than did Herophilus), noting the irreversibility of the flow through the valves and detailing the heart's pumping action. Second, his account of the brain includes descriptions of its four ventricles, the convolutions of the cerebrum and the cerebellum (which he linked to humans' superior intelligence), and the origin of the nervous system in the brain (or, as Erasistratus originally believed, in the dura mater, the outermost and toughest of the three membranes covering the brain and the spinal cord).

Three strikingly consistent features of Erasistratus's physiology are his use of mechanical principles rather than Aristotelian innate powers or invisible "faculties" to explain processes in the body, his willingness to verify hypotheses by means of experiments, and a teleological perspective (which he shared with Aristotle and others). In his version of the vascular system, the veins contain only blood, whereas the arteries transport only pneuma, a warm, moist, airlike substance ultimately derived from the atmosphere by respiration. From the lungs the "vein-like artery"—that is, the pulmonary vein—carries pneuma to the left ventricle of the heart, where it is refined into "vital" (life-giving) pneuma before being pumped into the arteries. If, however, the arteries contain only an airlike substance, how did Erasistratus account for the fact that blood flows from a punctured artery? Resorting to one of his favorite mechanical principles, he argued that when the artery is cut, its pneuma escapes, creating an empty space into which blood instantly rushes from the adjacent veins (veins being connected to the arteries throughout by means of *synanastomōseis*, or capillary-like communications). The underlying mechanical principle—"following toward what is being emptied," later called *horror vacui*—is that if matter is removed from a contained space, other matter will inevitably enter to take its place, because a natural massed void or vacuum is impossible. It is, therefore, blood from the veins, not from the artery, that escapes when a lesion of an artery occurs.

Erasistratus's similarly mechanical explanation of the pulse is closer to the truth than his view of the content of the arteries. Whereas Herophilus believed that a "fac-ulty," flowing from the heart to the arterial coats, draws or pulls a mixture of blood and pneuma from the heart into the arteries when they dilate, Erasistratus recognized that the heart functions as a pump: Every time the heart contracts, according to his account, its left ventricle pushes pneuma through a one-way valve into the aorta and the whole arterial network, causing the arteries to dilate. Because the left cardiac ventricle is empty after contraction, pneuma from the lung rushes into it again as it dilates, in accordance with the *horror vacui* principle, and thus the cycle continues, the systole of the heart always being simultaneous with the diastole of the arteries. Once in the arteries, the pneuma cannot return to or through the heart because of the one-way valves. After circulating through the arteries and providing the body with air, the pneuma apparently passes out of the body through the pores, making room for the fresh pneuma constantly being pumped into the arteries.

Erasistratus tried to prove experimentally that it is the heart, functioning as a pump, that causes pulsation, rather than some invisible "pulling" faculty in the arterial coat. After exposing an artery in a living subject, he tied a ligature around the artery. Below the ligature he made a lengthwise incision in the artery, into which he inserted a tube or hollow reed. The incised section of the artery was then ligated, with linen thread wound all around the tube and the surrounding tissue. When the ligature above the tube was undone, Erasistratus claimed, the pulse could be observed below the tube as well as above it, proving that the content of the arteries, pumped in by the heart, causes the pulse. The pulse could not, then, be attributed to a faculty in the incised, ligated, and hence "interrupted" coats of the arteries. (Galen, who reports this experiment, claims that he repeated it with opposite results.)

The central blood-making organ of the body, according to Erasistratus, is not the heart but the liver, where digested food finally is converted into blood. From the liver blood is carried as nourishment for the entire body through the veins. The largest vein in the body, the vena cava, carries blood into the right side of the heart through the tricuspid valve to nourish the heart. From the heart blood flows to the lungs through the pulmonary valve and pulmonary artery, or, as Erasistratus called it, the "arterial vein." The liver, however, cannot in and of itself account for the flow of the blood, since it has no pushing or pulling motion of its own. It is possibly for this reason that Erasistratus described the heart as the *archē* (origin, principle, or rule) not only of the arteries but also of the veins, despite his regarding the liver as the central blood factory. "The heart itself," Galen reports Erasistratus saying, after each contraction "expands like a blacksmith's bellows and draws in matter, filling itself up by its dilation." The *horror vacui* principle thus renders the heart responsible for the movement of blood into and from the heart and consequently, it would seem, for the motion of all blood through the veins, just as it is for the movement of pneuma through all the arteries (although blood is also absorbed into tissues throughout the body, thus creating space for fresh blood in the veins).

The nervous system, muscular activity, respiration, appetite, digestion, and the vascular system are all united by Erasistratus in a brilliantly coherent and comprehensive physiological model. External air moves into the lungs through the windpipe and bronchial ducts when the thorax expands. While the air (pneuma) is in the lungs, the left ventricle of the heart draws some pneuma into itself by its own expansion or diastole, contributing to the cycle described above. Excess air, having absorbed some of the superfluous body heat produced by the heart, is then exhaled by the lungs as the thorax contracts, after which the thorax expands once again, drawing in fresh air. The breathing cycle of the lungs thus both cools the body and provides the arteries with the pneuma they need for the body's life and health, whereas appetite and digestion—both of which are similarly explained in terms of the *horror vacui* principle—along with the liver, provide the veins with the food-derived nourishment that the body needs.

The nerves, like the arteries, carry pneuma that is ultimately derived from respiration, but it is a more highly refined version of air. Some of the vital pneuma produced in the left ventricle of the heart is carried by the arterial system to the brain, where it is refined into "psychic" pneuma, which in turn is distributed to the body through the nerves emanating from the brain. Not unlike Herophilus, Erasistratus distinguished between sensory and motor nerves; in his system, it is presumably by means of psychic pneuma that data and impulses are transmitted through the nerves to and from the brain.

Voluntary motion takes place through the muscles, which—like the nerves and perhaps all organic structures in the body—consist of triple-braided strands of veins, arteries, and nerves. Pneuma carried to the muscles by the arteries or nerves endows them with the ability to contract or relax—that is, to increase their width while simultaneously reducing their length, or vice versa, the speed of the muscular motions standing in direct relation to the amount of pneuma in the muscle at a given time.

Erasistratus's efforts in pathology were marked by some innovation as well. He emphasized three related causes of disease that, though not entirely inconsistent with humoral and other earlier theories, introduce some new perspectives. Plethora or hyperemia is a condition marked by excessive blood-nutriment in the veins, which can cause swollen limbs, diseases of the liver and stomach, epilepsy, spleen and kidney ailments, fever, inflammation, blockage of the arteries, and mental disorders (in part because excessive blood in the veins can spill over into the arteries through the *synanastomōseis* between veins and arteries, thus impeding the flow of vital pneuma). Second, disease can result from other disturbances of the arterial flow of pneuma, such as when blood enters a punctured artery (*horror vacui*) and some of it remains trapped in the artery after the wound has healed. Third, digestive dysfunctions cause the presence of sticky, bad moistures in the body that give rise to ailments such as apoplexy and paralysis. In Erasistratus's system, all bodily malfunctions, like all functions, must be understood in terms of the actions and interactions of matter, whose ultimate constituents are solid, possibly atomlike particles. Numerous diseases, their symptoms, and their causes were described by Erasistratus; his works, which are all lost, addressed subjects such as dropsy, diseases of the abdominal cavity, and fevers.

SIGNIFICANCE

In his *Hoi katholou logoi* (general principles) and other lost works, Erasistratus succeeded in accounting for practically all bodily functions within a single explanatory model whose economy, coherence, and scope are unmatched in antiquity except perhaps by those of Aristotle and Galen. Especially striking is his amalgam of mechanical principles and teleology. The latter is expressed in his Platonic-Aristotelian view of nature as a supreme artisan, whose providential care for living beings is revealed in the perfection and beautiful purposiveness of every part of the human body. Erasistratus's anatomical discoveries were, however, not as numerous as those of Herophilus, and there are some weak links in his system, such as his reproductive theory.

Bold in his theories, Erasistratus advocated restraint in practice. He assigned higher priority to preventive hygiene, on which he wrote a treatise, than to therapeutics, which, along with the study of symptoms, he regarded as a merely "stochastic," or conjectural, venture (in contrast to etiology and physiology). Proper treatment of patients requires the clear identification of the causes, both proximate and ultimate, of their diseases, as well as an individualized, mild therapy. Opposed to drastic cures, he also rejected the tradition of therapeutic bloodletting in all but a few cases, thereby provoking the notorious ire of Galen, who wrote an entire treatise against Erasistratus's views on bloodletting (and another against the Erasistrateans of Galen's own time, who were defending their patriarch). Instead of bloodletting, Erasistratus advocated drawing off morbid substances through fasting, vomiting, and inducing perspiration as well as through urine, plasters, poultices, steam baths, fomentations, fairly conventional dietary prescriptions, and exercise.

For all of their theoretical differences, Erasistratus and Herophilus shared this combination of theoretical audacity and clinical restraint, exceptional scientific originality and pragmatic conservatism. To a greater degree than in the case of Herophilus, Erasistratus's views—as transmitted through fragments and secondhand reports, since none of his works is extant—were met with the polemics of Galen. Even a hostile Galen could not refrain from repeatedly acknowledging Erasistratus's significant stature in the history of medicine. Galen also recognized his enemy's scientific honesty: Even in old age, he reports, Erasistratus stood ready to correct his errors in the light of fresh observations. In his search for a better understanding of the human body, the great theorist did not allow the systematic coherence of his theories to stand in the way of his own scientific progress.

— *Heinrich von Staden*

FURTHER READING

Galen. *Galen on Bloodletting*. Translated by Peter Brain. New York: Cambridge University Press, 1986. Includes translations of Galen's works against Erasistratus and the Erasistrateans, with extensive annotations.

_____. *On Respiration and the Arteries*. Edited by David J. Furley and J. S. Wilkie. Princeton, N.J.: Princeton University Press, 1984. Pages 26 to 37 offer an excellent introduction to Erasistratus's views on respiration, the heart, and the arteries. The volume also includes an annotated translation of three Galenic works that are important sources for Erasistratus's physiology.

_____. *Three Treatises on the Nature of Science*. Translated by Michael Frede and Richard Walzer. Indianapolis, Ind.: Hackett Publishing, 1985. A useful source for aspects of Erasistratus's theory of scientific method and his epistemology.

Harris, C. R. S. *The Heart and the Vascular System in Ancient Greek Medicine*. Oxford, England: Clarendon Press, 1973. Chapter 4 presents the most extensive analysis available of Erasistratus's description of the vascular system, with some attention to his theories of respiration and the nerves.

Jackson, Michael, and Amy Norrington. "An A to Z of Medical History: Part 1." *Student British Medical Journal* 10 (September, 2002): 317. This exploration of the history of medicine covers Erasistratus and his dissection techniques.

Lloyd, G. E. R. "A Note on Erasistratus of Ceos." *Journal of Hellenic Studies* 95 (1975): 172-175. Argues against Fraser (see above) that Erasistratus performed human dissection, was an outstanding anatomist, and worked for at least some time in Alexandria.

_____. *Science, Folklore, and Ideology*. Indianapolis: Hackett, 1999. Excellent observations throughout, especially on the standardization of anatomical terminology.

Pope, Maurice. "Shakespeare's Medical Imagination." *Shakespeare Survey* 38 (1985): 175-186. Traces the influence of Erasistratus's physiology on Renaissance poetry.

Smith, W. D. "Erasistratus's Dietetic Medicine." *Bulletin of the History of Medicine* 56 (1982): 398-409. Argues that attention to Erasistratus's own words, in the literal fragments preserved by Galen and others, reveals a less revolutionary, less contentious, and more conventional Erasistratus than the one suggested by Galen's polemics. Shows that his dietetics was a conservative development of an earlier tradition.

Von Staden, Heinrich. "Experiment and Experience in Hellenistic Medicine." *Bulletin of the Institute of Classical Studies* 22 (1975): 178-199. Relates the growth and decline of experimentation in Erasistratus's century to changing theories of scientific method; includes a close analysis of some of Erasistratus's experiments.

SEE ALSO: Alcmaeon; Arataeus of Cappadocia; Asclepiades of Bithynia; Diocles of Carystus; Dioscorides, Pedanius; Galen; Herophilus; Hippocrates; Seleucus I Nicator; Theophrastus.

RELATED ARTICLES in *Great Events from History: The Ancient World*: 6th-4th century B.C.E. (traditionally, 1st millennium B.C.E.), Suśruta, Indian Physician, Writes Medical Compendium; c. 500 B.C.E., Acupuncture Develops in China; c. 500-400 B.C.E., Greek Physicians Begin Scientific Practice of Medicine; c. 157-201 C.E., Galen Synthesizes Ancient Medical Knowledge.

ERATOSTHENES OF CYRENE
Greek scholar and inventor

Through his energetic directorship, Eratosthenes helped make the Library of Alexandria the greatest repository of learning in the Mediterranean world, and his varied contributions made him the most versatile scholar and scientist of the third century B.C.E.

BORN: c. 285 B.C.E.; Cyrene (now in Libya)
DIED: c. 205 B.C.E.; Alexandria, Egypt
AREAS OF ACHIEVEMENT: Literature, geography, mathematics

EARLY LIFE

Eratosthenes (ehr-ah-TAWS-theh-neez) was born in the Greek North African city of Cyrene about 285 B.C.E. The only surviving ancient biographical reference places his birth in the 126th Olympiad (276-273 B.C.E.), but this is too late to allow his reported meeting in Athens with Zeno of Citium, founder of Stoicism, who died around 261. His subsequent career suggests, moreover, that he was about forty years of age when he was called to Alexandria in 245; a birth date in the mid-280's therefore seems accurate. Because neither his name nor that of his father, Aglaus, is otherwise mentioned in Cyrenaean records, it seems that Eratosthenes was not of an especially prominent family.

While his family was not illustrious, his mother city had achieved considerable renown. Founded by Greeks from Thera before 600, Cyrene had prospered as an independent city-state. Following the death of Alexander the Great in 323, however, the Hellenistic Age brought a new political order in which large, bureaucratic monarchies dominated and absorbed the formerly autonomous city-states. Cyrene grudgingly accepted incorporation into the neighboring Ptolemaic kingdom of Egypt, which was ruled from Alexandria.

Founded by Alexander in 331, by Eratosthenes' time this harbor city was well on the way to becoming the commercial and cultural center of the Mediterranean world. Thanks to the generous subsidies of the Ptolemies, the city boasted the great Library and its adjunct Museum, a school of advanced studies that attracted scholars in literary and scientific studies, including Callimachus of Cyrene.

The most famous poet of the early third century and compiler of the Library's first catalog, Callimachus was the latest in a long line of Cyrenaean intellectual figures. Eratosthenes thus followed in a well-established tradition of Cyrenaean learning and scholarship when he undertook his early training at home with the renowned grammarian Lysanias. One might have expected him to pursue advanced studies in nearby Alexandria in the company of his countryman Callimachus, but the young man was primarily interested in philosophy, and for philosophy one went to the city of Socrates and Plato. Therefore, at age fifteen, Eratosthenes sailed to Athens, where he would remain for twenty-five years.

LIFE'S WORK

Eratosthenes later recalled that in Athens he found more philosophers than had ever been known to exist within the walls of one city. The eager student sampled all of their offerings and came away disappointed. He studied Stoicism with the aged Zeno, founder of the school, but he spent more time with Zeno's revisionist pupil, Ariston of Chios, who became the subject of one of Eratosthenes' earliest works, a biographical sketch titled *Ariston*. He also witnessed the flamboyant diatribes of Bion of Borysthenes, the son of a former slave and a prostitute, who preached the doctrines of Cynicism on street corners and dockside. Eratosthenes accused Ariston of not living true to his Stoic principles and Bion of adorning his philosophy to attract more attention, much like a tart in gaudy clothes.

Eratosthenes seems to have been more receptive to the Platonism that he learned from Arcesilaus, head of the Academy in this, its "middle" period. His first seriously intellectual work, the *Platonikos* (platonics), followed the dialogue format pioneered by Plato and explored traditional Platonic cosmological and mathematical themes. He also wrote another philosophical study titled *Peri agathon kai kakon* (on good and evil qualities), which has been lost. Eratosthenes' eclectic approach to his philosophical studies together with his criticisms of established philosophers provoked some later scholars to accuse him of dilettantism.

Less than satisfied with his experiences in philosophy, Eratosthenes fared somewhat better with poetry, the field in which he first achieved a degree of recognition. Although none of his early poetic pieces survives, two poems are known by name. The hexameter *Hermes* (c. 250) recalled the birth and career of that god, while the *Erigone* employed elegiac verse to portray the legendary suicide of an Athenian maiden. Both displayed the highly polished style of Callimachus, and the latter poem was later described as completely faultless. Without a doubt it was his early reputation as a poet, not his work in philosophy, that brought Eratosthenes' name to the attention of the royal patrons in Alexandria when the poet Apollonius of Rhodes retired from his position as librarian in 245.

Ptolemy III Euergetes must have considered other, equally famous poets for the position of librarian, but personal and political factors led him to invite Eratosthenes to Alexandria. While Eratosthenes had pursued his studies in Athens, his homeland had enjoyed a period of independence under the rule of Magas, a renegade Ptolemaic governor who had broken with the government in Alexandria and for several decades styled himself king of Cyrene. In 245 Cyrene had only recently returned to Ptolemaic rule, largely as a result of the conciliatory marriage of Ptolemy III to Berenice, the daughter of Magas. Less than a year on the throne, the young king sought a further gesture of reconciliation to Cyrenaean opinion. Many Cyrenaeans enjoyed Ptolemaic patronage in Alexandria, but none of them, not even the great Callimachus, had been offered the prestigious post of librarian. In addition, the aging Callimachus no doubt lobbied the king on behalf of his countryman Eratosthenes. Consequently, the invitation arrived in Athens, probably in 245, and Eratosthenes sailed for Alexandria to begin the greatest phase of his life.

In assuming the title of director of the Library, Eratosthenes accepted a post of huge prestige, one that brought great responsibilities as well as opportunity. In addition to serving as tutor to the royal children, he admirably fulfilled his primary obligation to maintain and develop the largest repository of learning in the world.

During his tenure, the Library acquired authentic texts of the great tragic dramas of Aeschylus, Sophocles, and Euripides and opened an entire section dedicated solely to the study of Homer. As competition for manuscripts developed with the founding of a rival institution at Pergamum, it may have been at Eratosthenes' behest that the Alexandrian harbor authorities began requiring all ships to surrender their books for inspection and possible duplication.

Despite his archival and tutorial duties, Eratosthenes found time to take advantage of the scholarly opportunities offered by his position—full access to the immense holdings of the Library and to the circle of resident scholars at the nearby Museum.

Because he refused to specialize and instead explored almost every area of learning, his admirers gave him the nickname "Pentathlos," for the all-around athletes of the Olympic pentathlon. His critics preferred to call him

"Beta," that is, second-best in many endeavors but never first. That he abandoned his original interest in philosophy in favor of other fields is understandable, for the intrigue-ridden court of an authoritarian monarch was not the place to pursue moral and constitutional questions. Although none of his works survives intact, it is possible to reconstruct the main lines of his achievement.

Eratosthenes' three-volume *Geographika* (geography) drew on the work of earlier geographers, but in two ways it represented a more scientific and systematic approach to the subject. He completely rejected the commonly accepted notion that writings such as Homer's *Odyssey* (c. 725 B.C.E.; English translation, 1614) contained reliable geographic information. He angered many established geographical authorities when he declared, "You will find the scene of the wanderings of Odysseus when you find the cobbler who sewed up the bag of the winds." Nor was Eratosthenes content merely to describe geographical phenomena and assign them to the various continents. Instead, by establishing distances and positions in relation to two primary axes intersecting at Rhodes, he created the first reasonably accurate map of the world. Admittedly crude, Eratosthenes' map anticipated the modern system of longitude and latitude, and it was the first to incorporate the knowledge of Eastern regions derived from Alexander the Great's expedition.

Eratosthenes' *Peri tes avametreoeos tes ges* (on the measurement of the earth) presented his most famous geographical achievement—a calculation of Earth's circumference. By means of a novel and elegantly simple application of two of Euclid's geometric propositions, Eratosthenes reasoned that the distance from Alexandria to Syene in Upper Egypt represented one-fiftieth of Earth's circumference. Coupling this figure with the known distance between the two cities, a measurement perhaps obtained at his request by Ptolemy's royal surveyors, Eratosthenes arrived at his figure of 252,000 stades (24,662 miles or 39,777 kilometers). Far more accurate than the then generally accepted estimate of 300,000 stades, Eratosthenes' result falls within 1 percent of the best modern measurements.

As he attempted to systematize geography, Eratosthenes also sought to replace the myriad local chronographical schemes with a universal chronology for all Greek history. A preliminary study, the *Olympionikai*, prepared an authoritative list of Olympic victors that could serve as a chronological yardstick. In his *Chronographiai* (chronological tables), which covered the period from the Trojan War to the death of Alexander, Eratosthenes placed events from various local and regional traditions in one coherent chronological system based on Olympiads.

In the field of mathematics, Eratosthenes is best known for his "sieve"—a method for discovering prime numbers—and for his solution to the "Delian Problem," the long-standing problem of doubling a cube. For the latter, Eratosthenes composed a proof and designed a mechanical instrument, his "mesolabe," to demonstrate it. In Alexandria he dedicated a monument bearing a model of the instrument, the proof, and his poem in praise of his patron, Ptolemy III. His longest mathematical treatise, *On Means*, of undetermined content, formed part of the Royal Mathematical Collection. Although Eratosthenes' mathematical work did not match his outstanding achievements in geography and chronography, it is worth noting that the greatest mathematician of his day, Archimedes, valued his opinion and corresponded with him on mathematical issues.

The most important of his works on literary subjects was the *Peri archaias komoidias* (on ancient comedy), in at least twelve books, which dealt with the foremost authors of that genre—Aristophanes, Cratinus, Eupolis, and Pherecrates. The few surviving fragments indicate that Eratosthenes was concerned with variations in the dialect and vocabulary of the plays as well as the history of their revisions and stagings.

A fragment of Eratosthenes' last work, the *Arsinoe* (biography of Arsinoe III), reveals the aging scholar's sympathy for the wife and sister of Ptolemy IV. Eratosthenes recalls that while walking with him at the palace during the rowdy "Feast of the Beakers," the queen shared with him her disgust over her husband's drunken celebrations. Shortly after the murder of this hapless queen in 205, Eratosthenes, at age eighty, met his own death, reportedly by voluntary starvation after he had gone blind. He was buried at Alexandria within sight of the Library.

SIGNIFICANCE

In his career, Eratosthenes perfectly exemplifies the apolitical cosmopolitan culture of the Hellenistic period. Uninterested in the political affairs of his city-state, he abandoned Cyrene for the cultural attractions of Athens, just as he later accepted the patronage of the Ptolemies. His work as librarian helped make Alexandria the outstanding center of learning in the Mediterranean world. Sadly, his remarkable scholarship had limited influence on later generations, and his reputation faltered. This circumstance is explained by his failure to produce students and by the envy that his exceptional versatility engen-

dered. The outstanding geographer and chronographer of his day, Eratosthenes also applied his powerful and independent intellect to important questions of mathematics and to literary studies. A polymath of extraordinary abilities, he definitely was no dilettante. Perhaps Eratosthenes is best recalled by the name that he coined to describe himself—*philologos*, a lover of human reason in all its various forms.

—James T. Chambers

FURTHER READING

Cunningham, Clifford J. "Updating Eratosthenes." *Mercury* 32, no. 2 (March/April, 2003): 10. Discussion of the measurement of the planet Earth.

Fraser, P. M. "Eratosthenes of Cyrene." *Proceedings of the British Academy* 56 (1970): 175-207. This article attempts to resolve the considerable chronological and source problems associated with Eratosthenes' life. An excellent single work on Eratosthenes' career.

_____. *Ptolemaic Alexandria*. 3 vols. Oxford, England: Clarendon Press, 1972. This monumental work provides a detailed view of Alexandrian society, politics, and intellectual life. It is especially good on the history of the Library and the Museum. Most valuable are its sensible reconstructions based on the fragments of Eratosthenes' lost works.

Grafton, Anthony. "Dating History: The Renaissance and the Reformation of Chronology." *Daedalus* 132, no. 2 (Spring, 2003): 74-85. Covers Eratosthenes in discussion of geography and chronology in the ancient world.

Heath, Thomas L. *A Manual of Greek Mathematics*. Reprint. New York: Dover, 1963. This volume places Eratosthenes in the context of the overall development of Greek mathematics, especially in chapters 7 and 11.

Lloyd, G. E. R. *Greek Science After Aristotle*. New York: W. W. Norton, 1973. Provides an excellent overview of Greek science in Eratosthenes' time but has only a brief reference to him in chapter 4. Includes a diagram of his measurement of the earth.

Pfeiffer, Rudolf. *History of Classical Scholarship: From the Beginnings to the End of the Hellenistic Age*. Oxford, England: Clarendon Press, 1976. This standard study of Greek scholarship in the classical and Hellenistic periods has an excellent chapter that briefly discusses the chronological problems associated with Eratosthenes' life and provides a complete catalog of the works attributed to him.

Tarn, W. W., and G. T. Griffith. *Hellenistic Civilisation.* 3d ed. London: Methuen, 1966. This classic study provides an overview of Eratosthenes' world, most notably in the chapters on Ptolemaic Egypt and Hellenistic intellectual life.

Thomson, James Oliver. *History of Ancient Geography.* New York: Cambridge University Press, 1965. Provides an overview of the evolution of geographical knowledge and theory from early Babylonia to the later Roman period. See chapter 4 for a discussion of Eratosthenes. Includes two excellent maps based on his theories.

SEE ALSO: Archimedes; Callimachus; Ctesebius of Alexandria; Hero of Alexandria; Herophilus; Hypatia; Pappus; Philo of Alexandria; Ptolemy (astronomer); Ptolemy Philadelphus; Ptolemy Soter; Sosigenes.

RELATED ARTICLES in *Great Events from History: The Ancient World*: 332 B.C.E., Founding of Alexandria; 323 B.C.E., Founding of the Ptolemaic Dynasty and Seleucid Kingdom; c. 300 B.C.E., Euclid Compiles a Treatise on Geometry; c. 275 B.C.E., Greeks Advance Hellenistic Astronomy; c. 250 B.C.E., Discoveries of Archimedes; 415 C.E., Mathematician and Philosopher Hypatia Is Killed in Alexandria.

EUCLID
Greek geometer

Euclid took the geometry known in his day and presented it in a logical system. His work on geometry became the standard textbook on the subject down to modern times.

BORN: c. 330 B.C.E.; probably Greece
DIED: c. 270 B.C.E.; Alexandria, Egypt
AREA OF ACHIEVEMENT: Mathematics

EARLY LIFE

Little is known about Euclid (YOO-klihd), and even the city of his birth is a mystery. Medieval authors often called him Euclid of Megara, but they were confusing him with an earlier philosopher, Eucleides of Megara, who was an associate of Socrates and Plato. It is virtually certain that Euclid came from Greece proper and probable that he received advanced education in the Academy, the school founded by Plato in Athens. By the time Euclid arrived there, Plato and the first generation of his students had already died, but the Academy was the outstanding mathematical school of the time. The followers of Aristotle in the Lyceum included no great mathematicians. The majority of the geometers who instructed Euclid were adherents of the Academy.

Euclid traveled to Alexandria and was appointed to the faculty of the Museum, the great research institution that was being organized under the patronage of Ptolemy Soter, who ruled Egypt from 323 to 283. Ptolemy, a boyhood friend of Euclid and then a lieutenant of Alexander the Great, had seized Egypt soon after the conqueror's death, become the successor of the pharaohs, and managed to make his capital, Alexandria, an intellectual center of the Hellenistic Age that outshone the waning light of Athens. Euclid presumably became the librarian, or head, of the Museum at some point in his life. He had many students, and although their names are not recorded, they carried on the tradition of his approach to mathematics. His influence can still be identified among those who followed in the closing years of the third century B.C.E. He was thus a member of the first generation of Alexandrian scholars, along with Demetrius of Phalerum and Strato of Lampsacus.

Two famous remarks are attributed to Euclid by ancient authors. On being asked by Ptolemy if there was any easier way to learn the subject than by struggling through the proofs in Euclid's work the *Stoicheia* (c. 300 B.C.E.; *The Elements of Geometrie of the Most Auncient Philosopher Euclide of Megara*, 1570, commonly known as the *Elements*), Euclid replied that there is no "royal road" to geometry. Then when a student asked him if geometry would help him get a job, he ordered his slave to give the student a coin, "since he has to make a profit from what he learns." In spite of this rejoinder, his usual temperament is described as gentle and benign, open, and attentive to his students.

LIFE'S WORK

Euclid's reputation rests on his greatest work, the *Elements*, consisting of thirteen books of his own and two spurious books added later by Hypsicles of Alexandria and others. This work is a systematic explication of geometry in which each brief and elegant demonstration rests on the axioms and postulates given previously. It embraces and systematizes the achievements of earlier mathematicians. Books 1 and 2 discuss the straight line, triangles, and parallelograms; books 3 and 4 examine the circle and the inscription and circumscription of triangles and regular polygons; and books 5 and 6 explain the theory of proportion and areas. Books 7, 8, and 9 introduce the reader to arithmetic and the theory of rational numbers, while book 10 treats the difficult subject of irrational numbers. The remaining three books investigate elementary solid geometry and conclude with the five regular solids (tetrahedron, cube, octahedron, dedecahedron, and icosahedron). It should be noted that the *Elements* discusses several problems that later came to belong to the field of algebra, but Euclid treated them in geometric terms.

The genius of the *Elements* lies in the beauty and compelling logic of its arrangement and presentation, not in its new discoveries. Still, Euclid showed originality in his development of a new proof for the Pythagorean theorem as well as his convincing demonstration of many principles that had been advanced less satisfactorily by others. The postulate that only one parallel to a line can be drawn through any point external to the line is Euclid's invention. He found this assumption necessary in his system but was unable to develop a formal proof for it. Modern mathematicians have maintained that no such proof is possible, so Euclid may be excused for not providing one.

Other works by Euclid are extant in Greek. *Ta dedomena* (c. 300-270 B.C.E.; *Data* in *Euclid's Elements of Geometry*, 1661) is another work of elementary geometry and includes ninety-four propositions. The *Optika* (c. 300-270 B.C.E.; *The Optics of Euclid*, 1945), by treating rays of light as straight lines, makes its subject a branch of geometry. Spherical geometry is represented by the *Phainomena* (c. 300-270 B.C.E.; *Euclid's Phaenomena*, 1996), which is an astronomical text based in part on a work of Autolycus of Pitane, a slightly older contemporary. Euclid wrote on music, but the extant *Katatomē kanonos* (known by its Latin title, *Sectio canonis*) is at best a reworking by some later, inferior writer of a genuine text by Euclid, containing no more of his actual words than some excerpts. Discovered in Arabic translation was *Peri diaireseon biblion* (c. 300-270 B.C.E.; *On Divisions of Figures*, 1915), for which the proofs of only four of the propositions survive.

Also discovered have been the names of several lost books by Euclid on advanced geometry: The *Pseudaria* (fallacies) exposed fallacies in geometrical reasoning, and *Konika* (conics) laid some of the groundwork for the later book of the same title by Apollonius of Perga. There was a discussion of the relationships of points on sur-

Euclid. (Library of Congress)

faces titled *Topoi pros epiphaneia* (surface loci), and *Porismata* (porisms), a work of higher geometry, treated a kind of proposition intermediate between a theorem and a problem.

In addition to the last two books of the *Elements*, there are works bearing Euclid's name that are not genuinely his. These include the *Katoptrica* (catoptrica), a later work on optics, and *Eisagōgē armonikē* (*Introduction to Harmony*), which is actually by Cleonides, a student of Aristoxenus. None of Euclid's reputation, however, depends on these writings falsely attributed to him.

SIGNIFICANCE

Euclid left as his legacy the standard textbook in geometry. There is no other ancient work of science that needs so little revision to make it current, although many modern mathematicians, beginning with Nikolay Lobachevski and Bernhard Riemann and including Albert Einstein, have developed non-Euclidean systems in reaction to the *Elements*, thus doing it a kind of honor. The influence of Euclid on later scientists such as Archimedes, Apollonius of Perga, Galileo Galilei, Sir Isaac Newton, and Christiaan Huygens was immense. Eratosthenes used his theorems to measure with surprising accuracy the size of the sphere of Earth, and Aristarchus attempted less successfully, but in fine Euclidean style, to establish the sizes and distances of the moon and the sun.

Other Hellenistic mathematicians, such as Hero of Alexandria, Pappus, Simplicius, and, most important, Proclus, produced commentaries on the *Elements*. Theon of Alexandria, father of the famous woman philosopher and mathematician Hypatia, introduced a new edition of the *Elements* in the fourth century C.E. The sixth century Italian Boethius is said to have translated the *Elements* into Latin, but that version is not extant. Many translations were made by early medieval Arabic scholars, beginning with one made for Harun al-Rashid near 800 C.E. by al-Hajjaj ibn Yusuf ibn Matar. Athelhard of Bath made the first surviving Latin translation from an Arabic text about 1120 C.E. The first printed version, a Latin translation by the thirteenth century scholar Johannes Campanus, appeared in 1482 in Venice. Bartolomeo Zamberti was the first to translate the *Elements* into Latin directly from the Greek, rather than Arabic, in 1505. The first English translation, printed in 1570, was done by Sir Henry Billingsley, later the lord mayor of London. The total number of editions of Euclid's *Elements* has been estimated to be more than a thousand, making it one of the most often translated and printed books in history and certainly the most successful textbook ever written.

—J. Donald Hughes

FURTHER READING

Euclid. *The Thirteen Books of Euclid's "Elements."* Translated by Thomas Little Heath. 3 vols. 1925. Reprint. New York: Dover, 1956. This English translation contains extensive commentary on Euclid's *Elements*. This admirable work supersedes all previous translations. It contains a full introduction, 151 pages in length, touching on all the major problems.

Fraser, P. M. *Ptolemaic Alexandria*. 3 vols. Oxford, England: Clarendon Press, 1972. Has a useful section on the intellectual background and influences of Euclid but is primarily valuable in providing a study of the cultural setting of Alexandria in Euclid's day.

Heath, Thomas Little. *From Thales to Euclid*. Vol. 1 in *A History of Greek Mathematics*. New York: Dover, 1981. Places Euclid in the context of the development

of ancient mathematics. A thoroughly dependable treatment.

Mlodinow, Leonard. *Euclid's Window: The Story of Geometry from Parallel Lines to Hyperspace*. New York: Free Press, 2001. In this history of geometry, reason, and abstraction, Euclid is represented as a major figure.

Mueller, Ian. *Philosophy of Mathematics and Deductive Structure in Euclid's "Elements."* Cambridge, Mass.: MIT Press, 1981. A study of the Greek concepts of mathematics found in the *Elements*, emphasizing philosophical, foundational, and logical rather than historical questions, although the latter are not totally neglected. Attention is directed to Euclid's work, not that of his predecessors. This monograph requires mathematical literacy, and the general reader may find it overly technical.

Reid, Constance. *A Long Way from Euclid*. New York: Thomas Y. Crowell, 1963. An explanation of how modern mathematical thought has progressed beyond Euclid, written for those whose introduction to mathematics consisted mainly of studying the *Elements*. Accessible to the general reader, this study takes Euclid as its starting point and shows that he did not provide the reader with all the answers, or even all the questions, with which mathematicians concern themselves.

Szabo, Arpad. *The Beginnings of Greek Mathematics*. Translated by A. M. Ungar. Boston: D. Reidel, 1978. Places Euclid within the context of the development of the Greek mathematical tradition.

SEE ALSO: Apollonius of Perga; Archimedes; Eratosthenes; Eudoxus of Cnidus; Hero of Alexandria; Hypatia; Pappus; Proclus; Pythagoras.

RELATED ARTICLES in *Great Events from History: The Ancient World*: c. 530 B.C.E., Founding of the Pythagorean Brotherhood; c. 500-400 B.C.E., Greek Physicians Begin Scientific Practice of Medicine; 332 B.C.E., Founding of Alexandria; c. 300 B.C.E., Euclid Compiles a Treatise on Geometry; c. 275 B.C.E., Greeks Advance Hellenistic Astronomy; c. 250 B.C.E., Discoveries of Archimedes; 46 B.C.E., Establishment of the Julian Calendar; 415 C.E., Mathematician and Philosopher Hypatia Is Killed in Alexandria.

EUDOXUS OF CNIDUS
Greek geometer

Eudoxus and his disciples resolved classical difficulties in the fields of geometry and geometric astronomy. Their approach became definitive for later research in these fields.

BORN: c. 390 B.C.E.; Cnidus, Asia Minor (now in Turkey)
DIED: c. 337 B.C.E.; Cnidus, Asia Minor
AREAS OF ACHIEVEMENT: Mathematics, astronomy

EARLY LIFE

As for so many ancient figures, little is known about the life of Eudoxus (yew-DAHK-suhs) of Cnidus. If one follows the account of the ancient biographer Diogenes Laertius (c. 250 C.E.), Eudoxus first visited Athens at age twenty-three to study medicine and philosophy. He soon returned home to Cnidus, however, and from there, joining the company of the Cnidian physician Chrysippus, he moved on to Egypt, where for more than a year he studied among the priests and engaged in astronomical investigations. Later, as he traveled and lectured in the wider Aegean area (specifically, Cyzicus and the Propontis), he built up a following and thus returned to Athens a man of considerable distinction. His main subsequent activity seems to have centered on Cnidus, where he was honored as a lawgiver. His renown extended to many areas, including astronomy, geometry, medicine, geography, and philosophy.

There is disagreement over his dates. The ancient chronicler Apollodorus sets Eudoxus's prime activity in 368-365 B.C.E. In general, the prime means age forty; if that holds here, Eudoxus's birth would be set c. 408. There is reason for doubt, however, because this early a date conflicts with other biographical data. G. L. Huxley favors c. 400; G. de Santillana and others argue for c. 390. Eudoxus is reported to have died at the age of fifty-three; the corresponding date would be 355, 347, or 337.

LIFE'S WORK

None of Eudoxus's writings survives, but fragments cited by ancient authors offer a reasonable impression of their diversity and significance. His principal efforts were in the areas of mathematics and astronomy, the former best represented in portions of Euclid's *Stoicheia* (c. 300 B.C.E.; *The Elements of Geometrie of the Most Auncient Philosopher Euclide of Megara*, 1570, commonly known as the *Elements*), the latter in astronomical discussions of the fourth-century cosmology of Aristotle and the ancient commentaries on it.

According to Archimedes (287-212 B.C.E.), Eudoxus was the first to set out a rigorous proof of the theorems that any pyramid equals one-third of the associated prism (that is, having the same height and base as the pyramid), and any cone equals one-third of the associated cylinder. Eudoxus also appears to have proved two other theorems: that circles are as the squares of their diameters and that spheres are as the cubes of their diameters. The proofs of these four theorems constitute the main part of book 17 of *Elements*, and the technique used there is likely to derive from Eudoxus.

To take the circle theorem as an example, one could imagine a regular polygon having so many sides that it seems practically indistinguishable from a circle. As two such polygons (with equally numerous sides) are proportional to the squares of their diameters, the same could be supposed for the corresponding circles. Presumably, an argument of this sort was assumed by geometers who used the circle theorem in the time before Eudoxus. In the strict sense, however, the reasoning would be invalid, for only by an infinite process can rectilinear figures eventuate in the circle.

In the Eudoxean scheme, one assumes the stated proportion to be false: If two circles are not in the ratio of the squares of their diameters, then one can construct two similar regular polygons, one inscribed in each circle, and one can make the difference between the polygon and its circle so small that the polygon is found to be simultaneously greater and less than a specified amount. Because that is clearly impossible, the stated theorem must be true. (This indirect manner for proving theorems on curved figures is often called, if somewhat misleadingly, the "method of exhaustion.")

A key move in this proof is making the polygon sufficiently close to the circle. To this end, one observes that as the number of sides is doubled, the difference between the polygon and the circle is reduced by more than half. The procedure of successively bisecting a given quantity will eventually make it less than any preassigned amount, however, as Euclid proves in *Elements*. According to Archimedes, however, it seems that Eudoxus took this bisection principle as an axiom.

The notion of proportion itself runs into a similar difficulty with the infinite. As long as quantities are related to one another in terms of whole or fractional numbers (for example, if one area is ⅞ of another area), their ratios can be specified from these same numbers (that is, the ratio of the one area to the other will be 7 to 5). Yet what if no such numbers exist? For example, it was found, a century or so before Eudoxus, that the diagonal and side of a square cannot equal a ratio of whole numbers. (In modern terms, one calls the associated number $\sqrt{2}$ "irrational"; its decimal equivalent 1.414 . . . will be nonterminating and nonrepeating.) Only by means of some form of infinite sequence can "commensurable" quantities (those whose ratio is expressible by two integers) equal the ratio of incommensurable ones. Geometers in the generation before Eudoxus had pursued the study of incommensurables with considerable interest, but Eudoxus was the first to see how the theorems on ratios could be rigorously proved when their terms were incommensurable.

It is usually supposed that Eudoxus's approach was identical to that given by Euclid in book 5 of *Elements*. Other writers, in particular Archimedes, however, knew of a different technique of proportions that seems more like what Eudoxus would have proposed. By this technique, one first establishes the stated theorem for the case of commensurable quantities. For the incommensurable case, one uses an indirect argument: If the proportionality does not hold, one can find commensurable terms whose ratio differs by less than a specified amount from the ratio of the given incommensurable terms—this is done by successively bisecting one of the givens until it is less than the difference between two others; when the commensurable case of the theorem (already proved) is applied, a certain term will be found to be simultaneously greater and less than another. Because that is impossible, the theorem must be true.

The defining notions of the proportion theory in Euclid's book 5 can be derived as a simple modification of this technique, for the role that the intermediate commensurable terms play in it is assumed by the Euclidean definition of proportion: that A:B = C:D means that for all positive integers m, n, if $mA > nB$, then also $mC > nD$; the same holds true if = or < is substituted for >. Proofs in this Euclidean manner do not require a division into commensurable and incommensurable cases, nor do they make use of the bisection principle; in general, they are rather easier to set up than in the alternative technique. It is thus possible to see Euclid's approach as an intended refinement of the Eudoxean.

In either the Eudoxean or Euclidean form, this manner of proportion theory can be made to correspond to the modern definition of real number, as formulated by the German mathematician Julius Wilhelm Richard Dedekind. In each example, the real term (possibly irrational) is considered to separate all the rationals into those greater and those less than it.

It seems likely that Eudoxus also contributed to the study of incommensurable lines. His predecessor Theaetetus (d. c. 369) had shown that if the squares of two lines are commensurable with each other but do not have the ratio of square integers, then the lines themselves will be incommensurable with each other; further, if two such lines A, B are taken, the lines A ± B will be incommensurable with them, not only as lines but also in square (lines of this latter type were called *alogoi*, literally, "without ratio"). The further study of the *alogoi* lines, as collected in book 10 of Euclid's *Elements*, divided into twelve classes all the *alogoi* formed as the square roots of R(A ± B), where R is a unit line, and A and B are commensurable with each other in square only. Presumably, Eudoxus and his followers played a part in this investigation.

Eudoxus's efforts are rooted in a concern for logical precision in geometry, and this interest may reflect his close association with the Platonic Academy at Athens. Two anecdotes (of questionable historicity) celebrate this connection. The first explains how Eudoxus came to be involved in seeking the cube duplication, the so-called Delian problem. To allay a plague, the citizens of Delos were commanded by the oracle to double a cube-shaped altar. When their attempts failed, they sent to Plato, who directed his mathematical associates Archytas, Menaechmus, and Eudoxus to solve it. When they did so, however, Plato criticized their efforts for being too mechanical. The solutions of a dozen different ancient geometers are known, but that of Eudoxus has not been preserved. It supposedly employed "curved lines" of some sort, and reconstructions have been proposed.

In a second story, Plato is said to have posed to Eudoxus the problem of "saving the phenomena" of planetary motion on the restriction to uniform circular motion. An account of Eudoxus's scheme is transmitted by Simplicius of Cilicia (sixth century C.E.) in his commentary on Aristotle's *De caelo* (before 335 B.C.E.; *On the Heavens*, 1777). From this account a reconstruction was worked out by the Italian historian of astronomy Giovanni Virginio Schiaparelli in 1875. The Eudoxean system reproduces the apparent motion of a planet by combining the rotations of a set of homocentric spheres. The planet is set on the equator of a uniformly rotating sphere. If a second sphere is set about the first, rotating with equal speed to the first but in the opposite direction and having its axis inclined, then the planet will trace out an eight-shaped curve (which the ancients called the *hippopede*, or horse fetter), so as to complete the full double loop once for every full revolution of the spheres. One superimposes over this a third spherical rotation, corresponding to the general progress of the planet in the ecliptic, and finally over this a fourth rotation, corresponding to the daily rotation of the whole heaven. In this way, each of the five planets requires four spheres, while the sun and the moon each take three.

Schiaparelli's exposition thus revealed the ingenuity of Eudoxus's scheme for reproducing geometrically the seemingly erratic forward and backward (retrograde) motion of the planets. Nevertheless, the model proves unsuccessful in some respects: Because the planets do not vary in distance from the earth (the center of their spheres), Eudoxus cannot account for their variable brightness or for asymmetries in the shape of their retrograde paths. Even worse, the values that Eudoxus had to assign for the rotations of the spheres do not produce retrogrades for Mars or Venus, and the sun and the moon are given uniform motions, contrary to observation. Apparently, the latter two defects were recognized, for Eudoxus's follower Callippus introduced seven additional spheres (two each for sun and moon, one each for Mercury, Venus, and Mars) to make the needed corrections.

The Eudoxean-Callippean scheme is enshrined in Aristotle's *Metaphysica* (c. 335-323 B.C.E.; *Metaphysics*, 1801), in which it serves as the mathematical basis of a comprehensive picture of the entire physical cosmos. Doubtless, Eudoxus proposed his geometric model without specific commitments on physical and cosmological issues. Nevertheless, it suited well the basic Aristotelian principles—for example, that the cosmos separates into two spherical realms, the celestial and, at its center, the terrestrial, and that the natural motions of matter in the central realm (for example, earthy substances moving in straight lines toward the center of the cosmos) differ from those in the outer (where motion is circular, uniform, and eternal). Ironically, these Aristotelian principles persisted in later cosmology, even after astronomers had switched from the homocentric spheres to eccentrics, epicycles, and other geometric devices.

Eudoxus also produced works of a descriptive and empirical sort in astronomy and geography. His *Phaenomena* (fourth century B.C.E.; phenomena) and *Enoptron* (fourth century B.C.E.; mirror) recorded observations of the stars—the basis, one would suppose, of a systematic almanac of celestial events (for example, solstices and equinoxes, lunar phases, heliacal risings of stars). He

adopted, as Diogenes and others report, an *oktaeteris*, or eight-year calendar cycle. As known to later authors, an *oktaeteris* is one of the cycles found to reconcile the solar year of 365.25 days with the period of the moon's phases (somewhat over 29.5), by parsing out the 2,922 days in eight years into ninety-nine lunar periods (fifty-one of thirty days and forty-eight of twenty-nine). However, it is unclear whether this was the arrangement used by Eudoxus. His geographical treatise, the *Gēs periodos* (fourth century B.C.E.; circuit of the Earth), systematically described the lands and peoples of the known world, from Asia in the east to the western Mediterranean region. A connection with his astronomical studies can be seen in the use of the ratio of longest to shortest periods of daylight for designating the latitudes of places.

SIGNIFICANCE

However interesting Eudoxus's contributions to calendarics, geography, and philosophy may be, they are secondary to his achievement in mathematics, for he may justly be viewed as the most significant geometer in the pre-Euclidean period. He advanced the study of incommensurables, introduced a new technique for generalizing the theory of proportion, and made exact the theory of limits with his new method of "exhaustion." Remarkable for the logical precision of his proofs, Eudoxus here set the standard against which even the foremost of the later geometers, such as Euclid and Archimedes, measured their own efforts.

Eudoxus's influence on geometric astronomy is more subtle. Already, early in the third century B.C.E., astronomers had discarded his system of homocentric spheres in their pursuit of viable geometric models for the planetary motions. If the shortcomings of Eudoxus's model were evident, however, it nevertheless defined for later astronomers the essence of their task: to represent the planetary phenomena by means of uniform circular motion. Eudoxus's success thus remains implicit in the later development of astronomy, from Apollonius and Hipparchus to Ptolemy.

—Wilbur R. Knorr

FURTHER READING

Charles, David. *Aristotle on Meaning and Essence.* Oxford, England: Clarendon Press, 2000. In this work on Aristotle, Charles is critical of his subject's analysis of Eudoxus and Callippus's astronomical conclusions.

De Santillana, G. "Eudoxus and Plato: A Study in Chronology." In *Reflections on Men and Ideas.* Cambridge, Mass.: MIT Press, 1968. A revised chronology of Eudoxus's life is argued on the basis of a detailed examination of the ancient biographical data and collateral historical evidence.

Knorr, W. R. *The Ancient Tradition of Geometric Problems*. Boston: Birkhäuser, 1986. Chapter 3 considers Eudoxus's studies of exhaustion and cube duplication, discussed in the wider context of pre-Euclidean geometry.

Neugebauer, O. *A History of Ancient Mathematical Astronomy*. New York: Springer-Verlag, 1975. All facets of Eudoxus's contributions to astronomy are covered; particularly detailed is the discussion of his planetary models. Includes an index.

Waerden, B. L. van der. *Science Awakening*. 4th ed. Princeton Junction, N.J.: Scholar's Bookshelf, 1988.

The author provides a brief, insightful review of Eudoxus's mathematical work.

SEE ALSO: Archimedes; Aristotle; Euclid.

RELATED ARTICLES in *Great Events from History: The Ancient World*: 600-500 B.C.E., Greek Philosophers Formulate Theories of the Cosmos; c. 500-400 B.C.E., Greek Physicians Begin Scientific Practice of Medicine; c. 380 B.C.E., Plato Develops His Theory of Ideas; c. 300 B.C.E., Euclid Compiles a Treatise on Geometry; c. 275 B.C.E., Greeks Advance Hellenistic Astronomy; c. 250 B.C.E., Discoveries of Archimedes; 46 B.C.E., Establishment of the Julian Calendar; 415 C.E., Mathematician and Philosopher Hypatia Is Killed in Alexandria.

EUPALINUS OF MEGARA
Greek architect

Eupalinus was the architect of the tunnel and aqueduct on the island of Samos that bear his name. Probably built for the tyrant Polycrates in the sixth century B.C.E., they still stand today as monuments to the engineering skills of the Greeks of the archaic period.

BORN: c. 575 B.C.E.; Megara, Greece
DIED: c. 500 B.C.E.; place unknown
AREA OF ACHIEVEMENT: Architecture

EARLY LIFE

Eupalinus (ew-PAW-lee-nuhs), the son of Naustrophos, was from the Greek city-state of Megara, in the district of Megaris, located between Athens and Corinth. No details of his life have been preserved, but much can be inferred from what is known about the history of his birthplace in the sixth century B.C.E. Eupalinus was born into a prosperous land. Megara had experienced much growth in the years before his birth and was the mother city of numerous colonies.

The young Eupalinus doubtless heard stories from his father and grandfather about the tyrant Theagenes, who had diverted water from the mountains to the city. The waterworks were still in operation, and the youth must have observed for himself the extensive underground conduit system that the tyrant had built to provide the city with water. The Megaris area was not well endowed with water, and the management of that precious resource was a prime concern. It is possible that a fountain house built in Megara toward the end of the century was designed by

Eupalinus. In any case, it is likely that he gained some reputation in hydraulic engineering before being called to Samos for the great tunnel project.

Education for boys of Megara in the sixth century was mostly a matter of training for military activities and of learning manners and politics from their elders during banquets and symposia (drinking parties). Eupalinus would also have observed the productions of some of the first comedies, for the Megarians were said to have invented this dramatic form during Eupalinus's youth. As a result of his upbringing, it is likely that he was cultured and comfortable among other citizens of privilege.

Eupalinus probably lived most of his life in the democracy that followed the tyranny but would have observed the many struggles between the wealthy conservative oligarchs and the poorer supporters of popular rule. The poetry of Theognis of Megara preserves many of the passions that this strife aroused. The differences between rich and poor were exacerbated by the introduction of coinage, which also took place during Eupalinus's lifetime, as did the *Palintokia*, or debt-relief measures meant to help farmers.

Eupalinus had firsthand experience with siege and warfare as well. Throughout the sixth century, Megara fought a series of wars with neighboring Athens. In one incident, the Athenian Pisistratus is said to have besieged and captured the Megarian harbor Nisaea. This background points to Eupalinus's later success in his life's work: He had a worldly background in politics and culture and a good knowledge of warfare and hydraulic engineering. These elements point to his future favor in the court of Polycrates.

LIFE'S WORK

Eupalinus is known from statements by Herodotus to have been the architect of the Eupalinos Tunnel, cut through the mountain bordering the capital city of the island Samos. Herodotus said that on Samos were the three greatest constructions of all the Greeks and listed the tunnel of Eupalinus first, describing its dimensions fairly accurately. The other two marvels of construction were Polycrates' great harbor works and the temple of Hera. Today, the tunnel is by far the best preserved of the three. Archaeological evidence points to a date somewhere between 540 and 530 B.C.E. for the beginning of the work. Scholars have inferred that the tyrant Polycrates called Eupalinus from Megara to direct the project.

The task facing Eupalinus was formidable: In order to keep the Samians supplied with water in time of siege, he was to bring water from a spring on the north side of Mount Ampelus (now called Kastro) into the walled city on the other side. His solution was ingenious, consisting of an 850-meter-long underground conduit (high enough for a man to walk) that led from the spring to the entrance of a straight tunnel cut almost one kilometer through the mountain. The conduit was circuitous, so as to make disposal of the fill easier on the hilly terrain and to make detection more difficult and thus secure the Samians' water supply. The tunnel not only had a channel for the water but also provided a convenient escape route should the city ever be taken. The system was so efficient that it continued to be used into Byzantine times, after which it fell into disrepair. The system was also well hidden; it lay undiscovered until 1853, when some of the conduit pipes were found, but the tunnel itself was not located by archaeologists until 1882, when a German team began excavations. The results of their work are still being published.

The tunnel was cut through solid limestone by workers using only hammer and chisel. It consists of two levels: an upper level on which people could walk—approximately two meters in height and width—and a deeper shaft on the east side up to seven and a half meters deep, where the water flowed in a channel made of ceramic tiles.

Eupalinus instructed his workers to divide into two teams, each of which began digging at opposite ends of the mountain. The method he used to ensure that they met in the middle has not yet been discovered. The teams

were only two meters apart when they could hear each other's chisels and abruptly turned east. The northern team then broke through into the southern tunnel at a right angle. It has been calculated that had the workers continued digging in a straight line, they would have met head-on, although the northern shaft was a bit higher than the southern one. A conduit within the town led from the south end of the tunnel, providing not only drinking water for the inhabitants but possibly also a steady stream to operate the town's water clock.

It is not known how long Eupalinus took to complete the tunnel—estimates range from five to fifteen years—nor is it known how many people he employed; certainly the size of the shafts would have permitted only a few workers on each team. It is obvious that Eupalinus took pride in his work and was something of a perfectionist, for the quality of the carving is very high, and there are niches carved in the walls to support lamps. In addition, Eupalinus saw to it that the tunnel was well provided with fresh air, which flowed through a ventilation hole and the conduits themselves.

It is likely that the tyrant Polycrates had ulterior motives when he hired Eupalinus. In addition to wanting the citizens of Samos to have a safe water supply and full employment, the tyrant was concerned that his people be occupied with large projects so as not to have time or desire to revolt against his power. Aristotle compares Polycrates' constructions to those undertaken by tyrants at Athens and Corinth. While the tunnel on Samos is the only undisputed work of Eupalinus, the similarity of the pipes used in its construction to those found in the Pisistratean aqueduct at Athens has led some to think that Eupalinus was the architect of that water system also, but no certain proof has yet been offered.

SIGNIFICANCE

Eupalinus was not the first of the ancients—or the last—to engineer an underground tunnel for water transport. His contribution was one not of originality but of quality: He proved that tunneling through a mountain for an aqueduct could be done efficiently with a simple technology. Although his northern team worked at a higher level than the southern tunnelers, and though the tunnel did not meet in a perfectly straight fashion, the work was nevertheless outstanding for its excellence: No other ancient tunnel matched its standards. Two hundred years earlier, a tunnel was constructed at Jerusalem between the Virgin's Pool and Siloam. Like Eupalinus's aqueduct, this construction was begun at both ends, but it was not as straight as the Samian tunnel. In fact, the Jerusalem tunnel wasted more than 150 meters on its winding way. A Roman tunnel project in northern Africa, at Saldae (modern Bejaïa), that used the two-team technique—more than five hundred years after Eupalinus—is also known. This project failed because the teams were unable to find each other. Their courses were so misdirected, in fact, that they dug a total distance that exceeded the mountain's width.

Eupalinus's engineering methods are not fully understood and probably combined the empirical (trial and error) with some surveying techniques that have yet to be discovered. He might have aligned poles carefully up one side of the mountain and down the other or used a method of triangulation that the engineer Hero of Alexandria described six hundred years later. It is also possible that Eupalinus kept the shafts straight by having his workmen keep their eyes on a light behind them at the end of the tunnel or shining through a hole cut in the roof. Whatever his methods were, they were effective, and the tunnel that bears his name stands as one of the most impressive engineering feats of antiquity.

—Daniel B. Levine

FURTHER READING

Burns, Alfred. "The Tunnel of Eupalinus and the Tunnel Problem of Hero of Alexandria." *Isis* 62 (Summer, 1971): 172-185. An excellent analysis of Hero of Alexandria's first century C.E. treatise, *Dioptra*, in relation to the tunnel, with diagrams from Hero's work compared with the Samian topography.

Figueira, Thomas J., and Gregory Nagy, eds. *Theognis of Megara: Poetry and the Polis*. Baltimore: The Johns Hopkins University Press, 1985. Provides historical background of archaic Megara. Includes a chronological table with extensive annotations as well as a discussion of Megarian society and education during Eupalinus's lifetime.

Goodfield, June. "The Tunnel of Eupalinus." *Scientific American* 210 (June, 1964): 104-110. An account of a scientific/photographic expedition to investigate the tunnel. Contains summaries of the German excavators' findings and engineering problems and excellent diagrams, photographs, and maps.

Humphrey, John William, John P. Oleson, and Andrew N. Sherwood. *Greek and Roman Technology: A Sourcebook*. New York: Routledge, 1998. Contains translations of Greek and Latin works and documents. One chapter covers hydraulic engineering.

Legon, Ronald P. *Megara: The Political History of a Greek City-State to 336 B.C.* Ithaca, N.Y.: Cornell University Press, 1981. A good source for the historical background of Eupalinus, discussing Megarian geography, tyranny, oligarchy, democracy, and commerce. Also treats the fountain house of Theagenes and Eupalinus's possible role in its construction.

Mitchell, B. M. "Herodotus and Samos." *Journal of Hellenic Studies* 95 (1973): 75-91. In the course of discussing Herodotus's relations with Samos and information about the town, Mitchell includes a concise and well-documented discussion of the tunnel, with speculations on date, manpower, rate of work, and use.

Rihll, T. E., and J. V. Tucker. "Greek Engineering: The Case of Eupalinos's Tunnel." In *The Greek World*, edited by Anton Powell. New York: Routledge, 1995. Volume of essays on ancient Greek civilization includes bibliography and index.

Shipley, Graham. *A History of Samos: 800-188 B.C.* Oxford, England: Clarendon Press, 1987. Contains an account of the tunnel of Eupalinus with a summary of scholarship on it.

White, K. D. *Greek and Roman Technology*. Ithaca, N.Y.: Cornell University Press, 1984. This book includes a section on hydraulic engineering with a discussion of the tunnel, comparative material from other ancient waterworks, and an extensive bibliography, as well as an explanation of Eupalinus's use of the channel on the east side of the tunnel. Discusses surveying problems and Hero of Alexandria's solution. Includes illustrations.

SEE ALSO: Archimedes; Hero of Alexandria; Pisistratus.

RELATED ARTICLES in *Great Events from History: The Ancient World*: 447-438 B.C.E., Building of the Parthenon; 312 B.C.E., First Roman Aqueduct Is Built; 312-264 B.C.E., Building of the Appian Way.

EURIPIDES
Greek playwright

Ranking with Aeschylus and Sophocles as a master of Attic tragedy, Euripides was the most "modern" of the great Greek tragedians, often criticizing traditional mythology and realistically working out the logical implications of ancient legends.

BORN: c. 485 B.C.E.; Phlya, Greece
DIED: 406 B.C.E.; Macedonia, Greece
AREA OF ACHIEVEMENT: Literature

EARLY LIFE

Little is known of the life of Euripides (yew-RIHP-uh-deez) because few records were kept in his time. Philochorus, a careful annalist who lived in the early third century B.C.E., wrote a biography of Euripides, fragments of which have survived; it is long on anecdotes but short on dates. What is reasonably certain is that Euripides' father, Mnesarchos, was an affluent merchant and that his mother, Cleito, was of aristocratic descent. When he was four years old, the great naval Battle of Salamis, in which the Greeks defeated the Persians, caused Euripides' family to flee the small town of Phlya for Athens. When the boy was eight, the ruined walls of Athens were rebuilt, after the Greeks had decisively defeated Persia on land as well as sea. Freedom had triumphed over despotism—only temporarily, as Euripides was to discover.

In 466, Euripides became officially a "youth," whereupon the state conscripted him for garrison duty in the frontier forts of Attica. Full military service ensued when he was twenty. He distinguished himself as an athlete, did some painting and sculpting, and undoubtedly participated in what may have constituted the greatest intellectual awakening in Western history. As the mother-city of the Ionian territories, Athens had become the harbor for a great influx of artists, poets, historians, philosophers, and scientists fleeing Persian repression. Euripides is known to have been involved with the Sophists, particularly Protagoras, author of the doctrine that "Man is the measure of all things" and a skeptic about the universal validity of science or religion. Euripides may also have associated with Anaxagoras, a philosopher concerned with theories of the mind; Archelaus, Anaxagoras's pupil; Diogenes of Apollonia; and Socrates. Sophocles was his contemporary; undoubtedly, the tragedians knew each other's works, but no evidence exists that they socialized with each other.

Euripides had his first play produced in 455, competing at the Great Festival of Dionysius one year after the death of Aeschylus and thirteen years after Sophocles' first victory. Titled *Peliades* (daughters of Pelias), it was a trial run of his later *Mēdeia* (431 B.C.E.; *Medea*, 1781); the manuscript is not extant.

LIFE'S WORK

Altogether, Euripides wrote 92 plays, of which 88 were entered in the Dionysian contests, although he won on only four occasions. Seventeen of his plays survive, compared with 7 out of 80 for Aeschylus and 7 out of 123 for Sophocles.

His earliest extant play is a tragicomedy, *Alkēstis* (438 B.C.E.; *Alcestis*, 1781), based on a folktale. It was placed fourth in a set of Euripidean plays, in the position usually accorded a comic satyr play, but its comic elements are minor. In this play, Admetus, a Thessalian king, has his young wife Alcestis agree to die in his place. The visiting Heracles, however, wrestles with Death and forces him to yield his beautiful victim. Euripides exposes the underside of this romantic legend: Admetus behaves as a warmly courteous host to Heracles and weeps over his "dead" wife, but essentially he is a coward. He lacks the courage to die at the time appointed for him, instead complacently allowing his wife to replace him. Moreover, he fails to admit his selfishness even to himself.

Euripides' next surviving drama was *Medea*, his most famous work. Athenians watching the first performance would have known the drama's mythic background: Medea, a barbarian princess and sorceress related to the gods, helped Jason the Argonaut to steal the Golden Fleece and even murdered her own brother so that she and Jason could safely escape pursuit. In the play's action, Medea's beloved Jason has tired of his dangerous foreign mistress and agreed to marry the daughter of Creon so that he can succeed to the throne of Corinth. Desolate and maddened, Medea pretends reconciliation with Jason's bride and sends her a poisoned robe that fatally burns both her and Creon. Medea proceeds to kill her two children by Jason and then sails away on a magic dragon-chariot sent by her grandfather Helius, god of the sun. Euripides' treatment of Jason and Medea renders their personalities in a rather modern fashion: He is calm, self-confident, and rational, but cold; she is devoted and kind, but her rage at being rejected transforms her into an elemental incarnation of vengeful hatred. Their arguments constitute brilliant fireworks of articulated feelings and clashing temperaments.

Hippolytos (428 B.C.E.; *Hippolytus*, 1781) is more restrained and economical. It was his second version of the Phaedra-Theseus-Hippolytus plot; the first has been lost. Framing the drama are a prologue spoken by Aphrodite and an epilogue spoken by Artemis. The tragedy consists of the conflict between them, as Phaedra is identified with love and lust, Hippolytus with chastity and a consequent neglect of Aphrodite's charms. The scorned Aphrodite causes Phaedra, Theseus's newest wife, to fall hopelessly in love with her stepson Hippolytus. Refused by him, she writes a letter falsely accusing him of having raped her; then she commits suicide. On reading the letter, Theseus curses Hippolytus, and Poseidon fulfills the malediction by having a monster fatally wound the young man. It is Artemis who reveals the truth to Theseus so that father and son can at least be reconciled before Hippolytus's death. Though Euripides magnificently celebrates the frustrated passion of his heroine, he permits the play to end in rhetorical commonplaces as Hippolytus and Theseus first argue, then forgive each other.

From a structural perspective, the most innovative achievement of *Hippolytus* is the freedom Euripides grants his characters to change their minds: Phaedra first resolves not to reveal her love, then does so; the nurse gives her mistress conflicting advice; and Hippolytus

Euripides. (Library of Congress)

first decides to reveal his stepmother's lust to his father, then chooses not to do so. In his focus on the unpredictability of his characters' wills, Euripides anticipates psychological dramas such as those of Henrik Ibsen and Luigi Pirandello.

Numerous relatively minor works were also first mounted in the 420's and 410's. Many of these reflect events of the Peloponnesian War, the decisive struggle between Athens and Sparta. While Athens had become a model of democracy under the leadership of Pericles, Sparta favored despotic oligarchies. Euripides, still subject to military service, presumably saw combat during the first years of this agonizing conflict, which eventually ended with Athens's capitulation.

Hērakleidai (c. 430 B.C.E.; *The Children of Herakles*, 1781), a mutilated text, presents a humane Athens as the protector of Heracles' children, standing for fairness, mercy, and right principles. *Hekabē* (425 B.C.E.; *Hecuba*, 1782) is a pacifist tragedy whose heroine, like Medea, is transformed by unbearable wrongs from dignified majesty to vindictive bitterness. *Ēlektra* (413 B.C.E.; *Electra*, 1782) is a melodrama that presents the protagonist as a slave princess in rags, morbidly attached to her dead father and inexorably jealous of her mother. *Andromachē* (c. 426 B.C.E.; *Andromache*, 1782) makes the Spartan king its villain; with its direct denunciations of Sparta, the play is virtually a wartime propaganda polemic. *Hiketides* (c. 423 B.C.E.; *The Suppliants*, 1781) also expresses Athenian wartime feeling, centering on the ceremonial lamentations of bereaved mothers over their sons' corpses.

Trōiades (415 B.C.E.; *The Trojan Women*, 1782) paints an even bleaker portrait of war's havoc. Only a few years earlier, Athens had emerged from an indecisive ten years' struggle with Sparta. In the spring of 415, Athens was but weeks away from launching the Sicilian expedition that would touch off the last, disastrous phase of the same war. The Sicilian venture had been voted when Euripides presented a trilogy of which only *The Trojan Women*, its concluding tragedy, survives. It shows the conquest of Troy by the Achaeans degenerating into calamity: The ancient Greeks have committed hubris by insulting the altars of the gods, killing all Troy's male inhabitants, and defiling virgins in holy places. The Trojan princesses must be the slaves of their Greek captors: Hecuba, Priam's widow, has been allotted to Odysseus; Cassandra, the virgin priestess, will be Agamemnon's concubine; Hector's widow, Andromache, will become slave to Pyrrhus, Achilles' son; and Hector and Andromache's son, the boy Astyanax, is taken from her arms and thrown to his death. Two of the mightiest scenes in Attic drama elevate this play to heartbreaking greatness: first, the parting between Andromache and Astyanax, and second, Hecuba's lament on receiving the boy's dead body after it has been flung from Troy's battlements. The work justifies Aristotle's designation of Euripides as "the most tragic . . . of the poets"; in this work, he is also the most nihilistic.

Euripides' later plays fall into two main divisions. One category consists of lighter, more romantic works with happy endings. These include *Iphigeneia ē en Taurois* (c. 414 B.C.E.; *Iphigenia in Tauris*, 1782), in which the heroine succeeds in saving her brother Orestes from the murderous Taurians; with this work, Euripides can be said to have written literature's first melodramatic thriller. *Iōn* (c. 411 B.C.E.; *Ion*, 1781) is Euripides' most intricately plotted and irreverent play: Apollo is treated as a selfish, mendacious rapist who is thoroughly discredited amid complex intrigues. *Helenē* (412 B.C.E.; *Helen*, 1782) is another melodrama, loaded with reversals: It was only Helen's ghostly double who went to Troy to start the Ten Years' War, while the substantive Helen takes refuge in Egypt and outwits its barbaric king. Her husband, Menelaus, arrives, and the two are able to escape.

An alternative line of development continues Euripides' ruthlessly probing tragedies. *Orestēs* (408 B.C.E.; *Orestes*, 1782) is a densely textured work focusing on Orestes' fate some days after he murdered his mother. He is intermittently mad and ill, nursed by Electra; both are imprisoned in the royal palace by an angry, rebellious populace and condemned to death for their matricide. A blazing climax—Orestes' party sets the palace on fire—leads to the intervention of Apollo, who orders Orestes to go to Athens, there obtain acquittal for his crime, and then marry Menelaus and Helen's daughter, Hermione, in order to restore peace to the House of Atreus. *Iphigeneia ē en Aulidi* (405 B.C.E.; *Iphigenia in Aulis*, 1782) was discovered after Euripides' death in incomplete form and finished by another hand. It shows an irresolute Agamemnon preparing to sacrifice his youngest daughter, Iphigenia, but a messenger's speech predicts the ending Euripides presumably would have written had he lived longer: Artemis's last-minute substitution of a deer as the victim.

Probably Euripides' finest tragedy is a play he did finish, though it, too, was produced posthumously: *Bakchai* (405 B.C.E.; *The Bacchae*, 1781). The work features Dionysius playing a central role as both actor and Fate. He is described in the opening scene as "of soft, even ef-feminate, appearance. . . . His long blond curls ripple down over his shoulders. Throughout the play he wears a smiling mask." His identity remains elusive as well as demoniac as he mingles gentleness with cruelty, flirtation with terror, coldness with passion. He presents himself as universal humanity, protean, both female-in-male and male-in-female, essentially amoral, blessing those who worship him and having no mercy on those who deny him. He personifies the bestial, primitive constituent of the psyche, free from ego constraint, at once superhuman and subhuman.

Dionysius's chief victim is the young ruler Pentheus, intemperate, self-willed, disdainful of tradition, and scoffingly arrogant. Pentheus masks his primitive instincts behind authority and orderliness, only to have Dionysus crack his shell of artificial self-control, maddening him into frenzies of voyeurism and sadism. The civilized, rational ruler is transformed into a bisexual Peeping Tom who costumes himself in women's clothes so that he can spy on the Bacchantes' orgies. His frenzied mother, Agave, takes her son for a wild lion and, in the grip of Dionysian delusion, slaughters him. Thus, Pentheus dies as both a convert to and a victim of the instinctual life. Dionysius has ruthlessly destroyed the self that is ignorant of its nature. Euripides in this way dramatized the pitiless drive of the unconscious and the precariousness of human existence.

Legend has it that Euripides in old age was a sad man who conversed little and sat for long hours in his cave by the sea on Salamis. In 408 he exiled himself to the court of King Archelaus in Macedonia. Details of his subsequent death, in the winter of 406, are unknown. Philochorus claims that when Sophocles introduced his chorus during the 406 Dionysian festival, he brought the men onstage without their customary garlands as a sign of mourning for his great rival.

SIGNIFICANCE

Anticipating such later playwrights as Henrik Ibsen and George Bernard Shaw, Bertolt Brecht and Jean-Paul Sartre, Euripides was an innovative, agile thinker who used the stage as a forum for his ideas about the world. The second half of the fifth century B.C.E. saw immense cultural convulsions involving the destruction of the Hellenic world's religious and political stability. Euripides recognized a world devoid of rational order and, hence, of Sophoclean notions of human responsibility and divine wisdom. He often highlighted the discrepancy between received traditions and experienced reality of human nature. Thus, his Admetus is shown as a shabby egotist, his Odysseus as a sly demagogue, his Agamemnon as an incompetent general, his Jason as an opportunistic adventurer. In contrast to the pious, conventional plays of Aeschylus and Sophocles, Euripidean drama is skeptical, rational, and diagnostic, stressing an often-difficult encounter between culture and the individual. It was this dramatic confrontation between mythic traditions and the elemental demands of the human psyche that chiefly interested Euripides.

His characters often find themselves captive to myths that strain their personalities: Euripides' Orestes murders his mother in an Argos that provides for judicial fairness; his Odysseus, Medea, Hermione, and Electra are all divorced from a culture in which their conduct was appropriate and are set instead in an alien time that distorts and misunderstands their choices. Euripidean personages tend to behave in self-contradictory and self-destructive ways, anticipating William Shakespeare's problematic Angelos, Claudios, and Lucios; August Strindberg's Miss Julie; and Eugene O'Neill's Cabots and Tyrones. Euripides' theater sabotages the conventions of ancient tragedy, replacing them with a challenging, turbulent, and revolutionary drama that bridges the gap between classical integration and contemporary chaos.

—Gerhard Brand

FURTHER READING

Conacher, D. J. *Euripidean Drama: Myth, Theme, and Structure*. Toronto: University of Toronto Press, 1967. Conacher conducts the reader on an erudite tour of Euripidean treatments of myths, beginning with such conventional texts as *Hippolytus* and ending with romantic melodramas such as *Alcestis*.

Kitto, H. D. F. *Greek Tragedy: A Literary Study*. New York: Routledge, 2002. This is a paperback reprint of a distinguished study first published in 1939. Kitto devotes five of his thirteen chapters to Euripidean tragedy.

Murray, Gilbert. *Euripides and His Age*. Reprint. London: Oxford University Press, 1965. The great British Hellenist's work remains vivid, vigorous, and lucid. His perspective is that of an Enlightenment liberal for whom religion is a form of superstition.

Segal, Erich, ed. *Euripides: A Collection of Critical Essays*. Englewood Cliffs, N.J.: Prentice-Hall, 1968. An anthology of ten essays by distinguished classical scholar/critics.

_____. *Greek Tragedy: Modern Essays in Criticism*. New York: Harper and Row, 1982. Segal reprints eight of the essays from the above-cited text and includes three additional articles of merit, one of which, by Jacqueline de Romilly, compares Aeschylus's and Euripides' treatments of fear and suffering.

Webster, T. B. L. *The Tragedies of Euripides*. London: Methuen, 1967. Webster's highly detailed study contains a vast amount of information, but his style is pedestrian and his focus on metrics may deter the reader who has not mastered ancient Greek.

SEE ALSO: Aeschylus; Anaxagoras; Aristophanes; Menander (dramatist); Protagoras; Socrates; Sophocles.

RELATED ARTICLES in *Great Events from History: The Ancient World*: c. 1600-c. 1000 B.C.E., City of Mycenae Flourishes; c. 750 B.C.E., Homer Composes the *Iliad*; c. 456/455 B.C.E., Greek Tragedian Aeschylus Dies; May, 431-September, 404 B.C.E., Peloponnesian War; June, 415-September, 413 B.C.E., Athenian Invasion of Sicily; 406 B.C.E., Greek Dramatist Euripides Dies; c. 385 B.C.E., Greek Playwright Aristophanes Dies.

EUSEBIUS OF CAESAREA
Caesarean pope and saint

Eusebius formulated the political philosophy of unity of church and state under the providence of God that became standard in the East.

BORN: c. 260 C.E.; probably Caesarea, Palestine (now Qisarya, Israel)
DIED: May 30, 339 C.E.; Caesarea, Palestine
ALSO KNOWN AS: Eusebius Pamphili
AREAS OF ACHIEVEMENT: Historiography, religion

EARLY LIFE

Relatively little is known of the early life of Eusebius (yew-SEE-bee-uhs). He was likely born near Caesarea to peasant parents. The church historian Socrates, writing in the fifth century, states that Eusebius received Christian teaching and baptism at Caesarea and was later ordained a presbyter there.

Eusebius's mentor, a presbyter from the church at Alexandria named Pamphilus, was one of the leading biblical and theological scholars of the day, a disciple of the Christian philosopher Origen. He founded a school in Caesarea and gathered a large library of both pagan and Christian works there. Eusebius read widely under his teacher's guidance. By 303 Eusebius had completed early versions of at least two of his most important historical works, *Chronicon* (c. 300, 325 C.E.; *Chronicle*, 1583) and *Historia ecclesiastica* (c. 300, 324 C.E.; *Ecclesiastical History*, 1576-1577, better known as Eusebius's *Church History*).

Eusebius grew very close to Pamphilus, eventually adopting the surname Pamphili (son of Pamphilus). During the persecution begun by the emperor Diocletian, Pamphilus was imprisoned for two years, eventually suffering martyrdom in 309 or 310. Before his teacher's death, Eusebius assisted him in completing five volumes of a six-volume defense of Origen.

It is possible that Eusebius was jailed for his faith for a short period in Egypt following Pamphilus's death. At the 335 Synod of Tyre, which dealt with the continuing Arian controversy, Eusebius was accused by Potammon, a rival bishop from Egypt, of having sacrificed to the emperor cult to avoid torture while in prison. The charge probably was false, judging by the harsh stance the Church took toward Christians who lapsed into such actions and by the honors Eusebius received immediately after the persecution. These honors included his consecration as bishop of Caesarea about 314, shortly after the proclamation of peace by Constantine and Licinius.

LIFE'S WORK

Eusebius lived during the period when one of the most dramatic events in the Church's existence occurred: the transformation of the Roman Empire, under Constantine's direction, from persecutor to supporter and protector of Christianity. Eusebius's work cannot be fully understood without recognizing the importance of this apparent miracle for his thought. The first editions of his works, however, were certainly composed before Constantine's rise, probably during the first years of Diocletian's reign. A cautious optimism pervaded Christian circles at that time as a result of the lack of persecution, and Eusebius seems to have developed his idea of Christianity as the culmination of the course of human history in the first editions of his *Chronicle* and *Ecclesiastical History*.

It was when the Church again came under attack in 303 that Eusebius felt compelled to set forth his views at length, doing so primarily in the works *Praeparatio evangelica* (c. 314-318; *Preparation for the Gospel*, 1903) and *Demonstratio evangelica* (after 314; *Proof of the Gospel*, 1920). Eusebius's notions of history and its meaning were greatly influenced by his work in and interpretation of the Scriptures. For him, the Bible was the key to a correct understanding of human history. His beliefs were deeply rooted in the study of the Old Testament, where he saw the beginning of Christianity—not in Judaism proper but rather in the earlier era of the patriarchs.

Christianity from its earliest days had been extremely sensitive to the charge that it was of recent origin. In *Kata Kelsou* (248; also known as *Contra Celsum*; *Origen Against Celsus*, 1660), Origen quoted the pagan writer Aulus Cornelius Celsus as scornfully saying, "A few years ago he [Christ] began to teach." The earliest Christian apologists tied Christianity to its Jewish roots and insisted that the loftiest ideas of paganism had actually been borrowed from the Hebrews. Eusebius did not consider that explanation to be adequate; he reinterpreted the biblical accounts to show that Christianity was, in fact, the most ancient of all the religions of humankind.

Eusebius, like Origen, saw history as having begun with a fall away from God, as illustrated in the Old Testament by the sin of Adam and Eve. Human beings after the Fall were characterized by savagery and superstition. There were some, however, who were able to see that God transcended the created world. These friends of God were the patriarchs, to whom were made known divine truths by the *Logos* (Christ). The patriarchs were the original Christians, knowing both God the Father and His Son, the divine Word. The unenlightened contemporaries of the patriarchs were the original pagans.

Judaism came into Eusebius's scheme as a purely transitional phase, to prepare the way for the new covenant of Jesus that would diffuse the religion of the patriarchs to all humankind. Following the period of the Mosaic law came the central period of history, which began with the nearly simultaneous appearance of Christ and Augustus, the foundation of Church and Empire. He saw the reign of Constantine as the culmination of human history, the last era before the end of the world. The whole story was a "salvation history" that set the Christian experience into a context of historical knowledge that was basically shared by all educated people in the ancient world.

The whole of Eusebius's *Ecclesiastical History* could be interpreted as the account of the Church's continual movement forward in the working out of its victory over the demoniac powers. He viewed Constantine as leading people into the way of truth, as preached by the Church. Under his influence, the Gospel could be preached everywhere, and when that was accomplished the end of the world and the return of Christ would take place. *Oratio de laudibus Constantini* (335-336 C.E.; *In Praise of Constantine*, 1976) and *Vita Constantini* (339 C.E.; *Life of Constantine*, 1845) contain several passages in which Eusebius seems to express hope of seeing the end in his own time.

It is likely that Constantine first took notice of Eusebius at the Council of Nicaea in 325. This council was called by the emperor to put an end to the strife in the Church over the doctrines of Arius, a presbyter of Alexandria, who taught that Christ was a created being and therefore not eternal. Although Eusebius had at first opposed action against Arius and evidently favored his subordinationist position, Eusebius was primarily interested in preserving unity in the Church. He was the leader of a moderate group at Nicaea, which attempted to steer a middle course between the position of Arius and that of his chief antagonist, Athanasius. Eusebius had been provisionally excommunicated by an earlier council in Antioch for his refusal to sign its strongly anti-Arian creed.

At Nicaea, Eusebius presented a creed used in Caesarea as proof of his orthodox beliefs and as a possible solution statement to the question of the relationship between the Father and Son in the Godhead. This Caesar-

ean creed, however, was expanded considerably before the bishops arrived at a final form. The most notable addition was of the term *homoousios* (Greek for "of the same substance" as God) to describe Christ. Although Eusebius reluctantly subscribed to the new creed for the sake of unity, during subsequent years he was involved in various actions against Athanasius, including the Synod of Tyre in 335, which formally condemned him.

Eusebius gained the respect of Constantine because of his peacemaking attitude; he enjoyed a rather close relationship with the emperor through the rest of his life. In 336, in celebration of the thirtieth anniversary of Constantine's accession, Eusebius praised the ruler in a lengthy speech that had as its theme the resemblance of Constantine to Christ. When Constantine died in May, 337, Eusebius immediately set about writing his *Life of Constantine*, which was left unfinished at his death in 339. His successor as bishop of Caesarea, Acacius, finished and published the book later the same year.

SIGNIFICANCE

Eusebius's approach to historiography is unique in several ways. He was the first Christian apologist to bring the literary-historical point of view to his works. While all other early opponents of paganism and heresy wished only to enter into polemical discussion, occasionally mentioning chronological facts when it served their argument, Eusebius fixed the dates of writers and cataloged their works, clearly grasping the concept of a Christian literature.

In the ancient world, Eusebius's *Ecclesiastical History* was so successful that no one tried to supersede it. Instead, 150 years after his death, three writers, Socrates, Sozomen, and Theodoret, continued Eusebius's history down to their own times. The approach of Eusebius was dominant in the writing of church history almost until the time of the Enlightenment in the eighteenth century. The *Ecclesiastical History* is classed as one of the four or five seminal works in Western historiography.

Eusebius's overriding theme was celebration of the success of Christianity in the Roman world. He produced the reformulation of Christian political theory necessitated by the legalization of Christianity under Constantine. In his reinterpretation, the government became a positive institution in which Christians could take a more active part and for which they began to take more responsibility. In the Eastern Roman Empire, his idea of the Church under the jurisdiction of a Christian ruler remained the norm until the fall of Constantinople in the fifteenth century.

Eusebius's optimistic theory of the general advance of human history under God proved to be the only real alternative to the historical views that would be developed in the fifth century by Saint Augustine of Hippo. Augustine was as much influenced in his comparatively pessimistic concept by the sack of Rome in 410 as Eusebius had been by the triumph of Constantine.

—Douglas A. Foster

FURTHER READING

Barnes, Timothy D. *Constantine and Eusebius*. Cambridge, Mass.: Harvard University Press, 1981. An extremely well-documented and interesting volume that the author describes as an "interpretive essay" on Eusebius and Constantine as individuals and their relationship to each other. Of the 458 pages, more than 180 contain helpful apparatus, including copious notes to the chapters, a bibliography, a list of editions of Eusebius's works, and a chronology of his life.

Chesnut, Glenn F. *The First Christian Histories: Eusebius, Socrates, Sozomen, Theodoret, and Evagrius*. 2d ed. Macon, Ga.: Mercer University Press, 1986. Details the historical work of Eusebius and the historians who followed him, placing them in the context of historiography in the pagan world of their times. Shows the importance of Eusebius's work in the development of a Christian historiography. Contains footnotes but no bibliography.

Drake, H. A. Notes to *In Praise of Constantine: A Historical Study and New Translation of Eusebius's Tricennial Orations*. Berkeley: University of California Press, 1976. Although focusing primarily on Eusebius's laudatory speech of 336, this slender volume of 191 pages is much more than simply a critical edition of the speech. It provides a number of valuable insights into the thought and actions of Eusebius throughout his life. Sixty pages of notes and bibliography make it very valuable for a study of Eusebius.

Eusebius. *The History of the Church from Christ to Constantine*. Translated by G. A. Williamson. New York: Penguin Books, 1989. This is Eusebius's most famous work. An introduction by the translator, a map, and several helpful appendices of names mentioned in the text make this volume of the Penguin Classics series a must for students of Eusebius.

Grant, Michael. "Eusebius." In *The Ancient Historians*. London: Duckworth, 1995. A chapter in Grant's monumental work, which, though only fifteen pages long, is valuable for its insights into Eusebius's place among historians of the ancient world. The book itself is lengthy, and it is more than most students need for a study of Eusebius alone but very valuable for a context of ancient historians.

Grant, Robert M. *Eusebius as Church Historian*. Oxford, England: Clarendon Press, 1980. An in-depth study of the *Ecclesiastical History* and an evaluation of Eusebius as a historian. Focusing on seven major themes (including apostolic succession, heretics, persecution, martyrdom, and the canon of Scripture), Grant points out both strengths and weaknesses of the first church historian's work. Footnotes and a brief bibliography are included.

Kofsky, Arieh. *Eusebius of Caesarea Against Paganism*. Leiden, Netherlands: Brill, 2000. Part of Brill's Jewish and Christian perspectives series; includes indexes and bibliography.

Mosshammer, Alden A. *The Chronicle of Eusebius and Greek Chronographic Tradition*. Cranbury, N.J.: Associated University Presses, 1979. A critical study of Eusebius's seminal work of historical chronology that details the possible sources for the work and places it in the context of early Greek chronography.

SEE ALSO: Saint Athanasius of Alexandria; Saint Augustine; Aulus Cornelius Celsus; Constantine the Great; Diocletian; Origen; Theodoret of Cyrrhus.

RELATED ARTICLES in *Great Events from History: The Ancient World*: 250 C.E., Outbreak of the Decian Persecution; c. 286 C.E., Saint Anthony of Egypt Begins Ascetic Life; 325 C.E., Adoption of the Nicene Creed.

EZANA

Aksumite king (r. c. 320-350 C.E.)

Ezana's rule brought the kingdom of Aksum to the highest level of power, influence, and cosmopolitanism it had ever enjoyed.

BORN: c. 303 C.E.; Aksum (now in Ethiopia)
DIED: c. 350 C.E.; Aksum
ALSO KNOWN AS: Ēzānā; Ezanas; Aezana
AREAS OF ACHIEVEMENT: Government and politics, religion

EARLY LIFE

Relatively little is known about the early life of Ezana (AY-zah-nah) and about the period in Ethiopia's history that he helped to shape. A tentative birth date is generally given as 303, although that date may be inaccurate by two or three years. For various reasons, 303 appears to be the latest year in which Ezana could have been born into the prominent and powerful family of Halen. He was the son of Ella Amida, king of Aksum, a kingdom in the highlands southwest of the Red Sea, which is now a part of northern Ethiopia, as well as several other principalities. Ezana acceded to the kingship at an early age, probably around six or seven, but in actuality did not serve actively as a full-fledged king until the early 320's, when he would still have been quite young. During that interim period, the boy's mother, Sofya, served as his regent. Ezana probably reached his majority around age seventeen or eighteen, at which time he would have assumed the kingship, very likely in 320 or 321.

In his youth, Ezana was tutored by Frumentius, who had served as one of Ella Amida's most trusted counselors prior to that king's death. Ezana's sustained association with his tutor was one of the most influential elements in his life. Frumentius, a cultivated man and a Christian, was from Syria. Eventually, Frumentius converted Ezana to the Christian faith. This conversion probably did not occur earlier than the mid-330's; more likely, it was not until the 340's. The change is noted both in Ezana's last inscription and in the symbols used in Aksumite coins issued late in Ezana's reign.

Following the king's conversion, Saint Athanasius of Alexandria named Frumentius, who had risen to a position of considerable power and responsibility in Aksum, bishop of the Ethiopian church, a position of considerable prestige. Much of Aksum, which by tradition had been largely Semitic, subsequently converted to Christianity, setting the stage for a desirable interrelationship between the Ethiopian church and the Egyptian Coptic church.

LIFE'S WORK

What is known about Ezana is derived largely from monolithic stele and obelisks, tall stone structures on which a record of historical events is carved. Some of these structures reached heights of seventy-five feet, towering over everything around them. The lettering on them was in three languages: Greek, Ge'ez (the language of ancient Ethiopia), and Sabean.

The inscriptions refer to Ezana as king of Aksum and of Himyar, of Raidan, of Aithiopia (the ancient spelling of Ethiopia), of Saba, of Siyanio, of Bega, of Salhen, and of Kasu. They also refer to Ezana as the king of kings. Other artifacts refer to various kinglets contemporary with Ezana, who probably ruled over portions of Ezana's domain. This would explain the designation, repeated in several inscriptions, of Ezana as "king of kings." Although there were regional kings, Ezana obviously was the king who ruled over all of them.

The first inscription attributed to Ezana recorded events early in his reign. The Bega people in the north had been attacking the trading caravans that passed near their territory. Ezana dispatched his younger brothers, Shai'azana and Hadefan, to the north to bring an end to the Began attacks, which were devastating to trade. It was with the success of this mission that Ezana demonstrated his exceptional skill as a negotiator and diplomat. He might have enslaved or inhumanely suppressed the people he had conquered, but instead of taking punitive action against them, he gave generously to them and resettled them in Matlia, one of the most fertile sections of Aksum, where they enjoyed considerable prosperity. These former adversaries eventually became supporters of Ezana, and the problem of Began attacks on caravans was brought under control.

It has been difficult for archaeologists to determine the exact extent of Aksum, although the kingdom was fairly large. Archaeologists, linguists, and historians have made various transcriptions from the period of Ezana's rule that mention places they cannot identify, partly because of an overall confusion in the terminology used.

Ezana is thought to have been an enthusiastic builder, probably the motive force behind the erection of some of the obelisks that stand to this day in Aksum. An inscription on one of the obelisks indicates that Ezana honored Ares, whom he figuratively calls his begetter, by erecting to him one statue of gold, one statue of silver, and three statues of copper. This inscription, composed after he had conquered and resettled the Bega, suggests that Ezana had not yet been converted to Christianity, inasmuch as Ares was a pagan god, a part of Ethiopia's old religion.

Immediately after the conquest of Bega, Ezana's brothers brought prominent people from Bega to Aksum along with their camp followers. The inscription on the obelisk indicates that these conquered people brought with them 3,112 cattle and 6,224 sheep. Ezana made a generous allocation of his spoils of war to the Bega captives, providing them as well with grain, wine, beer, and enough water to sustain them for a period of four months, which it apparently took them to journey to their resettlement area of Matlia. He also provided them with twenty-two thousand wheat cakes every day and with clothing. Ultimately, Ezana gifted the six kinglets mentioned in the inscription with 25,140 cattle, which in that part of the world at that time were the currency of the day.

The kingdom of Aksum was dependent for its survival on the brisk trade it had with Egypt and with the interior of Africa. Ezana had been instrumental in having a road erected between Aksum and the Nile to facilitate trade. He realized that the caravans on which his kingdom relied had to be protected at any cost if Aksum was to thrive. Although he shrank at the possibility of employing brutality in the achievement of his ends, he was quite capable of retaliating brutally when his kingdom's main enterprise was threatened.

An obelisk inscribed in Ge'ez relates how Ezana and his warriors subdued the Sarane of Afan in retaliation for their killing of a merchant traveling in a caravan. To achieve this vengeance, Ezana mustered the armies of Mahaza, Dakuen, and Hara, over all of which he ruled, and had them encamp in Alaha, whence they set out to bring retribution to the Sarane.

Ezana's men attacked four settlements of the Sarane: Sa'ne, Sawante, Gema, and Zahtan. A Serane leader, Alita, was taken as a prisoner along with his two children, after which a slaughter occurred. In Afan, 503 men and 202 women, a total of 705, were killed. Among Alita's camp followers, 40 men and 165 children, a total of 205, were taken prisoner.

The Aksumites claimed 31,900 cattle and 827 baggage animals from the Serane as part of their spoils. For his victory, Ezana offered as tribute to Mahrem, one of the gods he acknowledged, 100 cattle and 50 prisoners. The king, according to the transcription, returned safely to his people, assuming the throne at Shado, where he committed himself to the protection of Astar, Beher, and Meder. Having established his ability to exact vengeance,

Ezana vowed the he would destroy anyone who tried to overthrow or replace him as king, promising to confiscate such a miscreant's land, punish his family, and exile him from the country. Ezana also completely crushed the aggressive Kush when they began to threaten the economy of Aksum.

Ezana may have invaded and subsequently gained a degree of control over southern Arabia. Although the hieroglyphs that have thus far been uncovered and translated offer no definitive evidence that such was the case, there is some indication that he had been to territories east of the Red Sea. Ezana was familiar, as well, with countries at the eastern end of the Mediterranean Sea in the area now occupied by modern Lebanon, Israel, Saudi Arabia, Egypt, and other Mediterranean nations.

SIGNIFICANCE

Ezana's significance is found in the areas of religion, diplomacy, and commerce. By bringing Christianity to Aksum, he developed close associations with the Christian nations of the countries bordering the eastern end of the Mediterranean Sea. The alliances he established endured for several centuries, but eventually the rise of Islam isolated Aksum (later Christian Ethiopia) from much of the world. Its mountainous terrain made isolation easy for Aksum, although Ezana struggled to avoid being separated from the world at large. He established commercial ties with many nations and built a road to connect Aksum with the Nile River in order to promote trade.

A powerful king who did not shrink from conflict, Ezana sought to work with his adversaries in such ways as to bring them into his fold. When he was unable to do this, as with the Seranes and the Kush, his vengeance was swift and decisive. He was, however, quite willing, indeed eager, to work toward achieving accords with people such as the Begans.

—*R. Baird Shuman*

FURTHER READING

Budge, Sir E. A. Wallis. *A History of Ethiopia, Nubia, and Abyssinia*. London: Methuen, 1928. This venerable work offers insights into Ezana's rule and suggests the dates of his rule of the kingdom of Aksum drawn from the hieroglyphics on various stele. Despite its age, this book by one of Britain's leading writers on antiquity has held up very well.

Burstein, Stanley, ed. *Ancient African Civilizations: Kush and Axum*. Princeton, N.J.: Markus Wiener, 1997. Burstein reproduces inscriptions from three stele that contain information about Ezana and his accomplishments as king. His texts are simply transcriptions, but his endnotes are well worth exploring. Includes index and bibliography.

Davidson, Basil. *The African Past: Chronicles from Antiquity to Modern Times*. Boston: Little, Brown, 1964. Valuable for its transcription of Ezana's last inscription shortly before the end of his reign, this book offers a comprehensive glimpse of the ancient countries of Africa about which not a great deal has been written. Well documented; includes index.

Huntingford, George Wynn Brereton. *The Historical Geography of Ethiopia from the First Century A.D. to 1740*. New York: Oxford University Press, 1989. Touches briefly on the period during which Ezana ruled Aksum, offering some background for the period prior to Ezana's ascent. The main emphasis of the book is on the period following the twelfth century, but the material on the earlier period is useful. Includes bibliography and index.

Oliver, Roland Anthony, ed. *The Dawn of African History*. 2d ed. New York: Oxford University Press, 1968. George Wynn Brereton Huntingford's article "The Kingdom of Axum" focuses on the territory that Ezana ruled in the fourth century C.E. In addition, the first third of this book offers an exceptionally keen overview of the area and the period. Includes bibliography and index.

Pankhurst, Sylvia E. *Ethiopia: A Cultural History*. Essex, England: Lalibela, 1955. This general history of Ethiopia devotes considerable attention to Ezana. A valuable resource with a useful index and an extensive bibliography. Recommended for readers not well acquainted with the period.

Ullendorff, Edward. *The Ethiopians: An Introduction to Country and People*. New York: Oxford University Press, 1965. An excellent general overview of Ethiopia's history, including its earliest stages, when Ezana ruled Aksum. The documentation is impressive, the index useful.

SEE ALSO: Saint Athanasius of Alexandria.

RELATED ARTICLES in *Great Events from History: The Ancient World*: 8th century B.C.E., Kushite King Piye Conquers Upper Egypt; c. 712-698 B.C.E., Shabaka Reunites the Nile Valley; c. 6th century B.C.E.-c. 350 C.E., Meroitic Empire Rules from Southern Egypt to the Blue Nile; 1st century C.E., Kingdom of Aksum Emerges; 3d-5th centuries C.E., Giant Stelae Are Raised at Aksum; 4th century C.E., Ezana Expands Aksum, Later Converts to Christianity.

EZEKIEL
Hebrew prophet

As a visionary and prophetic leader, Ezekiel was one of a number of individuals who held the Jewish community together during the early years of the Babylonian Exile (586-538 B.C.E.). His visions and consolatory prophecies encouraged those in exile to look toward the day of the restoration of the temple in Jerusalem.

BORN: c. 627 B.C.E.; Jerusalem, Judah (now in Israel)
DIED: c. 570 B.C.E.; Babylonia (now in Iraq)
ALSO KNOWN AS: Ezechiel
AREA OF ACHIEVEMENT: Religion

EARLY LIFE

All knowledge about Ezekiel (ih-ZEEK-yuhl) is drawn from direct statements in the biblical book of Ezekiel or inferences from it. To develop a picture of his life, one must compare this material with that gathered from other books of the Hebrew Bible and additional contemporary texts. The twentieth century tendency to discount much of the book of Ezekiel as later editorial writing has given way to an acceptance of the bulk of the material as coming from Ezekiel; later revisions are assumed to have originated from Ezekiel himself or those close to him.

Ezekiel was born in Jerusalem around the time of the Josiah reforms (c. 627) to a priestly family of the Zadok line. His father's name is given as Buzi. Ezekiel in his writing shows great familiarity and concern with the temple cult, and it is likely that he was part of the priestly cult and an important member of the hierarchy.

Ezekiel's life and career were played out against the background of ancient Near Eastern world events. By the end of the seventh century B.C.E. Nebuchadnezzar II had helped his father, Nabopolassar, defeat the Assyrians and take over the southern part of that empire, including the kingdom of Judah. When Nebuchadnezzar succeeded his father as king, Judah, under King Jehoiakim, rebelled against Babylon (2 Kings 24:2). In 598, Nebuchadnezzar marched against Judah. Jehoiakim was assassinated, and his eighteen-year-old son, Jehoiachin (also known as Coniah), was placed on the throne. Three months later, defeated, he and his court were taken into exile in Babylon, and his uncle, Zedekiah, was given control of the state.

Ezekiel was one of those taken with King Jehoiachin into exile by Nebuchadnezzar in 597. This event was sufficiently important for Ezekiel to use it as the starting point for calculating the dates of his prophecies. Those prophecies that are dated are based on the number of years from the beginning of Jehoiachin's exile.

Ezekiel's marriage is attested by a reference to his wife's death in Babylonia. He had a residence that was sufficiently large to hold a gathering of the elders of the Israelites in Babylonia. His prophecies suggest that he was resident at Tel Aviv near Nippur in Babylonia. Ezekiel's mystic personality and his prophetic role should not be allowed to mask his position as an important member of the priestly establishment who continued to function in a leadership role in exile. While there is no direct proof, the linguistic similarities and priestly concerns exhibited in Ezekiel's writings are not inconsistent with his inclusion among the "priestly" writers who were responsible for the preservation of many of the Israelite traditions of history and worship, which culminated in the creation of the Torah.

LIFE'S WORK

Ezekiel's call to prophecy is dramatically described in the opening phrases of his book. He was thirty years old at the time, resident in Tel Aviv, and standing on the Chebar canal. Ezekiel, in his prophetic actions and utterances, is revealed to be a dramatic mystic. Some have described his condition as that of a catatonic schizophrenic, and his actions as reported by him are congruent with clinical descriptions of that condition.

After Ezekiel received his call, he apparently abandoned all normal discourse and spoke only to utter the words of the Lord, Yahweh, as revealed to him, accompanied on several occasions by graphic symbolic actions. In this first period, Ezekiel's prophecies centered on the forthcoming destruction of Jerusalem, the impious actions of Zedekiah (the regent in Jerusalem), the futility of depending on Egypt for deliverance, and the false nature of prophets who

predicted such deliverance. The prophecies were written in a mixture of poetry and prose notable for graphic imagery, dramatic vocabulary, and extensive parables. In addition to the prophecies against Jerusalem, the prophecies against foreign nations reserved most of their invective for Tyre and Egypt, the two allies of Zedekiah against Babylon. In all these matters, Ezekiel's prophecies were paralleled by those of Jeremiah writing from Egypt to Babylonia. In both cases, their prophecies stemmed from activities taking place in Jerusalem and the importance of the homeland for the exiles.

After the final fall of Jerusalem to Nebuchadnezzar in 586 and the entrance of the second wave of exiles into Babylonia, the general tenor of Ezekiel's prophecies changed from one of denunciation to one of hope and encouragement. It is assumed that at that time Ezekiel returned to normal, everyday activity. Even in this period, however, he seems periodically to have gone into a cata-

Ezekiel. (Library of Congress)

tonic state in which he claimed to have visionary and out-of-body experiences, which he then recorded in detail. Of these, the most famous are the vision of the valley of the dry bones and that of the restored temple and the city of Jerusalem. This extensive passage shows the idealized Temple under priestly control.

In the period after 586 there were several overreaching problems facing the Israelite (or Jewish) community. First, and most important, was gathering the community together and encouraging it to continue the ancestral belief in Yahweh and the covenant agreement. To the exile this was no small problem, for the destruction of the temple by the Babylonians would have been regarded universally as a defeat of Yahweh by the chief Babylonian god, Marduk, through the actions of Nebuchadnezzar. With Marduk having proved himself the stronger god, there would have been no compelling reason to continue the cult of Yahweh, particularly in exile. It was uniquely Ezekiel in Babylonia and Jeremiah in Egypt who interpreted the actions of Nebuchadnezzar as directed by Yahweh against his own people for not upholding the covenant agreement. The emphasis on the position of the deity in Ezekiel is made clear by the constant use in the prophecies of the phrase "Adonai Yahweh," which emphasizes his continuing power. (Because "Adonai" is usually translated as "Lord," most translations use "Lord God," which is the normal translation of the Hebrew "Adonai Elohim." Grammatically, the form in Ezekiel is usually described as an emphatic form.)

Ezekiel's prophecies either ceased or were not recorded after 571. There was a revision to the prophecy of the destruction of Tyre that suggests an unwillingness on the part of Ezekiel or his editor to change the wording of the earlier prophecy, preferring instead to add a corrected version. He may well have continued his nonprophetic activities after that date, including the preparation of the book of Ezekiel.

Evidence of Ezekiel's death, although recorded late and not from the most secure sources, should not be neglected. Evidence from the third century C.E. Dura Synagogue wall painting and the fourth century Christian work on the lives of the prophets suggests that Ezekiel was arrested by the authorities and executed under the orders of Jehoiachin. What brought this about is unknown, but given Ezekiel's orientation it is not hard to conclude that his words could have aroused official opposition. It has been suggested that Ezekiel had realistic expectations of the restoration of the temple in his lifetime. Only the death of Nebuchadnezzar and the incompetence of his successors postponed that event until

the reign of Cyrus the Great, the Persian liberator of Babylon.

SIGNIFICANCE

The personality of Ezekiel as expressed in his book is a forceful and enduring one that has become part of the religious heritage of Judaism and Christianity. He presents himself as a mixture of opposites. There is the mystic visionary and the priest concerned with minutiae of cult and religious law. He is a superb poet but at the same time can write in the most pedestrian prose. His words seem strange, even repulsive, but then reveal a sympathetic and sensitive nature. He revels in symbolic acts and elaborate allegories one moment and speaks with directness and bluntness the next. By uniting these contradictions, he has impressed himself on tradition.

Ezekiel was one of the primary architects of Judaism. Faced with a historical situation in which the abandonment of the covenant was a high probability, not only was Ezekiel one of the few who demanded that the Israelites keep the covenant, but he also outlined the procedures and methods for doing so in the exilic environment, thus laying the foundations for Judaism. In addition to emphasizing the importance of the covenant, Ezekiel was one of the first to stress the importance of individual responsibility over collective or familial responsibility. In the recognition of God working outside Judah and through non-Israelite rulers, Ezekiel developed a concept of a universal deity while still holding to particularistic practices that became basic to all subsequent Judaism.

The influences of Ezekiel on Christianity have been less obvious but are nevertheless significant. His concepts of salvation and divine grace point to the reinterpretations of the concepts by the Apostle Paul. The unique prophetic use of the term "Son of Man" (in Hebrew, *ben-adam*) to indicate Ezekiel's special position as prophet had a strong effect on early Christian writers. His general mysticism found its way into the writings of the Apostle John and the book of Revelation. This influence is most clear in Ezekiel's prophecies on Gog and Magog as the ultimate foes before the establishment of God's kingdom.

—*Michael M. Eisman*

FURTHER READING

Boccaccini, Gabriele. *Roots of Rabbinic Judaism: An Intellectual History, from Ezekiel to Daniel.* Grand Rapids, Mich.: Wm. B. Eerdman's, 2001. Examines early roots of the Rabbinic system of thought in the period from the Babylonian Exile to the Maccabean revolt, or from Ezekiel to Daniel.

Broome, Edwin C., Jr. "Ezekiel's Abnormal Personality." *Journal of Biblical Literature* 65 (September, 1946): 277-292. A fascinating and convincing account of the mental state of the prophet. Suggests that Ezekiel's visions and descriptions are not incompatible with his being able to remember them in detail and to function normally while not in such a condition.

Eissfeldt, Otto. *The Old Testament: An Introduction.* Translated by Peter Ackroyd. New York: Harper and Row, 1976. This volume, with its skilled exposition and clear analysis, is still an excellent introduction, of which there are many.

Goodenough, Erwin R. *Jewish Symbols in the Greco-Roman Period.* Vols. 9-11 in *Symbolism in the Dura Synagogue.* Princeton, N.J.: Princeton University Press, 1988. The short section in this rather large work concerned with the late Roman synagogue paintings at Dura is the best available clear exposition of the traditions of the death of Ezekiel.

Gottwald, Norman K. *The Hebrew Bible: A Socio-Literary Introduction.* Philadelphia: Fortress Press, 1985. Well-written and up-to-date analysis of the Hebrew Bible. Useful for information on Ezekiel and his background. Includes excellent bibliography.

Greenberg, Moshe. *Ezekiel, 1-20.* Garden City, N.Y.: Doubleday, 1983. A definitive translation, with extensive introduction, translation, notes on the translation and textual problems, commentary, and bibliography. The notes and comments are particularly extensive.

SEE ALSO: Cyrus the Great; Ezra; Jeremiah; Moses; Nebuchadnezzar II.
RELATED ARTICLES in *Great Events from History: The Ancient World*: c. 1280 B.C.E., Israelite Exodus from Egypt; c. 966 B.C.E., Building of the Temple of Jerusalem; c. 922 B.C.E., Establishment of the Kingdom of Israel; c. 607-562 B.C.E., Nebuchadnezzar Creates the First Neo-Babylonian State; 587-423 B.C.E., Birth of Judaism.

EZRA
Hebrew spiritual leader

As a "scribe skilled in the law of Moses," Ezra led a religious reform movement that transformed the identity of the Jewish community that had returned from exile to Jerusalem. This new identity of the Jewish people was premised on a return to observance of the law (Torah).

FLOURISHED: Late sixth or early fifth century B.C.E.; southern Mesopotamia (now in Iraq)
AREA OF ACHIEVEMENT: Religion

EARLY LIFE

Nothing of substance is known about the early years of Ezra (EHZ-ruh), though his genealogy is given in Ezra 7:1-5. There he is called the son of Seraiah, and he is presented in the priestly heritage, with his ancestral line traced all the way back to Aaron, the first high priest and brother of Moses. While in the Bible Ezra is never specifically called the high priest or chief priest, he is so referred to in Flavius Josephus's *Antiquitates Judaicae* (93 C.E.; *The Antiquities of the Jews*, 1773).

Ezra was born in captivity, under the yoke of the great Persian Empire. It actually had been about a century earlier, under the imperialistic policies of the Neo-Babylonian Empire in the early sixth century, that the stage had been set for several generations of Jews to be born in exile. Beginning in 597, when Jerusalem fell under the onslaught of Nebuchadnezzar II, the Babylonian king, a series of deportations was initiated in which large numbers of people within the kingdom of Judah were physically transported to Babylon and other tightly controlled sectors in southern Mesopotamia.

For almost six decades after 597, the exiles lived and worked under Babylonian control. Although sources describing the daily life of the exiles are meager, there is evidence that suggests that some were put to forced labor for various building projects; perhaps the greatest numbers were relocated to agricultural communities with a relative amount of freedom. Remarkably, the once-powerful Babylonian Empire was overthrown with ease. To the east of the empire, the Persians had been a growing threat for many years. By 539, the great city of Babylon was taken, virtually without a fight. Cyrus the Great, the Persian king, embarked on a series of military campaigns with the goal of securing the bulk of territory once controlled by the Babylonians. Within a year, much of the Near East was under Persian influence.

Cyrus determined to control his new empire via a novel approach: as liberator. Thus, the Assyrians and

Babylonians' traditional methods of terror and deportations were cast aside in favor of very tolerant policies. It is within this framework that Ezra 1:1-4 relates how Cyrus, in 538, issued a decree that allowed and even encouraged the exiled Jews to return to their homeland. Indeed, they did return. Under the leadership of Sheshbazzar, and later his nephew Zerubbabel, those who returned resettled and even commenced rebuilding the Temple, which had been destroyed by the Babylonians. Construction began in 520, and by 515 the work had been completed. Chapter 6 of the Book of Ezra relates the events of completing and dedicating the new Temple and the observance of Passover in the spring of 515. With this accomplishment, the stage was set for the return of even more exiles and the coming of Ezra to Jerusalem. Ultimately, Ezra would provide the leadership and spiritual direction needed by the Jewish community of Jerusalem in order to restore and invigorate its once-rich religious heritage.

LIFE'S WORK

Between the close of the biblical narrative in Ezra 6 and the introduction of Ezra himself at the start of chapter 7, a substantial number of years passed. It was probably early during this period, sometime after 515, that Ezra was born. With virtually no information concerning his early years, the real story of Ezra begins with his return to Jerusalem along with groups of other Israelites, as mentioned in Ezra 7:7. It is at this point that one of the more vexing problems in biblical studies arises: the dating of Ezra's return to Jerusalem. Artaxerxes I ruled the Persian Empire from 464 to 423. The text of Ezra 7:8 states that Ezra and his retinue arrived in Jerusalem in the fifth month of the seventh year of Artaxerxes' reign; by this reckoning, Ezra came to Jerusalem in 458. This straightforward calculation would place him in Jerusalem before Nehemiah. There is, however, some confusion surrounding the chronological relationship between Ezra and Nehemiah. For this reason, two other theories concerning the date of Ezra's return have been articulated. Some believe that a scribal error marred the biblical text and that "the seventh year" should read "the thirty-seventh year" of Artaxerxes. This would place the return of Ezra to Jerusalem in 428. Although supported by some, this position has not met with widespread acceptance. There is a third possibility: "The

Ezra gives a sermon. (Hulton|Archive by Getty Images)

seventh year of Artaxerxes" does not refer to Artaxerxes I but rather to Artaxerxes II, who ruled from 404 to 359. Accordingly, the seventh year would be 398. The thorny problem of dating Ezra's return has by no means been resolved. To deal pragmatically with the events of Ezra's life, however, the traditional date of 458 for his return to Jerusalem has been adopted here.

As a "scribe skilled in the law of Moses" (Ezra 7:6), Ezra received a special royal commission from the Persian king Artaxerxes. The document, which was written in Aramaic, is preserved in Ezra 7:12-26. This document presented Ezra with far-reaching powers to teach and enforce measures of the law among the members of the Jewish community residing in the Persian satraphy of Abar-nahara—thus including not only those in Palestine proper but also the Jews in the trans-Euphrates area. The idea that the Persian king would so empower a man to impose the law of Moses on Jewish subjects within the Persian Empire might seem on the surface to be unreasonable. However, many attested Persian documents clearly demonstrate that, indeed, most of the kings implemented such policies. There was a long-standing Persian commitment to giving official sanction to the various religious elements within the empire.

Armed with the royal decree, Ezra, on his return to Jerusalem, initiated a program of religious reform that was designed to renew loyalty to the law in the hearts and minds of Jews. He had been given explicit authority to appoint magistrates and judges and to teach those who had no knowledge of the laws of God. He was even granted authority to mete out punishment on those who did not comply with the law, as Ezra 7:26 states: "Whoever does not obey the law of your God and the law of the king must surely be punished by death, banishment, confiscation of property, or imprisonment."

There is great variance of opinion over the chronological order of the events that followed. What is clear is that Ezra initiated changes that brought about profound religious reforms and the reconstituting of the Jewish community along lines drawn within the law. Some scholars hold that the narrative of Nehemiah 8 probably reflects the events shortly after Ezra's arrival in Jerusalem. As priest and scribe, Ezra presented the law publicly to the people in what must have been a very solemn ceremony. Standing on a platform before an assembly of "men and women and all who were able to understand," Ezra read from the law from dawn until noon. The next day, Ezra, along with the heads of certain families and various priests and Levites, gathered to study the precepts of the law. They read about the Feast of Tabernacles, proclaimed in Leviticus 23. Realizing that the observance of this festival had long been neglected, Ezra immediately issued a decree throughout the country that the people were to gather materials necessary for the construction of the booths that were requisite for the celebration. The people's response was overwhelming: Nehemiah 8:17 states that "the whole company that had returned from exile built booths and lived in them. From the days of Joshua son of Nun until that day, the Israelites had not celebrated it like this. And their joy was very great." The reforms of Ezra were under way.

The public reading of the law and the celebration of the Feast of Tabernacles made a powerful spiritual impact on the people. They began fasting, wearing sackcloth, and confessing their sins as they came to understand the wickedness of their ancestors and their own role in Israel's recent and unfortunate history. In this very humbling circumstance the people were encouraged by the rehearsing of their place as God's chosen and as beneficiaries of redemptive works performed by God on their behalf throughout history. Their repentance and gratitude are articulated in a long penitential prayer recorded in Nehemiah 9. The spiritual underpinnings of the community were being reshaped as the law began to find a central place within the lives of individuals.

As the spiritual leader of a society that was reaping the consequences of years of abuse and neglect of the law of God, Ezra exerted remarkable influence in addressing a basic problem within Israelite culture: intermarriage. The law strictly forbade marriages between Jews and pagans, and clearly intermarriages had created innumerable problems throughout Israelite history. Marriage to foreigners did nothing but water down the worship of Yahweh and the observance of God's ordinances. When a contingent of elders reported that intermarriage was rampant and that certain leaders and officials had, in fact, led the way in this pattern of activity, Ezra reacted with the emotion of one understanding the true nature of God's holiness and his utter hatred of sin: "When I heard this, I tore my tunic and cloak, pulled hair from my head and beard and sat down appalled." The passion of Ezra for the law and holiness before God was further revealed as he prostrated himself and prayed:

> What has happened to us is a result of our evil deeds and our great guilt, and yet, our God, you have punished us less than our sins have deserved and have given us a remnant like this. Shall we again break your command and intermarry with the people who commit such detestable practices?

Ezra now moved in such a way as to penetrate the conscience of the entire community. Broken before God because of the calamity of intermarriage, Ezra prayed to God near the temple. As he was praying, weeping, and confessing this great sin, the people were moved. A large crowd gathered around him, spellbound by the realization of their sin. Masses began to weep bitterly and confess their sins. It was one of those few times in history when a solitary individual touches the inner recesses of an entire nation's soul. Ezra, the scribe, by revealing his contrition and weeping in anguish before the Lord and before the people, moved the nation of Israel that day.

Leaders from the community issued a declaration that all the exiles must assemble themselves in Jerusalem within three days. Anyone not complying would be removed from the ranks of Jewish community life. In what must have been an incredible scene, all the exiles gathered near the Temple in a driving rainstorm to hear Ezra's public rebuke and plea for change. The result was that the people did acknowledge their sin, and a program was established for separating themselves from the foreigners. Within three months, all mixed marriages had been dissolved. Once again, the law became foremost in the hearts of the people.

SIGNIFICANCE

Ezra did not become a long-standing force in the Jerusalem community. In fact, he was probably an active leader for only about a year after arriving in the city. He does not appear in any biblical narratives of later events. According to Josephus, after the accomplishment of his mission, Ezra died and was buried in the Holy City. How does one accurately judge the impact of Ezra? Certainly, his reputation in the succeeding generation suggests a level of awe and respect comparable to that afforded to Moses, the unquestioned hero of the faith. Yet reputation is not the proper criterion for judging an individual's significance. In this case, Ezra's pragmatic reforms, which reorganized and reenergized the struggling Jewish community, should serve as a measuring rod.

Undoubtedly, the elevation of the law to a place of centrality in the Jewish community was Ezra's paramount achievement. The primacy of the law in the lives of the people was a renewed force that enabled the Jews to survive as a separate entity. Although the stringency of the reforms concerning intermarriage may have seemed unreasonable to some, the observance of the law aided them in realizing anew their stature as a people chosen by God. The acceptance of the law as presented by the faithful scribe Ezra brought about a reorganization of the people that was desperately needed in the tumultuous years after the return from exile.

—*W. R. Brookman*

FURTHER READING

Bossman, D. "Ezra's Marriage Reform: Israel Redefined." *Biblical Theology Bulletin* 9 (1979): 32-38. The focus of this article is the intermarriage problem addressed by Ezra and the restructuring of Israel around the law. Bossman shows that cultic aspects of the Jewish community were purified through the reforms of Ezra.

Bright, John. *A History of Israel*. 4th ed. Louisville, Ky.: Westminster J. Knox Press, 2000. Chapter 10 of this work is a very useful overview of the Jewish community in the fifth century B.C.E. A full discussion of the problems involved in the dating of Ezra's mission to Jerusalem is included in an excursus to the chapter.

Childs, Brevard S. *Introduction to the Old Testament as Scripture*. Philadelphia: Fortress Press, 1979. Chapter 42 presents an in-depth bibliography of resources dealing with the Ezra-Nehemiah era. Although there is no focus on the life of Ezra specifically, short summaries are presented that address, among other issues, the chronological controversies and the reforms initiated by Ezra.

Fensham, F. Charles. *The Books of Ezra and Nehemiah*. Grand Rapids, Mich.: Wm. B. Eerdmans, 1982. Particularly valuable is the introductory matter, which presents a clear and concise discussion of the major issues, such as sources, historical background, and theology.

Hamilton, Victor P. *Handbook on the Historical Books: Joshua, Judges, Ruth, Samuel, Kings, Chronicles, Ezra-Nehemiah, Esther*. Grand Rapids, Mich.: Baker Book House, 2001. Thorough exposition of the ideology, theology, and content of these ancient Israelite histories, compiled by use of rhetorical criticism, archaeological data, and word studies, among other sources.

LaSor, William, David Allan Hubbard, and Frederic William Bush. *Old Testament Survey: The Message, Form, and Background of the Old Testament*. 2d ed. Grand Rapids, Mich.: Wm. B. Eerdmans, 1996. Chapter 50 of this book offers an excellent presentation of the crux of the Ezra and Nehemiah narratives. Among the gems to be discovered in this work are potent insights into the achievements and significance of Ezra.

SEE ALSO: Aaron; Cyrus the Great; Ezekiel.

RELATED ARTICLES in *Great Events from History: The Ancient World*: 587-423 B.C.E., Birth of Judaism; October, 539 B.C.E., Fall of Babylon; c. 538-c. 450 B.C.E., Jews Return from the Babylonian Captivity; c. 90 C.E., Synod of Jamnia.

FABIUS
Roman military leader

During the Second Punic War (218-202 B.C.E.) between Carthage and Rome, Fabius, nicknamed "the Delayer," using feint-and-run tactics, carried on a fairly successful war of attrition against Hannibal, the great Carthaginian general whose army ravaged the Italian peninsula and threatened Rome itself.

BORN: c. 275 B.C.E.; place unknown
DIED: 203 B.C.E.; possibly Rome (now in Italy)
ALSO KNOWN AS: Quintus Fabius Maximus (full name); Verrucosus; Cunctator ("the Delayer")
AREAS OF ACHIEVEMENT: Government and politics, war and conquest

EARLY LIFE

Quintus Fabius (FAY-bee-uhs) Maximus was born into the patrician Fabii *gens*, or clan, in about 275 B.C.E. Although the Fabii traced their ancestry back to a mythic origin, to Hercules, their actual origin is obscure. However, they became an important family group with a distinguished history in Roman affairs. Fabius was the great-grandson of Fabius Rullianus (fl. c. 325-290 B.C.E.), the first of the Fabii to append the title *Maximus* to his surname and the most famous of Fabius's forebears.

In his youth, Fabius seemed to show little promise. He was nicknamed Verrucosus ("Warty") because he bore disfiguring warts on his upper lip, and also Ovicula ("Lambkins") because he was docile and unassuming. He readily submitted to the will of childhood friends and to some of them seemed both slow and dim-witted. His apparent placidity would later mature into an admirable forbearance that served him well in the turmoil of Roman politics. In his deliberate, plodding manner, he studied and mastered military tactics and oratory, important disciplines for the public offices for which he quietly and diligently prepared himself. In time, perceptive colleagues came to see that his outward lethargy masked great inner strengths, including quiet persistence, fortitude, and a nearly inexhaustible patience.

Fabius's political career also proved slow in developing. He did not serve as consul until 234, when he was about forty, and even though he drove the Ligurians from Cisalpine Gaul in 233 and was awarded a triumph, he garnered little support from the Roman populace. He lacked the more flamboyant manner and aggressive style of many soldier-statesmen, and his cautionary counsel was often ignored. In fact, his political star rose rather late, starting in 221, when, in his fifties, he was elected dictator for the first time. Thereafter, with the military failures of rivals during the Second Punic War (218-201 B.C.E.), he gained prominence as the conservative leader in the Roman senate and the primary architect of a strategy designed to wear down Rome's great adversary, Hannibal of Carthage.

LIFE'S WORK

In 219, the Carthaginian warrior Hannibal provoked Rome by attacking its Spanish ally, Saguntum. The next year, in one of history's boldest military ventures, he crossed the Alps, invading northern Italy. Aided by Cisalpine Gauls, his army won battle after battle, including, in 217, a major engagement at Lake Trasimene, where the Roman army under Flaminius was destroyed.

Flaminius had been a proponent of an aggressive military policy opposed by Fabius, and his defeat and death prompted the reelection of Fabius as dictator. To the Romans, hunkering down in anticipation of Hannibal's imminent siege of the city, Fabius's defensive tactics finally made good sense.

Fabius's strategy was to erode Hannibal's strength by denying him access to supplies and fresh troops while constantly harassing his army with hit-and-run sorties against his flanks. Fabius knew that time was on Rome's side, and he studiously avoided a general engagement that promised less than certain victory. He kept his legions in the hills, protected by the terrain from assaults by Hannibal's vaunted calvary.

Fortunately for Rome, Hannibal deferred an assault on that city. Instead, he drove further down the Italian peninsula, hoping to capture Mediterranean ports and strengthen his army by turning or neutralizing Rome's allies. At first his strategy faltered, for Rome's allies remained steadfast.

Meanwhile, Fabius was nicknamed "Cunctator," or "the Delayer," an appellation used mockingly by his opponents. The nickname was not entirely just, however, for at one point, having Hannibal at a distinct disadvantage, Fabius was ready to risk a pitched battle. He had the Carthaginians outnumbered and trapped near Casilinum, on the Campania frontier; using a celebrated ruse, however, Hannibal escaped the snare. He had his soldiers attach burning kindling to the horns of two thousand oxen and drive the frantic animals against the bewildered Roman troops guarding his escape route. In the resulting confusion, Hannibal's army broke out of the trap and vanished.

As the threat of a siege of Rome faded, its citizens again clamored for a more aggressive policy, turning against Fabius's cautious strategy. Hannibal helped fuel the ire of Fabius's critics. By carefully protecting Fabius's provincial property from pillage and burning, he deliberately created the impression that Fabius, worse than a coward, was an out-and-out traitor in league with the enemy.

While the ever-hostile Roman tribunes fanned the flames of suspicion toward Fabius, the dictator's master of the horse, Lucius Minucius, acting against the express orders of his absent superior, sought open battle with a detachment of Hannibal's troops and achieved a minor victory. When word of Minucius's success arrived in Rome, Fabius, in the city on official business, came under vicious verbal attack from the tribune Metilius, a close friend and kinsman to Minucius. He wanted Fabius stripped of power, but the senate instead opted to give Minucius joint control of the army.

Fabius, on his return from Rome, rejected Minucius's demand that each of them assume command on alternate days. By then, Minucius was openly bragging of his su-

periority to Fabius in military strategy and leadership, and Fabius feared that his rival, when in command, would imperil the whole army through some rash venture. Fabius therefore would agree only to divide the army into two separate commands, each composed of two legions.

Minucius quickly justified Fabius's fears by leading his two legions into one of Hannibal's clever traps. Surrounded, with escape routes cut off, Minucius's army faced annihilation, but Fabius attacked and forced Hannibal's forces to retreat. Reportedly, the narrow escape from disaster humbled Minucius, who, apologizing for his imprudence, ceded supreme command of the army to Fabius alone.

In 217, momentarily assured that his defensive strategies would be followed, Fabius stepped down from his dictatorship. In 216, however, Terentius Varro, another headstrong but popular soldier, was elected consul and gained joint control of the army with his less popular co-consul, Lucius Aemilius Paulus. With the support of the senate, which authorized an offensive policy, he engaged Hannibal in an all-out battle at Cannae, a village located near the Aufidus River in southeastern Italy. Fabius had hoped that Paulus, whom he supported, could prevent Varro from making such a costly mistake. Because command of the army alternated between the commanders, however, Varro was able to ignore Paulus's advice. The result was the worst Roman debacle of the war, with the loss of upward of sixty thousand men. The defeat also allowed Hannibal to take Capua, the second most important city in Italy, and to roam freely through the rich provinces in the southern part of the Italian peninsula, forcing some of Rome's former allies into his camp.

The Roman senate, again fearing an attack on the capital, once more turned to Fabius. He quickly took measures to steel the citizens' resolve to survive the expected siege, stopping a panic and flight from the city. Fortunately for Rome, against the advice of his lieutenants, Hannibal once more passed up the opportunity to take advantage of his victory. Rome took heart and again sent Fabius into the field. His cautionary tactics soon found balance in the bolder stratagems of another general, Claudius Marcellus, who led attacks against the main body of Hannibal's army and in 211 captured Syracuse, greatly eroding the Carthaginian influence in Sicily. Marcellus and Fabius became known, respectively, as "the Sword and Shield of Rome." Marcellus was eventually led into one of Hannibal's tactical snares and killed. Fabius, meanwhile, eluded all traps that Hannibal set for

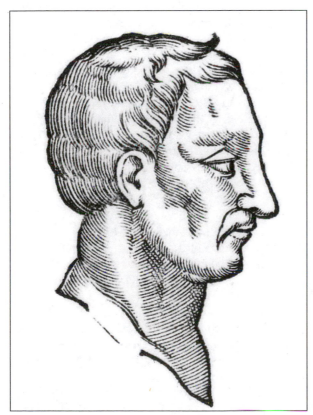

Fabius. (Library of Congress)

him and, in 209, during his fifth consulship, won an important victory at Tarentum, one of Hannibal's important strongholds. The tide of war by that time had turned in Rome's favor.

Up until his death, Fabius remained circumspect in his policies. He vigorously opposed the plans of Cornelius Scipio, who, after winning renown by driving the Carthaginians out of Spain, was elected consul in 205. Scipio proposed an invasion of Africa and, against the strong objections and blocking maneuvers of Fabius and his faction, undertook the expedition in 204. He defeated the Punic army in 203, with the result that Carthage, in the ensuing armistice, recalled Hannibal from Italy. Fabius died before Scipio's great victory over Hannibal at Zama in 202, the battle that effectively ended Carthage's Mediterranean dominance and earned for Scipio the cognomen "Africanus."

SIGNIFICANCE

The only blemish on Fabius's career came in his final years, when his caution and superstition led him to oppose Scipio, whose achievements would finally eclipse his own. By then, he was about seventy and securely bound to his delaying tactics by virtue of their past successes. He had sought to outlast Hannibal and to force his withdrawal from Italy when it became impossible for the invader to meet the logistical needs of his marauding army or win over Rome's unstable allies. Once shorn of him, Fabius saw little need to pursue Hannibal or attack Carthage.

Clearly, in his policies, Fabius placed a high value on the lives of his soldiers. He was unwilling to risk them for personal glory or political advantage. Legends concerning him relate that he also won the loyalty of his soldiers by a leniency uncharacteristic of Roman discipline. He was also generous; on one occasion, when the senate refused to honor an obligation, he sold some of his own lands to ransom 240 soldiers held prisoner by Hannibal. Moreover, Fabius seemed remarkably free of grudges, bearing with great patience the most vituperative political attacks on him. Although too vain for popular tastes, Fabius was an honorable man. He never abused his power by exacting revenge on his political adversaries.

Perhaps the greatest tribute to both his policies and his genius lies in the fact that it was in Fabius that Hannibal saw his greatest threat. He is said to have told his followers that Fabius was like a terrible cloud, ever hovering in the mountains, threatening to storm down on them with terrible destruction. The acknowledged fear of such

an enemy as Hannibal constitutes the highest kind of praise.

—John W. Fiero

FURTHER READING

De Beer, Sir Gavin. *Hannibal: Challenging Rome's Supremacy.* New York: Viking Press, 1969. A richly illustrated, approachable study treating its subject figure as tragic and inevitably doomed to fail in his efforts to save Carthage in the rise of Rome. Gives a solid account of the major battles and the part played by Fabius in Hannibal's Italian campaign.

Jones, Peter. "Ancient and Modern." *The Spectator* 291, no. 9113 (April 3, 2003): 21. Examines Fabius's military tactics and compares them with those employed by the Iraqi army in the 2003 conflict with the United States.

Livy. *The War with Hannibal: Books XXI-XXX of The History of Rome from Its Foundation.* Translated by Aubrey de Sélincourt and edited by Betty Radice. Baltimore: Penguin Books, 1972. A full account of the Second Punic War from the vantage point of a major Roman historian who flourished at the time Rome became an empire. Although prone to romanticizing the events and major figures, Livy's narrative is both vivid and detailed. Includes maps and a chronological index.

Plutarch. *The Lives of the Noble Grecians and Romans.* Translated by John Dryden and revised by Arthur Hugh Clough. New York: Modern Library, 1992. The famous work of a major first century Roman biographer and moralist, whose "parallels" included a comparison of Fabius with Pericles of Athens. Gives a very positive assessment of Fabius's character. Includes index.

Scullard, H. H. *Roman Politics: 220-150 B.C.* Westport, Conn.: Greenwood Press, 1981. An in-depth study of the various political factions in Rome at the time of the Second and Third Punic Wars. Devotes chapters to the patrician family groupings and the conservative strategies and politics of Fabius and his followers. Includes genealogical charts and year-by-year listings of consuls, censors, and praetors.

_____. *Scipio Africanus: Soldier and Politician.* Ithaca, N.Y.: Cornell University Press, 1970. A biographical study of Fabius's final rival. Useful for its analysis of Scipio's military success in Spain, leading to the final discrediting of Fabius's more timorous tactics and Scipio's expedition into Africa. Includes extensive notes, plus maps and photographs.

SEE ALSO: Archimedes; Hannibal; Scipio Africanus.
RELATED ARTICLES in *Great Events from History: The Ancient World*: 264-225 B.C.E., First Punic War; 218-201 B.C.E., Second Punic War; 202 B.C.E., Battle of Zama; 149-146 B.C.E., Third Punic War; 133 B.C.E., Pergamum Is Transferred to Rome; Early 1st century B.C.E.-225 C.E., Sātavāhana Dynasty Rises to Power in South India.

FAXIAN

Chinese Buddhist pilgrim and translator

Faxian journeyed from China to India to obtain a more complete version of the Buddhist monastic rules and participated in the translation of the Sanskrit texts into Chinese.

BORN: c. 337 C.E.; Wuyang, Shanxi Province, China
DIED: 422 C.E.; China
ALSO KNOWN AS: Fa-hsien (Wade-Giles); Gong (original name)
AREA OF ACHIEVEMENT: Religion

EARLY LIFE

Not much is known about the early life of Faxian (fah-shyahn). He was born c. 337 in Wuyang in Shanxi Province. His original name was Gong. He was admitted to the Buddhist orders at the age of three and received the name Faxian ("Manifestation of the Law").

LIFE'S WORK

In 399 C.E. the Buddhist Faxian decided to journey to India. His reason for making the journey was his concern that "not all the canon of the Monastic Rules was obtainable in China." He was not to return to China until 414. On his return he composed *Fo Guo Ji*, also known as *Faxian Zhuan* (fourth century C.E.; *Fo Koue Ki*, 1836; also known as *The Travels of Fa-hsien*), a journal of his travels. He also took on the task of translating the monastic rules and other works that he had brought back with him.

Faxian set out from Changan (now Xi'an) in 399 with fellow pilgrims, most notably Dao Zheng (Tao-ching). Along the way he was also joined by others, including Zheyan (Che-yen) and Baoyun (Pao-yun). These travelers separated and rejoined at various points in the journey. Some returned early. Others died. Dao Zheng traveled all the way to India and decided to remain there.

The group journeyed to Dunhuang (Tunhuang) and then passed on to Khotan, staying there for three months to see the Image Procession. From Khotan, Faxian arrived in Khalcha (modern-day Kashgar) just in time for the Great Five Year Procession (*Pañcavarsa*) in which the king bestowed offerings on the monks. Next Faxian crossed the Pamirs, stopping in Darada, Udyana, Suvastu, Gandhara, Taxila, Purusapura, Hilo, and Nagarahara. Many of these sites were the setting for the *Jātakas* (fifth-fourth centuries B.C.E.; translated into English as *Buddhist Birth-Stories*, 1925), stories about the former lives of the Buddha. For example Suvastu was where the *jātaka* of the hawk and dove is said to have taken place. Near Taxila was the setting of the Tiger *jātaka*. Near Darada, Faxian saw an 80-foot (24-meter) statue of Maitreya, the future Buddha. Buddhist relics were also found in these towns, including the Buddha's alms bowl in Purusapura and his skull in Hilo. The region around Nagarahara is well known for a cave where the shadow of the Buddha or the projection of his image had been preserved. Crossing the Safed Koh (Lesser Snow Mountains) he entered into north-central India.

Faxian called this region the Middle Kingdom, with Pataliputra (modern-day Patna) as its capital. He paints an idyllic picture of the region. Here he visited the major sites connected with the life of Śākyamuni Buddha. He first came to Śrāvasti, south of which city was the Jetavana Vihāra. The Buddha is said to have spent a longer time here than anywhere else. Faxian then passed on to Kapilavastu, where he saw the ruins of the palace of King Śuddhodana Gautama, the king into whose family the Buddha was born. Not far was Lumbinī, the birthplace of the Buddha. Also he traveled to Kuśinagara, where the Buddha entered *parinirvāna*. Most important, Faxian visited Gayā, which he described as desolate. Here he saw the Bodhi tree and the various stupas commemorating events leading up to and following the Buddha's enlightenment. He also noted three monasteries in the area. After Gayā he went to Vārānasī (Benares) and visited nearby Deer Park, where the Buddha delivered his first sermon. In addition to these sites related to the Buddha, Faxian stayed in Pataliputra, the capital of King Aśoka.

Faxian was disappointed that there were no written copies of the monastic rules in northern India, since these rules were handed down orally. He had to travel to central India to locate written texts. There he found copies in Sanskrit of the rules of the Mahāsānghika and the

Sarvāstivāda, the Saṃyuktabhidharma Śāstra, the Nirvāna and Vaipulyaparinirvāṇa sutras and the commentaries of the Mahāsāṅghika. Faxian then went to Tāmralipti on the east coast of India, where he spent two years copying more manuscripts and making drawings of images of the Buddha.

Sailing from Tāmralipti (modern-day Tamluk) he arrived in Sri Lanka. He spent two years on the island, where he saw the tree that was said to have been grafted from the Bodhi tree in Bodh Gayā. He also visited the Abhayagiri and Mahāvihāra monasteries. He observed the procession displaying one of the Buddha's teeth and the funeral of an arhat (a Buddhist who has obtained enlightenment). Here Faxian obtained copies in Sanskrit of the rules of the Mahiśāsikas, the Dīrghāgama, the Saṃyuktāgama and the Sannipata.

Faxian then decided to sail back home. On the voyage a typhoon arose and damaged the ship; he feared that his books would be thrown overboard. He prayed to Guan Yin (Kuan Yin), and thirteen days later the ship reached an island where it could be repaired. After ninety days they arrived in Yavadvipa (modern-day Sumatra), where Faxian boarded another ship bound for China. Due to rains, the ship drastically went off course. A trip that should have taken fifty days stretched out to seventy days. Supplies ran low. Finally they adjusted their course to the northwest and landed in northern China at Laoshan on the Shandong Peninsula in 413 C.E.

Faxian had intended to return to Chang-an to translate the writings that he had brought back with him, but he ended up in Jiankang (modern-day Nanjing). Here in 414 C.E. he wrote up his journal, *The Travels of Fa-hsien*. A postscript records how Faxian produced an expanded edition of the work at the insistence of monks in Jiankang who heard a reading of the journal.

Also in Jiankang, Faxian and the monk Buddhabhadra (359-429 C.E.) set about the task of translating the writings brought back from India. Buddhabhadra, who was said to be a descendant of the Buddha, had been invited to China by Zheyan, one of Faxian's fellow pilgrims who had stayed on in Kashmir to study. In 411 C.E., Buddhabhadra arrived in China and at the invitation of Emperor Liu Yu settled in Jiankang at the Daochang si (Tao-ch'ang ssu) temple. Baoyun, who accompanied Faxian up to Puruṣapura, aided Buddhabhadra in translating. By 418 C.E., the team had translated the rules of the Mahāsāṅghika and the *Mahāparinirvāṇa Sūtra*, as well as the Saṃyuktabhidharma Śāstra and the *Bhikṣuṇī Prātimokṣa* (c. third-fourth century C.E.). Later, Guṇabhadra translated the Saṃyuktāgama and Buddhajiva

translated the rules of the Mahiśāsikas, which were completed by Zheyan and Baoyun. These translations made a great impression on Chinese Buddhism.

In addition to Faxian's translation work, his journal is an invaluable source of information on the Buddhist countries of his time. He dutifully recorded all the monasteries of each region, the number of monks in each monastery, and whether the monks were Hīnayāna or Mahāyāna. He also noted all the stupas that he saw, relating the stories behind each stupa. Buddhist ceremonies also attracted Faxian's attention. He gave detailed descriptions of the image processions in Khotan and Pataliputra, the Great Five Year Procession in Khalcha, and the procession for the Buddha's tooth in Sri Lanka.

Faxian also showed interest in matters non-Buddhist. He occasionally noted the clothes worn by people in different regions. He also took notice of the vegetation. In Khalcha, for example, he recorded that the only crop that would grow there is wheat and that from this point onward he did not see plants that are found in China except for the bamboo, pomegranate, and sugar cane. Faxian also painted an idyllic picture of the Middle Kingdom, where the climate is temperate, and there were no taxes, currency, capital punishment, killing of animals, or alcohol. People did not eat onion or garlic. However he did record the presence of *candalas*, "who are known as 'evil men' and are segragated from the others. When they enter towns or markets they strike a piece of wood to announce their presence, so that others may know that they are coming and avoid them."

For the most part the text is written in a matter-of-fact style. Only occasionally does one find touches of emotion appearing. For example, a weeping Faxian lamented the death of one of his companions in the Safed Koh: "You have failed in your purpose. Yet such is fate!" He also wept when, having been away for so many years, he saw a Chinese fan as one of the offerings (probably by a Chinese merchant) at the Abhayagiri Monastery in Śrī Lanka.

SIGNIFICANCE

Faxian's journal is an invaluable source of information on the Buddhist regions of his time. Since the nineteenth century, the text along with the writings of Xuanzang (Hsuan-tsang) has served as a guide for identifying Buddhist ruins. The translations of Sanskrit works into Chinese played a major role in the development of Buddhism in China. In translating the various versions of monastic rules, Faxian accomplished what he had set out to do on his journey to India. The translation of the *Mahā-*

parinirvāṇa Sūtra in particular attracted a great amount of attention. While the doctrine of *śūnyatā* (emptiness) dominated Chinese Buddhist thought at this time, the *Mahāparinirvāṇa Sūtra* proclaimed that there is an element underlying the phenomenal world. Furthermore, in contrast to the rigid class structure in China, it maintained that all people could attain enlightenment.

—*Albert T. Watanabe*

FURTHER READING

Faxian. *A Record of Buddhistic Kingdoms*. Translated and annotated by James Legge. 1886. Reprint. New York: Dover, 1991. The introduction provides what little information we know about the life of Faxian as well as some historical background. Detailed notes in the translation along with the Chinese text.

_____. *A Record of the Buddhist Countries*. Translated by Li Yung-hsi. Peking: The Chinese Buddhist Association, 1957. This volume was published to commemorate the 2,500th anniversary of the Buddha's attainment of Nirvana. As with that of Legge mentioned above, the introduction tells of Faxian's life. Some notes in the translation. Map.

Tsukamoto, Zenryu. *A History of Early Chinese Buddhism*. Translated by Leon Hurvitz. 2 vols. New York: Kodansha International, 1985. At the end of volume 1, Tsukamoto provides the best available account in English of the translation activities of Faxian and Buddhabhadra. This book also provides comprehensive background of Buddhism in China at the time of Faxian's journey. Bibliography and indexes.

Tulku, Tarthang, and Elizabeth Cook eds. *Holy Places of the Buddha*. Berkeley, Calif.: Dharma Publishing, 1994. This book employs the accounts of Faxian and Xuanzang, among others, in examining the remains of Buddhist sites. Maps, bibliography and indexes.

SEE ALSO: Bodhidharma; Buddha.

RELATED ARTICLES in *Great Events from History: The Ancient World*: c. 60-68 C.E., Buddhism Enters China; 399 C.E., Chinese Monk Faxian Travels to India; c. 470 C.E., Bodhidharma Brings Chan Buddhism to China.

GALEN
Roman physician

Although not a first-rate philosopher, Galen was influential in formulating a powerful logical empiricism that took scientific axioms as self-evident rather than hypothetical. His greatest contribution was in medicine, where he made the best presentation of anatomical knowledge in the ancient world; his theories and practices remained dominant during the Middle Ages.

BORN: 129 C.E.; Pergamum, Mysia, Anatolia (now Bergama, Turkey)
DIED: c. 199 C.E.; possibly Rome or Pergamum
ALSO KNOWN AS: Galen of Pergamum; Galenos (Greek name); Galenus (Latin name)
AREAS OF ACHIEVEMENT: Medicine, philosophy

EARLY LIFE
Galen (GAH-luhn) was born on an estate in Pergamum (also known as Pergamon), a city situated on the mainland almost opposite the island of Lesbos in Asia Minor. Pergamum lay inland in a fertile valley, and its hilltops were crowned by temples and theaters. Pergamum's library rivaled Alexandria's. Another distinguishing feature was the Asclepieion, or medical temple dedicated to Asclepius, the god of healing. This was a combination religious sanctuary, sanatorium, and place of recreation. Pergamum was one of the great seats of Christianity and held one of the seven churches mentioned by John the Apostle in the Revelations (2:12-17). Because of these features, the city became one of the great pilgrimage and entertainment centers in the Roman world, and Galen grew up exposed not only to scholars but also to rhapsodists, musicians, tumblers, actors, and snake-charmers.

Galen's father, Nicon, was an architect and geometer. He was also a prosperous landowner with a farm that cultivated peas, beans, lentils, almonds, figs, olives, and grapes. Nicon himself came from a highly educated family and was able to provide his son with an education partly in the country and partly in the city. Galen (whose name derives from *galenos*, Greek for "calm" or "serene") was closer to his father than to his mother, who scolded the maids and quarreled almost incessantly with her husband. Galen compared her with Socrates' difficult wife, Xanthippe, but was able to keep his distance from her by accompanying his father to lectures in the city. His father provided or supervised Galen's education until the boy reached fourteen, then directed his son to philosophical studies.

There were four leading philosophical systems at the time—Platonism, Aristotelianism, Stoicism, and Epicureanism—and Galen was not prodded along any single path of knowledge. He had the benefit of a liberal education, although he found confusion in philosophy and had doubts about mathematics. His father wanted a state career for the boy, but after having a dream in which Asclepius directed attention to medicine, Nicon sent Galen, then seventeen, to study under the celebrated anatomist and Sophist Satyros.

LIFE'S WORK
When Nicon died, probably in 151, Galen worked with Pelops in Smyrna and with Numisianos in Corinth and Alexandria, where he wrote a treatise in three parts on the movement of the lungs and thorax. He remained in Alexandria for roughly five years, traveling in various parts of Egypt. There were six main medical sects at the time, three ancient (the Hippocratic, Dogmatic, and Empirical) and three "modern" (the Methodist, Pneumatic, and Eclectic). Galen, like many of his colleagues, was free to try combinations of these sects, and he devoted two treatises to the discussion of them.

On his return to Pergamum, he was appointed physician to the school of gladiators by the head priest of the Asclepieion. Galen's appointment lasted more than two years and was a useful experience. Because gladiators often received severe wounds, a physician was obliged to attend to the diet, exercise, and convalescence of these combatants in order to ensure that they were in good health and that they would recover in due course from certain injuries. Galen did not perform much surgery on the gladiators, and his knowledge of anatomy was derived exclusively from dissections on animals—particularly the Barbary ape (for which he was nicknamed the "ape doctor"). Slaves or students would prepare the cadavers of pigs, sheep, oxen, cats, dogs, horses, lions, wolves, birds, and fish by shaving and flaying them, and it is a wonder that Galen and other anatomists were not killed by infection.

Dissection led to insights about the general plan of the body, and Galen showed that this plan was essentially the same from creature to creature. He discovered that arteries contain blood and that a severed artery (even a small one) could drain all the body's blood in one-half hour or less. He showed that the right auricle outlives the rest of the heart and that there is a link between the brain and the larynx.

When a new war between the Pergamumites and the neighboring Galatians began, Galen left for Rome. His life and career coincided with the noble rule of Antoninus Pius and that of his son, Marcus Aurelius. Galen rented a large house, practiced as a physician, attended medical meetings in the temple of peace, and continued his interest in philosophy.

He respected the ancients, particularly Aristotle, Plato, and Hippocrates. He argued that all scientific knowledge begins with the senses, or mind, and he was opposed to the Skeptics, who taught their disciples to argue on either side of any point. Galen found it absurd to argue so freely while doubting, as the Skeptics did, the starting points of knowledge. Although somewhat "magical" or irrational in medical practice (he believed in the therapeutic value of excrement and amulets), he was a rationalist in his philosophical method, recognizing a role for syllogistic reasoning and admiring the purposiveness of all nature. He believed, with Aristotle, that nature never makes anything superfluous; he tried in *Peri chreias morion* (169-175, commonly known as *De usu partium corporis*

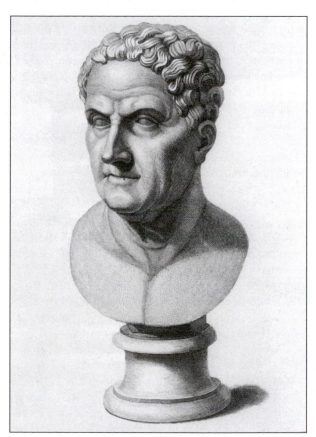

Galen. (Library of Congress)

humani; *On the Usefulness of the Parts of the Body*, 1907-1909) to justify the form and function of each organ of the body. He interpreted other philosophers (especially Plato, Aristotle, Theophrastus, Chrysippus, and Epicurus), but his many ethical treatises were lost, as was a series of works on lexicographical and stylistic problems.

He held a Platonic view of the soul, recognizing the three parts (nutritive, animal, rational) distinguished in Plato's *Republic* and opposing the Stoic doctrine of a single, indivisible soul. His treatise on the subject ascribes nutrition to the liver and veins, the pneuma or spirit to the lungs and heart, and sensation and muscular movement to the brain and nerves. It is easy to see how physiology and philosophy mixed in Galen's theories, especially in his pneumatic theory, which, though derived from Hippocrates and Anaximenes of Miletus, was an interesting revision of those older beliefs. According to Galen, each of the three fundamental members (liver, heart, brain) was dominated by a special pneuma or spirit: the liver by natural or physical spirit—a vapor from blood, which controlled nutrition, growth, and reproduction; the heart by vital spirit, transmitted in the veins and conveying heat and life; the brain by animal or psychical spirit, which regulated the brain, nerves, and feeling.

Galen believed that the habits of the soul were influenced by bodily temperament (rather than by climate, as Hippocrates had insisted). Galen's theory of the four humors (based on the four elements earth, air, fire, and water) went back to Empedocles but was a restatement of Hippocrates' theory of four qualities (dry, wet, hot, cold) and of another version of the four humors (blood, yellow bile, black bile, phlegm). This attempted reconciliation of medicine and philosophy was consistent with his claim that the best physician was also a philosopher.

Galen became a friend of the Aristotelian philosopher Eudemos, and when the latter fell ill, Galen was consulted—much to the hostility of the patient's other physicians. A contest of invective, suspicion, and tactlessness broke out between Galen and his rivals. Galen's outspoken and contemptuous criticism of those he considered charlatans put his life in danger; he decided to return to Pergamum.

His recuperation from Rome-weariness was short. He received a letter from the two rulers, Marcus Aurelius and Lucius Verus, ordering him to join the Imperial camp in Aquileia (a commercial and military center and one of the great cities of the west), where legions were gathering to march against the barbarians. These military preparations were disrupted by plague, a form of typhus or smallpox probably brought in from Syria and stubbornly resistant to health measures. The emperors decided to leave the army, but when Verus died in 169, Marcus returned to the field after ordering Galen back to Rome to take medical charge of Marcus's eight-year-old son, Commodus.

As court physician, Galen strengthened his position. He continued in office when Commodus succeeded his father as emperor in 180. Galen remained in Rome until 192, when a fire destroyed the Temple of Peace, as well as many libraries and bookshops. Many of his writings, especially some of his philosophical treatises, which existed only in a few copies, were annihilated.

Under Commodus, the climate for scholars and philosophers became intolerable. The emperor, a superior athlete who regarded himself as a reincarnation of Hercules, placed a premium on hunting and circus games rather than on intellectual pursuits. Galen returned to Pergamum in 192, where he had yet another encounter with the plague. He was saved by letting his own blood. Most of his time was devoted to meditation and writing, and he died about 199.

SIGNIFICANCE

Galen's writings were diverse and profuse. Although he did not have students of his own, nor did he found a school, his stature was large in his lifetime and larger after his death. His texts were translated into Syriac and Arabic as Greek culture spread throughout Syria and then into Persia and the Islamic world. From the eleventh century onward, Latin translations of Galen made their way into Europe, where the phenomenon of Galenism dominated the medicine of the Middle Ages, despite the plethora of other commentators and forgeries of Galen's texts.

As a medical practitioner and theorist, Galen mixed fact and speculation. Although a brilliant diagnostician, he relied on observations of "critical days," pulse, and urine for his prognoses. He had a deep distaste for surgery, except as a means to repair injuries or suppurations, and confined his operative surgery to nasal polyps, goiters, and tumors of fatty or fibrous tissues. His writing in the field, however, provides information on the use of caustics, unguents for healing wounds, and opium and other drugs for anesthesia. His anatomical knowledge suffered from the unavailability of human cadavers, so his errors were understandable. His physiology was strictly limited, but he was far ahead of his time in developing concepts of digestion, assimilation, blood formation, nerve function, and reproduction.

As a philosopher, he was hardly original, but he was useful for his commentaries on Plato and Hippocrates, and he wrote about logic, ethics, and rational psychology, arguing that "passions" were the result of unbridled energy opposed to reason, and "errors" of the soul were the result of false judgments or opinions. Galen believed that psychological troubles could be related more to the body's predisposition to disease than to disease itself, and so he recommended a daily self-examination as a preventative.

Galen erred in thinking that inadequate medical knowledge could be compensated by general knowledge. Nevertheless, he was versatile, producing works of philology (including two dictionaries) and an autobiography in addition to his more than one hundred treatises on medicine. His language was often repetitive and difficult, but he never assumed literary affectations, and he continually revised his work.

Despite the fact that the Renaissance saw the overthrow of many of his theories of anatomy, physiology, and therapy, Galen can be credited for several things: setting a high ideal for the medical profession; insisting on contact with nature as a condition for treating disease; stressing the unity of an organism and the interdependence of its parts; and realizing that a living organism can be understood only in relation to its environment. His fame and theories lasted for nine centuries, before being rivaled by those of the Muslim philosopher-physician Avicenna.

—Keith Garebian

FURTHER READING

Brock, Arthur John, trans. *Greek Medicine, Being Extracts Illustrative of Medical Writers from Hippocrates to Galen.* 1929. Reprint. New York: AMS Press, 1972. A good historical survey by one of the best English translators of Galen. Places Galen in historical context. Includes annotations.

Galen. *Galen on Bloodletting.* Translated by Peter Brain. New York: Cambridge University Press, 1986. Includes translations of Galen's works against Erasistratus and the Erasistrateans, with extensive annotations.

_____. *On Respiration and the Arteries.* Edited by David J. Furley and J. S. Wilkie. Princeton, N.J.: Princeton University Press, 1984. Pages 26 to 37 offer an excellent introduction to Erasistratus's views on respiration, the heart, and the arteries. The volume also includes an annotated translation of three Galenic works that are important sources for Erasistratus's physiology.

_____. *Three Treatises on the Nature of Science.* Translated by Michael Frede and Richard Walzer. Indianapolis, Ind.: Hackett Publishing, 1985. A useful source for aspects of Erasistratus's theory of scientific method and his epistemology.

Gilbert, N. W. *Renaissance Concepts of Method.* New York: Columbia University Press, 1963. Contains information on Galen's scientific methodology.

Nutton, Vivian. "Logic, Learning, and Experimental Medicine." *Science* 295, no. 5556 (February 1, 2002): 800-801. In this physician's profile, Nutton notes that, based on logic and experimental methodology, Galen's ideas dominated the field of medicine for centuries.

Porter, Dorothy. *Health, Civilization, and the State: A History of Public Health from Ancient to Modern Times.* New York: Routledge, 1999. Galen is covered as a Roman practitioner of medicine as well as an early figure in public health.

Sarton, George. *Galen of Pergamon.* Lawrence: University of Kansas Press, 1954. An accessible and read-able biography. Contains interesting historical background, but the discussion of philosophy is brief and takes some knowledge for granted.

Temkin, Owsei. *Galenism: Rise and Decline of a Medical Philosophy.* Ithaca, N.Y.: Cornell University Press, 1973. An authoritative overview of the phenomenon that so influenced medieval medicine and philosophy. Also contains a description of the various forgeries of Galen's texts.

SEE ALSO: Anaximenes of Miletus; Aretaeus of Cappodocia; Aulus Cornelius Celsus; Diocles; Empedocles; Herophilus; Hippocrates; Marcus Aurelius.

RELATED ARTICLES in *Great Events from History: The Ancient World*: 6th-4th century B.C.E. (traditionally, 1st millennium B.C.E.), Suśruta, Indian Physician, Writes Medical Compendium; c. 500 B.C.E., Acupuncture Develops in China; c. 500-400 B.C.E., Greek Physicians Begin Scientific Practice of Medicine; 332 B.C.E., Founding of Alexandria; 133 B.C.E., Pergamum Is Transferred to Rome; c. 157-201 C.E., Galen Synthesizes Ancient Medical Knowledge.

GENSERIC
Vandal king (r. 428-477 C.E.)

One of the most important Germanic rulers, the Vandal Genseric invaded North Africa, sacked Rome, and hastened the fall of the Western Roman Empire.

BORN: c. 390 C.E.; probably Slovakia
DIED: 477 C.E.; Carthage (now in Tunisia)
ALSO KNOWN AS: Gaiseric
AREAS OF ACHIEVEMENT: Government and politics, war and conquest

EARLY LIFE

Born into a tumultuous era, Genseric (GEHN-suh-rihk), or Gaiseric, was the son of the Vandal king Godigisel and his freed slave wife. By the time of Genseric's birth, the Roman Empire's unity, uneasily based on the mutual recognition of several emperors, had to be renewed constantly by force. The emperors' use of Germanic troops to combat discord among Romans eventually got out of control, and barbarian peoples meant to serve as nonpolitical military resources gained control over large areas. The Franks and Goths would be the most famous of these groups, while eastern Germanic peoples included the Vandals, Suebi, and Alans.

The polygamy, love of war, unsophisticated nature worship and often brutish customs practiced by Germans left lasting bad impressions on the Romans. The Roman historian Tacitus regarded the illiterate Germans as savages incapable of knowledge. However, the Germans were also characterized by their rejection of slavery. Their thirst for independence, fostered by poverty, overcame the sophisticated despotism of Rome. Militarized by the unstable situation, these peoples left an indelible mark. Many geographical names (including "France," "Burgundy," "Lombardy," and "England") originated with the Germans, who conquered them. Words such as "vandal" and "frankness" became part of the English language.

Little is known of the origins of the Vandals. Tacitus used "Vandilii" as a general term for eastern Germans. Two branches of the group are later mentioned, Silings and Asdings. Driven west by the Huns, they burst into the Roman Empire on December 31, 406, when, together with the Alans, Suevi, Alamanni, and Burgundians, they crossed the icebound Rhine River near Mainz. Genseric was in his teens when this migration marked the end of

Roman power north of the Alps.

This crisis began when Emperor Theodosius the Great died in 395, shortly after reconquering the West. The Empire was inherited by his underage sons, Arcadius in Constantinople and Flavius Honorius in Rome. Born in 384, Honorius was greatly influenced by his subordinates. Stilicho, a Vandal general who had married into the Theodosian Dynasty, claimed that Theodosius had bequeathed the regency of the entire empire to him. Many refuted his claim. Ambitious warlords played the opposing courts off against each other, but no one warlord had enough power to destroy his rivals. Discredited, Stilicho was assassinated in 408. Under their able leader Alaric, the Visigoths, who had crossed Rome's borders to avoid the Huns, invaded Italy three times and sacked Rome in 410. The security and plenty that Romans had enjoyed for centuries was lost.

Barbarian bands ravaged Gaul. By 409, the Vandals, Suevi, and Alans had moved into Spain, where they divided the spoils by lot. The Silings and Alans took the south, while the Asdings and Suevi occupied Galicia. In 411, they became *federati*, or Roman military allies. In 416, however, the Visigoths were sent by the emperor to evict the Silings and take Galicia from the Suevi. Warfare between the Suevi and the Visigoths would continue for eighty years.

Beset by barbarian warlords and hostile Imperial claimants, Honorius's court went into hiding in the heavily defended city of Ravenna. The fortifications on the Danube and Rhine Rivers were abandoned. Honorius was reduced to relying on armies raised by gifts to slaves and deserters. He died heirless in 423, ending a reign afflicted by revolts and usurpations. Not until 425 did his nephew Valentinian III restore the legitimate dynasty.

After the grant of Aquitaine to the Visigoths in 418, weak governments and ambitious generals regularly turned over provinces to warlords in exchange for support in whatever crisis arose. Around 420, the Asdings moved south to rejoin the Silings, who had suffered severely under Visigothic occupation. Raiding far and wide, the united Vandals were content to plunder rather than rule. Only when they had exhausted the riches of the southern Spanish region of Andalusia (Vandalusia) did they move on.

LIFE'S WORK

In 427 the Vandals were invited to Africa by a rebellious Roman official, Bonifacius, who recruited their support against Honorius's regent. Lured by the prospect of controlling rich North African lands, Genseric and his half brother Gunderic responded by organizing an expedition. Gunderic died before the plans were carried out, but in Genseric, the Vandals had a single leader of immense ability.

In 429, in the largest seaborne movement of Germanic peoples, some eighty thousand Vandals and Alans, including about twenty thousand warriors, landed near Tangier. Ignoring the interests of Bonifacius, Genseric

The Vandals descend on Rome. Genseric, their king, spared the city from destruction. (F. R. Niglutsch)

laid siege to the coastal city of Hippo Regius for fourteen months; shortly before its capitulation in the summer of 430, the seventy-five-year-old bishop Augustine died inside the besieged city. Genseric overran Mauretania and Numidia (Algeria), defeating Bonifacius's troops in 431. Seven provinces that had known peace and prosperity for centuries were given over to plunder and massacre. Although the Vandals' destructiveness has been exaggerated, Genseric seldom gave quarter to opponents. Torture was employed to force captives to reveal hidden wealth. Stern policies were backed by the frequent use of execution. The alleged wholesale destruction of olive trees and crops is improbable, given that the Vandals intended to settle in the region.

By 435 Genseric had concluded a treaty with Imperial authorities who made the Vandals *federati* in Numidia. Only Carthage held out. After the city's destruction following Rome's defeat of Hannibal, the great city of Carthage had been rebuilt as the capital of Roman Africa. The surrounding region, Africa Proconsularis, became vital to Rome's grain supply. Wealthy Romans maintained vast estates, which they rarely saw, in the region. By Genseric's time, decades had passed without an emperor having visited Africa. Africa's economic and strategic importance was taken for granted by the Romans but was well known to the Vandal invaders. Foreshadowing what was to come, the Roman general Gildo had cut off Rome's grain shipments during a dispute in 397.

In a surprise attack, Genseric captured Carthage on October 19, 439, giving the Vandals a major naval base and a stranglehold on Rome's food supplies. As feared as Attila's horsemen, Vandal fleets made Genseric master of the western Mediterranean. By 442, Rome was forced to acknowledge Genseric in a second treaty that gave the Vandals North Africa.

Having spent a generation harried by stronger groups throughout Europe, Genseric was determined not to be moved again. He therefore ran a regime that was aggressive externally and harsh domestically. Although he continued to use many Roman administrators, he asserted an independent stance toward the Empire, especially terms of religion. He confiscated estates belonging to the Imperial court and Roman landlords. His tyrannical regime was hated by both his Vandal subjects and the local inhabitants, who were crushed by heavy taxation. The kingship became hereditary, based on succession by the oldest living male. Consistent with his autocratic nature, he even attempted to establish a new chronological era dating from his capture of Carthage.

Meanwhile, Rome's decline continued. Like Honorius, Valentinian III had little political aptitude. His early years were beset with intrigues over succession. Spoiled, hedonistic, and overshadowed by his mother and his general Aetius, he ironically oversaw the accumulation of papal authority, particularly that of Leo the Great. Attempting to neutralize the Vandal threat, he betrothed his sister to Vandal prince Huneric. Having murdered Aetius to assert power in his own right, he himself was assassinated by members of his bodyguard in 455.

After his death, the decay of Rome accelerated. Northern Gaul fell to the Franks, the only Germans to succeed in building an enduring state. Southern Gaul and Spain were ruled by the Visigoths, and Africa by Genseric. Eventually, Ostrogoths captured Italy itself. Preserving classical civilization, Greek-speaking "Eastern Romans" ruled the eastern Mediterranean from Constantinople.

A few months after Valentinian's assassination, Genseric descended on Rome. Pope Leo was able to convince him to choose peaceful occupation over bloody massacre. Heaps of treasure were carted off to Carthage, and thousands of citizens, including the widow and daughters of the recently murdered emperor, were made captives. However, Genseric spared the city from destruction. In 468, Genseric crowned his achievements by destroying a naval expedition sent jointly by the Eastern and Western emperors.

Vandal and Roman societies were separated by religious differences. As a sign of independence and a way of avoiding domination by the Roman clergy, most Germanic groups had converted to Arianism, which questioned Jesus Christ's divinity. Genseric brought an organized Arian clergy to Africa. Allied with the Donatists, a rival Christian sect, he and his successors instituted vengeful persecutions against Catholics. Churches were burned, and all Catholic gatherings were forbidden. Bishops and priests were deported. After two decades of persecution, Valentinian III intervened, and Genseric allowed Catholic bishops to be installed. When the bishop of Carthage died two years after Valentinian's murder, the election of a new bishop was forbidden. Genseric presided over another twenty years of repression, particularly of Catholics surviving within the administration.

SIGNIFICANCE

After a fifty-year reign, Genseric died in 477 and was succeeded by his even more fanatical son, Hunneric. After Catholic bishops refused to convert to Arianism, Huneric applied Roman laws against heretics. The bishops were exiled. Members of the Catholic laity found every trade closed to them. Huneric died within months, but forced baptisms, martyrdoms, and tortures continued. African Catholicism was left with no bishops, no churches, and hardly any priests. Persecution ended only when Hilderic, the son of Huneric and a captive daughter of Valentinian III, came to power in 523. Meanwhile, Mauritania and Numidia were abandoned to the Moors.

The pro-Catholic Hilderic was half Roman, the last descendant of the old Imperial family of Theodosius. He enjoyed friendly relations with the emperor Justinian, and he recalled bishops and restored churches. Incurring the wrath of the Arian Vandal nobility, he was overthrown and murdered in 532. Justinian intervened with a large force. On September 14, 532, the Imperial general Belisarius defeated the Vandals at Ad Decimam, took Carthage, and easily subdued one district after another. By 539, Vandal rule in Africa had ended.

Unlike the Goths and Franks, the Vandals were unable to put down deep roots. They made no lasting cultural contribution and left almost no records. Those Vandals who survived became Roman slaves, intermingled with the peoples of North Africa, and disappeared from history. Nevertheless, Genseric was one of the most able, and unscrupulous, of all Germanic leaders. His conquest of Roman Africa irreversibly weakened the Empire and the North African church. A feeble Roman-Christian North Africa survived the barbarian onslaught, only to succumb to seventh century Muslim invasions, which permanently destroyed the unity of the Mediterranean world.

—*Randall Fegley*

FURTHER READING

Gibbon, Edward. *The History of the Decline and Fall of the Roman Empire*. Edited by J. B. Bury. 7 vols. New York: Modern Library, 1995. Although inaccurate in parts, Gibbon's classic work on Rome's fall contains much valuable information and commentary on the Vandals, the Alans, Germanic society in general, and Imperial intrigues.

Goffart, Walter. *Barbarians and Romans*. Norman: University of Oklahoma Press, 1983. A reprint of a 1928 work, Goffart's book emphasizes the ruthlessness of Genseric and the Vandals, who he argues played a key role in the collapse of the Western Roman Empire.

Gwatkin, H., and J. Whitney, eds. *The Cambridge Medieval History*. 8 vols. Cambridge, England: Cambridge University Press, 1964-1968. The first volume of this standard source includes an excellent section by Ludwig Schmidt, who offers a balanced look at the social, political, and military aspects of the Vandals from Genseric to Hilderic.

O'Donnell, James J. *Augustine*. Boston: Twayne, 1985. A biography of Augustine that contains much information about religious controversy within Roman Africa, Rome's decline, and Genseric's siege of Hippo Regius.

Tacitus. *Germania*. Translated by J. B. Rives. New York: Oxford University Press, 1999. Tacitus provides a representative Roman view of the society, politics, and customs of the Vandals and other Germans in the era prior to Rome's decline.

Todd, Malcolm. *The Early Germans*. Cambridge, Mass.: Blackwell, 1995. The society, organization, migrations, customs, and conquests of the Vandals and other Germanic groups are surveyed in this useful book, which sheds much light on a confused era.

SEE ALSO: Attila; Saint Augustine; Tacitus; Theodosius the Great.

RELATED ARTICLES in *Great Events from History: The Ancient World*: August 24-26, 410 C.E., Gothic Armies Sack Rome; 439 C.E., Vandals Seize Carthage; 445-453 C.E., Invasions of Attila the Hun.

GOŚĀLA MASKARĪPUTRA
Indian religious leader

Gośāla Maskarīputra founded the religious sect known as the Ājīvikas, which held to a doctrine of absolute determinism and became known as a an early competitor of Buddhism and Jainism.

BORN: Sixth century B.C.E.; Possibly Sarāvaṇa, Magadha (now in India)
DIED: c. 467 B.C.E.; Savatthi, Magadha (now in India)
ALSO KNOWN AS: Gośāla Makkhali (Pāli); Gośāla Mankhaliputta (Prakrit); Markali (Tamil); Goshala Maskariputra
AREAS OF ACHIEVEMENT: Philosophy, religion

EARLY LIFE

The life of Gośāla Maskarīputra (goh-SHAH-lah MAS-kah-ree-PEW-trah) is known primarily from the writings of Buddhists and the Jains, who considered him a heretic. It is difficult to judge how much historical truth about the founder of the Ājīvikas can be found in the texts of these other religions. The two primary sources on Gośāla's early life are the Jain *Bhagavati Sūtra* (c. fourth century C.E.; *Sudharma Svami's Bhagavati Sūtra*; 1973) and the *Samaññaphala Sutta* (fifth century C.E.), written by the Buddhist Buddhaghosa. Although the Ājīvika faith appears to have had characteristics in common with both Jainism and Buddhism, it was closest to the Jains. Both the Ājīvikas and the Jains held that humankind had been visited by twenty-three *tīrthaṅkaras*, or "ford-makers," who brought sacred truth. However, the Jains maintained that the twenty-fourth and last *tīrthaṅkara* was their sage Vardhamāna (c. 599-527 B.C.E.), while the Ājīvikas believed that Gośāla was the twenty-fourth *tīrthaṅkara*.

In the Jain version of Gośāla's life, Vardhamāna, the major proclaimer of the Jain faith, tells the story of Gośāla's birth. Vardhamāna relates that Gośāla's father was named Mankhali and his mother was named Bhadda. Mankhali is said to have been a *mankha*, the precise meaning of which is now unclear, but which seems to have referred to a wanderer who lived by singing religious songs and showing religious pictures. While visiting the village of Sarāvaṇa, Mankhali left his pregnant wife in the cowshed of a rich man named Gobahula. There the child was born, thus obtaining his name, which refers to a place where cattle are kept. This story may be pure fiction, told for the sake of discrediting Gośāla, although the specific identification of Sarāvaṇa may indicate that this was Gośāla's actual birthplace. The Buddhist version by Buddhaghosa agrees that Gośāla was born in a cowshed but maintains that Gośāla was a slave. Much of this story, also, may have been little more than an effort to discredit a rival religion.

As a young man, according to the account in the *Bhagavati Sūtra*, Gośāla took up his father's occupation as a *mankha*. It does seem likely that he was a wandering religious practitioner and that this way of life brought him into contact with Vardhamāna, the founder of the Jain religion. Jainism, which continues to have a following into the twenty-first century, teaches extreme renunciation of material things and nonviolence (*ahimsā*) to achieve the liberation of the soul. The *Bhagavati Sūtra* maintains that Vardhamāna was living in a shed at Nālanda when Gośāla went to the Jain sage and begged to be allowed to become Vardhamāna's disciple. After several rejections, Gośāla was accepted and the two holy men became companions for six years.

LIFE'S WORK

The true events of Gośāla's life and work are as difficult to ascertain as the circumstances of his childhood and upbringing, since so much of his biography has been passed down through hostile Jain and Buddhist writings. The Jain *Bhagavati Sūtra* tells that during their wanderings and adventures together, Gośāla was impressed by Vardhamāna's magical powers and wanted to acquire these kinds of powers for himself. After observing Vardhamāna's ascetic practices, Gośāla sat down by a lake facing the sun, with his hands raised above his head. He remained in this position for six months, eating only a handful of beans every three days. At the end of this period, Gośāla is said to have acquired the magical powers he desired. Since all sources indicate that Vardhamāna and Gośāla spent time together, it is probable that there were connections between these two religious teachers and that these connections were broken because they developed different doctrines. The story of sitting in one place to acquire powers is similar to accounts of how other holy men achieved enlightenment, so it is probably of the Ājīvika tradition regarding Gośāla.

For about sixteen years after the acquisition of his powers (or after his enlightenment), Gośāla stayed in the town of Sāvatthi (Śrāvastī, in Uttar Pradesh), in a pottery shop. His teachings attracted a number of disciples among the seekers of his age. The disciples who gathered around him at Sāvatthi were the first of the Ājīvika communities that were to spread and persist long after his

355

death. The meaning of the term "Ājīvika" is unclear, but many scholars believe that it can be translated as "one who follows the ascetic way."

The basic principle of Gosāla's teaching was the concept of *niyata*, which is translated as "order" or "fate." In his view, the universe is a system of interconnected forces in which every event happens by necessity. Gosāla accepted the common Indian idea of the rebirth of souls. However, while other Indian religions hold that rebirth is influenced by good or bad actions, Gosāla maintained that all sin and virtue had no effect. One's past, present, and future births and all other events were simply the working out of a completely determined destiny. It was not simply that one's will could change nothing: Free will itself was an illusion. Every individual was destined to go through a chain of births before ultimately ending in extinction. Faced with this utter powerlessness, the Ājīvikas believed that all one could do was to follow a life of simplicity and renunciation. Ājīvika doctrine also taught a perspective known as atomism, the view that all things are composed of much smaller building blocks. While determinism was clearly a part of Gosāla's original teaching, though, the atomism may have been a later addition.

It seems clear that this determinism was part of Ājīvika doctrine because this view appears consistently in all reports of Gosāla and his teachings. The Pāli language Buddhist texts frequently compare the teachings of the Buddha with those of "the six heretics," teachers of sects competing with Buddhism during the Buddha's lifetime. In the *Samaññaphala Sutta*, these six heretics are named and their teachings are discussed at some length. In this text, Buddhaghosa wrote that Ajatasattu, king of Magadha in northern India, fell into a spiritual crisis. The king's advisers suggested six teachers that he could visit for an answer to his questions. After receiving unsatisfactory answers from all six, he finally visited the Buddha and, before hearing a sermon, told the Buddha about the teachers. Ajatasattu identified Gosāla as the second of the six. He described Gosāla as teaching that there was no cause of either sin or purity, that destiny directs all occurrences, and that all beings necessarily go through repeated births and deaths.

Toward the end of his life, in the account given by the *Bhagavati Sūtra*, Gosāla was visited at Sāvatthi by six holy men known as the *disacaras*. This is apparently a reference to a conference or council held at Sāvatthi by Gosāla and his major disciples. The Ājīvika doctrines seem to have been discussed and refined at this conference, and it probably began the process of assembling the Ājīvika scriptures from earlier writings. These scriptures have been lost in the centuries since the disappearance of the Ājīvika religion, but selections from them have survived as disapproving quotations in Buddhist and Jain texts.

Gosāla is supposed to have visited Vardhamāna not long after the meeting with the six holy men. The Ājīvika sage was angry because the Jain leader had talked about Gosāla's lowly birth and about shameful incidents during the time the two were together. Gosāla threatened Vardhamāna with magic, but Vardhamāna simply answered that the magic would affect only Gosāla himself, who would soon be stricken with fever and die. Gosāla made his way back to his shed and fell into the foretold fever. During his sickness, he is said to have proclaimed some of the last doctrines of his religion. He then gave instructions for an elaborate funeral, during which his followers would proclaim the death of the last *tīrthaṅkara*. Before dying, however, Gosāla repented and announced that he was a fraud and that Vardhamāna was the true "fordmaker." The Ājīvika leader told his followers to tie a rope around his foot and to drag his body through the streets of Sāvatthi, praising Vardhamāna. The followers only drew a map of Sāvatthi on the floor of the pottery shop and, after dragging the body over the map, held funeral celebrations according to the original instructions before cremating the body. The tale of Gosāla's repentance and deathbed conversion should be regarded with skepticism, since it is the Jain version. Still, it does indicate that the Jains and the Ājīvikas had once been closely connected, possibly even members of the same sect, and that there was some bitterness when the two went their separate ways.

Gosāla's religion survived him for about a thousand years. The Ājīvikas committed to a religious profession followed a regimen of strict asceticism, begging their food and eating only a restricted diet. Sometimes they carried their asceticism to the point of starving themselves to death. The Ājīvika monks were supported by lay believers, in a manner similar to Buddhist monks. Stone inscriptions during the time of the Buddhist emperor Aśoka (c. 302–c. 238 B.C.E.) indicate that Ājīvika communities flourished by this time. There are various mentions of Ājīvika communities in Buddhist writings, most of which compare these communities unfavorably to those of the Buddhists. Over the centuries, the Ājīvika religion dwindled, while the rival Jain faith survived in India and Buddhism spread throughout Asia. Ājīvika communities maintained a hold in the southern parts of India, but these also gradually vanished, possibly absorbed into the complex and flexible system of the dominant Hindu religion.

SIGNIFICANCE

Gośāla Maskarīputra's life and teachings illustrate the variety of philosophical views that thrived in India at the time that Buddhism and Jainism emerged from Hinduism. He also propounded an early form of determinism that was similar in many ways to later determinist philosophies in other parts of the world, such as that of Baruch Spinoza (1632-1677 C.E.). Although Ājīvikism largely died out in northern India about two centuries after Gośāla's death, Ājīvika communities in southern India survived until about the fourteenth or fifteenth century C.E. Even after that, they may have left influences on the beliefs of Hindu sects in southern India.

—*Carl L. Bankston III*

FURTHER READING

Basham, A. L. *History and Doctrines of the Ajivikas: A Vanished Indian Religion*. 1951. Reprint. New Delhi: Motilal Banarsidass, 1981. An essential work on the Ājīvikas that contains an extensive discussion of the Buddhist and Jain versions of the life of Gośāla.

Charoborti, Haripada. *Asceticism in Ancient India: In Brahmanical, Buddhist, Jaina and Ajivika Societies (From the Earliest Times to the Period of Sankaracharya)*. Columbia, Mo.: South Asian Books, 1993. A useful work on the religious communities of ancient India and one of the few that devotes substantial attention to the Ājīvikas.

Dundas, Paul. *The Jains*. New York: Routledge, 2002. An excellent book on the history and practice of Jainism.

SEE ALSO: Ānanda; Asanga; Aśoka; Aśvaghosa; Bodhidharma; Buddha; Chandragupta Maurya; Kanishka; Vardhamāna; Vasubandhu; Vattagamani.

RELATED ARTICLES in *Great Events from History: The Ancient World*: 1500-1100 B.C.E., Compilation of the Vedas; 6th or 5th century B.C.E., Birth of Buddhism; 527 B.C.E., Death of Vardhamāna, Founder of Jainism; c. 467 B.C.E., Gośāla Maskarīputra, Founder of Ājīvika Sect, Dies.

GRACCHI
Roman statesmen

Although the Gracchi brothers were born into one of the wealthiest and most influential families in Rome, they dedicated their lives to the service of the people. In the waning years of the Roman Republic, when greed and the lust for power consumed the energies of many from the ruling class, the Gracchi tried, through a series of reforms, to restore the vigor of popular government. Many of their ideas were later adopted by rulers such as Julius Caesar and his nephew and heir, Augustus.

TIBERIUS SEMPRONIUS GRACCHUS

BORN: 163 B.C.E.; probably Rome (now in Italy)
DIED: June, 133 B.C.E.; Rome

GAIUS SEMPRONIUS GRACCHUS

BORN: 153 B.C.E.; probably Rome (now in Italy)
DIED: 121 B.C.E.; Grove of Furrina, near Rome (now in Italy)
AREA OF ACHIEVEMENT: Government and politics

EARLY LIVES

Tiberius Sempronius Gracchus (GRAK-uhs) and Gaius Sempronius Gracchus were among the twelve children born to Tiberius Sempronius Gracchus and Cornelia, the daughter of Scipio Africanus, the general who defeated the Carthaginian leader Hannibal in the Second Punic War. The elder Gracchus died when Tiberius was twelve and Gaius was barely two, but his widow raised the boys and their sister in the traditions of their ancestors and in the virtues responsible for the greatness of the Republic. She was assisted by Diophanes of Mitylene, a noted master of rhetoric, and Blossius, the famous Stoic philosopher. Ptolemy VI, the king of Egypt, sought to marry Cornelia, but rather than deny her duty to her children, she rejected his suit. Remaining in Rome, she set an example of simplicity and frugality that both amazed and confounded her friends.

A serious youth, Tiberius was quiet, gentle, and always obedient to his elders. To test his courage and further shape his character, he was sent to Africa during the final phase of the Third Punic War to serve under his brother-in-law, Scipio Aemilianus. At the age of sixteen, Tiberius distinguished himself by being the first to climb the walls of Carthage when the Roman army launched its final assault on the doomed city. Shortly thereafter the war ended, and he returned to Rome, where he was betrothed to and later married Claudia, the daughter of Appius Claudius, a man with tremendous influence and great wealth. In 137 Tiberius was chosen a quaestor, and in the Numantine Wars in Spain, which followed his election, he distinguished himself for his bravery and fairness in dealing with the enemies of the Republic. He was elected tribune in 133 at the age of twenty-nine.

Although Gaius Gracchus eventually proved himself to be a more effective politician than his brother, as a young man he had the reputation of being emotional, high-strung, fiery tempered, and extravagant. In his teens he, too, was sent to serve under his brother-in-law, Scipio the Younger, in Spain. When he was twenty, his brother selected him in absentia as one of the commissioners to conduct the redistribution of land under the provisions of the revised agrarian law, but the untimely murder of Tiberius rendered his appointment useless. Gaius returned to Rome, married the daughter of Publius Crassus, and assumed the character of a young man of fashion with very expensive tastes. The senators who were responsible for the death of Tiberius constantly anticipated the revenge of the younger Gracchus.

Goaded by the jibes of his family and friends, Gaius finally sought public office. Chosen a quaestor, he was sent to Sardinia to serve under Aurelius Orestes. Rather than considering his duty an exile, Gaius enjoyed it because at the age of twenty-seven he was not yet ready for a life in public service. Days spent on the march or in camp suited him well. The success of Gaius in Sardinia only deepened the suspicions of his enemies in the senate, and to keep him abroad they extended the term of Orestes and consequently those of his subordinates. This devious manipulation of the civil service infuriated Gaius, who returned to Rome, without permission, to confront his enemies. Accused of acting contrary to orders, a charge of which he was easily acquitted, Gaius began to consider entering public life. Against the advice of his mother, he offered himself as a candidate for the office of tribune, and in 123 he was elected to that position.

LIVES' WORK

While Tiberius may have been encouraged by his mother and his former tutors to seek a tribuneship, it was the plight of the poor that really moved him to forgo the quiet of private life for the stress and uncertainty of elected office. For decades the number of small family farms had been declining, and Tiberius wanted to reverse this trend. As the Romans conquered their neighbors, thereby laying the foundations of an empire, they increased the slave population by a tremendous percentage, as those who re-

sisted the power of the Republic were condemned to perpetual servitude. Many a wealthy Roman had grown even richer by investing first in slaves and then in both public and private land that could be devoted to agriculture. These *latifundia*, great estates worked by slave labor, yielded an enormous profit. Roman farmers were forced to sell their land when they discovered that they could not compete with the cheaper, slave-produced foodstuffs that flooded the market. In many instances, they sold their farms to the very men who had driven them to bankruptcy. By the thousands, these dispossessed men flocked to Rome with their families, hoping to find jobs, but there were none. Tiberius wanted to put this vast army of unemployed farmers back on the land, and his program of agrarian reform was designed to do exactly that.

In 376, the tribunes Licinius and Sextius had passed a law that limited the amount of public land that could be held by one individual to five hundred *iugera*, or 311 acres (152 hectares). This measure was ignored because no mechanism was ever created to enforce it. Tiberius sought not only to revive it but also to form a three-man commission to see that the letter of the law was fulfilled. On the advice of some of the most respected men in Rome, he sought not to punish those who had violated the law but merely to encourage them to abandon the land they occupied illegally. To make the task easier, compensation in the form of the fair market price of each acre abandoned was offered by the government.

The land-rich rejected the reforms of Tiberius and began to offer bribes to anyone they thought could help defeat the measure. Many a senator was counted among those who sold influence in exchange for gold, but an honest man, Marcus Octavius, was persuaded to stop Tiberius. Octavius was the fellow tribune of Tiberius, and he had the obligation to veto any bill proposed by his colleague that, in his opinion, violated the rights of the Roman people. The founders of the Republic had created this system of checks and balances to ensure honest government, but now this safeguard of liberty was unwittingly corrupted to serve greed. Octavius was convinced that the newly revised law was illegal; thus, he vetoed it. No amount of pleading could make him change his mind. Frustrated at every turn, Tiberius resorted to measures that were ill-advised, if not unlawful.

The mild law was withdrawn, and a new measure with no provision for compensation was substituted. Octavius naturally opposed this measure with more energy than he had the previous one, and thus Tiberius appealed to the people to vote Octavius out of office. This was an illegal move, but once aroused, Tiberius would not heed the advice of his family or his associates. When Octavius had been recalled, Tiberius had one of his close supporters elected in his place, and the agrarian law was finally passed. The three men quickly appointed to enforce the law were Appius Claudius, Gaius Gracchus, and Publius Crassus. Tiberius had originally reserved one of these places for himself, but he was persuaded to appoint his brother's father-in-law instead.

The method Tiberius used to finance his plan was ingenious. King Attalus III of Pergamum, a state in Asia Minor, had, in his will, left his kingdom and all of his treasure to the Roman people in the hope of sparing his subjects Rome's inevitable conquest. Tiberius now proposed to sell the treasures and use the profits to buy farm tools and livestock for those to receive land under the provisions of the new law. It was a very popular move with the people but not with the senate.

Just as Tiberius began to implement his plan, his term of office expired. Convinced that the success of the new agrarian law depended on him, Tiberius ignored tradition and stood for reelection. The senate responded to his challenge by goading the city mob into a frenzy. In the resulting riot, Tiberius was beaten to death, and his body was thrown into the Tiber River. Three hundred of his closest followers were arrested and condemned to death without a trial.

Thus, when Gaius was elected tribune ten years after his brother, the senators who had arranged the murder of Tiberius had reason to fear for their lives. Almost immediately after his election, Gaius proposed legislation to punish Octavius and Popillius, the magistrate who had unjustly sentenced Tiberius's associates to death. Only the intervention of Cornelia saved Octavius, but Popillius fled Rome. Gaius, who craved the adoration of the people and welcomed conflict, revived his brother's agrarian law in the face of certain senatorial opposition. That controversy was only the beginning.

While serving in Sardinia, Gaius had witnessed the privation of the average Roman soldier, who was ill-equipped and poorly fed. In quick succession, laws were passed to furnish each soldier with clothing proper to the season and climate at government expense. By law, boys under the age of seventeen were forbidden to enlist in the army. The market price of grain sold to the poor was lowered, and the government absorbed the difference. To curtail the control of the senate over the judiciary, he expanded the number of judges and then personally recruited them from the nonsenatorial orders. Roads and public granaries were built, giving jobs to the unem-

ployed. Then, as his first term of office ended, Gaius turned his attention to the founding of colonies as places of settlement for the landless.

When Gaius sought reelection, he met with no open opposition from his enemies in the senate, because he was too popular with the people. Unwisely, Gaius left Rome to supervise personally the laying of the foundations of a new colony on the site of Carthage. In his absence, his opponents began to undermine his policies. Returning to the capital, he found Rome on the verge of anarchy. The issue that led to the downfall of Gaius was his proposal to extend the benefits of Roman citizenship to the Italian allies. This reform would have seriously weakened the power and influence of the senate. Once again, he sought the endorsement of the people, but this time he lost at the polls. At last, his senatorial enemies had their chance. Gaius was declared an outlaw, and within a day the second of the remarkable Gracchi brothers was dead, the victim of a murder-suicide. Three thousand of his followers were judicially murdered, and an uneasy peace settled over Rome.

SIGNIFICANCE

In the middle of the second century before the Christian era, the Roman Republic faced a constitutional crisis that threatened to destroy the fabric of the state. Invincible on the field of battle, Rome suddenly enjoyed unbelievable wealth as the booty from a host of countries flowed into the capital, accompanied by thousands of captives who were reduced to servitude. Condemned to endless labor on the huge farms that dotted the Italian landscape, these slaves drove free Romans from their tiny family farms when they could no longer compete. As they swelled the mob of unemployed in the capital, the Gracchi brothers, Tiberius and Gaius, arose to give them hope. In their respective programs lay the last and best chance for the Republic, and their assassinations were its death knell.

An uneasy quiet descended on Rome after the murder of the Gracchi and their supporters, but within a generation the peace was shattered as two men, Gaius Marius and Lucius Cornelius Sulla, vied for control of the state. Marius was a successful general who modernized the Roman army, transforming it from a force formed of draftees into one filled with long-term volunteers. Most of these recruits were landless peasants who received a tract of land at the end of their service; thus, one of the proposals of the Gracchi was revived and became a permanent part of the Roman system. Marius led the Populares, the party of the Gracchi, while Sulla headed the Optimates, the party composed of the senatorial enemies of Tiberius and Gaius. In the ensuing civil war, thousands of innocent victims from both sides were butchered.

A slave rebellion, countless conspiracies, and another civil war followed in the wake of Sulla's victory. Then the Romans, weary of the bloodshed, turned to Julius Caesar for deliverance. Caesar used a number of the ideas of the Gracchi to win and retain popular support, a practice continued by his Imperial successors. The welfare system proposed by Gaius Gracchus thus became a political weapon and then a financial liability during the latter days of the Roman Empire. The distribution of public lands to veterans, however, settled thousands of responsible and loyal citizens on the frontiers of the Empire. Thus, the best that Rome had to offer survived despite the steady decline of the Imperial system.

With the rediscovery of classical culture during the Renaissance, the Gracchi once again caught the public's imagination, but it was not until the birth of popular republics in the United States and France that they regained their places in the pantheon of democratic heroes. Their deeds have become legendary, and their names are synonymous with reform and the best in the liberal tradition.

—Clifton W. Potter, Jr.

FURTHER READING

Badian, E. *Foreign Clientalae, 264-270 B.C.* New York: Oxford University Press, 1984. This scholarly work is extremely valuable because it enables the student to place the Gracchi in the context of Roman history. The bibliography serves as an excellent departure point for further reading.

Bernstein, Alvin H. *Tiberius Sempronius Gracchus, Tradition and Apostasy.* Ithaca, N.Y.: Cornell University Press, 1978. The author has written an excellent, well-balanced biography of the eldest of the Gracchi. Each step in the career of Tiberius is carefully examined and evaluated. The bibliography is comprehensive.

Perelli, Luciano. *Gracchi.* Rome: Salerno, 1993. A biography of the Gracchi that analyzes their environment. In Italian.

Plutarch. *Agis and Cleomenes, and Tiberius and Gaius Gracchus, Philopoemen and Titus Flaminus.* Vol. 10 in *Plutarch's Lives.* Translated by Bernadotte Perrin. Cambridge, Mass.: Harvard University Press, 1982-1990. Contains the Greek original and a very fine English translation. Plutarch supplies his reader with a clear, concise, and moving portrait of the two brothers who might have saved the Roman Republic.

Scullard, H. H. *From the Gracchi to Nero: A History of Rome from 133 B.C. to A.D. 68.* New York: Routledge, 1988. This work chronicles not only the rise and fall of the Gracchi but also the aftermath of their attempts to save the Roman Republic: the tragic decline of Roman liberty from the mid-second century B.C.E. to the reign of Nero.

Stockton, David. *The Gracchi.* Oxford, England: Clarendon Press, 1979. For those unfamiliar with the actual mechanisms by which the Roman Republic was governed, the author provides an excellent foreword. This slim volume offers a detailed treatment of the careers of the Gracchi as well as a series of useful appendices.

SEE ALSO: Augustus; Julius Caesar; Gaius Marius; Lucius Cornelius Sulla.

RELATED ARTICLES in *Great Events from History: The Ancient World*: 149-146 B.C.E., Third Punic War; 133 B.C.E., Tiberius Sempronius Gracchus Is Tribune; 107-101 B.C.E., Marius Creates a Private Army.

GREGORY OF NAZIANZUS
Greek theologian and poet

A consummate rhetorician, Gregory produced many orations, poems, and letters that provide much information on the religious and social life of Christianity in the second half of the fourth century. As a theologian, Gregory was influential in the formulation of orthodox doctrine regarding the divinity of the Holy Spirit.

BORN: 329 or 330 C.E.; Arianzus, Cappadocia (now in Turkey)
DIED: 389 or 390 C.E.; Arianzus, Cappadocia
ALSO KNOWN AS: Gregory Nazianzen
AREAS OF ACHIEVEMENT: Literature, religion

EARLY LIFE

Gregory (GREH-gor-ee of nay-zee-AN-zuhs) was born on the family estate of Arianzus, near Nazianzus, the son of Bishop Gregory, the Elder of Nazianzus. His mother, Nonna, a pious woman who had converted her husband to Christianity in 325, was a very formative influence on her son. Young Gregory was educated in the school of rhetoric in Caesarea in Cappadocia, then briefly in the Christian schools of Caesarea in Palestine and of Alexandria, where he became familiar with Christianized Platonism. On his sea journey from Alexandria, his ship encountered a great storm; realizing that he was not yet baptized, Gregory made a solemn vow to spend the rest of his life in the service of the Church if he survived. Finally, he went to the great secular university of Athens, where he spent nine years, becoming an outstanding student of the rhetoricians Prohaeresius and Himerius. There he became an inseparable friend of Basil of Caesarea (later Basil the Great), whom he commemorated at length in his famous autobiographical poem *Carmen de vita sua* (c. 382; *On His Life*, 1814).

LIFE'S WORK

In 362, Gregory's father ordained him a priest, against the young scholar's own will but by popular demand. Gregory subsequently fled to the desert, where he wrote a famous treatise on the priesthood, *Oratio apologetica de fuga sua* (*Apology for His Flight*, 1899), but he soon rejoined his father. He preached his first sermon on Easter Sunday, 362. In this sermon, he likened his father to the patriarch Abraham and himself to Abraham's son Isaac being led forth to sacrifice. Thereafter, he helped to administer his father's diocese. His school friend, Basil, now bishop of Caesarea, soon appointed him bishop of Sasima, "a bewitched and miserable little place," according to Gregory, who refused to take possession of the see. After his father's death in 374, Gregory administered the see of Nazianzus for a time.

In 375, he retired to a monastery in Seleucia, Isauria, but four years later he was invited to reorganize the dwindling Nicene community in Constantinople, a city rife with Arianism. In 380, Emperor Theodosius the Great formally inducted him into the Church of the Apostles in Constantinople, which he served until the middle of 381. His Forty-second Oration is a speech announcing his resignation from the see of Constantinople, which he characterized as a place "not for priests, but for orators, not for stewards of souls, but for treasurers of money, not for pure offerers of the sacrifice, but for powerful patrons." Though still in his early fifties, he retired, a prematurely old, sick, and very disillusioned man, to Cappadocia, where he died in 389 or 390.

Gregory's celebrated speeches defending the orthodox teaching on the Trinity against the heretical Eunomians and Macedonians are collected as the *Orationae* (362-381; *Theological Orations*, 1894). They earned for him the appellation "the Theologian." These orations represent brilliant defenses of the divinity of the Son and the Holy Spirit. *In laudem Basilii Magni* (381; *On St. Basil the Great*, 1953) is regarded as the finest piece of Greek rhetoric since the time of Demosthenes. Indeed, in Byzantine times Gregory was often called "the Christian Demosthenes." Also surviving are panegyrics on his father, his sister, his brother, and the church fathers Saint Athanasius of Alexandria and Saint Cyprian of Carthage.

Gregory's poetry, though rarely inspired, makes competent use of classical models. It deals didactically with a variety of topics, mainly theological. Some forty of the surviving four hundred poems are dogmatic, dealing with such themes as the Trinity and Divine Providence. Most of the poetry was composed in Gregory's final years of retirement.

Particularly important among his numerous letters, written in a very engaging classical style, are three—addressed to a certain Cledonius—which present a forceful refutation of the popular contemporary heresy of Apollinarianism. In writing to pagans, Gregory quoted authors such as Homer and Demosthenes as freely as he quoted from the Old and New Testaments when writing to Christians.

SIGNIFICANCE

Gregory was a man of great sensitivity and spirituality. His was a contemplative nature, very ill-suited to the rough and tumble of ecclesiastical politics in Constantinople at the time of the Second Ecumenical Council of 381. He had great rhetorical skills, and his lasting achievement is the surviving forty-five orations, evidencing a masterful synthesis of classical rhetoric and Christianity. Gregory was particularly adept at countering the logic-chopping of the later Arians, known as Eunomians. He was obviously well trained in Aristotelian and Stoic logic and dialectic. Moreover, his wide knowledge of Scripture enabled him to outwit his opponents in the deployment and interpretation of scriptural texts. The theological importance of the orations is especially evident in their Trinitarian and christological concerns.

Some of Gregory's autobiographical poems are as deeply spiritual and revealing as the *Confessiones* (397-400; *Confessions*, 1620) of Saint Augustine. A careful reading of the poems dealing with his brief tenure in Constantinople can contribute much to an understanding of the ecclesiastical politics of the time, the shallowness and wiliness of some of his fellow bishops at the council, and Gregory's dissatisfaction with the compromise statement on the divinity of the Holy Spirit that emerged in 381. One of Gregory's epitaphs on his father is equally applicable to himself:

> If there was one Moses privileged on the mountain
> to hear the pure voice, there was also the mind of great
>   Gregory,
> whom once God's grace called from afar
> and made a great high-priest.
> Now he dwells near the holy Trinity.

—Thomas Halton

FURTHER READING

Gregg, Robert C. *Consolation Philosophy: Greek and Christian Paideia in Basil and the Two Gregories.* Cambridge, Mass.: Philadelphia Patristic Foundation, 1975. A useful comparative study of the three great Cappadocians' consolatory letters and discourses, with a consideration of their biblical and Hellenistic background. Letters of consolation and panegyrics are examined in the light of the established rhetorical norms of Greek literature.

Gregory of Nazianzus. *Three Poems.* Translated by Denis M. Meehan, with notes by Thomas P. Halton. Washington, D.C.: Catholic University of America Press, 1987. These poems reveal Gregory's sensitivity and reflect his unrelenting quest for perfection in a world full of intrigue and corruption. Includes an introduction, bibliography, and notes.

Gregory of Nazianzus and Saint Ambrose. *Funeral Orations of Saint Gregory Nazianzen and Saint Ambrose.* Translated by Leo P. McCauley et al. Washington, D.C.: Catholic University of America Press, 1968. Particularly useful for the translation of *In laudem Basilii Magni.* Also includes the panegyrics on Gregory's father, brother, and sister.

Kennedy, George A. *Greek Rhetoric Under Christian Emperors.* Princeton, N.J.: Princeton University Press, 1994. Chapter 4, "Christianity and Rhetoric," includes a lengthy and sympathetic study of Gregory, described as "the most important figure in the synthesis of classical rhetoric and Christianity."

Quasten, Johannes. *The Golden Age of Greek Patristic Literature.* Vol. 3 in *Patrology.* 4 vols. Westminster, Md.: Newman Press, 1986-1992. Contains a well-documented and sympathetic account of one characterized as "the humanist among the theologians of the fourth century." Includes copious bibliographies.

Ruether, Rosemary R. *Gregory of Nazianzus, Rhetor and Philosopher.* Oxford, England: Clarendon Press, 1969. A careful examination of the Hellenistic influences apparent in Gregory's thought. Includes a particularly helpful examination of his early training. Ruether shows that Gregory became a master of numerous rhetorical devices taught in fourth century schools.

SEE ALSO: Gregory of Nyssa; Theodosius the Great.

RELATED ARTICLES in *Great Events from History: The Ancient World*: October 28, 312 C.E., Conversion of Constantine to Christianity; 313-395 C.E., Inception of Church-State Problem; 325 C.E., Adoption of the Nicene Creed; November 24, 326-May 11, 330 C.E., Constantinople Is Founded; 380-392 C.E., Theodosius's Edicts Promote Christian Orthodoxy; 428-431 C.E., Nestorian Controversy; October 8-25, 451 C.E., Council of Chalcedon.

GREGORY OF NYSSA
Greek prelate of Asia Minor

A profound thinker and theologian, as well as an eloquent preacher, Gregory was one of the brilliant leaders of Christian orthodoxy in the late fourth century. His influence led to the defeat of the Arian heresy and the triumph of the orthodox Nicene position at the Council of Constantinople in 381.

BORN: c. 335 C.E.; Caesarea Mazaca, Cappadocia (now Kayseri, Turkey)

DIED: c. 394 C.E.; Constantinople (now Istanbul, Turkey)

ALSO KNOWN AS: Gregorius Nyssenus (Latin name)

AREA OF ACHIEVEMENT: Religion

EARLY LIFE

One of ten children, Gregory (GREH-gor-ee of NIS-uh) was born in the city of Caesarea Mazaca, the capital of Cappadocia, to an important and wealthy Christian family that had suffered in the persecutions of the Roman emperor Diocletian. He was the third son and one of the youngest children of Basil the Elder and Amelia, the daughter of a martyr. Gregory was left fatherless at an early age and was raised largely by his older brother, Basil (later called "the Great"), bishop of Caesarea, and by his sister Macrina. Throughout his life, Gregory looked up to his brother with great affection and respect.

As a young man, Gregory was educated in his native city, attending secular pagan schools. His feeble constitution and natural shyness caused him to concentrate on scholarship rather than physical activities or public life. Thus, his intellectual prowess was enhanced by diligent private study.

While in his youth, Gregory became involved in church activities, but he did so without great conviction. Later in life, he recounted his reluctant, even unwilling, attendance at a ceremony given by his mother in honor of church martyrs. Wearied with his journey and the length of the service—which lasted far into the night—he fell asleep. A terrifying dream soon followed that filled him with a sense of remorse for his neglect of spiritual matters, and he became a lector, or reader of biblical passages in a Christian congregation.

Gregory's youthful years coincided with the last revival of pagan culture, which reached its peak under the emperor Julian the Apostate (reigned 361-363). Gregory was completely won over to the pagan humanistic ideal. Therefore, after a time, Gregory abandoned his church position and devoted himself to secular pursuits. Some-time after the year 360, he accepted a position as a teacher of rhetoric. This desertion from the Christian cause gave his friends and family great pain and brought to him accusations of all kinds.

At about this time Gregory married a woman named Theosebeia. She is believed to have been the sister of Gregory of Nazianzus, who was a family friend. In a letter written many years later, Gregory of Nazianzus, consoling his friend on the death of Theosebeia, extolled her as a true priestess, most fair and lustrous. In fact, Gregory's final conversion to the Christian faith undoubtedly resulted in part from the pleadings and remonstrations of both his wife and his friend.

Another contributing factor that led Gregory back to the Church was the increasing distaste he felt for teaching rhetoric. He became discouraged by the results of his efforts to inspire literary tastes among youths who, he complained, were more ready and better suited to enter the army than follow rhetorical studies.

Gregory abandoned his teaching sometime before 370. He then retired to a monastery at Pontus that was presided over by his brother Basil. There he devoted himself to the study of the Scriptures and the works of Christian commentators. He was especially influenced by Origen, as is evident from Gregory's own theological works.

While he was at the monastery, an episode occurred that may reveal a flaw in Gregory's judgment. A rift had arisen between Basil and an aged uncle, also named Gregory, over doctrinal matters. Acting as a self-appointed mediator, the younger Gregory forged some letters that purported to be from his uncle to his brother Basil offering peace. The deception was exposed, and Gregory received a stern but dignified rebuke from his brother.

LIFE'S WORK

Around the year 365, Basil had been summoned by Eusebius, metropolitan of Caesarea, to aid in repelling the assaults of the Arian faction of Christianity on the Nicene orthodox faith. During the next few years, the Arian believers were assisted and encouraged by the emperor Valens. Basil greatly helped orthodox resistance and in 370 was called, by popular voice, to succeed Eusebius on the latter's death.

To strengthen his position and surround himself with defenders of the orthodox faith in the outposts of his diocese, Basil persuaded Gregory (in spite of his protests) to accept the bishopric of Nyssa, an obscure town of Cappadocia, about ten miles from Caesarea. It was as bishop of Nyssa that Gregory achieved his greatest fame and realized his greatest accomplishments. When a mutual friend wrote to express his surprise at Basil's choosing such an obscure place for so distinguished a man as Gregory, Basil replied that his brother's merits did indeed make him worthy of governing the entire Church. Basil added, however, that the see should be made famous by its bishop, and not the bishop by his see.

Gregory was consecrated bishop in 372. Nevertheless, as soon as he arrived in Nyssa he faced grave difficulties. Arianism was strong in the city and was supported by the emperor. In addition, one of the emperor's courtiers had wanted the bishopric, and Gregory's appointment made for immediate hostility. A man named Demosthenes had been recently appointed governor of Pontus by the emperor and charged to do all in his power to crush the adherents of the orthodox Nicene faith. After some petty acts of persecution, a synod was summoned in 375 at Ancyra to examine charges made against Gregory, including embezzlement of church property and irregularities surrounding his consecration.

Though Gregory escaped from the band of soldiers sent to arrest him, his Arian enemies continued their persecution. Finally, in 376, another synod was summoned at Nyssa; this time the assembled bishops deposed Gregory. A successor was consecrated, and Valens banished Gregory from the city. For many months he traveled from place to place to avoid his enemies. Heartsick over the apparent triumph of Arianism, Gregory nevertheless encouraged his friends to be of good cheer and trust in God. This advice proved to be well-founded. In 378 Valens died, and the youthful emperor Gratian restored Gregory to his bishopric.

Soon afterward another event occurred that forever changed Gregory's life; Basil died in 379, and Gregory fell heir to his position of leadership. Basil had been a man of action and an organizer. Gregory was forced to stand on his own, carrying out the work of his brother and bringing it to completion.

From 379 onward, Gregory's activity was limitless. The next two years saw him preach tirelessly against heresies, Arianism especially. Named after Arius, a priest in Alexandria, Egypt, this doctrine denied the true divinity of Jesus Christ by maintaining that the Son of God was not eternal but created by the Father from nothing, that he, therefore, was not God by nature—being a changeable creature—and that his dignity as Son of God was conferred on him by the Father because of his abiding righteousness. During this time Gregory preached against

Eunomius (an Arian bishop); this preaching would lay the foundation for a major theological treatise titled *Contra Eunomium* (382; against Eunomius).

The spring of 381 marked the pinnacle of Gregory's career. It was then that the emperor Theodosius I convoked the Council of Constantinople. Gregory played a major role in the council. He gave the opening address, influencing many, and witnessed the complete victory of the orthodox Christian doctrines and ideas for which he and Basil had fought. Thus, the work of the Council of Nicaea (in 325) regarding the doctrine of Christ was ratified. The council condemned all varieties of Arianism and added clauses to the Nicene Creed that were supplied by Gregory himself.

After the Council of Constantinople, Gregory became one of the leading personalities of the church in the East. The council gave him jurisdiction, together with two other church leaders, over the regions of Cappadocia and Pontus. He was also sent to Arabia to mediate a dispute between two bishops, though he met with limited success. On his return, he visited the Holy Land, including the city of Jerusalem and the places associated with the life of Christ.

By the end of 381 Gregory was back in Nyssa. The following year, he produced two of his most important theological writings, *Contra Eunomium* and *Adversus Apollinarem* (382; against Apollinaris), in which he responded to heretical ideas and discussed the doctrines relating to Christ and His nature.

Gregory's influence outside the Church was also at its peak during the years from 381 to 386, and he enjoyed the favor of the Imperial court. When Gregory visited the Holy Land, the emperor provided a public chariot for his transportation. Following the success of the Council of Constantinople, Theodosius wanted to hold a council every year; in 383 Gregory was chosen by the emperor to give a major sermon on the divinity of the Son and the Holy Spirit at the convocation. In 385 he was chosen to deliver the funeral eulogies in honor of Empress Flacilla and her daughter Pulcheria, who had died shortly before her mother. At Constantinople, too, Gregory enjoyed the friendship of Olympias, one of the outstanding women of the age.

After 386, Gregory's influence began to decline. His ideas were called into question a number of times, and he had to defend himself against charges that his thinking was tainted with heretical notions. Finally, in Asia Minor, Gregory's prerogatives began to be restricted to his own diocese, and he increasingly came into conflict with Helladius of Caesarea.

In the year 394, Gregory was invited to attend a synod at Constantinople that was called to decide once and for all the claims of two bishops over the see of Bostra. At the request of Nectarius, who was the presiding official there, Gregory delivered his last recorded sermon. It is very likely that he did not long survive the synod, dying in Constantinople the same year as the meeting.

SIGNIFICANCE

Among church fathers and theologians, there is no more honored a name than Gregory of Nyssa. Besides receiving the accolades of his brother Basil and his friend Gregory of Nazianzus, Gregory of Nyssa was praised by biblical scholar Jerome for the sanctity of his life, his theological learning, and his strenuous defense of the Nicene faith. Gregory came to be regarded as one of the three Cappadocian Fathers of the Church, along with Basil the Great and Gregory of Nazianzus.

Though not considered as able an administrator as his brother, Gregory was highly appreciated for his eloquence in writing and speaking. He was chosen to deliver many discourses in the company of other theologians, and his writings show him to be well versed in the work of pagan philosophers as well as in Holy Scripture and the writings of Christian commentators. His works comprise some thirty letters; many sermons and exegetical writings; polemical treatises, including *Contra Eunomium* and *Adversus Apollinarem*; and several ascetic pieces.

Gregory's tireless championing of the Nicene faith and his battle against heresies, especially Arianism, are his greatest legacy. Indeed, his efforts seem to have made prophetic the statement of his brother Basil, spoken at the time of Gregory's consecration to the bishopric: Nyssa was ennobled and made famous by its bishop, and not the other way around.

—*Andrew C. Skinner*

FURTHER READING

Dunstone, Alan S. *The Atonement in Gregory of Nyssa*. London: Tyndale Press, 1964. Provides a succinct discussion of one of the most important themes of Gregory's christological writings and sermons. Its value lies in its concise analysis of Gregory's thinking on a complex theme.

Gregory of Nyssa. *From Glory to Glory*. Edited by Herbert Musurillo. Crestwood, N.Y.: St. Vladimir's Seminary Press, 1979. This volume comprises texts taken from Gregory's mystical and ascetical writings. It also contains a readable, well-organized introduction that presents a history of Gregory's life and work as well as an analysis of some of his writing. The notes and comments on the texts by the editor are also very enlightening. The selected texts have been translated into modern idiomatic English.

_____. *The Lord's Prayer, the Beatitudes*. Edited and translated by Hilda C. Graef. New York: Newman Press, 1954. This book is a compilation of various sermons given by Gregory on the subjects of the Lord's Prayer and the Beatitudes. They give the flavor of Gregory's style of preaching. The work contains an adequate introduction, including a sketch of the scholar's life. Gregory's sermons display his imaginative, rhetorical, and devotional talents.

Hardy, Edward Roche, and Cyril Richardson, eds. *Christology of the Later Fathers*. Philadelphia: Westminster Press, 1953-1966. This volume devotes almost half of its contents to the writings of Gregory of Nyssa. It provides an excellent biographical sketch of Gregory and a summary of his work. It also contains selections, translated into English, of his more important works. Its greatest value, however, lies in the bibliography of the works of Gregory as well as the biographies.

Jaeger, Werner, ed. *Two Rediscovered Works of Ancient Christian Literature*. Leiden, Netherlands: E. J. Brill, 1965. A scholarly volume containing critical notes and commentary on two important treatises by Gregory, this book presents the relationships between Greek theologians and Greek philosophy and Gregory's thought. It contains valuable commentary on the cultural context of Gregory's work.

Meredith, Anthony. *Gregory of Nyssa*. New York: Routledge, 1999. A diverse range of Gregory's writings is presented along with an accessible, well-organized introduction to Gregory's thought.

Schaff, Philip, and Henry Wace, eds. Introduction to *Gregory of Nyssa: Dogmatic Treatises*. Vol. 5 in *A Select Library of Nicene and Post-Nicene Fathers of the Christian Church*. Grand Rapids, Mich.: Eerdman's, 1974-1978. This is an important and informative introduction to Gregory's life and work, though the style is somewhat awkward. The selected texts from Gregory's compiled major works are supplemented by scholarly notes and references.

SEE ALSO: Eusebius of Caesarea; Gregory of Nazianzus; Origen; Theodosius the Great.

RELATED ARTICLES in *Great Events from History: The Ancient World*: 325 C.E., Adoption of the Nicene Creed; 361-363 C.E., Failure of Julian's Pagan Revival; 380-392 C.E., Theodosius's Edicts Promote Christian Orthodoxy.

GUDEA
Neo-Sumerian king (r. c. 2100-2070 B.C.E.)

Gudea ruled Lagash, rebuilt many temples there, and recorded transport of distant materials from as far away as what would now be Lebanon and the eastern coast of the Mediterranean Sea and the southern Persian Gulf.

BORN: c. 2120 B.C.E.; Sumer (now in Iraq)
DIED: c. 2070 B.C.E.; probably Lagash, Sumer (now Tello, Iraq)
ALSO KNOWN AS: Gudea of Lagash
AREA OF ACHIEVEMENT: Government and politics

EARLY LIFE

Almost nothing factual is known of his early life, so the origins of Gudea (gew-DAY-ah) are obscure. If inscriptions are any help, this possibly autobiographical statement on his Eninnu temple cylinder (*Gudea Cylinder A 3:6-8*) could shed some light: "I have no mother, you are my father. My seed you implanted in the womb; in the sanctuary you gave birth to me." Because his god Ningirsu is being addressed as a sort of divine ancestor, negating or superseding human ancestry, this interpretation is difficult. One idea suggests he was a temple orphan or descended from poor priests, especially if his birth in the sanctuary is to be taken literally. The autobiographical detail may be later propaganda to legitimize dubious family origins. Gudea instead may have come from a noble family like a member of the *awelum* in later Babylon (although this is a non-Sumerian word) or a member of a priestly caste like the *mushkenum* in the contemporary state of Eshnunna. While he is later noted as *en*-priest, this title is also concurrently translated along with *ensi*, kingship, and the title of governor.

On the other hand, priesthood is partly extrapolated from his likely literacy and later record of a dearth of military conquests, although these are speculative claims. Any putative background in youth or early adulthood as a priest, then, is unknown, although it is conceivable that his ultimate rise or claim to the throne of Lagash could have been partly a result of the religious reforms or religious ascendance he brought. His name Gudea means "the called one" or "the chosen one," and his Eninnu temple hymn inscription makes a pun on his name by repeating the prayer phrase "His call having been heard."

LIFE'S WORK

Whatever his past, Gudea became a great king (*ensi* in Sumerian) or god-king ("god of his city") and priest who ruled the independent state of Lagash after the collapse of the empire of Akkad (Agade) and its last great king, Naram-Sin. The survival of Lagash as an independent Sumerian state between the Euphrates and Tigris Rivers of southern Mesopotamia after the fall of Akkad, when nearly all other Mesopotamian cities were in chaos or engaged in conflict, may even have been because of Gudea.

Most information on Gudea comes from his inscriptions in cuneiform language texts, many of which are found on clay tablets, such as the clay Eninnu cylinders A and B, both of which are about a foot high. These cylinders describe his building a temple (Eninnu) to the Sumerian god Ningirsu. Ceramic foundation cones inserted at the base of temples during their dedication or consecration are another source of information on Gudea. The other primary source of details about Gudea's life and reign derive from his multiple statues of himself, which deserve special consideration.

These dozen diorite statues present Gudea as either seated or standing in formal Mesopotamian monumentality, with hands clasped together in authority. A convention in Mesopotamian art is depicting ruling males as bearded, but a beard is absent on Gudea in surviving statues, almost unique to his representation of kingship. Although speculative, several explanations have been offered. He may have been a eunuch. He may have instituted a new beardless convention that lasted only during his period, because male beardedness is representative for Mesopotamian rulers before and after him as a tradition for several millennia. Priesthood might also be inferred from the fact that some of his statues show his head to be shaved. Otherwise, he usually wears a caplike headdress with spirals or curls that scholar Michael Roaf suggests could be fur. It might be that these many statues—rare in late third millennium B.C.E. esopotamia—are even propaganda to solidify both his claimed divine kinship as well as kingship of Lagash.

Another interesting sculptural feature is that prior to Gudea, soft stone like calcite or a form of alabaster is more typical as the suitable medium for statuary. His near total use of diorite for these formal sculptures of highly artistic craftsmanship is remarkable for several reasons. First, southern Mesopotamia did not have a prior tradition or even a known craft for working hard stone, because it is an alluvial region where stone is so scarce that clay or mud brick is the dominant medium for architecture as well as for writing. Second, this use of diorite is fascinating because the source of this variety of hard igneous stone is the Horns of Makran at the south end of the Persian Gulf located at the straits of Hormuz (currently Oman), a then-distant region about 450 miles (725 kilometers) to the south. The workmanship of such hard stone may have necessitated a grinding agent, such as pulverized emery or emery powder, whose use seems to be known at contemporary and nearby Ur III from research conducted by Wolfgang Heimpel, which shows emery chips to be embedded in lead blocks for hand use. Little else would have sufficed to achieve the high polish these Gudea statues demonstrate. While Gudea may not

This statue of Gudea, in green calcite, depicts the king holding an overflowing vessel. (© Adam Woolfitt/Corbis)

have pioneered the use of emery, sources for emery in ancient Mesopotamia are known only in Armenia, far to the north over the Taurus and Caucasus Mountains, or even further away to the west on the Aegean island of Naxos—both very distant from southern Mesopotamia. An ability to bring luxury materials over a long distance attests to the wealth of Lagash. Thus, there are many reasons that these sculptures of Gudea are remarkable and even enigmatic.

The other important feature of Gudea's administration is his building or rebuilding of fifteen temples in the city of Girsu, the chief city of Lagash. This in itself suggests a religious reformer or a zealous and pious king. Known primarily from the two clay cylinders A and B, the most important of these temples, as mentioned, is the Eninnu structure to Ningirsu, the patron city god of Girsu.

Gudea claimed on the cylinders that the god Ningirsu gave him the plan for the temple in a dream, and his record therein of transporting materials reveals geographical breadth possibly rivaled before only by Akkadian examples. His workers and materials are recorded as coming from fairly diverse lands—not necessarily immediate neighbors—such as Elamites from Elam (to the east across the Tigris river, currently Iraq and Iran), Susians from Susa (east in the foothills of the Zagros Mountains, currently in Iran), and crafters, carpenters, and timber from distant Magan (currently Oman) and the very distant Meluhha (currently Pakistan), identified with the Indus River and Harappan civilization, possibly mediated through Magan.

Temple building materials listed on this record include cedar from "a path cut into the Cedar Mountains," in what he claims was the first exploitation of timber in "river transport like snakes" down the Euphrates River, as well as likely Aleppo pine brought by the same route. The use of these two timber sources as well as the Euphrates seems to have occurred contemporarily in Lebanon and Syria, which were then greatly distant, more than four hundred miles. He also claims to have been the first to exploit sources for stone quarrying and transport of blocks, repeating his "first to cut a path there" formula. He includes on his source list "red stones from Meluhha"—likely to be carnelian—as well as the Kimash copper mountain that brought him gold dust and silver ore, possibly also from Meluhha. Other imported materials include tin and lapis lazuli (although prior Mesopotamian importation of this distant stone source from current Afghanistan predates Gudea by around a millennium). His claim of pioneering certain quarries is consistent with his use of Makran diorite. Gudea appears not to have been militaristic or oriented to conquest—engaged in successful conflict only with Elam and Anshan—and his greatest successes seem to be greater as a ruler, trader, and builder. It is likely that Gudea and his dynastic successors made Lagash a stable and wealthy state.

Although previous Sumerian trade occurred at Ur and Sargon, and subsequent Akkadian rulers also had wide trade connections, Gudea claims several firsts, as noted above, for cedar timber and actual quarrying. As Akkad was an empire stretching over much of Mesopotamia and Lagash was only a small southern state of aggregate cities and land, it makes Gudea's accomplishments stand out even more. Thus, from his accounts and considering at least the materials necessary for sculpture, Gudea appears to be very sophisticated in utilizing international craftsmanship, trade, and source materials for the late third millennium B.C.E.

Sumerian epigraphy and language study has also benefited from Gudea's inscriptions. The listing of Gudea's titles and administrative actions are numerous from these clay cylinders, clay foundation cones, and the stone statues. Other examples from the above-mentioned clay cylinders alone include the following. His relationship with the gods is shown in these two statements: "Guardian deities of all the countries whose command is like an overflowing water, the one who would stem it is carried off." (*Gudea Cylinder* B 2:1-2); "The ruler being wise and eloquent, kissed the ground before the deities, with supplication and prayer, in humility, he prostrates." (*Gudea Cylinder* B 1:12-14). His building under the gods' patronage and the practice of making bricks is seen in the following lines: "He struck the brick mold and dropped the brick under the sun to dry." (*Gudea Cylinder* A 19:3); "He laid the foundation, set the walls into the ground." (*Gudea Cylinder* A 20:26).

SIGNIFICANCE

Part of Gudea's significance is due to his political and religious reinvigoration of Sumer after the Akkadian period of conquest, assimilation, and then decay. Another part of his importance can be found in the detailed accounts of Sumerian religious structure and ritual as well as elements of Sumerian cosmology and the names of deities and their domains. He would have been considered the primary patron of the arts of architecture and sculpture. His sculptures of himself are also fairly unique in that no other ruler of ancient Sumer has so many (twelve) surviving statues of himself, nearly all in hard diorite

stone. While this may seem egoistic, there may have been a need for justifying his reign or authenticating his claims to divine kingship. On the other hand, these sculptures are in many ways very important for helping to establish the canon of Sumerian art, particularly sculpture. By his own account, he would qualify as a reformer and zealous builder of temples. Another aspect of his importance can be seen in the geographical breadth of his accounts with materials brought via far-flung trade from all over Mesopotamia and even portions of the eastern Mediterranean coast.

Under Gudea it is most clear—possibly from Akkadian precedents—that even small Sumerian states are not just city-states but incorporated several cities and surrounding countryside. Thus, he is considered responsible for the golden age of Lagash, when this state rivaled Ur in Sumer, which became prominent under the kingship of Ur-Nammu (c. 2112-2095 B.C.E.) in Ur's Third Dynasty. His account of building Eninnu, the temple of the god Ningirsu, is the second longest extant Sumerian text up to that date, with more than 1,350 lines inscribed in cuneiform on two clay cylinders about a foot high, thus providing priceless material for reconstructing temple administration and, more important, this phase of the written Sumerian language. That Gudea could be called an administrative genius and possible artistic innovator for bringing Lagash into such prominence is not merely because of the selective nature of the archaeological record, which preserves some names and buries others in oblivion.

—Patrick Norman Hunt

FURTHER READING

Edzard, D. O. *Gudea and His Dynasty.* Toronto: University of Toronto Press, 1997. References many of Gudea's achievements and examines the inscriptions he left in various epigraphic media, such as clay and stone. Most of the above Sumerian translations are from Edzard.

Klein, J., and Y. Sefati. "Word Play in Sumerian Literature." In *Puns and Pundits: Word Play in the Hebrew Bible and Ancient Near Eastern Literature*, edited by S. B. Noegel. Bethesda, Md.: CDL Press, 2000. This scholarly article lists quite a few of Gudea's inscriptions as word plays and clever puns.

Roaf, M. *Cultural Atlas of Mesopotamia and the Ancient Near East.* New York: Facts on File, 2000. Describes Gudea's achievements in the light of other contemporary Mesopotamian rulers, especially his trade contacts and temple building.

Saggs, H. W. F. *Civilization Before Greece and Rome.* New Haven, Conn.: Yale University Press, 1989. Presents the anthropomorphizing nature of Gudea's religion, as seen from temple inscriptions—particularly a hybridized Ningirsu, who was described by Gudea as part bird in contrast to humanlike divinity—as a new development in Mesopotamia. Also examines Mesopotamian trade in its broader contexts.

SEE ALSO: Enheduanna; Sargon II; Ur-Nammu.

RELATED ARTICLES in *Great Events from History: The Ancient World*: c. 4000 B.C.E., Sumerian Civilization Begins in Mesopotamia; c. 3800 B.C.E., Cities and Civic Institutions Are Invented in Mesopotamia; c. 3000-c. 500 B.C.E., Elamite Empire Rises in Near East; c. 2340 B.C.E., Sumerian Uruk-Agina Makes Social and Political Reforms.

HADRIAN
Roman emperor (r. 117-138)

Hadrian succeeded in bringing a relatively peaceful period to the Roman Empire, in realizing much-needed domestic and civil reforms, and in leaving, through his architectural and artistic gifts, his stamp on Rome, Athens, and Jerusalem.

BORN: January 24, 76 C.E.; Italica (now in Spain)
DIED: July 10, 138 C.E.; Baiae, Bay of Naples (now in Italy)
ALSO KNOWN AS: Publius Aelius Hadrianus (Latin original name); Caesar Traianus Hadrianus Augustus; Adrian
AREA OF ACHIEVEMENT: Government and politics

EARLY LIFE

Hadrian (HAY-dree-uhn) was born in Italica, Spain, a Roman settlement, to Publius Aelius Hadrianus Afer, a distinguished Roman officer and civil administrator, and Domitia Paulina. Hadrian's parents, however, were not as influential in his development as Hadrian's cousin Trajan, the future Roman emperor who served as his coguardian after his father died when Hadrian was ten years old. Soon after his father's death, Hadrian was sent to Rome to further his education; during his stay in Rome, his study of Greek language, literature, and culture made him so much a Hellenist that he became known as the "Greekling." When he was fifteen, he returned to Italica, where he supposedly entered military service but actually spent his time hunting, a lifelong passion of his. As a result of the jealousy of his brother-in-law Servianus, who complained to Trajan of Hadrian's "dissipation," he was recalled to Rome in 93 and probably never saw Italica again.

In Rome, Hadrian continued his studies, laying the groundwork for a lifelong commitment not only to literature and art but also to music, architecture, astronomy, mathematics, law, and military science. In fact, few rulers have received such appropriate education and been so fortunate in their political connections. He had the support of Trajan and of Trajan's wife, Plotina, who helped to further his advancement. As Hadrian also began his public career in 93, he added practical experience in public service and in military affairs to his extensive educational background. Through Trajan's influence with Emperor Domitian, Hadrian became a decemvir, a minor magistrate in probate court, as well as a military tribune serving at a Roman outpost on the Danube River.

When Domitian was assassinated in 96, the Roman senate chose Nerva to succeed him. Nerva, in turn, adopted Trajan in 97, and when Nerva died in 98, Trajan became emperor. With his coguardian as emperor, Hadrian rose rapidly within the civil and military ranks, despite Servianus's interference. In 101 Hadrian was appointed quaestor and communicated Trajan's messages to the senate; in 107 he became praetor and governor of a province on the Danube; and in 108 he was elected consul and soon began writing Trajan's speeches.

As a provincial governor and as *legatus* of Syria during Trajan's Parthian campaign, Hadrian had military as well as civil responsibilities and he had already demonstrated his military talents during the second Dacian War. Moreover, because Trajan's ambitions had greatly, and precariously, extended Roman rule, Hadrian benefited from firsthand observations of a military conqueror.

On his return from the Parthian campaign in 117, Trajan died. On his deathbed, he apparently adopted Hadrian (there is considerable controversy about the "adoption"). The adoption practically guaranteed Hadrian's accession, and after the Syrian troops acclaimed him emperor, the senate quickly confirmed their action. At the age of forty-two, Hadrian became emperor, and his twenty-one-year rule was to be marked by policies and actions almost antithetical to those of his guardian, cousin, and mentor.

LIFE'S WORK

Hadrian commanded the largest Roman army at the time of Trajan's death, and his ties to the emperor had been close, but his position was far from secure. He had many enemies among the Roman senators, some of whom considered him a provincial upstart opposed to militaristic expansion and enamored of Greek culture. In fact, Hadrian's policy of peace, retrenchment, and reform was diametrically opposed to Trajan's expansionist policy.

Domestically, moderation was the order of the day as Hadrian attempted to convert his enemies by exercising restraint even in suppressing rebellious factions. In fact, when his coguardian Attianus became too zealous in his emperor's cause—he had four traitors executed—Hadrian eased him out of power. To gain the support of the Roman populace, Hadrian canceled all debts to the Imperial treasury, renounced the emperor's traditional claim to the estates of executed criminals, extended the children's welfare centers, and staged spectacular entertainments for the masses. In addition to these public relations measures, Hadrian accomplished a major overhaul of the administrative system—he created opportunities for the talented as well as the wealthy—and a thorough reform of the army. His domestic achievements culminated in the codification, under Julian's supervision, of Roman statutory law in 121.

Such reforms were necessary because Hadrian, who never felt at home in Rome, was intent on establishing his rule before leaving to tour the provinces, a task that occupied him, for the most part, from 120 to 131. In fact, Hadrian's travel was consistent with his Imperial policy of creating sister relations with areas in ways that made them bound to him as to a patriarch. (He assumed in 128 the title *pater patriae*, "father of the fatherland.") During his extensive travels, Hadrian determined not on expanding the empire but on consolidating it, even reducing where necessary, and establishing *limes*, definite physical boundaries that could be effectively defended.

Accordingly, after visiting Roman outposts on the Rhine River, Hadrian traveled through the Netherlands to England, where rebellious tribes were unwilling to be assimilated. As there was no natural defensive barrier against northern invaders, Hadrian's Wall was constructed. This human-made fortification, parts of which survive today, also served as a 73-mile (118-kilometer) road that facilitated the defense of the empire. Hadrian then traveled to Spain and Mauretania before he arrived in 124 in Ephesus, in what is now Turkey; there, Hadrian's Temple, one of the Seven Wonders of the ancient world, was constructed. Hadrian's next significant visit was to Bithynia, where he met Antinous, a young man who became his inseparable companion for the next nine years. After a trip to Athens, his intellectual and cultural homeland, Hadrian returned to Rome in 125.

Although he continued his travels, Hadrian's next four years were distinguished primarily by his architectural achievements and the rebuilding, or re-creation, of Rome and Athens. The renowned Roman Pantheon is Hadrian's work, as is his mausoleum, built in imitation of the tomb built for Augustus, the emperor who always served as a model for Hadrian. When he left Rome, he stopped in his beloved Athens, where he constructed bridges, canals, and an elaborate gymnasium.

In the autumn of 129, Hadrian went south, and after literally saving the famous cedars of Lebanon, he made a fateful error involving the Jews in Palestine. An ardent supporter of Hellenism, which was in philosophical

Hadrian. (Library of Congress)

conflict with Judaism, and a xenophobe who considered the Jews as foreigners, Hadrian enacted laws against circumcision and also determined to rebuild Jerusalem as a Roman city. Both actions infuriated the Jews, who were almost forced into another rebellion against Rome. After inciting the Jews, Hadrian traveled to Absandria; then, on a trip up the Nile River, he lost his beloved Antinous, who was drowned. It is not certain whether Antinous's death was an accident or suicide—the matter is controversial—but in any case it profoundly affected Hadrian. When he returned to Palestine, Hadrian found the reconstruction of Jerusalem interrupted by a Jewish uprising. Although the bloody rebellion was eventually ended in 134, his punitive actions against the Jews, many of whom were sold into slavery, were decidedly uncharacteristic.

The remaining years of Hadrian's life somewhat negated the positive image he had created. Despite his rebuilding of Rome, the Romans never really accepted their provincial ruler who openly preferred Athens. Hadrian's problems were compounded by the onset of debilitating health problems that transformed the athletic emperor into a weak as well as a cruel and vindictive ruler. The man who had used moderation and patience to establish his rule actually began to order some executions, and the troublesome Servianus was finally put to death. The only notable achievement of these troubled years was the villa he had begun to build at Tibur in 126. The villa, of immense proportions, was an architectural blend of Roman and Greek styles.

Hadrian's problems extended to the naming of his successor. Because his union with his wife, Sabina, had failed to produce an heir, Hadrian named Lucius Aelius, who was perhaps his illegitimate son. Lucius, however, died before Hadrian. Hadrian adopted Antoninus Pius, a loyal and capable supporter, and then required that Antoninus in turn adopt the younger Aelius as well as Marcus Annius Verus (the future philosopher and emperor Marcus Aurelius), Antoninus's nephew. When Hadrian died in 138, it was Antoninus, his successor, who was responsible for persuading a reluctant senate to deify the man whose last few years unfortunately clouded the real accomplishments of the early years of his reign.

SIGNIFICANCE

Because he succeeded the militaristic Trajan, who had trained him to be an emperor, Hadrian determined to bring peace to a war-weary Rome, which was already overextended. By consolidating and precisely fixing defendable boundaries, he was able to focus his considerable energies on much-needed civil reforms, among them the law code and the civil service. As a result of his artistic training and architectural expertise, he was able to transform Rome, Athens, and Jerusalem. While he is widely known for the Pantheon and Hadrian's Wall, Hadrian left his architectural stamp on many of the cities he visited in his extensive travels.

Through his rule and his adoption and appointment of Antoninus Pius as his successor, he also was largely responsible for establishing what many historians have regarded as a golden age that lasted through the reigns of Antoninus Pius and his successor, the celebrated philosopher and emperor Marcus Aurelius. (Because he had required Antoninus to adopt his successor, Hadrian was directly involved in Marcus Aurelius's appointment as emperor, even though it occurred after his death.) When an iron age began with the ascension of Commodus, son of Marcus Aurelius, the so-called Antonine Dynasty came to an end. Nevertheless, Rome had enjoyed approximately one hundred years of prosperity, greatness, and—with the exception of Trajan's reign—relative peace.

In fact, Hadrian's only significant military campaign, the suppression of the Jewish rebellion late in his reign,

also became the indirect cause of an ironic development Hadrian neither intended nor desired: the spread of Christianity throughout the Roman Empire. By banishing the Jews from Jerusalem, the site of both Judaism and Christianity, Hadrian inadvertently caused Christianity to be separated from the Christian Jews who had controlled the early Christian Church. Consequently, as scholar Stewart Perowne has suggested, Hadrian became the "unwitting forerunner of Constantine, and of the triumph of the faith in his own Rome." It seems both ironic and appropriate that Hadrian, an intellectual, artistic Hellenist and advocate of peace, should play such a role in the development of Christianity.

—Thomas L. Erskine

FURTHER READING

Gregorovius, Ferdinand. *The Emperor Hadrian: A Picture of the Greco-Roman World in His Time.* Translated by Mary E. Robinson with an introduction by Henry Pelham. New York: Macmillan, 1898. Places Hadrian within the cultural, literary, artistic, and philosophical contexts of his day. The book lacks a general thesis to account for Hadrian's individual arts or his apparently contradictory nature.

Henderson, Bernard W. *The Life and Principate of the Emperor Hadrian, A.D. 76-138.* London: Methuen, 1923. The acknowledged standard work in English on Hadrian, Henderson's book is a scholarly and gracefully written biography. Henderson succeeds in rendering Hadrian as a person, not merely a public figure, and his comments on "personalia" provide a glimpse of the man and an objective corrective to those too-lavish apologists for Hadrian.

Ish-Kishor, Sulamith. *Magnificent Hadrian: A Biography of Hadrian, Emperor of Rome.* New York: Minton, Balch, 1935. A sympathetic account of Hadrian's life, this book is also a heavy-handed psychological study designed to outline the "final tragedy of the homosexual temperament" in the relationship between Hadrian and Antinous. Ish-Kishor contrasts Trajan, the life-destroying father figure, with Hadrian, the life-building and life-restoring mother figure.

Perowne, Stewart. *Hadrian.* Westport, Conn.: Greenwood Press, 1976. This comparatively short, readable biography is accompanied by a map illustrating Hadrian's travels, a bibliographical essay, appropriate illustrations, and tables outlining the Roman emperors, Hadrian's ancestors, and the problem of succession. Perowne categorizes Hadrian's travels and policies as manifestations of a political philosophy unique in its day.

Speller, Elizabeth. *Following Hadrian: A Second Century Journey Through the Roman Empire*. New York: Oxford University Press, 2003. Historical tract also provides insight into the life of the then-most-powerful human being in the world.

See also: Augustus; Marcus Aurelius; Constantine the Great; Trajan.

Related articles in *Great Events from History: The Ancient World*: c. 50 C.E., Creation of the Roman Imperial Bureaucracy; September 8, 70 C.E., Roman Destruction of the Temple of Jerusalem; c. 110 C.E., Trajan Adopts Anti-Christian Religious Policy.

Hamilcar Barca
Carthaginian general and statesman

Hamilcar Barca led Carthaginian forces in the last stages of the First Punic War (264-241 B.C.E.) against Rome. He compensated for the loss of Carthage's colonies of Sicily, Sardinia, and Corsica by founding new ones rich in minerals and agricultural resources in Spain. Hannibal, his eldest son, was pledged by the father to continue the conflict and maintain the enmity of the Barcids against Rome.

Born: c. 275 B.C.E.; Carthage (now in Tunisia)
Died: Winter, 229/228 B.C.E.; central eastern Spain
Also known as: Amilcar Barca
Areas of achievement: War and conquest, government and politics

Early Life

The years from the end of the second millennium B.C.E. to the beginning of the first witnessed a fundamental economic and social transition in the ancient world. The Bronze Age gave way to the Iron Age, which emerged from a greater exploitation and distribution of mineral, agricultural, and manufactured resources.

Semitic peoples in the eastern Mediterranean port cities of northern Canaan were in a particularly advantageous position to take advantage of and contribute to this development. The ancient Greeks referred to this maritime coastal region as Phoenicia. The modern world knows it as Lebanon. The Phoenician city-state of Tyre, under the protection of its gods Melqart and Baal, opened maritime frontiers across the Mediterranean Sea, establishing trading stations in Crete, Sicily, Sardinia, northern Africa, and beyond Gibraltar, in Morocco and Spain.

During the ninth century B.C.E. a group of dissident elite from Tyre founded a port city in North Africa near present-day Tunis. Named Carthage, the new city flourished as the western flank of the Phoenician trading realm. Eventually it rivaled and surpassed the older Phoenician cities. A handful of families emerged to control the economic, military, and political affairs of the Carthaginian Empire. One of the later emerging families of this oligarchy, the landowning Barcids, came to produce some of the city's greatest military leaders. This leadership arose as the Empire faced its greatest threat in the third and second centuries B.C.E.—the advancing Roman Empire.

Some time during the mid-270's B.C.E., Hamilcar (huh-MIHL-kahr—"Aided by Baal") Barca (BAHR-kuh—"Lightning") was born. He was raised in a prominent and wealthy family and in a culture focused on maritime trade supported by naval and military prowess. During his childhood the first of the three Punic Wars began, in 264. The wars became a life-or-death struggle for Carthage and its empire against the advancing power of Rome across the Mediterranean. These struggles steeled Hamilcar Barca and his children to military leadership.

Life's Work

The heart of the struggle in the First Punic War was for control of Sicily. Lasting from 264 to 225 B.C.E., the war became a stalemate in which the Roman army could advance against Carthaginian land forces but could not achieve final victory for lack of Roman naval power. Romans even confronted the African elephants, capturing some, which the Carthaginians brought to battle. By steadily building ships and accumulating maritime skills, Rome eventually massed a considerable navy. Despite early defeats, even humiliations, this navy came to match and then decisively defeat the Carthaginian fleet, ending the war in Rome's favor.

By 247, after nearly two decades of war and having exhausted much of its armed forces, Carthaginian power in Sicily had become isolated to the far western region. Under such reduced circumstances, Carthage passed command of its army, overwhelmingly composed of non-

Carthaginian mercenaries, to Hamilcar Barca. Using guerrilla tactics, he became successful in reversing Carthaginian losses, challenged Roman forces, and raided along the Italian coast. However, Rome had by now mounted sufficient naval power to defeat Carthage on the sea.

Late in the winter of 241, a massive Roman naval force met its Carthaginian counterpart off the northwest tip of Sicily and decimated the fleet. Authorities in Carthage ordered Hamilcar to end his military efforts and sue for peace. When Hanno, admiral of the Carthaginian fleet, returned home, the same authorities ordered him crucified. Rome required that Carthage pay huge annual indemnities for ten years to cover the cost of the war. The Romans desperately needed these funds to finance their renewed conflicts with the warrior Celts (or Gauls) to the north of Rome.

The peace that Hamilcar obtained with Rome did not follow him to Carthage. There, unpaid mercenaries and impoverished peasant groups from the countryside besieged the city. Although victory had been denied Hamilcar in Sicily, it did not escape him on his home territory. He suppressed the uprisings and became the supreme authority of Carthage.

Hamilcar's last duties in Sicily were to return his mercenary troops to Carthage for payment of their back wages. However, Carthaginian finances were now in a dire situation. With rich colonies lost, ships decimated, and a huge indemnity due to Rome, Carthaginian officials could not pay the mounting number of unemployed soldiers entering the city or settling in outlying regions. Increasingly furious at the delays in receiving their back wages, the angered troops adhered to the leadership of a renegade Italian mercenary, Spendios, who appealed to them to lay siege to Carthaginian cities until the troops were paid.

The mercenaries were joined by thousands of native peasants whose own situation had worsened with the decline of the Carthaginian economy. These natives were led by Matho, who, joining the hordes of Spendios, created a mass of tens of thousands of rebels laying siege to Carthaginian cities. When Hamilcar returned to Carthage, he was entrusted with the task of suppressing this massive rebellion.

Hamilcar's task now was to combat the very soldiers he had once led. He had as recruits only the untrained citizen volunteers of Carthage, their experience as weak as their numbers against the rebel mass. Under such limited circumstances, Hamilcar nonetheless demonstrated how exceptional were his military and leadership skills.

Moving quickly and surreptitiously, as he had against the Romans, he defeated a large contingent of the rebel forces to the north of Carthage. Attracting back to himself the allegiance of some mercenaries who now deserted the rebels, Hamilcar enlarged his troops. He lured the besiegers of Carthage to move south of the city, where he trapped them in a gorge. Spendios was crucified and Matho, captured in a later battle, brutally tortured and killed. By 237, Hamilcar had subdued all rebellions on mainland Carthaginian territory, amassing great popularity. To many among the elite, there arose suspicions about his dictatorial potential. Hamilcar, though, was about to leave Carthage forever to find fortune for himself and his country in Spain.

Determined to restore the power and treasure of Carthage, he resolved with his sons to rebuild the Carthaginian Empire by expanding west into Spain. Once enriched and reinvigorated by colonies in that region, Carthage would be able successfully to renew its struggle with Rome for dominance of the Mediterranean.

In 237 he set out with his troops, trekking westward across North Africa. From what is today Morocco, he crossed the Atlantic, passing through the Straits of Gibraltar. In ancient times these straits were known as the Pillars of Herakles, guarding the entrance to the Mediterranean Sea. To Carthaginians, the Greek hero Heracles, son of Zeus, was associated with Melqart, the deity of Phoenician imperial expansion.

Hamilcar entered Spain at Gades (today, Cádiz), one of the oldest and largest Phoenician ports on the Atlantic. From there he moved eastward, encountering older Phoenician settlements or founding new Carthaginian ones. Along the Mediterranean coast he founded New Carthage (today, Cartagena). The allure of this southeastern territory of Spain lay in its minerals, including gold and silver, and rich agricultural land. The precious metals were mined and shipped to Carthage. Hamilcar also maintained a mint, producing coins that presented his profile as reminiscent of Herakles/Melqart.

To many in Carthage, he was virtually establishing a Barcid kingdom in Spain. However, such suspicions were set aside before the wealth he was returning to the city's coffers. Among the Romans, too, his rising wealth and power raised suspicions. However, such concerns were again cloaked. The wealth he sent to Carthage in good part passed on to Rome, paying the Carthaginian indemnity and financing Rome's Celtic wars.

In Spain Hamilcar found Celtic natives hostile to his incursions. An encounter with warriors of one of their tribes in the winter of 229-228 ended Hamilcar's life.

The exact time and circumstances of the death are lost. One tradition maintains he was struck as he retreated on horseback across the Jucar River (between Alicante and Valencia), trying to protect his sons Hannibal and Hamilcar the Younger from the enemy onslaught. If so, he was true, then, in death to his lifelong pledge: to preserve the forces of opposition to Rome.

SIGNIFICANCE

The life of Hamilcar Barca must be understood in conjunction with his sons, most famously Hannibal, whose lives were consumed in military efforts to counter the advance across the Mediterranean of the Roman Empire against the Carthaginian. The conflicts of the Punic Wars over two centuries were the most momentous in ancient Mediterranean history, changing the area from a Phoeno-Semitic region to a Hellenized Latin one. Only the rise of Islam in the seventh century eventually restored the southern Mediterranean to a Semitic character. The northern Mediterranean has maintained its Hellene-Latin characteristics to the present day. In the mid-third century B.C.E. Hamilcar Barca slightly stalled this direction of history by compensating for the loss of Carthaginian dominance in the central Mediterranean as he secured territory and dominance along the western part of the sea.

—*Edward A. Riedinger*

FURTHER READING

Goldsworthy, Adrian. *The Punic Wars*. London: Cassell, 2000. The first section of this three-part work masterfully elaborates the complex of military, naval, geographic, and historic details of the First Punic War.

Lancel, Serge. *Carthage: A History*. Translated by Antonia Nevill. Cambridge, Mass.: Blackwell, 1997. Richly detailed study of Carthage from its founding and rise in the early centuries of the first millennium to its defeat and Roman absorption by the end of the period. Lancel is a French scholar and among the foremost modern authorities on Carthage.

_____. *Hannibal*. Translated by Antonia Nevill. Malden, Mass.: Blackwell, 1998. Well-documented and detailed life of the son of Hamilcar Barca, the first chapters of the work detailing Hamilcar's family, military, and political background.

Lazenby, J. F. *The First Punic War: A Military History*. Stanford, Calif.: Stanford University Press, 1996. Based on close reading of primary sources, this work details the military action of the First Punic War, the last chapters concentrating on the efforts of Hamilcar Barca to retake the offensive against the Romans in the closing years of the conflict.

Vega, Luis Antonio. *Amílcar Barca, fundador de España = Amílcar Barca, Founder of Spain*. Madrid: Cultura Clásica y Moderna, 1960. Considered founders of ancient Spain, Hamilcar Barca and his family have received considerable scholarly attention in Spanish. The name of the city of Barcelona is derived from the Barca family name.

Wise, Terence. *Armies of the Carthaginian Wars, 265-146 B.C.* London: Osprey, 1982. This amply illustrated work displays the armor, dress, and environment of Carthaginian military personnel.

SEE ALSO: Dido; Hannibal; Hanno.
RELATED ARTICLES in *Great Events from History: The Ancient World*: c. 800 B.C.E., Phoenicians from Tyre Found Carthage; 264-225 B.C.E., First Punic War; 218-201 B.C.E., Second Punic War.

HAMMURABI
Mesopotamian king (r. c. 1792-1750 B.C.E.)

The Babylonian king Hammurabi stretched his control over the entire length of the Euphrates and Tigris river valleys, ultimately controlling all of Mesopotamia. The literary creativity of the age brought into being the Old Babylonian dialect, most fully exemplified in the codification of law remembered under Hammurabi's name.

BORN: c. 1810 B.C.E.; Babylon (now in Iraq)
DIED: 1750 B.C.E.; Babylon
ALSO KNOWN AS: Hammurapi
AREAS OF ACHIEVEMENT: Government and politics, law, war and conquest

EARLY LIFE

The founder of Babylon and the creator of the first Babylonian Dynasty was a nineteenth century B.C.E. Amorite chieftain named Sumu-abum. His ancestral predecessors are known by name back into the twenty-first century B.C.E., when Shulgi, king of the Third Dynasty of Ur in southern Sumer, first began to encounter the movements of Amorite-speaking Semitic peoples down the Euphrates River. A famine began to devastate the economy of the Sumerian city-states, weakening their defenses so that old centers such as Larsa and Isin passed directly into the newcomers' hands.

Another family within the same tribal grouping as Sumu-abum replaced his control, and with that shift came into being the dynasty that Hammurabi (ham-uh-RAHB-ee) recalled in his inscriptions. He was son of Sin-muballit, grandson of Apil Sin, great-grandson of Sabium, and great-great-grandson of the dynastic founder, Sumu-la-el. The rapidity of succession brought Hammurabi to the throne as quite a young man.

The initial years of Hammurabi's life were lived in the shadow of greater or longer-established chieftains of comparable ancestry. The region to the east along the Diyala River was centered on Ibal-pi-El II at Eshnunna. The region to the south was centered on Rim-Sin at Larsa. Rim-Sin's reign was long, but there are only a few inscriptions, mainly concerned with that piety of building for the gods that was one of the principal ways of proving one's greatness as a ruler in those times. Rim-Sin's thirtieth year, during which he captured Isin, was the year Hammurabi assumed the throne at Babylon.

During Hammurabi's father's reign, Babylon was in the shadow of Shamshi-Adad I, who had gained control of the capital of Assyria and had spread his influence not only up the Tigris River but also across the steppes and tributaries to the Euphrates River, placing his own son on the throne at the great trading center of Mari. Much of what is known about this earlier period comes from the vast archival records found in excavations at Mari beginning in 1929.

LIFE'S WORK

Hammurabi, on ascending the throne in 1792, found himself hemmed in on all sides by formidable powers. The political situation is well described in a letter from a Mari diplomat or spy to his king: "No one king is strong by himself. Ten to fifteen go after Hammurapi man of Babylon, similarly after Rim-Sin man of Larsa, similarly after Ibal-pi-el man of Eshnunna, similarly after Amut-pi-el man of Qatanum. Twenty go after Yarim-Lim man of Yamhad."

Thus, the whole country was split among petty chiefs joined together in leagues with some stronger figure nominally as head. Rather than being a clear-cut struggle between well-defined, uniformly large states, it was a situation requiring a constant shuffling of alliances among aggregations of minor rulers under some stronger chief as head. These combinations changed often. Economic issues played a major role in the formation of alliances.

From the variety of year-names of the various chiefs, it is possible to reconstruct an overall picture of the way Hammurabi was hemmed in at the time of his accession. The kingdom of Larsa, by conquering Isin in the south, covered almost all the territory that had once been Sumer.

At Mari, the situation had undergone change. In the middle of the nineteenth century, in the days of Sabium, great-grandfather of Hammurabi, Mari had been ruled by Iaggid-Lim. When Iaggid-Lim broke a treaty made with Ila-kabkabu, father of Shamshi-Adad I of Ashur, there was retaliation. The occasion was used effectively by Shamshi-Adad to take over rule in Mari, where he placed his son, Iasmah-Adad, on the throne. Mari was retained as long as Shamshi-Adad was alive, but in the days of his successor at Ashur, Ishme-Dagan, the old line at Mari was reinstated under Zimri-Lim. These latter two, neither as strong as his predecessor, were the ones with whom Hammurabi had to deal. From the time of Zimri-Lim, the district of Terqa, just to the north of Mari, was entirely denuded of trees, so that the lucrative timber trade came to an end, and the area received an ecological blow from which it never recovered.

When Hammurabi took over, Babylon was a small

principality. In his second year, Hammurabi established "righteousness in the land." He remitted debts and other obligations, allowing land to revert to original owners. In undertaking such measures, he was following the tradition of his royal ancestors. In 1787 Hammurabi captured Uruk and Isin, indicating that he and his allies were strong enough to challenge Rim-Sin in the latter's territory. It would appear, however, that the success was ephemeral: The cities were taken back. In 1783 Hammurabi destroyed Malgum on the Tigris, south of the Diyala. In 1782 he took Rapiqum on the Euphrates; it was close to a major caravan crossing and thus provided for him access to the west.

Mention of this achievement is the last reference to military accomplishments during this period in Hammurabi's official inscriptions, which thereafter focus on pious deeds of rebuilding walls and refurbishing temples. Their index illustrates, if not the extent of Babylonia, at least the increasing strength of its economic base. From Mari, letters give account of Hammurabi's diplomatic relations; messengers went back and forth between Mari and Hammurabi's court.

In the inscriptions for 1763, the chronicle of Hammurabi's military conquests is taken up once more, beginning with his defeat of Elamite troops at the boundaries of Mahashi, Subartu, Eshnunna, Gutium, and Malgum— all to his east. He successfully opposed a concerted attack of northern and eastern principalities surrounding him, though there is no reference to his annexation of territory. Hammurabi was intent on restoring the foundations of old "Sumer and Akkad."

These victories allowed Hammurabi to turn undivided attention to the south. In 1762 he fought successfully against the very old Rim-Sin of Larsa, who was brought alive in a cage to Babylon. With this termination of the independent dynasty of Larsa, all of southern Mesopotamia passed into Hammurabi's hands.

In 1761 a core of the old coalition of enemies was against Hammurabi again. He defeated the armies of Subartu, Eshnunna, and Gutium and conquered all the territory along the Tigris as far north as the border of Assyria. In 1760 he fought with Mari on the Euphrates and Malgum, south of Eshnunna. In 1758 he destroyed the walls of both Mari and Malgum. A change in relations with Mari occurred once more. Hammurabi had previously sent troops to assist Zimri-Lim, and the latter had been instrumental in his taking over Eshnunna. Now native rule at Mari ended. In 1755 the "great waters destroyed" Eshnunna; it is not clear whether the reference is to a natural disaster or to Hammurabi's damming up and diverting a river. In any case, the inscriptions make no further mention of Eshnunna until the time of Hammurabi's son.

In 1754 Hammurabi conquered all of his enemies as far as the land of Subartu, east beyond the Tigris. With this success, he was established as the dominant figure in all Mesopotamia. No further references to warfare are made in the chronicle of his reign. To this final period belongs the monumental edition of his law code, on which he is portrayed standing humbly before Shamash, the sun god and overseer of justice. Its prologue identifies his control over twenty-six cities, from each of whose deities, whose temples he adorned, he received powers to make justice in the land.

By intensive restructuring of the whole geographical area under his control, Hammurabi had inadvertently set in motion the forces that, during the next century and a half, were to terminate the dynasty and its Amorite leadership—a decline culminating in the Hittites' sacking of Babylon in 1595. The prosperity of Babylon depended on remuneration from its conquered territories for massive construction of buildings and

Hammurabi. (Library of Congress)

waterworks organized by Hammurabi with the help of appointed officials. Once a system of governors and palace dependents was created, however, this bureaucracy established itself in hereditary positions, so that the territories fed local rather than royal interests.

Already before Hammurabi's death, his son Samsuiluna reported in a letter to an official, Etil-pi-Marduk, that his father was ill and that he had to assume charge of what had become a real kingdom. Hammurabi was succeeded by Samsuiluna and his grandson Abi-eshu. There remained three further generations, Ammi-ditana, Ammizaduga, and Samsu-ditana, before Hammurabi's achievement was terminated by Kassite invaders, dividing the realm again into petty kingdom warring on relatively equal terms.

SIGNIFICANCE

Coming at the middle of the First Dynasty of Babylon, Hammurabi created out of a small principality not merely an imperial kingdom but a distinctive city whose name is not to be forgotten: Old "Sumer and Akkad" became thereafter Babylonia. From the many preserved Old Babylonian letters, especially those to or by Hammurabi, it is possible to understand the administrative structure of his power and that of Babylon. These letters document the lines of communication existing within the capital and out to the official governors appointed to administer annexed cities and territories. Two large collections are illustrative: those related to Sin-idinnam, Hammurabi's governor of Larsa after the defeat of Rim-Sin, and those related to Shamash-hazir, a lesser official, also at Larsa, who managed for the king the landholdings and the landholders.

Extensive economic records from the various cities, especially Sippar, provide details of royal involvement. At Sippar, Hammurabi's sister Iltani engaged in business transactions on behalf of the gods Lord Shamash and Lady Aja for more than fifty years, at least until 1755. She lived in that unique Old Babylonian institution the *gaga* (cloister), as one of the many *naditu*-women, among whom she ranked the highest. *Naditu*-women were dedicated to a god, often from youth; they were usually unmarried and were always forbidden to have children, but they frequently played significant economic roles.

The period was one of great literary creativity. Epic poetry, some of it based on Sumerian-derived sources, addressed central issues and problems of human existence. Two epics of the period, for example, took up issues of life and death in their glorification of the heroes Gilgamesh and Atra-hasis. Another remembered the ancient Etana. During this time, the chief god Marduk replaced older creator gods, just as Babylon had replaced the older Sumerian city-states.

Aside from the monumental copy of Hammurabi's code, clay tablet examples demonstrate that its text was regularly copied in both Babylonia and Assyria until the era of the Seleucid state at Uruk (third century B.C.E.). The great stela itself was carried off as a prize to Susa by the twelfth century B.C.E. Elamite king Shutruk-nakhunte I. There it remained until January, 1902, when its rediscovery changed Hammurabi from simply another ruler among many into a world-famous lawgiver with a status comparable to that of the biblical Moses or the Byzantine Justinian I.

The last great king of Assyria, the seventh century B.C.E. Ashurbanipal, sought texts of Hammurabi's era for his library at Nineveh. While no building attributable to Hammurabi has been excavated beneath the rubble of Babylon, it is known that its last king, Nabonidus (sixth century B.C.E.) knew of his work and remembered him.

—*Clyde Curry Smith*

FURTHER READING

Driver, G. R., and John C. Miles. *The Babylonian Laws.* 2 vols. Oxford, England: Clarendon Press, 1956-1960. Volume 1 provides a detailed commentary on all Babylonian law, with special focus on the Code of Hammurabi. Volume 2 contains the transliterated texts with full translation, philological notes, and glossary.

Harper, Robert Francis. *The Code of Hammurabi, King of Babylon.* Reprint. Stockton, Calif.: University Press of the Pacific, 2002. An English translation of Hammurabi's code, with a parallel transliteration of the original ideograms from the monument on which they were engraved. Includes facsimiles of all the original cuneiform tablets, glossary, index of subjects, lists of proper names, and tables of weights and currencies.

Leemans, W. F. *The Old Babylonian Merchant: His Business and His Social Position.* Leiden, Netherlands: E. J. Brill, 1966. Beginning from provisions in Hammurabi's code, and on the basis of texts coming from various archives, especially those of Larsa and Sippar, the nature, role, and function of the merchant class are described as independent but bound by the law of the king.

Munn-Rankin, J. M. "Diplomacy in Western Asia in the Early Second Millennium B.C." *Iraq* 18 (1956): 68-110. This major essay, working from the Mari archive, puts in perspective the historical situation and the interaction among major figures during Hammurabi's reign.

Pallis, S. A. *The Antiquity of Iraq: A Handbook of Assyriology.* Copenhagen, Denmark: Ejnar Munksgaard, 1956. This volume is a vast storehouse of information including a history of Babylon, a description of the city, an account of its rediscovery in the nineteenth century, and the subsequent excavations. Chapter 8 explains the chronological shift in dating Hammurabi, made possible by the discovery of the Mari archive and the correlation with Shamshi-Adad of Assyria. Chapter 10 provides a picture of Hammurabi and his age, with extensive discussion of the code.

Saggs, Henry W. F. *Babylonians.* Berkeley: University of California Press, 2000. In this college-level text, Saggs uses evidence from architecture, pottery, and metal works to provide a picture of life in ancient Babylon as well as the myths, languages, and lives of its inhabitants.

Yoffee, Norman. *The Economic Role of the Crown in the Old Babylonian Period.* Malibu, Calif.: Undena, 1977. This study is significant for its close analysis of economic texts from various urban archives, shedding light on the operations of Hammurabi's palace economy and the administration of conquered realms. Extensive bibliography.

SEE ALSO: Ashurbanipal; Sargon II.
RELATED ARTICLES in *Great Events from History: The Ancient World*: c. 2112 B.C.E., Ur-Nammu Establishes a Code of Law; c. 2000 B.C.E., Composition of the Gilgamesh Epic; c. 1770 B.C.E., Promulgation of Hammurabi's Code; c. 607-562 B.C.E., Nebuchadnezzar Creates the First Neo-Babylonian State; October, 539 B.C.E., Fall of Babylon.

HANFEIZI
Chinese philosopher

Hanfeizi wrote a Legalist work of twenty volumes and fifty-five chapters that had a profound influence on Chinese methods of organization and management.

BORN: 280 B.C.E.; the state of Han, China
DIED: 233 B.C.E.; the state of Qin, China
ALSO KNOWN AS: Han-fei-tzu (Wade-Giles)
AREA OF ACHIEVEMENT: Philosophy

EARLY LIFE

According to his biography in Sima Qian's *Shiji* (first century B.C.E.; *Records of the Grand Historian of China*, 1960, rev. ed. 1993), Hanfeizi (hahn-fay-dzu) was one of several sons from a noble family in the small state of Han. The ruling family of Han had formerly been high ministers in the state of Jin, but they gradually usurped power, divided the territory of Jin with two other noble families, and created three new states, Han, Zhao, and Wei. This event initiated a new era in ancient China called the Warring States Period (475-221 B.C.E.).

Among the seven states that existed during this period, the domain of Han was relatively small and its territory located in a mountainous area, so it was constantly threatened by strong neighbors, especially the powerful state of Qin. Worried about the dangerous condition of his own native state, Hanfeizi devoted himself to studying how to rule a state. Because he stuttered, he was unable to articulate his ideas with eloquence. He repeatedly submitted his suggestions for political reform to the ruler, but they were ignored. He therefore decided to write them into chapters, creating the *Hanfeizi* (latter half of third century B.C.E.; *The Complete Works of Han Fei Tzu: A Classic of Chinese Legalism*, 1939-1959, 2 vols.; commonly known as *Hanfeizi*), which became a part of the Legalist (*fa-jia*) tradition.

LIFE'S WORK

Fa-jia, a major school of Chinese philosophy, emerged in a chaotic and tumultuous age of ancient China. In the earlier Zhou Dynasty (Chou; 1066-771 B.C.E.), the nation had been ruled by the king of Zhou and his vassals. Their rights and duties were clearly defined by a system of feudalism. The sovereign not only commanded universal allegiance and tribute among his vassals but also exercised considerable control over their social affairs. He could even punish an offending vassal with force of arms.

When the Zhou capital was invaded by barbarians in 771 B.C.E., the ruler fled and re-established his court at Luoyang (Lo-yang) in the East. The power of the Eastern Zhou Dynasty declined rapidly, and the rulers of the feudal states were left with increasing freedom to ignore their customary duties to the sovereign and to expand their territories through military force. After a series of battles, five powerful feudal leaders emerged. They not only had to deal with the threat of influential noble families within their states but also vied for influence or even control of the Zhou king and tried to impose their power on the other feudal lords.

This historical context fostered the formation of the Legalist school. In order to acquire official positions for themselves, scholars offered various suggestions, on the basis of different philosophical grounds, on how to rule a state. Unlike the Confucians, the Legalists had no interest in preserving moral values or restoring traditional customs. Their only goal was to teach the ruler how to survive and prosper in a highly competitive world through various measures of administrative reform, such as strengthening the sovereign's power, increasing food production, enforcing military training, and establishing a merit system to replace the old aristocracy with a team of bureaucrats.

Disappointed with his own political career, Hanfeizi concentrated on studying the works of previous Legalists, including Guan Zhong, Shang Yang, Shen Buhai, and Shen Dao. Guan Zhong (Kuan Chung) was a minister of Duke Huan of Qi (685-643 B.C.E.). He suggested the ruler should carry out a series of reform programs that enriched the state, strengthened the army, and made Qi one of the five hegemonies. From Guan Zhong's chapter on *xin-shu* (literally, "art of mind") in his book *Guanzi* (fourth century B.C.E.; selections translated in *Economic Dialogues in Ancient China*, 1954; complete translation *Guanzi*, 1985), Hanfeizi adopted the doctrine of *xu-yi-er-jin* ("concentrate on one thing with a calm and serene mind") and argued that it is necessary for an enlightened ruler to cultivate his mental capability for recognizing the objective facts of an event by concentrating on them with a calm and peaceful mind.

Shang Yang (d. 388 B.C.E.) was originally from Wei. He went to serve Duke Xiao of Qin as a high minister and helped Qin to carry out a series of administrative reforms. Hanfeizi adopted many fundamental concepts of *fa* (law) from the *Shangjun shu* (also known as *Shangzi*; compiled 359-338 B.C.E.; *The Book of Lord Shang*, 1928) but noted a weakness in Shang's works. In ruling the state, Shang Yang strongly emphasized strict control of people with harsh laws as well as the encouragement of agricultural production and aggressive warfare. These policies enriched the state within a short period of time. Shang paid less attention to *shu* (the art of manipulation) and was unable to discriminate the cunning ministers from the loyal ones. Thus, Qin's reform program enhanced the ministers' power, but it brought few benefits to the ruler of the state.

Shen Buhai (Shen Pu-hai; d. 377 B.C.E.) was a Legalist who served at the court of Hanfeizi's native state and

taught the ruler how to manipulate subordinates with *shu*. Hanfeizi also criticized him for carelessness about the consistency of the law. Eventually there were many contradictions between newly issued rules and old laws, and many people took advantage of the confusion and used it to defend their own misconduct. Hanfeizi, therefore, paid great attention to these aspects in proposing his theory for constructing a legal system as well as its application.

From Shen Dao (Shen Tao; 350-275 B.C.E.), a Daoist-Legalist philosopher, Hanfeizi recognized the importance of *shih* (power). He agreed with Shen's argument that power for a ruler is like claws and teeth for a tiger. A tiger without claws or teeth can catch no animals, while a ruler without position and power cannot control his subjects.

In addition to these Legalists, Hanfeizi followed his teacher Xunzi (Hsün-tzu; c. 298-c. 230 B.C.E.), an eminent Confucian scholar who served as magistrate of Lanling, in adopting the idea that human beings are born evil, in direct opposition to the theory promoted by Mencius (Mengzi; Wade-Giles Meng-tzu; c. 327-c. 289 B.C.E.) that people are born good. However, unlike his teacher, he made no attempt to preserve the moral values or traditional ceremonies, and he looked on the fondness for such ceremonies as an omen of a doomed state.

Hanfeizi's theory of leadership was constructed on the basis of three core concepts, namely, *shih* (power), *fa* (law), and *shu* (technique of management). He argued that a ruler has to hold the two handles of punishment and favor tightly while situated in a ruling position, and then manipulate subordinates with *fa* and *shu*. Although Hanfeizi advocated that *fa* should be initiated by the ruler, he also insisted that it should be constructed on the basis of *dao* (the way), which is the origin and fundamental principle of operation for everything in the universe. The legal system thus constructed must be publicized and made known to everybody; it should be objective and fair to everybody; furthermore, it must be practical, compulsory, and feasible for everyone to carry out. One it was announced, it should be applicable to everyone in the state without exception.

Based on his concept of *fa*, Hanfeizi proposed several techniques (*shu*) for a ruler to manipulate subordinates. For example, he suggested that an enlightened ruler should assign competent talent to the right position, ask subordinates to propose projects for pursuing organizational goals, and follow up on the projects and check their effectiveness. Finally, the ruler should evaluate subordinates' contributions and grant rewards accordingly.

Some of Hanfeizi's works were sent to the king of

Qin, a young ruler with ambitions to conquer the whole country. The king read the chapters and told his minister Li Si (Li Ssu; 280?-208 B.C.E.), a former classmate of Hanfeizi under Xunzi's tutelage, "If I have a chance to make acquaintance with this author, I would die without any regrets!"

Li Si identified the author and persuaded the king to send troops to launch a fierce attack on Han. At the moment of crisis, the ruler of Han dispatched Hanfeizi as peace envoy to the king of Qin.

The king received Hanfeizi with great delight, but before Hanfeizi could earn the full confidence of the king, Li Si incriminated him by warning the ruler that, since Hanfeizi was a son of a noble family of Han, he would always be loyal to Han against Qin. If Hanfeizi were allowed to return home, he might become a barrier to Qin's plan of annexing other states, including Han. The king was persuaded. He ordered officials to arrest Hanfeizi for investigation. Before the ruler had a chance to regret his decision, Li Si sent poison to Hanfeizi, who was confined in prison and unable to communicate with the ruler to defend himself against the accusation of duplicity. Eventually, Hanfeizi was forced to commit suicide.

SIGNIFICANCE

Legalism is one of the major philosophies of the Chinese cultural tradition. Hanfeizi is a representative figure of Legalism who reviewed previous Legalist works and integrated them into a comprehensive theory of leadership. He used many idioms and metaphors to explain his ideas, which were widely circulated in Chinese society and frequently cited by Chinese scholars. Before the end of the nineteenth century, when China began to come in contact with Western culture, the philosophy of Legalism formed the worldview with which Chinese people understood the meaning of the legal system and how a legal system should operate. The influence of Legalist thoughts on Chinese social life is second only to Confucianism, although its contents are in direct opposition to Confucianism in many respects.

During the Han Dynasty, Dong Zhongshu (Tung Chung-shu; 179-104 B.C.E.) proposed the idea of "making judicial sentence by the Confucian classic of Spring and Autumn" and "utilizing Legalism as an instrument to consolidate the Confucian social system." Rulers of China began to use Legalist methods to defend their power and position and to control people, but retained Confucian doctrine to educate and discipline people. The two systems were merged to constitute the philosophical foundation of Asian despotism, and Chinese society became characterized by following Confucianism in public and Legalism in private.

—Kwang-Kuo Hwang

FURTHER READING

Chü, T'ung-Tsu. *Law and Society in Traditional China*. Paris: Monton, 1961. Chü explains the structure and functioning of traditional Chinese society, including family and *zu*, marriage, and social classes, in terms of the interplay between Confucian *li* and Legalist law. Bibliography and index.

Lundahl, Bertil. *Han Fei Zi: The Man and the Work*. Stockholm: Institute of Oriental Languages, Stockholm University, 1992. Lundahl presents an account of the historical and philosophical background of Hanfeizi's work, discusses the problems with the work, and analyzes its authenticity chapter by chapter. Bibliography, appendix, and index.

Waley, Arthur. *Three Ways of Thought in Ancient China*. Garden City, N.Y.: Doubleday, 1956. Waley presents three distinctive ways of thought representing Daoism, Confucianism, and Legalism in ancient China. In the third part of the book, the extracts from Hanfeizi's works are arranged in such a way, under the label of "Realism," that they appear to have a close parallel in modern totalitarianism. Appendices and index.

Wang, Hsiao-po, and Leo S. Chang. *The Philosophical Foundations of Han Fei's Political Theory*. Honolulu: University of Hawaii Press, 1986. Wang and Chang analyze and evaluate five chapters of Hanfeizi's works in an attempt to demonstrate that Hanfeizi adopted the salient strains of classical Chinese thought stretching back to Daoism and *Yijing* (eighth to third century B.C.E.; English translation, 1876; also known as *Book of Changes*, 1986). Appendix, footnotes, bibliography, and index.

Watson, Burton, trans. *Basic Writing of Mo Tzu, Hsun Tzu, and Han Fei Tzu*. New York: Columbia University Press, 1967. Watson translates twelve sections of Hanfeizi's works and also discusses his life, his thoughts, and the historical context in the introduction. Index.

SEE ALSO: Confucius; Laozi; Mencius; Mozi.

HANNIBAL
Carthaginian general

During the Second Punic War, Hannibal led an army of mercenaries across the Alps into Italy, where, for fifteen years, he exhibited superior generalship, defeating the Romans in one battle after another.

BORN: 247 B.C.E.; probably Carthage, North Africa (now in Tunisia)

DIED: 182 B.C.E.; Libyssa, Bithynia, Asia Minor (now in Turkey)

ALSO KNOWN AS: Hannibal Barca

AREA OF ACHIEVEMENT: War and conquest

EARLY LIFE

Hannibal (HAN-uh-buhl) was born in 247 B.C.E., probably in Carthage, of an aristocratic family that claimed descent from Dido, the legendary foundress of the city. Of his mother nothing is known, but his father, Hamilcar Barca, was for nearly twenty years the supreme military commander of the Carthaginian forces. Assuming this position in the year of Hannibal's birth, Hamilcar guided his country through the last difficult years of the First Punic War and then began the construction of a new empire in Spain. After his death in 229, Hamilcar's son-in-law, Hasdrubal, extended Carthaginian dominion northward to the Ebro River and founded New Carthage.

Little is known of Hannibal during these years. Livy, the principal source of information, notes that when Hannibal was nine years of age, he accompanied his father to Spain. Prior to their departure, Hamilcar invoked the blessings of the gods with a sacrifice at which Hannibal was compelled to swear that he would never be a friend to Rome. Such was the hostile atmosphere in which the youth was raised. Although little is known about the years of Hannibal's apprenticeship under his father and later under Hasdrubal, there can be little doubt that Hannibal would benefit immeasurably from the rigors of frontier life. When Hasdrubal was assassinated in 221, Hannibal, age twenty-six, was ready to assume command. That he had already distinguished himself as a warrior and a leader is indicated by the alacrity with which the army proclaimed him commander.

LIFE'S WORK

Hannibal was the epitome of a warrior. According to silver coins supposedly bearing his likeness, he had curly hair, a straight nose, a sloping forehead, a strong neck, and a look of determination in his eyes. A man with a mission, in his mid-twenties Hannibal was ready to

carry his father's dream to completion. All that was needed was an excuse. The opportunity presented itself in 219, when Rome violated a treaty with Carthage by intervening in the political affairs of the Spanish state of Saguntum. Hannibal dismissed a Roman commission sent to investigate the matter and then laid siege to the city, which fell eight months later. Rome's failure to aid its client state probably encouraged Hannibal to extend Carthaginian dominion northward to the Pyrenees. When Carthage refused to surrender Hannibal, Rome declared war.

The Roman strategy was to end the war quickly. One army was dispatched under the leadership of the consul Publius Cornelius Scipio to confront Hannibal in Spain, while the other consul, Tiberius Sempronius Longus, was to attack Carthage. In this matter, however, the Romans greatly underestimated the military genius and determination of Hannibal. In the spring of 218, Hannibal gathered his army of Numidians and Spaniards—variously estimated at forty thousand to sixty thousand men—and, in one of the most celebrated marches in history, crossed the Pyrenees, the Rhone River, and finally the snow-laden Alps to reach the Po River valley. It was a perilous five-month journey fraught with dangers of all sorts—hostile tribes, bad weather, impenetrable geographical barriers, and a scarcity of provisions. Thousands of Hannibal's soldiers and many of the elephants perished along the way. By journey's end, Hannibal's forces had been reduced to about twenty thousand infantry and six thousand cavalry, too few to undertake the conquest of Roman Italy. The success of the venture would depend on Hannibal's ability to lure many of Rome's disaffected allies to his side.

In the meantime, after hearing of Hannibal's departure from Spain, the two consuls rushed northward to meet the threat. Scipio, in a move of future importance, sent his army on to Spain to prevent reinforcements from joining Hannibal. In December, the two consuls joined forces to stop Hannibal's advance, but the Romans fell into an ambush in the frigid waters of the Trebia River. Approximately two-thirds of the Roman force was lost. Although Rome managed to conceal the defeat from its citizens, it was necessary to abandon the Po River valley to the Punic forces. Hannibal, to curry favor with the natives, released his Italian prisoners.

Hannibal wintered in northern Italy. During that time, his army grew, with the addition of Celtic recruits, to

Hannibal. (Library of Congress)

about fifty thousand in number. In the spring of 217, Hannibal moved southward into the peninsula. The Romans sent the consul Gaius Flaminius with orders to hold Hannibal at the Apennines. Hannibal, wily as ever, slipped around the Roman commander by sloshing through the marshes of the Arno River into Etruria. Along the way, Hannibal contracted malaria and lost the sight of one eye. Flaminius regained his composure and eventually caught up with Hannibal's forces, only to suffer a crushing defeat at Lake Trasimene. Flaminius and virtually all of his soldiers perished in the battle.

A second major defeat was more than Rome could endure. In desperation, Rome resurrected an old emergency procedure and appointed a dictator, Quintus Fabius Maximus, to handle the crisis. Nicknamed "the Delayer," Fabius refused to meet Hannibal in open battle, preferring hit-and-run tactics. He also used a scorched-earth policy to prevent Hannibal from living off the land. Although the strategy worked and restored Roman morale, public opinion favored more aggressive action. In 216, Rome felt strong enough to send the consuls Lucius Aemilius Paulus and Gaius Terentius Varro with an army of about sixty thousand men to engage Hannibal in open battle at Cannae in northern Apulia. Although numerically superior, the Romans fell prey once again to Hannibal's genius. While the Romans drove hard through the middle of the Carthaginian line, they were gradually encircled and destroyed. Only a fraction of the Roman force managed to escape. Hannibal's double-envelopment maneuver has since been copied many times by other generals.

The news of defeat threw Rome into chaos. Hannibal, contrary to the advice of his generals, refused to march on the panic-stricken city. The reasons for his cautious behavior are not clear, though he probably understood that Rome was strongly fortified, and he may have continued to hope that Rome's allies would now defect. The major rebellion for which he had hoped never occurred. There were, however, encouraging signs. Much of southern Italy, including Capua, second only to Rome in importance, went over to Hannibal's side. He also gained the support of Macedonia's King Philip V, who hoped to involve Rome in a war in the east.

Hannibal was supreme for the moment, but he had not broken the indomitable Roman spirit. There were also some encouraging signs for Rome. Many of Rome's allies, especially in central Italy, had remained faithful. Property qualifications for military service were lowered, and new armies were raised that returned to Fabius's successful tactics of the past. Furthermore, the decision to remain in Spain, coupled with Rome's continued mastery of the sea, made it difficult for Hannibal to receive reinforcements. While Hannibal moved his diminished, bedraggled army from one encampment to another without benefit of open battle, the Romans began to reconquer the lost cities and provinces. In 211, both Capua and Syracuse were retaken. Compounding Hannibal's problems was the fact that the alliance with Philip V had proved ineffectual.

In the meantime, Rome had gained the advantage in Spain through the efforts of the brilliant young general Publius Cornelius Scipio. In 209, New Carthage, the major city of Hannibal's Iberian empire, was captured by Scipio's forces, along with vast quantities of supplies. He could not prevent Hasdrubal, Hannibal's brother, from crossing the Pyrenees in an attempt to reach Hannibal in Italy, but the relief expedition was intercepted and defeated at the Metaurus River in 207. Nevertheless, Hannibal and his diminished army remained a threat. In 211, he appeared before the walls of Rome, though he took no action. He defeated and killed the consuls Gnaeus Fulvius and Marcus Claudius Marcellus in other battles. It was becoming increasingly obvious, however, that Hannibal could not win the war.

In 205, Scipio returned triumphantly from Spain to assume the consulship. Under his leadership, Rome was ready to take the offensive. In the following year, Scipio invaded Africa and after a brief campaign forced Carthage to capitulate. Hannibal and his army were recalled from Italy, ostensibly as a part of the peace agreement. Once he and his fifteen thousand veterans were on African soil, however, the Carthaginians broke off the negotiations and renewed the war. In 202, Scipio and Hannibal met at Zama in a titanic battle. Using tactics he had learned from Hannibal, Scipio was victorious.

Following Zama, a harsh treaty, termed a "Carthaginian Peace" ever since, was imposed on the defeated Carthage. Hannibal remained in the city for five years and worked hard to build a more unified and democratic state. His enemies would give him no rest, however, and in 196 he fled first to Syria and then to Bithynia, where he served briefly as commander of the army in a war with the Romans. In 182, Hannibal committed suicide rather than surrender to his enemies.

SIGNIFICANCE

The Second Punic War was, in large part, the biography of Hannibal of Carthage. Perhaps no other man in history has so thoroughly dominated a conflict. The historian Polybius observed that Hannibal was the architect of all things, good and bad, which came to the Romans and Carthaginians. His feats, although recorded by reliable ancient historians, are almost legendary. After inheriting his father's struggle with Rome, he crossed the Alps into Italy, where for fifteen years he moved about the countryside at will. He never lost a major battle, scoring decisive victories at the Trebia River, Lake Trasimene, and Cannae. Hannibal's impact was so great that the Romans were driven at times to desperate measures—the appointment of dictators, human sacrifice to appease the gods, and what today is known as guerrilla warfare.

Roman historians, through whose eyes the conflict must be viewed, were not subdued in their praise. Livy recounts with amazement the fact that Hannibal was able to hold his army of various nationalities and beliefs together for so long a time in hostile territory. That he succeeded was the result, in large part, of his courage, an element of recklessness, and an excellent rapport with his men. Yet, Livy continues, he was capable of great cruelty and had little respect for either gods or men. According to Polybius, on the other hand, while Hannibal might have been guilty of these things, he was forced by circumstances and the influence of friends to behave in this paradoxical manner.

Hannibal was, in the eyes of both his contemporaries and modern scholars, the perfect general. Yet, like Pyrrhus

before him, he was fighting an unwinnable war. Rome had the advantages of terrain, command of the sea, and inexhaustible reserves of men. In the end, he lost, and Rome, from which much of Western civilization is derived, remained in the ascendant for the next six centuries. Nevertheless, Hannibal remains one of the most fascinating figures in the annals of military history.

—*Larry W. Usilton*

FURTHER READING

Bradford, Ernle. *Hannibal: The General from Carthage*. New York: McGraw-Hill, 1981. One of the most recent studies, derived in large part from the accounts of Livy and Polybius. Provides excellent descriptions of the major battles at the Trebia River, Lake Trasimene, and Cannae. The author attempts to put Hannibal's career in better perspective through the use of modern examples.

Goldsworthy, Adrian. *The Punic Wars*. London: Cassell, 2000. The first section of this three-part work elaborates the complex of military, naval, geographic, and historic details of the three Punic Wars.

Lancel, Serge. *Carthage: A History*. Translated by Antonia Nevill. Cambridge, Mass.: Blackwell, 1997. Detailed study of Carthage from its founding and rise in the early centuries of the first millennium to its defeat and Roman absorption by the end of the period.

_____. *Hannibal*. Translated by Antonia Nevill. Malden, Mass.: Blackwell, 1998. Well-documented and detailed life of Hannibal.

Livy. *The Rise of Rome*. Translated by T. J. Luce. New York: Oxford University Press, 1998. Includes introduction, notes, bibliography, and index.

_____. *The War with Hannibal*. Translated by Aubrey de Sélincourt. Baltimore: Penguin Books, 1965. Written by a patriotic Roman historian who greatly admired Hannibal's military genius. Along with Polybius's work, it is the best source of information on the Punic Wars. Useful for the more knowledgeable reader. The Penguin edition has been taken from Livy's overall history of Rome.

Polybius. *The Histories of Polybius*. Translated by Evelyn S. Shuckburgh. 2 vols. Westport, Conn.: Greenwood Press, 1974. A history of Rome from the onset of the First Punic War in 264 B.C.E. to the destruction of Carthage in 146 B.C.E. One of the best sources of information about Hannibal.

Sinnigen, William G., and Arthur E. A. Boak. *A History of Rome to A.D. 565*. 6th ed. New York: Macmillan, 1977. One of the better surveys of Roman history. Includes a valuable chapter on the conflict with Carthage in which the chief events of Hannibal's career are mentioned. Useful for scholars and students alike.

Toynbee, Arnold. *Hannibal's Legacy.* 2 vols. New York: Oxford University Press, 1965. The beginning student will find it ponderous, but it is a valuable study that goes far beyond Hannibal.

SEE ALSO: Dido; Fabius; Hamilcar Barca; Hanno; Regulus; Scipio Africanus.

RELATED ARTICLES in *Great Events from History: The Ancient World*: c. 800 B.C.E., Phoenicians from Tyre Found Carthage; 264-225 B.C.E., First Punic War; 218-201 B.C.E., Second Punic War; 202 B.C.E., Battle of Zama.

HANNO
Carthaginian explorer

Hanno founded the first trading colonies along the western African coast and then pushed on to explore the coast at least as far as modern Sierra Leone. His account of his journey provided the only reasonably accurate account of Africa until the time of Prince Henry the Navigator.

BORN: c. 520-510 B.C.E.; place unknown
DIED: Date unknown; place unknown
AREA OF ACHIEVEMENT: Geography

EARLY LIFE

Hanno (HAN-oh) belongs to that lamentably large class of ancients whose names have survived the centuries for a single history-shaping deed but about whom little else is known. Apart from scattered, confused references to his voyage in a few ancient works, the main source of information on Hanno is his text known as the *Periplus* (*The Voyage of Hanno*, 1797; best known as *Periplus*). Consisting of just under 650 words of Greek, it purports to be a translation of the public inscription Hanno erected in the temple of Kronos at Carthage to commemorate his voyage.

The introduction to the *Periplus* calls Hanno a king. The Carthaginian constitution had no kings but placed supreme power in two *suffetes*. In any case, Hanno was surely of the ruling nobility of Carthage. The dating of his life depends on the dating of his voyage. Pliny the Elder asserts twice that the voyage was undertaken when the power of Carthage was at its peak; modern scholars have suggested a date just prior to 480 B.C.E. Before this time, Carthage enjoyed a period of prosperity and expansion in the western Mediterranean region. Just at the time the Persians were losing their war with the Greeks at Thermopylae and Salamis, so did the Carthaginians, led by Hamilcar Barca, fall decisively to Gelon of Syracuse at the Battle of Himera. Subsequently, it took several decades for Carthage to regain its former strength and influ-

ence. This fact, together with philological evidence dating the Greek text to the fifth century, makes it seem best to place Hanno's exploits prior to the Carthaginian defeat at Himera.

There are two men named Hanno known from this period, one the father and the other the son of the Hamilcar who died at Himera. The birth dates given above result from adding the probable age of a magistrate and state-sponsored explorer (between thirty and forty) to the upper limit of the date of the voyage (480). With this date, evidence seems to lean toward the younger Hanno, but there is ample room for doubt.

One can easily understand what may have inspired Hanno's career. As a member of the ruling class, he viewed at first hand the cosmopolitan activity of the trading town of Carthage. A young man could have been readily lured by the possibility of travel and exploration as he walked along the busy docks and through the hectic markets of Carthage, which traded with Etruria, Phoenicia, and countless Greek city-states and African nations. It can be assumed that Hanno received the best Punic education of his day. His inscription, translated though it is, remains the longest bit of Punic literature available to modern scholars.

LIFE'S WORK

The *Periplus* begins by stating that the Carthaginians instructed Hanno to sail "beyond the Pillars of Heracles" (the Straits of Gibraltar) to found Lybyophoenician cities. Modern scholars suggest plausibly that these cities were to serve as bases for trade with inner Africa, perhaps in precious metals.

The narrative claims that Hanno left with thirty thousand colonists and sixty oared ships. As such ships were small fighting craft, they must have served as a convoy for the colonists in transports. Two days beyond Gibraltar, Hanno founded his first city; five others followed in rapid succession. He then pushed along the western coast of Africa, stopping at Lixus River (now Wad Dra) to recruit interpreters before sailing along the coast of the Sahara Desert. He thereupon came to an island, which he named Kerne and on which he founded his seventh colony.

From there, his colonizing done, Hanno became an explorer. The *Periplus* tells of two excursions south from Kerne. On the first, Hanno encountered wild, skin-clad savages who pelted his crew with rocks. He discovered a river, filled with crocodiles and hippopotamuses, which he called the Chretes. On the second, apparently longer exploration, he eventually came to forests from which his crew heard the sounds of pipes, cymbals, and shouting. Terrified, they fled until they came to a burning country, filled with fragrant odors and from which burning streams flowed to the sea. In the midst of it stood a towering, blazing mountain that Hanno called the Chariot of the Gods, from whose summit fire shot up almost to the stars. Three days later, he reached an island inhabited by small, hairy "wild men" who threw rocks at the Carthaginians. The nimble males escaped, but Hanno's crew managed to capture three scratching, biting females, who were promptly skinned. According to Pliny the Elder, two of these skins were on display in the temple of Juno at Carthage until its destruction by the Romans in 146 B.C.E. Hanno's interpreters informed him that these creatures were called "gorillae." Following the account of this incident, the *Periplus* notes rather abruptly that Hanno ran out of supplies and returned home.

There is no persuasive reason to believe that the *Periplus* is either a forgery or a literary exercise. It is exactly what it purports to be—a public version, probably abridged, of an actual voyage. Its few sentences, however, have caused rivers of ink (and no small amount of vitriol) to flow, all in an attempt to determine where Hanno went. Nineteenth century investigators tended to shorten the voyage too much, even claiming that Hanno never got beyond the Atlantic border of Morocco. A confused Pliny the Elder went to the other extreme, stating that Hanno sailed from Cádiz to the borders of Arabia. Somewhere in between lies the truth.

The solution to this problem hinges on the identification of several key places mentioned in the text, and one must first be aware of its limitations. It is at best a translation of an abridgment, and in spots the text is in question. There are no consistent indications of distance from one point to another; where measurements are given, they are in days. How many hours a day were spent in sailing?

Were the explorers under sail or oars? Were they against or with the wind and currents?

Despite all these problems, a consensus seems to exist among many scholars on some matters. It is generally accepted that Hanno's first six colonies dotted the northwest Atlantic coast of Africa, all fairly close to the Pillars of Heracles. The location of the seventh colony, Kerne, reached in two days after the Lixus River, is as difficult as it is crucial. When "two" is emended to "nine," as it often is, it suggests a small island named Herne, lying opposite the Río de Oro off Western Sahara. Another candidate for Kerne is the Island of Arguin, farther still to the south.

One site of Hanno's first exploration is accepted without question. The river full of crocodiles and hippopotamuses can only be the Senegal. It is the first river he could have reached with the requisite wildlife, and Pliny the Elder elsewhere remarks that the name of this river was the Bambotum, a name plausibly explained as a corruption of *behemoth*, the Semitic word for hippopotamus.

In recounting his adventures farther south, Hanno's reports seem to take on a less believable tone. Nevertheless, his descriptions of aromatic, blazing lands, of the mountain called the Chariot of the Gods, and of the wild, hairy gorillas, once scorned as fictions, can be explained in such a way as to make them plausible.

An early report from the eighteenth century travels of explorer Mungo Park, for example, made clear that the fires Hanno saw sweeping the plains were the natives' annual burning of the fields to increase their fertility. Hanno's description of the "fiery streams" rushing to the sea and of the Chariot of the Gods with its fire reaching to the stars has prompted many, ancient and modern, to suppose a volcano is meant. Rather far to the south lies Mount Cameroon, a volcanic peak towering 13,353 feet (4,070 meters) over the plain and quite visible from the coast. The time given in the text for this leg of the trip, however, is clearly insufficient for Hanno to have reached this latitude. Other scholars, therefore, choose to see the Chariot of the Gods in the much closer Mount Kakulima in Guinea (on some maps called Souzos or Sagres). At 3,300 feet (1,005 meters), it is much less spectacular, but ablaze it could perhaps resemble a volcano. There are sound arguments for and against either site, and the choice is significant in determining the southern extent of the voyage. It is safest to say that Hanno reached at least as far as Sierra Leone.

Finally, there are the much-debated gorillas. One of the few things agreed on concerning this segment of the *Periplus* is that these are surely not gorillas in the modern sense of the word, for these animals are not found in this part of Africa. Most scholars believe that Hanno saw either chimpanzees or baboons, while a few hold to the earlier belief that they were pygmies or dwarfs. "Gorilla" in its modern sense was first used by Thomas Savage, an American missionary who happened to see some gorilla skulls and in 1847 announced to the world a new creature, locally called a *pongo*. Because this word was already in use scientifically, he recalled Hanno's hairy creatures and bestowed the name gorilla on his new find. Any attempt to claim that Hanno saw real gorillas—and thus to extend his voyage as far south as Gabon—is undoubtedly incorrect.

SIGNIFICANCE

Hanno's work itself seems not to have been widely acclaimed in antiquity, and his reputation could not have been helped by the fact that he was a Carthaginian. The authors who cited him were often confused, and several seem incredulous. Educated guesses about Hanno's dates and true identity are all that is possible. Hanno must be judged by his work.

Hanno was not the first to attempt a voyage down the western coast of Africa. Herodotus says that Pharaoh Necho II (early sixth century B.C.E.) engaged Phoenicians to circumnavigate Africa from east to west and that they did so in a three-year voyage. Most scholars treat the story with caution, and its lack of any precise geographical details does make it suspect. Herodotus also notes that in the fifth century King Xerxes I of Persia commuted the sentence of death by impalement of a certain Sataspes with the provision that he attempt to circumnavigate Africa from west to east. Sataspes returned a failure and, perhaps to appease the king, told a tale of dwarfish races he had seen. The ploy did not work, and Sataspes was promptly impaled. A third sailor, a Greek from Massalia named Euthymenes, claimed to have sailed south along Africa until he saw a river filled with crocodiles (the Senegal?). His date, however, is merest conjecture. These tales demonstrate at the least that the idea of such a voyage was in circulation before Hanno attempted it. Also, the fact that his charge was to establish settlements along the coast indicates that the Carthaginians knew at least the closer, northwestern shore of Africa.

These facts, however, do not detract from Hanno's accomplishments. His is the earliest believable and documented voyage of this scope. Moreover, later authors suggest that the colonies, including southern Kerne, continued to engage in trade up to the destruction of Car-

thage by Rome in 146. Furthermore, there are no records of any further voyages of this length along the African coast until the Middle Ages, when ships routinely turned back at the "impassable" Cape Bojador. It was not until the expeditions of Prince Henry the Navigator that ships went farther, and then it took them forty years to get as far as Hanno had done.

Thus, in one summer, Hanno traveled farther than anyone was to do for some two thousand years. Moreover, his written record of his voyages, flawed as it may be, remained the sole source for the geography of western Africa during all the intervening years. Few explorers since have had such an influence.

—*Kenneth F. Kitchell, Jr.*

FURTHER READING

Bunbury, Edward Herbert. *A History of Ancient Geography Among the Greeks and Romans, from the Earliest Ages till the Fall of the Roman Empire.* 1879. Reprint. Amsterdam: J. Gieben, 1979. Features a reasonable discussion of the *Periplus*, with a fine map. Identifies Herne as Kerne, Kakulima with the Chariot of the Gods, and chimpanzees as the gorillas.

Carpenter, Rhys. *Beyond the Pillars of Heracles.* New York: Delacorte Press, 1966. Includes a translation of the *Periplus* and a lucid discussion of the practical problems of sailing times. Carpenter emends the text to produce a new identification of Herne with Saint-Louis at the mouth of the Senegal. Excellent source.

Cary, Max, and E. H. Warmington. *The Ancient Explorers.* Rev. ed. Baltimore: Pelican Books, 1963. Provides treatments of Euthymenes, Hanno, Necho, and Sataspes. A map of northwest Africa, with major landfalls marked, is of great use. Balanced interpretation of the evidence for Hanno's itinerary.

Church, Alfred J. *The Story of Carthage.* 1893. Reprint. New York: Biblo-Moser, 1998. This illustrated volume describes the history of the extinct city. Includes maps.

Hyde, Walter Woodburn. *Ancient Greek Mariners.* New York: Oxford University Press, 1947. Includes an extended discussion of the gorilla question. Good summary of Hanno's text. The maps, however, are of low quality.

Thomson, J. O. *History of Ancient Geography.* New York: Biblo and Tannen, 1965. Good sections on Hanno and his predecessors. Excellent bicolored map shows various theories as to locations of Hanno's landfalls.

SEE ALSO: Dido; Hamilcar Barca.
RELATED ARTICLES in *Great Events from History: The Ancient World*: c. 800 B.C.E., Phoenicians from Tyre Found Carthage; 520-518 B.C.E., Scylax of Caryanda Voyages the Indian Ocean; c. 500-470 B.C.E., Hecataeus of Miletus Writes the First Geography Book; 480-479 B.C.E., Persian Invasion of Greece; 290-300 C.E., West African Gold First Reaches North Africa; 399 C.E., Chinese Monk Faxian Travels to India.

HATSHEPSUT

Egyptian queen (r. c. 1503-1482 B.C.E.)

Governing in her own right, Hatshepsut gave to Egypt two decades of peace and prosperity and beautified Thebes with temples and monuments.

BORN: c. 1525 B.C.E.; probably near Thebes, Egypt
DIED: c. 1482 B.C.E.; place unknown
ALSO KNOWN AS: Hatshipsitu; Hatchepsut; Maatkare
AREA OF ACHIEVEMENT: Government and politics

EARLY LIFE

Hatshepsut (hat-SHEHP-sewt), or Hatshopsitu, was the daughter of Thutmose I and his consort (the Egyptian title was "great royal wife") Ahmose. Little is known of Hatshepsut's early life. Although Thutmose I was the third king of the powerful Eighteenth Dynasty, he was probably not of royal blood on his mother's side; the princess Ahmose, however, was of the highest rank. During the period in Egyptian history known as the New Kingdom (from the Eighteenth to the Twentieth Dynasty; c. 1570-c. 1069 B.C.E.), royal women began to play a more active role in political affairs. Among her titles, the pharaoh's chief wife was called the "divine consort of Amen" (Amen was one of the principal Theban deities). Being the wife of a god increased her status, and her children were given a certain precedence over the children of minor wives or concubines.

In addition to Princess Hatshepsut, at least two sons were born to Thutmose I and Ahmose, but both of them died young. The male line had to be continued through a third son, born to a minor wife, who was married to his half sister, Hatshepsut. Thutmose II's claim to the throne was strengthened by this marriage; he succeeded to the throne around 1518.

A daughter, Neferure, was born of this union, but apparently no son was born. The ancient records are fragmentary and at times obscure, but there is evidence that Thutmose II was not very healthy and thus his reign was short, ending around 1504. Once more, there was no male of pure royal blood to become pharaoh; thus, the title passed to a son of Thutmose II by a concubine named

Isis. This boy, also named Thutmose, was at the time of his father's death between the ages of six and ten and dedicated to the service of the god Amen at the temple at Karnak. Because he was underage, the logical choice as regent was his aunt Hatshepsut, now the queen mother.

LIFE'S WORK

Hatshepsut soon proved to be a woman of great ability and large ambitions. The regency was not enough for her; she wanted the glory of being called pharaoh as well as the responsibility for Egypt and the young king. To realize this desire, however, seemed impossible. There had never been a woman pharaoh—only a man could assume that title, take a "Horus name," and become king of Upper and Lower Egypt.

For a time Hatshepsut looked for possible allies, finding them among the various court officials, the most notable being the architect and bureaucrat Senmut (or Senenmut) and among the priests of Amen. By 1503 her moment had come. Accompanied by young Thutmose, she went to Luxor to participate in one of the great feasts honoring Amen; during the ceremonies, she had herself crowned. There was no question of deposing Thutmose III, but he was, in effect, forced to accept a coregency in which he played a lesser part.

To justify this unique coronation, Hatshepsut asserted that she had been crowned already with the sanction of her father the pharaoh. To support this claim, an account was given of her miraculous birth, which was later inscribed at her temple at Dayr el-Bahrī on the west bank of the Nile River. According to this account, Amen himself, assuming the guise of Thutmose, had fathered Hatshepsut. With the approval of both a divine and a human parent, none could oppose the new pharaoh's will, while Thutmose remained a child and the army and the priests supported her.

Hatshepsut did not merely assume the masculine titles and authority of a pharaoh; she ordered that statues be made showing her as a man. In the stylized portraiture of

Egyptian royalty, the king is usually shown bare-chested and wearing a short, stiff kilt, a striped wig-cover concealing the hair, and a ceremonial beard. The number of statues commissioned by Hatshepsut is not known, but in spite of later efforts by Thutmose III to blot out the memory of his hated relative, several examples exist, showing Hatshepsut kneeling, sitting, or standing, looking as aloof and masculine as her predecessors.

Neferure, daughter of Hatshepsut and Thutmose II, was married to Thutmose III. This marriage served the dual purpose of strengthening the succession and binding the king closer to his aunt, now his mother-in-law. Hatshepsut then focused her attention on domestic prosperity and foreign trade, activities more to her personal inclination than conquest. Throughout Egypt an extensive building program was begun. At Karnak four large obelisks and a shrine to Amen were built. A temple was also constructed at Beni-Hasan in Middle Egypt. Several tombs were cut for her, including one in the Valley of the Kings. Her inscriptions claim that she was the first pharaoh to repair damages caused by the Hyksos, Asian invaders who had conquered Egypt in the late eighteenth through mid-sixteenth centuries B.C.E. with the aid of new technologies, such as war chariots pulled by horses. The usurpation of these foreign kings was an unpleasant and recent memory to the proud, self-sufficient Egyptians; Hatshepsut's restorations probably increased her popularity.

The crowning architectural triumph of her reign was her beautiful funerary temple at Dayr el-Bahrī. Built by Senmut, her chief architect and adviser, it was constructed on three levels against the cliffs; the temple, a harmonious progression of ramps, courts, and porticoes, was decorated in the interior with scenes of the major events of the queen's reign.

Probably the most interesting of the achievements so portrayed was the expedition sent to the kingdom of Punt, located at the southern end of the Red Sea. As the story is told, in the seventh or eighth year of her reign, Hatshepsut was instructed by Amen to send forth five ships laden with goods to exchange for incense and living myrrh trees as well as such exotic imports as apes, leopard skins, greyhounds, ivory, ebony, and gold. Pictured in detail are the natives' round huts, built on stilts, and the arrival of the prince and princess of Punt to greet the

Egyptians. The portrait of the princess is unusual because it is one of the rare examples in Egyptian art in which a fat and deformed person is depicted.

In addition to the voyage to Punt, Hatshepsut reopened the long-unused mines of Sinai, which produced blue and green stones. Tribute was received from Asian and Libyan tribes, and she participated in a brief military expedition to Nubia. Despite the latter endeavors, Hatshepsut's primary concern was peace, not imperialistic expansion. In this regard, her actions were in sharp contrast to those of her rival and successor Thutmose III, who was very much the warrior-king.

It would not be sufficient, however, to explain Hatshepsut's less aggressive policies on the basis of her sex. Traditionally, the Egyptians had been isolationists. Convinced that their land had been blessed by the gods with

Hatshepsut. (Library of Congress)

almost everything necessary, the Egyptians had throughout much of their earlier history treated their neighbors as foreign barbarians, unworthy of serious consideration. Hatshepsut and her advisers seem to have chosen this conservative course.

As Hatshepsut's reign continued, unpleasant changes began to occur. Her favorite, Senmut, died around 1487. In addition to the numerous offices and titles related to agriculture, public works, and the priesthood, he had also been named a guardian and tutor to Neferure. No less than six statues show Senmut with the royal child in his arms. At the end of his life, he may have fallen from favor by presuming to include images of himself in his mistress's temple. Most were discovered and mutilated, presumably during Hatshepsut's lifetime and with her approval—her names remained undisturbed.

Princess Neferure died young, perhaps even before Senmut's death, leaving Hatshepsut to face the growing power of Thutmose III. The king had reached adulthood: He was now the leader of the army and demanded a more important role in the coregency. His presence at major festivals became more obvious, although Hatshepsut's name continued to be linked with his until 1482.

It is not known exactly where or when Hatshepsut died or whether she might have been deposed and murdered. That her relations with her nephew and son-in-law were strained is evident from the revenge Thutmose exacted after her death: Her temples and tombs were broken into and her statues destroyed. Her cartouches, carved oval or oblong figures that encased the royal name, were erased, and in many cases her name was replaced by that of her husband or even of her father. She was eliminated from the list of kings. Thutmose III ruled in her stead and did his best to see that she was forgotten both by gods and by men.

SIGNIFICANCE

The nature and scope of Hatshepsut's achievements are still subject to debate. Traditional historians have emphasized the irregularity of her succession, the usurpation of Thutmose III's authority, and her disinterest in military success. Revisionist studies are more generous in assessing this unique woman, praising her for her promotion of peaceful trade and her extensive building program at home.

Her influence throughout Egypt, though brief and limited only to her reign, must have been profound. The considerable number of temples, tombs, and monuments constructed at her command would have provided work for many of her subjects, just as surely as the wars of her

father and nephew provided employment in another capacity. Art, devotion to the gods, and propaganda were inextricably mingled in the architectural endeavors of every pharaoh. Hatshepsut's devotion to the gods, especially the Theban deity Amen, and her evident need to justify her succession and her achievements enriched her nation with some of its finest examples of New Kingdom art.

Controversial in her own lifetime and still something of a mysterious figure, Hatshepsut continues to inspire conflicting views about herself and the nature of Egyptian royalty. She was a bold figure who chose to change the role assigned to royal women, yet at the same time, she seems to have been a traditionalist leading a faction that wanted Egypt to remain self-sufficient and essentially peaceful. Perhaps that was yet another reason that she and Thutmose III were so much at odds. His vision of Egypt as a conquering empire would be that of the future. She was looking back to the past.

—Dorothy T. Potter

FURTHER READING

Aldred, Cyril. *The Development of Ancient Egyptian Art from 3200 to 1315 B.C.* Reprint. London: Academy Editions, 1973. The title indicates the focus of the work. There are more than fifteen plates depicting Hatshepsut, other members of her family, and her adviser Senmut. Detailed explanations accompany each picture, and there is also an index and a bibliography.

"Egypt Completes Repairs to Pharaonic Sites." *The New York Times*, December 26, 2001, sec. A, p. 4. Describes the reopening in Egypt of part of the temple of Queen Hatshepsut, which contains reliefs of the pharaoh making offerings to the gods.

Gardiner, Sir Alan. *Egypt of the Pharaohs*. New York: Oxford University Press, 1969. Although a lengthy study, Gardiner's work is engagingly written, with balanced views of both Hatshepsut and her successor, Thutmose III. Provides a good background for the less knowledgeable reader. Includes an index, a bibliography, and a comprehensive chronological list of kings. Illustrated.

Nims, Charles F. *Thebes of the Pharaohs: Pattern for Every City*. New York: Stein and Day, 1965. The city of Thebes was extremely important to Hatshepsut and her family as both a political and a religious center. This book is helpful because it places the queen in her environment.

Tyldesley, Joyce A. *Hatchepsut: The Female Pharaoh*. New York: Viking, 1996. In this biography, archaeologist Tyldesley dismisses speculative attempts made by some scholars to suggest that Hatchepsut was a transvestite. This book will be primarily of interest to specialists.

Wenig, Steffen. *The Woman in Egyptian Art*. New York: McGraw-Hill, 1969. This book is extremely well illustrated with both color and black-and-white photographs as well as drawings. The period covered is from c. 4000 B.C.E. to c. 300 C.E. Contains a chronology and an extensive bibliography and is written for the general reader.

Wilson, John A. *The Burden of Egypt*. Chicago: University of Chicago Press, 1951. This extensive study is both detailed and well written; it deals with the impor-

tance of geography to Egypt. Includes maps, a bibliography, illustrations, and a chronology of rulers. Wilson's analysis of political theories and discussion of possible motivations of the pharaohs is very useful in understanding the conflict between Hatshepsut and Thutmose III.

SEE ALSO: Arsinoe II Philadelphus; Cleopatra VII; Nefertari; Nefertiti; Thutmose III; Tiy.

RELATED ARTICLES in *Great Events from History: The Ancient World*: c. 1570 B.C.E., New Kingdom Period Begins in Egypt; From c. 1500 B.C.E., Dissemination of the Book of the Dead.

SAINT HELENA
Roman empress

Helena was the mother of Constantine the Great, the first Christian Roman emperor. Her elevation to sainthood was conferred because, according to tradition, she set out on a pilgrimage to Palestine to discover the cross of Christ's Crucifixion and, on doing so, founded the Church of the Nativity and the Church of the Holy Sepulchre in the Holy Land.

BORN: c. 248 C.E.; Drepanum, Bithnyia, Asia Minor (now Helenopolis, Turkey)

DIED: c. 328 C.E.; Nicomedia (now İzmit, Turkey)

ALSO KNOWN AS: Helena, Flavia Iulia (original name); Helen; Helena of Constantinople; Augusta of the Roman Empire

AREA OF ACHIEVEMENT: Religion

EARLY LIFE

Historical fact and historical fiction intertwine in the writings regarding the life and times of Helena (HEHL-uh-nuh). The more authentic versions are believed to be those that are oldest, those being from Eusebius of Caesarea, Saint Ambrose, and Cassiodorus. Eusebius, Helena's contemporary, was bishop of Caesarea in Palestine and author of the four-book "eulogy" *Vita Constantini* (339 C.E.; *Life of Constantine*, 1845). Eusebius dedicated paragraphs 42-47 of Book 3 of *Vita Constantini* to the eastern provinces of the Empire and Helena's stay in Palestine.

Although little is known of her early life, the most common belief is that Helena was born of the humblest of origins and possibly started her life as a stable girl or servant at an inn. While a few accounts claim that she

married Constantius Chlorus, more often the interpretation has been that she was his concubine. In the Roman Empire of that time, concubinage was an accepted form of cohabitation. The relationship, however legal it may have been, began around 270; Helena gave birth to Constantine sometime near the period between 273 and 275.

Constantius was an officer in the Roman army when Helena met him. He rose to the position of caesar, or deputy emperor, in 293 and to the rank of augustus from 305 until his death in 306—but not before deserting Helena. He became caesar under Maximian in the west of the Roman Empire. Constantine's mother was cast off in order that Maximian could marry his stepdaughter Theodora to Constantius in 289. Constantius's marriage with Theodora was a prerequisite for a successful political career in Diocletian's newly introduced tetrarchy. Helena and her son were separated, and not until 306, when Constantine was named successor of his father, did she reappear in the historical accounts in her new role as the empress-mother at Constantine's court.

A definitive interpretation of historical writings on the era is not possible, but tradition says that during his rule, Constantine was struck with incurable leprosy. Pagan priests advised him to bathe in the warm blood of three thousand boys. When the children were gathered, Constantine responded to the anguished pleas from their mothers and freed them. For this act, he was visited by two emissaries from Jesus Christ. Constantine was baptized, catechized, and cured. This story was later popularized by the famous Italian painter Raphael (1483-

1520), whose interpretation of the event is captured in the painting *The Donation of Constantine*.

Helena, as the legend continues, challenged her son's conversion from pagan idolatry to Christianity, and a theological debate was established to resolve the dispute. Saint Silvester entertained the arguments of eleven leading Jewish scholars who protested the Christian faith. Silvester ultimately won when he brought back to life, in the name of Jesus Christ, a bull that the Jew Zambri had caused to drop dead. As the legend recounts, Helena, the Jews, and the judges all then converted. Another popular legend regarding Constantine's conversion to Christianity holds that the Christian Saint Silvester pardoned Constantine for the murder of his son and wife and won the leader to Christianity for doing so.

Constantine gave the first impetus to the Christianization of the Roman Empire and the eventual Christianization of Europe. He became sole ruler of the Roman Empire in 324, proclaimed Helena as augusta soon after and summoned the Council of Nicaea in 325. A prominent participant in this religious council, Constantine pushed for the dogmatic unity of the Christian religion. The bishops agreed on a common dogma expressed in the Nicene Creed. Constantine's focus on Christianization led to the building of many churches, including those over Christ's purported tomb and over the cave where Christ was said to have been born in Bethlehem. Both structures were credited to Helena's pilgrimage to those places.

During Constantine's reunification efforts following his victory in 324, he equated the harmonious unity of his family with the unity of the Empire. This position was lethal to his political leadership when, in 326, he executed his wife, Fausta, and his eldest son, Crispus, the young man who had been born to his concubine, Minervina. The most plausible justification was that a sexual relationship had developed between Fausta and Crispus, but the truth is obscure. Various accounts relate the pain experienced by Helena at the news of her favorite grandson's murder; her pilgrimage may have been in some part a response to the sin her son had committed in ordering the murder.

The scandal in the Constantinian family and the turmoil caused by Constantine's insistence on Christianity created unrest in the eastern parts of the Roman Empire. To appease the people of the eastern provinces, Helen set off to meet them. Her travels were marked by her piety and gracious giving to all whom she encountered. An old Anglo-Saxon poem by Cynewulf (c. eighth century) tells the legend of Saint Helena's journey to Jerusalem to search for the Cross.

LIFE'S WORK

Tradition says Helena discovered the True Cross. She discovered three crosses, and Pontius's inscription marked the True Cross, according to one tradition. In a more symbolic interpretation, historians have written that on finding three crosses, Helena turned to Marcarius, bishop of Jerusalem, for mediation. A mortally sick woman (in some tellings, one who had just died) was brought to the crosses. When she was touched by the first two, nothing happened; on the touch of the third cross, she was immediately healed. Thus, the holy wood of the True Cross was identified. More important, the healing symbolized the salvation of Christianity for those who believed in Christ.

Because of Helena's visit to the Holy Land, churches were erected at the cave where the nativity occurred in Bethlehem (the Church of the Nativity) and on the Mount of Olives, from which Christ is said to have ascended into heaven (the Church of the Assumption). The attachment of holiness (or unholiness) to something tangible was not inherent in Christianity, for nothing earthly was considered holy. The concept of churches as holy places was established by Constantine and Helena as part of the establishment of Christianity. The churches were thus structured to represent the places where earth and heaven met.

The bodies of the Three Magi, now shown at Cologne, Germany, are said to have been brought by Helena from the East and given to the Church of Milan. She is also said to have given the Holy Coat, the seamless robe of Christ, to the cathedral of Trier in Germany. In some accounts, she is also credited with finding the nails that fastened Christ's body to the Cross.

Legend reports she established Stavrovouni Monastery in Cyprus, where she stayed during her return journey from Jerusalem. She is said to have presented a piece of the True Cross in establishing the monastery. The monastery occupies the easternmost summit of the Troodos range of mountains, at a height of 2,260 feet (689 meters). Tradition describes the monastery as a fortress impregnable against pagan attacks.

To the southeast of Rome, a territory called *fundus Laurentus* was an estate belonging to Helena (acquired sometime after 312). The site was one of the first areas in Rome where the new Christian convictions of the members of the Imperial house were manifested.

Another historical legend, with some archaeological support, tells that Helena gave her Imperial palace in Trier to Agricius, at the time priest to Antioch, for use as Trier's cathedral. Legend also has it that she was involved in the foundation of the abbey of Saint Maximin at Trier.

SIGNIFICANCE

The sarcophagus of Saint Helena is in the Vatican Museum. Originally intended for Constantine, the sarcophagus is covered with reliefs celebrating military triumphs. More than one hundred churches have been dedicated to Saint Helena in England. By the end of the Middle Ages, her feast was kept in many churches on February 8. Throughout the world, her feast day is celebrated: by the Roman Catholic Church on August 18, by the Greeks on May 21, by the Ethiopians on September 15, and by the Copts on March 24 and May 4. She is the patroness of dyers, needlers, and nailsmiths.

Jan Willem Drijvers reported in his definitive book *Helena Augusta: The Mother of Constantine the Great and the Legend of Her Finding of the True Cross* (1992) that there may be two cameos depicting Helena: the so-called Ada cameo, preserved in the Stadtbibliothek in Trier, and a cameo in the Koninklijk Penningkabinet in Leiden, Netherlands. It is difficult to identify statues of Helena with any certainty. Because Helena's coiffure was well attested, it is typically the test for images. On the coin portraits that have been identified as depicting Helena, her hair is sleekly combed and worn in a knot over the middle of her head. Although her image is sometimes difficult to distinguish, her impact is not. For many empresses and queens who came to the throne after her, Helena Augusta became the perfect Christian empress whose humble piety was a model for all.

—*Tonya Huber*

FURTHER READING

Bietenhoiz, Peter G. *Historia and Fabula: Myths and Legends in Historical Thought from Antiquity to the Modern Age*. New York: E. J. Brill, 1994. Establishes a perspective from which to approach the "historical" study of Saint Helena as that concerned both with things that actually happened (*historia*) and things that are merely supposed to have happened (*fabula*).

Explores myths, legends, and historical thought surrounding Constantine the Great and his mother.

Burckhardt, Jacob. *The Age of Constantine the Great*. Translated by Moses Hadas. 1949. Reprint. Berkeley: University of California Press, 1983. Cited as the most meaningful history for the nonprofessional reader, Burckhardt's essay of nearly four hundred pages is a humanist reaction against the microscopic but less imaginative writings of scientific historians. Topical page headings and an extensive index make the book reader-friendly.

Drijvers, Jan Willem. *Helena Augusta: The Mother of Constantine the Great and the Legend of Her Finding of the True Cross*. New York: E. J. Brill, 1992. This book focuses on the task of distinguishing the history of Helena from the legend. Includes identification of coins and statues of Helena and an extensive bibliography.

Firth, John B. *Constantine the Great: The Reorganization of the Empire and the Triumph of the Church*. Freeport, N.Y.: Books for Libraries Press, 1971. The twenty-seven illustrations in this book include several depictions of Helena and others related to her. Includes a comprehensive index.

Grant, Michael. *Constantine the Great: The Man and His Times*. New York: Scribner's, 1994. A chronological table, maps, and illustrations enhance this telling of the impact of Constantine and Helena on Christianity.

Waugh, Evelyn. "Saint Helena Empress." In *Saints for Now*, edited by Clare Boothe Luce. New York: Sheed and Ward, 1952. Brief but highly readable and literary interpretation of Helena's life.

SEE ALSO: Constantine the Great; Eusebius of Caesarea; Jesus; Mary.

RELATED ARTICLES in *Great Events from History: The Ancient World*: October 28, 312 C.E., Conversion of Constantine to Christianity; 325 C.E., Adoption of the Nicene Creed; November 24, 326-May 11, 330 C.E., Constantinople Is Founded.

HENGIST

Kentish king (r. c. 456-c. 488 C.E.)

Hengist is reputed to have led the first Germanic invasion of Britain and to have established the first "English" kingdom in Kent.

BORN: c. 420 C.E.; probably Jutland (now in Denmark)
DIED: c. 488 C.E.; probably Kent, or near
    Knaresborough, Yorkshire (now in England)
ALSO KNOWN AS: Hengest
AREA OF ACHIEVEMENT: War and conquest

EARLY LIFE

Information on Hengist (HENG-guhst) is derived from oral tradition subsequently captured in written texts. Chief among these is the *Historia ecclesiastica* (731; *Ecclesiastical History of the English People*, 1723) of Bede, which was the basis for the relevant entries in *The Anglo-Saxon Chronicle* (c. 900) by an unknown author, the standard source for the story of Hengist. More detail can be found in the *Historia Britonum* (c. 830; *History of the Britons*, 1819) by Nennius, who drew on an earlier document, perhaps from the sixth century, known as the *Kentish Chronicle*, though this is clearly a mixture of fact and legend. Even less reliable is *Historia regum Britanniae*, (Vulgate version, c. 1136; *History of the Kings of Britain*, 1718) by Geoffrey of Monmouth. Yet Geoffrey's work cannot be dismissed out of hand, for he may have had access to sources no longer available.

A character called Hengist appears in *Beowulf* (eighth century) and in the related fragment *The Fight at Finnesburg* (perhaps seventh century). The contemporaneity of these events and the similarity of background with the works of Bede and Nennius are strongly suggestive that the two Hengists are the same. The references in *Beowulf* and *The Fight at Finnesburg* help scholars to date Hengist to the middle of the fifth century C.E., independent of Bede's *Ecclesiastical History*, which specifically dates Hengist's arrival in Britain to the period 449-457. Nennius also places Hengist's arrival in that period, citing it as forty years after the end of the Roman Empire in Britain, which is usually dated to 410 C.E.

Nennius provides a genealogy for Hengist, recording that he was the son of Wichtgils and grandson of Witta. Witta is recorded elsewhere as the ruler of the Swæfe, or Suebi, a tribe of Angles who lived in what is now southern Denmark. *Beowulf* and *The Fight at Finnesburg* fragment reveal that Hengist was a prince in exile, no doubt driven out of his homeland by interdynastic rivalries. He was probably of mixed Anglian/Jutish descent, as he

was one of an army of Half-Danes, a mercenary warband. Their leader Hnæf was killed in a fight at Finnesburg against the men of Finn, king of the East Frisians. Hengist survived the battle and became the leader of the Half-Danes. He agreed to winter at Finnesburg, but in the spring, the feud erupted again. Hengist's army defeated the Frisians, and Finn was killed.

This episode, referred to by Anglo-Saxonist J. R. R. Tolkien as the *freswæl*, or "Frisian massacre," doubtless established Hengist's reputation as a warrior. He was probably in his late twenties at this time, as he had been some years in exile and was old enough to be accepted as leader of the Half-Danes and to entreat with Finn on equal terms. It is possible that it was news of this episode that encouraged the British high king, Vortigern, to invite Hengist to Britain.

LIFE'S WORK

In the mid-fifth century, Britain was in a state of chaos, with civil wars between the native British punctuated by incursions by the Picts from the north and the Irish from the west. This disruption of the social fabric led to poor harvests and famine. In the midst of this turmoil, the Germanic invaders began to arrive, their forces peppering the eastern coastline of Britain from Bamburgh and the Forth estuary to Thanet and the Kentish coast. What marks Hengist's arrival as different is that he was invited and, in return for his services, was granted land. Whereas other Germanic colonies may have been won by conquest, Hengist's was, at least initially, authorized. Hengist was summoned at the request of Vortigern (whose real name may have been Vitalinus Vortigern, the latter a title that means "high king"). Bede is not specific about where Hengist settled, simply saying that it was in the "east of the island." The traditional landing place was Ebbsfleet, near Richborough in Kent, but this was probably the site of a later landing. Scholars David Dumville and John Morris, while disagreeing on many points, agree that the initial settlement was almost certainly in the north, probably around Bamburgh, a logical site for fighting the Picts. Hengist arrived with his brother Horsa in three boats, or "keels." Despite this small force, they were successful in pushing back the Picts. In gratitude, Vortigern granted Hengist and his men land in Thanet. According to Nennius, Hengist convinced Vortigern that he could be of greater assistance with additional warriors. Nennius reports that Hengist was able to appeal to the gullible

Vortigern by handing him his daughter, Reinwen, as his wife. Reinwen was probably only fifteen or so, and Hengist might have fathered her when he was about seventeen, which would place him in his early thirties, supporting the supposition that he was about thirty during the fight at Finnesburg.

Hengist brought to Britain his son Oisc, or Æsc (called "Octha" by Nennius), and his nephew Ebissa (possibly Horsa's son), along with forty ships. Oisc and Ebissa focused their efforts in the north, and the ensuing fighting evidently spread over several years. The *Anglo-Saxon Chronicle* suggests it lasted from 449 to 455, though the true date was probably later. At the end, Ebissa stayed in the north, but Oisc apparently joined his father in Kent. Later references suggest that Oisc remained in the north, so it is probable that he joined his father temporarily in order to provide reinforcements. The British, led by Vortigern's son Vortimer, were trying to drive the Jutes out of Britain. The sequence of events differs in the records, but all agree that there were a series of three or four battles in which the British gradually gained the upper hand. The most important of these was at Ægelesprep, or Aylesford, near Maidstone on the river

Medway, where Horsa was killed. The British may have claimed the victory, though the *Anglo-Saxon Chronicle* asserts that Hengist declared himself king of Kent after the battle. Perhaps negotiations set the river Medway as the frontier, with Hengist as ruler of the territory to the east. Vortimer continued to press Hengist's forces back. A third battle took place at an unknown location conjectured to be on the Wantsum, the river that once divided Thanet from mainland Kent. The victory again went to the British, and Hengist was forced back to Thanet and subsequently expelled from the island.

Vortimer, however, died soon afterward, reputedly poisoned by Reinwen, and Vortigern was too weak a king to resist Hengist. Hengist returned with more troops, and this time their advance was decisive. This may be the time of the Battle of Crayford, dated to 456 by the *Anglo-Saxon Chronicle* though it may have occurred as much as nineteen years later. Hengist's army routed the British and sent them fleeing to London. Hengist then called a peace conference. The British representatives were unarmed, but Hengist ordered his men to hide their knives in their boots. At his command, Hengist's men slaughtered the British, save only Vortigern. Most authorities regard this episode as fiction, but it is consistent with Hengist's character. The treachery is similar to that played on Finn and supports the argument that the two Hengists are the same and that he was the "shrewd and skilful" warrior Nennius described. Thereafter, Vortigern was forced to grant Hengist his wishes. According to the *Kentish Chronicle*, Hengist received not only Kent but also parts of what became Essex and Middlesex, including London. Hengist's triumph established his kingdom and opened up the Thames River route into the British heartland for the next wave of Saxons.

The final reference to Hengist in the *Anglo-Saxon Chronicle* is to the year 473, when, it is reported, he and his son again defeated the British and gained "innumerable spoils." Oisc succeeded to the kingdom in 488, which may be the year of Hengist's death; he would have been about sixty-eight, a remarkable age for a warrior. Bede, Nennius, and the *Anglo-Saxon Chronicle* remain silent on Hengist's fate, but Geoffrey of Monmouth reveals the full story with customary flair. He states that after Vortigern's death, Hengist was defeated by Aurelius Ambrosius (known otherwise as "Ambrosius Aurelianus") at Maisbeli, from where Hengist fled

Hengist, right, with Horsa, meets with British king Vortigern. (Hulton Archive by Getty Images)

to Kaerconan or Cunungeburg, identified by some as Knaresborough in Yorkshire. There, Hengist was captured, beheaded, and buried. Because Hengist's son Oisc was apparently still in the north of England, probably at York, at this time, Geoffrey's story remains within the realm of possibility, although certainly suspect.

It is because they were descended from Oisc that the members of the Kentish royal family were known as "Oiscingas." This raises the question of the relationship between Hengist and Oisc and the matter of Hengist's real name. "Hengist" means "stallion," while "Horsa" is interpreted as "wild horse." Some commentators have suggested that these were two names for the same person. However, the horse was probably an emblem of the brothers, and the names by which they were known could have been nicknames, not their real names. There is also some confusion in the genealogies over the name of Hengist's son. The *Kentish Chronicle* calls him "Octha," and the *Anglo-Saxon Chronicle* calls him "Æsc" or "Oisc." However, Bede states that Oisc's real name was "Oeric." It is possible that Bede's source confused these names. If Hengist's son was Oeric, then "Octha" might be Hengist's real name. This could account for Oeric's calling his own son "Octha," in memory of his father. The epithet "Oisc" (derived from *ossa*, meaning "gods") was a later veneration based on the tradition of ancestor worship, in which the forebears of the Angles were believed to be descended from the god Woden. Hengist may have been venerated in the same way, and Oeric was recognized as *Oisc*, the son of a god.

The argument about dates is far from resolved. John Morris proposed that Hengist arrived as early as 428, while David Dumville asserts that the correct date is closer to the year 480. The latter date is in keeping with errors in the early *Anglo-Saxon Chronicle* chronology, and it makes Oisc's age more realistic. He ruled for at least twenty-four years after 488, which suggests a birth date of no earlier than 450. Oisc's successors each ruled for around thirty years, a surprising span for those violent times. This unusual stability reinforces the view that Kent had been decisively won by Hengist, allowing its rulers to exist in relative peace.

SIGNIFICANCE

Although there were other contemporary Germanic invaders of Britain, such as Cerdic in Hampshire and Aelle in Sussex, their conquests were not decisive. The kingdom of the South Saxons was obliterated, and the West Saxons remained as a ragged series of confederate tribes for more than a century. Hengist enabled others to benefit

from a strong kingdom established by conquest and treaty and free from further British retaliation. Kent was the first of the Germanic kingdoms, and its early history, after Hengist, was relatively peaceful, allowing its people to trade, prosper, and develop a wealthy kingdom. Influential Frankish connections developed during the sixth century, almost certainly because of the strong base that Hengist established, and this paved the way for the arrival of Saint Augustine and the introduction of the Roman church to the English.

—Mike Ashley

FURTHER READING

Bassett, Steven, ed. *The Origins of Anglo-Saxon Kingdoms*. New York: Leicester University Press, 1989. Includes a chapter that looks specifically at the creation and early structure of the kingdom of Kent.

Kirby, D. P. *The Earliest English Kings*. New York: Routledge, 2000. A highly readable and remarkably integrated study of the development of early English kingships.

Morris, John. *The Age of Arthur*. Rev. ed. Chichester, England: Phillimore, 1977. A creative and often challenging study of Dark Ages Britain that throws new light on the Germanic invasion.

Tolkien, J. R. R., with Alan Bliss, ed. *Finn and Hengest: The Fragment and the Episode*. Boston: Houghton Mifflin, 1983. A detailed study of Hengist in *Beowulf* and his relationship to the Hengist of Bede. Challenging and original.

Witney, K. P. *The Kingdom of Kent*. Chichester, England: Phillimore, 1982. A thorough study of the first English kingdom, with a reasoned analysis of Hengist's contribution.

Yorke, Barbara. *Kings and Kingdoms of Early Anglo-Saxon England*. London: B. A. Seaby, 1992. Includes a detailed discussion on the origin of the Kentish kingdom and the roles of Hengist and Horsa.

SEE ALSO: Arminius; Boudicca; Genseric; Vercingetorix.

RELATED ARTICLES in *Great Events from History: The Ancient World*: c. 3100-c. 1550 B.C.E., Building of Stonehenge; c. 2300-c. 1800 B.C.E., Beaker People Live in Western Europe; 14th to 9th centuries B.C.E., Urnfield Culture Flourishes in Northwestern Europe; 15 B.C.E.-15 C.E., Rhine-Danube Frontier Is Established; 9 C.E., Battle of Teutoburg Forest; c. 3d-4th century C.E., Huns Begin Migration West from Central Asia; 449 C.E., Saxon Settlement of Britain Begins.

HERACLITUS OF EPHESUS
Greek philosopher

Heraclitus formulated one of the earliest and most comprehensive theories of the nature of the world, the cosmos, and the soul. His theory that the soul pervaded all parts of the universe and its inhabitants stood in contrast to the ideas of his more mechanistic contemporaries.

BORN: c. 540 B.C.E.; Ephesus, Greece
DIED: c. 480 B.C.E.; place unknown
AREA OF ACHIEVEMENT: Philosophy

EARLY LIFE

According to Diogenes Laertius, Heraclitus (hayr-uh-KLI-tuhs) was born in the city of Ephesus to an important family that had an ancient and respected reputation. Through his family, he inherited public office, but he resigned in favor of his brother. When his friend Hermodorus was expelled from Ephesus, Heraclitus protested publicly and subsequently withdrew from public life. Heraclitus was a man of great personal integrity whose main purpose in life was to find the truth and proclaim it for the benefit of humankind, irrespective of the consequences. He attacked the sacred festival of the Bacchanalia, condemned the worship of images of the gods, and spoke unkind words about Pythagoras, Xenophanes, Hecataeus, and Hesiod. His arrogance was legendary. Heraclitus insisted that he was the sole bearer of the truth. He thought that the multitude of common people were too weak of wit to understand the truth, claiming that his work was meant for the few who were intelligent.

To complicate the difficulty presented by this posture, his writings (those that survived) present special problems. Aristotle and Theophrastus observed that his statements were sometimes ambiguous, incomplete, and contradictory. It is no wonder that his contemporaries named him "The Riddler," "The Obscure One," and "The Dark One." Heraclitus was well aware of their criticism, but he was dedicated to his own high purposes.

LIFE'S WORK

Heraclitus's book was titled *Peri physeōs* (c. 500 B.C.E.; partial translation in *The Fragments of the Work of Heraclitus of Ephesus on Nature*, 1899). He dedicated the work to Artemis and left a scroll of it in her temple, an act that was not unusual in that culture. Heraclitus would not qualify as a scientist; his talent was more that of the mystic. He had the ability to see further into the nature of things than others did. He was the first to unify the nat-

ural and the spiritual worlds, while others saw only the discrete components of nature. Anaximander and Heraclitus both were impressed with the ceaseless change of the temporal world and formulated theories about the primal matter of the universe. Anaximander's primal matter was colorless and tasteless and otherwise had no characteristics. For Heraclitus, however, that which underlay the world of form and matter was not substance; it was process.

Heraclitus saw the world as a place where change, at every level and every phase of existence, was the most important phenomenon. The basic element of change, and at the heart of the process, was fire. The processes governing the world involved the four elements: fire, water, air, and earth. According to Heraclitus, fire was the element from which the others devolved, and it was always in motion. It was fire in the form of body heat that kept animal forms in motion; it was also able to transform and consume the other basic elements. In essence, air was hot and wet, water was cold and wet, earth was cold and dry, and fire was hot and dry. Under certain circumstances, each of the four elements could be transformed into another (enough water could quench fire; a hot enough fire could reduce earth to ash, or water to steam). All the possible transformations were happening at any given time somewhere in the universe, such as in the cooking of a meal, the thawing of the winter ice, the volcanism of Mount Etna—and even in phenomena unknown to Heraclitus, such as the atmospheric disturbances of the sunspot cycle or the explosion of a supernova.

Heraclitus described two fundamental directions of this change. In the downward path, some of the fire thickens and becomes the ocean, while part of the ocean dies and becomes land. On the upward path, moist exhalations from the ocean and the land rise and become clouds; they then ignite (perhaps in the form of lightning) and return to fire (presumably the fiery ether, which was thought to dwell in the heights of the sky). If the fiery clouds from which the lightning comes are extinguished, however, then there is a whirlwind (a waterspout, perhaps), and once again the fire returns to the sea and the cycle is complete.

All this change and transformation was not, however, simply random motion. There was a cosmic master plan, the Logos. Nothing in the English language translates "Logos" perfectly. As it stands in the beginning of the

Gospel of John, it is usually translated as the Word, which is clearly inadequate in context and requires a definition. In Heraclitus's time, Logos could mean reputation or high worth. This meaning devolved from another definition of Logos: narrative or story.

The flexibility of the word has been a source of considerable debate. The three most important meanings of the word are (1) general rule or general principle, (2) the carrying out of a general principle, and (3) that which belongs distinctly to the realm of humanness, the faculty of reasoning. First and foremost, the Logos is the universal law, or plan, or process, that animates the whole cosmos. The Logos is the cosmos; it inhabits the cosmos. It is also what makes the difference between the sleeping human and the awakened human. It is, in humans, the wisdom to perceive that the Logos (on the highest level of abstraction) is immanent in the cosmos, that it is the universe's governing principle. That is the fountainhead of true knowledge in Heraclitus's system: All humans have the Logos in common. What they specifically have in common is the realization or perception that they are a part of the whole, which is the Logos. Without that realization, they are fundamentally asleep. Within the slumbering human, the Logos lies dormant. Even if one is technically awake, however, one can still be subject to error if one follows one's own private "truth," that is, one's own inclinations, and prefers one's subjectivity more than one values the Logos. The self-dependence that one would call individuality could then be considered a violation of the Logos.

Though the physical senses are not attuned to the perception of the Logos, they are important in the process that leads to wisdom. For example, the ability to see is a prerequisite that may eventually lead to the perception that there is a plan to the universe. The senses are the mediators between that which is human and that which is cosmic. They are the windows that, during waking hours, connect the human with the portion of the Logos that can be perceived. During sleeping hours those channels are closed, and the direct participation in the cosmos ceases. Respiration then becomes a channel by which the direct access can be maintained; the act of breathing maintains minimal contact.

The Logos can be considered the soul of the universe. Each awakened human has a portion of higher enlightenment: the soul. Logos, Soul, and Cosmic Fire are eventually different aspects of the same abstraction—the everlasting truth that directs the universe and its conscious constituents. According to Heraclitus, the enlightened soul is hot and dry, like fire, which is why it tends up-

Heraclitus of Ephesus. (Library of Congress)

ward, in the direction of the fiery ether. Soul and ether are the same material.

Soul is linked to Logos, but its roots are in the human body that it inhabits. Soul is possibly the healing principle in the body: Heraclitus likened the soul to a spider that, when its web is torn, goes to the site of the injury. Soul is born from moisture and dies when it absorbs too much water. Drunkenness was to Heraclitus a truly bad habit: A moist soul had diminished faculties as its body was also diminished, in that its intellect was stunted and its physical strength lessened.

Though the body was subject to decomposition, some souls seem to have been exempted from physical death (becoming water). Certain situations, among them dying in battle, tune the soul to such a heightened state (with the soul unusually motivated and not weakened by illness and old age) that it merged directly with the world fire. After death, there seems to be no survival of personal identity, though it is likely that the soul-stuff is merged with the Logos and that the Logos is the source of souls that exist in the physical world. Evidently, soul material follows a cycling process of its own. Heraclitus saw that the world was a unity of many parts, but the unity was not immediately manifest. The oneness of the world was the result of an infinite multiplicity. Heraclitus thought that the key to understanding this multiplicity was to look on the world in terms of the abstract concept of Harmony.

Pythagoras had previously used musical harmony in explaining the attunement and orderliness that he saw in the universe. Heraclitus, however, used the concept of Harmony in a different way. He believed that Harmony existed only where and when there was opposition. A single note struck on a lyre has no harmony of itself. Any two notes struck together, however, form a tension or a contrast between the two sounds, creating a continuum of possible notes between the two that have been struck. In terms of a continuum of hot and cold temperatures, not only do the extremes exist, but so also does the continuum exist, bounded by the extremes. At every point between the extremes of hot and cold there is an identifiable point that has a specific temperature that is a function of both extremes.

Similarly, every virtue has a corresponding vice. Neither extreme on this scale is especially significant in human behavior: Few people, if any, represent extremes of either virtue or vice; most live in the continuum between. Ethical considerations motivate good individuals to tend toward the good in a choice between good and evil, and the measure of a person's soul is where one stands on the continuum defined by good and evil.

Heraclitus's most controversial statement on the subject was that the opposites that define the continuum are identical. Hate and love, therefore, would have to be one and the same. The absence of either defining term destroys the continuum, and without the continuum the two extremes cannot relate to each other. They define a world in which the people are passionate haters and ardent lovers, with no real people in between. The Harmony that Heraclitus discerned was dependent on the tension between two opposites. The cosmos was, for him, a carefully and beautifully balanced entity, poised between a great multiplicity of contrasting interests, engaged in continual strife. The sum total of all these contrasting interests, however, was the Harmony that no one saw except the truly enlightened souls. Only the Logos, which was One, and which created and tuned the Harmony, was exempt from the balancing of opposites.

Perhaps the best-known of Heraclitus's observations is that everything in the universe is incessantly moving and changing. He considered all matter to be in a state of constant transformation from one form to a different form and, at the same time, from one set of physical qual-

ities to another. Not only did he believe that the Logos bestowed life on all its parts, but he also believed that the forms of matter were intrinsically alive and that the flux was a function of the life within the matter. All life was caught up in the constant change: Everything was involved in processes of decomposition and in the reconstitution of new forms from the products of decay.

As the Greeks viewed the world, they saw only the portions of the movement that were available within the limits of their senses. Though they were not aware of the whole spectrum of movement, they were intelligent enough to extrapolate from what they could perceive. A continuous stream of water wearing away a stone was, to them, a good reminder of the fact that many processes of change were not perceptible in their time scale.

Heraclitus summed it up poetically in his famous analogy: "You cannot step twice into the same river, for fresh waters are flowing on." From one second to the next, the flux of things changes the world; though the river is the same river, the flux of things has moved its waters downstream, and new water from upstream has replaced the old. According to Diogenes Laertius and others, "The cosmos is born out of fire and again resolved into fire in alternate periods for ever." One line of interpretation is that the world is periodically destroyed by a universal conflagration. More plausible, however, is the assumption that this is a restatement of Heraclitus's doctrine that fire is the one primal element from which all others derive and into which all elements are eventually transmuted by the workings of the eternal flux. In support of this argument is a phrase from the remaining fragments of Heraclitus's work: "From all things one, and from one all things." In Heraclitus's cosmology, however, there was the concept of a Great Year that occurred every 10,800 years, at which time the sun, moon, and other heavenly bodies returned to a hypothetical starting place. These bodies, though they were not exempt from the principle of constant flux, were permanent in their forms and in their heavenly paths. Beyond the measured paths of their orbits was the fiery ether of the unmoving Logos.

SIGNIFICANCE

Heraclitus was quite unlike his contemporaries, both in terms of his personality and in the nature and scope of his thoughts. Whereas the works of his contemporaries were more in the line of primitive scientific inquiry, the endeavors of Heraclitus were more closely akin to poesy and perhaps prophecy. His aim was not to discover the material world but to seek out the governing principles within and behind the physical forms. In this respect, he was the most mystical of the Greeks.

Though the body of Heraclitus's work is faulted by time, by problems of interpretation, and by obscurity of the text (some of which was solely Heraclitus's fault), it is clear that he believed he had provided a definitive view of the processes that govern the cosmos and the workings of the human soul. His ideas were novel and daring in their time. At the center of his cosmos is the concept of constant change, which masks the concept of unity: All things are in balance, yet all things are in motion and transition, with fire playing the central role, and the Logos disposing and directing the parts. The Logos also governs human actions, reaching into the deeper parts of the personality, with the Oversoul touching the soul material within, fire outside calling to the fire within to awake, to look, to learn, to become, and to unite.

—Richard Badessa

FURTHER READING

Burnet, John. *Early Greek Philosophy.* 1892. 4th ed. London: A. and C. Black, 1963. Chapter 3 is devoted to Heraclitus and is probably the best of the nineteenth century English works that discuss Heraclitus. It has considerable insight and is readable without being dated.

Fairbanks, Arthur. *The First Philosophers of Greece.* London: K. Paul, Trench, Trübner, 1898. This volume has a good section on Heraclitus, including the Greek text of the fragments as well as an English translation. The discussion is short and basic and covers most of the important points.

Guthrie, W. K. C. *The Earlier Presocratics and the Pythagoreans.* Vol. 1 in *A History of Greek Philosophy.* New York: Cambridge University Press, 1978-1990. This volume is one of the best works on Heraclitus's contemporaries and contains an excellent extended discussion of Heraclitus.

Heraclitus. *The Cosmic Fragments.* Edited by G. S. Kirk. Cambridge, England: Cambridge University Press, 1975. A deep and thorough analysis of some of the Heraclitian fragments, this volume focuses on the "cosmic" fragments—those that are relevant to the world as a whole, the Logos, the doctrine of opposites, and the action of fire.

Kahn, Charles H. *The Art and Thought of Heraclitus: An Edition of the Fragments with Translation and Commentary.* New York: Cambridge University Press, 1979. This volume is a fine and useful scholarly tool, although not comprehensive. It includes the Greek text of the fragments and an English translation, as well as a short but very provocative appendix that discusses the possibility of a link between Heraclitus and the Orient.

Kirk, G. S., and J. E. Raven. *The Presocratic Philosophers: A Critical History with a Selection of Texts.* New York: Cambridge University Press, 1983. One of the chapters provides a very good short analysis of Heraclitus. The book itself is one of the very best on Greek thought and the individual Greek philosophers.

Mourelatos, Alexander. *The Pre-Socratics: A Collection of Critical Essays.* Princeton, N.J.: Princeton University Press, 1993. A collection of critical essays covering the major contemporaries of Heraclitus. Included in the book are four fine essays on Heraclitus.

Wheelwright, Philip. *Heraclitus.* Oxford, England: Oxford University Press, 1999. An excellent and well-written volume. Good bibliography.

SEE ALSO: Anaximander; Aristotle; Plato; Theophrastus.

RELATED ARTICLES in *Great Events from History: The Ancient World*: 600-500 B.C.E., Greek Philosophers Formulate Theories of the Cosmos; c. 530 B.C.E., Founding of the Pythagorean Brotherhood; c. 500-400 B.C.E., Greek Physicians Begin Scientific Practice of Medicine; c. 440 B.C.E., Sophists Train the Greeks in Rhetoric and Politics; 399 B.C.E., Death of Socrates; c. 380 B.C.E., Plato Develops His Theory of Ideas; c. 350 B.C.E., Diogenes Popularizes Cynicism; c. 335-323 B.C.E., Aristotle Writes the *Politics*; c. 300 B.C.E., Stoics Conceptualize Natural Law.

HERO OF ALEXANDRIA
Egyptian scientist and inventor

Hero wrote about mechanical devices and is the most important ancient authority on them. Some of these were his own inventions, including a rudimentary steam engine and windmill. He also investigated mathematics, where his most noted contribution was a method for approximating square roots.

FLOURISHED: 62 C.E.; Alexandria, Egypt
ALSO KNOWN AS: Heron of Alexandria
AREAS OF ACHIEVEMENT: Mathematics, science

EARLY LIFE

Virtually nothing is known about the personal life of Hero (HEE-roh), also known as Heron, of Alexandria, other than the fact that an eclipse of the moon visible from Alexandria and mentioned in one of his books occurred in 62 C.E. Under the Roman Empire, Alexandria flourished somewhat less than it had under the Ptolemies, but the famous museum was still a center of research and learning where scientists and philosophers were active. Technology also continued to make amazing strides, so that Hero found an atmosphere conducive to his own theories and inventions. His writings show that he was an educated man, familiar with Greek, Latin, Egyptian, and even Mesopotamian sources, and reveal a wide-ranging mind unusual for his time. There is no indication that he worked for either a Roman patron or the Roman government.

LIFE'S WORK

Hero's greatest renown results from the fact that many of his writings on mechanics and mathematics are extant. The mechanical works include the two-volume *Pneumatica* (*The Pneumatics of Hero of Alexandria*, 1851), on devices operated by compressed air, steam, and water; *Peri automatopoietikes* (*Automata*, 1971), on contrivances to produce miraculous appearances in temples; the three-volume *Mechanica*, surviving in Arabic, on weight-moving machines; *Dioptra* (partial English translation, 1963), on instruments for sighting and other purposes; *Catoptrica* (surviving in Latin), on mirrors; and two artillery manuals, *Belopoeïca* (English translation, 1971) and *Cheiroballistra* (English translation, 1971), on different types of catapults. Missing are other works on weight-lifting machines (*Baroulkos*, which might be a name for part of *Mechanica*), water clocks, astrolabes, balances, and the construction of vaults.

Of his mathematical treatises, there exist the three-volume *Metrica*, on the measurement and division of surfaces and bodies, and *Definitiones*, on geometrical terms. There are other works, more or less heavily edited by later redactors, such as *Geometrica*, *Stereometrica*, and *Peri metron* (also known as *Mensurae*), all treatises on measurement, as well as *Geodaesia* and *Geoponica* or *Liber geeponicus*, on the measurement of land. A commentary on Euclid is represented by extensive quotations in the Arabic work of an-Nairīzī.

The contents of Hero's mechanical works reveal the state of technological knowledge during the early Roman Empire, reflecting the heritage of the Hellenistic period and Ptolemaic Alexandria in particular. Later writers referred to him as "the mechanic" (*ho mechanikos*). In most cases, he gives the best or most complete description extant of ancient machines. In *Mechanica*, he gives attention to the simple machines—lever, pulley, wheel and axle, inclined plane, screw, and wedge—but he goes on to present others, there and in his other books, that are more complex.

Devices described by Hero include a machine for cutting screw threads on a wooden cylinder; a syringe; an apparatus for throwing water on a fire by hydraulic pressure, which is produced by a two-cylinder force pump (designed by the earlier Alexandrian mechanic, Ctesibius); and the odometer, for measuring distances by a wheeled vehicle. Of value to scholars, there was a pantograph for enlarging drawings and an automatic wick-trimmer for lamps. Hero provides a careful account of the diopter, a sighting instrument used in surveying and astronomy that contains sophisticated gears.

The automata mentioned by Hero are of fascinating variety, including singing birds, drinking animals, hissing serpents, dancing bacchants, and gods such as Dionysus and Hercules performing various actions. Some of these were activated by lighting a fire on an altar or pouring libations into a container, and their effect on worshipers when seen in temples can be imagined. Hero also described coin-operated machines to dispense holy water, a sacred wand that whistled when dipped into water, and a device powered by heated air that would open temple doors without any visible human effort. In order to invent such a device, Hero had to recognize that a vessel containing air was not empty but contained a substance that could exert force, a fact that he clearly explained in *The Pneumatics*. His demonstration depends on the observation that water will not enter a vessel filled with air unless the air is allowed to escape. He also was aware that air is compressible, which he said was the result of its being made up of particles separated by space.

The nonproductive character of some of the inventions just mentioned has led some modern critics to call Hero's technology impractical, but he also described demonstrably useful machines. Cranes, which could be used to lower actors portraying gods into theaters (the famous *deus ex machina*), also were available to help in heavy construction. There were other weight-lifting machines utilizing gears. Cogs and gears were highly developed even before Hero's day, as archaeological evidence such as the Antikythera Machine, a calendrical, mechanical analogue computer retrieved from the Aegean Sea, demonstrates. Hero also described a twin screw press. He knew the use of compound pulleys, winches, and cogwheels interacting with screws. Not merely theoretical, his catapults were effective in war, particularly in siege operations. There was also the *gastraphetes*, or "belly shooter," a kind of crossbow.

Hero's most famous invention was a prototype steam engine called the aeolipile. A free-spinning, hollow sphere was mounted on a pipe and bracket on the lid of a boiling vessel. Steam from the vessel came up through the pipe and escaped through open, bent pipes on the sphere's surface, causing the sphere to rotate. Less often remarked upon but also significant is his windmill, used to work the water pump of a musical organ. Both of these show that Hero recommended harnessing sources of power that were not actually exploited until centuries later. In the form in which he presented them, to be sure, these engines were extremely inefficient, and the industrial processes of the first century might not have allowed improvement to the point where they could have been widely used.

In mathematics, Hero emphasized pragmatic applications rather than pure theory. For example, he showed methods of approximating the values of square and cube roots. In his writings on geometry, he followed Euclid closely, making only minor original comments or improvements. The first book of *Peri metron* deals with the mensuration of plane and solid figures, and the second explains the ways to calculate the volumes of various solids. The third explains problems of the division of plane and solid figures.

SIGNIFICANCE

Hero of Alexandria looms large in the history of ancient technology because a considerable portion of his writings on mechanics still exists, while little else on the subject survives from the Greek and Roman world. He preserved much information that came to him from earlier writers whose works have been lost, and his own contribution has been downgraded by some modern scholars because it is unclear how much he owes to previous writers, including Archimedes, Strato of Lampsacus, Philon of Byzantium, and especially Ctesibius of Alexandria. This tendency is probably unfair, however, as his work reflects a systematic mind and tireless research. Moreover, some of his ideas, such as the harnessing of steam and wind power, were clearly ahead of their time.

Although he was interested in the principles of mechanics, Hero was not primarily a theoretician. His mechanics and his mathematics are presented in a way that would have made them useful to the practical engineer of his day. For example, in *Stereometrica*, he shows how to calculate the number of spectators a theater would hold and the number of wine jars that could be stacked in the hold of a ship of a certain size. Both are approximations intended for utilitarian needs.

Hero's writings were prized by later authors. Both Pappus of Alexandria (fourth century C.E.) and Proclus (fifth century) quoted from his works. Some of his works were translated and preserved by learned Arabs, and an-Nairīzī commented extensively on Hero's critique of Euclid. Four of Hero's shorter books on mechanics were published in Paris in 1693, and interest in Hero accelerated with the Industrial Revolution. In the twentieth century, he continued to receive attention, in histories of mechanics and mathematics.

—J. Donald Hughes

FURTHER READING

Drachmann, Aage Gerhardt. *The Mechanical Technology of Greek and Roman Antiquity: A Study of the Literary Sources*. Madison: University of Wisconsin Press, 1963. Contains translations of Hero's mechanical writings, with useful running commentary. Also including sections from Vitruvius and Oreibasios, this book gives a clear idea of the written evidence for ancient mechanical technology.

Heath, Thomas. *A History of Greek Mathematics*. 2 vols. New York: Dover, 1981. Volume 2 includes an excellent, detailed chapter on Hero's mathematical achievements.

Landels, John G. *Engineering in the Ancient World*. Berkeley: University of California Press, 2000. Hero is discussed in the context of the development of technology, and Landels provides a useful brief treatment of Hero and his major writings in the final chapter.

Marsden, E. W. *Greek and Roman Artillery: Technical Treatises*. Oxford, England: Clarendon Press, 1971. This book includes the texts and translation of Hero's two works on war machines, *Belopoïeca* and *Cheiroballistra*, with illuminating diagrams and helpful notes and commentary.

Singer, Charles Joseph, ed. *From the Renaissance to the Industrial Revolution, c. 1500-c. 1750*. Vol. 3 in *A History of Technology*. Oxford, England: Clarendon Press, 1954-1984. Despite its title, volume 3 contains an informative section on Hero's diopter.

SEE ALSO: Archimedes; Ctesibius of Alexandria; Euclid; Pappas; Proclus.

RELATED ARTICLES in *Great Events from History: The Ancient World*: 332 B.C.E., Founding of Alexandria; c. 300 B.C.E., Euclid Compiles a Treatise on Geometry.

HEROD THE GREAT
Judaean king (r. 37-4 B.C.E.)

As a loyal king of Judaea under Roman administration, Herod brought peace, prosperity, and a cultural flowering to the land he ruled. Nevertheless, negative aspects of his reign—including harsh dealings with family members and the inability to placate his Jewish subjects—have tended to overshadow these positive achievements.

BORN: 73 B.C.E.; probably Idumaea (now in Palestine)
DIED: Spring, 4 B.C.E.; Jericho, Judaea (now in Palestine)
ALSO KNOWN AS: Herodes Magnus (Latin name)
AREA OF ACHIEVEMENT: Government and politics

EARLY LIFE

Herod (HEHR-uhd) was born into a prominent family of Idumaeans, an Arab people whose capital was Hebron, a city south of Jerusalem. During the time of Herod's grandfather, Antipater, Idumaea had been conquered by Jewish armies and its citizens were forced to convert to Judaism. It is not clear, at that time or in subsequent periods, exactly how deeply the beliefs and practices of Judaism were ingrained into the lives of Idumaeans such as Herod's family.

At the time of the Idumaean conquest, the Jews of the Holy Land were politically independent and ruled over by a royal family known as the Hasmonaeans. They were descendants of Judas Maccabaeus and his brothers, who had led a successful revolt (beginning in 168 or 167 B.C.E.) against their Syrian overlords and for the continuance of the monotheistic faith of Israel. When the Idumaeans came under Jewish domination later in that century, Herod's grandfather served members of the Hasmonaean Dynasty with some distinction. Herod's father, also named Antipater, in turn was also closely allied to some of the Hasmonaeans. By the time of Herod's birth, a rift had developed in the Jewish royal family, with two brothers, Aristobulus and Hyrcanus, vying for the throne and the religiously significant position of high priest. Herod's father supported the elder of the brothers, Hyrcanus, but the matter was still in doubt when the rival claimants both appealed for support to the Roman general Pompey the Great, then in Damascus, Syria. That was in 63 B.C.E., when Herod himself was about ten years old.

Antipater's maneuvers were decisive in winning Pompey's support for Hyrcanus, whose personality seemed as weak and passive as Antipater's was aggressive and active. During the years that Herod was growing up, his father continued to show support for Hyrcanus. In fact, Antipater's actions were aimed as much at bringing his own family to the favorable notice of powerful Romans. These twin concerns—family and Rome—continued to be prominent in the subsequent career of Antipater's most famous son, Herod.

In the early 40's, Julius Caesar became a force in the Near East, and Antipater provided him with significant military support. For this, he was rewarded by Caesar, who confirmed his growing prestige while not totally displacing the Hasmonaean Hyrcanus. Antipater was able to name Herod as governor of the area of Galilee and to place others of his children (he had four sons and a daughter) in positions of power. Shortly after Caesar's death, Antipater was assassinated, a murder that Herod himself avenged. In the decade that followed, the confusion in Rome was mirrored in the provinces, and local leaders such as Herod had to be resourceful to retain power—and their lives. Herod succeeded admirably.

Hyrcanus's brother had been killed, but one of his nephews joined with the Parthians (eastern rivals to the Romans) to wrest the throne from Hyrcanus. The resultant civil war forced Herod to flee. This turned out to be but a temporary setback, however, for Herod ultimately reached Rome and gained the friendship and backing of the two most powerful individuals of the day, Marc Antony and Octavian (later Augustus). In response to their urging, the senate of Rome declared that henceforth Herod was to be king of Judaea. That was in the year 40 B.C.E., when Herod was in his early thirties.

LIFE'S WORK

On the basis of his family background and earlier achievements, it would appear that Herod was an ideal choice to occupy the kingship of Judaea—at least from the Roman point of view. He and his family had shown themselves to be loyal subjects and deft leaders. Herod, it seemed, could give the Romans what they wanted most: steady payment of taxes and other levies, military support against common enemies, and internal peace and stability within the lands he ruled. Moreover, Herod possessed physical characteristics that the Romans appreciated. He was tall, athletic, and able to enjoy and appreciate manly activities such as hunting and riding. Dressed in proper Roman garb, he looked and acted at home in the courts of the powerful Romans whom he had to please.

There is every reason to think that his Roman benefactors were very pleased indeed with Herod's initial actions. In 40 B.C.E., he became a king in name, but not in fact, for his capital, Jerusalem, was still in the hands of his rivals. Within three years, that is, by 37 B.C.E., he had regained control of his capital and the land that was now his kingdom. At this point, Herod probably looked forward to a long and relatively serene reign. He had longevity (approximately thirty-three years); serenity was to prove far more elusive.

From the beginning, there were substantial numbers of Jewish subjects who doubted the depth of Herod's commitment to Judaism. His Idumaean ancestry led to the taunt that he was but a half Jew. His commitment to Rome, with its polytheism and philosophical pluralism, was—in the opinion of many in Jerusalem—incompatible with the relatively austere monotheistic faith of Israel. Criticisms of Herod in this regard preceded his assumption of the kingship, and they undoubtedly increased as he consolidated power. A more pressing challenge, however, soon presented itself.

Herod was a king, and there was no mistaking it. However, the Jews still had their own royal dynasty in the surviving members of the Hasmonaean family. Hyrcanus, while essentially powerless, was still a potential rival. Herod sought to neutralize this threat, even turn it to his advantage, by marrying Hyrcanus's granddaughter, Mariamne. Now, he may have thought, people would at last tire of bringing up details of his past, for the children he and Mariamne would produce would be royal from both the Jewish and the Roman perspectives. If such were his thoughts, he erred grievously. Hyrcanus was too old to pose a threat, but Mariamne's mother, Alexandra, and eventually Mariamne herself were not. Then, too, there was Mariamne's brother Aristobulus, whom Herod was forced to appoint as high priest. One by one, these Hasmonaeans were to be eliminated by Herod, for faults real and imagined. His murder of Mariamne in 29 B.C.E. was especially unsettling for Herod and may have pushed him to—and over—the brink of mental disorder and instability. In his anti-Hasmonaean actions, Herod was generally supported by members of his Idumaean family and in particular by his sister, Salome.

The Romans were not overly concerned about Herod's domestic problems at this time. Herod had grown very close to Antony, who was the virtual ruler of the eastern portion of the Empire that included the lands Herod governed. When Antony did intervene, it was usually at the insistence of his queen, Cleopatra VII, who, according to one account, coveted the person of Herod as much as she did his lands. The civil war of the late 30's that pitted Antony against Octavian found Herod contin-

Herod the Great. (Hulton\Archive by Getty Images)

uing to provide vital assistance to his benefactor, Antony. It is a credit to Herod's extraordinary abilities as diplomat and as briber that Octavian allowed him to retain his position after Antony's resounding defeat.

The fifteen-year period from 28 to 13 B.C.E. was the high point of Herod's reign. The most visible sign of this prosperity was the ambitious building program that Herod undertook. Throughout his kingdom and beyond, he constructed temples, amphitheaters, and even an entire city (Caesarea, on the Mediterranean coast) to honor the Romans and the civilization they represented. Part of that civilization was the worship of many gods through sacrificial offerings, athletic and dramatic competitions, and a wide array of other public functions. Herod actively promoted such activities, partly because he knew that they were important to his Roman overlords and partly—it is fair to say—because he enjoyed them. The Romans and their gods had been good to him, and he was only giving them their due.

Herod was not without gratitude toward the God of Israel, whose people he ruled and whose favor he also solicited. Herod's rebuilding of the Temple of Jerusalem, a vast complex that stood at the very center of the Judaism of his day, was the most tangible expression of his concerns in this regard. Moreover, he sometimes was able to accommodate his own ambitions to the religious sensitivities of his subjects. For example, he generally refrained from setting up images—which would be seen as infringements of the Ten Commandments—in locations where they would attract attention. Nevertheless, most Judaean Jews were not as "broad-minded" as their monarch, nor did they regularly join in the praise Herod received when he aided Jewish communities outside Judaea.

During the last ten years of his life, domestic difficulties came to overshadow and almost cancel out all else. Herod had married ten times and had fathered numerous children. As he grew older, several of his sons grew bolder in their efforts to guarantee that they would succeed him. Some of them may even have plotted to hasten the day of their father's death. The most prominent players in this deadly game were Mariamne's sons, Alexander and Aristobulus, and Antipater, the son of Herod's first wife. Mariamne's sons, as the last heirs of the Hasmonaean Dynasty, were especially dangerous. They may well have been guilty of treasonous activities against the man who had killed their mother, uncle, grandmother, and great-grandfather. In this case, Augustus was unable to effect a final reconciliation between father and sons. Their execution occurred in 7 or 6 B.C.E.

Herod was almost seventy years old, in very poor health, and in need of an heir.

For most of the period until his death, that heir was Antipater. Unwilling to wait gracefully, he persisted in meddling in his father's plans to arrange the marriages of other offspring. More important, he grew impatient, and that impatience cost him his life and the throne just prior to Herod's own death in the early spring of 4 B.C.E. Herod managed to identify three of his sons whom he judged to be worthy of portions of his kingdom. When Augustus, who was a prime financial beneficiary of Herod's will, confirmed these choices, Herod's legacy was, in one sense, complete and secure. In another sense, there is much about Herod's legacy that is puzzling, even troubling.

SIGNIFICANCE

It is difficult for scholars to take the measure of Herod as a man and as a ruler. This difficulty is almost as old as Herod himself. Nearly everything that is known of Herod is contained in the works of the Jewish historian Flavius Josephus, who wrote almost a century after Herod's death. Josephus used both pro- and anti-Herod sources and was not without biases of his own. Moreover, Josephus described Herod's reign in two separate writings, *Bellum Judaium* (75-79 C.E.; *History of the Jewish War*, 1773) and *Antiquitates Judaicae* (93 C.E.; *The Antiquities of the Jews*, 1773), and the accounts are often contradictory. The problem described here is not unique to Herod. It recurs, for example, in the study of Alexander the Great, Julius Caesar, and other leaders of antiquity.

In the case of Herod, it does seem possible to affirm certain things. His loyalty to Rome and the values it espoused is beyond question. His ability to conceive and carry out large-scale building projects cannot be doubted. His success in organizing his kingdom to produce vast revenues for Rome, himself, and his supporters was an impressive, if not always welcome, accomplishment. All of this was compatible, in Herod's view, with a devotion to the Jewish religion and to the Jewish people. Herod undoubtedly believed that loyal support for Rome was the only hope for Jewish survival. Rebellion could only lead to disaster—a judgment that the Jewish revolts of the following centuries revealed as all too true.

Balanced against Herod's achievements was, first of all, a cruelty so monstrous that it led the author of the Gospel of Matthew to write that Herod had ordered the slaughter of innocent children (see Matthew, chapter 2). Many historians do not believe that such an event ever occurred. Nevertheless, a man who would slaughter close members of his own family was certainly capable of the actions Matthew attributed to him. It was actions of this sort that led Augustus to say, in a play on words in Latin, that he would have preferred to be Herod's pig than his son—or, one might add, his wife, his mother-in-law, or brother-in-law. Even in an admittedly violent age, it must be acknowledged, Herod's cruelty, perhaps the result of some mental disorder, stands out.

Herod's view of Judaism and Jewish survival was not without value. Still, it is hard to see what sort of Judaism Herod actually had in mind. His active support for polytheistic institutions would, it seems likely, have ultimately led to a dilution of Judaism's insistence on monotheism. A Jewish people may then have survived, but without the distinctive features of their ancestral religion.

Sometime in antiquity, the epithet "the Great" was first applied to Herod. Initially, it may have served to designate him as an older son of Antipater or to distinguish him from several other individuals named Herod who followed him. At some point, it came to describe certain elements of his personality and career. In that context, it is appropriate. In an overall evaluation of Herod, however, "great" is not the word most likely to come to mind for most observers of this complex and somehow fascinating man.

—Leonard J. Greenspoon

FURTHER READING

Grant, Michael. *Herod the Great*. New York: American Heritage Press, 1971. A straightforward account of the reign of Herod. Grant takes care to place Herod in the larger political and cultural context of first century B.C.E. Rome. Viewed from this perspective, Herod, while far from a saint, is not quite the total sinner that he is made out to be in many other modern accounts. Includes illustrations.

Hoehner, Harold W. *Herod Antipas*. Cambridge, England: Cambridge University Press, 1972. A detailed account of the reign of one of Herod's heirs. It is particularly valuable because of its extensive bibliography that fully covers the reign of Herod and his successors.

Josephus, Flavius. *Josephus*. Books 1-3. Translated by H. St. James Thackeray. Cambridge, Mass.: Harvard University Press, 1998. As described above, these are the primary ancient sources for the personal and public life of Herod. In this Loeb Classical Library edition, the original Greek text of Josephus is printed along with an authoritative English translation and notes. This is the essential starting point for all research on Herod.

Perowne, Stewart. *The Life and Times of Herod the Great*. 1956. Reprint. New York: Sutton, 2003. A balanced and sober account. Like Grant, Perowne makes the point that Herod was largely a product of his own time and must, to a degree at least, be judged by the standards of that period. Perowne continued his narrative in a second volume titled *The Later Herods*.

Roller, Duane W. *The Building Program of Herod the Great*. Berkeley: University of California Press, 1998. A systematic presentation of all the building projects known to have been part of Herod's architectural achievement. Each is discussed within a broad historical and cultural context.

Sandmel, Samuel. *Herod: Profile of a Tyrant*. Philadelphia: J. B. Lippincott, 1967. A clear and well-written account of the life and times of Herod. Sandmel attempts to re-create Herod's mental state at key moments, such as when he had Mariamne killed. The author's overall assessment of Herod is succinctly captured in the subtitle of his book.

SEE ALSO: Marc Antony; Augustus; Julius Caesar; Cleopatra VII; Jesus.

RELATED ARTICLES in *Great Events from History: The Ancient World*: 51-30 B.C.E., Cleopatra VII, Last of Ptolemies, Reigns; 43-42 B.C.E., Second Triumvirate Enacts Proscriptions; 27-23 B.C.E., Completion of the Augustan Settlement; c. 6 B.C.E., Birth of Jesus Christ; September 8, 70 C.E., Roman Destruction of the Temple of Jerusalem.

HERODOTUS
Greek historian

Herodotus is commonly called "the father of history" for having written the first work of history, a narrative that covered his world, from the age of myth to his own time.

BORN: c. 484 B.C.E.; Halicarnassus, Asia Minor (now Bodrum, Turkey)
DIED: c. 425 B.C.E.; Thurii, Lucania (now in Italy)
ALSO KNOWN AS: Herodotus of Halicarnassus
AREA OF ACHIEVEMENT: Historiography

EARLY LIFE

Herodotus (hih-RAHD-uh-tuhs) was born about 484 B.C.E. into a notable family of Halicarnassus, near the modern city of Bodrum, Turkey. He received the customary education available to well-born Greek men of his day. An intellectual and creative ferment was sweeping the Greek world, and Miletus, a major center of this enlightenment, was only about 40 miles (65 kilometers) from Halicarnassus. Such philosopher-scientists as Anaximander and Thales and the geographer Hecataeus influenced Herodotus. He read Hesiod, Sappho, Sophocles, Aeschylus, and Pindar, and also learned from the Sophists. The writings of Homer, in particular, shaped his worldview. If the intellectual atmosphere of the Greek world encouraged Herodotus to study the affairs of humans, it was probably Homer's masterpiece on the Trojan War, the *Iliad* (c. 750 B.C.E.; English translation, 1611), that caused Herodotus to recognize that the Persian invasion of Greece, which had occurred when he was a child, was the great drama of his own age.

His early surroundings also educated Herodotus. The rich diversity of cultures in Asia Minor provided the foundation for the remarkable cosmopolitan scope and tone of his writing. Travel further shaped his mind. According to tradition, he went into a brief exile to Samos after taking part in Halicarnassian political upheavals and later left his home city permanently. His travels took him to Athens, where intellectual and artistic life was flourishing in the age of Pericles. Around 443, Herodotus joined a Greek colony at Thurii, in Italy. From there, he probably continued the travels that provided the foundation for his history. He later said that he had interviewed people from forty Greek states and thirty foreign nations. No physical descriptions of Herodotus exist, but his travels in the ancient world testify to his physical vigor and strength and to his insatiable curiosity.

LIFE'S WORK

As Homer had preserved the stories of the Trojan War by rendering them into poetry, Herodotus came to realize that during his childhood another historic confrontation had occurred between the East and the West. The Persian War embodied all the drama and tragedy of human life, and its effects reverberated through his lifetime. He captured this human drama in one of the world's first great prose works and pioneered a new form of intellectual endeavor, history.

Herodotus states his intentions in the first sentence of *Historiai Herodotou* (c. 424 B.C.E.; *The History*, 1709):

> I, Herodotus of Halicarnassus, am here setting forth my history, that time may not draw the color from what man has brought into being, nor those great and wonderful deeds, manifested by both Greeks and barbarians, fail of their report, and, together with all this, the reason why they fought one another.

He intended to transmit to future generations the record of men and women's deeds in this dramatic era, and in so doing explore the tragedy of human existence. In Herodotus's worldview, people were subject to a cosmic order working by rules that they did not understand, an order in which fate or destiny destroyed those who aspired to excessive achievements. He would show that rationalism, a growing force in his age, could not protect against the contingencies of existence. Nevertheless, though humans could not change the cosmic order, Herodotus could combat the ravages of time by preserving the memory of their deeds. Herodotus was interested in people and in all of their diverse ways of living and acting. He used his history to contrast East and West, detailing the diversity of the peoples of the known world but finding common humanity beneath the differences.

Herodotus wrote a narrative history of his world, from the age of myth to his own time. He did not have available to him the kinds of written records on which modern historians rely but based his history on oral accounts. He placed most trust in his own experience and others' eyewitness accounts but used hearsay when he deemed it proper to do so. Regarding the latter, he wrote: "I must tell what is said, but I am not at all bound to believe it, and this comment of mine holds about my whole *History*." He sometimes recorded stories that he found dubious because he realized that just as time changed the fortunes of all people, it changed truth also. At times, he recorded material that seemed significant despite its questionable validity, because its meaning might become clear in the future. He was aware that there was a mythical element in much that people told him, but he realized as well that human myths carry a truth that makes them as important as other interpretations of reality.

Herodotus, the father of history, more than almost any of his offspring, was a master storyteller, able to hold the interest of his audience today as easily as he did thousands of years ago. He begins his story with Croesus, the last king of Lydia, who, after having begun the Asiatic incursion against the Greeks, trapped himself in the web of fate by believing himself the most blessed of humankind. Cyrus the Great conquered Croesus and began constructing the huge and powerful Persian Empire. Through the nine books of *The History*, Herodotus follows Cyrus, Cambyses, Darius the Great, and finally Xerxes I as these Persian rulers extended their power over the known world of Asia and Africa. Eventually, they turned to Europe and the Greeks.

As Herodotus follows Persian expansion, he begins his renowned "digressions" on the Lydians, Egyptians, Assyrians, Scythians, Libyans, Greeks, and others. In these digressions, which make up the bulk of *The History*, he describes the geography and economies of the various lands, the religious practices of the people, the roles of women, and the customs of everyday life. Human creations fascinated him, and he carefully described the pyramids, the walls surrounding Babylon, canal systems, and famous temples.

The so-called digressions are a carefully wrought expression of Herodotus's larger purposes in writing *The History*. A religious man, he wanted to show that all people, Greeks and Asians alike, were living in a cosmos that destroyed the excessive aspirations of even the best and greatest. Herodotus also intended to use the story of the Persian War as a backdrop to his study of the range of possibilities expressed by humans in their social, political, and spiritual lives. He seldom condemned any custom he described but gloried in the spectacle of life and in human achievements. The digressions, then, are part of his examination of the human condition. He knew that any custom, no matter how strange, had validity and meaning for the people who observed it: "As for the stories told by the Egyptians, let whoever finds them credible use them." The Persian ruler Cambyses revealed his madness, Herodotus believed, when he stabbed the Egyptian sacred bull. If he had not been mad,

> he would never have set about the mockery of what other men hold sacred and customary. For if there were a proposition put before mankind, according to which each should, after examination, choose the best customs in the world, each nation would certainly think its own customs the best. Indeed, it is natural for no one but a madman to make a mockery of such things.

Herodotus adds, "I think Pindar is right when he says, 'Custom is king of all.'"

Whether from the shadows of the pyramids or from the walls of Babylon, Herodotus's gaze always returned to the developing conflict of Greece with the steadily expanding Persian Empire. He gives attention to Darius's first probe into Europe, blocked by the Greeks at the Battle of Marathon in 490. Darius then laid careful plans to conduct a full-scale invasion, but he died before he could make another foray into the Greek world. In 480, his successor, Xerxes I, invaded with a huge force. The Greeks

Herodotus. (Library of Congress)

fought heroically at Thermopylae, and in such battles as Salamis and Plataea, Athens, Sparta, and other Greek city-states they defeated the Persians. It is here that Herodotus's history comes to a close. Most historians believe that *The History* was published in stages between 430 and 424, although a minority of historians believe it contains references to events as late as 421. Most scholars place Herodotus's death at about 425, in Thurii.

SIGNIFICANCE

Herodotus has attracted extravagant admiration. He has been commonly called the father of history, and some see him as an equally great geographer, anthropologist, and folklorist. He had his detractors also, one of whom called him "the father of lies." He was too cosmopolitan to fit well with the surge of Greek patriotism of later years. Some critics saw him as a detractor of the gods because he spoke so casually of religious practices that differed from the Greeks', but others, in more rational ages, regarded him as too superstitious. As the centuries passed, his admiration for the East and his breadth of sympathy for different cultures placed him out of step with the parochial West.

Herodotus always, however, had his admirers, who usually regarded him as a charming, if credulous, storyteller. His work was first translated into English in 1584, but scholars neglected him until the nineteenth century, when archaeology began to verify much of his account. Even then, his work was seen as a loose collection of moral tales of great actors.

His achievement became clearer as twentieth century historians traced the evolution of historical writing and more fully understood the intellectual breakthrough Herodotus had made in separating history from other intellectual endeavors. He established the methods that historians still use: gathering evidence, weighing its credibility, selecting from it, and writing a prose narrative. He assumed a role of neutrality, of objectivity; while expressing personal opinions, he never dropped his stance of universal sympathy. He tried to find the rational causes and effects of events, yet he was skeptical enough to understand that rationalism could not explain everything, perhaps not even the most important things, in human life. In recent years, admiration for him has grown as scholars have used literary analysis to show how tightly integrated were the famous Herodotean anecdotes and digressions into his larger purposes. His book is a literary masterpiece and one of the greatest works of history produced in the Western world.

—*William E. Pemberton*

FURTHER READING

Bakker, Egbert J., Irene J. F. De Jong, and Hans Van Wees, eds. *Brill's Companion to Herodotus*. Boston: Brill, 2002. Includes essays on Athens, oral strategies in the language of Herodotus, epic heritage and mythical patterns, the intellectual trends of Herodotus's time, the Persian invasions, and more.

De Sélincourt, Aubrey. *The World of Herodotus*. San Francisco: North Point Press, 1982. This work retraces Herodotus's literary journal based on twentieth century knowledge of his world. De Sélincourt translated *The History* for the Penguin Classics series.

Evans, J. A. *Herodotus*. Boston: Twayne, 1982. This biography covers the known facts of Herodotus's life and clearly explains the various scholarly controversies surrounding him.

Flory, Stewart. *The Archaic Smile of Herodotus*. Detroit: Wayne State University Press, 1987. An analysis of literary motifs in *The History*, showing the tightness of its structure and the larger purposes Herodotus had in mind, beyond chronicling the Persian War.

Herodotus. *The History*. Translated by David Grene. Chicago: University of Chicago Press, 1987. This translation includes a commentary that provides an excellent introduction to Herodotus. Illustrated with helpful maps.

How, Walter W., and Joseph Wells, eds. *A Commentary on Herodotus: With Introduction and Appendixes*. 2 vols. New York. Oxford University Press, 1989-1990. This is the standard commentary on Herodotus and provides almost a line-by-line analysis.

Hunter, Virginia. *Past and Process in Herodotus and Thucydides*. Princeton, N.J.: Princeton University Press, 1982. An analysis of the first two historians, finding great similarities in their worldviews.

Myres, John L. *Herodotus, Father of History*. Reprint. Chicago: Henry Regnery, 1971. Myres reveals the tight and deliberate construction of *The History*.

SEE ALSO: Croesus; Cyrus the Great; Darius the Great; Xerxes I.

RELATED ARTICLES in *Great Events from History: The Ancient World*: 520-518 B.C.E., Darius the Great Conquers the Indus Valley; 520-518 B.C.E., Scylax of Caryanda Voyages the Indian Ocean; September 17, 490 B.C.E., Battle of Marathon; 480-479 B.C.E., Persian Invasion of Greece; c. 450-c. 425 B.C.E., History Develops as a Scholarly Discipline.

HEROPHILUS
Greek physician

The first systematic dissector of the human body, Herophilus made numerous anatomical discoveries, laying the foundation for subsequent Western anatomy. Herophilus's analysis of the pulse and his dream theory also exercised a strong influence on medicine and psychology in later centuries.

BORN: c. 335 B.C.E.; Chalcedon, Bithynia (now Kadiköy, Turkey)
DIED: c. 280 B.C.E.; probably Alexandria, Egypt
ALSO KNOWN AS: Herophilus of Chalcedon
AREA OF ACHIEVEMENT: Medicine

EARLY LIFE

The sparse ancient evidence suggests that Herophilus (huh-RAHF-uh-luhs) left his native city of Chalcedon for an apprenticeship with the distinguished physician Praxagoras of Cos before settling in the recently founded North African city of Alexandria. An Athenian sojourn is implied by the report of Hyginus, a second century Roman mythographer, that a young Athenian woman, in guileful reaction against the exclusion of women from the medical profession, disguised herself as a man and completed an apprenticeship with Herophilus. As a consequence of her popularity with women patients, who alone knew that she was a woman, Herophilus's pupil was brought before an Athenian jury on charges of seducing and corrupting her women patients. In court she raised her tunic and revealed her gender. After she received assertive support from women, Hyginus relates, "the Athenians amended the law so that free-born women could learn the art of medicine." No independent evidence corroborates Hyginus's account—which formally belongs to the genre of invention fables—but it is worth noting that Herophilus's contributions to gynecology and obstetrics are richly attested.

LIFE'S WORK

The first scientist to violate the entrenched Greek taboo against cutting open a human corpse, Herophilus made spectacular discoveries in human anatomy. From classical antiquity until the early Renaissance, anatomical accounts were mainly based on comparative anatomy—Aristotle and Galen, in particular, dissected numerous animals—and on chance observations of the wounded or injured. While Herophilus continued this practice of dissecting animals, he and his contemporary Erasistratus apparently were the only pre-Renaissance scientists to

perform systematic dissections on humans. Furthermore, if the controversial but unequivocal evidence of several later authors is trustworthy, Herophilus also performed vivisectory experiments on convicted criminals.

Herophilus was able to break the spell of the taboo because of an exceptional constellation of circumstances in Alexandria. The combination of ambitious, autocratic patrons of science (the Ptolemies), bold scientists such as Euclid and Archimedes, a new city on foreign soil in which traditional Greek values initially were not accepted as intrinsically superior, and a cosmopolitan intelligentsia committed to literary, technological, and scientific frontiersmanship made it possible for Herophilus to overcome tenacious inhibitions against opening the human body. The native Egyptian practice of mummification, sanctioned by centuries of stable religious belief, might have been invoked as a precedent, although embalming was in fact very different from scientific dissection. The Egyptian embalmers, for example, scraped and drained the brain piecemeal through the nostrils of the corpse, mangling it beyond anatomic recognition, whereas Herophilus dissected the brain meticulously enough to distinguish some of its ventricles and to identify several of its smaller parts with unprecedented accuracy.

One of Herophilus's more noteworthy discoveries was that of the nerves. He distinguished between sensory and "voluntary" (motor) nerves, described the paths of at least seven pairs of cranial nerves, and recognized unique features of the optic nerve. He also was the first to observe and name the calamus scriptorius, a cavity in the floor of the fourth cerebral ventricle. His careful dissection of the eye yielded the discovery not only of the optic nerve but also of several coats of the eye (probably the sclera, cornea, iris, retina, and chorioid coat), an achievement all the more remarkable in the absence of the microscope.

Like his other works, Herophilus's main anatomical work, *Anatomika* (*Anatomy*, 1989), survives only in fragments and secondhand reports. From its second book, ancient sources have preserved the first classic description of the human liver: The shape, size, position, and texture of the liver as well as its connections with other parts are described with admirable accuracy. The pancreas and small intestine, or duodenum (a Latin version of the name Herophilus first gave it), are among the other parts in the abdominal cavity that he explored.

The third book of *Anatomy* appears to have been devoted to the reproductive organs. In the male, Herophilus distinguished between various parts of the spermatic duct system, meticulously identifying anatomical features previously unknown. As for the female, Herophilus seems to have abandoned the traditional theory of a bicameral human uterus, and, using the male analogy, to have discovered the ovaries (which he calls female twins or testicles), the Fallopian tubes (although he did not determine their true course and function), and several other features of female reproductive anatomy.

In the fourth book, Herophilus dealt with the anatomy of the blood vessels. Accepting Praxagoras's distinction between veins and arteries, he provided further anatomical precision and offered some basic observations on the heart valves, the chambers of the heart, and a variety of vessels and vascular structures. The torcular Herophili, a confluence of several great venous cavities or sinuses in the skull, was first identified by Herophilus and still bears his name.

In his physiopathology, Herophilus appears to have accepted the traditional theory of a balance or imbalance between humors (or moistures) in the body as the cause of health and disease, respectively, but he insisted that all causal explanation is provisional or hypothetical. One must start from appearances, or observation, he said, and then proceed on a hypothetical basis to what is not visible, including cause. The command center of the body is located in the fourth cerebral ventricle or in the cerebellum (which is indeed the center responsible for muscular coordination and maintenance of the equilibrium of the body). From the brain and spinal marrow, nerves—sensory and motor—proceed like offshoots. Neural transmission, at least in the case of the optic nerves, apparently takes place through pneuma, a warm, moist, airlike substance flowing through the nerves and ultimately derived from external air by respiration.

Among the involuntary motions in the human body (that is, ones for which the motor nerves are not responsible), Herophilus gave novel, detailed accounts of two: respiration, which he attributed to a natural tendency of the lungs to dilate and contract through a four-part cycle, and the pulse, which he attributed to a faculty that flows to the arteries from the heart through the arterial coats, causing the arteries to dilate and contract. His treatise *Peri sphygmōn* (*On Pulses*, 1989) is the first work devoted to the subject, and it became the foundation of all ancient and of much subsequent pulse lore.

Central to Herophilus's vascular physiology is the theory that the arteries transport a mixture of blood and pneuma (similar to the modern view that the arteries carry blood and oxygen), whereas the veins contain only blood. Here he parted ways with his teacher Praxagoras and his contemporary Erasistratus, both of whom believed the arteries contain only pneuma. The arteries, Herophilus believed, pulsate in such intricate, differentiated patterns that the pulse is a major diagnostic tool. Deploying sustained analogies between musical-metrical theory and pulse rhythm, Herophilus described nature's music in the arteries as successively assuming pyrrhic, trochaic, spondaic, and iambic rhythmic relations between diastole and systole as one passes through four stages of life—from infancy (pyrrhic) through childhood and adulthood to old age (iambic). Deviations from these rhythms indicate disorders.

Herophilus had such faith in the diagnostic value of the pulse that he constructed a portable water clock, or clepsydra, to measure the rate of his patients' pulses. The device could be calibrated to fit the age of each patient. One example of its clinical application suggests that it also functioned as a protothermometer: "By as much as the movements of the pulse exceeded the number that is natural for filling up the clepsydra, by that much Herophilus declared the pulse too frequent, i.e., that the patient had either more or less of a fever" (quoted from the second century Marcellinus). Herophilus's pulse theory represents an unusual attempt within ancient medicine to introduce measurement and quantification into nonpharmacological contexts. Besides rhythm and frequency, he used size, strength, and perhaps speed and volume to distinguish one pulse from another.

Reproductive physiology and pathology represent other strengths of Herophilus. He accepted, in general, Aristotle's view that male seed is formed from the blood and, according to Saint Augustine's acquaintance Vindician, Herophilus characteristically tried to defend this idea by arguments based on dissection. He wrote the first known treatise devoted only to obstetrics, *Maiōtikon* (*Midwifery*; also known as *On Delivery*), in which he tried to demystify the uterus, arguing that it is constituted of the same material elements as the rest of the body and is regulated by the same faculties. There is no disease peculiar to women, he asserts, though he concedes that certain "affections" are experienced only by women: menstruation, conception, parturition, and lactation. The causes of difficult childbirth, embryological questions (such as, is the fetus a living being, as it possesses involuntary but not voluntary motions?), and the normal duration of pregnancy are among the other subjects apparently explored by Herophilus. The church father Tertullian implied that the Alexandrian performed abortions and charged him with having possessed an instrument known as a "fetus-slayer" (*embryo-sphaktes*).

In his treatise *Pros tas koinas doxas* (*Against Common Opinions*, 1989), Herophilus also dealt with gynecological and obstetrical issues, attacking the common opinion that menstruation is good for every woman's health and for childbearing, and, characteristically, adopting a more discriminating view: Menstruation is helpful to some women, harmful to others, depending on individual circumstances. For all of his emphasis on the hypothetical nature of causal explanations, Herophilus tried to determine the causes of many individual disorders, including fevers, heart diseases, and pneumonia. He also described the symptoms of several physical and mental disorders and developed a semiotic system known as a "triple-timed inference from signs," which used a combination of the patients' past signs or symptoms, the present signs, and the "future signs" (inferences from what has happened to other similarly afflicted patients) for diagnostic, prognostic, and therapeutic purposes.

In *Die Traumdeutung* (1900; *The Interpretation of Dreams*, 1913), Sigmund Freud recognized Herophilus's importance in another area: dream theory. Dreams, Herophilus believed, belong to one of three classes by origin: "godsent" dreams occur inevitably or by necessity; "natural" dreams arise when the soul forms for itself an image of what is to its advantage; and "compound" or "mixed" dreams arise when one sees what one desires. Freud acknowledged Herophilus's emphasis on the fulfillment of sexual and other wishes in dreams as an important anticipation of his own theory. With modifications, Herophilus's tripartite classification of dreams reappears in the works of several pagan and Christian authors, thus representing another influential part of his legacy.

SIGNIFICANCE

The frequent lag between scientific discovery and clinical application, between theory and therapy, also characterized Herophilus's work. Despite his brilliant discoveries in anatomy and physiology, he was a traditionalist in practice. In his works *Diaitētikon* (*Regimen*, 1989) and *Therapeutika* (*Therapeutics*, 1989), Herophilus prescribed a preventive regimen, bloodletting, various simple and compound drugs (with at least some innovative ingredients), and a limited amount of surgical intervention (with a felicitous emphasis on checking hemorrhages).

He perhaps also prompted the influential Alexandrian tradition of exegesis of Hippocratic texts, to which several of Herophilus's adherents made major contributions by taking a keen, critical interest in Hippocratic works. One of Herophilus's pupils, Philinus of Cos, broke with him and became a leader of the powerful Empiricist school of medicine, but many others continued proclaiming themselves his followers. As the old taboos against human dissection reasserted themselves after Herophilus's death, the Herophileans abandoned this central part of the founder's legacy. However, the rich history of his school, both in Alexandria and in Laodicea-on-Lycus (Turkey), can be traced for at least three centuries after Herophilus's death. Through Galen's detailed acclaim of Herophilus's dissections and of his pulse theory, the Alexandrian's fame survived the polemics of those Christians and pagans who believed that what had been concealed by God or nature should not be revealed by humans.

—Heinrich von Staden

FURTHER READING

Fraser, P. M. *Ptolemaic Alexandria*. 3 vols. Oxford, England: Clarendon Press, 1972. An excellent comprehensive treatment of Alexandria at the time of Herophilus. Chapter 7 offers a good introduction to Herophilus and other Alexandrian physicians.

Lloyd, G. E. R. *Greek Science After Aristotle*. New York: Norton, 1973. Chapter 6 offers a useful general introduction to Hellenistic biology and medicine, with a valuable assessment of Herophilus's place in the history of science.

_____. *Science, Folklore, and Ideology*. Indianapolis: Hackett, 1999. Excellent observations throughout, especially on Herophilus's contributions to reproductive theory and the standardization of anatomical terminology.

Longrigg, James. "Superlative Achievement and Comparative Neglect: Alexandrian Medical Science and Modern Historical Research." *History of Science* 19 (1981): 155-200. A solid overview of the scientific views of Herophilus and Erasistratus by a classicist and historian of medicine.

Potter, Paul. "Herophilus of Chalcedon: An Assessment of His Place in the History of Anatomy." *Bulletin of the History of Medicine* 50 (1976): 45-60. A physician and historian of medicine subjects Herophilus's anatomical descriptions to thoughtful, informed scrutiny.

Von Staden, Heinrich. *Herophilus: The Art of Medicine in Early Alexandria*. New York: Cambridge University Press, 1989. The first comprehensive collection, translation, and evaluation of the ancient evidence concerning Herophilus. Part 1 includes extensive essays on his anatomy, physiopathology, therapeutics, and theory of method; part 2 traces his followers from 250 B.C.E. to 50 C.E.

SEE ALSO: Alcmaeon; Aretaeus of Cappadocia; Asclepiades of Bithynia; Diocles of Carystus; Pedanius Dioscorides; Erasistratus; Galen; Hippocrates; Tertullian.

RELATED ARTICLES in *Great Events from History: The Ancient World*: 6th-4th century B.C.E. (traditionally, 1st millennium B.C.E.), Suśruta, Indian Physician, Writes Medical Compendium; c. 500-400 B.C.E., Greek Physicians Begin Scientific Practice of Medicine; 332 B.C.E., Founding of Alexandria; c. 157-201 C.E., Galen Synthesizes Ancient Medical Knowledge.

HESIOD
Greek poet

Hesiod organized and interpreted the Greek myths that form the basis for European civilization and examined with moral conscience the working life of Greek society at the dawn of modern history.

FLOURISHED: c. 700 B.C.E.; Ascra, Greece
AREA OF ACHIEVEMENT: Literature

EARLY LIFE

In the centuries after his death, Hellenic historians and writers so embellished the life of Hesiod (HEE-see-uhd) that a moderately detailed portrait of him developed through commentary and speculation. The work of more recent classical scholars has demonstrated that most of this material cannot be substantiated through historical records. While it is not inconceivable that subsequent archaeological discoveries will provide additional information, it seems reasonable to assume that the autobiographical information provided by Hesiod himself in *Erga kai Emerai* (c. 700 B.C.E.; *Works and Days*, 1618) is the only basis for drawing an outline of his life. Like some of the work traditionally attributed to him, it is fragmentary and sketchy, but as one of Hesiod's best translators, Apostolos Athanassakis, contends, it is "better than all fanciful conjecture." Although some scholars maintain that even this work cannot be positively authenticated, without it, "there is no poet named Hesiod," as P. Walcot argues.

In *Works and Days*, four assertions about Hesiod's father are presented—that he made a living as a merchant sailor, that he came from the province of Cyme in Aeolis, that "grim poverty" drove him from Asia Minor, and that he settled in Ascra in the region known as Boeotia, an initially inhospitable but visually striking district near Mount Helicon. Considering the fact that others who followed this migration pattern moved on to establish Greek colonies in Italy when they were unable to make a living,

it is reasonable to assume that Hesiod's father was comparatively prosperous, an assumption corroborated by the story of the division of his estate between Hesiod and his brother Perses in *Works and Days*. Although Boeotia was thought to be something of a backwater by scholars possibly influenced by the prejudices of its neighbors, there is convincing evidence from artistic and poetic sources that it was actually more like a cultural center. Boeotian verse shared many of the traits of epic poetry associated with the Ionian region, and the area's geographic location on the trade route to the Near East provided many opportunities for cultural advancement, including an earlier adoption of the alphabet than that in many other parts of the Hellenic world.

In both *Works and Days* and the *Theogonia* (c. 700 B.C.E.; *Theogony*, 1728), the crucial moment of transformation in Hesiod's life is presented as a justification for his work. While tending sheep, probably in early manhood, Hesiod was visited by the Muses, who gave him the gift of song (that is, wisdom in poetic language) and charged him with the responsibility to instruct his fellow Boetians. Hesiod combines the perspective of the common person—the "country bumpkin," the "swag-bellied yahoo," whom the Muses address—with the poet's power to create pleasure that counters the pains of human existence, and the orator's eloquence, which reconciles citizens to the necessity for compromise in a social community. Thus, when Hesiod found himself in a dispute with Perses over the division of their father's estate, he took the occasion to criticize the nobles (or "kings") who presided as judges for accepting bribes and not rendering true justice. He developed *Works and Days* as a poem in which he counsels his brother and his fellow citizens about the kind of society in which, through the gods' justice, they may all have an opportunity to live relatively comfortably.

413

There are hints in *Works and Days* and *Theogony* that Hesiod lived much of his life as a bachelor, although he briefly speaks as if he had a son, and there is an account of a visit to Chalcis in Euboea for funeral games, in which he won a handsome prize. M. L. West argues that the poem he performed was the *Theogony*. Beyond that, a number of inferences may be made from the sensibility that emerges through his work. As West observes in explaining the style of his translation, "If I have sometimes made Hesiod sound a little quaint and stilted, that is not unintentional: He is." The obscurity that wreathes Hesiod's life is an intriguing invitation to conjecture. As long as it is based on a careful reading of the work in its known historical context, it is a kind of modern equivalent of the mentally active participation of the audience in that earlier era of oral communication.

LIFE'S WORK

Most of the poems that were originally attributed to Hesiod in the centuries after he lived have been designated the work of other writers by modern scholarship. From an original oeuvre consisting of eleven fragments and two titles, only the *Ehoiai* (c. 580-520 B.C.E.; *The Catalogue of Women*, 1983), describing heroic genealogies and appended to *Theogony*, and *Ornithomanteia* (divination by birds), which was appended to *Works and Days*, may have been based on something Hesiod wrote. Athanassakis mentions that both works, which were thematically connected and impressive imitations by anonymous writers, were often amalgamated into the work of a commanding literary figure, as is the case with Homer and Hippocrates. Athanassakis observes that the *Aspis Herakleous* (*Shield of Herakles*, 1928) is included in most standard editions of Hesiod, "thus paying homage to ancient tradition," but he makes a plausible case that it is a visionary poem of apocalyptic power that stands comparison with Hesiod's finest writing.

In any event, *Theogony* stands as the beginning of Hesiod's work. It carries out the Muses' injunction to "sing of the race of the blessed gods" and "tell of things to come and things past," in return for their fabulous gift. This gift, however, like most divine bounty, carries the burden of its own mystery, and *Theogony* is not only a form of thanks and worship but also an attempt to understand the import and consequence of the action of the gods in the affairs of humans.

To do this, Hesiod reaches back to the creation of time and space from an immeasurable, primordial flux to chart the origins of cosmic history. As he describes the beginning of the known universe, the elemental aspects of the cosmos, Earth (Gaia), Sky (Ouranos), and Sea (Pontos), are not only physical components of firmament and terrain but also are gods, with all the attributes of divinity (and humanity) common to the Hellenic vision of deity. This merging compels him, in composing a poem on the birth and genealogy of the gods, to create also cosmogony, or an account of the development of the shape and form of the universe through time. As a correlative, without actually identifying the precise moment of the emergence of the human race, *Theogony* also presents an early history of humanity set amid, and sometimes parallel to, the genealogy of the Olympian deities.

Because the eighth century B.C.E. was a time of rapid economic expansion and increasing mobility for Greece, with contacts with the Orient already in process for more than a hundred years, it is not surprising that elements of creation myths from the thirteenth century B.C.E. Hittite castration motif (known as *Song of Ullikummi*, 1952), the Babylonian *Enuma Elish* (twelfth century B.C.E.; *The Seven Tablets of Creation*, 1902), the Indian *Rigveda* (also known as *Ṛgveda*, c. 1500-1000 B.C.E.; English translation, 1896-1897), and even the Norse *Poetic Edda* (ninth to twelfth century; English translation, 1923) appear in *Theogony*. Hesiod was working at the apex of a tradition, but his singular contribution was to place—above the diversity of the separate families of gods, shaping the chaos of turmoil and struggle—the controlling power of Zeus's sovereignty. The argument of the poem is the rightness and justice of Zeus's reign, the intelligent ordering of what had been a saga of endless, almost random violence. The structure of the poem itself contributes to this sense of order, beginning with the world in Hesiod's time, then moving back to show the evolution from Chaos, and then concluding with a reaffirmation of Zeus's wise aegis.

The direction of cosmic evolution is from a focus on the form of the natural world to a concentration on the structure of an anthropocentric one. This is a reflection of the imposition of the will of Zeus, because, as Hesiod presents it, the first "beings"—Chaos (Void), Gaia (Earth), and Eros (immanent creative energy)—are essentially elemental impulses, unbound and undirected. Hesiod does not postulate what preceded this condition but sees Eros as a crucial catalyst to the proceeding procreation. First, Hesiod lists the progeny of Chaos and the progeny of Earth. The birth of the Mountains and the Sea by parthenogenesis, and then the birth of the Titans through Earth's incestuous union with her son Sky, are actions apparently without purpose, more impulse than vision. The lineage of Zeus is established with the castra-

Hesiod. (Hulton\Archive by Getty Images)

tion of Kronos (Time)—an act challenging order—who is the last of the Titans, son of Sky and father of Zeus. Parallel to this, the children of Chaos arrive, dark and gloomy, negative in impact, a plague to humankind.

The story of the ascendancy of Zeus involves a shift from the maternal line with an obscure partner to a patriarchal lineage much more in accordance with Hesiod's own society. Zeus, a male sky god, is ultimately evolved from Mother Earth, an evolutionary process directed toward male dominance, which Hesiod justifies as necessary for law and order. Zeus, "the father of gods and men," generates the seasons (emblems of regularity and predictability) by his second wife, Thetis, herself an embodiment of wisdom that he assimilates. Their children symbolize the constants of civilization: Eunomia (Law), Dike (Justice), and Eirene (Peace). Thus, the history of Zeus is also a progression from chaos to law, as Zeus stands in antithesis to his defeated but still dangerous rivals, who are expressions of wild energy. As *Theogony* concludes, Zeus divides his spoils—titles and spheres of influence—with some principles of fairness that lead gradually to a civilized order of governmental succession. The union of Zeus with noble women produced the race of heroes that drew humankind closer to the immortals, but as the children of Night remain on the scene, strife and sorrow will always be the lot of humans. For

this reason, the Muses have given the poet the gift of song to provide some relief.

Works and Days is a shift of emphasis from the cosmological and eternal to the local and specific. Hesiod examines the ways in which a man might lead a reasonably satisfying life. Working within the larger pattern of the universe as presented in *Theogony* and assuming a familiarity with it, Hesiod confronted the limitations imposed by often unfathomable forces and offered a program of sorts for survival. Because the only style of literary expression available was the dactylic hexameter of the Homeric epic, the poem follows that form, but it is essentially didactic in tone and style, a series of instructions regarding the proper conduct of a man's working life in an agricultural economy controlled by not always scrupulous nobles or "kings." The form is not ideal for Hesiod's purposes, and the poem tends to ramble, but it contains fascinating lessons designed as guidance for those who were prepared to commit their lives to productive industry proscribed by moral behavior.

Works and Days is developed out of the sense of divine justice elaborated in *Theogony*. It accepts the concept of order in human existence and sees work as "the action to fulfill that order." The rationale behind the poem is that conditions have steadily deteriorated since the Golden Age. As Hesiod tells it, humans have progressively weakened through the "Five Ages," their working conditions becoming harder, their physical strength diminishing, and such afflictions as hunger and disease, unknown in earlier times, now plaguing humankind in the Iron Age.

These banes occur as a consequence of human deviousness as expressed in the myths of Prometheus and Pandora. Hesiod sees violence and injustice emerging from Prometheus's challenge and, without being specific, names Pandora (meaning "all gifts") as a source of increasing complexity in human affairs for the introduction of sexual and artistic matters. Bound by the thinking of his era, he describes the feminine role as one of distraction, undermining a man's clarity of purpose and, by implication, his control. A woman's "glamor" and guile encourages dissipation and waste, which restricts independence. For Hesiod, woman is "the other," an outsider, who must be taught "right" ways. That is, she must eradicate the singularity in her nature that makes her different from a man. Once a similarity is achieved, she will become valuable property, because she contributes to the permanence of the home. The perspective is very male-oriented and very narrow. A larger view of the two myths suggests that Prometheus introduces the technical to the natural and Pandora introduces the beautiful or ecstatic to the rational, each complicating but also deepening human experience. In a sense, Zeus has used Pandora as a tactic in his contest with Prometheus, and both myths are part of Hesiod's explanation for the current condition of the world.

In order to overcome these unpleasant conditions, Hesiod stresses justice as the crucial virtue, the essential value in all endeavor. Focusing on his own life, he decries the local politicians, subject to bribes, who have unjustly favored his brother Perses in dividing their father's legacy. The entire poem is supposedly addressed to Perses, who is exhorted to follow a life of honest work because without it, men would scheme to gain riches and justice could not exist. The central text of the poem is a series of maxims, suggestions, folk sayings, and specific advice about how to function in a grain-growing or wine-making world.

Rather than a manual, however, it is more an outline of operations framed by a reliance on the right time of the year for a particular action. The purpose is really to inculcate a sense of appropriateness and propriety in everything. Similarly, the long, expressive descriptions of the harshness of winter and the pleasures of summer are designed to reconcile human nature to the larger patterns of the natural cosmos. The "works" section is a kind of astronomical guide for plowing, planting, and harvesting, that places man in harmony with his environment, thus putting him in synchronization with the will of Zeus. The part of the poem known as the "Days" is less impressive because it is rooted in the "science" or superstition of Hesiod's world. It is a forerunner of astrological prediction—an attempt to make sense of mysterious, perplexing aspects of existence. It represents a variety of superstitions, particularly numerology, in Mesopotamia and Egypt. Hesiod is recording the folk wisdom of the tribe, another valid task of the didactic poet.

SIGNIFICANCE

The fifth century judgment of Herodotus, that "Hesiod and Homer are the ones who provided the Greeks with a theogony, gave the gods their names, distinguished their attributes and functions, and defined their various types," is still valid. The mythic truth that Hesiod established is the basis for the origin of the European mind and worldview, the beginning of a definition of Western civilization. In his work, the strong thread of value and principle that distinguishes the most admirable attributes of culture can be traced back to its inception. The ultimate lessons of his philosophy, organized through reflection on astronomical phenomena, are to live in harmony with the visible, the regular, the knowable, and to acknowledge and forbear the illusive, the abrupt, the terrible. Speaking across the gulf of time, Hesiod remains the "great teacher and civilizer," the poet as embodiment of the divine voice that offers access to universal truth that humankind ignores at its own peril.

—*Leon Lewis*

FURTHER READING

Brown, Norman O. Introduction to *Theogony*, by Hesiod. New York: Liberal Arts Press, 1953. A detailed, interpretive introduction that contains perceptive commentary on the poem's meaning accompanies a reliable translation.

Burn, Andrew Robert. *The World of Hesiod: A Study of the Greek Middle Ages*. 2d ed. New York: B. Blom, 1966. An early study that examines the poet in his historical context. Includes much basic background information.

Evelyn-White, Hugh G., ed. and trans. *Hesiod, the Homeric Hymns, and Homerica*. 1914. Reprint. Cambridge, Mass.: Harvard University Press, 1982. The translation considered standard through most of the twentieth century.

Havelock, Eric. *Preface to Plato*. Cambridge, Mass.: Harvard University Press, 1982. An excellent discussion of "oral acoustic intelligence," the tradition in which Hesiod composed.

Hesiod. *"Theogony," "Works and Days," "Shield."* Translated by Apostolos N. Athanassakis. Baltimore: The Johns Hopkins University Press, 1983. An imaginative modern translation, combined with lucid, thorough notes and an incisive introduction. The translator's familiarity with historic and contemporary Greece enables him to offer many relevant details from folk culture. Includes bibliography.

Janko, R. *Homer, Hesiod, and the Hymns: Diachronic Development in Epic Diction*. Cambridge, England: Cambridge University Press, 1982. Solid scholarship and interesting speculation about the development of the hexameter tradition, with many theoretical assertions about dates and origins.

Lamberton, Robert. *Hesiod*. Fort Lauderdale, Fla.: Hermes Books, 1988. An accessible introduction to Hesiod's works. Historical background of the poems and problems of dating them are discussed. Major subsidiary works are analyzed.

Nelson, Stephanie A. *God and the Land: The Metaphysics of Farming in Hesiod and Vergil*. New York:

Oxford University Press, 1998. Shows how Hesiod as well as Vergil viewed the farming lifestyle as a religion unto itself.

Penglase, Charles. *Greek Myths and Mesopotamia: Parallels and Influence in the Homeric Hymns and Hesiod*. New York: Routledge, 1997. Examines how Mesopotamian ideas and themes influenced Greek religious mythological works, including the Homeric hymns to the gods and the works of Hesiod.

Pucci, Pietro. *Hesiod and the Language of Poetry*. Baltimore: The Johns Hopkins University Press, 1977. An extremely detailed examination of the meaning of words in Hesiod. Primarily for the specialist but clear in presentation.

Thalmann, William G. *Conventions of Form and Thought in Early Greek Epic Poetry*. Baltimore: The Johns Hopkins University Press, 1984. A comprehensive, carefully annotated examination of the form and structure of the poetry of Homer and Hesiod, illuminating parallel approaches in the work of both poets and pro-

viding many incisive comments on the meanings of their poems. An impressive assimilation and extension of much previous scholarship on the subject.

West, M. L. *The Hesiodic Catalogue of Women: Its Nature, Structure, and Origins*. New York: Oxford University Press, 1985. A definitive study of a work previously attributed to Hesiod.

SEE ALSO: Aesop; Enheduanna; Homer; Ovid.
RELATED ARTICLES in *Great Events from History: The Ancient World*: c. 3100 B.C.E., Sumerians Invent Writing; c. 2300 B.C.E., Enheduanna Becomes First Named Author; c. 2000 B.C.E., Composition of the Gilgamesh Epic; 1500-1100 B.C.E., Compilation of the Vedas; c. 1000-c. 200 B.C.E., Compilation of the Upaniṣads; c. 950 B.C.E., Composition of the Book of Genesis; c. 800 B.C.E., Phoenicians from Tyre Found Carthage; c. 700 B.C.E., Hesiod Composes *Theogony* and *Works and Days*; 600-500 B.C.E., Greek Philosophers Formulate Theories of the Cosmos.

HIPPARCHUS
Greek astronomer

Hipparchus was the greatest astronomer of ancient times. He was the founder of trigonometry, which he used to determine the distances from Earth to the moon and sun, and the first to use consistently the idea of latitude and longitude to describe locations on Earth and in the sky.

BORN: 190 B.C.E.; Nicaea, Bithynia, Asia Minor (now İznik, Turkey)
DIED: After 127 B.C.E.; possibly Rhodes, Greece
AREAS OF ACHIEVEMENT: Astronomy, mathematics

EARLY LIFE
Very little is known about the life of Hipparchus (hih-PAHR-kuhs). He was born in Nicaea, a Greek-speaking city in Bithynia (modern İznik, Turkey), in the northwestern part of Asia Minor. Calculations in his works are based on the latitude of the city of Rhodes, on the island of the same name, so many historians believe that he spent a major portion of his life there. Rhodes was a merchant center, a convenient port from which to make voyages. At least one of Hipparchus's observations was made in Alexandria, so it seems that he visited and perhaps spent time as a student or research scholar at that great nucleus of scientific inquiry. Because he was in-

tensely interested in geography, it is likely that he traveled to other places in the Mediterranean basin and the Near East. He seems to have been familiar with Babylonian astronomy, including eclipse records, but it is impossible to say how he came to know these.

LIFE'S WORK
Most of what is known of Hipparchus comes from the *Mathēmatikē syntaxis* (c. 150 C.E.; *Almagest*, 1948) of Ptolemy, whose work depends to a considerable extent on that of the earlier scientist, and from the *Geōgraphica* (c. 7 B.C.E.; *Geography*, 1917-1933) of Strabo. Of Hipparchus's own writings, only the *Tōn Araton kai Eudoxou phainomenon exigesis* (commentary on the phenomena of Eudoxus and Aratus) survives, in three books. It criticizes the less accurate placement of stars and constellations by two famous predecessors. It is certainly not one of his most important works, but it contains some information on his observations of star positions, which were the basis of his lost star catalog. Other lost works of Hipparchus include *Peri eviausiou megethous* (on the length of the year) and *Peri tes metabaseos tōn tropikon kai isemerinon semeion* (on the displacement of the solstitial and equinoctial points).

He is also credited with a trigonometrical table of chords in a circle, a work on gravitational phenomena called *On Bodies Carried down by Their Weight*, an attack on the geographical work of Eratosthenes, a compilation of weather signs, and some aids to computational astrology.

A number of achievements are attributed to Hipparchus by Ptolemy and other ancient writers. A new star appeared in the constellation Scorpio in July, 133 B.C.E. Hipparchus realized that without an accurate star catalog, it was impossible to demonstrate that the star was indeed new, so he set about producing a complete sky map with a table of the positions of the stars, including the angle north or south of the celestial equator (latitude) and the angle east or west of the vernal equinox point (one of the two intersections between the celestial equator and the sun's path, or ecliptic).

In order to do this, he needed a means of measuring celestial angles, which led him to invent many of the sighting instruments, including the diopter and possibly the armillary astrolabe, used by astronomers before the invention of the telescope in the seventeenth century. He also knew how to calibrate water clocks. Hipparchus's star catalog included about 850 stars, along with estimates of their brightness. He divided the stars into six categories, from the brightest to the dimmest, thus originating a system of stellar magnitude. He also made a celestial globe, showing the locations of the fixed stars on its surface.

In comparing his own measurements of positions of stars with those of earlier astronomers, Hipparchus discovered that there had been a systematic shift in the same direction in all of them. He noticed the phenomenon first in the case of the bright star Spica. In 283 B.C.E. Timocharis had observed the star to be eight degrees west of the autumnal equinoctial point, but Hipparchus found the figure to be six degrees. He found a displacement for every other star that he was able to check. These discrepancies, he established, were the result of a shift in the position of the equinoxes—and therefore of the celestial equator and poles. In modern astronomy, this shift is called the precession of the equinoxes and is known to be caused by a slow "wobble" in the orientation of Earth's axis. The spot to which the north pole points in the sky (the north celestial pole) describes a circle in a period of more than twenty-six thousand years. Hipparchus was first to describe and to attempt to measure this phenomenon. He was, however, unable to explain its cause, since he held the geocentric theory, which postulates a motionless Earth at the center of a moving universe.

From the beginning of theoretical astronomy, the geocentric theory had been the accepted one. It assumed that the sun, moon, planets, and stars were carried on vast transparent spheres that revolved at different but constant speeds around Earth. Unfortunately, in order to explain the observed motions of the planets, which vary in speed and sometimes are retrograde relative to the stars, astronomers had to postulate the existence of additional spheres, invisible and bearing no celestial bodies but interconnected with the other spheres and affecting their motions. An Alexandrian astronomer, Aristarchus, had proposed the heliocentric theory, which holds that Earth, with its satellite, the moon, and all the other planets revolve around the central sun. The main appeal of this theory was its simplicity; it required fewer imaginary spheres to make it work.

Hipparchus rejected the heliocentric theory and instead adopted modifications of the geocentric theory to make it accord better with observations, perhaps following Apollonius of Perga. The main feature of the Hipparchan system is the epicycle, a smaller sphere bearing a planet, with its center on the surface of the larger, Earth-centered sphere and revolving at an independent speed. He also postulated eccentrics, that is, that the centers of the celestial spheres do not coincide with the center of Earth. The geocentric system with epicycles is often called "Ptolemaic," as Ptolemy made observations to support the theory developed by Hipparchus. Aristarchus's heliocentric theory is closer to the picture of the solar system provided by modern astronomy.

In developing his astronomical system, Hipparchus observed the period of revolution of the celestial objects that move against the background of the stars. That of the sun, which is the year, he found to be 365 $\frac{1}{4}$ days, less $\frac{1}{300}$ of a day, a figure that was closer to the true one than that of any previous astronomer. He noticed the inequality in the lengths of the seasons, which he correctly attributed to the varying distance between Earth and the sun but incorrectly explained by assuming that the center of the sun's sphere of revolution was eccentric to the center of Earth. These conclusions were, perhaps, a step in the direction of recognizing that the relative motion of the two bodies describes an ellipse. He also achieved a measurement of the length of the lunar month, with an error of less than one second in comparison with the figure now accepted. The Roman scholar Pliny the Elder wrote that Hipparchus countered the popular fear of eclipses by publishing a list that demonstrated their regularity over the preceding six hundred years.

Hipparchus attempted to measure the distances of the

moon and sun from Earth by observing eclipses and the phenomenon of parallax (the shift in the apparent position of the moon against the background of the stars under changing conditions). His figure for the distance of the moon (60.5 times the radius of Earth) was reasonably accurate, but his estimate of the sun's distance (2,550 times Earth's radius) was far too small. (The true ratio is about 23,452 to 1.) In fairness to Hipparchus, it should be noted that he regarded his solution to the problem of the sun's distance as open to question.

In order to make the mathematical computations required by these problems, it was necessary for Hipparchus to know the ratios of the sides of a right triangle for the various angles the sides make with the hypotenuse—in other words, the values of trigonometrical functions. He worked out tables of the sine function, thus becoming, in effect, the founder of trigonometry.

Geography also occupied Hipparchus's attention. He began the systematic use of longitude and latitude, which he had also employed in his star catalog, as a means of establishing locations on Earth's surface. Previous geographers show evidence of knowing such a method, but they did not employ it consistently. Hipparchus was able to calculate latitudes of various places on Earth's surface by learning the lengths of the days and nights recorded for different seasons of the year, although the figures given by him were often in error. As the base of longitude, he used the meridian passing through Alexandria. He was especially critical, probably too much so, of the descriptive and mathematical errors in the work of Eratosthenes. He even had some quibbles with the famous measurement of the spherical Earth, which is the latter's most brilliant achievement. It may be Hipparchus, rather than Eratosthenes, who first described climatic zones, bounded by parallels of latitude north and south of the equator.

SIGNIFICANCE

Hipparchus was a careful and original astronomer whose discoveries, particularly that of precession, were of the greatest importance in the early history of the science. He was a meticulous observer who produced the first dependable star catalog and who determined the apparent periods of revolution of the moon and the sun with an exactitude never before achieved. As a mathematician, he originated the study of trigonometry, compiling a sine table and using it in an attempt to measure distances in space beyond Earth that was, at least in the case of the moon, successful. Both as astronomer and as geographer, he pioneered the systematic use of the coordinates of latitude and longitude. He devised instruments for use in these observations and measurements.

Unfortunately, almost all Hipparchus's writings have disappeared, so modern assessments of his work must depend on ancient writers who happened to mention him. His influence was important enough to cause several later scientists whose works survive to refer to and summarize him. Most notable among these were Ptolemy and Strabo. It is sometimes hard to tell when these authors, particularly Ptolemy, are following Hipparchus and when they are going beyond him to present their own conclusions. Ptolemy's work became the standard textbook on astronomy until the time of Nicolaus Copernicus in the sixteenth century; thus Hipparchus's name was deservedly remembered. One of Hipparchus's most important mathematical successors was Menelaus of Alexandria (fl. c. 100 C.E.), who developed the study of spherical trigonometry.

—*J. Donald Hughes*

FURTHER READING

Dicks, D. R. *Early Greek Astronomy to Aristotle.* Ithaca, N.Y.: Cornell University Press, 1985. Hipparchus is not given major treatment, although he does appear as an important figure in the history of astronomy. The discussion of his criticisms of Eudoxus and Aratus is particularly good.

Dreyer, John L. E. *A History of Astronomy from Thales to Kepler.* 2d ed. New York: Dover, 1953. This fine, accessible study places Hipparchus clearly in the context of the development of astronomy. Dreyer differs from common interpretation in crediting Ptolemy, not Hipparchus, with the theory of epicycles.

Heath, Thomas. *A History of Greek Mathematics.* 2 vols. Reprint. New York: Dover, 1981. Includes a section on Hipparchus in the second volume, emphasizing his probable contributions to the origin of trigonometry and establishing his place in the history of mathematics.

Lloyd, G. E. R. *Greek Science After Aristotle.* New York: W. W. Norton, 1973. Rather than giving a separate treatment to the subject, this work discusses the contributions of Hipparchus as they arise in a general study of ancient science from the fourth century B.C.E. to the end of the second century C.E. The attention given to Hipparchus is appropriate and appreciative.

Neugebauer, Otto. *A History of Ancient Mathematical Astronomy.* 3 vols. New York: Springer-Verlag, 1975. This work contains a section on Hipparchus in volume 1, briefly discussing what little is known about his life and chronology and devoting the rest of its space to a careful consideration of his astronomical work. There are some mathematical and astronomical symbols and formulas that the layperson may find difficult.

Ptolemy. *Ptolemy's "Almagest."* Translated by G. J. Toomer. Princeton, N.J.: Princeton University Press, 1998. Much of what is known about Hipparchus is based on Ptolemy's words. This fine translation has complete notes and a useful bibliography.

SEE ALSO: Apollonius of Perga; Eratosthenes; Eudoxus; Ptolemy (astronomer); Strabo.

RELATED ARTICLES in *Great Events from History: The Ancient World*: c. 275 B.C.E., Greeks Advance Hellenistic Astronomy; c. 250 B.C.E., Discoveries of Archimedes.

HIPPOCRATES
Greek physician

Hippocrates is credited with separating the practice of medicine from magic and superstition, inaugurating the modern practice of scientific observation, and setting the guidelines for high standards of ethical medical practice.

BORN: c. 460 B.C.E.; Island of Cos, Greece
DIED: c. 370 B.C.E.; Larissa, Thessaly (now in Greece)
AREA OF ACHIEVEMENT: Medicine

EARLY LIFE

Hippocrates (hihp-AWK-ruh-teez) was born in Cos; he lived during the period spanning the end of the fifth century and the first half of the fourth century B.C.E., according to two references to him in Plato's dialogues. Though little else can be thoroughly documented, many legends, possibly true in parts, have been offered by commentators regarding Hippocrates' early life. According to tradition, he was one of several sons of Praxithea and Heracleides. He probably had the education suitable to one of his background, which would include nine years of physical education, reading, writing, spelling, music, singing, and poetry. After another two years at a gymnasium, where he would have had intensive training in athletics, it is conjectured that Hippocrates studied medicine under his father, a member of the priest-physician group known as Asclepiads. This training was a form of apprenticeship in a medical guild.

In addition to his training, which consisted of following a physician and observing his treatment of patients, Hippocrates is believed to have traveled to the nearby islands of the Aegean Sea, to the Greek mainland, and possibly to Egypt and Libya, to study the local medical traditions. He is thought to have met the philosopher Democritus and the rhetorician Gorgias.

His sons Thessalus and Draco carried on the family tradition of medical practice. As testimony to his fame, legend also has it that King Perdiccas of Macedonia asked Hippocrates and another physician, Euryphon, to examine him and that Hippocrates helped him to recover from his illness.

Hippocrates was equally renowned as a teacher, giving rise to the image of the "Tree of Hippocrates," beneath which students sat and listened to him. Plato, a younger contemporary, referred to Hippocrates the Asclepiad as the very type of the teacher of medicine. Some historical accounts suggest that Hippocrates habitually covered his head with a felt cap, though the reason for this habit is only a matter of speculation. This description did, however, help twentieth century archaeologists to identify a likeness of him.

LIFE'S WORK

That Hippocrates was a well-known Greek physician who lived in the period of golden achievements in Greek history is undisputed. The rest of his achievements remain a matter of scholarly debate, centered on the problem of *Corpus Hippocraticum* (fifth to third century B.C.E.; Hippocratic collection), a substantial body of writings whose authorship seems to be spread out over different historical periods.

Thus the medical views expressed in this collection are carefully referred to as the ideas of Hippocratic medicine, acknowledging the complete lack of confirmation about the identity of his actual writings. Of the approximately seventy unsigned treatises that constitute the collection, only two are definitively known to have been written by Hippocrates' son-in-law, Polybus, because another famous ancient writer, Aristotle, quoted from them.

The normal historical tendency has been to attribute those that are written with authority and good sense and that seem to be of the approximately right time period to Hippocrates and the rest to other authors. The debate over the authorship of the *Corpus Hippocraticum* itself has produced an enormous body of scholarship; one tentative point of agreement is that the earliest essays are from the fifth century B.C.E. and the latest about two centuries later. To cloud the matter even further, the Hippocratic writings themselves are inconsistent, suggesting that the collection incorporates the thinking of different schools of medical practice.

The collection is historically important precisely because it had more than one purpose: to establish medicine as a practice distinct from philosophy and religion and, in furtherance of this goal, to collect information about this separate discipline in writing for the future edification of patients and physicians. Part of this effort involved debate with other schools of thought, such as the Cnidian school.

The centers of medical teaching were often in the temples of healing known as Asclepieions. The two most famous ones of the time were on Cos and Cnidus, between which there were both a traditional rivalry and a fundamental difference in approach to medical practice. The Cnidus practitioners, under the guidance of the chief physician, Euryphon, seemed to have been much concerned about the classification of diseases and continued the tradition of deductive knowledge of disease derived from the practice of ancient Greece, Babylonia, and Egypt. Hippocrates was of the Coan school, which worked more inductively, concentrating on observation and treatment of the entire patient and taking into account the mental as well as the physical state.

The first important contribution of the Hippocratic writers—to separate medicine from the shackles of religion, superstition, and philosophy—is apparent in the first text of the collection, *Peri archaies ietrikes* (fifth or fourth century B.C.E.; *On Ancient Medicine*, 1849), which is a reminder that medicine had previously been very much a matter for philosophical speculation. This essay establishes medicine as a branch of knowledge with its own rational methods and describes a practice that calls for skill and craft and art, one based on observation.

Hippocratic medicine recognized disease as a natural process and further suggested that most acute diseases are self-limited. The symptoms of fever, malaise, and other apparent sicknesses were not considered to be mysterious spiritual symptoms but merely the body's way of fighting off the poison of infection. Epilepsy, for exam-

Hippocrates. (Library of Congress)

ple, much feared as a mysterious, sacred affliction, is discussed as a medical problem. The focus of Hippocratic medicine was on regulation of diet, meaning not merely nutrition but exercise as well. The adjustment of diet to the physical state of the patient was thus viewed as the original function of medicine, and the importance of the kind of food and its preparation to treat sickness was recognized early.

The Hippocratic writers mention other ideas equally surprising in their modern relevance and influence, such as the notion that great changes, whether in temperature, periods of life, or diet, can lead to illness. Thus the collection of four books titled *Peri diaites oxeon* (fifth or fourth century B.C.E.; *Regimen, in Acute Diseases*, 1849) starts with the argument that health is affected by the totality of diet and exercise; the age, strength, and constitution of the individual; the seasonal changes; variations in wind and weather; and the location in which the patient lives. The Hippocratic idea that a local condition must be treated in conjunction with the general condition, the whole constitution (*physis*) and the complex relations to the environment, is also remarkably similar to the modern notion of holistic healing.

Though many of the other practices and theories have been discarded medically, some were influential for so long that they have been incorporated into the history of Western culture. For example, among the most influential theories set forth in the Hippocratic collection is the idea that the human body is composed of four fluid substances: blood, phlegm, yellow bile, and black bile. Perfect health results from the balance of these fluids in the body. Concomitantly, an excess or deficiency or imperfect mixture results in pain, sickness, and disease. The influence of this theory is apparent in many classics of Western literature, such as the plays of William Shakespeare and Ben Jonson.

Hippocratic medicine was also conservative, seeking primarily to help the sick when it would be beneficial. Medicine was defined by three purposes: It should relieve suffering, reduce the severity of the illness, and finally, abstain from treating that which was beyond the practice of medicine. The physician's job was to help the natural recovery process with diet and regimen, to be administered only after careful observation of the individual symptoms and the patient's constitution. The remedies recommended were mild and adapted to the various stages of the disease; drugs were relatively rare. Most important, sudden and violent measures to interrupt the natural course of the disease were forbidden.

The Coan school believed in prognosis, in predicting, from the experience of long and careful observation, the course of the disease and furthermore in telling the patients and their friends, so that they could be mentally prepared for what might follow, even if it were death. This dictum prevented the physician from prescribing ineffective or expensive treatments simply to remain busy; it is thought that the Hippocratic physician would not even undertake the treatment of a hopeless case, though he probably did his best to make the patient as comfortable as possible.

The most important view in the Hippocratic collection—the most important because it is still unchanged over the course of two thousand years—is the clearly expressed concept of the medical profession as it is summed up in the Hippocratic oath. The doctor is defined as a good man, skilled at healing. Perhaps for this definition alone, the man who is thought to have written or inspired the Hippocratic writings has been called the father of medicine, a title that suggests the ideal of the philosopher-physician—similar to the ideal of the philosopher-king—a person with moral character as well as practical skills.

SIGNIFICANCE

Hippocrates was a much admired physician whose contemporaries were also giants in their fields: Aeschylus, Sophocles, and Euripides in tragedy; Aristophanes in comedy; Thucydides in history; Pericles in government. Leaving aside the question of authorship of the Hippocratic writings, it is clear why the figure of Hippocrates, for whom the collection is named, is so revered: The keen observations of human behavior and health recorded in these pieces remain fruitful reading.

The Hippocratic writings include a book of more than four hundred aphorisms, pithy observations that have been absorbed, though sometimes in a mutilated form, into the English language, influencing those outside the medical field. The most famous of these, popularly remembered as "Life is short, Art long," started as

> Life is short, whereas the demands of the (medical) profession are unending, the crisis is urgent, experiment dangerous, and decision difficult. But the physician must not only do what is necessary, he must also get the patient, the attendants, and the external factors to work together to the same end.

Others reveal a common sense which has been proven over and over again: "Restricted or strict diets are dangerous; extremes must be avoided"; "People who are excessively overweight (by nature) are far more apt to die suddenly than those of average weight"; "Inebriation removes hunger (for solid foods)."

If much of the rest of the body of medical knowledge represented by Hippocrates has long since been surpassed, its spirit has not. Hippocrates and his colleagues changed the attitude toward disease, freeing medicine from magic and superstition and insisting on the importance of observation over philosophical speculation. The Hippocratic writings established medicine as a separate discipline with a scientific basis, setting down in writing the medical knowledge of the time regarding surgery, prognosis, therapeutics, principles of medical ethics, and relations between physicians and patients, thus laying the foundations and formulating the ideals of modern medicine.

—*Shakuntala Jayaswal*

FURTHER READING

Edelstein, Ludwig. *The Hippocratic Oath: Text, Translation, and Interpretation*. Baltimore: The Johns Hopkins University Press, 1943. This monograph argues that the Hippocratic oath represented the opinion of a small segment of Greek medical society, was based on Pythagorean principles, and served as a voluntary oath of conscience between teacher and student.

Goldberg, Herbert S. *Hippocrates, Father of Medicine*. New York: Franklin Watts, 1963. A short, simple overview of the life and work of Hippocrates, his times, and his relevance to modern health practice. Includes index.

Jones, W. H. S., trans. *Hippocrates*. 4 vols. 1923-1931. Reprint. New York: Putnam, 1995. Among the best English translations and critical editions of Hippocratic writings, this work is part of the Loeb Classical Library edition. Greek texts face their English counterparts.

King, Helen. *Hippocrates' Woman: Reading the Female Body in Ancient Greece*. New York: Routledge, 1998. Explores early gynecology as based on ideas about women taken from myths. King argues that doctors twisted ancient Greek texts into ways of controlling women's behavior.

Levine, Edwin Burton. *Hippocrates*. New York: Twayne, 1971. Levine introduces the problems of scholarship in identifying authorship of the Hippocratic writings. The discussion focuses on ideas presented in various selected essays. Includes notes, an index, and an extensive annotated bibliography.

Moon, Robert Oswald. *Hippocrates and His Successors in Relation to the Philosophy of Their Time*. New York: AMS Press, 1979. This work briefly categorizes the philosophies underlying the practice of ancient medicine before and after Hippocrates. Index.

Phillips, E. D. *Greek Medicine*. New York: St. Martin's Press, 1973. Phillips traces practical and theoretical achievements of Greek medicine up to Galen. Includes selected references to the Hippocratic collection, an appendix on the cult of Asclepius, illustrations, an extensive bibliography, and indexes.

Temkin, Owsei. *Hippocrates in a World of Pagans and Christians*. Baltimore: The Johns Hopkins University Press, 1995. Examines the ways in which Hippocratic practice helped establish a relationship between medicine and monotheistic worship.

SEE ALSO: Aretaeus of Cappadocia; Aristotle; Aulus Cornelius Celsus; Democritus; Diocles of Carystus; Galen; Herophilus.

RELATED ARTICLES in *Great Events from History: The Ancient World*: c. 500-400 B.C.E., Greek Physicians Begin Scientific Practice of Medicine; c. 157-201 C.E., Galen Synthesizes Ancient Medical Knowledge.

HIPPOLYTUS OF ROME
Roman bishop

Initiating Christian commentary on the books of the Old Testament, Hippolytus also provided the first systematic handbook regulating the ordination of the ministry and the conduct of worship. In addition, he elaborated the connections among the Greco-Roman philosophical schools and popular practices and the diversity of opinions that divided the Christian communities.

BORN: c. 170 C.E.; place unknown
DIED: c. 235 C.E.; Sardinia (now in Italy)
AREAS OF ACHIEVEMENT: Religion, philosophy

EARLY LIFE

While it remains impossible to construct an early life for Hippolytus (hihp-AHL-uht-uhs), it is possible to identify what he studied and when. It is instructive to compare his education with those of the great Alexandrians who were his contemporaries, Clement of Alexandria (c. 150-c. 220) and Origen (c. 185-c. 254). His style is more spirited and argumentative—perhaps more typical of his Western roots. Hippolytus wrote in Greek and was the last Christian author in Rome to do so. He is often thought to have been a student of Saint Irenaeus in Gaul; both tackled the subject of heresy, which at that time meant simply a variety of opinions or practices. Nevertheless, Hippolytus's work *Kata pasōn haireseōn elenkhos* (*The Refutation of All Heresies*, 1868, also known as *Against All Heresies*), written before 199, took on its own character.

Two special dimensions gave focus to his thought. In order to elaborate the catalog of heresies and extend it into his own time, Hippolytus sought the intellectual foundations for that "diversity of opinions." He looked to Greco-Roman philosophers, magicians, astronomical inquiries, and what he could learn of the inner working of the "mystery religions."

Hippolytus's study of astronomy and astrology preserved what had taken shape in the centuries immediately following the crucifixion of Jesus Christ. He cataloged details of horoscopes and their attempted applications as well as the calculations of the sizes of Earth and planets and their respective distances from one another. These calculations led to arithmetic considerations, including the interrelationship between numbers when expressed by letters of the alphabet and words or names. The role of magicians, with their amulets and contrivances for illusion, indicated other activities competitive with Christianity. His quotations from others' works, extensive though disjointed, remain a principal source for studies of pre-Socratic and later ancient intellectual tendencies.

The summary of these inquiries was not the primary focus of Hippolytus's concern, but he used his subjects' words as a basis for his theory that the Christian intellectual formulations at odds with his own teaching originated in this environment. His conclusion is that the truth is found by a method of intellectual contrast: Let the other side speak and demonstrate its own inherent falsity. His books belong to his mature years; his method illustrates how and what he learned in his early life.

The other dimension of his formative years was the practice of the so-called apostolic tradition. In it were both patterns for administering the internal core of Christian worship and the external requirements necessary for church structure. Hippolytus's later account of the tradition indicated the status of developments within the expanding Christianity of the second century, in which his religious practice was grounded, and the reason that in later years he critically opposed every alternative form with such vigor.

LIFE'S WORK

Hippolytus was already a mature thinker and author when he became well known. The Roman emperor Septimius Severus (r. 193-211) initiated a Christian persecution in 202, the tenth year after his power was secured against rivals. Hippolytus's response was a treatise on the Antichrist and a commentary on the Book of Daniel. These works illustrate how Hippolytus perceived that the Imperial demand for acts of obedience (emperor worship) violated the inhabitants of the Roman world. He reflected Greek concerns that went back to the power of the *demos* (urban people in *ekklesia*, or "assembly"). He recognized that the Roman state, with "feet of clay," had usurped the divine prerogatives, in a manner analogous to the example first propounded in the Book of Daniel.

His interpretation was cautioned by his own chronological considerations: Like others of his day, he affirmed the world to be not more than fifty-seven hundred years old, so that the millennium remained at least three hundred years in the future. His discussion of the Antichrist is the most comprehensive written in antiquity.

Severus's persecution was severe in Alexandria, where it touched the life of an adolescent whose father was executed and who, but for his mother's intervention, would have followed in his father's path. That youngster was the budding biblical scholar Origen, who became, in spite of his youth, the director of the greatest Christian school. Origen spent considerable time in hiding. Accompanied by his principal benefactor, Ambrose, Origen came to Rome to hear Hippolytus speak. When Origen returned to Alexandria, Ambrose provided funding for secretarial staffing and encouraged Origen to emulate Hippolytus in the production of biblical commentaries and other works against critics of Christianity, especially those of greatest intellectual impact.

Hippolytus is known for commentaries on many biblical books. A close examination of these studies reveals an emerging New Testament. He recognized twenty-two books as authoritative: four Gospels, thirteen of Paul's Epistles, one Acts of the Apostles, three catholic Epistles, and the Revelation. He also knew and used the Gospel of the Hebrews, the Epistle to the Hebrews, Second Peter, James, Jude, Shepherd of Hermas, Revelation of Peter, and Acts of Paul. The distinction seems to be based on what was allowed to be read in "our churches" and what, while proper for private reading, could not be publicly used because such had come into being "in our own times."

In the period of Severus's persecution and the following relative prosperity for the Church, Zephyrinus was bishop of Rome (198-217). By the early third century, urban Rome counted some one million people, with thirty to forty thousand estimated to be Christian. This number was spread throughout the metropolis and not located in any single area. The tradition of "house churches," which goes back before the Constantinian revolution in 325, provides evidence for this diversity of location, as does the development of catacomb burial grounds.

Hippolytus described Zephyrinus as "an ignorant and illiterate individual," one "unskilled in ecclesiastical definitions," "accessible to bribes and covetous," and "incapable of forming his own judgment or of discerning the designs of others." The bishop also apparently represented a theological stance, relative to the interrelationship of Father and Son within the Christian Godhead,

Hippolytus of Rome (foreground). (Library of Congress)

ing, and sentencing to the mines on Sardinia. While Victor was bishop of Rome (189-199), an Imperial concubine, Marcia, also a Christian, obtained release for the captives from Commodus. As a "martyr," Callistus came to the attention of Victor, who pensioned him to Antium. When Zephyrinus became bishop, he brought Callistus into his service to take charge of the clergy and of the one principal asset held by the churches—the cemetery catacombs.

At Zephyrinus's death, none of these men was any longer young. Callistus officially succeeded, but Hippolytus held a rival claim, leading directly to theological disputes. Callistus claimed that Hippolytus's view of the relation of Father and Son was "ditheistic," while Hippolytus accused Callistus of so unifying the Persons of the Godhead that the Father could be said to have suffered equally when the Son was crucified. Some of the confusion may have arisen from the difference between the Greek of Hippolytus and his followers and the Latin of Callistus and his followers. (There was a sizable Greek-speaking population in officially Latin Rome.)

which was at odds with Hippolytus's understanding, so that there were continual disturbances among the diverse Christians of the capital. The theoretical formulation developing during the third century that there was but one bishop for each conurbation prevented the ancient acknowledgment that Hippolytus was a rival bishop in Rome itself. In modern times, he receives the designation "first antipope."

His principal rival was Callistus, also known as Calixtus, who became bishop of Rome on the death of Zephyrinus. During the reign of the emperor Commodus (180-192) and his urban prefect Sejus Fuscianus, Callistus had been a slave to Carcophorus, a minor official in the Imperial household; both were Christian. Carcophorus handled money deposited by widows and others toward burial expenses, and Callistus was directed to make a profitable return on these deposits through banking transactions. A failure led to his flight and capture, a further confrontation with the law, scourg-

Conflict of theology moved into conflict of administration. The actual role of Hippolytus became more evident, especially in his linguistic use of the episcopal "we" for pronouncements against the decisions of Callistus. These decisions included permission for those married more than once to enter the clergy, for clergy to marry and remain in orders, for women to live in concubinage with slaves (Roman law did not permit full marriage to occur between slaves or between them and free persons), and for second baptism of those reconciling with the Church after lapse. In Hippolytus's opinion, such decisions were bad enough, but Callistus, on his own authority, determined that as bishop of Rome he could forgive any sin, including that of abortion.

Like his North African contemporary Tertullian, Hippolytus was a champion of old causes in a rapidly changing world; tradition was encountering a variety of internal opinions and external pressures. This conservatism is nowhere better illustrated than in *Apostolikē paradosis* (second or third century; *The Apostolic Tradition of Hippolytus*, 1934). This handbook contains the most ancient forms and prayers for the ordination of bishops, presbyters, and deacons; for the consecration of confessors; and for the appointment of widows and readers. It also contains instructions for catechumens for baptism and first participation in the Lord's Supper and for fasting and praying.

Callistus died naturally and was buried not in the catacomb that bears his name but in a crypt on the Via Aureliana; his feast day is October 14. Hippolytus outlived Callistus and his successors Urban and Pontian. When Maximinus became emperor in 235, severe persecution was resumed, going after the ranking leadership. Both Pontian and Hippolytus were sent to the mines of Sardinia, where they were worked to death. Anterus was bishop for three months during this upheaval, before Fabian, a layman, was elected directly into the episcopal office in 236.

Fabian was able to recover the bodies of both Pontian and Hippolytus and bring them back to Rome. Pontian was interred in the papal crypt of Saint Callistus. In 236 or 237, Hippolytus was interred in the cemetery on the Via Tiburtina that subsequently carried his name. The date of his burial, August 13, remains his feast day.

SIGNIFICANCE

The historical testimony to Hippolytus's role within the Church, even to location, became vague. The church historian Eusebius of Caesarea, writing less than a century later, identified Hippolytus as a bishop of "some" church; that vagueness might be excused were it not that Eusebius knew directly of Hippolytus's writings from the library at Aelia Capitolina (Roman Jerusalem) and of his contemporaneity with Zephyrinus and the Roman persecutions of that era. A century after Eusebius, the Latin biblical scholar Saint Jerome, in *De viris illustribus* (392-393; lives of illustrious men), repeats this vague affirmation of Hippolytus's bishopric—"the name of the city I have not been able to learn"—in spite of extending the list of publications and confirming the correlation with Origen, whom Jerome knew had called Hippolytus his "taskmaster."

In 1551 a statue of a person seated on a throne was discovered in Rome. Because the throne base had engraved on it Hippolytus's table for computing the date of Easter and a list of his writings, the statue was reconstructed with a bearded head—as though it were Hippolytus— even though the statue in body and dress is that of a woman, probably a follower of the philosopher Epicurus.

It was not until the mid-nineteenth century—an era refueled with conflict centering on the bishop of Rome and pronouncements of "infallibility"—that the personality and concerns of Hippolytus were rediscovered. Those of his works that had survived had in the interim been confused with the writings of others, and only a chance manuscript-discovery permitted his own works to be disentangled from the hodgepodge of other writings.

—*Clyde Curry Smith*

FURTHER READING

Eusebius. *The Ecclesiastical History and the Martyrs of Palestine*. Translated by Hugh Jackson Lawlor and John Ernest Leonard Oulton. 2 vols. London: Society for Promoting Christian Knowledge, 1927-1928. The text of Eusebius's history in English translation appears in the first volume. Eusebius sets in time, space, and circumstance the earliest Christian figures, including the "succession from the apostles" and the variety of alternative opinions as well as the Roman Imperial context with its intermittent persecutions. The second volume provides extensive notes.

Grant, Robert. *Augustus to Constantine: The Thrust of the Christian Movement into the Roman World*. New York: Harper and Row, 1970. By placing the history of early Christianity within its widest socioeconomic context, Grant provides the reader with an interpretation of Christianity within, rather than apart from, its world. Chapters 10 through 13 most concern Hippolytus, though he informs many other sections.

Hippolytus. *The Treatise on the Apostolic Tradition of St. Hippolytus of Rome, Bishop and Martyr*. Edited by Gregory Dix. Ridgefield, Conn.: Morehouse, 1991. Along with a readable edition of the text concerning the earliest Christian liturgical practice, this work provides a discussion of it with an account of its rediscovery and its centrality to Hippolytus's thought. Includes preface, bibliography, and index.

Quasten, Johannes. *The Ante-Nicene Literature After Irenaeus*. Vol. 2 in *Patrology*. Westminster, Md.: Newman Press, 1962-1966. This handbook presents in chronological and geographical order those Christian authors who provide the literature and thought of the ancient Church. Hippolytus is a major figure in this volume.

Wordsworth, Christopher. *St. Hippolytus and the Church of Rome in the Early Part of the Third Century*. Reprint. Eugene, Oreg.: Wipf & Stock, 2001. This first reconstruction of the life of Hippolytus is significant for the history of the Church in the mid-nineteenth century. A major feature is the Greek text and English translation of the ninth book of *The Refutation of All Heresies*, which includes autobiographical information.

SEE ALSO: Eusebius of Caesarea; Saint Irenaeus; Origen; Saint Paul; Tertullian.
RELATED ARTICLES in *Great Events from History: The Ancient World*: c. 50-c. 150 C.E., Compilation of the New Testament; c. 110 C.E., Trajan Adopts Anti-Christian Religious Policy; 200 C.E., Christian Apologists Develop Concept of Theology; c. 250 C.E., Saint Denis Converts Paris to Christianity; October 28, 312 C.E., Conversion of Constantine to Christianity; 313-395 C.E., Inception of Church-State Problem; 361-363 C.E., Failure of Julian's Pagan Revival; 380-392 C.E., Theodosius's Edicts Promote Christian Orthodoxy; October 8-25, 451 C.E., Council of Chalcedon.

HOMER
Greek poet

Homer wrote two Greek epic poems that played a crucial role in the birth of classical Greek civilization. These works greatly influenced history, theology, and literature in Greece and in the entire Western world.

BORN: c. early eighth century B.C.E.; possibly Ionia, Asia Minor (now in Turkey)
DIED: c. late eighth century B.C.E.; Greece
AREA OF ACHIEVEMENT: Literature

EARLY LIFE

The Greeks were not sure where Homer (HOH-muhr) was born, when he lived, or even if such a person actually existed. The name "Homer" may simply be a generic term denoting "one who fits a song together." Still, various sources provide some information about the provenance of the *Iliad* (c. 750 B.C.E.; English translation, 1611) and the *Odyssey* (c. 725 B.C.E.; English translation, 1614). The language of the poems is Ionic and Aeolic Greek, which points to an East Greek origin. (In antiquity, East Greece included the west coast of Asia Minor and neighboring islands.) Greek tradition named either the island of Chios or the town of Smyrna, both in eastern Greece, as Homer's birthplace. Chios boasted a guild of rhapsodists who recited the Homeric epics and who claimed, without any proof, to be directly descended from Homer. The geographical references in the poems, particularly in the *Iliad*, are most specific and correspond to the Ionian area and thus also support an East Greek origin.

Homer's precise dates are no easier to ascertain than his birthplace. At first sight, twelfth century features in the poems, the Mycenaean geography of the *Iliad*'s Catalogue of Ships, and ancient weapons such as Ajax's great body shield and Odysseus's curious boar's tusk helmet seem to suggest that the poems were composed around the time of the Trojan War. However, archaeological discoveries have shown that certain features of weaponry and warfare described in the poems were not in use before 900 to 700 B.C.E. For example, the shield of Achilles in book 18 of the *Iliad* clearly depicts the law courts and agricultural life of an eighth century city-state, not the twelfth century monarchy of Agamemnon. The internal evidence from the poems points to a poet working in the eighth century but trying to paint a picture of the Mycenaean era more than four hundred years before his own time. The fact that there are virtually no references to events after 700 B.C.E. indicates that the poems must have been completed by that date.

LIFE'S WORK

The obscurity surrounding the author of the *Iliad* and the *Odyssey* is partly a product of the conventions of the epic poetic genre itself. An epic poet was expected simultaneously to create and sing a poem on a heroic subject before an audience, without the help of writing. This astonishing feat was possible because generations of epic poets had developed traditional language, phraseology, and motifs with which to tell the stories of the great Greek heroes. Such poetry placed a premium on the ability to create poems orally, not on the development of a unique individual style. Hence, any trace of the personality of the author of the *Iliad* and the *Odyssey* has vanished.

Greek epic poets may have sung their songs at the dinner gatherings of the aristocracy, as do the bards in the *Odyssey*, as well as to members of their own artisan class. How the *Iliad* and the *Odyssey* moved from oral performance to their final written forms is not fully understood. The poems are clearly not an assemblage of stories stitched together by a collector. As both poems develop organically around a central theme and exhibit a sophisti-

Homer. (Library of Congress)

to the gods, possess a constant order of elements that is easily remembered. This regularity of events creates a strong sense that both nature and human life proceed along a carefully ordered path and makes anomalous behavior such as Achilles' seem especially jarring.

Even the major plot elements of both the *Iliad* and the *Odyssey* are very likely traditional. Both poems employ a "withdrawal-devastation-return" framework with a revenge motif at the end, a format typical of many epic poems. Scholars have found evidence for other earlier Greek epics that contained many of the thematic elements of both the *Iliad* and the *Odyssey*, but the Homeric poems are unique in their tight organization around one major theme: the *Iliad* around the wrath of Achilles, the *Odyssey* around the homecoming of Odysseus.

The action of the *Iliad* covers only fifty-three days in the last year of the ten-year siege of Troy, although the poet cleverly inserts references to the events of the previous decade that make the listeners believe they have experienced the entire war. The abduction of the Greek queen Helen by the Trojan prince Paris forms the backdrop for the events of the *Iliad*, which takes as its subject the wrath of one individual, Achilles, the greatest Greek warrior at Troy, and the devastation it wreaks on him and all heroic society.

cated handling of poetic techniques, they are most likely the creations of a single monumental composer at the end of a long poetic tradition.

In creating the *Iliad* and the *Odyssey*, Homer employed the various conventions of epic style in a skillful and flexible manner, which satisfied both aesthetic expectations and the need for fluent oral composition. The artificial dialect mixture of the poems was created for the epic and was never used by anyone in actual conversation. The mixture of dialect forms gives the language of the poems a unique "epic" quality and provides metrically convenient words for the poets to use in oral composition. Composition is also aided by ornamental epithets that are applied to divinities, people, and objects. Such adjectives not only satisfy metrical demands but also illuminate beautifully the unchanging nature of the heroic world. Thus, ships are "swift" even when standing still, and Odysseus is already "much-suffering" in the *Iliad*, before starting his ten-year trek home. Even the sequence of events in the poems is structured in a way that helps the poet compose aloud. Frequently repeated traditional scenes, such as arming for battle and sacrificing

The leader of the Greek army, Agamemnon, has taken away Achilles' concubine after he is forced to give up his own. Achilles responds to this slight by laying down his arms, a correct response according to the heroic code of honor. However, he errs when refusing the fabulous ransom Agamemnon offers him to return to battle. The result is devastation: Patroclus, Achilles' closest companion, dies at the hands of the Trojan hero Hector while trying to take Achilles' place. This catastrophe finally goads Achilles to return to battle. He is, however, now fighting not for the Greeks but for personal revenge, a crucial difference. He abandons the civilized humanity of the heroic code and crosses over into inhuman frenzy, which the poet likens to the uncontrollable force of nature. He kills Hector, the embodiment of the civilized humanity that Achilles has left behind. Achilles continues to rage out of control until the gods intervene to persuade him to give Hector's body back to the aged King Priam. Thus, the *Iliad* is more than a tale of heroic exploits: It is a profound meditation on life and death, culture and nature, and individualism and society.

The *Odyssey* tells the story of the return of Odysseus to his wife, Penelope, and son, Telemachus, on the island of Ithaca after ten years of fighting at Troy. It is the only surviving story of many that narrated the experiences of the Greek heroes returning home after the Trojan War. Odysseus's return itself took ten years, but, by using a technique seen in the *Iliad*, the poet compresses the time frame of the *Odyssey* into forty days in the tenth year of the journey, while casting many backward glances over the events of the preceding decade.

While the poem centers on the return of Odysseus from Troy, the content of the *Odyssey* is thematically more diverse than that of the *Iliad*, and its structure is correspondingly more complex. It contains four major themes: the journey of Odysseus on his way home, replete with fantastic monsters, beguiling sorceresses, and a trip to the underworld; a parallel journey of Telemachus, who is now twenty years old and trying to grow to adulthood despite an absent father; Odysseus's actual return to Ithaca and his winning back of home and wife; and his revenge, aided by his son and faithful retainers, on the suitors who were vying for Penelope's hand. The amalgamation of all these elements into a coherent whole is most skillfully accomplished. Frequent changes of scene and an exciting narrative of his adventures by Odysseus create suspense and keep the plot moving quickly.

The *Odyssey* paints a vivid picture of life in Greece. It focuses on the city-state Ithaca and, in particular, on the nuclear family represented by Odysseus, Penelope, and Telemachus. It also includes moving portraits of slaves and other nonaristocratic characters. The center of attention, however, is always Odysseus, who is not a tragic hero such as Achilles or Hector. He is a survivor who lives by his wits and his tongue. He confronts death on a daily basis but is never in danger of dying before accomplishing his goals. In later Greek literature, Odysseus became a symbol of persuasion, trickery, and deceit.

The *Iliad* and the *Odyssey* thus focus intently on the role of the individual in society. This theme is rooted in the events of the eighth century, the very beginnings of classical Greek society. The great Mycenaean Greek kingdoms had collapsed by 1150 B.C.E. for reasons that are not understood but that probably included intense internecine warfare. The absence of the palace bureaucracies forced small, separate groups of people to fend for themselves but ultimately allowed them to grow from 1150 to 800 B.C.E. into the city-states of classical Greece.

The ninth and eighth centuries, during which the heroic epic tradition probably took shape, saw the forma-tion of many city-states composed of individual households, much like that of Odysseus and in contrast to the extended Mycenaean family of the Trojan king Priam seen in the *Iliad*. Each member of such a household bore a great responsibility for its maintenance and, by extension, that of the city-state. Hence, the *Iliad* and the *Odyssey* devote much attention to the crucial question of the proper behavior of individuals in society.

An awareness of the common Greek heritage shared by all the city-states sprang up alongside the growth of the different separate political units. The Olympic Games, to which every city sent athletes, were founded in 776 B.C.E. The Panhellenic oracle at Delphi began dispensing political as well as personal advice around the same time. The Homeric epics, which record an expedition of many Greek heroes united against a common enemy, may be seen as both an affirmation of the connections between all the Greeks and support for the hero-founders of the new city-states.

SIGNIFICANCE

Homer bequeathed to the West the beginnings of its literature. Countless works have been inspired and influenced by the epics, in which may be found the seeds of narrative, comedy, and tragedy. The sheer genius of the *Iliad* and the *Odyssey* becomes obvious in comparison with other epic poems that have survived from ancient Greece. Fragments of other epics, known collectively as the Epic Cycle, indicate that the Homeric epics were the originals around which the poems of the cycle were fashioned. These other poems were much shorter and, judging from the scanty remains, inferior in scope and style.

Homer also gave both history and religion to the ancient Greeks, and through them to Western civilization. Little has been said here about the gods mentioned in the poems, because humans are so clearly the focus of the poet's interest. The gods, who have the same emotions and social structure as the struggling mortals, appear frequently as mirrors for human activities and emotions, but there is one essential difference. The gods will never die, whereas death is the inevitable portion of every hero. Heroic life is merely a brief and shining prelude to a long and shadowy afterlife in Hades. Immortality for humans is obtainable only in heroic song. The gods' immortality underscores the mortality of the heroes, adding emphasis and pathos. The gods watch avidly the events unfolding on the Trojan plain, but they cannot rescue anyone—even their own offspring—from death when it is fated.

—*Julie A. Williams*

FURTHER READING

Clarke, Howard. *The Art of the "Odyssey."* Englewood Cliffs, N.J.: Prentice-Hall, 1967. General introduction to the *Odyssey*, with a chapter comparing the *Iliad* and the *Odyssey*.

Homer. *The Iliad*. Translated by Robert Fagles. New York: Pengiun, 2003. Fagles's verse translation is accompanied by a long and detailed introduction by Bernard Knox. Includes glossary and textual notes.

_____. *The Odyssey*. Translated by Robert Fitzgerald. New York: Farrar, Straus, and Giroux, 1998. Poetic translation includes introduction by D. S. Carne-Ross and bibliographical references.

Kirk, G. S. *The Songs of Homer*. Cambridge, England: Cambridge University Press, 1962. The standard introduction to the Homeric poems, focusing on their language and composition. Illustrated.

Nagy, Gregory. *The Best of the Achaeans*. Rev. ed. Baltimore: The Johns Hopkins University Press, 1999. Sophisticated and stimulating analysis of the hero in Greek civilization and how the language of Greek epic defines his role.

Powell, Barry B. *Homer*. Malden, Mass.: Blackwell, 2004. A concise introduction by a professor of classics writing with students in mind. Considers the Homeric question by reference to recent scholarship. Good bibliography.

Schein, Seth. *The Mortal Hero: An Introduction to Homer's "Iliad."* Berkeley: University of California Press, 1984. An introduction to a literary interpretation of the *Iliad*. Explores questions of mortality, the gods, and heroism in detail. Excellent references.

Snodgrass, Anthony. *Archaic Greece: The Age of Experiment*. Berkeley: University of California Press, 1980. Economic and social history of the age in which the epics were composed, based on the archaeological evidence. Well illustrated.

Wace, Alan J. B., and Frank H. Stubbings, eds. *A Companion to Homer*. New York: St. Martin's Press, 1962. Essays on language, transmission of the text, and especially the archaeological evidence pertaining to the Homeric poems, by authorities in each field. Slightly dated but still authoritative. Illustrated, with many references.

SEE ALSO: Hesiod; Vergil.

RELATED ARTICLES in *Great Events from History: The Ancient World*: c. 2000 B.C.E., Composition of the Gilgamesh Epic; 1400-1300 B.C.E., Aqhat Epic Is Composed in Ugarit; c. 1250 B.C.E., Fall of Troy Marks End of Trojan War; 776 B.C.E., Olympic Games Are First Recorded; 775 B.C.E., Delphic Oracle Provides Guidance for City-States; c. 750 B.C.E., Homer Composes the *Iliad*; c. 700 B.C.E., Hesiod Composes *Theogony* and *Works and Days*; c. 550 B.C.E., Vālmīki Composes the *Rāmāyaṇa*; c. 400 B.C.E.-400 C.E., Composition of the *Mahābhārata*; 19 B.C.E., Roman Poet Vergil Dies.

HORACE
Roman poet

The most important Roman lyric poet, Horace took an appealing, deceptively casual approach to poetry. His poems became a beloved source of proverbial wisdom and a model for Renaissance and neoclassical poets throughout Europe.

BORN: December 8, 65 B.C.E.; Venusia (now Venosa, Italy)
DIED: November 27, 8 B.C.E.; Rome (now in Italy)
ALSO KNOWN AS: Quintus Horatius Flaccus
AREA OF ACHIEVEMENT: Literature

EARLY LIFE

Horace (HOR-uhs) was born in Venusia, a military colony in southern Italy. Nothing is known of his mother or siblings. His father was a freed slave whose profitable post as an auctioneer's assistant enabled him to buy land and to send his son to school in Rome. There, with the sons of senators and knights, Horace was educated in the Greek classics. Horace asserts in his *Satires* (35, 30 B.C.E.; English translation, 1567) that he received better education from his father, who accompanied him on walks through Rome's bustling marketplace while commenting on the character, appearance, and manners of passersby.

Sometime in his late teens or early twenties, probably in 45 B.C.E., Horace went to the Academy in Athens to study moral philosophy. As this education was unusual for a freedman's son, it is likely that Horace's father recognized his son's brilliance and wished to give him every chance for success. In Athens, Horace began to write

Greek poetry. In 44 B.C.E., Marcus Junius Brutus came to Athens after the assassination of Julius Caesar. He recruited young Romans studying there to fight with him against Caesar's successors, Marc Antony and Octavian. The call to fight for freedom and the Republic stirred Horace to join Brutus's forces in 43 B.C.E. Though young and inexperienced, he became military tribune (that is, an officer capable of commanding a legion) and probably rose at the same time to the social rank of knight. At the Battle of Philippi, in 42, Brutus was killed and his army defeated. Rather than continue a hopeless cause, Horace returned to Rome.

His prospects were not bright. He had chosen the losing side; his father was dead; and the farm in Venusia had been confiscated for distribution to a loyal legionnaire or officer. However, Horace still had equestrian rank and must have had some money because he soon purchased the post of scribe in the quaestor's office, where public financial records were kept. In 39 B.C.E., a general amnesty for Brutus's followers removed whatever stigma was attached to Horace's military service.

While a scribe, Horace began writing verse again, Latin imitations of the satirical, witty Greek poet Archilochus. A friendship was begun between Horace and the poet Vergil. The two were physical as well as poetic contrasts. Horace was short and stout; Vergil was tall and lean. The longevity of their friendship showed that these differences made them complements, not opposites.

Horace. (Kim Kurnizki)

LIFE'S WORK

What drew Horace and Vergil together was a common interest in poetry. Vergil was at work on the *Eclogues* (43-37 B.C.E., also known as *Bucolics*; English translation, 1575), idealized poems about rural life, while Horace was writing realistic, trenchant observations of urban mores. Though their topics differed, these young writers shared an interest in the craft of poetry. Vergil was acquainted with Gaius Maecenas, one of Octavian's counselors, who acted as patron to promising poets. In 39 or 38 B.C.E., Vergil introduced Horace to Maecenas. At their second meeting Maecenas invited Horace to join his literary circle. Horace, still without a published poem, accepted the offer. The decision shaped the rest of his life.

In late 35 B.C.E., Horace published the first book of *Satires*. It is a misleading title for most modern readers, who associate satire with ridicule and attack. To Horace, the word meant a mixture, or medley, indicating that the work lacked a narrative structure, consistent characters, and interrelated themes. Horace also referred to these poems as *sermones* (conversations), which suggests their casual tone and varied subject matter. One poem describes a trip with Vergil, another tells a ribald story about witches, a third is a fond remembrance of his father, and a fourth is a witty portrait of a boor. All the poems display a mastery of metrical form and reveal a good-humored and congenial persona. The poems are like conversations over dinner, and the poet is a most attractive host.

In 33 B.C.E., Maecenas rewarded Horace's skillful and popular poetry: He gave Horace land in the Sabine Valley. Prudently, Horace leased most of it to tenant farmers and built himself a house. The so-called Sabine Farm became his beloved retreat from the world, where he lived simply but comfortably amid attentive servants and good friends, with leisure to concentrate on writing. Maecenas also gave Horace property in Rome and a house in Tibur. All the evidence indicates that Horace and Maecenas not only were mutually useful acquaintances but also possessed a deep friendship based on a mutual love of literature.

Horace published two works in the year 30 B.C.E. One was a second book of *Satires*, less personal and more consciously literary in subject matter than the first book. This volume includes the famous story of the Country Mouse and the City Mouse as well as a parody of Homer's *Odyssey* (c. 725 B.C.E.; English translation, 1614). The second work was the *Epodes* (English translation, 1638), which was actually written ten or twelve years earlier. Shorter and more lyrical than *Satires*, these seventeen poems treat a miscellany of topics: the pains and pleasures of love, impatience with pretenders and sycophants, tribulations of the civil war. The poems reflect a variety of moods as well as topics, but this variety does not result in incoherence. Rather, the contrasts create the sense of balance, the portrait of personality that cannot be moved from the golden mean, either by life's follies or by its tragedies.

Horace himself testifies that these years were the happiest of his life. He spent most of the time at Sabine Farm, reading and composing. Maecenas's circle remained intact for more than a decade. Most educated Romans, including Octavian, who—after 27 B.C.E.—called himself Augustus, admired Horace.

During this productive period Horace worked on the *Odes* (23, 13 B.C.E.; English translation, 1621) and the *Epistles* (c. 20-15 B.C.E., English translation, 1567). The *Odes* display Horace's poetic virtuosity: Eighty-eight poems in a variety of traditional and experimental meters demonstrate his absolute control of language and his ability to suit expression to subject matter. Like previous works, the *Odes* treat a spectrum of political, personal, and social topics. Whatever the topic, the theme is that piety, moderation, and fellowship undergird the good life. The spirit of the *Odes* is autobiographical; the poems reflect Horace's contentment with life. Fortunately, contentment does not breed complacency or conceit in the poet. If life is good, it is not the poet's doing: Honest friends, a peaceful state, and kindly gods bestow this gift. It is somewhat surprising that Horace's contemporaries found the poems unsatisfactory, though perhaps that can be explained by the poems' unfamiliar style. Subsequent generations reversed the verdict and regarded the *Odes* as a personal and national masterpiece.

The *Epistles* return to the conversational tone of the early *Satires*. Addressed to friends, the poems engage Horace's companions, one by one, in reflection on literary and philosophical topics. Perhaps the verses were a return to the atmosphere of the Academy, where the pleasurable speculation on life's puzzles was interrupted by Brutus's politics. The *Epistles* are leisurely, intelligent

poems—indeed, compliments, tributes, and memorials to the discussions they record.

Ironically, the world these collections describe rapidly vanished. A plot against the life of Augustus was indirectly linked to Maecenas. He and his circle lost their privileged place near the ruler. Vergil died in 19 B.C.E., while Maecenas himself seems to have been distracted by a new favorite, the poet Sextus Propertius.

In 17 B.C.E., Augustus himself prompted Horace to begin writing again. Horace's relationship with Augustus was never easy. Though Horace admired Augustus's efforts to reunify the country after the civil war, he maintained his distance. Horace never flattered the emperor openly and obsequiously, as other poets did, though Augustus teased him about the omission. In this year, Augustus declared that Rome, the world's capital, would hold the Secular Games. He requested Horace to write a hymn for the gods' blessing. Horace's *Carmen Saeculare* (17 B.C.E.; *The Secular Hymn*, 1726), sung by a chorus of twenty-seven girls and twenty-seven boys, prays that fertility, morality, tranquillity, and glory may be the gods' gifts to Rome. The final book of *Odes*, published in 13 B.C.E., repeats this idea of festivity and ritual as bonding devices of community and celebrates poetry as itself a festive ritual.

Horace's last work was a second book of *Epistles*, also published in 13 B.C.E. These three long poems discuss the art to which Horace devoted his life. The first epistle calls on Augustus to be the patron of developing poets rather than to enshrine a set of classics. The second epistle is Horace's moving envoi to poetry: He senses that his career is done. The third epistle is the famous *Ars poetica* (17 B.C.E.; *The Art of Poetry*), in which Horace advises both readers and writers on the appreciation of poetry. It contains opinions (for example, that poetry should be pleasing as well as instructive and that a poet should set a work aside for nine years before trying to publish it) that subsequent generations would take, in very un-Horatian fashion, as a consistent philosophy of criticism. Maecenas died in the year 8 B.C.E., without having regained Augustus's full confidence. Horace died within months of his friend and was buried beside him.

SIGNIFICANCE

Horace was spokesman for a generation of the Roman leadership class. He expressed its fears, its hopes, its discontents, and its pleasures. Because his poems interwove autobiography, social commentary, philosophy, and politics, they provided succeeding generations with insights, precepts, and bons mots on topics of enduring interest. Horace was remembered, therefore, in fragments. Readers quoted him and poets imitated him on particular topics (such as love, sex, the gods, wine, and friendship) that overlapped with their own concerns. Horace appealed to different audiences for different reasons: to second century Romans for patriotism, to medieval monks for piety, and to seventeenth century gentlemen for rakish self-indulgence.

Beyond the classical period, Horace was most influential among aristocratic writers in European countries between 1500 and 1850. He appealed to them on several levels. His character showed how a congenial, generous temperament draws together like-minded and similarly talented individuals. His biography showed that one could become important and yet live independent of the world's demands. His career showed that art and politics were allies in fostering a sense of national identity and culture. His secular philosophy made clear that one could live morally without religious faith—an especially important idea to educated Europeans, who, for three centuries, watched Christian countries war with one another and split into hostile denominations. Thus, Horace was a poet whose life and art illustrated universal themes. When a society made urbanity and leisured culture its goals, its poets chose Horace as their guide.

In the twenty-first century, Horace attracts attention for an additional reason. Modern scholars appreciate him as a verbal craftsman; his work is valued for the scope of the whole more than for the cleverness or beauty of the parts. Criticism today tends to value poets less as seers and legislators of humankind than as fabricators, the makers of meaning out of confusion. Contemporary critics study Horace's work in search of the unity in each volume of *Odes, Epistles*, and *Epodes*. The diversity of subjects and moods is no longer the sign of miscellaneous disquisition but the sign of subtle coherence. Critics aim to recover the poet's reason for grouping his poems and to gauge their aesthetic impact on the reader. Like William Shakespeare and every great author, Horace is always freshest to those who encounter him again and again.

—*Robert M. Otten*

FURTHER READING

Commager, Steele. *The Odes of Horace*. Reprint. Norman: University of Oklahoma Press, 1995. Commager's book is widely regarded as the most substantial, incisive commentary on Horace's verse in English. He approaches Horace as a "professional poet," one committed to art as a vocation. Horace's distinctive characteristic is that he writes poetry about poetry, as if he wants to define the idea and demonstrate verbal craftsmanship at the same time.

Hadas, Moses. *A History of Latin Literature*. New York: Columbia University Press, 1964. The chapter on Horace demonstrates why he is the most beloved of Roman poets. It articulates the virtues of common sense, good fellowship, and literary pleasure that generations of European writers have found in the poetry.

Highet, Gilbert. *The Classical Tradition: Greek and Roman Influences on Western Literature*. New York: Oxford University Press, 1985. Through judicious use of the index, the curious student can survey European attitudes toward Horace's poetry since the Renaissance. Highet is an opinionated and lively critic who inspires a return to primary texts.

Horace. *The Complete Works*. Translated by Charles E. Passage. New York: F. Ungar, 1983. This volume offers an unusual translation: without rhyme, in the original meter, with notes about the context of and allusions in each poem. Passage makes Horace accessible to the new reader and offers a fresh perspective to readers familiar with other translations.

Levi, Peter. *Horace: A Life*. London: Duckworth, 1997. The first major biography since 1957, Levi's work considers Horace's personal life, including his father's status as a freed man and why the poet never married.

Oliensis, Ellen. *Horace and the Rhetoric of Authority*. New York: Cambridge University Press, 1998. This introduction to Horace covers the poet's entire career and all the genres in which he wrote.

Putnam, Michael C. J. *Artifices of Eternity*. Ithaca, N.Y.: Cornell University Press, 1986. Putnam presents a detailed analysis of Horace's last work, the final book of *Odes*. Traditionally the fourth book is considered not unified and is said to show Horace bowing to Augustus's influence. Putnam argues that Horace remakes Augustus as the poet sees him. The approach has interesting biographical implications for interpreting Horace's last years.

Reckford, Kenneth J. *Horace*. New York: Twayne, 1969. Reckford's brief, appreciative study attempts to chart the growth of Horace's imagination and thought by a survey of his poetry. The emphasis is on theme rather than poetic technique. Includes notes and bibliography.

Wilkinson, L. P. *Horace and His Lyric Poetry*. 2d ed. Cambridge, England: Cambridge University Press,

1968. Though this study is intended for the student who can read Latin, the first four chapters are accessible to the general reader. Wilkinson's *Horace* is neither the patriotic versifier of Augustus's policies nor the contented gentleman farmer addicted to ease and companionship. Wilkinson provides valuable summaries of Horace's thoughts on subjects ranging from religion to love to the state to poetry.

SEE ALSO: Augustus; Marcus Junius Brutus; Catullus; Clodia; Quintus Ennius; Martial; Plutarch; Sulpicia; Terence; Vergil.
RELATED ARTICLES in *Great Events from History: The Ancient World*: 43-42 B.C.E., Second Triumvirate Enacts Proscriptions; 27-23 B.C.E., Completion of the Augustan Settlement; 19 B.C.E., Roman Poet Vergil Dies; November 27, 8 B.C.E., Roman Lyric Poet Horace Dies.

HYPATIA
Egyptian scientist

A mathematician, astronomer, inventor, and teacher, Hypatia is best known for the manner of her death, which made her a symbol of courage in the face of an oppressive Christian Church.

BORN: c. 370 C.E.; Alexandria, Egypt
DIED: March, 415 C.E.; Alexandria, Egypt
AREAS OF ACHIEVEMENT: Mathematics, astronomy, science

EARLY LIFE

Almost nothing is known about the early life of Hypatia (hi-PAY-shyuh). Ancient Rome did not have the elaborate systems of record keeping found in the modern world, and no one in Hypatia's own time considered her worthy of biographical attention. Although she made significant contributions to at least three fields of study, Hypatia is more famous for the way she died than for what she accomplished in life. While many legends about her early life have sprung up over the centuries, none are considered reliable sources of information about Hypatia's youth.

What is known is that she was the daughter of the pagan Theon, an important astronomer and mathematician in Alexandria. Alexandria, the third largest city in the Holy Roman Empire, had once been the intellectual center of Greece and was the home of the first university three hundred years before the time of Christ. Mathematics was taught then by Euclid, whose ideas about plane geometry are still at the foundation of basic geometry courses more than two thousand years later.

Seven hundred years after Euclid, Theon was teaching mathematics in Alexandria and writing books of commentary on ancient mathematics. He may also have written several books on the occult. At the time of Hypatia's birth, the Roman Empire was suspicious of Greek mathematics and attempted to suppress it. The life of a pagan scholar was intellectually exciting but politically dangerous.

The traditional date for Hypatia's birth is 370, although most scholars now believe that she must have been born earlier. Nothing is known of her mother. Some stories tell that Theon supervised her complete education, demanding that she discipline her mind and body. According to this version of her life, Theon developed a rigorous system of exercises Hypatia performed every day and oversaw her training in public speaking and rhetoric. Probably he taught her mathematics himself. According to legend, Hypatia was Theon's most talented student, surpassing her teacher and eventually becoming his collaborator. She apparently never married but devoted herself to her studies.

LIFE'S WORK

Eventually Hypatia became a university lecturer herself, teaching mathematics and astronomy. According to historical accounts left by Socrates Scholasticus (c. 379-450), a contemporary of Hypatia, she was a charismatic teacher who attracted the best students from Asia, Africa, and Europe. They were drawn to her intelligence, her legendary beauty, and her reputation as an oracle.

In Hypatia's time, mathematics was a different type of inquiry than it is today. Although it dealt with the relationships between geometric shapes, such as spheres, ellipses, and cones, mathematics was used to discover the composition of the universe. A series of mathematical problems might seek to reveal such things as the locations of the planets or the location of the soul. The discipline was not far removed from astronomy, which was similar to what the modern world would consider to be astrology.

Although few of Hypatia's writings survive, much is known about her research, because descriptions of her work do survive in the form of letters and histories written by her students and followers. Her most important work was a thirteen-volume commentary on the *Arithmētika* (c. 250 C.E.; "Arithmetica" in *Diophantus of Alexandria: A Study in the History of Greek Algebra*, 1885) by Diophantus, who is sometimes called the "father of algebra." Diophantus, who lived in Alexandria in the second century C.E., was interested in equations that can be solved in more than one way, which are now known as "indeterminate" or "Diophantine" equations. He also studied quadratic equations. Hypatia proposed some new problems and new solutions to complement Diophantine's work. A fragment of her *Commentary on the Arithmetic of Diophantus* was found in the Vatican in the fifteenth century.

Her second major work was the eight-volume *Treatise on the Conics of Apollonius*. Apollonius, who lived in Alexandria in the third century B.C.E., was most interested in the geometry of cones, especially because conic sections such as the ellipse and the parabola could explain planetary orbits. Hypatia's commentary presents Apollonius's difficult concepts in a more accessible form, suitable for her students, and supplements the earlier work. Hypatia's text was the last important consideration of conic sections until the seventeenth century. Other writings thought to be Hypatia's include a commentary on Ptolemy's great second century compilation of all that was then known about the stars, the *Mathēmatikē syntaxis* (c. 150 C.E.; *Almagest*, 1948). She is also believed to have written, in collaboration with Theon, a discussion of the work of Euclid—the last important contribution to Euclidean geometry until the end of the sixteenth century.

In the late tenth century, a researcher named Suidas identified several more writings that he attributed to Hypatia, but no copies are known to exist today. According to letters written by one of her students, the philosopher Synesius, Hypatia was also skilled as an inventor. She is said to have developed a form of the astrolabe, used to measure the positions of planets and stars, and other instruments for the study of astronomy.

As a philosopher, Hypatia is identified as a member of the Neoplatonic school, a group based on the later teachings of Plato. Neoplatonism, the last major pagan philosophy, was founded by Plotinus a hundred years before Hypatia's birth; Neoplatonists saw reality as a hierarchical order with "the One" at the center, linked together by the "World Soul." During Hypatia's lifetime, Neoplatonism was, according to Greek thought, scientific and rational. Hypatia was as well-known as a philosopher as

she was as a mathematician, and she was frequently consulted on matters philosophical and political. She was a celebrated figure, sweeping through the city on her chariot on her way to the university or to the homes of important people. It was this fame that ultimately led to her death.

Western mathematics had long been dominated by the Greeks and held little interest for the Romans (imagine trying to do even simple algebra using Roman numerals). The increasingly Christianized Roman Empire believed that science and mathematics were heretical and evil. The Church leaders also felt threatened by Neoplatonism, which involved a focus on rationalism that contradicted the notion of faith. During Hypatia's life, Alexandria was locked in a struggle between the ancient Greek ways and beliefs and the changing ideas of the Roman Christians who now ruled the city.

For most of Hypatia's career, Alexandria had been under the control of the Roman prefect Orestes, a secular civil authority who admired Hypatia and her work. In 412, however, he was joined by Cyril, a Christian bishop who was determined to eliminate any threats to Christian domination. Cyril began an immediate campaign to eradicate all heretical teachings in Alexandria, including Judaism and Neoplatonism. Despite being warned, Hypatia refused to convert to Christianity or to stop teaching mathematics and Neoplatonism.

Many stories have been told of how Hypatia met her death, each more vivid and gory than the next. What seems irrefutable is that Cyril continued his oppression, inciting mob violence against those he labeled heretics. The city of Alexandria was in chaos, as Alexandrians were torn between loyalty to tradition and to the new rulers, between science and faith. According to one account, Cyril came to believe that he could increase his own standing by calling for a virgin sacrifice. Other accounts explain that Cyril saw Hypatia as an obstacle to his shared power with Orestes.

Whatever his reason, he let it be known that Hypatia was a Satanist, a witch whose charisma was the result of evil powers. One day during March in 415, as she made her way through the city in her chariot, Hypatia was surrounded by a mob of Christian fanatics, dragged to a nearby church, stripped naked, tortured, and killed. Her body was taken outside the city and burned. There is no real evidence that Cyril ordered her execution, but historians for sixteen centuries have assumed he was responsible. No investigation was ever performed; Orestes was replaced, and the Christian hold on Alexandria was advanced. Cyril was later named a Roman Catholic saint.

SIGNIFICANCE

Hypatia was a talented philosopher, mathematician, and astronomer and a gifted teacher of all three disciplines. None of her accomplishments in these areas changed the world, although her name has been held in high regard for nearly sixteen centuries. Perhaps her greatest significance is as a symbol of her age, a marker of changing times. Hypatia, often called the "Divine Pagan," is considered the last of the great pagan scientists; her death marked the end of an era. She was the last of the important Greek mathematicians; because of the fall of Alexandria shortly after her death, no important progress was made in Western mathematics for a thousand years. In the eighteenth and nineteenth centuries, with the publication of Edward Gibbon's *The History of the Decline and Fall of the Roman Empire* (1776-1788) and Charles Kingsley's historical novel *Hypatia* (1853), she was regarded as a symbol of courage in the face of an oppressive Christian Church.

For the women's movement that came of age in the late twentieth century, she has also emerged as an important symbol, this time as a "first": the first important woman philosopher, mathematician, and astronomer. The leading journal of feminist philosophy is titled *Hypatia*, and its editors have stated, "Her name reminds us that although many of us are the first woman philosophers in our schools, we are not, after all, the first in history."

—*Cynthia A. Bily*

FURTHER READING

Alic, Margaret. *Hypatia's Heritage: A History of Women in Science from Antiquity Through the Nineteenth Century*. Boston: Beacon, 1986. Examines biographical and scientific evidence to reveal the lives and accomplishments of women in natural and physical sciences and mathematics. The material dealing with Hypatia claims for her the roles of the last important pagan scientist in the Western world and the representative of the end of ancient science.

Cameron, Alan, and Jacqueline Long. *Barbarians and Politics at the Court of Arcadius*. Berkeley: University of California Press, 1993. A study of the Gothic rebellion and massacre under the reign of the Roman Emperor Arcadius in 399-400 C.E. Because one of the best contemporary accounts of these events was written by Synesius, a student of Hypatia, the book includes a clear and thorough discussion of Hypatia's philosophy and accomplishments.

Dzielska, Maria. *Hypatia of Alexandria*. Translated by F. Lyra. Cambridge, Mass.: Harvard University Press, 1995. Examines Hypatia as she appears in literature of the past sixteen hundred years and traces what can be confirmed of her biography. Also discusses her students and followers. Includes bibliography.

Kingsley, Charles. *Hypatia*. Chicago: W. B. Conkley, 1853. A historical romance novel based on Hypatia's life. Kingsley was involved in the Christian Socialism movement and was strongly anti-Catholic. His interpretation of Hypatia's death places the blame squarely on Cyril.

Molinaro, Ursule. "A Christian Martyr in Reverse: Hypatia." In *A Full Moon of Women*. New York: E. P. Dutton, 1990. Included in this volume's twenty-nine portraits of notable women is a feminist treatment of Hypatia's brilliance, her refusal to live according to convention, and her murder at the hands of a tyrannical patriarchy.

Osen, Lynn M. *Women in Mathematics*. Cambridge, Mass.: MIT Press, 1974. A historical study of women mathematicians from Hypatia through the early twentieth century and of the social contexts within which they worked. Includes a chapter devoted to Hypatia's life and accomplishments as well as a chapter on "The Feminine Mathtique," which discusses uses and abuses of stories of exceptional women.

Perl, Teri. *Math Equals: Biographies of Women Mathematicians and Related Activities*. Menlo Park, Calif.: Addison-Wesley, 1978. Includes a brief biography of Hypatia and a series of activities to familiarize students with the mathematics important to some of her written commentaries: Diophantine equations and the geometry of conic sections. Also offers mathematical games to introduce an overview of women in mathematics.

SEE ALSO: Enheduanna; Euclid; Ptolemy (astronomer); Sappho; Sulpicia.

RELATED ARTICLES in *Great Events from History: The Ancient World*: 332 B.C.E., Founding of Alexandria; c. 300 B.C.E., Euclid Compiles a Treatise on Geometry; 415 C.E., Mathematician and Philosopher Hypatia Is Killed in Alexandria.

IGNATIUS OF ANTIOCH
Antiochene bishop

Ignatius served as bishop of Antioch from the early 60's to the early 100's and was an important theologian and the exemplary martyr of the early Christian church. By his writings and example, Ignatius strengthened the office of bishop in the church hierarchy, clarified many central Christian doctrines, such as the Real Presence and the Virgin Birth, and formulated the strategy and tactics of voluntary martyrdom.

BORN: c. 30 C.E.; Antioch, Syria
DIED: December 20, 107 C.E.; Rome (now in Italy)
AREA OF ACHIEVEMENT: Religion

EARLY LIFE

Ignatius (ihg-NAY-shee-uhs) was born to pagan parents at Antioch, the capital of Syria, during the second quarter of the first century, about 30 C.E. One of the largest cities of the Roman Empire, the terminus of both Eastern caravan routes and Mediterranean sea-lanes, Antioch was the center of commerce and Greek culture in the eastern Mediterranean region. It contained a large Jewish refugee population but was also the site of the first gentile Christian community, which became the mother church of Christian churches throughout the Roman Empire.

According to the earliest traditions, Ignatius was converted to Christianity by the Apostle John, whose theology certainly profoundly influenced him, and in the early 60's was consecrated bishop of Antioch by Peter and Paul on their way to Rome and martyrdom under the emperor Nero. A charming but improbable story identifies Ignatius with the small child whom Jesus Christ presented to his disciples at Capernaum as a lesson in humility. It would appear that this story is a wordplay on the surname Theophorus (or "God-bearer"), which Ignatius took later in life; the tradition shows that Ignatius was believed to have been born before the death of Christ. Ignatius, the eager young Christian convert, was blessed with strong faith and great abilities; these qualities brought him quickly to prominence in the Christian community at Antioch and to the attention of Saint Evodius, bishop of Antioch, and Peter and Paul.

LIFE'S WORK

As bishop of Antioch in the first century, Ignatius presided in dignity over the early gentile church, leading the greatest Christian community in the Roman Empire. Here he furthered Paul's work in transforming Christianity from a Jewish sect into a world religion. Ignatius was an exemplary bishop who maintained Christian order in the community and orthodoxy in doctrine; like a good shepherd, he protected his flock from the wolves during the persecution under the emperor Domitian (81-96 C.E.).

Bishop Ignatius of Antioch suffered martyrdom not then but later under the humane, progressive, and just emperor Trajan. Though a pagan, the emperor was a good man and an enlightened ruler who regarded himself as the servant and protector of his people. So admirable was Trajan that there would arise a popular legend in the Middle Ages that Pope Gregory the Great had interceded with God and secured Trajan's salvation. In *La divina commedia* (c. 1320; *The Divine Comedy*, 1802), Dante, following this legend, placed Trajan, though a pagan, in Heaven alongside certain eminently just Christian rulers.

Trajan's policy toward Christianity was both moderate and legalistic. He strongly discouraged active persecution of Christians, though he allowed the legal prosecution of those who had been publicly denounced to the Roman authorities. Trajan laid down this policy explicitly in 112 in his correspondence with Pliny the Younger, the governor of Bithynia. Roman officials were forbidden to search out Christians. Those denounced to the state were to be prosecuted by their denouncers before Roman magistrates, but these Christians were given procedural guarantees and the opportunity and encouragement to recant Christianity and conform to the state religion. Thus, under Trajan, Christians could be punished if legally proved guilty and then only if obdurate in their belief.

Allegations against Christians included treason, sedition, unspecified crimes, impiety, depravity, and membership in illegal secret societies, but ultimately their real offense was their primary allegiance to the kingdom of God instead of to the Roman Empire. Ignatius could not, in good conscience, pay reverence to the Imperial cult and the divinities in the Roman pantheon because he believed them to be idols and demons. To the emperor Trajan, however, respect for the state religion was an important aspect of civic duty and a mark of patriotism; thus, to him, a gesture of respect was a very reasonable demand.

Ironically, Trajan's policy was probably more destructive than Domitian's and Nero's persecutions had been. It was neither sporadic nor localized but was spread throughout the Empire. It seemed reasonable, legal, and just. Nevertheless, Trajan's policy threatened to divide and demoralize Christian communities by encouraging apostasy and discrediting Christian martyrs. The prosecution that Ignatius of Antioch faced was much more insidious than other persecutions because it appeared humane and just.

Later Christian hagiographers imagined a dramatic personal confrontation between Ignatius and Trajan. Ignatius was prosecuted at a time when Trajan's recent victory in Dacia had occasioned enthusiastic displays of loyalty to the Roman gods throughout the Empire. Ignatius's trial, as described by his biographers, probably never occurred, but the fictitious confrontation did capture the global conflict between the city of God and the earthly city. In fact, not Trajan himself but one of his governors condemned Ignatius; Ignatius was sent to Rome rather than executed in Antioch simply because the many celebrations of Trajan's Dacian victory had caused a scarcity of gladiators and victims for the Roman games. Moreover, the Roman mob found it especially entertaining to watch the death of an old man such as Ignatius. Although mistaken in imagining the personal confrontation between Ignatius and Trajan, the hagiographers were perceptive in personifying the conflict between two cities, two systems of belief, and two ways of life. It was not so much good versus evil as the best of the temporal—Emperor Trajan—versus the best of the spiritual—Bishop Ignatius.

The most significant historical source for the life's work of Ignatius is the collection of his seven epistles, which he wrote around 107, during his journey under guard to Rome and his martyrdom. Ignatius's journey was triumphant and even ecstatic: Along the way, his Roman guards permitted him to visit important Christian communities in Asia Minor and the Balkans, where he preached, blessed, ordained, and was received enthusiastically. Pausing at Smyrna, Ignatius wrote four epistles, to the Christians of Ephesus, Magnesia, Rome, and Tralles. Traveling on to Lystra, he paused there and wrote three more epistles, to the Christians at Philadelphia and Smyrna, and in farewell to Polycarp, the bishop of Smyrna, who was Ignatius's protégé and later would himself suffer martyrdom. The contents of the seven epistles cover Christian beliefs and practices and stress Christian unity in doctrine and hierarchical organization. The most poignant of the letters is the epistle written to the Romans, in which Ignatius begged the Christian community at Rome not to try to have him reprieved.

Ignatius's eagerness and joy to be a martyr, that is, publicly to witness his Christian faith even unto death, appears to some modern psychoanalytical commentators

Ignatius of Antioch. (Hulton|Archive by Getty Images)

"disturbed" and "self-destructive." Ignatius welcomed not self-destruction but union with Jesus Christ, humbly and faithfully identifying his own martyrdom with Christ's sacrifice.

Ignatius anticipated his martyrdom, which he perceived in almost Eucharistic imagery. He would become as "God's wheat, ground fine by the teeth of the wild beasts, that he may be found pure bread, a sacrifice to God." Across the millennia ring his triumphant words:

> Come fire and cross, and grapplings with wild beasts, cuttings and manglings, wrenchings of bones, breaking of limbs, crushing of my whole body, come cruel tortures of the Devil to assail me. Only be it mine to attain unto Jesus Christ.

On December 20, 107, according to Greek tradition, on the last day of the public games, Ignatius of Antioch was brought into the Flavian Amphitheater, the infamous Colosseum, and thrown to the lions. He welcomed the two ravenous lions, which immediately devoured him, leaving in the bloody sand only a few of his larger bones.

Reverent Antiochenes gathered up the relics and took them to Antioch, where they were enshrined.

SIGNIFICANCE

Ignatius of Antioch was among the greatest of the early fathers of the Church. Admirable as the bishop of Antioch and brilliantly imaginative as a Christian theologian, his greatest contribution was doubtless his exemplary martyrdom. His fortitude, commitment, authenticity, love, joy, and ecstasy illustrate the maxim that the blood of the martyrs is the seed of the Church. Ignatius was an Apostolic Father, having met and been associated with the Apostles Peter and John and with Paul, the Apostle of the Gentiles. Ignatius proved the continuity and catholicity of the early Christian Church by bridging the distance between Jew and Gentile and between the Age of the Apostles and the Age of the Martyrs.

—*Terence R. Murphy*

FURTHER READING

Butler, Alban. *Butler's Lives of the Saints*. Edited by David Hugh Farmer. Collegeville, Minn.: Liturgical Press, 1995-2000. The standard hagiography in English, Alban Butler's eighteenth century collection is arranged according to feast days (Ignatius's day is February 1).

Eusebius of Caesarea. *The Ecclesiastical History of Eusebius Pamphilus*. Translated by Christian Frederick Cruse. Grand Rapids, Mich.: Baker Book House, 1955. The standard narrative primary source for the first three centuries of Christianity, Eusebius's account includes some information on Ignatius of Antioch.

Frend, W. H. *Martyrdom and Persecution in the Early Church: A Study of a Conflict from the Maccabees to Donatus*. Grand Rapids, Mich.: Baker Book House, 1981. A penetrating examination of the social and psychological dynamics of martyrdom. Includes an insightful discussion of Ignatius of Antioch.

Ignatius of Antioch, Saint. *The Epistles of St. Ignatius*. In *The Apostolic Fathers*, translated and edited by Kirsopp Lake. 2 vols. Cambridge, Mass.: Harvard University Press, 1976-1977. These epistles are the principal primary source for the life of Ignatius and also are important for the history of early Christianity.

Lane Fox, Robin. *Pagans and Christians*. San Francisco: HarperSanFrancisco, 1995. An ambitious synthesis of scholarship about the cultural and social context of early Christianity, Lane Fox's work is important for background information.

SEE ALSO: Jesus; John the Apostle, Nero; Saint Paul; Saint Peter.

RELATED ARTICLES in *Great Events from History: The Ancient World*: 64-67 C.E., Nero Persecutes the Christians; c. 110 C.E., Trajan Adopts Anti-Christian Religious Policy.

IMHOTEP
Egyptian physician and architect

Imhotep, the priest-physician who was deified as the Egyptian god of medicine, was also an architect and is credited with starting the age of pyramid building.

FLOURISHED: Twenty-seventh century B.C.E.;
Memphis, Egypt
AREAS OF ACHIEVEMENT: Architecture, medicine

EARLY LIFE

Little is known about the early life of Imhotep (ihm-HOH-tehp) except that his father, Kanofer, is believed to have been a distinguished architect and that his mother was named Khreduonkh. Imhotep was probably born in a suburb of Memphis, and his early training was most likely influenced by his father's profession. To judge by his later reputation, he received a liberal education and was interested and skilled in many areas.

That Imhotep was a real historical figure in an influential position and that he was evidently respected for his wisdom and talent is deduced from his position as the chief vizier for one of the most famous Egyptian kings, Zoser (c. 2700-c. 2650 B.C.E.), of Egypt's Third Dynasty. From what is known of the duties of viziers at a later period, it is likely that Imhotep had to be both efficient and extremely knowledgeable, for the vizier was in charge of the judiciary and the departments of the treasury, the army and navy, internal affairs, and agriculture. As a judge, Imhotep is reputed to have penned many wise proverbs, although unfortunately none is known to have survived.

The increasing stature of Imhotep during his lifetime is apparent in the changes in statuettes discovered. In some, he appears to be an ordinary man, dressed simply;

he looks like a sage, seated on a throne or chair with a roll of papyrus on his knees or under his arm, and is depicted as reading or deep in thought. When he achieved full god status, he was shown standing, carrying a scepter and the ankh, with the beard typically worn by gods. His mother was then regarded as the mother of a god and his wife, Ronpe-nofret, as the wife of a god; following what appears to have been a tradition of Egyptian deities, Imhotep was considered to be the son of the god Ptah as well as the son of the mortal Kanofer.

LIFE'S WORK

Imhotep's reputation is remarkable not only because he was accomplished in so many fields but also because he is credited for his accomplishments in two distinct fields and in two distinct periods: his achievement as an architect during his lifetime and his high position as priest-physician, for which he was accorded a divine status several hundred years after his lifetime. In his capacity as architect, Imhotep is credited with designing and implementing the building of the earliest large stone structure—the Step Pyramid of Saqqara—which inaugurated the age of pyramid building in Egypt.

A story much debated among scholars nevertheless reveals the reverence with which Imhotep was regarded. According to the Legend of the Seven Years' Famine, it happened that the Nile River had not risen to its usual level sufficient to irrigate the land for seven years, resulting in a shortage of food. King Zoser, distressed by the suffering of his subjects, consulted Imhotep about the birthplace of the Nile and its god. After absenting himself for a brief period of research and study, Imhotep revealed some unspecified "hidden wonders" that the king investigated; he offered prayers and oblations at the temple of the god Khnum and, promised by the god in a dream that the Nile would not fail again, endowed the temple of the god with land and gifts in gratitude.

Imhotep's achievement in the field of medicine is equally legendary. His reputation as a healer seems to be based almost entirely on his apotheosis from a wise and talented man who was a contemporary of Zoser, to a medical demigod, and then finally to a full deity of medicine in the period of Persian rule (about 525 B.C.E.). In the period of the Greco-Egyptian rule, he was called Imouthes and identified with Asclepius, the Greek god of medicine, resulting in a gradual assimilation of the two figures.

Imhotep's reputation as a wise healer is thus one that seems to have developed several hundred years after his death. The godlike status accorded him as a healer not only shows how he was revered but also points to the inextricable connection between medicine, magic, and religion in Egyptian medical practice. In addition to his other duties, Imhotep held an important position as the Kheri-Heb, or chief lector priest. Thus entitled to read holy religious texts that were believed to have magical powers, he served as a mediator and teacher of religious mysteries. Among the priest-physicians, two main classes predominated: the physicians who had some systematic training in medicine and the larger class of those who emphasized the power to cure with amulets and magic incantations. Because the names or achievements of other practitioners of medicine in ancient times have been discovered while the specific qualifications of Imhotep as a healer are not as clearly documented, it is thought that his duties as a priest who was regarded as a magician may have initiated his reputation as a medical man.

In all likelihood, his cumulative achievements as architect, physician, priest, sage, and magician led to the great reverence in which Imhotep was held and to his subsequent deification. The magic he was reputed to practice may well have been grounded in the considerably well-developed art of healing in ancient Egypt. A

Imhotep. (Library of Congress)

number of medical documents have survived in rolls of papyrus: the Ebers Papyrus, the Hearst Papyrus, the Berlin Medical Papyrus, the Kahun Medical Papyrus, the London Medical Papyrus, the Edwin Smith Papyrus, and another papyrus in Berlin. The Ebers Papyrus, the most important of these, was written about 1550 B.C.E. but appears to be a compilation of other books written centuries before. Parts of it were already in existence during Imhotep's lifetime and may therefore be construed to reflect the kind of medicine and magic Imhotep practiced.

The Ebers Papyrus lists many prescriptions for a variety of ailments. Approximately 250 kinds of disease are identified in the various papyruses. Doses of medication and modes of administration are specified, suggesting that clinical examination, diagnosis, and therapeutics were quite progressive. Drugs from herbs, vegetable products, minerals, and parts of animals were studied and administered in many forms, such as gargles, salves, lozenges, pills, and plasters. Simple surgery was performed, and fractures were successfully treated. The custom of mummification, involving the dissection of bodies to remove the viscera, undoubtedly provided the Egyptians with a better working knowledge of the internal organs and practical anatomy than existed elsewhere for many centuries afterward.

Although the papyruses demonstrate that empirical knowledge existed and medical treatment was widely practiced, they also reveal that such practical measures were always accompanied by magical formulas. Disease was treated primarily as a visitation of a malign spirit or god, not as a dysfunction of the body. The healer therefore had to identify the nature and the name of the evil spirit, determine how far it had invaded the body, take into account the times and seasons of the year in gauging the virulence of the attack, and then try to drive it out with every possible means—including magic, ritual, and material remedies. Some physicians would seek to differentiate between symptoms that called for drugs, magic, or temple sleep, suggesting that already in ancient times an elementary form of psychiatry was practiced.

Several legends show the importance of the Egyptian temples as a gathering place for the sick and the practice of incubation sleep as a form of cure. The writer of one of the Oxyrhynchus papyruses, written in Greek around the second century C.E., recounts two incidents involving Imhotep's power. The writer, a priest named Nechautis in the temple of Imhotep, and his mother both fell sick at different times. On both occasions, they went to the temple, where Imhotep appeared to them in dreams, suggesting a simple remedy; on waking, both were cured.

Other legends discovered by Egyptologists recount stories of infertile couples who sought help at the temple of Imhotep and conceived children afterward.

One explanation given for the demigod status of Imhotep during the New Kingdom (c. 1570-c. 1069 B.C.E.) was the religious revival that increased the magnificence and wealth of the Egyptian gods to such a degree that they became inaccessible to the common people. In search of a superhuman but sympathetic friend, it is conjectured, the common people selected new demigods from the national heroes of the past—including Imhotep, who had a reputation as a wise man.

In at least three temples built to honor him, the cult of Imhotep flourished. The first one, at Memphis, was famous as a hospital and school of magic and medicine and was referred to as the Asclepieion by the Greeks. Two other temples, one at Philae and one at Thebes, and a sanatorium are believed to have been devoted to the worship of Imhotep. Stories similar to the one related above illustrate the power of the practice of incubation at Egyptian medical temples. People with all sorts of illnesses as well as those seeking protection from accidents went to the temples for help. During this natural or drug-induced sleep, it was believed that either the deity or a priest acting on behalf of the deity would appear and indicate a remedy. Temple sleep served as a powerful form of faith healing, the most effective for very high-strung patients.

It is thought that a practical man of affairs such as Imhotep, with his interest in astronomy and other sciences, probably leaned toward the scientific treatment of illnesses. From the records about the cult of Imhotep that grew hundreds of years after his death, it is apparent, however, that his greatest public achievements were in the capacity of a faith healer.

SIGNIFICANCE

The name Imhotep means "he who cometh in peace"; the symbolic significance of the name is perhaps the best way to explain the enduring reputation of a person whom some scholars doubt even existed. For three thousand years, well into the Roman period, Imhotep was worshiped as the god of medicine, for a long time in temples devoted to him. This deification of a person who was not of the royal pharaohs was in itself a rare achievement, pointing to the great respect that a priest-physician could command. It is entirely conceivable, too, that the powerful fraternity of priest-physicians deliberately helped to create his reputation, spreading the word about the healing power of a man otherwise familiar to people as a wise and accomplished vizier in order to increase the contributions of the pharaohs to the temple coffers. The champions of Imhotep's reputation argue, on the other hand, that the civilization of ancient Egypt was unknown for hundreds of years, compared to the relative familiarity of scholars with Greek and Roman life and culture. According to this argument, Imhotep simply suffered the fate of the ancients, as the inexorable process of history dimmed his achievements and assimilated his fame with succeeding generations of medical practitioners.

Under the Ptolemies, six festivals were regularly held to honor the events of Imhotep's life, including his birthday on May 31 and his death on July 1, though there is no documentation to prove that these dates have any relation to real historical events. The elaborateness of the cult of Imhotep points, if not to his actual existence or achievement, to the power of his reputation as a healer. It is a recognition of the power that people in pain and suffering are willing to attribute to a distinguishable healing authority who, by virtue of that confidence in his skill, is able to bring them a measure of peace.

—*Shakuntala Jayaswal*

FURTHER READING

Asante, Molefi Kete. *The Egyptian Philosophers: Ancient African Voices from Imhotep to Akhenaten*. Chicago: African American Images, 2000. Imhotep and ten other African scholars are examined. Discusses Hippocrates' study of the works of Imhotep and the mention of his name in his Hippocratic oath.

Dawson, Warren R. *Magician and Leech: A Study in the Beginnings of Medicine with Special Reference to An-*cient Egypt. London: Methuen, 1929. A short account of Egyptian medicine, based on the study of the Egyptian papyruses relating to medicine and on the study of techniques of mummification. Contains illustrations and index.

Hurry, Jamieson B. *Imhotep: The Vizier and Physician of King Zoser and Afterwards the Egyptian God of Medicine*. Rev. ed. New York: AMS Press, 1978. The single most informative source about Imhotep, this monograph contains a short bibliography, an index, illustrations, and appendices referring to the construction and variants of the name Imhotep, his pedigree as architect, and the statuettes and murals depicting him.

Sigerist, Henry E. *Primitive and Archaic Medicine*. Vol. 1 in *A History of Medicine*. New York: Oxford University Press, 1967. Written by one of the most promising historians of medicine (although he did not live to complete the series), this book includes a substantial chapter on ancient Egypt. Contains illustrations, an index, and appendices on histories of medicine, sourcebooks and medical history, museums of medical history, and literature of paleopathology since 1930.

SEE ALSO: Galen; Hippocrates; Zoser.

RELATED ARTICLES in *Great Events from History: The Ancient World*: c. 2687 B.C.E., Old Kingdom Period Begins in Egypt; c. 2575-c. 2566 B.C.E., Building of the Great Pyramid; c. 1570 B.C.E., New Kingdom Period Begins in Egypt; 323 B.C.E., Founding of the Ptolemaic Dynasty and Seleucid Kingdom.

SAINT IRENAEUS
Roman bishop

As the first systematic theologian of the Christian church, Irenaeus laid the foundation for the development of church doctrine and effectively ended the threat that Gnosticism might substitute mysticism for faith in the resurrection of Christ.

BORN: Between 120 and 140 C.E.; probably Smyrna, Asia Minor (now İzmir, Turkey)
DIED: c. 202 C.E.; Lugdunum, Gaul (now Lyon, France)
AREA OF ACHIEVEMENT: Religion

EARLY LIFE

All that is known of the life of Saint Irenaeus (i-ree-NEE-uhs) derives from the *Historia ecclesiastica* (c. 300, 324 C.E.; *Ancient Ecclesiastical Histories*, 1576-1577; better known as *Church History*) of Eusebius and from occasional comments made by Irenaeus himself in his works. Because Eusebius was less interested in biography than in recording the development and growth of the Church, he offers only a few tantalizing details. Irenaeus was born sometime after 120, in or near the trading city of Smyrna on the southwestern coast of Asia Minor, which was at that time part of the Roman Empire. His parents, who were probably Greeks, were also Christians.

In the century that had passed between the crucifixion of Christ and the birth of Irenaeus, the Apostles of Jesus had spread his message throughout the Mediterranean world, and Peter and Paul, in particular, had transformed a minor Jewish sect into an established institution with churches, priests, and bishops throughout the Roman Empire. In fact, the rapid growth of the Church had frightened and angered the Roman authorities. Though most Christians tried to be good citizens of the Empire, they refused to worship the old Roman gods; as a result, they were often regarded as traitors and were frequently persecuted.

The early history of the Church is filled with heroic and miraculous tales of these martyrs. One of them was Polycarp, a renowned Christian teacher and bishop of Smyrna, who was burned at the stake in 156. As a young man, Irenaeus was apparently brought to Polycarp for instruction in the faith and was deeply influenced by him. Because Polycarp had known several of the Apostles, he was able to transmit their teaching with a personal vigor. Irenaeus's belief that the books of the Apostles accurately present the true message of Christ probably derived from Polycarp. In his later years, Irenaeus's memories of his old teacher were still so sharp that he could vividly describe Polycarp and the lessons he had taught. It may have been Polycarp who sent Irenaeus as a missionary to the city of Lugdunum in the Roman province of Gaul.

LIFE'S WORK

After his arrival at Lugdunum, Irenaeus was ordained as a priest by Pothinus, the bishop, and he soon began a life-long career of converting the pagans of southwestern Gaul to Christianity. In 161, however, the expansion of the Church was endangered by the appointment of a new Roman emperor, Marcus Aurelius. Though in many ways an admirable man, the emperor saw the Christians as a threat to the strength and unity of the Empire, and he initiated an especially cruel series of persecutions against them. In 177, it was the turn of the churches of Gaul, and it is said that the streets of Lugdunum ran with the blood of thousands of Christians who had been tortured and killed.

Fortunately, though, Irenaeus had been sent by the leaders of the Church on a mission to Pope Eleutherius at Rome, so he escaped the time of persecution. The purpose of the mission is somewhat unclear: Eusebius says only that Irenaeus acted as a mediator in a dispute over an issue related to Montanism, which was one of many heresies in the early Church. Montanists, who took their name from their leader, Montanus, believed that they were under the direct influence of the Holy Spirit, and their worship services, like those of the nineteenth century Shakers, were often characterized by emotional outbursts and "speaking in tongues." Some modern authorities have stated that the pope had become a Montanist and that Irenaeus tried to persuade Eleutherius to return to a more orthodox view. Others assert the opposite—that Irenaeus tried to convince the pope not to excommunicate the Montanists.

In any case, while in Rome, Irenaeus saw that heresies were threatening to tear the Church apart, and he determined that he would do everything he could to eliminate them. The problem of heresies had arisen, Irenaeus believed, because the Church had as yet no established body of doctrine accepted by all Christian churches. In the modern world, many Christian denominations coexist peacefully and are drawing closer together through the ecumenical movement. This degree of unity has been possible only because Christians of nearly every denomination acknowledge and share certain fundamental beliefs.

In the early days of Christianity, however, these common beliefs had not yet been clearly or systematically articulated. Without an authoritative body of doctrine, Christians could be led astray by religious leaders who claimed to have a new revelation or a superior interpretation of the Gospels. While Montanism was a relatively minor, and even tolerable, deviation from orthodoxy, Christianity itself was but one of several competitors in a great theological contest occurring throughout the Roman world. Among the others were the pagan religions, such as that of the old Roman state gods. Despite attacks from Roman Imperial authorities, Christianity had been making steady advances against these religions, because they offered no vision of eternal life. A much more dangerous threat to the Church came from the various sects called Gnostics.

Gnosticism comprised a vague system of ideas about the nature of the universe; these ideas predated Christianity and had spread throughout the Mediterranean world by the second century after Christ. A central feature of this system was a belief in the salvation of the soul through the acquisition of a gnosis, or secret knowledge. This mystical revelation of the origins and fate of the cosmos would be communicated by a "divine redeemer" to an elite group of individuals ready to receive it. Gnosticism had become popular, particularly among intellectuals, through a gradual process of absorbing elements of other religions as well as some aspects of Greek philosophy.

When Gnostics encountered Christianity, they attempted to integrate it into their system by identifying Christ as the "divine redeemer" and by accepting only those portions of the Scriptures that agreed with their views. In addition, they claimed to possess secret books that augmented and improved on the Christian message. Often, Gnostics even called themselves Christians. However, Christianity and Gnosticism were fundamentally opposed: For the Christian, salvation was achieved through faith in Christ's resurrection and cooperation with the will of God, rather than by gaining some body of esoteric knowledge.

Irenaeus had become especially distressed about Gnosticism during his visit to Rome because one of his childhood friends and fellow students of Polycarp, Florinus, had fallen under the influence of a Gnostic leader. Florinus had become a Roman consul and was thus in a position to do great harm to the Christians of the city. Irenaeus wrote his old friend a long letter explaining some of his objections to Gnosticism and reminding Florinus that Polycarp had taught them to adhere only to the teachings of the Church established by the Apostles. Unfortunately, Irenaeus was unsuccessful in dissuading Florinus from leaving the Church.

In 178, after returning to Lugdunum, Irenaeus was elected to replace Pothinus, who had been martyred, as bishop. Irenaeus also continued his missionary work. In 190, he again acted as a mediator for a new pope, Victor I, in a dispute between the churches of the eastern and western parts of the Empire over the determination of the proper date for the celebration of Easter. Irenaeus suggested that such differences were not particularly important and, in any case, would probably disappear eventually. Eusebius notes that through his efforts, Irenaeus certainly lived up to his name, which means "peacemaker."

The constant appearance of such controversies reinforced Irenaeus's belief that the Church must have a consistent body of doctrine. Throughout his career, the problem of heresy, and especially Gnosticism, continued to weigh on his mind. As a result, he wrote a large number of letters, treatises, and books, all building toward a clear exposition of orthodox Christianity and a refutation of heresy. Though most of these works have been lost, several Latin translations of Irenaeus's most important treatise, which was originally written in Greek, have been preserved. *Elenchou kai anatropes* is most commonly known by its Latin title, *Adversus haereses* (c. 180 C.E.; *Against Heresies*, 1868). Irenaeus began the work as a response to a request from a friend for information, but he continued to expand on his ideas during a period of several years. It was finally completed by about 190.

Against Heresies is the most important exposition of Christian theology prior to the Council of Nicaea in 325.

As the Greek title implies, it is both a detailed discussion of the doctrines and history of Gnosticism and a rigorous refutation of Gnostic theory. In the first section, Irenaeus demonstrates the inconsistencies and lack of logical coherence of Gnostic belief. The more important portion of the book, however, contains, in essence, the first complete and systematic articulation of Christian theology. This system is relatively familiar to every educated Christian, for it is, in essence, still the basis of Christian belief: There is only one God, of which Christ as the Son is a part. God created humanity in his image; yet, through the sin of disobedience, humanity fell away from God into the clutches of Satan, an angel who had been envious of humanity. God therefore sent His Son so that humanity might be saved from damnation and ultimately rejoin God. Through the Holy Spirit, people are drawn into Christ's victory over Satan and can ultimately attain salvation.

To Irenaeus, the biblical tradition is the only source of faith; no additional gnosis is necessary, nor is it compatible with biblical truth. The Old and New Testaments form a continuous unity with a clear purpose: The Old Testament predicts the coming of Christ, whose oral teachings were written down by the Apostles to form the books of the New Testament. They, in turn, established the Church, which preserves and disseminates the pure Christian message of redemption through faith. This apostolic tradition, passed on through the succession of bishops of the Church, ensures the correct interpretation of Scripture against the perversions and distortions of the Gnostics and other heretics. Thus, Irenaeus not only refuted heresy; in doing so, he also became the first theologian to defend the Church as an institution.

It is not clear how *Against Heresies* became well known, yet the fairly large number of Latin manuscripts containing it, a translation in Armenian made in the third or fourth century, and numerous fragments in other languages all testify to its popularity. The fact that Eusebius reproduced sizable portions of it in the *Ecclesiastical History* demonstrates that by the early fourth century it had become part of the standard canon of Christian dogma. Irenaeus's other works seem also to have been well known to the ancients, yet he himself drops out of sight after about 190. A tradition that originated in the fourth or fifth century states that Irenaeus was martyred in 202 in the general persecution orchestrated by the emperor Septimus Severus, but there is no solid evidence for this. On the other hand, no evidence contradicts the story, and it would be entirely consistent with Irenaeus's devotion to his faith.

SIGNIFICANCE

Irenaeus is regarded by most authorities as the most important Christian theologian of the second century as well as the founder of Catholic doctrine. Chronologically, he stands at a critical point in the history of the Church. The Apostles and their immediate disciples had founded Christian communities all over the Mediterranean world, but without any central doctrine or authority, some of these had begun to accept competing and very different theologies. The mystical-philosophical system of Gnosticism, as well as pagan religions newly arrived from the East, such as Mithraism, had begun to make inroads in Christian congregations, while Roman Imperial policy sought to wipe out Christianity. Irenaeus's coherent expression of Christian belief and his justification of the Church as an institution provided exactly the impetus toward consolidation needed by Christians to help ensure the survival of their faith.

What was required was a concept of what "the Church" meant to Christians. In *Against Heresies*, Irenaeus provided such a definition. He stated, first, that the Church is guided by the "rule of faith," a statement of belief to which all Christians subscribe, and he offered a creed that differs very little from the Apostles' Creed used to this day. Because the creed was given by the Apostles to the Church, it expresses a tradition descended directly from Christ's own disciples. Second, the churches were established by the Apostles themselves, who appointed their successors, the bishops. Thus, an unbroken line of succession was established that guarantees the rule of faith and guards against any notions of gnosis. If Jesus had been the "divine redeemer" of the Gnostics, surely he would have given the gnosis to his disciples, who would have passed it to their successors. Third, what the Church has instead of some secret knowledge is the Gospels of the Apostles, who were eyewitnesses to Christ's resurrection, which itself fulfills the predictions of the Old Testament.

Because many books claimed apostolic authorship, Irenaeus made an important contribution to the determination of what exactly would constitute the New Testament by limiting the Gospels to those written by Matthew, Mark, Luke, and John and using as accepted apostolic writings most of the other books now included in the New Testament. In developing this threefold definition of the Church, Irenaeus not only debunked heresy but, much more important, also provided the average Christian with dependable means through which to attain salvation: the Church, its rule of faith, and the Scriptures. According to Irenaeus, these means may be trusted because the rule of faith is the essence of apostolic teaching, because the Church has descended directly from the Apostles, and because the Scriptures were written by the Apostles. With this explanation of the sources of Christian theology, Irenaeus provided the fundamental structure of Church doctrine and ended the early period of uncontrolled Christian diversity.

—*Thomas C. Schunk*

FURTHER READING

Coxe, Arthur Cleveland, ed. *The Apostolic Fathers with Justin Martyr and Irenaeus*. Vol. 1 in *The Ante-Nicene Fathers*. 1884. Reprint. Peabody, Mass.: Hendrickson, 1994. Contains a complete English translation of *Against Heresies* and fragments of other works by Irenaeus. Also includes a useful introduction that explains the plan and ideas of *Against Heresies* and places the work in its historical context.

Eusebius. *The History of the Church from Christ to Constantine*. Translated by G. A. Williamson. New York: Penguin Books, 1989. Eusebius is the primary source for nearly all information on the life of Irenaeus, and the ecclesiastical history also reveals how other early Christian writers built on his work. Eusebius is an essential source for early Church history.

Hägglund, Bengt. *History of Theology*. Translated by Gene J. Lund. St. Louis, Mo.: Concordia, 1968. Treats the history of Christian doctrine topically, within a chronological context. While possibly difficult for a reader with no background in theological or philosophical study, Hägglund is worth the effort. Provides the clearest explanation of Irenaeus's reasoning in *Against Heresies* and helps to show how it relates to that of other early theologians.

Quasten, J. *The Beginnings of Patristic Literature*. Vol. 1 in *Patrology*. Westminster, Md.: Christian Classics, 1986-1992. A complete discussion of early Christian literature, including poetry and stories, in addition to theological works. Details on texts, translations, and history of editions of each work covered. Includes extensive bibliographies for each section. Contains an excellent discussion of *Against Heresies* and other works by Irenaeus.

Schaff, Philip. *Ante-Nicene Christianity A.D. 100-325*. Vol. 2 in *History of the Christian Church*. 3d ed. Peabody, Mass.: Hendrickson, 1996. Though extremely dated in both its approach and its style, Schaff's is perhaps the most complete history of the Church in English. This volume discusses in great detail all aspects of the growth and spread of Christianity and the development of the Church in the period covered. Contains helpful sections on early Christian heresies, including Montanism and Gnosticism, and a chapter on Irenaeus.

Tyson, Joseph B. *A Study of Early Christianity.* New York: Macmillan, 1984. An excellent and readable discussion of the historical and theological context in which Christianity developed, early Christian literature, the varieties of early Christianity, and the place of Jesus Christ in the development of the Christian tradition. Includes an evaluation of the contribution of Irenaeus.

Wolfson, Henry Austryn. *Faith, Trinity, Incarnation.* Vol. 1 in *The Philosophy of the Church Fathers.* Cambridge, Mass.: Harvard University Press, 1970. This massive study of the relationship of Greek philosophy and Old Testament theology to the development of Christian philosophy is extremely thorough and may therefore be more detailed than some readers need. Organized topically; thus, references to Irenaeus and his thought are scattered through several sections.

SEE ALSO: Saint Anthony of Egypt; Saint Athanasius of Alexandria; Saint Augustine; Saint Christopher; Saint John Chrysostom; Clement I; Saint Denis; Eusebius of Caesarea; Gregory of Nazianus; Gregory of Nyssa; Saint Jerome; Marcus Aurelius; Saint Paul; Saint Peter; Saint Simeon Stylites; Saint Siricius; Saint Stephen; Saint Thomas; Saint Vincent of Lérins.

RELATED ARTICLES in *Great Events from History: The Ancient World*: c. 50-c. 150 C.E., Compilation of the New Testament; January-March, 200 C.E., Christian Apologists Develop Concept of Theology; c. 286 C.E., Saint Anthony of Egypt Begins Ascetic Life; October 28, 312 C.E., Conversion of Constantine to Christianity; 313-395 C.E., Inception of Church-State Problem; 361-363 C.E., Failure of Julian's Pagan Revival; 380-392 C.E., Theodosius's Edicts Promote Christian Orthodoxy; c. 382-c. 405 C.E., Saint Jerome Creates the Vulgate; 413-427 C.E., Saint Augustine Writes *The City of God*; 428-431 C.E., Nestorian Controversy; c. 450 C.E., Conversion of Ireland to Christianity; October 8-25, 451 C.E., Council of Chalcedon.

ISAIAH
Judaean prophet

Because of his clear grasp of political reality and the power of his poetic utterances, Isaiah is generally considered to be the greatest of the Old Testament prophets.

BORN: c. 760 B.C.E.; Jerusalem, Judah (now in Israel)
DIED: c. 701-680 B.C.E.; probably Jerusalem, Judah
AREA OF ACHIEVEMENT: Religion

EARLY LIFE

Although there are sixty-six chapters in the book that bears his name, Isaiah (i-ZAY-uh), the great prophet of the eighth century B.C.E., probably wrote only the first thirty-nine of them. Stylistic and historical evidence indicates that the later chapters were written in the sixth century B.C.E., after the people of Judah had passed into the Babylonian captivity predicted at the end of Isaiah's own works. The author of chapters 40-55 is probably a single anonymous prophet, called for want of a name "Deutero-Isaiah" or "Second Isaiah." The final chapters, called "Trito-Isaiah" or "Third Isaiah," are probably by various hands. At any rate, although these later chapters are clearly in the tradition of Hebrew prophecy, they have no other claim to the name of the great prophet Isaiah. In actuality, they may have been attached to the earlier chapters simply for the sake of convenience.

Isaiah was the son of Amoz; evidently he was a native of Jerusalem. Beyond that, very little is known about the life of Isaiah before he was called to prophesy around 742. Because he obviously had access to the inner area of the Temple, some scholars conjecture that Isaiah was a member of a priestly family and may even have studied for the priesthood himself. As a young man, he might have been a "wisdom teacher." Certainly he was familiar with the wisdom literature that was so much a part of Hebrew education.

The tone of Isaiah's poetry suggests that he was of aristocratic background. His pronouncements regarding specific rulers and councillors, his comments on statecraft, and his exposures of international intrigues all reveal the knowledge of an insider. Although the prophet Isaiah, like Amos and Hosea, forecast doom if the people of Judah did not reform, his warnings were often addressed to the ruling classes in words that evidence firsthand knowledge of their self-centered, luxurious, and corrupt way of life.

Even if Isaiah had not been an insider in court circles, he would have attracted attention because of his intellectual brilliance and his poetic genius. His social status, however, gave him an additional sense of security in his dealings with councillors and with kings. Even when God himself spoke to him, Isaiah did not hide behind false modesty but volunteered with confidence for whatever mission God had in mind. It is undoubtedly this confidence that sustained him when God sent him out naked and barefoot, supposedly for three years, in order to attract the attention of his countrymen to the predictions that they had ignored.

Aside from this unusual episode, Isaiah seems to have lived a godly yet normal life. He was married—whether before or after his call is not clear. He had two sons, probably after he began to prophesy, as their names reveal his preoccupation with God's intentions toward his people. He maintained his court contacts, at times being called on to advise the king.

It is clear that when Isaiah became the prophet of Judah, he did not emerge wild-eyed from the wilderness, nor did he change except in the intensity of his dedication. The rulers of Judah could not complain that God had not given them every chance to turn to him; he had sent to them a prophet who spoke their language and understood their problems, a moderate, rational man who insisted only that private and public life should be subject to the will of God.

LIFE'S WORK

In the sixth chapter of Isaiah, the prophet describes the experience that directed his life. The moment is dated as falling within the year of King Uzziah's death (probably 742 B.C.E.). After seeing a vision of God enthroned, surrounded by angels, Isaiah's first reaction was the sense of his own uncleanness in the sight of God. After being forgiven, he heard God ask, "Whom shall I send? Who will go for Me?" Isaiah's immediate response was to utter the well-known words, "Here am I! Send me!"

During the next four decades, Isaiah took his advice, his satirical comments, his diatribes, and his predictions of doom to the people of Judah, later expanding his warnings to address the neighboring Jewish state of Israel as well as pagan lands ranging from Egypt and Syria to powerful Assyria. Because so many manuscripts were lost after the fall of Jerusalem to Babylon, scholars cannot be certain of the chronology of Isaiah's thirty-nine chapters. Specific historical references date some segments, however, while others reflect themes that clearly preoccupied the prophet throughout his life.

Shortly after Isaiah began his life of prophecy, Judah was threatened by the allies Israel and Syria, who had joined forces in the hope of conquering Judah and placing a puppet on the throne and eventually defeating the powerful nation of Assyria. Isaiah was troubled by the fact that Israel's intended puppet was not of the house of David; furthermore, he was convinced that Assyria was in the ascendancy with the permission of God. Thus, on both counts Israel and Syria were defying God.

Isaiah. (Library of Congress)

Given these convictions, it fell to Isaiah to convince King Ahaz that God would protect Judah. Taking his son Shear-jashub (whose name means "a remnant will return"), Isaiah went to meet Ahaz, carrying the reassurances that the king needed. Later, at the command of God, Isaiah fathered a second son, whom he named Maher-shalal-hash-baz (the spoil comes, the prey hurries). Isaiah then explained to the nervous king that the baby's name had been assigned by God, who thereby promised that before the child learned to speak, the defiant countries would be despoiled by Assyria.

Such messages from God, dictating specific directions that Judah's foreign policy should take in troubled times, evidently alternated with advice in domestic matters. God's protection could be depended on only if Judah obeyed his moral laws. At court, in the streets of Jerusalem, and on the outlying estates of the wealthy, Isaiah saw the real danger to Judah. In Isaiah 5:8-24, he points out the inner rottenness of his people: the atheism and drunkenness of its men, the triviality and extravagance of its women, the smugness and greed of its elite. In the country, the great landholders extended their properties, squeezing out the poor. In Jerusalem, corrupt judges dispensed injustice. At the Temple, priests offered worthless sacrifices that could not substitute for righteousness. At court, great officials served their own interests. Such a society, the prophet warned, would not be protected by the God to whom Judah gave lip service.

In chapters 10 and 11, Isaiah expresses his preoccupation with a later threat, that of Assyria, which was no longer threatened by alliances against it. Realizing its own vulnerable position, Judah was fearful. Again, Isaiah warned that military might and political stratagem would be useless; only God's intervention on behalf of a righteous people could save Judah.

The power of Isaiah's God, however, was not limited to dealings with Judah or even Israel. Isaiah's warnings were addressed to Moab and Samaria, to Egypt, and even to Assyria itself, a nation that he saw as the tool of God, powerful but destined eventually to be destroyed. In 711, Isaiah walked naked and barefoot through the streets of Jerusalem in order to point out the approaching fall of Egypt, which had betrayed a confederate to the Assyrians (Isa. 20:1-6). Not only their unrighteous cowardice but also their defiance of the governing plan of God had doomed the Egyptians.

For a country as defenseless as Judah, Isaiah's warnings about defying Assyria made sense. In 703 he advised King Hezekiah against sending an embassy to Egypt in order to plot against Assyria, which clearly would constitute a rejection of common sense as well as of God's plan (Isa. 30:1-7). In 701 the Assyrian king Sennacherib and his army were at the gates of Jerusalem. Isaiah urged Hezekiah to depend on patience and righteousness, not the Judaeans' inferior military forces, as the appropriate defense. When Sennacherib's men suddenly began to die, perhaps because of a plague, he withdrew, and Isaiah's God was appropriately credited with having saved the city.

Isaiah's role at Hezekiah's court is illustrated in chapter 38. Sick and believing that he was about to die, Hezekiah was visited by Isaiah, who brought a message from God: Put your spiritual house in order, and you shall be spared. The repentant king turned to God and was promised another fifteen years of life. Still, death would at last come to him, as it would to Jerusalem itself. Isaiah's portion of the book concludes with a prophecy of the Babylonian conquest and captivity, with the promise—reflected in the name of Isaiah's first son—that a remnant would return.

Isaiah's thirty-nine chapters contain no specific references to events in his life after about 700 B.C.E. Whether he continued his work into old age, whether he ceased to prophesy, or whether there is truth to the legend that he was cut in two during the reign of Manasseh is not known. It is ironic that this man who spent his life transmitting God's directions to the heads of nations should disappear so silently from the stage of history.

SIGNIFICANCE

Isaiah is considered the greatest of the Old Testament prophets not only because of the fact that so much of his work remains but also because of his stature as a poet and as a representative of the God he served.

Unlike prophets of a humbler station, Isaiah could speak to the aristocracy as one of them. He could rebuke the daughters of Zion for their frivolity with references to their tinkling anklets; he could rebuke the great landowners by detailing their greedy appropriation of land. No pretense, no hypocrisy was proof against his penetrating eye; no foreign intrigue was too complicated for his mind to fathom.

The exactness of Isaiah's perception is one of the qualities that makes him a great writer. It is not known whether all of his work was in poetic form or whether segments were deliberately written in prose. It is undisputed, however, that all of his work is evidence of a remarkable talent. His style is so individual that scholars have been able to separate his own words from later additions with a surprising degree of agreement.

Although Isaiah's words continue to be significant to the faiths that depend on the Judaic tradition, they would be far less significant if they had come from a lesser person. Even more important than the intellectual brilliance and the poetic genius of Isaiah is the quality of his obedience to God. When God asked who would go as his messenger, without hesitation his greatest prophet answered, "Here am I! Send me!"

—*Rosemary M. Canfield Reisman*

FURTHER READING

Church, Brooke Peters. *The Private Lives of the Prophets and the Times in Which They Lived*. New York: Rinehart, 1953. Though admittedly conjectural, a plausible reconstruction of the life of Isaiah based on a scholarly study of the chapters generally attributed to the prophet. Despite this skepticism about the text, the work is imaginative, readable, and useful.

Cohon, Beryl D. *The Prophets: Their Personalities and Teachings*. New York: Charles Scribner's Sons, 1939. In three chapters, the author treats the three separate bodies of work into which the Book of Isaiah is usually divided. Using fairly lengthy excerpts from the text, Cohon reconstructs the historical setting of the prophecies in prose.

Herbert, A. S. *The Book of the Prophet Isaiah 1-39*. New York: Cambridge University Press, 1973. Part of the Cambridge Bible Commentary on the New English Bible. A passage-by-passage explanation of the text. Clear and uncluttered. Contains a useful chronological table of events in the eighth century B.C.E., as well as a number of maps.

_____. *The Book of the Prophet Isaiah 40-66*. Cambridge, England: Cambridge University Press, 1975. Covers Deutero-Isaiah and Trito-Isaiah, the chapters attributed to writers of the sixth century B.C.E. Includes helpful maps, as well as a table of historical events from 626 B.C.E. to approximately 500 B.C.E.

Kraeling, Emil G. *The Prophets*. Chicago: Rand McNally, 1969. A scholarly work dealing with the prophets in chronological order. Emphasizes the prophets'

response to external and internal pressures. Includes chronology.

Motyer, J. Alec. *The Prophecy of Isaiah: An Introduction and Commentary*. Downer's Grove, Ill.: InterVarsity Press, 1999. Commentary by a lifelong student of Isaiah.

Phillips, J. B. *Four Prophets, Amos, Hosea, First Isaiah, Micha: A Modern Translation from the Hebrew*. New York: Macmillan, 1969. Casts four prophetic books in modern poetic form. The translation of First Isaiah ceases after chapter 35 because of the close parallel between chapters 36-39 and 2 Kings.

Sawyer, John F. A. *The Fifth Gospel: Isaiah in the History of Christianity*. New York: Cambridge University Press, 1996. Examines Isaiah's influence, from the cult of the Virgin Mary and anti-Semitism to Christian feminism and liberation theology.

Scott, R. B. Y. *The Relevance of the Prophets*. Rev. ed. New York: Macmillan, 1968. An excellent background study, ranging in subject matter from the definition of prophecy and the significance of prophecy in Hebrew life to the relation of the prophets to society, to history, and to conventional religious structures.

Smith, J. M. Powis. *The Prophets and Their Times*. 2d ed. Chicago: University of Chicago Press, 1941. An important study by a great biblical scholar. Places the prophets within their historical periods.

SEE ALSO: Cyrus the Great; Darius the Great; David; Ezekiel; Ezra; Jeremiah; John the Apostle; Moses; Samuel; Solomon.

RELATED ARTICLES in *Great Events from History: The Ancient World*: c. 1000 B.C.E., Establishment of the United Kingdom of Israel; c. 966 B.C.E., Building of the Temple of Jerusalem; 745 B.C.E., Tiglath-pileser III Rules Assyria; 701 B.C.E., Sennacherib Invades Syro-Palestine; c. 607-562 B.C.E., Nebuchadnezzar Creates the First Neo-Babylonian State; 587-423 B.C.E., Birth of Judaism; c. 538-c. 450 B.C.E., Jews Return from the Babylonian Captivity.

ISOCRATES
Greek philosopher

One of the ten Attic Orators, Isocrates made significant contributions to the development of rhetorical theory, philosophy, and education in ancient Greece. Isocrates' model of education, grounded in rhetoric, guided educators for centuries to follow.

BORN: 436 B.C.E.; Athens, Greece
DIED: 338 B.C.E.; Athens, Greece
AREA OF ACHIEVEMENT: Philosophy

EARLY LIFE

Isocrates (i-SAWK-ruh-teez) was born during the archonship of Lysimachus in 436 B.C.E. His father, Theodorus, was a wealthy flute maker. His father's wealth afforded Isocrates the finest education of the day. He studied under such luminaries as Protagoras, Prodicus, Gorgias, Theramenes, and Tisias and joined the circle of Socrates. In *Phaedros* (388-368 B.C.E.; *Phaedrus*, 1792), Plato described Isocrates as a "youth of great promise."

Isocrates desperately wanted to play an important role in Athenian politics. A powerful case of stage fright coupled with a weak voice precluded his participation in the public-oratory-driven Athenian Assembly. In 404, during the reign of the "Thirty Tyrants," Isocrates fled to the island of Chios, where he operated a small school of rhetoric. As a result of the Peloponnesian War, Isocrates' father, Theodorus, lost most of his property and wealth. Thus, in 403 Isocrates returned to Athens, where, as a result of financial need, he became a "forensic locographer," writing speeches for others to deliver in the courts. After only six speeches, Isocrates discovered that he lacked the practical gifts for winning cases and abandoned the profession. Isocrates would later disavow his career as a locographer, scorning the profession.

In 392, at the age of forty-four, Isocrates set himself up as a teacher of rhetoric. His academy, located near the Lyceum in Athens, became the first permanent institution of liberal arts education, preceding Plato's Academy by five years. Isocrates announced the school and his new profession while attacking his sophistic competition with his essay *Kata tōn sophistfū* (c. 394 B.C.E.; *Against the Sophists*, 1929)

LIFE'S WORK

Isocrates' main legacy is the impact of his teachings on future generations of oratory and education. Isocrates' Academy was the most successful of all the Grecian schools of rhetoric. Cicero holds that this was the school in which all the eloquence of Greece was perfected, and alumni of Isocrates' academy are among the greatest statesmen, historians, writers, and orators of their time. There is evidence that even Aristotle may have been a pupil of Isocrates. Cicero and Demosthenes used Isocrates' work as a model, and through their work, Isocrates shaped generations of rhetorical thought and practice. Isocrates' style was incorporated into the works of orators, writers, and historians and was passed down for more than nine centuries.

Isocrates would admit only those students who had mastered grammar and could demonstrate previous knowledge in mathematics and the sciences. He believed that this knowledge was necessary grounding for the mental gymnastics of rhetoric, philosophy, and civics. Isocrates also demanded that potential students must demonstrate promise in voice control, intellect, and confidence. He believed that there were three essential qualities necessary for learning: natural ability, training, and experience. The training included studies in composition, debate, literature, philosophy, math, and history. Isocrates was also the first educator to utilize imitation and models as educational tools. The *Panegyricus* (c. 380 B.C.E.; English translation, 1928) and the *Plataicus* (c. 373 B.C.E.; English translation, 1945) were written as model speeches for his pupils.

Isocrates' students were always expected to write and speak about cultural issues, with particular attention to the keeping of a panhellenic Greece above all nations. While style and diction were important, for the first time content was stressed in an academic setting. This content served to train the student in Isocrates' Hellenic ideology. The model orations that his students studied were propagandistic in that they professed Isocrates' political beliefs. Isocrates taught, and wrote in *Panegyricus*, that "Greek" denoted a man's education, not his race. Isocrates was sorely troubled by the petty squabbles that kept the various city-states at odds. He longed for a Greece that could stand united, and he planted this desire in his students.

In the light of Isocrates' patriotism, it is unremarkable that the primary focus of his educational plan was the development of citizen-orators. He considered political science and rhetoric nearly one and the same. Greek society was driven by oratory, and Isocrates taught that those who are the best users of speech are those of greatest wisdom. He held that all the great works of humankind are the result of rhetoric. As he wrote in *Antidosis* (c. 354 B.C.E.; English translation, 1929), "There is no institution devised by man which the power of speech has not helped to establish." Isocrates taught that proper speaking was a sign of proper thinking and that the properly educated citizen was conspicuous for his eloquence.

Although Isocrates' known works contain no definition of rhetoric, he did describe the functions of rhetoric: "With this faculty we both contend against others on matters which are open to dispute and seek light for ourselves on things which are unknown." For Isocrates, rhetoric was an epistemic, or knowledge-discovering, tool that guides thought and action and that demonstrates wisdom. In *Against the Sophists*, he taught that good oratory is speech that proves appropriate for an occasion while demonstrating proper style and originality. In *Panegyricus*, he added that timeliness was also a key to good oratory.

Another function of good oratory, for Isocrates, is eloquence, and he freed Greek prose from the stiff style of earlier periods. He created and mastered a smoothly rolling style of prose and elevated oratory to a formal art. His style involved precise vocabulary, few figures of speech, and many illustrations from history and philosophy. He believed that good oratory was very polished, as demonstrated by his taking ten years to refine *Panegyricus* for release.

Isocrates also professed that rhetoric is philosophic in that it teaches morals and politics. By "philosophy," Isocrates was describing a theory of culture. He believed that "philosophy" was the study of how to be a reasonable and useful citizen. Isocrates held that one should deliberate about both one's own affairs and the affairs of the state. He believed that a philosophic education should arouse intense patriotism as well as construct a personal philosophy close to the stoic ideal.

While Isocrates did not believe that virtue could be taught, he argued in *Against the Sophists* that it could be strengthened through training and practice in oratory. He argued that moral argumentation encourages right action because argumentation produces a historical narrative that uses historic events as precedents for present action. Therefore, one gains moral knowledge by studying public address as the art of oratory and by imitating the great speakers. As he wrote in *Antidosis*, the lessons made "by a man's life" are stronger than lessons furnished by words.

Isocrates also saw the relationship between morality and oratory as reciprocal. In *Antidosis*, Isocrates explained that the more one wishes to persuade one's fellow citizens, the more important it is that the orator have a favorable reputation among those citizens. This notion served as the basis for the Roman rhetorician Quintilian's definition of *ethos*, or credibility, as a good man speaking well.

The concept that rhetorical training is moral training is hinged on Isocrates' notion that the test of all virtue or truth lies in that which wins approval. For Isocrates, it is through rhetoric that one can approximate truth, or at least a consensual truth. One who is trained in rhetoric is trained in truth, and in the creation of that truth through oratory. In *Antidosis*, he writes that "thanks to speech, we educate the fools and put the wise to the test; for we consider the fact of speaking rightly as the greatest sign of correct thinking." Thus, for Isocrates, there is no absolute truth, only consensual truth created by rhetoric.

Isocrates also believed that rhetoric had a role to play in the study of history. He made the study of history an art, not a science as Aristotle would have it. Isocrates began the tendency for a writer or speaker to idolize the past and use examples of the past to guide political attitudes and actions in the present. He also promoted the practice of glorifying individual figures, heroes, as catalysts of history. The outstanding historians of the fourth century, Ephorus of Cumae and Theopompus of Chios, were both pupils of Isocrates, and they introduced Isocrates' rhetorical style into the construction of history. There is also evidence that Xenophon, the greatest of fourth century historians, was intellectually influenced by Isocrates' *Evagoras* (c. 365 B.C.E.; English translation, 1945). From Isocrates forward, history has been more than an objective recounting of events; history has been patriotic.

Ironically, the man that Cicero termed "the master of all rhetoricians" did not himself speak in public. In *Philippos* (c. 344 B.C.E.; *To Philip*, 1928), Isocrates explained that "nature has placed me more at a disadvantage than any of my fellow-citizens for a public career: I was not given a strong enough voice nor sufficient assurance to deal with the mob, to take abuse, and bandy words with the men who haunt the rostrum." As a result, his writings were meant to be read and are considered to be the earliest political pamphlets known. Through these oratorical pamphlets, Isocrates espoused a brand of Hellenism that would unite all Greeks together against a common foe. In his later years, Isocrates urged Philip II, king of Macedonia, to unite the Greeks under his leadership in a war against Persia.

Relatively late in his life, Isocrates married the daughter of Hippias, a Sophist. He died in the Archonship of Chaerondas in 338, reportedly starving himself to death at the age of ninety-eight after hearing the news of Philip's victory over Athens in the Battle of Chaeronea.

SIGNIFICANCE

Isocrates was the first of a series of great teachers who equated rhetoric and education. His method of teaching students to speak well on noble subjects, *vir bonus dicendi peritus*, remained the ideal of the ancient world. The creation of this ideal kept the rhetorical practices of the Greeks alive and passed that knowledge on to the Romans. Isocrates' significance rests, then, on the influence he had on those who followed him. His ideas were carried on through such luminaries as the Athenian general Timotheus; Nicocles, the ruler of Salamis, in Cyprus; the Roman rhetoricians Cicero and Quintilian; and the historians Ephorus, Theopompus, and Xenophon. *Against the Sophists* served as the prototype for Plato's *Gorgias* (399-390 B.C.E.; English translation, 1804), and Isocrates' name is mentioned more than that of any other rhetorician in Aristotle's *Technē rhetorikēs* (335-323 B.C.E.; *Rhetoric*, 1686).

The tradition of Isocrates runs silently through intellectual history, in that the art of the rhetorician is manifest in all human practices that are dependent on effective communication. The tradition of *vir bonus dicendi peritus* continues in all scholarship in the attempt to create consensual truth. Moreover Isocrates' refinement of the Greek ideal of educating the individual for an active life in the service of the state widened the bounds of education. Cicero reported Isocrates' style of teaching oratory through his writings, and it became the standard of excellence for rhetorical education in Europe until the Renaissance. Components of this broad-based "liberal arts" education remain in the curricula of many modern schools.

—*B. Keith Murphy*

FURTHER READING

Benoit, William L. "Isocrates on Rhetorical Education." *Communication Education* 33 (1984): 109-119. Provides a thorough analysis of Isocratean rhetorical study. Examines the whole of Isocrates' body of works and the impact that these works have had through the centuries.

Bury, J. B. *A History of Greece*. 4th ed. New York: St. Martin's Press, 1991. The standard history of Greece, providing a detailed account of Greek history from the dawn of Western civilization to the death of Alexander the Great.

Golden, James L., Goodwin F. Berquist, and William E. Coleman. *The Rhetoric of Western Thought*. 7th ed. Dubuque, Iowa: Kendall/Hunt, 2000. A thorough history of the development of rhetorical theory and practice; contains a chapter on Isocrates, Cicero, and Quintilian. The standard work in the field of rhetorical theory.

Grube, G. M. A. *The Greek and Roman Critics*. Toronto: University of Toronto Press, 1968. Complete coverage of the Greek and Roman philosophers, from Homer and Hesiod through Longinus. Delineates connections between individual thinkers and schools of thought. Clearly shows Isocrates' role in the broadening of rhetorical theory.

Poulakos, Takis. *Speaking for the Polis: Isocrates' Rhetorical Education*. Columbia: University of South Carolina Press, 1997. This study in rhetoric and communication includes bibliography and index.

Romilly, Jacqueline de. *Magic and Rhetoric in Ancient Greece*. Cambridge, Mass.: Harvard University Press, 1975. An unusual, enlightening treatment of the intellectual development of *logos* (rhetoric) and magic. Includes a section on the works of Isocrates.

SEE ALSO: Cicero; Demosthenes; Philip II of Macedonia; Socrates; Xenophon.

RELATED ARTICLES in *Great Events from History: The Ancient World*: 480-479 B.C.E., Persian Invasion of Greece; c. 440 B.C.E., Sophists Train the Greeks in Rhetoric and Politics; September, 404-May, 403 B.C.E., Thirty Tyrants Rule Athens for Eight Months; 359-336 B.C.E., Philip II Expands and Empowers Macedonia; August 2, 338 B.C.E., Battle of Chaeronea.

JEREMIAH
Judaean prophet

Though the people of Judaea failed to repent their ways despite Jeremiah's warnings until catastrophe overwhelmed them, his prophecies remained to comfort later generations of the people of Judah and to stand as a symbol of renewal for all people.

BORN: c. 645 B.C.E.; Anathoth, Judaea (now in Palestine)
DIED: After 587 B.C.E.; Egypt
AREA OF ACHIEVEMENT: Religion

EARLY LIFE

If Jeremiah (jehr-uh-MI-uh) was born about 645 (some authorities place the date later), he was born into a troubled world. Israel, the northern Jewish kingdom, had been utterly crushed by Assyria (though some of the people must have remained, for Jeremiah denounced their religious laxness), and Judah itself, under Manasseh, had accepted Assyrian overlordship. Perhaps with Assyrian encouragement, pagan cults had flourished alongside the worship of Yahweh—cults devoted to Baal and the "queen of heaven," involving temple prostitution and even human sacrifice.

With the decay of Assyrian power, however, King Josiah (r. c. 639-c. 609) was able to institute drastic reforms, which were encouraged by the finding in 622 of the book of the law (some version of Deuteronomy). The reforms involved not only the suppression of the cults but also the centralization of the Lord's worship in Jerusalem at the expense of local shrines, even those dedicated to the Lord. Presumably, Jeremiah supported these reforms, even though they meant the decline of the shrine of Anathoth, where he had been born into a priestly family, possibly descendants of Abiathar, a high priest who had been exiled from Jerusalem for an intrigue against Solomon. Jeremiah's support of Josiah would explain the plots that the men of Anathoth directed against him. The gloomy tone of his prophecies even after the reforms could have been justified by the lingering existence of the cults, but he was also saddened by the empty ritualism that he observed and by the failure of the revival to promote social justice.

It was in this atmosphere, at any rate, that Jeremiah grew up. Some authorities date his appearance as a prophet in 627, amid an impending invasion by Scythian barbarians, which Jeremiah prophesied. Had no invasion taken place, his powers of prediction could have been called into question. Jeremiah, however, was no mere fortune-teller: He was a preacher calling his people to abandon paganism, to worship only the Lord, and to practice social justice. Though sometimes a prophecy of disaster was unconditional, it was often a threat of a punishment that could be averted by repentance, and sometimes it was a promise of restoration, however far in the future.

As for the prophet, his was a heavy burden, for he was commanded by the Lord to deliver a message that was usually unwelcome. It was perhaps for this reason that Jeremiah never married and that his prophecies express a troubled relationship to the Lord and to his fellow Judaeans: "Why is my pain perpetual, and my wound incurable, which refuseth to be healed? Wilt thou be altogether unto me as a liar, and as waters that fail?"

LIFE'S WORK

In about 609, Josiah died in battle against the Egyptians, and Jehoiakim succeeded him as an Egyptian vassal. Jeremiah found little reason to be satisfied with the new king, who allowed the cults to return and, at a time when his subjects had to pay onerous tribute to Egypt, built a new palace with forced labor: "Woe unto him that buildeth his house by unrighteousness, and his chambers by wrong; that useth his neighbor's service without wages, and giveth him not for his work." Jeremiah's repeated denunciations of the social order (he prophesied that the king would be "buried with the burial of an ass") once brought him in danger of his life, and on another occasion he was beaten and put into the stocks overnight.

Nevertheless, in 604, as the Babylonians were becoming an increasing menace to Judah, Jeremiah dictated to his disciple Baruch a kind of final warning, a scroll that Baruch read aloud in the Temple. When some of the king's advisers had it read to him, Jehoiakim took a knife and hacked off bits as it was read and burned them. Jehoiakim temporarily accepted the overlordship of Babylon, but three years later, under his son Jehoiachin, Judah rebelled. After the fall of Jerusalem in 597, King Nebuchadnezzar II carried off an immense booty and a considerable number of the most prominent inhabitants. Zedekiah (r. 597-587) was permitted to take over the throne as a Babylonian vassal. Jeremiah, who had come to regard Nebuchadnezzar as the Lord's instrument of punishment, persistently urged Judah to submit quietly to Babylonian rule. Zedekiah may have been inclined to accept Jeremiah's advice, but he could not control his

Jeremiah. (Library of Congress)

reenslaved them, Jeremiah made an especially bitter prophecy:

Ye have not hearkened unto me, in proclaiming liberty, every one to his brother, and every man to his neighbor: behold, I proclaim a liberty for you, saith the Lord, to the sword, to the pestilence, and to the famine; and I will make you to be removed into all the kingdoms of the earth.

The end came in 587. The city fell; Zedekiah was blinded and his sons and many nobles executed; the city was destroyed, and its surviving inhabitants were deported to Babylon. Nebuchadnezzar took care that Jeremiah was treated kindly, offering him a special place in Babylon. Jeremiah elected, however, to cast his lot with Gedaliah, a native prince who had been appointed governor of the remnant "of the poor of the people, that had nothing, in the land of Judah," who had been left behind and given vineyards and fields. Some remnants of the army and the court and a number of other fugitives rallied to Gedaliah, but he was assassinated by diehards who regarded him as a turncoat. The survivors sought Jeremiah's advice, and he urged them to remain and submit themselves to Babylon, and under no circumstances to go into Egypt, where they would die "by the sword, by the famine, and by the pestilence." To Egypt they went nevertheless and carried Jeremiah with them. The last words of Jeremiah in Scripture are a report of his denunciation of some women who had sacrificed to the queen of heaven, but he had lost honor as a prophet, since the Lord had failed to save his people. According to one tradition, Jeremiah was stoned by the angry refugees.

SIGNIFICANCE

In terms of immediate results, it would be easy to term Jeremiah's life a failure. The prophecies against foreign states, which were made without promise of renewal, did indeed come true, though it needed no prophet to foresee them; the same is true of his prophecies against the northern kingdom of Israel. The reforms of Josiah apparently gave him imperfect satisfaction, for presumably the cults revived after Josiah's death. In any case, the issue came to be overshadowed by Judah's suicidal foreign policy, and Jeremiah suffered persecution and derision for urging more prudent behavior toward Babylon. When the survi-

ministers, and a rival prophet, Hananiah, promised the downfall of Babylon and the return of the captives. In 589, revolt broke out, and by 588 Jerusalem was under siege.

During the siege, Jeremiah was in considerable danger as a traitor and threat to morale. In spite of the hostility of the people of Anathoth, he had exercised a kinsman's right to redeem a piece of family land put up for sale there and had symbolically buried the dead against the time of restoration, when once again people should "buy fields for money, and subscribe evidences, and seal them, and take witnesses in the land of Benjamin." When, during an interlude in the siege, he tried to go into the land of Benjamin, he was arrested and beaten as a deserter. When he urged the people to surrender, he was cast into a muddy pit and might have died if he had not been rescued by an Ethiopian eunuch, and he was thereafter kept in custody, though less rigorously, throughout the siege.

After Zedekiah, in accordance with the law, had "proclaimed liberty" to all the Hebrew slaves in Jerusalem, and their masters pretended to let them go and then

vors of the consequent disaster elected to flee to Egypt, Jeremiah was powerless to deter them, and in Egypt he suffered a final humiliation when the Jewish women revived the worship of the queen of heaven, saying that as long as they had worshiped her in Judaea, they had been "well, and saw no evil." It is no wonder that "jeremiad" is a modern word for a dolorous tirade.

However, these original jeremiads are eloquent and beautiful (much of the text is in the form of Hebrew poetry), and even more impressive (though less lengthy) are the promises of restoration:

> After those days, saith the Lord, I will put my law in their inward parts, and write it in their hearts; and will be their God, and they shall be my people. And they shall teach no more every man his neighbor, and every man his brother, saying, Know the Lord: for they shall all know me, from the least of them unto the greatest of them, saith the Lord: for I will forgive their iniquity, and I will remember their sin no more.

Perhaps inspired by these words, years later some of the exiles returned and, under Persian protection, established a state that observed the Deuteronomic code and endured until its destruction by the Romans. Still later, such passages were interpreted as announcing the coming of Jesus Christ.

—*John C. Sherwood*

FURTHER READING

Ackroyd, Peter R. *Exile and Restoration: A Study of Hebrew Thought in the Sixth Century B.C.* Philadelphia: Westminster Press, 1968. Ackroyd's assumptions are that Old Testament prophecy is relevant to Christian theology, that the prophetic books should be viewed as a whole, and that this whole is unique and far-reaching in its influence.

Heschel, Abraham J. *The Prophets*. New York: Perennial, 2001. Attempts to attain an understanding of the prophet through analysis of his consciousness. This contrasts with an approach that either emphasizes supernatural truth or uses a psychological bias.

Perdue, Leo G., and Brian W. Kovacs, eds. *A Prophet to the Nations: Essays in Jeremiah Studies*. Winona Lake, Wis.: Eisenbrauns, 1984. An anthology representing the best modern scholarship on Jeremiah. Among the topics discussed are the date of the prophet's call, the identity of the enemy from the north, textual problems, and the composition and development of the book.

Rosenberg, Joel. "Jeremiah and Ezekiel." In *The Literary Guide to the Bible*, edited by Robert Alter and Frank Kermode. Cambridge, Mass.: Harvard University Press, 1987. Aside from comment on purely literary topics, this piece is chiefly valuable for making sense out of the confused chronology of the Book of Jeremiah. Includes valuable notes and bibliography.

SEE ALSO: Ezekiel; Ezra; Isaiah; Nebuchadnezzar II; Solomon.

RELATED ARTICLES in *Great Events from History: The Ancient World*: 701 B.C.E., Sennacherib Invades Syro-Palestine; c. 607-562 B.C.E., Nebuchadnezzar Creates the First Neo-Babylonian State; 587-423 B.C.E., Birth of Judaism; 547 B.C.E., Cyrus the Great Founds the Persian Empire; c. 538-c. 450 B.C.E., Jews Return from the Babylonian Captivity.

SAINT JEROME
Roman Christian monk, writer, and translator

Because of his scholarship, commentaries on and translation of the Bible into Latin, and role as a propagandist for celibacy and the monastic life, Jerome is numbered with Saint Ambrose, Saint Augustine, and Gregory the Great as one of the Fathers of the Church.

BORN: Between 331 and 347; Stridon, Dalmatia (now in Croatia)
DIED: Probably 420; Bethlehem (now in Palestine)
ALSO KNOWN AS: Eusebius Hieronymus (given name); Sophronius
AREAS OF ACHIEVEMENT: Scholarship, religion

EARLY LIFE

Saint Jerome (jeh-ROHM) grew up in a world in which the influence of Christianity was rapidly expanding. He was born Eusebius Hieronymus. The names of his mother and younger sister are unknown, but his father, Eusebius, was a wealthy landowner, and Jerome had a younger brother, Paulinianus. Jerome's parents were Christians, although apparently not fervent.

Jerome began his schooling in Stridon, Dalmatia. From Stridon he was sent to Rome for his secondary education. His parents were clearly ambitious for him: Rome was the most prestigious center of learning in the Latin-speaking part of the Empire, and Aelius Donatus, the most famous master of the day, was Jerome's instructor in grammar. For at least four years, Donatus provided Jerome with a fairly typical Hellenistic education, centering on grammar and the reading and analysis of classical literature. By his adult years, Jerome had an extensive knowledge of the Latin classics. He is generally considered to be the finest of all Christian writers in Latin. In Rome he probably also acquired an elementary knowledge of Greek.

From Donatus's school, Jerome went to a school of rhetoric, also in Rome. He seems to have studied some law during this period and later could cite the Roman law with great accuracy. One of his fellow students was the Christian Tyrranius Rufinus, who was later to translate many Greek Christian writings into Latin. He and Jerome were the closest of friends, although this friendship would later break down over a theological dispute. Jerome, as a young man, had already begun to acquire many books; in his subsequent journeys he carried his library with him.

LIFE'S WORK

Jerome's baptism at Rome, sometime before 366, signaled his deepening interest in Christianity. Nothing is known of his life from approximately 357 until 367. In the following five years, Jerome traveled in Gaul, Dalmatia, and northeast Italy, particularly to Aquileia, where Rufinus lived. Although this period is also very obscure, it is clear that Jerome had become interested in contemporary theological controversy. More important, during this period, he felt called to a more serious Christian life. For many of his contemporaries, this call was to an abandonment of the world and a life of asceticism or strict discipline. Monasticism—an institutionalized form of asceticism commonly centered on the abandonment of private property, various forms of self-denial, such as fasting and celibacy, and the attempt to live a life of perpetual prayer—had existed in the eastern part of the Roman Empire for more than a half century but had only recently appeared in the west. Jerome did not adopt this difficult lifestyle suddenly. Like his younger contemporary Augustine, he first renounced further secular ambitions and committed himself to a life of contemplation and study.

Apparently, Jerome's determination to follow the ascetic life, and his success in persuading his sister to follow suit, led to an estrangement from his parents. In 372, like many pilgrims of his day, Jerome left Rome for the East and Jerusalem. As it turned out, he was not to reach Jerusalem for some years. He remained a year in Antioch, Syria, plagued with illness but used his time there to improve his Greek and familiarize himself with the contemporary state of theological controversy on the nature of the Trinity.

Jerome was tormented by the fact that he still had not made a clean break with the world, and probably in 374 had his famous dream, in which a judge appeared and accused him of being a disciple of Cicero rather than of Christ. That was an expression of Jerome's inability to give up reading of the classical authors in favor of purely biblical studies. Jerome records that this dream ended with him swearing an oath no longer to possess or read pagan books. He was later to say that he could not be held permanently to an oath made in a dream, but the dream does seem to mark the point at which his life's work—the study of Christian literature—came into focus. He began the first in a series of commentaries on the books of the Bible; this earliest work is not extant.

As Jerome's health returned, with it came the desire to follow through on his ascetic intentions. Many desert hermits lived near Antioch, and Jerome chose a hermit cell for himself near Chalcis. He remained in the desert two or three years, increasingly frustrated by the abuse heaped on him by the quarreling Syrian theological factions, each wishing to convert him to its position. He had his large library with him and continued his studies, learning Hebrew from a Jewish convert. Shortly after his return to Antioch, in 376 or 377, he began the second of his sustained projects, a series of translations of Greek Christian writings into Latin. His fame was growing rapidly, and he was ordained a priest by the bishop of Antioch, although he was always to think of himself primarily as a monk.

By 379 or 380 Jerome was in Constantinople and suffering from a disease of the eyes. In 382 he was in Rome, in the service of Damasus I, the bishop of Rome, as secretary and adviser. Damasus commissioned what was to become the great labor of Jerome's life—the preparation of a standard Latin translation of the Bible. The intended scope of this project is unclear: He probably completed translations of the four Gospels and the Psalms while in Rome.

Jerome spent about three years in Rome, during which he became the spiritual guide for an extraordinary group of high-born girls and women committed to the ascetic life and led by the widows Marcella and Paula. Paula's third daughter, Eustochium, was to be at Jerome's side for the rest of his life. Throughout his life, Jerome tended to create conflict with his sarcastic and combative remarks and letters. Damasus died in 384, and Jerome left Rome in 385 under pressure from both clergy and lay people whom he had offended.

Paula, Eustochium, and Jerome settled in Palestine in 386. The rest of Jerome's life was to be spent in Bethlehem and the environs of Jerusalem in a penitential life of prayer and study. Two monasteries were built at Bethlehem, one for women and one for men, and there the three friends lived until their deaths. Jerome returned to the study of Hebrew and moderated his earlier condemnation of the study of the classics. More and more, in his commentaries on and works related to the Old Testament, he relied on rabbinical interpretation and turned from the Septuagint—the Greek translation of the Old Testament commonly used in Christian circles—to the Hebrew. Jerome became convinced that a Latin translation of the Old Testament should be based directly on the Hebrew, and in about 390 he set aside the work he had done and began a new version from the original texts. Jerome's translation met with opposition and charges of Judaizing. It was not until the ninth century that his work was fully accepted; his translation of the Old Testament

and Gospels, when added to translations of the remaining New Testament books by unknown scholars, became known as the Vulgate (common) Bible.

Jerome's last years were filled with tragedy. He continued to be in pain and poor health. Paula died in 404. The barbarians, who began their invasion of the Empire in 375, attacked the Holy Land in 405, and Rome itself was sacked in 410. Jerome interpreted the fall of Rome as the destruction of civilization. In 416, the monasteries at Bethlehem were burned and the monks and nuns assaulted. Jerome died in Bethlehem, probably in 420.

SIGNIFICANCE

Saint Jerome's Christianity was a religion that at once challenged the mind of the scholar and urged those "who would be perfect" (Matthew 19:21) to detach themselves from normal worldly expectations. That a monasticism both learned and ascetic was the central cultural institution of the Middle Ages is in no small part his heritage. Although he is not, as was once thought, responsible for the entire Latin Vulgate Bible, he is responsible for the Old Testament and Gospel books of that translation. The Bible in Jerome's translation was the basis for the Wycliffe translation in the fourteenth century and the Douay version in the sixteenth century. His work was to influence Western theology and church life for centuries.

Jerome was a Latin scholar in a Greek- and Hebrew-speaking world. At Bethlehem, he was one of the most important agents of cross-cultural transference the world has known. Very few ancient Christians, Greek or Latin, knew Hebrew, and contacts between Jew and Christian in the ancient world regularly led to conflict. Against this backdrop, Jerome, because he saw the necessity of tracing Christianity to its most ancient Jewish roots, cultivated personal and scholarly contact with learned Jews and offered a clearer vision than had ever existed of what united, and separated, the religions.

—*Glenn W. Olsen*

FURTHER READING

Courcelle, Pierre. *Late Latin Writers and Their Greek Sources*. Translated by Harry E. Wedeck. Cambridge, Mass.: Harvard University Press, 1969. One of the great achievements of twentieth century scholarship, this volume traces in detail the use and knowledge of Greek works by Latin writers. Makes clear the central importance of Jerome as a translator and agent of dissemination of Greek authors.

Hagendahl, Harald. *Latin Fathers and the Classics*. Göteborg, Sweden: Almqvist and Wiksell, 1958. This is a careful, thorough, generally reliable study of

Jerome's familiarity with and use of the pagan classics. Good on his dream of the judge and its effect on his later life.

Kelly, J. N. D. *Jerome: His Life, Writings, and Controversies*. Peabody, Mass.: Hendrickson, 1998. This excellent, complete book on Jerome may be criticized for holding its subject to a demanding modern standard of judgment, for a lack of sympathy for his spiritual ideals, especially when they involve celibacy, and for an insufficiently sophisticated presentation of the issues involved in the relation of the literal to the spiritual senses of Scripture.

Rebenich, Stefan. *Jerome*. New York: Routledge, 2002. Part of Routledge's Church Fathers series, this book

provides a representative selection of Jerome's vast literary output. Includes index and bibliographical references.

SEE ALSO: Saint Ambrose; Saint Anthony of Egypt; Saint Athanasius of Alexandria; Saint Augustine; Saint Christopher; Saint John Chrysostom; Saint Denis; Saint Helena; Saint Irenaeus; Saint Simon Stylites; Saint Siricius; Saint Thomas.

RELATED ARTICLES in *Great Events from History: The Ancient World*: c. 382-c. 405 C.E., Saint Jerome Creates the Vulgate; August 24-26, 410 C.E., Gothic Armies Sack Rome; September 4, 476 C.E., Fall of Rome.

JESUS
Judaean preacher

As the basis for a religious faith that has attracted many millions of adherents, Jesus' life and teachings have exerted an enormous influence on Western civilization.

BORN: c. 6 B.C.E.; Bethlehem, Judaea (now in Palestine)
DIED: 30 C.E.; Jerusalem (now in Israel)
ALSO KNOWN AS: Joshua (Hebrew name); Jesus of Nazareth; Christ Jesus
AREA OF ACHIEVEMENT: Religion

EARLY LIFE

Though his name is recognized by millions and his birthday is celebrated as a holiday across the Christian world, the early life of the man now known by the Greek version of his Hebrew name, Jesus Christ (JEE-zuhs KRIST) is shrouded in obscurity. Neither the day nor the year of his birth can be fixed with certainty. Some scholars think that Bethlehem was identified as the place of his birth merely to make his life conform to old prophecies. Objective study of his life is complicated by the fact that many people believe him to be the Son of God, as indicated by the appellation Christ, Greek for the Hebrew Messiah, or "anointed one."

The earliest Christian writer whose works are extant, the Apostle Paul (d. 64 C.E.), makes no reference to the historical life of Jesus, aside from quoting a few of his sayings. Although the near-contemporary historians Flavius Josephus and Tacitus mention him, they say little of substance. The four canonical Gospels are not, strictly

speaking, biographies of Jesus. They were written as aids to memorizing his teachings or as arguments in favor of his divinity; they do not purport to be complete accounts (John 20:30). The earliest of them, attributed to Mark (c. 70 C.E.), begins with the story of Jesus' baptism by John in the river Jordan. The two attributed to Matthew (80 C.E.?) and Luke (90 C.E.?) add a story about Jesus teaching in the Temple when he was twelve and give differing accounts of his birth and genealogy. John's Gospel (100 C.E.?) is a reflective memoir, differing in chronology and in its portrayal of Jesus as a Hellenistic teacher rather than a Jewish rabbi. Other gospels, not included in the New Testament, attempted to fill the gap in Christians' knowledge about Jesus' early life by concocting fantastic stories. There are no other historical sources for the study of his life.

Matthew and Luke agree that Herod the Great was king of Judaea at Jesus' birth. Herod died in 4 B.C.E. Since, in Matthew 2, he is reported to have slaughtered male children under the age of two in an effort to kill the infant Jesus, scholars conclude that Jesus may have been born as early as 6 B.C.E. (The error in calculation was made by a sixth century monk, who compared all the then-available chronological data to determine the time of Jesus' birth.) The date of December 25 was selected by the bishop of Rome in the late fourth century. Having a Christian festival at that time of year enabled the Church to distract its members from popular pagan festivals that occurred then. Before that time, Jesus' nativity was celebrated at various times of the year, if at all.

Jesus Christ is crucified. (Library of Congress)

Jesus grew up in Galilee, where Greek influences were stronger than in the southern territory of Judaea. Though his native language was Aramaic, which is related to Hebrew, he would have had to know Greek to conduct any business. His father, Joseph, is usually described as a carpenter. The Greek word actually means something more like "builder" or "general contractor."

LIFE'S WORK

The Jews of Galilee were less conservative than those of Judaea. Rabbinic traditions and regulations were challenged in the north by a greater interest in the prophetic side of Judaism. Jesus, while not trained as a rabbi, seems to have been familiar with the standard methods of argument. He engaged in debates over interpretation of Scripture where appropriate (Mark 12:13-34) but sometimes sidestepped hairsplitting questions (Luke 10:25-37). At some points, though, he showed flashes of originality. He is never recorded as basing his teaching on the opinions of earlier rabbis—the accepted technique of the day—but taught instead on his own authority (Matt. 7:29). Parables (story-comparisons) seem to have been the foundation of his teaching technique (Mark 4:33).

Judaism was a diverse religion in the early first century C.E. Flavius Josephus describes three sects, or schools, flourishing at that time: the liberal and popular Pharisees, the aristocratic and conservative Sadducees, and the monastic Essenes. The Pharisees were further subdivided into the school of Shammai, which urged resistance to Roman rule, and that of Hillel, which counseled accommodation. There were also radical fringe groups such as the Zealots, who hoped to provoke a confrontation with the Romans that would lead to divine intervention and the foundation of a new kingdom of Israel.

Jesus' sudden appearance in the "fifteenth year of the reign of Tiberius" (Luke 3:1), or 29 C.E., when he was "about thirty years of age" (Luke 3:23), fit in with the general mood of discontent that prevailed in Judaea at the

459

time. His message that "the kingdom of God is at hand" found a receptive audience. The eschatological tone was interpreted by some as an announcement of the overthrow of Roman hegemony. Even Jesus' closest disciples did not easily give up their hope for a reestablishment of the Davidic kingship (Acts 1:6).

Jesus does not, however, seem to have envisioned himself as a political revolutionary. His aim appears to have been to reform Judaism, which had become so weighted down with minute requirements that even the most scrupulous Jews had difficulty adhering to the Torah. Jesus accused the Pharisees of imposing their own restrictions on top of the commandments of the Torah (Luke 11:46) and of neglecting what he called "the weightier matters of the law: justice, mercy, and faith" (Matt. 23:23). Such utterances link Jesus with Old Testament prophets such as Amos (Amos 5:21-24), Jeremiah (Jer. 31:31-34), and Micah (Mic. 6:7-8), who criticized the legalism of Judaism in their day and urged that obedience to the law be a matter of inner motivation, not observance of external rituals.

Such a view was thus not a new creation of Jesus. Even his most familiar injunction, to love one's neighbor as oneself, was a quotation of Leviticus 19:18. In general, his teaching can be classed under three headings: criticism of the normative Judaism of his day (for example, Matt. 23), proposal of a new, interiorized ethic (Matt. 5-7, the Sermon on the Mount), and expectations of the imminence of the kingdom of God (Mark 13).

In addition to his teaching, the accounts of his life contain miracle stories, in which Jesus purportedly heals people with various infirmities or demonstrates his power over nature by calming storms and walking on water. The Gospels conclude with the greatest of the miracle stories, the account of Jesus' resurrection, which Paul saw as the proof of his divinity (Rom. 1:4). The other apostles also made it the center of their preaching (Acts 2:22-36).

These miracle stories are probably the major point of dispute between those who accept the divinity of Jesus and those who do not. Even those who find his ethical teachings attractive sometimes find it difficult to accept the supernatural accounts that surround them. The scientific orientation that has undergirded Western education since the mid-nineteenth century has produced an outlook on the world that makes the miracle stories seem more akin to fairy tales.

In the first century C.E., however, people were eager to believe stories of the supernatural. In Petronius Arbiter's *Satyricon* (first century C.E.), one of the characters tells a

werewolf story. At the end, a listener says, "I believe every word of it" and goes on to tell a ghost story of his own. Suetonius, biographer of the first century Roman emperors, recounts as fact a story that Vespasian healed two men in Egypt in the presence of a large audience. The philosopher and mystic Apollonius of Tyana, a contemporary of Jesus, was credited with healing, resurrecting the dead, and having his birth accompanied by supernatural signs.

A major difficulty with the Gospel miracles is the inconsistency of various versions of some of the stories. For example, in Matthew 14:22-33, when Jesus walks across the waves to his disciples' boat, Peter steps out of the craft and takes a few steps before, becoming fearful, he starts to sink. Mark 6:45-51 and John 6:17-21, however, make no mention of Peter's aquatic stroll. John's is the only version that says that as soon as Jesus got into the boat, it reached the other shore.

Perhaps too much attention is devoted to the miracle stories, distracting from the more central issues of Jesus' teaching. The Gospels record his reluctance to perform miracles (Mark 8:12) because the crowds paid more attention to them than to his teachings.

Recovering Jesus' own sense of his purpose is difficult because all the documents relating to him were produced by people who believed him to be divine. Modern scholarship has concentrated on probing under the layers of interpretation that his followers added to the story in consequence of their claim that he was resurrected (see John 12:16). Jesus seems to have seen himself as a final messenger to the Jews. He claimed to have greater authority than the prophets, just as a king's son has greater authority than his servants (Mark 12:1-11).

His message was essentially a warning that the Jews had exalted ritual observance of God's law to the point that they had lost sight of its moral implications. His criticism was directed especially against the Pharisees and scribes. They reacted predictably, by plotting to silence the troublemaker. With the collusion of one of Jesus' followers, Judas Iscariot, they seized him in a garden on the outskirts of Jerusalem.

The trial of Jesus has been a subject of much controversy as to its legality and the exact charges involved. The Romans normally left local matters in the hands of provincial officials, and the Sanhedrin had the right to try cases involving Jewish law. They do not seem to have had the power to condemn a prisoner to death. They found Jesus guilty of violating religious laws, especially those against blasphemy, but before Pontius Pilate, the Roman governor, they accused him of treason.

Pilate had been governor of Judaea for about three years at that time. According to Josephus, he had difficulty getting along with the Jews from the day of his arrival. His insensitivity to their religious traditions was a major part of the problem. His decision to crucify Jesus may have been made out of genuine concern that the man was a threat to the social order, but it was probably an effort to mollify the Jews, who had already complained to the emperor about him.

Within a few days of his death, Jesus' disciples were claiming that he had risen from the dead. Whatever one may think of that assertion, the disciples' belief in it had a remarkable effect on them. From a dispirited band of fishermen and peasants who had begun to scatter back to their homes, they were transformed into a fellowship of believers willing to undergo any difficulty or torment to proclaim their faith (Luke 24:13-35). Not even threats from the religious authorities of the day could silence them (Acts 5:27-32).

SIGNIFICANCE

If his goal was to reform Judaism, Jesus can hardly be judged successful. The Pharisees resisted his initial efforts and refused to recognize his followers as loyal Jews. Driven out of the synagogues, they founded a new faith that emphasized the spiritual values of Jesus' teachings. Jesus' assertion of the importance of love of God and of one's neighbors—even one's enemies—and the shunning of ceremonialism and class distinctions were not original but resulted from his stress on long-neglected facets of Jewish scripture. His is the Judaism of the prophets, not of the Torah and the Talmud.

However one may regard the claims made about his divinity, Jesus' impact on Western culture has been too profound to ignore. His teaching introduced an element of humaneness that even the Greeks and Romans found remarkable. Unlike their pagan neighbors, Christians did not procure abortions or abandon unwanted children after birth. They cared for their sick, and during plagues they cared for the sick and dying pagans who had been dumped in the streets. They did not seek vengeance on those who wronged them. Several pagan writers of the first four centuries, including Aulus Cornelius Celsus, Porphyry, and the Emperor Julian (sometimes called Julian the Apostate), grudgingly admired the despised Christians and urged pagans to live up to the Christian standards of charity and philanthropy.

In summary, then, Jesus' teachings laid the groundwork for the Western world's system of morality, however imperfectly it has been observed. If Socrates gave definition to the Western intellect, Jesus implanted in it a conscience.

—*Albert A. Bell, Jr.*

FURTHER READING

Bornkamm, Gunther. *Jesus of Nazareth*. London: Hodder and Stoughton, 1973. The book that reopened the question of how much can be known about the historical Jesus after a half century of pessimism engendered by Albert Schweitzer's *The Quest of the Historical Jesus* (see below).

Bowker, John. *Jesus and the Pharisees*. New York: Cambridge University Press, 1973. Comparison of the teachings of Jesus with those of the Pharisaic schools of his day. Bowker concludes that the content of much of Jesus' message was not new, but his interpretation of it was.

Grant, Michael. *Jesus: An Historian's Review of the Gospels*. New York: Collier Books, 1992. A moderate, scholarly review of the problems related to using the Gospels as historical sources.

Habermas, Gary R. *The Historical Jesus: Ancient Evidence for the Life of Christ*. Joplin, Mo.: College Press, 1996. Assessment of the historical facts surrounding the life of Jesus refutes those scholars who say Christ did not exist.

Jeremias, Joachim. *The Parables of Jesus*. Rev. ed. New York: Scribner, 1973. Regards the parables as the most accurately preserved part of the material relating to Jesus. Discusses principles and problems of interpretation, then analyzes the parables under subject headings.

Radin, Max. *The Trial of Jesus of Nazareth*. Delanco, N.J.: Notable Trials Library, 2001. Discusses the problem of evidence that makes the study of Jesus' trial so problematic. The Gospels cannot be studied as if they were legal transcripts; the biases of their authors must be understood first.

Robinson, James McConkey. *A New Quest of the Historical Jesus and Other Essays*. Philadelphia: Fortress Press, 1983. Survey of the debate over the question of how much one can know about the historical Jesus on the basis of the Gospels. Robinson suggests that it is possible to learn something about his life if one uses the sources advisedly.

Schweitzer, Albert. *The Quest of the Historical Jesus*. Edited by John Bowden. Minneapolis: Fortress Press, 2001. Originally published in German in 1906, this study surveys nineteenth century attempts at writing a biography of Jesus and concludes that, because of the nature of the sources, it is an impossible task.

Van Voorst, Robert E. *Jesus Outside the New Testament: An Introduction to the Ancient Evidence.* Grand Rapids, Mich.: Wm. B. Eerdmans, 2000. Evaluates evidence outside the Scripture for the life and teachings of Jesus. Includes bibliography and indexes.

SEE ALSO: Herod the Great; John the Apostle; Saint John the Baptist; Mary; Saint Paul; Saint Peter; Pontius Pilate.

RELATED ARTICLES in *Great Events from History: The Ancient World*: c. 200 B.C.E.-c. 100 C.E., Composition of the Intertestamental Jewish Apocrypha; c. 135 B.C.E., Rise of the Pharisees; c. 6 B.C.E., Birth of Jesus Christ; c. 30 C.E., Condemnation and Crucifixion of Jesus Christ; c. 30 C.E., Preaching of the Pentecostal Gospel; c. 50-c. 150 C.E., Compilation of the New Testament; 64-67 C.E., Nero Persecutes the Christians.

JIMMU TENNŌ
Legendary first Japanese emperor (traditionally r. 660-585 B.C.E.)

According to Japanese tradition, Jimmu Tennō established the Imperial Japanese line and founded the empire after conquering the Yamato region in central Japan.

BORN: Possibly the third century B.C.E.; Takachiho Palace, Hyūga (now in Miyazaki Prefecture, Japan)
DIED: Possibly the late third century B.C.E.; Kashihara Palace (now in Kashihara, Nara Prefecture, Japan)
ALSO KNOWN AS: Kamu Yamato Iware Hiko no Mikoto
AREAS OF ACHIEVEMENT: War and conquest, government and politics

EARLY LIFE

Legend has it that Kamu Yamato Iware Hiko no Mikoto was born on the Japanese island of Kyūshū in 711 B.C.E. as the son of King Hiko Nagisatake Ugaya Fukiaezu no Mikoto, a great-grandson of the sun goddess Amaterasu Ōmikami, and Tamayorihime, the daughter of the sea god. Much later, long after his death, he would be given the name of Jimmu Tennō (jeem-mew tehn-noh) or Emperor Jimmu, in the late eighth century C.E., and he has been known by this name in Japan ever since.

Most historians agree that the traditional dates given for Jimmu's life and reign are much too early, and many events of his life, as traditionally related, are clearly mythical. The reason for this was the desire to cite very ancient divine origins by Japan's nobility in the seventh and eighth centuries, when the first histories of Japan were actually written. Writing itself was not introduced to Japan from China through Korea until about 404 C.E., almost one thousand years after the presumed death of Jimmu. The first history of Japan was written in 621 C.E., its single copy lost in a fire soon after. The *Kojiki* (712; English translation, 1882) and *Nihon Shoki*, or *Shogi*

(720; *Nihongi: Chronicles of Japan from the Earliest Time to A.D. 697*, 1896), are the two oldest sources of Jimmu's life and reign and begin at the presumed date of the creation of the universe by the deities, continuing into the eighth century.

Until 1945, the official history of the Japanese empire treated these two traditional accounts of Jimmu's life as real history. Afterward, some scholars came to believe Jimmu to be a purely mythical figure, something like a Japanese King Arthur. By the early twenty-first century, a more balanced historical consensus had been established.

Scholars agree that by the third century B.C.E., in the Yayoi period of Japanese history, there existed a strong kingdom on Japan's southern island of Kyūshū. Sometime in the third century, people from Kyūshū seem to have conquered the Yamato region in the heart of the central Japanese island of Honshū, encompassing the present cities of Nara, Ōsaka, and Kobe as well as the ancient shrine of Ise, dedicated to Jimmu's mythical ancestor, the sun goddess Amaterasu.

Thus it is believed to be possible that Jimmu was an actual ruler of the third century, helping to establish a unified empire of Kyūshū and Yamato that gradually grew to hold most of modern Japan. Some scholars see in the traditional account of Jimmu references to the legendary tenth emperor, Sujin, famed for building a strong empire. They believe that Sujin may have been a historical ruler on whom Jimmu was modeled later. Another theory holds that Jimmu is a mythical projection of the genuine twenty-sixth historical emperor Keitai, who also had to fight his way into Yamato before he was enthroned in the sixth century.

Regardless of the ongoing historical debates about the historical qualities of Jimmu, the eighth century accounts of his life still hold sway over much of the Japanese sense of national history. While most stories of Jimmu are open to historical questioning, they are nevertheless seen at least as powerful myths describing the origin of an Imperial line dating back more than a millennium.

According to tradition, Jimmu grew up in his parents' Takachiho palace. He received the education of an imperial prince, which stressed both knowledge of and proficiency in sacred rituals and martial prowess. He was famous for his great intelligence and powerful will. At the age of fifteen, he was made official heir to the throne. He married a princess from Kyūshū, Ahiratsu Hime. Ahiratsu was only made consort of Jimmu, a rank beneath that of wife, even though together they had two children, Tagishimimi no Mikoto and Kisumimi no Mikoto.

LIFE'S WORK

As the Japanese sources state it, in 667 B.C.E., Jimmu gathered his household in his palace and revealed his plan to conquer the Yamato region, an island away from his native lands. Jimmu justified his planned invasion with his divine mandate that called for him to subjugate the plains of Nara, for it was held as the center of the universe, predestined for his rule. His brothers and sons agreed with this divinely ordained plan and collected a strong naval expeditionary force to accomplish the goal.

As Jimmu's expedition gathered, the future emperor picked up more followers, who would become the ancestors of Japan's noble families ruling in the seventh and eighth centuries. This pattern would continue throughout the events of his life and indicates why this traditional story was so popular among Japan's ruling elite seeking to establish their ancient roots.

In 666, Jimmu landed in the south of Honshū, in the present prefecture of Okayama. For three years, until 663, Jimmu rested in a temporary palace erected there and built up his huge fleet. He then sailed eastward across the Inland Sea and made landfall near today's city of Ōsaka. With his troops bunched up on a narrow road as they headed inland, Jimmu had to turn back at first and launch his invasion from a different route. Driven by his desire to subjugate and unify what he considered his empire, however, Jimmu soon attacked the local chieftain and powerful adversary Nagasune Hiko, who ruled the fertile Nara plains behind the coastal mountains.

In a first battle, Jimmu's forces were defeated at Ōsaka, and his brother Itsuse was mortally wounded by an arrow from a lowly enemy foot soldier. Retreating south by sea toward the tip of the Wakayama peninsula, Jimmu lost his remaining two brothers to the ferocious

sea. Angry that there should be storms at sea despite the status of their mother as sea goddess, both jumped into the ocean, whereupon one was turned into a god and the other brother reached the eternal land.

Landing in the south, after executing a local chieftain—as he did everywhere he faced opposition—Jimmu tried to lead his army across the mountains against Nara. Suddenly his troops were enshrouded by a poisonous vapor. The mist was lifted by the intervention of the sun goddess Amaterasu. She also sent Jimmu a three-legged sun-crow, Yatagarasu, to lead his army out of the mountainous wilderness nearby the shore and bring it in contact with the enemy.

By force and trickery, Jimmu and his most able officer, Michi no Omi, succeeded in subduing their various enemies. This involved inviting some opponents to a friendship banquet, only to have Jimmu's troops slaughter the drunken guests. Late in 663, Jimmu met up again with Nagasune Hiko. Their battles were inconclusive until a golden kite descended from heaven and blinded Hiko's soldiers, who abandoned the battlefield. As Nagasune Hiko asked Jimmu for mercy, he was killed by his own brother-in-law, who then submitted their army to the victorious Jimmu.

In 662, Jimmu cleaned the Nara area of bandits, among them some hideous earth spider people, who were summarily executed. In spring, he decided to found a genuine empire and civilize the land and his people. In 661, Jimmu married Hime Tatatara Isuzu Hime no Mikoto, a beautiful princess with a divine father from the Nara plains. This dynastic marriage to a local princess clearly underlines Jimmu's claims to both Kyūshū, site of his birth and that of his first consort, and Yamato, the conquered region where his new wife was born.

THE FIRST TEN LEGENDARY EMPERORS OF JAPAN, 660-30 B.C.E.	
Emperor	*Traditional Reign Date*
Jimmu	660-585
Suizei	581-549
Annei	549-511
Itoku	510-477
Kōshō	475-393
Kōan	392-291
Kōrei	290-215
Kōgen	214-158
Kaika	158-98
Sujin	97-30

In 660, in his newly built palace at Kashihara near to-day's city of Nara, Jimmu enthroned himself and his wife Tatatara as Japan's first emperor and empress. At that point the country was considered unified, and the Japanese nation was born, the crowning achievement of Jimmu, according to legend.

Subsequently, Jimmu rewarded his followers, and he had two more children, one of whom would succeed him on the throne. According to tradition, he reigned for seventy-five more years, as the country prospered and grew. The *Nihon Shoki* states that Jimmu died in 585, at the age of 127 (traditional calculations add a year to a person's age).

SIGNIFICANCE

Most contemporary scholars see in the legendary figure of Jimmu and the often fantastic accounts of his life and deeds a traditional rendition of the genuine, albeit much later, historical process of the beginning of the imperial system in Japan. Whether Jimmu actually existed as a person in history or is a purely legendary construct appears less significant than the agreement that in the third century B.C.E., central authority was established over two connected cultural centers, on Kyūshū and Honshū. This gave rise to the eventual establishment of the Japanese empire. Historically, Jimmu became important as Japanese civilization came into its own, imperial rule solidified, and the young nation sought to establish a worthy native counterpart to the much older Chinese culture.

Thus, the traditional date of Jimmu's accession as emperor is based on Chinese numerology rather than history. Calculating backward from the eighth century, 660 was considered a grand *kanoto tori*, a year in which universe-shaping events would take place. Consequently, the foundation of the Japanese nation was put into this special year. By projecting so far back the origin of the empire, ancient historians had to give impossibly long lives to the first fourteen legendary emperors, whose reigns had to cover a huge span of years, testing the limits of human longevity.

Regardless of the rather shaky historical basis for the person of Jimmu, the story of Japan's first emperor has enjoyed great popularity in Japan for many centuries. Misused by the militarists in World War II, the Jimmu legend was criticized in the postwar period. In its revived and revised form, it serves to remind the Japanese people of the long duration of their culture and preserves a nostalgic notion of an ancient, mythical past.

—R. C. Lutz

FURTHER READING

Aston, W. G., trans. *Nihongi: Chronicles of Japan.* 1896. Reprint. Rutland, Vt.: C. E. Tuttle, 1972. A translation of the Japanese text originally published in 720 and also called *Nihon Shoki* (or *Shogi*) that contains one of the two original accounts of Jimmu's life and work.

Brown, Delmer M., ed. *Ancient Japan.* Vol. 1 in *The Cambridge History of Japan.* New York: Cambridge University Press, 1999. Collection of essays covering the latest scholarship on the actual rise of early Imperial Japan, with an interesting reflection on ancient Japanese historical consciousness and the role played by the legendary first emperor, Jimmu.

Lu, David J. *Japan: A Documentary History.* Armonk, N.Y.: M. E. Sharpe, 1997. Contains an abridged account of Jimmu's accession to Japan's throne and related historical documents of the period.

Philippi, Donald L., trans. *Kojiki.* Princeton, N.J.: Princeton University Press, 1969. English translation of the first Japanese account of Jimmu's life and rise to power, originally published in 712. The reader has to get used to Philippi's unique style of transcribing ancient Japanese names into Roman letters, which alters the spelling of most.

Reischauer, Robert Karl. *Early Japanese History, c. 40 B.C.-A.D. 1167.* 1937. Reprint. Gloucester, Mass.: P. Smith, 1967. A pre-World War II compilation of Japanese sources telling of mostly legendary events.

Sansom, George B. *A History of Japan.* Stanford, Calif.: Stanford University Press, 1978. Still valuable study of the earliest, legendary period of Japanese history.

SEE ALSO: Jingū; Ōjin Tennō.

RELATED ARTICLES in *Great Events from History: The Ancient World*: 3d century B.C.E. (traditionally 660 B.C.E.), Jimmu Tennō Becomes the First Emperor of Japan; c. mid-3d century C.E., Himiko Rules the Yamatai; c. 300-710 C.E., Kofun Period Unifies Japan; 390-430 C.E. or later, traditionally r. 270-310, Ōjin Tennō, First Historical Emperor of Japan, Reigns.

JINGŪ

Japanese empress (traditionally r. 200-269 C.E.)

According to tradition, Jingū executed a prophecy of the sun goddess Amaterasu and conquered the three kingdoms of Korea.

BORN: Early fourth century C.E.; Kinai Region, Japan
DIED: Late fourth century C.E.; Wakazakura Palace, Japan
ALSO KNOWN AS: Jingō; Jingū Kōgō (full name); Okinaga Tarashi Hime no Mikoto (birth name); Jingō-kōgō
AREAS OF ACHIEVEMENT: War and conquest, government and politics

EARLY LIFE

Jingū (jihn-gew) is the name given to Okinaga Tarashi Hime no Mikoto after her death, by which she is commonly known. Most of her story comprises legendary events. According to Japanese tradition, Jingū was the great-granddaughter of the legendary ninth emperor, Kaika. Her father was Prince Okinaga no Sukune and her mother Princess Katsuragi (or Katsuraki) no Takanuka. As a young girl, Jingū was known for her intelligence, shrewdness, and great beauty. She grew up in the society of the Imperial court around the present cities of Ōsaka and Nara in central Japan.

Most scholars believe that Jingū is still a legendary, rather than a real, figure of Japanese history. The traditional dates for her amazingly long life of one hundred years have been shown to be fictitious. To claim ancient outside verification of the facts of their own history, thus making them more believable, the early Japanese historians of the eighth century wanted to identify Jingū with Queen Himiko. Himiko, an ancient shaman-ruler of Japan, is mentioned in written Chinese sources of the third century that are almost five hundred years older than the first written history of Jingū's reign. Indeed, like a shaman-priestess, Jingū is shown to often rely on her close contact with the gods when executing her rule. However, as later events of Jingū's life show, she cannot have lived when Himiko flourished, between 220 and 250 C.E.; the two must have been different persons. Modern scholars therefore believe that if Jingū was real, she lived about 120 years later than the traditional Japanese dates of her life and flourished in the fourth century C.E.

At age twenty-four, in February, 193 (according to legend), Jingū married the (likely legendary) emperor Chūai (also Chiuai) and was given the official rank of empress. Chūai, at age forty-four, already had two children from his first consort and later would have another son with a consort he took after his marriage to Jingū.

In the year of their marriage, Chūai decided to undertake a naval expedition to subjugate the rebellious Kumaso people of Kyūshū. From central Japan, Empress Jingū followed in a ship of her own. She joined Chūai at Kashihi palace on Kyūshū. In October, the emperor held a war council with his ministers. Now, according to legend, Jingū became possessed by the spirit of a god. Through Jingū as a medium, the god prophesied that Chūai should cease pursuing the Kumaso and direct his military energy toward Korea, which he would conquer. Chūai refused to believe this. Through Jingū's mouth, the angry god promised an early death for the emperor and that the boy child just conceived by Jingū would inherit Korea.

Japanese historical accounts differ on the year of the council and the death of the emperor. The *Kojiki* (712; English translation, 1882) has Chūai die suddenly on the day of the curse. The *Nihon Shoki* (720; *Nihongi: Chronicles of Japan from the Earliest Times to A.D. 697*, 1896) gives his death seven years later, either from an illness or in battle against the Kumaso. Scholars who believe in Chūai's existence place his death in 362 C.E.

LIFE'S WORK

After the death of the emperor, traditionally in March, 200 C.E., Jingū met with her imperial ministers and decided to keep his demise a secret, in order to avoid popular unrest. Prime Minister Takechi no Sukune gave the corpse a temporary burial. To restore order, Jingū commanded performance of a great exorcism.

One month later, Jingū performed a high ritual to learn the identity of the god who had prophesied to Chūai. After seven days, Jingū learned that it was the sun goddess Amaterasu, in addition to a variety of other deities. Now Jingū ordered their proper worship and sent a general to the Kumaso, who quickly submitted. Dressed as a male warrior, Jingū killed Hashirō Kumawashi, a legendary figure whose wings made him almost invincible. She also ordered the execution of a hideous earth spider princess before conducting various rituals for success against the Koreans.

In May, Jingū declared to her ministers that she would lead the Japanese army herself, dressed as a man. In October, her army could assemble—only after she built a new shrine and made offerings. When a scout sighted the mountains of Korea, Jingū addressed her troops in male attire and admonished them to keep discipline, fight the enemy, and show mercy to those who surrendered. A god sent two spirits to protect her. In order to delay the birth of her baby until her return to Japan, Jingū took one or two stones, either to insert into her vagina (*Nihon Shoki*) or to attach to her skirt (*Kojiki*).

In November, Jingū's fleet sailed from the island of Tsushima in the northeast of Japan to the coast of Korea, to conquer the kingdom of Silla. Silla occupied the eastern coast of Korea, including today's city of Pusan. Silla's king was so awed by the Japanese fleet that he surrendered his whole country. Bowing to the imperial ship of Jingū, Silla's king promised eternal loyalty and regular tribute in goods and slaves. When a Japanese soldier proposed to kill him, Jingū reminded her troops to show mercy to those who submitted and made the king her vassal.

The *Nihon Shoki* gives the name of Silla's king as Phasa Mikeun and states that he gave Jingū his son Micheul Kwichi Phachin Kanki as a hostage. Ancient Korean sources reveal that Phasa reigned Silla from 80 to 112, and Silla Prince Misăheun, the Prince Micheul of the Japanese account, was sent as hostage to Japan in 402. Clearly, Japan's historians compiled events that could be almost three hundred years apart and patched them together to form one coherent narrative, flattering to their nation. Scholars tend to agree that Japan was active in Korea in the fourth century C.E. and that many events ascribed to Jingū's reign are corroborated, although they generally happened 120 years later than Japanese history documents.

After taking the records and maps outlining the possessions and lands of Silla, Jingū symbolically subjugated the country by placing her spear at the gates of Silla's palace. Realizing that the Japanese forces were too strong for them, the kings of Paekche in western Korea (around today's Seoul) and of Koguryo or Kokuryo in North Korea submitted to Jingū's rule and promised tribute. Asserting her rule over Korea, Jingū returned to Japan. In the late fourth century C.E., in Kyūshū, she gave birth to her son Homuda, the future emperor Ōjin Tennō.

The sun goddess Amaterasu, seated at right. According to tradition, her spirit took possession of Jingū. (F. R. Niglutsch)

In spring of 201, Jingū faced a rebellion by the two princes born to Chūai's first consort. They did not want to obey her son and gathered an army. They and Jingū prepared two competing burial sites for the emperor's corpse, which remained in Jingū's possession. When one of the princes was killed by a wild boar, the other retreated east. To confuse her enemies, Jingū sent Takechi with her son separately to her capital. Reunited with Takechi, she ordered an attack. Takechi pretended to make peace. When the enemy rendered their bows inoperable, Takechi's troops fell on them. Defeated, the last prince drowned himself in Lake Biwa, east of Kyoto.

With her rule cemented, Jingū accepted the title of grand empress in 201. She was considered a regent for her son Homuda (Ōjin Tennō), rather than a reigning empress. However, she ruled until her death, long after Homuda reached maturity. In 202, the emperor was buried in his final tomb, and in 203 Homuda was designated next emperor. Jingū built the palace of Wakazakura, where she would govern for the rest of her life. There, she also enjoyed banquets and drinking games with her son and prime minister Takechi.

In 205 Silla's Prince Micheul escaped and went home, having tricked the empress into allowing him to leave. Enraged, Jingū's general burned Silla's envoys to death, conquered a Korean castle, and returned with captives to be settled in Japan.

For the years 239-243, the *Nihon Shoki* copies Chinese sources telling of the reign of Queen Himiko and (anachronistically) ascribes them to Jingū's rule. In 246 Jingū sent an emissary to the Japanese enclave of Mimana (Kaya in Korean) in South Korea, wedged between the two kingdoms of Paekche in the west and Silla in the east. The king of Paekche again sent valuable tribute.

In 247, Silla robbed Paekche of their tribute and passed it off as their own. Jingū sent Chikuma Nagahiko to Korea. Allied with Paekche, Nagahiko's forces defeated Silla in 249 and Jingū enlarged Paekche at the expense of their enemy in 250. In 252, in traditional chronology, Paekche's grateful king sent Jingū gifts, among them a seven-branched sword. This sword was actually identified resting in Isonokami Shrine in Nara in 1873. Made in 369 in reality, it was given by the king of Paekche to the Japanese. Its existence proves the authenticity of at least some of the events ascribed to Jingū's reign.

In 262, Silla failed to sent tribute. Jingū sent General Sachihiko to punish Silla. Sachihiko was seduced by two beautiful Silla women and attacked another kingdom in-stead. Enraged, Jingū sent another general to defeat Silla, and Sachihiko committed suicide. According to tradition, Jingū died in Wakazakura Palace in May, 269. She was buried six months later.

SIGNIFICANCE

The reign of Jingū marks the point where Japanese historical records leave the realm of legend. From then on, their events can actually be corroborated by histories written in other countries such as China and Korea, and by archaeological evidence. The dates given in Japanese accounts are predated, but some events clearly took place. Scholars notice how magic and ritual become less important later in Jingū's regency, when practical politics and a cheerful court life dominate.

To document Jingū's conquest, or at least involvement, in Korea, two archaeological artifacts are of crucial relevance. First, there is the sword presented to Jingū by Paekche. Second, in 1884 a Japanese officer discovered an inscribed stele on the banks of the Yalu River separating North Korea from China, which commemorates a war of Japan and Paekche against Koguryo in North Korea, ending with the utter defeat of the Japanese in 391. This proves Japanese military involvement in the region.

By 2003, scholars were still hotly divided over the true nature of Japanese-Korean relations in the fourth century, now agreed on as the time of Jingū's life. Japanese scholars believe that during this time, Japan established a colony at Mimana, while the Koreans dispute the existence of this state they call Kaya. While most Japanese read the inscription on the Paekche sword to mean that the king submitted to Jingū, many Korean scholars read it to mean a gift to the inferior Japanese. Similarly, the inscription of the stele on the Yalu River is disputed, and its location in Communist North Korea prevents independent scholarly access to it.

Even if Jingū was not a single historical person, there is historical evidence for many of the events described in her reign. She may well be a composite character created around a real person. Jingū's reliance on her spiritual powers early in her life corresponds to the existence of women shamans in Japan and is in line with the continuous importance placed on ritual by Japanese emperors.

—*R. C. Lutz*

FURTHER READING

Aston, W. G., trans. *Nihongi: Chronicles of Japan*. 1896. Reprint. Rutland, Vt.: C. E. Tuttle, 1972. English translation of the *Nihon Shoki* (or *Shogi*) that contains one of the two original accounts of Jingū's life.

Brown, Delmer M., ed. *Ancient Japan*. Vol. 1 in *The Cambridge History of Japan*. New York: Cambridge University Press, 1999. Chapter 2, "The Yamato Kingdom," contains an excellent historical account of the time of Jingū's life and discusses many of the controversies surrounding her presumed person and rule.

Farris, William Wayne. *Sacred Texts and Buried Treasures*. Honolulu: University of Hawaii Press, 1998. Chapters 1 and 2 discuss Japan's historical relationship with Korea in the time of Jingū's rule. Excellent scholarly discussion of the textual and archaeological evidence for the events of her regency. Illustrated; includes bibliography and index.

Philippi, Donald L., trans. *Kojiki*. Princeton, N.J.: Princeton University Press, 1969. An English translation of the first Japanese account of Jingū's life. Philippi's unique transcription of ancient Japanese names alters their English spelling.

Tarō, Sakamoto. *The Six National Histories of Japan*. Translated by John S. Brownlee. Vancouver: University of British Columbia Press, 1991. Translation of the 1970 Japanese study of the oldest Japanese histories. Chapter 2, on the *Nihon Shoki*, contains an excellent discussion on the source materials used by Japanese historians. Pages 61-63 deal directly with accounts of Jingū. Includes appendix, bibliography, and index.

SEE ALSO: Hatshepsut; Jimmu Tennō; Ōjin Tennō.

RELATED ARTICLES in *Great Events from History: The Ancient World*: 3d century B.C.E. (traditionally 660 B.C.E.), Jimmu Tennō Becomes the First Emperor of Japan; c. mid-3d century C.E., Himiko Rules the Yamatai; c. 300-710 C.E., Kofun Period Unifies Japan; 390-430 C.E. or later, traditionally r. 270-310, Ōjin Tennō, First Historical Emperor of Japan, Reigns.

JOHANAN BEN ZAKKAI
Judaean religious leader

After the destruction of Jerusalem by the Romans in 70 C.E., when the Temple cult—the center of Jewish life—lay in ruins, Johanan was responsible for reorienting Jewish life around faithful observance of the law (Torah).

BORN: c. 1 C.E.; Judaea (now in Israel)
DIED: c. 80 C.E.; Beror Heil, west of Jerusalem, Judaea (now in Israel)
AREA OF ACHIEVEMENT: Religion

EARLY LIFE

Little is known of the early life of Johanan ben Zakkai (joh-HAHN-uhn behn ZAK-ay-i). Of the three most important sources of information for Roman-occupied Judaea during the first century, two of them, Flavius Josephus's *Bellum Judaium* (75-79 C.E.; *History of the Jewish War*, 1773) and the New Testament, contain no reference to Johanan. The rabbinical writings from the Talmud, which constitute the sole source of information regarding the life of Johanan ben Zakkai, were compiled between the third and fifth centuries and at best testify to carefully handed-down memory.

The Talmud pictures Johanan as a leader among the Pharisees, a group of especially devout observers of the Torah (the first five books in the Hebrew Bible) who first came to prominence in the late second or first century B.C.E. and who, after the destruction of the Temple in 70 C.E. by the Romans, became the sole shapers of what is today normative Judaism. The main tradition concerning Johanan relates that he "occupied himself in commerce forty years, served as apprentice to the sages forty years, and sustained Israel forty years." He was one of four Jewish leaders believed to have lived for 120 years, the others being Moses, Hillel the Elder, and Rabbi Akiba ben Joseph. Johanan was considered to have been the last of eighty students of Hillel, who, in similar manner, "went up from Babylonia aged forty years, served as apprentice to the sages forty years, and sustained Israel forty years."

Johanan actually was born near the beginning of the first century and died during its last quarter, probably around 80. "Johanan" means "the Lord gave graciously"; Ezra and Nehemiah record 760 sons of Zakkai ("righteous man") among nearly forty-five thousand exiles returning to Jerusalem and Judah from Babylonian exile during the sixth century B.C.E. Johanan was descended from commoners rather than priests; his halakic (legal) rulings sternly criticize the conduct of the upper classes toward the poor. Some of his rulings reflect a detailed knowledge of business affairs and support the claim that he engaged in business in his early or mid-life. As a young man, he entered the rabbinic academy of Hillel in Jerusalem. Whether he studied under the Master himself is problematical; Hillel died probably around 10 C.E. or, at most, a few years thereafter.

What is certain is that, of the two great Pharisaic schools of Torah interpretation—those of Hillel and Shammai—Johanan was schooled in the traditions of Hillel, which are generally pictured as more irenic in approach to the law and more patient in dealing with students as well as more widely accepted among the middle classes. Hence, Johanan developed traits of flexibility in casuistry and gentleness toward students that enabled him to make a lasting contribution to the development of Judaism.

As a student, Johanan was famed for both intellectual acuity and self-discipline. He never traveled 4 cubits (6 feet, or 1.8 meters) without words of the Torah, even in winter. No one preceded him into the schoolroom, nor did he ever leave anyone behind there. "If all the heavens were parchment," said Johanan, "and all the trees pens, and all the oceans ink, they would not suffice to write down the wisdom which I have learned from my masters." One of his students later made a similar statement regarding his own education at the feet of Johanan. Tradition pictures Hillel endorsing Johanan, conferring as it were his own mantle on his young student. When he completed his studies in Jerusalem, Johanan moved to a village in the northern province of Galilee—the other end of the country from Jerusalem and far removed from its scrupulous observance of the Torah. There, with his wife and his young son, he undertook his career as a teacher, a missionary for the Torah. In the Pharisaic manner, he supported himself, probably in business, while he attempted to teach the Galileans.

LIFE'S WORK

A political event—the destruction of the Temple in 70 C.E. by the Romans—intervened in Johanan's life to thrust him, at seventy years of age, onto the center stage of Jewish history. Johanan had given his life to scholarship and teaching and was not involved in politics. His eighteen years in Galilee and the subsequent three decades that he spent as a teacher in Jerusalem together consumed his prime years. He reached the biblical "threescore and ten" offstage from history, and his decades of labor in Galilee and Jerusalem are historically noteworthy only as part of the story of a life made unexpectedly significant in the context of the destruction of the center of Judaism—the Temple—and the consequent reorientation of the Jewish religion around the law.

There is no specific evidence that Johanan's purpose in going to Galilee was to serve as a missionary of the To-

rah, but it is clear that this is the significance of the years he spent there. He resided in Arav, a small village in the hill country of central Galilee, where he generally failed to make an impression on the religious life of the region. During his entire stay he had only one student, Hanina ben Dosa, and only two cases of halakic law were brought before him for judgment. The Galileans, recent converts to the Jerusalem cult, sought a religion of miracle-working, messianic fulfillment, the piety of the Temple pilgrimage, and salvation in the next world. Johanan, by contrast, offered only the discipline of a humble life of faithful observance of the law set forth in the Torah. A third century Talmudic source records the closing of Johanan's ministry in Galilee: "Eighteen years Rabban Yohanan ben Zakkai spent in 'Arav, and only these two cases came before him. At the end he said, 'O Galilee, Galilee! You hate the Torah! Your end will be to be besieged!'"

Disappointed, Johanan took his ailing son and wife and returned to Jerusalem. There he set up a school near the site of the Temple and spent the next three decades patiently teaching the Torah. His quiet success is demonstrated in his rise through Pharisaic ranks. Pharisaic leadership had often been shared between pairs— Shemaiah and Abtalion, Hillel and Shammai. Two halakic rulings sent to Galilee from Jerusalem during this period bear the names of both Gamaliel I—the acknowledged leader of the Pharisees—and Johanan ben Zakkai, who probably served as his partner or deputy. Johanan, nearing his seventieth year, could look back with satisfaction on a life of quiet scholarship, but he had accomplished nothing to earn for himself a permanent niche in history.

Just at this point in Johanan's life, an explosion occurred in the political life of Judaea. Judaean independence had been won from the Greeks in 166 B.C.E., but after 62 B.C.E. the nation had had to live in uncertain peace under Roman occupation. The Pharisees, for whom the heart of Judaism lay in personal fidelity to the Torah rather than in political sovereignty, had accepted tenuous coexistence with Rome. From 5 B.C.E. onward, however, there had grown among the people a Zealot movement that anticipated messianic fulfillment in the overthrow of Roman rule and the establishment of a divine monarchy in place of Caesar's. In late 65 C.E., a contingent of Zealots ambushed and defeated the twelfth Roman legion, inaugurating what is in Roman annals the famous Bellum Judaicum of 66-70. In face of the Zealot revolt and the siege of Jerusalem by the Romans, Johanan made the most critical decision of his life—one that made him for a brief moment the single most important figure in Judaism.

In 68, Johanan abandoned the war and the Zealot-controlled city of Jerusalem, fleeing for safety to the camp of Vespasian. He allowed himself to be smuggled past the Zealot watchguards and out of Jerusalem inside a coffin borne by two of his rabbinical students. Pharisaic leaders such as Gamaliel I who remained behind with the Zealots perished in the massacre that followed the fall of Jerusalem to the Romans.

The main Talmudic tradition regarding what happened next represents the following encounter when Johanan arrived at the camp of Vespasian:

> They opened the coffin, and Rabban Yohanan stood up before him. "Are you Rabban Yohanan ben Zakkai?" Vespasian inquired. "Tell me what I may give you."
>
> "I ask nothing of you," Rabban Yohanan replied, "save Yavneh, where I might go and teach my disciples and there establish a house of prayer, and perform all the commandments."
>
> "Go," Vespasian said to him.

Moreover, Johanan allegedly predicted that Vespasian would become emperor, a prophecy fulfilled three days later.

A different interpretation has suggested that Johanan was held under house arrest at Yavneh by the Romans. Whether Johanan was Vespasian's guest or his detainee, however, he spent the decade following the fall of Jerusalem in the Roman-protected town of Yavneh, instructing a contingent of Pharisees who had survived the destruction. There he husbanded and nurtured the most important remnant of Pharisees, and in so doing patched together the torn fabric of Jewish national life and rescued Judaism as a law-centered community now that it could no longer continue as a temple cult.

The period of Johanan's service at Yavneh was brief, no more than a decade. The manifest yield of his labors was sparse; few chose to sit at the feet of one who seemingly had turned his back on the nation in its hour of need. So difficult was his reception that he was even compelled to remove from Yavneh to the neighboring settlement of Beror Heil, where he died, probably around 80, surrounded by a very small number of students.

Succeeding generations, however, proved the permanent worth of Johanan's years at Yavneh. His small academy laid foundations that guaranteed the survival of Pharisaism. Furthermore, his tenure there afforded sufficient time for Gamaliel II, the true successor of Gama-

liel I, to emerge from the political shadow of his family's support of the rebellion against Rome. The next decade at Yavneh—the 90's—was pivotal in the history of Judaism: Gamaliel II led five of Johanan's students, among others, in constructing the basis for what eventually emerged, in the vacuum remaining after the destruction of the Temple, as normative Talmudic Judaism.

SIGNIFICANCE

According to rabbinic tradition, Johanan ben Zakkai acted out the nation's response to the fall of the Temple: It was he who rent his garments on hearing the news. His physical appearance is undocumented; what is emphasized instead is the high rabbinical estimate of Johanan, whom the Jewish teachers ranked alongside Moses, Hillel, and Akiba ben Joseph as one who indeed "sustained all Israel." His title, "Rabban," indicates that he was considered the rabbi of primacy during his own period.

"My son," Johanan once replied to a student who despaired that the destruction of the Temple would mean that there could be no more atonement for sins, "be not grieved. We have another atonement as effective as this. And what is it? It is acts of loving-kindness, as it is said, *For I desire mercy, not sacrifice*." In accord with this principle, Johanan's halakic rulings at Yavneh readjusted the Jewish ritual calendar to suit the demands of the new situation in which the synagogue, rather than the Temple, would be the center of Jewish life.

In the age of a Judaism beset with messianic movements such as those of the Zealots themselves, of Jesus of Nazareth, and of Simeon bar Kokhba, Johanan set a standard of caution that became normative in Judaism through the succeeding nineteen centuries:

> If you have a sapling in your hand, and it is said to you, "Behold, there is the Messiah"—go on with your planting, and afterward go out and receive him. . . . Do not haste to tear down [the altars of Gentiles], so that you do not have to rebuild them with your own hands. Do not destroy those of brick, that they may not say to you, "Come and build them of stone."

So Johanan had cautioned the Zealots. His advice became the watchword of the tradition of political restraint necessary for survival during the long centuries of persecution and statelessness of the Jewish people between the fall of the second Jewish commonwealth in 70 C.E. and the establishment of the third in 1948.

—Marlin Timothy Tucker

FURTHER READING

Alon, Gedalyahu. *Jews, Judaism, and the Classical World: Studies in Jewish History in the Times of the Second Temple and Talmud.* Jerusalem: Magnes Press of Hebrew University, 1977. A series of articles on a wide variety of critical issues dealing with the history of the Jewish people from the first century B.C.E. through the third century C.E.

Ben-Sasson, H. H., ed. *A History of the Jewish People.* Cambridge, Mass.: Harvard University Press, 1976. Written by six eminent scholars, this is the best one-volume interpretive history of the Jewish people. Places Johanan ben Zakkai in the context of the entire stream of Jewish history.

Neusner, Jacob. *Development of a Legend: Studies on the Traditions Concerning Yohanan ben Zakkai.* Leiden, Netherlands: E. J. Brill, 1970. A detailed criticism of the Talmudic texts that are the sole source of evidence for the life of Johanan.

_____. *From Politics to Piety: The Emergence of Pharisaic Judaism.* Englewood Cliffs, N.J.: Prentice-Hall, 1973. A brief popular account of Pharisaic Judaism during the era of Johanan ben Zakkai.

_____. *A Life of Yohanan ben Zakkai, ca. 1-80 C.E.* 2d ed. Nashville, Tenn.: Abingdon Press, 1975. The single scholarly biography of Johanan ben Zakkai written in English. Neusner contests Alon's view that Johanan was under house arrest at Yavneh and argues for the more widely accepted tradition that he was allowed to reside in Yavneh as a favor from Vespasian.

Shanks, Herschel, ed. *Ancient Israel: From Abraham to the Roman Destruction of the Temple.* Englewood Cliffs, N.J.: Prentice Hall, 1999. History includes numerous color and black-and-white photos, maps, charts, and time lines.

Zeitlin, Solomon. *The Rise and Fall of the Judaean State: A Political, Social, and Religious History of the Second Commonwealth.* Philadelphia: Jewish Publication Society of America, 1978. An excellent narrative account of this period of Jewish history. One chapter treats the work of Johanan ben Zakkai at Yavneh.

SEE ALSO: Akiba ben Joseph; Jesus; Moses; Vespasian.

RELATED ARTICLES in *Great Events from History: The Ancient World*: 587-423 B.C.E., Birth of Judaism; c. 135 B.C.E., Rise of the Pharisees; September 8, 70 C.E., Roman Destruction of the Temple of Jerusalem.

JOHN THE APOSTLE
Christian theologian

John the Apostle was one of Jesus' most trusted disciples during his lifetime. After Jesus' death, John was a leader in the early Church and by his writings made important contributions to Christian theology.

BORN: c. 10 C.E.; probably Capernaum, Palestine

DIED: c. 100 C.E.; Ephesus, Ionia, Asia Minor (now in Turkey)

ALSO KNOWN AS: Saint John the Evangelist; Saint John the Divine

AREA OF ACHIEVEMENT: Religion

EARLY LIFE

Assuming John to have been a young man when he was called as a disciple of Jesus, he must have been born about 10 C.E., probably in Capernaum. His father was Zebedee and his mother Salome; he had a brother, James, also a disciple and presumably the elder of the two, because he is generally mentioned first, and John is often identified as the "brother of James." The family occupa-tion was fishing. They were presumably prosperous, as they owned their own boat and employed servants; they may have been a priestly family as well. Salome figures occasionally in the Gospels; she requested that her sons be given seats of honor beside Jesus in Heaven (Matt. 20), and she was one of the women who helped to support Jesus financially (Matt. 15).

James and John may have been cousins of Jesus, a fact that would explain their early call and the episode at the Cross in which Mary, Jesus' mother, was committed to the care of "the disciple whom Jesus loved," a term generally taken to refer to John, the son of Zebedee. The nickname "Boanerges" (sons of thunder or perhaps anger) bestowed on James and John by Jesus suggests a certain impetuousness and aggressiveness; James's early martyrdom suggests that he had the greater share of the quality. As for John, his occupation and his besting of Peter in the race to Jesus' tomb suggest a strong, athletic man.

LIFE'S WORK

It is with the call by the Sea of Galilee that John's recorded life begins. Having called Peter and Andrew to leave their nets and become "fishers of men," Jesus immediately proceeded to James and John, who left "the boat and their father" and followed him. In general, the position of John in Jesus' ministry is clear. He appears on lists of the Twelve and always among the first: "Simon who is called Peter and Andrew his brother; James the son of Zebedee and John his brother." When a smaller group is named, John is always among them; it is James and John who would have called down fire on a village of the Samaritans (Luke 9). Generally, however, John is linked to Peter in a subordinate role. Thus, he was present at the healing of Peter's mother-in-law (Mark 1) and of Jairus's daughter (Mark 5); he was present with Peter and James at the Transfiguration (Matt. 17) and again at Gethsemane (Mark 14).

Toward the end of the Gospel of John, there are numerous references to "the disciple whom Jesus loved," almost certainly John. He was the disciple whom Peter prompted to solicit Jesus' identification of the betrayer at the Last Supper (John 18). He was possibly the disciple who introduced Peter to the high priest's courtyard. He is the one to whose care Christ commended his mother. He is the one, along with Peter, to whom Mary Magdalene brought news of the Resurrection. Finally, "the disciple whom Jesus loved" clearly was present when the risen Jesus appeared at the Sea of Galilee, and the Gospel records a statement of Jesus that some interpreted as a prophecy that the disciple would not die before the Second Coming (John 21). John appears here, incidentally, in the same role in which Luke casts him at his first appearance: as a fishing partner with Peter.

After the Crucifixion and Resurrection, John seems to have filled much the same role as before: as a leader and spokesman for the infant Church, constantly in a subordinate role to Peter and sometimes also to his brother James, until the latter's martyrdom. John was with Peter when the lame man was healed (the first miracle performed after the death of Jesus); twice he was imprisoned, once with Peter, once with all the Apostles; he went with Peter to support the missionary effort of Philip of Samaria. Finally, he played a leading role when the Church had to decide whether Gentile converts were obliged to observe the Jewish ceremonial law, as some converted Pharisees had argued. Paul had gone to Jerusalem with Barnabas to confer on the matter and was cordially received by James (the Lord's brother) and Peter and John, "who were reputed to be pillars." At the

prompting of Peter, the Gentiles were released from the law, except with respect to unchastity and meat sacrificed to idols (Acts 15; Gal. 2). It was a crucial episode in the history of the early Church, for it meant that Christianity could no longer be regarded as a Jewish sect.

This episode took place some seventeen years after Paul's conversion and is the last biblical record of John, but church tradition suggests the shape of his later life. According to this tradition (which is not beyond dispute), John spent the latter part of his life in missionary activity at Ephesus. During the reign of Domitian (81-96), he was banished to the Isle of Patmos (an association that is still advertised in tourist literature). He is thought to have returned to Ephesus and to have lived on into the reign of Trajan (98-117). It was during this period that he is thought to have written the Gospel of John, the three Epistles of John, and (possibly) the Book of Revelation.

Some scholars would make John not so much the author of these works as the authority behind them; it is evident that another hand edited the manuscript of the Gospel, with John's certification "that this testimony is true" (John 21). Perhaps John should be envisioned as the respected leader of the community, whose disciples aided him in putting together his recollections of Christ; the Gospel apparently went through several editions as material was added, perhaps in accord with specific needs of the Church. The Epistles give evidence of dissension in the churches in the Ephesus area; if the heretics mentioned indeed denied that Christ came in the flesh, in "water and blood," they may have represented an early stage of Gnosticism (which is not to say, as some authorities have, that John at one stage was Gnostic). Revelation could well reflect this same troubled atmosphere; the church at Pergamos is accused of the same offenses that were discussed at the Council of Jerusalem: fornication and meat sacrificed to idols. The latter parts of Revelation, if indeed they are John's, would reflect his exile to Patmos. The manner and even the date of John's death are unknown.

SIGNIFICANCE

From the time of his calling (or even before), John's name was constantly associated with that of Peter—sometimes when together they were called aside by Jesus for moments that were confidential and intimate. His personality came to be defined in terms of Peter: Though he and his brother James were "sons of thunder," they almost always deferred to Peter as their spokesman. The relationship continued after the Crucifixion and through the history of the early Church. Eventually, there had to be a parting: Peter went to Rome and John to Ephesus, where he became the leader of the churches in the area. Here too he developed his theology, which differed in emphasis from that of the Synoptic Gospels (Matthew, Mark, and Luke), which at least in part were based on the preaching of Peter. Specifically, John favored a higher Christology that affirmed not only that Christ was the Son of God and the Messiah but also that he was the creator who had coexisted with God for all eternity. Apparently, some of his followers went beyond this to deny "the coming of Jesus Christ in the flesh" (2 John), like the later Gnostics. After John's death, these individuals presumably became Gnostics indeed, while John's church, which had pursued its own way apart from the "great church" of Peter and Paul, was absorbed into the greater church, taking with it the Gospel of John, which thus became canonical.

The whole issue may be summed up in the last chapters of the Gospel of John, which were apparently added in the last edition. Here John once more recalls his intimacy with Peter; there is an account of a final fishing expedition, and he records how the risen Christ charged Peter to "feed My sheep" and foretold Peter's death. Finally, as he asserted the divinity and coeternity of Christ at the opening of the Gospel, so here John asserts Christ's humanity in the striking image of his preparing a picnic breakfast for his disciples on the shore.

—*John C. Sherwood*

FURTHER READING

Alter, Robert, and Frank Kermode, eds. *The Literary Guide to the Bible*. Cambridge, Mass.: Harvard University Press, 1987. Contains an essay on John by Frank Kermode and another on Revelation by Bernard McGinn. Both are very fine essays, though by no means simple; they do not convey simply the author's own impressions but also contain historical surveys of past criticism.

Brown, Raymond E. *The Community of the Beloved Disciple*. New York: Paulist Press, 1979. Though it carries an imprimatur, this volume contains all sorts of improbable hypotheses concerning John and the church at Ephesus. It does offer a useful summary of the scholarship.

Culpepper, R. Alan. *John, the Son of Zebedee: The Life of a Legend*. Minneapolis: Fortress Press, 2000. This study examines many sources on John, from the New Testament through medieval sources and more recent scholars of early Christianity.

Dodd, Charles H. *Historical Tradition in the Fourth Gospel*. Cambridge, England: Cambridge University Press, 1963. Dodd argues that though the "quest for the historical Jesus" came to nothing and led many to despair of the historical approach, modern critical methods can lead to conclusions that have a high degree of probability.

Jacobus, Melancthon W., Elbert C. Lane, and Andrew C. Zenos, eds. *Funk and Wagnalls New Standard Bible Dictionary*. 3d rev. ed. Philadelphia: Blakiston, 1936. Offers a rather conservative view of the controversy surrounding John. John's authorship of the Gospel is elaborately defended, although his authorship of Revelation is questioned. There is a good summary of what is known of John's life.

Pollard, T. E. *Johannine Christology and the Early Church*. London, England: Cambridge University Press, 1970. Analyzes early theological controversies that grew out of the Gospel of John. Includes index and bibliography.

SEE ALSO: Jesus; Mary; Saint Peter.

RELATED ARTICLES in *Great Events from History: The Ancient World*: c. 6 B.C.E., Birth of Jesus Christ; c. 30 C.E., Condemnation and Crucifixion of Jesus Christ; c. 30 C.E., Preaching of the Pentecostal Gospel.

SAINT JOHN THE BAPTIST
Judaean prophet

According to the biblical narrative, John was the cousin of Jesus and played a central role in introducing Jesus' ministry to the people of Palestine.

BORN: c. 7 B.C.E.; near Jerusalem, Judaea (now in Israel)
DIED: c. 27 C.E.; Jerusalem, Judaea
AREA OF ACHIEVEMENT: Religion

EARLY LIFE

The main historical record for the life of John the Baptist is the Bible, specifically the New Testament, revered by Christians worldwide as an authoritative complement to the Old Testament. Each of the Gospels records significant portions of the life and ministry of John, and three of them actually begin with his birth rather than that of Jesus, who is the central figure of the New Testament. Historical tradition suggests that John was born in a village four miles west of Jerusalem around 7 B.C.E. to elderly parents, Zacharias, a Jewish priest, and Elizabeth, a relative of Mary, the mother of Jesus. The Gospel of Luke provides the most extensive treatment of the early life of John and indicates that he was probably born about six months before his cousin. Like those of other famous Old and New Testament patriarchs and heroes, John's birth, Luke relates, was foretold by an angel (in this case Gabriel, who also appeared to Mary and prophesied the coming of Jesus). Gabriel, in fact, suggested the name John, and friends and relatives were shocked at the time of John's circumcision and dedication to learn that he would not be named for his father, Zacharias (Luke 1:63).

Luke's account goes on to suggest that John's education continued along the path one might expect: John, like his father, prepared for the priesthood. Sometime in his late adolescence, however, John traveled on a pilgrimage to the deserts for study, meditation, and further consecration (Luke 1:66, 80). During this extended period, John took on the appearance and habits of other prophets of Israel, especially Elijah —to whom he was compared by Jesus (Matt. 11:12-14). John is said to have eaten wild locusts and honey and to have worn coarse garments of camel hair and a leather girdle—clear associations with Elijah (Matt. 3:4; Mark 1:6; 2 Kings 1:8). After this episode of ascetic discipline and study of the Scriptures, John emerged to begin his public ministry in "all the country about the Jordan River" (Luke 3:3), a ministry that began prior to that of Jesus by at least several months.

The message John presented to the people was in many ways unique to his ministry, but it was also linked thematically to that of the prophets of old. That message can be summarized as "prepare ye the way of the Lord." John believed unequivocally that he had been called to announce some cataclysmic work of God in the first century, to which he would be both witness and martyr. The message was twofold in purpose: It was a call both to radical repentance and to immersion in water for the forgiveness of sins. In his preaching, John used straightforward language, referring to some in his audience as "vipers" or "hypocrites" and imploring them to repent or change their ways and act justly toward their neighbors and manifest their love for God in obedience to the law. The insistence on full water-immersion gave John his unique label, "the Baptist," and indicated the necessary radical break with past lackluster adherence to the law of Moses. The repentant believer was to emerge from the water in some sense a new person, ready to behave and believe differently.

LIFE'S WORK

John's ministry attracted many followers, many more at one point than that of Jesus (Luke 7:29). In instructing his disciples, John taught them to pray and to fast (Luke 5:33, 11:1; Mark 2:18), but his work was not essentially preoccupied with personal devotion. Within and without his circle of disciples, his message was interpreted as an attack on organized religion—or the parody it had become. "The axe," he declared, "is laid at the root of the trees" (Matt. 3:10; Luke 3:9). His message focused on the necessity for a new beginning and on the emptiness of the Jews' continuing to claim some special merit as descendants of Abraham. The Coming One, or Messiah, John prophesied, would execute judgment on all but the loyal remnant of believers ready to embrace him. Late in an actually quite brief ministry, John suggested to his followers—many of whom would become Jesus' own most trusted associates—that John himself "must decrease, while [the Messiah he proclaimed] must increase." That is, as the time came closer for the Messiah to emerge, John's ministry would diminish in importance and finally come to an end.

John's ministry climaxed when Jesus came to be baptized by John "to fulfill all righteousness." John at first balked at baptizing "for the forgiveness of sins" the one who himself was regarded as sinless; earlier, John, on glimpsing Jesus across a street, had told an assembled crowd, "Behold the Lamb of God who takes away the sins of the world." Jesus insisted on this act of identification with humankind, and it was at this crucial event that the stunned crowd heard a voice from Heaven declare, "This is my beloved son in whom I am well pleased." This event signaled the beginning of Jesus' ministry and launched him on his itinerant preaching tours.

After this episode, John's ministry was abruptly interrupted and then ended by the antipathy he engendered in King Herod Antipas of Palestine. Herod had several motives for his displeasure with John. First, John's preaching drew large, enthusiastic crowds, a matter sure to perturb the Roman authorities at whose pleasure Herod served as a puppet ruler. More to the point, however, was John's radical insistence on the public morality of Israel's leaders; indeed, he had outspokenly denounced Herod for his adultery. When John refused to back down, Herod had him imprisoned, both to silence him and, in a sense, to protect him. Despite being humiliated by John, Herod was entertained by his gruff, quaint manner, much as Pontius Pilate was impressed with the sincerity and commitment of Jesus.

During his imprisonment, John sent some of his disciples to Jesus to confirm that he indeed was the coming Messiah; perhaps John wished to assure himself that his mission had been successful. Finally, during a particularly uproarious party, Herod was manipulated by his stepdaughter Salome into granting her any wish as payment for a lascivious dance she had performed (Matt. 14:6-12; Mark 6:21-28). Prompted by her mother, she requested that John be beheaded and that his head be brought to her on a platter. Herod reluctantly acceded.

At his death, John elicited the highest praise from Jesus as the greatest of all men who lived under the Old Covenant: "The law and the prophets were until John; since that time the kingdom of God is preached" (Luke 16:16). Throughout his later ministry, Jesus continued to pay tribute to the faith and example of John. While John's baptism provided a gateway into the messianic community, the Apostles later interpreted baptism as a sacrament, a reenactment of the death, burial, and resurrection of Jesus that united the believer with the saving work of Jesus on the Cross.

SIGNIFICANCE

The ancient Jewish historian Flavius Josephus adds historical perspective to John the Baptist's life outside the biblical account. Writing in the first century C.E., Josephus stated that John "was a good man who bade the Jews

practice virtue, be just to one another, and pious toward God, and come together by means of baptism." This latter comment regarding John's teaching on baptism indicates the force and strength of John's ministry to first century Jews and to Christians. Its appearance in a secular account suggests the impact John's ministry had on Jewish culture as a whole. His call to baptism—which

Saint John the Baptist. (Library of Congress)

gave to him the name "the Baptist" or the "one who baptizes"—represented a call to radical commitment, to withdraw from a complacent, "everyday" faith to a bolder, holier response to the God of Abraham, Isaac, and Jacob. Clearly, however, John was more dramatically an influence on the development of Christian thought and the ministry of Jesus. Jesus' appearance at John's baptisms stamped John himself as a true prophet of God in the eyes of first century Christians. Later, when arguing on his own behalf, Jesus invoked the baptism of John to corroborate his own authority to command baptism and healing.

Important as it was, John's baptism is presented in the New Testament account as something that would eventually be succeeded by a peculiarly "Christian" baptism that brought believers into the kingdom of God rather than merely "preparing" them for it. The power of John's message and ministry was so strong, however, that even into the second and third decades of Christian faith, approximately 45-55 C.E., pockets of believers adhering to "John's baptism" and needing further instruction in the baptism practiced by the Apostles after the death and resurrection of Jesus could be found. For example, the New Testament Book of Acts tells how a married couple, Priscilla and Aquila, drew aside the respected teacher Apollos and instructed him in proper Christian baptism. Later, the Apostle Paul encountered a group of believers who had never heard of Christian baptism—only John's—and he instructed them further.

Modern scholarship has attempted to locate the origins of John's teaching in his presumed association with the Qumran community. The teachings of this radical Jewish religious group became known to biblical scholarship with the discovery of the Dead Sea Scrolls in 1945. The Qumran community stressed strict adherence to a legal code to achieve a higher degree of righteousness before God and, curiously, a water baptism, something that traditional Judaism had required of all Gentile converts. Whatever influence John's exposure to such teaching may have had, it is clear that he intended to link his own message with the prophecy of a coming redeemer, a ministry of preparation that would turn the hearts of the faithless and the faithful to a religious belief

that transcended mere formalism and embraced an ongoing commitment to justice, righteousness, and peace. His mission, in his own words, was "to make ready a people prepared for the coming of the Lord."

—*Bruce L. Edwards*

FURTHER READING

Alexander, David, and Pat Alexander, eds. *Eerdmans' Handbook to the Bible*. Rev. ed. Grand Rapids, Mich.: Wm. B. Eerdmans, 1987. A helpful overview of the basic message of the New Testament, the life of Christ, and the relationship of John the Baptist to Jesus, his cousin. A succinct and very practical guide to the ministries of both John the Baptist and Jesus of Nazareth and their impact on first century culture.

Guthrie, Donald. *New Testament Introduction*. 4th ed. Downers Grove, Ill.: Inter-Varsity Press, 1990. A standard, scholarly overview of the entire New Testament that includes a thorough discussion of the life of John the Baptist and his ministry.

Hendriksen, William. *New Testament Commentary*. Grand Rapids, Mich.: Baker Book House, 1997. An important scholarly discussion of the Gospel of Matthew, which contains the longest narratives about the birth and destiny of John.

Malherbe, Abraham. *The World of the New Testament*. Austin, Tex.: R. B. Sweet, 1968. A brief but valuable overview of the entire New Testament period with special attention to the historical and theological events that served as the backdrop to the life and ministry of John the Baptist.

Thompson, J. A. *Handbook to Life in Bible Times*. Downers Grove, Ill.: Inter-Varsity Press, 1986. A standard work on the archaeology of the first century world; it continues to be one of the most comprehensive and informed overviews of the historical data gleaned from the ancient world.

SEE ALSO: Jesus; Mary; Saint Paul.

RELATED ARTICLES in *Great Events from History: The Ancient World*: c. 135 B.C.E., Rise of the Pharisees; c. 6 B.C.E., Birth of Jesus Christ; c. 30 C.E., Condemnation and Crucifixion of Jesus Christ; c. 30 C.E., Preaching of the Pentecostal Gospel.

FLAVIUS JOSEPHUS
Palestinian historian

Josephus's history of the Jewish revolt against Rome in 66 C.E., the fall of Jerusalem in 70, and the capture of Masada in 73 remains, despite patent exaggerations and questionable reporting, the primary source of information for this segment of world history.

BORN: c. 37 C.E.; Jerusalem, Palestine (now in Israel)
DIED: c. 100 C.E.; probably Rome (now in Italy)
ALSO KNOWN AS: Joseph ben Matthias (Jewish name)
AREAS OF ACHIEVEMENT: Historiography, scholarship

EARLY LIFE

Flavius Josephus (joh-SEE-fuhs) was born in Jerusalem into an influential priestly family. His Jewish name, Joseph ben Matthias, indicates that he was the son of Matthias, whom he asserts to have been of noble Hasmonaean (that is, Maccabean) lineage. He claims that he was consulted at the age of fourteen by high priests and leading citizens on the fine points of law and that, at the age of sixteen, he conducted inquiries into the relative merits of the Pharisees, Sadducees, and Essenes. Becoming a disciple of a Pharisee named Banus, he entered on an ascetic existence, living with Banus in the desert for three years and then returning, as a Pharisee, to Jerusalem at the age of nineteen.

Seven years later, by his account, he went to Rome as an emissary to plead for the release of some Jewish priests who were being held on what Josephus considered to be trivial charges. The sea voyage to Rome ended in shipwreck in the Adriatic Sea, with Josephus being one of eighty survivors out of the six hundred on board.

He reached Puteoli (modern Pozzuoli) and was befriended by a Jewish actor named Aliturius who enjoyed Nero's favor. Aliturius secured for Josephus an audience with Poppaea Sabina, Nero's wife, and with her assistance Josephus gained the release of the priests. He returned to Palestine a year or two later.

His homeland at this time (66 C.E.) was in a state of incipient rebellion against Roman occupation. Josephus was opposed to insurrection and sided with the moderate faction against the extremists. The insurgent nationalists, however, prevailed. The Roman garrison at Masada was captured, and the Roman contingent was expelled from Jerusalem. The Roman Twelfth Legion, sent to put down the revolt and restore order, was decisively defeated by Jewish patriots. By the end of 66, the war between the Jews and the Romans was a military reality. Josephus was pressed into service as the commander of the region of Galilee.

Although his talents were for the priesthood and research, Josephus, like many learned men in classical antiquity, proved to be capable in military affairs. He conceived defenses and trained fighting forces but refrained from taking the initiative in attack. In the spring of 67 C.E. the Romans moved into Galilee. Josephus's main fighting unit was routed, and he retreated to Jotapata, the most strongly fortified town in Galilee. Three Roman legions under Vespasian laid siege to Jotapata, captured it on the first of July in 67 C.E., and took Josephus prisoner.

LIFE'S WORK

The relationship of Josephus with Vespasian and the Roman Imperial entourage marks the major stage in his life. Vespasian's prisoner of war became his adviser and, in time, favored client. It is this sustained association with the dominant enemy of the Jews that clouds the attitudes toward Josephus taken by his compatriots and their descendants. In his early opposition to the Jewish revolt he had been suspected of complicity with the Romans, and in view of the perquisites accorded him by the Roman leaders after Jotapata, no apologist can effectively defend him against the charge of fraternization with the enemy.

He appears to have ingratiated himself with Vespasian by accurately predicting Vespasian's installation as emperor. He assumed the name of Vespasian's family, Flavius, when he Romanized his own. His account, published between 75 and 79 C.E., of the Jewish revolt against Rome carries the Greek title *Peri tou Ioudaikou polemou*, which in Latin is *Bellum Judaicum* (75-79 C.E.; *History of the Jewish War*, 1773). The significance of the title is that it denotes the Roman, not the Jewish, perspective, just as Julius Caesar's *Comentarii de bello Gallico* (45 B.C.E.; *The Gallic Wars*, 1609, translated in *Commentaries*) denotes the Roman, not the Gallic, perspective. Josephus had clearly cast his lot with the victorious Romans.

A telling incident prior to the fall of Jotapata makes it difficult for anyone to admire Josephus as a patriotic Jew. The besieged had agreed on a mass suicide pact as a means of avoiding capture by the Romans. Josephus relates his attempt to dissuade them, his failure to do so, and his alternate and subsequently accepted plan to draw lots whereby number two would kill number one, number three would kill number two, and so on until, presumably, the last person left would be the only one actually to commit suicide. Josephus concludes this story with a nod to divine providence or pure chance: He and one other

Flavius Josephus. (Library of Congress)

were the last two alive and, making a pact of their own, remained alive.

By contrast, Josephus's account of the mass suicide in the year 73 C.E. of the 960 Jews at Masada, the last citadel of resistance to the Romans, who had conclusively ended the revolt three years earlier, includes reference to no survivors, save two women and five children who had hidden in subterranean aqueducts. Comparison of the respective survivors of Jotapata and Masada lends no honor to the historian of both defeats.

After the Jewish revolt of 66-70 C.E., Josephus was granted living quarters and a regular income in Rome. Thus ensconced, he produced his history of the revolt. His claim that he wrote the work initially in Aramaic and then translated it into Greek need not be disputed, although no Aramaic text whatsoever remains in either small part or citation. The Hellenistic Greek in which this work and the other works of Josephus appear is faultlessly in character with the lingua franca of the time. The idiomatic perfection of Josephus's Greek may owe, in large part, to his employment of Greek-speaking assistants, but his own linguistic abilities were patently considerable.

History of the Jewish War was published between 75 and 79 C.E., the year in which Vespasian died and was

succeeded as emperor by his son Titus. It covers not merely the years 66 to 73 C.E. but also much of the history of the Jews, from the desecration of the Temple at Jerusalem by Antiochus IV Epiphanes in 167 B.C.E. through the events culminating in the capture of Jerusalem by Titus in 70 C.E. The work is composed of seven books, the first two of which outline the Hasmonaean, or Maccabean, revolt, the reign of Herod the Great, and the Roman occupation of Palestine up to the military governorship of Galilee by Josephus.

The five books dedicated to the details of the revolt are both exciting and graphic. Josephus mars his credibility with hyperbole and distortion of fact—for example, he describes Mount Tabor, which has an altitude of 1,300 feet (400 meters), as being 20,000 feet (6,100 meters) high, and his crowd counts are almost invariably exaggerated, one such noting thirty thousand Jews crushed to death in a panic rush—but, if his particulars are questionable and his narrative self-serving, his general survey of times and events has not lost its value.

Although it may tend to disqualify him as a scientific historian, his creative imagination undeniably enhances the grand movement of his history. In one respect, *History of the Jewish War* resembles the history by the more scientific Thucydides. Both works are informed by a major theme: In Thucydides' *Historia tou Peloponnesiacou polemou* (431-404 B.C.E.; *History of the Peloponnesian War*, 1550) that theme is Athenian hubris; in *History of the Jewish War* it is Jewish self-destructiveness. Josephus sees the factionalism of the Jews and their impractical unwillingness to yield to the overwhelming power of Rome as suicidal tendencies that make the Jews their own worst enemies. He underscores this theme with many images of suicidal conflict and with depictions of individual and mass suicides.

Josephus's pride in his heritage is evident in his work and transcends both his contempt for his Jewish rivals and enemies (especially Josephus of Gischala) and his deference to his Roman benefactors. His second work is a massive history of Judaism and the Jews titled *Antiquitates Judaicae* (93 C.E.; *The Antiquities of the Jews*, 1773). This work, in twenty hooks, or about three times the length of *History of the Jewish War*, begins with the Creation as recounted in Genesis and ends with the Palestinian war clouds of 66 C.E. The first eleven and one-half books cover Jewish history up to the tyranny of Antiochus IV Epiphanes. The latter eight and one-half books cover the same material as the first book and a half of *History of the Jewish War* but in greater detail and with many additions. The work is addressed to Epaphroditus, an otherwise unknown figure who seems to have succeeded the emperor Titus, dead in 81 C.E., as one of Josephus's patrons.

At the conclusion of *The Antiquities of the Jews*, Josephus claims, characteristically, that his work is accurate and that no other person, Jew or non-Jew, could have enlightened the Greeks on two millennia of Jewish history and practices as well as he. In quality, however, and in importance and readability, *The Antiquities of the Jews* is discernibly inferior to its predecessor.

It must be noted, however, that *The Antiquities of the Jews* offers passages that are of notable importance to Christians. For example:

> Jesus comes along at about this time, a wise man, if indeed one must call him a man: for he was a performer of unaccountable works, a teacher of such people as took delight in truth, and one who attracted to himself many Jews and many Greeks as well. This man was the Christ. And when Pilate sentenced him to crucifixion, after he had been indicted by our leading citizens, those who had been devoted to him from the start remained firm in their devotion, for he appeared to them alive again three days afterward, as it had been prophesied about him, along with countless other wonders, by holy men. And to our own time the host of those named, after him, Christians has not dwindled.

There is a passage on the aftermath of the execution of John the Baptist and another on the stoning of Jesus' brother James. Jesus is not mentioned in the Greek version of *History of the Jewish War*. There is, however, an Old Slavonic (that is, Russian) version with an independent late medieval manuscript tradition that contains references to the lives of John the Baptist and Jesus, one of them being a variation of the passage quoted above.

Josephus completed *The Antiquities of the Jews* in 93 C.E., at the age of fifty-six. His plans, announced at the end of the work, to produce an epitome of *History of the Jewish War*, a continuation of the same work, and a tetrad of books on the Jewish religion and laws appear not to have been realized. His brief autobiography is attached to the end of *The Antiquities of the Jews* and contradicts some of the statements made in *History of the Jewish War*, in the interest, it seems, of mitigating his early military opposition to the Romans and perhaps as a means of offsetting his rivals for the favor of the emperor Domitian.

The treatise that marks the end of Josephus's literary career is one that could warrant no complaint from his fellow Jews. It is called *Contra Apionem* (*Against Apion*, 1821). The work is an effective and stirring defense of the Jewish people and their religion and laws against scurrilous anti-Jewish writings of the past (by Manetho and Cheremon, for example) and by Josephus's older contemporary, Apion of Alexandria.

Having been favored by the emperors Vespasian and Titus and having enjoyed the patronage of Emperor Domitian and his wife, Josephus seems to have survived Domitian, who died in 96 C.E., by no more than a few years. Nothing is known of his reception by the emperors Nerva (ruled 96-98 C.E.) and Trajan (98-117 C.E.). It is significant that the last remaining works of Josephus are defenses—the autobiography a defense of his part in the Jewish revolt and *Against Apion* a defense of his Jewish heritage. It is not known whether these *apologiae*, also addressed to Epaphroditus, qualified him for a return to Judaea or, for that matter, for continued subsistence in Rome. His status with either Jews or Romans during his last years of life, as well as the actual place of his death, can only be conjectured.

SIGNIFICANCE

The latter part of Josephus's autobiography includes a digressive apostrophe to Justus of Tiberias, who had also written an *Antiquities*, which covered Jewish history from Moses through the first century of this era and which related the insurrection and revolt of 66 to 70 in such a way as to challenge Josephus and attempt to discredit him. Justus, for example, accused Josephus of actively fomenting the revolt against the Romans. This charge, made during the reign of Domitian, would have eroded Josephus's credibility at court were it to have gone without answer and may have done so in any case. The work of Justus stood in rivalry to that of Josephus at least until the ninth century, after which its readership, along with all traces of its actual text, disappeared. Josephus prevailed; the fact that he did attests his value, not as a benign and likable person or as an objective and fully credible historian but as a writer of great erudition and talent, whose narrative scope and magnitude and whose personal association with many of the figures and events in his narrative make him perennially readable and provide a veritable drama in complement to scientific history.

Of special value to general readers and to students of first century history are the detailed appraisals by Josephus of the zealotry, factions, and religious turmoil in Palestine, the political thrusts of the Roman aristocracy, and the complex relations between Rome and the Judaean principate.

—Roy Arthur Swanson

FURTHER READING

Bentwich, Norman. *Josephus*. 1914. Reprint. Folcroft, Pa.: Folcroft Library Editions, 1976. A consideration of Josephus from the Jewish point of view. The writer is harsh on Josephus, not only as a general whom he calls traitorous but also as a scholar, claiming that Josephus was not so learned and erudite as he claims to have been and is credited as having been. According to Bentwich, Josephus misuses words such as "Gamala," an error that may have been understandable for a Roman but not for someone Jewish.

Cohen, Shaye J. D. *Josephus in Galilee and Rome: His Vita and Development as a Historian*. Boston: Brill, 2002. This work is a scholarly study of Josephus and his sources, the literary relationship of the autobiography to *The Jewish War*, the aims and methods of the autobiography, and the historicity of Josephus's activities in Galilee and Rome.

Feldman, Louis H. *Josephus and Modern Scholarship, 1937-1980*. New York: Garland, 1986. A massive achievement in its comparative summaries of Josephan scholarship and in bibliographical research. This work is chiefly of interest, and is indispensable, to the Josephan scholar.

Josephus, Flavius. *The Jewish War*. Translated by G. A. Williamson. New York: Dorset Press, 1985. This, in its estimable revision by E. Mary Smallwood, is the definitive English translation. Its introduction, notes, maps, and appendices are edifying to both the student and the general reader.

Smallwood, E. Mary. *The Jews Under Roman Rule: From Pompey to Diocletian*. Leiden, Netherlands: Brill, 1981. The first twelve chapters of this study, particularly chapters 11 and 12, provide an informative reprise of the world in which Josephus was elevated to greatness and offer an appreciable survey of his place in history.

Tcherikover, Victor A. *Hellenistic Civilization and the Jews*. Translated by S. Applebaum. Peabody, Mass.: Hendrickson, 1999. Comprehensive exposition of the confluence of the Judaic and Hellenistic traditions; essential to an understanding of the cultural crucible in which the political identity of Josephus was formed.

Whiston, William. *The Life and Works of Flavius Josephus*. Reprint. New York: Holt, Rinehart and Winston, 1977. This translation of the complete works of Josephus, for all its faults and verbosity, remains an important part of the Josephan tradition in the English-speaking world. Both G. A. Williamson and M. I. Finley mention its being kept alongside the family Bible in Victorian homes.

SEE ALSO: Johanan ben Zakkai; Nero; Poppaea Sabina; Vespasian.

RELATED ARTICLES in *Great Events from History: The Ancient World*: 168 B.C.E., Revolt of the Maccabees; c. 30 C.E., Condemnation and Crucifixion of Jesus Christ; September 8, 70 C.E., Roman Destruction of the Temple of Jerusalem.

JULIA DOMNA
Roman empress

Julia Domna helped two emperors rule the Roman Empire. As patron, she promoted learning and helped preserve classical culture.

BORN: c. 167 C.E.; Emesa, Syria
DIED: 217 C.E.; Antioch, Asia Minor (now in Turkey)
ALSO KNOWN AS: Augusta
AREAS OF ACHIEVEMENT: Government and politics, art and art patronage

EARLY LIFE

Julia Domna (JEWL-yuh DAHM-nuh) was born in Emesa, a city that had been a petty princedom before being absorbed into the Roman province of Syria. Her father, Julius Bassianus, was a high priest of the cult of Elagabal, a dominant religion in the area. Although Bassianus was classified as a plebeian, he came from a royal line, and he had impressive family connections. Four years before Julia's birth, one of his relatives, formerly a Roman senator and consul, had been crowned king of Armenia. Clearly, Julia Domna and her younger sister, Julia Maesa, expected to marry men of high rank.

Julia Domna had a privileged childhood. Because Emesa was a wealthy city, surrounded by productive farmland and on an important trade route, she was certainly exposed to the best that civilization had to offer. The people of Emesa were bilingual, speaking both Greek and Aramaic. As a member of the ruling class, Julia Domna may well have known Latin, too.

It is likely that during Julia Domna's youth, her future husband, Septimius Severus, who was a native of Roman Africa, visited the great temple at Emesa. On that occasion, he would have become acquainted with the high priest, but it is not known whether he met Bassianus's young daughters.

Shortly after Septimius was appointed governor of Gaul, his wife died, leaving him without heirs. Septimius, who was already over forty, needed to remarry as soon as possible. He began his quest by looking into the horoscopes of prospective brides. In Syria, he heard, there was a woman whose horoscope predicted that she would marry a king. She was Julia Domna. Because he was still at Lugdunum in Gaul, Septimius first approached her father through friends, then sent him a letter proposing marriage. The proposal was accepted, and in the summer of 187 Septimius and Julia Domna were married. Septimius found his bride to be not only beautiful but also gifted with good judgment and a high degree of intelligence.

LIFE'S WORK

A son was born on April 4, 188, at Lugdunum. His first name is not known, but he was given the *cognomen*, or family name, of his grandfather Bassianus; at seven, he would be renamed Marcus Aurelius Antoninus. Early in 189, Julia Domna had a second son. He was given the name of Septimius's father and brother, Publius Septimius Geta. When Septimius rose to the rank of proconsul, the family relocated in Sicily.

Septimius's next appointment, as governor of a province just north of Italy, put three legions at his disposal. Rome was in turmoil. Two emperors had been assassinated within less than three months, and none of those proposed as their successors seemed equipped to take over. Septimius waited long enough to make sure that Julia and his sons were safe, then gathered his forces and marched on Rome. After taking the city without bloodshed, he seized power and moved into the palace. Within a month, he had organized matters well enough so that he felt he could leave on the first of many military campaigns against either rivals or rebels.

Julia Domna, who now had the title augusta, or empress, accompanied her husband as an adviser, as she would often do during his reign. Septimius recognized her contributions to his success by giving her the title *mater castrorum*, or "Mother of the Camp," at a ceremony on April 14, 195. Another important member of his entourage was his wife's brother-in-law, the husband of Julia Maesa, who was very close to her sister.

Julia Domna. (Hulton|Archive by Getty Images)

However, Fulvius Plautianus, a relative of Septimius, was also along on that first expedition. Already he had begun intriguing to replace Julia Domna as Septimius's primary counselor. On campaigns or in Rome, Plautianus seldom left the emperor's side. In public, he treated Julia Domna with contempt. In private, he spread rumors about her conduct and reported her supposed infidelities to the emperor. Evidently Septimius discounted or ignored what Plautianus said about Julia Domna. The emperor continued to take her with him on his expeditions, such as a trip to Egypt; at other times, he displayed his trust in her by leaving her in Rome to administer the Empire on his behalf. He had assessed Julia Domna correctly: She was both intelligent and capable. Moreover, both she and her sister had a political shrewdness and a steely resolve that enabled them to survive at times when one misstep could be disastrous.

FAMILY OF JULIA DOMNA (SEVERAN DYNASTY)		
Family Member	*Vital Dates*	*Reign Dates*
Julia Domna	c. 167-217	193-217
Julia Maesa, *sister*	died 226	218-226
Septimius Severus, *husband*	146-211	193-211
Marcus Aurelius Antoninus (Caracalla), *son*	188-217	211-217
Publius Septimius Geta, *son*	189-212	211-212
Elagabalus, *great-nephew*	c. 204-222	218-222
Severus Alexander, *great-nephew*	208-235	222-235

As the emperor's favorite, Plautianus was now recognized as one of the most powerful men in Rome. He murdered his enemies at will. He tortured noble women in order to gather evidence against Julia Domna, whom he considered his primary enemy. He even arranged to have her son Antoninus, the emperor's heir, marry his daughter, though the boy loathed his bride as much as he detested her father.

About 200 C.E., when Plautianus was at the height of his power, Julia Domna found a refuge from his malice by studying philosophy and rhetoric. Most of what is known about her informal "circle" of scholars comes from the works of the sophist Philostratus. It was at her request, he notes, that he wrote a biography of the legendary miracle worker Apollonius of Tyana; probably she intended to have pagans worship him instead of Christ. At the gatherings of her circle, which included sophists, philosophers, and geometricians, Julia Domna evidently participated as an equal in discussions on such subjects as the relative merits of philosophy and rhetoric. She also commissioned works to be written on subjects that interested her. Moreover, as a patron, she was able to arrange rewards for her scholarly friends, such as a chair of rhetoric in Athens that one sophist obtained during the reign of her son Antoninus, who is often referred to by his nickname, Caracalla. Julia Domna's interest in intellectual matters and her involvement on behalf of her learned friends continued until her death.

Meanwhile, Julia Domna's archenemy had finally been exposed and eliminated. In 205, Caracalla, who in 198 had been named "augustus," or coemperor, arranged for evidence to be presented to Septimius that Plautianus was plotting to kill both emperors. When Plautianus arrived to defend himself, Antoninus started to kill him but, when his father protested, had a retainer finish him off instead. Julia, who was in the next room, did not know what was going on. However, it is reported that when she was taking some hairs from Plautianus's

beard to prove that he was indeed dead, she was clearly delighted.

Antoninus and Geta had now progressed from being rivals in outrageous acts to bitter personal enmity. Hoping that military action might take their minds off their hatred of each other, in 208 Septimius embarked for Britain, taking with him his sons and their mother. Because of crippling gout or arthritis, Septimius did most of his traveling by litter. In the winter of 210, he became much worse. He died at Eboracum (now York) on February 4, 211.

Although their father had told his sons that he wished them to rule together, for years Antoninus had been planning his brother's death and perhaps even that of his father. Before they left Britain, Julia Domna tried to reconcile the brothers. On their return to Rome, however, they remained apart, while their followers were rallying supporters. In February, 212, after Antoninus convinced his mother that he was ready for a reconciliation, Julia Domna summoned Geta to her apartment in the Imperial palace. Antoninus had Geta stabbed to death in his mother's arms. He then issued an order forbidding anyone to grieve for Geta. Subsequently, he had thousands of Geta's followers killed.

Although he was popular with his soldiers, Antoninus, or Caracalla, has gone down in history as one of the most bloodthirsty tyrants ever to rule Rome. However, even if he was mentally ill, as some believe, he was shrewd enough to rely on the advice of Julia Domna. In fact, her name appeared along with his in letters to the senate. Like his father, Caracalla left Julia Domna to administer the Empire when he was absent from Rome. However, she was in Antioch in April, 217, when her son, then fighting the Parthians, was assassinated by an army officer. Caracalla's successor, Macrinus, had undoubtedly planned the murder.

Julia Domna may already have been ill with breast cancer. In any case, she is believed to have been so devastated by the report of her son's assassination that she decided on suicide. It is said that she starved herself to death. However, Julia Maesa, who had been at her sister's side throughout all those years in Rome, was not yet ready to give up. Withdrawing to Emesa, she plotted the downfall of Macrinus and even participated in the battle near Antioch in which he was defeated. After the execution of Macrinus, Julia Maesa arranged for her older grandson to become emperor. When he was killed three years later, she had him replaced immediately by her younger grandson. Both sisters were deified after death.

SIGNIFICANCE

For more than two decades, Julia Domna was one of the most influential women in Rome. Two emperors, one her husband, the other her son, relied on her for advice. During their lengthy absences, she administered a vast empire. She remained resolute even when she was attacked by her enemies, even when she saw her sons turning on their father and on each other. Julia Domna is also admired for her love of learning, which led her not only to expand her own knowledge but also to inspire and to aid the scholars she gathered around her. As their patron, she is credited with having done much to preserve her culture.

—*Rosemary M. Canfield Reisman*

FURTHER READING

Birley, Anthony R. *Septimius Severus: The African Emperor*. Rev. ed. New Haven, Conn.: Yale University Press, 1989. In this definitive biography of Septimius Severus, his relationship with Julia Domna is explored at length, and the significance of her role as a patron is discussed. Also contains information about her family background. Includes maps, photographs, genealogical chart, bibliographies, and index.

_____, trans. *Lives of the Later Caesars: The First Part of the Augustan History, with Newly Compiled Lives of Nerva and Trajan*. Harmondsworth, England: Penguin, 1976. A work of unknown authorship, almost certainly written in the fourth century C.E. and considered an important source of factual material. Footnotes by the translator point out the occasional fictions. Includes charts, maps, and index.

Hemelrijk, Emily A. *Matrona Docta: Educated Women in the Roman Élite from Cornelia to Julia Domna*. London: Routledge, 1999. Julia Domna and the various theories as to her circle are discussed at length in a chapter on "patronesses of literature and learning." Illustrations, voluminous notes, extensive bibliography, and index.

Oliver, J. H. "Julia Domna as Athena Polias." In *Athenian Studies, Presented to William Scott Ferguson*. New York: Arno Press, 1973. After she intervened with her husband on their behalf, Athenians identified Julia Domna as an incarnation of their goddess Athena and honored her accordingly. An interesting example of her historical importance.

SEE ALSO: Agrippina the Younger; Antonia Minor; Arria the Elder; Arria the Younger; Julia Mamaea; Julia Soaemias; Julia III; Lucretia; Valeria Messallina; Poppaea Sabina.

RELATED ARTICLES in *Great Events from History: The Ancient World*: c. 2600 B.C.E., Leizu Discovers Silk Making; c. 2300 B.C.E., Enheduanna Becomes First Named Author; c. 10th century B.C.E., Queen of Sheba Legends Arise; 509 B.C.E., Rape of Lucretia; 60 C.E., Boudicca Leads Revolt Against Roman Rule.

JULIA MAMAEA
Roman empress, regent of the Roman Empire

Julia Mamaea effectively ruled the Roman Empire throughout the reign of her son, Severus Alexander, cementing the power of the Severan Dynasty while achieving needed reforms.

BORN: Second century C.E.; Emesa, Syria
DIED: March 10, 235 C.E.; Moguntiacum (now Mainz, Germany)
ALSO KNOWN AS: Julia Avita Mamaea
AREA OF ACHIEVEMENT: Government and politics

EARLY LIFE

Born the younger daughter of Julia Maesa, Julia Avita Mamaea (JEWL-yuh ah-VEE-tuh MAH-mee-uh) married Gessius Marcianus. Julia Mamaea's entire family on the maternal side was connected to the worship of the Syrian solar deity, Elagabal, for whom her grandfather was high priest at Emesa. Indeed, her nephew the emperor Elagabalus (named for the god) brought the cult to Rome formally. Though many of his efforts were undone after his death, the import of the cult, like Elagabalus's magnificent buildings, was one of the key factors in Julia Mamaea's early life.

For some time Julia Mamaea was overshadowed by her ambitious and gifted mother, the augusta (or empress) Julia Maesa, and her older sister, Julia Soaemias. As a niece of the empress Julia Domna, wife of Emperor Septimius Severus, she was prominent as a member of the Severan Dynasty. While her mother and sister conspired successfully to place her nephew Elagabalus on the throne, she carefully saw to the education of her son, Alexianus. Her constant care in this regard lasted the rest of her life; even as emperor, he enjoyed the best instruction as well as a maternal vigilance over his personal customs and pastimes. In fact, her life and career may be seen as largely devoted to his success as a good emperor, even if she herself virtually ruled.

Julia Mamaea's prudence and dignity were said to contrast with the lax reputation of her elder sister, who, in the plot to raise Elagabalus to the throne, put forth the notion that he was an illegitimate child of the murdered Emperor Caracalla. Julia Mamaea was prepared, for her own son (originally named Marcus Julius Gessius Alexianus Bassianus) and the dynasty's sake, to play along with the story that he, too, was a son of Caracalla.

LIFE'S WORK

After the assassination of her sister Julia Soaemias (who had been raised to the rank of augusta) and that of her nephew Emperor Elagabalus in 222 C.E., Julia Mamaea's son, known to history as Emperor Severus Alexander, was chosen ruler. He had already been formally adopted by his cousin as "caesar," or heir-designate. Now, following the precedents of her mother, Julia Maesa, and sister Julia Soaemias, Julia Mamaea became augusta on the accession of her son. This rank, one primarily honorific, had come to denote something much more under the Severan Dynasty: a powerfully effective regency for the throne. Thus, Julia Mamaea enjoyed the important benefit of succeeding her older sister, while yet sharing the honor with Julia Maesa, who had survived the downfall of Julia Soaemias and Elagabalus.

Unlike Julia Soaemias, Julia Mamaea appears to have been a faithful wife to her husband. Also unlike Julia Soaemias, she protected her son from a lascivious lifestyle. These differences, no doubt, exacerbated the friction between Julia Mamaea and her sister, but details are lacking. One way in which Julia Mamaea followed her sister's lead was in the free exercise of power behind her

son's throne. Again unlike Julia Soaemias, she remained a model for the young ruler throughout his reign. In addition, the mother's earlier care for the son's education continued in a broader way. Ulpian, the great contributor to the field of law, was made Alexander's personal guardian, in addition to his promotion by the new augusta to the post of Praetorian Prefect. For his part, Ulpian advanced the theory that an augusta could receive prerogatives from the emperor.

To assist her son in governing the Empire, Julia Mamaea created a Council of Sixteen from among the senators. Though this body lacked decisive constitutional dimensions (its deliberations were not binding), she had created an efficient mechanism for her son on one hand, and on the other she had made an impressive showing of restoring the senate's ancient prestige. Unfortunately, part of the equilibrium the augusta created was upset for a time because of the machinations of Epagathus, a wealthy freedman with a personal grudge against Ulpian. He succeeded in bribing some of the Praetorians to kill Ulpian—as it turned out, in the presence of both Julia Mamaea and Alexander. However, after ostensibly raising Epagathus to the governorship of Egypt, the augusta avenged Ulpian's death when the culprit was executed onboard a ship bound for Crete.

Knowing that Dio Cassius, the historian and politician, was unpopular for his severity with the soldiers, Julia Mamaea was able to help raise him to the consulship but avoid trouble by having him reside at Rhegium for most of his term. Further courting good relations with the senatorial nobility, she arranged her son's marriage to Barbia Orbilia. When this caused unwanted friction after Alexander promoted his father-in-law to the rank of caesar, Julia Mamaea first drove the younger augusta from the palace. Afterward, when her father, Orbilius, took refuge with the Praetorians, Alexander himself soon arrived at their camp accompanied by troops, and both father and daughter were arrested. Julia Mamaea soon had the caesar executed and the girl exiled.

WOMEN OF THE SEVERAN DYNASTY		
Name, Relationship	*Severan Emperors*	*Years of Influence* (C.E.)
Julia Domna, *wife and mother*	Septimius Severus and Caracalla	193-217
Julia Maesa, *grandmother*	Elagabalus and Severus Alexander	218-226
Julia Soaemias, *mother*	Elagabalus	218-222
Julia Mamaea, *mother*	Severus Alexander	222-235

Julia Mamaea's frugal manner came to be expected likewise of the emperor; for example, he was said to have paid the costs of his various birds through selling their eggs and young fowl. However, her reputation came to be that of parsimony and greed. On at least one occasion she managed to confiscate a considerable inheritance. Practically speaking, such moves may well represent her shrewd efforts to disarm potential mutinies by depriving would-be conspirators of financial means.

The augusta's reforms were effective. Apparently following an older precedent from the reign of Pertinax in the late second century, she saw to it that small landholders survived the pressures of the wealthy landlords who had the benefit of slave labor. Loans were available at very low interest rates in select circumstances. On one occasion she solved a meat shortage by an Imperial decree that prevented the slaughter of female animals. The keepers of the livestock soon restored the supply. In another move, one designed to win the favor of the nobility, she saw to it that customary spectacles were financed by the state. It had been the traditional burden of new office holders to pay for these. Further, the costs of establishing new governors in office was likewise assumed by the state: Transport and baggage animals, servants, clothing, silver services, and concubines were all now provided.

When the aggression of Ardashīr I, architect of the renewed Persian Empire, brought Alexander to war in the East, Julia Mamaea accompanied him. They first attempted energetically to negotiate with the Persians, but after enduring effrontery from a heavily armed Persian embassy, they entered the war in earnest. Unfortunately, the main column of the Roman force, hindered by camp disease and the heat, was slow, and Ardashīr achieved successes over other troops before the Imperial plan could be carried out. In spite of this significant setback, the Roman frontiers were, after all, soon restored, and mother and son returned to Rome. Following amphitheater games and the distribution of gifts, it was clear that the popularity of the reign was not diminished. Alexander established youth organizations named in Julia Mamaea's honor, called the Mamaeani.

Unfortunately, the confusion that accompanied the troop movements in the East had brought crisis to the German frontier, so in response to the governors of that region, the emperor and his mother again left Rome for a military campaign abroad. Alexander was successful in crossing the Rhine River and impressing the Germans with a show of force and then in negotiating peace with a large payment. Ironically, these very successes were the immediate causes for the downfall of the dynasty. Now soldiers of the German frontier, motivated by jealousy of some of the eastern troops, as well as the idea that Julia Mamaea was generous with the enemy but not the Roman forces, brought about a mutiny. A personal grudge is also cited. The general Maximin had previously suggested the marriage of his son to Alexander's sister Theoclia, and Julia Mamaea instead had arranged the girl's marriage to a senator. Maximin led the rebellion, and on March 10, 235, his troops entered Alexander's headquarters at Moguntiacum and killed both Julia Mamaea and her son.

SIGNIFICANCE

After the downfall of her sister and nephew, Julia Mamaea, with her son, stepped forward to fill the place vacated by a coup, as natural heirs in a dynastic succession. However, her individual accomplishments were meritorious and deserving of respect apart from her role as one of "the four Julias." If she lacked her mother's political charisma, she worked diligently for the welfare of the state, even when it brought her difficulties and the occasional, severe setback, for example, the downfall of Ulpian. Her eventual demise, like that of her son, may be fairly attributed to the complexities of the military emergencies that arose swiftly, rather than any failure of capable and energetic leadership.

Julia Mamaea's importance, on a grand scale, is simple. She ruled the Roman Empire, in effect, throughout the nominal reign of her young son. However, on closer scrutiny, she ruled vigorously and decisively. Her reforms were grounded in prior experience and practical necessity. She succeeded in gathering individuals of outstanding qualification for her son's regime, men like Ulpian, the great jurist. Ironically, even Maximin, the general who eventually unseated her, had capably risen in the ranks during her administration, and the outcome may have been quite different had the Persian War gone according to plan. At the time of her death in 235, the Roman Empire was efficiently administered, thanks to her vigilance. Its treasury was not depleted, thanks to her frugality. In fact, the reign of her son and her own regency were models of governance for the Empire—and not only in hindsight provided by the subsequent period of anarchy.

In other arenas, too, she provided examples not often emulated. For example, in her pursuit of ecumenical religious knowledge, represented by her conference with the Christian Origen (at Antioch during the Persian War), her actions were suggestive of a tolerance that subsequent rulers were far from capable of advancing. Such tolerance, fostered already by the other Julias, was a portion of her dynasty's legacy that did not long survive.

—*Malcolm Drew Donalson*

FURTHER READING

Brauer, George C., Jr. *The Decadent Emperors: Power and Depravity in Third-Century Rome*. New York: Barnes and Noble, 1995. Brauer chronicles in vivid detail the reigns of the series of young emperors who ruled from 193 to 244 C.E. The four Julias, including Mamaea, receive much attention here as powers behind the throne.

Dio Cassius. *Roman History*. Translated by Earnest Cary. 9 vols. Cambridge, Mass.: Harvard University Press, 1961. Though this history survives intact only for earlier times, the Byzantine epitomist Xiphilinus fortunately preserved the material in his condensed form. This is valuable in that Dio Cassius was an eyewitness to many of the events.

Herodian. *Historiae*. Translated by C. R. Whittaker. 2 vols. Cambridge, Mass.: Harvard University Press, 1969. In this history covering the period from the death of Marcus Aurelius to the year 238—all within the author's lifetime—the facts may be less than trustworthy, yet Herodian's own sources may have been better than is often suggested.

Turton, Godfrey. *The Syrian Princesses: The Women Who Ruled Rome, A.D. 193-235*. London: Cassell, 1974. Turton here focuses, unlike Brauer, on the women of the Severan Dynasty who determined much of the destiny of the Empire. Julia Mamaea receives the principal attention in the final two chapters. A bibliographical appendix includes useful discussion of primary sources and some relevant modern works.

SEE ALSO: Agrippina the Younger; Antonia Minor; Arria the Elder; Arria the Younger; Julia Domna; Julia Soaemias; Julia III; Lucretia; Valeria Messallina; Poppaea Sabina.

RELATED ARTICLES in *Great Events from History: The Ancient World*: c. 2600 B.C.E., Leizu Discovers Silk Making; c. 2300 B.C.E., Enheduanna Becomes First Named Author; c. 10th century B.C.E., Queen of Sheba Legends Arise; 509 B.C.E., Rape of Lucretia; 60 C.E., Boudicca Leads Revolt Against Roman Rule.

JULIA SOAEMIAS
Roman empress

Julia Soaemias exercised political influence within the Roman Imperial family of the Severans through manipulation of familial, religious, and governmental resources at a time when women were officially excluded from political power.

BORN: c. 180 C.E.; Apamea, Syria
DIED: 222 C.E.; Rome (now in Italy)
ALSO KNOWN AS: Julia Soaemias Bassiana (sometimes spelled "Soaemis")
AREA OF ACHIEVEMENT: Government and politics

EARLY LIFE

Knowledge of the life of Julia Soaemias (JEWL-yuh soh-I-mih-uhs) derives principally from three literary sources. First is the Roman history of Dio Cassius, which was written in Greek in the third century C.E. Dio was a political insider whose work was a comprehensive Roman history that is only partially preserved. Fortunately, many details of the Severan Dynasty under which Dio had pursued his own political career are preserved. The second main literary source is the Roman history from the time of Marcus Aurelius written (also in Greek) by Dio's slightly younger contemporary, Herodian of Syria. Finally, the *Historia Augusta* (c. 325 C.E.; *The Scriptores Historiae Augustae*, 1921-1932) is a Latin work of unknown authorship that dates from the late third or early fourth century C.E. and that relies on numerous other sources that are now lost. Although generally considered the least reliable of the three literary sources for information about the Severan Dynasty, the *Historia Augusta* can, nevertheless, supply some verifiable, or at least potentially correct, information. In addition, a wealth of information has emerged from the careful study of inscriptions and coins. Still, one must note that there is often substantial disagreement among these sources regarding the details of events. Nevertheless, the general outline of the role played by Soaemias under the Severans can be sketched with some certainty.

Julia Soaemias was born into an influential Syrian family whose members were the wives and mothers of the "Severan" Roman emperors, who (with the exception of Macrinus, 217 C.E.-218 C.E.) held the chief position in the Roman government from the accession of Septimius Severus (193 C.E.) until the death of Severus Alexander (235 C.E.).

A brief account of the genealogy of Julia Soaemias must precede any discussion of her character and activities because she grew up amid an extraordinary group of women and could not help but be influenced by the pervasive character of her family. Julia Soaemias's aunt was Julia Domna, the second wife of the emperor Septimius Severus. Her grandfather, Julius Bassianus, served as high priest of the cult of Baal in the city of Emesa (now Homs) on the Orontes River in the Roman province of Syria Phoenice. Although Emesa had·become a part of Roman Syria under Domitian (r. 81 C.E. -96 C.E.), the cult of Elagabal, along with its famous temple, was independently administered by priest-kings who passed down control of the cult within their family. Because the cult attracted many worshipers and lavish gifts, Soaemias's family had available political and monetary resources from this association. Further, the women in Soaemias's family were well-educated and ambitious; they wielded broad influence throughout the years that the Severan emperors ruled. As the wife of the emperor, Julia Domna advised Septimius Severus, especially in matters of religion, and developed a reputation as an intellectual among the Roman aristocracy.

Along with her sister, Soaemias's mother, Julia Maesa, cultivated close ties with the Imperial court and was mindful of the future of her two daughters, Soaemias (the elder) and Mamaea. Soaemias was born in Apamea in 180 to Maesa and Julius Avitus, a man of consular rank. In 193 Maesa moved to the Imperial court at Rome with her sister. Soaemias married Varius Marcellus, an influential proconsular official of equestrian rank who served in various positions under Septimius Severus and Caracalla.

Although she spent most of her young life in Syria, Soaemias traveled to Rome at least once and probably participated in the Secular Games there among the wives of influential equestrians. In 204, at the age of twenty-four, she gave birth to a son whom she named Avitus. His full name was Varius Avitus Bassianus, but he is best known as Elagabalus, after the god whom he served as a priest. When Septimius Severus was succeeded in 211 by his son (with Julia Domna) Caracalla, Julia Domna, who had shared many official duties with her husband during his life, began to exercise greater power within the government. Soaemias's mother, Maesa, was also making contacts within the Imperial household and acquiring greater personal wealth. The influence of her mother

and aunt must have had considerable effect on the shaping of Soaemias's character because the Severan women worked closely together to guarantee their family's prestige in the Imperial government and were, no doubt, in constant communication.

It is not known if Soaemias actually lived at Rome with her mother during the reigns of Severus and Caracalla, as some have conjectured, but she may have visited frequently. There is evidence of her being at Rome near 204, the year that her son, Elagabalus, was born. It is reasonable to suppose, however, that she spent much of her time at Emesa soon after that; Elagabalus was highly trained in the priestly duties at an early age.

Despite the closeness of the family, however, any plans on which Maesa and Domna may have entered to establish an Imperial dynasty at Rome were interrupted in 217 when a Praetorian Prefect and sometime lawyer named Macrinus conspired with the army to assassinate Caracalla and to become emperor. He saw those plans to fruition. Shortly after hearing of Caracalla's death, Domna died also, perhaps by her own hand; the sources are unclear. Following the coup, Macrinus ordered Maesa to return to Syria. However, he allowed her to do so in full possession of her property, which she had much augmented during her years in the capital. When Soaemias's mother returned to Emesa, she was equipped with wealth, contacts, and knowledge about the machinations of Imperial government. These tools would not go to waste; Maesa now turned her attention to her daughters, Soaemias and Mamaea, and to her Imperial aspirations for the family.

LIFE'S WORK

At the time Maesa returned to Emesa from Rome, her husband, Julius Avitus, had died of old age. Soaemias's husband was also dead (in 217 C.E., or shortly before that), and her son, Elagabalus, was thirteen years old. Both Soaemias and Elagabalus had caught the attention of soldiers from a Roman legion, the Legio III Gallica, which was stationed not far from Emesa. Elagabalus had been consecrated as a priest to the sun god El-Gabal, or Elagabal, as his hereditary obligation. Mamaea's son, Alexianus (six years younger than Avitus) was also so dedicated. Elagabalus, however, was most zealous in the performance of his duties, dancing and performing rites for the god. A handsome young man known for his especially fervent performances at cult observances, Elagabalus was much admired by the soldiers from the legion who made frequent trips to the temple at Emesa. Further, Soaemias had entered into a relationship with a man of local influence whose name was Gannys, with whom she may have even lived as though he were her husband.

Maesa and Soaemias could not mistake the opportunity that these circumstances afforded them. Pointing to the uncanny resemblance of Elagabalus to Caracalla, they spread the story that the handsome youth was, in fact, the son of the late emperor. Whether or not this story is true, it is, at very least plausible; Soaemias had likely been in Rome at the Secular Games near the date of Avitus's birth (c. 204 C.E.). Soaemias's relationship with the influential Gannys gave the family hope that the soldiers, who had become increasingly disillusioned with the treatment that they were receiving under Macrinus, could be swayed to proclaim Elagabalus emperor.

On the evening of May 15, 218 C.E., Soaemias, Elagabalus, Mamaea, Alexianus, and Maesa came secretly onto the military base of Legio III Gallica. Dio reports that only Avitus was brought into the camp, but both the *Historia Augusta* and Herodian agree that the entire family came immediately into the company, and under the protection of, the army. The legion proclaimed Elagabalus the new emperor under the title Marcus Aurelius Antoninus Pius Felix Augustus. On receipt of this news, the Roman senate understood that the threat was not one posed by a single usurper but rather one orchestrated by Soaemias, Mamaea, and Maesa. As a result, the senate declared war not only against Avitus but also against Soaemias, Mamaea, Maesa and the youthful Alexianus.

The Legio III Gallica was joined by Legio II Parthica after its defection, and the combined forces, under the command of Gannys, began to move northward toward Antioch to oppose the Praetorian forces under Macrinus that were hastening to crush the rebellion. They met on June 8, 218, outside Antioch. Numerous defections to Avitus's side had preceded this engagement, and Macrinus's reinforcements had not yet arrived. Thus, the numbers on each side were similar, and the battle was closely contested. Gannys had only limited military experience, and his troops began to flee as they met the experienced praetorian forces under Macrinus. At this juncture, Soaemias and Maesa leapt from their carriages and managed to give heart again to the soldiers in flight. These soldiers then returned to the battle and defeated Macrinus's troops.

It remained only for Soaemias and Maesa to reach Rome with Elagabalus and to install him on the throne. Maesa, knowing the political elite, orchestrated the assassination of numerous members of the government who were then replaced by chosen men of the equestrian order who would remain loyal. A series of dispatches were sent to Rome outlining the legitimacy of Elagabalus's claim and informing the senate that he would be hailed, when he arrived at Rome, not under his Imperial title but under his priestly name: *Deus Sol Elagabalus*. From this time on, Soaemias's son would be known to history only as Elagabalus. Gannys, whom Elagabalus had at first chosen as caesar (heir to Imperial power), was slain within the year, apparently in order to focus all loyalty and authority on Elagabalus and his family. On July, 14, 218, the senate officially recognized Elagabalus as the emperor. Elagabalus, his mother, and family were delayed at Nicomedia over the course of the winter, arriving in Rome about a year later.

At Rome, Soaemias held considerable prestige as a result of her position as mother of the emperor. Further, inscriptional evidence indicates that she was even invited into the meetings of the senate. Soaemias, although politically capable, was less than successful in preserving the alliances within her own family that could have reinforced the power wielded by the dynasty. Elagabalus fell out of favor, perhaps because of personal excesses (no doubt exaggerated by hostile historical sources) or administrative incompetence. At very least, it does seem true that the real interests of Elagabalus were not directed toward dynastic succession but rather focused on instituting the sun god Elagabalus as the supreme deity of the Roman world.

As a result, the stability of his rule was threatened, and Maesa, the family matriarch, determined that Mamaea's son Alexianus was a potentially more capable ruler than Elagabalus. Soaemias championed Elagabalus against the interests of Mamaea and Alexianus, and the two factions became rivals. Soaemias was able to convince her son to adopt Alexianus in order to appease the army, which he did in June of 221. Alexianus (Severus Alexander) shared power with Elagabalus in 222, but the adoption had been one that even Elagabalus had mocked, and the rivalry between the two factions of the family continued. Maesa and the Praetorians took the side of Mamaea in the dispute but, at first, tolerated Elagabalus as the emperor. However, when it came to light that Soaemias and Elagabalus had been conspiring to assassinate Alexander, the Praetorians demanded that Elagabalus appear in their camp with the uninjured Alexander. He did so, but this scene repeated itself a short time later and on that occasion, after the Praetorians saw that Alexander was safe, they killed both Elagabalus and Soaemias. The Praetorians and populace viewed Soaemias as being equally guilty with Elagabalus of misgovernment and treachery; both their bodies were desecrated, hers eventually tossed away by the side of the road and his disposed of in the river Tiber. The maltreatment of Soaemias in death was a grisly testimony to the power that she had held in life.

SIGNIFICANCE

The roles played by Soaemias, her mother, and her sister display the extent to which women were able to make decisions that influenced the destiny of an empire that, in many of its functions, denied any official political function to women. As at few other times in the history of the Roman Empire, women were among the most important political actors on the stage during the reign of the Severans.

—Wells S. Hansen

FURTHER READING

Brauer, George C. *The Young Emperors*. New York: Crowell, 1967. A well-written, albeit factually strained, look at the lives of the Severan circle.

Dio Cassius. *Dio's Roman History*. Translated by Earnest Cary. 9 vols. Cambridge, Mass.: Harvard University Press, 1970-1987. Greek text with facing English translation. Includes excellent introduction and summaries of each book.

Grant, Michael. *The Severans: The Changed Roman Empire*. New York: Routledge, 1996. Grant details the lives and times of the Severans with ample historical evidence, a clear discussion of the sources, and numerous plates showing numismatic, inscriptional, and other ancient witness to the period.

The Scriptores Historiae Augustae. Translated by David Magie. Cambridge, Mass.: Harvard University Press, 1979-1982. Latin text with facing English translation. Includes thorough introduction detailing theories regarding the authorship and date of the work.

Whittaker, C. R., trans. *Herodian*. 2 vols. Cambridge, Mass.: Harvard University Press, 1969-1970. Greek text with facing English translation. Includes clear introduction and numerous historical notes.

SEE ALSO: Agrippina the Younger; Antonia Minor; Arria the Elder; Arria the Younger; Julia Domna; Julia Mamaea; Julia III; Lucretia; Valeria Messallina; Poppaea Sabina.

RELATED ARTICLES in *Great Events from History: The Ancient World*: c. 2600 B.C.E., Leizu Discovers Silk Making; c. 2300 B.C.E., Enheduanna Becomes First Named Author; c. 10th century B.C.E., Queen of Sheba Legends Arise; 509 B.C.E., Rape of Lucretia; 60 C.E., Boudicca Leads Revolt Against Roman Rule.

JULIA III
Roman noblewoman

Julia, the daughter of Emperor Augustus, promoted her father's political agenda through marriage alliances and by having sons. Her unconventional behavior contributed to the enmity between the Julian and Claudian branches of the Imperial household and deeply grieved Augustus, indirectly influenced his political decisions, and furthered the rift between the Julians and the Claudians.

BORN: 39 B.C.E.; Rome (now in Italy)

DIED: 14 C.E.; Rhegium (now Reggio di Calabria, Italy)

ALSO KNOWN AS: Julia, daughter of Augustus; Julia the Elder

AREA OF ACHIEVEMENT: Government and politics

EARLY LIFE

Most information about Julia (JEWL-yuh) III, daughter of Augustus, comes from Roman historians writing after her death. Of these, Velleius Paterculus is her nearest contemporary, but the account by Suetonius is the most comprehensive. The fifth century C.E. Christian writer Macrobius, the only biographer who purports to record Julia's own words, is some four centuries removed from her life.

Julia was the only child of Octavian (later Augustus, emperor of Rome) and Scribonia, whom her father wed after a brief, unconsummated marriage to Marc Antony's stepdaughter Claudia. Octavian divorced Scribonia on the day of Julia's birth, claiming that he could not bear her nagging. Soon thereafter, Octavian took the pregnant Livia Drusilla from her husband Tiberius Nero and remained happily married to her until his death in 14 C.E. Julia received a strict, conservative upbringing in her father's household. She was taught weaving and spinning and was expected to conduct herself modestly at all times. Octavian became emperor when Julia was eight years old and assumed the honorary title Augustus in 27 B.C.E. Because he had no male heir, Augustus betrothed his daughter to M. Claudius Marcellus, son of his sister Octavia, in effect designating Marcellus his successor.

LIFE'S WORK

Julia married Marcellus in 25 B.C.E. When she was widowed three years later, Augustus married her to his friend and adviser Marcus Vipsanius Agrippa, twenty-three years Julia's senior and also married to Marcellus's sister. With Agrippa, Julia had five children: Gaius Julius Caesar (II), Lucius Julius Caesar (IV), Julia (IV, or the Younger), Vipsania Agrippina (II, or the Elder), and Agrippa Julius Caesar (Agrippa Postumus). Augustus adopted Gaius and Lucius soon after Lucius's birth in 17; in doing so, he fulfilled the requirements of the *de maritandis ordinibus*, his own law requiring every citizen to produce three children, and at the same time designated Gaius and Lucius, respectively, as his successors. In 13 B.C.E., Augustus symbolized this designation and honored his daughter as a mother by issuing a coin with his own idealized image on the front and a portrait of Julia, flanked by her sons, on the reverse.

Julia was a cultured, intelligent woman whose kind and gentle nature made her extremely popular. The first Latin woman to be apotheosized in the east, she was called "divine" in Paphos, "the new Aphrodite" in Mytilene, and "Aphrodite Genetrix" in Eressus. However, Julia's unconventional ways caused her father anxiety. Macrobius preserves a number of anecdotes that illustrate this father-daughter conflict as well as demonstrate Julia's wit and independence. There and elsewhere, the free-spirited Julia is often compared to the more traditional and conservative Livia. Some scholars even posit a rivalry between the two, prompted by Julia's ambition and resulting in a rift between the Claudian branch of the Imperial family, represented by Livia and preferred by the older generation, and the Julian branch, represented by Julia and favored by the younger, more progressive generation. Sometime during this period, Julia embarked on a number of adulterous affairs with young noblemen in her circle. Augustus was initially suspicious but wanted to believe his daughter chaste. Reassured by her children's resemblance to Agrippa, he decided that Julia was simply lighthearted and liked to say that he had "two somewhat wayward daughters—the Roman Republic and Julia," as quoted by Macrobius. The explanation for Julia's appearance of fidelity is also preserved by Macrobius, who reports that when asked how she man-

aged to produce only legitimate children, Julia replied, "I never take on a passenger unless the ship is full."

Agrippa died in 12 B.C.E., and Augustus settled on Tiberius, Livia's son from her first marriage, as Julia's next husband. At the time, Tiberius was married to Vipsania, whom he loved dearly, but Augustus saw this as an opportunity to unify the Julians and Claudians and compelled a divorce. After their marriage in 11 B.C.E., Tiberius at first acted as a good husband to Julia; they had one child together, but it died in infancy. Soon, Tiberius learned that Julia had resumed relations with one of her lovers. Although he was indignant and cut off marital relations, he did not accuse her publicly, out of respect for Augustus and the scandal it would cause.

When Julia's son Gaius assumed the *toga virilis*—the "toga of manhood"—in 5 B.C.E., he was admitted to the senate, given the title *princeps iuventutis* (prince of youth), designated as a consul in advance for the year 1 B.C.E., and allowed to serve prematurely as commander in the provinces. Soon afterward, Tiberius requested permission to withdraw from politics and retire to the Greek island of Rhodes. The historian Tacitus identifies Tiberius's soured relations with Julia as his primary motive for this move, a possibility echoed by Suetonius. Tiberius later claimed that he desired to avoid the appearance of rivalry with Gaius and Lucius. Regardless of his reasons, the loss of an experienced soldier and capable administrator like Tiberius both angered Augustus and damaged Tiberius's reputation. Thus, the rift between the Julians and the Claudians, which Augustus had tried to mend with his daughter's marriage, was instead enlarged.

In 2 B.C.E., Augustus was confronted with evidence of his daughter's indiscretions and compelled to invoke the *Lex Julia de adulteriis*, which provided harsh penalties for adultery, against his daughter. According to Seneca, Augustus sent a letter to the senate stating that Julia

> had been accessible to scores of paramours, that in nocturnal revels she had roamed about the city, that the very forum and the rostrum, from which her father had proposed a law against adultery, had been chosen by the daughter for her debaucheries, that she had daily resorted to the statue of Marsyas, and, laying aside the role of adulteress, there sold her favours, and sought the right to every indulgence with even an unknown paramour.

Of the men implicated in Julia's affairs, Iulus Antonius was either executed or committed suicide, while the others were exiled. Julia was banished to the island of

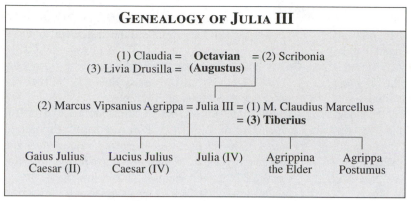

GENEALOGY OF JULIA III

(1) Claudia =   **Octavian**   = (2) Scribonia
(3) Livia Drusilla =   **(Augustus)**

(2) Marcus Vipsanius Agrippa = Julia III = (1) M. Claudius Marcellus
= **(3) Tiberius**

| Gaius Julius Caesar (II) | Lucius Julius Caesar (IV) | Julia (IV) | Agrippina the Elder | Agrippa Postumus |

Note: Emperors appear in boldface. Cardinal numbers represent spousal order.

Pandateria, deprived of every sort of luxury, and forbidden male visitors unless they were first thoroughly scrutinized by Augustus. Julia's mother, Scribonia, voluntarily accompanied her daughter in exile. Augustus, however, having long attempted through the passage of laws and by his own example to promote conservative values, was deeply grieved by his daughter's downfall and refused visitors for some time. After Phoebe, one of Julia's freedwomen also implicated in the scandal, hanged herself in disgrace, Suetonius reports that Augustus proclaimed, "I should have preferred to be Phoebe's father!" When Tiberius learned of Julia's banishment and that Augustus had sent her a divorce decree with his name on it, he was pleased but nonetheless wrote to Augustus urging a reconciliation. The Roman people also lobbied on Julia's behalf, provoking the relentless Augustus to rail at them in assembly, "If you ever bring up this matter again, may the gods curse you with daughters as lecherous as mine, and with wives as adulterous!," according to Suetonius.

Augustus suffered further blows in 2 and 4 C.E. with the deaths of Lucius and Gaius, respectively. With Julia and her sons out of the way, Tiberius requested permission to return to Rome. Although Augustus was initially reluctant, he soon agreed, because the political climate required a man of Tiberius's experience and capabilities. Moreover, as he was now left without an heir, Augustus adopted Tiberius, along with Julia's youngest son, Agrippa Postumus.

Augustus's family problems were not over, however: Agrippa Postumus's behavior soon became offensive, and Augustus disinherited and banished him. Additionally, Julia's daughter Julia the Younger was caught in breach of the same law as her mother and, like her mother, was banished. The poet Ovid was also exiled at this time, and

while the causes are unknown, his assertion in *Tristia* (after 8 C.E.; *Sorrows*, 1859) that "two sins . . . ruined me, my poem and my grave error" has caused speculation that he was complicit in this scandal. Augustus was terribly grieved by his family's disgraces. He often wished aloud to have remained childless and frequently referred to the two Julias and Agrippa Postumus as "my three boils" or "my three running sores," according to Suetonius.

Julia had been transferred to Rhegium on the Italian mainland in 4 C.E. and her conditions improved slightly. When Augustus died, however, he omitted both Julias from his will and instructed that they be excluded from the family mausoleum. Tiberius, now emperor, cut off the stipend Augustus had allowed Julia and ordered the execution of both Agrippa Postumus and Sempronius Gracchus, an exile since his implication in Julia's scandal fourteen years earlier. Tiberius also made Julia's conditions harsher, so that she died of malnutrition in 14 C.E. Tacitus suggests that Tiberius intended this outcome, presuming that "she had been banished for so long that her death would pass unnoticed."

SIGNIFICANCE

As a young woman, Julia functioned as a pawn, serving her father's political agenda. In choosing her three husbands, Augustus was motivated by the need to designate a successor or to enhance the power and prestige of the Imperial family. Augustus also manipulated his daughter's public image to promote traditional values and reinforce her sons' positions, as is indicated by the numismatic portrait of Julia and her sons. Another coin portrays Julia in the manner of the goddess Diana, an attempt to exalt the Imperial family and reinforce Augustus's power. That the public embraced the idealized image of Julia that Augustus promoted is demonstrated in Propertius's fourth book of poetry (ca. 15 B.C.E.), where a deceased Roman matron laments, "My bones are defended by Caesar's grief./ He mourns the death of a fit sister for his own daughter."

After her downfall, Julia's image suffered a sharp reversal: ancient historians vilified her; Seneca called her "shameless beyond the indictment of shamelessness," and Velleius Paterculus characterized her downfall as "shameful to narrate and dreadful to recall." Modern scholars, too, have often cast Julia as a licentious wanton who stands in contrast to Livia, the ideal Imperial matron. Only recently have scholars acknowledged that the ancient sources are biased by the knowledge of her terrible end and by Augustan propaganda and, following Ronald Syme in 1939, begun to view Julia as either a victim of male political agendas or as a strong, independent woman promoting her own interests within the constraints of the patriarchal system.

—*Kirsten Day*

FURTHER READING

Dio Cassius. *Dio's Roman History*. Translated by E. Cary. Cambridge, Mass.: Harvard University Press, 1968-1980. Greek text accompanied by parallel English translation. Includes bibliographical references and indexes.

Fantham, Elaine, Helene Peet Foley, Natalie Boymel Kampen, Sarah B. Pomeroy, and H. A. Shapiro. *Women in the Classical World: Image and Text*. New York: Oxford University Press, 1994. Fantham et al. pay surprisingly little attention to Julia. The space they do devote to her demonstrates sympathy for Julia's position and admiration for her independence.

Ferrero, Guglielmo. *The Women of the Caesars*. Translated by Christian Gauss. New York: Century, 1912. Ferrero oversimplifies by casting Julia as a foil for the virtuous Livia, and his work additionally suffers from conservative bias, moral squeamishness, and inadequate references. Nonetheless, his account is more comprehensive than most and readily accessible to the nonspecialist.

Kleiner, Diana E. E., and Susan B. Matheson, eds. *I, Claudia: Women in Ancient Rome*. New Haven, Conn.: Yale University Art Gallery, 1996. Kleiner and Matheson provide a general overview of Julia's adult life and briefly examine the political agenda promoted on Augustan coinage.

Macrobius. Excerpt from *Saturnalia*. In *Women's Life in Greece and Rome: A Source Book in Translation*, edited by Mary R. Lefkowitz and Maureen B. Fant. 2d ed. Baltimore: The Johns Hopkins University Press, 1992. The writings in this collection from ancient Greece and Rome, all by men, focus on women's lives. Includes bibliography and index.

Pomeroy, Sarah B., ed. *Women's History and Ancient History*. Chapel Hill: University of North Carolina Press, 1991. Discusses Augustus and Julia's relationship and the emperor's motivations in choosing husbands for his daughter. Includes index and bibliography.

Propertius, Sextus. *The Poems*. Translated by Guy Lee. New York: Oxford University Press, 1996. Includes notes, introduction, bibliography.

Richlin, Amy. "Julia's Jokes, Gallia Placidia, and the Roman Use of Women as Political Icons." In *Stereotypes of Women in Power: Historical Perspectives and Revisionist Views*, edited by Barbara Garlick, Suzanne Dixon, and Pauline Allen. New York: Greenwood Press, 1992. Richlin examines first and fifth century political motivations behind the preservation of Julia's witticisms.

Seneca, Lucius Annaeus. "De Beneficiis." In *Moral and Political Essays*, by Seneca. Edited and translated by John M. Cooper and J. F. Procopée. New York: Cambridge University Press, 1995. This volume of selections from Seneca includes bibliography and index.

Suetonius. *Lives of the Twelve Caesars*. Translated by Robert Graves. New York: Welcome Rain, 2001. Includes an introduction by Michael Grant as well as illustrations, maps, indexes, and bibliography.

Syme, Ronald. *The Roman Revolution*. Reprint. New York: Oxford University Press, 2002. Syme says that Julia was a pawn, serving her father's political purposes. Includes bibliography and index.

Tacitus, Cornelius. *The Annals of Imperial Rome*. Translated with an introduction by Michael Grant. Rev. ed. New York: Penguin Books, 1996. Translator Grant provides an introduction to this work, which also contains illustrations, maps, genealogical tables, indexes, and bibliography.

Velleius Paterculus. *Compendium of Roman History*. Translated by Frederick W. Shipley. Cambridge, Mass.: Harvard University Press, 1998. Text in Latin and English. Includes a biographical addendum about the author and bibliography.

SEE ALSO: Marcus Vipsanius Agrippa; Augustus; Livia Drusilla; Gaius Maecenas; Ovid; Tiberius.

RELATED ARTICLES in *Great Events from History: The Ancient World*: 43-42 B.C.E., Second Triumvirate Enacts Proscriptions; 27-23 B.C.E., Completion of the Augustan Settlement; November 27, 8 B.C.E., Roman Lyric Poet Horace Dies; 9 C.E., Battle of Teutoburg Forest; c. 50 C.E., Creation of the Roman Imperial Bureaucracy.

JUVENAL
Roman poet

Juvenal expanded the dimensions of poetic satire in savage works that lashed out at humankind's vices and corruption.

BORN: c. 60 C.E.; Aquinum (now in Italy)
DIED: c. 130 C.E.; place unknown
ALSO KNOWN AS: Decimus Junius Juvenalis (full name)
AREA OF ACHIEVEMENT: Literature

EARLY LIFE

Juvenal (JEW-vuhn-uhl) was born around 60 C.E. in the small town of Aquinum (now in Italy). It is thought that his family was wealthy and that Juvenal entered the army to make a career in service to the emperor. Unsuccessful in his endeavors to achieve a position of responsibility, however, he turned to literature to establish or simply to express himself. He was a friend of the well-known poet Martial during this period and wrote his first satires against the flatterers and hangers-on in the Imperial court. For this scathing attack, Emperor Domitian confiscated Juvenal's property and exiled him to Egypt.

Juvenal returned to Rome after the death of Domitian in 96 and wrote, recited, and published his *Saturae* (100-127 C.E.; *Satires*, 1693) during the years that followed. Most of the satires written at this time do not refer to contemporary events but to the abuses of the earlier reign of Domitian. For several years, Juvenal was very poor, but eventually his financial problems were alleviated by a gift from Emperor Hadrian.

LIFE'S WORK

Juvenal's achievement can be found in the five books of satires he produced during his lifetime. There are sixteen satires in the collected works of Juvenal, and the first book contains the first five. These five satires have as their subject matter the corruption and immorality that Juvenal perceived among Roman aristocrats and leaders of his time. He considered that they were interested in wealth and sexual excess rather than the personal virtue and rectitude befitting leaders of the Roman Empire.

The first satire in book 1 is an introduction to the whole work; it is a justification for the literary mode that Juvenal created. There had been satire before Juvenal, but it did not have the tone, subject matter, or structure that Juvenal employed. Earlier satires, such as those of Horace, tended to laugh tolerantly at humankind's social foibles rather than rage about their vices. The tone set by Juvenal, then, was new:

> Must I be listening always, and not pay them back? How
>   they bore me,
> Authors like Cordus the crude, with the epic he calls the
>   Theseid!

Juvenalian satire is an attack on those who have offended him; its realm is not the heroic but the low and the mean. He directs his hearers to the disgusting Roman scene and declares: "Then it is difficult *not* to write satire." He points to such absurdities as a eunuch marrying and Juvenal's former barber becoming richer than any patrician. Although his satire has the sweep of epic, covering "everything human" from the earliest times, its special province is contemporary life: "When was there ever a time more rich in abundance of vices?"

At the end of the poem, Juvenal brings up the problem of whether he will "dare name names," meaning real names rather than invented ones. If he does, he is likely to end up "a torch in a tunic" in these corrupt times. He determines therefore to use only the names of the dead and reveal the type of vice, if not the specific example.

The second satire is against not only homosexuality but also the hypocrisy of homosexuals who set themselves up as moral censors of society. The poem opens with a typical Juvenalian hyperbolic exclamation of frustration:

> Off to Russia for me, or the Eskimos, hearing these fellows
> Talk—what a nerve!—about morals, pretend that their virtue
> Equals the Curian clan's, while they act like Bacchanal
>   women.

A list of odious examples follows this opening, the most important being that of Gracchus, a descendant of the republican Gracchi who defended the rights of the Plebeians. This Gracchus has given a large sum of money to a musician and married him in a bizarre ceremony. Once more, the target of Juvenal's wrath is members of the aristocratic class, who should be offering models for the rest of society instead of pursuing debauchery. Even the great feats of Roman arms are mocked: "An Armenian prince, softer than all of our fairies" ends up in the arms of a Roman tribune, an act that Juvenal calls "the Intercourse Between Nations."

The third satire, against the city of Rome, is one of Juvenal's greatest works. The speaker in the poem is not Juvenal but his friend Umbricius. Umbricius is leaving Rome because he is "no good at lying" and therefore cannot possibly survive in Rome. One aspect of Roman life that he finds especially offensive is that the old republican Rome has become a "Greekized Rome," filled with subtle Greeks who can adapt to any role and thus are displacing the native aristocracy. Another target is the great value now given to wealth; poverty "makes men objects of mirth, ridiculed, humbled, embarrassed." In addition, Rome is a dangerous place; if its resident does not catch a disease, then he is likely to die in a fire or be killed by a burglar at night. The only sane course is to flee the city and relocate in a country town where civic virtue is still possible and one can live an honorable life.

The fourth satire contains two episodes. In the first, Curly the Cur spends an absurdly large sum of money for a red mullet that he devours by himself. Juvenal remarks that he could have bought the fisherman for less than he paid for the fish. This excess is paralleled by an incident involving Emperor Domitian. Domitian is given a huge turbot because his subjects fear that by purchasing it they would incur the wrath of the "baldheaded tyrant." There is no pot large enough for the fish, however, and a council of state is called to decide what to do. The councillors are all terrified of saying the wrong thing and ending up dead, so they treat the problem as a question of war. One suggests that the emperor will capture a monarch as great as the fish, while a craftier one suggests that a huge pot to cook the fish whole be created and from henceforward, Great Caesar,/ Let potters follow your camp!" The motion is carried, and the councillors nervously depart. Juvenal adds a comment at the end of the poem to sum up the reign of Domitian: "Nobles he could kill. He was soaked in their blood, and no matter./ But when the common herd began to dread him, he perished." Once more, the Roman aristocrats are ineffectual or corrupt, and only the mob can bring down a vicious (and here ridiculous) emperor.

The fifth satire satirizes both the proud and overbearing patron and the submissive client who acquiesces to, and even encourages, this situation. The poem is structured as a description of a typical dinner with a patron. The patron drinks the best wines while the client is given wine that would make blotting paper shudder. The patron dines on a choice mullet, the client on an eel that looks like a blacksnake. The reason for such shameful treatment is the client's poverty; if he were rich, the daintiest

morsels would be placed before him. Juvenal suggests to such clients that if they persist in seeking and accepting such treatment, "some day you'll offer your shaved-off heads to be slapped." If the client acts like a slave, the patron will surely treat him like a slave.

Book 2 of the *Satires* is composed of one long poem attacking Roman women; it is the longest and most ambitious of Juvenal's satires. His charges against women are similar to those he made against Rome's nobility: They have fallen into decadence, they care only about money, and they have forsaken old ways in favor of current fashions and modes. Women are no longer to be trusted, because so many have poisoned their husbands for wealth or convenience. Finally, even if a man were to find the perfect woman, she would not do because her perfection would be unbearable. It is an amusingly unbalanced, excessive, and effective poem.

The third book is made up of three poems. The subjects are again poverty, nobility, and ways of gaining a livelihood in first century Rome. The poor wretches in satire 7 are poets, historians, and teachers, occupations that had once been honored but are now despised. The poem piles negative example on example, but it does offer some hope for a decent life; "Caesar alone" can provide the help the public refuses to give. The eighth satire contrasts nobility of character with nobility of family; Juvenal cites examples of debased scions from famous families and declares: "Virtue alone is proof of nobility." The most telling contrast is between the noble heritage of Catiline (Lucius Sergius Catilina), who attempted to enslave the Roman people, and the relative obscurity of Cicero, who thwarted Catiline's designs and saved the Republic.

The ninth satire has as a speaker, not Juvenal or one of his spokesmen but a homosexual, who is complaining about the difficulties he finds in his work as a prostitute. He is consoled at the end by a cohort who assures him that "there'll always be fairies/ While these seven hills stand." Because this is so, he can be content with a contingent of slaves, a villa of his own, and a sum of money equivalent to a thousand dollars—amenities unavailable to most poets of the time.

The highlight of book 4 of the *Satires* is "The Vanity of Human Wishes," in which Juvenal poses the question of the proper petitions of humans in their prayers to the gods. He inventories the usual requests that people make—for wealth, beauty, or power—only to find that their attainment produces dangerous results. The wealthy man, for example, has to fear the poison in the jeweled cup, while the poor man is free from such fears. The powerful man has to watch out for envy and hatred, while the weak man can be at peace. Even the desire for a long life is not appropriate, because the man to whom such a request has been granted must face burying his wife, children, and all those dear to him while he withers into a lonely old age. What, then, should people pray for? "A healthy mind in a healthy body, a spirit/ Unafraid of death, but reconciled to it." The rest must be left to the gods, for human beings do not know their own best interests.

The last book of satires contains only one important poem, "On an Education in Avarice." It deals not only with the dangers of the desire for great wealth but also with how the example of the parents influences the children. There is a surprising tenderness in Juvenal's tone when he speaks about the vulnerability of children.

> To a child is due the greatest respect: in whatever
> Nastiness you prepare, don't despise the years of your
>   children,
> But let your infant son dissuade you from being a sinner.

People should desire only enough to feed, clothe, and shelter themselves; the rest is not only unnecessary but corrupting.

Juvenal's last book of satires was published in 127. He died shortly after its publication.

SIGNIFICANCE

Juvenal's satires retain their power nearly two thousand years after they were written. Their powerful moral vision and the freshness of their language permit them to transcend the local and specific occasions that they address. Juvenal's solutions or consolations are not unusual; similar Stoic advice can be found in the writings of Horace or Sextus Propertius. No other poet of the period, however, exposed so much so fully. Some have complained that Juvenal went too far in his condemnation of humankind and that his poetic vision is unbalanced. These critics fail, however, to relate Juvenal's vision to the social and political systems of the time and to take into consideration the special social role of the satirist in this period. Juvenal believed epic and lyric poetry to be entirely inappropriate forms for a corrupt age. Instead,

his time demanded exactly the sort of fiercely agitated satires that he produced.

—*James Sullivan*

FURTHER READING

Duff, J. Wight. *A Literary History of Rome in the Silver Age: From Tiberius to Hadrian*. 1927. Reprint. Westport, Conn.: Greenwood Press, 1979. A broad historical survey of the literature of the period, with a specific discussion of satire as a literary form in Juvenal's time.

_____. *Roman Satire: Its Outlook on Social Life*. Berkeley: University of California Press, 1936. Reprint. Hamden, Conn.: Archon Books, 1964. Duff relates Juvenal's poems to the literary and social contexts, but he does not analyze the poems in any detail. A brief but useful introduction to the poet.

Freudenberg, Kirk. *Satires of Rome: Threatening Poses from Lucilius to Juvenal*. New York: Cambridge University Press, 2001. This study of Roman verse satire highlights the mounting pressure in ancient Rome of Imperial oversight.

Highet, Gilbert. *Juvenal the Satirist: A Study*. New York: Oxford University Press, 1961. Includes a cogent discussion of each of Juvenal's satires and of their influence on later literature. The book is very thorough but accessible to the general reader.

Jenkyns, Richard. *Three Classical Poets: Sappho, Catullus, Juvenal*. Cambridge, Mass.: Harvard University Press, 1982. This detailed study of Juvenal's style and poetic effects brings to light the satirist's techniques and methods. It is well written, but it is directed toward an academic audience.

SEE ALSO: Catiline; Cicero; Hadrian; Horace; Martial; Sextus Propertius.

RELATED ARTICLES in *Great Events from History: The Ancient World*: 159 B.C.E., Roman Playwright Terence Dies; 54 B.C.E., Roman Poet Catullus Dies; 51 B.C.E., Cicero Writes *De republica*; 19 B.C.E., Roman Poet Vergil Dies; November 27, 8 B.C.E., Roman Lyric Poet Horace Dies; 8 C.E., Ovid's *Metamorphoses* Is Published; 100-127 C.E., Roman Juvenal Composes *Satires*.

KĀLIDĀSA
Indian poet and dramatist

Recognized as the author of no more than three plays and four poems, which fuse together themes of nature and love within the framework of Hinduism, Kālidāsa is generally regarded as India's greatest poet and dramatist.

BORN: c. 340 C.E.; west-central India
DIED: c. 400 C.E.; west-central India
AREA OF ACHIEVEMENT: Literature

EARLY LIFE

The play *Mālavikāgnimitra* (c. 370 C.E.; English translation, 1875) by Kālidāsa (KAL-ee-DAS-uh) has as its hero Agnimitra, a historical king of the Śunga Dynasty who reigned from 151 to 143 B.C.E. In addition, inscriptions found in the Deccan at Mandasor (dated 473 C.E.) and Aihole (dated 634 C.E.) quote from Kālidāsa's poetry and laud his genius. These firm evidences are all that establish a chronological range for Kālidāsa's life. The rest is conjecture. Though the Śunga was an important successor to the great Maurya Dynasty and led a cultural revival, opinion holds that Hindu culture had not sufficiently developed and the times were too disturbed to accommodate a talent such as that of Kālidāsa. Thus scholars suggest that the Gupta Dynasty (c. 321-c. 550 C.E.), the golden age of India, marked by serenity and sophistication, was more in line with the spirit and style of Kālidāsa. It is quite possible that Kālidāsa flourished during the reign of Chandragupta II (r. c. 380-413), with whom a congenial relation of court poet to patron can be readily conceived. Still, students of Kālidāsa tend to attach two date ranges to his works to acknowledge the uncertainty.

Just as little is known of his dates, little is known of Kālidāsa's life—except by inference from his writings and the legends concerning him. Identified in various stories as an orphan, idiot, laborer, and shepherd, Kālidāsa may have had a difficult early life. His knowledge of religion, philosophy, the sciences, and Sanskrit probably marks him as a Brahman and a devotee of the cult of Śiva. (Indeed, his name means "servant of Kali," one of the consorts of that god.) His aristocratic sensitivity, grasp of court etiquette, and familiarity with Indian geography suggest that he was not only a court poet to Vikramāditya I, his patron at Ujjain, but also a traveler and an ambassador (possibly to Kuntala, a kingdom inland from the Malabar coast). The erotic overtones in his works make it easy to accept the legend of a princess as his lover and spouse. It is not difficult to believe that his life ended, at sixty or eighty years of age, by foul play at the hands of a courtesan in Sri Lanka, as another legend would have it.

The order of his works (rejecting the twenty or so spurious works sometimes attributed to him) is unknown. Hypothetical reconstructions have been made, even to the degree of correlating the writings to his biography, but the writings are too impersonal to do this with any accuracy. Perhaps the two lyrics are early, the two epics somewhat later, while the plays are scattered at different phases of his life—*Abhijñānaśākuntala* (c. 395 C.E.; *Śakuntalā: Or, The Lost Ring*, 1789) being the product of maturity.

LIFE'S WORK

Nearly all Kālidāsa's works were written in Sanskrit, a highly inflected language learned by an aristocratic elite—the word literally means "perfected." Sanskrit was written as poetry (*kavya*), either lyric or epic, according to precise rules of grammar. The poetry, combined with other factors, created the visual immediacy of drama. Kālidāsa, using twenty-six different meters, was the king of similes, drawing from religion and nature in a style distinguished by a grace and economy that made music.

The *Rtusamhāra* (c. 365 C.E.; English translation, 1867) is a pastoral poem mirroring a newly married man's joy of nature during the six Indian seasons (summer, the rains, autumn, early winter, winter, and spring); it is composed of 140 stanzas divided into six cantos. Though popular with the young, it is regarded as a piece of juvenilia, generally neglected by the literary critics. Yet this "lover's calendar," because of its romance, may have been innovative at its first appearance.

The *Meghadūta* (c. 375 C.E.; *The Cloud Messenger*, 1813), much adored by the German Romantic poet Johann Wolfgang von Goethe, is an elegiac monody of 111 to 127 verses, according to various recensions; it is cast in a series of seventeen-syllable quatrains in a single meter. A *yaksa*, a sensual demigod, separated from his wife for a year by a curse, asks a rain cloud to transmit a love message to her. The first part of the poem contains a sweeping and detailed picture of the subcontinent via the hypostatized cloud; the second part focuses on its delivery to the wife in a celestial city of the Himalayas. The lyric plays on the pathos of love with full intensity of mood. The travels of the cloud and its detour over Ujjain lend credence to the idea of Kālidāsa as a traveler and diplomat. The poem is original and subjective; indeed, Kālidāsa pioneered a new genre. The traditional court epic (*Mahākāvya*) Kālidāsa found riddled with stereotype and convention. However, he was able to condense, deepen, and stylize his works into epics of aristocratic appeal, combining elevated themes with emotional verity.

The epic *Kumārasambhava* (c. 380 C.E.; *The Birth of the War-God*, 1879) is incomplete at eight cantos, covering the courtship and marriage of Śiva and Pārvatī only. (The birth of their son Kumāra, and his exploits, are recounted in ten additional cantos that were found not to be Kālidāsa's work.) The material is drawn from the Purāṇas (the epic elaborating and expanding on the great epic *Mahābhārata*). Mount Himalaya's daughter Pārvatī falls in love with the meditative Yogi god Śiva. Menaced by the demon Taraka, the gods determine that only a son by Śiva and Pārvatī can defeat the demon; they send Kāma, the god of love, to bring about the union, but Śiva burns Kāma with his third eye. Pārvatī then abandons sensuality for spiritualism, emaciating herself. Śiva, in disguise, dissuades her from her course, and they come lovingly together. Thematically, self-abnegation leads to the highest form of love. Symbolically, Śiva, who is Truth, combines with Pārvatī, Beauty, to produce Kumāra, Power. The risqué depiction of the lovers' honeymoon led to the charge that canto 8 is sacrilegious.

In the epic *Raghuvamśa* (c. 390 C.E.; *The Dynasty of Raghu*, 1872-1895), Kālidāsa traces a line of kings descended from the sun god over nineteen cantos, dwelling on the varying aspects of the ideal king in terms of *dharma* (moral duty): Dilipa, the ascetic; Raghu, the warrior; Aja, the lover; and Rāma, the *avatāra* (incarnation) of Vishnu. Yet the line ends with Agnivarna, the consumptive voluptuary: Does this reflect the poet's tragic vision of lost ideals, or is the epic merely incomplete? Much of the poem is a brilliant summary of the classical epic *Rāmāyana*. The first nine cantos of that classic deal with Rāma's forebears, cantos 10 through 15 with Rāma, and cantos 16 through 19 with his descendants. One critic wonders whether Kālidāsa preferred Raghu to Rāma, who shuns the pregnant Sītā as unclean after her abduction by Rāvana the demon. When one compares these epics, *The Birth of the War-God* has singleness of legend, theme, structure, and philosophy, while *The Dynasty of Raghu* is a multifaceted pageant and chronicle.

The *Mālavikāgnimitra*, a spirited, musical harem intrigue for a spring festival, involves the love of Agnimitra, a historical figure, for a princess disguised as a maiden, Mālavikā, against the opposition of his two queens, the mature Dhārinī and the accomplished Iravati. In winning her in this parallelogram of relationships, Agnimitra has the aid of a jester, a nun, and good luck, as well as an Aśoka tree that responds to those that touch it by flowering or not. Perhaps the key element of the plot is Dhārinī's final acceptance of Mālavikā into the harem.

Vikramorvaśiya (c. 384 C.E.; *Vikrama and Urvaśī*, 1851), probably intended to be sung at a royal coronation, concerns the love of a semidivine hero, Purūravas, for an immortal nymph, Urvaśī, a tale drawn from Vedic legend. Though their love is opposed by Purūravas's queen and subjected to a divine curse that separates them, the gods bring the couple together in the end. Thus, love (*kāma*), supported by wealth (*artha*), issues in progeny (*dharma*, moral duty). Act 5, in which the grief-maddened king wanders in the woods apostrophizing nature, is a famous scene.

It was the eighteenth century Calcutta judge Sir William Jones, the founder of comparative philology by his "discovery" of Sanskrit, who brought Kālidāsa to the attention of the West by rendering the first English translation of *Abhijñāānaśākuntala* in 1789. The play remains one of the world's masterpieces. Its story of love spanning Earth and Heaven must have appealed to Europeans, as the Romantic movement was then in its infancy. Drawn from the *Mahābhārata*, the play centers on star-crossed lovers: the tender, tortured ruler Dushyanta and the natural, selfless Śakuntalā, daughter of a sage and a nymph. Their match is destroyed by a curse that erases the king's recognition of his spouse when she comes to him at his palace after a separation. Only his ring, lost and swallowed by a fish, can recover his memory of love. When the ring is found, the lovers are reunited via the aerial chariot of the god Indra, and they live happily together with their child Bharata, the first legendary emperor of India. Throughout, the play contrasts the demands of public life and the sorrow of frustrated love to the serenity of simple values and the conception of ideal love.

SIGNIFICANCE

The drama of Kālidāsa can only be understood within its own cultural context. The theater was part of the palace complex, playing to sensitized aristocratic audiences. It combined poetry, music, dance, song, mime, and characterization in a highly stylized presentation shorn of scenery and props, with most actions occurring offstage. The absence of evil—indeed, the fusing of Heaven and Earth into a happy ending—is unique to Indian thought. The transmigration of souls, the demand of moral duty, and the consequences of fate make the cosmos ultimately moral and purposeful and eliminate the role of chance. The plays are dominated by psychological rather than plotting factors, by the power of a basic mood, or emotion (*rasa*), and the characters fill roles assigned by the cosmos rather than marked by individualism. Thus, Kālidāsa was actually a traditionalist, a believer in a finally beneficent world order (politically, he subscribed to benevolent monarchy). With such ideals as *maya* (illusion of reality), *mokśa* (enlightenment), and *santa* (tranquillity) and a view of love encompassing sensual, aesthetic, and spiritual levels in different lives and worlds, Kālidāsa contributed to literature an elucidation of the cosmic pervasiveness of love.

—*Ralph Smiley*

FURTHER READING

Dimock, Edward C., Edwin Gerow, C. M. Naim, A. K. Ramanujan, Gordon Roadarmel, and J. A. B. van Buitenen. *The Literatures of India: An Introduction.* Chicago: University of Chicago Press, 1978. This critical study complements historical and sociological approaches of earlier Orientalists. It was a cooperative venture mostly of University of Chicago faculty for the Asia Society. Covers full sweep of Indian literature. See especially sections on the epic, drama, poetics, and the lyric. Scholarly, invaluable insights.

Horrwitz, E. P. *The Indian Theatre: A Brief Survey of the Sanskrit Drama.* 1912. Reprint. New York: Benjamin Blom, 1967. An old but evocative description of the Indian theater. A court theater of Ujjain and imaginary performances of Kālidāsa's plays are especially well described.

Kālidāsa. *Theater of Memory: The Plays of Kālidāsa.* Translated by Edwin Gerow, David Gitomer, and Barbara Stoler Miller. 1984. Reprint. Columbia, Mo.: South Asian Books, 1999. Contains three brilliant chapters: "Kālidāsa's World and His Plays" (by Miller), "Sanskrit Dramatic Theory and Kālidāsa's Plays" (by Gerow), and "Theater in Kālidāsa's Art" (by Gitomer). The texts of the three plays are freshly translated and accompanied by copious annotations. Most valuable.

Krishnamoorthy, K. *Kālidāsa.* New York: Twayne Publishers, 1972. Literary and scholarly introduction by an Indian scholar, written in the light of both Indian and Western criticism. The author attempts a biographical analysis based on a supposed order of the works. Comprehensive but tends toward the Romantic-Victorian school of literary appreciation and consequently suffers from Kālidāsian hagiography. Includes full references to translations of all of his works.

Shastri, Satya Vrat. *Kālidāsa in Modern Sanskrit Literature.* Columbia, Mo.: South Asian Books, 1992. Explores the influence of Kālidāsa on later writers.

SEE ALSO: Aśvaghosa; Chandragupta Maurya; Vālmīki.
RELATED ARTICLES in *Great Events from History: The Ancient World*: c. 550 B.C.E., Vālmīki Composes the *Rāmāyaṇa*; c. 400 B.C.E.-400 C.E., Composition of the *Mahābhārata*; c. 321 B.C.E., Mauryan Empire Rises in India; c. 380-c. 415 C.E., Gupta Dynasty Reaches Its Peak Under Chandragupta II; c. 400 C.E., Kālidāsa Composes Sanskrit Poetry and Plays.

KANISHKA

Kushān ruler (r. c. 127-c. 152 C.E.) and patron of the arts

Kanishka, the greatest ruler of the Kushān Empire, administered an extensive realm that embraced much of modern India and Pakistan and parts of Central Asia and China. Kanishka's patronage was responsible for the introduction of Mahāyāna Buddhism into China and for a remarkable flowering of Buddhist iconography.

BORN: First or second century C.E.; probably west-central Asia

DIED: c. 152 C.E.; probably northern India

ALSO KNOWN AS: Kaniśka

AREAS OF ACHIEVEMENT: Government and politics, religion, art and art patronage

EARLY LIFE

Considering the fame of Kanishka (kuh-NIHSH-kuh), remarkably little is known of his life, certainly not enough to construct a proper biography. Symbolic of this gap in history is the fact that the 6-foot (1.8-meter) statue of him in the archaeological museum in Mathura, Uttar Pradesh, India, is headless. The scarcity of data is further compounded by the tangled, obscure complexities of the wider history of Inner Asia and northern India during the first centuries C.E. What is known regarding Kanishka and his achievements has been gleaned principally from folklore and archaeological artifacts dating from this period. Inscriptions, coins, sculpture, architecture, legend, and Chinese and Iranian literary sources are the raw materials from which scholars have attempted to reconstruct an understanding of Kanishka's life and times.

Even the time frame of Kanishka's reign has been the subject of much discussion; indeed, two scholarly conferences (in 1913 and 1960) were convened in London to explore the issue. One long-accepted reckoning places it roughly between 78 and 103 C.E., but more recent scholarship (agreeing with an earlier line of thought) places it between 127 and 151 C.E. Kanishka's reign has been associated, probably mistakenly, with the Saka Era dating system, which was initiated in 78 C.E. and which ultimately became the basis of the modern Indian governmental calendar.

The precise origin of the Kushāns is also an open question, as they arose out of a welter of Central Asiatic races and languages in a region of complex migrations. They could have been Turkic or Iranian or, more probably, a mixture of the two. They can be traced to the Yuezhi (Yüeh-chih, or Indo-Scythians) in Chinese Turkistan on the frontier of Han China. Displaced by the Xiongnu (Hsiung-nu, or Huns), the Yuezhi crossed the Jaxartes River (modern Syr Darya) and occupied Sogdiana (Transoxiana) at the expense of the Saka (Iranian nomads) by 150 B.C.E. Then, having crossed the Oxus River (modern Amu Darya) by 130 B.C.E., they conquered the Indo-Greek Bactrian kingdom. The Bactrians' development of a trading economy and their advanced culture had a deep influence on their nomadic conquerors. One of the five tribes among these conquerors, the Kushāns, rose up to assert dominance and establish political unity under Kujūla Kadphises (r. c. 30-80 C.E.). For unknown reasons, the Kushāns eventually gravitated to the east to the Hindu Kush region and ultimately to northwest India, a world of petty states floundering in a political vacuum after the end of the Maurya Empire in 185 B.C.E.

LIFE'S WORK

Details of how, when, and how deeply the Kushāns penetrated northwest India are not entirely clear, nor are the roles of Kujūla, his successors Vima Takhto, Vima Kadphises I, and Kanishka. Until the coming of the Muslims in the twelfth century, however, no foreign power after the prehistoric Indo-Aryans gained control over as much of India—and held it for as long—as did the Kushāns. There is some suggestion that Kanishka was not in the line of the Kadphises. It is thought that Kanishka may have begun a new line of succession. He may have invaded India from the north (Khotan in Xinjiang according to one authority), or he may have been one of several chiefs in India engaged in a struggle for the succession. When Kanishka came to power, he apparently used co-optation, for he shared rule with a junior, Vashishka (either his brother or his son), who ultimately succeeded him; he may have had other corulers as well.

A statue of Kanishka at Mathura shows him in Turkic warrior garb. Images of him on gold coins of the time render him as a bearded man with large, thoughtful eyes and thin, determined lips. He seems to have had a forceful personality, yet in cultural and religious matters he was more tolerant and accommodating than rigid and austere.

The Kushān Empire reached its zenith under Kanishka. An inland realm with its capital at Puruśapura (modern Peshawar, Pakistan) at the foot of the Khyber Pass leading to Kabul and the Hindu Kush region, it centered on the upper Indus and the upper Ganges valleys (in modern Iran and India). It seems in India to have embraced Pataliputra (Patna) to the east, Sānchi to the south, and Bahāwalpur on the Sutlej River, but its key southern city was Mathura on the Yamuna River. To the north, beyond the Pamirs, the Kushāns dominated the caravan city-states of eastern Turkistan, especially Khotan, and held Bactria; to the west, in what is now Afghanistan, they held sway over Begram and Balkh. This location enabled the Kushāns to connect India with China, Persia, and the Roman Empire via the Old Silk Road opened in 106 B.C.E. across Central Asia, combined with the old Mauryan royal highway between Taxila and Pataliputra and then through the Ganges Delta (where a Roman ship is known to have arrived about 100 C.E.). Other roads led to the Arabian Sea ports of Barbaricum and Barygaza (modern Broach). The Kushāns, with their command of animal power and soldiery, held the routes together and exacted great revenues through transit dues. In this way, the Kushāns maintained a network of international trade that also allowed for a wide-ranging exchange of art and ideas. Within the empire, though agriculture remained important, trade profits gave rise to an urban society of guilds and merchants.

Not surprisingly, the Kushān Empire, comprising as it did many peoples, religions, and belief systems—such as Hellenism, Mithrism, Hinduism, and Buddhism—was marked by attitudes of coexistence and syncretism. The Kushāns, who had spoken Bactrian (an Iranian tongue) and then Greek, in India began to adopt Sanskrit. Kujūla Kadphises had been a Buddhist, Vima Kadphises a Hindu; Kanishka was a Buddhist. Such cosmopolitanism was a product not only of their history and economy but also of their role as foreigners faced with the inflexibilities of *karma* (destiny) and *jati* (caste) within the Hindu system, within which the Kushāns could be treated as "fallen *Kśatriya*" (warriors). Their low position within the stratified social classes of Hinduism helps to explain the Kushān tendency to embrace Buddhism (though later rulers such as Huvishka and Vasudeva were Hindu).

Such a huge and complex empire could only be governed by a feudal system allowing for significant regional autonomy. The emperor did, however, appoint satraps (provincial governors), *meridareks* (district officers), and *strategoi* (military governors). The ruler ascribed to himself a divine origin and borrowed such appellations as "King of Kings" (from Bactria), "Great King" (from India), "Son of Heaven" (from China), and "Emperor" (probably from Rome). After death, emperors were deified and temples were dedicated to them.

Religiously eclectic, to judge by his coins bearing images of a variety of gods, Kanishka came to favor the

RULERS OF THE KUSHĀN DYNASTY	
Ruler	*Reign (C.E.)*
Kujūla Kadphises	c. 30-c. 80
Vima Takhto	c. 80-c. 100
Vima Kadphises I	c. 100-c. 127
Kanishka	c. 127-c. 152
Huvishka	c. 152-c. 192
Vasudeva I	c. 192-c. 223

emerging Mahāyāna form of Buddhism over Hinduism, probably because he found the former to be more cosmopolitan and more amenable to mercantilism. It is not clear whether he underwent a genuine conversion or simply found embracing Buddhism to be politically expedient. In any case, Kanishka gave official support to Buddhist proselytization by means of education and iconography, stimulating the spread of Buddhism through Central Asia into China. Under his auspices, the Sarvāstivādins, a sect of monks who favored the nascent Mahāyānist Buddhism, organized the fourth Buddhist council (a gathering that cannot be called ecumenical, for the Hīnayānists in the south called a separate fourth council in Sri Lanka). Rejecting Pāli (the Hīnayāna or Theravāda language) in favor of Sanskrit, the monks spent twelve years in Kashmir (or in Punjab) writing commentaries on the Buddhist canon, in the process probably launching Mahāyāna Buddhism. The records of this gathering, inscribed on copper plates in stone boxes, are found today only in Chinese translation.

In old age, Kanishka may have sent an army of seventy thousand over the Pamirs to oppose Chinese military thrusts into Central Asia, a venture that failed miserably. The date and circumstances of Kanishka's death are unknown.

SIGNIFICANCE

Kanishka's policies were responsible for generating a new style in Oriental sculpture, a style that combined Greco-Roman and Iranian elements with Indian ideology to lay the basis for a Buddhist representational art with a popular appeal. The Gandhara school (in Puruśapura, Taxila, and Bāmiān) produced more naturalistic Buddhas mostly in schist, while the Mathura school turned out more stylized images in sandstone, suggesting a Western versus an Indian inspiration in the respective schools.

Throughout the historic Punjab and modern north-central Afghanistan east of Balkh and Kandahār, more than in the Hindustan, can be found the monumental ruins of Kanishka's building projects. He erected a 638-foot (194-meter) stupa to Buddha at Peshawar, a monument celebrated throughout Asia: a five-stage, 286-foot (82-meter) diameter base, surmounted by a thirteen-story carved wood structure topped by an iron column adorned with gilded copper umbrellas (*chhatras*). In decay by the seventh century, the relic casket bearing an effigy and inscription of Kanishka was found in situ in 1908 and now may be seen in the Peshawar Museum.

The most important Kanishka inscriptions are those found on a monolith before a temple-acropolis in Greco-Iranian style at Surkh Kotal (Baghlan) in the Kunduz River Valley of northeast Afghanistan. The structure, excavated between 1952 and 1964, suggests a dynastic Zoroastrian fire-temple. In Begram (now Kāpīsā), north of Kabul, Kanishka built a monastery (*vihara*) to house Chinese royal hostages. At Bāmiān, in the high passes at the Hindu Kush west of Kabul, two colossal rock Buddhas, though carved well after his time, may have been modeled on Kanishka. These statues were destroyed by the Taliban in 2001. Further records of Kanishka's reign are numerous coins minted during his time, many of gold, bearing images of a variety of Greek, Iranian, and Indian gods. The first Buddha coin also dates from this period.

Not only was Kanishka another Aśoka the Great in his championship of Buddhism, but he also seems to have been a patron of scholarship and the arts. It is thought that such distinguished men as the Sanskrit poet-dramatist and Buddhist popularizer Aśvaghosa (who wrote the conciliar commentaries) and the physician and medical writer Caraka may have been at his court. Imperious in nature, Kanishka could launch an army against China and carry off Aśvaghosa from Vārānasi. Yet, when demanding huge booty at Vārānasi, he could accept instead a begging bowl of Buddha. Kanishka stood at a crossroads of world civilization, keeping the way open for the cross-fertilization of Eastern and Western economics and culture. His patronage of Mahāyāna Buddhism, however, though it brought about the introduction of Buddhism to Central Asia and China, may have weakened that religion in India, for Kanishka was regarded as a foreigner, and his religion was therefore alien as well. Hinduism correspondingly came to be accorded status as India's indigenous religious system.

—*Ralph Smiley*

FURTHER READING

Davids, T. W. Rhys. *Buddhist India*. London: T. Fisher Unwin, 1903. Reprint. Delhi, India: Motilal Banarsidass, 1997. Chapter 26 constitutes a full discussion of Kanishka's historic role. Based on the ancient sources, it examines socioeconomic, political, and religious aspects of the Buddhist ascendancy from a non-Brahman point of view.

Geoffroy-Schneiter, Berenice. *Gandhara: The Memory of Afghanistan*. New York: Assouline, 2001. Nearly all of the monumental Gandharan Buddhas were destroyed during the Taliban's rule of Afghanistan. This well-illustrated book describes the importance of Gandharan art in world history and provides images of works now destroyed.

Raychaudhuri, Hemchandra. *Political History of Ancient India: From the Accession of Parikshit to the Extinction of the Gupta Dynasty*. Rev. ed. New York: Oxford University Press, 1996. This political history covers the Kushān period and also includes an appendix on the dating of Kanishka's reign.

Yarshater, Ehsan, ed. *The Seleucid, Parthian, and Sasanian Periods*. Vol. 3 in *The Cambridge History of Iran*. 1983. Reprint. New York: Cambridge University Press, 1993. See especially chapter 5, "The History of Eastern Iran," by A. D. H. Bivar, and chapter 26, "Buddhism Among the Iranian Peoples," by R. E. Emmerick, for fully updated scholarship and comprehensive examinations of the historical regions of Iran.

Zwalf, Wladimir. *Catalogue of the Gandhara Sculpture in the British Museum*. Chicago: Art Media Resources, 1997. A massive work documenting the British Museum's entire Gandharan collection. In addition to photographs of the objects, the catalog includes a useful historical introduction, bibliography, and indexes.

SEE ALSO: Aśoka; Buddha; Chandragupta Maurya; Menander (Greco-Bactrian king).

RELATED ARTICLES in *Great Events from History: The Ancient World*: 6th or 5th century B.C.E., Birth of Buddhism; c. 250 B.C.E., Third Buddhist Council Convenes; c. 245 B.C.E., Diodotus I Founds the Greco-Bactrian Kingdom; 2d century B.C.E., Silk Road Opens; 1st century B.C.E.-1st century C.E., Compilation of the *Lotus Sutra*; c. 100-c. 127 C.E., Kushān Dynasty Expands into India; 1st century C.E., Fourth Buddhist Council Convenes.

LAOZI
Chinese philosopher

Laozi is widely recognized as the premier thinker of Daoism, the second of China's great philosophical schools.

BORN: 604 B.C.E.; Quren, State of Chu, China
DIED: Sixth century B.C.E.; place unknown
ALSO KNOWN AS: Lao-tzu (Wade-Giles); Li Er (Pinyin); Lao Dan (Pinyin), Lao-tan (Wade-Giles)
AREA OF ACHIEVEMENT: Philosophy

EARLY LIFE

The *Dao De Jing* (possibly sixth century B.C.E., probably compiled late third century B.C.E.; *The Speculations on Metaphysics, Polity, and Morality of "the Old Philosopher, Lau-Tsze,"* 1868; better known as the *Dao De Jing*) is the name of a slim volume from China's classical era that forms a principal text of the Daoist school of philosophy. The title literally means "Old Master," and the book has traditionally been ascribed to the "Old Master" himself—or, at least, it has been thought to reflect faithfully the philosophy of someone known as Laozi (lowdzih). This Laozi is, however, the most shadowy of all classical Chinese philosophers, and nothing at all can be said with any certainty about him.

The earliest attempt to write a biography of Laozi was made in the first century B.C.E. by the great historian Sima Qian (Ssu-ma Ch'ien; c. 145-c. 86 B.C.E.), but even at that early date the historian was only able to assemble a few scraps of information concerning Laozi, many of which are mutually contradictory. Sima Qian attempted to merge the stories of at least three different individuals into his biography of Laozi, since he was uncertain which one was "the real Laozi," and in the end the various stories proved impossible to reconcile. As Sima Qian concluded, "Laozi was a reclusive gentleman," and it is perhaps fitting that he remain forever elusive.

Among the few facts that are alleged about Laozi are that his family name was Li, his given name Erh, and his "style" Dan. He was supposedly born in the southern state of Chu; indeed, Laozi's thought does typify the lush, mystical, romantic, and sometimes erotic southern side of ancient Chinese culture that contrasts so starkly with the stern moralism of northern Confucianism.

Sima Qian says that Laozi served as Historian of the Archives in the court of the Zhou Dynasty (Chou; 1066-256 B.C.E.) and that Confucius (Kong Qiu; 551-479 B.C.E.) personally sought instruction from him in the rites. At age 160, or perhaps 200, disappointed with the decline of civilization in China, Laozi departed. The Keeper of the Xiangu Pass detained him on his way out and required him to commit his wisdom to writing in the book that came to be known as the *Dao De Jing*, before permitting him to continue his westward journey. According to a later legend, Laozi subsequently went to India, where his teachings gave birth to Buddhism.

None of this information is historically reliable, however, and many modern scholars doubt that Laozi is a historical figure at all. It seems more likely that there were several "old masters" in ancient China who taught ideas similar to those of the *Dao De Jing* than that no such man ever existed at all. In either case, however, it ceases to be meaningful to say that Laozi wrote the book that is sometimes called by his name.

The best evidence indicates that the *Dao De Jing* was compiled sometime during the fourth or third century B.C.E., probably incorporating earlier fragments, and that it did not settle into its present form until the middle of the second century B.C.E. It may be that it is largely the product of one hand, but it can also be plausibly viewed as a jumble of anonymous Daoist sayings assembled by an editor or editors during this period.

LIFE'S WORK

The *Dao De Jing* has been translated into English more often than any book except the Bible, and in China hundreds of commentaries have been written on it. The explanation for all this attention is that, aside from the great intrinsic appeal of the work, it is a very cryptic book that defies definitive interpretation. Each reader finds something different in the *Dao De Jing*, and, despite deceptively simple grammar and vocabulary, it is often possible to argue at great length even about the meaning of individual sentences.

For example, the famous opening line of the *Dao De Jing* could read, in English, "Any way that you can speak about is not The Constant Way." Alternatively, it could also read: "The way that can be treated as The Way is not an ordinary way," or, "The way that can be treated as The Way is an inconstant way." Multiply this kind of ambiguity by the more than five thousand Chinese characters in the book, and it becomes easy to understand why so many different translations of the *Dao De Jing* are possible.

The work is divided into two sections and eighty-one brief chapters; more than half of it is written in rhyme, and it is suffused throughout with a distinct poetic atmosphere. There appears to be no particular order to the chapters, and even individual paragraphs may be unrelated to their context, thus reinforcing the impression of the *Dao De Jing* as an anthology of Daoist maxims rather than a systematic treatise.

Interpretation of the *Dao De Jing* must hinge, in part, on the date one chooses to assign for its composition. Its pointed ridicule of Confucian sanctimoniousness, for example, is puzzling if the legend is true that Laozi was older than Confucius, but would make sense if it was really compiled in the post-Confucian period. At least one scholar claims that the *Dao De Jing* was not compiled until the late third century B.C.E.; he bases his argument on signs of opposition he sees in it to the Legalist school that was then developing.

More critical is the *Dao De Jing*'s position within the chronology of the Daoist movement itself. Tradition gives the *Dao De Jing* pride of place as the oldest Daoist work, but there are grounds for speculation of greater age for the other great Daoist text, the *Zhuangzi* (traditionally c. 300 B.C.E., compiled c. 285-160 B.C.E.; *The Divine Classic of Nan-hua*, 1881; also known as *The Complete Works of Chuang Tzu*, 1968; commonly known as *Zhuangzi*, 1991). Not knowing which book was written first makes it difficult to determine which book influenced which and seriously cripples scholars' ability to analyze the development of Daoism.

The principal philosophical difference between the *Dao De Jing* and the *Zhuangzi* is that the former advocates understanding the laws of change in the universe so as to conform to them and thereby harness them to work for one's benefit; *Zhuangzi*, on the other hand, contends that a true understanding of the laws of change reveals all transformations to be equally valid and all differences to be ultimately relative. Hence the wise man does not try to manipulate the Dao (pronounced "dow"), but simply accepts what it brings.

The Dao is the central concept of all Daoist philosophy. The basic meaning of the word is "road" or "way," and by extension it came to refer to "the way" of doing various things. Philosophers of all Chinese schools of thought (even the Confucians) used this word and considered it to be important, but only the Daoists treated it as a universal absolute. For Confucians, the Dao is the moral Way of proper human behavior; to a Daoist, it is an amoral principle of nature.

The Dao is the constant law (or laws, since the Chinese language has no plurals) that governs the otherwise incessant change of the material universe. It is thus the one permanent, immutable thing in existence, the hub at the center of the wheel of life. Since the Dao is absolute, however, it is impossible to break it down for analysis. The mere act of giving it a name, such as Dao, is misleading, because it implies that the Dao is a thing that can be critically examined and labeled. The Dao actually transcends all humanly imposed conceptual models.

Because the Dao cannot be logically analyzed or described in words, it therefore can only be perceived holistically through intuition. This gives the *Dao De Jing* its mystic tone and helps explain the frustrating statement in chapter 56 that "he who knows does not speak; he who speaks does not know." Ultimate truth is beyond the capacity of speech to convey. For this reason, one third century C.E. wag remarked that Confucius actually understood the Dao better than Laozi, since Confucius was wise enough to keep silent about the subject.

Laozi. (Hulton|Archive by Getty Images)

Laozi's favorite theme is the disparity between intention and result. "Reversal is the action of the Dao," he wrote (chapter 40). Striving to make oneself strong eventually exhausts and weakens a man; striving for wealth leads to poverty in the long run. The wise man instead conforms to the Dao and aligns himself with the weak, the humble, and the poor.

This philosophy was in large part a reaction to the highly competitive environment of the Warring States Period in Chinese history (475-221 B.C.E.), when conflict was continuous and life itself uncertain. Amid such surroundings, *Dao De Jing* taught that survival came through not competing. The solution to the problem of how to preserve life and happiness was simply to be content.

The *Dao De Jing* contains wisdom for all people, but much of the book is directed in particular toward the ruler. It teaches a kind of laissez-faire approach to government: The state will function best if left to run itself naturally, and strenuous efforts on the part of the ruler can only cause greater confusion and disorder. The more the ruler acts, the more work he creates for himself, and the more impossible it becomes to do everything that is necessary. Far better to do nothing. The *Dao De Jing* calls this form of government *wuwei*, or "nonaction."

As a concrete application of this principle, the *Dao De Jing* criticizes attempts to improve the state through moral codes or laws. The very existence of laws produces lawbreakers, and moral codes result in pretense, competition, and the very kinds of immorality they were intended to discourage. Far better, says Laozi, to return to the childlike condition of original innocence that prevailed before the awakening of desires.

SIGNIFICANCE

Laozi the man is a will-o'-the-wisp—an insubstantial legend. Even a legend, however, can have important consequences. During the common era, religious Daoism emerged under Buddhist influence out of earlier immortality cults. This Daoist religion adopted very little of the philosophical content of the *Dao De Jing*, but its adherents came to venerate Laozi himself as a god.

By the second century C.E., Laozi was being worshipped as a progenitor of the universe, an incarnation of the Dao itself. The deified Laozi became one of the most important members of the native Chinese religious pantheon, and the eighty-one earthly manifestations he was ultimately said to have taken included the Buddha (Siddhārtha Gautama; c. 566-c. 486 B.C.E.) and Mani (Manes; c. 216-276 C.E.), the Persian founder of Manichaeanism.

The religious Daoist canon includes more than fourteen hundred separate titles, but the *Dao De Jing*—often badly misunderstood, to be sure—ranks at the top. Even for Chinese who remained skeptical about this native religious movement, the *Dao De Jing* continued to be regarded as an outstanding guide for living and a delightful work of literature.

The *Dao De Jing* and *Zhuangzi* represent the native Chinese tradition of true metaphysical speculation (as opposed to the political and social philosophy of Confucius and others) and as such have contributed immensely to the subsequent development of Chinese thought. Chan Buddhism (Japanese Zen), for example, owes much to Daoist influence. Daoist philosophy has always been the natural consolation of the Chinese gentleman in retirement or disgrace. The *Dao De Jing*, one of the most profound and baffling books ever written, is a principal text in China's perennial "other" school of thought: the playful, mystical, Daoist alternative to staid and conventional Confucianism.

—Charles W. Holcombe

FURTHER READING

Kohn, Livia, ed. *The Daoism Handbook*. New York: E. J. Brill, 2000. An excellent introduction, summarizing virtually every aspect of Daoism.

Kohn, Livia, and Harold D. Roth, eds. *Daoist Identity: History, Lineage, and Ritual*. Honolulu: University of Hawaii Press, 2002. A collection of essays exploring the many ways in which Daoism has functioned as a religion.

Laozi. *Tao te Ching*. Translated by Stephen Mitchell. New York: HarperCollins, 1988. An excellent translation.

Oldstone-Moore, Jennifer. *Taoism*. New York: Oxford University Press, 2003. A concise introduction to the religious and cultural history of Daoism.

Yu, David C. *History of Chinese Daoism*. Lanham, Md.: University Press of America, 2000. Discusses the relationships between Daoism and other Chinese religions, Daoism and the state, and Daoism's position in relation to social class.

Zhuangzi. *Zhuangzi*. Translated by Burton Watson. Reprint. New York: Columbia University Press, 2003. A classic translation of Daoism's second most important text.

SEE ALSO: Buddha; Confucius; Hanfeizi; Mencius; Sima Qian.

RELATED ARTICLES in *Great Events from History: The Ancient World*: 479 B.C.E., Confucius's Death Leads to the Creation of *The Analects*; 3d century B.C.E. (traditionally 6th century B.C.E.), Laozi Composes the *Dao De Jing*; 285-160 B.C.E. (traditionally, c. 300 B.C.E.), Composition of the *Zhuangzi*; 139-122 B.C.E., Composition of the *Huainanzi*; 142 C.E., Zhang Daoling Founds the Celestial Masters Movement; c. 3d century C.E., Wang Bi and Guo Xiang Revive Daoism; 4th century C.E., Ge Chaofu Founds the Ling Bao Sect of Daoism; c. 405 C.E., Statesman Tao Qian Becomes Farmer and Daoist Poet; c. 470 C.E., Bodhidharma Brings Chan Buddhism to China.

LEONIDAS

Spartan king (r. 490 B.C.E.-480 B.C.E.)

The bravery and supreme sacrifice of Leonidas and his men at Thermopylae sent a surge of pride through all Greece, made the Greeks aware of their heritage, and stiffened their resolve to face—and, eventually, to prevail over—what seemed to be overwhelming odds.

BORN: c. 510 B.C.E.; Sparta, Greece
DIED: August 20, 480 B.C.E.; Thermopylae, Thessaly, Greece
AREA OF ACHIEVEMENT: War and conquest

EARLY LIFE

When Leonidas (lee-AHN-uhd-uhs) was born, it was not expected that he would be king. Leonidas's father, King Anaxandrides, and his wife at first had no children. In order that the royal line not die out—for it was said to be directly descended from the mythical hero Hercules—the Ephors, or administrators of Sparta, asked the king to take a second wife, with whom he had a son, Cleomenes. The king's first wife then had three sons: Dorieus, Leonidas, and Cleombrotus. When Anaxandrides died, Cleomenes was named king—to the indignation of Dorieus, who considered himself better qualified.

Not wishing to stay in Sparta under the rule of Cleomenes, Dorieus went to Sicily to found a colony, and he died there. Cleomenes was a controversial king; some considered him mentally ill. He forced his coruler Demaratus into exile, then tried to expand and consolidate his limited power to the extent of attempting to bribe the sacred oracle at Delphi. His policies aroused so much controversy that he was forced to leave Sparta. When Cleomenes returned, Leonidas, now king, had him arrested and imprisoned. Cleomenes was later found in his cell badly mutilated, and he died soon after. It was said he had bribed his jailer to give him a knife with which to commit suicide. Others maintained that Leonidas had a hand in his half brother's death. Leonidas subsequently married Cleomenes' daughter, Gorgo.

In appearance, Leonidas was a typical Spartan, possessing a lean body hardened by years of gymnastics and military exercises, free of physical defects. (No Spartan infant with deformities was permitted to live.) A characteristic of Spartan warriors was their long hair, which they took care to groom, especially if they were about to die on the battlefield. Like all young Spartans, and the more so because of his royal status, Leonidas, from the age of seven, spent his life in military training. He became king in 490 B.C.E., the year of the first Persian War, in which a small Greek force defeated a much larger Persian army on the plain of Marathon. The victory belonged mainly to Athens. Sparta, Greece's most formidable military power, did not participate because its citizens were celebrating a sacred festival. Leonidas was determined, should a second Persian attack occur, that Sparta and its army would participate.

LIFE'S WORK

Leonidas's life's work and short reign as king revolved around the preparation for and participation in one important battle, one of the most significant in Western history. Humiliated by the defeat of his forces by the Greeks in 490 B.C.E., Darius, the Persian king, ruler of one of the world's largest and richest empires, was determined to avenge the defeat, but he died in 486 B.C.E. His mission became that of his son Xerxes I, who began assembling the largest military force known to the ancient world to defeat the Greeks. The exiled Demaratus, who was living at the court of Darius, sent a message to the Spartans, concealed under a layer of wax on a table, warning them of the danger. The message was reportedly discovered by the sharp eye of Queen Gorgo.

The Panhellenic League was formed at a military conference held in Corinth the fall of 481 by those Greek states willing to take a stand against Xerxes. Leonidas was given command of the army. Athens had the most powerful fleet, and naval activities were largely under the command of the Athenian Themistocles. Greece at the time consisted of many independent, often warring states. The Greeks, however, shared a language and value system, and, as the war was to prove, they could act in unison if necessary.

In the early spring of 480 B.C.E., Xerxes and his mighty army began the slow march to the Greek mainland. The Persians crossed the Bosphorus, the waterway between the Black and Mediterranean Seas, by constructing pontoon bridges. Skirting the Aegean Sea and marching parallel to his fleet, Xerxes sought to capture Athens in central Greece. The land through which he marched could not support such a mighty army, and Xerxes was therefore dependent on his ships to replenish supplies. Without the necessary naval support, the expedition would fail.

The Persians prepared to enter central Greece in August, again the time of the festival that had kept the Spar-

tans home ten years before. Leonidas marched nevertheless with only three hundred Spartans, expecting to pick up allies en route and to be joined by the rest of the Spartan army once the festival was over. It was decided to try to check the Persian advance by holding the pass of Thermopylae between northern and central Greece. Only about fifty feet wide, the pass lay between high cliffs and the Malian Gulf.

By the time he reached Thermopylae, Leonidas had assembled a force of about seven thousand men. He reconnoitered the area, laid waste the valley through which the Persians would have to pass, and coordinated his activities with Themistocles and the fleet. The bodies of water bordering Thermopylae are among the most complex and dangerous in the Mediterranean region. It was an area the Greeks knew well. They also knew that the Aegean in August was subject to violent, unexpected windstorms, and storms did occur with extraordinary force and frequency, destroying a significant portion of

Leonidas, left, meets an ambassador of Xerxes. (Library of Congress)

the Persian fleet. The naval battle of Artemisium, which coincided with the land battle of Thermopylae, gave the Greeks a small victory and valuable experience.

Leonidas deployed his forces to the rear of the pass and the adjoining mountains, leaving mainly the Spartans to face the Persians. The Persians called on the Spartans to lay down their arms; Leonidas shouted back that the Persians would have to come and get them. On August 18, Xerxes gave the order to attack. Wave after wave were sent against the Greeks, but the first encounters proved how badly equipped the Persians were for close-quarter fighting. Their armor was too thin; their shields were too small and weak; their short spears were ineffective against the Greek long spears; and their arrows dashed harmlessly against the great bronze shields of the Spartans. Successive attacks only succeeded in piling up bodies in the narrow pass and made no progress in dislodging the Spartans and their allies.

At the end of the second day of fighting, Xerxes ceased his attacks in favor of another plan. A Greek traitor revealed the existence of a path through the mountains that led around and behind the Greek position. Xerxes dispatched the captain of his best troops to lead a contingent of chosen soldiers along the path and thus cut off Leonidas's forces from the rear. Leonidas, who had learned of the path soon after he reached Thermopylae, had sent an inexperienced contingent of Greek soldiers to guard it, for he could spare no Spartans. The soldiers fled as the Persians approached, and word came to Leonidas that before noon of the third day he would be trapped between enemy forces. After a hurried conference and with the road to the south still open, Leonidas sent away most of his troops, leaving only the Spartans and some hand-picked soldiers. As his men sat down to eat their last meal, Leonidas with wry humor told them to eat heartily, for they would next dine in Hades.

The little band was determined to fight to the last. In order to kill as many of the enemy soldiers as possible, Leonidas had his men leave the defensive wall behind which they had been fighting and prepare for hand-to-hand combat. Seeing how few the defenders were in number and realizing that their resistance could at last be broken, Xerxes ordered column after column of Persians to sweep down on the Greeks. Four times the Spartans and their allies flung them back. Shouts from the rear told the Greeks that the escape route was closed, so the heroic remnant gathered for a last stand on a small knoll. Leonidas was among the first to fall, and a struggle for his body ensued. Fighting without their leader, their weapons broken, those Greeks still standing fought with their fists and even their teeth until the last of the Spartans was killed. Xerxes had his men find the body of Leonidas, cut off the head, and impale it on a pole to show his army that the great warrior was mortal.

SIGNIFICANCE

Why the heroic stand of Leonidas and his men? Retreat and regrouping were permitted a Spartan commander; cowardice and surrender were not. Legend has it that Leonidas willed his own death because the Delphic oracle had warned him that either a king or Sparta must fall. Closer to the truth is probably that Leonidas realized that the manner of his death would be a source of inspiration to other Greeks, enabling them to resist the Persian foe. His assessment was correct, for Leonidas almost instantly became one of Greece's greatest heroes. His sacrifice imbued the Greeks with the pride and confidence necessary for them eventually to expel the enemy.

The Greek naval forces shared in the confidence. The knowledge gained of the composition and tactics of the Persian navy enabled the smaller, more maneuverable Greek ships to ram and sink so many Persian ships in a later naval battle that the Persian navy was no longer an effective fighting force. Even the windstorms served to bolster Greek confidence, for they believed their gods of the wind and sea were supporting their cause.

The Greco-Persian War made Europe possible. It enabled Western civilization to develop its own political and economic life, its tradition of democratic government, and its emphasis on the rights of the individual, as opposed to the theocratic absolutism and social orientation of the East. In its aftermath, Greece entered its golden age of art, philosophy, literature, and science, the single greatest influence on the development of Western civilization.

—*Nis Petersen*

FURTHER READING

Bowra, C. M. *Classical Greece*. New York: Time-Life Books, 1965. Using a pictorial approach to history, the book is rich in details such as models of the Greek ships and the pontoon bridges across the Bosphorus.

Bradford, Ernle Dusgate Selby. *Thermopylae: The Battle for the West*. New York: Da Capo Press, 1993. Despite its detailed and thorough research on the battle, Bradford's account is easy to read and is presented in a chronological format. Also of value is the discussion of the sequel to Artemisium and Thermopylae at the battles of Salamis and Platea, which brought an end to the Persian menace.

Durant, Will. *The Life of Greece*. New York: MJF Books, 1992. A comprehensive yet easy-to-read work on Greek civilization. Chapter 4 contains an excellent description of Sparta; book 3 examines Greece's golden age.

Herodotus. *The History of Herodotus*. Translated by George Rawlinson. 2d ed. Chicago: Encyclopaedia Britannica, 1994. Much of the knowledge of the Persian Wars, including the Battle of Thermopylae, is from Herodotus. Known as "the father of history," Herodotus, although detailed, is remarkably easy and interesting to read. Book 7 deals with the Battle of Thermopylae; book 5 contains background information on Leonidas. Includes maps and an index.

SEE ALSO: Cleomenes; Darius the Great; Themistocles; Xerxes I.

RELATED ARTICLES in *Great Events from History: The Ancient World*: 520-518 B.C.E., Darius the Great Conquers the Indus Valley; September 17, 490 B.C.E., Battle of Marathon; 483 B.C.E., Naval Law of Themistocles Is Instituted; 480-479 B.C.E., Persian Invasion of Greece; May, 431-September, 404 B.C.E., Peloponnesian War.

LIVIA DRUSILLA
Roman empress

Livia was an active partner with Augustus in the creation and maintenance of the Roman Empire and the Imperial family.

BORN: January 30, 58 B.C.E.; place unknown
DIED: 29 C.E., Rome (now in Italy)
ALSO KNOWN AS: Julia Augusta
AREA OF ACHIEVEMENT: Government and politics

EARLY LIFE

No ancient literary source focuses entirely on Livia Drusilla (LIH-vee-ah drew-SIH-lah), but at least four major sources include information on her. They are Suetonius's *De vita Caesarum* (c.120 C.E.; *History of the Twelve Caesars*, 1606); Dio Cassius's *Romaika* (probably c. 202 C.E.; *Roman History*, 1914-1927); the *Annales* of Velleius Paterculus (c. 29 C.E.; *Compendium of Roman History*, 1924); and Tacitus's *Ab excessu divi Augusti* (c. 116 C.E., also known as *Annales*; *Annals*, 1598).

Alfidia gave birth to Livia Drusilla in late January of 58 B.C.E. About Alfidia little is known except her name and that her father must have been wealthy. More can be said of Livia's father, Marcus Livius Drusus, who was born into the family Claudii and adopted into the family of the Livii Drusi. Through her father's family ties, Livia was a member of two of the most prestigious and oldest of all Roman families. This fact has more meaning than simple biographical information, for, like that of all ancient Romans, Livia's role was to be defined by the family into which she was born.

Although the specifics of her education are not known, as an upper-class girl belonging to the highest social and political spheres in the Roman world, Livia was surely taught reading, writing, mathematics, the management of a household, and perhaps even rhetoric. This education was meant to prepare her to take her place as the wife and mother of males in the upper echelon of the Roman sociopolitical world. At a young age Livia was betrothed to Tiberius Claudius Nero, a cousin who was about fifteen years her senior, from another branch of the Claudian family. When she was about fifteen years old she married him. Under normal circumstances, Livia could have expected Tiberius to rise to the highest offices in Rome. She could also have expected to play an active role in his success through the maintenance and creation of political alliances behind the scenes. Livia, however, did not live in normal times.

She was only nine or ten years old when, in 49 B.C.E., Julius Caesar marched his troops across the Rubicon River and started the civil wars that would last for almost a quarter of a century and would bring the Republic to an end. During these wars, every elite family was forced to choose sides. Livia's father sided with the ill-fated Pompey the Great against Julius Caesar. Nonetheless, the family weathered that first storm. In the next phase of the wars, beginning with the assassination of Caesar on the ides of March in 44, her husband repeatedly allied himself with the losing side. Because of this, he was forced to flee for his life several times.

The details of the relationship between Livia and her first husband are unknown, but the evidence of other women suggests that Livia had a choice: She could choose to stay with her husband, or she could choose to turn him over to his opponents. Livia chose loyalty to him and it nearly cost her her life. For example, at one point

Tiberius and Livia, with their young son, Tiberius (the future emperor), had sought refuge in Sparta. When they were suddenly forced to flee Sparta (the reason is unknown) Livia, clinging to her young son, ran into a forest fire, and the two barely escaped with their lives—as Livia's scorched clothing and hair attested.

The period of the civil wars from 49 B.C.E., and especially from 44 to 27 B.C.E., were chaotic for all Romans, and while Livia's path may not have been more terrifying than the paths of her contemporaries, her story is the most ironic. In 40-39 B.C.E. Octavian created a general amnesty in Rome, and Tiberius and Livia returned to the city. Some time shortly after their return Octavian met Livia, and for reasons personal—he allegedly fell in love with her—as well as political—her good family name—he decided he wanted to marry her. He asked Tiberius to divorce Livia and asked Livia to marry him. All parties agreed, and Livia, pregnant with what would prove to be her second and last son, divorced Tiberius and married Octavian (January 17, 38). Her first husband even gave her away at the wedding ceremony.

It is in her marriage to Octavian, who would become Augustus, the first emperor of Rome, and subsequently in her position as mother of the second emperor that Livia's life's work was carried out. Livia, raised as she had been to play a political role in the life of her husband, would play a more important and more public role than any woman in Rome before her day and arguably more than any woman after her.

LIFE'S WORK

In 31 B.C.E. Livia's second husband defeated Marc Antony and Cleopatra VII at the Battle of Actium. The following year Antony and Cleopatra committed suicide, and Octavian became sole ruler. Three years later, Octavian ostensibly gave up his official post and, without holding any political office, he became the de facto ruler of the Roman Empire. In that same year he was granted the honorary title of Augustus ("revered"). Augustus spent the rest of his forty-one years refining his administration of the Empire and his representation of himself and his family as rulers of that empire. One of the key elements of Augustus's plan was a massive propaganda campaign returning Rome to "traditional" Roman values. In carrying out his agenda he had a willing and capable partner in Livia.

Livia Drusilla. (Hulton|Archive by Getty Images)

Before examining the specifics of Livia's participation in her husband's agenda, it is worth considering how her precise role in these events was colored by her gender. As a woman she was traditionally limited to the private sphere, but as the wife of the First Citizen she played a remarkably public role, unique in Roman history. With Augustus's emphasis on traditional values, Livia's public role might have appeared somewhat anomalous. She was, however, able successfully to present herself as a public benefactor of Rome through wifely and motherly virtue: She became the ideal Roman *matrona*.

Livia's commissioning of public buildings and consecrating of shrines and temples reflect her active participation in Augustus's agenda and also reflect the specific character of that participation. The public buildings that she erected were connected with the sphere of the *matrona*. For example, in the Porticus Liviae—the colonnaded, covered walkway that bears her name—Livia consecrated the Shrine of Concordia, a shrine to the harmony between husband and wife. Furthermore, the date of the consecration of the shrine was June 11, 7 B.C.E. June 11 was also the festival of the Matralia, one manifestation of the mother goddess.

Livia intentionally represented herself as a mother of the Imperial family and as a mother of Rome. She served as a patron to various womanly causes: supplying dowries to deserving young women whose families were unable to ensure a suitable marriage for them and providing money for the support of orphans. One poet even referred to Livia as *princeps* of the class of *matronae*. *Princeps*, though not of *matronae*, was the same title that Augustus had received, demonstrating Livia's role as mother and as partner with her husband.

Livia's generosity continued even after her husband died in 14 C.E. Indeed, when Augustus died he left a large portion of his wealth to her, as much as was legally permitted, enabling her to make even further benefactions. He also adopted her in his will, which meant that she was able to take the feminine form of his family name: Julia. At the same time, the senate granted her the title of augusta, one of the few privileges offered by the senate that her son, Tiberius, was willing to allow her. Despite Tiberius's famous stinginess when it came to honorific titles for his mother, it is clear that she continued to play an active role in the Roman political world even during his reign.

Not only did Livia's involvement in the public sphere continue but Tiberius's piety toward her was also officially sanctioned by the senate. The most striking example of the role of Livia as mother of the emperor and deserving of piety comes during the trial of Gnaeus Piso. Piso and his wife Plancina were implicated in the killing of Germanicus, nephew and adopted son of Tiberius. Plancina, fearful that her husband would not survive the trial, sought the help of Livia. Livia was able to intercede on her behalf, and when the senate published the results of the trial—carved on bronze tablets and posted all over the Roman Empire—the senators recorded the fact that Plancina was acquitted because of the respect the senators had for the *princeps*' extreme piety toward his mother.

In the context of Germanicus's death, Livia's undeserved reputation for poisoning all of the potential heirs to her husband's power requires attention. Most scholars today view these accusations as, at best, unsubstantiated. The accusations exist for two reasons. Tiberius did inherit Augustus's position, and a remarkable number of potential heirs did predecease Augustus. More interestingly, though, the accusations of poisoning provide insight into the difficult path that Livia had to walk and the ambivalence that walk engendered. As a woman, she was expected to be involved behind the scenes. As the wife (then mother) of the most important man in Rome, she had to play a public role. Men, uncomfortable with the extent of authority wielded by this woman, may have been expressing that discomfort by spreading rumors of her killing off other members of the family.

Livia died in 29 C.E., when she was almost ninety years old. Her son, Tiberius, though still emperor, was in self-imposed isolation on the island of Capri and did not return to attend her funeral. Her grandson, the future emperor Caligula, gave her eulogy. Her death inspired the senators to proclaim multiple honors for her, the vast majority of which Tiberius forbade. They even proposed that she be consecrated as a goddess, thus demonstrating that, despite the ambivalent response to Livia in some of the extant sources, at the time of her death she was revered and admired by the Romans.

SIGNIFICANCE

The emperor Claudius I's deification of Livia, as one of his earliest acts as emperor, reflects the continued popularity of the first First Lady of Rome. By deifying his grandmother, Claudius reinforced his own authority. Furthermore, the consecration of Livia took place on January 17, 42, the anniversary of her wedding to Augustus. This makes particular sense because Claudius, though he was the grandson of Livia, was not biologically related to Augustus. Livia was made a goddess through her role as the ideal Roman *matrona* and because of her relationship to Augustus. The cultivation of this identity and this relationship, created as they were by Augustus and Livia and subsequently fostered by their descendants, helped Livia to remain in the hearts and minds of the Roman people for centuries to come.

—*Judy E. Gaughan*

FURTHER READING

Barrett, Anthony. *Livia: First Lady of Imperial Rome.* New Haven, Conn.: Yale University Press, 2002. Barrett has written a complete English-language biography of Livia. Includes nineteen appendices, notes, an extensive bibliography, and an index.

Bartman, Elizabeth. *Portraits of Livia: Imaging the Imperial Woman in Augustan Rome.* New York: Cambridge University Press, 1999. Bartman attempts to identify portraits of Livia and to place them in their social and political context. Includes 194 images, two catalogs, notes, three appendices, a select bibliography, and three indexes.

Kleiner, Diana E. E., and Susan B. Matheson, eds. *I, Claudia: Women in Ancient Rome*. New Haven, Conn.: Yale University Art Gallery, 1996. Kleiner and Matheson provide a collection of essays that use images of women in art to flesh out the roles of women (including Livia) in Roman society. Includes genealogy charts, glossary, and select bibliographies.

_____. *I, Claudia II: Women in Roman Art and Society*. Austin: University of Texas Press, 2000. Continues the work of the first *I Claudia*. No ancient literary source focuses entirely on Livia, but these are major sources that include information on Livia.

Severy, Beth. *Augustus and the Family at the Birth of the Roman Empire*. New York: Routledge, 2003. Severy argues that Augustus's ultimate method for establishing and maintaining his new form of government was to base it on the Imperial family. Includes notes, an extensive bibliography, and an index.

SEE ALSO: Augustus; Caligula; Claudius I; Tiberius.

RELATED ARTICLES in *Great Events from History: The Ancient World*: 43-42 B.C.E., Second Triumvirate Enacts Proscriptions; September 2, 31 B.C.E., Battle of Actium; 27-23 B.C.E., Completion of the Augustan Settlement.

LIVY
Roman historian

Livy preserved many of the legendary traditions and mythology dealing with the earliest phase of ancient Roman history. Because many of the authors and sources he used have long been lost, his work assumes particular importance.

BORN: 59 B.C.E.; Patavium (now Padua, Italy)
DIED: 17 C.E.; Patavium
ALSO KNOWN AS: Titus Livius (full name)
AREA OF ACHIEVEMENT: Historiography

EARLY LIFE

Titus Livius, or Livy (LIHV-ee), was born in 59 B.C.E. in Patavium, northern Italy, according to the theologian Saint Jerome. Livy makes only a few brief references to his homeland, but they indicate a patriotic pride. Unfortunately, nothing certain is known about his youth, but it is assumed that he was schooled in his native town. This idea is based on a comment made by Asinius Pollio that Livy's style was provincial. This criticism, however, is largely negated by the excellent Ciceronian style of most of Livy's historical writings.

Livy's early education must have included philosophical studies, as his writings contain many allusions and direct references to traditional Stoic values. Also, his frequent comments about religion show that he was familiar with the traditions and rituals of the Roman cults.

Livy probably did not begin writing his history of Rome until he was about thirty years old. Presumably, he had had adequate time in the previous years to read and research in preparation. By the age of thirty, he had probably moved to Rome, but regarding this there is no sure evidence. By the year 5 B.C.E., Livy was definitely in Rome, as at this time he was criticized by Emperor Augustus for being a "Pompeian," a person who was biased in favor of the aristocratic, senatorial views. Augustus seems not to have meant this remark too seriously, for there is ample evidence to suggest that the emperor counted Livy as a friend and took an interest in his work. Indeed, it is known that about 8 C.E. Livy helped the future emperor Claudius in his historical studies.

LIFE'S WORK

Livy's great history was written in Latin and is generally known as *Ab urbe condita libri* (c. 26 B.C.E.-15 C.E.; *The History of Rome*, 1600), literally meaning "from the founding of the city" (of Rome). The work was exceptionally long, containing 142 books (scrolls); this length has been estimated to be equivalent to twenty-four or twenty-five crown-octavo volumes of three hundred pages each.

Probably as a result of the extreme length of the original work, abridgments and summaries were made in antiquity. Most of these have survived, but much of the original work has been lost. Only 35 of the 142 books have survived the ravages of time, including books 1-10 and 31-45. These surviving books deal chronologically with events between the years 753 and 243 B.C.E. and between 219 and 167 B.C.E. From the surviving summaries and fragments, it is clear that the work included information about Rome from its traditional foundation date in 753 through 9 B.C.E. The last twenty-two books were probably not published until after the death of Augustus in 14 C.E. The surmised reason for this is that Livy was fearful of publishing information about contemporaneous people and events.

Most scholars who have studied Livy's work in detail have noted certain distinctive features of his great history. These include intensely personal psychological portraits of major military and political figures, speeches of uncertain origin interwoven with the chronological narrative to reflect certain political or religious perspectives of ancient Romans, lengthy discourses on cultic religion, including references to miracles and prodigies, frequent references to the virtuous morals and ethics of the early Romans in contrast to the degeneration of morals in the more recent age, a clear sympathy with Stoic views on the providential determination of history, and a patriotic bias in favor of aristocratic, republican conservatism.

Of these features, greater scholarly attention has been devoted to two aspects: Livy's use of speeches and his emphasis on religion and morals. With regard to Livy's use of speeches, it should be noted that he was not alone among ancient historians in the use of oratorical devices. The Greek historian Thucydides, like most other ancient historians, made the most of rhetoric in his accounts. In each case, the scholar must ask whether the speeches reflect the beliefs and attitudes of the author or of the one being quoted. Unfortunately, the question cannot be resolved with certainty. Most scholars have concluded that the speeches are not verbatim (though shorthand methods of taking dictation were known) but that they represent the historian's artful summary of what he assumed must have been said on the occasion. In the particular case of Livy's history, there is evidence that Cicero was used consciously with regard to style. There are 407 major speeches in Livy's extant volumes, and if indirect speeches and minor exhortations are included, the number rises to more than 2,000. These statistics, obviously, are only based on the surviving books of Livy.

One of the longest of his speeches deals with Livy's other chief preoccupation, religion. Marcus Furius Camillus, who has been called the second founder of Rome, was the man who prevented the Romans from abandoning the site of Rome, which had been badly damaged by warfare with the Gauls. Though the Romans had finally defeated the Gauls, many citizens of Rome wanted to migrate to the city of Veii, which had earlier been taken from the Etruscans. Camillus convinced them, however, that such a move would be a sin, a sacrilege, according to Livy's report.

Most scholars believe that references to ancient religious beliefs, whether occurring in an alleged speech or in the narrative, reflect traditional views of the time more than Livy's personal beliefs. Regardless of scholarly controversy, however, Livy's history is so full of references to religion, morals, and ethical concerns that it seems difficult to believe that he simply repeated them to fill space. Instead, he probably did believe that his age had degenerated from earlier, more austere times. Examples of dramatic concern for morality include the stories of the rape of Lucretia, the execution of the vestal virgin Minucia, the debauchery of Hannibal's army at Capua, and the introduction of the worship of the Greek god of wine, Dionysus-Bacchus.

The frequent references to religion and morals in Livy have led many scholars to conclude that he had Stoic sympathies or perhaps was actually a Stoic. Evidence for this conclusion is Livy's frequent use of such terms as *fatum* (fate), *fortuna* (chance), *felicitas* (good fortune), *virtus* (virtue, bravery), *fors* (luck), and *causa* (cause), which may indicate some sympathy with the Stoic concept of the universe.

Having enjoyed years of productive work in Rome, Livy retired to his hometown, Patavium, near the end of his life. An Augustan tomb inscription discovered in the modern city of Padua honors the memory of a Titus Livius. Some scholars believe that he died as early as 12 C.E., although Saint Jerome records his death as occurring in 17.

SIGNIFICANCE

The popularity of Livy in ancient times cannot be denied. He is also customarily covered in modern scholarly accounts of great ancient historians of Greece and Rome. The fact that he did have religious and political biases does not negate the fact that he did occasionally record his sources of information and make comments about their reliability. The ancient historian Valerius Antias is mentioned by name thirty-six times, Claudius Quadrigarius twelve times, Coelius Antipater eleven, Licinius Macer seven; Calpurnius Piso, Polybius, and Fabius Pictor are mentioned six times. In most cases, Livy tried to evaluate his sources in regard to probable accuracy and truthfulness.

Livy did, however, have undeniable weaknesses as a historian: occasional anachronisms, mistaken chronology, and topographical and geographic confusions, especially in accounts of battles. Furthermore, his patriotism makes him seem a bit prejudiced against other nations and peoples, most notably the Greeks.

—John M. Lawrence

FURTHER READING

Duff, John W. "Augustan Prose and Livy." In *A Literary History of Rome: From the Origins to the Close of the Golden Age.* New York: Barnes and Noble, 1960. A brief but good analysis of Livy and other literary figures of the age of Augustus, with special emphasis on the Ciceronian literary style of Livy.

Feldherr, Andrew. *Spectacle and Society in Livy's History.* Berkeley: University of California Press, 1998. Feldherr's analysis of several episodes in Livy's history shows how Livy uses specific visual imagery to give his reader the sense of being a participant in the events described.

Frank, Tenney. "Republican Historiography and Livy." In *Life and Literature in the Roman Republic.* Berkeley: University of California Press, 1971. An excellent summary and analysis of Livy's predecessors in writing Roman history. Special emphasis is placed on archaeological discoveries that have confirmed some of the early legends about the founding of Rome mentioned by Livy.

Grant, Michael. "Livy." In *The Ancient Historians.* London: Duckworth, 1995. Grant summarizes the contents of Livy's history and emphasizes his historio-graphical methods and aims, concluding that Livy deserves credit as a great historian.

Laistner, M. L. W. "Livy, the Man and the Writer" and "Livy, the Historian." In *The Greater Roman Historians.* Berkeley: University of California Press, 1966. A detailed treatment of Livy as an adherent of a Stoic view of history in which religious signs were considered valid.

Walsh, P. G. "Livy." In *Latin Historians*, edited by T. A. Dorey. New York: Basic Books, 1966. Describes Livy's themes, such as the decline of Roman morality, his political views (senatorial and conservative), and his philosophical views (Stoic). Walsh also points out Livy's weaknesses: He is too rhetorical and too concerned with individual psychological factors in history.

SEE ALSO: Augustus; Cicero; Claudius I; Hannibal; Lucretia.

RELATED ARTICLES in *Great Events from History: The Ancient World*: c. 450-c. 425 B.C.E., History Develops as a Scholarly Discipline; c. 300 B.C.E., Stoics Conceptualize Natural Law; 1st century B.C.E., Sima Qian Writes Chinese History; 51 B.C.E., Cicero Writes *De republica*.

LUCIAN
Roman orator

Lucian turned the philosophical dialogue into a form for satirizing ideas and manners. Lucianic satire became a mainstay of European literature in the Renaissance.

BORN: c. 120 C.E.; Samosata, Commagene, Syria (now Samsat, Turkey)
DIED: c. 180 C.E.; probably Egypt
ALSO KNOWN AS: Lucianos (Greek); Lucianus (Latin); Lucinus (Latin)
AREA OF ACHIEVEMENT: Literature

EARLY LIFE

Almost nothing is recorded about the life of Lucian (LEW-shuhn), outside his own works. Because most of these are satires, full of topical allusions and semiautobiographical asides, readers must be cautious before accepting the claims he makes. By his own account, Lucian was born in Samosata (modern Samsat) on the Euphrates River. It was a strategic point in the Roman province of Syria but far from the centers of culture. His father was a middle-class citizen, poor enough to suffer the tedium of life at the edge of the Roman Empire but wealthy enough to send his son to school.

Lucian left school for a while to apprentice with his uncle, a successful stonecutter and sculptor. His master beat him, however, and Lucian thought again about the value of education. He was good at Greek, the language of learning and commerce in the eastern part of the Roman world, and he developed an elegant prose style. In conversation, he may have had a provincial accent—he may have spoken a Semitic language at home—but in writing, he showed exceptional purity.

Lucian's training qualified him to work as a public speaker—also called a *rhetor* (the Greek word) or an orator (the Latin word). Citizens who took a case to the law courts, or who had to defend themselves, would hire an orator who knew the finer points of law and who could argue their cases in memorable language with a voice that would carry in a large public gathering. As his reputation grew, Lucian began to give public performances of his oratorical skills, which included the ability to improvise on a theme, to speak eloquently, and to entertain large, paying crowds. He says he was a great success, but he made his appearances on the fringes of the Roman Empire—in Ionia (modern Turkey) and Gaul (modern France) rather than Athens or Alexandria—and no other orators referred to him. Several of his early orations survive, including a speech in praise of a fly and two seriocomic defenses of a tyrant named Phalaris and the officials at the oracle of Delphi who accepted the tyrant's bribe. When Lucian was approximately forty, he stopped traveling and began a new career as a writer of satires.

LIFE'S WORK

Having made his fortune as an orator, Lucian retired to Athens and enrolled in the school of the Stoic philosopher Demonax. He studied philosophy during a great revival of interest in ancient Greek thought known as the Second Sophistic. He became acquainted with the leading ideas of all the philosophical schools, including the Cynics and the Epicureans. He may have called himself a philosopher, but the main thing he learned was the dialogue form developed by Plato (427-347 B.C.E.). In such works as the *Symposion* (c. 388-368 B.C.E.; *Symposium*, 1701), Plato used dialogue and other dramatic devices to voice philosophical ideas—and to challenge them. In Lucian's *Symposion* (*The Carousal*, 1684), the ideas are used for comic effect. Lucian always goes for the laugh.

Lucian was not the first to adapt the philosophical dialogue for satiric purposes. A Cynic named Menippus developed the satiric dialogue a century after Plato's death. Menippus called himself a dog, for he wrote biting satires, and Lucian used him as his alter ego or persona. The *Nekrikoi dialogoi* (*Dialogues of the Dead*, 1684) followed Menippus into the underworld and recorded the questions he put to the gods of the dead and the heroes of old. There were conversations between the Greek and Trojan heroes Ajax and Agamemnon; between Philip of Macedon and his son, Alexander the Great; among Alexander and the general Hannibal and the Cynic philosopher Diogenes; and between Diogenes and the comic dramatist Crates.

Lucian's dialogues have survived in several collections. Much as he satirized popular views of heroes and heroism in the *Dialogues of the Dead*, he satirized religious beliefs and practices in the *Theōn dialogoi* (*Dialogues of the Gods*, 1684), calling attention to the artifices of a state-sponsored revival of the Olympian religion. Greek philosophers back to Socrates (c. 470-399 B.C.E.) had questioned the morality of the Olympian gods. Lucian did not raise serious objections, though; he was too busy having fun, and he was prepared to challenge the sobersided philosophers.

One of Lucian's longest dialogues, *Bion Prasis* (*Philosophies for Sale*, 1684), put the famous philosophers of Greece in the marketplace, where each one hawked his wares. Philosophers are supposed to be above all that, but in fact they competed fiercely for private students as well as for positions in the best towns and schools. If anything, the competition grew fiercer during the Second Sophistic. Lucian knew how to expose their rivalries. His philosophers in the dialogue, like the pedants in comedies, are their own worst enemies. They unwittingly reveal their human weaknesses.

Eventually, Lucian's savings gave out, and he had to perform in public to support himself. It was common for readers to perform Plato's dialogues as minidramas, and

Lucian. (Library of Congress)

it seems likely that Lucian performed his own dialogues, perhaps doing all the voices himself. (Most dialogues are short skits that would take only five or ten minutes to perform.) He also used elements from the old Attic comedy of Aristophanes (c. 450-c. 385 B.C.E.). For example, his *Hetairikoi dialogoi* (*Dialogues of the Courtesans*, 1684) presented comic scenes that might arise among prostitutes and their clients. Although Lucian wrote down the dialogues—perhaps for sale to members of the audience—he probably improvised extensively. Indeed, his dialogues may remind modern readers of the sometimes improvisational comedy associated with such television shows as *Monty Python's Flying Circus* and *Saturday Night Live*.

Lucian traveled again, reprising his success as a public speaker who could improvise something to say on any topic for any occasion. He also tried his hand at a new literary form, the prose romance. Two stories attributed to him are among the first forerunners of the novel. *Alēthon Diēgēmaton* (*A True History*, 1634) tells the outrageous story of his journey to the Moon. It is the first in a series of imaginary travels that includes Sir Thomas More's *Utopia* (1516), Jonathan Swift's *Gulliver's Travels* (1726), and Samuel Butler's *Erewhon* (1872). *Loukios e Onos* (*Lucius: Or, The Ass*, 1684) is a story of a young man's transformation into an ass. It may not be Lucian's work, however, and at any rate it became famous only in the extended Latin reworking, *Metamorphoses* (second century; *The Golden Ass*, 1566) by a contemporary, Lucius Madura (c. 125-170).

Lucian says he married, but he says nothing about his wife nor does he mention children. Presumably, he traveled alone. Occasionally, he sought a permanent position. Perhaps it was at this time that he applied for a post as the public speaking teacher in a Greek-speaking city, a well-paid position in the civil service. He was not successful and lampooned the new teacher in the satiric speech, *Rhētorōn didaskalos* (*A Professor of Public Speaking*, 1684). Lucian traveled through Italy and into Egypt, where he found work as a public official in the law courts. He was still writing dialogues, and he described himself as an elder statesman. While in Egypt he died, in relative obscurity, at about the age of sixty.

Lucian's contemporaries and near-contemporaries probably thought of him as a clever entertainer who was also a bit of a braggart and clown, rather than as a serious philosopher. They probably regarded his writings as "low" exercises in prose satire and comedy rather than "high" examples of poetic epic and drama. They liked his

works enough to preserve a great many of them—some eighty works attributed to Lucian survive in some twelve dozen manuscripts—but they did not mention him in histories of philosophy and literature. Ironically, the works of Lucian's model Menippus have not survived, though the name appeared often enough in ancient works on literature. The type of satire that Lucian wrote—the tough intellectual dialogue, full of gossip and farce—is most commonly known today as "Menippian" satire and less frequently as "Lucianic." Very occasionally, it is called Varronian after the Latin writer Marcus Terentius Varro (116-27 B.C.E.), who modeled his satires on those of Menippus.

Some scholars think that Lucian may have known other great writers of Greek, including the Roman emperor Marcus Aurelius (121-180 C.E.), but the emperor was a true Stoic and would have preferred Lucian's prose style to his sense of humor. There is more reason to think that Lucian influenced the emperor Julian the Apostate (331-363 C.E.), who wrote a Menippian satire about the Caesars. Julian, though, attempted a last revival of the Olympian religion—for which he became known as "the Apostate"—and could not have approved of Lucian's levity in the *Dialogues of the Gods*.

SIGNIFICANCE

With the revival of interest in Greek culture during the Renaissance, Lucian's writings caught the interest of such humanist scholars as Desiderius Erasmus (c. 1468-1536). Soon they were translated into Latin and the modern European languages. One of the first printed books in Germany was a Latin translation of *Lucian, Or, The Ass*, printed in Augsburg c. 1477. One of the favorite books of Renaissance scholars was a Latin translation of selected dialogues made by Erasmus, who imitated Lucian's style in the celebrated *Moriae Encomium*, 1511 (*The Praise of Folly*, 1549). Erasmus's friend Sir Thomas More (c. 1478-1535) translated four dialogues into English and showed Lucian's influence in *De Optimo Reipublicae Statu, deque Nova Insula Utopia* (1516; *Utopia*, 1551), which used the dialogue form to tell of an imaginary voyage. The religious reformer Martin Luther scolded Erasmus for translating such an irreligious, indeed anti-Christian, author, but Luther was in the minority.

Lucian has influenced many other writers of English, from Geoffrey Chaucer (c. 1343-1400) to Ben Jonson (1573-1637) and Henry Fielding (1707-1754). His influence is also apparent in the works of French writers from François Rabelais (c. 1494-1553) to Voltaire (1694-

1778). The literary critic Northrop Frye discussed Lucian and the "Menippian" satire in *Anatomy of Criticism: Four Essays* (1957), one of the most influential books of literary theory to appear in the twentieth century. Frye saw this form of satire persisting in such unlikely places as *The Complete Angler*, by Izaak Walton (1653), and *Alice's Adventures in Wonderland*, by Lewis Carroll (1865). Frye suggested replacing the rather cumbersome term "Menippian satire" with the word "anatomy" and so placed his own book, with all its clever comments on the classics, within the tradition of Lucian. The writer who was almost forgotten by his contemporaries has thus become an important name in the history of European literature.

—Thomas Willard

FURTHER READING

Branham, R. Bracht. *Unruly Eloquence: Lucian and the Comedy of Traditions*. Cambridge, Mass.: Harvard University Press, 1989. Discusses Lucian's relation to Epicurean philosophy and to comic traditions. Emphasizes the role of laughter in a successful life.

Branham, R. Bracht, and Marie-Odile Goulet-Cazé, eds. *The Cynics: The Cynic Movement in Antiquity and Its Legacy*. Berkeley: University of California Press, 1995. Collection of essays examines the ethical, social, and cultural practices inspired by the Cynics. Includes introduction, appendices, index, and annotated bibliography.

Gay, Peter. *The Bridge of Criticism: Dialogues Among Lucian, Erasmus, and Voltaire on the Enlightenment*. New York: Harper, 1970. Written by an influential historian, this book shows how the satiric tradition has contributed to the freedom of thought.

Highet, Gilbert. *The Anatomy of Satire*. Princeton, N.J.: Princeton University Press, 1967. A history of satire, written by a great classicist. Offers a good introduction to the Menippian satire written by Lucian.

Jones, C. P. *Culture and Society in Lucian*. Cambridge, Mass.: Harvard University Press, 1986. A careful study of social satire in Lucian's dialogues. Discusses his historical context and his comments on the writing of history.

Payne, F. Anne. *Chaucer and Menippean Satire*. Madison: University of Wisconsin Press, 1981. Provides background on Lucian's tradition in satire and his influence on the greatest English poet of the Middle Ages.

Relihan, Joel C. *Ancient Menippean Satire*. Baltimore: The Johns Hopkins University Press, 1993. Discusses the early development of the sixteenth century literary genre Menippean satire, including its continuity from early classical roots. Covers Menippus, Seneca, Lucian, and other writers. Includes bibliography and index.

Robinson, Christopher. *Lucian and His Influence in Europe*. Chapel Hill: University of North Carolina Press, 1979. A study of Lucian's times and works, with attention to his influence on the Renaissance and Enlightenment. Includes chapters on Erasmus and Fielding.

SEE ALSO: Juvenal; Marcus Aurelius; Plato.

RELATED ARTICLES in *Great Events from History: The Ancient World*: c. 380 B.C.E., Plato Develops His Theory of Ideas; c. 350 B.C.E., Diogenes Popularizes Cynicism; 100-127 C.E., Roman Juvenal Composes *Satires*.

LUCRETIA
Roman matron

Lucretia embodied Roman virtue and catalyzed the overthrow of the Roman monarchy by committing suicide after being raped by her husband's royal relative.

BORN: Sixth century B.C.E.; place unknown
DIED: c. 509 B.C.E.; Collatia, Latium (now in Italy)
ALSO KNOWN AS: Lucrece; Lucresse
AREA OF ACHIEVEMENT: Government and politics

EARLY LIFE

The traditional story of Lucretia (lew-KREE-shee-uh), in its earliest extant form, is recounted in Latin by the Roman historian Titus Livy (59 B.C.E.-17 C.E.), in the first book of his monumental Roman history, *Ab urbe condita libri* (c. 26 B.C.E.-15 C.E.; *The History of Rome*, 1600). In the course of his narrative, Livy records Lucretia as the daughter of Spurius Lucretius Tricipitinus and as the wife of Lucius Tarquinius Collatinus. No details about Lucretia's early life are known, as it is in her death, rather than in life, that she performed the heroic act that made her a paradigmatic figure for the Romans and subsequently a prolific symbol for numerous productions in Western literature, art, and music.

LIFE'S WORK

The suicide of Lucretia marks the end of the Roman monarchy and the beginning of its Republic because, in avenging her honor, her father, Lucretius, and her husband, Collatinus, contribute to the fall of the Tarquin family from absolute power at Rome. Ironically enough, it is not Collatinus but his companion, Lucius Junius Brutus, who, while Lucretia's husband and father are distracted with mourning, emerges to swear himself Lucretia's primary avenger and shortly thereafter to become the founder of the Roman Republic.

If Collatinus steps up a bit too slowly to avenge the violation and death of his wife, he hurries to praise her beauty and virtue far less slowly while she is still alive. In fact, it is Collatinus's boasting that precipitates the first fateful meeting between Lucretia and Sextus Tarquinius, the youngest son of Tarquinius Superbus, monarch of Rome.

With the Roman army encamped about Ardea during a prolonged blockade of the city, Sextus Tarquinius holds a feast in his quarters at which is present Collantinus with a number of other members of the royal family. After some time of drinking, the soldiers all begin to praise their own wives to one another. Collatinus insists that his wife is clearly the most deserving of their praises and suggests that they ride off to their homes and check up on their wives unexpectedly, to prove who is the best. The group travels first to Rome, where they find that all the royal princesses are feasting and enjoying themselves late into the night. From Rome, the soldiers turn to Collatia, where they find Lucretia and her maids engaged in the domestic business of spinning, even late into the night by candlelight. Collatinus exults in the superior virtue of his wife and invites his companions into his house, paving the way for Sextus Tarquinius to become completely captivated by the unrivaled beauty and virtue of Lucretia and to conceive an insurmountable evil desire for her.

It is only a few days later that Sextus returns to the house of Collatinus, this time unaccompanied by his host. Welcomed by Lucretia as a guest of her husband, Sextus secures a meal, a guest room, and the opportunity to act on his evil intentions. In the middle of the night he visits Lucretia's room and awakens her with a sword pressed against her chest. Alternating his threats with entreaties, he attempts to have his way with her, but she refuses to yield to him. Finally he prevails, but only when he threatens to kill her and place beside her in her bed the naked body of a murdered slave as evidence that she had been caught in the act of adultery with one of the lowest members of her household. Fearing this taint on her reputation, Lucretia relinquishes her chastity.

While Sextus departs, thinking he has successfully achieved this object of his desire, Lucretia sends messages to her husband at Ardea and to her father at Rome, summoning them each to come with one trusted friend to her house because a terrible thing has happened. When the four men arrive, they find Lucretia mourning in her bedroom with a knife concealed under her clothes. She reports what has happened to her, names her assaulter, and extracts a pledge that they will avenge her defiled body. They assure her that crime is committed by the mind, not by the body, and that her pure intentions defy any guilt on her part. In book 1 of Livy's *The History of Rome*, Lucretia responds:

> You will see to what that man deserves. I absolve myself from the crime but not from punishment. There will not be any woman who lives unchaste because of the precedent of Lucretia.

(Vos . . . videritis quid illi debeatur: ego me etsi peccato
absolvo, supplicio non libero; nec ulla deinde impudica
Lucretiae exemplo vivet.

As she finishes speaking, Lucretia stabs herself with the
concealed weapon and dies before the eyes of her husband and father. While they are mourning her death, the
companion of her husband, Lucius Junius Brutus, picks
up the bloodied knife and makes a promise to drive the
royal Tarquin family out of Rome in punishment for the
deed committed by Sextus Tarquinius.

SIGNIFICANCE

Not only has Lucretia's brave and selfless act influenced
many subsequent versions and depictions of her story,
but her suicide also functioned as a powerful symbol
for Roman political change directly following her death.
Her body was paraded first through Collatia and then
through Rome, provoking the outrage of the Roman people against Sextus Tarquinius and spurring them on to
take up arms against the tyrants of the Tarquin family.
At Rome, Brutus made a speech to the Roman public
emphasizing the violence, lust, and arrogance of the
monarchy, using Lucretia's body as an object lesson for
the Roman people. Literally written on her body were
the assaults of the young Tarquin. The Roman people,
compelled both by her virtue and by her victimization,
subsequently drove the Tarquins out of Rome, thereby
dismantling the Roman monarchy and establishing the
beginnings of the Roman Republic.

Even under the Roman Empire, Lucretia remained a
symbol of the highest form of Roman female chastity
and as an example of the greatest Roman virtue, whether
female or male. Later Roman poets seize on the prolific material of her story to formulate sections or make
references in larger works. Ovid (43 B.C.E.-17 C.E.), in his
Fasti (c. 8 C.E.; English translation, 1859), a poetic synthesis of astronomy, religion, legend, and history, includes Lucretia's story among the patriotic legends of
early Rome, seeming to rely more or less on Livy's
version of the events. Shortly thereafter, Silius Italicus
(c. 26-101 C.E.) in his *Punica* (after 88 C.E.; *The Second
Punick War Between Hannibal and the Romans*, 1661)
includes Lucretia as one of the ghosts of famous Roman
women whom the Sibyl points out to Scipio on his trip
through Hades. Here Lucretia is called *decus pudicitiae*,
"the glory of chastity." Her story is also recorded by the
Greek rhetorician Dionysius of Halicarnassus in *Antiquitates Romanae* (c. 7 B.C.E.; *The Roman Antiquities of
Dionysius Halicarnassensis*, 1758), by the Greek writer

Plutarch ("Life of Publius Valerius Publicola," from his
Bioi paralleloi, c. 105-115 C.E.; *Parallel Lives*, 1579), by
Dio Cassius (*Romaika*, early third century C.E.; *Dio's
Roman History*, 1914-1927), by Diodorus of Sicily
(*Bibliotheca historica*, c. 60-30 B.C.E.; *The Historical
Library of Diodorus the Sicilian*, 1700), by Valerius
Maximus (*Factorum et dictorum memorabilium libri IX*,
c. 31 C.E.; *Romanæ antiqæ descriptio: A View of the Reli-
gion, Laws, Customs, Manners, and Dispositions of the
Ancient Romans, and Others*, 1678), and by Lucius
Annaeus Florus (*Epitome de T. Livio bellorum omnium
annorusm DCC libri duo*, second century C.E.; *The His-
tory of the Romans*, 1658).

While Lucretia has been celebrated by many ancient
authors for her beauty, chastity, and virtue, the rationale
for her suicide has raised questions about guilt and sin
that have provoked even deeper consideration of her motives. Saint Augustine discusses her chastity and guilt in
his Christian treatise *De civitate Dei* (413-427; *The City
of God*, 1610), while in the medieval period John Gower,
Geoffrey Chaucer, and Thomas Heywood (the first two
in verses; the third in dramatic form) revisit her story as a
paradigm of woman's virtue in the face of man's lust.
William Shakespeare, too, devotes a long poem to portraying the episode, though his perspective is also more
moralistic than political. From the Renaissance on, the
story of Lucretia has been the subject of countless paintings, sculptures, and sketches with a flurry of artistic activity occurring in the sixteenth, seventeenth and eighteenth centuries. Perhaps most famous is the 1570 Titian
painting *Tarquin and Lucretia*. More recently, Lucretia
has served as the subject of Benjamin Britten's 1946 opera *The Rape of Lucretia*, based on André Obey's play *Le
viol de Lucrèce* (pr. 1931; *Lucrece*, 1933).

Lucretia's legacy in artistic representation has been
put to further use by scholarly work in various academic
fields, as critics have drawn on the material in her legend
to develop and support provocative arguments in political theory, cultural studies, literary criticism, and other
humanities disciplines. Lucretia has become a prolific
symbol for generating ideas in the spheres of feminism
and humanism and in discussions of heroism and sexism.
The significance of her suicide has been continuously reinterpreted from the beginnings of the Roman Republic
to modern times. While Lucretia may have prevented
herself from becoming a precedent for the existence of
unchaste women, she has nevertheless offered herself as
a striking paradigm for the social and political behavior
of both sexes in a plethora of cultural contexts.

—Janie Anne Zuber

FURTHER READING

Bowen, Anthony. *The Story of Lucretia: Selections from Ovid and Livy*. Oak Park, Ill.: Bolchazy-Carducci, 1987. Provides Latin text, vocabulary, notes, and useful discussion of the two versions of Lucretia's story in Livy and in Ovid.

Chaucer, Geoffrey. *The Legend of Good Women*. Translated by Ann McMillan. East Lansing, Mich.: Colleagues Press, 1995. Includes Chaucer's version of the Lucretia legend in modern English.

Donaldson, Ian. *The Rapes of Lucretia: A Myth and Its Transformations*. Oxford, England: Clarendon Press, 1982. Critical analysis of the Lucretia story, with attention to each of the Latin authors who retold her story. Also considers Saint Augustine's remarks about her and the role of Brutus. Especially useful for its compilation (reproduced in black-and-white photographs) of artistic renditions of Lucretia from the sixteenth, seventeenth, and eighteenth centuries, including Titian's well-known *Tarquin and Lucretia* (1570).

Gower, John. *Confessio Amantis*. Edited by Russell A. Peck. Buffalo, N.Y.: University of Toronto Press, 1997. Includes his Middle English version of Lucretia in the seventh book.

Heywood, Thomas. *The Rape of Lucrece: A True Roman Tragedy.* London: John Raworth, 1638 (reprint 1824). Dramatic version of the Lucretia story.

Jed, Stephanie H. *Chaste Thinking: The Rape of Lucretia and the Birth of Humanism*. Bloomington: Indiana University Press, 1989. Interpretation of the Lucretia legend as symbolic of the development of humanism, with special attention to ethics, feminism, and Coluccio Salutati's Renaissance version of Lucretia.

Matthes, Melissa M. *The Rape of Lucretia and the Founding of Republics: Readings in Livy, Machiavelli, and Rousseau*. University Park: Pennsylvania State University Press, 2000. Investigates the relationship between the Lucretia story and the establishment of the Roman Republic, taking its cue from Livy's version of Lucretia and the beginnings of the Roman Republic.

Shakespeare, William. *The Poems: Venus and Adonis, The Rape of Lucrece, The Phoenix and the Turtle, The Passionate Pilgrim*, edited by John Roe. New York: Cambridge University Press, 1992. Includes Shakespeare's lengthy poem about the Lucretia story.

Trout, D. "Retextualizing Lucretia: Cultural Subversion in *The City of God*." *Journal of Early Christian Studies* 2, no.1 (1994): 53-70. Critical analysis of Saint Augustine's remarks about Lucretia in *The City of God*, book 1, chapter 19, where this early Christian writer tries to rationalize Lucretia's guilt in terms of contemporary Christian women.

SEE ALSO: Agrippina the Younger; Antonia Minor; Arria the Elder; Arria the Younger; Boudicca; Cleopatra VII; Clodia; Julia Domna; Julia Mamaea; Julia Soaemias; Julia III; Valeria Messallina; Ovid; Tarquins; Zenobia.

RELATED ARTICLES in *Great Events from History: The Ancient World*: 509 B.C.E., Rape of Lucretia; c. 509 B.C.E., Roman Republic Replaces Monarchy; 8 C.E., Ovid's *Metamorphoses* Is Published.

LUCRETIUS
Roman philosopher

Though he in no sense offered an original philosophical outlook, Lucretius's major work synthesized primary tenets of Greek Epicureanism and atomism and offered a rational, nontheological explanation for the constituents of the universe; all this he accomplished in Latin hexameter verse, and he developed a philosophical vocabulary required for the task.

BORN: c. 98 B.C.E.; probably Rome (now in Italy)
DIED: October 15, 55 B.C.E.; Rome
ALSO KNOWN AS: Titus Lucretius Carus (full name)
AREAS OF ACHIEVEMENT: Literature, natural history, philosophy

EARLY LIFE

It is much easier to show why most of what has been written about the life of Lucretius (lew-KREE-shee-uhs) is incorrect, doubtful, or malicious than it is to arrive at a reliable account. Relatively little can be deduced from his poem, and there are no substantive contemporary references to him. Consequently, too much credence has been given to the jumbled biographical note written by Saint Jerome, which itself was derived from an unreliable account by the Roman historian Gaius Suetonius Tranquillus. Jerome miscalculates Lucretius's dates of birth and death; also, it is unlikely that Lucretius was driven insane by a love potion and wrote *De rerum natura* (c. 60 B.C.E.; *On the Nature of Things*, 1682) during periods of lucidity. The latter story seems to have arisen from Lucretius's treatment of love in section 4 of the poem.

Several details of Lucretius's early life can, however, be inferred with relative certainty. His name is a strange combination that implies both servile (Carus) and noble origins (from the kinship grouping *Gens Lucretia*), but he was likely closer to the middle class of his contemporary Cicero. Though Cicero himself did not emend Lucretius's poetry, as Jerome reports, it is likely that his brother Quintus Cicero oversaw its publication. Like Cicero, Lucretius appears to have evinced an early interest in philosophy, influenced by the Alexandrian movement, though his own poetry has an old Roman spirit reflecting his readings of Quintus Ennius. Cicero considered that Lucretius had the genius of Ennius and the art of the Alexandrians.

Lucretius lived through the turmoil caused by the civil war between aristocrat Lucius Cornelius Sulla and populist Gaius Marius as well as the conspiracy of Lucius Sergius Catilina. He also witnessed the consequent decline of Roman republican government. Perhaps this political uncertainty directed him to the comfortable philosophy of Epicurus, which held that the goal of human existence should be a life of calm pleasure tempered by morality and culture. The atomism of Democritus and Leucippus, which held that the material universe could be understood as random combinations of minute particles (*atomoi*), provided a rational and scientific means of explaining the cosmos and avoiding what Lucretius came to see as the sterile superstitions of religion.

In all, the impressions one has of Lucretius at this early stage in his life are of a young man, of good background and a good education, who is eager not for the political arena or personal advancement but to explain the world in a reasonable way to Romans with similar education who would read his verse. In addition, he aimed to make living in that rationally explained world as pleasant an experience as possible.

LIFE'S WORK

One can guess how Lucretius lived during the years he was writing *On the Nature of Things* from its dedication to Gaius Memmius. Memmius held the office of praetor in 58 B.C.E. and fancied himself a poet, primarily of erotic verse in the style of Catullus. Memmius's shady political dealings eventually caught up with him, and he was driven into exile; nevertheless, it is reasonable to assume that Lucretius received some financial support from him. Memmius figures less importantly in the body of the poem, however, and his name is used in places only for metrical convenience.

Details of the poem show the kind of atmosphere Lucretius wished to escape, essentially that of his own city in the final years of the Republic. The world is filled with gloom, war, and decay. The poet wishes to stand on a hill, far removed from wickedness and ambition, and watch the waste and destruction. Passages such as these reveal a man who yearned for tranquil anonymity. Other writers, such as Cicero, would find themselves propelled into a political maelstrom that would ultimately destroy them; Lucretius was determined to avoid this fate.

The times in which Lucretius lived cried out for reasonableness. Educated Romans saw the obvious conflict between their elaborate mythology and their religion, which glorified deities who did everything from seducing women to causing mildew. Even so, Rome continued to fill the various priestly colleges, to take auspices as a means of determining favorable outcomes, and to celebrate public games in honor of these very deities. A century later, Rome would deify its emperors, partly to shift its religious observances to personalities who were incontestably real, and partly to curb the spread of imported cults such as Mithraism and what came to be known as Christianity.

Lucretius had solved this problem, for himself at least, and outlines his position on religion in *On the Nature of Things*. The creative force of nature is real; it is personified in the goddess Venus. The deities are simply personifications of various aspects of nature, and human beings can free themselves of superstition by seeing the world as constantly recombining *atomoi*. Death itself is nothing more than atomic dissolution, a preparation for new arrangements of atoms and new creation. If human beings can accept death in these terms, they can cast aside the fear that binds them to religious superstition. This acceptance will prepare them to see that life's purpose is to maximize pleasure and minimize pain.

Neither of these theories is new; they are derived from the atomism of Democritus and Leucippus and the teachings of Epicurus. What is new is Lucretius's synthesis and his offering it as rational scientism to educated Roman readers. One reason almost nothing is known about Lucretius's personal life is undoubtedly his determination to practice these ideas. Removing himself from the fray to seek philosophical calm necessarily results in a lack of contemporary biographical references, but it is precisely on this score that Lucretian Epicureanism is most misunderstood. It is just the opposite of egocentric gratification, because Lucretius couples it with the mechanics of atomism. Seen in this way, the individual is merely a part in the world machine; immortality exists, but only in the myriad indestructible *atomoi* that constitute each part.

One can only guess how Lucretius first encountered Epicureanism. There were Greek professors in Rome during the first century B.C.E. who taught the theories of Epicurus. Cicero mentions non-Greek Epicureans who wrote treatises Lucretius might easily have read. The ease with which Lucretius deals with the technical vocabulary of atomism suggests that he was accomplished in Greek. (This would be expected of any educated Roman.) He no doubt read Epicurus, Democritus, and Leucippus in the original language.

Reading Greek gave Lucretius access to other sources such as Empedocles, the philosopher-poet who wrote *Peri physeōs* (fifth century B.C.E.; *On Nature*, 1908). What the modern world calls natural selection comes to

Lucretius through Empedocles, as does the principle of attraction and repulsion, which Lucretius sees as love and hate. Lucretius's hexameter meter is used by Empedocles but also by Homer. Indeed, Lucretius borrows from Homer, Euripides, Thucydides, Hippocrates, and various early Roman poets.

Though his philosophy is Greek, Lucretius maintains a very Roman insistence on the primacy of law. In *On the Nature of Things*, for example, he notes that human beings moved from primitive status to society only after they had agreed on a social contract. Language improved on gesture, and social order prevailed. It is worth noting that similar ideas later appear in the creation account of Ovid in *Metamorphoses* (c. 8 C.E.; English translation, 1567). Though Lucretius failed to convert the Roman masses, he obviously made inroads among his successors in poetry. Vergil read him, too, and while Vergil's work is more elegant, there can be little doubt that he was impressed by Lucretius's descriptions of nature; one can easily see their influence in Vergil's pastoral poems.

The random nature of the *clinamen* ("swerve") that atoms make when they recombine must have troubled Lu-

Lucretius. (Hulton|Archive by Getty Images)

cretius, as he is generally insistent on the orderly cycle of nature. This bothered others, too, but it is the only way to explain natural differences atomically. The *membranae* ("films"), which are thrown from objects and thereby produce visual impressions, are another artificial means of describing a natural phenomenon, but *On the Nature of Things* is, on the whole, free of such difficulties.

The poem's six books show evidence of unfinished composition, but one cannot deduce Lucretius's premature death from this fact. The Victorian poet Alfred, Lord Tennyson, perpetuated Suetonius's marvelous fiction of Lucretius's mental illness and death by a love potion, but the author of *On the Nature of Things* was a very sane man whose entire reason for living was to bring rationality to an irrational world.

SIGNIFICANCE

Lucretius noted the creative force of nature, but he in no sense resembled the English Romantic poets in their wonderment at its powers. He was the rare combination of natural scientist, philosopher, and poet, and he strove for clarity and reasonableness in what he wrote. He clearly was not the gaunt, love-crazed, mad genius of Suetonius and Jerome but an evangelizer who appealed to an educated audience, much like twentieth century writers of popular science.

Lucretius thus became a symbol that served the purposes of those who wrote about him. Because the facts of his life remained a mystery, even to the generation that immediately followed his own, he could be portrayed by Suetonius as foreshadowing the Empire's vice, by Jerome as representing pagan degeneracy, and ultimately by Tennyson as typifying egocentric gratification. Even so, as is true of many great lives, work overshadows personality, and this is clearly what Lucretius intended, for *On the Nature of Things* opened a world of what would otherwise have remained esoteric Greek philosophy to a popular audience. What is more important, Lucretius presented these ideas as a means of dealing with his own troubled world.

Were one to cancel out Lucretius's masterly synthesis of Epicureanism and atomism, his contribution to both Roman poetry and the Latin language would remain. Nearly one hundred technical words adapted from the Greek appear within six books of hexameter verse, the epic meter of Homer and of Lucretius's fellow Roman Ennius. That Lucretius's work inspired the succeeding generation of Roman poets, which included both Vergil and Ovid, attests its immediate influence. The modern reader, armed with contemporary science and psychol-

ogy, can object only to the mechanics of the natural phenomena Lucretius discusses; his plea to cast aside superstition and fear strikes a welcome note.

—*Robert J. Forman*

FURTHER READING

Bailey, Cyril. "Late Republican Poetry." In *Fifty Years (and Twelve) of Classical Scholarship*, edited by Maurice Platnauer. New York: Barnes and Noble Books, 1968. This article discusses Lucretius with special emphasis on editions and translations of his poem, possible sources, textual criticism, and Lucretian thought, philosophy, and natural science.

Duff, J. Wight, and A. M. Duff. *A Literary History of Rome from the Origins to the Close of the Golden Age.* New York: Barnes and Noble Books, 1960. This companion volume to the Duffs' study of Silver Age Latin literature devotes a sizable chapter to Lucretius. It records the basic meager details of Lucretius's life, analyzes his poem, and makes several interesting cross-references to English Romantic and Victorian poets.

Johnson, W. R. *Lucretius and the Modern World.* London: Duckworth, 2000. In this description of Lucretius's influential poem, Johnson surveys major texts from the eighteenth and nineteenth centuries in the works of John Dryden, Voltaire, Alfred, Lord Tennyson, and others. Emphasizes Lucretius's version of materialism and his attempt to devise an ethical system appropriate to the universe.

Latham, R. E., trans. *Lucretius: On the Nature of the Universe.* Harmondsworth, Middlesex, England: Penguin Books, 1971. This accurate translation has the great virtue of an introduction that discusses what is known about Lucretius's life and, more, outlines his poem section by section with line references. It is, by far, the best introduction to Lucretius for one unable to read Latin.

Lucretius. *On the Nature of Things.* Translated by Martin Ferguson Smith. Indianapolis: Hackett, 2001. Includes introduction and notes by the translator in addition to bibliography and index.

SEE ALSO: Cicero; Democritus; Empedocles; Quintus Ennius; Epicurus; Ovid; Vergil.

RELATED ARTICLES in *Great Events from History: The Ancient World*: Late 63-January 62 B.C.E., Catiline Conspiracy; 54 B.C.E., Roman Poet Catullus Dies; 51 B.C.E., Cicero Writes *De republica*; 19 B.C.E., Roman Poet Vergil Dies; 8 C.E., Ovid's *Metamorphoses* Is Published.

LYSIPPUS
Greek sculptor

A sculptor whose career spanned virtually the entire fourth century B.C.E., Lysippus was not only a major transitional figure between classical and Hellenistic styles but the most renowned portraitist of the century as well.

BORN: c. 390 B.C.E.; Sicyon, Greece
DIED: c. 300 B.C.E.; place unknown
AREA OF ACHIEVEMENT: Art and art patronage

EARLY LIFE

Though relatively little contemporary evidence survives about the man or his life, a considerable amount is known about the era in which Lysippus (li-SIHP-uhs) produced his art and about the key events and a number of the significant individuals that helped shape his career. Lysippus was born in Sicyon, in southern Greece. His early work is said to have reflected certain values and preoccupations of the fifth century B.C.E., when Greek civilization, led by Athens, defined for the West the essence of the classical in art. With the work of his later career, Lysippus's artistic concerns show dramatic change, as he established himself as perhaps the most renowned portraitist of antiquity, defining forever in sculpture the essence of Alexander the Great. There is perhaps no other ancient artist whose style evolved more dramatically or whose work more clearly reflects the significant changes of an era.

Subsequent to the great wars with Persia (490-478 B.C.E.), the Greek city-states, though independent political units, fell generally under the influence of either Sparta or Athens. These two city-states had achieved their ascendancy chiefly by force of arms; Sparta had been the dominant military power in Greece since at least the sixth century B.C.E., and Athens had converted an alliance of coastal and island states in the early fifth century B.C.E. into a naval empire. Although it eventually fell to Sparta in 404, Athens for the last half of the fifth century was the cultural and intellectual center of all Greece. Here was defined the classical in the arts, notably in architecture (chiefly by the Parthenon) and in sculpture.

The fourth century witnessed in its early decades a series of attempts by different city-states to repeat the fifth century achievements of Athens and Sparta. Internally divided and weakened by constant warfare, the city-states by the mid-fourth century began to be pressured by the ambitions of outsiders, including Mausalus, dynast of Caria in Asia Minor, Jason of Pherae in Thessaly,

and finally, Philip of Macedonia. Abruptly and decisively, the uncertainties of the mid-fourth century Greek world were brought to an end in 338, when Philip and his eighteen-year-old son, Alexander, overwhelmed a Greek allied army at Chaeronea in central Greece. With defeat, the states of Greece were obliged to follow the lead of Macedonia, and during the next sixteen years stood, cowed and helpless, as Alexander succeeded his father and marched east, conquering by the time of his death in 323 most of the then-known world. By the time of his death, Alexander had been formally acknowledged a god by the Greeks, though his kingdom quickly suffered irreparable division at the hands of his successors. All of this Lysippus witnessed, from the attempts early in the century to replicate the achievements of the classical era to the partitioning of Alexander's empire in the last decades of the century. What Lysippus witnessed is reflected in his art.

LIFE'S WORK

While Lysippus is said to have been especially prolific during the course of his long career—it is claimed that he produced as many as fifteen hundred pieces—none of his works is known in fact to have survived, a consequence in part of his having worked primarily in bronze. What has survived is written testimony about a number of his more important pieces—mainly in the work of the first century C.E. Roman encyclopedist Pliny the Elder—and some stone copies, which in subject matter and manner of execution seem consistent with what is known of Lysippus's work.

Lysippus's style early in his career is said to have been influenced by the work of Polyclitus, also a southern Greek and unquestionably one of the most important sculptors of the fifth century B.C.E. Polyclitus in his sculpture is said to have sought to express a sense of the good and the beautiful; that is, he attempted to represent in sculpture abstract values. It was Polyclitus's belief that there existed an underlying order in the universe and that this order could be understood in terms of mathematical ratios, much as the order of music can be understood. Polyclitus wrote a treatise (now lost) detailing his views and executed a piece that was to embody them, titled the *Doryphorus* (c. 450-440 B.C.E.; *Spear Bearer*). This statue of an athlete standing, poised with spear held over his left shoulder, of which only stone copies survive, was so sculpted that each element stood in what Polyclitus

A copy of the quadriga, thought to be the work of Lysippus, sits atop the Carousel Arch at the western entrance to the Louvre in Paris, France. (© Annebicque Bernard/Corbis Sygma)

judged to be a perfect ratio to every other element. Thus it possessed a perfect order and expressed Polyclitus's ideal of the good and the beautiful. Such preoccupation with form, with principles of organization, and with effecting a tension between the abstract and the concrete, the universal and the individual, became central characteristics of fifth century Greek classical style.

As he matured, Lysippus moved away from conformity to the classical norms of Polyclitus. Though no copies of his earlier works survive, those copies that survive of works from the middle part of his career mark a turning from the abstract and universal toward a more explicit expression of the individual, the concrete, and the momentary. Not only is the statue of the athlete scraping himself with a strigil (called the *Apoxyomenos* and dated c. 330) executed in proportions more elongated (and thus visually more realistic) than those of the *Doryphorus*, but the statue is also fully three-dimensional: The arms are outstretched and actually intrude into the viewer's space and thus make more immediate the relationship be-

tween figure and viewer. Indeed, the action of the figure, cleansing after exercise, is intimate and private. Here, then, in the uncertainty of the mid-fourth century, the confidence that had been expressed by classical form gives way to the exploration of the momentary and transient.

Exploration of the individual in sculpture is effected most naturally through portraiture. In his later career, Lysippus became the master of this medium. An example that has survived, though again only in stone copies, is the statue of the seated Socrates. There is nothing in this statue to suggest the idealization of the human form. The philosopher, balding, eyes bulging, with satyrlike features and an exposed upper torso exhibiting the physical softening brought on by old age, sits gazing ahead in reflection or in mid-dialogue. The effect of realism is genuine and remarkable, especially because Socrates had been tried and executed in Athens in 399 B.C.E. and thus would never have been seen by Lysippus. As illustrated by this statue, Lysippus's portraiture sought to capture the essence of the subject. Like Polyclitus, Lysippus explored beneath the surface of things, but whereas Polyclitus sought with his art to define the ideal, Lysippus sought to define the real.

Such became the reputation of Lysippus that he was retained by the Macedonian court and later in his career served as the official sculptor of Alexander the Great. So prized was Lysippus's ability to capture Alexander's character that the young Macedonian king is alleged to have allowed no one else to render a likeness of him. Again, stone copies constitute the only visual evidence, but these are suggestive. Consistently in these copies, Alexander's head is turned to the side, tilted slightly upward, eyes deep-set and gazing, and hair folded back in waves. The essence captured is of a man in search, looking longingly beyond the present—an attitude attributed to Alexander by the historian Arrian. Lysippus would have seen Alexander, and thus there is reason to believe the likeness truer to the person than is the portrait of Socrates. Confirmation comes from a story told by the ancient biographer Plutarch, who notes that Alexander's former rival and successor, Cassander, while walking in the sanctuary at Delphi, encountered a statue of Alexander, presumably by Lysippus, and was seized by a shuddering and trembling from which he barely recovered.

The realism of Lysippus's work was heightened, so it seems, by the attention he devoted to detail. He was recognized throughout his career as an especially skilled craftsman. In fact, Pliny notes that Lysippus was said to have been a student of no one but originally to have been a coppersmith. Other of his works known from copies are the *Agias* of Pharsalus, the copy of which is nearly contemporary with the original; a series of works on Heracles, who, like Alexander, attained the status of a divinity as a consequence of his heroic exploits; as well as depictions of a satyr; the god Eros; and Kairos (Fortune) made a divinity. Of Lysippus's other works, only written testimony survives.

SIGNIFICANCE

With the death of Alexander the Great in 323 B.C.E., a new era dawned in the eastern Mediterranean region. Alexander's kingdom, lacking a designated heir, quickly was divided among his generals and companions into a series of rival monarchies and remained so until absorbed by Rome in the second century B.C.E. With the defeat at Chaeronea, the city-states of Greece had ceased to exercise internationally significant political or military influence. Greek culture, on the other hand, during this

so-called Hellenistic era was suffused throughout the entire Mediterranean. Much that was characteristic of Hellenistic visual art had been anticipated by Lysippus in the fourth century. In brief, Hellenistic sculpture explored the unique and the individual; it investigated internal emotional states and sought to extend the appreciation of form beyond the canons of the classical. Beyond the particular achievements of his own career, Lysippus may also be regarded as one of the significant transitional figures in the history of art.

—*Edmund M. Burke*

FURTHER READING

Beazley, J. D., and Bernard Ashmole. *Greek Sculpture and Painting to the End of the Hellenistic Period*. Cambridge, England: Cambridge University Press, 1966. This is a standard, scholarly handbook on Greek sculpture and painting from the early archaic period to the Hellenistic era. The text is concise; the illustrations are numerous and of excellent quality. There is a separate chapter on the sculpture of the fourth century.

Boardman, John. *Greek Art*. 4th ed. New York: Thames and Hudson, 1996. The volume surveys systematically and with numerous illustrations the arts of Greece, major and minor, from the post-Mycenaean through the Hellenistic eras. Lysippus is examined in two chapters, one on classical sculpture and architecture, the other on Hellenistic art.

Carpenter, Rhys. *Greek Sculpture: A Critical Review*. Chicago: University of Chicago Press, 1960. Although a survey of sculpture from the archaic to the Hellenistic eras, the work also focuses on the evolution of style in sculpture. Consequently, it makes no claim to completeness. The plates are excellent, though there are none of Lysippus's work.

Hammond, N. G. L. *A History of Greece to 322 B.C.* 3d ed. New York: Oxford University Press, 1986. An excellent standard survey, detailed and clearly written, of ancient Greek history: political, military, and cultural. Lysippus is noted in a chapter on the intellectual background of the fourth century.

Johnson, Franklin P. *Lysippos*. 1927. Reprint. New York: Greenwood Press, 1968. This remains among the most complete works on Lysippus available, though it is somewhat dated. The appendix is especially valuable, because it preserves all the ancient notices on Lysippus with English translations. Includes numerous plates.

Pliny the Elder. *The Elder Pliny's Chapters on the His-*

tory of Art. Translated by K. Jex-Blake. Chicago: Ares, 1992. Pliny is the principal ancient source on Lysippus.

Pollitt, J. J. *Art and Experience in Classical Greece.* New York: Cambridge University Press, 1999. This is an excellent analysis of Greek classical art, chiefly sculpture and architecture, and the intellectual and cultural context in which it was produced. Lysippus is examined in some detail. The plates are numerous and of a high quality.

Richter, Gisela Marie Augusta. *The Sculpture and Sculptors of the Greeks.* 4th ed. New Haven, Conn.: Yale University Press, 1970. This remains the standard volume on Greek sculpture from the early archaic through the late Hellenistic eras. As the title suggests, there are two main sections, one on sculpture, the other on known sculptors, including Lysippus. Includes three hundred pages of plates.

SEE ALSO: Alexander the Great; Philip II of Macedonia; Pliny the Elder; Polyclitus; Socrates.

RELATED ARTICLES in *Great Events from History: The Ancient World*: 480-479 B.C.E., Persian Invasion of Greece; 359-336 B.C.E., Philip II Expands and Empowers Macedonia; August 2, 338 B.C.E., Battle of Chaeronea; 336 B.C.E., Alexander the Great Begins Expansion of Macedonia; c. 323-275 B.C.E., Diadochi Divide Alexander the Great's Empire.